Encyclopedia of Prisoners of War and Internment

Encyclopedia of Prisoners of War and Internment

Second Edition

Jonathan F. Vance, Editor

Grey House Publishing
Millerton, NY 12546

PUBLISHER: Leslie Mackenzie
EDITORIAL DIRECTOR: Laura Mars-Proietti
PRODUCTION EDITOR: Toby Raymond
MARKETING DIRECTOR: Jessica Moody

Grey House Publishing, Inc.
185 Millerton Road
Millerton, NY 12546
518.789.8700
FAX 518.789.0545
www.greyhouse.com
e-mail: books @greyhouse.com

First Edition printed 2000
Second Edition printed 2006
Printed in the USA

Publisher's Cataloging-In-Publication Data
(Prepared by The Donohue Group, Inc.)

Encyclopedia of prisoners of war and internment / Jonathan F. Vance, editor. -- 2nd ed.

p. : ill. ; cm.

ISBN: 1-59237-120-5
Originally published: Santa Barbara, Calif. : ABC-CLIO, 1996.
Includes bibliographical references and index.

1. Prisoners of war--Encyclopedias. 2. Concentration camps--Encyclopedias. I. Vance, Jonathan Franklin William, 1963- II. Title: Prisoners of war and internment

UB800 .E53 2006
355.1/13

Encyclopedia of Prisoners of War and Internment

Second Edition

DETAILED TABLE OF CONTENTS

ENCYCLOPEDIA OF PRISONERS OF WAR AND INTERNMENT

SECOND EDITION

SECTION ONE: ENTRIES

A

B

C

D

S

T

U

V

W

Y

Preface and Acknowledgments

In this encyclopedia, it has not been possible to discuss the nature of captivity in every war, or to describe the attitudes toward captivity that have prevailed in every society throughout human history. This would have produced an immense volume but, more significantly, one with far too much repetition. To cite just one example, the European states fought dozens of campaigns against indigenous peoples in Africa and Asia during the nineteenth century, but there were few differences in the treatment of captives from campaign to campaign. The Afghan or Sikh Wars, then, stand as examples of how captivity issues evolved in imperial conflicts. By the same token, the Wars of the Spanish and Austrian Successions were certainly significant in European geopolitics, but there was little about captivity in those wars to distinguish them from the Seven Years' War. Nor has it been possible to cover captivity issues in all non-European societies. Instead, a number of societies (like the Aztecs of central America) have been chosen more or less arbitrarily to illustrate attitudes toward prisoners.

The entries in this encyclopedia are intended to be self-contained, but cross-references to other, related entries have been provided wherever possible. Suggestions for further reading have also been included; many entries are followed by a short list of books or articles that relate directly to the subject. The only exceptions are 11 of the large entries: Escape; Korean War; United States Civil War; Vietnam War; War Crimes; Women; World War I—Eastern Front; World War I—Western Front; World War II—Far East; World War II—North America; and World War II—Western Europe. These topics are covered in the comprehensive bibliography, which also includes general sources on POWs and internment.

While extensive, this bibliography is not exhaustive. Of the thousands of published sources on captivity in wartime, I have selected those that are most significant and most likely to be easily obtainable. Readers looking for more detailed source lists should consult the excellent bibliographies in Robert C. Doyle's books *Voices from Captivity: Interpreting the American POW Narrative* and *A Prisoner's Duty: Great Escapes in U.S. Military History*. Readers interested in sources covering the Holocaust, which has yielded a massive literature, are advised to consult one of the many published bibliographies on the subject. Abraham J. Edelheit and Hershel Edelheit's *Bibliography on Holocaust Literature*, second edition (Boulder, CO: Westview Press, 1990) remains one of the most comprehensive listings available.

My first debt is to the dozens of writers who have given of their time and expertise to contribute to this volume. Not only did they provide entries, but they also made suggestions for broadening the coverage of the book and helped out with information on illustrations and sources. For this revised edition, I have made every effort to locate the original contributors, and many took the opportunity to update their entries to reflect new research. Regrettably, I was unable to trace everyone. In most cases, their original entries have been reprinted without change, but where important new details or publications have become available, I have taken the liberty of making minor additions to their entries.

I am also grateful to my friends and colleagues Mike Bechthold, Tim Cook, Sarah-Jane Corke, Jean Daudelin, Serge Durflinger, Kent Fedorowich, Luz Maria Hernández-Sáenz, Linda McKnight, Bob Moore, Kim Nossal, and Nevin Williams for their assistance in filling gaps in the work. I am indebted to Bob Neville for giving me the opportunity to work on the encyclopedia. He first came up with the idea for this project and provided sound and patient guidance through the entire process of putting together the first edition. I am also grateful to Grey House Publishing for their interest in doing a revised edition, and to Toby Raymond for making it happen on a tight deadline. Finally, I must thank my family for their patience and indulgence. I have spent some 20 years engaged in the study of POWs and captivity, and my wife and children have been part of that odyssey (sometimes reluctantly). I couldn't have done it without their tolerance and encouragement.

—Jonathan F. Vance

Introduction

Captivity is as old as war itself. It has existed for centuries and has profoundly affected the lives of millions of people, including some of the most influential figures in history. Politicians such as Winston Churchill and Charles de Gaulle, and writers such as Miguel de Cervantes and P. G. Wodehouse have all endured imprisonment in wartime. It might even be argued that captivity, which historically has affected entire populations, has been more universal than combat, which usually involves only the warriors of any society. W. Wynne Mason, a historian of New Zealand POWs, has estimated that one person in every thousand was interned at some point during World War II. Even in that global conflict, armed combat occurred in only a few regions. Internment, on the other hand, occurred in all nations, belligerent and neutral, and affected the lives of people thousands of miles from the firing lines.

Any discussion of captivity in wartime must account for the fact that, throughout history, there have been many kinds of prisoners, each of which experienced different treatment. Most notable (and certainly most glamorous in terms of modern culture) have been prisoners of war, called POWs, members of a recognized military body captured during wartime. *POW* is apparently a straightforward classification that should admit of little controversy, but even within this group, a number of subcategories have evolved. Guerrilla fighters and merchant mariners are, to varying degrees, combatants, but their status as POWs has been the subject of considerable debate. The status of camp followers, civilians who attach themselves to armies to provide services or for personal reasons, has also been unclear. Even legitimate POWs have sometimes found their status called into question. The Allied powers in World War II created other categories to cope with the massive numbers of enemy soldiers captured. Some of them were classed as Disarmed Enemy Forces (DEF) or Surrendered Enemy Personnel (SEP), artificial distinctions that relieved the Allies of according them all the rights of official POWs. By the same token, Italian soldiers captured by the Allies were often classified not as POWs but as military internees, another dubious distinction that owed more to the demands of the moment than anything else. Finally, war captivity has also involved civilians who have been interned for a variety of reasons. While they are not prisoners of war in the strictest sense, they have certainly been prisoners in wartime.

Over the millennia, there have been many changes in captivity as it affected these various groups. Most striking are the improvements in international law, which have created a broad and complex network of largely nongovernmental organizations to monitor and improve the conditions of captivity during wartime. But these improvements make it easy to lose sight of a more sobering reality: that, despite the Enlightenment, notions of progress, and the evolution of a humanitarian spirit, there is far more continuity than change in the institution of war captivity.

For centuries, all people were vulnerable to enslavement or massacre. War was total war, waged by societies rather than armies; soldiers were captured, but so, too, were women, children, the elderly, and the infirm. The population of a vanquished city was essentially a kind of plunder, no different from gold or oxen or implements, that belonged to the conquering armies. If the victorious commander had a use for his human trophies, either as slaves or to augment his own community's population, they would live. If not, or if they had offended him by resisting conquest, they would be quickly dispatched. Human history is full of accounts of entire populations being taken into slavery or put to the sword.

In the early modern era, and particularly with the great liberal revolutions in America and France, the situation began to change. Following trends that originated with international jurists, there evolved a distinction between combatant and noncombatant, and between combatant and commander. Wars were fought by people's armies, but no longer was it assumed that a subjugated population was one of the spoils of war. Civilians, provided they took no active part in hostilities, were deemed to be inviolate. Furthermore, it was recognized that the soldier was essentially an employee of his commander. Military considerations demanded that soldiers be removed from action if captured, but humanity demanded that they not be treated unduly harshly. After all, the opposing leader was the real enemy; the soldier was merely a worker.

Despite occasional lapses (Napoleon Bonaparte, for example, had no compunction about interning British civilians in France or slaughtering thousands of Arab prisoners at Jaffa in 1799), such notions persisted until the world wars of the twentieth century. During these global conflicts the distinction between combatant and noncombatant was broken down, a development that had been foreshadowed by events of the Philippine-American and Boer Wars. In World War I, civilians were once again vulnerable to internment, and World War II took the process to new lengths, with the imprisonment, enslavement, and massacre of millions of people, combatants and noncombatants alike. On the surface, this might seem to be a characteristic of an alarming new trend in warfare, but in fact it was merely a throwback to centuries-old practices.

There is now one new element in the mix, however: ethnicity. When wars were primarily political or ideological struggles, it was relatively easy for captives to change sides. For centuries, prisoners were encouraged to join the armies of their captors. For the detaining power, this was a simple method of securing new soldiers after a costly campaign; for the captives, it was a way to save their own lives while continuing to receive a soldier's wage. In the modern world, this would be considered defection, but in reality it was simply an expedient that allowed countless prisoners to escape death.

Defection was also encouraged in ideological wars; to convert or "turn" a prisoner to one's side was a propaganda victory that proved not only the appeal of one's own ideology, but also the bankruptcy of the enemy's ideology. Germany, the Soviet Union, and Japan all went to great lengths to convert prisoners to their own ideologies during World War II. In practical terms, their efforts largely failed; tens of thousands of POWs were turned, but they tended to make poor soldiers in the service of their erstwhile enemies and were rarely an asset on the battlefield. In propaganda terms, however, the numerical results were thought to justify the effort, for each convert was proof of the superiority of National Socialism, Communism, or the Great East Asia Co-Prosperity Sphere.

Generally speaking, changing sides is no longer an option in the increasingly ethnic and racial conflicts of the post-1945 era. One cannot simply change one's ethnicity in the event of capture; indeed, it is the very fact of ethnicity that distinguishes friend from foe. Furthermore, it is increasingly clear that there is no such thing as a noncombatant in ethnic wars. The genocides in Rwanda and the former Yugoslavia reveal the degree to which all people, regardless of age, gender, and combatant status, are vulnerable to imprisonment, abuse, and execution. But here again, even though race is a modern notion, there is a strong sense of continuity. If there is one striking feature of these genocides, it is the degree to which they are reminiscent of the attitudes toward captives in the ancient world.

As the international community has had to come to terms with racial or ethnic aspects of captivity, it has also had to come to terms with cultural factors. Simply put, not all societies share the Western belief in the sanctity of a prisoner's life. This reality has historically been troublesome to Western armies that encountered other societies, whether it be in the Americas, Africa, or Asia. Does one adopt the enemy's often brutal practices in dealing with prisoners, or does one attempt to instill in the enemy a respect for captives' lives? Typically, Western armies adopted the former course, maintaining that natives expected to be treated brutally and took anything else as a sign of weakness. But developments in international law have tended to advance the latter course and to force other societies to accept Western notions of acceptable conduct. The conundrum here is obvious. It is all well and good to lament the fact that Japan did not abide by the Geneva Convention in its treatment of prisoners during World War II, but scholars have pointed out that the treatment was an outgrowth of Japanese cultural and military traditions dating back hundreds of years. In this sense, international law, while attempting to protect POWs, has incidentally attempted to legislate away centuries-old cultural practices. Some observers have seen this as progress, while to others it smacks of cultural imperialism.

There is another cultural dimension to captivity that bears mention. The fact that captivity has been such a universal experience has made it a ubiquitous presence in popular culture, where the images are instantly recognizable to millions. Steve McQueen attempting to leap into neutral Switzerland on his motorcycle after escaping from Stalag Luft 3 *(The Great Escape)*, Alec Guinness destroying the bridge that he and his fellow POWs had labored so hard to build *(The Bridge on the River Kwai)*, even Sergeant Schultz insisting, "I know nothing, nothing!" *(Hogan's Heroes)*—these are all part of the lexicon of modern culture. That some of them bear only the faintest resemblance to reality has been largely irrelevant to the viewers.

But even this is not a new trend in popular culture. In the seventeenth and eighteenth centuries, European settlers in North America used the captivity narrative as an object lesson; such narratives were published by the hundreds, almost always with the same basic elements. After the U.S. Civil War, the treatment of POWs by the Confederacy was transformed into a bloody shirt to be waved at every conceivable opportunity. After World War I, the British turned the escape story into a minor literary genre not unlike the colonial captivity narrative. The escape story, too, was in effect a simple morality play that pitted British pluck and ingenuity against German or Turkish perfidy and oafishness. All of these trends foreshadowed the dominance of captivity in popular culture after 1945.

The emergence of television, however, has added a new ingredient into the mix. Images of captivity—from the bruised faces of captured United Nations airmen during the Persian Gulf War to scenes from Bosnian detention camps to images of Western hostages held in Iraq—now come directly into our homes in a way that they could not in earlier times. These images, in all their harsh realism, have served to temper our often distorted views of prisoners. What impact this will have on captivity over the long term remains to be seen. Even the most violent regimes of the twentieth century have been aware of the importance of good public relations. The Japanese in World War II had no qualms about brutalizing prisoners, but they were very keen to ensure that the brutalization was hidden from the prying eyes of neutral observers; the same was true of Nazi Germany. But it is also true that prisoners can be used as trophies, as they often were in ancient history. Putting them on display on the television or the Internet is a way for captors to demonstrate their ability to strike at will or, in effect, to thumb their noses at their enemies. The technology is new, but the reality behind it is not: The prisoner is always the most powerless of pawns.

The fact remains that, even with the improvements in international law and the increasing difficulty of committing crimes in secret, prisoners remain at the mercy of their captors just as they were thousands of years ago. A government that is benevolent toward POWs will be benevolent with or without legislation or inspection; a regime that is determined to mistreat prisoners will do so regardless of any strictures or sanctions. This fact does not make the attempt to protect prisoners any less worthy, but it does put it into the proper perspective.

CONTRIBUTORS

Michael J. Allen
North Carolina State University
Raleigh, North Carolina

Richard H. Beal
Oriental Institute
University of Chicago
Chicago, Illinois

Victoria Belco
University of California
Berkeley, California

Alexander M. Bielakowski
Command and General Staff College
Fort Leavenworth, Kansas

Christopher Blackburn
The University of Louisiana at Monroe
Monroe, Louisiana

Scott Blanchette
San Diego, California

Lori Bogle
United States Naval Academy
Annapolis, Maryland

Michael Booker
Mitcham, Surrey, England

Jorg Bottger
Hamburg, Germany

Wayne Bowen
Ouachita Baptist University
Arkadelphia, Arkansas

Graham Broad
The University of Western Ontario
London, Ontario, Canada

Kara Brown
Thames Valley District School Board
London, Ontario, Canada

Jon Brudvig
University of Mary
Bismarck, North Dakota

Colin Burgess
Bonnet Bay, Australia

Andrew Burtch
Carleton University
Ottawa, Ontario, Canada

Roger Chapman
Lincoln Trail College
Robinson, Illinois

Tim Clarkson
University of Manchester
Manchester, England

Craig T. Cobane
Western Kentucky University
Bowling Green, Kentucky

Steve Cocks
2nd Battalion Scots Guards
Falkland Islands, 1982

Tony Dawes
(1921-1998)
Prisoner of war, Italy and Germany,1941-1945

Tanya Demjanenko
Toronto, Ontario, Canada

Guillaume de Syon
Albright College
Reading, Pennsylvania
Laurent Ditmann
Atlanta, Georgia

Robert C. Doyle
Franciscan University
Steubenville, Ohio

Mark A. Eaton
The University of Western Ontario
London, Ontario, Canada

Lars Ericson
Military Archives
Stockholm, Sweden

Sarah Fishman
University of Houston
Houston, Texas

Max Paul Friedman
Florida State University
Tallahassee, Florida

Douglas G. Gardner
Miami University Hamilton
Hamilton, Ohio

Daniel German
Library and Archives Canada
Ottawa, Ontario, Canada

Wendy Jo Gertjejanssen
Twin Cities, Minnesota

Sarah Glassford
York University
Toronto, Ontario, Canada

Matthew Gonzales
Saint Anselm College
Manchester, New Hampshire

Julie V. Gottlieb
University of Sheffield
Sheffield, England

Amanda Green
The University of Western Ontario
London, Ontario, Canada

David S. Green
University of Nottingham
Nottingham, England

Dorotea Gucciardo
The University of Western Ontario
London, Ontario, Canada

Wesley Gustavson
The University of Western Ontario
London, Ontario, Canada

B. Alan Guthrie III
Delmont, Pennsylvania

Bertil Häggman, LL.M.
Swedish Authors' Union
Helsingborg, Sweden

William T. Hartley
University of Tennessee
Knoxville, Tennessee

Susan M. Hawthorne
Brynteg School
Bridgend, Wales

David Hay
University of Lethbridge
Lethbridge, Alberta, Canada

Jennifer Ho
Mississauga, Ontario, Canada

Craig Howes
University of Hawai'i at Moanoa
Honolulu, Hawai'i

Teresa Iacobelli
The University of Western Ontario
London, Ontario, Canada

Andrew Iarocci
Wilfrid Laurier University
Waterloo, Ontario, Canada

Alexander Ingle
University of Michigan
Ann Arbor, Michigan

Mark Janson
Brockville, Ontario, Canada

Ronald J. Joy
Dartmoor Prison Historian (retired)
Tavistock, Devon, England

Betje Black Klier
Latin Gulf South Research
Austin, Texas

Arnold Krammer
Texas A&M University
College Station, Texas

Robert S. La Forte
University of North Texas
Denton, Texas

Mark L. Lilleleht
University of Wisconsin
Madison, Wisconsin

Erik R. Lofgren
Bucknell University
Lewisburg, Pennsylvania

Brad Lucas
Texas Christian University
Forth Worth, Texas

Elaine McKinnon
University of West Georgia
Carrollton, Georgia

S.P. MacKenzie
University of South Carolina
Columbia, South Carolina

John Maker
University of Ottawa
Ottawa, Ontario, Canada

J. Peters Mersereau
Dalhousie University
Halifax, Nova Scotia, Canada

Dwight R. Messimer
California State University
San Jose, California

Anne M.E. Millar
The University of Western Ontario
London, Ontario, Canada

Esmorie Miller
Research in Motion
Waterloo, Ontario, Canada

Stephen M. Miller
University of Maine
Orono, Maine

Tracy Moore
CityTV
Toronto, Ontario, Canada

Reinhard Nachtigal
University of Freiburg
Freiburg, Germany

Simon Nantais
University of Victoria
Victoria, British Columbia, Canada

Robert D. Necci
Vietnam Veterans of America
National POW/MIA Committee
Bohemia, New York

Tom Nichols
United States Naval War College
Newport, Rhode Island

Patrick M. O'Neil
Broome Community College
Binghamton, New York

Rüdiger Overmans
Freiburg, Germany

Forrest D. Pass
The University of Western Ontario
London, Ontario, Canada

Matthew E. Pearson
Vancouver, British Columbia

Gervase Phillips
Manchester Metropolitan University
Manchester, England

Alon Rachamimov
Tel Aviv University
Tel Aviv, Israel

David Ray
Rugby School
Rugby, Warwickshire, England

William S. Reeder Jr.
Prisoner of war, Vietnam, 1972-1973
Seabeck, Washington

Roy Robson
University of the Sciences in Philadelphia
Philadelphia, Pennsylvania

Charles G. Roland
Hannah Professor Emeritus, History of Medicine
McMaster University
Hamilton, Ontario, Canada

Charles W. Sanders, Jr.
Kansas State University
Manhattan, Kansas

Margaret Sankey
Minnesota State University
Moorhead, Minnesota

Elizabeth D. Schafer
Loachapoka, Alabama

Aldona Sendzikas
The University of Western Ontario
London, Ontario, Canada

George Sheppard
Upper Canada College
Toronto, Ontario, Canada

E.P. Smith
(1919-1999)
Prisoner of war, Singapore and Japan, 1942-1945

J.W. Smith
The Ohio State University
Columbus, Ohio

Thomas L. Smith
Major, U.S. Army, Retired
Gonzaga University
Spokane, Washington

Kevin A. Spooner
Wilfrid Laurier University
Waterloo, Ontario, Canada

Anthony Staunton
Department of Veterans' Affairs
Woden, Australia

Gaius Stern
University of California
Berkeley, California

Geoffrey C. Stewart
The University of Western Ontario
London, Ontario, Canada

Eva-Maria Stolberg
Institute of East European and Russian History
Bonn, Germany

Robert Talbot
University of Ottawa
Ottawa, Ontario, Canada

Andrew Theobald
Queen's University
Kingston, Ontario, Canada

Karim Tiro
Xavier University
Cincinnati, Ohio

Liam van Beek
The University of Western Ontario
London, Ontario, Canada

Andrea Vandenberg
Information Niagara
St. Catharines, Ontario, Canada

Robert Ventresca
King's University College
The University of Western Ontario
London, Ontario, Canada

Wolfram von Scheliha
Hohen Neuendorf, Germany

Vasilis Vourkoutiotis
University of Ottawa
Ottawa, Ontario, Canada

Gillian Weiss
Case Western Reserve University
Cleveland, Ohio

Darryl Wiggers
Corus Entertainment
Toronto, Ontario, Canada

Richard D. Wiggers
Department of Education
Fredericton, New Brunswick, Canada

Gaye Wilson
University of Sydney
Sydney, Australia

Nathan Andrew Wilson
Dalhousie University
Halifax, Nova Scotia, Canada

Yücel Yanīkdağ
Virginia Commonwealth University
Richmond, Virginia

Andrew C. Young
Canadian War Museum
Ottawa, Ontario, Canada

Charles S. Young
Rutgers University
Highland Park, New Jersey

Rafael A. Zagovec
University of Heidelberg
Heidelberg, Germany

Jelica Zdero
The University of Western Ontario
London, Ontario, Canada

Pingchao Zhu
University of Idaho
Moscow, Idaho

Encyclopedia of Prisoners of War and Internment

Entries A - Z

A

Abu Ghraib Prison (Baghdad Correctional Facility)

Abu Ghraib is a city in Iraq approximately 30 kilometers west of Baghdad where the government of Iraq built a 280-acre prison facility in the 1960s. Under Saddam Hussein, Abu Ghraib became a symbol of the ruling Ba'ath party's tyranny. Saddam's security services dispatched countless thousands of real and suspected enemies of the state there during his 24-year reign. In 2004, the prison became the focal point of an enormous scandal involving American abuse of prisoners following the U.S.-led invasion that liberated Iraq from Saddam's regime.

For decades, Abu Ghraib figured prominently in human rights reports from Iraq. In the 1980s, Amnesty International catalogued thousands of reported cases of abuse, brutal interrogation, forced starvation, and torture, as well as innumerable "disappearances" and extrajudicial executions occurring inside Abu Ghraib. Conditions did not improve after Iraq's defeat in the 1991 Gulf War; if anything, the regime's survival emboldened it to take even more repressive measures against dissent. In the 1990s, thousands of alleged enemies of the state (including large numbers of Sh'ia Muslims and Kurds who had risen against Saddam following his army's expulsion from Kuwait in March 1991) were sent to Abu Ghraib, and reports of torture and execution continued. In 1998, Amnesty International reported that several hundred inmates, many of them political prisoners of the regime nearing the end of their sentences, had been suddenly executed there the previous November. As late as 2001, approximately 15,000 inmates were held in the prison, many for political reasons. However, with war against the United States imminent, Saddam Hussein announced a general amnesty, and in October 2002 most prisoners throughout Iraq were released. Abu Ghraib was largely abandoned, and files pertaining to past prisoners were hurriedly burned by prison officials and staff. Hence, it is probable that the fate of many who "disappeared" inside Abu Ghraib will never be known.

In March 2003 an American-led military coalition invaded Iraq, quickly brushing aside Iraqi military opposition and seizing Baghdad. Saddam's government disintegrated within three weeks, although Saddam himself was not apprehended until December. Subsequently, Abu Ghraib, renamed with typical bureaucratic loquaciousness the "Baghdad Central Confinement Facility," was reactivated by the Americans to serve as a detention center for Iraqi prisoners of war, insurgents, and suspected terrorists. By year's end, more than 5,000 Iraqis were held in the facility.

In January 2004 the U.S. Army commenced an investigation into reports of abuse and torture being committed by American military personnel at Abu Ghraib after receiving testimony and a compact disc of photographic evidence from a member of the military police. In late April, the American television program *60 Minutes II* and the journalist Seymour Hersh, writing in the online edition of *The New Yorker,* exposed to the public the abuse and torture of Iraqi prisoners by American military personnel. Thus began a series of revelations that engulfed the U.S. armed forces, the Department of Defense, and the Presidency itself in scandal. Published photographs of U.S. service personnel intimidating, sexually humiliating, and in some cases beating prisoners or threatening them with dogs shocked many Americans accustomed to regarding their armed forces as defenders of human rights. In addition, the revelation of these crimes did incalculable damage to the moral credibility of the American cause. Henceforth, the claim that the United States had invaded Iraq to liberate its citizens from tyranny would, throughout much of the world, be dismissed as self-serving hypocrisy.

In some cases the instances of abuse and torture occurred during interrogations to extract "actionable intelligence" from prisoners, but in others it appears to have had no motive apart from abject sadism. While decrying the incidents, U.S. President George W. Bush and Secretary of Defense Donald Rumsfeld stressed that only a handful of poorly trained and ill-supervised individuals were directly responsible for the abuse (neither Bush nor Rumsfeld would deign to use the word "torture"). Subsequent accusations regarding similar incidents in American detention facilities in Iraq, Afghanistan, Cuba, and, indeed, at various "secret" facilities utilized in the War on Terror, have led many to suspect that the Abu Ghraib incidents may have been more systemic.

In all, 17 soldiers were relieved of duty and seven charged under military law. The prison's commanding officer, Brigadier General Janice Karpinsky, was demoted to colonel, while as of December 2005 two soldiers, Specialist Charles Garner and Private Lynndie England, have received jail terms of 10 and three years, respectively.

For opponents of the war, Abu Ghraib has become a symbol for everything morally and pragmatically wrong with U.S. policy in Iraq. The irony, however, is that American treatment of prisoners in Abu Ghraib, appalling though it was, actually constituted an improvement over the former regime's, but few opponents of the Iraq War had ever heard of the facility before April 2003.

See also Hussein; Saddam Iran-Iraq War; Gulf War; Iraq War; Torture; War on Terror

References

Abu Ghraib: The Politics of Torture (Berkeley, CA: North Atlantic Books, 2004).

Amnesty International, *International Report 1980, 1984, 1989, 1998, 2005* (London: Amnesty International Publications).

Seymour Hersh, *Chain of Command: The Road from 9/11 to Abu Ghraib* (New York: HarperCollins, 2004).

Human Rights Watch, *Human Rights in Iraq* (New Haven, CT: Yale University Press, 1990).

Michael Martin, *The Iraqi Prisoner Abuse Scandal* (Farmington Hills, MI: Lucent Books, 2005).

National Commission on Terrorist Attacks Upon the United States, *The Taguba Report – Article 15-6: Investigation of the 800th Military Police Brigade* (New York: Cosimo Books, 2004).

Steven Strasser, ed., *The Abu Ghraib Investigations: The Official Independent Panel and Pentagon Reports on the Shocking Prisoner Abuse in Iraq* (New York: Perseus Publishing, 2004).

—*Graham Broad*

Accommodation

Detaining powers face many challenges when handling prisoners of war and civilian internees, not the least of which is the need to provide accommodation, or living quarters for captives. In some conflicts, belligerents are able to make advance preparations, but more often, arrangements must be made much more hastily. As a result, prisoners have usually been housed in structures that have been hurriedly converted to prisons rather than in camps specially designed for internment.

For centuries, belligerent nations have agreed on a number of practices for the release of prisoners, all of which have been intended, in part, to solve the problem of having to provide accommodation. Until the twentieth century, there was widespread use of parole, whereby, upon giving a pledge not to fight again, prisoners would be released, either to their home country or to arrange their own lodging in the enemy state. Many prisoner exchanges, often on the basis of numerical equality, also allowed prisoners to return to their homes. At the other end of the spectrum, it was not uncommon for prisoners to be massacred. This, like exchange and parole, was a way to

A typical hut that accommodated Allied POWs on the Burma-Thailand Railway in World War II (Australian War Memorial 157878)

relieve a belligerent state of the burden of housing prisoners.

However, if exchange or parole could not be agreed upon and if execution offended the sensibilities of the state, it had no choice but to provide accommodation for prisoners. In the worst-case scenario, when an enemy collapsed suddenly or an offensive was more successful than predicted, a belligerent government would suddenly be faced with masses of prisoners to house. This was the case at certain points during the U.S. Civil War, during the German spring offensive in the summer of 1918, after the fall of France in 1940, and after the fall of Germany in 1945. In each instance, prisoners bore the brunt of the lack of preparations. They endured long and exhausting treks, only to discover there were no buildings to shelter them. When the first Union prisoners reached Andersonville, Georgia, in February 1864, there were no barracks; POWs slept in the open air, dug holes in the ground, or cobbled together rude shelters from scraps of lumber they found. The situation was the same for the hundreds of thousands of German soldiers who surrendered when the Nazi state collapsed in 1945; there were simply not enough buildings available to house them, so many spent weeks living in open fields without shelter. Prisoners of the Japanese in World War II, sent to Thailand to work on the Death Railway, found that they had to build their own camps. Their captors provided the tools, but they had to clear the jungle and erect the barracks themselves.

Wherever possible, detaining powers have adapted other structures to serve as prisons. Of course, there is nothing inherently wrong with this practice: Provided there is sufficient time to complete the arrangements, a converted camp can be quite adequate. Indeed, millions of prisoners have been incarcerated in camps that had once been something else. Perhaps the most common practice has been to convert a military establishment into a prison camp. During World War I, the German government did this at a former cavalry school at Bischofswerda and at a former training school for noncommissioned officers at Friedberg. Disused industrial buildings were also used frequently, although they were not particularly well suited to the task. They were large and could easily accommodate many prisoners, but considerable effort was generally required to make them habitable, and the detaining power was often not willing to expend that effort. In the U.S. Civil War, the prison at Cahaba, Alabama, had once been a cotton warehouse. British POWs confined in Halle in World War I were dismayed to discover that their camp had once been an iron foundry; there were no proper sanitary facilities, and the room that served as a mess hall had a dirt floor. Castles have also been natural choices: Portchester Castle in England held French POWs during the Napoleonic Wars, and during World War II, the German military made prison camps out of many castles, including Colditz, Königstein, Spangenberg, and Laufen. But there were also many strange conversions. In World War I, the British government converted London's Alexandra Palace, a huge, glass-roofed exhibition hall, into a prison for 5,000 civilian internees. Oflag 21B at Schubin in eastern Germany was a former girls' school that held Allied POWs during World War II. Cu Loc prison in southwest Hanoi (known to its American inmates as "the Zoo") had been a film studio before it was converted to hold American POWs captured in the Vietnam War.

Conditions in POW camps have obviously varied, but this variation is largely related to issues unconnected with the nature of the camps themselves; virtually any converted structure can be made comfortable, provided that the detaining power is inclined to do so. The only type of prison camp that is by its nature less than inhabitable is, oddly enough, the converted military fortress. British prisoners captured during the Napoleonic Wars lived in a number of French fortifications, like Verdun citadel and the fortresses at Bitche, Valenciennes, Arras, Besançon, and Auxonne. Fortresses in eastern Germany, like Thorn (Torun), Zinna, Posen (Poznan), and Graudenz (Grudziadz), held Allied prisoners during both world wars. In such places, cold, damp, and dank conditions were undeniably inimical to prisoners' health.

Less significant numerically but equally important in historical terms were camps built specifically as prisons. These have a longer lineage than might be imagined, and as a consequence, it is not unknown for prison camps to be used in more than one war. Mill Prison in Devon, in southern England, had first served as a POW camp during the War of the League of Augsburg (1688–1697). Later, permanent buildings were erected there to house prisoners during the War of the Austrian Succession (1740–1748), and those same buildings housed American prisoners during the American Revolution. Lamsdorf, in eastern Germany, served as a prison camp in both World War I and II, and conditions were equally bad in both wars. One unlucky British prisoner even had the misfortune to be imprisoned in Lamsdorf in both wars.

However, most camps built as prisons were never intended to be permanent. Dozens of camps in Nazi Germany, for example, were built according to a standard plan and consisted of the same basic elements: long wooden barracks divided into small sleeping and common rooms; high barbed-wire fences, often with a low warning wire running around the inside of the fence to create a danger zone close to the wire; guard towers around the perimeter; a lavatory block; common buildings to be used for recreation or study; and adjacent compounds for the punishment block and the camp staff offices. Camps of roughly the same design were constructed in Britain, Canada, the United States, and Australia, so that it is almost possible to speak of a common style of prison-camp architecture for this period. Most of these camps were dismantled soon after the war, although some have been retained (either whole or in part) as museums.

International law has gradually been improved to ensure that POWs are housed in the most favorable conditions possible. The 1907 Hague Convention allowed that prisoners "may be interned in a town, fortress, camp, or other place" (Article 5), but it did not specify that these places of internment should be healthy or safe. The 1929 Geneva Convention Relative to the Treatment of Prisoners of War was a considerable improvement. It stipulated that prisoners should be lodged "in buildings or in barracks affording all possible guarantees of hygiene or healthfulness" and that the quarters should be dry, heated, lighted, and protected against fire. The dormitories themselves, with respect to the bedding, floor space, and area, should be comparable to the dormitories of the detaining power's own troops (Article 10). The 1949 Geneva Convention Relative to the Treatment of Prisoners of War went even further to allow for cultural differences, requiring that detaining powers should make allowances for the habits and customs of prisoners; should the accommodation provided for their own troops be insufficient to maintain the health of their POWs, they were bound to improve the standards for prisoners (Article 25).

—Jonathan F. Vance

AFGHAN WARS

The series of imperial conflicts called the Afghan Wars, which spanned over a century, witnessed tremendous variations in the treatment of prisoners. The treatment meted out to captured Afghan tribesmen, British soldiers and civilians, Indian sepoys, and prisoners captured during recent Russian and United States operations in Afghanistan is a study in contrasts.

During the first British campaign into Afghanistan (1839–1842), undertaken to ensure that the region did not fall under the sway of Russia or Persia, the British Army of the Indus had neither the supplies nor the inclination to intern the 1,600 Afghan fighters captured at the Battle of Ghazni, near Kabul; they were simply disarmed, rebuked, and released. The Afghans themselves were not so lenient. Captured Indian sepoys were typically massacred on the spot (for example, after the sieges of Kahan and Charikar), along with any women, children, and camp followers unlucky enough to be with them. The same fate often awaited British officers and soldiers who fell into Afghan hands, although the more valuable of them were retained for ransom. Perhaps the most famous hostages of the war were in a group that included Lady Florentia Sale, the wife of a senior general in the Indian Army. Captured with dozens of other prominent hostages after the retreat from Kabul in January 1842, she remained a captive in generally tolerable conditions until September 1842, when a relief column led by her husband freed her and the 121 surviving hostages.

Britain launched the second Afghan war in 1878, for much the same reasons as the first, and the conflict saw a deterioration in the treatment of prisoners. In the Afghan attack on the British Resident in Kabul and his escort in September 1879, the entire garrison was killed, moving British General F. S. Roberts to embark upon a campaign of retribution when he recaptured Kabul in October. He admitted to ordering the execution of 87 Afghan hostages (the actual figure may well have been higher) as punishment and was also accused of a host of other abuses, including denying quarter and torturing prisoners. Roberts strenuously denied these charges, and they have never been satisfactorily proven.

A century later, the Soviet invasion of Afghanistan in December 1979 wrote a new chapter in the ill-treatment of prisoners. Soviet soldiers and civilian workers captured by the mujahideen, the Afghan freedom fighters, were routinely tortured and executed (a few were spared when they converted to Islam), despite the urging of the International Committee of the Red Cross that the Geneva Convention be observed. The rebels argued that, since the Kabul government treated captured mujahideen as political prisoners rather than as prisoners of war, captured Soviets did not deserve protection under the laws of war. Eventually, the mujahideen were convinced to trade some Soviet prisoners for weapons and supplies and to transfer others to Switzerland, where they would be held on parole for two years or until the occupation ended. As of November 1988, the Soviets were still seeking information on 311 missing soldiers. For their part, the mujahideen inquired about some 35,000 of their fighters, who were either dead or in Afghan jails. Not until December 1991 did the first formal prisoner releases take place: four Soviet POWs were released in exchange for 100 political detainees held by the government in Kabul.

The most recent invasion of Afghanistan occurred in the wake of the terror attacks on the United States on 11 September 2001. The Taliban regime that controlled Afghanistan was known to be sympathetic to the terrorist organization known as Al Qaeda, and had allowed its training camps to operate in the country. U.S. President George W. Bush issued an ultimatum to the Taliban demanding that they turn over all Al Qaeda leaders, close the training camps, and release all foreign nationals (including a number of American Christian missionaries) they were holding captive. The Taliban refused to accede to the demands, and U.S. and British air strikes began on 7 October 2001. The aerial campaign against military, communications, and command and control targets continued until 9 November, when ground troops of the anti-Taliban Northern Alliance began a land offensive. On 7 December, the last major city controlled by the Taliban, Kandahar, fell to the Alliance, marking the end of the first phase of the war. Since then, U.S., Afghani, and coalition forces have been deployed to eliminate pockets of Taliban resistance, search for Al Qaeda members, and return peace and stability to Afghanistan.

Afghanistan was the first battleground in the so-called War on Terror, and it brought into focus many difficult issues regarding the treatment of captives in this new kind of conflict. There was the general question of whether prisoners taken in Afghanistan were to be considered as POWs, with the protection of the Geneva Convention. The U.S. government definitively answered this question on 7 February 2002 when a White House spokesman declared that neither Taliban soldiers nor Al Qaeda fighters would be granted POW status, although they would be treated humanely in the spirit of international law. This would include meals that accorded with Muslim dietary law, opportunities to perform religious observances, the ability to send and receive mail, and monitoring visits from representatives of the International Committee of the Red Cross (ICRC). Prisoners would be held in two detention facilities in Afghanistan, at Bagram military air base and in Kandahar, although suspected Al Qaeda members were transferred to the facility at Guantánamo Bay, Cuba.

From the beginning of the war, however, there were reports of prisoner abuse, starting with the summary execution of over 500 captured Taliban fighters by troops of the Northern Alliance in the city of Mazar-e-Sharif. There were allegations, still unconfirmed, that in December 2001, Northern Alliance and U.S. troops were responsible for the deaths of hundreds of Taliban prisoners as they were being transferred from the fallen city of Kunduz to a prison in northern Afghanistan. In June 2004, a Central Intelligence Agency (CIA) contractor became the first civilian to face criminal charges relating to the abuse of prisoners of Afghanistan; he was charged with four counts of assault in the death of a prisoner at an American base the previous July (in November 2005, his request for new legal counsel was rejected by a judge, who ordered the trial to proceed). In February 2005, the American Civil Liberties Union released documents alleging that Taliban prisoners held near another American base were abused and made to endure mock executions.

But the most controversial episode occurred at Qala-i-Jangi, a nineteenth-century fortress that had been converted into a makeshift prison. On 24 November

2001 hundreds of Taliban soldiers surrendered to a Northern Alliance general and were transported to Qala-i-Jangi. But the guards had neglected to search the prisoners for weapons, and in separate attacks, two Taliban captives blew themselves up with grenades, also killing two Alliance commanders. The following day, a delegate of the ICRC arrived to register the prisoners and gain assurances that they would be treated humanely. At the same time, two American CIA agents also arrived at Qala-i-Jangi to identify Al Qaeda members, but instead the agents were overwhelmed by the prisoners; one was killed, while the other escaped to warn the Alliance forces that the prisoners had taken over Qala-i-Jangi and, more dangerously, its armory. Facing a determined enemy that was now heavily armed, the local U.S. commander called in missile strikes on the prison. The strikes, augmented by air attacks, continued until 27 November, when it was determined that the surviving prisoners were incapable of further resistance. U.S., British, and Alliance soldiers entered the prison, where, according to a correspondent from *TIME* magazine, they found only 86 of the captives left alive. One of the survivors was the now notorious "Taliban American," John Walker Lyndh.

See also Guantánamo Bay Detention Centre; Lyndh, John Walker; War on Terror

References

Dayna Curry and Heather Mercer, *Prisoners of Hope: The Story of Our Captivity and Freedom in Afghanistan* (New York: Doubleday, 2002).

Vincent Eyre, *Journal of an Afghanistan Prisoner* (London: Routledge and Kegan Paul, 1976 [1842]).

T. A. Heathcote, *The Afghan Wars, 1839–1919* (London: Osprey, 1980).

Edgar O'Ballance, *Afghan Wars: What Britain Gave Up and the Soviet Union Lost* (New York: Brassey's, 1993).

Florentia Sale, *The First Afghan War* (Harlow: Longmans, 1969 [1843]).

Philip Smucker, *Al Qaeda's Great Escape: The Military and the Media on Terror's Trail* (Dulles, VA: Potomac Books, 2004).

—*Jonathan F. Vance*

Agincourt Massacre

The Agincourt massacre, which occurred during the Hundred Years War between England and France, was indicative of the often harsh treatment meted out to prisoners during the Middle Ages. In the late stages of the Battle of Agincourt, on 25 October 1415, the English King Henry V gave an order to kill those prisoners who had already been taken. This action was provoked by a raid on the English baggage train and the massing of French troops by the counts of Masle and Fauquemberghes, apparently to charge the disorganized English line. The French prisoners, standing on a battlefield strewn with discarded weaponry, posed a potential threat should this attack have developed.

However, Henry's noble men-at-arms refused to carry out his instructions, either because they were pledged to protect the lives of men whose surrender they had accepted or because they feared the loss of their prisoners' ransoms. In any event, it was 200 archers who set about the grim task. It is most likely that the intention was not actually to kill large numbers of the captives but to terrorize them into obedience and to hustle them away from the battlefield. It is unclear how many men were killed, but the majority of captives certainly survived the battle. When it became apparent that no French counterattack would take place, Henry immediately ordered the killings to stop.

None of Henry's contemporaries saw fit to condemn him over the fate of those prisoners who had died. One French chronicler blamed his own countrymen, arguing that their futile late rally had made the slaughter inevitable. Indeed, the French themselves had unfurled the Oriflamme, the red war-banner that proclaimed that they did not intend to give quarter. Brutal as this killing of captives undoubtedly was, contemporaries did not judge it unlawful, nor did it necessarily run counter to their notions of chivalry. By the harsh standards of fifteenth-century warfare, the killing of the prisoners was accepted as a tactical necessity.

See also Hundred Years War

References
Alfred H. Burne, *The Agincourt War* (London: Eyre and Spottiswoode, 1956).
John Keegan, *The Face of Battle* (London: Jonathan Cape, 1976).
Michael Prestwich, *Armies and Warfare in the Middle Ages: The English Experience* (New Haven: Yale University Press, 1996).

—*Gervase Phillips*

ALLEN, ETHAN (1738–1789)

The son of Connecticut farmers, Allen gained his first military experience during the French and Indian War, but developed a reputation as something of a troublemaker among the elites of New York for his efforts to settle the Green Mountain district. He remained an outlaw until May 1775, when he and a few hundred irregular troops from Vermont, known as the Green Mountain Boys, captured Fort Ticonderoga from the British in one of the first successful battles of the American Revolution. Emboldened by this success, Allen looked north to Montreal, where he believed he could strike the British with an attack against the weakly defended city. But the September 1775 operation, which involved New Englanders, discontented French Canadians, and native warriors, was ill advised and poorly organized, and Allen soon found himself a prisoner.

The British disliked their new captive, as much for his victory at Ticonderoga as for his attempts to raise natives and French Canadians against them, and General Robert Prescott's first instinct was to shoot him on the spot. Cooler heads prevailed, however, and Allen was clapped in irons and imprisoned in the hold of a ship with some of his men. Not knowing what to do with their famous prisoner, the British shuttled him around—to Ireland, Madeira, North Carolina, Halifax—before landing him in New York, where he joined the 3,000 other prisoners who had recently been captured at Fort Washington. Eventually, Allen and other officers were granted parole and the leader of the Green Mountain Boys settled on Long Island to await his exchange. But he chafed at the inactivity, and turned to drinking and brawling to pass the time. Then, after learning that his son had died of smallpox, he simply wandered away, thereby breaking his parole. Allen was quickly arrested as a parole violator and placed in solitary confinement in New York. With this, he reached his lowest point. Depressed that the war was passing him by and that, as a prisoner, he was prevented from joining "the list of illustrious American heroes," as he put it, Allen slipped into a deep despair that was not even relieved when he was exchanged for a British colonel in May 1778.

He found solace, however, in writing his memoir, *A Narrative of Colonel Ethan Allen's Captivity*, a hugely popular work that went through eight editions in the two years following its publication in 1779. It was part propaganda (full of virtuous American prisoners and vicious British jailers) and part therapy, for it allowed Allen to cast himself as a hero in captivity who gallantly resisted the British at every turn and whose spirit would not be crushed by abuse. He returned to an active role in Vermont politics, taking control of its military forces from 1778 to 1784 and devoting his energies to fighting for Vermont statehood, but his reputation among his contemporaries was damaged by his resolute and very public atheism. The man who called himself a "clodhopper philosopher" died at Colchester, Vermont, shortly before the outbreak of the French Revolution, of which he would surely have approved.

See also American Revolution

References
Ethan Allen, *A narrative of Col. Ethan Allen's captivity: from the time of his being taken by the British, near Montreal, on the 25th day of September, in the year 1775, to the time of his exchange, on the 6th day of May 1778* (Boston: Draper and Folsom, 1779).
Michael A. Bellesiles, *Revolutionary Outlaws: Ethan Allen and the Struggle for Independence on the*

Early American Frontier (Charlottesville: University Press of Virginia, 1993).
Hugh Moore, *Memoir of Col. Ethan Allen; Containing the Most Interesting Incidents Connected with his Private and Public Career* (Plattsburgh, NY: O.R. Cook, 1834).

—*Jonathan F. Vance*

ALTMARK INCIDENT

On 16 February 1940 a boarding party from the British Royal Navy seized the German supply ship *Altmark* in the territorial waters of then-neutral Norway and freed a number of British POWs. This incident contributed to Nazi Germany's plan to invade Denmark and Norway.

The *Altmark* was a 14,367-ton German tanker converted into an auxiliary warship with a cruising speed of 25 knots and armed with three six-inch guns. In the fall of 1939, it operated as a supply ship for the pocket battleship *Admiral Graf Spee* in the South Atlantic and the Indian Ocean. In addition, the *Altmark* functioned as a transport for the captured crews of British ships sunk by the *Graf Spee*. On 6 December 1939, the *Altmark* separated from the *Graf Spee*, which was scuttled on 17 December 1939 off the coast of Montevideo, Uruguay, in the wake of the Battle of the River Plate. The *Altmark*'s commander, Captain Heinrich Dau, ordered it to set course for home on 24 January 1940. For three weeks the *Altmark*, carrying almost 300 captured British soldiers, went undetected by the British until a reconnaissance plane caught sight of the vessel on 14 February 1940, heading south in Norwegian territorial waters. On 16 February, a British force consisting of the light cruiser *HMS Arethusa* and five destroyers led by *HMS Cossack*, under the command of Captain Phillip Vian, sighted the *Altmark* off the coast of Norway, under escort by two Norwegian patrol boats. An attempt by the British to board the *Altmark* failed because it refused to stop and, instead, took refuge in the Jossing Fjord. The *Cossack* followed it and Vian demanded the release of the POWs, but the Norwegians responded that they had boarded the *Altmark* earlier and had not found any POWs. Vian returned into international waters and requested further instructions from his superiors in London. The First Lord of the Admiralty, Winston Churchill, ordered Vian to offer to escort the *Altmark* and the Norwegian patrol boats back to the port of Bergen and to conduct a search of the German ship there. If this offer was refused, Vian should board the *Altmark* anyway. Vian reentered Jossing Fjord, determined to accomplish his mission even against Norwegian resistance. The Norwegians refused to cooperate but did not prevent the *Cossack* from putting alongside the *Altmark*. An assault party boarded the German vessel. In a short firefight, four Germans were killed and five wounded, and, most importantly for the British, 299 British sailors were freed. The next day, the *Cossack* returned to England.

The Norwegian government protested the violation of its territorial waters by British warships. The British countered the accusation, insisting that Norway had violated international law by allowing a German warship with POWs on board to pass through neutral waters. The *Altmark* incident also raised doubts in Nazi Germany about Norwegian neutrality. As a result, Adolf Hitler demanded an acceleration of preparations for the invasion of Norway.

See also Transportation by Sea

References
Willi Frischauer, *The Altmark Affair* (New York: Macmillan, 1955).
Richard Wiggan, *Hunt the Altmark* (London: Robert Hale, 1990).

—*Jorg Bottger*

AMERICAN CIVIL WAR

See United States Civil War

AMERICAN REVOLUTION (1775–1783)

Military and civilian prisoners of war proved problematic for both the rebellious colonists and the British during the

American Revolution. Neither side had considered how to deal with captured soldiers, officers, and camp followers. The British envisioned a quick victory over the colonists and did not foresee that they would seize and then have to maintain prisoners for an extended time. Because they did not recognize the colonists as being independent, the British government viewed them as traitors and pirates instead of prisoners of war.

The first Revolutionary prisoners were 27 colonists captured at the Battle of Bunker Hill in June 1775. By early 1776, the British had taken numerous colonial POWs during the failed invasion of Quebec. Lord Dunmore's forces in Virginia and General Sir Guy Carleton's troops in Canada seized more American soldiers. According to official reports, the maximum number of colonial prisoners of war held by the British at one time was 5,500. During the periodic lulls in the fighting, the colonial POW population dipped below 1,000.

Most prisoners were immediately paroled if they promised not to rejoin the army, or they were exchanged for British prisoners held by the colonists. If there were suitable buildings close to the battlefield, they were often converted into prisons. If not, the British constructed prisons, as they did at Philadelphia, Charleston, and Savannah. Because the British did not occupy any area but New York City for a lengthy duration, these prisons were abandoned as the troops moved to new theaters of war, and the captives were released, exchanged, or transported. Similarly, the colonists held British prisoners in buildings, stockades, and hastily erected prisons wherever the Americans occupied territory or participated in major engagements. Some captured British officers were allowed to stay in colonists' homes.

British officers recognized that their methods were insufficient to handle the large number of prisoners captured during the summer and autumn of 1776. After his victorious campaigns in New York and New Jersey, General Sir William Howe reported on 13 December 1776 that his troops had gathered 4,430 colonial prisoners, including officers and enlisted soldiers. Although Howe did not mention civilians, any camp followers attached to the colonial forces probably accompanied them to their place of confinement. Realizing that a systematic approach to managing prisoners of war was necessary, leaders from both sides reevaluated how to undertake prisoner collection and maintenance. The administration of POWs was no longer an issue they could ignore.

Howe established the position of Commissary General of Prisoners in 1776 to supervise prisons and arrange for more jails. The commissioner was responsible for developing a code to cover prisoner treatment, rations, medical attention, and supplies of clothing and blankets, and was expected to pursue prisoner exchanges with the colonial forces whenever possible. Howe named a Massachusetts Loyalist, Joshua Loring, as the first commissioner, and Loring had a daily influence on how prisoners were handled. Colonial prisoners of war received daily food equivalent to two-thirds of a British soldier's ration, but most food was of poor quality. Because prisoners complained they were mistreated, colonists vilified Loring, but in reality, Loring did not systematically abuse or neglect prisoners. His poor management, a lack of supplies, and the inadequate state of eighteenth-century medical knowledge resulted in their distress. British military leaders attempted to reform prisons and secure better circumstances for prisoners of war but were unsuccessful during the Revolution. Both sides had corrupt prison administrators; Loring, for example, sold prisoners' provisions for profit, thereby worsening the prisoners' circumstances.

Throughout the war, New York City was the nucleus for British military prisons on land and sea. Initially, American war prisoners were confined in the town's Old Jail, which the British improved and renamed the Provost. A second local jail, New Bridewell, also housed colonial prisoners of war. The influx of colonial prisoners in 1776 swelled the population in these two prisons, and the British adapted sugar warehouses on the waterfront as staging points for newly arrived prisoners. Inmates complained about the intolerable conditions in these poorly ventilated buildings that were not intended to shelter humans. Some prisoners were placed in churches, and structures at King's College and City Hall were converted into temporary prisons to address the shortage of space for colonial war prisoners. Two years later, when fewer prisoners were in the city, these buildings were used as hospitals to care for wounded British soldiers. British leaders willingly paroled American officers who agreed to live in Loyalists' homes around New York City and on Long Island. This arrangement eased crowding in prisons and assured better living quarters for the parolees while they waited to be released.

The British also used prison ships to provide more space for prisoners. When the colonists began privateering raids against British shipping, many American sailors were captured and either impressed into service with the British or kept as prisoners. The British navy, like the army, was not ready to care for prisoners. Officers decided to use an antiquated ship, the *Whitby*, as a prison, removing its fittings to make room for prisoners and securing the craft at Remsen's Mill on western Long Island. Realizing that housing prisoners would be a useful role for ships not sturdy or swift enough for combat, British naval officers ordered more vessels to be prepared and anchored at Long Island's Wallabout Bay and on the Hudson River. Twenty-six prison ships and three hospital boats alleviated some of the pressure to shelter prisoners. Similar ships also moved to other areas of the colonies that the British occupied, such as Charleston, but most prisoners of war were relocated to ships in New York City. The floating prisons were miserable places where men lived in dark, dank cells and endured strict discipline from guards. Diseases spread quickly through the ships' prisoner population, and an estimated 700 prisoners died on these ships.

Colonial crews caught in non-American waters were taken to Great Britain to be confined at Forton Prison in the Portsmouth area or Mill Prison near Plymouth. The prisoners referred to these prisons as "Mill and Fortune." These fortifications were more permanent than floating prisons and contained seamen from Allied nations, such as France, as well as colonial prisoners. Records do not state exactly how many prisoners of war were held on ships and in Great Britain, but scholars estimate that there were as many as 2,500 prisoners in 1777 and 5,300 by 1780. David Sproat, the British Commissary General of Naval Prisoners, worked in New York, deciding the terms for naval prisoners' confinement and arranging exchanges for British sailors. Most colonists found him loathsome, stressing that his policies encouraged guards to be neglectful. During the Revolution, British and colonial leaders constantly disagreed about how prisoners were treated and possible means of exchange. Descriptions of prisons, guards, and prisoners were often biased and tinged by emotion.

The Continental Congress created its own Commissary General of Prisoners to monitor the needs of colonists held in British prisons and to mitigate the harsh conditions they faced. Elias Boudinot, the first Commissary General of Prisoners for the colonists, was commissioned as a lieutenant colonel in the Continental Army. He immediately convinced the British to allow an agent to live permanently in New York City as his representative. This agent, Lewis Pintard, secured and distributed clothes, food, money, and fuel to prisoners to supplement British rations. Such relief work was limited by finances. John Beatty and John Franklin replaced Boudinot and Pintard as commissioner and agent before the Revolution ended. Their efforts helped some New York City prisoners, but those in England were less fortunate. Benjamin Franklin, serving as a diplomat in Paris, decided to locate people in England who would deliver aid to colonial prisoners. He asked David Hartley in Parliament to gauge the prisoners' conditions, offering to refund him any money he gave them. Presbyterian preacher Thomas Wren at Portsmouth and William Hogson, a merchant in London, also took money to the prisoners. Franklin requested more money from Congress, which only granted limited funds. At least one of his agents embezzled relief funds, and guards still served watered-down beer and maggoty beef.

Prisoners could secure their release from captivity in a number of ways. Some tried to escape, but punishment upon recapture was severe and could involve being placed in irons; most prisoners lacked the physical strength and courage to attempt such a feat. Others secured release by enlisting in the enemy's army or navy. British recruiters visited prisons, and some prisoners mistakenly believed that their captors intentionally created awful environments so that inmates would want to enlist or would be so afraid or depressed they would accept any alternative to imprisonment. Many prisoners accepted a parole, agreeing to cease fighting until they were exchanged. Parolees who went home promised to remain neutral and to return to prison if requested. In one instance, Isaac Hayne, a South Carolina militia colonel, was executed for violating parole. Prisoners were exchanged only infrequently because the British refused to establish a policy for routine prisoner repatriations. They feared that acquiescence to such a policy might be seen by other European powers as an acknowledgment of the colonists' independence, and these countries might decide to aid the colonies. George Washington scheduled several conferences, endeavoring to establish formal exchange policies, but the British insisted on partial exchanges in which arrangements for each transfer of prisoners were determined separately, on a case-by-case basis. Washington sought a cartel in which prisoners were regularly and consistently exchanged, but because the British held more colonial prisoners than the colonists held British captives, the Americans lacked the bargaining power to bring this proposal to fruition.

The colonists had been overwhelmed by the need to detain thousands of prisoners from the Convention Army after General John Burgoyne surrendered at Saratoga in 1777, but these prisoners did give the colonists some leverage in discussions about exchanges with the British. In the following years, Britain agreed to a number of exchanges involving several thousand prisoners. At Tappan, New York, on 6 May 1783, after a series of conferences, General George Washington and General Sir Guy Carleton agreed to exchange all remaining prisoners. Two months later, Washington told Secretary of War Benjamin Lincoln that only a few Hessians were still imprisoned. At the same time, Franklin announced that the American prisoners in British prisons had also been freed.

Prisoners of the American Revolution kept diaries during confinement and wrote autobiographies and histories that have been useful primary sources for scholars. Famous prisoners such as Ethan Allen and Nathan Hale became heroes to Americans, while thousands of prisoners returned to homes in America, Britain, Canada, France, and other locations to resume their lives, having been profoundly influenced physically and emotionally by their time spent as prisoners of war.

References

Francis Abell, *Prisoners of War in Britain, 1756–1815* (London: Humphrey Milford, 1914).

Larry G. Bowman, *Captive Americans: Prisoners during the American Revolution* (Athens: Ohio University Press, 1976).

George Carey, ed., *A Sailor's Songbag: An American Rebel in English Prisons, 1777–1779* (Amherst: University of Massachusetts Press, 1976).

Sheldon S. Cohen, *Yankee Sailors in British Jails: Prisoners of War at Forton and Mill, 1777–1783* (Newark: University of Delaware Press, 1995).

William N. Dabney, *After Saratoga: The Story of the Convention Army* (Albuquerque: University of New Mexico Press, 1955).

William R. Lindsey, *Treatment of American Prisoners of War during the Revolution* (Emporia, KS: School of Graduate and Professional Studies of the Kansas State Teachers College, 1973).

Charles Metzger, *The Prisoner in the American Revolution* (Chicago: Loyola University Press, 1971).

Louis Arthur Norton, *Joshua Barney: Hero of the Revolution and 1812* (Annapolis, MD: Naval Institute Press, 2000).

Catherine M. Prelinger, "Benjamin Franklin and the American Prisoners of War in England during the American Revolution," *William and Mary Quarterly* 32 (1975): 261–294.

Richard Sampson, *Escape in America: The British Convention Prisoners, 1777–1783* (Chippenham, UK: Picton Publishing, 1995).

—*Elizabeth D. Schafer*

ANDERSONVILLE

The prisoner of war camp at Andersonville, Georgia, was operational for only 15 months, but it was by far the largest and most notorious such facility operated by the Confederacy during the American Civil War. Over 41,000 Union captives were interned there, and almost one-third of that number died while confined within its walls.

The origins of the prison can be traced to the summer of 1863, when chronic food shortages and repeated raids by federal cavalry prompted Confederate legislators to seek measures that would ease the logistical crisis in Richmond, Virginia, and render it more secure. One solution that promised to address both of these concerns simultaneously was to transfer the 12,000 Union prisoners confined in the capital to prisons outside the city. In November, Brigadier General John H. Winder, Richmond's provost marshal and commander of its prisons, ordered his subordinates to choose a suitable location for the construction of a new prison in Georgia. The site selected lay about a mile east of the small village of Andersonville.

Many of the horrors that would soon characterize Camp Sumter, as the prison at Andersonville was officially known, can be traced to the fact that the facility was less than half completed when the first captives arrived on 24 February 1864. As there were no barracks for the healthy prisoners and no hospital for the sick, the prisoners were simply herded into the open stockade and left to fend for themselves. Camp officials could do little more than guard their charges. Such would be the case throughout the tragic history of the facility.

Camp Sumter eventually grew into a double-stockaded open pen covering 26 acres. A small stream that cut diagonally across the enclosure was the prisoners' only supply of water, and shelter could be found only in the rude huts soldiers cobbled together from bits of wood and fabric or in simple holes dug in the red Georgia clay. Sanitation was virtually nonexistent. Inmates polluted the compound indiscriminately, and such human waste and refuse as were collected were simply dumped into the stream. Pneumonia, scurvy, dysentery, diarrhea, typhoid, smallpox, and other diseases ravaged the prisoners without respite, and although a large camp hospital was eventually erected, the surgeons were overwhelmed from the beginning. Most of the sick died in the dirt where they collapsed. Over 1,500 died in the first three months, and much worse was yet to come.

Winder had been warned that adequate rations for a facility the size of Camp Sumter would be difficult to supply, and that prediction was based on a maximum prisoner population of only 10,000 men. By 2 May the pen held 12,000, and the influx of captives taken in the Union army's Overland Campaign swelled that number to over 15,000 by the end of the month. Captain Henry Wirz, commander of the stockade since March, petitioned the Richmond government unceasingly for sufficient rations, but a combination of scarcity, bureaucratic squabbling, and naiveté on the part of senior Confederate officials combined to ensure that slow starvation would be the lot of Sumter's prisoners.

In June, Winder was ordered to assume personal command of the camp, but there was little he could do to improve the conditions significantly. Although the camp's ill-trained guard force ruthlessly enforced measures intended to prevent escapes, it was too small to maintain discipline within the stockade. Gangs of Union thugs (dubbed "raiders") robbed and murdered their fellow soldiers at will until outraged prisoners began trying and hanging the raiders for their crimes.

Sanitary conditions and medical care also continued to deteriorate, and assistance from Richmond was paltry, when it came at all. The Union's decision to terminate prisoner exchanges closed that option for reducing the number of captives, and in August the population peaked at almost 33,000, an incredible 1,269 prisoners per acre. Almost 3,000 men died that month—97 in a single day. Relief finally came with the resumption of exchanges and the transfer of inmates to newly established Confederate prisons, but by the time the last of the captives departed at war's end, Camp Sumter had claimed the lives of almost 13,000 prisoners. Ironically, the final casualty of the prison at Andersonville was the camp's warden, Henry Wirz. Following a carefully scripted trial, he was found guilty of atrocities and hung, the only soldier executed for his role in Civil War prisons.

See also Elmira; Libby Prison; United States Civil War

References

Leon Basile, ed., *The Civil War Diary of Amos E. Stearns, a Prisoner at Andersonville* (Rutherford, NJ: Fairleigh Dickinson University Press, 1981).

William Marvel, *Andersonville: The Last Depot* (Chapel Hill: University of North Carolina Press, 1994).

John Ransom, *Andersonville Diary* (New York: Berkley Publishing, 1986 [1881]).

Ezra Hoyt Ripple, *Dancing Along the Deadline: The Andersonville Memoir of a Prisoner of the Confederacy* (Novato, CA: Presidio Press, 1996).

William B. Styple and John J. Fitzpatrick, eds., *The Andersonville Diary and Memoirs of Charles Hopkins, 1st New Jersey Infantry* (Kearny, NJ: Belle Grove Publishing, 1988).

—*Charles W. Sanders, Jr.*

ANGOLAN CIVIL WAR (1975–2002)

The west African nation of Angola gained its independence from Portugal in 1975, after a 10-year war waged by the Popular Movement for the Liberation of Angola (MPLA). But even as Angolans were celebrating their nationhood, the seeds of a longer and more destructive conflict were germinating.

The roots of the Angolan Civil War lay in the failure of a power-sharing agreement between the MPLA and its two rivals, the National Front for the Liberation of Angola (FNLA) and the National Union for the Total Independence of Angola (Unita). Complicating matters was the fact that Unita and the FNLA enjoyed the active support of South Africa, the United States, and Zaire, while the MPLA relied on backing from Cuba. In August 1975, South African troops invaded Angola from the south, while the FNLA and its Zairean allies invaded from the north; the MPLA responded by calling on Cuba, which sent 650 combat soldiers (in addition to the 450 Cuban military instructors who had been despatched in response to the attack by South Africa). By this time, there were over 17,000 foreign troops in Angola.

Eventually, the MPLA was successful in pushing back its rivals, allowing it to proclaim independence in November 1975. But so, too, did Unita and the FNLA, although neither made any attempt to form a government. Soon, all three groups were at each other's throats; the stage was set for a three-decade civil war that would see hostage-taking, crimes against prisoners, and the impressment of POWs into military service.

After the apparent triumph of the Marxist MPLA, Unita's powerful and charismatic leader, Jonas Savimbi, decided to take the war in a different direction. To impress upon his American backers the strength of his anti-communism, he arranged for an all-female firing squad to execute 17 Cuban POWs in March 1976. Suitably impressed, the Central Intelligence Agency expanded its support of Unita, save for a short period in the late 1970s, when the United States Senate voted to suspend aid to Angolan opposition groups. South Africa, too, remained largely behind Unita. Savimbi's terror campaign, then, would not have been possible without the active support of Washington and Pretoria.

Unita's plan was to fight a guerrilla war against the MPLA, using whatever tactics seemed most likely to cause disruption. In 1982, for example, it targeted foreign workers (upon which Angola's economy was heavily reliant), warning them all to leave the country or risk being kidnapped. The first hostages were taken shortly afterwards, although Unita did not intend to execute them. Instead, they were to be marched to the movement's headquarters at Jamba and released in a series of public relations spectacles. The first of these occurred in September 1982 and involved the release of 15 foreign prisoners, including a Swiss nurse. In 1983, Unita captured 66 Czech technicians from a paper factory at Alto Catumbela; later, they took 16 British, 40 Portuguese, and 50 Filipino workers from a diamond mine at Lunda. By 1986, Unita was taking 150 or 200 foreign hostages at a time, both to destabilize Angola's economy and to demonstrate its ability to strike at will. In time, Unita became less discriminating in whom it captured: Election officials, rival politicians and military leaders, foreign diplomats and businessmen, civilians, and even a United Nations observer were all imprisoned for varying periods as propaganda tools. But the hostages were not always used in this way. In January 1992, a Unita fringe group captured and executed four tourists, three from Britain and one from New Zealand.

Savimbi was able to keep up this ruthless campaign against the MPLA, not only because of American and South African support, but because of his willingness to use captives to replenish Unita's armies. Rather than seek volunteers of the kind that had filled the ranks in the early 1970s, a decade later Savimbi's soldiers were routinely kidnapping thousands of young Angolan men to fight in the Unita army, as well as thousands of young women to serve as their "wives." These prisoner-soldiers were kept in place by the threat of execution, and by the policy of transferring them to units far from their homes, to make escape more difficult. After the war, the United Nations estimated that as many as 80 percent of Unita's soldiers may have been kidnapped and forced to serve against their will.

Both sides also employed mercenary soldiers in the Angolan Civil War, and these individuals were particularly vulnerable if captured. Savimbi offered a bounty of $25,000 for the capture of one of the Russian soldiers of fortune rumored to be fighting in Angola, and it is not difficult to imagine the fate of such fighters if captured. Mercenaries employed by Unita were in the same position. After the MPLA's victory, the government tried and executed four soldiers-for-hire, three Britons and an American, who had been captured while fighting for Unita. In one of the more bizarre twists of contemporary African geopolitics, a South African commando officer was captured in an attack on an American-owned oil refinery that was being defended by Cuban soldiers.

The Lusaka Accords of November 1994 brought the civil war to a temporary halt, but localized fighting eventually spread, and by 1998 the country had again drifted into all-out war. It continued until 2002, when Savimbi was killed in a gun battle with government troops. A cease-fire was quickly agreed to, and the now-dictatorless Unita decided to demobilize its army and become a political party. The cost of the 27-year civil war was tens of thousands of Angolans killed, hundreds of thousands maimed (Angola has more amputees than any country in the world, mostly because of Unita's landmines), millions displaced, and a country that, for much of its independent history, could not be considered a functioning nation-state.

See also Mozambican Civil War

References

Victoria Brittain, *Death of Dignity: Angola's Civil War* (Chicago: Pluto Press, 1998).

Karl Maier, *Angola: Promises and Lies* (London: Serif, 1996).

William Minter, *Apartheid's Contras: An Inquiry Into the Roots of War in Angola and Mozambique* (New York: Zed Books, 1994).

—*Jonathan F. Vance*

APACHE WARS (1861–1886)

The Apaches, Athapaskan speakers who lived in scattered bands from present-day Texas to Arizona, fought bravely from 1861 until 1886 to live undisturbed in their homeland. Many ultimately found themselves as prisoners of the U.S. government, and some endured many years in captivity.

After a series of skirmishes with Cochise, a Chiricahua chief wrongfully accused of theft and kidnapping in 1861, General James H. Carleton received orders to join forces with Colonel Christopher (Kit) Carson in the southwest. Determined to take control of the region, Carleton established Fort Bowie and sent 4,000 Mescalero Apaches to Bosque Redondo, a barren reservation along the Pecos River. In January 1863, Carleton captured Mangas Coloradas, a Chiricahua chief, under a flag of truce. During the night, soldiers killed the Apache leader. Enraged Apaches responded by attacking settlements throughout Arizona and New Mexico.

During the 1870s, Arizona became the center of intense military and diplomatic activity. Eskiminzin, chief of the Pinal and Aravaipa Apaches, wanted a lasting peace with the Americans. In 1871, he accepted an offer to settle down and plant crops in the vicinity of Camp Grant, near Tucson. The plan worked well until a Tucson mob attacked the peaceful camp and murdered 144 Apaches. The vigilantes later sold 29 captured children into slavery in Mexico. In an attempt to bring order to the region, General George Crook met with the Apache leaders and insisted that Apaches move to the reservations. Crook's tireless campaigning, his use of Indian scouts, and his reliance on Apache fighting methods eventually restored order by 1875.

However, hostilities had erupted two years earlier at the San Carlos Agency, a barren tract of land along Arizona's Gila River, and Delshay, a Tonto Apache leader, was accused of harboring Apache fugitives accused of killing a white officer. Rather than submit to arrest, Delshay fled in 1873 and was killed the following year. Eskiminzin's people also found peace to be elusive. Although they wanted to rebuild their lives at Camp Grant, they were transferred to San Carlos in 1873. Following the murder of a young lieutenant during a summer uprising, General Crook ordered Eskiminzin's arrest, but the cagey chief escaped. He and his followers surrendered a few months later and were detained as prisoners of war at Camp Grant.

After Crook left Arizona, bureaucrats unwisely decided to confine all Apaches on one reservation at San Carlos, but many bands opposed the move. Rather than relocate, Victorio, Geronimo, and other Apache leaders terrorized settlements from 1877 until 1880. Colonel Edward Hatch's Ninth Cavalry eventually restored order after Victorio's death in an ambush at Tres Castillos in Chihuahua, Mexico. Although 30 warriors managed to escape, soldiers detained 68 women and children as prisoners of war.

Although the uprising had been tamed, San Carlos Agency festered with discontent. Fearing that they might be killed, angry warriors followed Juh, Naiche, and Geronimo to Mexico in 1881. From their mountain hideout, the Apaches conducted one raiding party after another. Panicked officials recalled General Crook in September 1882 to deal with the renegades. His soldiers and Apache scouts pursued the them and ultimately convinced them to return to San Carlos in 1883.

Once there, however, the renegade Apaches realized that agency conditions had not improved, and they fled the reservation in May 1885. Undeterred, Crook once again pursued the elusive warriors into Mexico. His constant pressure gradually wore down the tired Apaches, who surrendered at Cañon de los Embudos in March 1886. All went well until Crook and his captives encountered a trader whose lies prompted Geronimo and 31 other Apaches to escape. As a result of this escape, Crook resigned his post and was replaced by General Nelson A. Miles. When Miles finally reached his elusive quarry in September 1886, he had

Lieutenant Charles Gatewood, a trusted leader of Apache scouts, inform the warriors that resistance was unwise. The renegades soon learned that Miles had shipped the other Chiricahuas from the reservation to a military prison in St. Augustine, Florida. Hoping to rejoin their loved ones, the renegades surrendered for the last time at Skeleton Canyon, Arizona, on 4 September 1886.

A short time later, the captives were loaded onto trains and sent to three Florida internment camps to be reunited with their families; even Apache scouts who had served with Crook and Miles were sent to Florida. Eskiminzin and his peaceful Aravaipas later joined the Chiricahuas in Florida. Whichever side they fought on, the Apaches were now prisoners of war. Life in Florida was not pleasant. Several of the leading men were isolated from their families at Fort Pickens, a hard labor camp. The region's humid heat, combined with homesickness and disease, resulted in the deaths of more than 100 Apache prisoners of war. To make matters worse, parents watched helplessly as their children were sent off to boarding schools.

After repeated public protests condemning the treatment of the Apache prisoners, the government reunited the 375 Apache exiles at an abandoned army barracks in Mount Vernon, Alabama, in 1887. In time the Aravaipas were allowed to return to San Carlos, but Arizona residents refused to allow the Chiricahuas to return. Kiowa and Comanche leaders responded to the situation by inviting the Chiricahuas to share part of their reservation at Fort Sill, Indian Territory. Geronimo and nearly 400 other surviving Apache exiles arrived there in 1894 and made the most of their confinement by farming and ranching. Although he consistently lobbied for his return to Arizona, Geronimo died at Fort Sill on 17 February 1909, still a prisoner of war. Congress released the last of the Apache prisoners in 1913. Some 187 Chiricahuas responded to the news by moving to the Mescalero Apache Reservation in New Mexico, while 78 chose to remain at Fort Sill.

See also Plains Indian Warfare; Seminole Wars; Sioux Wars; Wounded Knee Massacre

References

Eve Ball, *In the Days of Victorio* (Tucson: University of Arizona Press, 1970).

Max L. Moorhead, *The Apache Frontier* (Norman: University of Oklahoma Press, 1968).

Dan L. Thrapp, *The Conquest of Apacheria* (Norman: University of Oklahoma Press, 1967).

John Anthony Turcheneske, Jr., *The Chiricahua Apache Prisoners of War: Fort Sill, 1894–1914* (Niwot: University Press of Colorado, 1997).

Robert M. Utley, *The Indian Frontier of the American West, 1846–1890* (Albuquerque: University of New Mexico Press, 1984).

—*Jon Brudvig*

ARAB-ISRAELI WARS

Israel has fought five major wars (six, if the War of Attrition of 1967–1970 is considered) with its Arab neighbors between 1948 and the present. The periods between these wars have not been peaceful, and saw a continuous cycle of Arab guerrilla *fedayeen* attacks against Israeli targets, followed by Israeli retaliatory raids. The first *Intifada*, 1987–1993, of Palestinians living under Israeli occupation was followed by the second *Intifada* from 2000 onwards, that was characterized by suicide bomber attacks against Israeli citizens, followed by Israeli Defense Forces (IDF) raids against targets in the occupied West Bank and Gaza Strip. All of these conflicts have involved the capture of prisoners of war by both sides, as well as the displacement of thousands of Palestinians from their homes.

Despite the constant state of war between Israel and its Arab neighbors (only Egypt and Jordan have signed peace treaties with Israel; Lebanon and Syria have not), an almost regularized pattern of prisoner of war exchanges was established between the two sides. At the end of any one of the outbreaks of fighting, Israel would invariably negotiate

Arab woman with forms allowing them to visit relatives in Israeli captivity (©ICRC/A Meier)

prisoner exchanges with each Arab state that held any of its soldiers or civilians captive (this included the remains of dead Israeli soldiers). These exchanges always involved the release of a much greater number of Israeli-held prisoners than Arab-held prisoners, as Israel has generally been the victor in its wars with the Arab states.

While the exchange of POWs between the state of Israel and other Arab states resembles that of other states exchanging prisoners at the end of hostilities, this has rarely been the case in the Middle East. These exchanges have more frequently acknowledged that a temporary ceasefire was in effect, with fighting to resume at a later date. The release of hundreds or even thousands of "terrorists" by Israel in exchange for a handful of Israeli soldiers has often looked liked "giving in to terrorists demands" and is often portrayed as such in the Israeli press. The pressure to recover Israeli soldiers held in captivity is strong, however, and time and again the Israeli government has agreed to these lopsided prisoner exchanges.

The Israeli government places a great deal of importance on recovering its soldiers captured during operations and on the return of the remains of fallen Israeli Defense Forces personnel. Following the 1973 Yom Kippur War, the Unit for IDF Soldiers Missing in Action was created in the Personnel Directorate of the General Staff of the IDF. The Unit is charged with recovering MIAs from all of Israel's wars, and uses open and clandestine sources of information in its work, as well as liaisons with governmental and non-governmental organizations involved with prisoner of war issues, such as the International Committee of the Red Cross.

The actual negotiating for release of POWs is done by a team attached to the Israeli Prime Minister's Office. The Israeli public follows these prisoner exchanges closely. The swaps have resulted in heated debate in the Israeli press about the merits of releasing hundreds of "terrorists" in exchange for one or two captured Israeli soldiers. Generally, though, if a deal can be made, whatever the imbalance in numbers, the Israeli government has been prepared to make it.

The First Arab-Israeli War (known to the Israelis as the War of Independence) took place in 1948–1949, and established Israel as an independent state after the end of the British Mandate. Israeli forces, after much heavy fighting, were able to defeat the combined forces of Lebanon, Syria, Jordan, Egypt, and Iraq, and Palestinian irregulars. The Arab armies attempted to crush the new state of Israel, but their attacks were uncoordinated and badly organized. After an armistice period allowed Israel to rearm, the new country launched a series of counterattacks that secured its existence, with international recognition, but not, of course, from the Arab world.

At the end of the First Arab-Israeli War, the Arab states held 884 Israeli POWs and

Israel held 6,346 Arab POWs. The first exchanges took place during the armistice negotiations. On 26 February 1949, the Egyptian Brigade encircled in the Faluja pocket was allowed to evacuate its positions in return for five Israeli captives held by the Egyptians inside the pocket. One of the Egyptian officers trapped inside this pocket was Anwar Sadat, who would later become the president of Egypt. By July 1949 a full exchange of prisoners of war had taken place between Israel and Egypt, Syria, Lebanon, and Jordan.

Between the end of the war in 1949 and the Sinai Campaign of 1956, a low-level conflict between Israel and its Arab neighbors simmered. Clashes were of two basic types: *fedayeen* attacks against Israeli civilian and military targets; and IDF clashes with regular Arab army formations during Israeli retaliatory strikes. Several incidents during this period resulted in Israelis being taken captive; many Palestinians and other Arab nationals were also captured by Israeli forces. On 13 April 1952, the Egyptians ambushed an Israeli patrol, killing one soldier and taking two prisoner. The Israeli soldiers were returned after three days. An Israeli raid on the Arab Legion compound at Azzun, Jordan, resulted in the capture of one Israeli soldier, who was held for almost a year before being released by the Jordanians. On 30 September 1954, Egyptian authorities boarded the Israeli-registered ship *Bat Galim* at the southern entrance of the Suez Canal. The voyage of the *Bat Galim* was part of an Israeli campaign to involve the international community in its assertion of free right of passage through the Suez Canal and Straits of Tiran, a right the Egyptian government denied. The Egyptians detained all 10 sailors on board, but finally released them in January 1955. On 8 December 1954, five Israeli soldiers were captured while operating on Syrian territory in the Golan Heights. One of the soldiers (Uri Ilan) committed suicide on 13 January 1955, and his body was returned to Israel the next day. The other four soldiers were eventually released in exchange for 40 captured Syrian soldiers. The Israeli public was shocked at the mental and physical state of these released soldiers, who had obviously been tortured while in Syrian captivity.

The Sinai Campaign of 1956 was, in reality, a combined British-French and Israeli operation. The Anglo-French governments hoped to regain control of the Suez Canal region, which they lost after President Nasser nationalized the canal on 26 July 1956. Israel hoped to launch a preemptive strike to destroy powerful Egyptian army units stationed near its borders in the Sinai. American and Soviet diplomatic pressure forced the British and French to withdraw ignominiously. The Israelis, too, grudgingly agreed to withdraw from Egyptian territory after a United Nations Emergency Force (UNEF) was established to act as a buffer force between Egyptian and Israeli troops.

During the brief Sinai Campaign of 29 October to 5 November 1956, Israel captured over 5,500 Egyptian troops, while one Israeli pilot was taken by the Egyptians. By 5 February 1957, a full Israeli-Egyptian prisoner exchange was completed, including troops captured by both sides before the Sinai Campaign commenced (this included 77 Egyptian and three Israeli POWs from earlier operations).

Between 1961 and 1963 there were three notable prisoner exchanges between Israel and its neighbors. On the night of 16–17 March 1961, an Israeli raid on the Syrian strongpoint of Kukeib left a dead Israeli soldier behind; one Syrian soldier was captured during the operation. On 21 February 1962, the body of the Israeli soldier, Hannan David, was exchanged for the captured Syrian. On 24 September 1962, an Israeli truck with 14 female cadets took a wrong turn and drove over the border into Lebanon. The women were taken prisoner by the Lebanese but were released the following day. Finally, on 21 December 1963, 11 Israelis were exchanged for 18 Syrians. The Israelis, both civilians and soldiers, had been in Syrian custody for various lengths of time.

The 1967 War (or the Six-Day War) was Israel's most impressive campaign in the

Arab-Israeli Wars. Fearful of an eventual Arab attack, especially after Nasser announced a re-imposition of the blockade on the Straits of Tiran on 21 May 1967, Israel decided to strike first. On 5 June 1967, the Israeli air force launched a devastating surprise attack on the Egyptian air force, destroying 309 out of 340 operational aircraft. From that moment onward the war was a disaster for the Arab armies, for with Israel enjoying air superiority, the Arab forces had no chance of winning. Israel launched a series of lightning advances that in turn captured the Gaza Strip and Sinai Peninsula from Egypt, the West Bank from Jordan, and the Golan Heights from Syria. In active, mobile operations, which lasted from 5 to 10 June 1967, Israel captured 4,338 Egyptian soldiers and 899 civilians, 533 Jordanian soldiers and 366 civilians, and 367 Syrian soldiers and 205 civilians. The Arab armies only captured 15 IDF personnel: 11 by Egypt, one by Syria, two in Iraq (both of them pilots), and one in Lebanon.

POW exchanges between Israel and Egypt were completed on 23 January 1968, and in February 1968 members of Israeli intelligence captured by Egyptian authorities in what was known as the Lavan Affair were returned to Israel. The Israeli authorities also released 428 Jordanian prisoners in return for two Israeli pilots who were shot down while attacking the H3 airbase in western Iraq. The Israelis released 572 Syrian POWs in return for one Israeli pilot, the bodies of two other pilots, and the body of one Israeli civilian who had been kidnapped by the Syrians and died in prison. Syria, however, refused to release the remains of Eli Cohen, an Israeli spy who had earlier been hanged in Damascus.

Allegations of Israeli soldiers killing Egyptian prisoners surfaced in 1995. Aryeh Yitzhaki, a former employee of the IDF history department, claimed in a radio interview on 16 August 1995 that the *Shaked* (Almond) reconnaissance unit had killed hundreds of Egyptian POWs in the Sinai desert during the 1967 war. The unit's acting commander at the time was Binyamin Ben-Eliezer, who was, in 1995, the housing minister in the Labor government. Other former Israeli army officers came forward and claimed that Yitzhaki was merely trying to divert attention away from his own involvement in the execution of 49 Egyptian soldiers during the 1956 Sinai campaign. Either way, the arguments around these killings did nothing for Israel's reputation internationally. Later in 1995, Elli Dayan, Israel's Deputy Foreign Minister, traveled to Egypt and made an offer to compensate the families of the victims. Israel has maintained that the 20-year statute of limitations has expired on these crimes and no one will be directly punished for the executions. Documentation that could shed further light on the execution of Egyptian POWs by Israeli soldiers has yet to be released by the IDF.

The Yom Kippur War of 1973 saw Israel on the receiving end of an Egyptian-Syrian offensive. The Egyptians attacked across the Suez Canal and dug in a few kilometers from the eastern bank of the Canal. The Syrians' armored divisions stormed across the Golan Heights, almost breaking into northern Israel. This time, Soviet surface-to-air missiles negated the superior Israeli air force. Things looked bleak for Israel but eventually the IDF adapted its tactics and was able to gain the upper hand in the fighting. Nevertheless, the Egyptian and Syrian armies showed great tenacity and the Egyptians did regain control of the Suez Canal. The war led to the Camp David Peace Accords in which Israel returned the Sinai Peninsula to Egypt in return for a peace treaty.

During the Yom Kippur War, 231 Israeli soldiers were captured by Egypt, 62 by Syria, and two by Lebanon; another six Israelis were subsequently captured after the ceasefire. The IDF took 8,372 Egyptians, 392 Syrians, six Moroccans, and 13 Iraqis prisoner. A POW exchange with Egypt occurred over the period 15–22 November 1973; prisoners captured during the War of Attrition (1967–1970) were also exchanged at this time. The POW exchange with Syria was held between 1 and 6 June 1974; Moroccan and Iraqi POWs were also released by the Israelis at this time. On 4 April 1975, the

Egyptians released the remains of 39 Israeli soldiers killed in the Yom Kippur War; in return, Israel released 92 security prisoners (civilians) from its custody.

Israeli military involvement in Lebanon, notably the 1978 invasion and the even more massive 1982 Israeli invasion (which reached Beirut) have generated numerous prisoner of war exchanges between Israel and various Arab governments and armed militias. Some of the prisoner exchanges that took place included the 23 November 1983 exchange of six Israelis for 4,700 "terrorists" held at the Ansar detention center in Lebanon, as well as another 65 held in Israel. On 21 May 1985, three Israeli soldiers held by Ahmad Jubril's organization were exchanged for 1,150 detainees. An exchange with Syria on 28 June 1984 returned six Israelis and the remains of five others in return for 291 Syrian soldiers, 13 Syrian civilians, and the bodies of 74 Syrians. On 21 July 1996, Israel returned the bodies of 123 "terrorists" to Hizb'Allah in return for the bodies of two Israelis abducted on 17 July 1986.

Other prisoner releases of Palestinian detainees in the years after 1990 have occurred on numerous occasions, some of them routine, others as part of a public relations campaign by the Israeli government to show support for this or that peace initiative. Despite these prisoner releases, no lasting, effective deal has brought peace between Israel and the Palestinian people. Israel also remains in a state of war with two of its neighbors, Syria and Lebanon.

See also Intifada; Lebanese Civil War

References

Jeremy Bowen, *Six Days: How the 1967 War Shaped the Middle East* (New York: Simon & Schuster, 2003).

Hussein of Jordan, *My "War" with Israel* (London: Peter Owen, 1969).

Amia Lieblich, *Seasons of Captivity: The Inner World of POWs* (New York: New York University Press, 1994).

Benny Morris, *Israel's Border Wars, 1949–1956* (Oxford: Oxford University Press, 1997).

John B. Quigley, *Palestine and Israel: A Challenge to Justice* (Durham, NC: Duke University Press, 1990).

Robert G. Rabil, *Embattled Neighbors: Syria, Israel, and Lebanon* (Boulder, CO: Lynne Rienner, 2003).

Indar Jit Rikhye, *The Sinai Blunder* (London: Routledge, 1980).

—*Andrew C. Young*

ARBEITSKOMMANDOS

During World War II, the German army established work detachments, or *Arbeitskommandos*, to detain prisoners of war who were put to work in factories, farms, mines, and other industries. Under the terms of the 1929 Geneva Convention (Articles 27 to 34), countries at war were permitted to utilize the labor of prisoners of war so long as that labor was not directly related to the production of war materials. Officers could not be forced to work but could be given supervisory jobs, if they so requested. Noncommissioned officers could be forced to do supervisory work, unless they requested regular work for pay. The majority of POWs, being private soldiers, had no choice but to work for pay and were placed in *Arbeitskommandos* for this purpose.

Arbeitskommandos were administrative subunits of the main POW camps, but because they were often located away from the main camps and closer to the places of work, they often functioned with a considerable degree of independence. As it was difficult for neutral inspectors and delegates of the International Committee of the Red Cross (ICRC) to visit all the work detachments, conditions were, in many cases, substandard. The prisoners of an Arbeitskommando usually elected a leader, known as the Man of Confidence, whose duties included ensuring that the food rations were regular, clothing stocks were sufficient, medical attention was adequate, and the work being assigned was not directly related to the war effort. In the event of complaints or queries, the Man of Confidence would contact his counterpart at the main prison camp, who would take the matter up with the German commandant and, if necessary, with the neutral authorities or the ICRC.

Although the POWs were effectively leased to a company or factory, they remained under the disciplinary authority of the German military guards who supervised them. As the war progressed and Germany's economic circumstances became more desperate, the military assigned a new responsibility to these guards: In addition to ensuring that the prisoners obeyed the lawful requests of their employers, the guards were also required to ensure that they worked as hard as possible. In some cases, the material conditions under which the prisoners worked or lived were so bad that they threatened illegal strikes. Because the requirement to work carried the weight of a military order, refusal to work was legally considered mutiny. Consequently, the German guards were permitted to force the prisoners to work at gunpoint, if necessary. If the prisoners' behavior was too unruly, they could be arrested and charged with disciplinary infractions. Nevertheless, threats of mutiny as a result of poor working or living situations did occur, and some *Arbeitskommandos* faced virtual starvation in the final chaotic year of the war.

Conditions were bad for American and British Commonwealth POWs, but at least they were rarely forced to labor in industries that produced war materials. French, Polish, and especially Russian prisoners fared considerably worse. The German government employed them directly in war-related work, such as in munitions factories or the construction and maintenance of military installations. The *Arbeitskommandos* for Soviet POWs, furthermore, were run as slave-labor camps, with conditions sometimes on a par with those in concentration camps. The use of these prisoners of war in illegal labor was considered a war crime at the postwar Nuremberg Trials; *Arbeitskommandos* were the vehicle for the commission of this crime.

See also Labor; Lamsdorf; Nuremberg Trials

References
Sam Kydd, *For You, The War Is Over* (London: Bachman and Turner, 1973).
Claire E. Swedberg, *Work Commando 311/I: American Paratroopers Become Forced Laborers for the Nazis* (Mechanicsburg, PA: Stackpole Books, 1995).
Elvet Williams, *Arbeitskommando* (London: Victor Gollancz, 1975).

—*Vasilis Vourkoutiotis*

ARDEATINE CAVES MASSACRE

The Ardeatine Caves massacre was the first major atrocity committed by German forces in Italy during World War II as a reprisal for partisan actions. On the afternoon of 23 March 1944, in Rome's Via Rasella, a group of 16 urban partisans of the Patriotic Action Group ambushed and bombed a German police unit that was part of the German occupation forces. Thirty-two policemen were killed and several others (one of whom died shortly thereafter) were injured.

Although no formal written order appears to have been made, there followed a nearly immediate verbal order to execute 10 Italian citizens for every German killed. The order is believed to have originated from Adolf Hitler himself, passed through Field Marshal Albert Kesselring, the commander of all German forces in Italy, to SS Obersturmbannführer Herbert Kappler, who directed the massacre and composed the list of people to be executed. It consisted of 260 civilians already under German arrest and in custody for various charges, including black marketeering, possessing false documents, agitating for strikes, hiding Jews, or otherwise being "enemies of the regime." The final list also included 75 Jews awaiting deportation to concentration camps in Germany. None of those listed had been involved in the bomb attack.

The massacre took place on the afternoon of 24 March 1944 in caves on the Via Ardeatine just south of Rome. Five SS soldiers escorted five prisoners at a time to the mouth of the cave. As the victims entered the cave, SS Captain Erich Priebke checked off their names from Kappler's list. With their hands tied behind their backs, the prisoners were made to kneel and then were shot in the back of the head. After all had been shot, the entrance to the cave was blasted shut with explosives.

On 27 March 1944, a young priest and several relatives of the victims found an entrance to the caves and were able to ascertain what had happened. Learning of this, the Germans reblasted and resealed the cave and its tunnels. Not until after the Allied liberation of Rome in June 1944 were Italian and American officials able to open the cave, exhume the bodies, and attempt to identify them. On the fifth anniversary of the massacre, the caves were consecrated as a national monument.

For what would be one of the last World War II war crimes trials, Priebke was extradited from Argentina in 1995 to stand trial in Italy for his role in the Ardeatine caves massacre. After a second trial and appeal, his conviction was upheld and he was sentenced to life imprisonment—under house arrest.

See also Lidice Massacre; Oradour-sur-Glane Massacre; Reprisals

References
Attilio Ascarelli, *Le fosse Ardeatine* (Bologna: Canesi, 1965).
Robert Katz, *Death in Rome* (New York: Macmillan, 1967).
Richard Lamb, *War in Italy: A Brutal Story* (New York: Da Capo Press, 1996).

—*Victoria C. Belco*

ASHANTI WARS (1824–1831, 1869–1873, 1896–1900)

The Gold Coast of West Africa was the site of a series of punitive expeditions launched by Britain against the Ashanti (Asante) people during the nineteenth century. These expeditions were intended to ensure Britain's control of the territory and the safety of its trade and, like many imperial conflicts, frequently involved the taking and freeing of hostages. Since the early part of the century, there had been minor skirmishes between Britain, which had established a protectorate along the coast, and the Ashanti, who inhabited the region some 50 miles inland. In 1824, during the First Ashanti War (1824–1831) the Ashantis inflicted a signal defeat upon the British; the governor was killed and his colonial secretary captured, his release only gained through the intervention of a Dutch diplomat. As part of the peace treaty that ended the war, the Ashanti were compelled to turn over two members of the royal family as hostages.

There followed a period of relative calm, but in 1869 Ashanti armies began raids on outposts in the protectorate. In June, a raiding party captured a group of German and Swiss missionaries, who were treated with relative generosity by their captors while negotiations for their release were set in motion. The opposing sides still had not been able to agree on a ransom when in 1873 a much larger Ashanti army swept into the protectorate, burning and plundering villages on its way south. British Major General Sir Garnet Wolseley was given the task of bringing the Ashantis to heel and freeing the missionaries. When Wolseley's column of British regular and native troops was halfway to the Ashanti capital of Kumasi, the hostages were released, bearing a note that informed the British that, as the hostages had been freed and the ransom waived, the campaign need not continue. The entreaty was refused, the British instead demanding that the Ashanti king send his mother and heir as hostages for his good behavior. This demand, which was quite impossible to meet, was wisely forgotten when it came time for both sides to sign the Treaty of Fomena that ended the Second Ashanti war.

The Third Ashanti War constituted yet another attempt to impose control over what some British regarded as a barbaric and lawless land. In January 1896, an expedition delivered an ultimatum to the Ashanti king, Prempeh, at Kumasi. He agreed to perform an act of submission to the British, but when he was unable to produce the demanded amount of gold, the British promptly arrested Prempeh and most of his royal household. They were taken to the coast by a heavy guard of British regulars, placed aboard the *HMS Racoon*, and conveyed into imprisonment on the coast. Later, the hostages were moved to Sierra Leone and, ultimately, to the Seychelles. The shock of seeing their royals clapped in irons pacified the Ashanti for a time, but in 1900 their resentment had reached a boiling point and they turned on the British. Ashanti armies laid siege to the British fort at Kumasi, and only a prolonged and bitter campaign in the summer of 1900 vanquished the Ashanti and secured British rule in the area. King Prempeh was not released and permitted to return to Kumasi until 1923.

References
Alan Lloyd, *The Drums of Kumasi: The Story of the Ashanti Wars* (London: Longmans, 1964).
Leigh Maxwell, *The Ashanti Ring: Sir Garnet Wolseley's Campaigns, 1870–1882* (London: Leo Cooper, 1985).
Frederick Myatt, *The Golden Stool: An Account of the Ashanti War of 1900* (London: William Kimber, 1966).

—*Jonathan F. Vance*

ASSURANCE

Assurance was a legal procedure, common in the Anglo-Scots border country during the early decades of the sixteenth century, by which contracting parties agreed to a period of truce during which they would refrain from the pursuit of blood feud and raid. During the "Rough Wooing," the Anglo-Scots war of 1542–1550, this practice was adapted by the English to create a body of Scottish collaborators who would support dynastic union via the marriage of Edward, Prince of Wales (from 1547, Edward VI), to the infant Mary, Queen of Scots. Men captured in battle or living in areas garrisoned by the English were given the opportunity to assure; this involved swearing allegiance to the English crown, supplying English forces in the field, and sometimes, fighting alongside them. In return, assured Scots received protection, pensions, land, and trading privileges. This was a novel development, for although many Scottish nobles had long had dealings with England, now men of all ranks were encouraged to assure.

The motives for taking assurance varied. Many were genuinely committed to the principle of dynastic union, particularly those whose religious sympathies favored Protestant England over Scotland's ancient ally, Catholic France. Others assured merely as an expedient for so long as the fortunes of war favored England. Personal and regional quarrels were also factors. Andrew Kerr, laird of Ferniehurst, endured three months of captivity before agreeing to assure. Yet once he had done so, he pursued with vigor his own feud with Walter Scott of Buccleuch, under the banner of St. George. Similarly, when the town of Dumfries was captured by the English, the townsfolk took assurance and then spearheaded the attack on neighboring Kirkcudbright, their longstanding commercial rival.

The loyalty of assured Scots was, however, always suspect. English forces were defeated at Ancrum Moor (27 February 1545) and Drumlanrig (20 February 1548) because bodies of assured Scots changed sides in mid-battle. The whole system of assurance became largely untenable following the arrival of French troops in Scotland in the spring of 1548. Since English garrisons could no longer offer protection, they became instead the means to coerce the local population, a process that inevitably alienated their assured allies.

Following the collapse of the English war effort in 1550, the French urged reprisals against those who had taken assurance. Few, however, were actually punished. In an age of religious and social upheaval, there would have been little justice in pursuing individuals who had been caught up in a complex conflict of loyalties.

References
M. L. Bush, *The Government Policy of Protector Somerset* (London: Edward Arnold, 1975).
George MacDonald Fraser, *The Steel Bonnets: The Story of the Anglo-Scottish Border Reivers* (London: Collins Harvill, 1989).
Marcus Merriman, "The Assured Scots," *Scottish Historical Review* 47 (1968): 10–34.

—*Gervase Phillips*

ATTILA THE HUN (D. 453)

Attila the Hun was the most powerful ruler of the Hunnic Empire. He ascended the throne alongside his older brother Bleda, after the death of their uncle Rua in 434. Bleda died in approximately 445, and some historians allege that Attila murdered him to become the empire's sole ruler, which he remained until his death in 453.

Nothing is known about Attila's childhood and little about the first five years of his life as leader of the Huns. However, we do know the details of his first treaty with the East Romans in 434, the Peace of Margus. Attila and Bleda had inherited tense relations with the Romans from their belligerent uncle; Rua had demanded that if the Romans did not return escaped POWs, he would declare war. Before his threat was realized, however, Rua died. The subsequent treaty negotiated between his nephews and Roman ambassadors stipulated that the Romans were either to return the prisoners or pay eight soldi for each. After 435, the price for Roman soldiers was increased to 12 soldi.

After Bleda's death, Attila helped transform the empire from tribes of roving bandits into a strong and cohesive military power. Although he himself was never a prisoner of war, Attila led his troops on military campaigns against the Romans and ruthlessly took prisoners with them along the way. POWs became Attila's property and were only released if sold or ransomed. Evidence suggests that ransoming captives was lucrative for Attila; however, the exact amount of gold he received for these transactions is unknown.

During the summer of 452, Attila led his troops against the Roman General Flavius Aetius, a former hostage of the Huns. Three cities—Aquileia, Mediolanum (now Milano, Italy), and Ticinum (now Pavia, Italy)—fell to the Hunnic Empire. Those who could not escape were either killed or taken into captivity. Sometimes captives were made into slaves and participated in religious ceremonies; some slaves of Christian households were even baptized. Whether or not this baptism was forced is unclear, but evidence suggests that the Roman slaves were well-treated.

References

C.D. Gordon, *The Age of Attila: Fifth-Century Byzantium and the Barbarians* (Ann Arbor: University of Michigan Press, 1960).

J. Otto Maenchen-Helfen, *The World of the Huns: Studies in Their History and Culture* (Berkeley: University of California Press, 1973).

E.A. Thompson, *A History of Attila and the Huns* (Westport, CT: Greenwood Press, 1975).

—*Dorotea Gucciardo*

AUSCHWITZ

Auschwitz (in German) or Oświęcim (in Polish) was the largest and most notorious German concentration camp during World War II. Located 37 miles west of Kraków in Poland, Auschwitz would eventually contain three main camps and 45 subcamps. Originally built as a military barracks, Auschwitz I received its first prisoners in June 1940 with the arrival of 700 Polish Catholic political prisoners. Birkenau (or Auschwitz II) opened in October 1941 and was designed to accommodate 100,000 prisoners. Birkenau contained four gas chambers, and the majority of the people murdered at Auschwitz were killed here: one million Jews and 500,000 Polish Catholics, Gypsies, and Soviet POWs. Monowitz (or Auschwitz III) grew out of a camp that supplied slave labor for the nearby I. G. Farben synthetic rubber and oil plant.

Captivity at Auschwitz began with the arrival of new prisoners at the railroad station in Birkenau. After having been transported like cattle for many hundreds of miles, the prisoners were forced to form quickly into two lines, one for men and the other for women. The lines moved to a point where camp officers separated the prisoners again, this time into inmates who would become slave laborers and those who would be gassed immediately. As the new arrivals endured the selection process, a detachment of prisoners gathered up the possessions that had been left in the railroad cars. These possessions would eventually be sent to Germany to serve the war effort or to increase the wealth of high-ranking SS and Nazi Party officials.

The prisoners who were not sent to the gas chambers were first sent to the quarantine camp. There, the prisoners' last remaining possessions were taken away from them, their heads were shaved (both men and women), and they were issued striped prison uniforms. Each prisoner was also registered and received an identification number, which was tattooed on the left arm. The life expectancy of these prisoners once they started working as slave laborers was only a few months. All told, 405,000 people worked as slave laborers at Auschwitz.

The daily routine of the slave laborers at Auschwitz began when they woke up at dawn and were forced to stand at attention for the roll call. Any prisoners who could not remain standing for the roll call were immediately sent to the gas chambers. Prisoners then worked in the factories all day, received one wholly inadequate meal, stood for the evening roll call, and finally were allowed a few hours of sleep before the process started all over again. Some prisoners were neither gassed immediately nor sent to join the slave-labor force. These unfortunate individuals were the subjects of medical experiments carried out by camp doctors, the most notorious of whom was Dr. Josef Mengele, the "Angel of Death."

Despite the horrific conditions that existed in the camp, the prisoners constantly resisted their oppressors and 667 prisoners (almost all of them Poles) actually managed to escape from the camp; 270 of the these were later recaptured and killed. In 1943, photographs of the mass executions taking place in Auschwitz were smuggled out by two Polish prisoners who managed to escape. Despite the fact that these photos reached the Allied powers in London, the Allies refused to believe that they were authentic. The mass killing in Auschwitz continued until November 1944, when the SS began to dismantle the camp in the face of Soviet advances. When the Red Army liberated Auschwitz on 27 January 1945, only 7,650 sick prisoners remained.

See also Buchenwald; Concentration Camps; Dachau; Extermination Camps

References

Rebecca Camhi-Fromer, *The Holocaust Odyssey of Daniel Bennahmias, Sonderkommando* (Tuscaloosa: University of Alabama Press, 1993).

Jozef Garlinski, *Fighting Auschwitz: The Resistance Movement in the Concentration Camp* (Greenwich, CT: Fawcett Crest Books, 1975).

Martin Gilbert, *Auschwitz and the Allies* (New York: Holt, Rinehart and Winston, 1981).

Yisrael Gutman and Michael Berenbaum, eds., *Anatomy of the Auschwitz Death Camp* (Bloomington: Indiana University Press, 1994).

Laurence Rees, *Auschwitz: A New History* (New York: Public Affairs, 2005).

Lilka Trzcinska-Croydon, *The Labyrinth of Dangerous Hours: A Memoir of the Second World War* (Toronto: University of Toronto Press, 2004).

—Alexander M. Bielakowski

AVITAMINOSIS

Avitaminosis or, more properly, *hypovitaminosis,* apparently first coined in 1914, is a blanket term covering a variety of deficiency diseases caused by a diet that does not provide sufficient vitamins and minerals to maintain health. Because of reduced diets, prisoners of war have traditionally been vulnerable to beriberi, pellagra, and other deficiency diseases. The terrible suffering they can cause becomes even more tragic when it is realized that such diseases can be remedied relatively easily.

It is a misconception that diseases related to avitaminosis have been confined to POWs in the Far East during World War II or the Korean War, for these diseases are not peculiar to certain geographical areas. It was in the Japanese camps, however, that avitaminosis in all its variations was most readily visible and where its symptoms were most acute. Beriberi, caused by a deficiency of vitamin B1, occurred in two forms, wet and dry, each of which had different symptoms. Dry beriberi is more painful but less hazardous to life; with wet beriberi, the patient retains fluid, swells up, and ultimately

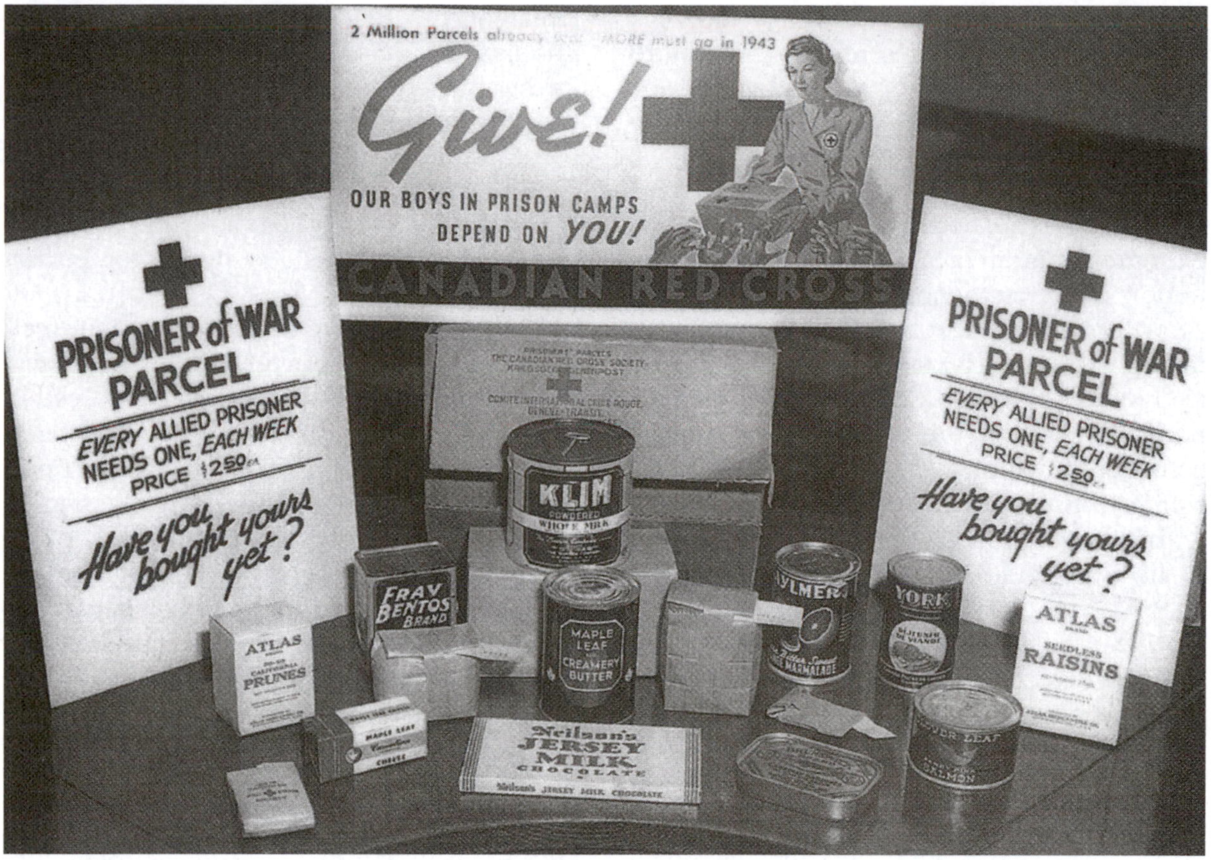

The contents of Red Cross food parcels were intended to prevent the onset of avitaminosis (Special Collections, Hamilton Public Library)

often dies of heart failure. Another condition all too common among Far East POWs is a deficiency disease known as "electric feet," in which the prisoner suffers agonizing burning or shooting pains in the feet. Pellagra results from a deficiency of vitamin B3 and produces painful scaling of the skin, loss of vision, and in its later stages, dementia. With all of these conditions, the most immediate symptoms disappear relatively quickly once the proper vitamins are added to the diet. As thousands of former Far East POWs discovered, though, the secondary effects of the disease are permanent. Impaired vision or premature blindness, circulatory problems, cardiovascular disorders, and skin diseases struck them in later life, legacies of the avitaminosis they had endured while in captivity.

See also Epidemics; Health

References

Kenneth J. Carpenter, ed., *Pellagra* (Stroudsburg, PA: Hutchinson Ross, 1981).

Robert R. Williams, *Towards the Conquest of Beriberi* (Cambridge, MA: Harvard University Press, 1961).

—*Jonathan F. Vance*

AZTECS

Captives were of paramount importance in the Aztec Empire, which reigned over central Mexico in the fifteenth and sixteenth centuries. Because of the religious and social significance of captives, military campaigns were frequently entered into for the sole purpose of capturing prisoners. Religion and expansion went hand in hand; territories were conquered to secure captives, who could then be offered as sacrifices to the gods.

The strategy of Aztec warriors was to capture rather than kill their enemies on the battlefield because the taking of prisoners was a way for a warrior to move up in the military hierarchy. When a youth took his first captive, he was presented to the king to be awarded ceremonial paint and garments, and there were similar ceremonies for the second and third captive. After four captives, the honors depended upon the reputation of the enemy who had been captured. In the extremely hierarchical Aztec military, these honors were tremendously significant; one could not ascend through the ranks without taking captives. The taking of prisoners was also a way for a new king to display his martial prowess. For the captives' part, it was considered dishonorable for a captured warrior to return home. For this reason, Aztec warriors were reluctant to allow themselves to be captured and usually fought to the death rather than become imprisoned.

After a battle had concluded, special troops would rush to the field to bind the prisoners and secure them for transport. Most would be conveyed to Tenochtitlán, the Aztec capital, or to one of the other large cities, but it was traditional for the first prisoner taken to be sacrificed on the spot. Once they had been brought back to the city, captives were used for a variety of purposes. The king would determine who would assume ownership of the captives; nobles he reserved for himself, captured military leaders were awarded to his own leaders, and other combatants were awarded to the warriors who had captured them. In the event of a dispute in which no warrior had clear claim to the prisoner, the captive would be allotted to Huitcalco temple, where slaves were sacrificed. Some prisoners were killed in gladiatorial combat, but sacrifice was the fate of most prisoners taken by the Aztecs; few were released or ransomed. Prisoner sacrifices were held as part of the festivals held at the beginning of each month, at the New Fire ceremony, which marked the end of the Aztec century, or at any of the other religious festivals. At the festival of Coailhuitl, the feast of the earth, for example, each of the towns was expected to supply prisoners it had captured to be sacrificed. On some occasions, the sacrifices could reach epic proportions. At the dedication of the main temple to Huitzilopchtli, the god of war, in Tenochtitlán, it is said that 80,400 captives were sacrificed. Priests carried out the actual sacrifices, and then the bodies were returned to those who had captured them in the first place. At each captor's home a ritual feast was then held in which the body would be eaten and the bones displayed in the house, to signify the importance of the captor.

All captives were important in that they demonstrated the power of the king, but because there was little challenge involved in capturing noncombatants, only captured enemy warriors conferred social status upon those who captured them. Consequently, civilians were not always taken into captivity. If cities gave up before being attacked, their inhabitants would likely be spared, but there are accounts of cities being sacked and their inhabitants slaughtered. In a war against Cuetlachtlán, for example, the Aztecs massacred the elderly, women, and children until the enemy nobles begged them to stop and promised to provide tributes. In another episode, King Ahuitzotl, while campaigning on the south Pacific coast, ordered that all prisoners be killed because of the difficulty in transporting them back to the Aztec capital.

The accuracy of statistics regarding captives in Aztec warfare has been debated, but it seems that prisoners were taken in far greater numbers than in European warfare. King Ahuitzotl is reputed to have taken 100,000 prisoners on his campaign in Huaxyacac, and the taking of more than 10,000 captives in a single campaign was far from unusual.

References

Inga Clendinnen, *Aztecs: An Interpretation* (Cambridge: Cambridge University Press, 1991).

Geoffrey W. Conrad and Arthur A. Demerest, *Religion and Empire: The Dynamics of Aztec and Inca Expansionism* (Cambridge: Cambridge University Press, 1984).

Ross Hassig, *Aztec Warfare: Imperial Expansion and Political Control* (Norman: University of Oklahoma Press, 1988).

—Jennifer Ho

B

Bader, Douglas Robert Steuart (1910–1982)

Douglas "Tin Legs" Bader was a highly decorated British fighter ace who became one of the most famous and uncompromising POWs to fall into German captivity during World War II. Born 21 February 1910, Bader became a cadet in the Royal Air Force (RAF) at age 18 and was assigned to 23 Squadron in 1930. The qualities that made him an outstanding athlete also made him an exceptional pilot. However, on 14 December 1931, during a flying demonstration that went terribly wrong, Bader crashed his Bristol fighter, sustaining injuries that necessitated the amputation of both legs. His indomitable spirit not only helped him survive this tragic accident, but also imbued him with a fierce determination to return to the air. Fitted with artificial legs, he fought to fly again and stubbornly challenged his discharge from the RAF. With the outbreak of war he finally won back his wings. An inspired and courageous squadron leader, he also evolved fighter tactics that helped win the Battle of Britain. Shot down over France in August 1941, he soon fell into German hands, but within days he had made the first of many persistent but unsuccessful escape attempts. He became the scourge of his German captors at several prison camps, including Colditz and Stalag Luft 3, and was liberated in April 1945. His life story was told in the book and film *Reach for the Sky*.

Douglas "Tin Legs" Bader, photographed before his capture in 1941 (Imperial War Museum)

For his personal bravery and inspiring leadership, Bader was awarded the rare combination of the Distinguished Service order and Bar, Distinguished Flying Cross and Bar, the Legion d'Honneur, and the Croix de Guerre. A prodigious inspiration for the disabled, he became a Commander of the British Empire in 1956 and was knighted by Queen Elizabeth II in 1976. He died on 4 September 1982.

See also Colditz; Stalag Luft 3

References

Douglas Bader, *Fight for the Sky: The Story of the Spitfire and the Hurricane* (London: Doubleday, 1973).
Paul Brickhill, *Reach for the Sky* (London: Collins, 1954).
P. B. Lucas, *Flying Colours* (London: Hutchinson, 1981).

—Colin Burgess

Barbary Wars

The first foreign military interventions carried out by the United States, the Tripolitan War (1801–1805) and the war with Algiers (1815), came at the end of a centuries-long battle between Europe and the Ottoman Empire for control of the Mediterranean. For generations, Ottoman-sponsored corsairs from Tripoli, Tunis, Algiers, and Morocco had preyed on European coasts and shipping, and carried thousands of captives back to North Africa. By the late eighteenth century, military intervention, bilateral treaties, and the efforts of two religious orders, the Trinitarians and Mercedarians, had greatly diminished the threat of Barbary corsairs and reduced the number of Europeans held in North Africa.

When the United States declared its independence from Britain, however, it lost immunity from attack on the high seas. A 1778 commercial treaty with France brought protection against North African corsairs, but after the American Revolution, the fledgling nation had to negotiate its own agreements. Only Morocco settled for a treaty without tribute, resolving in 1787 to cease attacks on American vessels for a period of 50 years. The other Barbary States demanded money in exchange for security, and the United States capitulated, judging even large indemnities less costly than war. Pressured to defend American commerce and citizens against North African privateering, Congress appropriated millions of dollars to appease the Barbary States and ransom approximately 150 American captives, and the Senate ratified peace treaties with Algiers (1795), Tripoli (1796), and Tunis (1799). Their punishing terms stirred resentment in the United States and support for the subsequent wars.

The Tripolitan War, memorialized in the Marine Hymn, began on 14 May 1801 after the United States refused to increase its agreed payments to the pasha (sometimes spelled bashaw). At first, all the Barbary powers aligned with Tripoli, but a successful blockade and repeated bombardments by the U.S. Navy, led by Captains Richard Dale and Edward Preble, convinced Tunis and Algiers, and later Morocco, to break ranks and renew treaties with the United States. Tripoli did not surrender until Captain William Eaton led an American land force across the desert to Derna in April and turned back a counterattack in May 1805. A month later, Tripoli signed an accord to accept a small settlement and free all Americans held captive in Algiers.

In 1815, the United States entered its second war against a Barbary power and sent the navy to Algiers. After seizing an Algerian galley off the coast and threatening to besiege Algiers on 30 June 1815, Captain Stephen Decatur compelled the dey to release all American captives, renounce all tributes, and pay compensation. Then he exacted similar agreements from the rulers of Tunis and Tripoli.

The North African practice of enslaving captives had been in the public eye long before the hostilities broke out. Readers in the United States followed the military engagements in press reports and learned from published accounts about Americans who met this fate. These Barbary captivity narratives drew upon an established genre of firsthand accounts of captivity among American Indians and sometimes used the example of European slavery in the Barbary States to argue for abolishing African slavery in the United States. During the late eighteenth and early nineteenth centuries, European and American leaders proposed cooperative measures to stamp out Barbary corsairs and to free European captives. Thomas Jefferson suggested the formation of a league of maritime nations, and Britain's Sir Sidney Smith established a society for the abolition of white and black slavery in North Africa. In the end, France struck out alone to stamp out the Barbary corsairs. Ending Barbary piracy and captivity formed an important pretext for French invasion and subsequent colonization of Algeria in 1830.

References

Robert J. Allison, *The Crescent Obscured: The United States and the Muslim World, 1776–1815* (New York: Oxford University Press, 1995).

Paul Baepler, ed., *White Slaves, African Masters: An Anthology of American Barbary Captivity*

Narratives (Chicago: University of Chicago Press, 1999).
Michael Kitzen, *Tripoli and the United States at War: A History of Relations with the Barbary States, 1785–1805* (Jefferson, NC: McFarland, 1993).
Franklin Lambert, *The Barbary Wars: American Independence in the Atlantic World* (New York: Hill and Wang, 2005).
Richard B. Parker, *Uncle Sam in Barbary: A Diplomatic History* (Gainesville: University Press of Florida, 2004).

—*Gillian Weiss*

Barbed-wire Disease

Barbed-wire disease (also known as "barbed-wire-itis" or "stalag syndrome") is the name commonly given to a psychological condition that affects POWs and civilian internees. The term seems to have been coined by A. L. Vischer, who published the first detailed study of the subject in 1919.

Vischer identified a number of symptoms of the disease, including intense irritability, difficulty in concentration, restlessness, memory failure, moodiness, extreme lethargy or listlessness, and depression. In addition, he argued that prisoners' latent feelings of guilt at being captured (regardless of the circumstances of capture) often drive them to find fault with everything around them and to attempt to elevate their own status over that of other prisoners. The same feelings might drive a prisoner to display intense hatred of other prisoners, or self-loathing based on a feeling of utter uselessness. By the same token, affected prisoners might display feelings of suspicion bordering on paranoia, as they attribute evil or malicious motives to everyone around them, guards and other prisoners alike.

According to Vischer, a number of factors combine to produce this state of mind. The first is simply the loss of freedom, the prisoners' inability to do as they please, when they please. The very fact that the captor is in control of so much of the prisoner's life is, in Vischer's eyes, one of the most pernicious influences. Monotony, the realization that every day is the same as the last, is also a factor. This lack of variety is complicated by the fact that it is indefinite. A criminal in a penal institution at least knows the length of his sentence and so can look forward to a certain date of release. The POW has no way of knowing if his captivity will last weeks or months or years; there is no release date to look forward to, and this accentuates the prisoner's feeling of helplessness. The lack of privacy is also important. In the cramped confines of a prison camp, it is virtually impossible to get a moment to oneself, a period of silence to be alone with one's thoughts. Indeed, many prisoners intentionally have committed minor infractions simply to get themselves placed in solitary confinement, where they can have a few days away from their fellow prisoners. Finally, Vischer identified sexual deprivation as a factor in barbed-wire disease, although later writers have placed less emphasis on this element. The absence of actual sexual intercourse was probably less important in this regard than the lack of other forms of interaction with members of the opposite sex, such as simple conversation.

Interestingly, Vischer argued that ill-treatment in captivity has little to do with the onset of barbed-wire disease. Civilian internees living in relatively comfortable camps showed the same incidence of the condition as did prisoners in the most brutal work camps. Furthermore, he stated that the condition does not disappear once captivity ends; a period of therapy and readjustment is necessary, and even then the symptoms might never entirely disappear. Indeed, they might be joined by other symptoms, including irresponsibility (a product of living in an environment where one is absolved of responsibility for making decisions concerning one's life), dishonesty (a carryover of the prisoner's tendency to be less than honest with his captors), and fear of crowds or feelings of embarrassment when in groups of people. The condition might also manifest itself in emotional outbursts, acute discontent, alcoholism, chronic apathy, and in extreme cases, complete withdrawal from society.

Lack of privacy, a factor in barbed-wire disease, is a major source of psychological stress for POWs (Jonathan F. Vance)

See also Rehabilitation

References
Pascal Daudin and Hernán Reyes, "How Visits by the ICRC Can Help Prisoners Cope with the Effects of Traumatic Stress," in Yael Danieli et al., eds., *International Responses to Traumatic Stress* (Amityville, NY: Baywood Publishing, 1996): 219–255
Manfred Jeffrey and E. J. G. Bradford, "Neurosis in Escaped Prisoners of War," *British Journal of Medical Psychology* 20 (1946): 422–435.
Brian H. Kirman, "Mental Disorder in Released Prisoners of War," *Journal of Mental Science* 92 (1946): 808–813.
P. H. Newman, "The Prisoner-of-War Mentality: Its Effect After Repatriation," *British Medical Journal* 1 (1 January 1944): 8–10.
A. L. Vischer, *Barbed Wire Disease: A Psychological Study of the Prisoner of War* (London: John Bale, Sons, and Danielsson, 1919).

—*Jonathan F. Vance*

BASIL II BULGAROCTONUS (958–1025 C.E.)

The Byzantine Emperor from 976 to 1025, Basil II solidified the empire's presence in the Balkans, Mesopotamia, Georgia, and Armenia, and at the same time exerted greater control over the military aristocracy and the church than had his predecessors. He is known in history by the sobriquet "Bulgaroctonus" (the Bulgar Slayer), which derives in part from his treatment of enemy prisoners of war.

On 29 July 1014, Basil fought a Bulgar army at the Pass of Chimbalongus in the valley of the river Struma in Macedonia. The Bulgar Tsar Samuel escaped, but Basil captured almost all of the remainder of his army, between 14,000 and 15,000 soldiers. Before releasing the prisoners, Basil ordered that 99 out of every 100 prisoners be completely blinded, and that every one hundredth prisoner be blinded in one eye. When this woeful remnant of his army returned to Samuel at Prespa in Macedonia, he collapsed and died at the sight. In subsequent campaigning in 1016 to subdue the Bulgars, Basil blinded every Bulgarian he captured. He completed the eradication of the Bulgarian Empire in 1018, and, despite his sobriquet, treated the captured Bulgarian royal family with great restraint. He died while in the process of planning a recovery of Sicily from the Arabs.

References
Sir Steven Runciman, *A History of the First Bulgarian Empire* (London: G. Bell and Sons, 1930).

—*B. Alan Guthrie III*

BATAAN DEATH MARCH

One of the most notorious atrocities committed against POWs in the Pacific theater of World War II, the Bataan Death March took American and Filipino troops to prison camps in the northern Philippines after they surrendered to the Japanese on the Bataan Peninsula on 9 April 1942. As a result of their three-month defense of the peninsula, American forces were already physically and mentally exhausted, having been forced to subsist on half rations or less and suffering from a variety of diseases, including malaria, scurvy, beriberi, and dysentery. At the time of capitulation, the American commander, General Edward P. King, asked that he be allowed to organize the movement of troops out of the peninsula, but the Japanese refused, having developed their own two-phase plan. Under their program, captives would first be assembled at Balanga, a town about halfway up Bataan on a main road near the east coast. The bulk of American troops were located in the area of Mariveles on the southern tip of the peninsula and moved up the main highway, which ran east, then north along the coast. A smaller number marched up a secondary road near the west coast and then crossed eastward to the assembly point. Since the defenders were scattered at the time of surrender, some traveled only a few miles, but many walked 20 miles or more to get to Balanga. After this first phase was completed, a second phase began, with the captives moving north along the east coast highway to its intersection with Route 7, where their path turned east to the railhead at San Fernando, a trek of about 31 miles. From San Fernando they rode

25 miles by train to Capas, then hiked another nine miles overland to Camp O'Donnell, a former Filipino army base in central Luzon and their final destination. They were to be fed periodically along the way and rested at established intervals. Those needing medical services were to be treated at field hospitals set up in Balanga and San Fernando.

Both parts of the plan quickly unraveled. Lieutenant General Masaharu Homma, the overall Japanese commander, left its execution up to two subordinates, who failed to coordinate their efforts. Many other problems developed as well. The plan estimated that 35,000 prisoners would be taken, but twice that number surrendered—12,000 Americans and 66,000 Filipinos. Nor did the Japanese appreciate the malnourished and dispirited condition of their captives. Supplies that were to be used for the prisoners were used instead to support the Japanese attack on Corregidor, which began at the same time as the evacuation. During that attack, some POWs were killed by friendly fire at Mariveles when the removal began. Many who died along the way succumbed to exhaustion (their guards expected them to march much faster than they could), exposure, disease, hunger, and thirst. A portion of the suffering was the result of thoughtlessness, but Japanese cruelty also took its toll as men were beaten, robbed, bayoneted, shot, beheaded, run over, mutilated, and even buried alive. One incident of mass murder occurred near Balanga when Japanese soldiers executed 350 to 400 men of the Ninety-first Philippine Army Division. The train trip from San Fernando to Capas was a different kind of hell for the prisoners as they were crammed into metal railroad cars whose doors were then sealed. The stench of dying men and the heat generated by the metal cars made the journey unbearably oppressive. However, Japanese treatment was inconsistent; some prisoners rode in trucks to Camp O'Donnell while their compatriots suffered bitterly along the march.

In total, between 600 and 650 Americans and 5,000 to 10,000 Filipinos perished in the Death March, which ended in late April. American officials did not learn of the fate of their men until mid-1943 and waited until early 1944 before informing the American public. Demands for retribution were swift, and when President Harry S Truman explained the use of the atomic bombs on Hiroshima and Nagasaki in August 1945, he mentioned the atrocities at Bataan. After the war, General Homma was tried by the International Military Tribunal of the Far East for war crimes committed by his men, and he was executed in 1946.

See also Cabanatuan; Sandakan-Ranau Death March; World War II—Far East

References

Anton F. Bilek, *No Uncle Sam: The Forgotten of Bataan* (Kent, OH: Kent State University Press, 2003).

Stanley L. Falk, *Bataan: The March of Death* (New York: Norton, 1962).

Preston John Hubbard, *Apocalypse Undone: My Survival of Japanese Imprisonment during World War II* (Nashville, TN: Vanderbilt University Press, 1990).

Donald Knox, ed., *Death March: The Survivors of Bataan* (New York: Harcourt Brace Jovanovich, 1981).

—*Robert S. La Forte*

BERGEN-BELSEN

In April 1945, British forces liberated Bergen-Belsen, a concentration camp complex located near Hanover, Germany. The contents of the "Horror Camp" shocked and disgusted hardened soldiers and medics alike. As a result of extensive British film and press coverage of conditions in the camp, Belsen was held up as a symbol of the cruelty of the Nazi regime, and provided further evidence to the Allies of the Nazis' program to exterminate European Jewry.

Bergen-Belsen was not originally intended to serve as an extermination camp. Unlike Auschwitz-Birkenau, Belsen's installations did not include gas chambers or large crematoria. Belsen was originally built to house prisoners of war near German Army barracks constructed in 1935, but by 1942 the camp was nearly empty after epidemics decimated the

Bergen Belsen prior to 1945

primarily Russian prison population. In April 1943, slave laborers were used to rebuild the Bergen-Belsen site as the result of an agreement between the German Foreign Office and the SS, who planned to detain 30,000 Jews for use in an exchange program. The *Austauschjuden*, or "Exchange Jews," were prominent Jews or those holding dual nationalities, held ransom in exchange for German prisoners held by Allied governments. Approximately 7,000 exchange Jews from Poland, Greece, Spain, Holland, and Hungary were sent to Belsen from July 1943 to early 1944, although many of the Poles were sent to Auschwitz-Birkenau the following year. Prisoners were housed in subdivisions of the camp complex by nationality or political status.

As in other camps, work was mandatory. Prisoners labored for long hours salvaging leather from shoes, working in the kitchen, and extracting valuables from corpses. The SS guards often withheld food from prisoners or administered brutal beatings as punishment for failure to meet their quota. During the first year of their internment, Hungarian exchange Jews received comparatively lenient treatment, since they did not have to work or attend roll calls, and were permitted to wear civilian clothing.

In the first half of 1944, food was inadequate but endurable; prisoners were given a daily ration of thin soup, bread, and turnips. There was inadequate sanitation, no privacy, and no medication available for prisoners despite an improvised hospital section in the camp. Despite the hardships, a limited cultural life was pursued by healthy inmates, and some groups maintained Jewish law to provide a measure of structure and government in the camp. Most maintained the hope of escaping the camp through the exchange program. Ultimately, very few Jews were successfully rescued from the camp by diplomatic means.

In March 1944, as a result of a decision by the SS that the complex was underutilized, Bergen-Belsen was designated a reception camp for sick prisoners, and a section of the camp was set aside for this purpose. In the deceptively named *Erholungslager* (convalescence camp), tuberculosis sufferers were housed in bare huts with no blankets, mattresses, or medical attention. Many of these prisoners died shortly thereafter. The population of the camp exploded as German forces retreated from Poland and the SS evacuated forced laborers and political prisoners from the eastern extermination camps by train or in death marches. In December 1944, Belsen was transformed into a concentration camp under the brutal command of SS Captain Josef Kramer, a former commander at Auschwitz-Birkenau. Prisoners were forced to attend a roll call in freezing temperatures, resulting in many deaths. Captives arrived by the tens of thousands; overcrowding, malnourishment, and exposure fed a typhus epidemic. Huts meant to house 60 people were crammed with 600 prisoners. The crematorium was inadequate to the task, and corpses littered the ground in piles outside the squalid, overcrowded huts and tents, causing further disease. It is estimated that over 35,000 prisoners died of starvation and disease between January and April 1945, including Anne Frank.

On 12 April 1945, German forces in the area surrendered to the advancing British 2nd Army. The Germans deceptively portrayed Belsen as a quarantined prisoner of war camp afflicted by typhus; as a result, it was not liberated until 15 April 1945. British soldiers of the 63rd Anti-Tank Regiment discovered over 10,000 unburied corpses and 50,000 emaciated survivors in various stages of starvation, guarded by German and Hungarian SS troops. The prisoners were fed barely 400 calories daily in the final weeks before liberation, but had gone without nourishment since the German surrender. There was evidence of cannibalism. British soldiers were incredulous when they found tons of untouched Red Cross food and medical supplies at a nearby German Army training school. Inmates remained in camp to receive treatment and nourishment, but 14,000 more died before doctors could gain control over outbreaks of typhus and dysentery. In a ceremony on 21 May 1945, the last vestiges of Bergen-Belsen were burned to the ground by the British.

Though reports had been received from the Red Army of the horrors at extermination camps, Bergen-Belsen was the first concentration camp to be extensively photographed and filmed by the British. Over radio broadcasts, in print, and in movie theaters, the horrific story of conditions within Bergen-Belsen was widely circulated to demonstrate the inhumanity of the Nazi regime and provided further moral justification to the Allies' war effort.

See also Auschwitz; Buchenwald; Concentration Camps; Dachau; Extermination Camps; Frank, Anne

References

Azriel Eisenberg, *Witness to the Holocaust* (New York: Pilgrim Press, 1981).

Martin Gilbert, *The Holocaust: The Jewish Tragedy* (London: Collins, 1986).

Eberhard Kolb, *Bergen-Belsen: From "Detention Camp" to Concentration Camp, 1943-1945* (Göttingen: Vandenhoeck & Ruprecht, 1986).

Anita Lasker-Wallfisch, *Inherit the Truth, 1939-1945: The Documented Experience of a Survivor of Auschwitz and Belsen* (London: Gilles de la Mare, 1996).

Joanne Reilly, *Belsen: The Liberation of a Concentration Camp* (New York: Routledge, 1998).

Ben Shepard, *After Daybreak: The Liberation of Belsen, 1945* (London: Jonathan Cape, 2005).

—Andrew Paul Burtch

BERGER, GOTTLOB (1896–1975)

Gottlob Berger, a senior general of the Waffen-SS, commanded the entire German prison camp organization for the last months of World War II. He had previously been the head of the SS recruitment section, but was reassigned in the wake of the attempted assassination of Adolf Hitler on 20 July 1944. That plot exposed the disloyalty of officers of the Reserve Army, the branch responsible for the administration of prisoner-of-war camps, and gave Hitler the excuse to appoint SS chief Heinrich Himmler to the military post of commander of the Reserve Army. This legal fig leaf was designed to maintain the illusion that the armed forces, rather than the SS, still retained authority over POWs, as required by the Geneva Convention.

On 1 October 1944, Himmler appointed Berger to run the prisoner-of-war branch of the Reserve Army. Much to Himmler's later surprise, Berger proved to be a fair administrator who showed concern for the plight of at least the Western POWs. He openly disagreed with Himmler on the rate of distribution of Red Cross parcels to POW camps and, directly disobeying orders from Berlin, personally escorted some of the Prominenten (prominent prisoners who were either close relatives of high-ranking Allied officials or significant personalities in their own right) to Swiss custody, rather than send them to Berlin where they would have been used as hostages by the increasingly desperate Nazi leadership. Berger also personally organized the surrender of POW camps to advancing Allied armies.

At his trial at Nuremberg, Gottlob Berger received many testimonials from high-ranking Allied officers in appreciation for his efforts on behalf of the prisoners, and he was released from prison in 1951. He was later honored by a group of American former POWs, led by Major Generals Delmar T. Spivey and Arthur W. Vanaman, for "his humanity . . . and the protection and care he gave Prisoners-of-War during the critical last days of World War II."

See also British Free Corps

References
Bernd Wegner, *Chef OKW: Das Kriegsgefangenenwesen unter Gottlob Berger* (Lindhorst, Germany: Askania, 1984).

—*Vasilis Vourkoutiotis*

BESLAN

September 1 is the first day of school for Russian children, and from Soviet times into the post-Communist period, the day is treated as a virtual secular holiday. Every school in the Russian Federation celebrates the so-called "Day of Knowledge," when children, dressed in their finest clothes and, accompanied by their parents and siblings, go to school to the sounds of music to hear speeches from administrators, teachers, and older students. On 1 September 2004, approximately 30 heavily armed fighters, of mostly Chechen and Ingush descent and dressed in camouflage uniforms and black masks, took advantage of these events and seized control of School Number One in the city of Beslan, in the North Ossetian region of Russia, taking over 1,300 schoolchildren and adults hostage.

Since Vladimir Putin rose to power, first as Russia's prime minister in 1999 and subsequently as the country's president, the conflict between Russia and Chechen separatists evolved, as Peter Baker and Susan Glasser put it, "from a nationalist struggle for independence into a blood feud in which both sides terrorized civilians with wanton cruelty." Russian forces have dropped more ordnance on the capital of Chechnya, Grozny, than any European city has endured since World War II, resulting in many civilian casualties. International human rights organizations have criticized the practice by Russian security forces of *Zachistki* (cleansing operations), known locally as "disappearances," which allegedly involve the capture, torture, and in some cases execution of Chechen men of fighting age.

Unable to match federal forces with conventional methods, Chechen fighters rely on terrorist acts against mainly civilian targets. Several events foreshadowed the Beslan hostage crisis. On the night of 21 August 2004, for example, a week before scheduled presidential elections in Chechnya, several hundred well-armed Chechen fighters carried out a large military operation in Grozny, killing and injuring dozens of federal troops and citizens. An increasingly common practice has been the use of female suicide bombers known as *shakhidki*. On 24 August, two *shakhidki* boarded two planes at Domodedovo Airport in Moscow—one paid an airline official a paltry bribe of 1,000 rubles to bypass airport security—setting off explosions within minutes of each other, killing themselves and all 90 passengers on board both planes. And on 31 August, a *shakhidki* blew herself up outside the Rizhskaya metro station in Moscow, killing nearly a dozen civilians.

The next day, the armed Chechen and Ingush fighters (including two *shakhidki* covered with explosives) drove into the Beslan School compound and surrounded the crowd of children and adults assembled for the "Day of Knowledge" celebrations. They forced the hostages into the gymnasium and covered it with explosives. The most powerful bomb was connected to spring-loaded trigger pedals, the hostage-takers telling the captives that if either of the two men pressing down the pedals removed their feet, the bombs would explode. The fighters also killed several hostages in the early stages of the crisis. Some were executed in order to intimidate the other hostages; a group of men was executed after they had been forced to build barricades around the school.

For nearly a day and a half, efforts to negotiate with the hostage-takers failed. Authorities then turned to Ruslan Aushev, a Soviet Afghan war hero, former president of Ingushetia, and a rival of Putin. Aushev had good relations with some Chechen leaders and was therefore allowed to enter the building, where the hostage-takers gave him a note addressed "To his Excellency, President of the Russian Federation Putin, from the servant of Allah, Shamil Basayev." The radical Chechen separatist leader Basayev, who later assumed responsibility for the seizure, listed a series of demands, including that Russian troops withdraw from Chechnya and that Chechnya be granted its independence. The release of prisoners would begin only after Putin signed a decree ordering the pull-out. The hostage-takers also warned that if federal authorities captured their relatives, they would kill half of the hostages. If the demands were not met, they threatened to blow up the school.

Aushev convinced the hostage-takers to release nursing infants and their mothers, and upon leaving the school he confirmed what many already suspected—that many more than the officially reported 354 people were being held. He reported that conditions inside the gymnasium had become intolerable; the heat was unbearable, and because the hostage-takers refused to receive food and water, many of the captives had resorted to drinking urine. During the trial of the lone-surviving hostage-taker, Nur-Pashi Kulayev, children testified that the women hostages told the boys to urinate into bottles for the younger children to drink.

In the afternoon of 3 September, the hostage-takers agreed that medical workers could remove the bodies of some of the victims from the school grounds. As the removal team, composed of FSB (Federal Security Service, formerly the KGB) officers, began removing the bodies, explosions occurred inside the school. The hostage-takers opened fire on the security forces surrounding the school, and an intense battle ensued. A portion of the gymnasium roof collapsed as a result of the explosions, killing several civilians. As the battle raged, hostages attempted to escape through the barrage of gunfire being exchanged by the hostage-takers, police and security forces, and armed civilians; many died in the attempt.

It took security forces four hours to make their way into the school. By the time the chaotic battle ended, over 330 people had been killed, including 186 children, and hundreds of civilians suffered injuries. Only two of the 32 hostage-takers survived. One was viciously killed by an angry mob of citizens while being escorted away. The other, a Chechen carpenter named Nur-Pashi Kulayev, is currently standing trial on charges of murder, kidnapping, banditry, and terrorism in a North Ossetian court.

Putin's government has been severely criticized for its handling of the Beslan school crisis. His two closest security officials, Nikolai Patrushev (head of the Federal Security Service) and Rashid Nurgaliev (head of the Interior Ministry), arrived secretly in Ossetia but remained away from the scene. The Kremlin's hand-picked North Ossetian president Aleksandr Dzasohov waited for word from Moscow and rejected requests from the hostage-takers to negotiate, as did Ingush president General Murat Ziazikov, another Putin ally. Putin remained silent throughout the crisis, and paid only a brief visit to a hospital in the regional capital Vladikavkaz early on the morning of 4 September. In his speech to the nation shortly after the siege, Putin accepted no responsibility for the manner in which the crisis unfolded, downplayed the link between his Chechnya policy and the hostage-taking, and instead linked the event to international terrorism.

The relatives of the victims of the Beslan massacre have organized in order to pressure the Russian government to determine exactly what happened during the crisis. The Beslan Mothers' Committee, made up of mothers who lost relatives, is a constant fixture at the trial of Nur-Pashi Kulayev. In August 2005, the organization staged a daylong sit-in protest in the North Ossetian courthouse where the trial is being held. The organization has accused Putin of attempting to conceal official incompetence in carrying out negotiations and failing to prevent the siege, and on 1 September 2005, the Committee refused to allow Putin to attend memorial ceremonies in Beslan on the anniversary. Later the same month, several mothers traveled to Moscow and met with Putin; however, they believe they will never get answers to questions about how dozens of heavily armed gunmen dodged military checkpoints around North Ossetia's borders, how they made it into the city of Beslan undetected, why negotiations failed to resolve the crisis, who is to blame for the first explosion, and why security forces used tank shells and flame-throwers during the siege, which the women believe resulted in many unnecessary deaths. In December 2005, the Voice of Beslan (made up of Beslan Mothers' Committee members) sent a statement to European Union and U.S. leaders asking for assistance in investigating what really happened during the siege. Specifically, they asked the U.S. government to declassify satellite images of the school during the siege.

In the wake of the crisis, the Russian and North Ossetian governments organized commissions to investigate the events surrounding the siege. In November 2005, a North Ossetian parliamentary commission report criticized law enforcement agencies for failing to prevent the seizure of the school. The commission head, Stanislav Kesayev, stated that a large number of heavily armed people should not have been able to gain access to a major transportation hub such as Beslan. A Federal Parliamentary Commission is also interviewing hundreds of witnesses, ostensibly to determine the actions of Russian officials and security forces during the crisis. Its report was published on 26 December 2005, and it concluded that Chechen terrorists, not Russian forces, were responsible for the death of over 300 hostages.

See also Hostages

References

Peter Baker and Susan Glasser, *Kremlin Rising: Vladimir Putin's Russia and the End of Revolution* (New York: Scribners, 2005).

Lilia Shevtsova, *Putin's Russia*, revised edition (Washington: Carnegie Endowment for International Peace, 2005).

—Mark Eaton

Biafran War (1967–1970)

On 30 May 1967, the Military Governor of Eastern Nigeria proclaimed the region to be the sovereign and independent Republic of Biafra. A three-year civil war with Nigeria's Federal Military Government (FMG) ensued, claiming at least a million lives. Once praised as Africa's new "model for democracy," Nigeria had embodied the West's hopes for stability in the region. American press accounts described it as "one of the most promising African nations" and "a magnet for Western investment." In

1967, seven years after gaining its independence from Great Britain, Nigeria's promise seemed unlikely to be fulfilled.

By December 1964, Nigeria's economic and political development had come to a halt during the nation's first post-independence general election. The following year, anti-government violence erupted again during the Western region's election. On 15 January 1966, Nigeria's government was overthrown in a military coup. During the coup, Nigeria's federal prime minister, Sir Abubakar Tafawa Balewa, and two of the country's regional prime ministers, Sir Ahmadu Bello of the Northern region and Chief Samuel Akintola of the Western region, were murdered. Following the coup, Major General Aguiyi-Ironsi, an Eastern Ibo, became Nigeria's new head of state. In May, the North's Muslim Hausa population retaliated for Bello's murder and killed hundreds of non-Hausa-Fulanis, primarily Ibos, living in the Northern region.

Although a majority of the southern populations had supported the January coup, Northerners came to view it as an Ibo conspiracy to control Nigeria's government. Ironsi's abolition of the tribal-based federal system, coupled with military promotions that favoured Ibos, alienated Northerners and led to anti-Ironsi demonstrations in the North. On 28–29 July, Northern soldiers led a military coup and killed Major General Ironsi and approximately 200 Ibo officers.

In the aftermath of the coup, the federal military appointed Lieutenant-Colonel Gowon, a Northern Christian, as Nigeria's new head of state. By August, Lieutenant-Colonel Odumeguw Ojukwu, the Ibo military governor of the Eastern region, predicted the imminent secession of the East. Between September and October, feuding between the two tribal populations led to the slaughter of 100,000 people, and initiated the exodus of approximately two million Ibos from the North.

Gowon's efforts to prevent Nigeria's disintegration failed. On 6 July, the first military actions of the Nigerian civil war erupted. The initial victories belonged to the FMG with the capture of the Biafran towns of Ogoja on 6 July and Nsukka on 15 July. Later that month, the FMG captured Bonny Island and its offshore oil installations. On 9 August 1967, the FMG's apparent military victory was reversed when, under the leadership of Brigadier Victor Banjo, the Biafran military gained control over the entire mid-Western region of Nigeria without a shot. Two days later, Banjo announced the secession of the region from Nigeria. These events shocked Gowon out of his complacency. Biafra's military achievements in the mid-West were short-lived. By the end of September, the FMG's forces expelled the Biafran military and returned the secessionist state to its original size. Armed with modern weapons from the Soviet Union and the United Kingdom, the FMG was able to capture Enugu, Biafra's capital, and cut off the secessionist state's border with Cameroon by November. Despite the newfound strength of Gowon's forces, the Biafran military refused to capitulate. Instead, along with Biafra's citizens, it moved deeper into the interior. By 12 January 1970, Nigeria's civil war was over and Biafra's secessionist attempt had failed.

As the population in the interior region grew, members of the international press and aid workers increasingly observed evidence of malnutrition and starvation. By the war's end, approximately one million people, predominately children, had died from starvation. In an attempt to gain international support for Biafran secession, the Biafran government had accused the FMG of carrying out a deliberately genocidal military campaign against the Ibos. In order to refute this accusation, the FMG invited international observers from Britain, Canada, Poland, and Sweden as well as representatives from the Organization of African Unity and the United Nations to visit Nigeria's war zones. By July 1969, after approximately one year of investigation, the observers found no evidence to substantiate the Biafran government's claim, and even praised the FMG's forces for their behavior in the war zones and their generally good treatment of prisoners of war.

Before the arrival of observers in Nigeria, however, journalists and aid workers had discovered that both the FMG and Biafran forces had not in all cases abided by the Geneva Convention for the humane treatment of prisoners. The International Committee of the Red Cross (ICRC) had voiced concern about reports that the FMG forces had executed three prisoners of war and massacred numerous civilians. In a public appeal, the ICRC urged both forces to abide by the Geneva Convention. By January 1968, it appeared as though the ICRC's request had fallen on deaf ears. An American artist and a French filmmaker, accused of being mercenaries, narrowly avoided execution by the FMG. Later that year, a British film crew witnessed the interrogation and execution of a Biafran soldier by a Nigerian army lieutenant. The lieutenant himself, however, was subsequently executed for this infraction. Events such as these appeared to have been rare and were generally carried out by individuals who abused their authority over prisoners of war; such actions did not reflect an official policy of either side. Most often, civilians were the victims of human rights abuses. In spite of the claims made by the international observers, federal and Biafran forces were responsible for illegally seizing property, rape, torture, and murder. At times, soldiers murdered hundreds of civilians in a single day.

Although the Nigerian government acted quickly following the war to reconstruct its national economy, and to reconcile its peoples by implementing a program entitled "No Victor, No Vanquished," successive Nigerian governments neglected to investigate officially the vast human rights abuses committed by each side's military until President Olusegun Obasanjo established the Human Rights Violation Investigation Commission in March 1999. According to its mandate, the head of HRVIC, Justice Chukwudifu Oputa, was to investigate all human rights abuses committed in Nigeria since 1966. In May 2002, after approximately three years of investigations, Oputa submitted his report to Obasanjo's government. According to the report, prisoners of war during the Nigerian civil war were at times severely ill-treated; however, of the 340 petitions (of some 10,000 received) concerning human rights violations reviewed by the commission, none were brought forth by former civil war POWs. Nigeria's government neither acted on its recommendations nor disclosed its contents to the public. Rather, the Nigerian Democratic Movement, a Washington-based organization, in cooperation with Nigeria's Civil Society Forum, released it to the international public in January 2005. Due to the Nigerian government's stance on human rights, as demonstrated by its unwillingness to disseminate the Commission's report, full details pertaining to the treatment of POWs in the Nigerian Civil War have yet to be revealed.

References

Herbert Ekwe-Ekwe, *The Biafra War: Nigeria and the Aftermath* (Lewiston, NY: Edwin Mellen Press, 1990).

Dan Jacobs, *The Brutality of Nations* (New York: Alfred A. Knopf, 1987).

Joseph E. Thompson, *American Policy and African Famine: The Nigeria-Biafra Civil War, 1966–1970* (New York: Greenwood Press, 1990).

—Amanda Green

BICYCLE CAMP

One of several Japanese prisoner-of-war camps on Java during World War II, Bicycle Camp was located in Koenigplein, a suburb of Batavia (now Jakarta, Indonesia), and occupied an area of approximately 700 by 900 feet. Named by the POWs, it was formerly the home of the Tenth Battalion of the Dutch colonial army, a bicycle force. The camp, one of the better facilities used by the Japanese to house prisoners, was surrounded by a high brick wall and composed of several large, two-story brick barracks that held approximately 300 men each. Their construction was typical of the tropics—open-air, breezeway-type buildings with verandas and unscreened windows. Three or four men were usually assigned to a cubicle or room. There were no beds, but the prisoners improvised them. Each barracks had water and electricity. Sanitation was adequate and kitchens were well equipped but food, as always, was in short supply. The prisoners established a canteen where, if they had money, they could purchase food or other useful items. POWs regularly worked in the surrounding area, in gardens, on the docks, or in factories. Men with special knowledge and skills gave lectures, held classes, put on plays, held boxing matches, or engaged in other recreational activities. Some had clandestine radios and, at great risk, kept abreast of what was happening.

Although treatment by Japanese guards could be brutal, in retrospect many of the POWs (a large number of whom later worked on the Burma-Thailand Railway) considered the Bicycle Camp to be among the least objectionable camps. Prisoners were segregated by nationality into groups that were separated by barbed-wire fencing. In April 1942, the camp housed Indian, British, Dutch, American, and Australian POWs, but in October the Japanese began to send prisoners north, leaving 2,600 men, primarily Australians, in the camp. During the next several months, the population dwindled to slightly more than 100, mostly Dutch, but a few Americans and Australians remained. In August 1943, however, some 4,000 captives were shifted to the camp, taxing its capacity. The number of POWs held there continued to fluctuate until early 1945, when most were shipped to Changi in Singapore. Nevertheless, Bicycle Camp continued to operate until the war's end.

See also Bataan Death March; Changi; Sandakan-Ranau Death March; World War II—Far East

References

Frank Fujita, *Foo: A Japanese-American Prisoner of the Rising Sun* (Denton: University of North Texas Press, 1993).

Rohan D. Rivett, *Behind Bamboo: An Inside Story of the Japanese Prison Camps* (Sydney, Australia: Angus and Robertson, 1946).

—*Robert S. La Forte*

Big Switch, Operation

Big Switch was the code-name for the large exchange of prisoners of war during the Korean War in 1953. It was preceded by Operation Little Switch, which involved the exchange of sick and wounded prisoners.

Negotiations aimed at securing the release of POWs, or at the very least the exchange of sick and wounded, began early in the Korean War but were bogged down over the question of voluntary repatriation, or whether or not a prisoner had the right to refuse repatriation to his home country. These talks dragged on until March 1953, when Chinese Premier Chou En-Lai stated on Peking radio that the Communist governments were prepared to discuss an exchange of sick and wounded POWs under the terms of the 1949 Geneva Convention Relative to the Treatment of Prisoners of War. The agreement was signed on 11 April 1953, with Operation Little Switch beginning on 20 April at Pánmunjŏm. In total, the operation freed 684 United Nations Command (UNC) prisoners in exchange for 6,670 from the North Korean and Chinese forces.

After Little Switch, UNC negotiators continued to press for the release of the rest of their prisoners, and in June 1953 another agreement was signed that paved the way for Operation Big Switch. This operation, which took place from 5 August to 6 September 1953 in a neutral zone near Pánmunjŏm, involved the exchange of 12,773 prisoners (primarily South Koreans) for 70,183 North Korean and 5,640 Chinese POWs. In accordance with the ideological nature of the Korean War, the UNC prisoners were received at a compound named Freedom Village.

See also Korean War

—*Jonathan F. Vance*

United Nations POWs arrive at Freedom Village during Operation Big Switch, August 1953 (National Archives of Canada PA128831)

Black Hole of Calcutta

On 16 June 1756, the troops of Siraj-ud-Dawla, the Nawab of Bengal, attacked the British fort at Calcutta for reasons that are still disputed. The fort surrendered on 20 June after the governor and many high officials had escaped to British ships offshore. After the fall of Calcutta, the Nawab's troops confined those British who had surrendered to a military prison known as the Black Hole—a room measuring 18 feet by 14 feet. Only 23 of the 146 prisoners were alive when the dungeon was opened the next day. Some historians in the early twentieth century cast doubt on the historical accuracy of the event, but today few question its historicity.

Robert Clive, the deputy governor of Madras, was entrusted with the command of the punitive expedition sent out to avenge the atrocity. After inflicting some minor reversals upon the Nawab, Clive forced him to sign a treaty restoring English trading privileges, returning plunder, and granting the English the right to fortify Calcutta and to coin rupees.

The British East India Company entered into a secret treaty with Mir Ja'far, a subordinate of the Nawab, promising him the throne of Bengal in exchange for military assistance to the British cause. On 23 June 1757, Clive and an army of 3,000 defeated the Nawab at the battle of Plassey. Mir Ja'far then became Nawab, executing the deposed ruler. Clive's victory at Plassey laid the foundation of British rule in India, and British outrage over the violation of the rules of war in the incident of the Black Hole seems to have contributed to the British resolution that led to that signal victory.

References
Noel Barber, *The Black Hole of Calcutta: A Reconstruction* (New York: Dorset Press, 1965).
H. H. Dodwell, ed., *The Cambridge History of the British Empire*, vol. 4, *British India*, 1497–1858 (Cambridge: Cambridge University Press, 1929).
Lawrence James, *Raj: The Making and Unmaking of British India* (New York: St. Martin's Press, 1998).

—*Patrick M. O'Neil*

Blue Division

The Blue Division was a unit of Spanish soldiers that fought alongside German forces on the Eastern Front during World War II. Between 1941 and 1945, the Soviet Union captured just over 300 Spaniards on the Eastern Front. These anticommunist soldiers, serving in the German army and Waffen-SS, had volunteered to fight the Red Army to repay the Soviet Union for its attempts to export Communism during Spain's Civil War (1936–1939), when Soviet leader Josef Stalin provided weapons, pilots, training, and political guidance to the Spanish Communists.

At 16,000 strong, the Blue Division was the largest Spanish unit that fought along the Eastern Front during World War II. Incorporated into the German army, it defended positions near Novgorod and Leningrad from late 1941 to late 1943. It was followed in late 1943 by the Blue Legion, a unit of approximately 1,500, which was finally withdrawn under Allied pressure in March 1944. From the withdrawal of the Blue Legion until the end of the war, several hundred Spaniards also served in the Waffen-SS, against the will of the Spanish government. During the course of the war, 30 Spaniards deserted to the Soviet army, most of these while serving with the Blue Legion. Another 350 were captured—almost 100 during just one battle, at Krasni Bor, in February 1943.

Upon capture, Spanish prisoners of war were sent to camps throughout the USSR, often in small groups or together with Germans, Italians, Hungarians, and others. Because Spain was one of the most anticommunist nations in the world, and because Stalin identified the Franco regime as one that had defied him, the Spaniards were not treated humanely. Instead, many were tortured, denied basic essentials, or ordered to labor in dangerous conditions, including mining and forestry operations in the harsh Siberian climate. Many of the prisoners refused to serve as forced laborers, organizing strikes, fasts, and sabotage to avoid aiding the nation that was their persecutor.

After World War II, Spanish soldiers were not included in the repatriations that covered nations officially at war, instead remaining prisoners of the Soviets, even as Germans and Italians were sent home. Spain and the Soviet Union did not establish diplomatic relations until the late 1960s, but indirect negotiations began through the offices of the International Committee of the Red Cross (ICRC) in 1949 to effect the return of the Spanish prisoners, at this time numbering just over 300. With the intensification of the Cold War and the beginning of the Korean War, however, the Spanish government made little progress with its efforts. After the death of Stalin in March 1953, the Spanish government, with the continued assistance of the ICRC, continued its efforts, offering wheat and other commercial considerations indirectly to the USSR through Poland. Finally, in early 1954, the Soviet leadership ordered the release of the remaining Spaniards, in exchange for the proffered Spanish economic concessions. On 2 April 1954, the 286 surviving Spanish POWs arrived at the port of Barcelona on the passenger ship *Semiramis*. More than 50 of the original prisoners had died in the Soviet Union as a direct or indirect result of mistreatment.

References
Gerald Kleinfeld and Lewis Tambs, *Hitler's Spanish Legion: The Blue Division in Russia* (Carbondale: Southern Illinois University Press, 1979).
Luis Suarez Fernandez, *Franco y la URSS* (Madrid: Ediciones RIALP, 1987).
Fernando Vadillo, *Los Prisioneros* (Madrid: Ediciones Barbarroja, 1996).

—*Wayne Bowen*

BOER WAR (1899–1902)

In June 1901, in the midst of the war that pitted the armies of the British Empire against the Afrikaans republics of South Africa, the future prime minister of Great Britain, Sir Henry Campbell-Bannerman, asked the question, "When is a war not a war?" He answered, "When it is carried on by methods of barbarism." No British act of "barbarism" gained more notoriety than the use of concentration camps in South Africa.

The Boer War had not opened well for the British. Due mostly to political constraints, the British army lacked necessary numbers, equipment, and intelligence. To make matters worse, strategy had been determined not by the generals, but by an angry public, spurred on by the yellow press, which demanded the relief of besieged British garrisons. The result was the disastrous "Black Week" of mid-December 1899, when all three British armies were stopped in their tracks. In response to these reverses, supplies were

A group of Boer prisoners after capture at the battle of Paardeberg in 1900 (National Archives of Canada C24627)

readied, volunteers were recruited, more divisions were mobilized, and popular generals were sent to South Africa.

Over the next year, the British advance succeeded in relieving the besieged towns and capturing the capital of the Orange Free State, Bloemfontein, and the major political and economic centers of the Transvaal, Johannesburg, and Pretoria. However, the Boer units in the field (known as commandos) refused to surrender and turned to guerrilla tactics: destroying railroads and telegraph lines, attacking isolated British outposts, and always staying one step ahead of their less mobile pursuers. In early 1901, the new British commander in chief, Lord Kitchener, decided to employ two counterinsurgency techniques to break Boer resistance. One involved a series of blockhouses that would slowly pen in the Boer guerrillas. The other was meant to strip the Boers of their resources: Orders were given to burn their lands, seize their cattle and sheep, and prevent their families from supplying aid by concentrating them in camps originally designed to house refugees. Although the concentration camp had been used a few years earlier by the Spanish in their war with Cuba, it was during the Boer War that its use became widespread and well known.

During the course of the war, the British constructed some 50 camps, eventually housing more than 150,000 men, women, and children. This population included more than 40,000 black African refugees as well. Although most British officers simply deposited their captives into the camps because they were told to do so, some, such as General Lord Methuen, believed that they were removing women and children from harm's way. By the end of the war, however, it was clear to all that the most dangerous place for these civilians was inside the camps. The camps were poorly situated, often far from water sources and from the railway, resulting in long and arduous journeys aboard uncovered and cramped wagons. Shelter, usually tents, was limited and of poor quality, and fuel, both coal and wood, were only haphazardly supplied. Sanitation was insufficient and garbage and human waste became breeding grounds for disease. With few doctors and nurses, epidemics of typhoid and measles resulted. Perhaps most devastating to the camp populations were the insufficient quantity and poor quality of food. The diet, which consisted primarily of flour and mealies, and included neither vegetables nor fruit, led the self-appointed advocate of the South African Women and Children Distress Fund, Emily Hobhouse, to describe the ration as "starvation rate."

Conditions improved only after a great deal of pressure was put on the British government by Hobhouse and others. Among the Boer population, mortality rates in the camps were extremely high through 1901, only starting to drop near the end of the year. The rate of death among the black Africans continued to rise well into 1902. Historians estimate that as many as 28,000 Boers and more than 14,000 Africans died in the concentration camps, most of them women and children.

Nearly 30,000 Boer burghers captured in combat and sympathizers who surrendered during the war were sent to POW camps, located mostly outside of South Africa at places such as the island of St. Helena, Amritsar in India, and Ceylon. Although many of these prisoners died in exile, life for the survivors was certainly better than it was for the civilian population held in concentration camps. The quality of shelter, sanitation, and food was acceptable, schools and churches were established, and a wide range of cultural and sporting activities was promoted. When the war ended, any prisoner willing to sign an oath of allegiance to King Edward VII and agree to accept the Treaty of Vereeniging, which ended the war, was permitted to return home.

The Boers also took British prisoners during the conflict. In the early stages of the war, they were held at racecourses, in schoolhouses, and in other structures far from the fighting. Winston Churchill, Britain's most famous prisoner and a future prime minister, was held at the Model School in Pretoria until he managed to escape. As the British advance strengthened, Boer commanders were forced to take their prisoners with them as they fled across the veldt. In the closing months of the war, a Boer commando led by General J. H. de la Rey was able to capture General Lord Methuen after defeating his force at Tweebosch. A seriously wounded Methuen was returned to the British without any demand.

Not all exchanges were this civil. Throughout the war, both sides complained that the other abused the white flag by continuing to fire after it had been raised. On more than one occasion, prisoners were summarily executed for this abuse. The most notorious execution of prisoners was the killing of twelve Boers captured by the Bush Veldt Carbineers, an Australian unit. Its officers, Lieutenants Harry "Breaker" Morant and Peter Handcock, were court-martialed and put to death by firing squad in February 1902. At their court martial, they claimed in their own defense that shooting prisoners had become an accepted practice and that they were being made "scapegoats for empire." Three months later, the war ended.

See also Churchill, Winston Leonard Spencer; Concentration Camps

References
Aylmer Haldane, *How We Escaped from Pretoria* (London: William Blackwood, 1900).
Emily Hobhouse, *The Brunt of the War and Where It Fell* (London: Methuen, 1902).
Stephen M. Miller, *Lord Methuen and the British Army* (London: Frank Cass, 1999).
Thomas Pakenham, *The Boer War* (New York: Random House, 1979).
S. B. Spies, *Methods of Barbarism* (Cape Town: Barber and Rousseau, 1977).

—*Stephen M. Miller*

BONAPARTE, NAPOLEON (1769–1821)

Napoleon Bonaparte was born to minor nobility in Ajaccio, Corsica, on 15 August 1769. As fate had it, France acquired the island of Corsica from Genoa just before Napoleon's birth. As a result, the Bonaparte family gained access to French institutions and soon sent the young Napoleon to the military academy at Brienne in 1779. Given his apparent natural abilities and aspirations, it was no surprise that Bonaparte was promoted to the Parisian Royal Military Academy in 1784. After completing his formal education, Bonaparte was commissioned into a French artillery regiment. His fortunes were forever changed by his formative years in France, as he received a thorough education in both military science and Enlightenment doctrine. Napoleon's own military ambitions coupled with his Enlightenment values to form an ideal French Revolutionary soldier.

Bonaparte's meteoric rise through the French ranks began as a Revolutionary captain of artillery at Toulon in 1793 and ended with his coronation as emperor of France in 1804. As emperor, Napoleon directed every facet of government, from commanding the military and making political appointments to managing the writing of his *Code Napoléon* and administering the national infrastructure. While his time as emperor brought unprecedented domestic reforms to France, it also brought about disastrous international conflict. Napoleon's personal ambitions drove him to attempt the military conquest of Europe and the imposition of the French revolutionary ideals of *liberté, egalité, and fraternité* upon all Europeans. His policies and military practices led to almost incessant warfare during his time as emperor.

Despite numerous successful campaigns, the French armies were eventually worn down and defeated by a coalition of Great Britain, Russia, Prussia, Spain, Portugal, Austria, and Sweden in October 1813. A few months later Napoleon was forced to surrender unconditionally, and was "given" the tiny Mediterranean island of Elba on which to live out his remaining days in the vicinity of his native Corsica. By 1815, Napoleon was restless and bored living in exile far from events of Paris. In the spring, Bonaparte gave in to his impulse and began the period known as the Hundred Days by taking his Elba bodyguard and returning in

'Napoleon's prison on the island of Elba' (from Désiré Lacroix, Histoire de Napoléon [Paris, 1902])

force to the south of France. As Napoleon marched toward Paris, the recently returned King Louis XVIII evacuated the capital and left it in the hands of the returning emperor. Most of Europe quickly moved against France and mobilized for war. The Hundred Days did not go according to Napoleon's plan, however, and resulted in the catastrophic Battle of Waterloo.

The French defeat at Waterloo prompted Napoleon to flee the continent by surrendering to the first available British naval vessel. Unlike the favorable conditions of Bonaparte's first surrender in 1814, his second abdication saw him stripped of all titles, rank, and wealth, and exiled to the minuscule South Atlantic island of Saint Helena, where he died on 5 May 1821.

See also Napoleonic Wars

References

Robert Asprey, *The Reign of Napoleon* (New York: Basic Books, 2001).
Alexander Grab, *Napoleon and the Transformation of Europe* (New York: Palgrave, 2003).
Paul Johnson, *Napoleon* (New York: Penguin, 2002).
Alan Schom, *Napoleon Bonaparte* (New York: HarperCollins, 1997).

—*Christopher Blackburn*

BOSNIAN WAR (1992–1995)

The war for control over Bosnia, which lasted from April 1992 to October 1995, was characterized by a campaign of mass expulsions and detainments. While Serbian, Croatian, and Muslim factions all participated in brutal ethnic clashes, most reports have identified Serbian forces as the key proponents of ethnic cleansing. Former Bosnian Serb leader Radovan Karadzic targeted Muslims in a campaign that involved harassing and terrorizing civilians through torture, rape, mutilation, murder, confiscation of personal goods, and the desecration of Muslim mosques, libraries, and schools.

In a crisis focused on achieving ethnic purity, people became each warring group's most precious commodity. The exodus of Muslim and Croat Bosnians was reminiscent of the expulsion of Jews throughout World War II. By 1994, of the 536,000 Muslims and Croats who once populated northern Bosnia, only 40,000 to 60,000 remained. By the end of the war, Banja Luka, the second-largest city in Bosnia, held only 4,000 of the 20,000 Muslims who once lived there.

While thousands of Muslims and Croats were expelled, many others were detained as prisoners of war. Because the three parties frequently altered alliances, POWs were sometimes traded among the warring factions. Irfan Ajonivic, the former deputy speaker of parliament in the old Yugoslav federation, was initially captured by Croats but then given to Serbs during the war. Throughout the crisis, the International Committee of the Red Cross (ICRC) was only allowed access to Serb-held "conflict-related prisoners." Reports claim that these prisoners were used in exchanges for Serb POWs. Contrary to the Geneva Convention, Serb POWs were sometimes detained in the same facilities as common criminals. The POWs held by Serbian forces reported a range of incidents while in captivity. Some accused the Bosnian Serb Army of regularly engaging in torture, including the use of electric shock. Some were captured after having played dead among executed civilians. Others reported of being forced to carry the dead bodies of children to makeshift burial sites. Some POW survivors of the Serbian capture of Srebrenica, an eastern Bosnian enclave, had no reports of ill-treatment in captivity beyond bad food.

Military action in Croatia, NATO bombing in Bosnia, and international diplomatic efforts led to the signing of the Dayton Agreement in 1995. The accord created a new dual Bosnia, with the Muslim-Croat Federation controlling 51 percent and the Serbian Republic 49 percent. The agreement also stipulated that the 900 POWs detained during the war be freed by 19 January 1996. A series of POW exchanges occurred in the months following Dayton. In the first of these exchanges, the Bosnian government released about 115 Serbs in return for 132 of the Serbs' prisoners, most of whom had disappeared from Srebrenica after Serbs overran the city during the war. In southwestern Mostar, 127 Serbs were loaded onto buses and driven to Sarajevo's airport for their release. The largest exchange took place on 5 October 1995, when 295 Serbs were released in exchange for 166 Bosnians. In the majority of these exchanges, Bosnian civilians from ethnically cleansed areas of Serb-held territory were exchanged for Serbian POWs.

Trials of alleged war criminals have proceeded since the end of the war in Bosnia. For example, in October 2003 a local Bosnian Serb official, Miroslav Deronjic, pleaded guilty to ordering an attack on the Muslim village of Glogova in eastern Bosnia. Some 60 male villagers were killed, and the women and children deported. He was sentenced to 10 years in prison under a plea-bargain agreement, with the sentence to be served in a prison in Sweden, according to agreements between the International Military Tribunal for the former Yugoslavia and various European governments.

See also Kosovo War

References

Norman L. Cigar, *Genocide in Bosnia: The Policy of "Ethnic Cleansing"* (College Station: Texas A&M University Press, 1995).

Slavenka Drakulic, *They Would Never Hurt a Fly: War Criminals on Trial in The Hague* (Harmondsworth: Penguin UK, 2005).

James Gow, *The Serbian Project and Its Adversaries: A Strategy of War Crimes* (Montreal: McGill-Queen's University Press, 2003).

Carol Rogel, *The Breakup of Yugoslavia and the War in Bosnia* (Westport, CT: Greenwood Press, 1998).

—*Tracy Moore*

BOULLE, PIERRE (1912–1994)

Pierre Boulle was a French novelist whose experiences in Asia during World War II provided the inspiration for the film *The Bridge on the River Kwai*. Born in Avignon on 20 February 1912, Boulle went to Malaya in 1936 to work on a rubber plantation. When the war broke out, he enlisted in the French armed forces in Indochina, joining the Free French forces after the fall of France in 1940. Trained as a saboteur, Boulle entered Indochina to make contact with resistance groups, but after only five days was captured by Thai villagers, who turned him over to the Vichy French authorities. In October 1942, Boulle was court-martialed by the Vichy government, found guilty of treason, deprived of his French citizenship, and sentenced to hard labor. He spent nearly two years in prison until the tide of war turned in the Allies' favor; then, Boulle's captors allowed him and his fellow Free French captives to escape. After the war, Boulle turned to fiction writing. He published *The Bridge over the River Kwai* in French in 1952 (the English edition appeared in 1954) and later wrote the screenplay for the Oscar-winning motion picture. Although Boulle had no firsthand knowledge of conditions endured by the POWs who built the railway that linked Burma and Thailand, some of the book's characters, not to mention the values that it explores, can be traced back to Boulle's wartime experiences in Indochina.

See also The Bridge on the River Kwai; Burma-Thailand (Death) Railway

References

Lucille Frackman Becker, *Pierre Boulle* (New York: Twayne Publishers, 1996).

Pierre Boulle, *My Own River Kwai* (New York: Vanguard, 1967).

—*Tanya Demjanenko*

Boxer Rising (1900)

The Righteous Harmony Society, better known by their English sobriquet, the Boxers, waged a brutal uprising against the European presence in China at the end of the nineteenth century. The violence was confined largely to the northern region, and was provoked by the determination of foreign powers to extend their political and economic influence throughout the country. The Boxers were also deeply disturbed by attempts to Christianize China, and so Western missionaries were particularly targeted.

The conflict was sporadic until June 1900, when Boxer forces and soldiers from the imperial Chinese army laid siege to the foreign quarters of Beijing (written as Peking in contemporary accounts) and Tianjin (Tientsin). Foreigners, including diplomats, merchants, and missionaries, and their Chinese converts took refuge in the embassy district in Beijing, which was hastily fortified against the attackers. Similar preparations were made in Tianjin, and in both cities foreigners endured almost constant barrages of gunfire and took heavy casualties. The governments of the United States, Great Britain, France, Germany, Russia, Japan, Austro-Hungary, and Italy immediately began to prepare a relief expedition, eventually assembling an army of over 50,000 soldiers from eight countries. In a difficult campaign, they relieved Tianjin on 14 July 1900 and Beijing a month later. The death toll was over 230 foreigners; there is little agreement on the number of Boxers, Chinese soldiers, and Christianized Chinese who died, but it is certainly in the tens of thousands.

The rebellion was noted for the almost unimaginable abuse of captives by both sides. The Boxers had begun to capture and execute foreign missionaries as early as 1897, but the spark that ignited the rising may have been struck by the German minister in Beijing, Baron von Ketteler, who beat and captured a young Chinese boy he found in a cart belonging to a Boxer. Violent reprisals broke out in the city almost immediately; a few days later, von Ketteler was shot dead in the street by a Chinese officer and the rest of the foreigners retreated to their fortified compounds. Any who ventured out were almost invariably captured and executed by Boxers or Chinese soldiers, and any soldiers who fell into the hands of the foreigners met the same fate; they were usually bayoneted to death because the besieged defenders could not spare the bullets to shoot them.

Meanwhile, as the cities remained under siege, the Boxers stepped up their attacks against Christian missions in the countryside. The missionaries, mostly British, American, and Swedish, were hunted down and butchered, sometimes by the very people they had recently taught. Englishwoman Emily Whitchurch and New Zealander Edith Searell, who between them had spent 21 years teaching in the schools of the China Inland Mission, were beaten to death by Boxers while they prayed in the remote village of Xiaoyi

(Hsiao-I) in Shanxi (Shansi) province on 29 June 1900. But there was no safety in numbers. On 9 July 1900, a large party of Protestant and Roman Catholic missionaries, teachers, and their families who had been imprisoned at Taiyuan (T'ai-yuen-fu) were executed on the orders of the district governor. In all, 46 men, women, and children were put to death, most of them beheaded. A group of 10 missionaries from Fenzhou (Fen-Cho-fu) were led to believe that they were being evacuated to the coast under the protection of the imperial army; in fact, they were already doomed. At each village they entered, the military commander gave the villagers a choice: They could pay a hefty bribe, or their village would become the site of a massacre. Most of the villagers were willing to pay, but some 20 miles into their march, one village refused to be cowed. In short order, all 10 prisoners, including two children, were hacked to death by the soldiers.

The killing of so many teachers and missionaries outraged public opinion outside China, and calls to avenge these new Christian martyrs, as they were usually styled, became more strident. On 27 July 1900, in a speech at Bremerhaven, Kaiser Wilhelm of Germany promised that no quarter would be given to Chinese soldiers; they would not be taken prisoner, but were to be executed immediately. The various armies of the relief force were not all so bloodthirsty—the British and American units preferred to use the Chinese soldiers they captured as laborers, but contemporary sources note that French and Japanese units were more likely to mutilate and execute prisoners. But after the Boxers were defeated and the Chinese government humbled, little mercy was shown to captives. In Beijing, soldiers of the Royal Welch Fusiliers often marched out 50 to 100 prisoners each morning to be beheaded by a Chinese executioner. Contemporary reports suggest that German units preferred to have Boxer prisoners dig their own grave trenches; they were then forced to stand beside the trench and were shot to death.

In some instances, there was a judicial proceeding of sorts. In March 1900, two men were apprehended and charged with the murder of missionary S.M.W. Brooks; they were executed after a short trial. In August and September 1901, two large groups of supposed Boxers were executed by Chinese officials for their part in the murders of missionaries. The German government preferred to take its own action against the Chinese officer responsible for the death of von Ketteler; when he was captured by Japanese soldiers, the Germans brought him to the exact location of von Ketteler's death, and there he was beheaded.

It is ironic that such abuses occurred just a few months after the Hague Convention of 1899, an effort to create legislative protection for prisoners of war, was signed by the major powers. Clearly, such legislation could do nothing to protect captives in undeclared wars or uprisings.

References

Robert Coventry Forsyth, *The China Martyrs of 1900: A Complete Roll of the Christian Heroes Martyred in China in 1900, with Narratives of Survivors* (London: The Religious Tract Society, 1904).

Diana Preston, *Besieged in Peking: The Story of the 1900 Boxer Rising* (London: Constable, 1999).

Eva Jane Price, *China Journal, 1889–1900: An American Missionary Family during the Boxer Rebellion* (New York: Charles Scribner's Sons, 1989).

Frederic A. Sharf and Peter Harrington, *China, 1900: The Eyewitnesses Speak* (London: Greenhill Books, 2000)

—*Jonathan F. Vance*

BRAINWASHING

See Indoctrination

BRÄNDSTRÖM, ELSA (1888–1948)

A Swedish Red Cross nurse and the daughter of the Swedish ambassador in Petrograd, Elsa Brändström supervised the distribution of relief to over two million Austro-Hungarian and German POWs interned in Russia during World War I. Under her management, 1,016 vanloads of shoes and clothing were supplied to poorly clad prisoners in Siberia, European Russia, and Russian Central Asia (Turkestan). She used her extensive contacts in Russia to ease bureaucratic restrictions and acquire the necessary rolling stock at a time of great shortage. The efforts of the Swedish Red Cross and other neutral philanthropic societies such as the Danish Red Cross and, until 1917, the American Young Men's Christian Association probably saved the lives of thousands of prisoners. Because of Brändström's activity on behalf of POWs, they gave her the nickname "the angel of Siberia." She continued with her mission to the prisoners during the Russian Civil War, despite her own arrest in the summer of 1918 and the execution of four of her colleagues. After the war, she lectured about her work in Russia and raised money to ease the reintegration of prisoners into civilian society. She also opened sanatoriums for disabled POWs and orphanages for their children in Marienborn and Schreibermöhle in Germany for the children of dead prisoners.

See also Russian Civil War; World War I—Eastern Front

References

Elsa Brändström, *Among the Prisoners of War in Russia and Siberia* (London: Hutchinson, 1929).

—*Alon Rachamimov*

The Bridge on the River Kwai

The building of the infamous Burma-Thailand (Death) Railway for the Japanese during World War II is the setting for one of the most celebrated of war films. The film is primarily an illustration of the dangers of the obsessive military mind. Based on the novel by Pierre Boulle, the story focuses on the battle of wills between a Japanese POW camp commander (Sessue Hayakawa) and a British colonel (Alec Guinness) over how a strategic bridge will be built. The project is soon transformed from a product of slave labor to a monument to British pride, even though its successful construction will only benefit the Japanese war effort. Meanwhile, an escaped American prisoner (William Holden) agrees to help a group of British commandos in their mission to blow up the bridge. The convergence of these parallel stories becomes the film's adventure-filled climax. In the book, the bridge is left standing as a symbol of the futility of war. The film's most popular moment occurs during the opening scene with the whistling of the "Colonel Bogey March." Veterans of World War II will remember its scurrilous lyrics that began with "Hitler has only got one ball." Made for $3 million, the film grossed $30 million at the box office and marked the beginning of American-financed "British" films. Filmed in Sri Lanka, The *Bridge on the River Kwai* won seven Academy Awards, including Best Picture of 1957, Best Director for the legendary British film-maker David Lean, and Best Actor for Guinness. It also won Best Screenplay for Pierre Boulle, the author of the novel, even though the actual writers were blacklisted writers Carl Foreman and Michael Wilson. The Writer's Guild of America officially restored their names in 1996.

See also Pierre Boulle; Burma-Thailand (Death) Railway; World War II-Far East

References

Pierre Boulle, *The Source of the River Kwai* (London: Secker & Warburg, 1966).

—*Darryl Wiggers*

British Army Aid Group

The British Army Aid Group (BAAG) was created in free China in 1942 to assist members of the Allied forces in Japanese captivity during World War II. Its founder was Lieutenant Colonel Lindsay Ride (1898–1977), a physician and physiologist who had commanded the Hong Kong Field Ambulance during the three weeks of fighting in Hong Kong. After the colony surrendered, Ride successfully escaped from Sham Shui Po Prison Camp in Kowloon in January 1942.

By the time Ride arrived in Kukong (Shaoguan), in free China, some weeks later, he had given much thought to ways to provide succor to those left behind in Hong Kong. He concluded that there must be some productive way to carry on the fight against the Japanese, both directly and indirectly, as well as to provide medical supplies to the thousands interned in POW and civilian camps and to assist some of those thousands to escape. Senior British officers in China agreed and were able to persuade the Chinese to cooperate. Ride, who became known to his Chinese associates as "the Smiling Tiger," received verbal orders to proceed by the end of February 1942. Written confirmation in detail came on 16 May 1942, by which time the organization was already formed. Temporary headquarters were established, first in a Methodist mission in Kukong, then for a time in a boat that had recently been a brothel. Forward posts were set up at Wuchow (Wuzhov) and in the villages close to Kowloon (the BAAG also created a unit that served with distinction in Burma). The unit needed a cryptic name, and after consultation with the Chinese, "Ying Kwan Fuk Mo T'uen" was chosen; the literal translation is "British Army Aid Group." Ride chose the scarlet pimpernel as its emblem.

One chief function of the BAAG was communicating with and supplying the POW camps and Stanley Internment Camp in Hong Kong. Chinese agents trained in clandestine operations gradually set up message drops and found locals who worked for the Japanese and had legitimate reasons to enter the various camps, for example, as truck drivers. Being loyal to the Allies, these persons carried items into the camps or met with camp inmates on work details outside. All these individuals functioned under threat of exposure, torture, and death, and for many, that threat was realized. One of Ride's companions in his original escape from Kowloon, Francis Lee Yiu Piu, served in BAAG with distinction throughout its history, receiving the Military Medal in 1945.

One ambitious scheme devised by Ride was a mass rescue of prisoners from Hong Kong. The War Office gave its approval, and preliminary contact was made in the camps about this plan in mid-1942. An officer in Sham Shui Po, the largest of the military camps, managed to send out a message indicating their willingness to participate in a rescue attempt. The plan was contingent on a commitment to rescue all the POWs, since any left behind would be subject to severe reprisals. This was a major deficit in the plan, since the number of extremely ill men who would somehow have to be transported across enemy-held territory increased with every month. Whether the plan could have ever worked soon became moot. In June 1943, the Japanese discovered the scheme and arrested two BAAG agents, other contacts, some Formosan guards, and even a Japanese officer. Shortly after this, several POW officers were taken away by the Kempei Tai, the Japanese secret police. Several of them were executed after months of appalling torture.

On 31 December 1945, the BAAG was officially disbanded after operating for just over three and a half years. It had assisted approximately 200 Allied escapees, including many whose escapes it had engineered, and also provided aid to 40 American evaders, mostly downed airmen. Materials of many kinds and messages were sent into the Hong Kong POW camps, and via messages sent out, officials were able to reassure worried relatives about the whereabouts of husbands and sons. Hundreds of civilians of many nationalities were helped, and in some cases, supported financially.

See also World War II—Far East

References

Edwin Ride, *BAAG: Hong Kong Resistance, 1942–1945* (Hong Kong: Oxford University Press, 1981).

—*Charles G. Roland*

British Free Corps

The British Free Corps (BFC) was a German army formation made up of British Commonwealth POWs who had been recruited to serve the Nazi war effort during World War II. The British traitor John Amery first conceived of the idea early in the war, envisioning a unit that would be used largely for propaganda purposes. But in the fall of 1943, when Germany's manpower shortage became acute, Gottlob Berger, the head of recruiting for the SS, decided instead to raise a regiment or brigade of Commonwealth prisoners to serve with the Waffen-SS against the Soviets on the Eastern Front. Members of the unit would receive standard German pay but would not be subject to German military law. According to the terms of enlistment, the unit would be sent into combat as soon as it recruited 30 men, the strength of an infantry platoon. Under these terms, the BFC officially came into being on 1 January 1944.

Recruitment began immediately, but by June 1944, the strength of the BFC stood at only 23 prisoners of war. They came from all parts of the Commonwealth, including the United Kingdom, Australia, New Zealand, South Africa, and Canada. However, only a handful of them were committed fascists; the rest were an odd mixture of opportunists, malcontents, mental defectives, and men hoping to escape penal sentences they had received for civil infractions. They were coaxed into treason by a variety of means, including promises of better food, greater liberty, and a chance to fight communism.

In October 1944, the BFC was sent to Dresden to begin infantry training, and in January 1945 it reached its peak strength of 27 members. Shortly after the Allied bombing raid on Dresden in February 1945, the unit was arrested en masse after one of its members boasted that he had advance knowledge of the raid. The political masters of the BFC secured their release and decided to send them into action immediately, although the unit had not yet reached platoon strength. Accordingly, 11 of the most able BFC members began intensive training and were eventually attached to a divisional armored reconnaissance battalion. However, suspicion that the members of the BFC would be completely unreliable in battle convinced their superiors to withdraw them from the front lines.

The BFC never did see action, and its members were eventually rounded up in northern Germany by advancing American troops. Many of the renegades were tried for treason by their own governments after the war, receiving sentences that ranged from a few months to life in prison. In the final reckoning, these POWs-turned-traitors contributed nothing to the German war effort; on the contrary, the BFC consumed considerable resources that the German government could well have put to other uses.

See also Berger, Gottlob; Defection

References

Brendan Murphy, *Turncoat: The True Case of Traitor Sergeant Harold Cole* (London: Macdonald, 1987).

Ronald Seth, *Jackals of the Reich* (London: New English Library, 1972).

Adrian Weale, *Renegades: Hitler's Englishmen* (London: Weidenfeld and Nicolson, 1994).

—*Jonathan F. Vance*

Brussels Declaration

On 27 August 1874, delegates accredited by the major powers completed the Brussels Declaration, intended to clarify and expand the rules of war to protect nonbelligerents and to diminish the evils of war. The treatment of sick and wounded prisoners was regulated by the Geneva Convention of 1864.

The declaration had a number of important provisions. Populations of non-occupied territory who, on the approach of the enemy, took up arms to resist were to be treated as prisoners of war if they respected the laws and customs of war, just as the combatants and noncombatants of the regular armed forces were to be. The murder of an individual who had laid down arms and surrendered was strictly forbidden, and anyone who operated secretly or under false pretenses could be treated as a spy. Prisoners were to be treated humanely and provided with supplies sufficient for their basic needs, were to retain their property rights, and were not to be compelled to take part in or to assist with operations of war. They might be compelled to labor, but not excessively, and they might be punished for insubordination, under the regulations of the armed forces. Prisoners must declare their true name and rank and must observe the conditions of their parole, which their own governments could not cause them to violate. Civilians, such as reporters, contractors, and others who accompanied armies, were entitled, when captured, to be treated as prisoners of war.

The declaration was not ultimately ratified by the powers, but many of its proposals were incorporated into the Hague Conventions of 1899 and 1907.

See also Geneva Conventions of 1864 and 1906; Hague Conventions of 1899 and 1907; International Law

—*Patrick M. O'Neil*

BUCHENWALD

Buchenwald concentration camp in Germany operated from 1937 to 1945, during which time tens of thousands of inmates were put to death by the SS, including several thousand Soviet POWs and a number of Allied intelligence officers.

On 19 July 1937, the SS established Buchenwald concentration camp on the Ettersberg Hill, five miles north of the city of Weimar, Thuringia. Until 1939, the inmate population consisted primarily of German political prisoners, criminals with multiple convictions, Jehovah's Witnesses, and homosexuals. After the beginning of World War II, more and more prisoners from German-occupied Europe arrived in the camp and would eventually vastly outnumber German inmates.

Although Buchenwald was not an extermination camp, mass killings (or "special actions") and other atrocities committed by SS personnel and guards occurred frequently. One of the most notorious special actions was directed against Soviet POWs. The chief of the Security Police and Security Service, Reinhard Heydrich, issued two decrees on 17 and 21 July 1941 whereby special detachments of his agency would comb POW camps in search of communists, political commissars of the Red Army, functionaries of the Soviet state and party, and Jews. Those POWs selected were sent to various concentration camps in the Reich for "special treatment" (execution). From September 1941, transports of Soviet POWs arrived at Buchenwald and were liquidated in the so-called horse stable, an installation that had been specifically designed for this gruesome task. A unit of the SS known as Commando 99 carried out the executions by shooting the victims in the back of the neck. At least 7,000 soldiers of the Red Army fell victim to this killing operation.

On 18 October 1941, some 2,000 Russian POWs were transferred from a POW camp near Hamburg to Buchenwald, where they were interned in a special compound separated by barbed-wire from the rest of the camp. By the end of 1942, only 1,200 of these men were still alive, and some 800 survived until early 1945. On 10 April 1945, the SS sent the remaining Russian POWs on a death march. Another special action involved 37 members of Allied secret services (British, Canadian, and French) who had served as liaison officers to the French resistance movement. The Gestapo brought these men to Buchenwald on 17 August 1944. Between early September and mid-October, 34 of them were hanged by the SS in the camp crematorium; three men survived by going into hiding in the camp, with the aid of other camp inmates. In the fall of 1944, 168 Allied airmen (82 Americans, 48 British, 26 Canadians, 9 Australians, 2 New Zealanders, and 1 Jamaican) were held at Buchenwald for a few months.

On 11 April 1945, advance units of the U.S. Third Army liberated Buchenwald. Approximately 250,000 women and men were held in the camp between 1937 and 1945, and more than 50,000 of them perished there.

See also Auschwitz; Concentration Camps; Dachau; Extermination Camps

References

Colin Burgess, *Destination Buchenwald* (Kenthurst, Australia: Kangaroo Press, 1995).

Gedenkstätte Buchenwald, *Konzentrationslager Buchenwald 1937–1945: Begleitband zur ständigen historischen Ausstellung* (Göttingen: Wallstein Verlag, 1999).

David A. Hackett, ed., *The Buchenwald Report* (Boulder, CO: Westview Press, 1995).

John D. Harvie, *Missing in Action: An RCAF Navigator's Story* (Montreal: McGill-Queen's University Press, 1995).

—*Jorg Bottger*

BULLET DECREE

A secret order issued by the German army, the Bullet Decree stated that escaped and recaptured POWs were to be handed over to the Gestapo for execution. The Bullet Decree was based on an order of the German Armed Forces High Command (Oberkommando der Wehrmacht, or OKW) dating from early 1944. It stipulated that escaped and recaptured POWs (officers and nonworking NCOs), with the exception of British and Americans, were to be turned over to the chief of the Security Police and Security Service (CSSD) under the code name "Stage Three" (Stufe III). Subordinate Gestapo offices were informed of this order by a decree of 2 March 1944 and a telex of 4 March, which also instructed them to maintain strict secrecy. The local Gestapo offices were to inform the International Committee of the Red Cross that these POWs had escaped and not been recaptured. Escaped and recaptured British and American POWs were to be kept in detention outside POW camps, and their fate was to be determined on an individual basis by the OKW's chief of POWs.

The POWs who fell under the decree were transferred under extraordinary security measures to Mauthausen concentration camp in Austria. The POWs were not registered as inmates, and were detained in a special block inside the camp. Most starved to death, but others were gassed, shot, or tortured to death by the SS camp personnel in an operation code-named "Bullet Action" (Aktion Kugel). On 2 February 1945, several hundred POWs, mostly Soviet officers, made an escape attempt, and 419 reached the area beyond the camp perimeter. Many were too weakened to escape, however, and were quickly finished off. The Nazi authorities initiated a huge manhunt, which was eagerly supported by parts of the local populace. Recaptured POWs were shot on the spot and many were clubbed to death. All in all, 17 men successfully escaped. Nine of them survived the end of the war by reaching Soviet lines in Czechoslovakia or hiding with Austrian and Czech farmers. It has been estimated that some 5,040 POWs (4,300 Russians) fell victim to the Bullet Decree. The original document with the exact date of the Bullet Decree has never been located. Its existence and contents are reproduced verbatim, however, in excerpts of the 4 March 1945 telex of the CSSD.

See also Arbeitskommandos; Gestapo

References

Szymon Datner, *Crimes against POWs: Responsibility of the Wehrmacht* (Warsaw: Zachodnia Agencja Prasowa, 1964).

Gordon J. Horwitz, *In the Shadow of Death: Living Outside the Gates of Mauthausen* (New York: Free Press, 1990).

Evelyn Le Chêne, *Mauthausen: The History of a Death Camp* (London: Methuen, 1971).

Christian Streit, *Keine Kameraden: Die Wehrmacht und die sowjetischen Kriegsgefangenen 1941–1945* (Bonn: J.H.W. Dietz, 1997 [1978]).

—*Jorg Bottger*

BURMA-THAILAND (DEATH) RAILWAY

Built in 1942 and 1943 by Allied prisoners of war and native slave labor, and extending from Ban Pong, Thailand, to Thanbyuzayat, Burma, the Burma-Thailand railway was intended to supply Japanese forces fighting in Burma. As World War II progressed, American submarines and Allied aircraft had increasingly threatened Japanese cargo ships in the Indian Ocean. Japanese military planners assumed that an all-land route from Bangkok to northern Burma would improve the chances of supplies reaching the front. Accordingly, a railway was planned to link two existing lines—one that ran west from Bangkok to Ban Pong in Thailand and then south along the Gulf of Siam to Singapore, and another that ran entirely in Burma from Ye, on the Andaman coast, north to Thanbyuzayat and then to Rangoon (Yangon). When completed, the new road was 261 miles (421 kilometers) long and followed the Mae Klong and Kwae Noi Rivers across some of the most inhospitable terrain in the world—dense jungle, rugged mountains, swift streams, and monsoon-flooded plains. Time

Australian prisoners of war laying track on the Burma-Thailand railway, 1943 (Australian War Memorial P406/40/8)

would demonstrate that the Japanese had been wrong in pinning such hopes on the new railway; Allied bombers began interrupting traffic even before it was completed and continued their devastation until the Japanese abandoned the line in early 1945.

The Japanese regarded POWs as an ideal work force for the project. They had captured many more than expected and did not want to feed what they considered to be a useless rabble. As a consequence, the railway became the largest single use of POWs by the Japanese in World War II; among the approximately 61,000 Allied prisoners who worked on it were 13,000 Australians and New Zealanders, 30,000 British and British colonials, 18,000 Dutch and Indonesian-Dutch, and 668 Americans. The conditions under which they labored were unbelievably cruel. Many of the guards were Koreans pressed into duty, and most of the supervisors were the incompetents and misfits of the imperial army. One Scottish POW, Ernest Gordon, who for years after his ordeal was dean of the chapel at Princeton University, described conditions cogently: "The Japanese military violated every civilized code. They murdered prisoners overtly by bayoneting, shooting, drowning, or decapitation; they murdered them covertly by working them beyond human endurance, starving them, torturing them, and denying them medical care." Men suffered malnutrition, dysentery, beriberi, jungle ulcers, malaria, and many other maladies, and more than 12,000 of the POWs died or were killed during construction, a death rate of one in five or about 55 POWs per mile. The estimated death rate by nationality was one in three Britons, one in four Anzacs, one in five Americans, and one in six Dutch and Indonesians. Although figures are hard to ascertain, perhaps 250,000 native conscripts worked on the railway and 125,000 of them perished. It has been written that one worker died for every sleeper (cross-tie) laid.

After the road was finished, the Japanese erected a pyramidal, 25-foot cenotaph as a memorial, a structure that one American POW called "the greatest travesty of all. It denied, the very date it was dedicated, all the freedoms, liberties, and human dignity that men should accord one another." Another memorial was the 1957 Oscar-winning movie *The Bridge on the River Kwai*, which, although unable to project the suffering and cruelty adequately, remains an extremely effective reminder of the building of the Death Railway.

See also Boulle, Pierre; *The Bridge on the River Kwai*; Labor; World War II—Far East

References
Idris James Barwick, *In the Shadow of Death: The Memoir of a Prisoner of War on the Burma Railway* (Barnsley, UK: Pen & Sword Books, 2005).
Brian Best, ed., *Secret Letters from the Railway: The Remarkable Record of Charles Steel, Japanese POW* (Barnsley, UK: Pen & Sword Books, 2004).
Joan and Clay Blair, Jr., *Return from the River Kwai* (New York: Simon and Schuster, 1979).
Ernest Gordon, *Through the Valley of the Kwai* (New York: Harper, 1962).
Clifford Kinvig, *River Kwai Railway: The Story of the Burma-Siam Railroad* (London: Brassey's, 1992).
Robert S. La Forte and Ronald E. Marcello, eds., *Building the Death Railway: The Ordeal of American POWs in Burma, 1942–45* (Wilmington, DE: SR Books, 1993).
Gavan McCormack and Hank Nelson, eds., *The Burma-Thailand Railway: Memory and History* (St. Leonards, Australia: Allen and Unwin, 1993).
Chaim Nussbaum, *Chaplain on the River Kwai: The Story of a Prisoner of War* (New York: Shapolsky Publishers, 1988).
Ray Parkin, *Into the Smother: A Journal of the Burma-Siam Railway* (London: Hogarth Press, 1963).
Loet Velmans, *Long Way Back to the River Kwai* (New York: Arcade Publishing, 2004).

—Robert S. La Forte

BUSHELL, ROGER JOYCE (1910–1944)

Regarded by his captors as one of the most dangerous escape leaders in Germany, Roger Joyce Bushell was largely responsible for planning the Great Escape, the most famous mass escape of World War II. Born in South Africa, Bushell was educated in Johannesburg and in England, and studied law at Cambridge University. He joined the Royal Auxiliary Air Force in 1932, and in October 1939 was posted to command 92 Squadron, which later flew Hawker Hurricanes. On 23 May 1940, Bushell was captured when his aircraft was shot down over Boulogne.

He immediately threw himself into escape work, and made his first escape in June 1941, when he slipped away from the recreation field at Dulag Luft; he was recaptured the following day near the Swiss frontier when a German border guard refused to believe that he was a drunken skiing instructor. In October 1941, Bushell escaped again, from a train transferring prisoners between camps. This time, he and his partner, a Czech airman named Jack Zafouk, remained at large until May 1942, when they were recaptured in Prague.

Bushell's next enterprise was his most ambitious: assuming leadership of the escape organization at Stalag Luft 3 Sagan. In that role, he coordinated dozens of small escapes and was the prime architect of a plan that involved constructing three large escape tunnels and scattering hundreds of escaped airmen throughout occupied Europe. Only one of the tunnels was ever used: on the night of 24–25 March 1944, 79 airmen (including Bushell) crawled to temporary freedom through the tunnel code-named Harry. Although Bushell spoke flawless German, his last escape was short. He and his French partner, Lieutenant Bernard Scheidhauer, were among the first of 79 to leave the tunnel, and on the morning of 26 March they had reached Saarbrücken, near the German-French border. There, police discovered a fault in their forged papers and arrested the pair. It was common knowledge that the Gestapo had marked Bushell as a troublemaker and would not tolerate further escapes. So, his fellow prisoners were not surprised to learn that he was among the 50 airmen murdered after the Great Escape; he and Scheidhauer were shot in a field near Saarbrücken on 29 March 1944.

See also Dulag Luft; Great Escape; Stalag Luft 3

References
Jonathan F. Vance, *A Gallant Company: The True Story of "The Great Escape"* (New York: Simon & Schuster/iBooks, 2000).

—Jonathan F. Vance

C

Cabanatuan

The largest concentration of American prisoners of war in the Far East in World War II, Cabanatuan consisted of three camps near Cabu village, five to 15 miles northeast of Cabanatuan City in south central Luzon, Philippine Islands. Originally built to house the 91st Philippine Army Division, the prison camp occupied about 100 acres of land, most of which was surrounded by a high barbed-wire fence. The camp consisted of several wooden buildings and thatched barracks made of nipa palm and cogon grass with bamboo-slat floors.

The first POWs, the sick and wounded who had been left behind in Bataan, arrived at Cabanatuan and were assigned to Camp No. 3 on 26 May 1942. They were joined three days later by more than 6,000 prisoners from Corregidor, men who had been held at Bilibid Prison. Camp No. 3 having reached its capacity, an additional 1,500 Corregidor prisoners were sent to Camp No. 2, but because its water supply was over 1,000 yards from the camp, these men were immediately moved to Camp No. 1. The high mortality rate at Camp O'Donnell, where Bataan Death March captives had initially been sent, caused the Japanese to begin shifting O'Donnell's prisoners to Cabanatuan No. 1; Donald Knox estimates their number at 5,850 men. Filipino prisoners of war remained at O'Donnell until their release in late 1942. As the Japanese began transferring men to work details elsewhere in the Philippines and overseas to Manchuria and Japan, Camp No. 3 was closed in October 1942 and its remaining POWs, about 3,000, were sent to Camp No. 1.

Terrible conditions prevailed at Camp No. 1 during much of 1942. Food supplies were insufficient, medical treatment was haphazard and generally poor, and Japanese conduct was erratic. Conditions improved in 1943 and mortality rates dropped significantly. A black market thrived for those with money, and smuggling as well as some trading allowed by the Japanese provided badly needed supplies. Farming, which became the main occupation for the camp's inmates, also helped increase the amount of food available. Entertainment and recreation programs were developed and life became as normalized as possible in a Japanese-run prison camp. During 1944 conditions worsened again as the Japanese reduced rations and cracked down on smuggling. As American forces approached the Philippines in mid-1944, the Japanese began to ship POWs deemed able to endure hard labor to Japan in the so-called "death ships." Only about 500 prisoners were left at Cabanatuan when a daring raid, carried out by the U.S. 6th Ranger Battalion, the 6th Army's "Alamo Scouts," and local guerrilla groups, liberated the camp on 31 January 1945. In 2005, the raid was transformed into a movie based on William Breuer's book and starring Benjamin Bratt.

See also Bataan Death March; Transportation by Sea; World War II—Far East

References

William B. Breuer, *The Great Raid on Cabanatuan: Rescuing the Doomed Ghosts of Bataan and Corregidor* (New York: John Wiley and Sons, 1994).

John S. Coleman, Jr., *Bataan and Beyond* (College Station: Texas A&M University Press, 1978).

Forrest Bryant Johnson, *Hour of Redemption: The Heroic WWII Saga of America's Most Daring POW Rescue* (New York: Time Warner, 2002).

Donald Knox, *Death March: The Survivors of Bataan* (New York: Harcourt Brace Jovanovich, 1981).

Mario Machi, *Under the Rising Sun: Memories of a Japanese Prisoner of War* (Miranda, CA: Wolfenden, 1994).

Hampton Sides, *Ghost Soldiers: The Epic Account of World War II's Greatest Rescue Mission* (New York: Doubleday, 2001).

Stanley W. Smith, *Prisoner of the Emperor: An American POW in World War II* (Niwot: University Press of Colorado, 1991).

—*Robert S. La Forte*

Camp Followers

Civilians accompanied military forces from the earliest known wars through nineteenth-century conflicts. These individuals, known as camp followers, sometimes became prisoners of war because of their proximity to battlefields and enemy forces. The stereotypical camp follower is a prostitute or a woman following her man, but in reality, camp followers were a much more diverse group, including all civilians voluntarily attached to military troops, men as well as women.

Civilian men, women, and children attached themselves to armies for a variety of reasons. Many women went to war with their husbands or with their fathers, brothers, sons, other male relatives, or romantic partners because they wanted to care for them. Some women also needed the protection and shelter the military offered to soldiers' often nomadic families who lacked a permanent home. Not surprisingly, children traveled with their mothers. Other women considered the troops as a means of economic survival, agreeing to cook, do laundry, sew, nurse, or provide other services in exchange for payment or bartered food and goods. Male sutlers and merchants who moved with troops, selling them essential items, and nonmilitary personnel who received administrative appointments with armies were also considered camp followers and were at risk of capture.

Treatment of imprisoned camp followers varied, depending on the war, the region, and the individual commander's policies. The fates of these captives were often unknown, as no military laws regulated the imprisonment of camp followers and so they were vulnerable to the whims of their captors. Few records of imprisoned camp followers have been preserved, but comments about individuals in official reports and letters provide details about who was captured and what their imprisonment entailed. Some of the earliest known accounts of captured camp followers come from the French and Indian War (1754–1763). Three women accompanying British troops under Edward Braddock in the expedition against Fort Duquesne were captured by the French and sent to Canada to be sold as servants. A group of 100 women and children surrendered to the French at the British garrison at Oswego. Imprisoned for complaining about her husband's officers, one Martha May petitioned Colonel Henry Bouquet for a pardon in 1758, declaring "I have been a Wife 22 years" and "have traveld with my Husband every Place or Country the Company marcht too and have workt very hard ever since I was in the Army."

Captured camp followers of the American Revolution have been the most thoroughly documented. Although most camp followers who became prisoners were seized by enemy soldiers, some were arrested by officers of their own side, court-martialed, imprisoned, and sometimes publicly flogged. These camp followers were found guilty of illicit acts, such as stealing, spying, or selling liquor. Other camp followers were drummed out of camp rather than imprisoned, to reduce the military's responsibility for feeding and housing them.

Although camp followers on both sides were captured during the American Revolution, most records describe British and Hessian prisoners. The Journals of the Continental Congress noted the colonial leaders' decision "that the women and children belonging to prisoners be furnished with subsistence." The largest group of camp follower prisoners, totaling several hundred people, was captured with the Convention Army after General John Burgoyne's 1777 surrender at Saratoga. These camp followers were British, Canadian, German, and Loyalist, and represented both anonymous, illiterate peasants and prominent aristocrats such as Frederica, Baroness Riedesel, the wife of a German general in British service, who later wrote about her experiences. Traveling 200 miles to Cambridge, Massachusetts, the camp followers suffered in the frosty November weather. British Lieutenant Thomas Anburey witnessed a woman giving birth on a baggage cart during a snow storm, observing "It maybe said that women who follow a camp are of such masculine nature they endure hardships." In the correspondence of Boston resident Hannah Winthrop we find a letter to her friend, the poet and historian Mercy Otis Warren, describing the camp followers "who seemed to be the beasts of burthen, having a bushel basket on their back, by which they were bent double." She noted they had bare feet and were "cloathed in dirty rags" and "such effluvia filld the air while they were passing, had they not been smoaking all the time, I should have been apprehensive of being contaminated by them." The captive camp followers frequently eluded sentries and wandered through Boston, where the city council passed an ordinance stating "that these wenches were not to show themselves outside of camp for fear the pregnant women in Boston should be marked" (authorities feared that camp followers might spread diseases such as smallpox). One year after their capture, the Convention Army prisoners were moved to Virginia and then to Pennsylvania. Some camp followers escaped during these moves, while others willingly accompanied the POWs and remained in captivity until the war ended.

Other known Revolutionary camp follower prisoners included British officers' wives and mistresses who were captured at sea. In 1782, when French forces seized his ship, British Captain James A. Gardner reported that the baggage and the soldiers' wives were the only losses sustained. General Lafayette remarked that these prisoners worried they would be forced to become prostitutes or servants, but General George Washington permitted some women to return to their husbands and provided funds to board others.

Camp followers continued to risk capture in nineteenth-century conflicts such as the U.S. Civil War and the Crimean War. In the twentieth century, changes in the practices of modern warfare (including an expansion in a modern army's support units and the employment of women in military roles) discouraged camp followers from attaching themselves to armies in the field.

See also Children; Women

References

Walter Hart Blumenthal, *Women Camp Followers of the American Revolution* (Philadelphia: George S. MacManus Company, 1952).

Piers Compton, *Colonel's Lady & Camp-follower: The Story of Women in the Crimean War* (New York: St. Martin's Press, 1970).

William M. Dabney, *After Saratoga: The Story of the Convention Army* (Albuquerque: University of New Mexico Press, 1955).

Linda Grant De Pauw, *Battle Cries and Lullabies: Women in War from Prehistory to the Present* (Norman: University of Oklahoma Press, 1998).

Paul E. Kopperman, "The British High Command and Soldiers' Wives in America, 1755–1783," *Journal of the Society for Army Historical Research* 60 (1982): 14–34.

Noel T. St. John Williams, *Judy O'Grady and the Colonel's Lady: The Army Wife and Camp Follower since 1660* (Washington, DC: Brassey's, 1988).

—*Elizabeth D. Schafer*

THE CAPTIVE HEART

This 1946 British feature film from Ealing Studios, directed by Basil Dearden and starring Michael Redgrave and Derek Bond (himself a former POW), was filmed on location at a former German prison camp for naval officers (Marlag at Westertimke) from a script cowritten by Guy Morgan, also a former prisoner. *The Captive Heart* is the most true-to-life of the British POW movies dealing with World War II. The central plot, involving the love letters between a Czech refugee and the wife of the dead British army officer he is impersonating, is fictional, and POW life in general is at times somewhat romanticized. However, many of the background events covered in the film, including the long march into captivity, the lean times before the arrival of food parcels from the International Committee of the Red Cross, enemy propaganda efforts, the shackling incident, and other reprisals, are all based on actual events. Hundreds of soldiers of the famous Scottish infantry regiments, the Argyll and Sutherland Highlanders and the Black Watch, served as extras, adding extra veracity to the look of the film. The stresses of captivity are highlighted more than escape attempts, and unlike most POW films, *The Captive Heart* features Other Ranks (in the form of orderlies) prominently.

See also Film

References

Charles Barr, *Ealing Studios* (London: Cameron and Tayleur, 1977).

Derek Bond, *Steady, Old Man! Don't You Know There's a War On?* (London: Leo Cooper, 1990).

Jack Warner, *Jack of All Trades* (London: W. H. Allen, 1975).

—*S. P. MacKenzie*

CASEMENT, ROGER DAVID (1864–1916)

This enigmatic Irish nationalist was born in Dublin to a Catholic mother and a Protestant father. Throughout his career, Casement worked in the British consular service in Africa and Brazil, and was an outspoken critic of human rights abuses in these regions. In 1911 he was knighted for his efforts to improve conditions for native workers, but after returning to Ireland in 1913, Casement fervently took up the Irish national cause. He arrived in the United States shortly before the outbreak of World War I to engage in fundraising for the Clan na Gael, an Irish republican organization dedicated to securing the independence of Ireland.

In October 1914 Casement traveled to Berlin to foster support for an uprising in Ireland and raise an Irish brigade from the ranks of prisoners of war interned in German camps. Casement achieved little during his 18-month visit. He found the General Staff uncooperative, and was unable to elicit any meaningful support from the 2,500 Irishmen who were held at Limburg-an-der-Lahn. On the contrary, prisoners jeered Casement's recruiting efforts, and even physically attacked him. Only about 50 men volunteered for the brigade, most of whom were simply seeking to escape German captivity. Deep in despair, Casement returned to Ireland in April 1916 hoping to stop the Easter Rebellion, which he now felt was doomed to fail. In an ill-advised maneuver, he was landed on a County Kerry beach by the German submarine U-19 and promptly arrested by the Royal Irish Constabulary.

Sir Roger's first hours in custody bordered on the comical, but his circumstances worsened after he was transferred to the Tower of London. He had not washed or changed clothes since his arrest, and was in very poor condition. After more than a week of rough treatment, Casement was transferred to Brixton Prison, where his living conditions improved. In a highly publicized four-day trial, Casement was found guilty of treason, and was hanged in August at Pentonville Prison. The controversy surrounding Casement's activities did not end with his execution. The implications of the so-called "Black Diaries"—which allege that Casement was gay—remain unresolved.

References

Reinhard R. Doerries, *Prelude to the Easter Rising: Sir Roger Casement in Imperial Germany* (London: Frank Cass, 2000).

Brian Inglis, *Roger Casement* (London: Coronet Books, 1974).

Seán McConville, *Irish Political Prisoners, 1848-1922: Theatres of War* (London: Routledge, 2003).

B.L. Reid, *The Lives of Roger Casement* (New Haven: Yale University Press, 1976).

Roger Sawyer, *Casement: The Flawed Hero* (London: Routledge & Kegan Paul, 1984).

—*Andrew Iarocci*

CAVELL, EDITH (1865–1915)

Edith Cavell was an English nurse whose execution by the Germans during World War I, on charges that she had assisted

This photograph of Edith Cavell was widely publicized after her execution in 1915.

British soldiers in escaping from occupied Belgium, created an international uproar. She was born at Swardeston in Norfolk on 4 December 1865, and as a young woman she developed an interest in medical care and nursing. She worked in various infirmaries in London and in 1906 went to Brussels to establish a school for training nurses in the English system. When the Germans occupied Brussels in 1914, they allowed Cavell to remain at work and her nursing institute became a Red Cross hospital that served both German and Allied wounded. However, she also gave what aid she could to Allied soldiers who had been cut off behind German lines or who had escaped from captivity. On 5 August 1915, she was arrested and informed that she would face a German military court-martial for these activities.

Certainly unadvisedly, Cavell confessed to the offenses with which she was charged, and in so doing, sealed her fate. She was convicted of "conducting soldiers to the enemy" and sentenced to death. Despite strenuous appeals for mercy by many intermediaries, Cavell was executed on 12 October 1915. She immediately became a martyr to the Allied cause and in death became a weapon for Allied propagandists, something she could not have done in life.

See also Nurses

References

Rowland Ryder, *Edith Cavell* (London: Hamish Hamilton, 1975).

—*Kara Brown*

Central POW Agency

For over a century, the Central Prisoner of War Agency of the International Committee of the Red Cross (ICRC) has, under a variety of names, acted as the main clearinghouse for information on POWs and civilians interned by all belligerent nations. It was borne of the humanitarian belief that the mental suffering of prisoners and their families could be partly eased by the provision of reliable, current information on the status of prisoners.

The agency has its roots in the International Agency for Aid to Sick and Wounded Military Personnel, commonly known as the Basle Agency. The Basle Agency first served during the Franco-Prussian War of 1870–1871, initially as an intermediary, forwarding as many as 300 letters a day from prisoners held by each side. Later in the war the agency attempted to arrange for an exchange of lists of POWs between France and Germany. However, the German government, which held the vast majority of prisoners taken during the war, claimed that it was unable to provide lists of all of the nearly 100,000 French soldiers in its prison camps, and so the agency confined itself to handling information on wounded French prisoners.

During the Balkan Wars that preceded World War I, the Belgrade Agency of the ICRC handled information on POWs captured by Serbia, Bulgaria, Greece, and Turkey. However, for a variety of reasons, the agency's work was unsatisfactory. Red Cross officials believed there had been

250,000 prisoners taken by all sides, but the agency received the names of only 17,000. The names of another 70,000 were received after the conclusion of hostilities, but by then they were of little use to anyone.

At the 9th International Conference of the Red Cross at Washington, DC, in 1912, member delegates agreed that in peacetime, national Red Cross societies should organize commissions that could be activated to serve in wartime as clearinghouses for information about prisoners. In due course, arrangements were made by most national societies, so that when World War I began in August 1914, the ICRC was able to announce the immediate opening of the International POW Agency. Again, the Agency focused on securing from all combatants complete lists of the prisoners they captured. Typically, these lists were transmitted to Geneva through intermediaries, either the American embassies (for Britain, France, and Germany) or the Danish Red Cross (for Germany and Russia). When the lists reached Geneva, they were collated into an immense color-coded card index. There were also regimental and topographical cross-indices that allowed clerks to locate prisoners in the event of a misspelled name or inadequate information. The card indices were used to respond to inquiries from the general public about missing relatives or friends. On average, the agency received around 3,000 letters each day, but during major offensives that number could grow to as many as 30,000 a day. Another section of the agency handled the transmission of correspondence, parcels, and money to prisoners, and it, too, made prodigious efforts to assist captives. During the course of the war, this section handled over 1.8 million individually addressed parcels and forwarded the equivalent of 18 million Swiss francs to prisoners. Other departments were responsible for the welfare of prisoners who had been transferred to neutral countries and for inquiries regarding civilians, both interned and at liberty. In 1923, having amassed over 7 million index cards on individual prisoners, the agency concluded its work.

The Central POW Agency (as it was now called) was reactivated in September 1939 and continued working until after the end of World War II. Its organization and procedures were roughly similar to those used in World War I, but new sections were added to handle medical personnel, Jewish refugees, internees in Switzerland, and displaced families. Although the procedures were the same, the work certainly had a broader scope, as the following statistics demonstrate: At its peak, the agency had 2,528 workers, the majority of whom were volunteers. These workers handled an immense volume of material: over 110 million separate pieces of mail and over 560,000 telegrams; nearly 24 million civilian messages (transmitted on special forms); the personal effects of 90,000 individuals; and 36 million index cards, over 10 million for German prisoners alone.

In general, the agency received full cooperation from combatant governments regarding prisoners of war; there was less compliance from most governments regarding interned civilians, particularly the inmates of concentration camps. Furthermore, the Soviet government never submitted complete lists of German prisoners it captured, and the Japanese government was also slow to comply. By June 1943, for example, Tokyo had forwarded to Geneva the names of less than one-third of the Australian POWs it had captured.

Although the agency officially concluded its work in June 1947, for all intents and purposes it has continued to operate, changing its name one more time. Now the Central Tracing Agency of the ICRC, the agency still acts as an information clearinghouse for prisoners in conflicts around the world, including the Algerian War, the Arab-Israeli War, and the India-Pakistan wars. As the nature of international conflict has changed since 1945, so, too, has the agency. It now relies even more heavily on flexibility, adaptability, and the good will of belligerent states to carry out its vital work in support of prisoners and their families.

See also Information Bureaus; International Committee of the Red Cross

References

Gradimir Djurović, *The Central Tracing Agency of the International Committee of the Red Cross: Activities of the ICRC for the Alleviation of the Mental Suffering of War Victims* (Geneva: Henry Dunant Institute, 1986).

—*Jonathan F. Vance*

Central Registry of War Criminals and Security Suspects (CROWCASS)

In late 1944, Allied authorities in Paris began contemplating the creation of an organization to track and catalogue persons who might be of interest for the war crimes trials that were anticipated to be held once the war in Europe had been won. The result of these deliberations was the Central Registry of War Criminals and Security Suspects (CROWCASS), established at the Supreme Headquarters of the Allied Expeditionary Force at Versailles. CROWCASS was intended to maintain wanted lists of known war criminals, suspected war criminals, and individuals who were wanted for questioning or to serve as witnesses in potential trials; these lists would be made available to Allied authorities, particularly those in charge of the growing prisoner of war camps, to ensure that wanted individuals did not slip through the cracks. They were also to be used (and added to) by the teams of investigators that the Allies had put together to begin identifying suspects for future trials. These teams established three separate camps in the Normandy region to house people on the CROWCASS lists.

Using its own staff and information submitted by war crimes investigators in other countries, the registry collected some 70,000 names in its first three weeks, but it was hampered by poor management and a lack of resources. As a result, the first list was not published until July 1945, and even then it included the names of many individuals who had already been identified in earlier United Nations War Crimes Commission lists or who were already in custody. Furthermore, the July 1945 list was not fully distributed until October, making it of limited utility to prison camp commanders who had to cope with the tens of thousands of surrendered German soldiers, sailors, and airmen who had to be classified. By the end of 1947, four volumes of lists (comprising some 50,000 names) had been published, but the problems in the registry were by now manifest. It had become clear early in the process that identifying "security suspects" was a tedious and time-consuming task, and that part of CROWCASS's mandate was soon dropped so that personnel could concentrate on war criminals. Furthermore, investigators came to doubt the accuracy of the registry's information, and were hampered by the fact that it often failed to differentiate between people who were suspected of serious crimes against humanity, and low-ranking members of the armed forces who were simply wanted for interview about a possible war crime. If, for example, one infantry unit had been implicated in a potential crime, it was customary for the registry to list all members of that unit, even those who were not present when the events occurred. Finally, CROWCASS was criticized for stating the obvious, such as its decision to put Adolf Hitler at the top of the list, even though most people accepted the fact that he had committed suicide in May 1945.

Still, 60 years later the CROWCASS list remains a fascinating document to read. It even returned to the headlines briefly in 1986 when the World Jewish Congress revealed that the name of former United Nations secretary-general and president of Austria Kurt Waldheim had been found on one of the lists, with the notation that he had served with an army unit in the former Yugoslavia that had waged a violent war against anti-Nazi partisans and that had been implicated in atrocities against captured partisans. An international investigation eventually cleared Waldheim of any role in war crimes, although the very fact that his name had once been noted by CROWCASS cast a pall over the rest of his political career.

See also Nuremberg Trials; War Crimes

References

Richard Mitten, *The Politics of Antisemitic Prejudice: The Waldheim Phenomenon in Austria* (Boulder, CO: Westview Press, 1992).

Supreme Headquarters, Allied Expeditionary Force, *CROWCASS: Central Registry of War Criminals and Security Suspects Lists* (Uckfield, UK: Naval and Military Press, 2005).

—*Jonathan F. Vance*

CERVANTES, MIGUEL DE (1547–1616)

Spain's most famous writer, Miguel de Cervantes Saavedra, spent five years as a captive in Algiers. Before the beginning of his literary career, Cervantes served as a soldier, fighting the Turks in the Battle of Lepanto (1571) and laying siege against Corfu (1572), Tunis (1573), and La Goleta (1574). This military interlude came to an end in 1575 during a return voyage from Italy to Spain. On 26 September, off the coast of Catalonia, a storm separated the galley *El Sol* from its convoy and a fleet of Algerian pirate ships attacked. Carried into slavery with his brother, who was rescued two years later, Cervantes joined an estimated 25,000 Christian slaves in Algiers.

Unlike other passengers sold at the slave market, Cervantes remained in the custody of one of the corsairs who had captured him, a Greek renegade named Dali Mami, nicknamed "El Cojo" (the cripple). Convinced that Cervantes must be an important personage because he was carrying royal letters of recommendation from Don Juan of Austria, his captor demanded an exorbitant ransom: 500 escudos in Spanish gold (roughly equivalent to US$17,000). Cervantes made four unsuccessful escape attempts over both land and sea. In the meantime, his family took desperate measures to raise the necessary sum; his two sisters reportedly even sacrificed their dowries and joined a convent. Finally, the Trinitarians, a religious order devoted to liberating Christians in Muslim lands, negotiated his release and he set sail for Spain on 26 September 1580. Cervantes's experience as a slave in Algiers influenced several episodes in *Don Quixote (El ingenioso hidalgo Don Quixote de la Mancha)*, notably the interpolated novel *Captive's Tale (La historia del cautivo)*, probably written in 1590. His impressions of cruelty and humanity, sexual libertinism, and religious freedom in Barbary captivity also provided fodder for two plays, *Life in Algiers (El trato de Argel)* and *The Bagnios of Algiers (Los Baños de Argel)*.

See also Barbary Wars

References

Jean Canavaggio, *Cervantes*, trans. J. R. Jones (New York: Norton, 1990).

Ellen G. Friedman, *Spanish Captives in North Africa in the Early Modern Age* (Madison: University of Wisconsin Press, 1983).

Maria Antonia Garces, *Cervantes in Algiers: A Captive's Tale* (Nashville: Vanderbilt University Press, 2002).

Miguel de Cervantes Saavedra, *The Captive's Tale (La historia del cautivo)*, trans. by Donald P. McCrory (Warminster, UK: Aris and Phillips, 1994).

—*Gillian Weiss*

CHAD CIVIL WARS

A former French colony, the North African nation of Chad began self-rule in 1960 but for much of its history, it has been embroiled in civil war that pitted the largely Muslim north, which resented French involvement in the nation's affairs, against the dominant south, which relied on French support to remain in control. Indeed, conflicts between rival groups have been so persistent that war has almost become the normal state for most Chadians.

The unrest began soon after independence, with a revolt in the northern provinces that simmered for years as a low-intensity war, but in 1975 the army rebelled, killed the president, and took over the country. French forces returned, and a cease-fire negotiated in February 1978 lasted just two months before fighting broke out again. Soon a new army, under Hissène Habré, was in the ascendant, persuading Libya to drive its forces further into Chad to cement its hold on the country. But Habré's forces were up to the task, and in April 1979 drove the Libyans from their gains, capturing many Libyan and Arab prisoners in the process. There were then two attempts at forming transitional governments, neither of them successful, and then a second civil war from October 1981 to October 1982, this one revolving around Libya's desire to annex Chad. From then on, the fighting was virtually continuous, with rival factions attacking each other, foreign governments supplying arms and money to various groups, and the eventual partition of Chad, which brought two years of relative peace. That lasted only until February 1986, when fighting resumed, again with foreign assistance, particularly from Libya and the Soviet Union on one side, and France and the United States on the other. This time, a Chadian army under Habré won a series of stunning victories, and agreed to a cease-fire in September 1987. It generally held, with the exception of a few border raids into Libya, until March 1990, when forces allied to rival Chadian groups and assisted by Libya invaded from the Sudan. Habré was deposed and a new leader, Idriss Debey, took over the country and instituted a multi-party system that, if corrupt, has at least maintained the country's fragile peace. A new revolt broke out in northern Chad in 1998 that was tempered only slightly by two cease-fire agreements, in 2002 and 2003, between the government and rebel leaders.

Unlike many civil wars, abuse of prisoners, although it certainly occurred, was not the most notable feature of the long war in Chad. Rather, two episodes stand out. In April 1974, Habré arranged the capture of a French anthropologist, Françoise Claustre; a French aid official, Marc Combe; and a German doctor, Christian Staewen, and demanded arms in return for their release. A French officer who was sent to broker a deal was murdered by Habré's men, and Claustre's husband Pierre was also imprisoned when he arrived to visit his wife. The German government paid the ransom in 1974 and Staewen was freed, but the French hostages remained in captivity until 30 January 1977, when the Libyan government intervened to secure their release.

The other episode involved Libyan POWs. Habré's offensives of 1987 were a great success; in addition to capturing as much as $1 billion worth of Soviet weapons, they also took nearly 2,000 Libyan prisoners. Upon inspection, it turned out that these soldiers were mostly mercenaries from the Sudan, Lebanon, Mali, Benin, and Nigeria; there were even two Yugoslavs and an East German. Displeased by the presence of so many mercenaries, Habré refused to release them after the cease-fire took effect, holding them as bargaining chips to force Libya to renounce all territorial claims to parts of Chad. Had Debey not ousted Habré and released the last of the prisoners, they may well still be in captivity.

References

J. Millard Burr and Robert O. Collins, *Africa's Thirty Years War: Libya, Chad, and the Sudan, 1963–1999* (Boulder, CO: Westview Press, 1999).

Pierre Claustre, L'Affaire Claustre: Autopsie d'une Prise d'Otages (Paris: Karthala, 1990)

Benjamin Neuberger, *Involvement, Invasion and Withdrawal: Qadhdhafi's Libya and Chad, 1969–1981* (Tel Aviv: Shiloah Centre for Middle Eastern and African Studies, 1982).

—Jonathan F. Vance

CHANGI

A large prison-camp complex opened by the Japanese during World War II to house POWs captured on Singapore, Changi was set on nearly 16 square kilometers of undulating hills at the eastern end of Singapore. After the island's fall on 15 February 1942, more than 15,000 Australian and 35,000 British prisoners were herded into Changi Prison, formerly the magnificent Selarang Barracks and lately home to the Gordon Highlanders, a Scottish regiment. Now Changi was ostensibly a hospital center, but in fact it served as a massive POW camp. The barracks were badly damaged by shelling. As more and more prisoners filed into Changi, overcrowding became an ongoing problem. Within two months, 8,000 prisoners were without shelter. There was also no water, lighting, or sewage facilities, and clouds of flies were a constant annoyance. Food stores rapidly diminished and the men were placed on strict rations.

Surprisingly, there was only a nominal Japanese presence inside the vast compound, the guards mostly staying outside the confines of the camp. Changi's administrative staff had warned the prisoners that, apart from a rice ration, they had to be self-supporting, so the prisoners were placed under the management of their own senior officers. The officers in turn encouraged the men to clear drains to prevent the breeding of malaria-bearing mosquitoes, and they supervised efforts to dig latrines, scrounge for food, and obtain wood for cooking fires. Army engineers began to repair the shattered plumbing and restore electricity. Lieutenant-Colonel Glyn White of the Australian Army Medical Corps managed to smuggle in hospital equipment, drugs, and medicines, and soon the camp was functioning reasonably well. Gardens were sown to provide fresh food, and eventually 10 truckloads of green vegetables were being harvested every week. A poultry farm was established as well and fresh eggs were distributed under the direction of doctors.

With the camp running smoothly, the men began to look for other diversions. They attended lectures on a variety of subjects, studying such things as history, geography, engineering, and business. An Australian concert party was formed, and well-attended shows (which continued until July 1945) gave the men some relief from the boredom and uncertainty of prison life. During one early show an Australian comic named Harry Smith coined a melancholy slogan that will forever be associated with Changi: "You'll never get off the island!"

The Japanese soon began drawing on their prisoner population for local work parties, and more than 8,000 men labored on tasks such as filling bomb craters and gathering scrap metal for export to Japan. In May 1942, around 3,000 prisoners known as A Force were taken out of Changi to work on the Burma-Thailand railway. Two months later, a further 1,500 were shipped to Sandakan in British North Borneo to begin work on an airfield, while others went to labor camps in Japan. In August, the Japanese removed all the camp's senior officers above the rank of lieutenant-colonel and shipped them to Formosa.

As prisoner numbers dwindled, the whole camp, including the hospital, was moved to Selarang. Conditions there worsened dramatically and by war's end, Changi's POWs were in a pitiful state—diseased, starved, their bodies reduced to skin and bone. Today the Selarang Barracks still stands, while Changi itself is now home to Singapore's huge, modern international airport.

See also Bicycle Camp; Burma-Thailand (Death) Railway; Cabanatuan; *King Rat*; World War II—Far East

References

Patsy Adam-Smith, *Prisoners of War* (New York: Viking, 1992).

Kevin Blackburn, "Changi: A Place of Personal Pilgrimages and Collective Histories," *Australian Historical Studies* 30 (1999): 152–171.

Russell Braddon, *The Naked Island* (London: T. Werner Laurie, 1952).

Philippa Poole, ed., *Of Love and War: The Letters and Diaries of Captain Adrian Curlewis and His Family, 1939–45* (New York: Lansdowne Press, 1982).

—*Colin Burgess*

Chaplains

According to international law, chaplains are considered to be protected personnel who are not subject to internment as POWs. They are to be released as soon as possible by their captors and returned to their own forces. Many chaplains, however, have elected to stay with their captive flocks and have provided essential solace to POWs facing the challenges of captivity.

International law throughout the twentieth century has stipulated that chaplains be given every opportunity to minister to their fellow prisoners; this is one article of international law that seems to have been honored widely in the world wars. The 1929 Geneva Convention Relative to the Treatment of Prisoners of War stated that POWs should be at liberty to exercise their religious beliefs; the 1949 Geneva Convention Relative to the Treatment of Prisoners of War reiterated this point, adding that the detaining power is obliged to provide suitable space for worship. Other agreements stipulated the number of chaplains to be retained for prison-camp duties, ranging from one per thousand (as laid down in an agreement between the United States and Germany) to four per thousand (terms reached by Germany and South Africa). Should chaplains from one's own forces be unavailable, the 1949 Geneva Convention allowed that a chaplain from the local area could be appointed to work with prisoners. Furthermore, the chaplain was to be allowed further liberties, including freedom to travel between camps to visit POWs and freedom to correspond with ecclesiastical groups that assist in his work.

In World War II there were no German chaplains in captivity because German units did not include chaplains, as did most Allied units. Therefore, most of the religious work in POW camps in Canada and the United States was done by local or neutral chaplains. Despite the Nazis' official distaste for religion, many German POWs were receptive to the work of the American and Canadian religious organizations that were active in the camps, like the National Catholic Welfare Council, the Lutheran Commission for Prisoners of War, the World Council of Churches, and the Ecumenical Commission for Chaplaincy Service to Prisoners of War. Indeed, there were reports of dramatic increases in church attendance among German POWs within the first few months after a religious organization began work in a camp.

On the other side of the wire, few captured Allied chaplains reported any difficulty in carrying out their work in World War II. For example, Eugene Daniel, an American Presbyterian minister who became a POW in North Africa in 1943, was originally denied permission to remain with the enlisted ranks of his unit in captivity. Instead, he was transferred to an officers' camp that already had 21 padres on staff. Quickly pointing this out to his captors, Daniel was just as quickly on his way back to Stalag 7A at Moosburg, Bavaria, where the men of his unit had been imprisoned.

Shortages of religious materials were sometimes a problem, but the Young Men's Christian Association was very active in supplying church furnishings to prison camps. Padres found attendance at church services was spotty, but they could always be guaranteed a good crowd on important days. J. Ellison Platt, a Methodist chaplain taken prisoner at Dunkirk in 1940, organized four services on Christmas Eve and Christmas Day in Oflag 4C (Colditz) in 1944. All were well attended, despite the fact that the temperature in the unheated theater-cum-chapel had dropped to –11 degrees Celsius. The padre in captivity spent as much time counseling his fellow prisoners as preaching to them, for many troubled men would turn to the chaplain when the burdens of captivity grew too heavy. But chaplains themselves were also vulnerable to despair. Douglas Thompson, a Methodist chaplain captured in North Africa in World War II, found himself ministering to a fellow padre who had been captured in Greece and who had become unhinged as a result of his experiences in captivity. Thompson was able to keep the man from deteriorating further while he awaited repatriation home.

The situation was very different during the Korean War, when chaplains of the United Nations Command were singled out for particularly brutal treatment by the North Korean regime. Three U.S. Army padres—Kenneth Hyslop, Emil Kapaun, and Wayne Burdue—died in captivity, in part because of their selfless determination to serve their fellow prisoners, and a British chaplain, the Reverend S. J. Davies, was decorated for his devotion to his men. In each case, it was clear that the chaplain played a major role in helping his men to survive captivity.

See also Religion

References

Eugene L. Daniel, *In the Presence of Mine Enemies: An American Chaplain in World War II German Prison Camps* (Attleboro, MA: Colonial Lithograph, 1985).

Margaret Duggan, ed., *Padre in Colditz: The Diary of J. Ellison Platt* (London: Hodder and Stoughton, 1978).

William L. Maher, *Shepherd in Combat Boots: Chaplain Emil Kapaun of the 1st Cavalry Division* (Shippensburg, PA: White Mane, 1997).

Douglas Thompson, *Captives to Freedom* (London: Epworth Press, 1955).

—*Jonathan F. Vance*

CHECHEN WARS

In the wake of the dissolution of the Soviet Union in 1991, Chechnya, an oil-rich and largely Muslim region in the northern Caucasus, was the only former Soviet republic that did not conclude a political accord with the government of the Russian Federation in Moscow. Three years of low-level violence ensued as pro- and anti-Russian elements in Chechnya struggled for control of the region. Finally, in December 1994, Russian President Boris Yeltsin sent in the Russian army to pacify the separatists and install a government that was sympathetic to Moscow. But Russian commanders mismanaged the campaign and their army became involved in an increasingly brutal, two-year struggle with an enemy that offered surprisingly tough resistance. It was a war in which prisoners became pawns to be used for political advantage.

The prisoners included military POWs and civilian hostages, some taken in action and others in carefully organized kidnappings involving a handful or hundreds of captives. The Russian government admitted to capturing 471 Chechens, but never revealed whether these were soldiers or civilians. Few, if any, of these prisoners were visited by humanitarian organizations, and the chief of the Russian general staff claimed to be under no obligation to take prisoners at all, because Chechen fighters were simply bandits who, according to international law, could be shot on the spot. Conversely, the Russian military insisted that its soldiers who fell into Chechen hands were hostages rather than POWs, because to admit that they were POWs would be to legitimize the Chechen resistance. Instead, Russia was determined to see the conflict as a rebellion, Chechen fighters as members of "criminal formations," and their own captured soldiers as hostages held captive by gangsters.

The Chechens, however, treated captured Russian soldiers as POWs, interning them first in the basement of army headquarters at the Presidential Palace in the Chechen capital, Grozny. They were evacuated only when fighting reached the city. By then, however, the Chechens had begun to take a harsher attitude toward Russian prisoners. For example, in May 1995, a Chechen commander announced that five Russian prisoners would be killed for every day that the Russian army bombarded a village in the Shatoisky region.

The Chechens had also moved toward mass hostage-takings as a tactic. The first of these involved the capture by Chechen fighters of as many as 1,500 civilian hostages at Budennovsk in southern Russia in June 1995; they were eventually released when Russian authorities agreed to a ceasefire and peace negotiations. However, the Chechens did retain a number of hostages to use as human shields to safeguard their passage back across the border into Chechnya. Then, in January 1996, Chechen fighters seized another 1,500 civilians at Pervomayskoye, on the border with the neighboring district of Dagestan. Once more, negotiations with Russian authorities secured the release of most of the hostages, but the Chechens again kept a small number as shields to guarantee their safe return to Chechnya. It should be noted that the Russian army also used civilian hostages as human shields to protect their military vehicles, which were vulnerable to Chechen small arms fire.

It did prove possible to negotiate a number of prisoner exchanges, but this was not as positive as it seems. The Russian government almost invariably exchanged Chechen civilians for Russian soldiers, and it seems fairly certain that when the Russian military learned that some of its members were in enemy hands, it simply kidnapped a similar number of Chechen civilians and negotiated an exchange. Often, these civilians were detained at what was called a "filtration camp" at Mozdok in the region of Ossetia. Survivors of Mozdok reported to Human Rights Watch that they were held in railway cars (known as "Stolypin wagons," after the pre-Russian Revolution prime minister who first used sealed railway cars to transport prisoners), sometimes 70 people to a car, and subsisted on rations of water, bread, and the occasional tin of sardines in tomato sauce. Some of these individuals were exchanged for Russian soldiers (one such exchange was a January 1995 swap of 43 Russian POWs for a similar number of Chechen civilians), while others were eventually transferred to camps deeper inside Russia. Eventually, Chechen authorities refused to continue the exchange process until it started receiving back some of its captured soldiers.

Furthermore, family members of captives were often told that they had to take responsibility for facilitating the exchanges. Russian authorities told the relatives of one detained Chechen that he could be exchanged for a Russian POW, but that they would have to find the POW themselves. When they protested that they could not afford to buy a Russian soldier from a rebel cell that might be holding one, they were told that their relative would be freed in exchange for the remains of three Russian officers killed in the fighting around Grozny. This time, they were able to locate the bodies and secure the release of their imprisoned relative.

In May 1996, Russian and Chechen leaders concluded another peace treaty that, among other things, promised the release of all prisoners within two weeks of the end of hostilities. But the Russian government was not satisfied with the results and, on 8 July, issued an ultimatum to Chechen authorities: If all prisoners were not released by the following day, the Russian military would take "adequate measures." The captives did not materialize, and tensions between Moscow and Grozny remained high, even after Russia withdrew its troops from Chechnya.

There followed a period of increasing Chechen terrorist activity inside Russia, and in September 1999 the Russian military again began operations against Chechnya. The following year, new Russian President Vladimir Putin reestablished formal rule over Chechnya, but the violence continued in what became known as the Second Chechen War. Once again, civilians were the primary targets, most notably in two bloody hostage-taking incidents: the seizure by Chechen terrorists of a Moscow theater with over 700 civilians inside in October 2002 (many died when Russian special forces stormed the building); and the assault on Beslan school, in which Chechens took hostage over 1,000 civilians, primarily women and children (more than 300 of them died in the relief operation). Still, despite calls for a ceasefire in February 2005, the fighting in the region continued.

The passage of time did not clear up the mystery surrounding the numbers of prisoners captured by either side. In 1998, Russian press reports suggested that some 1,300 Russian soldiers were still missing in action from the first Chechen war, and that perhaps 10 percent of them were POWs in Chechen hands. Those same reports suggested that the release of a Russian soldier could be secured by paying a ransom of as much as US$100,000, an astronomical sum for most Russians. In February 2003, a Russian presidential commission determined that 832 soldiers remained unaccounted for in Chechnya, but could not (or would not) say whether these men were captured or dead. What has become clear, however, is that if more prisoners are to be released, it will have to be through the efforts of their relatives.

See also Beslan

References

Matthew Evangelista, *The Chechen Wars: Will Russia Go the Way of the Soviet Union?* (Washington, DC: Brookings Institution Press, 2003).

Tracey C. German, *Russia's Chechen War* (New York: Routledge, 2003).

—J.W. Smith

CHIETI

Campo 21 at Chieti, on the Adriatic coast near Pescara, was typical of the prison camps operated by the Italian armed forces during World War II. The camp consisted of eight single-story barracks, each in a U-shape, with additional buildings serving as cookhouse, mess hall, hospital, guard barracks, and administrative office. The entire camp was ringed by a 12-foot-high brick wall that was foreboding but did not prevent prisoners from enjoying a wonderful view of the Apennines Mountains.

Chieti housed officers captured in North Africa, including British, Australian, New Zealand, and South African army officers and American airmen. On the whole, conditions in the camp were good. Food, clothing, and water were always in short supply, but recreational opportunities were excellent. There were five bands, a theater, film screenings, hikes in the countryside, and swimming in a nearby river. Perhaps most importantly, relations between the prisoners themselves were extremely amicable, something that was not true in all camps.

On 21 September 1943, after the capitulation of Italy, German troops arrived in Chieti to move the prisoners northward to captivity in Germany. On 24 September, the evacuation began, and many prisoners were sorry to leave Campo 21. As James Chutter, a former inmate, wrote, "All who knew Chieti hold it in kindly memory."

References
James B. Chutter, *Captivity Captive* (London: Jonathan Cape, 1954).
Odell Myers, *Thrice Caught: An American Army POW's 900 Days Under Axis Guns* (Jefferson, NC: McFarland & Co., 2002).

—*Tony Dawes*

CHILDREN

Children have been on the periphery of battlefields and have actively participated in warfare throughout military history. Many soldiers in their teens and younger, both male and female, have lied about their ages to enlist, disguised themselves, or served as drummer boys and in auxiliary military roles. In some cultures, it was expected that teenaged and young boys would perform military service. In other situations, noncombatant children accompanied female camp followers, either their mothers, sisters, or other relatives, to assist their soldier fathers. As a result, children often became prisoners of war. Joan of Arc and Anne Frank are probably the most famous child prisoners.

Perhaps the best documented child prisoners were captured during the American Revolution. Colonial officials counted several hundred children among the camp follower prisoners in the Convention Army after the British defeat at Saratoga during the American Revolution. Most of the young prisoners were peasants, but several, such as General Friedrich Riedesel's daughters (two of whom were born during the war and named Canada and America), were officers' children or teenaged maids and servants. In November 1777, the Convention prisoners, including British, German, Canadian, and Loyalist children, marched or rode in wagons, covering 200 miles in two weeks, from Saratoga to Boston, where they were imprisoned. Boston resident Hannah Winthrop described how the prisoners carried supplies with "children peeping thro' gridirons and other utensils," including "some very young Infants who were born on the road." She noted the young prisoners were barefoot and dirty. British Lieutenant Thomas Anburey reported hearing children squealing as they stumbled through snowstorms. The shelters on Prospect and Winter Hills where the children lived were unstable, and snow drifted through holes in the walls and roofs. As Sergeant Roger Lamb commented, "It was not infrequent for thirty or forty persons, men, women and children, to be indiscriminately crowded together in one small, miserable, pen hut, a scanty portion of straw their bed, their own blankets their only covering." The children spent most of their time with female prisoners and the sick and wounded, and so were exposed to contagious diseases. Boston citizens disliked the fact that the children escaped from their quarters to roam the city's streets. The young prisoners were moved with their families, first to Virginia and then Pennsylvania. During their travels, children were often the only prisoners who were given food by sympathetic local residents. Although the Continental Congress demanded that children of prisoners be furnished with subsistence, many suffered malnutrition because of poor rations.

The child prisoners of the American Revolution are particularly well documented, but young soldiers were captured in other pre-twentieth-century wars. For example, on 14 August 1756, approximately 100 women and children were in the British garrison at Oswego that surrendered during the French and Indian War. During the American Civil War, child inmates were reported to have been seen at prison camps, including even Andersonville.

In World War II, millions of children became prisoners in Europe, Asia, and North America. Like the American Revolution prisoners, these children's experiences have been well recorded. For instance, when the Japanese interned Dutch citizens in the Dutch East Indies in 1942, children accompanied their mothers or female guardians to the prison camps, which eventually held some 80,000 women and children. While incarcerated, the children were forced to live and work in difficult conditions, which involved overcrowded barracks, meager rations, unsanitary water, and outbreaks of tropical diseases, which killed many of the malnourished children. Young prisoners helped grow gardens to supplement rations and also interacted with local residents, but by 1944, the children's diets became even more impoverished as a result of shortages throughout the Japanese occupation zone. Mothers decided that children should eat things like lizards and snakes to provide the protein necessary for growth, and medical personnel interned in the camps tried to treat children with herbal medicines. Unfortunately, many children's growth was stunted, and other health problems were either caused or exacerbated by their wartime imprisonment. Ten thousand Dutch women and children died while interned in the Dutch East Indies, and the survivors would require years to recover physically and mentally.

The situation was better in the Philippines, where child prisoners at Santo Tomas Internment Camp participated in a variety of recreational activities and also attended a well-organized school. When they first arrived at the camp with their baggage, the children were reunited with their mothers, who had been transported separately. Many of the upper-class mothers had previously relied upon servants to care for the children, and so internment was a time of learning how to perform such simple tasks as preparing a meal or changing a diaper. Children lived with their mothers in a crowded building and obeyed the 6:30 curfew every night, with lights out a half hour later. The prison camp established a dental clinic and children's hospital as well as a playground especially for the young prisoners. Some children lived temporarily with residents in nearby Quezon City, which gave them access to better food and more room to play. Despite a lack of basic educational materials like textbooks and chalk, volunteer teachers at the Santo Tomas school taught elementary and high school students. Parents supported the school because it provided a structure for their children's lives and enabled them to continue their education and prepare for college and the future. Attendance was voluntary, and almost 90 percent of the camp's children took classes in English, science, mathematics, languages, and history. Twenty pupils graduated from the camp's high school.

The civilian children in Japanese camps were isolated from the world and from their fathers. When a stunned wife received news of her husband's death in another prison camp, she was comforted by her children, who bonded with their widowed mother. This grieving was a shared experience, due to the lack of privacy in camp. This bothered some adult prisoners but was less of a concern for children, who were unaccustomed to individual isolation. In the prisoner-of-war camps, children learned to play and communicate among themselves much like children anywhere, and this socializing served to recreate an atmosphere of normality in an abnormal situation and to boost their spirits and pass the time. Younger children likely did not comprehend the seriousness of war and may have perceived imprisonment as just another game.

Despite the horrible conditions, child prisoners in Asia were often able to maintain some of the more routine aspects of their peacetime lives. They did not encounter the terrifying situations faced by Jewish children (as well as Gypsy children, children from other targeted ethnic groups, or those deemed to be mentally inferior) in Europe. Initially confined to ghettos, Jewish children and youth were stripped of their identities, removed from their homes, and shipped to concentration camps to endure unspeakable misery. Two of the best known non-Jewish child prisoners were college students Hans and Sophie Scholl, who led the White Rose resistance movement in Germany. Imprisoned and executed for their beliefs, they represent the idealism of children who matured during World War II and resisted political and cultural repression.

See also Camp Followers

References

Irena Grudzin Gross, ed., *War through Children's Eyes: The Soviet Occupation of Poland and the Deportations, 1939–1941* (Palo Alto, CA: Hoover Institution Press, 1981).

Shirley Fenton Huie, *The Forgotten Ones: Women and Children Under Nippon* (Pymble, Australia: Angus and Robertson, 1992).

Ing Jens, ed., *At the Heart of the White Rose: Letters and Diaries of Hans and Sophie Scholl*, trans. J. Maxwell Brownjohn (New York: Harper and Row, 1987).

Hildegard Schmidt Lindstrom, *Child Prisoner of War* (Ann Arbor, MI: Proctor Publications, 1998).

Carol M. Petillo, ed., *The Ordeal of Elizabeth Vaughan: A Wartime Diary of the Philippines* (Athens: University of Georgia Press, 1985).

—Elizabeth D. Schafer

CHINESE CIVIL WAR (1927–1949)

The treatment of prisoners of the Chinese Civil War can be examined in two stages. The first stage looks at the period during the war and takes into consideration how both the ruling Nationalists and the insurgent Communists dealt with their prisoners. The second stage concerns how Nationalist fighters and supporters were treated after the Communists took power.

During the war, both sides were indiscriminate in the tactics each used against the other, absorbing some members of the opposite side into their ranks, while choosing to eliminate others. At times, those individuals absorbed were foot soldiers, while those executed were officers; on other occasions, it was the foot soldiers who were killed and officers integrated. This was true of both sides. After the Communist victory, however, the state was more systematic in its approach and implemented a formal system of guidelines on how to treat prisoners, treatment that was described in all accounts as brutal.

In 1911, revolutionaries overthrew China's traditional political system but did not replace it with a working alternative. A lack of proper leadership, compounded by China's geographic size, saw the country fall increasingly under the influence of local strongmen known as warlords. These individuals would claim a certain area of territory and then defend it as their own, and with no central government in place, there was no one to stop them.

Like its political system, China's economy was also in chaos. Around this time, a significant proportion of China's population lived in rural areas. Many citizens were poor peasants who had no central state mechanism; thus, there was no system of social support to provide aid, if necessary. Instead, landlords who charged them high rent even in times of poor harvest governed peasants under a feudal system, and peasants had nowhere to seek accountability in the face of poor treatment. As the situation worsened, the society became deeply divided.

It is within this context that the Nationalists and the Communists began to gain momentum as political entities, each offering to build a China that was stable and unified. In 1916 the revolutionary Sun Yat-Sen established the independent Republic of South China under the banner of Nationalism. Sun set out to unite and stabilize China using the three principles of democracy, socialism, and nationalism. By the 1920s the Republican Government found support with the then newly formed Communists, working together to formulate ideas to wrest China from the factionalism of the feuding warlords.

However, around 1925 the Nationalists severed their informal alliance with the Communists. The split came about when the Nationalists began to fear that their Communist counterparts were heeding Soviet advice about how to advance the Chinese political process at the expense of Chinese unity. The change came about when the executive committee of the Nationalists party declared the formation of the National Revolutionary Army with party member Chiang Kai-Shek as the head. With the formation of the Army under Chiang, the committee declared that its intention was to unify the country by force, to counter the effects of the post-revolutionary era. However, Chiang was no longer willing to work with Communists because he did not trust the Soviet influence they heeded.

In response, the Communist leadership attempted to take power by endorsing the overthrow of the Nationalist government through a populist revolt. The attempt failed, as the Nationalist government was better equipped to defend its position than the Communists were to fight for it. In the face of the Communist failure, the Nationalist counterattacked, and from 1927 to 1949 the two parties engaged in a civil war.

The Chinese Civil War was a struggle for power that took place amidst a population in need of economic, political, and social unity and security. It was a struggle to determine whether the Nationalists or the Communists could unite the vast and regionalized country, and gain the power and influence that such control promised. It is within this context that one can begin to provide an account of how POWs were treated, beginning with an account of the war years and ending with an outline of how the Communists treated prisoners in the post-civil war era.

During the war, the preferred method for dealing with prisoners was death by execution or starvation, or by assimilation into the captor's ranks. For example, in 1927 during a Communist insurrection known as the "Canton Commune," the Nationalist government suppressed, captured, and executed every individual in the city whom they could prove was a Communist. This swift and harsh treatment was a testament to the Nationalist government's plan to unify China at all cost; dissenters were removed as roadblocks.

By the same token, the Communists committed their fair share of abuses toward prisoners during the civil war years. For instance, in 1931 the Communists successfully defended themselves against two Nationalist offensives known as the "Bandit suppression extermination campaign." Throughout these offensives, the Communists overwhelmed the Nationalists, inflicting severe casualties and capturing a significant number of prisoners. After the fight, the Communists killed every commanding officer captured.

The decision to execute high-ranking soldiers marked a clear pattern of intimidation carried out with increasing intensity in the later years of the war. In another case designed to hasten the surrender of a Nationalist battalion, the Communists held the Manchurian city of Chanchung under siege and watched as civilians and Nationalist soldiers in the captive city starved to death as their food supply ran out. Some accounts surmise that the Communists were indiscriminate in their brutality toward their captives. As Nationalist soldiers and civilians starved, the Communists allowed individuals who had material possessions of value (such as weapons) to leave the city if they were willing to trade them for their freedom. This action encouraged surrender and compliance to Communist will; scholars argue that this sort of pitilessness was one of the greatest Communist weapons.

In 1949, the Communists took power and consolidated their victory over the Nationalists. In this period, the treatment of POWs manifested itself as organized and brutal, flowing from leader Mao Tse-tung's doctrine on the political process. As part of his goals for China, Mao wanted harmony and stability, a policy he set out to achieve by ideologically remolding, through forced labor and torture, those who did not agree with his ideology. Most notably, he used this practice to remold, mentally, political dissenters, or POWs.

An example of the use of this practice on prisoners involves a nationwide network of camps called the *Laogai*. Meaning reform through labor, the *Laogai* were used by the Communists to re-educate prisoners in Communist ideology. Though 90 percent of all prisoners were members and soldiers of the defeated Nationalist government, the state classified the captives not as prisoners of war, but as counterrevolutionaries, or *Fangeming Fenzi*. In the *Laogai* system, these counterrevolutionaries often experienced torture through a combination of beatings and excessive physical labor. Most prisoners encountered starvation and appalling living conditions, including mice, lice, and disease. Many Nationalist POWs died and were buried by the state in unmarked graves. The state classified those killed during re-education as suicides, placing the responsibility for their deaths on each individual prisoner.

Not all prisoners died, however; some showed signs of being successfully re-educated by playing an integral role in such areas as the creation of economic, social, and other forms of infrastructure. For example, many prisoners were farmers and were responsible for international and domestic food production. Meanwhile, others helped build up China's plastic and nuclear industry.

However, *Laogai* reform sometimes did not end after the Communists considered the prisoner of war to be ideologically remolded. Instead, a common practice was the process of *Juiye*, where a prisoner would be kept in captivity, always acknowledging so-called crimes in a demonstration of constant reform. This proved to the state that the reform tactics it employed to change prisoners from within were indeed effective. In this sense, the Communist government considered *Laogai* tactics to be part of a public security measure to inspire and maintain society's safety from rouge elements.

Perhaps the most noteworthy exception to Communist brutality toward a POW involved Nationalist leader Chiang Kai-Shek. Betrayed by a group of his officers, Chiang was captured by the Communists in 1936. According to accounts, Mao Tse-tung himself ensured that Chiang was treated with respect and that he was not abused or hurt in the manner of other Nationalist prisoners. This was remarkable, given that Chiang was said to be uncooperative while in custody. Furthermore, Mao agreed to Chiang's release and safe passage back to his position as leader. Chiang's treatment while in Communist custody, it must be noted, is not typical Communist action toward prisoners of the civil war or counterrevolutionaries. It was a rare exception of kindness in a time of cruelty.

Both the Communists and the Nationalists would argue that each was involved in the civil war to save China from factionalism and divisiveness. Yet ironically, though this should be a story about the search for unity, history records it as a story of how the search for unity was derailed into civil war and the abuse of the people it was intended to protect.

References

Jung Chang and Jon Halliday, *Mao: The Unknown Story* (New York: A.A. Knopf, 2005).

Edward L. Dreyer, *China at War, 1901–1949* (New York: Longman, 1995).

Trevor N. Dupuy, *The Military History of The Chinese Civil War* (New York: Franklin Watts, 1969).

Colin Mackerras, *China in Transformation, 1900–1949* (New York: Longman, 1998).

Kate Saunders, *Eighteen Layers of Hell: Stories From the Chinese Gulag* (London: Cassell, 1996).

Hongda Harry Wu, *Laogai – The Chinese Gulag* (Boulder, CO: Westview Press, 1992).
Jun Zhan, *Ending The Chinese Civil War: Power, Commerce, and Conciliation between Beijing and Taipei* (New York: St. Martins Press, 1993).

—*Esmorie Miller*

CHURCHILL, WINSTON LEONARD SPENCER (1874–1965)

Although future British prime minister Winston Churchill referred to himself as a prisoner of war in his memoirs, he was in fact a civilian internee when he was captured during the Boer War on 15 November 1899. He was in South Africa as a correspondent for the London *Morning Post* and was accompanying an armored train headed toward Colenso when it was ambushed by Boer riflemen. Churchill and 51 soldiers were captured. They were sent to Pretoria, where Churchill and the officers were imprisoned in the State Model School. He immediately began to deluge Boer authorities with requests that he be released as an unarmed accredited correspondent, but the Boers refused; because he had played a leading role in resisting the attack on the train, they considered him a legitimate POW. Realizing he was not likely to be released, Churchill turned his efforts toward escape and convinced two officers to include him in their enterprise. However, when they made their attempt on 12 December 1899, only Churchill succeeded in getting out of the prison and began the lonely journey toward Portuguese East Africa and freedom. He traveled part of the way by freight train and was fortunate enough to knock at the door of a sympathetic mine manager, who hid him in a mine while formulating a plan for his escape. On 19 December, Churchill was concealed among some bales of wool on a freight train heading toward Portuguese East Africa. Two days later he was free and aboard a steamer bound for Durban.

Churchill later wrote a number of accounts of his escape, and he was dogged by accusations that he had broken his parole in escaping. But these accusations are unfounded because his captors had never accepted his pledge to not attempt escape. Despite this controversy, it is clear that Churchill the writer got remarkable mileage out of a captivity and escape that lasted less than five weeks.

See also Boer War

References

Randolph S. Churchill, *Winston S. Churchill*, vol. 1, *Youth, 1874–1900* (London: Heinemann, 1966).
Winston S. Churchill, *My Early Life: A Roving Commission* (London: Butterworth, 1930).

—*Jonathan F. Vance*

CIVILIAN INTERNEES—WORLD WAR I

All belligerent nations interned varying numbers of enemy civilians during World War I. They might have been tourists traveling on holidays, students going to school abroad, businessmen and their families, missionaries, merchant seamen, resident aliens, or simply people caught on the wrong side of the border when war broke out. Historically, it was the tradition to allow civilians a grace period to tidy up their affairs and return home, but during World War I, many civilians were not given this chance. Altogether, some 400,000 civilians were interned in Europe alone.

Internment policies varied greatly from country to country. The French government began interning civilians from the Central Powers almost immediately after the declaration of war. In addition to Germans and Austro-Hungarians, civilians from other "unfriendly" regions, like Czechoslovakia, Greece, Poland, Armenia, Alsace, and Lorraine, were liable to internment. These prisoners, however, were treated more favorably by the French in the belief that they might be convinced to join the Allied side. For German and Austro-Hungarian civilians, conditions were rather worse than those endured by prisoners of war. One camp, an old convent at Monleon Magnaoc, lacked heat and running water, and the internees slept on piles of straw on the stone floor. Able-bodied internees were forced to work, and others were condemned to months of inactivity in dreary camps. The French government interned German civilians in two distinct classes. Enemy women, children, and elderly men were held in camps run by the Ministry of the Interior. The majority of these people were tourists who had been vacationing in France when the war began or relatives of businessmen working in France. The other group, men of military age who were passing through France on their way back to Germany (many of them from the United States) were held in camps operated by the War Ministry.

In Britain, there were some arrests early in the war but general internment did not begin until July 1915, and then as a result of public pressure. Neutral delegates reported that conditions in most camps were very good and that the inmates had little reason to complain. Many articles in the press complained bitterly about "pampered prisoners." Paul Cohen-Portheim, a German-born painter interned in camps at Knockaloe and Wakefield for much of the war, recalled that although conditions were not as favorable as the British press claimed, he had fond memories of his internment, did not believe that it harmed him in the least, and looked back on his internment as a very valuable experience.

The internment of enemy civilians in Germany began on 6 November 1914, when the government ordered that all British males between the ages of 17 and 55 be imprisoned. Men from other parts of the British Empire, which did not at that time intern German civilians, were left at liberty until January 1915. By the end of the war, there were roughly 110,000 civilians interned in Germany. A few of these were held in well-known camps like Ruhleben, which had been constructed at a racecourse in a suburb of Berlin, but most were detained in military camps with prisoners of war. For example, Wallace Ellison, an Englishman living near Frankfurt, was arrested in the first week of the war and placed in Sennelager, a prison camp that then held thousands of Belgian POWs. He and his fellow internees were put to work for a few weeks, released, and then rearrested in November 1914. Because he was a persistent escaper, Ellison spent most of his captivity in military prisons and was rarely in the company of civilian internees.

Internment was also a feature of life for enemy aliens outside of Europe, although it was much more limited in scope. The United States adopted a very selective policy of internment, arresting only those civilians who were deemed to be a threat to security; in the end only one out of every 1,100 enemy aliens in the United States was interned. Over the course of the war, some 2,300 civilians and a similar number of merchant seamen were imprisoned in places like Hot Springs, North Carolina, where a resort area had been turned into an internment camp. The selective policy had its drawbacks, however. Those people who were interned were deemed, for various reasons, to be troublemakers. Occasionally this label was unjustified, but in other cases, civilians who were recalcitrant or difficult created discipline problems within the camps. Still, neutral delegates reported that, as in Britain, camp conditions in the United States were very good. The situation was similar in Canada, where a government decree of 28 October 1914 allowed for the internment of enemy aliens if they failed to abide by certain directives. In total, 8,579 civilians were interned in Canada, primarily recent immigrants from the Austro-Hungarian Empire. Most of these individuals were eventually posted to various public-works projects across western Canada; the internees from Germany proper were generally held in internment camps in eastern Canada. As in the United States, living conditions were relatively decent compared to the conditions endured by some internees in Europe.

Indeed, those internees who were put to work may have been better off than the idle ones, for they avoided the debilitating inactivity that burdened so many internees in Europe. This idleness, combined with the regimentation of camp life, probably weighed more heavily on civilian internees than it did on POWs, who were to some degree accustomed to these aspects of the military lifestyle.

See also Civilian Internees—World War II; Isle of Man; Ruhleben

References

Henri S. Béland, *My Three Years in a German Prison* (Toronto: William Briggs, 1919).

Paul Cohen-Portheim, *Time Stood Still: My Internment in England, 1914–1918* (New York: E. P. Dutton, 1932).

Wallace Ellison, *Escapes and Adventures* (London: William Blackwood and Sons, 1928).

James Farney and Bohdan S. Kordan, "The Predicament of Belonging: The Status of Enemy Aliens in Canada, 1914," *Journal of Canadian Studies* 39 (2005): 74–89.

Bohdan S. Kordan, *Enemy Aliens, Prisoners of War: Internment in Canada During the Great War* (Montreal: McGill-Queen's University Press, 2002).

Lubomyr Luciuk and Borys Sydoruk, *"In My Charge": The Canadian Internment Camp Photographs of Sergeant William Buck* (Kingston, ON: Kashtan Press, 1997).

Bryce and Mary Lyon, eds., *The "Journal de Guerre" of Henri Pirenne* (New York: North-Holland Publishing, 1976).

Jonathan F. Vance, "Dr. Henri Béland: Nobody's Darling," *American Review of Canadian Studies* 28 (1998): 469–487.

Bill Waiser, *Park Prisoners: The Untold Story of Western Canada's National Parks, 1915-1946* (Calgary: Fifth House, 1995).

—*Jonathan F. Vance*

CIVILIAN INTERNEES—WORLD WAR II

Just as in World War I, thousands of civilians found themselves facing internment during World War II in virtually every belligerent state. Their treatment ranged from the positively munificent to the abusive, but in most cases civilian internees were significantly better off than military POWs.

The Germans interned thousands of civilians in Europe during the war (this group is distinct from those civilians imprisoned in concentration camps), in conditions that were Spartan but generally not cruel. The earliest internees were crowded into an old convent at Wülzburg that lacked sufficient light, water, and food, but the situation improved when they were moved to Tost in October 1941. Two years later, these prisoners were transferred to two camps, Kreuzberg (now Kloczbork, Poland), and Giromagny, a dank and unpleasant French military barracks near the Swiss border. Frontstalag 221 at Vittel in France held some 2,400 internees in relative comfort, in a series of hotels and guest houses.

Conditions for Allied nationals interned in Japan and Japanese-held territories were considerably worse but still superior to those endured by Allied POWs. Roughly 12,100 Americans were interned there (6,000 in China, 1,100 in Japan, and 5,000 in the Philippines), as were 8,000 internees from Britain and the Commonwealth, primarily in China, Hong Kong, and Singapore. Orders for internment affected civilians in different areas at different times. In Hong Kong, 250 men, women, and children were placed in Stanley Internment Camp as early as January 1942, and civilians in Singapore were placed in Changi jail shortly after the Japanese conquest the same year. This latter group was moved to Sime Road Camp in May 1944. Similarly, civilians in the Philippines faced internment soon after the Japanese arrived; by January 1942, Santo Tomas Internment Camp already held 3,300 internees. In Sumatra, civilians were detained in a street of small houses in the town of Palembang. Their greatest problem was overcrowding, since up to 30 internees were packed into a house designed for a couple with one child. Eventually this group was transferred to Banka Island and then Muntok, where conditions were even worse and where shortages of food and medicine resulted in many deaths.

The situation was different in Japanese-occupied China. There was no general internment immediately after December 1941, and many mission compounds, though placed under Japanese guard, were left to function with little interference. The internment of civilians did not begin until November 1942, when roughly 300 males were sent to Haiphong Road Camp in Shanghai. In early

1943, the majority of other Allied nationals were interned, followed in 1944 by the elderly and infirm, who until then had been left at liberty. Still, conditions remained fairly good, in part because the facilities were in good repair. Lunghwa Civilian Assembly Center had been a university campus, while the camps at Yu Yuen and Great Western Road had been British military barracks. In these three camps, the internees at least enjoyed relative comfort in a physical sense. Furthermore, the internment camps in China were operated by the Japanese Consul General, which was more sympathetic to the needs of captives than was the military.

The other reason internees were better off than POWs is because they were better supplied. Internees in China were permitted to bring in their personal belongings, such as recreational equipment, books, and other comforts. The Japanese provided them with better rations than POWs received, allowed them to grow vegetables and to raise small animals for food, and permitted local civilians to send in parcels of foodstuffs. An internee with some means, then, could arrange to receive sufficient food to prevent the worst of the deficiency diseases that plagued POWs. Even when food supplies dwindled toward the end of the war, the situation was less dire than that in POW camps. At Shantung Compound in Weihsien, which held Allied civilians from the Weihsien and Canton regions of China, internee rations were cut to about 1,200 calories per day toward the end of the war, a minuscule allotment to be sure, but still twice the caloric intake that many POWs were receiving.

Civilian internees held by the Allied powers lived lives of comparative ease. In New Zealand, Somes Island, which had held civilian internees in World War I, was put back into commission, receiving its first German, Austrian, and Italian internees in December 1939. They were later joined by so many German and Japanese civilians from the Pacific islands that all internees were moved in January 1943 to larger quarters on the mainland of New Zealand. Later, when some of the Japanese internees were released in prisoner exchanges, the Somes Island facility was reopened and the internees spent the rest of the war there. Neutral officials reported that conditions in both camps were excellent; indeed, there was some concern in New Zealand over the treatment of civilian internees, who received more butter and meat than did New Zealand civilians.

It must also be said that the same spirit of cooperation that saved the lives of countless POWs did not necessarily prevail in civilian internment camps. In the absence of military discipline, it proved difficult to force internees, many of whom had enjoyed considerable economic or social status before the war, to cooperate with each other for the good of the community. In some camps, food shortages led not to a realization that rations had to be shared equally, but to bitter bickering over the division of rations. Sadly, deprivation among civilian internees seems to have produced more greed and selfishness than it did among POWs, who were bound together by notions of comradeship and unit esprit de corps.

See also Civilian Internees—World War I; Liddell, Eric Henry; Wodehouse, Sir Pelham Grenville

References

Margaret Bevege, *Behind Barbed Wire: Internment in Australia during World War II* (St. Lucia: University of Queensland Press, 1993).

Lynn Z. Bloom, "'Till Death Do Us Part': Men's and Women's Interpretations of Wartime Internment," *Women's Studies International Forum* 10 (1987): 75–83.

Dieuwke Wendelaar Bonga, *Eight Prison Camps: A Dutch Family in Japanese Java* (Athens, OH: Center for International Studies, 1996).

Charles B. Burdick, *American Island in Hitler's Reich: The Bad Nauheim Internment* (Menlo Park, CA: Markgraf Publishers, 1988).

James T. Carroll, "Sentenced to Death – Destined for Life: Catholic Religious and Japanese Occupation," *American Catholic Studies* 113 (2002): 57–74.

Frances B. Cogan, *Captured: The Japanese Internment of American Civilians in the Philippines, 1941–45* (Athens: University of Georgia Press, 2000).

Jean Gittins, *Stanley: Behind Barbed Wire* (Hong Kong: Hong Kong University Press, 1982).

Ernest Hillen, *The Way of a Boy: A Memoir of Java* (New York: Viking Penguin, 1995).

Agnes Newton Keith, *Three Came Home* (Boston: Little, Brown, 1947).
Elfreida Read, *Congee and Peanut Butter* (Toronto: Oberon Press, 1990).

—*Jonathan F. Vance*

CIVILIAN INTERNEES—WORLD WAR II—BRITAIN

At the outbreak of war in 1939 there were upwards of 75,000 Germans and Austrians living in Britain. As in World War I, the British government began contemplating internment as soon as war was declared. Enemy aliens were subject to Defence Regulation 12 (5A), the Aliens Order. Within the first weeks of the war, some 73,400 foreigners appeared before tribunals and were divided into three classes. Those placed in Class A were marked for immediate internment. Those in Class B were subject to restrictions of their liberty, while those in Class C were left entirely at liberty. Early on, in October 1939, just under 200 persons were classified Class A, and the majority were classified as "refugees from Nazi oppression" and left at liberty, for the time being at least.

Indeed, the majority of these foreigners were people who had escaped persecution under the Nazi regime. Among the genuine asylum seekers were Jews, pastors, socialists, and those the Nazis pejoratively labeled "decadent artists." Many had already survived Nazi concentration camps. Many German women—mostly Jewish—had been able to escape Nazi Germany during the mid-1930s by obtaining work permits as domestic servants in England. These women would soon be especially suspect, as they had access to the homes of the upper and middle classes in Britain. When Sir Neville Bland, British minister to the Dutch government at the Hague, returned to Britain two days after Germany's invasion of Holland on 14 May 1940, he busied himself with drafting a report on the "Fifth Column Menace." In his report he claimed that "the paltriest kitchen maid not only can be, but generally is, a menace to the safety of the country."

The British government's civilian internment policy took a sharp turn in May 1940 just as the false security engendered by the period of Phoney War gave way to a phase of Axis territorial gains and accelerated encroachment. On 10 May 1940, Winston Churchill replaced Neville Chamberlain as British prime minister. The same day, Germany attacked the Netherlands, and Holland's Queen Wilhelmina and her government fled to London. The Home Office did not delay, and on 12 May the home secretary, Sir John Anderson, ordered the temporary internment of all German and Austrian males between the ages of 16 and 60 who were living on the east coast of the British Isles, including those who had been classified C. The main fear here was that enemy aliens might assist in German coastal landings. On 15 May, Holland formally surrendered to Germany. On 16 May, the Home Office responded to the growing invasion panic within Britain by interning all Class B enemy aliens. On 10 June, Italy declared war on Britain and arrests extended to include Italians. At a Cabinet meeting following Mussolini's declaration of war, Churchill uttered the now famous command "Collar the lot!" and some 4,000 Italian men were interned. During the course of World War II, Britain interned 23,000 German and Austrian men, 4,000 German and Austrian women, 4,000 Italian men, and 16 Italian women.

The Home Office was placed in charge of rounding up enemy aliens subject to orders of internment, while the War Office was given the authority to organize and administer internment camps and control the movement of internees. Whereas most internees were placed in camps within the British Isles, fears of invasion made the government apprehensive about having so many enemy aliens in their midst. As a result, contingents of enemy alien men were deported to the Dominions. Canada agreed to take in 4,000 internees and 3,000 prisoners of war, and in June and July 1940, four ships sailed, including the ill-fated *Arandora Star*. On 2 July 1940, the *Arandora Star* embarked from Liverpool to

Canada and was struck by a torpedo from a German submarine off the east coast of Ireland. On board were 473 German and 717 Italian internees; approximately 146 Germans and 453 Italians drowned.

Significantly, enemy alien women were never scheduled for deportation overseas, an important indication of the different provisions made for male and female internees. The internment of enemy alien women was a lower priority, demonstrated by the fact that the first order to intern German and Austrian men between the ages of 16 and 60 was issued on 12 May 1940, while the first order issued to arrest women came two weeks later on 27 May 1940.

As in World War I, the majority of internees were placed in camps on the Isle of Man. Men's camps were built at Ramsey, Douglas, Ochan, and Peel, while separate camps for women and children were set up in Port St. Mary and Port Erin. A camp for married couples was also established at Mereside, Douglas. Port Erin was a pleasant Edwardian seaside resort, where internee women were either lodged in boarding houses or billeted by locals. Since most internees arrived during the summer months, the prospect of internment was not so dire, and some women recalled that upon settling in at their boarding house, they put on their bathing suits and went for a swim. Just as in World War I, many of the internees did adjust to life behind the barbed-wire and built temporary communities and support networks. Because the internee population included children, internees set up their own schools and classes. Life was far from idyllic, however, and one of the most unpleasant aspects of internment was that Nazis and anti-Nazis found themselves imprisoned in the same camps and often sleeping in the same barracks, if not in the same bed. In the women's camp, for instance, there were reports of some very awkward occasions; when they were short of beds a Nazi woman and a German Jewish woman had to share the same bed.

Few enemy aliens were held for the entire course of the war, and the review of cases and the release of many detainees began shortly after the implementation of the internment policy. For instance, in May 1941, the number of women interned on the Isle of Man fell from 5,000 to between 3,000 and 4,000. Of the 4,000 Italians interned, only 573 were still being held in May 1945. Of the British 18B prisoners, those who had been detained as potential threats to national security, only a dozen were still under detention when peace was declared.

See also Civilian Internees—World War I; Defence Regulation 18B; Holloway Prison; Isle of Man

References

David Cesarani and Tony Kushner, eds., *The Internment of Aliens in 20th-Century Britain* (London: Frank Cass, 1993).

Peter and Lilly Gillman, *'Collar the Lot!': How Britain Interned and Expelled Its Wartime Refugees* (London: Quartet Books, 1980).

Miriam Kochan, *Britain's Internees in the Second World War* (London: Macmillan, 1983).

Francois Lafitte, *The Internment of Aliens* (London: Libris, 1988 [1940]).

Livia Laurent, *A Tale of Internment* (London: G. Allen and Unwin, 1942).

Panikos Panyani, *Minorities in Wartime: National and Racial Groupings in Europe, North America, and Australia during the Two World Wars* (Oxford: Berg, 1993).

—*Julie V. Gottlieb*

Civilian Internees—World War II—North America

During World War II, the governments of the United States and Canada both interned enemy aliens because of the perceived threat they posed to the nation. The internments, which in some cases were carried out on a large scale, were frequently unjust and often had more to do with misinformation and personal animosity than threats to national security.

On the day that U.S. President Franklin D. Roosevelt declared war against Japan, 7 December 1941, the director of the Federal Bureau of Investigation (FBI), J. Edgar Hoover, unveiled a well-prepared plan, compiled a year earlier by his secret Special

Amerindians move into the barracks formerly occupied by Japanese—American internees at Poston, Arizona (National Archives and Records Administration)

Defense Unit, to identify and round up domestic enemies, real and imagined. While Congress had established provisions for the arrest and internment of enemy aliens in the event of war or threatened invasion as early as 1938, there is much evidence that Hoover's lists of enemies were often based on little more evidence than a neighbor's complaint, a business partner's greed, or an ex-wife's ire. The FBI logged 78,000 such accusations in 1939 alone. However, it must be noted that there were many genuinely dangerous people in America at the time: members of the vocal, pro-Nazi "German-American Bund," German nationalists, and real spies of every political stripe. Because of concern about the gathering war clouds in Europe, all foreign citizens residing in the United States, known as aliens, were required to register in August 1940, at which date the government calculated that there were 315,000 German citizens, 695,000 Italians, and 91,000 Japanese citizens living in America. The Department of Justice and the military's Adjutant General's Office, alarmed at the number of potential enemies, began making plans for a large-scale internment.

With the Japanese attack on Pearl Harbor, hundreds of FBI agents and local police, often acting on unsubstantiated charges or suspicions of disloyalty, awakened families in the middle of the night and took them by buses to be brought before local citizens' tribunals, called Hearing Boards, that determined if they were to be released, placed on parole, or sentenced to an internment camp for the duration of the war. In mid-1942, internments resulted in about 50 percent of the cases heard; 33 percent were placed on parole, and 17 percent were released. One year later, as passions cooled, the trend was reversed as most of those arrested were released. Thus was born the Enemy Alien Internment Program (EAIP), headed by Attorney General Francis Biddle, Immigration and Naturalization Service chief Earl Harrison, and the director of the Enemy Alien Control Unit, Edward J. Ennis. The EAIP (not to be confused with the War Relocation Administration, which forcibly evacuated some 120,000 Japanese and Japanese-Americans from the West Coast to 10 inland camps) operated from 1941 to 1948 and ultimately imprisoned 31,275 people: 16,849 Japanese (not counting the 120,000 relocated Japanese), 10,905 Germans, 3,728 Italians, 52 Hungarians, five Bulgarians, 25 Romanians, 161 assorted others, and several thousand Germans and Japanese who were brought from as far away as Haiti and Peru.

The internees were taken to one of eight federal internment facilities, several of which had been used for identical purposes during World War I: Fort Missoula, Montana, for Italians; Fort Lincoln, North Dakota, for Germans and Japanese; Kooskia Internment Camp, Idaho, and Santa Fe Internment Camp, New Mexico, for Japanese; Kenedy Internment Camp, Texas, for Germans imported from Latin America, Italians, and Japanese; Seagoville Internment Camp, Texas, for female alien enemies; Crystal City Internment Camp, Texas, for Germans, Italians, and Japanese; and Fort Stanton Internment Camp, New Mexico, a segregation camp for the most rabid Nazis. In addition to these eight large camps, there were more than 25 smaller facilities across the country, from Seattle, Washington, to San Juan, Puerto Rico.

During their years of incarceration, the internees managed as well as possible. Some took the opportunity to learn a trade or volunteered to work for local farmers, but the majority surrendered to the stultifying boredom. Each camp boasted its own weekly newspaper, a clinic, a mess hall, even a canteen and beer hall. The larger family camps maintained a school program for the youngsters, where many finished high school. These camps were small cities behind barbed-wire—people were married, babies were born, and the elderly died. Unlike military prisoners of war who were protected by the provisions of the 1929 Geneva Convention, the arrested enemy aliens had few rights and little recourse to legal protection. Interestingly, perhaps due to the frustration of incarceration or the close contact of numerous German nationalists, the level of pro-Nazi sentiment among the internees appears to have increased as the war progressed.

The experiences of these internees were very similar, but the circumstances of their repatriation varied greatly. Even before the end of the war, some were selected for involuntary repatriation to Germany; others, embittered by their unwarranted arrest, volunteered to go back to Germany. Between October 1944 and February 1945, entire families were placed on Swedish ships, the *Gripsholm* or the *Drottningholm*, or on American Victory ships and transported unceremoniously to Germany.

With the end of the war came the question of release or deportation back to Germany. Some who had been deported remained in Germany after the war, while others returned to the United States. A few were lost in the bureaucratic shuffle and actually remained in custody until 1948, but most simply picked up the threads of their prewar lives. A small number found that their wartime imprisonment was an employment obstacle and lost their jobs when their bosses learned about their imprisonment for supposed disloyalty. Yet there were also numerous exceptions. Many were never confronted by their past, and a handful spent their lives in the military, several even working on top-secret projects. Unlike the relocated Japanese from the West Coast, the Germans received neither an official apology for their treatment nor financial reimbursement for their losses. Many are still resentful of the treatment they underwent during the war and see themselves as unknown casualties of the war.

The fate of enemy aliens in Canada was not quite so dire. In 1914 about half a million, or six percent, of Canada's eight million residents had been German or Austro-Hungarian in origin, and these people were seen by Canadians as possible agents of the Kaiser. As in the United States, the Canadian population had turned against its German immigrants with shocking hostility; they were harassed, tormented, and routinely forced to demonstrate their loyalty to Canada. Thousands were arrested and interrogated, and 8,500 enemy aliens were shipped to internment camps for the duration of the war. This experience set the stage for the next war.

Although the Japanese living along the west coast of Canada were relocated, as in the United States, German aliens were in a different situation in World War II. There were 600,000 residents of German origin in Canada in 1939. Most did not live in the large cities and could not be seen as threats to defense plants, military bases, or seats of government. Moreover, Canada had halted immigration at the beginning of the Great Depression and those people who had entered the country before that time were either anti-Nazis or too distant from their German roots to cause any concern.

There were other reasons for the lenient treatment of German-Canadians. The Canadian prime minister, W. L. Mackenzie King, liked Germans. He began his political career by representing a heavily German constituency around the city of Kitchener (formerly Berlin), Ontario. In any case, Canada's Germans had proven their loyalty during World War I. Another reason for Canada's initial lack of concern was that, in sharp contrast to 1914–1918, Canadian war casualties were mercifully light, at least at first. Lastly, even if there had been indications of subversive activity, the Royal Canadian Mounted Police (RCMP) was simply unprepared to root it out. In 1939, the total strength of the RCMP consisted of only 2,541 officers, and they had been trained as policemen, not intelligence agents. Through 1939, only 303 Germans and German-Canadians were interned, and eventually all but the most dangerous were released.

Everything changed in May 1940, when Canada watched in horror as Hitler invaded Scandinavia, Belgium, Holland, and France. Public hysteria turned against Germans and German-Canadians, and rumors flew about German spies, saboteurs, and Fifth Columnists. Regulations were passed to restrict the rights of Germans who had been naturalized as far back as 1922, and by the end of 1940 the Canadian government had interned 1,200 people. As in the United States, many were released as the courts examined each case. By mid-1941 the number of internees had dropped to 780, and by the end of 1942, to 411. When the war ended, the Canadian government held only 22 enemy aliens. Forty other German-Canadians were denaturalized—stripped of their citizenship—and 12 German women and children were exchanged for the same number of Canadians who had been captured at sea. Ninety-eight others were repatriated to Germany. However difficult their lives during the war in Canada, enemy aliens were not treated as harshly as their counterparts in the United States.

See also Civilian Internees—World War I

References

Eric Koch, *Deemed Suspect: A Wartime Blunder* (Toronto: Methuen, 1980).

Arnold Krammer, *Undue Process: The Untold Story of America's German Alien Internees* (Lanham, MD: Rowman and Littlefield, 1997).

Panikos Panyani, *Minorities in Wartime: National and Racial Groupings in Europe, North America, and Australia during the Two World Wars* (Oxford: Berg, 1993).

—*Arnold C. Krammer*

Code of Conduct

In 1955, the United States Department of Defense introduced the Code of Conduct program after it was revealed that 21 U.S. soldiers subjected to communist "brainwashing" in Korean POW camps had defected to the enemy. While there was no proof that Americans behaved any less patriotically in Korea than they had in any other war (this was the first war in which a policy of voluntary repatriation was enacted), the Department of Defense claimed that a strict guideline was needed because the nation's homes, schools, and churches had failed to teach traditional American values. Secretary of Defense Charles Wilson appointed the Burgess Committee to investigate the Korean scandal and draft a new code of conduct to replace the old Geneva regulations that dictated proper POW treatment. The U.S. Air Force recommended writing a compassionate code that would take into account the fact that many men would give more than their name, rank, and service number when tortured. The final code, however, reflected the majority opinion that an uncompromising guideline was needed to "toughen up" the American character, which ostensibly lacked the strength to fight an ideological battle with communism.

After distributing copies of the Code of Conduct to all members of the armed forces, the Department of Defense joined forces with other governmental agencies to include training about the code in public citizenship education efforts. Such efforts proved ineffective, however, after the Code of Conduct program was combined with an Americanism program known as Militant Liberty, which had

The Code of Conduct

Article 1
I am an American, fighting in the forces which guard my country and our way of life. I am prepared to give my life in their defense.

Article 2
I will never surrender of my own free will. If in command, I will never surrender the members of my command while they still have the means to resist.

Article 3
If I am captured I will continue to resist by all means available. I will make every effort to escape and to aid others to escape. I will accept neither parole nor special favors from the enemy.

Article 4
If I become a prisoner of war, I will keep faith with my fellow prisoners. I will give no information or take part in any action which might be harmful to my comrades. If I am senior, I will take command. If not, I will obey lawful orders of those appointed over me and will back them in every way.

Article 5
When questioned, should I become a prisoner of war, I am required to give my name, rank, and service number, and date of birth. I will evade answering further questions to the utmost of my ability. I will make no oral or written statements disloyal to my country or its allies or harmful to their cause.

Article 6
I will never forget that I am an American, fighting for freedom, responsible for my actions, and dedicated to the principles which made my country free. I will trust in my God and in the United States of America.

been promoted by a number of evangelicals in the Department of Defense. Thereafter, it was only during basic training that the military instructed its personnel in POW behavior using the Code of Conduct. Personnel were also required to carry a copy of the Code on their person at all times.

During the Vietnam War, the Department of Defense, after learning that U.S. prisoners in Vietnam were tortured beyond their ability to withhold information, reinterpreted the code to reflect the compassionate stance the Air Force had first suggested.

References

Lori Bogle, "Creating an American Will: Evangelical Democracy and National Security" (Ph.D. diss., University of Arkansas, 1997).

Thomas Alfred Palmer, "Why We Fight: A Study of Indoctrination Activities in the Armed Forces" (Ph.D. diss., University of South Carolina, 1971).

Michael Walzer, "Prisoners of War: Does the Fight Continue After the Battle?" *American Political Science Review* 63 (1969): 777–786.

—Lori Bogle

COLDITZ

Perhaps the most famous German prison camp of World War II, Colditz Castle in Upper Saxony was taken over by the German High Command in October 1939 and transformed into a special POW camp for officers, designated Oflag 4C. Its purpose was to hold those prisoners who had proven themselves to be a nuisance at other camps, either because of repeated attempts to escape or by their general attitude toward their captors. At Colditz the guards outnumbered the prisoners and, extraordinarily for wartime Germany, the camp was floodlit by night. Initially the Germans boasted that Oflag 4C was escape-proof, but they were wrong. By the end of the war there had been more escapes from Colditz than from any other prison of comparable size during either world war.

A castle was first built on the site around 1080, but having survived centuries of battles and sieges, it was razed to the ground by Hussites in 1430. The present-day castle was built on the ruins of another dating back to the sixteenth century, situated atop a great rock promontory overlooking the river Mulde, between Leipzig and Dresden. Prior to the Nazi seizure of power in 1933, Colditz had been used as a prison and an insane asylum, and it later served as an offshoot of Buchenwald concentration camp and a Hitler Youth training camp. Massive rock walls with sheer drops, steep terraces, and a dry moat all lent the castle a daunting air of impregnability. The castle was divided into two main sections, each built around two small courtyards; the Germans occupied the southern part, while the slightly larger northern courtyard, ringed by towers, turrets, and lofty buildings three stories high, held the prisoners.

With the outbreak of war in 1939, Colditz became a transit camp for Polish officer POWs and then a permanent prison camp for Belgian and French prisoners. The first British prisoners to reach Colditz arrived on 5 November 1940, and from the outset they cooperated fully with the other resident nationalities in planning and executing a series of brilliant escapes. In one such effort, British Lieutenant Airey Neave and Dutch Lieutenant Tony Luteyn disguised themselves as German officers and walked through the gates of Colditz. They both reached neutral Switzerland.

As more inmates found ways out of Colditz, the already rigid security was tightened even more. Microphones were hidden all over the castle, roll calls were frequent, and guards were planted at every corner, by every wall, and on every battlement and terrace. But escape was still paramount for the inmates, and their ingenuity even extended to secretly building a full-size glider in a disused attic.

The record of escapes from Colditz is an impressive one, standing as its own tribute to the sheer audacity of its inmates: 300 prisoners were caught in various escape attempts, 130 actually got clear of the castle, and 30 successfully reached neutral territory—14 French, eight British, six Dutch, one Pole, and one Australian. The castle has recently fallen on hard times, with the state

Colditz Castle (Colditz Society)

government desperately looking for investors to refurbish the badly deteriorated fortress, but the name Colditz remains synonymous with high adventure and escape in wartime.

See also Escape; Sinclair, Albert Michael

References

Jack Champ and Colin Burgess, *The Diggers of Colditz* (St. Leonards: Allen and Unwin, 1985).

Gris Davies-Scourfield, *In Presence of My Foes: A Memoir of Calais, Colditz and Wartime Escape Adventures* (Barnsley, UK: Pen & Sword Books, 2004).

P. R. Reid, *The Colditz Story* (London: Hodder and Stoughton, 1952).

———, *The Latter Days* (London: Hodder and Stoughton, 1953).

———, *Colditz: The Full Story* (London: Macmillan, 1984).

Jim Rogers, *Tunnelling into Colditz: A Mining Engineer in Captivity* (London: Robert Hale, 1986).

J. E. R. Wood, ed., *Detour: The Story of Oflag IVC* (London: Falcon Press, 1946).

—*Colin Burgess*

THE COLDITZ STORY

This best-selling book by P. R. Reid, which described the exploits of Allied prisoners of war in a camp for inveterate escapers, spawned a movie, a television series, and a host of other spin-offs that form the core of what might be called the Colditz Castle industry. The original 1952 book, which itself inspired a number of sequels and remains in print today, was brought to the screen by British Lion in 1955. A number of obstacles had to be overcome to produce the film, not the least of which was the fact that the castle was in East Germany and therefore unavailable for location shooting. Instead, Shepperton Studios built a replica of the castle's courtyard and filmed other outdoor scenes at Stirling and Edinburgh Castles in Scotland. Shot in black and white, the film admirably captured the cold, dark, depressing conditions under which the prisoners actually lived. With popular actors like John Mills, Eric Portman, and Lionel Jeffries, it conveyed an image of heroism that appealed to a British public who had lived through six years of war and a decade of economic and political upheavals.

Nearly 20 years after the movie was first screened, Reid and writer Brian Degas sold the idea of a Colditz television series to the British Broadcasting Corporation. Starring such well-known actors as Robert Wagner and David McCallum, it first aired in 1972 and was sufficiently well received by viewers and critics to be followed by a second series in 1974. With the success of the television series, the Colditz industry really took off. A plastic model of the Colditz glider that had been constructed by POWs for a possible escape attempt, an action figure, and a board game were produced for the children's market; the board game was later repackaged to sell to adults. Audio books, a computer game, T-shirts, castle souvenirs, and even Colditz beer followed in the effort to capitalize on the public interest in the castle. At the same time, books on the castle have continued to appear, and Reid's 1952 bestseller now shares the shelves with dozens of other accounts of escape from the now legendary castle prison camp.

Three significant Colditz books were published in the new millennium: *Colditz: A Definitive History* by television producer Henry Chancellor; *The Colditz Myth* by American professor Paul Mackenzie; and *Collecting Colditz and Its Secrets* by Michael Booker. The last complemented a major exhibition at London's Imperial War Museum that was launched in October 2004, the first and possibly the last occasion that artifacts relating to the Great Escape, the Wooden Horse escape, and Colditz were displayed together, along with major items loaned by the Sagan and Colditz museums. The popularity of the exhibition resulted in an extension until June 2006. Of special interest to young visitors was a display of models exhibited as prizes in relation to a competition related to *Chicken Run*, an animated "escape" film. Unfortunately, the storage warehouse that housed models from all the animated films made by the company was destroyed in a fire in 2005, making the exhibition models particularly desirable.

A further revelation in 2005 was a report in *The Times* newspaper that the Colditz Association, made up of ex-prisoners of the camp, was to disband. But Colditz remains in the public consciousness. A two-part drama appeared on British television over the 2005 Easter weekend. Simply titled *Colditz*, it was billed as a tale of love and betrayal, causing some controversy among ex-POWs and historians. The general public's reaction, however, was to see it as a drama with no relation to fact. Colditz fiction had already been published in 2002 by the prolific author of war books Leo Kessler; *Murder in Colditz* has an impressive dust cover, even though it places the camp in the wrong position relative to the bridge. Finally, Colditz is still used in the British press for its symbolic connotations. A front-page story appeared in *The Mail* in 2005 with the headline "Colditz Camp for families from hell," referring to families that cause mayhem with their neighbors being moved to a more controlled environment. Another national newspaper printed a column headed "Fergie – It's like Colditz to us," quoting Sir Alex Ferguson, the manager of Manchester United soccer team, referring to the team's home field, Old Trafford. So, the passage of time and the demise of the Colditz Association has certainly not dampened the interest in this eleventh-century castle POW camp.

See also Colditz; Film

Reference

Michael Booker, *Collecting Colditz and Its Secrets: A Unique Pictorial Record of Life Behind the Walls* (London: Grub Street, 2005).

S.P. MacKenzie, *The Colditz Myth: The Real Story of POW Life in Nazi Germany* (New York: Oxford University Press, 2004).

—Michael Booker

Colonial Captivity Narratives

Colonial narratives of captivity were accounts of whites seized by American Indians. Generally appearing in pamphlet form, they constituted America's first bestsellers as well as the first distinctly

This early illustration shows a European prisoner surrounded by his native captors (from John Frost, Pictorial History of Indian Wars and Captivities *[New York, 1873])*

American literary genre. The popularity of these narratives afforded the captivity experience a prominent place in Anglo-American consciousness well into the nineteenth century. Although some of these narratives were fictionalized and most exhibited a thoroughly anti-Indian bias, those based on actual events provide important testimony of the experiences of captives, particularly women.

The genre's formula was established by the account of Puritan Mary Rowlandson, *The Sovereignty and Goodness of God*. Rowlandson's narrative was so popular that it made her arguably the most celebrated prisoner of war in American history. First published in 1682, her account of captivity during Metacomet's (or King Philip's) War became a runaway bestseller. It went through four editions in its year of publication and scores more over the next 200 years, under a variety of titles.

The enduring popularity of captivity narratives lay in their ability to thrill readers with stories of individuals or families enduring great stress, stories that were replete with exoticism and action. However, these narratives functioned at deeper levels as well. In the seventeenth century especially, they served a serious religious purpose. The captivity experience was understood as an affliction imposed by God for the betterment of souls and thus carried with it many important lessons about divine providence.

For this reason, ministers helped publish and promote many early narratives as spiritual guides and inspirational texts. Upon his release from captivity during Queen Anne's War, Reverend John Williams felt obligated to share his experience with others for their edification and published *The Redeemed Captive, Returning to Zion* (1707). As Williams and others saw it, captivity should prompt reflection, so it was the duty of those who returned to share their experience and the duty of all others to listen to or read about it.

These narratives were more than calls to worship; they were also calls to arms. Captivity narratives customarily employed inflammatory language to describe Indians while ignoring white provocations of Indian actions. By recounting Indian depredations against women and children in graphic detail, the genre provided ready-made justification for violence against Native Americans. While both the religious and propagandistic functions of the captivity narrative were present in the seventeenth and eighteenth centuries, the latter function had permanently gained preeminence by the end of the colonial period. This trend was amply reflected in the title of Charles Saunders's captivity narrative, *The Horrid Cruelty of the Indians* (1763).

Individual works occasionally transcended the genre's Indian-hating tendencies. While white audiences were fixated upon the "savage" nature of Indian culture, they could not deny the fact that many white captives had refused to return to Euro-American society even when the opportunity was made available to them. The narrative of Mary Jemison, a Scotch-Irish woman captured by the Shawnee in 1755 and adopted by the Seneca, conveyed a more sympathetic view of Indian life. She clearly demonstrated that the Shawnee took captives primarily to replace deceased kinfolk, rather than for ransom or enslavement, as was the case among Europeans. Her narrative, like many others, detailed the methodical fashion in which Native peoples encouraged captives to internalize a new identity, transforming them into full-fledged members of Indian communities.

In general, however, the genre became increasingly fictionalized and sensationalistic during the nineteenth century, as it legitimized the expansion of Euro-American populations into the American West. Moreover, as the United States sought an identity distinct from Europe, writers such as James Fenimore Cooper seized upon Indian captivity as a uniquely American experience and made it into a recurrent theme in U.S. literature. As a result, interest in early American captivity continued even in those areas where the threat had long since passed.

See also Mather, Cotton; Plains Indian Warfare

References

James Axtell, "The White Indians of Colonial America," in *The European and the Indian: Essays in the Ethnohistory of Colonial North America* (New York: Oxford University Press, 1981).

Sarah A. Carter, *Capturing Women: The Manipulation of Cultural Imagery in Canada's Prairie West* (Montreal: McGill-Queen's University Press, 2003).

John Demos, *The Unredeemed Captive: A Family Story from Early America* (New York: Alfred A. Knopf, 1994).

Evan Haefeli and Kevin Sweeney, *Captors and Captives: The 1704 French and Indian Raid on Deerfield* (Amherst: University of Massachusetts Press, 2003).

Kathryn Zabelle Derounian-Stodola and James Arthur Levernier, *The Indian Captivity Narrative, 1550–1900* (New York: Twayne Publishers, 1993).

Grace E. Meredith, *Girl Captives of the Cheyennes* (Mechanicsburg, PA: Stackpole Books, 2003 [1874]).

June Namias, *White Captives: Gender and Ethnicity on the American Frontier* (Chapel Hill: University of North Carolina Press, 1993).

—*Karim M. Tiro*

COMFORT WOMEN

See Sexual Violence

COMMANDO ORDER

The *Kommandobefehl*, or Commando Order, was a prime example of the systematic abuse of POWs by the Nazi state during World

War II. As a result of German reports of Allied crimes committed against prisoners during the Canadian raid on Dieppe in August 1942, Adolf Hitler ordered on 18 October 1942 that "all enemies on so-called Commando missions in Europe or Africa challenged by German troops, even if they are to all appearances soldiers in uniform or demolition troops, whether armed or unarmed, in battle or in flight, are to be slaughtered to the last man. It does not make any difference whether they are landed from ships and aeroplanes for their actions, or whether they are dropped by parachute. Even if these individuals, when found, should apparently be prepared to give themselves up, no pardon is to be granted them on principle." The order was not applicable to small groups of soldiers captured in the immediate area of land or sea battles or to those who bailed out of airplanes or abandoned their ships following military engagements.

The order was carried out with the full complicity of all branches of the German armed forces in all theaters of war, and it was confirmed in subsequent orders. Among the more significant instances of these killings were the October 1942 execution of seven British and Canadian commandos captured after a raid on Glomfjord, Norway; the November 1942 execution of 14 British commandos captured in an abortive operation against hydro installations in Norway; the execution of six British commandos captured in December 1942 during an operation against German shipping in Bordeaux harbor; and the March 1944 execution of 15 U.S. Army soldiers captured while attempting to blow up the railway tunnel between La Spezia and Genoa, Italy.

Establishing the existence of the Commando Order and its implementation proved to be of great importance at the Nuremberg trials of the German military and political leadership for war crimes. Furthermore, many lower-ranking German officers were imprisoned or condemned to death in subsequent proceedings for their involvement in executions carried out under the Commando Order.

References

Stephen Schofield, *Musketoon: Commando Raid, Glomfjord, 1942* (London: Jonathan Cape, 1964).

Richard Wiggan, *Operation Freshman: The Rjukan Heavy Water Raid, 1942* (London: William Kimber, 1986).

—*Vasilis Vourkoutiotis*

COMMISSAR ORDER

The Commissar Order, or *Kommissarbefehl*, decreed by the German government during World War II, passed a death sentence on political officials and leaders who were captured while serving with Russian units.

The order grew out of Adolf Hitler's determination to see the war on the eastern front as a clash of ideologies; the war against the Soviet Union was a war against communism, and every effort had to be made to destroy communism. Chief among the Nazis' targets were the commissars, the political leaders attached to units of the Red Army to provide political education to the soldiers. On 6 June 1941, the German Armed Forces High Command issued "General Instructions for the Treatment of Political Commissars," which stipulated that commissars were not to be treated as prisoners of war and were not to be sent back to POW camps; they were to be "liquidated" as soon as possible after capture. There was some discussion of softening the order to apply only to higher political officials, but Hitler refused and decreed that all commissars, of whatever rank, were to be executed.

The application of the order, however, was uneven. Because it clearly contradicted the rules of war as they pertained to prisoners, many army (as opposed to SS) field commanders had serious reservations about the order, as well as with a parallel decree that directed troops to execute any civilians deemed to pose a threat to the German army. A significant number even refused to transmit the Commissar Order to their subordinates. The troops of the 12th Infantry Division, for example, were read the order on the eve of the German invasion of Russia in June 1941, but immediately after, they were read an order from the divisional commander stating that the Commissar Order did not apply to the 12th Division. The *Abwehr*, the Nazi intelligence service, also criticized the order, arguing that it merely strengthened the will of Russian soldiers to fight and that it robbed the German armies of potentially valuable sources of information.

Because of this opposition, Wilhelm Keitel, head of the German high command, later ordered that all copies of the original order be destroyed; he hastened to point out, however, that this did not mean the spirit of the order should be ignored. When it became clear that the army would continue to resist implementation of the order, responsibility for executing political commissars was turned over to Reinhard Heydrich, the head of the Reich main security office, who created a number of *Einsatzgruppen* (action groups) to carry out the killings. Even so, because there were no clear criteria for determining the identity of political leaders, many of the commissars fell through the cracks and ended up in German prison camps. As many as possible were laboriously weeded out and sent to their deaths.

In the final consideration, the Commissar Order probably accounted for only a small percentage of the Soviets who died in German captivity. Nevertheless, it was an important example of the degree to which established norms in the treatment of POWs in World War II were made secondary to political imperatives.

See also Buchenwald

References

Alexander Dallin, *German Rule in Russia, 1941–1945: A Study of Occupation Policies* (Boulder, CO: Westview Press, 1981).

Hans-Adolf Jacobsen, "*The Kommissarbefehl and Mass Executions of Soviet Russian Prisoners of War,*" in *Anatomy of the SS State,* ed. Helmut Krausnick et al. (London: Collins, 1968).

Theo J. Schulte, *The German Army and Nazi Policies in Occupied Russia* (New York, 1989).

—Jonathan F. Vance

CONCENTRATION CAMPS

Although most commonly associated with Nazi Germany, concentration camps are generally thought to have originated during the Cuban War of Independence. In February 1896, the Spanish government assigned General Valeriano Weyler to the task of quelling the uprising. One of his first acts was to issue a decree of reconcentration, which required all inhabitants of certain districts to move to camps established near military headquarters. Once the *reconcentrados* were settled in the camps, they would be unable to assist the insurgents and Weyler's program of pacification could proceed. The camps, however, were badly overcrowded and lacked sufficient food and sanitary facilities; as many as 100,000 Cubans died, causing an uproar in the United States and Europe.

In turn, the United States itself adopted a similar expedient during the Philippine-American War. In December 1901, Brigadier General J. Franklin Bell ordered that Filipino civilians in sparsely settled zones be relocated to camps or barrios near towns; they would bring their crops and livestock with them, thereby denying sustenance to the insurgents. As a tool against the uprising, the camps achieved Bell's purpose, but again the cost was high. As many as 11,000 Filipino inmates may have perished due to the overcrowding, lack of food, and inadequate sanitary arrangements in the camps.

The British government also adopted the concentration camp model to deal with the guerrillas in the Boer War in South Africa. In March 1901, to prevent civilians from aiding the guerrillas, General Lord Kitchener ordered that Boer noncombatants be moved to concentration camps until the guerrillas could be captured and disarmed. At first, conditions in the 24 camps were adequate, but as the camp populations increased, so, too, did the death rates among inmates. By June 1901, the camps held over 118,000 civilians and the death rate was climbing steadily, eventually reaching over 3,000 a month, an annual mortality rate of over 30 percent. The outcry in Britain moved the government to establish the Fawcett Commission to study and report on the camps. When the commission's recommendations were acted upon, death rates in the camps soon started to drop, and eventually fell below the rate for some British cities.

In each of these cases, concentration camps were literally that: places where civilians were concentrated and prevented from having any impact on hostilities. The concentration camps of Nazi Germany were of an entirely different order. Adolf Hitler had predicted their use as early as 1921, and in 1933 the Nazis opened the first concentration camps, at Nohra, Oranienburg, and Dachau, to hold political opponents of the regime, especially communists. More camps opened in 1935, and the range of inmates expanded beyond political opponents to include Gypsies and criminals. By this time, the camps were fulfilling another role beyond incarcerating enemies of the state; they were used to provide labor, and the siting of camps such as Mauthausen and Flossenbürg was determined by the needs of local industry.

In 1940, responsibility for the concentration camps was transferred to the Waffen-SS, and the expansion of the system continued with the opening of new camps like Natzweiler, Neuengamme, Auschwitz, and Majdanek; the last two, originally constructed to house POWs, eventually became extermination camps. Over the next two years, the Nazis focused their attention on building extermination camps, which were constructed for the sole purpose of murdering Jews and other "undesirables" en masse. In 1942 the concentration camp system was reorganized to provide for more intensive use of prisoner labor. New camps were added and old camps were expanded, and in January 1945, over 700,000 prisoners were on the concentration camp rolls. They included political prisoners, homosexuals, Gypsies, Jews, Soviet soldiers, recaptured escapers, resistance members, and prominent prisoners whom the Nazis believed could be useful as hostages.

By this time, however, the camp system had already begun to collapse. Majdanek was liberated in July 1944, and in January 1945, other camps were evacuated and their inmates transferred to camps in central Germany. Many thousands of people either died in these transfers or were executed so that they did not have to be transferred. All told, as many as 600,000 inmates (of the 1.6 million people held in the camps between 1933 and 1945) died, in addition to the millions who perished in the extermination camps. The April 1945 liberation of the major concentration and extermination camps, like Buchenwald, Bergen-Belsen, and Dachau, and the shocking newsreel footage that it generated horrified the world more than almost any other aspect of the war. Because of the notoriety of the Nazi system, the term concentration camp has rarely been used in subsequent conflicts, although there are internment facilities (for example, in the Bosnian War) that are concentration camps in everything but name.

See also Auschwitz; Bergen-Belsen; Buchenwald; Dachau; Extermination Camps

References

Eugen Kogon, *The Theory and Practice of Hell: The German Concentration Camps and the System Behind Them* (New York: Farrar, Straus and Cudahy, 1950).

Brian McAllister Linn, *The U.S. Army and Counterinsurgency in the Philippines, 1899–1902* (Chapel Hill: University of North Carolina Press, 1989).

Thomas Pakenham, *The Boer War* (New York: Random House, 1979).

Joseph Smith, *The Spanish-American War: Conflict in the Caribbean and the Pacific, 1895–1902* (London: Longman, 1994).

—Jonathan F. Vance

COWRA INCIDENT

In 1944, Japanese POWs at a camp in Cowra, Australia, were involved in a suicidal mass escape attempt that left hundreds of prisoners dead. The camp, designated Number 12 Prisoner of War Group, Cowra, was situated 100 miles northwest of the Australian capital, Canberra. In August 1944, it contained 1,100 Japanese and 2,000 Italians in an area of some 28 hectares that was divided by two internal roads into four separate compounds. The north-south road, known as Broadway, was 50 yards wide and 700 yards long with heavy wooden double gates at each end. It was well lit at night. Each compound contained about 20 huts and was enclosed by three high, barbed-wire fences. Japanese noncommissioned officers and other ranks lived in B Compound (the northeast quarter), and Japanese officers were in D Compound (the southeast quarter).

On Friday, 4 August, in accordance with the provisions of international law, notice was given of a transfer of all Japanese prisoners below the rank of lance corporal to Hay POW Camp the following Monday, 7 August. At approximately 1:50 a.m. on Saturday, 5 August, an unauthorized bugle call was heard in B Compound. Immediately thereafter over 900 prisoners rushed from their huts, which they had set on fire, and attacked the fences of their compound. They wore baseball gloves or other specially prepared gloves, towels, or pads of toilet paper to protect their hands while negotiating the barbed-wire fences, and they threw blankets over the wire to assist them in breaking through. Many of the prisoners were wearing two or three sets of clothing, had towels wound round their bodies, and were carrying lengths of rope that they had manufactured from rice sacks. They had armed themselves with an assortment of weapons, including mess knives that they had ground down, pointed, and sharpened or serrated, swords fashioned from a dismantled bread cutter, baseball bats, and improvised clubs. Only the Japanese in B Compound were involved in the escape.

Large parties of prisoners broke through the camp's perimeter fence in two places. Another party breached the fence separating their compound from Broadway, split into two groups, and rushed the gates at either end. Approximately 50 prisoners succeeded in entering D Compound and remained there until apprehended at daybreak.

At daybreak, search parties armed only with bayonets began rounding up the escaped Japanese. At approximately 5:30 p.m., an Australian officer was killed in a brutal attack with knives and clubs. Two other Australians manning a machine gun outside the camp were killed by the escapers and were posthumously awarded the George Cross for their "outstanding gallantry and devotion to duty in their fight to death against an overwhelming onslaught by fanatical Japanese."

In the nine days after the escape, 309 escaped POWs were recaptured. Of the 231 who were killed, 183 died from gunshot wounds while attempting to escape and 48 committed suicide or were killed by other Japanese; another 108 POWs were wounded. Eight Australian guards were killed or wounded.

The conditions at Cowra prior to the escape were exemplary and fully in accordance with the provisions of the 1929 Geneva Convention Relative to the Treatment of Prisoners of War. The camp was frequently inspected by the representatives of the neutral nations and the International Committee of the Red Cross. An Australian military court of inquiry concluded that the escape was carried out according to a plan premeditated and concerted by prisoners in B Compound. Their objective was to overthrow the camp and to forfeit their own lives in suicidal combat. Alternative theories argue that it was an attempted mass suicide, a planned escape, or a spontaneous response to the transfer order.

See also Featherston Incident; World War II—Far East

References

Teruhiko Asada, *Night of a Thousand Suicides: The Japanese Outbreak at Cowra*, trans. and ed. Ray Cowan (Sydney: Angus and Robertson, 1970).

Charlotte Carr-Gregg, *Japanese Prisoners of War in Revolt: The Outbreaks at Featherston and Cowra during World War II* (New York: St. Martin's Press, 1978).

Hugh Clarke, *Break-Out!* (Sydney: Horwitz Publications, 1965).

Harry Gordon, *Die Like the Carp! The Story of the Greatest Prison Escape Ever* (Stanmore: Cassell Australia, 1978).

Harry Gordon, *Voyage from Shame* (St. Lucia: University of Queensland Press, 1994).

—*Anthony Staunton*

CRIMEAN WAR (1854–1857)

For the most part, information about prisoners in the Crimean War is fragmentary, and can be gleaned primarily from a few long-out-of-print sources. We know that some Russian POWs were held in Constantinople, in a long row of barracks in a district near the port area that was then known as Kassim Pasha. Some who were captured by the French were sent to France to labor on the fortifications at Toulon, and upon their return they complained bitterly about the conditions. If they failed to complete the allotted number of tasks on any given day, for example, they received no rations that day. Russian POWs who were sent to England, on the other hand, had nothing but praise for their captors. Most were held near the town of Lewes in Sussex; they were not forced to work, had comfortable accommodation and sufficient food, and even received a small allowance so they could visit local pubs. Toward the end of the war, one English soldier reported encountering a Russian POW who was sorry to be returning to Russia because he had enjoyed himself so much in captivity in England.

We do, however, have a very small number of remarkable narratives from British soldiers who fell into Russian hands. Two of the best were written by Sergeant George Newman of the Royal Welch Fusiliers, who was captured at Inkerman on 5 November 1854, and by Robert Farquharson of the Fourth Light Dragoons, who became a prisoner after the infamous Charge of the Light Brigade. Newman, Farquharson, and the other British prisoners were kept in a variety of civilian prisons, and then were eventually gathered together and marched some 550 miles to Voronesh, a trek that took them roughly three months. Conditions at Voronesh were acceptable—the food was rather scanty, consisting largely of thin soup, boiled beef or mutton, and a pound and a half of bread daily, but the prisoners could purchase treats such as butter, honey, milk, and tobacco from local merchants. They could also purchase alcohol, something which occasionally got them into trouble. One POW, Private Donoghue of the 4th Heavy Dragoons, died of injuries sustained in a drunken brawl. However, they were left largely to their own devices, spending most of the day playing cards. They were even given responsibility for disciplining themselves. When two prisoners insulted a Russian woman and an officer on the street, the police commander gave them the option of accepting punishment from their fellow captives, or from the Russian police. Wisely, they chose the former, and each was given 24 lashes from another POW.

Also held in captivity, though kept separate from the other prisoners, were soldiers who had deserted from British units. Some were willing to serve in the Russian forces, but the Russians were not interested in employing turncoats and promptly imprisoned them. They lived a grim existence, shunned by the other British and despised by their guards. The jailers, however, were not permitted to mistreat the prisoners. On one occasion, two police officials badly beat a British prisoner; when his fellow captives complained to the higher authorities, the police officials were promptly dispatched to the front lines as punishment.

In August 1855, the prisoners in Voronesh received word that they were to be released, in exchange for Russian POWs held in French and British hands. They embarked on another trek, this time southward to Odessa, which they reached in late September. A month later, they were collected by a British ship and returned home. Farquharson eventually went back to his native Scotland, where he published his memoir of captivity. Newman remained in the army; his unit was ordered to China in February 1857, but on 1 January Newman had been granted leave. At that point, he disappears from the historical record.

References

Robert S. Farquharson, *Reminiscences of Crimean Campaigning and Russian Imprisonment* (Glasgow: Evening Times, 1883).

David Inglesant, ed., *The Prisoners of Voronesh: The Diary of Sergeant George Newman, 23rd*

Regiment of Foot, The Royal Welch Fusiliers, Taken Prisoner at Inkerman (Old Woking, UK: Unwin Brothers, 1977).

Sir Harry Attwell Lake, *Kars and Our Captivity in Russia, With Letters from General Sir W.F. Williams; Major Teesdale; and the late Captain Thompson* (London: R. Bentley, 1856).

—*Jonathan F. Vance*

CRUSADES

Although some scholars have argued that only expeditions to the Holy Land qualify as "true" Crusades, the people of the Latin Christendom themselves considered a wide variety of campaigns to have been Crusades. These included offensives of the Spanish Reconquest, wars against non-Christians and orthodox Christians in Eastern Europe, assaults on "heretics" and schismatics within Latin Christendom itself, and attacks on the Mamluk and Ottoman Sultanates (not to mention the Byzantine and Holy Roman emperors). Given this diversity of theaters and opponents, conditions of captivity could vary considerably.

Nevertheless, generally speaking it can be said that during the Crusades, prisoners usually faced one of three fates: execution, enslavement, or ransom. Of the three, outright execution seems to have been the least common. To be sure, massacres did occasionally occur. The First Crusaders killed many of their prisoners after they had captured Jerusalem in 1099, Saladin executed members of the Christian military orders after the Battle of Hattin in 1187, and King Richard I of England massacred 2,600 prisoners after the fall of Acre in 1191. At times, execution even seems to have approached the status of standard policy in the Crusades against the "heretical" Albigensians, Waldensians, and Hussites within Europe itself. On the other hand, it should be noted that many of the most famous incidents of execution have been considerably exaggerated in the interests of pro- or anti-Christian propaganda and that executions were often nothing more than ad hoc solutions to pressing strategic, tactical, or logistical exigencies. At Jerusalem in 1099, for example, the crusaders' order to execute the remaining prisoners was intended to ensure the security of the city in light of the impending arrival of a Fatimid relief army, while similar considerations were alleged to have motivated King Richard I at Acre. Under less trying circumstances, execution was of limited appeal to captors because it prevented them from profiting materially from their captives, a significant limitation on the extended campaigns of crusading warfare, where many soldiers were not receiving pay but were providing for themselves out of their own pockets. Thus, when Saladin wanted to execute the Templars and Hospitallers after Hattin, he first had to purchase them back (at 50 dinars apiece) from his own troops, who were loath to part with such valuable prisoners.

Enslavement, which converted prisoners of war directly into booty, was therefore a far more popular option than execution. While Christian and Muslim law discouraged (with varying degrees of rigor and success) the enslavement of fellow Christians and Muslims, respectively, and while captives were sometimes freed upon conversion, both religions sanctioned the enslavement of persons of other faiths. Since civilians were no more protected from enslavement than were soldiers, vast numbers of slaves could be taken when a town fell to the enemy, as at Antioch in 1098 and Tripoli in 1289. In such situations, women and children tended to make up the bulk of the captives, not only because they comprised the majority of the population but also because many of the men had been killed in defending the city. Rich and noble prisoners sometimes escaped enslavement altogether, but poorer prisoners were usually bound with ropes or chains and led off to prison. They could be deprived of food and water and were sometimes tortured, especially when they were believed to be concealing their wealth. Women and young boys were routinely raped. The newly enslaved were then either put to work or sold on the slave market. The medieval slave trade was a large scale, international enterprise, and slave raiding was a regular feature of the crusading borderlands. The first Mamluk rulers of Egypt had been purchased as non-Muslim slaves; they subsequently converted, were given a military education, and were manumitted. The Ottoman Janissaries had a similar background.

Unlike the Mamluks and Janissaries, however, most POWs captured during the Crusades were neither converted nor freed but lived out the remainder of their days as slaves. Of those few lucky enough to regain their freedom, most did so through ransom. This was particularly true of the wealthier or more noteworthy captives, who were capable of paying out large sums of money or granting major military and political concessions in return for their release. Poorer prisoners, on the other hand, generally had difficulty in producing ransoms and lived as slaves unless they were freed by the kindness of others. Responsibility for raising alms for the redemption of the poor, which was recognized as a charitable act by all the major religions, usually devolved upon the captives' families and communities, with the clergy, military orders, and the bequests of private individuals also contributing significant funds. Merchants frequently acted as the middlemen, traveling to foreign lands and haggling for captives' release, although in the Christian West religious orders and lay fraternities, such as the Mercedarians and Trinitarians, combined the two functions of raising of alms and actually purchasing captives. These orders usually expected those whom they had redeemed to serve them for a specified term in order to make up for the sum that they had paid out on the captives' behalf.

Alternative routes to freedom included escape, exchange, and entreaty. Escape was difficult and dangerous because POWs were usually transported deep within enemy territory and rarely had knowledge of the local languages, customs, or terrain. However, the dramatic escape of Joscelin, Count of Edessa, from Kharput (in what is today central Turkey) in 1123 proves that it was not entirely impossible. Prisoner exchanges did occur in the crusading borderlands, although it was often only the rich who were exchanged; King Richard writes that he spared a few of the more noble prisoners from the massacre at Acre in order to use them to win back certain Christian captives and the "True Cross." (This relic, supposedly the very cross upon which Christ was crucified, had been used to inspire Christian troops for decades until it was captured by Saladin's forces at the Battle of Hattin. Thereafter, it became a bargaining chip—much like other captives—in negotiations between Christians and Muslims.) Finally, some captors simply let their prisoners go out of pity, charity, or the desire to be seen as magnanimous, but such acts were generally as rare as they were kind. All things considered, most of those who were taken prisoner during the course of the Crusades endured a harsh captivity without much hope of ever regaining their freedom.

See also Slavery

References

James William Brodman, *Ransoming Captives in Crusader Spain* (Philadelphia: University of Pennsylvania Press, 1986).

Yvonne Freidman, "Women in Captivity and Their Ransom during the Crusader Period," in *Cross Cultural Convergences in the Crusader Period*, ed. Michael Goodich et al. (New York: Peter Lang, 1995).

Fulcher of Chartres, *A History of the Expedition to Jerusalem, 1095–1127*, trans. Frances Rita Ryan (Knoxville: University of Tennessee Press, 1969).

Francesco Gabrieli, *Arab Historians of the Crusades: Selections and Translations from Arabic Sources*, trans. E. J. Costello (Berkeley University of California Press, 1969).

—*David Hay*

CUMMINGS, EDWARD ESTLIN (E. E.) (1894–1962)

The American poet known as e. e. cummings contributed to the canon of captivity literature with his memoir *The*

Enormous Room, describing his internment in France during World War I. Born in Cambridge, Massachusetts, Cummings joined the Norton-Harjes Ambulance Corps in April 1917 and proceeded to France almost immediately. His time at the front was frustrating, for a personality conflict with a superior consigned him to the motor pool, where he spent his days washing ambulances. The same conflict probably resulted in Cummings's arrest. On 23 September 1917, Cummings and his friend William Slater Brown were arrested by French police, whose suspicion was aroused by an unfavorable report from Cummings's superior and by Brown's letters to his family. Because Cummings refused to dissociate himself from Brown, he too was imprisoned, eventually in a seminary-turned-prison in La Ferté-Macé in Normandy.

The enormous room that inspired Cummings's book was a large cell housing some 40 prisoners of all nationalities. In it, he found more of interest than he had ever found with the ambulance unit, and so he declined to be placed in an individual cell. Cummings sketched, wrote poetry, and observed the idiosyncrasies of his fellow inmates, eventually collecting his observations into what he called the "French notes," which he began shortly after his release from prison on 19 December 1918. He completed the manuscript in October 1920, but it was rejected by a number of publishers before being accepted by Boni and Liveright of New York. *The Enormous Room* appeared in 1922 and has been in print continuously since then. It remains one of the most absorbing accounts of captivity to be published in the twentieth century.

References

Richard S. Kennedy, *Dreams in the Mirror: A Biography of E. E. Cummings* (New York: Liveright Publishing, 1980).

Christopher Sawyer-Laucanno, *E.E. Cummings: A Biography* (London: Methuen, 2005).

—*Kara Brown*

CYPRIOT CONFLICT

Cyprus is a large island (9,251 sq. km.) located at the eastern end of the Mediterranean just south of Turkey. Its population consists of approximately 80 percent Greek Cypriots (Greek Orthodox), 18 percent Turkish Cypriots (Muslim), and two percent other ethnicities. Exact population figures are not possible, as the Turkish administration in the northern part of the island refuses to hold a census.

The island was conquered by the Turkish (Ottoman) Empire in 1570 and remained Turkish for the next three centuries. In 1878 Great Britain gained control of the island when it signed the Cyprus Convention with the Ottoman Empire. The British declared Cyprus to be a Crown Colony in 1925.

The British withdrew their military from Egyptian bases in 1954, seeing Cyprus as a fall-back position from which to maintain a permanent military presence in the Eastern Mediterranean. Archbishop Makarios III, the spiritual and political leader of the Greek Cypriots, sought independence from Great Britain, to be followed by immediate union with Greece (*enosis*). Naturally, the Turkish Cypriot community did not favor *enosis*. Both Greece and Turkey supported their respective "co-nationals" on the island.

A guerrilla movement of Greek Cypriots was created, the EOKA (Ethniki Organosis Kyprion Agoniston) or National Organization of Cypriot Fighters, under Colonel George Grivas, a Cyprus-born Greek Army officer. Rioting by Greek Cypriots who wanted Britain out of Cyprus developed into a serious, if low-level, insurgency by the spring of 1955. The Turkish Cypriots established their own self-protection organizations but they were often badly outnumbered. Prisoners were rarely taken by these groups, and if they were, they were held for quasi-criminal reasons like ransoms. When the British authorities captured EOKA terrorists they were apt to treat them as dangerous criminals rather than prisoners of war.

In March 1956, the British arrested Makarios and exiled him from Cyprus, sending him to the Seychelles Islands in the Indian Ocean. This made Grivas the de facto leader of the Greek Cypriots. Turks and Greeks continued to commit atrocities against each other and the EOKA waged its guerilla campaign against British targets throughout the island.

A tentative agreement for the independence of Cyprus was reached in Zurich and London in 1959. The British were to maintain control of two Sovereign Base Areas on Cyprus; Turkey, Greece, and Great Britain were guarantors of the new Cyprus constitution. Both Greece and Turkey were allowed to station a limited number of troops on Cyprus. The Turkish minority was guaranteed a proportion of the legislative seats and the vice presidency, as well as other rights in the constitution. *Enosis* was prohibited, as was any separation of the Turkish-dominated north of the island. On 16 August 1960, Cyprus became an independent republic with Makarios III as the president.

The constitution proved unworkable (at least from the Greek Cypriot point of view), and Makarios pushed for revisions that would abolish the minority rights guaranteed to the Turkish Cypriots and institute simple majority rule. The Turkish Cypriots (backed by Turkey) rejected these proposals. Fighting between Greek and Turkish Cypriots flared up again in 1963–1964, threatening to bring two NATO allies, Greece and Turkey, into the conflict. A Greco-Turkish war was avoided when the United Nations Peacekeeping Force in Cyprus (UNFICYP) was dispatched to the island in 1964, where it remains to the present day. The United Nations intervention stabilized the situation on Cyprus for 10 years until a new crisis exploded in 1974.

A coup d'état by the Cypriot National Guard overthrew the Makarios government in the summer of 1974, an action that prompted a Turkish invasion of Cyprus on 20 July 1974. A second major Turkish thrust across the island on 14 August brought 40 percent of Cyprus under Turkish Army control. Today Cyprus has been de facto partitioned, with the self-proclaimed Turkish Federated State of Cyprus in the northern part of the island (only Turkey recognizes this government as legitimate).

Shortly after the end of hostilities, over 6,000 military and civilian internees were exchanged between Greek Cypriot and Turkish forces under the auspices of UNFICYP. Approximately 200,000 Greek Cypriots were displaced by the Turkish invasion and fled or were expelled by the Turkish Army and local Turkish Cypriot militias. By comparison, the 1963 communal fighting on the island led to the displacement of 25,000 Turkish Cypriots.

A continuing source of friction between the two sides is the unexplained disappearance of over 1,600 Greek Cypriots in the aftermath of the 1974 fighting. This number includes both soldiers and civilians, as well as a small number of other nationals, including five Americans. The Cyprus government claims that many of these missing persons were last seen alive and well in the custody of Turkish soldiers, sometimes months after their initial capture, by other Greek Cypriot prisoners. The Turkish government's response to these accusations has varied from denial that it ever held the prisoners, to a generalized statement that they all must have been killed in the initial fighting, to insisting that the matter should be referred to the Turkish Federated State of Cyprus (which, of course, the Greek Cypriots do not recognize).

Most analysts have concluded that these missing Greek Cypriots were probably killed some time after their capture by regular Turkish forces or Turkish Cypriot militias.

Repeated court cases brought before the European Commission of Human Rights by Cyprus against Turkey have found Turkey to be unresponsive and inadequate in providing information about these missing individuals. The stand-off over the "missing" captives is symbolic of the fact that Cyprus remains a divided island, despite numerous diplomatic initiatives over the years to resolve the problems separating the two ethnic communities.

References
Andrew Borowiec, *Cyprus: A Troubled Island* (Westport, CT: Praeger, 2000).
Charles Foley, ed., *The Memoirs of General Grivas* (London: Longmans, 1964).
Dan Lindley, *UNFICYP and a Cyprus Solution: A Strategic Assessment* (Cambridge, MA: Center for International Studies, Massachusetts Institute of Technology, 1997).

—*Andrew C. Young*

CZECH LEGION

The Czech Legion was a military force established during World War I in Russia and composed primarily of Czech and Slovak prisoners of war. In its heyday in the spring and summer of 1918, the Czech Legion consisted of some 40,000 POWs who effectively challenged the nascent Red Army.

Formed in August 1914 by orders of the Russian General Staff, the Czech Company (as it was originally known) was intended to be a small intelligence-gathering unit that recruited Czechs and Slovaks who had settled in Russia before the war. However, the capture by the Russian army of an estimated 250,000 Czech and Slovak soldiers from the Austro-Hungarian army created a manpower pool that Czech émigré politicians wanted to use as the nucleus of a future Czechoslovak army. Despite half-hearted support for this project from the Tsarist government, the unit grew into a regiment by February 1916 and a brigade four months later.

Following the first revolution in Russia in March 1917, the chairman of the Czech National Committee, T. G. Masaryk, arrived from Paris and launched a massive recruiting drive among the prisoners. This was helped by the conduct of the Czech Legion during the Kerensky offensive (June 1917), in which the legion outperformed most of the Russian units it fought alongside. The enthusiastic support received now from the Russian Provisional Government resulted in a fivefold increase in the size of the legion, to approximately 40,000 soldiers. However, the Bolshevik Revolution in November 1917 and the advance of the German army into the Ukraine and the Baltic areas in the winter of 1917–1918 created an extremely precarious situation for the Czech Legion. The Czech National Council (as the committee had been renamed) now decided to transport the legion to the western front, where it would contribute to the military effort of the Entente and gain support for an independent postwar Czechoslovakia. In February 1918, the French government recognized the Czech Legion as part of the French army and approved its transfer to France via the far eastern Russian port of Vladivostok.

Despite Masaryk's assurance to the Bolshevik leadership that the Czech forces had no wish to intervene in the internal affairs of Russia, the legion clashed in May 1918 with Red Guards in the Ural town of Chelyabinsk and was ordered by Trotsky to disarm completely. The Czech soldiers who were already en route to Vladivostok seized control of the Trans-Siberian Railroad and easily defeated the ill-organized Red Army units sent against them. During the spring and summer of 1918, the Czech Legion constituted the most significant military force within Russia and provided military protection to various anti-Bolshevik forces in Siberia and eastern Russia. Although not an integral part of the White or the allied interventionist forces, the Czech Legion played a crucial role in the Russian Civil War by exposing the initial weakness of the Red Army. It constituted an important bargaining chip for Czech politicians negotiating the postwar settlement, and was instrumental in the establishment in October 1918 of independent Czechoslovakia.

During 1919, the involvement of the Czech Legion in the Russian Civil War became negligible, and the successes of the Red Army forced the legion's leadership to reevaluate its position. Thus, in February 1920, an armistice agreement was signed between the Czech Legion and the Soviet forces, and the head of the White government in Siberia, Admiral Aleksandr Kolchak, was handed over to the Bolsheviks to be executed. The Czech Legion finally sailed from Vladivostok in September 1920 and became the core of the Czechoslovak army.

See also Defection; Russian Civil War

References

John Bradley, *The Czechoslovak Legion in Russia, 1914–1920* (New York: Eastern European Monographs, 1991).

Josef Kalvoda, "Czech and Slovak Prisoners in Russia during War and Revolution," in *Essays on World War I: Origins and Prisoners of War*, ed. Samuel R. Williamson and Peter Pastor (New York: Columbia University Press, 1983).

Thomas G. Masaryk, *The Making of a State: Memoires and Observations, 1914–1918* (New York: Frederick A. Stokes, 1927).

—Alon Rachamimov

D

Dachau

As the first Nazi concentration camp, Dachau set the tone for all subsequent facilities of this type. The rationale for the establishment of the camp followed the suspension of the German democratic constitution on 28 February 1933, with the ensuing "protective custody" measures against all critics of the Nazi regime. On 21 March 1933, Heinrich Himmler announced the opening of the Dachau concentration camp, northwest of Munich, to accommodate 5,000 prisoners. A transition period followed, during which the Bavarian State Police administered the facility before handing it over to the SS. Mistreatment of prisoners began early, with the first murders occurring in May 1933. Even though civilian prosecutors opened inquiries questioning Nazi reports of suicide and attempted escape, these and subsequent investigations of other deaths were quickly quashed. Theodor Eicke became the camp's first SS commandant in June 1933 and set about implementing protocols and rules of operation that would influence the functioning of all other Nazi detention camps. By October 1933, the commandant's office had issued a strict disciplinary and penal code that included flogging and solitary confinement for offenses as minor as failing to salute a guard. All prisoners, regardless of nationality, also had to correspond in German with their families.

Throughout its existence, Dachau served as a camp for political prisoners, primarily communists and Social Democrats, but also anyone deemed critical of the Nazi regime. Eventually, other types of prisoners would join the political detainees, especially common criminals and so-called anti-socials. This shift in the nature of the prisoner groups was also intended to further humiliate political prisoners. Following the implementation in 1935 of the Nuremberg Laws for the protection of German blood, Jews were also brought to Dachau, but they were eventually shipped east to death camps.

As of 1938, additional barracks were constructed, including the camp entrance building. When completed, Dachau was a self-contained entity that housed an SS Death's Head unit. Several notorious careers began in this unit, including those of Josef Kramer (the last commandant of Bergen-Belsen), Rudolf Höss (later commandant of Auschwitz), and Adolf Eichmann.

In wartime, Dachau became a principal camp, to which 33 subsidiary camps and several smaller units were attached. Prisoners worked either on the camp grounds or, later, in the war industry, especially in aircraft factories around Munich. In some cases, they were put to work in the stone quarries of Flossenbürg and Mauthausen concentration camps. As of 1941, Dachau became the site of human medical experiments, including those carried out for the Luftwaffe on hypothermia and high-altitude exposure. A gas chamber and crematorium were constructed in 1940 with the intent of using these to kill mentally handicapped patients under the wartime euthanasia program. Two years later, *Baracke X*, a bigger plant with a gas chamber and four incinerators, was completed. Neither gas chamber was used, as handicapped prisoners were shipped to Hartheim castle near Linz for discreet termination. Other victims, however, were shot.

As of the summer of 1944, Dachau began receiving prisoners from other camps in the east and west that were being evacuated, resulting in a huge congestion of prisoners and worsening living conditions. Dachau held some 40,000 prisoners on the day it was liberated by American troops. Since it opened, 206,206 prisoners had entered the camp; according to official records, 31,591 of these died on camp grounds. The fate of countless others remains unknown.

See also Auschwitz; Bergen-Belsen; Buchenwald; Concentration Camps; Extermination Camps

References

Concentration Camp Dachau 1933–1945 (Brussels: n.p., 1978).

Wolfgang Benz and Barbara Distel, eds., *Dachau Review: History of Nazi Concentration Camps—Studies, Reports Documents* 1 (1987).

Henry Friedlander, "The Nazi Concentration Camps," in *Human Responses to the Holocaust: Perpetrators and Victims, Bystanders and Resisters*, ed. Michael D. Ryan (Lewiston, NY: Edwin Mellen Press, 1981).

Harold Marcuse, *Legacies of Dachau: The Uses and Abuses of a Concentration Camp* (Cambridge: Cambridge University Press, 2001).

Paul Martin Neurath et al, *The Society of Terror: Inside the Dachau and Buchenwald Concentration Camps* (Boulder, CO: Paradigm Publishers, 2005).

—*Guillaume de Syon*

DARTMOOR

Now a prison for criminal offenders, Dartmoor, in southwestern England, originally served as a prisoner of war camp during the Napoleonic Wars and the War of 1812. During the Napoleonic Wars, the thousands of French prisoners captured by the British were taken to England and housed in various prisons and in old ship hulks moored off the coast, especially off Plymouth in Devonshire. The prisoners in the hulks were a constant source of worry to the British government because of their proximity to the Royal Navy dockyard at Plymouth. In view of this, a prison was constructed about 18 miles north of Plymouth, on Dartmoor, at a height of 1,500 feet above sea level. The facility, designated the Dartmoor Depot, comprised five separate war prisons and the necessary barracks for troops acting as guards. The first 2,500 French prisoners were marched to the Dartmoor Depot on 24 May 1809. Since new POWs were arriving constantly, two additional prisons were built by the French prisoners. The seven prisons were designed to hold 1,000 prisoners each, but the population soon reached 1,500 in each.

Soon after the beginning of the War of 1812 between Britain and the United States, thousands of American POWs arrived in England. Many were put in the hulks off Plymouth, but the same concerns regarding security at the naval dockyard arose. So on 2 April 1813, the first 250 American prisoners were marched up to the Dartmoor Depot and housed in Number 4 War Prison. By the end of April, some 1,700 Americans, mostly seamen, were held in Dartmoor. There were many problems in the prison, as the French and American POWs did not get along well together, and fights and disturbances were common. At least 218 of the prisoners died in captivity, some as a result of escape attempts or ill-treatment but the majority of disease; over 100 American prisoners died in Dartmoor hospital between 1813 and 1815, and another 70 perished in a smallpox outbreak that struck the prison in March and April 1815.

Upon the cessation of hostilities with France after the defeat of Napoleon at Waterloo, the French prisoners were marched to Plymouth for embarkation back to their native land. This left the prison well under capacity. Since Dartmoor Depot was capable of holding more than 7,000 men, it was decided that all the American prisoners still held in England and elsewhere should be brought to Dartmoor. Very soon the prison's population approached 9,000, with more than 1,000 troops in barracks. With the signing of the Treaty of Ghent on 24 December 1814, the American prisoners were returned home, with the last leaving in July 1815, seven months after the peace treaty had been signed. Since 1850, Dartmoor prison has housed convicts.

See also Napoleonic Wars; War of 1812

References
Charles Andrews, *The Prisoners' Memoirs, or, Dartmoor Prison* (New York: privately published, 1852).
L. Catel, *La Prison de Dartmoor* (Paris: n.p., 1847).
Ron Joy, *The Complete Illustrated History of Dartmoor Prison: At Her Majesty's Pleasure* (Tiverton, UK: Halsgrove, 2002).
A.J. Rhodes, *Dartmoor Prison* (London: John Lane, 1933).
Basil Thomson, *Dartmoor Prison* (London: William Heinemann, 1907).
Brad R. Tuttle, "Death at Dartmoor," *American History* 37 (2002): 30–36.

—*Ronald J. Joy*

DEAN, MAJOR GENERAL WILLIAM F. (1899–1981)

Major General William F. Dean was the highest-ranking American POW during the Korean War. When captured by North Korean forces in 1950, Dean possessed the most electrifying intelligence imaginable: the details of the surprise landing planned for Inch'on. Although Dean kept this secret, his case reveals how troublesome the standards of resistance are for POWs.

Born in Carlyle, Illinois, Dean was a career soldier who served in World War II and went to Korea in 1947 to serve as military governor of southern Korea. He took command of the 24th Division in October 1949 but was separated from his unit during the fighting around Taejŏn in July 1950. He hid behind enemy lines for 36 days before he was apprehended on 25 August. After capture, Dean was never assaulted but was questioned nonstop for days on end. He did not stick to name, rank, and service number but instead talked endlessly about trivia. He later explained that he was trying to divert his captors from resorting to torture. Although he did sign two propaganda statements, he attempted suicide to avoid divulging real secrets. Dean received the Congressional Medal of Honor while still listed as missing. He was released after the war and was given a hero's welcome.

After Korea, there were accusations that POWs had cooperated too easily with the enemy. Dean, however, felt this controversy was inflated, believing that soldiers should be more concerned about how to fight and less concerned about how to conduct themselves if captured. Dean was a sympathetic witness at a legal inquiry for Colonel Frank Schwable, who had assisted an enemy propaganda campaign about germ warfare. The general supported the notion that a POW should provide only name, rank, and service number as an ideal to be striven for, but he admitted that he had not had the strength to stick to it, even though he had had an easier time in captivity than men like Schwable.

See also Code of Conduct; Interrogation; Korean War

References
William F. Dean, *General Dean's Story* (New York: Viking Press, 1954).
John Toland, *In Mortal Combat: Korea, 1950–1953* (New York: Quill, 1991).

—*Charles S. Young*

DEATH CAMPS

See Concentration Camps; Extermination Camps

DEATH RAILWAY

See Burma-Thailand (Death) Railway

DECREE CONCERNING PRISONERS OF WAR (1792)

Enacted by the National Assembly in France on 4 May 1792, the Decree Concerning Prisoners of War reflected a humanitarian desire to improve the treatment of POWs, a spirit that was not always adhered to in practice. It stipulated that, because the prisoner was in the power of the French state, rather than under the control of an individual, the state had an obligation to provide protection from violence and insults.

Captives were to be detained well away from the fighting and were to be paid on the same scale as French soldiers. They could gain the limited freedom of parole by pledging not to fight again and parolees were to enjoy the same rights under the French common law as any other citizen, including the right to practice a trade and to seek legal remedy from the courts in the event of disputes. Subsequent decrees stipulated that the French government would abide by notions of reciprocity in its treatment of captured enemies and that exchanges of prisoners were to be negotiated on a man-to-man basis, irrespective of rank. This provision clearly owed a debt to the ideology of egalitarianism that flourished during the French Revolution.

The limitations of these decrees, however, were made clear by one of the most notorious atrocities committed against prisoners during this period, Napoleon Bonaparte's mass execution of some 3,500 Arab prisoners at Jaffa in 1799. His excuse was that his army was too weakened to spare soldiers to guard the prisoners. By the same token, historians credit Napoleon with effectively destroying the exchange system that had secured freedom for countless POWs in earlier wars. However noble the motives behind these decrees, they were rendered nugatory by the exigencies of the moment.

See also Napoleonic Wars

—*Jonathan F. Vance*

DEFECTION

For centuries, POWs have changed sides with relative ease. Triumphant armies often enrolled captured enemies as a way to fill their ranks after combat or to take advantage of the military prowess of their enemies. For the prisoners themselves, changing sides might be the only alternative to execution, enslavement, or starvation. In premodern armies, soldiers whose commitment to political ideals might be weak were probably not too particular about which side they fought for, as long as they were paid and fed. In modern terms, this would be considered defection, but historically it was just a part of warfare.

Since the nineteenth century, however, prisoners who change sides have been increasingly stigmatized. In the Mexican-American War of 1846–1848, for example, American General Zachary Taylor argued that POWs who enlisted in the enemy's army should be publicly humiliated because they were not worth the powder and shot required to execute them. In the world wars, defections were virtually unknown among combatants in western Europe. In 1943–1944, for example, a Nazi attempt to recruit British and Commonwealth prisoners for the British Free Corps produced only a few dozen defectors. In eastern Europe, on the other hand, defections have been much more common. During World War I, the Czech Legion, made up of Czech and Slovak soldiers captured while serving with the Austro-Hungarian army, fought on the eastern front against their former allies in the German army. During World War II, the Germans were successful in recruiting hundreds of thousands of Russian POWs to fight as German allies; among these were the famous Cossack cavalry regiments, which were first formed in 1942 and eventually grew to a strength of 70,000 men. However, this so-called Russian Liberation Army, unlike the Czech Legion, was largely a failure; the units posted to northwest Europe and Italy proved so unreliable that they had to be pulled from the front, and the units that served in the east, under the nominal command of former POW Andrei Vlasov, were scarcely more satisfactory. Many of them switched sides again in the closing weeks of the war.

The subject of defections among POWs became even more contentious during the Cold War. The second half of the Korean War was unusual in that it was fought more over POWs than over territory. After the conflict was stalemated in 1951, both sides used prisoners to fight a publicity war. Many prisoners held by the United States were disgruntled with their communist leaders. Contrary to the 1949 Geneva Convention, which committed detaining powers to return all prisoners to their homelands, they were invited to stay in South Korea or go to Taiwan after the war. This policy, known as voluntary repatriation, achieved its objective of embarrassing the Chinese side; a staggering 83,000 POWs did not go home.

Voluntary repatriation also had a humanitarian element; it was feared that POWs might be killed or imprisoned at home. This was known to have happened to some prisoners returned to the Soviet Union after World War II. This humanitarian impulse, however, was not well implemented because "voluntary repatriation" was often not truly voluntary. Rival gangs—communist and anticommunist—brutally controlled prisoner barracks. In anticommunist compounds, countless homesick prisoners did not dare choose home, except "clandestinely and in fear" of murder, according to a neutral overseer from India. Conversely, a few secret anticommunists could not go to Taiwan or South Korea because they were stranded in communist-controlled compounds. These men lost any chance of a choice after the camp's American commander stopped accepting defections. This occurred in June 1952 to speed armistice talks and calm riots in the compounds. On the other hand, the Chinese were able to secure only a few defections; just 21 Americans and 1 Briton went to live in China, but even this number horrified their compatriots. All of them eventually returned to the west, except one who died.

See also British Free Corps; Czech Legion; Indoctrination; Vlasov, Lieutenant General Andrei

References
Rosemary Foot, *A Substitute for Victory: The Politics of Peacemaking at the Korean Armistice Talks* (Ithaca, NY: Cornell University Press, 1990).
Jon Halliday and Bruce Cumings, *Korea: The Unknown War* (New York: Pantheon, 1988).
Virginia Pasley, *21 Stayed: The Story of the American GI's Who Chose Communist China—Who They Were and Why They Stayed* (New York: Farrar, Straus and Cudahy, 1955).
Jürgen Thorwald, *The Illusion: Soviet Soldiers in Hitler's Army, trans. Richard and Clara Winston* (New York: Harcourt, Brace, Jovanovich, 1975).
Morris R. Wills, *Turncoat: An American's 12 Years in Communist China* (Englewood Cliffs, NJ: Prentice Hall, 1966).

—Charles S. Young

DEF/SEP STATUS

The question of whether captured enemy personnel were given POW status or status as either Disarmed Enemy Forces or Surrendered Enemy Personnel was at the heart of much of the controversy surrounding the treatment of prisoners in World War II. To benefit from the protection of the Geneva Convention, a soldier must first be recognized as a "lawful belligerent" and granted POW status when taken into custody by an enemy power. Though they remain at the mercy of the detaining power, the captured soldiers who gain POW status are transformed into third parties to the conflict, protected by established norms of law until the conclusion of a peace treaty or repatriation to their state of origin.

During World War II, Nazi Germany employed various legal rationales to deny POW status and treatment to captured military personnel of Poland, Yugoslavia, the Soviet Union, and Italy. The Japanese did the same in the Pacific theater. But even as they prosecuted Axis officials for these and other violations of international law, the Allied governments themselves tried to circumvent the Geneva Convention through a newly created category known as Disarmed Enemy Forces (DEF) or, in the British case, Surrendered Enemy Personnel (SEP).

The Allies wanted to take advantage of the unconditional surrender of Germany and Japan, a circumstance not foreseen by the framers of the 1929 Geneva Convention. The newly formulated legal status of DEF/SEP was planned before the end of the war for use on the masses of German and Japanese service personnel taken into custody after the expected collapse of those regimes. The introduction of this new designation had multiple purposes: to ensure that the German army experienced the full humiliation of defeat, to deny generous Geneva Convention standards of food in a period of serious shortages elsewhere in Europe, and to permit the prolonged detention of millions of captured military personnel as postwar reparations laborers who could be assigned tasks, such as mine clearing, that would otherwise be in clear violation of the Geneva Conventions. DEF/SEP status also permitted captured units to be maintained under their own command structures, facilitating movement out of liberated territories, disarmament, and provisioning.

During the closing weeks of the war, discretion to declare captured enemy personnel DEF/SEP rather than POWs was left to individual Allied commanders. In the end, most Japanese military personnel who laid down their arms in the Pacific theater were so designated. In Europe, 1.8 million captured Germans were declared DEF/SEP immediately, and by September 1945, all POWs still in Allied custody in Germany were also assigned DEF/SEP status. The International Committee of the Red Cross was disturbed by the precedent, however, and protested vigorously. Finally, in March 1946, Allied authorities eliminated the DEF/SEP distinction and returned all German military personnel still in their custody to POW status.

In the negotiations that preceded the signing of the 1949 Geneva Conventions, DEF/SEP status was even more resolutely consigned to historical oblivion. In Article 4 of the expanded treaty, POW status and treatment are guaranteed to all enemy personnel taken into custody by a detaining power in future conflicts. Article 5 stipulates that enemy personnel must keep their POW status until final release and repatriation, or if reinterned for any reason by the detaining power. Finally, Article 6 provides that no special agreements or political changes, including the disappearance of a state that ostensibly formed the legal basis for a DEF/SEP designation, could adversely affect POW status.

See also War on Terror

References

Royce L. Thompson, *Military Surrenders in the European Theater of Operations: World War II* (Washington: Office of the Chief of Military History, 1955).

U.S. Army, *Disarmament and Disbandment of the German Armed Forces* (Frankfurt: Office of the Chief of Military History, 1947).

Richard D. Wiggers, "The United States and the Denial of Prisoner of War (POW) Status at the End of the Second World War," *Militärgeschichtliche Mitteilungen* 52 (1993): 91–104.

Rene Jean Wilhelm, *Can the Status of Prisoners of War Be Altered?* (Geneva: International Committee of the Red Cross, 1953).

—Richard D. Wiggers

Defence Regulation 18B

During World War II, the British government invoked Defence Regulation 18B, which eventually allowed for the detention of people perceived to be threats to national security. In response to the partly mythical, partly justified Fifth Column panic, the government put in place a number of legislative provisions to guard against subversion, espionage, and sabotage on the part of British nationals and civilians. The first legislative steps in defense of the realm were taken with the Emergency Powers (Defence) Act, which was passed by both houses of Parliament on 24 August 1939, and an Order-in-Council affecting the freedom of political discussion and the press, which came into effect on 1 September 1939. Further changes were provoked by the German invasion of Denmark and Norway in May 1940, coupled with the discovery on 22 May 1940 of subversive activities by Tyler Kent, a cipher clerk in the American embassy in London, and Anna Wolkoff, a leading member of Captain Maule Ramsay's pro-German Right Club. An Order-in-Council amending Defence Regulation 18B was made with immediate effect on 22 May 1940, and under 18B (1A), the home secretary was empowered to detain any person who posed a threat to national security by being a leader or a member of any organization that was presumed to be under foreign influence or control.

From 1940 to 1945, a total of 1,826 people were interned under Defence Regulation 18B. Sir Oswald Mosley's British Union of Fascists and National Socialists was outlawed, its publications banned, and 747 of its leaders and rank-and-file members interned. Mosley himself was arrested on 22 May 1940 and held in Brixton and later in Holloway Prison until November 1943. The legal basis for executive detention and the administration of the defense regulations troubled 18B detainees and civil liberty advocates alike, as internees were detained indefinitely with no charges filed against them and were denied habeas corpus and rights under the Magna Carta.

See also Civilian Internees—World War II—Britain; Holloway Prison

References

Mike Cronin, ed., *The Failure of British Fascism: The Far Right and the Fight for Political Recognition* (London: Macmillan, 1996).

Barry Domvile, *From Admiral to Cabin Boy* (London: Boswell Publishing, 1947).

A. L. Goldman, "Defence Regulation 18B: Emergency Internment of Aliens and Political Dissenters in Great Britain during World War II," *Journal of British Studies* 12 (1973): 120–136.

Diana Mosley, *A Life of Contrasts: The Autobiography of Diana Mosley* (New York: Times Books, 1978).

Oswald Mosley, *My Life* (London: Nelson, 1968).

A. W. Brian Simpson, *In the Highest Degree Odious: Detention without Trial in Wartime Britain* (Oxford: Clarendon Press, 1992).

Richard Thurlow, *The Secret State: British Internal Security in the Twentieth Century* (Oxford: Blackwell, 1995).

W. J. West, *Truth Betrayed* (London: Duckworth, 1987).

—*Julie V. Gottlieb*

DOOLITTLE RAID

On 18 April 1942, 16 American medium bombers commanded by Colonel James Harold Doolittle took off from the aircraft carrier USS *Hornet* to bomb Tokyo. The raid was a great success in propaganda terms, but eight of the aviators fell into Japanese hands. Given the shock that the raid caused in Japan, it is not surprising that the airmen were harshly treated from the beginning. Beaten and denied medical attention and sufficient rations, they were also bullied into signing confessions stating that they had intentionally bombed hospitals and civilian homes or strafed school children.

The Japanese leadership was split on whether the airmen should be treated as prisoners of war or war criminals. The chief of the general staff considered them to be war criminals and demanded their execution, but Prime Minister Hideki Tojo was reluctant to accede, instead ordering the authorities to pass a statute allowing Japan to impose the death penalty on captured aviators. This measure, he believed, would be a sufficient deterrent against future raids. However, under pressure from the military, Tojo eventually relented; there would be a show trial in Shanghai, after which the airmen would be executed. On 28 August 1942, in a trial that included no defense counsel, no interpreters, and no witnesses, death penalties were handed down to all eight men. However, Tojo, still uncomfortable with the sentences, appealed to Emperor Hirohito, who commuted five of the sentences to life in prison. The other three, whose "confessions" included admissions that they had attacked school children, would still face the death penalty. On 15 October 1942, Lieutenants Dean E. Hallmark and William G. Farrow and Sergeant Harold A. Spatz were executed by firing squad. Lieutenant Robert J. Meder died in solitary confinement in December 1943. Lieutenants Chase J. Nielsen, Robert L. Hite, and George Barr, and Corporal Jacob DeShazer survived over three years in solitary confinement to be liberated in August 1945. In 1946, four former Japanese soldiers were tried for their part in the executions of Hallmark, Farrow, and Spatz. All were found guilty, but the light sentences handed down, ranging from five to nine years in prison, outraged many Americans.

References
James Doolittle, *I Could Never Be So Lucky Again: An Autobiography* (New York: Bantam, 2001).
James M. Merrill, *Target Tokyo: The Halsey-Doolittle Raid* (New York: Rand McNally, 1964).
Craig Nelson, *The First Heroes: The Extraordinary Story of the Doolittle Raid – America's First World War II Victory* (New York: Penguin, 2003).
Duane Schultz, *The Doolittle Raid* (New York: St. Martin's Press, 1988).

—*Jonathan F. Vance*

DULAG LUFT

Dulag Luft, the German prison camp through which tens of thousands of Allied airmen captured in western Europe passed, was the most efficient interrogation center of World War II. Dulag Luft (the word is a corruption of the German *Durchsgangslager Luftwaffe*, or air force transit camp) was located near the town of Oberursel, about 10 miles northwest of Frankfurt-am-Main in western Germany, where it occupied a large, pleasant-looking farmhouse that had once been part of an experimental farm. The first prisoners arrived in December 1939, and in April 1940 they were moved to barracks in an adjacent compound. In early 1941, the interrogation center, consisting of 129 solitary confinement cells, was opened. The center, designated *Auswertestelle West*, or Evaluation Center West, later grew to about 200 cells, many equipped with electronic listening devices. In September 1943, the barracks, by now overcrowded with incoming prisoners, were moved to a public park in the center of Frankfurt, where it remained until March 1944, when the camp was hit by Allied bombs. It was then relocated to the nearby city of Wetzlar, where the prisoners were forced to live in tents until the barracks were completed in July. (Through these changes, the interrogation center remained at Oberursel.) The Wetzlar camp was evacuated to Nuremberg on 25 March 1945 in the face of advancing Allied armies; when American troops reached the site a month later, Dulag Luft was empty. It was later transformed into Camp King, a U.S. transport depot, the interrogation block becoming the officers' mess.

The camp population was relatively small. There were rarely more than 150 prisoners at Oberursel at any one time, while the Frankfurt camp held as many as 350. The Wetzlar camp was bigger still, holding as many as 500 POWs on any given day. Generally, conditions were good: neutral inspectors reported that food, medical attention, sanitation, washing facilities, and accommodations were often excellent, in part because of the Germans' belief that prisoners who were well treated in the first days of their captivity might let down their guard and reveal useful military intelligence.

The camp's purpose was to prepare prisoners for their transfer to a permanent camp. This involved helping them to acclimatize to life in captivity, a process that was assisted by a committee of long-term prisoners known as the Permanent Staff. Before this process began, however, prisoners were held at the interrogation center, where a variety of means were used to extract any useful information from them. Every prisoner was presented with a questionnaire, ostensibly from the German Red Cross, which asked a wide range of questions, many military in nature. Prisoners were told that failure to complete the form would result in delays in informing their next of kin of their whereabouts. In some cases, they were threatened with physical violence or exposed to high temperatures or constant light in order to convince them to talk. All were interviewed by skilled interrogators (the center had 55 experienced interrogators in a staff of over 300), who would soften them up with American cigarettes and English matches, then show them a thick file full of information on their own squadron. This frequently convinced the new prisoner that his captors knew everything about him and his unit and that there was no harm in answering any questions.

By 1944, the Luftwaffe had opened another interrogation center at nearby Dietz-an-Lahn to cope with the growing number of captured Allied airmen. Other, smaller centers were established in Holland, northern and western France, and Verona, Italy, so that by 1944, only those airmen of special technical interest were forwarded to Dulag Luft. The German army and navy also operated transit camps that served a dual purpose as intelligence-gathering centers, but none were as sophisticated and successful as Dulag Luft.

See also Interrogation; World War II—Western Europe

References

James L. Cole, "Dulag Luft Recalled and Revisited," *Aerospace Historian* 19 (1972): 62–65.

Eric Cuddon, ed., *The Dulag Luft Trial* (London: William Hodge, 1952).

Philip Plammer, "Dulag Luft," *Aerospace Historian* 19 (1972): 58–62.

Sydney Smith, *Wings Day: The Story of the Man Who Led the RAF's Epic Battle in Captivity* (London: Collins, 1968).

Raymond Toliver, *The Interrogator: The Story of Hans Scharff, the Luftwaffe's Master Interrogator* (Fallbrook, CA: Aero Publishers, 1978).

—Jonathan F. Vance

E

Education

Captivity is a time of enforced leisure, and prisoners naturally seek ways to fill that time usefully. One of the most productive ways has been in studying, either to gain basic literacy or to learn a trade or profession. Historically, before captivity came under the rule of international law, the provision of educational opportunities to prisoners was rare. It was a lucky prisoner who came in contact with a captor or agent willing and able to provide assistance in this regard. During the American Revolution, prisoners at Forton Prison in southern England were assisted by the Reverend Thomas Wren of Portsmouth, whose sympathy for the revolution moved him to procure educational supplies for the American captives. Their fellow inmates at Mill Prison were left largely to their own devices but still managed to provide each other with rudimentary instruction in ciphering and navigation. During the Napoleonic Wars, the Reverend R. B. Wolfe established in Givet Prison in France a school that taught reading, mathematics, and navigation to some 500 captive British soldiers. During the U.S. Civil War, even the horrific conditions in Andersonville prison camp in Georgia did not prevent the Union inmates from passing the time with study of such subjects as algebra and languages.

Not until the twentieth century were educational programs for prisoners put on a formal footing. During World War I, the British Prisoners of War Book Scheme (Educational) was launched to provide POWs with the reading matter necessary to improve their education. The interested prisoner could request a syllabus of examination from any one of a number of institutions—including Oxford and Cambridge Universities, the Royal Society of Art, and the Institute of Chartered Accountants—and would receive in due course the required texts and course materials. He could then study at his own pace, write the necessary examinations, and become fully accredited and able to start work upon his release from captivity. In a camp for Austro-Hungarian POWs in Khabarovsk in Siberia, the Swedish Red Cross provided materials to equip what the prisoners called the Peasant University, staffed by POWs who had been on faculty at some of central Europe's finest universities. A whole range of courses, from Esperanto to theoretical physics to paleontology, was available for interested inmates. Similar arrangements could be made on a more informal basis. Canadian composer Sir Ernest MacMillan, for example, worked on his doctoral thesis in music while interned in Ruhleben camp in Berlin. The value of such schemes was recognized in a 1918 agreement between the United States and Germany that stipulated that qualified prisoners could give educational lectures and courses, so long as study did not interfere with the work required of prisoners. This was the first time that the provision of educational opportunities for POWs was covered by international treaty.

The 1929 Geneva Convention was less specific than the 1918 agreement, simply asking belligerents to "encourage intellectual diversions" among prisoners (Article 17), but nevertheless educational opportunities were much broader and more widely available during World War II. The International Committee of the Red Cross created an Advisory Committee on Reading Matter for

Prisoners to coordinate the educational program and to act as a controlling committee for a number of bodies, including the World Alliance of Young Men's Christian Associations (YMCAs), the International Bureau of Education, and the International Federation of Library Associations. War Prisoners' Aid of the YMCA was particularly active in providing textbooks, pencils and paper, course materials, and classroom equipment to prison camps in Germany, Japan, Great Britain, North America, and Australia. YMCA representatives would visit each camp to assess the prisoners' needs, then request the necessary supplies from headquarters in Geneva. Most of the material was held in depots in Switzerland or New York, and the majority of books were produced in the United States; by April 1945, the YMCA had published over four million books in the United States for distribution to prison camps. The actual teaching was done by qualified prisoners, although correspondence courses were also available. Some prisoners took the courses merely to pass the time, but others received credit for high school equivalency, university entrance, or even bachelor's degrees for work done in prison camp. There are many examples of successful "barbed-wire universities." In Oflag 64 in Germany, courses were available in law, languages, mathematics, social science, English grammar, and science; in 1944, 30 POWs there passed their university entrance examinations. Teachers in Oflag 6B offered courses in 20 different subjects, and prisoners could learn any of 22 different languages. In camps in the United States, as many as half of the German POWs were enrolled in educational courses, and over 17,000 Italian prisoners learned to read and write in captivity. One study estimated that officer prisoners spent an average of two and a half hours a day in study, more than in any other daytime activity.

The provision of educational opportunities was again stipulated in the 1949 Geneva Convention, but in subsequent conflicts (Korea and Vietnam, for example), education was less prevalent than reeducation, or the indoctrination of POWs with the political values of the detaining power. Still, education is one of the few success stories of twentieth-century captivity. Educational opportunities allowed hundreds of thousands of prisoners to put to good use time that might have been wasted and to gain education that they might not otherwise have received.

See also Libraries

References

A. R. Dearlove, "Enforced Leisure: A Study of the Activities of Officer Prisoners of War," *British Medical Journal* (24 March 1945): 406–409.

Ralph Pierson, "The Barbed Wire Universities," *School and Society* 62 (8 September 1945): 156–158.

—Jonathan F. Vance

EGYPT, ANCIENT

Captives taken in war were depicted in many ways in ancient Egypt: on royal footstools, on the soles of royal sandals, on thrones, statues, and figurines, on floor tiles, and on monumental architecture. In the case of royal furniture, footwear, and flooring, the symbolism was clear: the pharaoh sat or walked upon the prisoners, crushing them, and by association, crushed the countries from which they were taken. Statues and figurines of prisoners of war were often captioned with magical texts (the so-called Execration Texts) that were meant to cause death to the countries and enemies they represented, and these also acclaimed the pharaoh's political dominance in the region.

Temples such as Medinet Habu, the funerary temple of Rameses III (1194–1163 B.C.E.) at Thebes, depict battles and their aftermath on the walls, and these monuments provide details not only of wars led by the pharaoh, but also of the entire range of the processes of war, from the preparation of troops, to the battles, to the capture and return to Egypt of booty and its subsequent distribution into Egyptian society. Booty included noncombatant men, women, and children, as well as prisoners of war. Since the captured combatants are rarely distinguished in the records from captured noncombatants, it is difficult to distinguish between the treatment of the two groups.

Egyptian sources record large numbers of prisoners of war in various campaigns. One of Amenhotep II's campaigns recorded over 100,000 captives; Thutmose III's (1479–1425 B.C.E.) Megiddo booty lists (as such records are known in Egyptological literature) note 340 living prisoners, 43 officers, 84 children, 1,796 male and female slaves including children (these were presumably already slaves), and 103 pardoned persons who had surrendered; Merenptah's (1224–1214 B.C.E.) troops captured more than 9,000 people in the war against the Libyans; and the temple estates in the reign of Rameses II had nearly 5,000 workers "of his majesty's capturing." One campaign of Amenhotep II (1427–1401 B.C.E.) took so many captives that he ordered a palisade to be built in order to contain them until he could deal with them, an unusual occurrence. While some of these numbers were probably inflated for propaganda purposes, it is clear that ancient Egyptian wars produced many prisoners.

When battle was over, victorious Egyptian soldiers systematically checked the battlefield for the dead, the dying, and the living. Enemy soldiers who had fled the battle site were rounded up and brought back. The dead were counted, the dying were executed, and the prisoners, including those who had surrendered, were processed. Not only combatants were captured; whole families, and sometimes whole towns, were captured and treated as booty, along with their livestock and other possessions.

The prisoners of war were presented to the pharaoh, sometimes in large groups and sometimes individually, by the soldiers who had captured them. Prisoners automatically belonged to the pharaoh, who had the power of life and death over them, as over all other war booty, and they were disposed of in several different ways. In some cases, prisoners were returned as slaves to their captors as a reward. In other cases, the prisoners were allowed to plead for their lives and were given their freedom after taking an oath of loyalty to the pharaoh. These men thus became vassals of the Egyptian administration and were returned to their homes after being disarmed.

Several temple walls display scenes of prisoners of war being executed, and others show that captured high officials or royalty were ceremonially executed and their bodies paraded throughout both the conquered country and Egypt as illustrations of the pharaoh's power. Other royal captives were returned to Egypt as laborers or as hostages to guarantee the good behavior of the vassals. Defeated soldiers were sometimes allowed to join the Egyptian army after swearing loyalty to the Egyptian pharaoh. One such group was the Sardinians, who were captured by the troops of Rameses II and then fought the Hittites at the Battle of Kadesh (c. 1295 B.C.E.) as part of the Egyptian army.

Those prisoners whom the pharaoh decided to keep as workers were branded and then transported to Egypt, either by forced march or by boat. That the forced marches caused hardships for the captives, especially the women and children, is made clear in the Papyrus Deir el-Medina from the Twentieth Dynasty: "The captives going to Egypt are handed over to His Majesty. The foreign woman faints because of the marching. She is placed on the soldier's shoulder. His haversack is cast aside; others take it-he is saddled with the captive."

In Egyptian temple scenes, prisoners of war are typically depicted bound with their elbows touching behind their backs or above their heads, positions that would be impossible unless their shoulders were dislocated. Since this would cause the prisoners to be injured and unable to work, this is probably an exaggeration; the bonds were probably not tight enough for the elbows to actually meet. Statues of prisoners show them tied at the elbow, with the arms as far back as they could go, but without the elbows actually touching. Other methods of restriction included a type of wooden handcuff, attached to the captive's hands and neck, by which the captive was often linked to others. The prisoners were bound during transport to ensure they did not escape. These methods of containment are described in the Harris Papyrus I (77.4–6): "I have brought back in great numbers those that my sword has spared, with their hands tied behind their backs before my horses, and their wives and children in tens of thousands, and their livestock in hundreds of thousands. I have imprisoned their leaders in fortresses bearing my name, and I have added to them chief archers and tribal chiefs, branded and enslaved, tattooed with my name, and their wives and children have been treated in the same way."

On arrival in Egypt, prisoners of war were presented by the pharaoh to the gods of Egypt, who were believed to have brought victory to the Egyptian forces. Here the chiefs of the prisoners were expected to plead for their lives and to pledge allegiance to the pharaoh in public. They were then allocated to their new lives in captivity: to quarries as miners, to temple estates as field laborers or animal herders, to the army as slave soldiers. Women joined the pharaoh's harem or worked as weavers, clothing makers, or house servants, and presumably their children went with them. Large groups were often kept together in settlements of their own, but with food and supplies provided by the pharaoh in return for their labor. Full repatriation as we know it did not occur; most prisoners of war who survived became members of Egyptian society. Some of them even rose to positions quite high in the Egyptian administration.

The influx of large numbers of prisoners of war and other war captives over the many years of ancient Egyptian military activity ultimately influenced Egyptian language and culture, even though the prisoners were forced to learn and speak Egyptian. They brought to Egypt foreign gods, and foreign words, customs, and values, thereby enriching the culture of their adopted homes.

See also Slavery

References

James Henry Breasted, *Ancient Records of Egypt: Historical Documents from the Earliest Times to the Persian Conquest*, 5 vols. (Chicago: University of Chicago Press, 1906–1907).

William F. Edgerton, *Historical Records of Ramses III: The Texts in Medinet Habu, Volumes I and II, Translated with Explanatory Notes* (Chicago: University of Chicago Press, 1936).

Geoffrey Thorndike Martin, *The Memphite Tomb of Horemheb, Commander-in-chief of Tut'ankhamun*, vol. 1, *The Reliefs, Inscriptions, and Commentary* (London: Egypt Exploration Society, 1989).

Donald B. Redford, *Egypt, Canaan, and Israel in Ancient Times* (Princeton, NJ: Princeton University Press, 1992).

John W. Wells, "War in Ancient Egypt" (Ph.D. diss., University of Maryland, 1986).

John A. Wilson, *The Culture of Ancient Egypt* (Chicago: University of Chicago Press, 1951).

—*Gaye Wilson*

ELMIRA

Elmira, New York, was the site of one of the most notorious Union prison camps of the U.S. Civil War. Almost 3,000 of the 12,000 Confederate soldiers imprisoned there in 1864 and 1865 died, a death rate that made "Hel-mira" the prison camp of choice for postwar Confederate polemicists looking for a comparison to the suffering of Union prisoners at Andersonville, Georgia. Many of the camp's survivors would later publish books and articles in *Confederate Magazine* and other pro-Confederate publications.

The Elmira facility had been a rendezvous and training camp for Union troops, but in May 1864, empty barracks were set aside for use as a prison camp. Most exchanges of prisoners had been suspended the previous year, forcing both armies to scramble to find room for tens of thousands of prisoners. Colonel Seth Eastman, commander of the Elmira military depot, prepared for 5,000 prisoners, though he was warned repeatedly that as many as 10,000 were coming. The selected 30-acre site on the banks of the Chemung River was swampy and unhealthful. The wooden barracks, hastily erected to house transient troops, looked more substantial than they were.

The first prisoners arrived in early July, and by mid-August, the population stood at 9,600. The logistical problems of feeding so many men were almost overwhelming.

Rations were cut in retaliation for conditions in Southern prisons, and rat became a much-sought-after delicacy. Union authorities several times delayed issuance of clothing and blankets to the prisoners. Overcrowding forced thousands of prisoners to sleep in the open air. Foster's Pond, a one-acre stagnant pool, served as sewer and garbage dump, one surgeon calculating that 2,600 gallons of urine a day were discharged into it; the odor, especially in the summer heat, was indescribable. Not until late October did Eastman's successor (Eastman had resigned due to ill health), Benjamin F. Tracy, receive permission to construct an adequate drainage system.

These conditions caused incalculable damage to the health of men, who were in many cases already ill-fed, ill-clothed, sick, and wounded upon arrival at Elmira, and Elmira became a death trap. Defeated by the camp's distance from the South and from potential escape routes, very few prisoners attempted escape. One of the stranger aspects of the camp was the observation platforms erected by private parties outside the walls of the camp, where for 15 or 50 cents (accounts vary) the curious could view the Confederate prisoners.

Too many of the physicians and other officers assigned to Elmira were of mediocre ability at best; some were charged by prisoners with deliberate cruelty. An October 1864 effort to exchange some of the sickest Elmira prisoners was badly bungled, resulting in dozens of horrific deaths. The winter of 1864–1865 was particularly harsh, only adding to the suffering and causing the camp to flood in March 1865. After the end of the war in April, the prison camp was emptied by 5 July, the last prisoner leaving the hospital in September 1865. The camp cemetery is maintained by the federal government.

See also Andersonville; Libby Prison; United States Civil War

References

Clay W. Holmes, *The Elmira Prison Camp: A History of the Military Prison at Elmira, N.Y., July 6, 1864 to July 10, 1865* (New York: G.P. Putnam's Sons, 1912).

Michael Horigan, *Elmira: Death Camp of the North* (Mechanicsburg, PA: Stackpole Books, 2002).

A. M. Keiley, *In Vinculis; or The Prisoner of War* (New York: Blelock, 1866).

James I. Robertson, "The Scourge of Elmira," in *Civil War Prisons*, ed. William B. Hesseltine (Kent, OH: Kent State University Press, 1962).

—Douglas G. Gardner

English Civil War (1641–1649)

The term *English* when used in reference to this conflict is somewhat of a misnomer: While the English played a major role in the events that occurred in the British Isles during this period, they were not alone in doing so, nor did the military engagements occur only in England. The civil wars of Britain were waged on battlefields across the breadth and depth of all of the British Isles, from Kerry in Ireland to John O'Groats on the northern tip of Scotland. The reasons for the conflicts also varied, and included political, religious, and even ethnic causes. Although the conflict normally referred to as the English Civil War lasted from 1641 until 1649, the larger war of which it was one part actually occurred between 1638 and 1651, with some isolated outbreaks of violence extending the dispute until 1658. The war was rooted in religious and political disagreements over who should govern the British Isles, and these disagreements were reflected in the treatment of prisoners of war on either side.

By the start of this civil war, the British Isles had come under one political umbrella, that of the Stuart kings. Ireland, a crazy quilt of petty kingdoms, came under English sway in the twelfth century, and the loose control England exerted over that island was strengthened in the sixteenth century by the Tudor kings of England, whose support for the Protestant Reformation had left many of the primarily Roman Catholic Irish politically impotent. In Scotland, much of the populace had become Protestant, but theirs was a form of Calvinism that contrasted strangely with the episcopal form of Protestantism practiced in England. At the beginning of the seventeenth century, the death of Elizabeth I, the last Tudor monarch, left the throne to her distant cousin, James Stuart of Scotland, and the three kingdoms were united under one throne.

By the 1630s, James's son, Charles I, was on the throne, and civil war was brewing. Charles was a reserved individual with a strong belief in a hierarchy that included both monarchs and bishops. At the time, the rise in mercantilism, joined to a reformist Protestantism called Puritanism, had resulted in deep divisions in England, which Charles attempted to rule without the benefit of any Parliamentary interference. As an adherent of the state-supported Church of England, Charles attempted to establish a similar episcopal system in the church in Scotland. This caused the so-called First and Second Bishops Wars in 1638, in which there was widespread mobilization of the Scottish nobility, gentry, and clergy, who signed a National Covenant in opposition to Charles's actions. Little real fighting took place at that time, but the opposition forced Charles to call a Parliament in England to pay for the war, and that Parliament refused to be disbanded. In 1641, the pressure was increased when the disenfranchised Irish Catholics rose in rebellion, and word soon spread of general massacres of Protestant English settlers. In response, Parliament became more intransigent, and in 1642 this, in turn, resulted in a break between those who supported the Crown and those whose allegiance was to Parliament.

The fate of any prisoners depended on the faction they supported—English Royalist, Parliamentarian, Irish Catholic, or Scottish Covenanter. Prisoners generally were held on an ad hoc basis, with little provision made for their care or treatment. In England, prisoners taken by either the Crown or the Parliament were usually clapped into the nearest jail and encouraged to change sides, or if the prisoner was an officer, he was allowed to give his parole not to fight again. For example, following the battle of Naseby, Royalist prisoners were housed in the local church prior to being marched to London where they were put on display. In Ireland and Scotland, where religion was joined to political and ethnic factors (many of those who supported Charles in Scotland were Roman Catholic, while in Ireland both Catholic and Protestant factions claimed at one time or another to be supporters of the king), ordinary soldiers could receive short shrift, with many being killed out of hand. This was quickly extended to England, where fears that Charles was receiving Catholic aid from Ireland led to a Parliamentary ordinance making it a capital crime for Irish or Catholics from Ireland to serve in Charles's forces in England. This led to reprisals by Royalists; when Shrewsbury was taken by Parliament, 13 men were executed under this ordinance, to be followed soon after by the execution of 13 prisoners held by the Royalists. At sea, though, there was no chance of reprisal. When ships were captured in the Irish Sea by Parliamentary vessels, they were searched for Irish soldiers, who, if found, were swiftly thrown overboard.

On other occasions, the bitterness inherent in a civil war led to a general mistreatment of any prisoners taken. Many were stripped of their possessions or imprisoned in hulks. In 1644, some 70 prisoners held in the hold of one such ship appealed to Parliament for relief from what they referred to as "hunger, cold nakednes, noisome smels, with many other calamities that dwell with us in this our louthsome Dungeon." Of course, prisoners on both sides had an option at their disposal: switching allegiance. Many common soldiers were strongly encouraged to change sides, with some success; after the Royalists took Cirencester and moved to Oxford, they took with them some 1,100–1,200 prisoners, almost all of whom joined the Royalist army. Those who did not were put to work building fortifications. Officers, if paroled, could return home, but if they were recaptured while under arms they were liable to be executed, as happened at the taking of Woodhouse, where 14 were hung for breaking parole.

As the war dragged on, it became more bitter; in 1649, even a captured King Charles I was executed by his Parliamentary captors. While this resulted in the support of the Scottish Covenant for his son, Charles II, in the end the English were triumphant. In Ireland, the English Parliamentary army broke the Irish rebellion, killing all who resisted, with a notable massacre at the storming of Drogheda. In this case, ethnic cleansing became a factor, as Parliament offered the Irish in many areas a choice between removal to Connaught, the most inhospitable of the four provinces of Ireland, or death. The attitude toward prisoners was reflected in the battle-cry of "Connaught or Hell."

Following Parliament's victory, adherents to the Royalist cause could either move to the continent or pay hefty "composition" for the crime of supporting the losing side. Prisoners taken in the wars were eventually released, but a series of minor plots continued to provide the Parliamentary forces with experience in handling captives. Most of the prisoners taken during this period remained as captives, were executed, or were transported to colonies in the West Indies. It was only in 1660 that the last prisoners were released upon the return of the Stuart monarchy, reestablished under a promise that there should be a blanket amnesty for those who had fought for Parliament. Only a few "regicides," those deemed to have had primary responsibility for the execution of the king, were omitted from this pardon; most of those fled and died in exile.

References

Charles Carlton, *Going to the Wars: The Experience of the British Civil Wars, 1638–1651* (New York: Routledge, 1992).

Barbara Donagan, "Prisoners in the English Civil War," *History Today* 41 (1991): 28–35.

Christopher Hibbert, *Cavaliers and Roundheads: The English at War, 1642–1649* (London: HarperCollins, 1994).

Joyce Lee Malcolm, *Caesar's Due: Loyalty and King Charles, 1642–1646* (London: Royal Historical Society, 1983).

—Daniel German

EPIDEMICS

In the twentieth century, the most direct menace to the life and health of prisoners of war and internees came from epidemic diseases. In previous centuries epidemics had posed one of the major threats to the fighting armies and the civilian population, but substantial improvements in medicine and hygiene considerably reduced the peril to both groups in most belligerent societies by the nineteenth century. Since prisoners in former wars were not interned in large camps for long periods of time, they had been affected by epidemics in much the same way as civilians or serving soldiers. This changed fundamentally during the great wars of the twentieth century. Insufficient sanitation and hygienic facilities in huge camps crammed with prisoners were combined with malnutrition, avitaminosis, and infected drinking water or food to play a decisive role in the outbreak of epidemics such as typhus (typhus abdominalis), dysentery, and typhoid fever (typhus exanthematicus). Other epidemic or endemic diseases with regional backgrounds in peacetime played a negligible role in war captivity; these included cholera, diphtheria, influenza, smallpox, and plague, with the exception of endemic malaria. Captives taken from besieged fortresses, such as Metz in the Franco-Prussian War (173,000 POWs); Przemyśl in World War I (117,000 POWs); and Stalingrad in World War II (about 100,000 POWs), were particularly prone to epidemic disease. Clearly, epidemics among captives have become a phenomenon of the age of mass warfare, fostered by large prison camps with insufficient medical facilities or indifferent administrations.

In modern times, the first experiences of epidemics among internees came during the U.S. Civil War (1861–1865), the Franco-Prussian War (1870–1871), and even more acutely during the Boer War (1899–1902). In the Boer War, the British detaining power erected so-called concentration camps and interned civilians in these cramped places. Many of the inmates were women and children, interned to prevent them from giving support to the Boer soldiers, and conditions in these camps resulted in enormous loss of life. More serious outbreaks occurred during World War I, with mass epidemics affecting all belligerents, particularly those in eastern and southeastern Europe. Whereas most of the western Allies and the Central Powers had sufficient hygiene and medical equipment (especially for vaccinations), Russia did not, despite the many endemic and chronic diseases among its population. During the war, Russia was cut off from medical and vaccination equipment, most of which had been previously supplied by Germany. In addition, the country's notoriously poor administrative organization contributed much to the misery endured by its captives and its own citizens alike. Thus, captivity and internment in Russia became fatal for hundreds of thousands of captured soldiers and some 250,000 civilian captives, as well as for Russian refugees from the theater of war, who in most cases suffered from typhus and typhoid fever. Though Germany and Austro-Hungary were subject to a tight food blockade by their enemies, the death tolls among Allied POWs in those countries were no higher than in Britain and France.

In Russia, huge losses from epidemics among POWs and civilian internees (including its own citizens) persisted in succeeding decades. In Nazi Germany, too, epidemics struck prisoner of war and concentration camps during World War II. It must be said that this infection was, to some degree, deliberate. The idea of reducing the captives' physical constitution in order to prevent escape attempts and to foster the captives' willingness to work for additional food had not been unknown during World War I. In Nazi Germany, however, some 5.7 million Soviet prisoners of war, together with inmates of concentration camps, were subjected to a racial policy of extermination. This was achieved by a lethal combination of starvation, lack of hygiene and medical care, and extensive forced labor. The eventual result was epidemics and mass deaths. British, French, Belgian, and American prisoners in German detention, on the other hand, received Red Cross parcels from their home countries, enabling them to improve their diet and so retain greater resistance to disease.

After the surrender of the German armies early in May 1945, epidemics spread among civilians in central Europe, several million of whom fled from the advancing Soviet army, and among the soldiers of the Wehrmacht, who had surrendered and were interned in huge makeshift camps operated by the Allies.

See also Health

References

Kenneth F. Kiple, ed., *The Cambridge World History of Human Diseases* (New York: Cambridge University Press, 1993).

Reinhard Nachtigal, *Kriegsgefangenschaft an der Ostfront, 1914–1918: Literaturbericht ze einem Forschungsfeld* (Frankfurt-am-Main: Peter Lang, 2005).

Anton Sebastian, *Dictionary of the History of Medicine* (New York: Parthenon, 1999).

Matthew Smallman-Raynor and Andrew D. Cliff, "The Geographical Transmission of Smallpox in the Franco-Prussian War: Prisoner of War Camps and Their Impact Upon Epidemic Diffusion Processes in the Civil Settlement System of Prussia, 1870–71," *Medical History* 46 (2002): 241–264.

Paul Weindling, *Epidemics and Genocide in Eastern Europe 1890–1945* (Oxford: Oxford University Press, 1999).

—*Reinhard Nachtigal*

ESCAPE

When members of the armed forces are captured in time of war it is their duty, by all possible and reasonable means, to attempt escape from the enemy. Whether or not an individual does indeed attempt escape is related to a number of factors, including opportunity, state of health, the security arrangements made by the captor, and personal motivation.

History is full of tales of daring escapes from captivity. In 1264, the future King Edward I of England, captured by his enemy Simon de Montfort at the battle of Lewes, escaped from Hereford Castle, an exploit that convinced waverers to join his ranks and defeat de Montfort. In 1716, the Earl of Nithsdale, captured the year before in the Jacobite Rising in Scotland, escaped from the Tower of London, dressed in woman's clothes that his wife had smuggled in for him. During the American Civil War, the largest escape occurred on 9 February 1864, when 109 Union officers escaped through a tunnel at Libby Prison in Richmond, Virginia; in all, 48 of them reached freedom.

Historically, however, only a small percentage of POWs ever make persistent attempts to escape. Once their basic instinct for survival reasserts itself, most accept captivity and try to endure life as a prisoner, however unpleasant, with stoical cheerfulness. Despite this, many prisoners in both world wars engaged themselves in escape activity, both as a means of defiance and as a way of occupying the long tedious days. Men worked diligently on shafts and tunnels, more often than not in the knowledge that the schemes had little, if any, chance of success. But in working on a tunnel, tailoring escape clothing, making maps or forging documents, the men felt useful once again, and part of a team effort.

During World War I, escapers were usually a small esoteric group who kept any escape plans to themselves. One notable exception was a 60-meter tunnel dug over two months beneath the barbed wire at Holzminden, through which 29 Allied officers wriggled free, with 10 eventually reaching neutral Holland and freedom. Getting out of German camps was relatively easy for any determined escaper, as escape techniques and knowledge accumulated with each attempt. In the later years of the war, when communication was established with friends and relatives back home, the possibilities of escape increased as prisoners were allowed to receive clothing items that they could convert into civilian outfits. Prisoners also learned how to forge German passes and make rubber stamps that they used to cover fake papers with impressive-looking Prussian eagles and other adornments.

Once out of the German camps, the prisoners generally headed for neutral Holland, Switzerland, or Denmark or, in some cases, traveled by boat to Sweden. Having reached freedom, many escapers wrote books about their experiences, inspiring and guiding prisoners in the war of 1939–1945. But they also unwittingly assisted the Germans, who by reading the same books, gained valuable intelligence about POW tricks and techniques and applied this information when setting up security in their World War II camps.

Of all the service personnel who fell into enemy hands during World War II, airmen were the most singularly unprepared. They generally had an unshakable belief in their own ability, or that of their pilots or crew, and imprisonment did not rate highly in their day-to-day expectations. They tended to treat training lectures on escape and evasion tactics as a waste of time. Most airmen did not even consider the possibility of capture until they found themselves alone in enemy territory after being shot down. Once they were taken prisoner, they would spend countless hours trying to recapture their freedom.

By far the most favored method of escape from captivity in World War II was the digging of tunnels. The Germans were cognizant of this and, armed with the information gleaned from World War I escape books, were constantly on the alert. They employed special equipment to detect underground tunnels, such as listening devices sunk into the grounds of new camps, while in established compounds snap hut searches were carried out and random trenches dug to expose tunnels.

The persistence of the prisoners was occasionally rewarded by success. Once the barbed wire had been breached, the escaper's energies turned to fleeing across a hostile nation toward heavily guarded frontiers. Success depended on good planning and guile, an adequate disguise, and forged papers. Ahead could lay weeks or even months spent traversing enemy territory, eating whatever could be obtained by stealth, sleeping for the most part in the open through all conditions or in lice-ridden barns, and generally living like a tramp. Even at the end of all this, the prospect of crossing a frontier safely was daunting. With all these factors weighing heavily upon the escaper, it was not uncommon for some to feel a form of relief when recaptured. Some, at the thin edge of desperation, hungry and cold, even turned themselves in.

The preferred method of travel was by rail, which, despite wartime conditions, was generally efficient and reliable. The main inducement was its speed, but to use the railways the escaper had to be equipped with first-rate forged papers and remain continually on his guard through repeated and meticulous identity checks. Fortunately, the massive movement of seven million legitimate foreign workers around Germany meant that an ignorance of the vernacular was not a serious handicap. Bluff and a strong story supported by official-looking documents was the essence of all such escapes. The more falsified endorsements on a travel pass, the better; the Germans had an uncritical confidence in officialdom. Habits of a lifetime had to be scrupulously avoided since such simple mannerisms as the way a man walked or gestured could betray his origins. Unthinking actions such as smoking or eating Red Cross supplies in public caused many a downfall.

Following the tragic aftermath of the Great Escape in March 1944, when 50 Allied airmen were executed by the German police after being recaptured, the senior officers in most German POW camps advised their men that escaping could no longer be considered a sport. There were many instances of recaptured prisoners being murdered by their military and civilian captors. With an Allied victory becoming more certain all the time, most prisoners heeded the grim message and set aside escape plans to wait for the inevitable liberation.

Meanwhile, the Japanese-held prisoner of European descent faced severe obstacles in any bid for freedom, the most obvious being his appearance. Another was the vastness of the Asian theater, with any escape requiring passage through pestilential jungles and across vast tracts of water in extreme and unpredictable tropical weather conditions. Furthermore, in many areas, local villagers turned in runaways for the generous rewards offered by the Japanese. Added to these difficulties, escapers faced hunger, which exacerbated an already generally weakened physical condition resulting from starvation diets and medical neglect, as well as a lack of escape aids and information on Allied positions, insidious tropical diseases, and little more than a vague idea as to their destination. For many there was also the omnipresent concern that their escape could incur severe reprisals on those they had left behind. But most daunting of all was the grim prospect that recapture would likely end in death by decapitation.

In general, Allied prisoners during the two world wars were more active escapers than other groups of prisoners. German POWs did attempt escape on a number of occasions; some of the more well-known incidents include the successful escape in 1941 of German pilot Franz von Werra from Canada into the then neutral United States; the Faustball tunnel, which five German naval POWs used to escape (albeit only for a short time) from Camp Papago Park, near Phoenix, Arizona, in December 1944; and the mass escape of German officers from the Island Farm prison camp in Wales in 1944. That so few German and Italian prisoners attempted escape is likely related to the generally comfortable conditions that existed in their prison camps. Japanese POWs, on the other hand, did stage a number of suicidal mass escape attempts, most notably at Cowra, Australia, and Featherston, New Zealand, which resulted in the deaths of hundreds of prisoners.

In other wars, a variety of factors constrained prisoners from attempting to escape. In the Korean and Vietnam Wars, escapers had the greatest success if they made attempts in their first days of captivity. Once they reached permanent camps, security was much tighter and the distances to be covered to safety were so much greater that the chances of success were slight. At other times, for example, in the Falklands War or the Arab-Israeli Wars, there have been few escape attempts because captured conscripts considered themselves lucky to be out of the fight and had no wish to offer resistance to their captors.

See also Colditz; Cowra Incident; Featherston Incident; Great Escape; Wooden Horse

—*Colin Burgess*

ETHIOPIAN CIVIL WAR (1974–1993)

The most direct cause of this devastating conflict in one of the most impoverished regions of Africa lay in Ethiopia's annexation, with the blessing of the United Nations, of Eritrea in 1962. A decade later, with Ethiopian Emperor Haile Selassie slowly losing his faculties, the country drifting into a ruinous drought, and rebel groups in Eritrea growing in size and strength, the Ethiopian army grew restive. It began a series of mutinies in January 1974, and in September, Selassie was deposed and replaced by Major Mengistu Haile Mariam. Mengistu's first problems were the growing revolt in Eritrea, and the fact that the commander of the army advocated withdrawing and writing off the annexation of Eritrea as an unfortunate mistake. In response, Mengistu had the commander executed, along with as many as 80 captives he had taken in the coup, including ministers, princes, generals, and members of Selassie's family. Not until May 1988 were the surviving prisoners, including seven royal princesses and Selassie's 79-year-old daughter, released from captivity.

Mengistu soon found himself fighting a civil war on three fronts. The Eritrean People's Liberation Front (EPLF), along with the older Eritrean Liberation Front (ELF), mounted against Ethiopian troops a series of offensives that came close to toppling the Mengistu regime; he was saved only by significant intervention from the Soviet Union. But his attempts to root the EPLF out of its strongholds in the north of the country, in eight separate offensives between 1973 and 1988, were all defeated with heavy losses, and the EPLF was able to go on the offensive itself. In March 1988, after a successful winter campaign, the Eritreans found themselves with huge stocks of enemy weapons and over 16,000 Ethiopian POWs, including three Soviet officers.

At the same time, Mengistu was facing a rebellion in Tigray, a northern province of Ethiopia, where famine had driven the people to revolution and caused the formation of the Tigrean People's Liberation Front (TPLF), and uprisings among the Oromo people, who made up the largest ethnic group in Ethiopia. In 1989, Mengistu temporarily gained the upper hand; he put down an army coup directed against him, executing 14 captured generals in the process, and accepted a cease-fire with the Eritreans and Tigreans so that a lasting solution could be negotiated. But the failure of the talks convinced the Eritreans to reopen their offensives, and by May 1991, EPLF and TPLF forces had captured much of Ethiopia, forced Mengistu into exile in Zimbabwe, and were closing in on the capital, Addis Ababa. On 27 May, the TPLF took over Ethiopia. Two years later, after a referendum, Eritrea formally proclaimed its independence.

Through the civil war, Mengistu's forces dealt with captured rebels in the way one might expect. They were held in prisons, either facilities dating from the Italian colonial period or newer detention centers like Expo, the commercial exhibition grounds in Asmara that had been converted to hold prisoners. Rebel captives were routinely tortured and executed in such numbers that one prison, in Addis Ababa, was known as Alem Bekagne, or the End of the World. Rebel forces, on the other hand, tended to be surprisingly lenient with their POWs. The Ethiopian government refused to recognize the existence of its soldiers in rebel hands, and the rebel armies, because they were not officially recognized, could not secure aid from the International Committee of the Red Cross (ICRC). As a solution, the EPLF allowed POWs to grow their own food, while at the same time subjecting them to re-education, which in some cases was successful in convincing the prisoners to defect. Still, the EPLF found itself with thousands of Ethiopian POWs on its hands, and was consistently frustrated in its efforts to repatriate them. In November 1983, it released 3,000 POWs but, because the Ethiopian government would not guarantee safe conduct and the ICRC would not provide aid, the men were simply released behind EPLF lines to do as they wished. As of 1985, the EPLF still held some 8,000 POWs, and the successful offensive of 1988 brought the total to over 100,000. With no other alternatives, the rebels began releasing POWs unilaterally, 10,000 in December 1989, 2,500 the following January, 8,000 more in May 1990, and over 30,000 in early 1991 (many of these soldiers, when they returned to Ethiopia, were either imprisoned or sent directly back into the army). After the Ethiopian capital fell to the Eritreans in May 1991, a further 86,000 POWs were freed, with the last 900 officers being released in July 1992.

As a memorial to executed Eritrean, Tigrean, and Oromo prisoners (estimates of the death toll run as high as 100,000), the notorious Maryam Ghimbi prison in Asmara was opened to the public between December 1991 and June 1992. Then, to erase the last physical traces of the abuses that had occurred there, it was pulled down to be used as a storage yard for municipal vehicles.

References

Tim Killion, *Historical Dictionary of Eritrea* (Lanham, MD: Scarecrow Press, 1998).

—*Jonathan F. Vance*

EXCHANGE

For hundreds of years, one of the few ways a prisoner could be freed before the conclusion of hostilities was through an exchange negotiated between the belligerent governments. During the eighteenth and nineteenth centuries, prisoner exchanges became the norm in international conflicts. Typically, exchange was tied to parole. Prisoners would be returned home on parole and would pledge not to participate in the war until they were officially exchanged. For example, one belligerent government might free 50 enemy prisoners on parole on the understanding that they would not perform military service. As soon as the opposing government freed 50 prisoners, all 100 could return to service. This was a pragmatic solution to the problem of housing and feeding large numbers of prisoners, and it only functioned as long as states were willing to rely on the honor system.

When a state was deceitful or unreliable, however, the process did not function. An attempt at exchange during the Napoleonic Wars, for example, came to nothing. Early efforts at negotiation were fruitless, but in 1810, with a huge increase in the number of POWs because of the Peninsular campaign, Britain and France elected to try again. The talks were complicated by the fact that most of the British prisoners were civilian internees, or *détenus*, but eventually an exchange rate was agreed upon that set out the military ranks to be exchanged for social ranks. For example, an imprisoned British peer of the realm was deemed to be equal to a French general or admiral, a baronet was equal to a commander, lieutenant colonel, or major, and so on. However, the agreement collapsed when Napoleon began attaching conditions, and exchange was not considered again until Napoleon proposed a mass exchange of all prisoners on all sides, in batches of 1,000 each. The British government duly dispatched the first batch, only to discover that the French had had a change of heart and no longer wished to participate in a mass trade. In the end, only about 40 British prisoners were exchanged during the conflict.

During the twentieth century, with the decline of the institution of parole, exchanges of able-bodied prisoners all but disappeared,

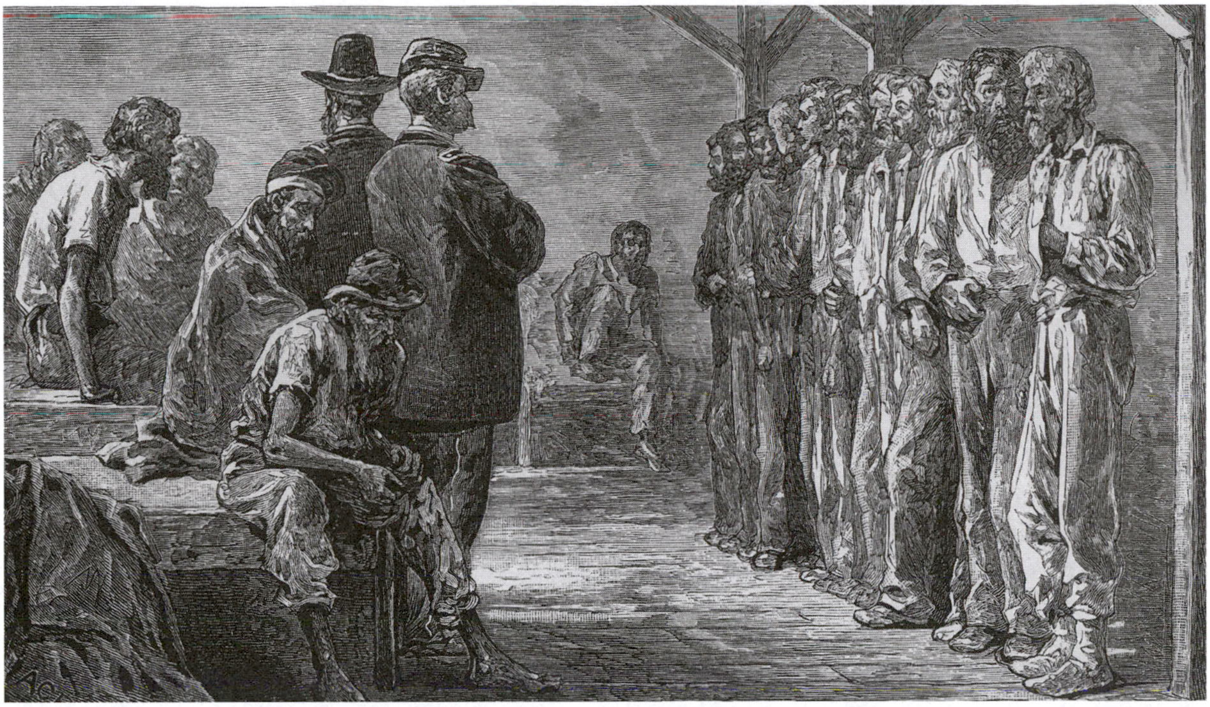

Sick POWs during the US Civil War being inspected for exchange (from R.R. Stevenson, The Southern Side, or Andersonville Prison *[Baltimore, 1876])*

to be replaced by the repatriation of the sick and wounded. Attempts to negotiate the exchange of interned civilians, however, did see some success, particularly in World War I. In October 1914, Germany and France agreed to exchange all women and all men older than 60 or younger than 16. This agreement was expanded two years later to cover males under 17 or over 55, an agreement that meant freedom for some 20,000 interned German civilians. Germany made similar advances to the British government, offering in August 1914 the exchange of all civilians on both sides. Because the offer would release 50,000 Germans in exchange for 5,000 Britons, it was declined, but Britain responded with a proposal to release all women and all men under 16 or over 46; military-age men could also be released if they gave their parole not to accept military service. The release of women and children went forward, but the provisions for males produced more dissent. Not until January 1917 did the two sides agree to exchange all men over the age of 45; this freed about 7,000 Germans and 700 Britons.

Successful exchanges were even more rare during World War II, for a variety of reasons. Early negotiations produced some small exchanges. For example, in 1941 a group of Canadian women who had been interned in France was released after the government gave assurances that Canada did not intern German women based on nationality alone, but only if they contravened the Defense of Canada Regulations. The following year, the government in Ottawa secured the release of another category of civilian internees, eight women from the Egyptian ship *Zam Zam*, which had been bound for South Africa with a complement of missionaries when it was sunk in the South Atlantic and its passengers interned. Two larger exchanges negotiated among Germany, Italy, and the United States, involving civilians and diplomatic personnel, brought home some 1,200 American civilians. Later in the war, a few civilians were added to the repatriation operations that brought home sick and wounded POWs, but there were no more general exchanges of civilians. This was largely because the major players could not agree on a formula for exchange. The United States wanted to repatriate all civilians, a policy that found favor with the German government, but Britain and the International Committee of the Red Cross believed that exchange should include only certain categories of civilians, such as women and children, men of nonmilitary age, doctors, and clerks. This inability to agree on principles made civilian exchanges more difficult to negotiate in the European theater.

Surprisingly, in light of the general treatment of POWs and internees by the Japanese, there was rather more success with exchanges in the Pacific theater. The governments of Japan and the United States were able to come to two agreements for the exchange of civilians. The first, in July 1942 at Lourenço Marques in Mozambique (Maputo), brought back to the United States 268 diplomatic officials and some 2,500 other civilians in exchange for a similar number of Japanese diplomats and interned civilians. A second exchange occurred in October 1943 at Mormugão in the Portuguese Indies, this one involving 1,340 Japanese (including 737 from Latin America) for about the same number of Americans, Canadians, and Latin Americans. A third civilian exchange was discussed in 1944, but the negotiations were fruitless. These were the last exchanges accomplished in the traditional mode, and in the post-1945 conflicts it has proven difficult enough to secure the release of POWs and internees at the conclusion of hostilities, let alone negotiate prisoner exchanges while conflicts are still in progress.

However, there have been some limited successes. During the Lebanese Civil War, the Israeli army was involved in operations in southern Lebanon, arresting many Lebanese and Palestinian fighters and losing some of their own soldiers as POWs in the process. So strong was Israel's determination to retrieve its soldiers that the government was willing to enter into what might appear to be lopsided exchanges. In March 1979, for example, one Israeli soldier who had been held captive for almost a year was exchanged for 76 Palestinian fighters. In November 1983, six Israeli soldiers taken prisoner at an outpost a year earlier were exchanged for 4,700 suspects held in the Ansar Detention Centre in Lebanon and another 65 who had been transferred to Israel. Another exchange, this time with Syria, occurred in June 1984, when three Israeli soldiers, three civilians, and the remains of five soldiers were traded for 291 Syrian soldiers, 13 civilians, and the remains of 74 Syrian soldiers. These operations suggest that, if the two sides can find sufficient community of interest, POW exchanges are still possible, even between bitter enemies.

See also Parole; Repatriation

References

Frances Ridgway Brotzen, "Marmagão Exchange," *Diplomacy and Statecraft* 14 (2003): 175–182.

P. Scott Corbett, *Quiet Passages: The Exchange of Civilians between the United States and Japan during the Second World War* (Kent, OH: Kent State University Press, 1987).

Bruce Elleman, *Japanese-American Detention Camps and Prisoner Exchanges During World War II* (New York: Routledge, 2005).

Kent Fedorowich, "Doomed from the Outset? - Internment and Civilian Exchange in the Far East: The British Failure Over Hong Kong," *Journal of Imperial and Commonwealth History* 25 (1997): 113–140.

Michael Lewis, *Napoleon and His British Captives* (London: George Allen and Unwin, 1962).

Eugene Nadeau, *La perle au fond du gouffre:* Zam Zam *et barbelés* (Montreal: Fides, 1963).

Jonathan F. Vance, "The Trouble with Allies: Canada and the Negotiation of Prisoner of War Exchanges," in *Prisoners of War and Their Captors in World War II*, ed. Bob Moore and Kent Fedorowich (Oxford: Berg, 1996).

—Jonathan F. Vance

EXTERMINATION CAMPS

To accomplish the elimination of Europe's Jews, the Nazi state created a number of special camps, known as extermination or death camps, to serve as factories of death. These were distinct from concentration camps, which were not designed primarily for mass killings. Having found that shooting their victims was too slow and required too much manpower, the Nazis experimented with poison gas, carrying out the first tests on 600 Russian prisoners of war at Auschwitz on 3 September 1941. This method of killing, in which victims were led into what they believed was a shower room but was in fact a gas chamber, was eventually employed almost exclusively at the extermination camps. So, too, was the practice of cremating the bodies of victims in specially designed ovens.

The first death camp to open was at Chełmno (Kulmhof), near Lódz in north-central Poland on 8 December 1941. It operated until April 1943, when it closed temporarily, to reopen for a short time in the summer of 1944. Roughly 320,000 people were murdered at Chełmno in gas vans, in which a truck's engine exhaust was funneled into the sealed cargo area of the truck, where the victims had been placed. Chełmno was followed by Auschwitz, Belzec (where some 600,000 Jews were killed between March and December 1942), Sobibór (which operated from April 1942 to October 1943 and killed some 250,000 Jews), and Treblinka (where 870,000 Jews were killed between July 1942 and August 1943). Gross-Rosen, in western Poland, and Majdanek, in eastern Poland, were also used as extermination camps at various times.

Despite the appalling conditions at these camps, the inmates were able to mount resistance. On 2 August 1943, a mass escape occurred at Treblinka; it was followed by a similar revolt at Sobibór on 14 October. A year later, on 7 October 1944, Jewish slave workers at Auschwitz rose against their captors; most of them died in the uprising.

The extermination camps were operated by the SS, through the same office that administered the concentration camps. After the war, the perpetrators were called to justice in dozens of separate trials, and the legal pursuit of death camp guards continues to this day.

See also Auschwitz; Bergen-Belsen; Buchenwald; Concentration Camps; Dachau

—Jonathan F. Vance

F

Falklands War (1982)

The Falklands (or Malvinas) War occurred from April to June 1982, pitting Britain against Argentina for control of an isolated group of islands that few people outside of the south Atlantic region had ever heard of.

At 4:30 a.m. on 2 April 1982, 60 men of the Argentine special forces landed by helicopter near the Falklands capital, Port Stanley. The long years of negotiation between the British and Argentine governments with regard to the sovereignty of the Falkland Islands and the frantic efforts to broker a last-minute peace deal had failed, and Argentina had resorted to the military option. Barely two months later, on 14 June 1982, the final surrender document was signed and hostilities came to an end after a campaign in which the British fought and won a war against a numerically superior enemy 8,000 miles from their home bases. The cost was 255 British and 750 Argentine dead.

The initial invasion of the islands resulted in the capture of the British forces defending Port Stanley. An 80-man Royal Marine unit resisted as best as it could, but, facing some 700 Argentine troops, defeat was inevitable. To avoid needless bloodshed, the marines surrendered. They were treated with great respect and transported to Bahía Blanca naval base, where they were landed on 13 April. After being interviewed by a tribunal of senior naval officers, on 16 April they were flown to Uruguay and handed over to British authorities. This was the only significant group of prisoners captured by the Argentine forces, and all of them returned to fight during the conflict as Company J, attached to 42 Commando. The only other British prisoner taken during the conflict was Flight Lieutenant Jeff Glover, whose helicopter was downed on 21 May 1982. His injuries were treated carefully at an Argentine hospital, but he was kept in virtual solitary confinement, not realizing that he was the only POW in Argentina. He was, however, visited by a delegate of the International Committee of the Red Cross (ICRC), who provided books and writing material. Glover was taken to Montevideo in Uruguay and released on 8 July.

The battles for the recapture of the Falkland Islands were a series of hard-fought actions that saw individual battalion assaults on key objectives as well as skirmishes between special forces. In conditions of freezing winds, snow, rain, and mud, the opposing forces fought each other for control of the high ground and strategic points around Port Stanley. Once British troops occupied that ground, the Argentine commander, General Mario Menendez, had little option but to capitulate. The fighting came to an end, and 12,978 Argentine soldiers surrendered.

I remember vividly my first sight of a live Argentine soldier. Having been in combat all night, I was exhausted, cold, wet, and a little in shock from the events of the last 14 hours of fighting. The platoon was sitting in a large semicircle in the lee of a large rocky outcrop to keep out of the wind and snow. The smell of battle was still strong despite the wind, and we were all covered in filth from the fighting. I looked to my right and saw a group of enemy soldiers being escorted off the battlefield. Suddenly two prisoners were carried to where we were sitting and unceremoniously dumped on the ground. They looked very scared and seemed to be in a lot of pain due to crudely bandaged leg wounds. They lay there avoiding eye contact, a very sorry sight. We all just stared for what seemed to be an eternity. Then with hardly a word being said, some of our boys got up and walked over to the prisoners and asked them if they were all right. Minutes earlier we were killing them; now we fell over ourselves trying to make them comfortable with a sleeping bag, hot tea, cigarettes, and a helmet under each of their heads.

Many of the prisoners were in poor physical condition due to the terrible field conditions, shortage of food, and injuries. There was simply nowhere to put them, as the only tents that the British had sent to the Falklands had gone down when a supply ship was sunk. Some 8,000 prisoners were moved to the area around the airport at Port Stanley, where they could easily be watched, and efforts were made to improvise shelter. However, there was no provision for such a large number of prisoners, and it became a top priority to repatriate them as quickly as possible. Two days after the fighting ended, 4,167 prisoners were taken onto the liner *Canberra*, and on 19 June they were disembarked at the Argentine port of Puerto Madryn. On 21 June, another ship returned an additional 2,047 prisoners. Most of the remaining prisoners were repatriated on Argentine ships. It is ironic that the defeated arrived home earlier than the victors, who had to wait another three weeks before they began the journey home.

One group remained on the islands: 593 prisoners who were being held at Ajax Bay, living in primitive conditions inside a bomb-damaged refrigeration plant. This group, which consisted of General Menendez, pilots, officers, and other specialist troops, were known as Special Category prisoners. They were considered to be key personnel who would not be released until the Argentines had formally recognized that hostilities were at an end. This detention was legally questionable, as Article 118 of the Geneva Convention states that POWs must be "repatriated without delay after the cessation of active hostilities."

The prisoners were kept in five large rooms, one for officers, one for senior NCOs, and three for the *chicos*, the other ranks. The groups were kept apart, as they didn't like each other very much. The officers were very correct in their manner, disciplined and quiet. They said Mass regularly and sat in small groups and chatted. The NCOs were very sullen and withdrawn; as their room was off to one side, we had little contact with them. The other ranks were noisy and happy that the war had ended. They made ingenious things out of old tin cans and bits of rubbish. One group that sat by the main guard post had quite a decent chess set. We didn't have a Spanish speaker among us, so one of the Argentine conscripts, known as George, volunteered to translate. He had a lot of fun, as he was responsible for choosing the ever popular fatigue parties. Three ICRC delegates visited to inspect camp conditions, and they were very upset with the lack of showers and demanded that we provide washing facilities. The fact that even our men didn't have access to washing facilities didn't seem to matter, so British engineers placed a plastic water bowser on top of an old shed and diverted an icy stream into it. Then four Scots Guards with hard brooms were positioned around the shed while groups of naked prisoners were marched across the snow in subzero temperatures and given a cold shower and scrubbed with the brooms. The Geneva Convention doesn't mention that the water had to be hot. I must say the Red Cross was not very popular after that.

On 30 June, the remaining Argentine prisoners were transferred to the MV *St. Edmund*, and on 13 July they finally set sail for home.

References

Nicholas van der Bijl, *Nine Battles to Stanley* (London: Leo Cooper, 1999).

Michael Bilton and Peter Kosminsky, eds., *Speaking Out: Untold Stories from the Falklands War* (London: Andre Deutsch, 1989).

David Brown, *The Royal Navy and the Falklands War* (London: Leo Cooper, 1987).

Martin Middlebrook, *Task Force* (Harmondsworth, UK: Penguin, 1987).

Derek Oakley, *The Falklands Military Machine* (New York: State Mutual, 1991).

—*Steve Cocks*

FAMILIES

The ripple effects of war captivity are felt far beyond the field of battle and the prison camp. The families of prisoners of war undergo an experience that can be as difficult as that of the prisoners, who at least have each other for support. Families adjust three separate times, first to the separation, then to the absence, and then, for the lucky ones, to the return. The hardships, both emotional and material, follow a series of phases.

By far the most traumatic phase is the period from capture to notification. Once captured, soldiers usually cannot directly contact their families and must depend on an agency like the International Committee of the Red Cross to notify next of kin. Families thus totally lose contact with their soldiers, going for weeks, even months, without knowing whether their loved ones are alive or dead. Once contact has been established, families often experience a brief period of hope for a rapid return, then establish an equilibrium, adjusting to the separation and maintaining contact through letters and packages. However, the censorship of mail and the inspection of packages allow for little privacy or intimacy. Many families find ways to disguise messages, using code words or hiding secret notes and materials, if not to provide escape information, then at least to maintain some privacy.

Family life at home presents a series of challenges to all members of a POW's family—parents, spouses, and children. Perhaps the greatest strain is on spouses, who become single heads of households under very difficult circumstances. In many cases, governments assist families by replacing part of the prisoner's income, but the amounts usually do not equal the contribution of this person, who often had been the family's primary breadwinner. Spouses who did not work outside the home before the captivity often will be forced to do so, or to take over a family business or farm alone. Those families living in a war zone are also alone in facing the material hardships: rationing, shortages, and threats like air raids and combat. Wives (and, more recently, husbands) with children carry the additional burden of single parenthood, which requires greater material resources and thus very often necessitates work outside the home and also means handling all the responsibilities related to caring for, disciplining, and making school/occupational decisions for their children with little input from their spouses.

Depending on their age, the children of a prisoner may suffer the same set of traumas, without much understanding of why their parent is gone and what it means to be a POW. Adults in the family must explain the prisoner's status to the children and facilitate communication between the absent prisoner and the children, encouraging children to write letters or contribute to care packages. Older children have a better understanding of the situation but may have a harder time readjusting to the prisoner's return.

Not much is known about the challenges facing the husbands of POWs, but it is clear that social attitudes about the families of prisoners of war, and particularly about their wives, have often made life more difficult rather than less difficult. Because of a simple lack of understanding of the special difficulties prisoners' families face, prisoners' wives in some cases face suspicion and mistrust. Their ambiguous status as both married and alone sets them apart from both married couples and single people. Prisoners' wives have reported being shunned by couples they had socialized with before the war, who see them as "on the prowl" for a man, and those with children have felt treated like unwed mothers.

In response to the public's lack of sympathy, families and wives have created mutual support groups on both local and national levels. For example, in World War II France, a national Federation of Prisoners' Wives formed out of an assortment of local groups that had developed independently. Seeking mutual assistance and moral support from each other, POW family groups often get involved in politics, lobbying the

This French illustration, from a prison camp newspaper in World War II, was used to illustrate the stresses caused by separation from family (Sarah Fishman)

local and even national authorities about issues of concern to them and their imprisoned loved ones.

The final phase for prisoners' families follows the prisoners' return. Most families, in adjusting to survival without the prisoner, have created new routines and carved out new roles during the absence. After the return, the family must to readjust to the prisoner's renewed presence and recreate a place for the prisoner. There are psychological challenges for both the prisoner and the family. Depending on the length of captivity, the prisoner is likely to have become somewhat of a stranger, especially to younger children. In addition, the prisoner himself (or herself) also often suffers emotional and physical repercussions of captivity that complicate readjustment to civilian and family life. Social, economic, and political changes that have taken place during the prisoner's captivity mean returning to a homeland quite different from the one remembered or idealized in prison camp. Some prisoners receive a hero's welcome on their return, but not all. Prisoners of war are captured soldiers, and some societies hold capture to be dishonorable. For instance, prisoners of war were tainted by France's humiliating defeat of June 1940, an attitude the returning prisoners bitterly resented. Thus, for families, the initial excitement of a prisoner's return is often followed by a difficult period of reacquaintance and readjustment.

The incidence of family breakdown owing to captivity has varied from war to war. A number of factors influence the divorce rate, including the length of captivity, the general social atmosphere after the return, and attitudes toward divorce. After World War II, with heavy social stigma attached to divorce and patriarchal norms dictating that wives subordinate their own needs and make every possible effort to help their husbands readjust to ensure a successful reunion, most families stayed together. In post-World War II France, it is estimated that about 10 percent of the couples divorced. In contrast, divorce rates were relatively high after Vietnam. Many U.S. POWs in Vietnam remained captive for a very long period of time. Their absence from the late 1960s through the early 1970s coincided with an era of rapid social change, and the civil rights, antiwar, and women's liberation movements together with a rebellious youth counterculture transformed American society. The soldiers returned to a very different society, with reduced stigma for divorce and changed ideas about appropriate roles for wives and mothers. Within five years of their return, nearly one-third of their marriages had ended in divorce.

See also Camp Followers; Rehabilitation

References

Sarah Fishman, "Waiting for the Captive Sons of France," in *Behind the Lines: Gender and the Two World Wars*, ed. Margaret Higonnet et al (New Haven, CT: Yale University Press, 1987).

———, *We Will Wait: Wives of French Prisoners of War 1940–1945* (New Haven, CT: Yale University Press, 1991).

Reubin Hill and Elise Boulding, *Families Under Stress: Adjustment to the Crises of War Separation and Reunion* (New York: Harper Brothers, 1949).

Edna Hunter, "Treating the Military Captive's Family," in *The Military Family: Dynamics and Treatment*, ed. F. Kaslow and R. Ridenour (New York: Guilford, 1984).

Aphrodite Matsakis, *Vietnam Wives: Women and Children Surviving Life with Veterans Suffering Post Traumatic Stress Disorder* (Kensington, MD: Woodbine House, 1988).

Julius Segal et al, "Universal Consequences of Captivity: Stress Reactions among Divergent Populations of Prisoners of War and Their Families," *International Social Science Journal* 28 (1976): 594–597.

Jonathan F. Vance, "Canadian Relief Agencies and Prisoners of War, 1939–45," *Journal of Canadian Studies* 30 (1996): 133–147.

—*Sarah Fishman*

Featherston Incident

Like a similar outbreak of violence at Cowra, Australia, the incident at Camp Featherston, New Zealand, was an example of active resistance carried out by Japanese POWs against their captors during World War II. Camp Featherston was opened in September 1942 to house Japanese prisoners captured at Guadalcanal, and by early 1943, it held just over 800 POWs: roughly 500 members of a labor force, many from minority groups such as Japanese of Korean descent; and nearly 300 NCOs and other ranks from the Imperial Japanese Navy. Soon after the camp received its first inmates, the naval prisoners began to mount various forms of passive and active resistance against the camp staff, particularly by refusing to complete work assignments. The situation came to a head on 25 February 1943, when the senior Japanese NCO refused to supply a work detachment, demanding instead that the camp commandant address a series of demands. The adjutant, a New Zealand army officer, summoned reinforcements from the guard company and attempted to remove from the naval compound two Japanese officers, whom the camp staff believed were inciting the resistance. Negotiations continued for well over an hour, until the adjutant fired a warning shot over the heads of the prisoners. The POWs responded with a barrage of stones, whereupon the adjutant fired again, wounding one of the Japanese officers. A large group of prisoners, perhaps as many as 250, immediately rushed the adjutant and the 40-man guard company in the compound. The guards opened fire, and 48 prisoners were killed and 63 wounded.

According to historian Charlotte Carr-Gregg, the Japanese resistance probably stemmed from a belief that the work assignments merely compounded the guilt the prisoners felt at being POWs; they may not have understood that those assignments were perfectly legitimate under international law, fearing instead that the New Zealand authorities were only trying to humiliate them. For their part, the camp staff probably did not appreciate the Japanese perceptions of the stigma of captivity or their imperfect knowledge of the 1929 Geneva Convention Relative to the Treatment of Prisoners of War. In the final reckoning, the Featherston incident is perhaps best interpreted as a manifestation of cultural differences with respect to attitudes toward captivity.

See also Cowra Incident; World War II—Far East

References
Charlotte Carr-Gregg, *Japanese Prisoners of War in Revolt: The Outbreaks at Featherston and Cowra during World War II* (New York: St. Martin's Press, 1978).

—*Jonathan F. Vance*

FILM

For many years representations of POWs and their circumstances have been staples of both films and television. The stories in both media have typically treated the reality of POW life in a somewhat cavalier fashion, at times presenting more or less completely implausible plots and situations. Hence historical inadequacies in such media depictions are inevitable, but so too is the recognition that historical dramatizations tend to be more reflective of the values and assumptions of the times in which they were produced—and where—than the events they purport to chronicle.

The POW genre had a meager beginning. As with most early cinema, the stories were typically melodramas showing strong affection, if not romantic love, between opposites. *The Splendid Sinner* (1918) is one of the earliest known examples, with a propagandist spin, in which an America woman must choose between the love of the German POW who deserted her before the war, and the love of her country. Similarly *Barbed Wire* (1927), based on the 1923 war novel *The Woman of Knockaloe* by Sir Thomas Henry Hall Caine, follows the story of a French farm girl who falls in love with a German POW. But these films were soon eclipsed by the release of *Grand Illusion* (1936). Its title is cryptic, but its purpose was clear. With Nazi Germany on the road to war and anti-war sentiments high elsewhere, Jean Renoir had hoped his film—about WWI POWs and their disparate class differences—could express his deep feelings for the cause of peace and perhaps prevent war. In retrospect, it seems that the "grand illusion" was held by the film-maker who thought that a work of art could change the world.

After World War II the melodramatic and anti-war POW films gave way to exciting, "based-on-a-true-story" escape films where clever Allied prisoners outsmart and mock their not-so-smart captors. *The Wooden Horse* (1950), based on an actual 1943 escape, shows how three British POWs made their exit through a wooden vaulting horse. In *Stalag 17* (1953) the prisoners pass the time pulling pranks on their dim-witted guards. More humor is evident in the escape adventure *The Colditz Story* (1955), derived from the personal experiences of Major P.R. Reid (the 1970s introduced a grimmer version of events through the BBC television series *Colditz*). Similar is *The Password is Courage* (1962), which gleefully capitalizes on the bizarre adventures of British POW Charles Coward, notably when he was unwittingly awarded the Iron Cross by a German officer (the only Allied soldier ever to receive such an honor). *The Great Escape* (1963), however, was the most popular of them all. Rich with action and adventure, stars and charm, the film is pure entertainment. As with most of these films, the milieu is more akin to a boarding school than a POW camp. The spartan conditions, clean clothes, and well-fed faces trivialize what was really a horrible and degrading experience. But such soft depiction was typical of mid-twentieth-century cinema and, with its uplifting "true" story of escape from submission, it is understandable why even cynics still love this film. *Von Ryan's Express* (1965) was an exciting, though purely fictional, adventure that became the last in this chapter of the genre. In the wake of *The Great Escape*, the escape genre arguably peaked. The POW setting eventually evolved into pure comedy via the popular television series *Hogan's Heroes* (1965-71). With its cozy and fun-filled atmosphere, it was easy to imagine why these sitcom prisoners never wanted to escape.

The first major POW film set in the Pacific theater of operations, *The Bridge on the River Kwai* (1957) was a huge success with fans and critics. Winner of multiple awards, it is still considered one of the greatest films ever made. Unlike the escape subgenre, there is little to laugh about in Far East prison camps. Because escape usually meant sure death in the jungle, the stories tended to be about co-operation and survival, instead of resistance. In *King Rat* (1965) the title character tries to live more comfortably by bribing the guards. The under-rated *Merry Christmas, Mr. Lawrence* (1983), a Japanese/British co-production, even suggests homosexual interest between the Japanese commandant and a British POW. *Captive Hearts* (1987) harks back to the "forbidden love" stories that started the genre, with a cliché-ridden story of an American prisoner falling in love with a Japanese woman. The only significant dramatization of the plight of Japanese POWs appears in the Australian mini-series *Cowra Breakout* (1984). Dramatizing the August 1944 escape from the Australian camp in Cowra, the sorrow of their death and capture is maximized. Another Australian-specific focus is evident in *Prisoners of the Sun* (1990), based on the Laha massacre of Australian and Dutch POWs on Ambon Island in WWII, which deals with its grisly subject matter by focusing on the post-war trial of the Japanese officials responsible.

Notable films about German POWs include *The One That Got Away* (1957), based on the true story of the only German to escape successfully from an Allied prison camp in World War II. *McKenzie Break* (1970), based on the novel by Sidney Shelley, follows the daring escape of 600 German POWs from a camp in Scotland. Forbidden romance returned in the made-for-TV production of *The Summer of My German Soldier* (1978) starring Kristy McNichol. Based on a Betty Greene novel, McNichol is a Jewish girl in Georgia who falls in love with an escaped German POW. Another look at complicated relationships is found in *The Brylcreem Boys* (1996). Set in neutral Ireland, it dramatizes the true circumstance of Allied and German prisoners being detained in the same camp.

POW stories set during the Korean War are rare, but they all share a common obsession. During the Red Scare of the 1950s, and immediately following the war, *The Bamboo Prison* (1955) and *Prisoner of War* (1954), starring Ronald Reagan, reinforced communist paranoia with their tales of brainwashing. *The Manchurian Candidate* (1962) also exploits the brainwashing element but it is less about POWs and the trauma of captivity, than it is a taut thriller and political satire of its possible, though fantastical, consequence. Re-released in 1987, during the Reagan era, its communist threat elements were still timely.

Films that focus on the return from captivity make up a minor sub-genre. *The Captive Heart* (1946), though mostly set in a POW camp, was more a story of impossible love, ending in an emotional homecoming. *The Forgotten Man* (1971) is a made-for-TV film about a Vietnam POW who returns home to find out that the life he once had no longer exists. His business is gone, his family scattered, and his wife has remarried. *Rolling Thunder* (1977) follows the same premise but adds a violent, vengeful twist. The bitter Vietnam vet character eventually became an American icon in the 1980s beginning with *First Blood* (1982), based on the novel by David Morrell. The film was originally to end with the death of former POW John Rambo, but instead of a fitting conclusion to a story about injustice in a country ashamed of its vets, the film saved its character and sparked a new genre of films about "finishing the job."

Uncommon Valor (1983) was the first film to deal in earnest with the subject of MIAs (soldiers who had been posted as missing in action). But, as with most examples of this genre, the POWs became mostly nameless extras, the stories emphasized cartoon action, and the villains were typically heinous communists. They fit perfectly in an era when Reagan was warning of totalitarianism and an evil empire. *Missing in Action* (1984), followed by *Missing in Action 2* (1985), and the most famous of MIA films, *Rambo: First Blood, Part 2* (1985), did little except sabotage legitimate efforts to locate actual MIAs and ensure their release. Outside of this genre the only films to deal exclusively with POWs in Vietnam were *The Hanoi Hilton* (1987) and *When Hell Was in Session* (1979), based on the book by Jeremiah Denton and Ed Brandt. In *When Hell Was in Session* Hal Holbrook plays Jeremiah Denton, Jr., who tried to organize a resistance movement during his eight years as a POW. The film concludes with a recreation of his famous homecoming in 1973.

As screen violence became more prevalent after the 1960s, film portrayals of POWs also became more graphic. *The Deer Hunter* (1978) was the first to fully exploit the deadly potential of this circumstance. Though the Russian Roulette scenes are often dismissed because they lack historical credence, there is little denying the disturbing quality of the first such scene in a POW camp. Even more graphic is the POW camp scene in *Bullet in the Head* (1990). Made in Hong Kong by director John Woo, and filled with many of his usual flamboyant action scenes, the POW sequence depicts extensive scenes of brutal violence such as random executions. Like *The Deer Hunter,* the scene is pure fiction yet its impact arguably falls closer to the realm of realism compared with earlier based-on-a-true-story tales.

Gritty portrayals of POWs is also evident in the made-for-TV *Andersonville* (1996) based on the famous U.S. Civil War camp. Polish Television produced the melodramatic *Bride of War* (1997) from the autobiographical story of Welsh POW John Elwyn who secretly married a Polish girl in a Nazi labor camp in 1941. The Russian film *Prisoner of the Mountains* (1996), though set during contemporary times, is based on Leo Tolstoy's nineteenth century story entitled *The Prisoner of the Caucasus.* The story of two Russian POWs in the custody of a Muslim captor mostly stresses the cultural divide between the opposing parties, a divide so old that 100 years since Tolstoy wrote the story, little has changed.

The release of *Three Kings* (1999) became the first example of Gulf War POWs, though only as a minor subplot. Similarly the POW experience in *Black Hawk Down* (2001)—a dramatization of the deadly conflict between U.S. Rangers and Somali civilians in the city of Mogadishu in 1993—is not a major plot element but, as with *Prisoner of the Mountains* and *Three Kings,* it allows for a dialogue between both sides of the conflict that strives to bridge their cultural differences.

The made-for-TV movie *Saving Jessica Lynch* (2003), inspired by the dramatic rescue of an army supply clerk from an Iraqi hospital that same year, is largely viewed as more fiction than fact, but it remains a rare

POW chronicle of an ongoing conflict. Coincidentally, *The Great Raid* (2005) was another movie being produced that year that also dealt with the military rescue of POWs, though it wasn't released for another two years. This time the inspiration was the 1945 raid on the Cabanatuan Japanese POW camp, which resulted in the liberation of more than 500 prisoners.

Altogether these dramatized tales cover a wide range of tones and a varying dedication to historical accuracy, mostly because the expectations and tolerances of audiences have changed over the years. Modern viewers are more likely to reject melodramatic perspectives, as typified by early cinema, and embrace greater ambiguity and gritty reality, as evidenced by more recent films. In addition, as a medium dedicated to entertaining its audience, it is perhaps inevitable that liberties with the facts are necessary. But, as with most historical drama, this has been a factor throughout film history.

See also The Bridge on the River Kwai; The Captive Heart; The Colditz Story; Grand Illusion; The Great Escape; King Rat; The Manchurian Candidate; Merry Christmas, Mr. Lawrence; Prisoners of the Sun; Slaughterhouse Five; Stalag 17; Von Ryan's Express.

—*Darryl Wiggers*

FOOD

See Rations

FORCIBLE REPATRIATION

The question of whether released prisoners of war and internees should be forcibly returned to their homelands after the conclusion of hostilities has bedeviled legislators through the twentieth century. How does one balance the right of a POW or refugee who desires repatriation with the equally fundamental right of another to choose asylum? In a century dominated by global wars, internal upheaval, and the displacement of vast populations, this question remains contentious. Yet the body of international humanitarian law continues to say surprisingly little about the obligation of detaining states to repatriate or the rights of civilians and especially POWs to choose asylum. During the American Civil War, the Union armies recognized that southern slaves captured while serving in Confederate uniform had a right to seek asylum in the north. But throughout the twentieth century, no such escape clause for POWs preferring asylum to repatriation has existed in international law.

According to the 1907 Hague Convention (Article 20), repatriation was to be carried out "as quickly as possible after the conclusion of peace." Those governments that signed this agreement assumed that a peace treaty would be concluded soon after hostilities ended and that repatriation would follow, but that did not happen after World War I. Article 75 of the 1929 Geneva Convention, therefore, insisted that repatriation take place "with the least possible delay" after the de facto end of hostilities, even in the absence of a formal treaty. The unconditional surrender of Germany and Japan in 1945 and the prolonged detention of millions of POWs as Allied reparations laborers demonstrated the need for further revision. So Article 118 of the 1949 Geneva Convention Relative to the Treatment of Prisoners of War insisted that release and repatriation be carried out "without delay after the cessation of active hostilities," even unilaterally if necessary.

None of these clauses included provisions for POWs who might prefer asylum. If anything, each successive change in the wording of the relevant clauses hastened the pace of repatriation and tightened the requirement to include all without exception. It was simply assumed that most captives would desire to return to their state of origin after hostilities ended. Negotiators for the 1949 Geneva Convention did consider an amendment to guarantee asylum to POWs who requested it, but most states were reluctant to obligate themselves to grant asylum in a future war, or they assumed that it would be granted when necessary and need not be formally entrenched. Delegates were also unwilling to leave an escape clause that might allow an unscrupulous detaining power to delay or prevent the repatriation of POWs in its custody. In essence, the rights of the minority who might seek asylum were sacrificed in favor of a tightly worded clause intended to better protect the rights of the majority who wanted to return. The issue was ignored again in the Geneva Convention Additional Protocols of 1977.

State practice has been equally inconsistent. At the end of World War I, the western powers prohibited Germany from forcibly repatriating Russian POWs or White Russian refugees unwilling to return to their state of origin. Although humanitarian considerations were employed as a rationale, the real motive for postponing repatriation and granting asylum was the desire of these states to prevent reinforcement of the Bolshevik armies.

After World War II the situation was different. Nearly one million Soviet nationals served in German uniform during the war, and millions more were taken to Germany as POWs or slave laborers. The British began to segregate and forcibly repatriate them to the Soviet Union as early as August 1944, but American authorities initially refused to do the same, arguing that they could not ignore the POW status and Geneva Convention protection of Soviet nationals captured in German uniform. But they assured Stalin that once the war ended and the fear of retaliation against their own POWs passed, all claimants to Soviet nationality would be repatriated, even against their will.

The repatriation accords concluded at the Yalta conference in February 1945 and a agreement in Halle in May formalized this policy. As soon as the war ended, fear of German retaliation passed, and a legal carte blanche over Germany was assumed by the Allied governments. Soviet nationals were segregated, and repatriation operations commenced. British and American officials were determined to rid themselves of a terrible humanitarian and administrative burden. Soviet nationals, along with humanitarian and legal considerations, were sacrificed on the altar of friendly postwar relations as the western Allies sought to strictly fulfill all covenants with Stalin. Most individuals who were subjected to forcible repatriation had been captured in German uniform. Some committed suicide rather than return, while the remainder were handed over to Soviet custody and executed outright or sentenced to long terms in the Gulag.

Only a few years later, the western position on repatriation was reversed again during the Korean War. When the armistice talks began in 1952, almost half of the 132,000 Chinese and North Korean POWs held by United Nations forces were expected to oppose repatriation. U.S. officials, led by President Harry S Truman, feared that a repeat of the postwar repatriation operations would harm the psychological warfare strategy of the United States. They now wanted to be seen as the standard-bearer of individual rights and humanitarianism in a global struggle against Communism, and so they permitted the peace negotiations to be stalemated for 15 months over their refusal to conduct forcible repatriation operations.

The communists actually had a more convincing legal case, arguing that Article 118 of the 1949 Geneva Convention obligated a detaining power to repatriate any and all POWs in its care as soon as possible after the cessation of hostilities and without exception. But in December 1952, the UN General Assembly voted overwhelmingly in favor of a resolution that emphasized the refugee provisions over the POW provisions of the 1949 Geneva Convention. It eschewed forcible repatriation, promising that "no violence to their dignity or self-respect shall be permitted in any manner or for any purpose whatsoever." Although this resolution had no legal standing, its passage demonstrated the international consensus that had developed in favor of a more humanitarian interpretation of repatriation obligations. The logjam in the Korean truce negotiations broke during the spring of 1953, and a Neutral Nations Repatriation Commission ensured that POWs on both sides were given the choice of asylum or repatriation when they were released later that summer.

Similar disputes emerged during the India-Pakistan and Vietnam Wars, as well as in the wake of the Gulf War, when thousands of Iraqi POWs were granted political asylum. The processing and screening of Iraqi POWs during 1991 was even modeled on the Korean precedent and demonstrated that human rights and asylum laws—which had continually evolved since passage of the Universal Declaration of Human Rights of 1948—are being taken more seriously into account when dealing with POW issues.

See also Liberation

References

Jan P. Charmatz and Harold M. Witt, "Repatriation of Prisoners of War and the 1949 Geneva Convention," *Yale Law Journal* 62 (1952–1953): 391–415.

Christiane Shields Delessert, *Release and Repatriation of Prisoners of War at the End of Active Hostilities: A Study of Article 118, Paragraph 1 of the Third Geneva Convention Relative to the Treatment of Prisoners of War* (Zurich: Schulthess Polygraphischer Verlag, 1977).

Mark R. Elliott, *Pawns of Yalta: Soviet Refugees and America's Role in Their Repatriation* (Urbana: University of Illinois Press, 1982).

Manuel R. Garcia-Mora, *International Law and Asylum as a Human Right* (Washington, DC: Public Affairs Press, 1956).

Jaro Mayda, "The Korean Repatriation Problem and International Law," *American Journal of International Law* 47 (1953): 414–438.

—*Richard D. Wiggers*

FRANCO-PRUSSIAN WAR (1870–1871)

The Franco-Prussian War, the last of the wars of German unification, led to the foundation of the German empire and constituted a turning point in the history of captivity in wartime. It combined practices typical of *ancien régime* warfare, characterized by feudal arrangements, with features of modern warfare involving masses of soldiers and captives that would characterize the great wars of the twentieth century.

Right from the beginning of the war in August 1870, events went against the imperial French army, which was poorly led and hit hard by epidemics, particularly in fortresses. Both the fortresses of Sedan and Metz housed huge armies that surrendered after few weeks of combat and siege: Sedan on 2 September 1870 with some 100,000 soldiers and Metz on 27 October with 173,000 soldiers. These big catches in the early stage not only determined, to a large extent, the outcome of the war, but in the immediate term created problems in transportation and accommodation for the German states. The officers captured at Sedan were released and sent home upon giving their word of honor not to fight again in that war. Under a similarly feudal arrangement, France's most prominent war captive, the emperor Napoleon III, was interned in Wilhelmshöhe Castle near Kassel in the state of Hesse.

Germans in French detention numbered some 8,000 over the course of the war, while there were about 724,000 French prisoners. Roughly half of the French prisoners were interned in the German states until a few weeks after the peace treaty of May 1871. Some 372,000 rank and file and 11,860 officers were shipped to makeshift camps, mostly fortresses, barracks, and other military establishments, in Germany. There they spent the winter and spring of 1871. The German military administration took care of them as best they could, and most of the captives enjoyed relative freedom. Besides homesickness and boredom, they complained to visiting care committees from the French, German, or International Red Cross about the lack of white bread and red wine in their diet. Though epidemics did occur, the death toll among French captives was tolerably low, below four percent. Local German commanders tried to encourage the use of POWs as a labor force, but this was resisted by industry; this resistance, combined with the short duration of captivity and the fact that it spanned the winter season, meant that POWs were rarely put to work. French prisoners captured in the final stage of the campaign, like the 250,000-man garrison of Paris, were no longer shipped to Germany, but were interned in France.

This war mixed practices originating in feudal times, such as the release of captive officers in exchange for their word of honor not to escape, with new phenomena, like volunteer irregulars, or *franc-tireurs*. Furthermore, the mass of prisoners taken by Germany brought an unprecedented logistical challenge that foreshadowed the wars to come. At the same time, humanitarian arrangements between the powers began to have an impact on the lives of prisoners. The experience of the Franco-Prussian War, in which prisoners benefited from organized medical and Red Cross services, contributed to the emergence of the codification of prisoner of war treatment in the Hague Conventions of 1899 and 1907.

References
Manfred Botzenhart, "French Prisoners of War in Germany 1870–71," in *On the Road to Total War: The American Civil War and the German Wars of Unification, 1861–1871*, ed. Stig Förster and Jörg Nagler (Cambridge: Cambridge University Press, 1997).

—*Reinhard Nachtigal*

FRANK, ANNE (1929–1945)

Arguably the most famous inmate of the Nazi concentration camps of World War II, Anne Frank was born in Frankfurt-am-Main, Germany, on 12 June 1929, the second daughter of a successful businessman. In March 1933, when Nazi candidates won seats on Frankfurt's municipal council and anti-Semitic demonstrations quickly followed, Otto Frank decided that the family might no longer be safe in Germany. He received an offer to open a business in the Netherlands, and in February 1934 moved his family to a suburb of Amsterdam.

After the Germans invaded the Netherlands in May 1940, restrictions against Jews were soon implemented. For the two Frank daughters, Margot and Anne, the immediate consequence of the new policy of segregation was having to leave their Montessori school and enroll in a Jewish school. In July 1942, Margot, then 16 years old, was ordered to present herself to the authorities to be transported to a work camp, and Otto Frank put into action a plan that he had been organizing for some months. The family would move into a number of small, secret rooms at his company's premises. Otto left clues that the family had escaped to Switzerland, and on 5 July, wearing as much clothing as they could without attracting attention, the Franks walked from their apartment to their new hiding place, which they called the *achterhuis*. In late July, they took in three members of another Jewish family, and in November another friend of the family joined them in hiding. Only a handful of people knew about the *achterhuis*, and they kept the fugitives supplied with food and other essentials.

Their secret remained safe for over two years, but on 4 August 1944 German police units, tipped off by an unknown informant, arrived at the company offices, found the *achterhuis*, and arrested the fugitives and two of their helpers. They were sent first to the transit camp at Westerbork, and on 2 September 1944 were transferred to Auschwitz concentration camp. All children under the age of 15 were sent directly to the gas chambers; Anne had turned 15 three months earlier and so was temporarily saved, along with the rest of her family. On 28 October, Anne and Margot were moved to Bergen-Belsen concentration camp, which was swept by a typhus epidemic in early 1945. Both Frank sisters died, probably a few days apart, although the exact dates are not known.

Anne Frank's story was far from unique, but it came to prominence after the war, when Otto Frank, the only survivor of the family, was given the diary that Anne had kept while in the *achterhuis*. The first attempts to publish it were unsuccessful, but it eventually appeared in 1946, with the first U.S. edition coming out in 1952 as *Anne Frank: The Diary of a Young Girl*. A stage play followed, which won the 1955 Pulitzer Prize for drama, and then a motion picture in 1959. The diary itself has been reprinted many times, in dozens of different languages; notably, editions published after 2001 contain a number of pages that Otto Frank kept from the original volume because they shed an unflattering light on the Franks' marriage.

The building where the Frank family hid, saved from demolition by the Anne Frank Foundation in 1957, was opened to the public in 1960, and remains one of Amsterdam's most visited tourist attractions. It is also a research institute dealing with issues of racism, right-wing extremism, and racial discrimination. The legacy of this teenaged victim of the Holocaust, then, has been remarkably varied and long-lasting.

See also Auschwitz; Bergen-Belsen; Concentration Camps; Extermination Camps

References

David Barnouw and Gerrold Van der Stroom, *The Diary of Anne Frank: The Revised Critical Edition* (New York: Doubleday, 2003).

Carol Ann Lee, *Roses From the Earth: The Biography of Anne Frank* (London: Penguin, 1999).

Willy Lindwer, *The Last Seven Months of Anne Frank* (New York: Pantheon, 1991).

Ernest Schnabel, *The Footsteps of Anne Frank* (London: Pan, 1988 [1958]).

—*Jonathan F. Vance*

Fraustadt-Grodno Massacres

This series of massacres of Russian POWs by the Swedes during the Great Northern War (1700–1721) reflected an escalation of violence against prisoners that was all too frequent in early modern warfare. The Swedish army defeated Danish, Russian, and Polish-Saxon forces in a number of battles between 1700 and 1703, and in early 1706 it prepared to meet the main Russian army of 34,000 men, stationed in Grodno in eastern Poland. The Swedish forces managed to crush a combined Polish-Saxon and Russian army at Fraustadt on 3 February, and all the Russian prisoners (the exact figure is not known, but it was certainly many hundreds, and perhaps even many thousands) were executed. The Poles and Saxons, however, were spared. Shortly thereafter, the Russian army at Grodno was surrounded by the Swedes. On 25 March, the Russians tried to break out of the encirclement and make their way back to Russia, across the river Njemen. During a month-long pursuit, almost 17,000 Russian soldiers were killed, many of them slaughtered after they had surrendered to their pursuers. Swedish troops had been given orders to take no prisoners, since "they only cause trouble." Preserved diaries written by Swedish officers describe how the massacres were carried out, and reveal that wounded Russians were systematically targeted for execution.

—*Lars Ericson*

French Revolution, Wars of the (1792–1799)

Although France was racked by domestic revolution in 1789, the foreign wars associated with the French Revolution did not commence until three years later, with a French declaration of war on Austria in April 1792. The ensuing violence began more than two decades of almost uninterrupted warfare between revolutionary France and her neighbors. By the outbreak of the war in 1792, the other European monarchies recognized the inherent dangers of both the ideas and the aggressive tendencies of revolutionary France. Accordingly, the courts of Europe feared the central ideals of the revolution, *liberté, égalité, fraternité* (liberty, equality, fraternity), as they were highly exportable and applicable to all of Europe.

The French began the war with several embarrassing defeats; however, at the battle of Valmy (20 September 1792), the French repelled a Prussian invasion and began a period of military conquest. To discourage further invasions of France and to make the victories of war more permanent, the traditional ransoming of prisoners of war was prohibited by the French decrees of September 1792 and May 1793. A French diplomat reportedly warned the king of Prussia: "You can only repair your losses by training at great expense new recruits at home; one thousand soldiers will cost you as much as one hundred thousand of the French." The diplomat's statement also suggests the coming of the newly created French Republican Army. By 1793 the glut of revolutionary volunteers did not provide sufficient manpower, and the French turned to wholesale conscription. In August of that year, the Jacobin-dominated government ordered a national *levée en masse,* which directed all able-bodied males between the ages of 18 and 25 to the front, while securing the labor of all other men, women, and children in the domestic war effort. The revolutionary army now swelled to an estimated one million men, surpassing any previous army in history.

With the *levée en masse* in place, the radical French leadership continued to press for the complete destruction of both foreign and domestic enemies of the revolution. To further this policy, Maximilien Robespierre, the radical leader of the Reign of Terror, decreed that all French counterrevolutionaries caught fighting on the side of France's enemies should be summarily executed. This manifestation of the French Terror resulted in some battlefield executions, but more significantly, it contributed directly to the deaths of some 300 imprisoned counterrevolutionaries. Shortly before his own execution in 1794, Robespierre went on to abandon the traditional rules of warfare by decreeing that no quarter or mercy be shown to wounded or captured British and Hanoverian troops. The French National Convention subsequently ordered that no more Spanish soldiers were to be taken prisoner; rather the military should offer no quarter and simply kill all enemy personnel on the battlefield. This extraordinary policy resulted in the slaughter of some 9,000 Spanish troops in 1795. With the collapse of the radical National Convention and the rise of the moderate French Directory government, the officially endorsed execution of enemy prisoners came to an end. Until the final overthrow of the Directory by Napoleon Bonaparte in 1799, the French kept captured prisoners in mass camps and offshore prison ships awaiting their eventual exchange.

References

Alan Forrest, *Conscripts and Deserters: The Army and French Society during the Revolution and Empire* (New York: Oxford University Press, 1989).

———, *The Soldiers of the French Revolution* (Durham, NC: Duke University Press, 1990).

John Lynn, *The Bayonets of the Republic: Motivation and Tactics in the Army of Revolutionary France, 1791–94* (Urbana: University of Illinois Press, 1984).

—*Christopher Blackburn*

Fresnes Prison

When it was constructed in Paris between 1895 and 1898, to a design by architect Henri Poussin, Fresnes represented a new innovation in prison architecture; it would later be called the telephone-pole design, because the wings of cells running off a central corridor made it resemble, when viewed from above, a telephone pole with cross-arms. The style was later used in many North American prisons, including Riker's Island in New York City.

During World War II, the German security service took over Fresnes shortly after Paris fell to the Nazis. From the summer of 1940 until the French capital was liberated in August 1944, Fresnes served as the Germans' main high-security prison in France. It was the temporary home to a variety of prisoners: French civilians who had broken civil laws; suspected spies and members of resistance organizations; downed Allied airmen who had been captured in the company of resistance workers; German soldiers who had committed military infractions; and anyone else who had fallen afoul of the Nazi occupation forces.

When Peter Churchill, an Englishman working in France with resistance groups, was captured and transferred to Fresnes in the spring of 1943, it had roughly 3,000 inmates, some of whom quickly initiated him in the prison's routine. Prisoners who had just arrived, were just about to leave, or who had been deemed of limited interest to the Nazis were kept in larger communal cells; everyone else was put into small cells measuring roughly six feet wide by 15 feet long. The only furniture consisted of a bed (with a straw mattress), table and chair (all of which were secured to the floor), and a sink and flush toilet in one corner. The windows were covered with thick, opaque glass and iron bars, and there was a small slot in the door through which trays of food could be passed. At that time, as Churchill discovered, there were only three ways out of Fresnes for inmates connected to the resistance: they could be transferred to a concentration camp (which was Churchill's fate); they could be killed, either in the prison itself or at a nearby site reserved for executions; or, if they had access to some 300,000 francs, they might bribe a staff member to release them.

Canadian airman John Harvie was a different kind of prisoner: he arrived at Fresnes in July 1944 after being arrested while in the company of resistance workers who were trying to help him to evade capture. When Harvie arrived, the regime at Fresnes had become, if anything, ever tougher. Rations were limited to a mug of acorn coffee for breakfast and dinner, and a bowl of thin soup and a slice of bread for lunch. Contact with other prisoners was strictly forbidden, even during exercise period, when a dozen or so inmates at a time were allowed out into one of the exercise pens adjacent to the prison. Harvie's time at Fresnes, however, was brief; just a month after arriving, he, too, was shipped off to a concentration camp.

By that time, Allied forces were nearing Paris and the Germans began to clear Fresnes of its inmates; those who might be of further use to them were moved to Germany, but many more were executed, some within days of the liberation of the city. Ironically, the prison was soon put to use by the Allies, who imprisoned convicted and suspected collaborators there. One was the automobile magnate Louis Renault, who was accused (some have argued unjustly) of collaborating with the Nazis and who died under suspicious circumstances in October 1944; witnesses reported seeing him being beaten over the head by a Fresnes guard not long before he died in hospital. Another inmate was Paul Touvier, a former police official tried and convicted in absentia in 1946 of treason and collusion with the enemy; tried again in 1994, this time in person, for complicity in crimes against humanity, he died two years later of natural causes in Fresnes, where some of the French men and women he betrayed had died more than 50 years earlier.

Fresnes remains in use as a civilian prison, and has been updated to suit modern principles of penology. But in 1945, French writer Henri Calet toured the facility to make a record of the messages that inmates had scratched into the whitewashed walls of its cells (including one by John Harvie). His book, *Les Murs de Fresnes* (*The Walls of Fresnes*) remains a remarkable testament to the indomitable spirit of the people who were imprisoned there: "Arrived May 6 44 one meal a day Pig food"; "If they took the bugs out of the soup—we would all starve to death, and dry up and blow out of the window"; "If you are a first Lieut. in the USAAF and the war lasts 2 years, you will have saved approximately 7,500 dollars"; and, all too frequently, inscriptions like "Menigoz Jules d'Argenteuil condamné à mort le 8 juin 1944 34 ans 9 enfants" ("Menigoz Jules d'Argenteuil, condemned to death 8 June 1944, 34 years, 9 children").

References

Henri Calet, *Les Murs de Fresnes* (Paris: Viviane Hamy, 1993 [1945]).

Peter Churchill, *The Spirit in the Cage* (London: Hodder & Stoughton, 1954).

John D. Harvie, *Missing in Action: An RCAF Navigator's Story* (Montreal: McGill-Queen's University Press, 1995).

Jerrard Tickell, *Odette: The Story of a British Agent* (London: Chapman & Hall, 1949).

—*Jonathan F. Vance*

Fryatt, Charles Algernon (1872–1916)

Charles Algernon Fryatt was an English merchant captain who was executed by the Germans during World War I, and his fate revealed the complex status of merchant seamen who fell into enemy hands. Fryatt was born in Southampton on 2 December 1872 and took to the sea at an early age. When the war began in 1914, Fryatt was a steamer captain on the route between Harwich and Antwerp. On one voyage in March 1915, he ordered his ship to ram a German submarine that had been pursuing it; both boats were undamaged, but Fryatt was hailed as a national hero in England. The German government, however, considered Fryatt to be a guerrilla, a civilian who had unlawfully taken part in an act of war. On 22 June 1916, his ship was ambushed off Holland and the entire crew captured. All of the crew except Fryatt were sent to Ruhleben internment camp; the captain was sent to Bruges in Belgium, where he was court-martialed, condemned, and, on 29 July 1916, executed.

Like the execution of British nurse Edith Cavell, Fryatt's death caused an outrage in Britain. Historians and jurists have since agreed that his conviction was unjust and that it underlined the need to define the status of merchant seamen under the laws of war: was Fryatt indeed a guerrilla who operated outside the protection of the law, or should he have been considered a lawful combatant entitled to protection as such? This dilemma was finally resolved with the Geneva Convention of 1949, which stated that merchant seaman were indeed combatants and therefore must receive the protection due to prisoners of war.

See also Merchant Seamen

—Jonathan F. Vance

G

Games

The first game based on the experience of captivity was probably *Escape from Colditz Castle,* a simple board game produced by Invicta Games in England in 1972. A year later came the more complicated *Escape from Colditz,* a Parker Brothers game (designed with the assistance of Colditz escaper P.R. Reid) in which players must collect various kinds of escape gear in order to break out of the castle. It was followed in 1995 by *Skedaddle!,* a Canadian-manufactured game that drew heavily from the earlier versions. Once again, players could either attempt to escape from Colditz, or take the role of the commandant and try to prevent escapes.

When video and computer games started to grow in popularity, POW and escape games became more common. An early arcade-style video game was *P.O.W.: Prisoner of War,* manufactured by SNK Corporation in 1988. Set in southeast Asia, it involved two prisoners named Snake and Bart who had to escape from their camp and assassinate an enemy general. The following year, Konami began manufacturing *M.I.A.: Missing in Action,* which was set in the Vietnam War. In this arcade game, the player had to progress through four stages before reaching a POW compound; once there, the prisoners had to be freed and safely evacuated from the camp by helicopter. In both games, however, the captivity element was largely incidental; they were primarily primitive action games like dozens of others then available in arcades.

Recent technological advances have allowed games to become more sophisticated, and therefore more ambitious in their content. The first major advance was Apogee Software's *Wolfenstein 3D* (1992), an adaptation of two earlier games, *Castle Wolfenstein* (Muse Software, 1983) and *Beyond Castle Wolfenstein* (Muse Software, 1984), which has been credited with playing a large part in popularizing the first-person shooter computer game. The game opens with William "B.J." Blazkowicz escaping from Wolfenstein Castle during World War II so he can overthrow the Nazi regime; it has been followed by a handful of sequels, most of which begin with the same prison-escape scenario, and imitators, such as *Vietnam: POW Rescue,* a first-person shooter game developed by ValuSoft. *Rising Sun,* in the popular *Medal of Honor* series, includes a mission in which the gamer must destroy a bridge built over the River Kwai by POW labor; in a sense, the player becomes the William Holden character from the movie *The Bridge on the River Kwai* (1957). Similar is *Commandos 2: Men of Courage* (2001), which includes a number of scenarios based on POW movies such as *The Colditz Story* (1955) and *The Bridge on the River Kwai.* More recently, Kuma Reality Games of New York has begun online distribution of computer games based on current events. In one mission, the gamer must rescue six British soldiers who have been taken prisoner by rebels in the west African country of Sierra Leone; two other missions involve firefights inside the walls of Baghdad's Abu Ghraib prison.

Two of the most popular computer games are set during World War II. *P.O.W.,* released by Codemasters in 2002, features American airman Captain Lewis Stone, who must escape from a number of famous prison camps, including Stalag Luft 3 and Colditz Castle. While its grasp of historical detail is somewhat shaky, it does provide the gamer with what are, for the most part, historically accurate game spaces in which to play. *The Great Escape*, released by Gotham Games in 2003, is based on the popular 1963 movie of the same name. Although Steve McQueen and his character Virgil Hilts are featured prominently on the packaging materials, the game is a mixture of scenarios taken directly from the film and others that have been specially formulated for the game.

Significantly, these games, whether they are for personal computers or game systems, are all first-person games. Strategy games about the POW experience, as typified by the Colditz board game, have not made the transition to digital gaming. One of the few exceptions was Digital Magic's *Escape from Colditz*, made for the Amiga game system (1991) and based directly on the Parker Brothers board game. However, the taking of prisoners is a minor part of battle in many popular strategy games. For example, in the successful *Age of Empires* series, enemy soldiers can be captured and converted to fight on the side of their former enemies. Microsoft's *A Bridge Too Far* (1997) also allows virtual soldiers to be captured and removed from the game. But in neither case does captivity become a significant element of the game play.

—*Jonathan F. Vance*

GAULLE, CHARLES-ANDRÉ-MARIE-JOSEPH DE (1890–1970)

The most influential French statesman of the twentieth century, General de Gaulle embodied the spirit of resistance to Germany's occupation of France during World War II and to the policy of collaboration personified by Marshal Philippe Pétain. A 1913 graduate of the military academy at Saint-Cyr, de Gaulle received his first commission in a regiment commanded by Pétain. Engaged in frontline operations during the first year and a half of World War I, he was wounded twice. In March 1916 during an action near Verdun, he was wounded a third time and captured. His five escape attempts earned him 120 days in solitary confinement and a new billet at the maximum security prison of Ingolstadt, where he met French air ace Roland Garros and future Soviet Marshal Mikhail Tukhachevsky. De Gaulle was to remain a captive until the 1918 armistice. Some biographers have argued that de Gaulle's imprisonment was seminal to his belief that any form of action is better than incarceration.

After the war, de Gaulle dedicated much time to staff teaching and research, envisioning a renewed French army articulated around professional, mechanized forces. His unconventional beliefs pitched him against the French military establishment in which Marshal Pétain was of paramount importance. In May 1940, in the midst of the German blitzkrieg, Paul Reynaud's beleaguered government called Colonel de Gaulle to the position of under-secretary of war. In this capacity, de Gaulle left for London, where he proclaimed himself leader of the Free French Forces, calling upon all French people to continue the struggle against the Nazi occupier. For this, he was sentenced to death by the Vichy regime, which believed that there was no point in resisting Nazi Germany in light of the two million French prisoners of war it held as hostages. Creating alliances across ideological barriers, de Gaulle created viable resistance networks within France and fighting forces in its colonial empire. By D-Day, he had become the Allies' only French partner and as such took over as France's leader by the end of the war. Yet his regime did not last long, and he resigned as prime minister in April 1947. He was recalled from retirement to solve the French-Algerian crisis of 1954–1962. De Gaulle was elected president of France's Fifth Republic in 1958 and remained in power until 1969.

References
Max Gallo, *De Gaulle* (Paris: Laffont, 1998).
Jean Lacouture, *De Gaulle: The Rebel, 1890–1944*, trans. Patrick O'Brian (New York: W.W. Norton, 1990).

Charles Williams, *The Last Great Frenchman: A Life of General de Gaulle* (New York: J. Wiley and Sons, 1993).

—*Laurent Ditmann*

GENEVA CONVENTION ADDITIONAL PROTOCOLS (1977)

The product of four international conferences held between 1974 and 1977, the Protocols Additional to the Geneva Conventions of 1949 were designed to supplement and extend international humanitarian law in response to new types of conflict that had emerged since World War II, and to extend the protection of the Geneva Conventions to civilian victims of war.

The type of "total war" practiced during World War II had created enormous danger and misery for civilians, for which reason the International Committee of the Red Cross (ICRC) proposed a conference for the purpose of protecting civilians as early as 1957. A complete revision of the 1949 Geneva Conventions was deemed too risky—the progress made in 1949 might have been reversed—as well as unnecessary, since the existing Conventions were still relevant and valuable. Instead, two draft protocols were drawn up by the ICRC to fill in gaps and extend the reach of the 1949 Conventions. In 1974 the Government of Switzerland convened the first session of the Diplomatic Conference on the Reaffirmation and Development of International Humanitarian Law applicable in Armed Conflicts; in attendance were 124 nations and observers representing 14 national liberation movements, 35 inter-governmental and non-governmental organizations, the League of Red Cross and Red Crescent Societies, and a number of national Red Cross societies. Unlike the original Geneva Conventions of the late nineteenth and early twentieth centuries, the Additional Protocols were debated by an international community that extended well beyond the borders of Europe, including many underdeveloped countries. Three more sessions of the conference followed over the ensuing three years, and in 1977 the plenipotentiaries of 102 states adopted the two protocols in a solemn (but non-binding) signing ceremony.

Protocol I contains 102 articles relating to the protection of civilian populations against the effects of hostilities, intended to spare civilians the kind of suffering that had marked World War II and to protect them from the increasingly common wars of liberation, guerrilla tactics, and use of sophisticated and indiscriminate weapons. This protocol alters the definition of a combatant (who is thereby entitled to POW status) to encompass guerrilla or freedom fighters of national liberation movements who cannot conform to the conditions specified in the 1949 Geneva Conventions. The new definition has been criticized as too vague and obscure, and some argue that it could entirely blur the distinction between combatants and civilians which is one of the chief concerns of international humanitarian law.

Protocol II contains 28 articles relating to the much more controversial subject of internal armed conflicts. It does not set out any special POW status for parties in internal conflicts. Instead, all parties, civilian or otherwise, are guaranteed a basic standard of humane treatment.

Although the Additional Protocols entered into force on 7 December 1978, the ratification process was lengthy. The vast majority of states initially hesitated to ratify because the two global superpowers, the United States and the Soviet Union, made no moves to accede to the protocols. As with the previous Geneva Conventions, questions of national sovereignty and the security of the state were obstacles to the ratification of the Additional Protocols. Intense media scrutiny of the 1990–1991 Gulf War brought to bear the pressure of international opinion, and although many countries still had not ratified the Additional Protocols at the time, their provisions were clearly evident in the language and conduct of the war. The ratification process finally gained momentum in the early 1990s, with the collapse of the

Soviet Union. By 1993 the Russian Federation and most of the former Communist Bloc nations and newly independent Soviet republics had ratified the protocols. Other nations followed suit.

By 2005 there were 191 states represented in the United Nations, of which 163 had ratified Protocol I and 159 had ratified Protocol II. Among those who had not acceded to either of the Additional Protocols were Israel, Pakistan, Iran, Iraq, and the United States. As with all the Geneva Conventions, the future success of the Additional Protocols will depend upon the signatories' willingness to uphold and respect them.

See also Geneva Convention of 1929; Geneva Convention of 1949; International Law

References

Joan Beaumont, "Protecting Prisoners of War, 1939–1995," in *Prisoners of War and Their Captors in World War II*, ed. Bob Moore and Kent Fedorowich (Oxford: Berg, 1996).

Françoise Bory, *Origin and Development of International Humanitarian Law* (Geneva: ICRC, 1982).

Basic Rules of The Geneva Conventions and Their Additional Protocols (Geneva: ICRC, 1987).

—*Sarah Glassford*

GENEVA CONVENTION OF 1929

The Geneva Convention Relative to the Treatment of Prisoners of War governed the conditions of captivity during World War II, replacing the Hague Convention of 1907 as the most important international convention dealing with the protection of POWs. The distinction between Geneva and Hague law is significant: the latter attempts to regulate the means of war (for example, by prohibiting the use of exploding bullets), while the former confines itself to the protection of the victims of war.

The movement to amend international law in light of the experience of World War I began even before the Armistice, when in February 1918 the International Committee of the Red Cross (ICRC) suggested a diplomatic conference to supplement and clarify those aspects of the Hague Convention of 1907 and the Geneva Convention of 1906 relating to POWs. In the early 1920s, a number of organizations prepared draft codes for the treatment of prisoners, and in August 1925, the Swiss government proposed a diplomatic conference to revise the 1906 Geneva Convention for the Amelioration of the Wounded in Time of War and to prepare a similar document for POWs. The conference, which ran from 1 to 27 July 1929, was divided into two sections, one to consider the sick and wounded convention and the other to work on the POW convention. Different governments approached the convention in different ways. The British government, for instance, believed that the articles should not be too specific and that the force of the conventions should come instead from its statement of the minimum conditions achievable and the assumption that general standards of humane treatment should improve on this whenever possible. Other governments preferred a more rigid codification that would translate general principles into specific practices.

The convention that was eventually agreed upon tended more toward the British view. It ran to 97 articles and elaborated upon many of the provisions of the Hague Conventions that had been proven inadequate by the experience of war. Once again, the basic assumption was that POWs should be considered on par with the detaining power's garrison troops with respect to rations, clothing, living space, and other necessities. Reflecting those areas that had proven troublesome during World War I, the sections dealing with work, punishment, and relief operations were all expanded, as was the section on repatriation; an annex giving a draft agreement for the repatriation of prisoners of war, similar to those reached by the major powers during World War I, was also included. Finally, the article covering the speedy evacuation of POWs after the close of hostilities was made more explicit.

Over 40 nations became signatories to the Geneva Convention before World War II, but just as important were the nations that did not. The Soviet Union declined to take part in the negotiations or to be bound by the agreement, with the result that Soviet POWs in German hands or German and Japanese prisoners in Soviet hands did not enjoy its protection. Japanese delegates to the conference signed the convention, and the government in Tokyo later ratified the sick and wounded convention. The POW convention, however, was not ratified by Japan for a number of reasons: the Japanese military did not expect its soldiers to be taken prisoner, and so assumed that the convention would be unilaterally binding on Japan; it was feared that the leniency implicit in the convention might encourage Japan's enemies to undertake bombing raids on Japan, knowing that they had little to fear from being captured; there was opposition to the notion of unsupervised visits of prison camps; and the punishments prescribed for POWs were considerably more lenient than the punishments meted out to Japanese soldiers convicted of the same offenses. The Japanese government pledged in 1942 to observe the spirit, if not the letter, of the convention, but in light of the abuses committed against Allied POWs in Japanese hands, this pledge was clearly insincere.

See also Geneva Convention of 1949; Geneva Convention Additional Protocols; Geneva Conventions of 1864 and 1906; Hague Conventions of 1899 and 1907; International Committee of the Red Cross; International Law

References

Charles G. Roland, "Allied POWs, Japanese Captors and the Geneva Convention," *War & Society* 9 (1991): 83–101.

—*Jonathan F. Vance*

GENEVA CONVENTION OF 1949

The 1949 Geneva Convention Relative to the Treatment of Prisoners of War was created to replace the 1929 version, whose inadequacies had been made manifest during World War II. Significantly, it was accompanied by the Geneva Convention Relative to the Protection of Civilian Persons in Time of War, the first comprehensive effort to provide legislative safeguards to noncombatants, and it also introduced the notion that international law should apply equally to civil wars.

Even before the end of World War II, the International Committee of the Red Cross (ICRC) began making official approaches to all national Red Cross societies regarding revisions to the 1929 Geneva Convention. The signatories to that agreement were then invited to participate in the process, and most governments began to assemble teams of diplomats and experts to consider the matter. Two gatherings were eventually convened to lay the groundwork for the upcoming conference in Geneva: the April 1947 Conference of Experts, held in Geneva, and the Seventeenth International Red Cross Conference, held in Stockholm, Sweden, in August 1948. Official invitations to the main conference were circulated in the late summer of 1948, with the conference itself being held from 21 April to 12 August 1949. It was attended by delegates representing 59 governments and observers from four other governments, who eventually agreed on four separate conventions covering the sick and wounded; wounded, sick, and shipwrecked members of armed forces at sea; prisoners of war; and civilians.

The discussions on the POW convention were overshadowed by other, more contentious issues (particularly the applicability of the conventions to conflicts that were not declared wars between belligerent states), and the POW code that emerged was not radically different from the 1929 version. It grew to 143 articles, with the largest single section covering the definition of a POW. This definition was an attempt to address the inconsistencies in the treatment of captured partisans, guerrillas, and irregular soldiers during World War II. Just as in 1929, the specific changes were intended to address matters that had proven particularly difficult during the previous global conflict. As of 1992, 175 governments had bound themselves to the conventions, albeit some with specific reservations.

The 1949 convention did not solve all of the problems that had been manifest during World War II. Perhaps the most contentious issue involved the release of POWs at the conclusion of hostilities. The ICRC attempted to insert a clause prohibiting forcible repatriation, but various governments resisted, insisting they did not wish to bear responsibility for sheltering unknown numbers of prisoners. However, in the ideological conflicts of the post-1945 era, the repatriation of POWs against their will became a major bone of contention. In the Korean War, for example, bitter negotiations centered on whether Communist POWs should be returned to North Korea or China against their will. Eventually, the understanding that prisoners should have the right to choose whether or not to return to their home country upon release has been widely accepted.

See also Geneva Convention of 1929; Geneva Convention Additional Protocols; Geneva Conventions of 1864 and 1906; Hague Conventions of 1899 and 1907; International Committee of the Red Cross; International Law; Repatriation

References

Joan Beaumont, "Protecting Prisoners of War, 1939–95," in *Prisoners of War and Their Captors in World War II*, ed. Bob Moore and Kent Fedorowich (Oxford: Berg, 1996).

G.I.A.D. Draper, *The Red Cross Conventions* (New York: Praeger, 1958).

J.M.E. Duchosal, "The Revision of the Geneva Conventions," *Political Quarterly* 19 (1948): 32–40.

—*Jonathan F. Vance*

GENEVA CONVENTIONS OF 1864 AND 1906

The Geneva Conventions for the Amelioration of the Wounded in Time of War, though they were not primarily addressed at the treatment of POWs, reflected a recognition that prisoners should be treated as a separate category of combatant in international law relating to warfare.

The 1864 convention contained a single provision (Article 6) relating to POWs, which stipulated that wounded and sick soldiers should be returned to their own forces either immediately after a battle or once their health had improved. If they were permanently incapacitated, they need provide no guarantee to the original detaining power, but if their health was fully restored, they would be returned home upon pledging to take no further part in hostilities. Significantly, the convention also spawned the International Committee of the Red Cross, which would go on to play a major role in improving the conditions of captivity for countless prisoners.

The 1906 convention expanded the consideration of POWs to seven articles, adding some new provisions to its predecessor. It provided for the internment of sick and wounded prisoners in a neutral state and stipulated that protected personnel, such as doctors, medical orderlies, and chaplains, were not to be made prisoners but were to be returned to their own forces without delay. Although the 1906 Geneva Convention was in force at the time of World War I, the Hague Convention of 1907 was more important during that war because it covered a much broader range of issues. The 1906 Geneva Convention was eventually superseded by a convention signed in 1929 that was devoted entirely to the protection of POWs.

See also Geneva Convention of 1929; Geneva Convention of 1949; Geneva Convention Additional Protocols; Hague Conventions of 1899 and 1907; International Committee of the Red Cross; International Law

—*Jonathan F. Vance*

GERARD, JAMES WATSON, III (1867–1951)

The American ambassador to Germany from 1913 to 1917, James W. Gerard III was instrumental in aiding Allied prisoners of war detained on the European continent during World War I. Born in Geneseo, New York, on 25 August 1867, Gerard was a lawyer who left a successful private practice to become a New York Supreme Court justice in 1908. In 1913, he accepted the position of U.S. ambassador in Berlin, a post he held until the United States entered the war in April 1917. Because the United States was designated as the Protecting Power with responsibility for safeguarding the interests of the British Empire in Germany, Gerard and his embassy staff became deeply involved in the conditions endured by POWs in German camps. He and his deputies inspected many camps during the war, negotiating with the camp staff, interviewing the prisoners, and doing everything possible to ensure that they were treated according to international law. He remained in close contact with the British government and kept them constantly updated with reports on camp conditions. Though it is difficult to quantify the impact of Gerard's efforts, most historians agree that his intervention was significant in improving the lives of POWs from the British Empire.

Gerard remained active in public life after the war, serving in an advisory capacity to both Presidents Franklin Delano Roosevelt and Harry S Truman. He died at Long Island, New York, on 6 September 1951.

References

James W. Gerard, *My Four Years in Germany* (New York: George H. Doran, 1917).

—*Andrea Vandenberg*

GESTAPO

The Gestapo (*Geheime Staatspolizei*, or Secret State Police) grew from a Prussian police office in existence before the rise of the Nazis to become the principal organization responsible for the internal political security of the Nazi state. As such, it played a significant role in the administration of POWs and civilian internees. The Gestapo reported to Hermann Göring in his role as Prussian minister of the interior at the start of the Nazi era, but in 1936 it was taken over by *Reichsführer* Heinrich Himmler, who had been appointed by Adolf Hitler as the chief of German police and of the SS. By the time World War II began, Gestapo agents had almost unlimited power to investigate, arrest, torture, deport to concentration camps, or kill. Because Soviet and Polish prisoners of war (who formed, indeed, the significant majority of Allied soldiers in German captivity) were not deemed by Germany to be covered under the Geneva Convention, they were the first to feel the ruthlessness of the Gestapo. Responsible for internal prison camp security, the Gestapo weeded out "political" POWs in the camps, and recaptured and usually executed prisoners of these nationalities who had escaped. The POWs from other countries occupied by Germany (such as France, Belgium, and the Netherlands) fared moderately better but, because those states held no German prisoners for potential reprisals, their captives suffered from the Gestapo's attentions as well. In one significant incident, captured French generals were executed by the Gestapo and SS. Prisoners from the United States and the British Commonwealth fared considerably better; given the number of German POWs in those countries, the Nazi leadership was more reluctant to turn them over to the Gestapo.

Though the German *Wehrmacht* (armed forces) was the legal authority over enemy POWs, the fact that escaped prisoners were by definition also a threat to the internal security of the state meant that the Gestapo was often involved in their recapture, with their influence increasing as the war progressed. Himmler coveted the chance to expand his influence in a realm dominated by the military, and the number of escapes gave him some leverage in arguing his case with Hitler. Thus, the military commandants of POW camps found themselves ordered, as early as 1942, to coordinate their security measures with the local Gestapo detachments in attempts to recapture escaped inmates. The height of the Gestapo's influence, before Himmler finally gained control of the POW apparatus, occurred in mid-July

1944, when the German high command issued an order that fundamentally threatened the legal protection offered by the Geneva Convention: prisoners of war could henceforth be dismissed from the legal state of captivity "if necessary or ordered" and turned over to the Gestapo.

By late 1944, Hitler's patience with the military had finally run out, firstly as a result of the steadily increasing number of escapes (costing the Reich hundreds of thousands of lost man-hours) and then after the disloyalty of the army was exposed by the 20 July 1944 assassination attempt. Himmler's later appointment to the head of the *Ersatzheer* (Reserve Army) gave him control of the administration of prison camps, and the influence of the Gestapo over POWs increased accordingly. By January 1945, complaints to German military officers about the pervasiveness of the Gestapo fell on deaf ears. As a commandant told a Swiss delegate, "The Gestapo has become an integral part of the Wehrmacht since the Reichsführer-SS has taken over the Supreme Command of the Ersatzheer." Thus by the war's end, the Gestapo exercised influence over American and British prisoners of war as well.

References

George C. Browder, *Hitler's Enforcers: The Gestapo and the SS Security Service in the Nazi Revolution* (Oxford: Oxford University Press, 1996).

Jacques Delarue, *The Gestapo: A History of Horror* (New York: Morrow, 1964).

Eric Johnson, *The Nazi Terror: Gestapo, Jews and Other Germans* (London: John Murray, 2000).

—Vasilis Vourkoutiotis

GIRAUD, HENRI-HONORÉ (1879–1949)

A graduate of the French military academy at Saint-Cyr, General Henri-Honoré Giraud emblematized the officer corps of France's elite colonial troops in the first half of the twentieth century. A frontline officer, he was captured by the Germans during World War I but escaped to return to the front. In the interwar years, he built a reputation as a pugnacious officer against Moroccan rebels. At the outbreak of World War II, he commanded the 9th Army in Northern France. Like many general officers, he was captured near Sedan during the German blitzkrieg of May–June 1940. A captive along with two million other Frenchmen, he became an instant hero in occupied France by escaping in April 1942. In November of the same year, after the Allied landings in North Africa, he was appointed high commissioner for North and West Africa and, in June 1943, co-president of the Committee of National Liberation. While opposed to Marshal Philippe Pétain's policy of collaboration with Nazi Germany, he was not willing to pledge allegiance to Charles de Gaulle's London-based Free France. He saw de Gaulle as a rival too amenable to the Communists' demands, and himself as the apolitical leader best able to marshal the French military and ideological forces necessary to liberate the country. He allegedly despised de Gaulle for having left France in June 1940 instead of undergoing the trial of captivity. Conversely, de Gaulle isolated Giraud politically and ultimately forced him to resign his command in April 1944.

See also Gaulle, Charles-André-Marie-Joseph de

References

Guy de Girard de Charbonnières, *Le Duel Giraud–de Gaulle* (Paris: Plon, 1984).

—Laurent Ditmann

GRAND ILLUSION (LA GRANDE ILLUSION)

Based on an original script by filmmaker Jean Renoir and Charles Spaak, this 1937 film centers on the complex rapport existing among World War I French POWs, as well as between the French and their German captors. Divided into three narrative phases, it first chronicles a few months in the lives of recently captured French officers. Thus are introduced aristocratic Captain de Boieldieu

(Pierre Fresnay) and plebeian Lieutenant Maréchal (Jean Gabin), both sent to a prison camp where they meet bourgeois Lieutenant Rosenthal (Marcel Dalio). Together they start planning their escape but are separated before their plans come to fruition. The second narrative phase starts when, a few months later, they meet again in the fortress camp of Wintersborn, commanded by Captain Von Rauffenstein (Erich von Stroheim in a now legendary neck brace). While Maréchal and Rosenthal continue to plan for their deliverance, de Boieldieu strikes up a friendship of sorts with his captor. However, realizing that men of his caste are no longer suited for modern warfare and its implications, de Boieldieu sacrifices himself to allow his fellow officers to make good their escape. The third phase of the film chronicles Rosenthal's and Gabin's circuitous journey to Switzerland, during which their friendship is tested by circumstances as well as by ideological differences.

Released at a time when the generation it portrays was caught between pacifism and the rise of Nazi Germany, this film, often considered Renoir's finest, touches on issues as diverse as soldierly camaraderie, chivalry, heroism, and anti-Semitism. Some of its crucial scenes, especially de Boieldieu's "last charge" to the tune of "Il était un petit navire" played on a fife, have become textbook examples of great filmmaking. It has been argued that such scenes created a sort of cinematic POW aesthetic that was to be perceptible in French World War II films (Henri Verneuil's 1959 *La vache et le prisonnier*, Alex Joffé's 1962 *Les culottes rouges*) but also in Anglo-American productions (Billy Wilder's 1953 *Stalag 17*, John Sturges's 1963 *The Great Escape*).

See also Film

References

Ronald Bergan, *Jean Renoir: Projections of Paradise* (Woodstock, NY: Overlook Press, 1994).

Leo Braudy, *Jean Renoir: The World of His Films* (Garden City, NY: Doubleday, 1972).

Jean Renoir, *My Life and My Films* (New York: Da Capo Press, 2000).

—*Laurent Ditmann*

Great Escape

Perhaps the most famous escape of World War II, the Great Escape was the brainchild of Roger Bushell, a South African–born fighter pilot who had been shot down and captured in 1940. Bushell spent his years in captivity planning escapes as a way to create disruption in occupied Europe. His most ambitious plan called for the construction in Stalag Luft 3 Sagan of three escape tunnels, code-named Tom, Dick, and Harry; he reasoned that the Germans might find one or even two tunnels, but they would be unlikely to find all three. These were to be the most sophisticated tunnels ever constructed in a prison camp, equipped with electric lighting, ventilated by a system of air lines and pumps, and serviced by wooden trolleys to facilitate ease of movement. On the first night of the escape, 200 airmen would be sent out, each outfitted with forged papers, civilian clothes, food supplies, maps, and compasses. If the tunnel was undiscovered, it would be used again later.

Work on the tunnels began in April 1943, when a large group of airmen was transferred to Sagan's new North Compound. The escape leaders carefully surveyed the camp to determine the best locations for the traps, devised a system of lookouts and diversions, and then began work on the tunnels themselves. They soon encountered two obstacles. The sand was very soft and collapsed easily, convincing Bushell that the entire length of all three tunnels would have to be fully shored with wood. Furthermore, the tunnel sand was a different color than the compound's surface sand, forcing the organizers to devise elaborate ways to disperse the 240 tons of sand the tunnels would eventually yield.

The organizers initially decided to concentrate on Tom, but in September 1943 the tunnel was accidentally discovered by camp guards. At 260 feet long and 25 feet deep, it was 40 feet short of its planned length and weeks away from being used. Once the furor over the discovery of Tom died down, Harry became the primary focus and Dick was converted into a storage tunnel. By March 1944, Harry stretched roughly 335 feet and was 28 feet underground at its deepest point. The 200 escapers had been selected and were fully equipped with civilian clothing, food, maps, compasses, and in some cases, forged papers and German money. All they required was the proper weather conditions.

On the morning of 24 March, Bushell and his lieutenants decided that conditions were as favorable as they were ever likely to be and that the escape would proceed that night. Unfortunately, the breakout was plagued by problems. Because of errors in surveying, Harry was shorter than planned and broke in an open field instead of the forest; the escapers had to use signal ropes to move men out of the tunnel without being seen by patrolling guards. Then, an air raid on Berlin caused the camp's electricity to be cut off, and the tunnel plunged into darkness. This caused further delays, as did a number of minor cave-ins, so that by dawn fewer than half of the waiting escapers had descended into the tunnel. Around 5:00 a.m., the escape leaders decided that it was too light to send more men, and they opted to shut down the operation. Shortly after, a patrolling guard spotted the tunnel mouth and raised the alarm. Three airmen were apprehended at the tunnel mouth, but 76 got away from the camp.

German police began recapturing the escapers within days, and only three men reached safety: two Norwegians who stowed away on a ship bound for Sweden and a Dutchman who eventually reached Spain with the help of resistance groups. Of the remainder, 11 returned to Sagan and others were scattered around various concentration camps. Outraged by the escape, which he believed was the prelude to a rebellion of prisoners of war and slave laborers in occupied Europe, Adolf Hitler ordered that the majority of the escapers be executed. A police official selected 50 names, and the Gestapo shot the victims at various places in the weeks following the escape. The human cost of the escape was considerable, but so too was the disruption it caused. Tens of thousands of German soldiers and civilians were diverted from other tasks to search for the escapers, and the executions poisoned relations between the German security services on the one hand, and the military and the Reich Foreign Ministry on the other. Bushell's plan, then, achieved precisely what it set out to.

See also Bushell, Roger Joyce; Escape; *The Great Escape*; Stalag Luft 3; Wooden Horse

References

Paul Brickhill, *The Great Escape* (London: Faber, 1951).

Anton Gill, *The Great Escape: The Full Dramatic Story with Contributions from Survivors and their Families* (London: Review, 2002).

Jonathan F. Vance, *A Gallant Company: The True Story of "The Great Escape"* (New York: Simon & Schuster, 2003).

—*Jonathan F. Vance*

The Great Escape

This 1963 feature film, directed by John Sturges for United Artists and filmed on location in southern Germany, was based on Paul Brickhill's 1951 best-seller about *the Great Escape* from Stalag Luft 3 in 1944. Because one of the principal escape organizers, chief tunnel engineer Wally Floody, acted as historical consultant for the film, the physical details were highly accurate, particularly with respect to the layout of the camp and the appearance of the tunnel. The sequence of events is also reasonably authentic, although the timing has been compressed so that the events, which in reality took place over the course of a year, seem to occur in a single summer. The characters were less true to life; most were composites of two or three real individuals, and only the Richard Attenborough role was patterned directly on an actual person, escape leader Roger Bushell. The most famous character in the film, the inveterate American escaper Virgil Hilts (played by Steve McQueen) was completely fabricated, as was his daring motorcycle escape across the Alps. The picture, made at a cost of $3.8 million, was intended to capitalize on the success of the studio's popular western *The Magnificent Seven*, and even included some of the same actors, like McQueen, James Coburn, and Charles Bronson. Also featured were British actors Donald Pleasence, who had been a POW himself toward the end of World War II, and James Donald, who had also starred in the POW epic *The Bridge on the River Kwai*. Critics generally lauded *The Great Escape*; it made a modest profit for United Artists and also elevated McQueen and James Garner to the status of major stars. It was followed in 1988 by a vastly inferior (and historically inaccurate) television remake, *The Great Escape II: The Untold Story*. Paul Brickhill, who had a number of his other best-sellers translated to the screen, did not care for either version.

References

Tino Balio, *United Artists: The Company that Changed the Film Industry* (Madison: University of Wisconsin Press, 1987).

Raymond Strait, *James Garner* (New York: St. Martin's Press, 1985).

Marshall Terrill, *Steve McQueen: Portrait of an American Rebel* (Kelso, WA: Plexus Press, 2005).

—Jonathan F. Vance

GREAT NORTHERN WAR (1700–1721)

Between 1700 and 1721, Sweden fought against a coalition formed by Russia and (at various times) Denmark-Norway, Poland-Saxony, Hannover, and Prussia, before the final collapse of the Swedish Baltic empire and the rise of Peter the Great's Russia. During these two decades a large number of POWs were taken by all participants in three distinct campaigns: in Poland, in the fighting between Sweden and Denmark, and in the fighting between Sweden and Russia.

During the Polish campaign from 1701 to 1706, 15,000 Poles and Saxons were captured and transported to Sweden. Included were a large number of women and children, eventually as many as 15 percent of the total number. Most of them were placed in small towns and were forbidden to move around. In keeping with the customs of the time, the officers were allowed to keep their swords, and many POWs were used as paid labor. In 1705, roughly 100 prisoners were exchanged for Swedish POWs in Poland-Saxony. After the peace of Altranstädt in 1706, most of the remaining POWs were released, but Sweden did raise one regiment and three battalions of former Saxon soldiers. It was clearly stated that this recruitment was open only to Saxons, not Poles, Lithuanians, and Cossacks, "no less any Russian"—distinctions that say something about how the Swedes regarded the different nationalities they held captive. These units were used on the eastern front against Russia and against Denmark in the south. Of the 2,700 men in the Saxon units, only a few seem to have survived to return home.

The conflict between Sweden and Denmark reached its peak in 1710, when a failed Danish invasion of southern Sweden resulted in the capture of 3,000 Danes. In general, the Danes were treated relatively well in Sweden, and a number of Danish soldiers placed in small country towns became burghers. In 1713, the tables were turned when the Danes captured almost 10,000 Swedes at Tönningen in northern Germany.

The Swedish victory at Narva, Estonia, in November 1700 crushed the Russian army, but several thousand Russian POWs were released immediately after the battle; only the highest-ranking officers were sent to captivity in Sweden. During the following years, the number of Russian POWs grew steadily. Most of them were sent to inland Sweden, to small towns and to the island of Visingsö in Lake Vättern. The Russians began to attack Swedish positions in the Baltic provinces from 1701, taking a number of military prisoners as well as Estonian and Livonian (Latvian) civilians. Many were sent to the mansions of the Russian nobility to work, while others were thrown into dark dungeons in different towns. After the disaster at Poltava, Ukraine, in June 1709, when the main part of the Swedish army was wiped out by the Russians, some 20,000 prisoners, including Swedes, Finns, Germans, Estonians, and Livonians, were taken by the victorious forces of Tsar Peter. At least 20 percent of them were women and children. After participating in a victorious parade in Moscow, they were sent to Tobolsk and a number of other towns in Siberia. Many worked in the shipyards at Voronezh, and others labored in the construction of the city of St. Petersburg, founded in 1703. A few remarkable Swedes even journeyed deep into Siberia, toward the Chinese border and other areas, and produced maps that are still of value to today's historians. When the peace came in 1721, only 3,000 of the Swedes who had been interned in Russia returned home.

See also Fraudstadt-Grodno Massacres; Swedish-Russian Wars

References

Alf Åberg, *Prisoners' Misery: The Karolingians in Russia, 1700–1723* (Stockholm: Natur och Kultur, 1991).

—*Lars Ericson*

GREECE—BRONZE AGE TO THE HELLENISTIC PERIOD

The evidence of Greek POWs, especially for the earlier periods, is scattered and fragmentary. Enough survives, however, to conclude that the acquisition of human beings as booty was an avowed goal of Greek warfare, apparently from the earliest times. By the fourth century, Aristotle in his *Politics* considered war, as a kind of hunting, to be a "natural mode of production." War was simply the hunting of humans and other movable goods, and enslavement in war was a law (*nomos*), "a sort of agreement under which the things conquered in war are said to belong to the conquerors" (1255a–1256b). For both soldier and civilian, then, capture in war meant almost certain enslavement or worse, as summary execution of both combatants and noncombatants was not uncommon throughout Greek history. In some instances, political and/or social considerations allowed captives to be ransomed, but in general, Greek prisoners of war became part of the vast pool of slave labor that underlay the ancient economy. This is perhaps not surprising when we consider the persisting pride of place slaveholding held in the Greek estimation of wealth.

Our evidence for POWs in the Greek Bronze Age is distressingly scant. The earliest evidence among Greek-speaking peoples in the southern Balkan peninsula is found in the Linear B texts found in archives at Pylos, Mycenae, Thebes, Tiryns, and elsewhere. The scribes of these archives concerned themselves primarily with economic matters, recording the exchange of various valuables and lands between the palace and individuals. Among the items accounted for in these tablets are individuals referred to as *douloi*, or slaves. At Pylos, 1,268 menial workers are ethnically identified as Milesian, Knidian, Lemnian, Chian, and Assuwan (Asian, that is, Anatolian). A small number of the women in the same list are described as *ra-wi-ja-ja*, or captive. There is good archaeological and Hittite textual evidence for Mycenaean military and colonial activity in the eastern Aegean islands and Anatolian mainland, but some of the places mentioned, Miletos in particular, are probable Mycenaean settlements. It is thus unclear whether these souls were brought to Pylos as prisoners of war from Miletos or Knidos, or bought in slave markets at these places. The separation of the captives from the other women may indicate that the former were acquired in war or piracy, while the latter were bought from slave emporia in the eastern Mediterranean.

The end of the Mycenaean palatial system around 1200 B.C.E. brought the end of literacy throughout the Greek world. The intervening four centuries, known as the Dark Age, provide no written record, and our next evidence are the Homeric epics, first codified in the seventh and sixth centuries B.C.E. While the precise historical value of these epics is still debated, most scholars agree that they preserve a picture of Greek Dark Age society. Thus, the *Iliad* and the *Odyssey*, with their ubiquitous tales of war and plunder, can provide some evidence for Greek attitudes toward and treatment of POWs during the Dark Age. The opening scene of the *Iliad* is the attempted ransoming of a POW, the daughter of Chryses, priest of Apollo. Chryses had come to ransom his daughter from Agamemnon, but the king haughtily refused and taunted the priest with the girl's future as a slave in Argos. When Agamemnon relents and restores Chryses's daughter, he demands compensation for his loss from the Greek troops. The rebuke of the king by Achilles is telling. "Honored son of Atreus, most grasping of men, how shall the great hearted Achaeans give you a prize? For we see no great heaps of loot lying about. That which we took from the cities, has been shared out. But collect it? Call it back from the fighting men? That would be a disgrace. So give the girl back to the god, now. For the Achaeans will pay you back three and four fold, if Zeus should grant us to sack the high citadel of Troy" (1.121–129).

This familiar story illustrates again the importance of loot, especially human beings, in Greek Dark Age warfare. Nor is this an isolated episode. Odysseus has no qualms telling his Phaecian hosts of his plundering on his way home. "From Ilion the wind bore me close to the Kikones at Ismaros. Thereupon I sacked the city and killed them—but we took their wives and many of their possessions, and divided them between ourselves" (*Odyssey*, 9.39–32). This is perhaps the earliest mention of a process for which the later Greeks developed a specific word, *andrapodismos*, the killing of the male population and enslavement of the women and children. We see from this tale that ransom was simply not an option for many POWs, since those who would have normally ransomed them, their family or fellow citizens, were either dead or enslaved themselves. Moreover, even when ransom was a likely and lucrative prospect for the captor, there was no guarantee of its acceptance. Both Menelaus (*Iliad*, 6.45–65) and Achilles (*Iliad*, 21.74–114) refuse ransom offers and kill their captives, both sons of Priam, on the battlefield. This bleak picture of POWs in Greek antiquity does not change fundamentally as we move into the historical period.

The seventh and sixth centuries B.C.E., known as the Archaic Age, saw a renaissance of Greek civilization, as the arts and trade between the city-states flourished, but the harsh fate of POWs persisted. An important source for this period is Herodotos of Halikarnassos, known as "the Father of History." Among his many tales is that of the rise of the tyrant Polykrates of Samos, who elevated that island to a formidable Aegean power in the later sixth century. In the course of his rise to regional hegemony, he fought and subdued many of the neighboring islands and towns along the Anatolian coast. Herodotos tells us (*History*, 3.39) that many captives of Polykrates' victory over the Lesbians and Milesians were enslaved and forced to dig a large trench around the fortifications of his capital, and POW work on public works is well attested elsewhere in Greek history. Another source for this period, the magnificently inscribed law code from the city of Gortyn in central Crete, records provisions for the ransoming of citizens captured in war. This ransoming was financed privately by fellow citizens, after which the ransomed citizen became a de facto slave of the ransomer. Servitude persisted until the benefactor deemed the debt repaid. This process was apparently the practice throughout Greek history, even in democratic Athens, as the fourth-century orator Demosthenes ransomed many Athenians captured by Philip of Macedon, apparently expecting the debt to be repaid. Ransom prices varied, but one or two minae (15–30 oz. troy) was customary.

Our sources for the fifth century are voluminous compared to those of earlier periods, yet nothing in them permits the view that Greek practice or attitudes toward POWs changed significantly. Indeed, as warfare became endemic, the methods of war and subsequent treatment of captives, both soldiers and noncombatants, became increasingly harsh. The pages of Thukydides, who recorded the 28-year Peloponnesian War between Athens and Sparta in his *Histories*, include numerous instances of *andrapodismos*. The small city-states Plataia, Melos, Torone, and Scione all suffered this fate at the hands of Athens or Sparta. The fate of Plataia offers perhaps the most telling instance of this phenomenon. An ally of Athens since 490 B.C.E., Plataia found itself besieged by Theban and Spartan forces in 428. Cut off from Athenian aid and faced with starvation, the city surrendered, on the terms that its citizens would receive a fair trial by the Spartans. The Plataians had committed no offense against Sparta in the current war and Plataia had been allied to Sparta since the Persian invasion of 480. Thukydides describes (3.68.1) the Spartan trial for each Plataian male: "Have you done anything to aid the Spartans or their allies in the war? As each man answered 'No,' he was taken away and put to death, no exceptions being made. Not less than 200 of the Plataians were killed in this way, together with twenty five Athenians who had been with them in the siege. The women were made slaves." Thukydides also describes imprisonment—for instance, the 120 Spartans whom the Athenians captured at Pylos in 424 B.C.E. But these prisoners were meant to be leverage in peace negotiations with the Spartans. In the absence of compelling political-economic incentive, the fate of the non-Athenians captured after the failure of the Athenians' Sicilian expedition in 413 is more typical. The POWs, numbering approximately 7,000, were herded into the Syrakusian quarries without adequate food or water and subjected to physical abuse from their captors for 10 weeks, after which they were sold as slaves.

The fourth century saw the eventual eclipse of the fractious Greek city-states by Philip II of Macedon. Philip showed himself to be no stranger to Greek practice in 349 when he razed Olynthos to the ground and enslaved its inhabitants. This period did see the increasing use of mercenaries by cities and individuals, but this affected the lot of POWs little. Mercenaries, when captured, were still liable to execution or enslavement, and victorious mercenaries expected human loot as part of their reward for service.

References

John Chadwick and Michael Ventris, *Documents in Mycenaean Greek* (Cambridge: Cambridge University Press, 1973).

Coleman Phillipson, *The International Law and Custom of Ancient Greece and Rome* (New York: Arno Press, 1979).

W. Kendrick Pritchett, *The Greek State at War*, vol. 5 (Berkeley: University of California Press, 1991).

T. Rihill, "War, Slavery, and Settlement in Early Greece," in *War and Society in the Greek World*, ed. John Rich and Graham Shipley (New York: Routledge, 1995).

—Matthew Gonzales

GREECE—HELLENISTIC PERIOD

The era after the death of Alexander the Great brought numerous changes to the role and status of the soldier taken POW. First and foremost, many of the soldiers captured in battle were no longer citizen militia fighting to protect their own *polis* (city-state), but rather were mercenary troops fighting for hire. Consequently, their loyalty to their general was often fleeting. There were many mercenaries about, and many were willing to desert for higher wages, especially if that choice was offered to them after capture, when the only alternative was execution. This constant shifting of sides became the dominant feature of captivity in the Hellenistic world.

For the most part, Hellenistic warfare occurred between the two Greek armies of either the large Greek-dominated empires (Ptolemaic, Seleucid, etc.) or the larger Greek states and leagues. These Hellenistic states were pitted against non-Greeks in occasional spurts of conquest, such as Lysimachus's failed Thracian campaign, Antiochus III's eastern reconquests, or the Spartan and Epirote incursions into Italy, but for the most part they warred with one another. Therefore it is important to recognize that there was continuity in that Greeks were still fighting fellow Greeks, but that a break from the past had occurred in that Hellenistic warfare was often characterized by conflicts between large empires.

For a variety of reasons, prisoners during this period were more apt to switch sides if the opportunity presented itself. In the first place, most soldiers were no longer fighting for their polis' preservation but frequently for a warlord/king. Quite often the troops' loyalty lasted only as long as their general won. As soon as he was defeated or the situation was jeopardized, the troops might defect, or even murder him. Thus Perdiccas was slain in Egypt, Euemenes was betrayed to Antigonus, Aecides was slain by his own men, and so on. Old friends found themselves fighting one another in wars of domination. Alexander's entire empire soon disintegrated in a series of civil wars and ever-shifting alliances. The question of loyalty became far more acute, as thousands of troops were captured in battle and their fates hung in the balance, to be determined by their former friends. Very often these former friends gave them a chance to defect, but sometimes they did not. Those who were spared and recruited might later face the prickly situation of being recaptured by their original commander.

As the generation that had served with Alexander passed on, a new set of rules began to form, reaching its completed state by the mid-third century. Now it was the king or his son who led an army into battle. Because the idea of a king was somewhat unnatural to Greeks outside Sparta, the mental frame of reference had to be expanded from polis to empire. This led to significant changes in political thought and patriotism. In some cases, the result was a diminishment of political investment, allowing soldiers to defect far more easily than in the Classical era. For this reason, we see far more defections from the troops of the major dynasts, while native troops almost never defected from the leagues or the city-states.

One practice that spread after Alexander's death concerned captured mercenaries, who were very often recruited to bolster the captor's army instead of being executed. As professional soldiers, they were useful, and loyalty or reliability seems to have been less of a concern than it was in the Roman world. In a time when much larger armies could be raised and marched against the rival empire, soldiers began to take on new significance for the king. It was time-consuming to execute thousands of POWs, a practice that in any case could toughen enemy resistance in the future. On the other hand, recruiting an enemy prisoner was as valuable as hiring two men: it increased the size of one's own army while decreasing the enemy's forces. So, defection and desertion of POWs became more prevalent; there are far more incidents of this in the Hellenistic era than in the Classical Era. If offering wages to POWs increased one's odds of victory, it was worthwhile.

Another factor was the increased ability of the *diadochoi* (successors) and others to bid for power with a realistic chance of success. While few had dared to challenge Alexander, after his death many of his generals made themselves kings. The feudal Macedonian politics of conspiracy and assassination assumed a much grander scale, and the vast number of troops available made the ambitions of the various generals possible. The rumor that an army or a city had defected from one general to another could create a momentum that could sweep a ruler into or out of power, as Antigonus II Gonatus knew from sad experience. The ability to win over an opponent's army by force of personality had great value in this era, though it had almost never been possible in the Classical era.

As the different generals began to joust for pieces of Alexander's empire, their own goals came into conflict with the ancestral ties that had traditionally put a brake on warfare. Most of the *diadochoi* had campaigned together under Alexander, and turning on one another represented a drastic break from the traditions they had grown up with and practiced all their military careers. Perdiccas had difficulty bringing himself to fight Ptolemy, who had been his comrade of old. The first time Antigonus captured Eumenes, he could not bring himself to execute him (the second time, however, he did). Seleucus also held his son-in-law Demetrius I Poliorcetes hostage for years before executing him.

The stakes grew once the *diadochoi* realized that Alexander's empire was not to be preserved for his son. Advantage began to trump old friendships. In his *Bibliotheca historica*, Diodorus Siculus reveals the ever-changing status of alliances in Greece from the time of the Lamian War to the murder of Alexander IV among the factions of Cassander, Polypserchon, and Antigonus. As the leadership began to break with their traditional attitudes and adherence to traditions, faith, and honor, the foot soldier, too, began to see the world in a very different light. Old traditions about limited warfare could not be maintained or expected out of the common foot soldier when the general himself was making war on his former comrade, brother-in-law, or even brother. As a result, the Hellenistic era saw a general degeneration of the standards of fair play in warfare, including more frequent breaking of alliances, violations of international law (attacking heralds and temples), and the return to power of several unusually savage tyrants who repeatedly committed atrocities of all sorts.

Although more and more POWs were recruited rather than executed, this does not mean that humanitarian motives were stronger. As W. K. Pritchett points out, Greeks hardly ever spared captives for humanitarian reasons; profit was always foremost in their minds. When a body of troops could be turned against their former masters, they were twice as useful—for the information they could bring and for reducing the opponent's army. However, survival by defection was not always offered. On some occasions, the POWs were enslaved or executed on the spot. Those in the Upper Satrapies who rebelled immediately after Alexander's death were put to death by Macedonian troops following Perdiccas's orders, even though they had surrendered. A survey of the number of occurrences of massacre shows that respect for POWs, even those who were Hellenes, had not increased dramatically since the Classical era. As Polybius remarks (5.9.8), when Antigonus III Doson defeated Cleomenes III of Sparta, Antigonus "had whatever authority he might wish to use the city and the citizens any way he chose," revealing that, even in this changing world, the rights of the victor had altered little.

Another factor that warns against assuming humanitarian motives is the relative infrequency with which besiegers punished only the ringleaders of a rebellion. From a practical point of view, this alternative should have been widely practiced. Mass reprisal carried the risk of inflaming the opinion of others against the aggressor and had the effect of persuading resistance to the bitter end, since surrender was futile. However, Greeks generally continued to regard humanitarianism as a sign of weakness. A few of the Hellenistic kings engaged this policy at the start of their reigns, but few maintained it for long.

Therefore we begin to see more examples of voluntary surrender after the sacrifice of the ringleaders in return for better treatment. Two factors led to this. In many cases, a garrison was holding a city and the population rose against them; the people had no reason to be loyal to a group of mercenary jailers. Secondly, a general mood of practicality on the part of the victor and besieged came about. Diodorus says (21.14.3) that "in many cases, indulging one's heart to fight with spirit to the end should be checked. For at times it is profitable to lay off and to pay money for safety and to esteem forgiveness above revenge." Polybius (18.37) encourages Greeks to be more moderate in victory, though there were many incidents where this was not the case. As Pritchett observes, humanitarianism was by far the lesser factor involved.

In Hellenistic times, the lot of civilian POWs had little improved since Homeric times, and they continued to suffer. Greeks often preferred to treat for terms and surrender rather than perish, and those who fell into enemy hands felt less shame than their Roman counterparts. (The lofty ideals of death before dishonor were mostly cast aside in the Hellenistic era. Whether this was due to the changing role of the individual in a cosmopolitan world or from a general degeneration of values varies from case to case.) However, in many cases civilian prisoners were violated, enslaved, or at least stripped of their possessions by the victor. Determined to resist to the bitter end, Abydos refused to surrender to Philip V and the population committed mass suicide, as the people of Saguntum had done just a few years earlier. There were incidents of clemency, unexpectedly dealt out by kings hoping to win over the sentiments of observers, and new rulers might attempt to create a good reputation by treating generously the civilians whose towns they had assailed. Philip V began his reign by offering clemency to cities he had attacked. However, he later revealed his true colors and committed many violations of international law, even attacking the temples of the gods. Clearly, kings were fearful of encouraging future rebellions by appearing to be weak. Thus, they often resorted to harsh punishments and exacted revenge from civilians, despite the ill repute such actions incurred. As Cicero reminds us, the operative sentiment was, "Let them hate so long as they fear."

Thus we must acknowledge that our sources suggest a decline in atrocities against POWs, but perhaps the decline was less significant than it seems. It may well be a sign of the limitations of our extant sources rather than a product of an era of more civilized warfare. Polybius says of the Aetolians (4.67), "they knew no limits in war or peace," meaning that they were as ruthless in 200 B.C.E. in their treatment of POWs as they had been 400 years before. Polybius had a strong anti-Aetolian prejudice, for he repeatedly mentions their atrocities and even defends the enslavement of their Mantinean allies. If we had the account of Phylarcus, whom Polybius criticizes for being overly dramatic in his description of the sack of Mantinea, we might also have a long list of atrocities committed by the Macedonians and Achaeans. So although our sources have to be accepted, it is with the warning that they may reveal too little of the real story in ancient warfare.

The simultaneous careers of Pyrrhus and Ptolemy Ceraunus illustrate well the conflicting values of the Hellenistic world. The former treated his POWs humanely and sent all of the Romans home to celebrate the Saturnalia. He was regarded as a man of chivalry and daring in a turbulent world. The latter was regarded as the ultimate opportunist, with no sense of loyalty or fair play. Repudiated by his father, he murdered the king who gave him hospitality and later seized Macedon and murdered his nephews after taking an oath to protect them. Since kings of such varying natures now ruled the Hellenistic world, the fate of all men, especially POWs, was subject to such random forces of caprice that the only safe policy was one of flexibility. Today's POW sometimes became tomorrow's captor. Therefore it paid to consider leniency: the tables might one day be turned, and help might be needed from where it was least expected.

References

F. Hultsch, *The Histories of Polybius*, trans. Evelyn S. Shuckburgh (Bloomington: Indiana University Press, 1962).

W. Kendrick Pritchett, *The Greek State at War* (Berkeley: University of California Press, 1971).

Diodorus Siculus, *The Bibliotheca Historica*, trans. John Skelton (London: Oxford University Press, 1956–1957).

—*Gaius Stern*

GROTIUS, HUGO (HUIGH DE GROOT) (1583–1645)

The Dutch jurist Hugo Grotius was the author of *The Law of War and Peace* (1625), widely considered to be the first treatise on international law. He had personal experience with captivity: imprisoned in 1618 for his political views, he escaped from Loevestein Castle in a crate of books in 1621 and went into exile in Paris.

A committed humanist who studied in France and served as a diplomat on behalf of Sweden, Grotius used biblical and classical sources to support the idea of a *jus gentium* (law of nations). Predicated on a purported natural law, his legal system extols the virtue of political restraint while advocating minimal recourse to the destruction of property and life in the conduct of war.

Grotius's central contention is that war is a socially natural, unavoidable evil that, to be just, must be kept in check. One the most fundamental consequences of war is the capture of property by either belligerent. In keeping with Roman law, which posited slavery as an alternative to the indiscriminate killing of captives and their families, Grotius describes prisoners of war as similar to slaves and, as such, to simple property. He submits that natural decency and equity demand that vanquished soldiers be treated with clemency, provided they have surrendered unconditionally and beg for mercy. Grotius grants slaves the right to escape while war is still being waged. The termination of hostilities, however, warrants their staying with their victors until killed or unilaterally freed. He also suggests that a modern, law-abiding state should limit the practice of slavery and revert as systematically as possible to the practices of hostage-taking and ransom.

References

Christian Gellinek, *Hugo Grotius* (Boston: Twayne Publishers, 1983).

Onuma Yasuaki, ed., *A Normative Approach to War: Peace, War, and Justice in Hugo Grotius* (Oxford: Clarendon Press, 1993).

—*Laurent Ditmann*

GUANTÁNAMO BAY DETENTION CENTER

Guantánamo Bay (commonly referred to as Gitmo in U.S. military parlance) is a small U.S. naval base on the eastern end of the island of Cuba, bordering on Oriente Province, that the Americans acquired as a result of the Spanish-American War of 1898. United States' possession of the Guantánamo Bay area (116 sq. km.) was not formalized until a 1903 treaty between Cuba and the U.S. leased the base area and Bahia Honda to the Americans; Bahia Honda was subsequently abandoned but Guantánamo Bay has remained in U.S. possession. The treaty of 1903 was affirmed in another formal treaty signed in 1934, which gave the United States complete jurisdiction and control over the territory, although formal sovereignty still resided with Cuba. In return for this lease the United States provided Cuba with a small remittance of $4,085.00 per year. The 1934 treaty cannot be abrogated by one side alone; thus, the U.S. government is legally entitled to retain possession of the area as long as it wishes.

The base was an obscure backwater between the two world wars but became a major training and anti-submarine center during World War II. With the assumption to power of Fidel Castro in Cuba in 1959, Guantánamo became one of many sources of friction between the U.S. and Cuba.

The first large-scale use of Guantánamo as a detention center came in 1994 when hundreds of Cuban and Haitian refugees, picked up off the coast of Florida, were held at the base. This detention of foreign nationals was challenged in federal court, with the court ruling that it had no jurisdiction to hear the case because the action was taking place on Cuban and not U.S. territory. This was a useful ruling for any U.S. administration seeking to remove the U.S. courts from overseeing their detention of foreigners in any future conflict, and one the Bush Administration sought to employ in 2002.

The 11 September 2001 terrorist attacks against targets in the United States led directly to the overthrow of the Taliban regime in Afghanistan. The Americans held the Taliban regime indirectly responsible for the 9/11 attacks because the Taliban refused to surrender Osama Bin Laden and other Al Qaeda leaders suspected of masterminding the terrorist strikes.

It was not long before hundreds of suspected Taliban and Al Qaeda figures, captured in Afghanistan in 2001 and 2002, began to arrive at Guantánamo Bay for interrogation and incarceration. The normal procedure for soldiers who are captured by United States' armed forces is for the rights of prisoners of war under the Geneva Convention to be guaranteed. The Bush Administration established the position that the Geneva Convention did not apply to captured Taliban or Al Qaeda "operatives" because the Taliban was not a legitimate government and Al Qaeda had no government affiliation at all.

U.S. government officials began to use the term "unlawful combatants" rather than POWs when referring to captured Taliban or Al Qaeda fighters. The term has no definition under international law, and its use was an early sign that the administration of President George W. Bush would not be held to the terms of the Geneva Convention when dealing with Taliban and Al Qaeda prisoners. Later, U.S. authorities adjusted their position somewhat and declared that captured Taliban prisoners would receive POW status, but captured Al Qaeda prisoners would not.

The Bush Administration also stated that non-U.S. citizens captured in the War Against Terror could face trial by military commissions (military tribunals), a process that would have greatly reduced due process mechanisms (in comparison to a civilian court or even a military court-martial procedure). President Bush issued an executive order on 13 November 2001 authorizing the establishment of military commissions to prosecute unlawful combatants captured in armed conflicts. The presidential order was specifically directed at Al Qaeda for violations of the laws of war and other applicable laws, but no definition of these violations was given.

A bloody prisoner uprising in November 2001 at a prison compound near Mazar-e-Sharif in Afghanistan led to the death of Central Intelligence Agency operative Michael Spann, the first known U.S. fatality in the war in Afghanistan. The problem of controlling Taliban and Al Qaeda prisoners was one of the reasons why the U.S. government began to transport selected prisoners out of Afghanistan to other locations, including Guantánamo Bay, Cuba. The first 20 detainees left Afghanistan by air for Guantánamo on 11 January 2002. After that first movement, the transport of prisoners to Guantánamo was a regular occurrence; by the end of the year, over 600 detainees were held in U.S. custody there.

Conditions at Camp X-ray (the detention center at Guantánamo) drew severe criticism by human rights groups and the international press. The prisoners were kept in individual 1.8-by-2.4-meter cells that were constructed of concrete floors, metal roofs, and exposed chain-link fences for the outside walls. The detainees, the vast majority of whom were Muslim males, were allowed to pray but were forced to shave their beards. Pictures showing the prisoners shackled and hooded while being moved also drew international protests, although Vice President Dick Cheney was of the opinion that the detainees were being treated better than they deserved.

Secretary of Defense Donald Rumsfeld's January 2002 announcement that the prisoners at Guantánamo Bay would not be given POW status created a huge outcry with human rights groups. The International Committee of the Red Cross flatly repudiated the American position, stating that all prisoners were to be given status as POWs under the terms of the Geneva Convention.

Reports showed that there were internal disagreements over the status of the Guantánamo prisoners within the Bush Administration. Secretary of State Colin Powell argued for POW status for both Al Qaeda and Taliban prisoners, and for dropping the whole concept of "illegal combatant." Such disagreements pointed to a lack of clarity at this time over the actual legal status of the prisoners being held at Guantánamo.

Several court challenges in the United States have failed to bring the Guantánamo detainees back into the orbit of the American justice system. U.S. federal courts hearing such cases have ruled either that the courts have no jurisdiction over anything that happens in the "sovereign" territory of

Cuba, or that those attempting to represent the prisoners have no standing with the courts; in other words, representatives have no legal right to bring a suit on behalf of the prisoners. In 2005, the Supreme Court agreed to hear a case that will determine the legality of the military tribunals in trying and convicting foreign nationals, many of whom are held at Guantánamo.

The Bush Administration, for its part, has consistently denied that any treaty of any kind signed by the U.S. has any application to the Guantánamo detainees, and has continued to promise that they would be treated humanely. There have been several reports of attempted suicides, and the prisoners have also attempted an organized hunger strike to protest their status. Despite the fact that a number of detainees have been released, the issue of the prisoners' status under U.S. law remained a hot political topic, both domestically and internationally. Critics of Guantánamo Bay claim that Camp X-ray has done more harm than good in the War on Terror, while defenders of the Bush Administration's policies have stated that it was a necessary evil.

See also Abu Ghraib Detention Center; Afghan Wars; Iraq War; War on Terror

References

Jeremy Rabkin, "After Guantánamo: The War Over the Geneva Convention," *National Interest* 68 (2002): 15–26.

Michael Ratner and Ellen Ray, *Guantánamo: What the World Should Know* (White River Junction, VT: Chelsea Green Publishing, 2004).

David Rose, *Guantánamo: The War on Human Rights* (New York: New Press, 2004).

W. Frederick Zimmerman, ed., *Basic Documents About the Treatment of the Detainees at Guantánamo and Abu Ghraib* (Ann Arbor, MI: Nimble Books, 2004).

—*Andrew Young*

Guatemalan Civil War (1960–1996)

The civil war had its roots in the political chaos that plagued Guatemala through the 1940s and 1950s, a period of dictatorships, invasions from neighboring countries, and failed coup attempts. The last of these before the outbreak of open civil war occurred in 1960, when a group of junior military officers attempted to overthrow the autocratic regime of General Ydigoras Fuentes. They failed, but the survivors went into hiding and became the instigators of a civil war that would last 36 years. Like most such conflicts in central America, it would pit left-wing guerrilla groups, backed by Cuba and the Soviet Union, against right-wing government forces, supported by the United States; the biggest losers, as always, would be the country's civilian population.

Over the course of the war, hundreds of thousands of civilians and suspected leftist guerrillas were imprisoned by the government, and many more were slaughtered out of hand. By 1982, the presidency had been assumed by Efrain Rios Montt, a lay pastor and retired general who quickly set about trying to crush the leftist opposition. He used conscription to create local civilian defense patrols, which worked in cooperation with the army to sweep away resistance in guerrilla-held territory. In this they were largely successful, but at enormous cost. The Conference of Catholic Bishops accused the army and militia of countless massacres of civilians, accusations that appeared to have been borne out by Rios Montt's declaration to his people, quoted in the *New York Times* in July 1982: "If you are with us, we'll feed you; if not, we'll kill you." The declaration obviously had the desired impact, for on 18 July government troops descended on the village of Plan de Sánchez and began an orgy of torture, rape, looting, and murder that left over 250 villagers, mostly women and children, dead.

That this was the policy of successive Guatemalan governments was made clear in a 1998 report issued by the Archbishop's Office on Human Rights, under its Recovery of Historical Memory project. The report detailed the many abuses committed by government troops and local militias, including the murder of unarmed civilians, the torture of guerrilla fighters, and the kidnapping of security suspects. The report admitted that the left-wing factions had not been blameless in this regard, but that over 80 percent of the war crimes had been committed by soldiers and militiamen on the government side. In the eyes of many observers, the allegations made in the report were validated two days after its release, when Bishop Juan Gerardi, who coordinated the Recovery of Historical Memory project, was assassinated by three military officers.

The peace accords signed in 1996 formally ended the civil war, but the violence continued, and was not limited to politically motivated assassinations. In 2001, the United Nations Verification Mission in Guatemala (MINUGUA) reported that the government was continuing its campaign against political opponents, using illegal detention, kidnappings, and summary execution to eliminate the opposition. This officially sanctioned violence, when combined with the increase in drug trafficking, prison revolts, hostage-takings, and petty crime, plunged the country into a public security crisis from which it has not yet emerged.

In December 2005, new information on the fate of detainees held by the government during the civil war came to light with the discovery of a large collection of files from the country's notorious National Police. The files included the names of thousands of civilians, with notations such as "disappeared," "assassinated," or "political detainee." It will take months to collate and examine the files, but many Guatemalans hope the results will shed light on the fate of the 40,000 civilians who disappeared during the civil war, and who have been presumed to have died in government custody.

References
Daniel Wilkinson, *Silence in the Mountain: Stories of Terror, Betrayal, and Forgetting in Guatemala* (Durham, NC: Duke University Press, 2004).

—*Jonathan F. Vance*

GUERRILLAS

Also called partisans, irregulars, and *francs tireurs,* guerrillas (the term means, literally, "small wars," and was coined in Spain in the early nineteenth century) are soldiers who engage in limited offensive actions. Traditionally, guerrilla units are small, loosely organized groups of men and women who lack the strength of numbers or equipment to engage in regular face-to-face combat against the enemy. Instead, avoiding and evading large, decisive battles, guerrillas use surprise attacks and ambushes to kill, to sabotage, to raid enemy bases, and to interrupt enemy lines of communication and supply.

Guerrilla warfare originally consisted of military operations carried out by irregular bands or forces against the rear of an enemy army or by local inhabitants against an occupying or invading force. Guerrillas, however, have operated as members of regular armies, and guerrilla warfare has been carried out as an adjunct to larger, world wars. Guerrillas have fought against invading or occupying forces, in revolutions, civil wars, and popular uprisings.

The instances of guerrilla warfare are too numerous to list completely. Indeed, guerrilla tactics and guerrilla warfare have existed for centuries. Roman General Fabius Maximus used guerrilla tactics against Hannibal in 217 B.C.E., as did Judas Maccabaeus in the Maccabaean revolt against Syria in 166 B.C.E. Maccabaeus and his followers lived in "secret places in the wilderness." Operating at night, they attacked towns and cities, setting them on fire and slaughtering the enemy. In modern times, nearly without interruption from 1775 to the present, guerrillas have been in action somewhere in the world. "Swamp Fox" Francis Marion and Thomas Sumter engaged in guerrilla warfare against the British during the American Revolution. French citizens acted as guerrillas during the French Revolution, and then used guerrilla tactics against the French Republic in the Vendée in 1793.

It was in Spain that the word *guerrilla* first came into use. After Napoleon defeated the regular Spanish armies in 1808, irregular independent bands, named "guerrillas" by the Spaniards, continued fighting against the French occupation forces. Guerrillas in

Southern Italy, the Tyrol, and Russia also slowed Napoleon's advance in those countries. Guerrilla warfare occurred in the Latin American wars of independence (ca. 1810–1821), and in the nineteenth-century wars of independence in Greece, Poland, and Italy. Native people used guerrilla tactics against Europeans in the many nineteenth-century colonial wars on the African and Indian continents. In North America, Amerindians used guerrilla methods against other tribes, and later warriors such as Black Hawk and Chief Joseph used the tactics against white invaders. During the U.S. Civil War, Ranger John S. Mosby, John Hunt Morgan, and Nathan Bedford Forrest of the Confederacy melded European cavalry tactics with the irregular tactics of Native Americans to create raiding forces against the Union.

The Franco-Prussian War of 1870–1871 had a guerrilla component, while guerrilla revolts in Cuba between 1868 and 1878, and again in 1895, led to the Spanish-American War. The Boer War pitted Dutch-Boer guerrilla fighters against British forces attempting to employ effective counter-guerrilla measures. Pancho Villa and a force of about a thousand guerrillas crossed the international border and raided Columbus, New Mexico, in March of 1916.

World War I produced two great guerrilla leaders: German General Paul von Lettow-Vorbeck, whose small European force and larger native force fought the British for four years in Central Africa; and Colonel T. E. Lawrence, who helped organize an Arab national rising against the Turks to support the British in the Middle East. Guerrillas operated in Russia during and after the Russian Revolution. The Irish Republican Army used guerrilla tactics to fight the British Black-and-Tans until 1922, and British occupiers since then.

During World War II, partisan guerrillas adjunct to regular troops fought the Germans in the Soviet Union, Yugoslavia, Poland, Greece, France, and Italy and fought the Japanese in China and the Philippines. Guerrilla warfare continued in post–World War II wars of decolonization in Indochina, Malaya, Algeria, Cyprus, Suez, Palestine, and Kenya. Guerrilla war was virtually uninterrupted in Vietnam, first against the French, then against United States troops for nearly 20 years.

Guerrillas continued, and still continue, to fight national, ethnic, separatist, and religious wars in Israel and the Middle East, throughout much of Africa, Northern Ireland, Afghanistan, and Latin America. The 1970s saw the phenomenon of modern urban guerrillas: the Italian Red Brigades, the German Bader Meinhoff, and the Symbionese Liberation Army in the United States. In Kosovo, in the former Yugoslavia, guerrillas carried out brutal warfare and massacres against civilians.

Guerrillas must be mobile, able to escape and disappear when challenged by the enemy. Thus, guerrilla warfare has been carried out more successfully in difficult mountainous or forested areas, particularly in terrain with which the guerrillas are familiar and are able to use to their advantage against larger bodies of regular troops. The great German military theorist Carl von Clausewitz advised guerrillas to operate in rough country and away from the seacoast. So that they are not recognized by the enemy and can quickly blend in with the civilian population, guerrillas generally do not wear a recognizable uniform or insignia identifying them as members of any organized force.

Guerrilla warfare also involves the local civilian population. Civilians may make up part or the bulk of a guerrilla force. In addition, local civilians—willing or unwilling—are often called upon to provide food and shelter to guerrillas in the area. Guerrilla war thus frequently brings reprisals, not only against the guerrillas themselves, but against the civilian population among whom the guerrillas live and operate.

Whether or not guerrillas should receive POW status and therefore protection under international law has preoccupied legislators since the early nineteenth century. In the Napoleonic era, states usually refused to treat guerrillas as POWs unless they fought openly in organized units under the public authorization of their government. The Lieber Code of 1863 also adopted this position: unless guerrillas belonged to and wore the uniform of their government's army, they were to be treated as "highway robbers or pirates." During the Franco-Prussian War of 1870–1871, the Germans demanded that French *francs-tireurs* possess written orders from the French government if they wished to be treated as POWs. Summary execution was the fate of guerrillas without such orders. Beginning with the Brussels Declaration of 1874 and continuing with the Hague Convention of 1907 and the Geneva Convention of 1929, however, lawmakers gradually accepted the notion that guerrillas should be granted POW status, provided they met four criteria: that they are commanded by an individual responsible for his subordinates, carry arms openly, bear an emblem visible from a distance, and respect the laws and customs of war. During World War II, the German government argued that resistance groups operating in occupied territory were not eligible for POW status, even if they fulfilled the four conditions. The 1949 Geneva Convention addressed this matter by stating that guerrilla forces operating in occupied territory should indeed receive recognition as POWs, provided they met the four conditions.

References

Robert B. Asprey, *War in the Shadows: The Guerrilla in History* (London: Macdonald, 1976).

Lewis H. Gann, *Guerrillas in History* (Stanford: Hoover Institution, 1971).

Anthony James Joes, *Guerilla Warfare: A Historical, Biographical, and Bibliographical Sourcebook* (Westport, CT: Greenwood Press, 1996).

Walter Laqueur, *Guerilla: A Historical and Critical Study* (Boulder, CO: Westview, 1984).

—*Victoria C. Belco*

GULAG

Gulag (Chief Administration of Corrective Labor Camps) was the official designation of the forced labor camps in the Soviet Union that were originally established to hold opponents of the Soviet Russian regime. Under Soviet leader Josef Stalin, the Gulag became the pillar of the Communist system of oppression, a gigantic source of free labor in support of the Soviet economy.

The system was established under the rule of Soviet leader V. I. Lenin. By 1934, under the Soviet secret police, the NKVD, the camps had several million inmates, including political prisoners, religious dissenters, and criminals. At the height of Stalin's terror, the number of arbitrary arrests increased. A religious observance or a remark that was critical of the regime could be enough for the individual concerned to be sentenced to indefinite confinement in Gulag.

Conditions in the camps were very harsh. The prisoners were forced to participate in huge construction projects such as the White Sea–Baltic Canal, the Moscow-Volga Canal, the Baikal-Amur railroad, hydroelectric stations, strategic roads, and industrial enterprises. Prisoners were also employed in mines; for example, the gold mines in the remote Kolyma region in Siberia were said to have been the center of the worst camps, where confinement led to certain death. The prisoners were inadequately fed and badly clothed. At the same time, weather conditions were severe and the long working hours, combined with disease and malnutrition, contributed to a very high death rate. A reduction of the Gulag population started after Stalin's death in 1953, but some camps were open until the end of Soviet leader Mikhail Gorbachev's rule in 1991.

Aleksandr Solzhenitsyn's massive, three-volume study of Gulag brought knowledge of the camp system to the public in the 1970s, although experts in the West had known for many years about the camps. An estimated 60 million people died as a result of Lenin's and Stalin's policies of terror and repression, of which Gulag was an important symbol and tool.

References

Robert Conquest, *Kolyma: The Arctic Death Camps* (New York: Viking Press, 1978).

Alexander Solzhenitsyn, *The Gulag Archipelago, 1918–1956: An Experiment in Literary Investigation* (New York: Harper and Row, 1985).

—*Bertil Häggman*

GULF WAR (1990–91)

The war in the Persian Gulf, precipitated by Iraq's invasion of Kuwait in August 1990 and brought to a close by an invasion of Iraq by a large coalition of members of the United Nations, brought captivity issues into the homes of millions of television viewers. The treatment of Coalition POWs was particularly controversial because it was so widely publicized.

Forty-seven members of the Coalition forces, including 20 Americans, 12 Britons, nine Saudis, and two Italians, were captured during the war, along with over 4,000 Kuwaiti servicemen. Many of the western POWs were immediately turned into symbols in a propaganda campaign launched by their captors. British, American, Saudi, and Italian airmen, who had been shot down and captured in raids on Iraq, appeared on Iraqi television looking dazed and beaten, and a number of them mumbled statements that they had been wrong to attack Iraqi civilians. Later, their captors announced that they would be dispatched to strategic centers to act as human shields, in the hope that their very presence would deter the Coalition from bombing those centers (an unconfirmed report in January 1991 claimed that a Coalition prisoner had been killed in a bombing raid). Both of these actions were widely condemned by other governments. Using prisoners as human shields is expressly forbidden by the 1949 Geneva Convention Relative to the Treatment of Prisoners of War (Article 3), as is exposing prisoners to acts of violence or to public curiosity (Article 13). The International Committee of the Red Cross (ICRC) stated that broadcasting prisoners' images (and parading them through angry crowds, as the Iraqis reportedly did) contravened Article 14 of the Geneva Convention, which stipulates that prisoners are entitled "in all circumstances to respect for their persons and their honor." Coalition leaders made the return of the POWs (and of western civilians who had been interned since before the war began) a priority in negotiations aimed at ending the war, and this aspect of the negotiations produced little conflict between the two sides.

On the other side, the Coalition captured 86,743 Iraq officers and men: 63,948 by American forces, 16,921 by Arab units, 5,005 by the British, and 869 by the French. They were detained in 11 camps, such as the British-operated a camp called Maryhill near the town of Al Qaysumah. There, the prisoners were treated according to the dictates of the Geneva Convention: they were provided with special tinned food that had been prepared under Muslim law; 69 wounded POWs were treated at British medical facilities; they were interrogated by Kuwaiti civilians brought in from the United Kingdom; and they were not asked to work, with the exception of repairing tents blown down by sandstorms. In January 1991, to avoid duplication of facilities, Iraqis captured by British forces were transferred to American control; later, they were turned over to the Saudis, after an agreement regarding their proper treatment had been reached.

Resolution 686 of the United Nations called on all sides to release their POWs with the assistance of the ICRC, despite the fact that Saddam Hussein apparently did not want all the Iraqi soldiers back and some of them expressed little wish to return to Iraq. Nevertheless, ICRC delegates played an active role in the repatriation of POWs after the conclusion of hostilities. Some 70,000 Iraqi prisoners expressed a desire to be repatriated to their homeland, and the Red Cross began organizing these operations in March 1991. At the same time, the Committee administered the repatriation of over 5,000 Kuwaiti military personnel and civilians who had been captured during the Iraqi invasion of Kuwait and were detained in

Iraq, and of the Coalition POWs captured during Operation Desert Storm, as well as 1,436 civilians from seven countries who had been interned by Saddam's government.

Still, doubt remained about the completeness of these operations. Kuwait claimed that Iraq had not released all of its detainees, something that Iraq vehemently denied at first. But in September 1994, Baghdad admitted that it did have information on 45 Kuwaiti POWs, and later acknowledged that it held 126 Kuwaitis, although the government maintained that it had lost track of them. As of 1999, Kuwait was still pressing Iraq for information on the whereabouts of 605 of its citizens who had been reported in Iraqi detention but who had not been heard from since the war's end. By the same token, questions still surround the fate of Lieutenant Commander Michael Speicher, an American airman shot down on 17 January 1991. Investigation of the wreckage of his aircraft suggested that Speicher had ejected safely, and some believe that he was made a POW by the Iraqis but never reported as such; indeed, there is credible evidence that he was in Iraqi captivity. After much public pressure, the U.S. military changed his status from "Killed in Action" to "Missing/Captured."

Civilian internment was also a feature of the Gulf War. In a controversial measure, the British government imprisoned 35 Iraqis living in the United Kingdom, on the grounds that they were serving members of the Iraqi military. They were held at the recently converted Rollestone prison camp in southern England, where British authorities considered each case individually to determine if detention was warranted. Four were released shortly thereafter, on the grounds that sufficient doubt existed as to whether they were members of the Iraqi military, and three more were released after examination by tribunals. The rest were indeed, in the view of British officials, Iraqi servicemen, and they remained imprisoned in Rollestone until the conclusion of hostilities. In addition, the British government ordered the internment of 75 Iraqi civilians living in Britain who were deemed to represent security risks. They were held at civilian prisons such as Pentonville and Wormwood Scrubs while their cases were considered; some were released under restrictions, while others were issued with deportation notices. The majority of the 75 remained interned until the end of the war, when they were released.

See also Human Shields

References

Charles Allen, *Thunder and Lightning: The RAF in the Gulf* (London: HMSO, 1991).
Peter de la Billière, *Storm Command: A Personal Account of the Gulf War* (London: HarperCollins, 1992).
John Peters and John Nichol, *Tornado Down: Their Gulf War Ordeal* (London: Penguin, 2004).
Peter Rowe, ed., *The Gulf War 1990–91 in International and English Law* (London: Routledge, 1993).

—Jonathan F. Vance

H

Hague Conventions of 1899 and 1907

In response to an invitation by Czar Nicholas II of Russia, all of the great powers and most of the lesser powers sent representatives to a conference convened at the Hague in the Netherlands on 18 May 1899. That conference was intended to take up not only issues related to the size of military and naval establishments, but also those concerning the introduction of new weapons of war, refinement of diplomatic mechanisms for the avoidance of war, and rules for the conduct of war, including the treatment of combatants and noncombatants.

The completed convention provided for a permanent court to hear cases in international law, and it established procedures for arbitration and mediation in international disputes. Traditional rules of land and sea combat were reaffirmed and clarified while new ones were adopted, including the inviolability of hospital ships, a five-year ban on bombing from balloons, and a ban on poison gases and dumdum bullets in war.

Concerning prisoners of war, the 1899 convention established rules providing that all combatant and noncombatant members of the armed forces enjoyed the status of prisoners of war. Confinement of prisoners was to be no more restrictive than absolutely necessary for safety, and prisoners were to retain property rights in all possessions other than implements of war and military papers. Prisoners could be utilized for labor only if it was neither excessive nor involved in military operations, and reimbursement for the value of this labor, minus the cost of maintaining the prisoner, was to be paid to the detaining power at the end of the war. Belligerent powers were obliged to maintain prisoners on a par with their own soldiers in regard to food, clothing, and shelter, and they might impose their own military regulations upon prisoners in inflicting punishment for insubordination. Escaped prisoners recaptured after rejoining their own forces or quitting the captor's territory were not subject to disciplinary punishment, and a spy captured after rejoining his own forces enjoyed the status of a prisoner. Every prisoner was bound to declare his true name and rank and to observe scrupulously any condition of parole. His own government was barred from requiring violations of these conditions. Reporters and others assigned to the army were entitled, upon producing a certificate of their status, to be treated as prisoners of war. A bureau of information on prisoners was to be established by each belligerent, and relief societies were permitted to inspect places of internment. Prisoners were to receive free postage and to enjoy freedom of religion. Wills, death certificates, and burials had to accord with regulations for comparable ranks in the captor's forces. The provisions of the Geneva Convention of 1864 governed the treatment of sick and wounded prisoners. Neutral states had the right and duty to intern, under humane conditions, troops of the belligerent armies that entered their territory, and at the conclusion of peace these states were entitled to reimbursement of the expenses for such internment.

In 1906, the Russian Foreign Office issued letters to independent nations proposing another conference, and on 15 June 1907, that conference convened at the Hague, with delegates signing an international convention on 18 October. Besides significant changes in other policies, the 1907 Convention established some important alterations in the rules regarding prisoners and internees. Captured officers were exempted from mandatory labor. Forced service against one's own country was never to be required, even when a foreign national had served in the capturing country's forces before hostilities. For example, a German who had served with British forces in the Boer War (1899–1902) and was captured by the British while serving with the German forces in World War I (1914–1918) could not be forced to serve in the British forces again. Crew of a merchant ship enlisted as a ship of war were granted status as prisoners of war, provided that the ship was properly marked, the crew was under military discipline, and the captain was commissioned by the state. Repatriation of prisoners and internees from neutrals and belligerents alike was to be as expeditious as possible at war's end, and bureaus of information concerning prisoners were required to provide far more detailed information about all persons who were interned or captured.

Virtually all of the independent powers of the world ratified the Final Act of the Hague Convention of 1907, with only Ethiopia, Liberia, Costa Rica, Honduras, and Paraguay absent. This fact was significant, given that it was the 1907 Convention that governed captivity during World War I.

See also Brussels Declaration; Geneva Convention of 1929; Geneva Convention of 1949; Geneva Convention Additional Protocols; Geneva Conventions of 1864 and 1906; International Law

References

Calvin DeArmond Davis, *The United States and the First Hague Peace Conference* (Ithaca, NY: Cornell University Press, 1962).

———, *The United States and the Second Hague Peace Conference: American Diplomacy and International Organization, 1899–1914* (Durham, NC: Duke University Press, 1975).

William I. Hull, *The Two Hague Conferences and Their Contribution to International Law* (Boston: International School of Peace/Ginn and Co., 1908).

James Brown Scott, ed., *The Hague Conventions and Declarations of 1899 and 1907* (New York: Carnegie Endowment for International Peace/Oxford University Press, 1915).

—*Patrick M. O'Neil*

HANOI HILTON

The Hanoi Hilton became infamous during the Vietnam War as the prison where many American POWs were held captive. The edifice, which predated the Vietnam War by many years, was built by the French as a prison and officially labeled by the North Vietnamese government as Hoa Lo. Americans later dubbed it the Hanoi Hilton. It sat near the center of the city, an impressive structure taking up an entire, irregularly shaped city block. The prison was virtually escape-proof. The 16-foot-high walls were massively thick and capped by thousands of pieces of broken glass imbedded into cement. This imposing array of forbidding ragged glass points was topped by several strands of barbed and electric wire. Interspersed along the top of the wall were several guard towers, each with a commanding view. Upon arrival, prisoners were placed in one of four separate areas of the camp—Heartbreak, Las Vegas, New Guy Village, or Camp Unity—where they lived in cells of various sizes, normally sleeping on wooden boards, their feet sometimes clamped in metal shackles. Here, prisoners of war and American and European civilian detainees were held, interrogated, and tortured.

The Hanoi Hilton was only the best known of the prison camps operated by the North Vietnamese government. Other POW camps in the system included Plantation Gardens, the Zoo, and Alcatraz, all within the city of Hanoi, and Briarpatch Son Tay, Faith, Skidrow, D-1, the Rockpile, and Dogpatch in the North Vietnamese countryside.

See also Vietnam War

—*William S. Reeder, Jr.*

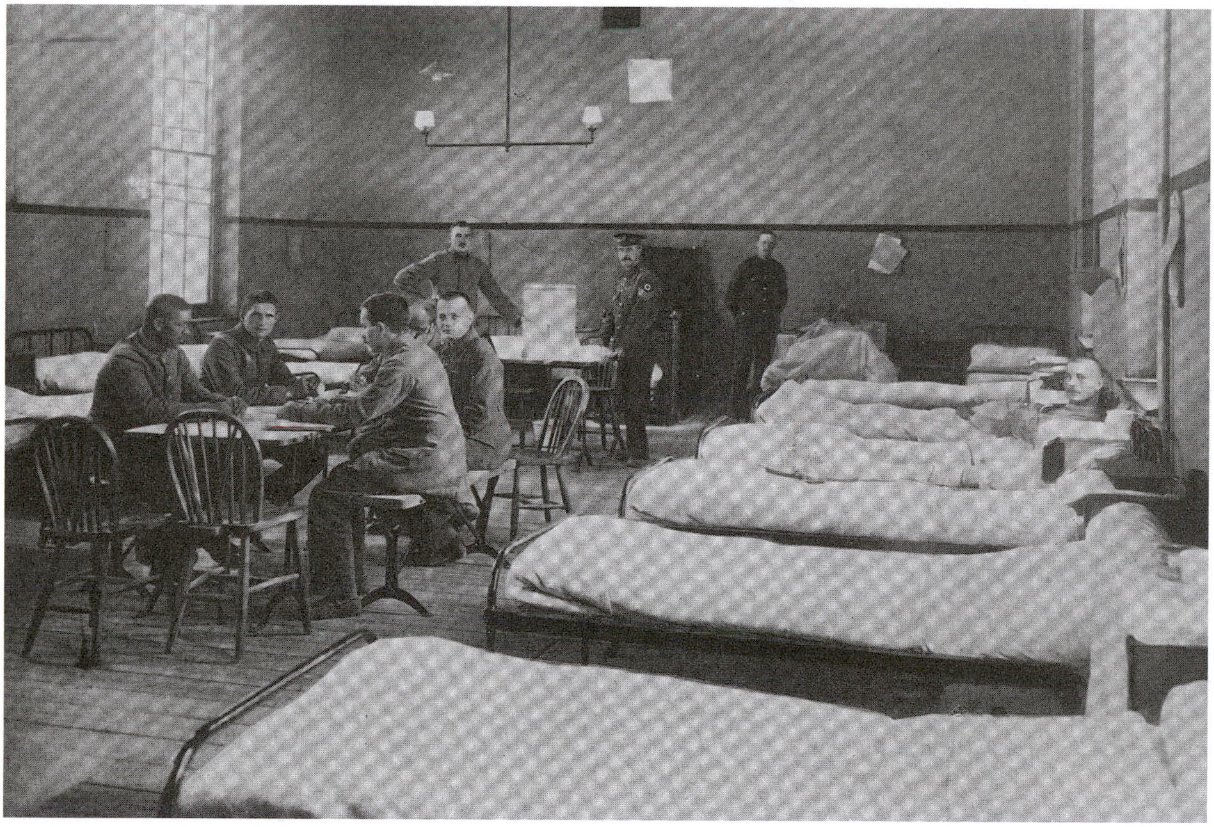

The hospital at Dorchester prison camp in England in World War I (from German Prisoners in Great Britain *[London, n.d.])*

HEALTH

The health of POWs and civilian internees has long been dependent upon a number of factors: quality of living space, sanitary facilities, working conditions, rations, and the availability of medical care. Since all of these factors are, to a greater or lesser degree, in the control of the detaining power, the prisoner must ultimately rely on the captor for the maintenance of health.

Ideally, the accommodation made available to prisoners should provide sufficient shelter from the elements, as long-term exposure might be injurious to their health. The barracks need not be luxurious, but they should be dry, properly ventilated, and adequately heated and should provide shelter from the rain, wind, or snow. They should also be spacious enough to prevent overcrowding, which can encourage the spread of disease. When these conditions are met, there is a reasonable chance that the health of POWs will not suffer unduly as a result of their confinement. However, shortcomings in any of these areas can cause significant hardship. For example, Allied prisoners who were moved to Japan late in World War II found that their huts provided inadequate shelter from the bitter Japanese winters. Thin walls and an almost total absence of heating equipment meant that prisoners, already weakened by malnutrition and overwork, suffered terribly from frostbite and circulatory ailments. By the same token, it would be impossible to calculate how many Soviet and German POWs froze to death in their camps because their captors failed to provide adequate heating.

Adequate sanitation is just as essential to the maintenance of prisoners' health, and both the 1929 and 1949 Geneva Conventions Relative to the Treatment of Prisoners of War bound detaining powers to take all possible steps "to ensure the cleanliness and healthfulness of camps." Neutral inspectors had discovered during World War II that many prisoners lacked access to toilet facilities at night, so the 1949 convention stipulated that clean and hygienic toilet facilities had to be accessible 24 hours a day. By the same token, the 1949 convention included an article stating that bathing facilities must be provided; the earlier convention had only said they were to be made available where possible. These measures are crucial to the maintenance of prisoners' health, for diseases like dysentery tend to be self-perpetuating in ill-equipped camps; afflicted prisoners place a strain on camp latrines, and when the sanitary arrangements are overwhelmed, the disease can easily spread to more prisoners, which in turn deepens the disease cycle. On the other hand, such outbreaks are rare in camps that have adequate sanitary facilities. As a further safeguard against epidemics, the 1949 convention obliged and authorized the detaining power to provide vaccinations or inoculations to prevent or stem outbreaks of infectious diseases.

Because in many conflicts the majority of POWs have been used as laborers, working conditions also have a significant impact on health. Prisoners who are sent to work on farms often thrive in the healthy surroundings of the countryside; in many cases, they live as well as their civilian overseers. Prisoners in mines, quarries, or industry, however, are often subject to terrible conditions. Exposure to toxic chemicals, poor ventilation, dangerous machinery, or brutal supervisors takes its toll on health, and many a prisoner has been permanently crippled while assigned to this kind of work. The threat of work-related illness or injury has been even greater because over the centuries many detaining powers have used POWs for the most hazardous work and had little incentive to provide medical care, since prisoner-slaves were often easier to replace than to treat. Indeed, not a few prisoners have died from otherwise minor injuries that were left untreated.

By far the most significant determinant of health is rations. It is a truism: a well-fed prisoner is a healthy prisoner. In contrast, the malnourished prisoner is less able to fight off minor infections, is more susceptible to infectious diseases, and is less able to resist those diseases when they strike. The most common ailments afflicting POWs historically have been deficiency diseases, in which a shortage of vitamins and minerals in the diet produced a wide range of physical problems, from nerve damage to blindness to dementia. One postwar study of POWs from Hong Kong determined that fully 68 percent of the study group were suffering from beriberi at the time of their liberation. Such health problems were virtually unknown in prison camps where the daily caloric intake was sufficient, and where a varied diet provided a full range of vitamins and minerals.

It goes without saying that the existence of medical practitioners who are well supplied with equipment and medicine has a major impact on prisoners' health. Again, standards and conditions have varied widely. The medical treatment of POWs by the western Allies in both world wars has generally been exemplary, and many prison camps in Germany were also well stocked with doctors, equipment, and medicine. Indeed, some of Britain's finest surgeons were captured in the fall of France in 1940 and carried on their vocation in captivity. When these renowned doctors performed surgery (sometimes using procedures that were very advanced), it was not uncommon for them to have an audience of admiring German physicians. Conditions were not always so favorable, however. There seems to have been an abundance of medicine and hospital supplies available from captured sources in the Pacific theater in World War II, but the Japanese military was reluctant to issue these supplies to prisoners. As a consequence, doctors were forced to make do with worn-out instruments and the small amount of medicine that could be smuggled into the camps; there is no question that they could have saved many more lives had they had access to the supplies of their own hospital units, which the Japanese had captured in 1941 and 1942. The situation was similar during the Korean War, when the Chinese withheld medical treatment from United Nations POWs who were not receptive to Communist indoctrination and who had been branded reactionaries.

Since 1945, exhaustive studies of the health of former POWs have been carried out in Britain, the United States, Canada, and Australia, and the general consensus is that captivity in Germany and Japan during World War II shortened the life expectancy of prisoners, in some cases dramatically. Prolonged vitamin deprivation and long periods of intense mental strain combined to weaken their health, so that many former prisoners died prematurely, many while still in middle age.

In the final analysis, the health of prisoners often depends in large part upon the value that the detaining power places on their lives. A single example from World War II is revealing. When epidemic diseases struck compounds of Russian prisoners, the German staff usually simply sealed off the compounds, let the disease run its course, and then sent in other prisoners to clear out the bodies. But when typhus struck a camp of British prisoners in November 1941, the German response was quick and efficient: all gatherings were canceled, every prisoner was shaved and disinfected, and a curfew was imposed. As a result of these measures, only three prisoners died. Clearly, the German authorities were interested in maintaining the health of British prisoners; the health of Soviet prisoners, on the other hand, was of no concern to them.

See also Epidemics; Rations

References

George Dunning, *Where Bleed the Many* (London: Elek Books, 1955).

John A. Glusman, *Conduct Under Fire: Four American Doctors and Their Fight for Life as Prisoners of the Japanese, 1941–1945* (New York: Viking, 2005).

P. Jones et al, "Health of Prisoners-of-War Evacuated from Hong Kong," *Lancet*, 17 November 1945, 645–646.

Leslie Le Soeuf, *To War without a Gun* (Perth, Australia: Artlook, 1980).

Aidan MacCarthy, *A Doctor's War* (Cork, Ireland: Collins Press, 2005).

George Moreton, *Doctors in Chains* (London: Howard Baker, 1970).

—*Jonathan F. Vance*

HELL SHIPS

See Transportation by Sea

HESS, WALTHER RICHARD RUDOLF (1894–1987)

Rudolf Hess was a prominent member of the *Nationalsozialistische Deutsche Arbeiterpartei* (NSDAP, or the Nazi Party) who rose to the rank of Deputy Führer before spending the second half of his life as an Allied prisoner. Born in Alexandria, Egypt, on 26 April 1894, Hess, the son of a successful merchant, was 14 years old before his family returned to Germany. During World War I, he enlisted in the German army, was wounded at Verdun, and subsequently joined the flying corps. After the war, Hess was drawn to right-wing movements, actively involved in the Freikorps, and then in the fledgling Nazi Party. In 1923 he took part in the failed Beer Hall Putsch and was jailed for seven and a half months alongside Adolf Hitler in Landsberg Prison. There, Hitler dictated to Hess much of his political treatise, *Mein Kampf*. In 1925 Hess became Hitler's private secretary and thereafter rose to other prominent Party positions, ascending to deputy party leader in 1933. However, over the course of the Third Reich and into World War II, Hess played an increasingly diminished role within Hitler's inner circle.

On 10 May 1941, Hess left Germany on a solo flight to the United Kingdom, allegedly on his own initiative, to broker a peace settlement with King George VI. After parachuting into Scotland, he was arrested and held first at Mytchett Place and then in the Tower of London. Following his flight and capture, Hess was disowned and declared mentally incompetent by Hitler and the Nazi leadership. He was brought back to Germany in 1945 to stand trial for war crimes before the International Military Tribunal at Nuremberg, where he was convicted and sentenced to life imprisonment. With six other prominent Nazis, Hess was incarcerated behind the walls of Spandau prison. Designated Prisoner Number 7, he spent his time behind bars plagued by bouts of hypochondria, paranoia, amnesia, and lethargy. However, during periods of lucidity he claimed to regret nothing and maintained an unwavering loyalty to his Führer. In 1966 he became the prison's sole inmate and, despite deteriorating mental and physical health, was never released. At the age of 93, Hess committed suicide in Spandau on 17 August 1987.

See also Nuremberg Trials; Spandau Prison; Tower of London

References

Eugene K. Bird, *Prisoner # 7 Rudolf Hess: The Thirty Years in Jail of Hitler's Deputy Führer* (New York: Viking Press, 1974).

Roger Manvell and Heinrich Fraenkel, *Hess, A Biography* (London: MacGibbon & Kee, 1971).

—*J. Peters Mersereau* and *Nathan Andrew Wilson*

HITTITES

The Hittites ruled a kingdom in the central part of what is now Turkey from around 1800 to 1175 B.C.E. Although they spoke an Indo-European language, their culture was largely a combination of the indigenous Hattian and the Mesopotamian Sumerian and Akkadian civilizations.

Prisoners of war were known by the Hittite word *appantes*, literally "seized ones." The first mention of POWs dates from the earliest known Hittite kings. Anitta, king of Kussara and Kanes, brought captured enemy troops back to his capital, a pattern that was repeated down through the centuries. The term seized ones is first mentioned in the Deeds of Suppiluliuma I (ca. 1350–1323 B.C.E.), a king who reigned at least 18 generations after Anitta: "The enemy died en masse and he [Suppiluliuma] took many appantes and brought them back to Samuha." The annals of Suppiluliuma's younger son, Mursili II (ca. 1322–1290 B.C.E.), record that "General Nuwanza defeated 10,000 infantry and 700 horse-troops who stood for battle against him. Many of them were killed and many of them became POWs." Later in the same text, the king reports an interesting division of war booty: "When I returned, the booty, civilian-captives-to-be-resettled (*arnuwales*), cattle and sheep which I took and the POWs whom they [the army] took, I deposited in Altanna, while I went to Mt. Kassu." Keeping large numbers of POWs could in itself be dangerous to the captors: "He [Crown Prince Arnuwanda] defeated the infantry and horse-troops of Egypt. When he was bringing back to Hatti the POWs whom he had seized, a plague broke out among the POWs and they began to die. When the POWs arrived in Hatti, the POWs brought the plague to Hatti, and from that day there has been continual dying." The death shortly thereafter of Suppiluliuma and soon after that of Arnuwanda is probably to be blamed on this particularly unfortunate group of Egyptian POWs.

The annals of Tudhaliya II, Suppiluliuma I's great-grandfather, reveal the fate of another group of POWs: "When I destroyed Assuwa [a western Anatolian kingdom from whose name is derived the later Roman province of Asia], I returned to [the capital] Hattusa. I brought back to Hattusa 10,000 infantry and 600 chariot-fighters and drivers and settled them in Hattusa. Piyamarunta, Kuggulli, and Ma-[. . .]-ziti, in-law of Piyamarunta along with their sons and grandsons I brought to Hattusa. When I arrived in Hattusa I gave Piyamarunta and Maziti to the Stormgod of the Portico in the portico. But I took Kukkulli into my service and left him free. Later Kukkulli revolted. He incited the Assuwan 10,000 infantry and 600 chariot-drivers and they revolted. The gods handed them over to me. The [Assuwan] plot came to light and the gods disposed of them and killed Kukkulli."

The fate of POWs brought to Hatti is mentioned in only a few cases. Queen

Puduhepa, wife of Mursili II's son, Hattusili III (ca. 1262–1240 B.C.E.), donated a large number of peasant households to a sanctuary. Several of the households happened to be headed by women, and it is noted that a POW was handed over to these women, presumably to assist them. Another source refers to a festival in which the young men present were divided into two groups—Hittites and Masans—and they staged a mock battle (the former with bronze weapons and the latter with reed weapons). When the Hittites won they took a POW and presented him to the deity. Thus slavery in the service of gods and soldiers was probably a typical fate of POWs.

A letter, dating from the period between Tudhaliya II and Suppiluliuma I, from a high official in the major Hittite city of Sapinuwa, demands that the recipient official in the border town of Tapigga return to him the blind men who had fled from the city to the border town. They had apparently been under some coercion, grinding grain (usually women's work) in an establishment in the city. Although the text does not call them POWs, the evidence of coercion and flight toward the periphery suggest that these were prisoners wounded in battle; that they were intentionally blinded to render them harmless cannot be ruled out, but this would be inconsistent with Hittite practice. Another text from Tapigga lists individually named men, some "blind," others "seeing," and gives figures for the numbers of men, women, children (some said to be hostages), oxen, and nanny-goats needed to ransom each one.

A curious and probably untypical fate for POWs was to become an ingredient in a magic ritual. One sadly incomplete list of ritual ingredients includes, among other things, a prisoner, followed immediately by a piglet and a dog. While the tablet breaks before we get to the ritual proper, one fears that this is the list of ingredients for a ritual similar to the following: "When the troops are defeated by the enemy, they perform the behind-the-river ritual as follows: Behind the river they sever a person, a billy-goat, a puppy and a piglet. They place half on one side and they place [the other] half on the [other] side. In front they build a gate of hawthorn. They stretch a hemp-rope[?] across the top. Then, in front of the gate on one side they light a fire, and on the other side they light a fire. The troops go through. When they reach the river-side, they splash water on them [literally, sprinkle upwards]. Afterwards they do the battlefield ritual." That is, whatever impurity caused the defeat was magically removed from the troops by the hawthorn's and rope's scraping, the fire's burning, the water's purification, and the power of the severed corpses. The soldiers were then magically reinducted into soldiering, using the standard battlefield ritual. They could thus put their defeat behind them and, with morale high again, look forward to their next victory.

A better fate awaited other POWs who became ingredients in Hittite rituals. When the king had defeated the enemy but found his people decimated by a plague inflicted by an angry enemy deity, there was a ritual to ameliorate the situation. The Hittites located a POW and a woman taken from the vanquished land. On the road on which the king returned from that land, before the assembled lords, the king removed his fine garment and placed it on the POW, while the woman was dressed in the female equivalent. The POW was then defined as a substitute, equal in every way to the king. The god was asked to relent and look favorably on the Hittites, and the substitute was told to convey the plague back to the enemy land. This was repeated for the woman and for a bull and ewe. All four of them were then driven across the border, back to their homeland. In another ritual to avert the prediction of the imminent death of the king, a POW was not only dressed as king but even anointed as king. He was also given gold, silver, tin, iron, and lead before being sent back to his homeland.

Distinct from POWs were *arnuwales* or civilian captives, literally "those caused to arrive/those transported." Captured civilian populations became the property of the victorious Hittite army and were divided among the king, his officers, and enlisted men. Many were then transported to older parts of the empire, where members of the king's share, at least, were either donated to temples to do the god's manufacturing or farming or were given land, provisions, and a several-year tax break, in an attempt to turn them into regular Hittite peasantry.

References

Richard H. Beal, *The Organisation of the Hittite Military* (Heidelberg: Carl Winter-Universitätsverlag, 1992).

———, *"Hittite Military Rituals,"* in *Ancient Magic and Ritual Power*, ed. M. Meyer and P. Mirecki (Leiden: Brill, 1995).

Trevor R. Bryce, *The Kingdom of the Hittites* (Oxford: Clarendon, 1998).

William W. Hallo, ed., *The Context of Scripture* (Leiden: Brill, 1997).

Harry A. Hoffner, "The Treatment and Long Term Use of Persons Captured in Battle According to the Maat-Texts," in *New Perspectives in Hittite Archaeology*, ed. H.G. Güterbock et al. (Winona Lake, IN: Eisenbrauns, 2002.)

—Richard H. Beal

Ho Chi Minh Trail

During the Vietnam War, the Ho Chi Minh Trail served both as the infiltration and resupply route of the insurgent communist Viet Cong guerrillas and the regular North Vietnamese forces operating in South Vietnam and as a back-haul route for wounded communist soldiers, special category civilian detainees, and prisoners of war. Traveling the trail was a tough experience for all and particularly grueling for prisoners, who were badly malnourished and often wounded. For the American prisoners, it was a world as alien as they could imagine.

The Ho Chi Minh Trail was actually a network of foot trails and vehicle roads that carried a large volume of foot, bicycle, and truck traffic. It had no set beginning or designated terminus. The trail originated at any of several mountain passes crossing from North Vietnam into Laos, and it ended along any number of infiltration routes that ran into South Vietnam from neighboring Laos or Cambodia. The trail was several hundred miles long and was well defended; it was also heavily bombed by American warplanes.

The prisoners who were assembled for the trek north would normally have been held in bamboo cages in crude jungle camps for several months or years before beginning the trip. All suffered from malnutrition, and many still nursed serious combat wounds that had not been adequately treated in the jungle. Disease was rife along the route, and many men contracted multiple strains of malaria, dysentery, intestinal parasites, and a variety of jungle fevers, rashes, boils, and fungi. There were also lice, leeches, and poisonous snakes to contend with along the way. Prisoners often had no shoes and endured on a diet almost exclusively of rice.

The American prisoners who were moved north along the Ho Chi Minh Trail were captured in one of the northern two corps areas of South Vietnam. Most crossed into North Vietnam over Mu Gia Pass and then worked their way up a series of roadways and trails inside North Vietnam to the capital city of Hanoi. Those prisoners captured in the southern two corps regions of South Vietnam were never moved to Hanoi and did not, therefore, share the Ho Chi Minh Trail experience. The prisoners who were moved north suffered greatly along the way, but for those who survived the journey, conditions in Hanoi were very much improved over what they had endured in bamboo cages in the south.

Approximately 100 American prisoners of war were force-marched north to Hanoi along the trail during the conflict. Many South Vietnamese prisoners were also pushed north on this route. For many it was a death march. It is difficult to determine how many prisoners died along the way, but the number is significant. From one group of 27 prisoners, eight died before their three-month ordeal up the trail came to an end. It will likely never be known how many others died singly, or in small groups caught under a hail of bombs.

See also Vietnam War

References
Marjorie A. Clark, *Captive on the Ho Chi Minh Trail* (Chicago: Moody Press, 1974).
John Prados, *The Blood Road: The Ho Chi Minh Trail and the Vietnam War* (New York: J. Wiley and Sons, 1998).
William S. Reeder, Jr., "Captured," *Field Artillery Journal* 42 (1974): 44–49.

—*William S. Reeder, Jr.*

HOGAN'S HEROES

In the world of television situation comedies, the American series *Hogan's Heroes* proved that life in a German POW camp during World War II could be fun. The commandant of Stalag 13 was the incompetent, monocled Colonel Klink (Werner Klemperer), and his head guard was the equally inept Sergeant Schultz (John Banner). Under the leadership of American Colonel Robert Hogan (Bob Crane), the prisoners were in complete control of the camp. Enjoying easy access in and out of camp through an elaborate tunnel, they fed classified information to the Allied forces, helped fugitives escape to freedom, printed counterfeit money, and did anything else imaginable to confound the Germans. It worked to their advantage that apparently every Nazi effort and strategy made its presence known at Stalag 13. The prisoners' living conditions were more reminiscent of a fancy hotel than a POW camp. They had a French chef, steam room, barbershop, and more comforts than home. With such fun and luxuries at their disposal, the prisoners had no desire to escape. Obviously, the program had numerous historical inaccuracies, not the least of which was the camp's location. With their camp set in Hammelburg, Bavaria (where a German prison camp had in fact been built), Hogan and his "heroes" used a submarine as a ferry. Yet the real Hammelburg is 420 kilometers away from the nearest open sea.

The popular series (which ran for a total of 168 episodes, from September 1965 to July 1971) did bear a resemblance to the play and movie, *Stalag 17*—a resemblance that drew an ultimately unsuccessful plagiarism suit against series creators Albert S. Ruddy and Bernie Fein. Ironically, John Banner, who played Schultz, was actually Jewish, and Robert Clary, who played the prisoner LeBeau, had been interned in Nazi concentration camps as a child.

See also Stalag 17

References
Robert Clary, *From Holocaust to Hogan's Heroes: The Autobiography of Robert Clary* (New York: Madison Books, 2002).
Brenda Scott Royce, *Hogan's Heroes: Behind the Scenes at Stalag 13* (New York: St. Martin's Press, 1998).

—*Darryl Wiggers*

HOLLOWAY PRISON

During World War II, Holloway Prison in London, England, was the main internment site for women held under Defence Regulation 18B, which empowered the British government to detain without charge or trial anyone deemed to be a member of an organization that was under foreign influence or control. Among those political organizations targeted were the British Union of Fascists (BU), the Right Club, the Imperial Fascist League, and the Link. Women members of these pro-German and antiwar fascist organizations in Britain were regarded by the authorities in much the same light as their male counterparts and were equally suspect as potential subversives or collaborators in the event of a Nazi invasion of Britain. Of the 747 BU members arrested after May 1940, 100 were women.

Holloway Prison already had a notorious reputation as the women's prison that had held militant campaigners for women's issues before World War I. Ironically, Norah Elam, one of the leading members of the BU

London's Holloway Prison, photographed in 1896

and an 18B internee during World War II, was already well acquainted with Holloway Prison through her experiences as a suffragette before World War I. As a suffrage campaigner, Elam had been arrested for militant acts; imprisoned in Holloway, she had participated in hunger strikes and had endured force-feeding at the hands of her jailers.

In Holloway, separate wings were made available for 18B women internees, and 18B women gradually won certain concessions and privileges that were denied remand prisoners. By 1941, the policy of internment was being eased: some women were released under restriction orders; others were moved to the women's camp on the Isle of Man starting in June 1941; and by the end of 1941, after repeated requests on the part of internees to be reunited with spouses who were also interned, a separate wing of Holloway prison was set aside for four 18B married couples, including Sir Oswald and Diana Mosley, the main figures of the BU. Holloway Prison is still used to this day as a prison for women criminal offenders.

See also Civilian Internees—World War II—Britain; Defence Regulation 18B

References

Julie Gottlieb, "Suffragette Experiences through the Filter of Fascism," in *A Suffrage Reader: Charting Directions in British Suffrage History*, ed. Claire Eustance et al. (New York: Leicester University Press, 1999).

Tony Kushner and Kenneth Lunn, eds., *The Politics of Marginality: Race, the Radical Right and Minorities in Twentieth-Century Britain* (London: Frank Cass, 1990).

Joan Miller, *One Girl's War: Personal Exploits in MI5's Most Secret Station* (Dublin: Dingle, 1986).

Diana Mosley, *A Life of Contrasts: The Autobiography of Diana Mosley* (New York: Times Books, 1978).

—*Julie V. Gottlieb*

HOLZMINDEN

The German prison camp at Holzminden, rashly described as "escape-proof" by its commandant in 1917, is best known for being the scene of one of the most successful escapes of World War I. The camp, a former cavalry barracks, was situated on the Weser River near Hanover, 160 kilometers from then neutral Holland.

Breaking into a partitioned area between the officers' and orderlies' quarters, Canadian Lieutenant W. G. Colquhoun discovered a wooden staircase leading up to the attic and down to a basement. Beneath a ground-level staging platform was sufficient room to conceal a party of tunnelers and the resultant spoil. Work began in November 1917, with shifts of diggers hacking a 45-centimeter hole through the yellow clay and layers of stone. Nine months later, the 60-meter tunnel was ready. On the evening of 24 July 1918, an officer broke the tunnel into a bean patch 50 meters from the camp wire and crawled away. Others followed, until a section of the tunnel collapsed around 4:00 a.m., effectively ending the escape. Two mud-stained officers were spotted trying to return to their quarters, and the alarm was raised. The full extent of the escape only became known after a hasty roll call revealed that 29 men, including the senior British officer, Lieutenant-Colonel C.E.H. Rathbone, had fled the camp. In order to locate the entrance point of the tunnel, the Germans had to excavate the tunnel backwards. Of the escapers, 10 (including Rathbone) managed to reach Holland and subsequently England. The mass escape of prisoners through the Holzminden tunnel was the first of its kind, setting an example for those men captured in World War II.

See also Escape; World War I—Western Front

References

Hugh Durnford, *The Tunnellers of Holzminden with a Side Issue* (Cambridge: Cambridge University Press, 1920).

Barry Winchester, *Beyond the Tumult* (London: Allison and Busby, 1971).

—*Colin Burgess*

HOMECOMING, OPERATION

Operation Homecoming was the name given to the repatriation of America's Vietnam War POWs, as negotiated in the 27 January 1973 Paris Peace Accords. The arrangements were relatively straightforward. The ill or seriously injured POWs would leave first, followed by the rest in order of capture. As it unfolded, however, the operation became more complicated. Of the 116 POWs who left in the first phase on February 12, the North Vietnamese insisted on releasing two officers widely considered to be collaborators, despite the fact that they had been captured after others who would remain in captivity. Another departure from the plan came six days later, when the North Vietnamese marked the visit of the U.S. Secretary of State Henry Kissinger by releasing 20 randomly chosen POWs. U.S. officials then had to order these "Kissinger 20" to leave out of turn.

The second release came in two installments. On 4 March, 106 American and two Thai POWs left; 34 military and civilian POWs, mostly captured in the South, left on 5 March. During the third release, 108 prisoners left on 14 March and 32 on 16 March. The fourth and last release, which began on 27 March, included the last 107 POWs held in Hanoi, some POWs captured in the South, and the 10 POWs who proved to be the only returnees from Laos. A single POW released on 1 April brought the total to 600: 591 Americans (77 Army, 138 Navy, 325 Air Force, 26 Marines, 25 civilians) and nine foreign nationals.

Though apprehensive about their reception, the POWs arrived at Clark Air Base to a heroes' welcome. The suspicions, interrogations, and accusations that had greeted the Korean War POWs were nowhere in sight; getting the returnees back to their families was clearly the priority. Once home, the POWs' words of thanks and praise for America, its commander in chief, and its military were met by equally fervent displays of welcome. The homecoming parades, corporate and private gifts, and massive public ceremonies and tributes culminated in May 1973 with the largest event ever held at the White House.

Two early suicides raised fears that the depression and dysfunction observed in some POWs from other wars would appear also among this group, and many Vietnam returnees were disgusted by the government's refusal to pursue charges that the senior POWs had lodged against a handful of their fellow POWs. For the most part, though, Operation Homecoming was a remarkable success—especially when we remember that over 300 of the returnees had been POWs longer than any previous Americans.

See also Vietnam War

—*Craig Howes*

HOMOSEXUALITY

Homosexuality has existed as long as recorded history, and undoubtedly before. It certainly existed in prisoner of war camps during World War II, but the scale of such activities is impossible to calculate. Since there were so few women incarcerated in World War II prison camps, lesbianism is not discussed here, only male homosexuality.

During World War II, many societies were much more closed toward homosexuality than they are now, and in the armed services of many nations, homosexuality was labeled a serious crime. American military officials defined homosexuals as sexual psychopaths and attempted to keep them out of the service. Nevertheless, many succeeded in enlisting. Inevitably cliques were formed of like-minded individuals, and these groups had to go to great lengths to avoid suspicion and exposure, which would mean either a dishonorable discharge or court-martial and imprisonment. In Canada, buggery was technically punishable by death in the 1940s, and it had been since at least 1892. In Hong Kong just before the war, a British officer was cashiered and given two years at hard labor after being convicted of homosexual acts.

In POW camps, homosexuality occurred both among the prisoners themselves and between the prisoners and their captors. Homosexual guards were not uncommon among POW camp staffs. The record includes the case of an Australian sergeant who was killed by a guard for refusing to participate in sexual acts, and in another case, at Singapore, an Indian guard raped a POW and was killed by the Japanese for this offense.

Consensual homosexual activity was much more common. Such acts represented the expression of genuine preference for one's own gender, but other pressures existed also. For some prisoners, homosexual sex was simply a way to pay for food or drugs, both of which were vital to survival; the individuals who initiated such trades were often men who had more than ordinary access to limited supplies—for example, members of the commissariat and cooking staff, prisoners with outside jobs providing access to stolen food or other material, or officers.

Homosexual activity was certainly more notably present in some camps than in others. A particularly notorious example was Fukuoka Camp 17 in Japan. Several of the Allied medical officers who were there made official postwar reports on the situation; Australian doctor Ian Duncan described homosexuality as "probably the greatest psychological problem in the camp." This activity was present in all national groups in Camp 17. For example, in his memoir, Geoffrey Adams (who was not a medical officer) described finding an American medic engaged in homosexual activities with a guard who, he noted, was "fulfilling the woman's role."

Given the official repudiation of homosexuality and the subsequent hidden nature of the practice, it is not surprising that many men who were not themselves involved would not know whether homosexuals existed in their camp or barracks. Extensive interviews with POWs from both the European and Pacific theaters of war have revealed a consistent pattern among answers to questions about homosexuality. Almost all of the men discount the occurrence of this form of sexual activity in terms of their personal experiences. But most concede that it might have happened, and some admit to certainty. Subjects of frequent suspicion, perhaps unfairly in many cases, were those who participated in camp theatricals; especially singled out were those playing the female roles, often with affecting realism aided by convincing costumes and padding.

The propinquity of prisoners held in confined space has been suggested by some as increasing the likelihood of homosexual activity. However, the opposite may be the case, since overcrowding made privacy almost unattainable. The inadequate diet of prisoners held on low rations has been identified as a strong deterrent to any kind of sexual activity. Evidence supporting this contention comes from observations that the incidence of both homosexuality and masturbation increased perceptibly when extra food parcels became available. The efficacy of this factor alone is doubtful, however; the often immediate resumption of sexual activity after the war ended suggests that dietary suppression of sexual function may be as much a mental as a physical entity.

Buggery was reported among the British troops in Hong Kong before the fighting started in 1941. Many of these men survived the fighting to become POWs, at which time presumably the same orientation was in effect. And Captain Archie Cochrane, a British medical officer who was a POW in Europe, believed that POWs treated homosexuals more sensibly than did civilians. Certainly a negative but relaxed approach is suggested in one poem quoted by Canadian POW Robert Prouse:

We'd rather face the foe again,
Be blasted by their mortars,
Than have our 'nature's turn-about'
And land in 'married quarters!'

Many observers believe that the less repressive attitude toward homosexuality that has emerged since World War II owes some of its impetus to the commingling of so many homosexual individuals in the armed forces of the various belligerents. Whether the relatively small numbers of involved POWs contributed to this change is a moot point. A proper history of these times and events remains to be written.

See also Sexual Relations; Sexual Violence

References
Geoffrey Adams, *No Time for Geishas* (London: Leo Cooper, 1973).
A.L. Cochrane, "Notes on the Psychology of Prisoners of War," *British Medical Journal* 1 (1946): 282–284.
Ian L. Duncan, "Life in a Japanese Prisoner-of-War Camp," *Medical Journal of Australia* 1 (3 April 1982): 306.
A. Robert Prouse, *Ticket to Hell via Dieppe: From a Prisoner's Wartime Log, 1942–45* (Toronto: Van Nostrand Reinhold, 1982).

—Charles G. Roland

HOSTAGES

A hostage is a person unlawfully detained by one party for the purposes of extracting a concession or ransom from another party. Hostage-taking should be distinguished from kidnapping, which is a term originally used for abducting children and has been extended to the taking of any human being against his or her will, sometimes for ransom. A noteworthy distinction between the two is the hostage-takers' desire to have their actions and intentions widely communicated. Consequently, the media has often played a crucial role in disseminating the hostage-takers' messages. Also, the location of a kidnapped victim is typically unknown to authorities, whereas in a hostage situation, authorities are usually made cognizant of the captive's whereabouts. Hostages are often released once an agreement has been reached; however, at times they are killed.

The contemporary definition of "hostage" is largely a twentieth-century phenomenon. Hostage-taking has a long association with warfare; historically, the taking of hostages was an accepted tool of diplomacy between two warring nations. A hostage, often an individual of high social status, could be presented or demanded by one side as a pledge of good faith. A General

Order issued during the U.S. Civil War (1861–1865) defined a hostage as "a person accepted as a pledge for the fulfillment of an agreement concluded between belligerents during the war." The word "accepted" is important because it reinforces the voluntary nature of the hostage transaction. For example, after the 1748 Treaty of Aix-la-Chapelle that ended the war of Austrian Succession, two British peers were willingly sent to France as hostages until Cape Breton Island was reinstated as a French colony. Typically, diplomatic hostages were provided with ample living conditions and released once the terms of the agreement had been fulfilled.

The usage of voluntary hostages to ensure the fulfillment of an obligation remained paramount until the mid-nineteenth century, but there were exceptions. Hostages were sometimes used for strategic purposes, as proven by the Athenian capture of Spartan troops during the Battle of Sphacteria. By the Middle Ages, taking hostages to collect ransom became rife in Europe. Warring nations extended this practice to their POWs by keeping them captive until a requested payment was received. Hostages were also taken as a reprisal for the illegal behavior of other parties, as is evidenced by the retaliatory nature of the War of 1812. During the conflict, British and American troops took POWs as hostages in response to each other's actions, until over 200 POWs were held captive on both sides. During the nineteenth century, the precedent of taking civilians hostage was established, and evidence suggests that some hostages were executed in retaliation against the perceived illegal actions of opposing parties.

By the turn of the twentieth century, warring nations no longer "accepted" hostages—they took them. During the Franco-Prussian War (1870–1871), for example, the Germans took civilians hostage and placed them on trains to deter the enemy from damaging the trains or destroying bridges. The British followed suit by boarding hostages on trains to ensure safe transport during the Boer War (1899–1902). When hostilities broke out once again, in 1914, there was widespread uncertainty among European powers as to the legitimacy of using civilian hostages to prevent a possible attack on a military target. Hugo Grotius had accepted the use of hostages on a voluntary basis in his seventeenth-century treatise, but he condemned putting a hostage to death because of actions undertaken by another. The two Hague Treaties of 1899 and 1907 attempted to codify the rules for proper warfare, but neither treaty specifically mentions hostages. However, it should be noted that the subsequent Hague Rules upon the Laws and Customs of War, which came into force in January 1910, declares that "the lives of private individuals must be respected." Despite its obvious intentions, however, this broad generalization did little to safeguard the rights of civilians in warfare.

During the twentieth century, the practice of accepting high-profile hostages disappeared and was largely replaced with the taking of civilians by force. During both world wars, civilians were seized and became what is referred to as prophylactic hostages, to shield both troops and military objectives from attack by an opposing force. The Germans became notorious for their practice of taking civilians hostage during World War II. At times of high resistance from rebellious groups in Belgium, for example, German forces seized lawyers, doctors, and university professors, and used them as human shields by boarding them on trains to ensure loyalty among the Belgians. Along with taking prophylactic hostages, German authorities used civilians for reprisal in retaliation for attacks against their troops. On 12 February 1942, for example, the German military took 45 civilians hostage and ordered their execution unless the individuals guilty of attacking and killing German soldiers in the two occupied cities of Tours and Rouen were found. On 9 March 1942, 20 of the hostages were killed because no culprit was found for the killing of a German sentinel at Tours.

There was growing concern among some European nations about the execution of hostages. For example, on

13 January 1942, a series of resolutions was passed by representatives-in-exile of Belgium, Czechoslovakia, France, Greece, Luxembourg, The Netherlands, Norway, Poland, and Yugoslavia, which condemned the killing of seized civilians. The governments agreed that principal among their war aims would be to punish anyone found responsible for participating in the execution of hostages. Out of World War II came the first concerted efforts to establish an international criminal code of law regarding the treatment of civilians. Members of the Nuremberg Tribunal maintained that individuals, along with states, fell under the jurisdiction of international law. Tribunal members agreed that the killing of hostages constituted a war crime, and Article Six of the 1945 Nuremberg Charter notes that individuals can be held responsible for the killing of hostages.

The Fourth Geneva Convention relative to the Protection of Civilian Persons in Time of War (1949) was the first international legislative attempt to safeguard the rights of noncombatants in war. The Convention comes into effect at the outbreak of any military operation and ceases operation at the end of hostilities. It is principally related to the 1948 U.N. Declaration of Human Rights because it posits that civilians have the right to be spared direct military attack. The taking of civilians as hostages and using hostages as a form of retaliation are considered grave breaches under the provisions of the Fourth Convention. If a crime is considered a grave breach, it means that it falls under universal jurisdiction and is subject to prosecution in every nation. In 1977, two additional protocols were adopted, which prohibit the taking of civilian hostages by a warring nation in any type of war, whether international or non-international. Two years later, the International Convention Against the Taking of Hostages was created, which requires every state party to make hostage-taking a nationally punishable offense. Furthermore, it calls for states to either prosecute or extradite anyone on their territory alleged to have taken a hostage.

Despite these safeguards, hostage-taking continues. Into the twenty-first century, hostage-taking has been increasingly linked with political terrorist activity. Civilians have been seized for many of the same reasons that hostages have been taken in the past, although civil wars have replaced interstate wars as the principal kind of conflict. The situation has been particularly dangerous in postwar Iraq, where the taking of western hostages has become an endemic problem. However, it is difficult to determine whether individuals have been taken by terror groups for political reasons, or by criminals interested only in financial gain. In July 2005, for example, Iraqi-Canadian businessman Zaid Meerwali was abducted by individuals who demanded $250,000 in ransom; he was murdered before the family could pay the ransom, and security officials in Iraq concluded that this was a case of criminal kidnapping. Most foreigners, however, have been taken hostage for political reasons. Filipino truck driver Angelo de la Cruz was captured in July 2004 and freed when his government acceded to his captors' demands, that all Filipino troops be withdrawn from Iraq. The terrorists who abducted Italian journalist Giuliana Sgrena demanded the removal of all foreign troops from Iraq, but ultimately released her after the Italian government paid a ransom rumored to be more than $6 million. Many other hostages have not been so lucky. Over 50 are known to have been murdered by their captors as of December 2005, and many others remain in the hands of terror or criminal groups.

References

Clive C. Aston, *A Contemporary Crisis: Political Hostage Taking and the Experience of Western Europe* (Westport, CT: Greenwood Press, 1982).

H. Wayne Eliott, "Hostages or Prisoners of War: War Crimes at Dinner," *Military Law Review* 149 (summer 1995): 241–274.

Isaac Cronin, ed. *Confronting Fear: A History of Terrorism* (New York: Thunder's Mouth Press, 2002).

Micah Garen and Marie-Hélène Carleton, *American Hostage: A Memoir of a Journalist Kidnapped in Iraq and the Remarkable Battle to*

Win His Release (New York: Simon & Schuster, 2005).

Webb Garrison, *Civil War Hostages: Hostage Taking in the Civil War* (Shippensburg, PA: White Mane, 2000).

Thomas Hammill and Paul T. Brown, *Escape in Iraq: The Thomas Hammill Story* (Accokeek, MD: Stoeger Publishing, 2004).

Richard Shelly Hartigan, "Noncombatant Immunity: Reflections on its Origins and Present Status," *Review of Politics* 29 (April 1967): 204–220.

Arthur K. Kuhn, "The Execution of Hostages," *American Journal of International Law* 36 (April 1942): 271–274.

—Dorotea Gucciardo

HULKS

See Prison Ships

HUMAN SHIELDS

Throughout the history of war, prisoners of war have occasionally been used as human shields, deliberately placed in the line of fire to deter their own forces from attacking. Though of dubious effectiveness and contrary to international law, the practice has persisted to the present day.

Before the twentieth century, international law did not explicitly cover this form of abuse, but it certainly occurred. During the U.S. Civil War, General Sam Jones, the military commander of the city of Charleston, South Carolina, asked for 50 Union prisoners, including a general, to be housed in an exposed part of the city to discourage the Union artillery from shelling the area.

Because of incidents like this, the 1929 Geneva Convention Relative to the Treatment of Prisoners of War stipulated that "no prisoner may, at any time, be sent into a region where he might be exposed to the fire of the combat zone, nor used to give protection from bombardment to certain points or certain regions by his presence" (Article 9). However, this did not stop the government of Nazi Germany from resorting to this tactic in World War II. Robert Wagner, a high Nazi Party official in Baden, twice proposed to concentrate POW camps in urban areas, industrial zones, and near dams, but both plans were rejected on the grounds that they might lead to reprisals against German POWs. However, in August 1943, Hermann Göring, the head of the German air force, suggested that POW camps be erected in residential neighborhoods in endangered cities. He believed that this would convince the Allies to suspend bombing; if it did not, at least some Allied POWs would be killed along with German civilians. The German high command approved the plan almost immediately, and Dulag Luft, a transit camp for newly captured Allied airmen, was the first to be moved. On 10 September 1943, it was transferred to a site in a residential quarter of the city of Frankfurt, barely a mile from the main railway station. Neutral authorities and Allied governments protested strongly, but to no avail. The camp was only moved again when it was bombed (with several POW casualties) in March 1944. A number of other camps were sited near industrial establishments: a POW hospital was placed near a tank assembly plant, Stalag 2D was placed near an important airfield, and six work detachments attached to Stalag 6G were housed in a synthetic oil refinery. Between November 1944 and March 1945, prison camps were bombed by Allied forces on 10 separate occasions, resulting in the deaths of over 150 POWs; one camp, Stalag 6C, endured its sixth bombardment on 29 November 1944. However, it is unclear if these locations were chosen as part of Göring's plan, or simply so the prisoners could be closer to the factories in which they labored.

Similar situations occurred in the Far East. Most of the camps that held POWs laboring on the Burma-Thailand (Death) Railway were situated close to the line, many near bridges of strategic importance. There were certainly practical reasons for these locations, but they also put POWs in the position of serving as de facto human shields. As a result, there were many casualties. In September 1944, for example, Non Pladuk Camp was hit by Allied bombs; 95 POWs were killed and over 300 wounded. This was the most deadly of such incidents, but deaths and injuries from Allied bombs were not uncommon in camps along the Death Railway.

Despite the fact that the 1949 Geneva Convention Relative to the Treatment of Prisoners of War reiterated the prohibition of using POWs as human shields (Article 28), they are still vulnerable to being so used by an unscrupulous enemy. This was made clear when a Canadian peacekeeper in the former Yugoslavia was captured by Bosnian Serbs. He was handcuffed to a pole near their base, and his captors freely admitted that he had been placed there to safeguard the base from attack. The whole scene was broadcast widely on television, giving viewers a very modern example of an old danger faced by POWs.

References

Glenda Lockwood, *Diary of a Human Shield* (London: Bloomsbury Publishing, 1992).

—*Jonathan F. Vance*

HUNDRED YEARS WAR (1337–1453)

Prisoners of war were an atypical yet highly significant element in the Hundred Years War, a conflict that was marked by regular shifts in the dominance of the chief protagonists, England and France. This did not mean that prisoners were only taken by the forces that happened to be victorious at the time. For instance, there were individuals fighting for the English at the battle of Poitiers (1356), which was a decisive victory for the Anglo-Gascons, who were unfortunate enough to be captured by the French.

Comparatively few people were made prisoner during this war, and these were almost invariably aristocrats or royalty. Consequently, their capture could be of great political and financial significance. Prisoners would only be taken if they were of sufficient value, and the treatment of defeated opponents who were not worth ransoming could be extremely brutal. However, as armies became more socially diverse, with the increased use of archers, crossbowmen, and infantry troops, even enemy knights could suffer greatly at the hands of the opposition since there was not the same sense of class consciousness and comradeship.

Since it was essentially a practice reserved for the knightly community and those ranked above them, the system of ransoming was bound up with the strictures of chivalry. It was this system that played a part in maintaining hostilities for such an extended period. Although armies were no longer solely raised by traditional, "feudal" means and soldiers were paid for their military service, a primary motivation for participating in a campaign was the expectation of acquiring booty and spoils. The most significant elements in the plunder from any campaign were ransoms. Therefore, the system of ransom encouraged war by both increasing the potential for financial reward and reducing the physical threat from combat, a knight tending to be worth more alive than dead. However, this was not always the case, and in a number of battles, orders were given that no captives should be taken. The battle of Crécy (1346) was fought under such conditions (*bellum hostile*), and it was estimated that over 1,500 nobles died in the conflict. By comparison, the casualties at Poitiers were much fewer, as no such orders were issued and many of the French aristocracy were taken prisoner, the most significant of whom was Jean II, the king of France. A ransom was supposed to be set at a level that would not ruin a captive, but such niceties were not always observed. The great nobles and kings were worth a very great deal of money. For example, Edward III of England received about £268,000 for three ransoms in the period 1360–1370. After the battle of Nájera (1367) Edward the Black Prince captured Bertrand du Guesclin, who was assisting the pretender to the throne of Castile. When the Black

Prince asked du Guesclin what sum he should ask for his ransom, Bertrand suggested the enormous figure of 100,000 francs, at which point Edward released him for half the amount and sent him to find the remainder of the sum.

The Hundred Years War was an Anglo-French confrontation encouraged by points of argument over Gascony, Normandy, and Scotland, enflamed by economic factors, and surmounted by a dynastic struggle for the throne of France. However, it was not restricted to military action only in these areas; other regions and elements were drawn into it as well. A civil war in Brittany was galvanized when the English and French offered support to the opposing sides. Prisoners also had a role to play in these exchanges. In June 1347, the English knight Sir Thomas Dagworth captured in battle Charles de Blois, one of the contenders for the duchy of Brittany. He was brought to the Tower of London, where he was held alongside David II, king of Scotland, who had also fallen into English hands at the battle of Neville's Cross (1346). The Iberian peninsula also became involved in the Hundred Years War, again due to a civil war, this time in Castile. Pedro the Cruel, with English support, engaged his half-brother, Enrique of Trastamara, in battle at Nájera in 1367. Pedro was victorious, and after the battle he demanded that the noble prisoners be killed, but the Black Prince, who led the English army as prince of Aquitaine, refused and allowed them to be ransomed. The effect of failing to keep du Guesclin under lock and key became apparent when Bertrand became involved in the subsequent ouster of Pedro, which left Aquitaine with an enemy on its border. Before long, du Guesclin, a future constable of France, was leading French forces against the principality itself when the Hundred Years War restarted in 1369.

The conditions under which these prisoners were held could vary a great deal, although in general they were well treated. Jean II, on his return to France from captivity in 1360, needed 12 wagons to transport all his goods. Tournaments were held in his honor during his captivity and his status was very much that of a great prince in exile, rather than a prisoner of war. On the other hand, the treatment meted out to the Earl of Pembroke after his capture by the Castilian fleet at the battle of La Rochelle (1372) resulted in his death shortly after his release. The conditions in which prisoners were held, like all military conventions, were laid down in the "laws of war" (*jus in bello*), which recognized that captives could expect a certain level of treatment. These laws also laid down strictures about the division of booty, although these provisions were sometimes overridden by individual contracts and indentures of retainer that were drawn up between an officer and the men he recruited to serve under him. In general, a recruiting captain was entitled to a third of all booty taken by his men, although sometimes as much as a half of all the spoils, including ransoms, was demanded. Such regulations were further formalized in the late fourteenth and throughout the fifteenth centuries in England and France through the issues of royal ordinances.

See also Jean II of France; Ransom; Tower of London

References

C.T. Allmand, *The Hundred Years War: England and France at War, ca. 1300–ca. 1450* (New York: Cambridge University Press, 1988).

Richard W. Barber, *The Knight and Chivalry* (Rochester, NY: Boydell Press, 1995).

—David S. Green

HUSSEIN, SADDAM (1937–)

Born in the Iraqi town of Tikrit, Saddam joined the Iraqi branch of the Arab Ba'ath Socialist Party in 1956. Forced into exile after a failed Ba'athist coup attempt in 1959, he returned to Iraq after the overthrow of Prime Minister Abdul al-Karim Qassem in 1963. By 1969 Saddam had become the Ba'ath party's general secretary and deputy chairman of its Revolutionary Command Council. He formally assumed the presidency of Iraq in 1979.

Saddam's 24-year reign was marked by an aggressive foreign policy (he eventually waged war against five of Iraq's six neighbors) and exceedingly repressive domestic politics. Hundreds of thousands of Iraqi Kurds, Shi'a Muslims, and other political opponents were murdered by his armed forces and security services. Many more were swept into Saddam's prisons, never to be seen again.

Saddam's armed forces fought Iran to an eventual stalemate in the 1980–1988 Iran-Iraq War but were decisively beaten in the 1991 Gulf War following Iraq's invasion of Kuwait. His government, however, survived the war—Saddam delighted in the irony that he remained president of Iraq while his Gulf War adversary, George H. W. Bush, was defeated in the 1992 American presidential election—and its brutal repression continued. Several coup attempts, a crippling United Nations embargo, and repeated skirmishes with the United States appeared only to strengthen Saddam's grip on power. Nonetheless, his regime effectively collapsed within three weeks of the American-led invasion in March 2003.

For several months following the cessation of the "formal" stage of the Iraq War, Saddam was missing. Observers wondered if he had escaped, perhaps to Syria; others presumed he had been killed by American bombs. On 13 December 2003, however, Saddam was captured in a makeshift bunker near his hometown of Tikrit by American Special Forces. He was subsequently imprisoned in an American holding facility near Baghdad International Airport. A special tribunal, responsible to the post-Saddam Iraqi government was established to try Saddam and other surviving members of the Ba'ath regime for their crimes. Saddam's own trial was delayed several times, in part owing to the killing of two of his defense lawyers, but was underway as of December 2005.

Measured even by the standards of the twentieth century, Saddam must surely be judged as one of the modern period's cruelest dictators. Iraqi expatriate Kanan Mohamed Makiya wrote that Saddam absorbed all the lessons in cruelty that Hitler and Stalin offered and added his own refinements to them, creating an amalgam of Stalinesque personality cult and National Socialist death fetishism, underscored by a profoundly anti-Semitic variety of Arab nationalism. Saddam's tyranny was at once systemic, in the sense that it perpetually threatened all enemies of the Ba'ath state, and arbitrary, in that even Saddam's family, friends, and faithful allies never knew if or when the instrument of the purge would be turned on them. Efforts by the International Committee of the Red Cross and other organizations to raise concerns about Saddam's treatment while in captivity, including the fact that he had been photographed in his underpants, have therefore met with little sympathy.

See also Abu Ghraib Prison; Gulf War; Iran-Iraq War; Iraq War

References

Kanan Mohamed Makiya (pseud. Samir al-Khalil), *Republic of Fear: The Politics of Modern Iraq* (New York: Pantheon, 1998).

John Keegan, *The Iraq War* (New York: A.A. Knopf, 2004).

—*Graham Broad*

I

Imma (fl. 679 c.e.)

Imma was one of the earliest prisoners of war to be referred to in the early Anglo-Saxon chronicles. The sole reference to him occurs in Bede's *Historia Ecclesiastica Gentis Anglorum* of c. 731, which describes Imma as an aristocratic warrior in the service of the king of Northumbria. We know nothing of Imma's birthplace or date of birth, but he was certainly a young man when, in 679, he fought in the Northumbrian army against the Mercians at the battle of the river Trent.

The Northumbrians were defeated, and in the aftermath, according to Bede, Imma found himself wandering dazed and wounded around the battlefield. He was seen by a roving band of Mercian soldiers and taken as a captive to their chief. Imma knew that under the Anglo-Saxon code of blood-feud, a high-status Northumbrian warrior could expect to be killed in revenge for the slain kinsmen of the Mercian lord. He therefore told the Mercians that he was neither a nobleman nor a soldier, but a peasant who had merely brought food supplies to the Northumbrian army. Initially, the Mercians believed his story and spared his life.

Imma's wounds were tended by his captors, who afterward held him as a prisoner, chaining him to prevent his escape. Eventually, the soldiers guarding him realized from his bearing that he was not in fact of peasant stock. Their lord, however, respected his earlier decision to spare the young Northumbrian's life, and sold him as a slave to a trader in London, who later gave Imma leave to seek a ransom for himself. Imma made his way to the royal court of Kent, where King Hlothere, the nephew of a Northumbrian queen whom Imma had once served, put up the necessary payment and secured the captive's freedom.

References

Bertram Colgrave and R.A.B. Mynors, eds., *Bede's Ecclesiastical History of the English People* (Oxford: Clarendon Press, 1969).

J.M. Wallace-Hadrill, *Bede's Ecclesiastical History of the English People: A Historical Commentary* (Oxford: Clarendon Press, 1988).

—*Tim Clarkson*

Indian Mutiny

Beginning with incidents on 29 March and 24 April 1857, widespread revolts of sepoys—the native soldiers in the service of the British East India Company—erupted across the Indian subcontinent. Although Muslim and Hindu concerns that cartridges for new rifles were greased with the fat of cows and pigs was the trigger for the uprising, underlying nationalistic and religious tensions had clearly been festering, as the desecration of Christian churches and cemeteries and the slaughter of native converts to Christianity indicated.

The insurgents ultimately proclaimed Bahadur Shah II, the aged king of Delhi, as their leader, but the rebellion failed, largely because of the loyalty of soldiers such as the Sikhs and Gurkhas to their British officers. The British government also acted with dispatch in transporting regiments to India, and several important native princes remained loyal to the company.

Although atrocities were doubtless exaggerated in some instances, between 2,000 and 3,000 British were massacred in the early stages of the rebellion. On 10 May, for example, European men, women, and children, soldiers and civilians alike, were murdered at Meerut by rebel troops of the 3rd Bengal Light Cavalry. In many cases, British officers were killed by their native regiments, but it was the killing of women and children, often accompanied by rape and torture, that inflamed British sentiments. The worst instances of such atrocities were the general slaughter of civilians at Delhi and the massacre at Cawnpore. At Cawnpore, General Hugh Wheeler accepted terms from rebel leader Nana Sahib, nawab of Awadh, which allowed the British to evacuate by boat downriver to Allahabad. On 27 June, however, rebel sepoys, by order of the nawab, ambushed the refugees as they embarked, killing and capturing many.

For the British imagination, the defense of the regency at Lucknow, where a British regiment and hundreds of refugees from the surrounding countryside endured a long and brutal siege by rebel forces, and its eventual relief by a column under Major Henry Havelock, came to symbolize British courage and resoluteness in the face of native betrayal and savagery. British opinion at home and in India was driven to fury by reports—some true and some false—of crimes against prisoners by the rebels, and British troops frequently took terrible retribution upon alleged perpetrators of atrocities, often without regard for sufficient proof or due process. To the standard practice of execution by firing squad or hanging, some British officers added death by dismemberment, with rebels chained to and fired from a cannon's mouth. In some instances Muslim prisoners were defiled with pork fat and Hindu prisoners with beef fat before execution, and individual British soldiers and loyal sepoys sometimes took direct revenge with bayonets or with fire. In contrast, Bahadur Shah was simply deposed and exiled to Burma.

Charles Lord Canning, the governor-general of India, granted a general clemency to rebels who had not been connected with outrages, both in the interest of humanity and to reduce the likelihood of further rebel resistance. As a direct consequence of the mutiny, the India Act of 1858 transferred India and its attendant territories from the care of the British East India Company to direct administration by the Crown, with Lord Canning installed as the first viceroy. For as long as the British ruled India, however, haunting images of the mutiny and its suppression hung as a shadow over Anglo-Indian relations.

References
H.H. Dodwell, *The Cambridge History of the British Empire*, vol. 5, *British India, 1858–1918* (Cambridge: Cambridge University Press, 1932).
Brian Gardner, *The East India Company: A History* (New York: McCall Publishing, 1971).
Christopher Hibbert, *The Great Mutiny: India, 1857* (New York: Viking, 1978).
Lawrence James, *Raj: The Making and Unmaking of British India* (New York: St. Martin's Press, 1988).
John Keay, *The Honourable Company: A History of the English East India Company* (New York: Macmillan, 1991).

—Patrick M. O'Neil

India-Pakistan Wars (1965–1971)

The wars fought between India and Pakistan in the last quarter of the twentieth century were noteworthy less for the treatment of prisoners in captivity than for the controversy surrounding their release at the conclusion of hostilities.

The first India-Pakistan War was fought in August and September 1965 over the status of Kashmir, and it produced roughly 1,000 POWs from both sides. Most were granted POW status, received visits from officials of the International Committee of the Red Cross (ICRC), and were permitted to correspond with their families—all rights guaranteed under international law. A number of POWs, however, were denied POW status for varying lengths of time: Pakistani paratroopers, merchant seamen, and Pakistani guerrillas who had crossed the border into Kashmir. The Indian government threatened to shoot on sight members of this latter group, although it is not clear if this was done; at least 100 of these guerrillas were taken prisoner by India and detained. The Tashkent Declaration of January 1966 temporarily resolved the issues of the war, and the exchange of prisoners began that month; the largest single exchange occurred in March 1966, involving 583 Indian and 552 Pakistani POWs. Thereafter, the ICRC visited former camp sites in Kashmir to ensure that all POWs and civilian internees had been released.

A second war occurred in November–December 1971, this time over the independence of East Pakistan. On 16 December, Pakistani forces surrendered to India and the new state of Bangladesh, putting some 73,000 POWs and 17,000 civilian internees into captivity. Generally speaking, the treatment of these prisoners was in accordance with international law. They received mail and parcels, took advantage of recreational opportunities, received their regular military pay, and were not required to perform labor. Regular visits by ICRC officials ensured that conditions in the 50-odd camps housing Pakistani prisoners were acceptable. The 600 Indian prisoners detained by Pakistan also seem to have been well treated by their captors. Civilians interned by both sides, unfortunately, did not benefit from the same protection.

Negotiations for the release of these prisoners were long and complex, for a number of reasons. Bangladesh and India took the position that Pakistani forces had committed war crimes against civilians in East Pakistan; punishment for these crimes became their precondition for the release of Pakistani prisoners. At the same time, the government of Pakistan leveled charges that its prisoners had been abused in Indian camps. The ICRC concluded that there was some merit to these charges, and that harsher measures were adopted by camp guards to deal with escape attempts and other forms of unrest that became more prevalent in camps in the summer of 1972. Finally, Bangladesh refused to release any prisoners until Pakistan recognized its existence as an independent state. Because of these thorny issues, it was not until 1 December 1972 that the first large-scale release of prisoners occurred, involving 616 Indian and 540 Pakistani prisoners who had been captured on the western front. In August 1973, the Delhi Agreement provided for the repatriation of the remaining prisoners. The exchange operation began on 28 September 1973, but not until 30 April 1974 did the last of the 72,795 POWs and 17,186 civilian internees return to Pakistan.

References

Zahid Said, "The Indo-Pakistan Conflict of 1971: Legal Aspects," *Pakistan Horizon* 25 (1972): 78–97.

Siddiq Salik, *Witness to Surrender* (Karachi: Oxford University Press, 1977).

S.P. Salunke, *Pakistani POWs in India* (New Delhi: Vikas Publishing, 1977).

—*Jonathan F. Vance*

INDOCTRINATION

The notion that prisoners might be indoctrinated with the ideology of their captors is a relatively modern one, dating from the post–World War II period. There are fragmented accounts of indoctrination from earlier periods, but it was generally a feature of captivity during the Cold War.

For centuries, prisoners have been encouraged to change sides, but this had nothing to do with politics and everything to do with economics or survival. During World War I, the Germans tried to seduce Irish POWs into joining their side, but the attempt was such a failure that it hardly bears mention. A similar attempt in World War II was equally unsuccessful, as were attempts by the Germans to indoctrinate French colonial prisoners, and by the Japanese to sway Indian prisoners into turning against the British Empire and joining the Greater East Asia Co-Prosperity Sphere. The German attempt to indoctrinate Soviet prisoners was considerably more successful. Many of these prisoners may have had a weak commitment to Communism in the first place and so were easy prey for the German officials who tried to convince them to join the crusade against Josef Stalin's communist regime. As many as one million Russian prisoners joined the German army; they obviously had many motives, but a good many of them were doubtless subjects of indoctrination. For their part, the Soviets seem to have had some success in indoctrinating Japanese POWs, many of whom returned home as ardent communists and worked to spread the message in Japan. The Allied campaign to "denazify" German POWs might also be considered indoctrination.

During the Korean War, indoctrination became even more controversial. Certainly United Nations officials did their best to try to convince North Korean and Chinese POWs of the supremacy of democracy, and the fact that so many of those prisoners eventually declined to return home after the conclusion of hostilities suggests that the UN enjoyed considerable success. The other side was less successful. UN prisoners were frequently subjected to indoctrination sessions. British and American POWs were targeted, while those of other nations were largely spared. Turkish and French-Canadian prisoners resisted reeducation by claiming to speak no English and, as some historians have pointed out, indoctrination becomes more difficult when it has to be done through an interpreter. For British and American prisoners, however, the pressure could be unrelenting. Early in their captivity, they were divided into two classes: those marked as "progressive" were assigned for indoctrination, while those classed as "reactionary" were subjected to physical and psychological abuse to break their will. Progressives received better food and more liberal treatment, but it was assumed that in return they would help their captors to spread the gospel of Communism. Only 21 Americans and one Briton elected to remain in China after the war, but it is difficult to say how many others were successfully indoctrinated. Certainly, UN officials were concerned about this, and most belligerent states put their returned prisoners through extended debriefings. There were few formal "de-indoctrination" programs (the British Commonwealth Forces in Korea, for example, decided that the best way to reeducate returned prisoners was to put them back in their normal domestic environment for a few months), but there was great effort to identify prisoners who might have been "turned."

See also Reeducation

—*Jonathan F. Vance*

Information Bureaus

The establishment of information bureaus to act as clearing and exchange houses for information about POWs and internees has brought significant improvement to the lives of prisoners since the late nineteenth century. Information bureaus were initially organized by the belligerent powers, but more recently they have been administered by neutral bodies.

In premodern wars, any information about POWs exchanged between belligerents usually occurred during negotiations for ransom, parole, or exchange. In these cases, information passed through diplomats who acted as government agents responsible for prisoners' welfare. As the use of ransom, parole, and exchange declined and it became more common to detain prisoners until the conclusion of hostilities, the need to establish information bureaus became more acute. During the Austro-Prussian War of 1866, the government in Berlin established a bureau to disseminate information on wounded and sick prisoners. The bureau was reactivated during the Franco-Prussian War of 1870, with separate departments for German and French prisoners. The 11 members of the French department handled 60,000 inquiries, forwarded 186,000 letters to and from French POWs, and prepared lists of sick, wounded, and deceased prisoners. Similarly, during the Russo-Turkish War (1877–1878), the Russian government regularly dispatched lists of prisoners to the Turkish government. In 1893, the government of France was the first to issue regulations calling for the establishment of bureaus by each belligerent government to provide information on POWs, whether or not they were wounded. This provision was adopted into international law with the Hague Conventions of 1899 and 1907.

During the Russo-Japanese War of 1904–1905, both governments established POW information bureaus. The Japanese bureau was considerably larger than the Russian, because the bulk of the prisoners in the war (some 70,000) were captured by Japan. That bureau was especially efficient, dealing with 50,000 inquiries, forwarding over 215,000 pieces of mail to and from prison camps, and exchanging lists of prisoners with its Russian equivalent on a regular basis.

In 1912, during the Balkan War, the International Committee of the Red Cross (ICRC) suggested that a central information bureau be established in a neutral country to act as an intermediary between the national information bureaus. The suggestion was enshrined in international law with the Geneva Conventions of 1929 and 1949, and as a result a Central POW Agency was established at Geneva, Switzerland, to collate information about prisoners and internees. In principle, each belligerent state was to provide space, equipment, and staff to operate its own bureau and was to provide the Central Agency with full lists of POWs without undue delay. Then, it was to keep the agency fully informed of each prisoner's movements, including transfers to other camps, release, repatriation, escape, admission to hospital, or death.

In practice, this system has not always functioned as intended. During World War II, the Japanese government claimed to have opened an information bureau as soon as it entered the war, but it did not transmit lists of prisoners until at least 18 months later. The Soviet government also refused to compile and transmit lists of prisoners, as did the communist governments involved in the Korean and Vietnam Wars. In both of these cases, western nations learned the identities of all of their citizens who had been captured only when they were released at the end of hostilities. Despite such lapses, the information bureaus have provided a valuable service in ensuring that the fate of individuals who are taken prisoner is communicated to their governments, and thence to their families.

See also Central POW Agency; International Committee of the Red Cross

References
Ronald F. Roxburgh, *The Prisoners of War Information Bureau in London* (London: Longmans, Green, 1915).

—*Jonathan F. Vance*

INTERNATIONAL COMMITTEE OF THE RED CROSS (ICRC)

For over 130 years, the International Committee of the Red Cross (ICRC) has been the single most influential body in ameliorating the conditions of captivity for POWs and civilian internees. By providing food, recreational equipment, and basic necessities and by inspecting camps, negotiating for the release of prisoners, and acting as a neutral arbiter, the ICRC and its national member societies have improved immeasurably the lives of millions of captives.

The mission of the ICRC began in 1863, when Jean-Henri Dunant and four other Swiss businessmen constituted themselves as the International Committee for the Relief of Military Wounded. The committee's goal was to provide aid and comfort to the victims of war, without distinction of nationality. To do this, it encouraged the creation of national relief societies and asked states to bind themselves to the effort to aid the sick and wounded in time of war. Its first great success was an international conference in 1863, followed by the adoption of the 1864 Geneva Convention for the Amelioration of the Condition of the Wounded in Armies in the Field, the first international humanitarian agreement. The Convention stipulated that a red cross on a white field would be the symbol for assistance to the victims of war.

The ICRC has recently focused its efforts on securing the freedom of POWs in post-colonial wars, like these men recently freed from captivity in Sudan (©ICRC/L. Brander)

In 1867, the First International Conference of the Red Cross, bringing together nine governments and 16 national committees, was convened, and in 1876 the International Committee for the Relief of Military Wounded was renamed the International Committee of the Red Cross.

However, the committee was not yet directly concerned with POWs. This development came during the Franco-Prussian War of 1870–1871, when the ICRC created a special subcommittee for POWs (with a green cross as its symbol). However, aid for POWs remained a tangential task; the ICRC did not yet see its mission as including able-bodied combatants, even if they were in captivity. An expansion in this direction was discussed at the Red Cross conference in London in 1907, but not until the 1912 conference in Washington did member states unanimously accept a French proposal that the ICRC include in its mandate assistance to POWs.

During World War I, the ICRC took a direct and comprehensive role in ameliorating the conditions of captivity. It established the International POW Agency in Geneva, which acted as a central clearinghouse for information about prisoners of war and civilian internees. Using a huge card index, the agency kept track of millions of captives of all nationalities, responding to queries from anxious relatives and handling mail to and from prisoners. It was involved in campaigns to secure the exchange or repatriation of captured medical personnel and sick, wounded, and over-age POWs and civilian internees. It received complaints of abuses committed against POWs and used its good offices to encourage belligerent states to abide by the spirit, as well as the letter, of international law. It strongly condemned the use of reprisals against prisoners. In 1916, for example, Germany had threatened to send French POWs to occupied Russia in retaliation for France's transfer of German prisoners to Cameroon and Togo; on the intervention of the ICRC, both sides backed down. ICRC delegates visited hundreds of prison camps in all countries to monitor their adherence to international law. And at the conclusion of hostilities in 1918, the ICRC provided experienced administrators and medical teams to assist in the return home of thousands of prisoners.

The ICRC was kept busy during the interwar period with tasks such as in facilitating the exchange of prisoners and civilian internees in the war between Greece and Turkey, but the greatest effort was devoted to the revision of the Geneva Convention. As early as 1918, the ICRC began to suggest that states assemble to discuss those aspects of the Hague and Geneva Conventions that dealt with POWs and internees, and in the early 1920s, a number of organizations produced draft codes for the treatment of prisoners. In August 1925, the Swiss government suggested an international conference to revise the 1906 Geneva Convention for the Amelioration of the Wounded in Time of War and to prepare a separate convention devoted to POWs. The conference was duly convened on 1 July 1929, and within a month, delegates had agreed upon the Geneva Convention Relative to the Treatment of Prisoners of War. This agreement recognized the ICRC's vital work on behalf of POWs; indeed, it was the only nongovernmental body explicitly recognized in the convention.

As in 1914, the ICRC was fully prepared for the coming of World War II in 1939 and established the Central POW Agency almost immediately. Again, the committee was involved in a wide range of activities for the benefit of prisoners. The Central POW Agency acted as a central information bureau, collating details on millions of prisoners from all nations. ICRC delegates around the world performed a total of 11,175 prison camp inspections, monitoring the conditions of captivity and seeking to improve them wherever possible. It served as a diplomatic intermediary and participated in negotiations involving exchanges, repatriations, and reprisals. Perhaps most importantly, it coordinated an immense campaign that shipped millions of food parcels to prisoners around the world. It was difficult and demanding work, and not without its dangers. In December 1943, the ICRC delegate in Borneo, Dr. Mattaeus Vischer, and his wife were executed after having been found guilty of plotting against the Japanese army. Also, 27 ICRC employees died in attacks on ships carrying food parcels for prisoners. But these losses were negligible when compared to the lives that were saved by their efforts.

The 1949 Geneva Convention Relative to the Treatment of Prisoners of War restated the commitment of the international community to the ICRC's work on behalf of POWs and internees, and the committee and its member societies continued to play a valuable role. Negotiations for the release of Japanese POWs held in China were concluded in 1956 after having been carried out largely by the Japanese and Chinese Red Cross societies. During the Vietnam War, the Cambodian Red Cross agreed to act as an intermediary in conveying mail to downed U.S. airmen in North Vietnam.

However, World War II and subsequent conflicts have also revealed the most significant obstacle to the committee's work: detaining powers that are most likely to mistreat prisoners are also most likely to refuse the ICRC access to its camps. Russia denied ICRC delegates access to its prison camps during World War II; Japan allowed access only infrequently and under certain stringent conditions. It is no coincidence that these two regimes witnessed some of the worst abuses of POWs. By the same token, the ICRC had great difficulty gaining access to POWs held by North Korea, the People's Republic of China, and North

Vietnam. Sadly, recent experience has proven that the prisoners who are most in need of ICRC assistance are least likely to get it.

Since the end of World War II, however, the greatest challenge facing the ICRC has been the proliferation of non-international armed conflicts, including civil wars, insurrections, and rebellions. The Russian Civil War (1917–1921) was the first such conflict in which the ICRC played an active role in visiting and assisting prisoners, and this activity has constituted the bulk of the Committee's activities in recent decades. This is despite the fact that there is no guarantee in international law for the ICRC to have such access to prisoners; it relies entirely on its international reputation for neutrality and on the willingness of Detaining Powers to allow access. Part of the reason that governments and quasi-governments allow access is the ICRC's insistence that a visit to a detainee does not constitute the *de facto* granting of POW status to that individual under international law, nor is it a legitimation of the cause espoused by one side or the other.

The range of prisoners assisted has grown to include not only combatants belonging to either government or rebel forces but also civilians arrested by government or rebel forces because of their support, whether real or perceived, active or passive, for the opposition. Individuals in this group are generally referred to as political prisoners or security detainees; this group includes, for example, Iraqi nationals living in Britain, Italy, and France who were interned there at the beginning of the Gulf War in 1990 or Palestinians detained by Israeli occupying forces. Regardless of the kind of prisoner involved, the ICRC has devoted its efforts to using visits to detainees as a way to ensure that the conditions of captivity are as favorable as they can be.

The Committee has established five conditions governing its visits: It must be able to visit all detainees of the class to which the Detaining Power has granted access; it must be able to tour every part of the facility in which the individuals are detained; it must receive authorization for repeat visits, to provide for constant monitoring; it must be allowed to speak freely and in private with any detainee; and it must be able to compile a list of all detainees of the class to which the Detaining Power has granted access. Each of these is vitally important to the ICRC's mission. The registration of detainees, for example, is crucial to prevent their disappearance of extrajudicial execution; once a prisoner has been registered with the Committee, which will then monitor that individual's well-being in future visits, it is assumed that the Detaining Power will be less likely to order his or her execution.

To ensure its continued access to detainees through a schedule of prison visits, the ICRC has accepted a number of principles. It does not seek to gain the release of individual prisoners, except in extreme medical or humanitarian cases. It does not concern itself with the reasons for which the detainee has been imprisoned; whether the individual has been accused of sabotage, terrorism, subversion, or dissidence, he or she is still entitled to the same assistance from ICRC inspectors. By the same token, the ICRC does not pass judgment on the legitimacy of the detention, merely on the conditions of captivity; whether the individual has been detained under established penal law, martial law, or in violation of any law is immaterial. Finally, in contrast with past precedent, reports of visits are considered confidential, to be shared only with the detaining power. This principle was adopted because the publication of reports of visits in Algeria (1960), Greece (1969), Pakistan (1972), Chile (1975), and Iran (1979) were released and used for political and propaganda purposes, thereby jeopardizing the Committee's work; more recently, the ICRC raised concerns when the *Wall Street Journal* published lengthy extracts from a report on detention sites in Iraq that had been written in January 2004 and the *New York Times* published similar extracts from confidential reports on internment conditions in Guantánamo Bay. The Committee's position on such leaks has remained consistent: If it is to do its work for the benefit of detainees, its reports cannot be allowed to become politicized or propagandized, or to stigmatize one side or the other. It will only publish reports as a corrective if extracts that are selective or misleading have been leaked and printed. In this sense, the most important capital that the ICRC possesses is its neutrality, something that the Committee guards very jealously.

With the proliferation of armed conflict, either internal or interstate, the work of the ICRC in protecting prisoners continues to grow dramatically. In 2000, 170,000 prisoners were visited and registered; in 2003, delegates of the Committee visited nearly 470,000 detainees in over 1,900 prisons in around 80 countries. For many of these detainees, the ICRC delegate is the only sympathetic person that they encounter while imprisoned.

See also Central POW Agency; St. John Ambulance; Young Men's Christian Association

References

Alain Aeschlimann, "Protection of Detainees: ICRC Action Behind Bars," *International Review of the Red Cross* 87 (March 2005): 83–122.

Pierre Boissier, *From Solferino to Tsushima: History of the International Committee of the Red Cross* (Geneva: Henry Dunant Institute, 1985).

André Durand, *From Sarajevo to Hiroshima: History of the International Committee of the Red Cross* (Geneva: Henry Dunant Institute, 1984).

David Forsythe, *Humanitarian Politics: The International Committee of the Red Cross* (Baltimore: Johns Hopkins University Press, 1977).

John F. Hutchinson, *Champions of Charity: War and the Rise of the Red Cross* (Boulder, CO: Westview Press, 1996).

International Committee of the Red Cross, *Deprived of Freedom* (Geneva: ICRC, 2002).

Marcel Junod, *Warrior Without Weapons* (London: Jonathan Cape, 1951).

Caroline Moorehead, *Dunant's Dream: War, Switzerland and the History of the Red Cross* (London: HarperCollins, 1998).

—Jonathan F. Vance

INTERNATIONAL LAW

For centuries, the treatment meted out to captives was largely dependent on the whim of the captor. Many were put to death, either as a simple expedient or as part of a post-battle ritual. At times, prisoners were used as slave labor, as long as they could be fed without putting undue pressure on the resources of their captors. Conquered peoples might also be assimilated into the captor's society or taken into the captor's army to augment its fighting strength. If they were of no use to their captors, prisoners might be either paroled—if a commander felt that their word was a sufficient safeguard against them taking up arms again—or ransomed—if their status was high enough to induce their compatriots or family to pay for their freedom. During the Middle Ages, the practice of ransoming became the most widespread method of dealing with prisoners. Any high-ranking soldier or civilian could be ransomed or sold to the highest bidder; in either case, prices varied greatly, depending on the status of the prisoner and the wealth of those who made the purchase or paid the ransom. If an entire ransom could not be raised at once, it was common practice to release a prisoner on parole until the full amount was paid.

Summary execution, enslavement, parole, and ransom, though, were all purely pragmatic solutions for dealing with prisoners of war; none of them grew out of any moral or legal trend toward regulating or improving the conditions of captivity. The needs of the captor, and little else, determined how prisoners would be treated. In fact, it was not until the eighteenth century and the appearance of Emmerich de Vattel's *Le droit de gens* (1758) that a comprehensive discussion of theories of captivity was attempted. One of the most significant themes of Vattel's treatise was his assertion that the captor did not have rights to the prisoner's life after surrender. Vattel extolled the virtues of erring on the side of mercy when dealing with prisoners and deplored as unjust and savage past practices that assumed that the captor held the power of life and death over his prisoners. However popular and significant Le droit de gens was, it remained within the realm of philosophy and was not translated into judicial practice.

It was not until the great revolutions of the eighteenth century that some attempt was made to put Vattel's ideas on a more legalistic footing. Unfortunately, these efforts reflected not so much a concern for POWs for their own sake as an interest in improving the quality of life in a wider sense. The 1785 Treaty of Amity and Commerce between Prussia and the United States included a number of articles dealing with captivity, but neither broke new ground in establishing a code of conduct; no new theories were advanced, and the restrictions on the use of manacles and prison hulks showed that the treaty was primarily a reaction against some practices adopted during the American Revolution. The French National Assembly's Decree Concerning POWs (1792) was more wide-ranging, but, as Geoffrey Best points out, it was more an aberration than the beginning of a trend; it should be viewed as an outgrowth of late Enlightenment philosophy and not as an attempt to ameliorate the lot of POWs for their own sake. Implicit in the decree is the Enlightenment notion that wars are fought between bad monarchs and good people, and that there is no reason why captives should suffer unduly for the transgressions of their monarchs.

In the nineteenth century came the first significant attempts to establish norms for ameliorating the conditions of captivity, but it would be misleading to suggest that POWs in themselves were deemed worthy of consideration, even at this late date. The improvement of conditions for captives occurred not in isolation but as part of a wider movement for social reform. It became fashionable to show concern for the welfare of the disadvantaged, including the common soldier, and POWs were apparently suitably pitiful objects of charity. The first of the important documents of the nineteenth century related to POWs, now known as the Lieber Code, was formulated in 1863 by Dr. Francis Lieber, a Prussian jurist at Columbia University, at the request of the commander of the Union Armies in the U.S. Civil War. The Lieber Code was followed by the Brussels Declaration of 1874, which reiterated the provisions of the Lieber Code (even going so far as to echo some of the language used in the 1863 document) but was far more limited in scope. There was the same concern for the determination of belligerent status and the provision of parole, and there was equal emphasis on humane treatment. The Brussels Declaration also allowed that prisoners might be put to work, provided that the employment was not connected to the war effort and was not excessive or humiliating. Like the Lieber Code, however, the Brussels Declaration had no force of law through ratification, even though it was widely sanctioned by armies around the world.

The Hague Conventions of 1899 and 1907 were the most well known of the early attempts to codify the law of POW treatment. Yet the first convention was considerably more limited in scope than either the Lieber or Brussels documents, while the second was virtually identical to its predecessor. Because of the exemplary treatment of prisoners in the Boer and Russo-Japanese Wars, international lawmakers concluded that the conventions drafted at the Hague were adequate. However, the many additional agreements reached by the belligerents during World War I proved that major modifications were necessary.

The Geneva Conventions of 1864 and 1906 had made brief mention of the treatment of prisoners, but only with respect to the sick and wounded. It was not until 1929 that all POWs became the subject of Geneva law, which was directed at protecting the victims or war and not at legislating the means of war, as Hague law did. With 97 separate articles, the Geneva Convention of 27 July 1929 was the most extensive codification of POW law yet attempted, and it addressed many of the issues that had arisen during World War I. However, the experience of World War II pointed out the shortcomings of the 1929 convention, and it was replaced by the Geneva

Convention of 1949, which repeated much of the earlier convention but tried to prevent some of the problems that had proven particularly thorny during World War II, like determining what kind of combatant was eligible to receive protection as a POW. Significantly, there was also a convention to protect the civilian victims of war, the first time that international lawmakers had been able to agree on the safeguards that should be afforded this most vulnerable group.

International law with respect to POWs and civilian internees continues to evolve. In 1977, governments agreed upon the Geneva Convention Additional Protocols, which extended the convention's protection to victims of civil war and other types of non-international conflict. Notably, Israel, Pakistan, Iran, Iraq, and the United States declined to ratify the 1977 Additional Protocols, for a variety of reasons. In the case of the United States, columnist William Safire argued in the *New York Times* that the Additional Protocols would give rights to terrorists and allow them to claim the same status and protection as the uniformed soldier. "Once the line between civilian and soldier is blurred," wrote Safire, "no civilian is safe."

The recent upsurge of international terrorism, which made it clear that no civilian is indeed safe, has reopened many debates surrounding prisoners of war and internees, debates that have yielded more questions than answers. What should be the position of terror suspects who are captured, and by what legal mechanism should they be tried? Some people have argued that they deserve no special protection under international law, beyond that they be treated humanely, while others hold that secret detention facilities, trial by military commission rather than in open court, and an insistence that, by their very conduct, such individuals have placed themselves outside of the protection of international law is misguided, counter-productive, and at variance with the legal traditions of most western nations.

At root, the question revolves around how to classify, as a form of conflict, the so-called War on Terror (in its various guises). Legal scholar Jordan Paust argues convincingly that the actions of Al Qaeda fail the test of even the lowest level of international conflict, an insurgency, because it meets none of the criteria for that classification (an insurgent group, under international law, should have some kind of government, an organized military force, and a relatively stable population, or at least a body of supporters, that occupy a distinct geographic territory). The war in Afghanistan against the Taliban regime, in contrast, was an armed conflict of an international character because of the involvement of other states, such as Pakistan and the United States; all of the laws of war, including the 1949 Geneva Convention, then, should have applied to the war in Afghanistan. Still, Paust concludes that, where captivity issues are concerned, there is no need to change international law in the wake of the 11 September attacks, for the Conventions now in force can cope with the new realities of the struggle against terrorism. "Mean-spirited denials of international legal protections," writes Paust, "would not merely be unlawful, but would also disserve a free people."

See also Brussels Declaration; Geneva Convention of 1929; Geneva Convention of 1949; Geneva Convention Additional Protocols; Geneva Conventions of 1864 and 1906; Hague Conventions of 1899 and 1907; Lieber Code.

References

M. Cherif Bassiouni, *International Criminal Law*, 2nd ed. (Ardsley, NY: Transnational Publishers, 1999).

Geoffrey Best, *Humanity in Warfare* (New York: Columbia University Press, 1980).

———, *War and Law Since 1945* (Oxford: Clarendon Press, 1994).

W.E.S. Flory, *Prisoners of War: A Study in International Law* (Washington, DC: American Council on Public Affairs, 1942).

Howard S. Levie, *Prisoners of War in International Armed Conflict* (Newport, RI: Naval War College Press, 1979).

———, ed., *Documents on Prisoners of War* (Newport, RI: Naval War College Press, 1979).

Jordan J. Paust, *There Is No Need to Revise the Laws of War in Light of September 11th* (Washington, DC: American Society of International Law Task Force on Terrorism, 2002).

Guy B. Roberts, "The New Rules for Waging War: The Case Against Ratification of Additional Protocol I," *Virginia Journal of International Law* 26 (1985): 109-178.

Nigel S. Rodley, *The Treatment of Prisoners under International Law*, 2nd ed. (Oxford: Clarendon, 1999).

Allan Rosas, *The Legal Status of Prisoners of War: A Study in International Humanitarian Law Applicable in Armed Conflicts* (Helsinki: Suomalainen Tiedakatemia, 1976).

Malcolm N. Shaw, *International Law*, 5th ed. (Cambridge: Cambridge University Press, 2003).

—*Tony Dawes*

INTERNATIONAL MILITARY TRIBUNAL

See Nuremberg Trials

INTERNATIONAL MILITARY TRIBUNAL FOR THE FAR EAST

See Tokyo War Crimes Trials

INTERROGATION

Prisoners of war have always been regarded as vital sources of information by the armies that capture them, but not until the twentieth century were techniques for the interrogation of POWs systematized and rendered more efficient. The practices adopted by Germany during World War I were copied by other nations and provide an excellent illustration of nonviolent means by which information can be extracted from prisoners.

The Germans conducted an efficient POW interrogation system using techniques that included examining personal effects and pieces of equipment, conducting highly sophisticated interviews, and using hidden microphones. Contrary to the suggestions of wartime propaganda, there is no recorded incident in which the Germans used torture to extract information from POWs. The information sought by the Germans included unit identification, order of battle, technical information on weapons and equipment, descriptions of troop morale, and the level to which enemy troops were motivated to carry on the war. The range of methods the Germans used depended on the type of POW under interrogation.

The first level of interrogation took place immediately after the soldier was captured. German frontline troops searched each prisoner thoroughly, confiscating personal items such as letters, diaries, photographs, and pieces of personal equipment on which the soldier had written any identifying information. The frontline troops quickly sent the seized material to an intelligence officer behind the front lines. At the same time, a German NCO or officer would ask each prisoner for his name, rank, and unit identification and attempt to get the prisoner to link his unit to the other units that had been operating in his area. This phase of interrogation was subject to limitations imposed by the number of prisoners, but at some point before he arrived in a permanent POW camp, each prisoner was asked those questions.

Throughout the war, the Germans showed a much greater interest in officers than enlisted prisoners. Officers were generally better educated, had greater access to valuable information, and saw more of what went on around their units than did enlisted men. But the Germans did not attribute equal importance to all captured officers. Senior officers were obviously more valuable than were first and second lieutenants. Doctors were of relatively little importance, whereas aviators, regardless of rank, were very valuable. A tank officer had much greater value to the Germans than did an infantry officer. As they had done with the enlisted men, the Germans first confiscated the officer's personal belongings. But from that point on, the Germans treated the officers entirely differently. The Germans first took the prisoner to an intelligence officer who was situated a mile or two behind the front. The intelligence officer was fluent in the language of the prisoners with whom he worked, either French or English. By the time the POW met his

German interrogator, the German already had all the POW's personal items that had been seized by the frontline troops. The initial interrogation was usually brief, militarily correct, and limited to questions to which the Germans already had the answers. This was the so-called softening-up phase. At this level, the Germans often accused aviators, especially American aviators, of having explosive rounds in their machine gun belts—something that was prohibited by international law. The rounds in their belts were actually tracer rounds, which the pilot knew did not qualify as an explosive round. Still, the Germans pressed the issue, threatening to have the pilot shot for a war crime if he did not cooperate. The fact that the Germans frequently used the ploy is well documented, but there was no instance in which the Germans shot any airman over the issue of explosive rounds.

A common feature at all levels of interrogation, especially the interrogation of officers, was the conversational nature of the interview. The interrogator adopted the pose of a professional soldier passing the time with another soldier. It was the interrogator's job to establish a bond with the POW that would get him talking. Once the prisoner started talking on any subject, the information the Germans wanted started to come out.

The second interrogation stage was more elaborate and more sophisticated than the first. In the second stage, the interrogator was often an expert in the same specialty as his prisoner. For example, German officers who interrogated aviators were often fliers themselves. Regardless of the type of officer he was interviewing, the German was fully prepared for the interview. He usually knew enough about the prisoner's unit to be conversational, and he was often able to convince the prisoner that he already knew as much as the prisoner did. The conversation was always friendly and nearly always centered on how the war was progressing and how much longer it might last. The Germans always asked American prisoners why the United States had entered the war. In both stages, the purpose was to get the prisoner to talk. From those conversations the Germans learned a great deal about the enemy's morale and degree of motivation. And as the discussion rambled on, the Germans picked up valuable military information too.

The most sophisticated German interrogation technique was carried out at the so-called Listening Hotel in Karlsruhe. The German army had converted this former tourist hotel into a wired intelligence-gathering center. They had planted microphones throughout the hotel and could listen to and record the prisoners' conversations. The technique was to put two to six prisoners in a room and listen to what they said. Sometimes they put men together who knew one another. Other times they put men together based solely on common language, for example British and American prisoners. Other times they put one Frenchman in a room with five British officers, one of whom spoke French. Or they reversed the mix, putting a lone Englishman among a group of French. Sometimes the prisoners found the microphones and tore them out. Other times the prisoners remained silent. But throughout its three-year career, the Listening Hotel proved to be a gold mine of information for the Germans. After three days to a week, the Germans transferred the prisoners to a distribution camp, and the interrogations were over.

These methods were further refined during World War II, when the German air force opened a carefully designed camp, called Dulag Luft, specifically for the interrogation of captured Allied airmen. By all accounts, the operation at Dulag Luft was every bit as successful as that developed at the Listening Hotel.

See also Dulag Luft

References

Robert Jackson, *The Prisoners, 1914–1918* (New York: Routledge, 1989).

Kevin Jones, "'From the Horse's Mouth': *Luftwaffe* POWs as Sources for Air Ministry Intelligence During the Battle of Britain," *Intelligence and National Security* 15 (2000): 60-80.

Dwight R. Messimer, *Escape* (Annapolis: Naval Institute Press, 1994).

Michael Moynihan, ed., *Black Bread and Barbed Wire: Prisoners in the First World War* (London: Leo Cooper, 1978).

U.S. Department of the Army, *U.S. Army Intelligence and Interrogation Handbook: The Official Guide on Prisoner Interrogation* (Guilford, CT: Lyons Press, 2005).

—*Dwight R. Messimer*

INTERROGATION IN DEPTH

Interrogation in depth was used on prisoners captured by the British military in colonial insurgencies in Palestine, Malaya, Cyprus, Malaysia, and elsewhere. When it was applied in the conflict in Northern Ireland, which was already complicated by the debate over whether captured members of the Irish Republican Army (IRA) were POWs (as the IRA claimed) or criminals (as the British government usually assumed), its use became even more controversial.

On 9 August 1971, British security forces swept through Northern Ireland and arrested 342 individuals without charge. The arrested were sent to various holding centers throughout Ulster for questioning, and a small group were selected for interrogation in depth, also known as the Five Techniques: (1) forcing the detainee to stand spread-eagled against a wall while using a baton to encourage him to stay in position until he collapsed, whereupon he is lifted back into position, (2) placing a heavy black hood (kept in place except during the questioning) over the detainee's head to produce sensory deprivation, (3) submitting the detainee to a continued and monotonous high-pitched noise of a volume meant to enhance a sense of isolation, (4) submitting the detainee to days of enforced sleep deprivation, and (5) depriving the detainee of food and water except for a small amount of bread and a pint of water at six-hour intervals.

Public outrage over the treatment of some detainees led to an official British inquiry, headed by Sir Edmund Compton. The inquiry concluded that interrogation in depth had taken place but had reached only the level of "physical ill-treatment" and not "physical brutality" as the term was understood. A second inquiry, under Lord Parker, was appointed to consider whether the interrogation methods should be continued. Contrary to the final recommendations of the Parker Report, the British government terminated the use of the Five Techniques and paid compensation to the victims.

The Republic of Ireland took the issue before the European Commission of Human Rights, contending that the interrogation techniques constituted torture and inhumane treatment and violated the European Convention on Human Rights. The commission unanimously upheld both of these contentions. The Irish government then petitioned the European Court of Human Rights to find that the British government had committed breaches of the convention and that the Five Techniques amounted to torture. The court proceeded to deal with the distinctions between inhumane treatment, degrading treatment, and torture, and to craft definitions for the future. The court concluded, in Ireland v. United Kingdom, that the Five Techniques, while inhumane, did not give rise to the "very serious and cruel suffering" that is needed to reach the threshold of torture. The victims of the Five Techniques would likely beg to differ.

The British security services claimed that interrogation in depth was an effective method of obtaining information that could not have been acquired by any other means. They also stated that, through use of the interrogation procedures, many lives were saved. Therefore the security establishment saw the episode as a tactical success—terrorists were captured and lives were saved. However, the security services were never able to support this claim with firm evidence in the context of Northern Ireland.

Time has clearly demonstrated that the situation in Ulster is enormously complex and the simple application of military tactics to a long war of attrition are counterproductive. The conflict in Northern Ireland is not a military struggle but a political struggle, involving propaganda, symbolism, and strategic political planning. On the whole, this episode was a political setback for security forces and a propaganda victory for the IRA with significant international political repercussions.

See also Northern Ireland; Torture

References

Frank Kitson, *Low Intensity Operations: Subversion, Insurgency and Peacekeeping* (London: Faber, 1971).

John McGuffin, *The Guineapigs* (Harmondsworth, UK: Penguin, 1974).

Tim Shallice, "The Ulster Depth Interrogation Techniques and Their Relation to Sensory Deprivation Research," *Cognition* 1 (1974): 385–405.

N. Wad, "Technology in Ulster: Rubber Bullets Hit Home, Brainwashing Backfires," *Science* 176 (1972): 1102–1105.

—*Craig T. Cobane*

INTIFADA

The ongoing violence in Israel has gone by many names. To Palestinians, it is part of the *intifada* (taken from the Arabic verb meaning to shake loose), an uprising intended to free them from Israeli control and lead to the establishment of a Palestinian state. Successive Israeli governments have regarded Palestinian resistance as either terrorism or criminal action, being very careful not to give the uprising any form of recognition that might confer on it standing under international law. The disagreement over the nature of the conflict has been paralleled by disputes over the status that should be granted to prisoners taken by either side.

The uprising began in earnest in December 1987, with demonstrations by Palestinian youths; Israeli patrols met the rocks and bullets with bullets, and the cycle of violence began. The first year of the intifada saw over 360 Palestinians killed and 20,000 wounded, while 11 Israelis died in the same period. By the time the fifth anniversary of the uprising came, the death toll had risen to over 600 Arabs and dozens of Israeli civilians and soldiers, but it was to rise much higher as Palestinian resistance groups, some well known (such as Hizb'Allah), some more shadowy, stepped up their terror campaign against the Israeli state. The lists of suicide bombings and retaliatory attacks that have plagued the region since 1989 makes depressing reading, particularly since they suggest that certain groups are not in fact interested in achieving peace, but are quite content to continue with a policy of sowing terror. The Palestinian conundrum remains one of the most challenging problems in international relations today.

The existence of prisoners taken by both sides has not helped the issue. Hizb'Allah, Hamas, and other aligned groups have been keen to take prisoners in the form of hostages, who could be exchanged for imprisoned leaders or for political concessions. In 1992, Hamas kidnapped an Israeli police official in the hopes of exchanging him for its spiritual leader, Sheikh Ahmed Yassin, then in Israeli detention. When Israel refused the exchange, the police officer was murdered. But Israel has used the same tactic. In July 1989, soldiers kidnapped a Lebanese Shi'ite religious leader, Abdul Karim Obeid, whom they believed was a leader in Hizb'Allah and played a role in the kidnapping and murder of U.S. Marine Corps Colonel William Higgins in Lebanon.

Israel has been far more active in arresting Palestinian fighters and other security suspects. The first captives were some 5,000 young Palestinian men arrested in the first year of the *intifada* and placed in detention facilities, such as the camp in the Negev. Such mass arrests would continue throughout the uprising, although Israel has been reluctant to confirm exactly how many Palestinians it holds at any given time.

In July 2003, the Israeli government indicated that it would begin to release prisoners as part of the Aqaba peace process. It began by freeing over 50 captives, although not the captives that Palestinian groups wanted; the leaders of the militant group Islamic Jihad insisted that the first prisoners to be freed should be those who had been in custody the longest; according to Palestinian authorities, there were roughly 460 Palestinians who had been in Israeli jails for more than 20 years. However, the Israeli cabinet had already decided its criteria for freeing prisoners: It would only release those individuals who did not have "blood on their hands." This meant that anyone who had personally participated in attacks in which Israelis or foreign nationals were killed or injured, who had been responsible for sending terrorists out to attack targets (regardless of whether the attacks had actually occurred), or who had been apprehended in the process of attempting to carry out a suicide attack would not be released.

How this criteria would operate in practice became apparent in November 2003, when Israel released nine Jordanians who had been convicted of possessing arms and illegally entering Israel. In December 2004, Israel released another 159 "low-security" captives in exchange for the Egyptian government releasing an Israeli national who was being held in Egypt on charges of espionage. Three months later, the government of Israel pledged to free 900 imprisoned Palestinians as a goodwill gesture on the eve of the Sharm al-Sheikh summit. In each case, none of the freed prisoners had been accused of involvement in any specific violent acts.

But the "blood on their hands" policy was not absolute, much to the chagrin of right-wing Israelis. In October 2000, three Israeli soldiers were abducted and subsequently murdered by Hizb'Allah fighters; anxious to retrieve their remains, and to secure the freedom of kidnapped businessman Elhanan Tannenbaum, the Israeli government accepted German mediation, which paid off after four years when Israel returned more that 400 Palestinian, Lebanese, and other Arab prisoners, including a small number who had been convicted of killing Israeli soldiers in southern Lebanon, in exchange for Tannenbaum and the remains of the three soldiers. More controversial were reports that Israel was willing to consider trading a Lebanese man, Samir Kantar, for information on the whereabouts of Israeli air force officer Ron Arad, who had gone missing in 1986 and was suspected to have been in Hizb'Allah hands at one point. The fact that Kantar was serving a 542-year prison sentence for killing three Israelis, including a child, outraged many people, and confused the Jordanian government, which was lobbying hard (and thus far unsuccessfully) for the release of four Jordanians convicted of killing an Israeli soldier in a 1990 attack.

Clearly, the Arab detainees have become pawns in the larger geopolitical game. By themselves, they are of little interest to the Israeli government, even, in spite of the "blood on their hands" policy, if they have been convicted of terrible crimes. However, they are very useful for other purposes. Hundreds of Palestinians for one Israeli (or the remains of one Israeli) is regarded as a fair trade. Prisoners can be released to gain allies internationally, to demonstrate good faith at the outset of wider peace negotiations, or to placate potentially sympathetic Arab states; they can even be used to deal with the enemy, like Hizb'Allah, and gain concessions that might not be secured under any other circumstances.

See also Arab-Israeli Wars; Lebanese Civil War

References

John Collins, *Occupied by Memory: The Intifada Generation and the Palestinian State of Emergency* (New York: New York University Press, 2004).

Anthony H. Cordesman, *The Israeli-Palestinian War: Escalating to Nowhere* (Westport, CT: Praeger, 2005).

Lisa Hajjar, *Courting Conflict: The Israeli Military Court System in the West Bank and Gaza* (Berkeley: University of California Press, 2005).

—*J.W. Smith*

IRAN-IRAQ WAR (1980–1988)

Known to the rest of the world as the Iran-Iraq War, this conflict is known by different names in Iran and Iraq. For Iraqis, it is the Qadisiya War, named after the seventh-century campaign of Muslim Arab invaders fought against the Zoroastrian Sasanian (Persian) Empire, the capital of which was not far from modern Baghdad. For Iranians, it is the Imposed War. Launched on 22 September 1980 by Iraq, the war was fought for a number of reasons; notably, Iraq wanted to regain control of the Shatt al-Arab waterway, the boundary between the two countries near the Persian Gulf. Also, Iraq aimed to put an end to Ayatollah Khomeini's anti-Ba'athist and anti-Saddam Hussein rhetoric and calls for rebellion directed toward Iraq's Shi'a majority. The United States, the Soviet Union, and many European and Arab states, especially the Gulf countries, supported Iraq in this war; it is often argued that the U.S. encouraged Hussein to attack Iran.

More than one million people were killed or injured in this war between the two Muslim countries. Most conservative western estimates put the number of dead on the Iranian side at 262,000 and Iraqis at 105,000. In addition, between 400,000 and 700,000 Iranians are thought to have been maimed by the war, at least half of whom are believed to be permanently disabled. Significantly lower than Western estimates are the statistics released by the Iranian government, which specified that 160,000 Iranians, including 11,000 civilians, died in the war.

The number of prisoners in this conflict totaled 100,000, with approximately 70,000 Iraqis held in Iran and 30,000 in Iraq. Significant Iranian POW camps were located in Arak, Bojnoord, Davoudieh, Ghouchan, Gorgan, Heshmatieh, Kahrizak I, Kahrizak II, Manjil, Mashad, Mehrabad, Parandak, Sari, Semnan, Takhti, and Torbate-Jam, but Iran was also accused of having secret prison camps. Approximately 13 Iraqi POW camps, identified by number, were located mostly around the cities of Mosul and Ramadi.

Early International Committee of the Red Cross (ICRC) reports accused both countries of committing grave violations, such as the summary executions of captive soldiers both at the fronts and behind the lines, and the abandonment of enemy wounded on the battlefield. Each country accused the other of committing mass murder of prisoners at or subsequent to the time of capture. The Iraqi side was generally more insistent on such charges against Iran and provided on more than one occasion photographs of dead Iraqi soldiers with their hands and legs tied; some Iraqi POWs corroborated witnessing their comrades being killed after capture. Although both sides professed to adhere to accepted international norms regarding the treatment of POWs, prisoners always accused their captors of not observing such norms. Neither country provided adequate mental or physical activity for the prisoners to keep them occupied. When recreational activities were allowed, the prisoners of each side complained it only amounted to listening to daylong radio programs with explicit political propaganda against their countries' leaders. While the physical ill-treatment of prisoners was more common in Iraq, psychological ill-treatment—mostly the religious and ideological pressure by authorities—was more common in Iran.

Looking more specifically to Iran, ICRC memoranda charged that Iraqi POWs in that country were subjected to ideological and political pressure. The Iranian government declared that it provided "spiritual guidance" to POWs under the responsibility of the Cultural Committee, purported to be organized and elected by the prisoners themselves. Iranian authorities claimed that, as far as possible, they grouped together Iraqi prisoners with commonalities in each camp; while this practice included putting together prisoners from same region of origin, it also meant separating pro-Iraqi "loyalists" from pro-Iranian "believers," presumably Iraqis who professed Shi'a Islam and others who were successfully indoctrinated. Yet, there were camps containing both "loyalists" and "believers." In such situations, various violent conflicts broke out between the two sides, or other factions that might have formed in each camp, which in some cases resulted in significant loss of life among the prisoners. Of course, from the point of view of the prisoners, "spiritual guidance" took the form of brainwashing and indoctrination. One ICRC mission that visited a number of camps in Iran was struck by the behavior of what it assumed to be Iraqis who had been through the "spiritual guidance" and were now "believers." The mission claimed to encounter in each camp it visited "fanatical, hysterical, and sometimes violent demonstrations" by the Iraqi prisoners who chanted pro-Islamic slogans that disparaged Saddam Hussein and flattered Ayatollah Khomeini. Iranian authorities claimed that they organized "visits" to holy places such as Qom, presumably for Shi'a Iraqis. Along with, or perhaps as part of the "spiritual guidance" which the Iraqi prisoners received was an opportunity for illiterate Iraqis to acquire literacy skills. Using educated POWs as teachers, Iran claimed that 13,000 illiterate Iraqi prisoners learned to read and write in prison camps. However, it is likely that these opportunities of travel and schooling were only open to "believers" who seem to have dominated the camps in which they were interned and may have intimidated "loyalists." In some camps, prisoners complained of sentences imposed on them by Islamic courts, namely the sentencing to death of some captured Iraqi pilots for having carried out raids on civilian centers—a charge the Iranian authorities denied.

In Iraq, the situation was only somewhat different. The ICRC mission visiting the camps found significant evidence of psychological pressure on the Iranian prisoners by the Iraqi authorities. However, the mission found no evidence of systematic indoctrination and concluded that the cause of psychological problems may have lain with the prisoners' longtime captivity and ill-treatment as a consequence of guard violence. Among the Iranian POWs in Iraq were teenage soldiers, some as young as 13. Both Iran and Iraq accused each other of physical ill-treatment toward the prisoners they held. However, such accusations against Iraq by the Iranian government and POWs were noticeably more common and consistent. Iranian POWs protested about being whipped, beaten with truncheons and heavy cables, and subjected to electric shocks; a considerable number of prisoners complained of becoming nearly or completely deaf after numerous and simultaneous blows on both ears. One ICRC mission confirmed the marks and scars of such ill-treatment when it visited camps in Iraq. Some POWs who had passed through interrogation centers accused the Iraqi officials of torture, either as punishment or to extract information. Common accusations were being suspended upside down from ceilings or ventilators, having the soles of their feet beaten, withstanding electric shocks, burning with cigarettes, and undergoing mock executions. While many such things took place in camps in Ramadi, some Iranian prisoners revealed that they had been to Abu Ghraib prison themselves, or knew people who had been there.

Along with POWs, Iraq also held as captive large numbers of civilians. These were ethnic Persians, ethnic Kurdish-Iranians (30,000), and Iranian citizens of Arab origin (25,000). Iran accused Iraq of holding as many as 75,000 of these civilians in miserable conditions. Iraqi authorities, however, described 25,596 Iranian civilians, almost exclusively Kurds, in their country as refugees who could leave Iraq if they chose to do so. While living inside barbed-wire "villages," some of these internees held jobs in Ramadi.

The war never officially ended, but the ceasefire was declared on 20 August 1988. From 1996–1998, some of the Iraqi prisoners captured in 1980 were released after 16 to 18 years of captivity. Although Iran claimed to have returned what it maintained was the last of the prisoners twice before, more Iraqi POWs were repatriated in May 2003. The last of the Iranian prisoners in Iraq were repatriated in 1998.

References

Ige F. Dekker and Harry H.G. Post, *The Gulf War of 1980–1988: The Iran-Iraq War in International Legal Perspective* (The Hague: Martinus Nijhoff, 1992).

J. Anthony Gardner, *The Gulf War : A Bibliography* (New York: Macmillan, 1989).

Lawrence G. Potter and Gary G. Sick, *Iran, Iraq, and the Legacies of War* (New York: Palgrave, 2004).

—*Yücel Yanīkdağ*

IRAQ WAR

In October 1998, United States President Bill Clinton signed into law the Iraq Liberation Act, which stated that it would be the policy of the United States to change the government of Iraq. Very little progress towards "regime change" was made, however, until after the 11 September 2001 attacks. Under the auspices of the recently declared War on Terror, the Administration of President George W. Bush began to seriously—and very publicly—plan for the removal of Saddam Hussein from power.

No war since the Vietnam War had so divided the American people. Advocates of regime change pointed to Saddam's brutally repressive rule, his aggression against Iraq's neighbors (Iraq had waged war against five of the six countries it bordered), his apparent links to international terrorism, and his continued dominance of the world's second-largest oil reserves. The antiwar left, however, argued that Saddam's worst atrocities had been committed while his government was receiving political, economic, and military support from the United States; that Iraq was effectively contained and no longer threatened its neighbors; that Saddam had no substantive ties to terrorists (let alone those who committed the 9/11 attacks), and that the war, if it came, would be fought principally on behest of American oil interests. Significantly, a pro-war left emerged, making the case for regime change on humanitarian grounds, while a substantial number of antiwar conservatives argued that the planned intervention would not serve the immediate political and economic interests of the United States (and perhaps quietly preferred the old policy of complicity with Saddam's regime).

But no issue was more central to the debate over intervention than weapons of mass destruction (WMDs). In the months before the war, the Bush Administration staked its case for regime change on the claim that Saddam harbored a vast arsenal of WMDs he had concealed from United Nations weapons inspectors. Secretary of State Colin Powell referred to these WMDs as "a threat to civilization." At times, the Administration went so far as to allege that Iraq might be on the verge of producing nuclear weapons. Opponents rebutted that Iraq had been stripped of its WMDs following the 1991 Gulf War, that it had little means of delivering a weapon of any sort over a great distance, and that, Saddam's WMDs, if they existed at all, would consist mostly of chemical weapons of the kind widely used in the First World War, and would hardly pose a "threat to civilization."

While a broad coalition of NATO and Arab states, backed by an unambiguous United Nations mandate, had supported the 1991 liberation of Kuwait, in 2003 George W. Bush found support for the planned invasion of Iraq more difficult to rally. Traditional American allies including France, Turkey, and Canada opposed the invasion, as did most Arab states, including Saudi Arabia, which had been the launching pad for the 1991 war. Consequently, the United States and its closest military ally, the United Kingdom, invaded Iraq in March 2003 with forces a good deal smaller than had been the case a dozen years earlier. What Bush called "the coalition of the willing," those states which had supported regime change, made only token contributions. Approximately 98 percent of all Coalition forces were either American or British.

Although the 1991 Gulf War had been one of the most lopsided military contests in history, many observers in 2003 predicted that Coalition forces were too light to accomplish the overthrow of Saddam's regime without very heavy casualties of their own. In fact, by 2003, the military calculus had in most respects shifted even further in favor of the United States. Saddam's forces were mostly worn out, while the Americans had absorbed all the lessons of the Gulf and Kosovo wars and developed a lean, tactically proficient force without peer. In technology, leadership, training, organization, and above all control of information, the American-led forces were in every way vastly superior to Saddam's. In particular, the advent of the global positioning system and the satellite guided bomb, when mated with stealth aircraft, enabled airpower, finally, to accomplish what its apostles had been hoping for since the First World War. Dire predictions by armchair strategists and "expert" media commentators about heavy American casualties proved false. Many Iraqi divisions did not turn out to fight (it was subsequently revealed that some senior Iraqi officers had been paid to defect), others were decimated by airpower or by American armor, and no serious battle for Baghdad occurred. Saddam's regime survived three weeks. Bush declared an end to "major combat operations" on 1 May 2003. As had been the case in 1991, Coalition losses were remarkably low: About 150 American and Coalition troops had been killed. Estimates of Iraqi casualties varied enormously. However, American planners had not foreseen the almost immediate emergence of an insurgency led by remnants of the Iraqi army, Ba'ath supporters, and foreign terrorists. By December 2005, this insurgency had claimed more than 2,000 American lives and the lives of many thousands of Iraqi civilians, police, and government officials.

The 1991 Gulf War had witnessed the lurid spectacle of coerced war crime "confessions" made by captured Allied airmen broadcast over Iraqi television. Only a handful of Coalition troops were captured in the 2003 invasion, however, and American officials warned that anyone mistreating Coalition prisoners would be treated as a war criminal. Consequently, only a few Coalition POWs were paraded before Iraqi cameras in 2003.

Given the size of the Iraqi army in 2003 (perhaps three-quarters of a million troops on paper), the Coalition took very few Iraqi prisoners. Much of the Iraqi army simply melted away in the face of the Coalition advance, and those units that did surrender tended to be fairly small and were detained for only a short time. Iraqi POWs were held mostly at the U.S. Theater Internment Facility Camp Bucca near Umm Qasr, a port on Iraq's narrow Persian Gulf coast. At its peak the camp held some 7,000 Iraqi POWs. However, among the first acts undertaken by the occupiers in the newly liberated Iraq was to disband the Iraqi army. While this decision is now generally regarded as a mistake because many former Iraqi soldiers joined the growing insurgency, it meant that there was no need for the Coalition to maintain very large prisoner of war or internment facilities.

While neither side took many prisoners during the brief period of formal hostilities, one of the paradoxes of the Iraq War is that prisoners would, along with WMDs, dominate the media's attention for most of the next two years. One incident concerning an American POW that received enormous media attention was a raid that American special forces mounted in April to rescue 19-year-old Private First Class Jessica Lynch, the survivor of an ambush on an army maintenance unit in late March. Conflicting and, as Lynch herself later revealed, highly sensationalized accounts of her capture and rescue were made in the media and in a hastily produced made-for-television movie. But no event so dominated the airwaves as an enormous scandal that emerged in April 2004 regarding American abuse of Iraqi prisoners at one detention facility in particular, the Abu Ghraib Prison. Lurid photographs of the physical and sexual abuse of Iraqi prisoners by U.S. soldiers were widely disseminated by the news media and on the Internet. The incident did enormous damage to the moral credibility of the American occupiers.

In the aftermath of the invasion, a spate of kidnappings of foreign journalists, military and civilian contractors, and in some cases military personnel by Iraqi insurgents began. Subsequently, the victims were made to plead for their lives in videotaped releases, or to issue a list of demands, usually for an end to the Coalition occupation, on behalf of their kidnappers. In a few cases the hostages were released; in most others they were executed, often by decapitation, on camera. Grisly videos of these decapitations found their way onto the Internet. The kidnappers showed little discrimination in their choice of victims, who included foreign aid workers and journalists who had opposed the war. Of these, the most prominent was British national Margaret Hassan of the aid agency CARE International, who had lived in Iraq since 1972.

Subsequent events have revealed that the Bush Administration's major case for war—that Saddam's regime harbored WMDs—was mistaken at best and consciously deceitful at worst. Postwar investigations revealed fewer WMDs than even skeptics had predicted, although there is little doubt that Saddam's government continued to seek to procure or develop WMDs until its last days in power.

In October 2004, a study published in the British journal *Lancet* concluded that as many as 100,000 Iraqis had been killed or had died prematurely in the wake of the invasion. While this figure was dismissed by many critics, in December 2005, Bush admitted that some 30,000 Iraqi civilians had been killed since the invasion. Against this must be weighed the end of Saddam Hussein's dictatorship and the fact that several elections since his fall have been quite successful, featuring voter participation rates higher than in recent federal elections in most Western nations, including the United States. Such facts, coupled with ongoing controversy over the Abu Ghraib scandal, continue to make the Iraq War immensely controversial.

See also Abu Ghraib Detention Center; Gulf War; Hostages; Iran-Iraq War; Lynch, Jessica; Saddam Hussein

References

Hans Blix, *Disarming Iraq* (New York: Pantheon, 2004).

Thomas Cushman, ed., *A Matter of Principle: Humanitarian Arguments for War in Iraq* (Berkeley: University of California Press, 2005).

Gwynne Dyer, *Ignorant Armies: The Coming New World Order* (Toronto: McClelland & Stewart, 2004).

Christopher Hitchens, *A Long Short War: The Delayed Liberation of Iraq* (New York: Penguin, 2003).

John Keegan, *The Iraq War* (New York: A.A. Knopf, 2004).

—*Graham Broad*

ISLAND FARM

Prisoner of War Camp 198, known as Island Farm, was located at Bridgend in south Wales and was the scene of the largest escape attempt by German POWs in Britain during World War II. Near the end of the war it became known as Special Camp Eleven and held some of the Third Reich's highest-ranking officers prior to their appearance at the Nuremberg war trials.

Island Farm Camp was originally built as a hostel for workers employed at the munitions factory in Bridgend. The authorities had believed that the female workers would rather stay nearby than travel as much as 30 miles home each day. However, the women preferred to travel than stay in the dreary barrack conditions of the hostel, so the camp remained empty until 1943, when it was used to accommodate American troops who would be involved in the invasion of France.

The large number of POWs taken in Europe meant that the authorities had to find suitable accommodation for them, and Island Farm was a logical choice. The prefabricated concrete huts surrounded by open fields were ideal, although the barracks had to be converted and barbed wire fences erected. This work had not been completed by the time the first batch of prisoners arrived, so the prisoners were put to work completing the conversion.

Island Farm was designated as Camp 198 and was to hold almost 2,000 prisoners. The first POWs were a mixed bag of Italian and German troops, but the War Office soon decided that the camp was too comfortable for enlisted men and that German officers should be held there. The first officer prisoners arrived in November 1944, one local observer noting that "their bearing and swagger were far removed from the popular conception of the cowed and captured prisoner."

The POWs soon turned their efforts to escape. Two tunnels were dug in the camp, but the first was discovered in January 1945. The second tunnel survived, although excavating it was not easy because of the heavy clay soil upon which the camp was built. To overcome this problem, cans, meat tins, and even knives were taken from the canteen to use as digging implements. The soil was hauled out of the tunnel on a makeshift skip and put into kit bags. At first, prisoners carried the soil in their pockets to the long-jump pit or garden plots. Others kneaded clay into balls and dropped them through a hole in a false wall they had constructed in an unused room in one of the huts. To support the tunnel roof, oak benches were stolen from the canteen and bed legs were cut down when supplies of wood were depleted. Ventilation was provided by a pipeline made from condensed milk tins; air was then forced through by a hand-operated fan.

The escapers were divided into groups, each of which was equipped with a map, homemade compass, and food. Each person within the group also had the necessary identity papers, which had been produced in the camp. All these preparations required tremendous organization, yet it is not known who actually organized the escape. For security purposes, each escaper's identity was known only to the others in his small group. This anonymity protected them against betrayal and prevented discovery of the full extent of the escape. On the night of 10 March 1945, 67 prisoners tunneled toward freedom. All were recaptured, some being found within a few miles of the camp. Others managed to travel considerable distances to places like Birmingham and Southampton, over 150 miles away.

Only three weeks after the escape, on 31 March 1945, the authorities suddenly transferred all 1,600 officers out of Island Farm Camp. It was then designated Special Camp Eleven and prepared to receive senior German officers, many of whom had been captured in France and were awaiting trial at Nuremberg. In all there were 160 officers holding the rank of general, admiral, or field marshal, including a number of Hitler's closest advisers: Field Marshal Gerd von Rundstedt, commander in chief of the German armies in the campaign against France in 1940 (because of his status, von Rundstedt received certain privileges at the camp, including his own private suite, consisting of a sitting room and bedroom); Field Marshal Erich von Manstein, who established the operation plans for Hitler's successful campaign in the west and commanded the Eleventh Army, which conquered the Crimea and Sevastopol on the eastern front; and Field Marshal Walther von Brauchitsch, who was named commander in chief of the German army by Hitler in 1938 and who was instrumental in the planning and execution of attacks on Poland, the Netherlands, Belgium, France, Yugoslavia, Greece, and the Soviet Union.

Many of the prisoners were staunch SS men, and others were members of the German aristocracy. In fact one prisoner, witnessing the arrival of the officers in the mess room, commented that it resembled a family reunion, as so many were related to one another. However, this did not mean that they were all on friendly terms. Differences ran deep—the SS officers, for example, refused to mix with other prisoners. But not all prisoners held in Island Farm were staunch Nazis. As one former prisoner commented, "The difficult part of coming to terms with being a prisoner is that you serve a sentence and you don't know how long the sentence is going to be. You are not individuals, you are there to serve other people's purposes. Purposes which are not visible to you which are rather barbaric and inhuman."

Island Farm Camp finally closed in 1948, when the last prisoners were returned to Germany.

References

Susan M. Hawthorne, *Island Farm Special Camp Eleven* (Bridgend: Brynteg Comprehensive School, 1980).

Herbert Williams, *Come Out, Wherever You Are: The Great Escape in Wales* (Llandsuyl, Wales: Gomer Press, 2004).

—*Susan M. Hawthorne*

Isle of Man

During both world wars, the British government established the Isle of Man as an internment center for enemy alien civilian internees. While in peacetime this island in the Irish Sea was a popular resort, between 1914 and 1919 some 29,000 men of German and Austrian heritage were detained there, and between 1940 and 1945 tens of thousands of German, Austrian, Italian, Hungarian, Finnish, Japanese, and British men and women were held on the Isle of Man, and housed either in makeshift camps or billeted in former hotels and guest houses.

During World War I, the Aliens Restriction Act was passed on 5 August 1914, and the internment of enemy aliens began almost immediately. By September 1914 some 10,500 male civilians were detained. Against the backdrop of a generalized "Spy Fever," the principal rationale for internment was protecting the realm against subversion, but an alternative argument was also posited, claiming that internment was a means of protecting foreigners from anti-alien hostility and mob violence. The sinking of the passenger liner *Lusitania* by German submarines on 7 May 1915 was the trigger for the government's decision to intern all enemy alien men who were still at liberty. Two camps were established for the internees, one at Knockaloe and the other at Douglas, Isle of Man. Gradually, the men built their own communities under the strict gaze of camp guards and were permitted to replicate certain aspects of their lives on the outside. While they suffered from austere rations of bland food, poor housing in tents and overcrowded barracks, and the restlessness of hours of idleness, they were able to provide their own forms of recreation and engaged in sports, mounted musical and theatrical performances, and set up their own schools with the help of the many teachers among the internees.

During World War II, the Isle of Man was again transformed from a holiday resort into a prison camp for enemy alien and British civilian internees. The situation this time was somewhat different, as prisoners included not only German and Austrian men, but also enemy alien women, as well as British nationals detained under Defence Regulation 18B 1(a), which allowed for the detention of people perceived to be threats to national security. Furthermore, it is estimated that some 75 percent of the enemy aliens were Jews fleeing Nazi persecution, and problems of administration arose when internees and those concerned with the plight of the refugees repeatedly lodged complaints that Nazis and anti-Nazis were being held behind the same barbed wire and were therefore forced to interact with one another. In 1940, camps were set up for the male internees at Ramsey, Rushen, Douglas, Onchan, and Peel, all on the Isle of Man, and separate camps for women and their children were established in Port St. Mary and Port Erin. The British 18B internees, most of them members of Britain's outlawed fascist organizations, began to arrive on the Isle of Man in May 1941; the men were held in Peveril camp, and the women at Port Erin. The presence of subversives and potential saboteurs on the island raised the hackles of Manx islanders, many of whom feared the taint of associating with those under suspicion for disloyalty to the Allied cause. While the policy of detention remained in force throughout the war, most civilian detainees were released well before 1945 in response to the ameliorated military situation and the easing of the invasion panic by 1943.

See also Civilian Internees—World War II—Britain

References

David Cesarani and Tony Kushner, eds., *The Internment of Aliens in 20th Century Britain* (London: Frank Cass, 1993).

Yvonne Cresswell, ed., *Living with the Wire: Civilian Internment in the Isle of Man during Two World Wars* (Douglas: Manx National Heritage, 1994).

Miriam Kochan, *Britain's Internees in the Second World War* (London: Macmillan, 1983).

François Lafitte, *The Internment of Aliens* (London: Libris, 1988 [1940]).

Livia Laurent, *A Tale of Internment* (London: George Allen and Unwin, 1942).

—*Julie V. Gottlieb*

ITALIAN UNIFICATION, WARS OF (1848–1870)

The Wars of Italian Unification, including the first war of 1848–1849, the second of 1859–1860, and the third of 1866, transformed Italy from a geographic expression to a genuine nation-state. Many hundreds of Italian, Austrian, and French soldiers died in these wars, and thousands were taken prisoner by both sides. Civilians were subjected to intimidation, imprisonment, or worse in the pursuit of the elusive dream of a united Italy.

The First War of Unification began with a series of popular uprisings in 1848 that culminated in the Five Days of Milan (18–22 March), during which the Milanese ousted the Austrian forces under the command of Field Marshal Johann Josef Radetzky. The success of the Milanese uprising encouraged the king of Piedmont, Carlo Alberto, to lead a campaign for the liberation of all of northern Italy. Between 1848 and 1849, the Piedmontese and the Austrians fought a number of bloody battles. The first serious clash took place at Pastrengo on 30 April 1848, when the army of Carlo Alberto captured close to 400 prisoners. A month later at Montanara and Curtatone, the Austrians had their revenge. On 29 May, Radetzky's forces launched a massive assault, taking over 1,000 Italian prisoners. They were imprisoned in Innsbruck and Prague until the end of the war. At the Battle of Custozza on 24 July 1848, the Austrians surrendered over 1,000 prisoners to the Piedmontese, while at the Battle of Mortara in 1849, the Piedmontese lost as many as 2,000 of their men to the Austrians.

The experiences of prisoners taken on both sides during the First War of Unification varied from brutal to benign. In April 1848, a small group of Austrian soldiers of Italian nationality who changed sides to support the Italian cause were captured by the Austrian forces near Vezzano; they met a quick but brutal end—the soldiers were taken to Trento and executed. This was standard Austrian practice with captured enemy soldiers. In fact, at the start of the war, the Austrians had been ordered to take no prisoners: any captured enemy soldier was to be summarily executed. But the Austrians soon changed the way they dealt with enemy soldiers in their care. A few days after the execution of the Austro-Italian prisoners at Trento, 29 Italian prisoners captured by the Austrians near Vicenza were immediately released by Radetzky. He ordered his generals to follow his example and put an end to the practice of executing enemy prisoners or deserters; this, he said, was a gesture of Austrian generosity.

The fact that the Wars of Unification were fought on Italian soil, albeit before there was a political entity called "Italy," influenced the experiences of civilians during the wars. Support for the Piedmontese cause outside Piedmont had Austrian officials constantly worried that Italian civilians might help Piedmontese forces. There was good reason to worry. When a group of captured Italian soldiers were imprisoned at Rovereto, Trento, home of the notorious Kuffstein Prison, the local population showered the prisoners with special treatment. There was even discussion among some civilians of helping the prisoners to escape. Because of such episodes, officials at Innsbruck ordered the reinforcement of the Austrian position at Trento. The castle of the city was put on a state of alert, and the cannons of the fortress were targeted on the city below. Many civilians were also arrested and sent to the prison at Kuffstein.

Italian patriots told alarming tales of Austrian treatment of civilians. Churches were damaged or destroyed, and livestock was stolen or killed. Many civilians were taken hostage, including women, many of whom were raped by Austrian troops. Civilians suspected of helping the Piedmontese saw their homes pillaged and destroyed, while other civilians faced threats, had their homes searched without warning, and endured the suppression of civil liberties.

The Second War of Unification in 1859–1860 witnessed some of the most brutal fighting of all the wars, with the largest number of prisoners taken by either side. At the Battle of San Martino in June 1859, close to 9,000 Austrians were taken prisoner or ended up missing. The French forces of Napoleon III, who had come to help the Piedmontese, surrendered over 1,000 prisoners to the Austrians, while the Piedmontese themselves surrendered under 800 men. Over a year later, at the Battle of Volturno in October 1860, Franco-Italian forces went down to defeat at the hands of the Austrians and a day later faced the humiliating capture of over 2,000 men by the Austrians at Caserta.

The most costly battles of the Third War of Unification in 1866 took place at Custozza in the north, and at Rome in the south. At Custozza on 24 June 1866, the Italian forces surrendered over 4,000 prisoners, while the Austrians lost about half as many. In the campaign of the Agro Romano, volunteers led by Garibaldi battled with the papal army and its French allies for control of Rome. The campaign ended with the Battle of Mentana on 3 November 1866, during which 1,600 of Garibaldi's volunteers were taken prisoner. By most accounts, Garibaldi's men were treated exceptionally well while in papal hands. The injured prisoners were diligently cared for by the very best doctors and nurses. Prisoners were allowed to write and to receive letters and entertain visits from family and friends. Pope Pius IX himself regularly visited the hospitals and jails, blessing his adversaries. The pope may have hoped to convert the enemy prisoners to the papal cause, but in 1870 Garibaldi's men returned to seize Rome and make it the new capital of the united Kingdom of Italy.

References

Frank Coppa, *The Origins of the Italian Wars of Independence* (New York: Longman, 1992).

Harry Hearder, *Italy in the Age of the Risorgimento, 1790–1870* (New York: Longman, 1983).

Edgar Holt, *Risorgimento: The Making of Italy, 1815–1870* (New York: Atheneum, 1970).

Piero Pieri, *Storia militare del Risorgimento. Guerre e insurrezioni* (Turin: Einaudi, 1962).

Denis Mack Smith, ed., *The Making of Italy, 1796–1870* (New York: Macmillan, 1968).

—Robert Ventresca

J

Jacobite Risings

The term Jacobite denotes supporters of the exiled King James II of England and his branch of the Stuart royal family. Including the revolution of 1688, Jacobitism generated four armed risings against the British government. The disposition of prisoners in these incidents varied depending on the nationality of the participants, their social rank, and the inclination of the government to view Jacobites as legitimate soldiers or as traitors.

Prisoners of the revolution of 1688 fell into two categories. First, Catholic and Irish soldiers left behind in England when James II fled were interned on the Isle of Wight, which was provisioned as a giant army encampment. Second, captured participants in James II's invasion of Ireland were held in local jails, and those who surrendered when James again fled were offered quarter under the Treaty of Limerick. All prisoners, whether Irish, French, or Scots, were offered the chance to lay down their arms and return home peacefully or to leave the British Isles under arms for service in Europe. Two boatloads of detainees from the Isle of Wight chose to enlist with the Holy Roman Empire against the Ottomans, while 11,000 Irish soldiers enlisted in French service.

Prisoners of the 1715 rising were divided by nationality. While French soldiers were paroled, Scottish prisoners were held at Stirling and Edinburgh before being tried at Carlisle. Although many of the Scots were found guilty of treason and sentenced to death, only one was hung; the rest were either released as being insufficiently important or were transported to the American colonies. English participants, however, felt the full wrath of the government. Sent in chains to the Tower of London, Fleet, or Newgate prisons, depending on their social status, the prisoners were jeered by rowdy London crowds. Twenty-two soldiers were hung, while two peers were drawn and quartered. Numerous prisoners effected escapes by bribing their jailers, walking out in women's clothing, or staging armed breakouts. Any prisoners remaining in jail were freed by the 1717 Act of Grace, but not before the expenses of imprisonment had ruined many Jacobite families.

The 1719 rising took place with the backing of Spain, which was fighting Britain as part of the War of the Quadruple Alliance. After defeat at Glen Shiel, the Scots disbanded and all 274 Spanish soldiers sent to assist the Jacobites surrendered to British forces. While holding them in Edinburgh, the British government paid the Spanish only their regular wage, which was not enough to cover the extra amenities available in eighteenth-century jails. Local Jacobites donated money, and moneylenders loaned funds to cover drink, women, and comfortable quarters until the Spanish ambassador to the Netherlands produced bills of exchange sufficient to pay the prisoners' debts and their passage back to Spain.

Mindful of the previous treatment of prisoners, participants in the 1745 rising sought to be classified as French auxiliaries. Actual French soldiers, assuming they would be treated as prisoners of war, covered the Scottish retreat at Culloden, thereby assuring their own capture. While the government respected their status and paroled them, the Scots were again treated as traitors. Reports of British soldiers killing prisoners are greatly exaggerated in Jacobite history, as British army surgeons cared for incoming Jacobite wounded for days after the battle, even farming them out to local private houses. However, Jacobites in custody were packed into Edinburgh castle, then into prison ships for transport to London, where the prisoners drew lots to determine the one out of twenty men who would be tried for treason. Of those found guilty, 120 were actually executed, including a young piper whose instrument the court deemed to be "an instrument of war" and members of the English Manchester Regiment, who were held to have mutinied in joining the Jacobites. The remaining prisoners were paroled or transported, 750 of them joining understrength British army units in Antigua, Jamaica, or Cape Breton, where the need for men outweighed any apprehension about their previous affiliation.

References
Bruce Lenman, *The Jacobite Cause* (Glasgow: National Trust for Scotland, 1986).
Stuart Reid, *1745: A Military History of the Last Jacobite Rising* (Staplehurst, UK: Spellmount, 1996).
Margaret Sankey, *Jacobite Prisoners of the 1715 Rebellion: Preventing and Punishing Insurrection in Early Hanoverian Britain* (Aldershot, UK: Ashgate, 2005).
Christopher Sinclair-Stevenson, *Inglorious Rebellion: The Jacobite Risings of 1708, 1715 and 1719* (London: Hamilton, 1971).

—Margaret Sankey

JANISSARIES

See Ottoman Empire

JEAN II OF FRANCE (1319–1364)

The King of France from 1350 to 1364, Jean II was captured by an Anglo-Gascon army, led by Edward the Black Prince, at the battle of Poitiers in 1356. This marked the second great English victory in the Hundred Years War (1337–1453), and Jean's capture gave the English a great political advantage. It is uncertain to whom the king surrendered: either Denis de Morbecque or Bernard de Troy, French knights and allies of the English. It may be that de Morbecque lost the royal prisoner in the confusion and that Jean II was retaken by de Troy. The resulting lawsuit between the pair was never settled and they both received a pension from Edward III.

On the night after the battle, the Black Prince treated his captive as his status deserved when, at dinner, he served the king personally and refused to sit at the same table as "so great a prince." Immediately after the Anglo-Gascon army returned to its base at Bordeaux, negotiations for a ransom treaty began. These resulted in the so-called Treaties of London of 1357 and 1358. The terms were harsh and it is possible that King Edward III of England (1327–1377) wanted an excuse to resume the war and try to win the throne of France. After the French were unable to fulfill the terms of the first treaty, which included the large-scale secession of lands and a sizable ransom, Edward increased the ransom to 4,000,000 florins, of which 600,000 had to be paid before the king would be released. Again the French were unable or unwilling to pay and the war resumed. However, the tide of English successes had turned; the Reims campaign of 1359–1360 ended in failure and a treaty was reached at Brétigny in 1360.

Jean II was released from captivity and returned to France, but he returned voluntarily into English hands when a number of the surrogates he had left in his place also crossed the channel without leave and the ransom payments fell into arrears. Yet Jean's captivity was not onerous. He was held at the Savoy, Berkhamsted Castle, and elsewhere, and great efforts were made to see to his comfort. He died in captivity on 8 April 1364. Installments of his ransom continued to be paid until the resumption of war in 1369.

See also Hundred Years War

References
Richard W. Barber, *Edward, Prince of Wales and Aquitaine: A Biography of the Black Prince* (London: Allen Lane, 1978).
Dorothy M. Broome, "The Ransom of John II, King of France, 1360–70," *Camden Miscellany* 14 (1926).

—David S. Green

JOAN OF ARC (1412–1431)

A teenage peasant girl and French national heroine who rose from obscurity to lead the French to a string of victories during the Hundred Years War, Joan of Arc had a brief but remarkable career as a military commander until she was wounded and captured by the Burgundians in 1430 and sold to the English. Joan spent a year held captive in the towers of a series of Burgundian chateaux, notably Beaurevoir castle, from one tower of which she leapt, achieving neither death (as she had sought) nor escape (as was the right of any prisoner of war, under the chivalric code). For nine months she was then constrained by iron shackles and guarded night and day by several male guards. The Duchess of Bedford, wife of the English regent in France, tried to protect Joan's virginity by forbidding guards, soldiers, and men of rank from touching Joan.

Joan claimed to be divinely led by the voices of saints who charged her to deliver France from the English. This claim, along with her male attire, earned Joan the charge of heresy from her captors—an accusation easy to make and difficult to disprove. Intent on judging and burning Joan for political reasons, the English provided her with the best available medical care when she fell ill. In the course of her lengthy trial for heresy in Rouen, Joan was interrogated on 12 separate occasions by two judges and a fluctuating roster of some 100 clerics. Near the end of the proceedings she was threatened with torture. The pious Joan also faced spiritual deprivation, as her captors denied her the solace of confession and the Eucharist.

Joan eventually confessed to heresy and put on women's clothing, but subsequently resumed her male attire and recanted her confession. She was promptly convicted, excommunicated, and burnt at the stake. Joan's case was posthumously re-tried by the French in the 1456 Rehabilitation Trial, in which she was cleared of the charges. In 1920 she was canonized by the Catholic Church.

See also Hundred Years War

References

Pierre Rocolle, *Un prisonnier de guerre nommé Jeanne d'Arc* (Paris: Editions S.O.S., 1982).

Bonnie Wheeler and Charles T. Wood, eds., *Fresh Verdicts on Joan of Arc* (New York: Garland, 1996).

—Sarah Glassford

A Romantic rendering of Joan of Arc in prison (from Andrew Lang, La Poucelle de France: Histoire de la vie et de la mort de Jeanne d'Arc *[Paris, no date (1895?)])*

K

KARBALA

Karbala, located in southern Iraq, is the site where al-Husayn, (c. 629–680) the son of the fifth Caliph Ali and grandson of Prophet Muhammad, and some of his followers were massacred by the men of the Umayyad Caliph. While living in Mecca, al-Husayn had been invited to the city of Kufa by the Shi'ites to lead their movement, and so he moved toward that city with approximately 70 of his male followers and family. After his refusal to swear fealty attracted the attention of Yazid, the new Umayyad caliph, al-Husayn was intercepted by about 4,000 of the caliph's men, led by the governor of Iraq, as he camped near Karbala. Al-Husayn anticipated the support of Kufan Shi'ites, but they were cowed into staying in Kufa by the new governor. On 10 October 680, al-Husayn rejected another solicitation for his surrender. Fighting ensued and al-Husayn's followers were killed one by one in individual battles with the caliph's men. Finally, al-Husayn's turn came; he was wounded numerous times, then finally killed. He and his male followers, with the exception of his young son, were decapitated; their bodies were buried in Karbala and the heads were sent to Damascus along with the captive female members of al-Husayn's party. Some versions of the Karbala massacre suggest that during the battle, at least one of al-Husayn's men was taken captive by the caliph's men, but eventually all were killed. According to tradition, al-Husayn's young son, Ali, and female members of his family were treated courteously by Yazid in Damascus and sent back to Medina. The massacre of the Prophet's grandson was condemned by both the Shi'a and Sunni Muslims. The events of Karbala were not written down until mid-eighth century. The Shiites consider al-Husayn a martyr of their movement, and the site of Karbala, where this watershed event for the Shiites took place, is now a city and a major shrine for them.

References

Heinz Halm, *Shi'a Islam: From Religion to Revolution* (Princeton, NJ: Markus Wiener, 1997).

al-Ţabarī, *The History of al-Ţabarī (Ta'rīhk al-rusul wa'l mulūk)*, vol. 19, *The Caliphate of Yazid b. Mu'awiyah*, trans. I.K.A. Howard (Albany: SUNY Press, 1985).

Julius Wellhausen, *The Religio-Political Factions in Early Islam* (New York: American Elsevier, 1975).

—Yücel Yanīkdağ

KATYŃ FOREST MASSACRE

The massacre of Polish prisoners of war by Soviet army units in 1940 created a controversy that persisted into the 1990s. Following the Nazi-Soviet partition of Poland in September 1939, hundreds of thousands of Polish soldiers, sailors, and airmen became prisoners of the Soviet Union. While enlisted men were detained in at least 26 POW camps and possibly hundreds of forced labor camps in Siberia, Polish officers were interned in 3 principal camps: Starobielsk, near Kharkov, housed 4,500 officers; Kozielsk, east of Smolensk, housed 3,800 officers; and Ostashkov, near Kalinin (Tver'), held 380 officers.

After the German invasion of the Soviet Union on 22 June 1941, the Soviet Union opened diplomatic relations with the Polish government-in-exile in London and agreed to allow a Polish army to be formed in Russia from the prisoners who were being detained there. The Poles discovered that approximately 4,000 Polish priests, policemen, professors, politicians, and diplomats, along with 11,000 Polish military officers and a quarter of a million other Polish servicemen, had been taken prisoner by the Soviets in 1939. By March 1942, only 80,000 Poles, many of them women and children, had made their way to the Polish headquarters at Buzuluk, near the border with present-day Kazakhstan. In that group of Poles, only 400 were officers who had been interned in the three main Soviet camps, and the Soviet authorities refused to provide any additional information concerning the whereabouts of the rest of the officers. On 19 August 1942, 115,000 Polish soldiers and civilians weretransported to Iran, where the British wereable to provide adequate food and equipment in order to train these troops for combat.

On 15 April 1943, the German propaganda ministry broadcast the news of the discovery of mass graves of Polish officers in a forested area, known as Katyń, near Smolensk. The Soviet Information Bureau issued a statement announcing that the Polish POWs had been captured by the Germans in 1941 and subsequently executed. In the end, three separate medical commissions examined the bodies at Katyń. The International Committee of the Red Cross, the Polish Red Cross, and an international commission drawn from 12 countries other than Germany all came to the same conclusion: the Polish soldiers at Katyń had been murdered by the Soviets in early 1940. Without exception, all the victims had been shot in the back of the head. Upon exhumation, some of the bodies were shown to have bayonet wounds in the back and stomach, or their jaws smashed by blows, presumably from the butts of rifles. Of the bodies exhumed, 2,914 were positively identified. They included three generals, one rear admiral, 100 colonels and lieutenant colonels, 300 majors, and over 2,000 captains, first and second lieutenants, and officer cadets. About half of the group were reserve officers, who included among their number 21 university professors and lecturers, 300 surgeons and physicians, 200 lawyers, and 300 engineers, as well as teachers, journalists, writers, and industrialists. Ironically, the Soviet government used the reports of the international commissions as an excuse to break off diplomatic relations with the Polish government-in-exile in London.

On 12 April 1990, the Soviet Union finally admitted its guilt in the Katyń Forest Massacre. Moscow radio, quoting the official Soviet press agency Tass, said that the NKVD, the Soviet secret police, was responsible for the deaths of the Poles. Although this admission was a great step forward, most Poles were still not satisfied, because Joseph Stalin was still not held directly accountable for the crime. Finally on 14 October 1992, Russian President Boris Yeltsin released Minutes No. 13 of the Politburo meeting on 5 March 1940. The notes referred to "a total of 11,000 people, whose cases must be considered in keeping with a special procedure and who must be subject to the supreme punishment—execution by a firing squad." The notes had been initialed by Josef Stalin. With the release of these documents, one of the most controversial episodes in Polish history was finally put to rest.

References

Crime of Katyń: Facts and Documents (London: Polish Cultural Foundation, 1989).

Jozef Garlinski, *Poland in the Second World War* (New York: Hippocrene Books, 1985).

Allen Paul, *Katyń: Stalin's Massacre and the Seeds of Polish Resurrection* (Annapolis, MD: Naval Institute Press, 1991).

George Sanford, *Katyń and the Soviet Massacre of 1940: Truth, Justice and Memory* (New York: Routledge, 2005).

Steven Stewart, *The Poles* (New York: Macmillan, 1982).

J.K. Zawodny, *Death in the Forest: The Story of the Katyń Forest Massacre* (Notre Dame, IN: University of Notre Dame Press, 1962).

—Alexander M. Bielakowski

KAZEMI, ZAHRA (1948–2003)

Zahra Kazemi was an Iranian-Canadian journalist who died in Iranian custody on 11 July 2003. Born in Shiraz in 1948, Kazemi studied film direction in Tehran before moving to Paris in 1974. In 1993 she emigrated to Montreal, where she became a Canadian citizen and worked as a freelance photojournalist. Her work focused attention on the daily life of destitute Palestinians in refugee camps in the Middle East. In June 2003, after covering an assignment in Iraq, Kazemi entered Iran. On 23 June, Kazemi was arrested for taking photographs of a student protest in front of the Evin Detention Center in Tehran. Between 23 and 27 June, Iranian security officials interrogated Kazemi for 77 hours. She was admitted to the hospital in the early morning of 27 June, and her death was announced on 12 July. The circumstances of her death were made the subject of an Iranian ministerial inquiry the following day.

The Iranian government produced conflicting accounts of her treatment and death. On 16 July 2003, Vice President Mohammad Ali Abtahi announced that Kazemi had died of a skull fracture after sustaining a blow to the head while in custody. On 22 September, Reza Ahmadi, an Intelligence Ministry Agent, was arrested and charged with Zahra Kazemi's murder. His closed trial began on 17 July 2004, but it was abruptly terminated the following day, and Ahmadi's acquittal followed. On 28 July, Iran's judiciary declared that Kazemi's death was an "accident." In a press conference in Ottawa on 31 March 2005, Dr. Sharham Aazam, a former emergency room doctor in Tehran, stated that he had examined Kazemi after her interrogation and found signs of torture. Kazemi suffered from multiple broken bones, internal bleeding, and evidence of a brutal rape. Unfortunately, the Canadian government, pressured by Kazemi's family, was unable to verify the cause of her death. The Iranian judiciary rejected demands to release her body for an independent examination on the grounds that Zahra Kazemi was an Iranian citizen.

Kazemi's death, and the Iranian judiciary's refusal to permit open and independent investigation, highlighted Iran's long record of human rights abuses, and caused a major diplomatic irritant between Canada and Iran. However, in November 2005, an Iranian appeals court accepted the opinion of the Canadian government that the original trial had been flawed, and ordered the reopening of the case. It did not dispute the acquittal of Ahmadi, but ordered further investigation "due to the possibility that some other people were involved" in Kazemi's death.

—*Andrew Paul Burtch*

KEELHAUL, OPERATION

Operation Keelhaul (the term keelhaul refers to an old method of punishment at sea that involved dragging an individual along the barnacled hull of a sailing ship) was the label selected by U.S. Army historians in 1948 when they compiled a dossier on the postwar forcible repatriation of thousands of Soviet nationals by Anglo-American troops in postwar Europe. As World War II drew to a close, approximately two million Soviet nationals were liberated by Anglo-American armies. Most were POWs or slave laborers brought to work in Germany, and many returned voluntarily to their homeland during the summer of 1945. Thousands of others, some captured in German uniform, were unwilling to return home and were segregated by the Allies. Though many successfully evaded repatriation, force was used in other instances to return them to Soviet custody, where most met a brutal fate. Two of the more famous operations took place in Fort Dix, New Jersey (June 1945), and Plattling, Germany (January 1946). Except for individual cases, most repatriation operations directed against Soviet nationals ended in 1948.

The term Operation Keelhaul has since been popularized in the writings of Stanford scholar Julius Epstein and British writer Nikolai Tolstoy. Epstein struggled for two decades in the U.S. Congress and legal system to declassify government documents relating to the repatriations. Tolstoy, meanwhile, focused on the British role in the return of Cossack and Yugoslav collaborators and civilians from postwar Austria, and he lost a 1989 lawsuit for allegations he made about a former British official reputed to have played a role in the process.

See also Forcible Repatriation; Liberation

References
Nicholas Bethell, *The Last Secret: Forcible Repatriation to Russia, 1944–47* (London: Coronet Books, 1977).
Russell D. Buhite, "Soviet-American Relations and the Repatriation of Prisoners of War, 1945," *The Historian* 35 (1973): 384–397.
Mark R. Elliott, *Pawns of Yalta: Soviet Refugees and America's Role in Their Repatriation* (Urbana: University of Illinois Press, 1982).
Julius Epstein, *Operation Keelhaul: The Story of Forced Repatriation from 1944 to the Present* (Old Greenwich, CT: Devon-Adair, 1973).
Nikolai Tolstoy, *Victims of Yalta* (London: Hodder and Stoughton, 1977).
———, *The Minister and the Massacres* (London: Century Hutchinson, 1986).

—Richard D. Wiggers

King Rat

Set in a World War II Japanese POW camp in Singapore's Changi jail, this 1965 film adaptation of the James Clavell novel (which incorporated some of his own experiences as a POW) tells the story of an American corporal who operates a number of rackets by bribing his Japanese captors. In his first starring role, George Segal plays a character who is called "*King Rat*" because he breeds rodents to serve as food for his fellow British, American, and Australian prisoners who are sickly because of insufficient rations. The nickname is also an unflattering label for his personality, since he is primarily concerned with his own well-being and lives more comfortably than the other prisoners. The interest of the film lies in the portrayal of this thoroughly unscrupulous opportunist. When King learns that British officer Marlowe (James Fox) speaks the language of their Malaysian guards, he enlists his help in expanding his operation outside the confines of the camp to include trading with the Japanese officers. But when Marlowe becomes gravely ill, King finally demonstrates that beneath his selfish exterior is a character ultimately concerned about the welfare of others, as he wangles precious antibiotics from the guards. Much like the film "Stalag 17," with Segal taking the William Holden role as the cynical collaborator and fixer-upper, "*King Rat*" similarly sets out to demonstrate that survival is the primary objective in captivity but, as with similar tales, evolves into the pursuit of dignity with oneself and respect in the eyes of one's peers. The film received Academy Award nominations for Best Cinematography and Best Art Direction.

See also Changi; World War II—Far East

References
James Clavell, *King Rat* (New York: Dell, 1962).

—Darryl Wiggers

Koje Incident

Koje Island, located off the southwest coast of the Korean Peninsula, was the site of a facility in which the United Nations Command (UNC) held prisoners of war from Communist China and North Korea during the Korean War. By April 1951, about 150,000 communist prisoners were jammed into the 32 compounds on the island. Conflict between the rival factions of POWs—the die-hard communists, who opposed the screening process by which the UNC attempted to separate those prisoners who wished to be repatriated from those who did not, and the anti-communists—often led to riots, beatings, and even killings. Clashes between prisoners from communist-controlled compounds and camp guards also created difficult situations that often ended in bloodshed. In one such incident, on 7 May 1952, Brigadier General Francis T. Dodd, commandant of Koje Island camp, was kidnapped by communist prisoners in Compound 76. The communist POWs requested that the UNC stop the screening process and reverse the principle of voluntary repatriation. After three days of hectic negotiations, General Dodd was released after he and Brigadier General Charles F. Colson, who briefly succeeded Dodd, issued a joint statement assuming responsibility for the recent mêlée and assuring there would be no further occurrences. For these actions, both Dodd and Colson were later reduced in grade to colonel.

In the wake of the Dodd incident, the UNC adopted tougher measures against the Koje POW compounds. In early June, the new camp commandant decided to move the POWs from the old quarters to newly constructed enclosures. Refusing to be relocated, the communist prisoners resisted the camp guards. On 10 June 1952, crack American paratroopers from the 187th Airborne Regiment were sent in to engage the POWs, particularly those in Compound 76. It was reported that the communist POWs were using homemade gasoline grenades, knives, hatchets, and other tools as the paratroopers, supported by tanks, moved into the compound. By the end of the day, 40 prisoners were dead and 130 wounded; one paratrooper was killed and 14 wounded.

The Associated Press journalist at the scene reported that the bodies of over a dozen prisoners who had been tortured and garroted were found in other compounds during the evacuation. They were likely victims of the kangaroo court run by the communist prisoners in an attempt to punish those who refused repatriation. Communist sources, however, portrayed the incident in a rather different way. They reported that the paratroopers entered the compound with flamethrowers while machine guns strafed the prisoners. The communist delegation at P'anmunjŏm cease-fire talks used the Koje incident to condemn UNC atrocities and its voluntary repatriation policy, and because of the violence, international opinion began to question the UNC screening process.

See also Repatriation

—*Pingchao Zhu*

KOMOROWSKI, TADEUSZ BOR (1895–1966)

Tadeusz Komorowski was born a child of partitioned Poland on 1 June 1895. His family resided in the small town of Chorobrów, near Lwów, in the heart of the Austro-Hungarian portion of partitioned Poland. A precocious and inquisitive child, at the age of 10 Tadeusz's parents sent him to the secondary school in Lwów to continue his education. In 1913, Komorowski graduated from the Lwów school and immediately entered the Austrian Army. Due to his intelligence and ambition, the Austrian military sent Komorowski to receive additional military training at the Franz Joseph Military Academy in Vienna.

In 1915, Tadeusz was given command of a platoon and saw action on both the Russian and Italian fronts during World War I. The end of the war in 1918 meant not only the rebirth of an independent Poland, but also the opening of numerous opportunities for men with military training. Komorowski spent the interwar years rising through the ranks of the Polish military and eventually becoming commander of the Grudziądz Cavalry School. After taking part in the defense of Poland following the German invasion of September 1939, Komorowski helped organize the Polish underground in the Kraków region of southern Poland. By 1942, he was given the position of deputy commander of the Polish Home Army (Armja Krajowa or AK) and the following year was elevated to the rank of Brigadier-General and appointed sole commander of the Home Army.

The Polish underground, or Home Army as it was known, was made up of approximately 500,000 soldiers scattered throughout the Polish lands. Like other members of the Home Army, General Komorowski often used pseudonyms or false names to protect himself and his associates from the Germans. The most common pseudonym associated with Komorowski was Bór, but he was also known by the names Korczak, Lawina, Prawdzic, and even Jerzy Korabski during the war.

In 1944, as Soviet-led Red Army units advanced into Poland, the Polish government-in-exile in London ordered Komorowski to initiate an armed uprising against Nazi forces in Warsaw. The London Poles reasoned that a successful rebellion in Warsaw would allow their exiled government to return to a capital liberated by Poles rather than by Stalin's Soviet forces, thus preventing the Communist occupation of Poland. The uprising began successfully on 1 August 1944, with the insurgents of the Home Army rising from the sewers and underground passages to seize control of most of central Warsaw. Despite a promising beginning, Komorowski was forced to surrender to the Germans on 2 October 1944, after two months of fighting. Following the battle, German demolition teams emptied the city of its inhabitants and systematically destroyed it.

General Komorowski was treated as a prisoner of war and imprisoned in Colditz Castle until the end of the war. After the war, he resided in London and became prime minister of the powerless Polish government-in-exile from 1947 until 1949. He died on 24 August 1966, in Bletchley, England.

See also Colditz

References
Norman Davies, *Rising '44: The Battle for Warsaw* (New York: Viking, 2003).
Tadeusz Komorowski, *The Secret Army* (London: Victor Gollancz, 1950).
Stefan Korbonski, *The Polish Underground State: A Guide to the Underground, 1939–1945* (New York: Hippocrene Books, 1981).
Jan Nowak, *Courier from Warsaw* (Detroit: Wayne State University Press, 1982).

—Christopher Blackburn

Korean War (1950–1953)

The POW issue of the Korean War was characteristically complicated. The United Nations Command (UNC) forces, which included troops from 16 of the 60 UN member nations, entered the Korean conflict on the side of the South Korean government to fight against North Korean Communists, who were soon joined by the Chinese People's Volunteer (CPV) military forces. The three-year, indecisive war in Korea produced a huge army of POWs, especially on the communist side. By July 1953 when the Korean War Armistice Agreement was signed, there were 13,803 UNC prisoners of war and 105,097 communist prisoners, including 21,374 Chinese and 3,746 Americans.

The UNC initially held communist captives in transit camps in locations such as Ch'ungju, Taegu, Inch'ŏn, and Taejŏn in South Korea. The POWs were then transferred to several permanent camps in Pusan, Koje Island, and Cheju Island, all located in the southernmost areas of the Korean Peninsula. Most of the sick and wounded prisoners were detained in camps in Pusan. Later, the UNC segregated communist and anticommunist POWs in different compounds. By July 1952, all of the Chinese POWs were sent to Cheju Island, where some 6,000 were held in separate compounds. The communist side established their POW camps along the south bank of the Yalu River in locations such as P'yŏngan-bukdo and Changsŏng, with P'yoktŏng as the headquarters. Prisoners of the South Korean Army (ROK) were also segregated from the rest of the UNC captives. Major General William F. Dean of the 24th Division of the U.S. Army was captured by the North Korean Army on 25 August 1950 in Taejŏn to become the highest-ranking UNC officer in communist hands. During most of his captivity, he was held under heavy guard in Camp Number 16, about 10 miles from the North Korean capital of P'yŏngyang. Wu Chengde, the political commissar of the 180th Division of the CPV force, was the highest-ranking communist officer in UNC custody.

As part of the negotiation process to secure the release of POWs, representatives from the International Committee of the Red Cross were allowed to visit the camps on both sides to inspect rations, living conditions, and medical arrangements. Life behind barbed-wire was reported differently by the communists and the UNC. According to CPV accounts, the monthly ration of UNC POWs included bleached wheat flour, rice, sugar, cooking oil, meat, and cigarettes, equivalent to the rations of a CPV regimental commander. They were also issued with blue cotton coats, pants, hats, rubber-soled boots, gloves, cotton comforters, and blankets. Medical facilities were slow to improve, and they remained insufficient. There were charges that the CPV's movement of UNC POWs from the battlefields to permanent camps resembled the Bataan Death March, which claimed the lives of hundreds of American and Filipino POWs during World War II. The CPV denied such accusations.

Inspection by Red Cross representatives revealed that in general the UNC provided prisoners with sufficient blankets, comforters, and wraps. They received the standard ration for South Korean troops, which included rice or rice flour, barley, fish or canned meat, seaweed leaf, Kokochon (Korean pepper sauce), and cigarettes. There was even a cash allowance to allow the POWs to purchase goods in the local markets, according to the UNC reports. Neither the UNC nor the communist side has given positive evaluations of the other's treatment of their POWs in custody. Both sides, for example, accused each other of resorting to brainwashing in an attempt to win over the captives.

In July 1951, the UNC and communist delegations began to negotiate a cease-fire. One of the major issues under discussion was the exchange of POWs. On the one hand, the Chinese and North Korean delegates demanded total repatriation of their POWs according to the principles of the 1949 Geneva Convention. The UNC, on the other hand, insisted on "voluntary repatriation," a proposal that was based on the humanitarian argument. The UNC had noted the particular composition of the POWs from both China and North Korea; the Chinese CPV forces consisted of a large number of quondam Nationalist soldiers, who surrendered to communist troops in 1949 when the latter took over mainland China. Less motivated to fight in Korea, they soon accounted for 70 percent of the Chinese POWs. Similarly, many South Korean soldiers, who were captured by the North Korean army and then recruited to serve in the North Korean troops, soon were taken captive by the UNC. Viewed as being "demoralized," most of these former Nationalist and South Korean soldiers refused to be repatriated. The UNC argued that it would be inhumane to force this group of POWs to return to Communist China or North Korea, where they would face persecution similar to that experienced by Russian POWs who returned to the Soviet Union after World War II. Through most of the negotiations, neither the UNC nor the communists were willing to budge from the extremes of total repatriation and voluntary repatriation.

Through lengthy and difficult discussion, the two sides came to agree to screen all POWs in order to separate those who wanted to be repatriated from those who did not. The screening process, which began in April 1952, led to frequent disturbances inside the UNC prison camps. The communist prisoners staged various demonstrations and protests to resist the screening (the most notable outbreak being the Koje Incident on 10 June 1952), and they convened kangaroo courts to prosecute those who did not wish to be repatriated. There were great discrepancies in the way the screening process and the riots were reported by U.S. and Chinese sources; each side accused the other of committing atrocities and of carrying out inhumane POW policies. Despite such difficulties, the results of the screening showed that while 90 percent of the 83,376 North Korean POWs chose to be repatriated, nearly two-thirds of the Chinese captives decided not to return to mainland China.

On 20 April 1953, Operation Little Switch exchanged sick and wounded POWs on the negotiation site at P'anmunjŏm. The UNC delivered 5,640 North Koreans and 1,030 Chinese soldiers and the communist side released 684 UNC POWs, including 149 Americans and 471 South Koreans. The final stage of POW repatriation, known as Operation Big Switch, took place between 5 August and 6 September 1953 and saw

70,183 North Koreans, 5,640 Chinese, and 12,773 UNC POWs exchanged in a neutral zone at Kaesŏng, about five miles west of P'anmunjŏm. Later, 440 more Chinese prisoners decided to be repatriated after further persuasion. In addition, toward the end of the negotiations the UNC also released over 71,000 detainees who had been reclassified as civilians or citizens of South Korea and, therefore, had not been listed as POWs.

Both the UNC and communist sides were greatly disturbed by their nonrepatriates; 14,704 Chinese and 7,900 North Koreans chose not to return home. Most of the Chinese soldiers went to Taiwan and many were recommissioned in the Nationalist army. The Americans were especially shocked to learn that 21 U.S. soldiers and one British marine decided to stay in Communist China. The United States military gave all 21 men dishonorable discharges. The U.S. secretary of defense soon appointed the 10-man Advisory Committee on Prisoners of War to investigate the misconduct and moral behavior of American POWs in captivity. On 17 August 1955, President Dwight D. Eisenhower signed Executive Order 10631, which created a Code of Conduct to ensure that every member of the U.S. armed forces "shall be provided with specific training and instruction designed to better equip him to counter and withstand all enemy efforts against him . . . during combat and captivity." During the following decades, all but one of the American soldiers who had not repatriated either returned to the United States or left China for Europe. The fate of the 7,110 returned POWs in mainland China was especially disheartening. Most of them were purged, and many were expelled from the Communist Party, deprived of employment opportunities, forced to divorce, or sent to do hard labor in rural areas. It was not until 1980 that the Chinese government began to rehabilitate their reputations, a process that is still underway.

See also Big Switch, Operation; Code of Conduct; Dean, Major-General William F.; Defection; Koje Incident; Repatriation

—*Pingchao Zhu*

Kosovo War (1998–1999)

Serbian attempts to "Serbianize" Kosovo began in the late nineteenth century. The year-long Kosovo War, which commenced in 1998, continued the legacy of Serbian aggression in the Balkans. The conflict began as a Serb government campaign against the separatist Kosovo Liberation Army (KLA). It quickly evolved into a systematic program to ethnically cleanse the Serbian province of Kosovo of its roughly 1.7 million ethnic Albanian residents. Because Serbian authorities have denied international monitors access to Kosovo, documentation of the campaign has been largely based upon refugee accounts and details coming to light in war crimes tribunals.

A key part of Serbian President Slobodan Milosevic's campaign against Kosovar Albanians was the forced expulsion and detention of thousands of ethic Albanians. Approximately 700,000 Kosovars fled to the neighboring states of Albania, Bosnia-Herzegovina, the former Yugoslav republic of Macedonia, and the republic of Montenegro. At the same time, Serbian forces took thousands of military-aged men from their families and held them in mass detention sites, such as a cement factory in Djeneral Jankovic, the Ferro-Nickel factory in Glogovae, a school in Vučitrn, and in Srbica, where as many as 20,000 ethnic Albanians were used as human shields for Serbian tanks.

Many of the prisoners of war who were not placed in mass detention centers became the victims of summary executions. Refugee accounts suggested that at least 4,000 Kosovars were executed. In some instances, Serbian forces would order an unarmed Kosovar POW to run away in order to shoot him from behind. Killings took place in at least 70 towns and villages throughout Kosovo. Mass graves were reported in Drenica, Kaaniku, Rezalla, Malisevo, Pusto Selo, Izbica, and in the Pagarusa Valley.

The majority of Kosovo War POWs were internally displaced people (IDPs). As many as 600,000 people were driven from their homes by Serbian forces such as the Ministry of Internal Affairs Police (MUP) or the Yugoslav army (VJ). Clusters of IDPs were scattered throughout the province, making crude encampments in isolated forests and mountains. Many suffered from malnutrition and health problems due to food shortages. In early 2000, the number of displaced Kosovar Albanians had risen to 600,000 IDPs in Kosovo, 404,000 in Albania, 62,000 in Montenegro, 38,000 in Bosnia, and 160,000 in other countries. Since the end of the war, remaining and returned Kosovar Albanians have launched revenge attacks against civilian Serbs, which has in turn resulted in the exodus of 200,000 Serbs.

For ethnic Albanian women who were detained or chose to remain in Kosovo, rape was a miserable reality of war. Refugee accounts described the organized and systematic nature of attacks against women by Serbian forces in Djakovica and Peć. Albanian women were reportedly separated from their families and sent to an army camp near Djakovica, where Serbian soldiers repeatedly raped them. In Peć, refugees alleged that Serbian forces rounded up young Albanian women and raped them repeatedly at the Hotel Karagac. Gang rapes in village homes and alongside the roads were also reported.

NATO intervention in the war brought soldiers from other nations to Kosovo and put them at risk of capture. On 31 March 1999, American Staff Sergeant Andrew A. Ramirez, Staff Sergeant Christopher J. Stone, and Specialist Steven M. Gonzales, part of the NATO peacekeeping force assigned to patrol the Yugoslav-Macedonian frontier, were captured when their vehicle was attacked by Serb soldiers; the Serbs maintained that they were on the Yugoslav side of the border, while the three soldiers insisted that they were still in Macedonia. All were severely beaten by their captors and, the following day, their images were broadcast on Serb television. Their captors immediately promised that the three would be tried as spies or terrorists, but subsequently agreed to treat them as prisoners of war. Although the three did receive a few amenities from the International Committee of the Red Cross, they were very roughly interrogated and were kept in isolation from one another. Meanwhile, diplomatic efforts were underway to secure their release. An intervention by Cypriot leader Spyros Kyprianou failed, but on 2 May 1999, all three were freed after the Reverend Jesse Jackson led a multi-faith delegation to press Serb leader Slobodan Milosevic for their release.

See also Bosnian War; Sexual Violence

References

Ivo H. Daalder, *Winning Ugly: NATO's War to Save Kosovo* (Washington: Brookings Institution Press, 2000).

Reginald Hibbert, *The Kosovo Question: Origins, Present Complications and Prospects* (London: David Davies Memorial Institute, 1999).

Tim Judah, *Kosovo: War and Revenge* (New Haven, CT: Yale University Press, 2000).

Noel Malcolm, *Kosovo: A Short History* (New York: New York University Press, 1998).

U.S. Department of State, "Erasing History: Ethnic Cleansing in Kosovo" (May 1999), online, available: http://www.state.gov/www/regions/eur/rpt_9905_ethnic_ksvo_3.html.

—*Tracy Moore*

L

Labor

Only in the wars of the twentieth century did the labor of prisoners of war become a significant factor in the economy of the belligerent powers, and thus a part of the enemy's war effort. In ancient times, war captives were often turned into slaves, unless they were released or exchanged under specific conditions. In early modern times, princes and kings tended to exchange prisoners soon after their capture for their own captured subjects, or to enlist prisoners in their own armies, a technique that was extensively practiced by Frederick the Great of Prussia in the eighteenth century.

Only with the emergence of modern warfare, with masses of soldiers and captives engaged in protracted wars, did prisoners' labor become an economic necessity. However, this shift did not occur immediately after the beginning of World War I, a period that in most societies was characterized by transitional unemployment due to the suspension of peacetime economic activity. The use of prisoners as laborers was first instituted in Germany, not for economic reasons, but to distract Entente prisoners from the negative psychological effects of internment. However, as the demand for soldiers and workers grew, the practice became more widespread, appearing in most of the

A party of POW workers, their German guards, and civilian overseers in World War I. Few POW labor projects were as pleasant as this (National Archives Canada PA182546)

belligerent states after 1915, although to a lesser extent in Britain. In some countries, the extensive use of POW labor was essential to the war effort. For example, in the absence of an efficient state that might have used modern machines and industrial practices, Russia relied heavily on captive labor, using prisoners to develop transport facilities and community infrastructure, as well as in agriculture and the war industry. After World War I, the victorious powers, particularly France and Belgium, continued to make use of such labor for clearing the battlefields and reconstructing the war zone's devastated infrastructure.

In Nazi Germany, prisoner of war labor took on an even greater significance right from the beginning of World War II. The Third Reich became the leader in the exploitation of forced labor, drafting not only POWs from Poland, France, Belgium, Britain, and after 1941, from the Soviet Union and the United States, but also millions of foreign civilian workers, or *Fremdarbeiter*, from occupied countries for Germany's war industry. It is estimated that, in the last years of the war, fully half of all laborers in the German economy were foreigners, and so were employed under coercion. In the Nazi hierarchy of prisoners, internees, and other forced laborers, the most terribly abused were Soviet POWs and the inmates of concentration camps, which housed political enemies of the Nazi regime, Jews, and a variety of racial and social minorities. The bulk of captured laborers were no longer occupied in peaceful agricultural work, as was typical before World War I, but in the war factories of the Third Reich. In Germany, some 5.7 million Soviet soldiers constituted the overwhelming majority of all prisoners of war. One million of these were turned into auxiliaries, or *Hilfswillige*, who received limited privileges in return for services to the German armies, or into combat soldiers of the German armies. Soviet war captives were largely denied the legal status of prisoners of war and instead were exposed to conditions that almost preordained their extermination by excessive labor, malnutrition, and disease. Human losses among them thus were the highest of all prisoners of war (some 3.5 million). Those who collaborated with Nazi Germany fared little better and were often brutally treated by the approaching Soviet army in 1944 and 1945.

After the war, forced labor of surrendered and interned German personnel continued to be used to some extent by the Allies in western Europe, and more broadly in the USSR, which had an established prewar tradition of forced labor in its Gulag system. After 1941, a similar system for the exploitation of the labor power of POWs and displaced persons (primarily civilian captives after the war) was simply grafted on to the Gulag system. From 1945 on, there were some four million captive laborers in the USSR, of whom hundreds of thousands did not survive their work in the reconstruction of the Soviet war zone and the industrial infrastructure. In violation of international law, the Soviet Union retained tens of thousands of captives for labor until 1955, long after German prisoners had been released by all other Allied powers.

In the more localized conflicts after World War II, forced labor by war captives did not play the same role as it had during the world wars; the extensive use of POW labor seems to be a characteristic of global warfare rather than regional conflicts. Moreover, it may lose its significance because the expansion of technology demands a workforce of highly skilled experts, rather than masses of physical laborers.

See also Arbeitskommandos; Burma-Thailand (Death) Railway; Murman Railway

References

Gerald H. Davis, "Prisoners of War in Twentieth-Century War Economies," *Journal of Contemporary History* 12 (1977): 623–634.

Ulrich Herbert, "Labour and Extermination: Economic Interest and the Primacy of Weltanschauung in National Socialism," *Past and Present* 138 (1993): 145–195.

Edward L. Homze, *Foreign Labor in Nazi Germany* (Princeton, NJ: Princeton University Press, 1967).

Stefan Karner, "Prisoners of War in the Economy of the Former Soviet Union, 1941–45," in *The*

System of Centrally Planned Economies in Central Eastern and South Eastern Europe after World War II and the Causes of its Decay, ed. Vaclav Prucha (Prague: Vysoka Skola Ekonomicka, 1994).

Stefan Karner and Barbara Marx, "World War II Prisoners of War in the Soviet Union Economy," *Bulletin du comité internationale d'histoire de la deuxième guerre mondiale* 27/28 (1995): 191–201.

Walter Struve, "The Wartime Economy: Foreign Workers, 'Half Jews,' and the Other Prisoners in a German Town, 1939–1945," *German Studies Review* 16 (1993): 462–482.

—*Reinhard Nachtigal*

LAMSDORF

Officially designated Stalag 8B, Lamsdorf was one of the largest and most disliked German POW camps of World War II. Located in a bleak part of Upper Silesia near the site of a POW camp built in 1915 to hold British and Russian prisoners, Lamsdorf was opened in the summer of 1940 to accommodate over 5,000 British army POWs captured during the Battle of France. There were originally six compounds, each with four to six brick barrack huts, with each hut housing between 150 and 240 men who slept first on straw and then on standard three-tier bunks. Although large numbers of prisoners were sent out to work camps (*Arbeitskommandos*), the total camp population rose to over 12,000 men and the number of compounds to 11 by the end of 1941, with the arrival of British Empire prisoners captured in Greece and Crete and the opening of a compound for Royal Air Force aircrew. Lamsdorf later came to hold many of the Canadian prisoners captured at Dieppe as well as Soviet POWs, who, as elsewhere, were treated abominably by the guards. At any given time from 1942 through 1944, between 10,000 and 20,000 prisoners were in residence in the camp.

Living conditions and morale in Lamsdorf were particularly bad in the first and last months of the camp's existence, as disruption of communications caused the influx of Red Cross food parcels to cease and theft consequently rose alarmingly. However, even in the years of relative stability (1941–1944), when sports and education facilities as well as a hospital were in place, Stalag 8B had an evil reputation. German rations, winter fuel, and building upkeep were all minimal, and this was not entirely unintentional. The harsh conditions were meant to encourage army prisoners—including NCOs, who were not legally required to work under the Geneva Convention—to volunteer for transfer to an *Arbeitskommando*, where conditions would supposedly be better. Dozens of *Arbeitskommandos* were supplied with labor from Lamsdorf. The sheer size of the camp also posed serious administrative difficulties for the camp authorities, and organization and discipline was left to British noncommissioned officers. Some of these NCOs worked solely for the benefit of prisoners in general, but others took advantage of their position to set up rackets whereby they received more food and clothing than the men they were supposed to help. There were also "Glasgow razor gangs"—groups of thugs and petty thieves who terrorized their fellow prisoners—that neither the British nor the German authorities were able to control. On the other hand, escape efforts were made (with the RAF contingent well to the fore) and German spies were not tolerated, as the mysterious appearance in 1944 of an unidentified body floating in one of the fire pools graphically indicated.

In November 1943, after months of complaints by neutral inspectors, the Lamsdorf complex was reorganized; thousands of prisoners were moved to the camp at Teschen (which took the name Stalag 8B), while Lamsdorf was redesignated Stalag 344. Conditions improved, but the camp was evacuated in January 1945 as the Soviet army approached. Several hundred POWs lost their lives in the subsequent weeks on the road due to lack of food, exposure, exhaustion, disease, and accidental strafing by Allied aircraft before the bulk were liberated in western Germany by American forces.

See also Arbeitskommandos; World War II—Western Europe

References
John Castle, *The Password Is Courage* (New York: Norton, 1955).
Robert Gale, *Private Prisoner* (Wellingborough, UK: Patrick Stephens, 1984).
Cyril Rofe, *Against the Wind* (London: Hodder and Stoughton, 1956).
Jonathan F. Vance, "The Politics of Camp Life: The Bargaining Process in Two German Prison Camps," *War and Society* 10 (1992): 109–126.

—*S.P. MacKenzie*

LEBANESE CIVIL WAR (1975–1990)

Although it is usually referred to as a civil war, the conflict that wracked Lebanon for 15 years was, in fact, much wider, involving active participation by the military forces of France, Britain, Italy, and the United States, and invasions by Israel and Syria. This, combined with the wide range of Christian and Muslim factions involved in the struggle, made it one of the most complicated conflicts in a region that is known for seemingly intractable disputes.

The civil war, the second in Lebanon's modern history, began in April 1975, when a Christian militia group killed a busload of Palestinians who were traveling through a Christian village. The Palestine Liberation Organization (PLO) retaliated in kind by slaughtering Christian civilians, and soon the country was plunged into a downward spiral of violence, as massacres were followed by reprisals, which in turn drew counter-reprisals. In 1976, as their forces were slowly losing ground to Muslim militias, Christian leaders called on Syria for aid; the government in Damascus, ostensibly to prevent left-wing anarchy from taking over Lebanon, responded with a full-scale invasion. Two years later, Israel became involved, occupying the southern part of the country and launching air and missile strikes against Palestinian targets in northern Lebanon. In June 1982, Israeli forces moved farther north, besieging the city of Beirut and inflicting heavy casualties on the Syrian army. Shortly thereafter, a multinational force consisting of troops from the United States, France, Italy, and Great Britain entered Lebanon to protect refugee camps and attempt to bring some stability to the region so that a peace deal could be brokered. The intervention was not a success. In October 1983, two separate car-bomb attacks killed over 300 U.S. and French soldiers, and in January 1984 most Western troops, except for a small French observer group, were pulled from Lebanon. The next six years were characterized by bitter power struggles within and between Christian and Muslim camps, political assassinations, massacres of civilians, and terrorist bombings. Not until 1991 was a ceasefire brokered that finally brought a fragile peace to the region, and though isolated attacks continued, Lebanon began to rebuild.

The Lebanese Civil War, in terms of the treatment of prisoners, was similar to many conflicts that were raging at the same time in Africa and Asia. Westerners were the targets of hostage-takers from the early days of the civil war; on 29 June 1975, the first U.S. hostage, Colonel Ernest Morgan, was taken by a Palestinian group called the Popular Struggle Front, who demanded that food, clothing, and building materials be delivered to a Beirut slum as ransom. Morgan was released on 12 July under pressure from the PLO and after an unknown group had delivered 12 tons of food to the slum. In September 1976, four Palestinians took over a Damascus hotel and captured 90 hostages. A Syrian army attack resulted in the deaths of four hostages and one of the Palestinians; the other three were hanged in public the following day. Hostage-takings increased in the mid-1980s, and most were blamed on the extremist group Islamic Jihad. In 1985, terrorists hijacked TWA Flight 847, en route from Athens to Rome, brought it to Beirut, and held the passengers and crew as hostages. The hijackers demanded the release of hundreds of Muslim prisoners, and murdered a U.S. navy diver when their demands were ignored. Eventually, after secret negotiations, the Israeli government began to release some of its prisoners, and eventually the hijackers freed all of the remaining hostages. (In December 2005, the German government released Mohammad Ali Hammadi, one of the two hijackers, after he had served 18 years in prison for the crime; the U.S. government was outraged, and has vowed to bring Hammadi to justice in the United States.) The following year, after U.S. forces bombed Libya, a Lebanese splinter group responded by killing two British and one American hostage. The terrorist groups were ambitious in their choice of victims, who included William Buckley, the CIA station chief in Beirut; U.S. Marine Corps Lieutenant-Colonel Williams Higgins (both of whom were murdered by their kidnappers); various employees of the American University of Beirut, including professors, the librarian, and the president, David Dodge; Catholic missionary Father Martin Jenco; CNN Bureau Chief Jeremy Levin; American journalist Terry Anderson; British television producer John McCarthy; Indian teacher Mithileshwar Singh; and Church of England envoy Terry Waite. The last hostages to be released were German aid workers Thomas Kemptner and Heinrich Struebig, who were freed in June 1992 after three years in captivity. Perhaps the most controversial aspect of the hostage-takings was the Iran-Contra deal, under which the United States would sell weapons to Iran in exchange for that country's intervention in gaining the release of U.S. hostages, and the proceeds of the sale would be turned over to the Contra guerrillas fighting to overthrow the leftist Sandinista regime in Nicaragua. The deal was widely criticized, both on ethical grounds and on the fact that it succeeded in gaining the release of only three hostages.

There were also captives who could properly be considered prisoners of war. On 4 December 1983, a U.S. pilot, Lieutenant Robert Goodman, was shot down while attacking Syrian missile sites, but was freed on 3 January 1984, after the Reverend Jesse Jackson intervened with the Syrian president on his behalf. The fate of Syrian and Lebanese POWs, however, was rarely so happy. In some instances, they were simply released. For example, in July 1976, a group of civilians and soldiers who surrendered to Christian forces laying siege to the Palestinian refugee camp at Tel-al-Zataar were briefly questioned and then turned over to delegates from the International Committee of the Red Cross. However, POWs were just as likely to be slaughtered, especially if the troops who captured them had lost family members in earlier attacks. As one Christian militia commander said, it was not their policy to mistreat POWs, "but if a PLO fighter fell into the hands of a man whose family had been killed, or whose sister had been raped, or whose home had been destroyed by them, he would take his revenge."

As with many such conflicts, attention has now focused on the return of prisoners, by both sides. It is estimated that as many as 17,000 people went missing during the conflict, many of whom can probably be classed as "forced disappearances," which the United Nations defines as "persons arrested, detained, or abducted against their will or otherwise deprived of their liberty by officials of different branches or levels of government, or by groups and individuals acting on their behalf." The distinguishing feature in such cases, according to the U.N., is "a refusal to disclose the fate or whereabouts of the persons concerned." Human Rights Watch and Amnesty International both insist that hundreds of Lebanese are still being held in Syrian prisons, while the Paris-based group Support of Lebanese in Detention and Exile has a list of 640 individuals who may have disappeared into Syrian custody. The group estimates that in October 1991 alone, as many as 150 Lebanese, mostly soldiers, were transported to Syria as political prisoners; a number of these individuals have subsequently been seen in Syrian prisons, although not until 1998 did the government in Damascus admit that it was still detaining Lebanese nationals. In that year, Syria released 121 Lebanese prisoners, and nearly

50 more were freed in 2001. However, Damascus insists that any other Lebanese in its prisons are being punished as terrorists. On the other hand, the Syrian government claims that nearly 800 Syrian nationals are missing in Lebanon, and in May 2005 a Lebanese-Syrian commission was created to investigate the alleged disappearances.

References

Terry Anderson, *Den of Lions: A Startling Memoir of Survival and Triumph* (New York: Ballantine Books, 1994).

Joseph Cicippio and Richard W. Hope, *Chains to Roses: The Joseph Cicippio Story* (Waco, TX: WRS Publications, 1993).

Robin Higgins, *Patriot Dreams: The Murder of Colonel Rich Higgins* (Central Point, OR: PSI Research, 2000).

David Jacobsen and Gerald Astor, *Hostage: My Nightmare in Beirut* (New York: Donald I. Fine, 1991).

Lawrence Martin Jenco, *Bound to Forgive: The Pilgrimage to Reconciliation of a Beirut Hostage* (Notre Dame, IN: Ave Maria Press, 1995).

Brian Keenan, *An Evil Cradling: The Five-Year Ordeal of a Hostage* (New York: Viking, 1993).

Magnus Ranstorp, *Hizb'Allah in Lebanon: The Politics of the Western Hostage Crisis* (New York: Palgrave, 1997).

Tom and Jean Sutherland, *At Your Own Risk: An American Chronicle of Crisis and Captivity in the Middle East* (Boulder, CO: Fulcrum Publishing, 1996).

—Jonathan F. Vance

LIBBY PRISON

Libby Prison, in Richmond, Virginia, was one of the largest and most well-known prison camps operated by the Confederacy during the U.S. Civil War. At the beginning of 1862, the Libby and Son ship chandlery was just one of the many buildings located in the warehouse district of Richmond. By the end of that year, however, the word *Libby* had become synonymous throughout the North with charges of southern atrocities and prisoner abuse, and Libby prison was well on its way to becoming one of the most notorious prisons of the war.

The coming of the Civil War found both the Union and the Confederacy woefully unprepared for managing large numbers of prisoners. Because Richmond was a major rail center, early plans called for prisoners to be shipped to the capital for distribution to prisons throughout the South. No one, however, expected the influx of captives to be very large, and the thousands of prisoners taken in the war's first year completely overwhelmed Confederate planners. Brigadier-General John H. Winder, the provost marshal of Richmond, scrambled for additional buildings to house the flood of Union captives, and in March 1862, he commandeered the Libby warehouse and directed that the Union officers and civilians confined in the capital's jails and other makeshift facilities be transferred there.

The warehouse was a large, three-storey structure on the bank of the James River. Each floor of the building was divided into three 45- by 90-foot rooms, and it was in these rooms on the top two floors of the building that prisoners were incarcerated. Conditions in the facility were deplorable by any standard. Prisoners suffered from stifling heat in the summer and only two stoves per room were provided to ward off the numbing cold of winter. The rooms contained no furniture, and lighting and ventilation were poor. Prisoners who ventured near the windows for fresh air risked being shot by the guards patrolling outside the building. There was no systematic effort to keep the rooms clean, and the men slept on floors encrusted with several inches of filth and teeming with vermin. Rations were always scanty, and by 1863 the daily allotment for each prisoner had shrunk to two ounces of meat, eight ounces of bread, and a cup of either beans or rice.

The most serious problem at Libby, however, was overcrowding. Each of the rooms held just over 100 men when the facility opened, but when prisoner exchanges were suspended in 1863, the population had burgeoned to over 400 men per room. At its peak occupancy, more than 4,000 prisoners were tightly packed into the prison's dank, dark confines. This crush prevented the men from moving about during the day and forced them to sleep spoon-fashion at night.

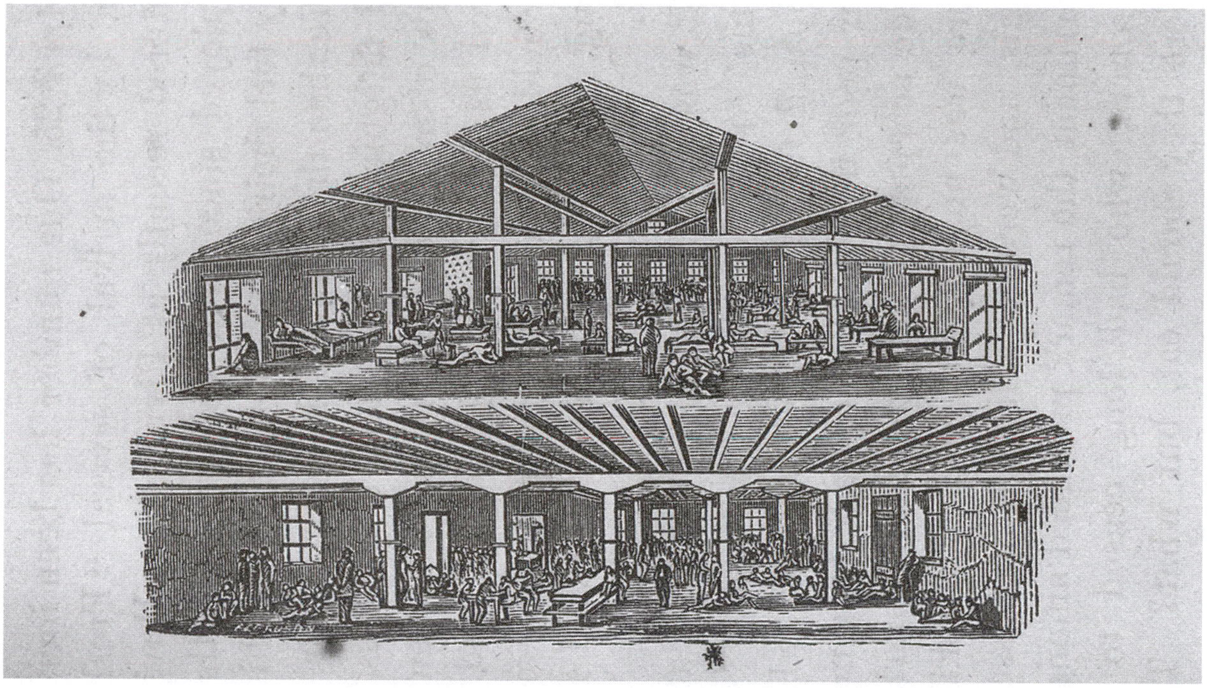

An interior view of Libby Prison (from Willard W. Glazier, The Capture, the Prison Pen and the Escape *[Albany, 1866])*

Scurvy, chronic diarrhea, pneumonia, and dysentery thrived in these conditions.

In the midst of these terrible surroundings, however, a surprisingly vibrant social life flourished. The prisoners elected their own governing body, competed in chess tournaments and debating clubs, formed foreign language and religious study groups, and even published their own newspaper, the *Libby Prison Chronicle*. They also plotted and executed numerous escape attempts, the most famous occurring in February 1864 when Colonel Abel D. Streight led 109 prisoners through a 60-foot-long tunnel to freedom. This exploit sparked fears that prisoners would aid raiding Union cavalry and led Confederate officials to order the facility mined and destroyed along with the prisoners should such a threat materialize.

Libby continued to hold Union prisoners until end of the war. The warehouse survived the fire that ravaged the city as Union forces entered in April 1865, and in 1890 the building was torn down and reassembled in Chicago as part of a Civil War museum.

See also Andersonville; Elmira; United States Civil War

References

Thomas M. Boaz, *Libby Prison and Beyond: A Union Staff Officer in the East, 1862–1865* (Shippensburg, PA: White Mane, 1999).

Daniel Patrick Brown, *The Tragedy of Libby and Andersonville Prison Camps: A Study of Mismanagement and Inept Logistical Policies in Two Southern Prisoner-of-War Camps* (Ventura, CA: Golden West Historical Publications, 1980).

Frank L. Byrne, ed., "A General Behind Bars: Neal Dow in Libby Prison," in *Civil War Prisons*, ed. William B. Hesseltine (Kent, OH: Kent State University Press, 1962).

Emory O. Thomas, *The Confederate State of Richmond: A Biography of the Capital* (Austin: University of Texas Press, 1971).

—*Charles W. Sanders, Jr.*

LIBERATION

At the conclusion of hostilities, one of the most significant issues facing combatant nations has been the release and return of

This poster was designed to give publicity to the fact that countless German POWs remained in Soviet captivity after the end of World War II. (Bundesarchiv Koblenz)

liberated POWs and internees. Availability of resources, advance planning, ideological factors, and the will of the detaining power have all played a role in determining how promptly prisoners are returned to their homes.

Before the twentieth century, when the number of prisoners was relatively small, the matter was fairly simple. Where the combatants had detained POWs until the end of hostilities (as opposed to executing, paroling, exchanging, ransoming, or enslaving them), treaties almost invariably stipulated the prompt release of all prisoners. The Treaty of Westphalia (1648), which ended the Thirty Years' War, for example, stipulated that all prisoners "without distinction of the gown or of the sword" were to be released. In some cases, a time limit was set; for instance, the Treaty of Badajoz, signed by Portugal and Spain in 1801, allowed 15 days for the release of prisoners, and the Treaty of River Seiwa of 1813 bound the governments of Persia and Russia to free all prisoners within three months. In any case, it was up to each government to make its own arrangements for prisoners' transportation home.

In the wars of the twentieth century, however, a number of factors complicated liberation procedures, most significantly, the scale of the problem and the impact of ideology. The prompt release of POWs was still a cornerstone of international law, but it became an ideal rather than a guarantee. The difficulties involved became clear during World War I. In the spring of 1918, Allied military officials drew up a preliminary plan for the handling of liberated prisoners once they reached their own territory. Missing from the plan, however, were any arrangements for getting them out of the prison camps in the first place. The immediate repatriation of all Allied POWs was stipulated in the armistice agreement, but the conditions of repatriation were left to be determined at some time in the future. That prisoners might try to make their own way home apparently did not occur to anyone until after the armistice was signed, when the British army issued instructions that returning prisoners would be gathered at forward collecting centers in France and Belgium to await onward transfer. They would then be moved to camps at Calais, Boulogne, or Dunkirk, and from there to their home countries.

These arrangements, however, applied only to the roughly 32,000 POWs who had been held immediately behind the front lines. The hundreds of thousands of Allied POWs scattered throughout the rest of Germany proved a bigger problem. To address the issue, a subcommission of the Permanent International Armistice Commission was established to finalize the liberation arrangements. The commission agreed that prisoners in Germany should be collected at points on the Oder, Elbe, Weser, and Rhine Rivers to be moved by water to embarkation ports such as Rotterdam. At those ports, they would be met by reception parties, provided with new gear, and escorted to the docks for the homeward voyage.

However, the agreement proved difficult to put into force, for a number of reasons. German intransigence was a factor, but a genuine lack of resources, especially railway cars to transfer POWs to collection points, was also a problem. Furthermore, there was no organization left in Germany that could hand over liberated prisoners, so most of the work had to be done by the commission itself. This task was made more difficult by the reluctance of prisoners to remain in their camps until advised otherwise, as they had been instructed to do through notices in German newspapers. In fact, the delays encountered in the return of prisoners became a considerable bone of contention in the post-armistice discussions, and although Allied officials believed that Germany was doing all it could to rectify the situation, the Allies threatened more exacting terms if the POW question was not solved satisfactorily. These threats seemed to have some effect, but it was late January 1919 before the last large groups of British ex-prisoners reached Britain. Other nationalities had to wait even longer. By February 1919, only 200,000 of the 1.4 million Russian POWs in Germany had been returned home. It was not until June 1922 that all of the German and Austro-Hungarian POWs held by the Russians were released.

Anxious to avoid a repetition of the confusion that had surrounded these liberation arrangements, Allied officials in World War II began contemplating the problem as early as March 1942. By October, they had agreed on the necessity of a stay-put order instructing prisoners to remain in their camps once hostilities had ended. In December 1942, the British War Office circulated its own draft plan for the postwar return of POWs, but by the summer of 1944, it was clear that all of the Allies would have to work in concert. As a result, Britain accepted an American proposal that planning for the liberation be left to the Supreme Commanders. Part of "Eclipse," the code name given to Allied arrangements for dealing with a German surrender, the plan assumed that liberated POWs would remain in their camps after the capitulation until specially trained liaison teams arrived to control the evacuation process. After hostilities had ceased, these teams would make an accounting of all Allied POWs, take any steps needed to ensure their safety and food supply, and prepare them for the evacuation. To avoid the need to ship large quantities of food to the camps, the evacuation would be done largely by air. The evacuation of prisoners liberated by the Soviets created a different set of problems. The British and American governments knew that diplomatic approaches to Moscow on the subject would be difficult, and prolonged negotiations were necessary to reach an agreement on the repatriation of former POWs from the eastern zone. The Soviet government's insistence that liberated prisoners be put to work until they were evacuated was the most serious obstacle to an accord, but all parties eventually came to terms and signed a treaty covering the matter at the Yalta Conference.

On a more practical level, Germany's apparent determination to fight to the death soon made it evident that much of the planning had been fruitless. Most Allied POWs were liberated before Eclipse conditions prevailed, so the exhaustive plan was quickly jettisoned in favor of hastily improvised arrangements. Once liberation troops reached a camp, the liaison officer contacted the leader of the POWs to procure accurate statistics of the camp's population and arrange for temporary supplies while an airlift was organized. When transport aircraft had been assigned, the liberated POWs were assembled at the nearest airfield, to be flown either directly to England or to one of three staging airfields at Le Havre, Rheims, and Brussels. Flights left continually, as long as weather permitted, and once the camp had been cleared, liaison officers remained behind to collect any stragglers and direct them to one of four Recovered Allied Military Personnel (RAMP) camps at Namur, Épinal, Rheims, and Brussels, established as concentration points for stragglers recovered by forward units.

The situation was even more complicated in the Pacific theater, where Allied planning for liberation was virtually nonexistent for much of the war. Not until April 1945 did Britain's War Cabinet decide that the time was ripe to make plans for the liberation of POWs in the Far East, and then it advised that the protection, maintenance, and evacuation of all POWs be left to the commanders of forward units. Each government would assemble statistics on its prisoners in the Far East and prepare to transmit to forward commanders information on the estimated requirements of all POWs. The draft plan envisaged that recovered Allied POWs and internees (RAPWI) would be moved to central collecting depots to be fed, clothed, and medically examined and that they would remain at those centers until they were well enough to travel. Since their health would be worse than that of European POWs, most of them would have to remain at the depots for a fortnight.

With this directive, the repatriation operation was finally clarified. Because it would take time for each camp to be reached and evacuated, they were first to be contacted by small British, American, or Australian recovery teams and supplied by air drops of food, medical supplies, and clothing. The teams would organize the evacuation operation from the camps so that it could proceed swiftly once air, ground, or water transport was available to take the POWs to reception centers elsewhere. Able-bodied Commonwealth POWs were to be transported from Forward Disposition Centers near their camps to main reception centers in Hong Kong and Singapore. From there, Allied ships would ferry the former prisoners to the Philippines, where personnel would be processed and examined before returning to their homelands. Sick POWs were to be taken by American hospital ship directly from the Forward Disposition Centers to the Philippines or the Marianas, and from there to North America. POWs in Japan would be carried on U.S. hospital ships, which spent September 1945 shuttling up and down the coast of Japan, picking up prisoners at various ports along the way.

As in World War I, the victorious side's POWs benefited most. Despite the obstacles, the liberation of Allied prisoners in Europe and the Far East ran very smoothly, some POWs reaching their homes within a few days of leaving their prison camps. German POWs were not so lucky. On 30 June 1947, the U.S. government freed the last German POW in its custody, becoming the first major Allied nation to do so. The French and British governments, rather than freeing all German POWs, converted some of them into civilian workers and continued to use their labor in mines and farms. The last German prisoner was not released from captivity in Britain until July 1948. In 1950, there were still nearly two million German POWs in the Soviet Union awaiting liberation; many of these would in fact never be liberated.

During the Korean War, negotiations over POW liberation—complicated by the issue of "non-forcible repatriation" whereby POWs could refuse to return to their original commands when liberated—dominated the final 15 months of armistice talks aimed at ending hostilities. The United Nations Command (UNC) hoped to win a propaganda victory if large numbers of Chinese and North Korean prisoners refused repatriation, but Chinese and North Korean negotiators rightly suspected that such a refusal would result from coercion and indoctrination rather than free choice and feared the embarrassment that massive defection would bring. The two sides debated liberation arrangements until a breakthrough was reached that allowed for the exchange of 7,200 sick and wounded POWs in Operation Little Switch between 20 April and 4 May 1953. Little Switch accelerated negotiations leading to the signing of the armistice that ended the war on 27 July 1953. The armistice was quickly followed by the general prisoner liberation called Operation Big Switch, carried out between 5 August and 6 September 1953, during which time the UNC released 75,801 Chinese and North Korean POWs to their original commands while the Chinese and North Koreans transferred 12,773 POWs to the UN. The roughly 23,000 remaining POWs who refused liberation were then transferred to the custody of the Neutral Nations Repatriation Commission for a 90-day "explanation" period beginning on 23 September 1953. During this period, few nonrepatriates changed their minds, leading to the final prisoner liberation of the Korean War on 20 January 1954, when the remaining POWs, including 21 Americans and one Briton, returned to their captors rather than their homelands, ostensibly the liberation of their choosing.

Disagreement over POW liberation also prolonged the Vietnam War. From 1969 onward, the uncertain status and suspected mistreatment of American POWs was frequently cited by the American president, Richard Nixon, as justification for prolonging the war. He argued that he could not end the war until all American POWs were liberated, otherwise the Vietnamese would have no incentive to return them. The Vietnamese responded that they would not free American prisoners of war so long as Americans remained combatants. This stalemate continued until 27 January 1973, when both sides grew so desperate to end the war that they agreed to a cease-fire agreement requiring the return of all prisoners to their original commands within 60 days of its signing. In the months following the peace agreement, 591 American POWs were liberated and returned home in the elaborately staged Operation Homecoming. This number was much smaller than the public had been led to expect and seemed to confirm Nixon's suspicions that the Vietnamese would retain American POWs after the war ended, fueling persistent allegations that Americans were being held captive in Southeast Asia after the war ended. These charges remain unproven despite 25 years of public and private investigations.

Since the Vietnam War, the problem of securing the release of prisoners after the end of hostilities has become more intractable. Although the International Committee of the Red Cross has no mandated role in this process, it has often been called upon by the United Nations or individual states to use its good offices to secure the freedom of prisoners. Still, the time and effort involved has been enormous. For example, the Iran-Iraq War ended by cease-fire in July 1988, but talks over the release of prisoners were sporadic; two years passed before both sides agreed to release some 40,000 POWs each. Not until 1997 was any substantial further progress made; the following year, the negotiations reached the point where the Red Cross was able to broker the release of more than 6,000 Iraqi and 300 Iranian POWs. In 1999, the ICRC supervised three more release operations that brought home 715 Iraqi POWs, two operations in 2002 returned a further 527 Iraqis, and another 882 Iraqis were released in March 2003; significantly, in keeping with ICRC policy against forcible repatriation, each prisoner was interviewed to determine if he actually wanted to return home.

Even more unfortunate have been the Moroccan soldiers held captive by the Polisario Front, a loosely organized liberation army that is seeking the separation of the Western Sahara from Morocco. In February 2003, the Red Cross secured the release of roughly 100 sick and elderly Moroccan soldiers, and in September of that year another 243 Moroccans were freed after prolonged negotiations; one had been held captive in Algeria since January 1975. A complicating factor in this process, in addition to the political issues, was the fact that the Moroccans were not considered POWs, because the Polisario Front was not a sovereign state.

References

Peter N. Carroll, *It Seemed Like Nothing Happened: America in the 1970s* (New Brunswick, NJ: Rutgers University Press, 1982).

Dorothy M. Davis, "Processing and Caring for Prisoners of War," *American Journal of Nursing* 46 (1946): 152–153.

Rosemary Foot, *A Substitute for Victory: The Politics of Peacemaking at the Korean Armistice Talks* (Ithaca, NY: Cornell University Press, 1990).

Bob Moore and Barbara Hately-Broad, eds., *Prisoners of War, Prisoners of Peace* (London: Palgrave, 2005).

Callum MacDonald, "'Heroes Behind Barbed Wire': The United States, Britain and the POW Issue in the Korean War," in *The Korean*

War in History, ed. James Cotton and Ian Neary (Atlantic Highlands, NJ: Humanities Press International, 1989).

Hank Nelson, "'The Nips Are Going for the Parker': The Prisoners Face Freedom," *War and Society* 3 (1985): 126–143.

Robert D. Schulzinger, *A Time for War: The United States and Vietnam, 1941–1975* (New York: Oxford University Press, 1997).

—*Michael J. Allen*

LIBRARIES

It has long been recognized that boredom is one of the greatest threats to the psychological well-being of POWs and internees, and that recreational activities are essential if captivity is to be made bearable. The provision of reading matter, through well-stocked prison camp libraries, has lessened the burden of captivity for millions of prisoners.

Before the twentieth century, there was no concerted effort to ensure that prisoners had access to reading material. Officers were expected to provide their own recreational materials, and enlisted men generally lacked a sufficient level of literacy to use libraries. So, any reading material that was available was organized on an ad hoc basis. During the U.S. Civil War, for example, Pennsylvania POWs in the camp at Andersonville, Georgia, organized an informal lending library that was available to prisoners from Pennsylvania. One indication of the library's popularity is that books, magazines, and newspapers were read until they literally fell to pieces.

There was a move to formalize such arrangements in the late Victorian era, when the British army began to view libraries as a way to assist in the moral improvement of soldiers. Reading, in this logic, was preferable to the other activities, such as drinking and carousing, that soldiers typically engaged in. During World War I, the same logic was applied to captivity: from the captor's point of view, it was far better for a POW to read than to attempt escape, and from the prisoner's point of view, reading was much preferable to going insane. As a result, a variety of organizations sprang up that were devoted to ensuring that prison camps had fully stocked libraries. The Camps Library Foundation in Britain, for example, began supplying books to prison camps in Germany early in the war and was later joined by the British POW Book Scheme, which eventually supplied libraries to over 190 prison camps in Germany, Austro-Hungary, Turkey, and elsewhere. In 1917 alone, the Book Scheme sent over 55,000 books to Allied POWs on the continent. At Wakefield, a camp in Britain for interned German civilians, the YMCA set up a large tent that was used as a library and reading room. Thanks to the efforts of these organizations, some camps were able to build large libraries. As early as December 1915, for example, the camp at Göttingen had a library of 7,000 books in several languages; Ruhleben camp for civilian internees also had a large library, which covered its expenses by issuing fines for overdue books. There were also traveling libraries that served prisoners held in small or isolated camps.

These efforts expanded considerably in scope during World War II. The War Prisoners Aid (WPA) of the YMCA, headquartered in Geneva, Switzerland, eventually grew into the largest organization supplying books to POWs of all nationalities. Using information received from senior prisoners, the WPA prepared shipments for individual camps and catered as much as possible to the interests of the inmates. In 1944, the American WPA alone shipped over 1.2 million books to Geneva, and hundreds of thousands more to camps in the United States. Aside from books, the WPA also provided wood for shelving (in fact, the crates in which books were shipped were specially designed to be easily converted into bookshelves), cards for cataloguing, and bookbinding supplies for repair work. With this material, camps were able to establish libraries that ranged in size from a few hundred to over 100,000 volumes. Traveling libraries again served prisoners in small or isolated camps, and other camps maintained what were known as "shadow

The library at Handforth prison camp in England in World War I (from German Prisoners in Great Britain *[London, n.d.])*

libraries": collections of books owned by individual prisoners who were willing to loan them to their camp-mates.

The provision of libraries to POWs reached its peak during World War II. Although international law still stipulates that detaining powers must assist in maintaining the intellectual well-being of POWs, the provision of reading matter has recently been colored by attempts at indoctrination. During the Korean and Vietnam Wars, for example, American prisoners found that camp libraries were stocked, not with books they wanted to read, but with books that would assist in their conversion to Communism.

Sometimes the reading interests of prisoners are surprising, however. News reports revealed that in the detention center at Guantánamo Bay, Cuba, which houses suspects detained in the War on Terror, the most popular books in the camp library are the fantasy novels in the Harry Potter series, by Scottish novelist J. K. Rowling.

See also Education

References

Valerie Holman, "Captive Readers in the Second World War," *Publishing History* 52 (2002): 83–94.

Jean Langdon-Ford, "Prisoners of War as Library Users," *Canadian Military History* 6 (1997): 92–94.

David Shavit, "'The Greatest Morale Factor Next to the Red Army': Books and Libraries in American and British Prisoner of War Camps in Germany During World War II," *Libraries and Culture* 34 (1999): 113–134.

Herbert Gay Sisson, "Books Behind Barbed Wire," *Library Journal* 65 (15 April 1944): 328–331.

—*Jonathan F. Vance*

LIDDELL, ERIC HENRY (1902–1945)

Eric Liddell was a famed Olympic runner, immortalized in the film *Chariots of Fire*, who was interned by the Japanese during World War II. Born in 1902 in Tientsin (Tianjin),

China, to missionary parents, Liddell was educated in England, where he showed impressive athletic ability, particularly as a runner. Success in university sports propelled him to a berth on the British Olympic team, and at the Paris Olympics of 1924, Liddell gained as much notoriety for his victory in the 400-meter dash as he did for his refusal to compete in the 100-meter dash because it was being run on a Sunday. In 1925, when his celebrity status was at its height, he returned to China to take up missionary work. Liddell served as a teacher at the Anglo-Chinese College and as an itinerant missionary, but shortly after World War II began, he volunteered for service in the Royal Air Force. Rejected on account of his age, he and his family returned to Tientsin. In May 1941, Liddell sent his family out of China and in December, he and six other missionaries were effectively placed under house arrest by Japanese troops occupying Tientsin. They remained there until March 1943, when all enemy nationals in the city were ordered to the Civil Assembly Center in Weihsien (Weifang), south of Beijing. The small internment camp was to be Liddell's home for the rest of his life. Conditions in Weihsien were not bad, but acrimonious relations between the internees poisoned the atmosphere in the camp. For Liddell, whose life had been built on tolerance and compassion, the situation was immensely difficult. The mental strain, in combination with malnutrition, began to take a toll on his health, and in January 1945 he was struck with influenza, sinusitis, and paralyzing headaches. His condition failed to improve, and on 21 February 1945 he collapsed and fell into a coma from which he never emerged. An autopsy revealed that Liddell had died from a brain tumor.

See also Civilian Internees—World War II

References

Langdon Gilkey, *Shantung Compound: The Story of Men and Women under Pressure* (New York: Harper and Row, 1966).

Sally Magnusson, *The Flying Scotsman: A Biography* (New York: Quartet Books, 1981).

David McCasland, *Eric Liddell: Pure Gold* (Grand Rapids, MI: Discovery House Publishers, 2003).

D. P. Thomson, *Scotland's Greatest Athlete* (Crieff, UK: The Research Unit, 1970).

—*Kara Brown*

Lidice Massacre

Along with a similar incident at Oradour-sur-Glane in France, the Lidice massacre was one of the most notorious reprisals committed by the Nazis against civilian hostages in World War II. In September 1941, Adolf Hitler appointed Reinhard Heydrich as Reich Protector of Bohemia-Moravia (now the Czech Republic). Even by the standards of the Third Reich, Heydrich was renowned for his reign of terror. Soon a plan, code-named Operation Anthropoid, was put in train to parachute Czech agents into Bohemia to assassinate him. On 28–29 December 1941, the operation commenced, and on 27 May 1942, two agents attacked Heydrich's Mercedes limousine in a Prague suburb. He lingered near death for days, eventually dying on 4 June. The Nazi reaction was swift and brutal. A state of emergency and a curfew were imposed on Prague, followed by arrests. Nazi officials discussed the number of civilian hostages to be killed, but Hitler was determined on a comprehensive act of vengeance.

The police in Slaný, a small town 30 kilometers northwest of Prague, had discovered a letter that they believed pointed to clandestine activity in the nearby village of Lidice on the day of the assassination. Lidice had featured before in Gestapo files, so the Germans decided that the village would be the main target of reprisal. Karl Hermann Frank, the Nazi secretary of state for Bohemia-Moravia, ordered that Lidice be obliterated from the earth. On 9 June 1942, the Gestapo and SS cordoned off the village, removed anything of value, herded the men into a farm, and burnt every building to the ground. In groups of ten, 199 men were led out of the farm and shot, while 195 women were deported to Ravensbrück concentration camp and 95 children were taken to institutions. Hitler ordered the complete destruction of everything at Lidice; even streams were diverted. Four parachutists of the Anthropoid group were eventually trapped in the crypt and choir gallery of a Prague church; all died in a gun battle on 18 June. Only 143 women of Lidice returned in 1945 and only 16 children were traced and repatriated to Czechoslovakia. For ordering the massacre, Frank was executed in 1946.

As far as is known, Lidice had no connection with any of the Anthropoid agents; the atrocity seems to have been part of a deliberate policy to terrorize the Czechs into submission. A new Lidice was built overlooking the old site, and after the war many countries renamed old towns or named new ones in memory of Lidice.

See also Ardeatine Caves Massacre; Oradour-sur-Glane Massacre; Reprisals

References

Alan Burgess, *Seven Men at Daybreak* (New York: E.P. Dutton, 1960).

Callum MacDonald, *The Killing of Reinhard Heydrich: The SS "Butcher of Prague"* (New York: The Free Press, 1989).

—David Ray

LIEBER CODE

Created by Columbia University jurist Francis Lieber at the request of the general in chief of the Union armies, Henry W. Halleck, during the U.S. Civil War, the Lieber Code was the most ambitious attempt yet to codify the treatment of prisoners of war.

Lieber's draft of the code was amended and approved by a board of officers and then submitted to U.S. President Abraham Lincoln for approval. On 24 April 1863, the code was promulgated as General Orders #100 of the U.S. War Department. There were 57 separate articles covering the treatment of prisoners, making it broader in scope than any subsequent convention until the 1929 Geneva Convention Relative to the Treatment of Prisoners of War. Lieber's provisions guaranteed the basic rights that today are taken for granted: protection of a prisoner's private property, adequate medical attention, "plain and wholesome" food, and humane treatment without being forced to endure "intentional suffering or indignity." However, these were innovative and far-reaching articles in 1863. Certainly neither side in the U.S. Civil War was able to live up to them in their entirety, and the 1874 Brussels Declaration, which repeated many of the articles, was deemed by all signatories to be too far-reaching and therefore unsuitable for ratification. Despite the fact that its practical impact was fairly limited, the Lieber Code was a significant step forward in providing international lawmakers with an ideal to strive for in the early years of the twentieth century.

See also Brussels Declaration; International Law; United States Civil War

References

Frank B. Friedel, Jr., *Francis Lieber: Nineteenth-Century Liberal* (Baton Rouge: Louisiana State University Press, 1947).

Richard Shelly Hartigan, *Lieber's Code and the Law of War* (Chicago: Precedent, 1983).

—Jonathan F. Vance

LIVINGSTON, CAMP

Located on the grounds of a U.S. army training center near Alexandria, Louisiana, Camp Livingston was a typical internment facility for German prisoners of war in the United States during World War II. In January 1945, Livingston held more than 8,000 German POWs, the majority in a system of about 20 branch camps spread all across southern Louisiana.

Built in early 1942, Camp Livingston first housed over 1,000 relocated Japanese civilians and all 62 of the Japanese POWs detained in the United States during that year. The camp then appeared on the U.S. provost marshal general's initial list of 17 proposed camp sites designed to accommodate the expected influx of Axis prisoners from the European battlefields. It consisted of 10 compounds, each with a capacity of 500 men and surrounded by four guard towers. In addition, a hospital with 200 beds had been built. The first 3,000 German POWs, all veterans of the Afrika Korps, arrived in July and August 1943 and immediately set out to beautify the grounds, organize educational courses, and initiate extensive sports and cultural programs. Surrounded by pine trees, the camp soon looked like a health resort, according to one prisoner. Internal camp affairs were handled by German NCOs who rewarded the autonomy granted to them by American authorities with an effective organization of the work program. Under their supervision, Livingston practically became a German enclave, both culturally and politically.

As in all other POW camps in the United States, American authorities at Livingston placed the greatest emphasis on the work program. The first prisoners worked only on maintenance jobs and on the adjacent U.S. Army post, but by October 1943, some 450 of them picked cotton on private farms in the vicinity. More importantly, the powerful American Sugar Cane League soon succeeded in its lobbying efforts aimed at the utilization of prisoner labor in Louisiana's sugar fields. By the end of 1943, Camp Livingston established seven subcamps west and southwest of New Orleans with a combined total of almost 2,500 laborers. While contracting problems, overguarding, and the Germans' unfamiliarity with the work at first hampered performance, the labor program began to pay off for the farmers in the following two years. More subcamps were built in 1944, and frequent transfers between them ensured that the sugar, rice, and cotton regions of the Bayou State received the maximum number of laborers during their respective harvesting seasons. Less luxurious than the base at Livingston, the subcamps nonetheless were laid out in accordance to Geneva Convention regulations, thus including dayrooms, canteens, and athletic fields. The relations between POWs and local contractors were generally harmonious, at times even cordial.

As was typical for German POWs in American captivity, ideological divisions and political dispute caused much unrest among them. One of Livingston's compounds, Company 10, as well as one of the branch camps, Camp Lockport, became segregation facilities for anti-Nazi prisoners who felt threatened by the politically loyal majority of their comrades. Hard-core Nazi agitators were sent to Camp Alva, Oklahoma. These measures somewhat pacified the prisoner population until the end of the war, when the news of the dramatic events in Europe once more heightened tensions. Thus American attempts at democratic reeducation made little headway until late in 1945. At that time, a newly staffed German leadership, a political workshop, and Livingston's democratic camp newspaper, the Echo, had begun to exert some influence on the prisoners' political views.

Camp Livingston ceased operations in April 1946, but some of its subcamps continued to house German POWs until the end of the sugar cane harvest in May 1946. In June 1946, the last German POWs left Louisiana, many to spend further time in captivity in France, Belgium, or Great Britain.

See also World War II—North America

References

Matthew J. Schott, "Prisoners Like Us: German POWs Encounter Louisiana's African-Americans," *Louisiana History* 3 (1995): 277–290.

William L. Shea and Merrill R. Pritchett, "The Wehrmacht in Louisiana," *Louisiana History* 23 (1982): 5–19.

—*Rafael A. Zagovec*

Los Baños Raid

The dramatic American raid on the Japanese internment camp at Los Baños in the Philippines took place on 23 February 1945. The successful rescue mission is noted for its remarkably quick planning and heroic execution, making it one of the most celebrated internment camp raids of World War II.

The Los Baños camp, which housed 2,147 internees, was located across a large lake some 30 miles southeast of Manila. Although principally American civilians, the internees of Los Baños comprised a variety of nationalities and professions. A large number of Catholic missionaries were interned at the camp, along with other civilians who had been working in the Philippines in medicine, business, and education. Like most Japanese prison camps, conditions inside Los Baños were dreadful. Malnourishment and disease were rampant and Japanese guards enforced rigid curfews and restrictions on movement within the camp. However, apart from these restrictions, internees enjoyed relative autonomy. They elected an executive committee to govern themselves and negotiate conditions with the Japanese, organized dormitory monitors, and held classes, dances, sporting events, and religious gatherings.

As the regional war came to favor the United States with the victory in Manila in early February 1945, American military officials, taking the lead from General Douglas MacArthur, began to express serious concern over the possibility of prisoner-of-war massacres. In response to reports of an impending slaughter of internees at Los Baños, American officers quickly drafted plans for a raid on the camp with the help of detailed intelligence reports obtained from Filipino guerillas and several escaped internees. Intelligence suggested their mission would not be easy. Los Baños lay 25 miles behind Japanese lines and a mere eight miles from the 8,000 troops of the Japanese 8th Division. A barbed-wire fence, 10 guard posts, and several machine gun turrets surrounded the camp. Eighty Japanese soldiers lived on-site, with at least 100 others manning posts in the surrounding area. However, American intelligence did uncover the camp's crucial weakness: The Japanese guards on lookout were the only armed soldiers in the compound, as the weapons of off-duty soldiers were locked in their barracks.

Although barred from contact with the outside world, internees at Los Baños became aware of the shifting tide of the war in early February as they heard rumors of American victories, saw American planes overhead, and tasted the fresh American cigarettes that had recently been smuggled into the camp. While encouraging, these developments also raised the specter of provoking a retaliatory prisoner massacre by the Japanese, who had long boasted to the prisoners of Japan's invincibility. Compounding these worries were rumors that the camp's food supply had been exhausted and that Japanese soldiers had begun digging a large grave-like ditch outside the camp.

Two days before the scheduled attack, a reconnaissance platoon of 30 elite soldiers from the 11th Airborne Division of the United States Army furtively crossed the lake and made contact with Filipino guerillas. Together, they took cover in a series of strategic positions in the hills surrounding the camp in preparation for the attack on the guard posts. The attack was launched at 7:00 a.m. on 23 February, at the exact moment that a second force of 125 American paratroopers made a low-altitude jump from nine C-47 planes into a small nearby drop zone that was flanked by high-voltage power lines, a barbed-wire fence, and large trees. The coordinated attack by the reconnaissance platoon, the guerillas, and the paratroopers killed the on-duty guards, and the Americans managed to use their weapons to beat the unarmed guards, sending them running to the hills. By this time, a third force of 54 amphibious tractors that had crossed the lake and landed at a beach two miles north of the camp came crashing through the main gates of Los Baños. The elated internees were quickly loaded onto the tractors and transported in two shifts back across the lake to safety behind American lines. The last of these transports left the beach in the early afternoon amidst heavy shelling from approaching Japanese forces.

The raid on Los Baños was a remarkable success. All of the 2,147 internees were rescued safely and the Americans did not lose a single soldier in the raid on the camp. Two Filipino guerillas were killed in the raid, along with approximately 70 Japanese soldiers.

The darker side of the Los Baños story was the brutal attacks on local Filipinos by Japanese forces that occurred in the days following the raid, in which an estimated 1,400 civilians were killed for their supposed role in helping the Americans. While there is a debate as to whether these massacres were direct reprisals for the raid, they nevertheless raised questions about the need to look beyond the walls of prison camps to the civilian populations nearby who often bore hardships as an indirect result of internment.

References

Anthony Arthur, *Deliverance at Los Baños* (New York: St. Martin's Press, 1985).

William B. Breuer, *Retaking the Philippines: America's Return to Corregidor and Bataan, October 1944–March 1945* (New York: St. Martin's Press, 1986).

Edward M. Flanagan, Jr., *Angels at Dawn: The Los Baños Raid* (Novato, CA: Presidio, 1999).

—*Mark Janson*

LUBYANKA PRISON

Located in downtown Moscow on Lubyanka Square, the Lubyanka was one of the most notorious prisons in the Soviet Union. Seized from an insurance company by the Bolsheviks after the October Revolution, its original cellar and office space were transformed into prison cells (approximately 120), many still with their polished parquet floors. It also functioned as the headquarters for the Soviet secret security services, from the All-Russian Extraordinary Commission for the Struggle Against Counter-Revolution, Sabotage, and Speculation (Cheka), founded by Felix Dzerzhinsky in 1917, to the KGB (Committee for State Security). Under the watchful gaze of Dzerzhinsky's massive statue in the square below, Soviet security chiefs from Lavrenty Beria to Yuri Andropov oversaw and directed the Soviet police state from the same third-floor office. In a strange juxtaposition, located across the square from this infamous symbol of state terror and repression is *Dyetsky Mir* (Children's World), once the Soviet Union's premier children's store.

Like the secretive Lefortovo prison, the Lubyanka served as a site for the incarceration, interrogation, and often the execution of thousands of prisoners. Countless others passed through the complex on their way to the prison and labor camps of the Soviet Gulag. Among its high-profile political prisoners was the Bolshevik intellectual Nikolai Bukharin, who wrote his lengthy prison manuscripts there in 1937 and 1938 while awaiting execution on Stalin's order. Others include the author and playwright Isaac Babel, who was executed in the prison's basement in January 1940 despite official claims to the contrary. Raoul Wallenberg, the Swedish diplomat whose efforts saved thousands of Hungarian Jews during World War II, likely died or was murdered there in 1947 while in Soviet custody. After publishing the dissident magazine *Syntax* in 1959, Alexander Ginzburg was arrested by the KGB and placed in Lubyanka prison. Alexander Solzhenitsyn was also held at Lubyanka before being transferred to the Gulag, and the prison features in his classic account of the Soviet prison system, *The Gulag Archipelago*. One of the last prisoners held at Lubyanka was Gary Powers, the American U2 pilot shot down over Soviet airspace in May 1960.

Closed as a prison in the 1960s, Lubyanka continued to operate as the headquarters of the KGB until the Soviet Union's collapse. It now houses the KGB's successor, the Russian Federation's Federal Security Service (FSB) in addition to a dining hall, offices, a warehouse, and a museum of the state security services that is open to the public. Dzerzhinsky's statue was torn down shortly after the failed August 1991 coup and a stone slab from a labor camp in the Solovetsky Islands was erected nearby as a memorial to the victims of totalitarianism.

See also Gulag

References

Anne Applebaum, *Gulag: A History* (New York: Doubleday, 2003).

Alexander Solzhenitsyn, *The Gulag Archipelago*, trans. Thomas P. Whitney (New York: Harper & Row, 1974).

Wesley C. Gustavson

LYNCH, JESSICA (1983–)

A supply clerk serving with the U.S. Army's 507th Maintenance Company in the Iraq War, Private First Class Jessica Lynch became one of the most famous POWs in U.S. history following her capture by Iraqi forces and much publicized rescue nine days later.

A native of Palestine, West Virginia, Lynch enlisted in the military in 2001. On 23 March 2003, the convoy in which she was traveling was ambushed after taking a wrong turn near the southern Iraqi city of Nasiriya. The 5′3″, 100-pound, blonde 19-year-old became an unlikely hero and sudden celebrity when initial press reports, citing U.S. military sources, claimed Lynch had suffered multiple gunshot and stab wounds in the ambush, yet continued to bravely fight off her Iraqi attackers. Later reports revealed that Lynch's M-16 had, in fact, jammed, and that the injuries she had sustained consisted mainly of fractures and a head wound caused when the vehicle she was riding in had overturned.

Lynch was treated at an Iraqi military hospital, then transferred to Saddam Hussein General Hospital in Nasiriya. After an Iraqi civilian alerted U.S. Marines to her presence, U.S. Special Forces launched a dramatic airborne assault on the hospital on the night of 1 April 2003, rescuing Lynch as well as recovering the bodies of nine other U.S. soldiers from the hospital grounds, and videotaping the operation. Contrary to initial reports, it was soon revealed that the rescuers had not come under fire during the rescue and had met no resistance; there were no Iraqi troops in the hospital at the time of the rescue, only medical staff. In media interviews upon her return to the U.S., Lynch herself claimed that the U.S. military had filmed her rescue and exaggerated events in an effort to increase public support for the war in Iraq. Initially a symbol of American military heroism in action, Lynch became a symbol of wartime media manipulation.

Lynch was awarded the Bronze Star, the Purple Heart, and the Prisoner of War medal. In 2005 she began teacher education training at West Virginia University.

See also Iraq War; Women

References

Rick Bragg, *I Am a Soldier, Too: The Jessica Lynch Story* (New York: Alfred A. Knopf, 2003).

—Aldona Sendzikas

LYNCHING

Lynching refers to the assault or murder of individuals by civilians as an alternative to turning them over to military authorities. It should be distinguished from the execution of POWs by military units at the time of or shortly after capture. The most notorious recent case of lynching occurred during World War II, when the German government condoned the killing of downed Allied airmen by the civilian populace.

The Nazi policy had its roots in a March 1940 directive, issued for the guidance of civilians, which said that enemy soldiers who entered German territory by parachute should be arrested or "made harmless." This perhaps innocuous order became more serious in August 1943, when German security chief Heinrich Himmler ordered that police officials were not to interfere if civilians saw fit to attack downed airmen. Even so, documented cases of the lynching of downed airmen are very rare from this period. However, in April 1944, the order was strengthened with the provisos that airmen who resisted could be executed, and that any civilian who assisted an airmen out of "evil intention" or "misplaced sympathy" could be committed to a concentration camp. This order was later toned down somewhat and made to apply only to airmen who were accused of strafing attacks on civilians; they were to be housed in a prison camp at Oberursel in western Germany and, if their guilt was established, would be turned over to the civilian populace so justice could be enacted. Then, in May 1944, the Nazi Party informed its local posts that there had been a number of cases of lynching, and that the local police had taken no action; this was an implicit statement of the fact that the regime approved of civilians enacting vigilante justice on downed airmen. The reasons for this order are not related simply to revenge. The German command also believed that publicized accounts of lynchings might deter the Allies from pressing the strategic bombing offensive.

Lynching could take many forms. There are documented cases of airmen whose parachutes became entangled in trees or the upper storeys of tall buildings; rather than assisting them down, civilians were known to simply cut the parachute lines and allow them to fall to their deaths. In other cases, they dragged wounded airmen from the wreckage of their aircraft and beat them to death, or pulled them away from military guards and shot them. In one incident, near the city of Pforzheim in March 1945, some 50 civilians, many screaming for revenge, gathered outside a school where seven airmen were being temporarily held. They quickly overpowered the single guard on duty, dragged out four of the airmen, and shot them.

Given the fierceness of that bombing campaign in the last year of the war, it is not surprising that civilians vented their rage on downed airmen, especially when their leaders encouraged them. Robert Wagner, the gauleiter of Baden and Alsace, issued orders that all Allied airmen who came down in his district were to be executed, a decree that many local residents took to heart. In March 1945, seven Allied airmen came down near Baden-Baden when their aircraft was destroyed. They were beaten by local civilians before being confined in a cellar, but before long a mob swarmed the cellar, dragged out the airmen, and shot five of them. The guards assigned to the prisoners did not intervene. Clearly this was not an infrequent incident in Wagner's area, for in 1946 he was sentenced to death by a French military court, in part for his role in encouraging the lynching of Allied airmen. Britain, the United States, and Canada also prosecuted German citizens for attacks on downed airmen. However, those cases did not often involve groups of outraged civilians attacking and killing airmen; most of the documented lynchings were carried out by local Nazi Party or police officials.

Lynching probably occurred in the Pacific theater as well. In 1942, the Japanese government passed the Enemy Airmen's Act, which stipulated that anyone who participated in a raid against nonmilitary targets or who violated international law could be executed. In May 1944, Adolf Hitler advised a Japanese diplomat that Japanese civilians should hang every American airman who fell into their hands. Again, it is difficult to determine how often this happened, but there were certainly many documented cases in which downed airmen were summarily executed by their captors.

Allied governments were diligent in pursuing those responsible for these lynchings, and dozens of civilians were tried and executed after the war; many more soldiers, local Nazi Party officials, and policemen were also brought to justice. And the investigation of these cases continues. In 2005, a German-Canadian solved the case of a previously unidentified Canadian airman who was beaten to death by a group of civilians near the city of Chemnitz in March 1945; according to eyewitnesses, the guard on duty stood by and watched as the murder occurred.

References

Oliver Clutton-Brock, *Footprints on the Sands of Time: RAF Bomber Command Prisoners-of-War in Germany, 1939-1945* (London: Grub Street, 2003).

Peter Hessel, *The Mystery of Frankenberg's Canadian Airman: An Eye-Witness to Terror Bombing and the Quest for Truth, Justice and Reconciliation in Canada and in Germany* (Toronto: James Lorimer, 2005).

—Jonathan F. Vance

M

Mail

Prisoners of war and internees have long relied on communication with home and family as a way to boost morale and lessen the pain of isolation. As a result, international law has been increasingly aware of the need to guarantee a prisoner's ability to communicate with the outside world by mail.

In the premodern era, communication was usually confined to whatever message a prisoner could smuggle out of captivity. Because of the difficulties this entailed, not to mention the relatively low level of literacy among soldiers, many prisoners were entirely cut off from home for the duration of their captivity. Not until the eighteenth century was communication put on a more formal footing, with provisions for government agents to convey messages in and out of prison camps. Attempts to codify this practice in international law occurred during the nineteenth century, with the result that prisoners generally enjoyed reasonable access to mail facilities. During the U.S. Civil War, for example, Andersonville prison camp in Georgia had a small mailbox near the main gate. Prisoners could deposit one-page letters for delivery to friends and family in the north, and each day, a clerk would post a list of those prisoners who had received letters.

Mail regulations during World War I were in fact remarkably lax, at least for prisoners captured by either side on the western front. The Hague Convention of 1907 had set general guidelines for the dispatch and receipt of mail by prisoners, and the detaining powers allowed considerable latitude in determining what items could be received by POWs through the mail. Some prisoners even received large hampers of food, including jars of preserves, fruit, alcohol, and cooked turkeys, from the mail-order departments of large stores in London, Berlin, and Paris.

The Geneva Convention of 1929, which was in force during World War II, stipulated that prisoners be allotted two letters and four postcards per month to communicate with friends and relatives, a limit put in place largely to speed up the censorship of outgoing mail. Some governments placed further restrictions; Japan, for example, ruled in 1943 that prisoners' letters were limited to 25 words each. All mail, whether it was destined for Allied or Axis prisoners, followed certain set routes. In the Pacific theater, mail traveled either in neutral ships used occasionally for the exchange of prisoners or along an overland route via Tehran, Iran, and Siberia to Tokyo. In Europe, mail to be exchanged was flown initially to Lisbon, Portugal, and Berne, Switzerland; later, a sea route was opened and mail went from Lisbon to Marseille, France, and then to Genoa, Italy, with the mail being moved across the continent by train. Although the stoppage of mail was not supposed to be used as a penal sanction, it did occur. Similarly, some prisoners, particularly those who had been captured on the eastern front or who were held in Japanese camps, received mail rarely, if at all. When prison camps in Japan were liberated, it was not uncommon for Allied troops to find sacks containing thousands of pieces of mail, which had reached the camp years earlier but had never been distributed. In one camp in Japan, POW officers decided that two-year-old shipments of mail would be destroyed rather than delivered; the

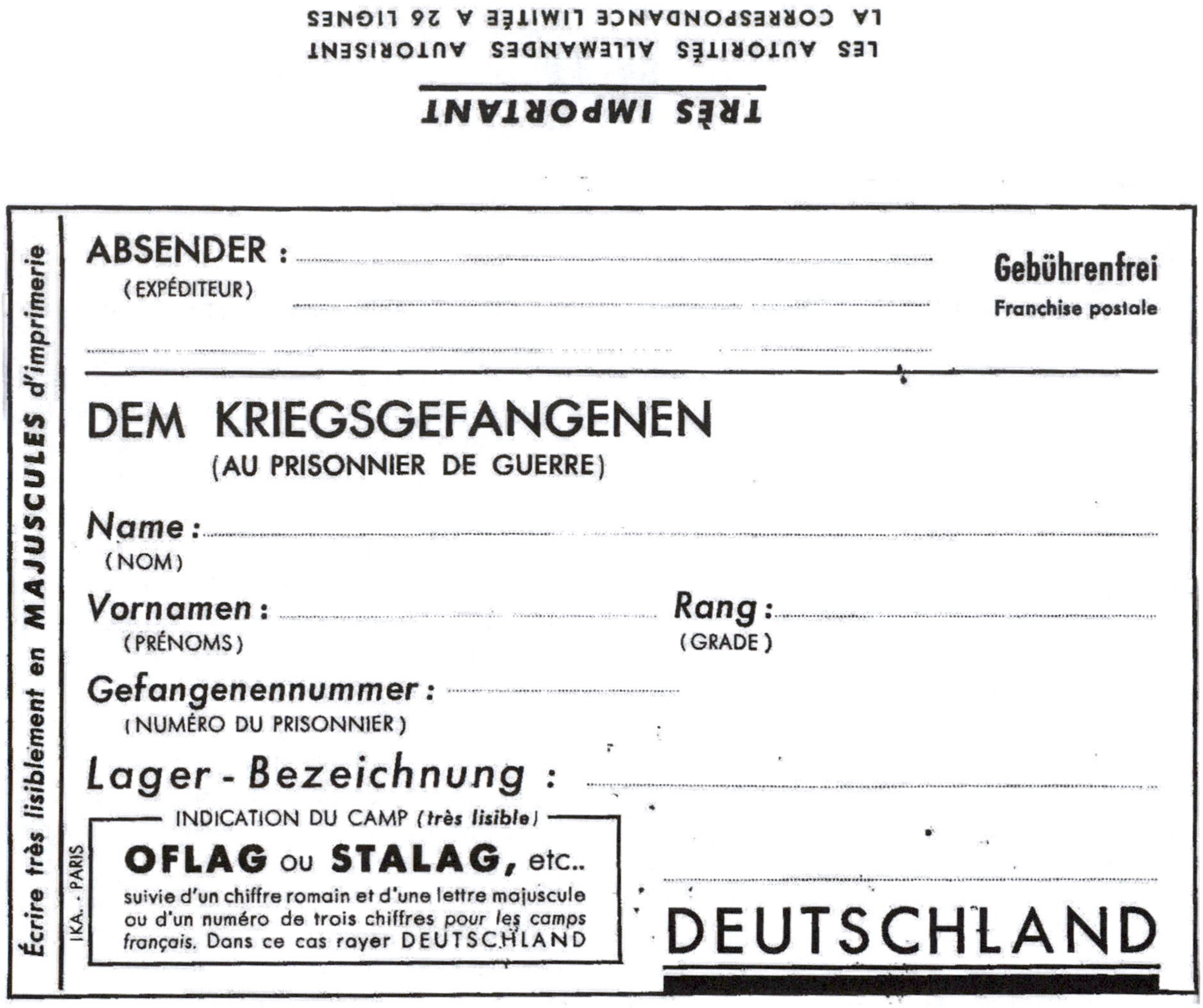

TRÈS IMPORTANT
LES AUTORITÉS ALLEMANDES AUTORISENT
LA CORRESPONDANCE LIMITÉE A 26 LIGNES

ABSENDER : (EXPÉDITEUR)

Gebührenfrei
Franchise postale

DEM KRIEGSGEFANGENEN
(AU PRISONNIER DE GUERRE)

Name : (NOM)

Vornamen : (PRÉNOMS)

Rang : (GRADE)

Gefangenennummer : (NUMÉRO DU PRISONNIER)

Lager - Bezeichnung :

INDICATION DU CAMP (très lisible)
OFLAG ou STALAG, etc..
suivie d'un chiffre romain et d'une lettre majuscule ou d'un numéro de trois chiffres pour les camps français. Dans ce cas rayer DEUTSCHLAND

DEUTSCHLAND

Écrire très lisiblement en MAJUSCULES d'imprimerie

IKA. - PARIS

The letter form provided for the use of French POWs in Germany during World War II (Sarah Fishman)

reminder of home was often too much for a prisoner whose morale was already fragile, and not receiving a letter was just as damaging to a prisoner's mental state.

In subsequent conflicts, the delivery of mail has depended less on international law (the 1949 Geneva Convention merely refined the provisions of the 1929 convention) than on the whim of the captors. United Nations prioners in the Korean War had irregular access to mail, which depended on government policy and on the conduct of individual POWs. When the North Korean government adopted a policy of treating prisoners leniently, mail privileges were extended; at other times, prisoners could only send or receive mail if they were not deemed to be "reactionaries" by their captors. During the Vietnam War, the North Vietnamese government initially refused to deliver any POW mail whatsoever, but it later relented in the face of a massive letter-writing campaign by the families of American prisoners. Even then, mail delivery remained uncertain. In contrast, in the India-Pakistan Wars of 1965 and 1971 and the Arab-Israeli Wars, it does appear that mail privileges were extended to prisoners captured by both sides, with the International Committee of the Red Cross handling the physical transfer of mail.

References

Norman Gruenzner, *Postal History of American POWs: World War II, Korea, Vietnam* (State College, PA: American Philatelic Society, 1979).

—*Jonathan F. Vance*

Malmédy Massacre

The execution of American prisoners of war near the Belgian town of Malmédy in 1944 represented one of the largest massacres of Allied troops in the west during World War II. On 16 December 1944, the German army launched a devastating surprise attack in the Ardennes forest, and the subsequent Battle of the Bulge decimated unprepared American units, forcing the large-scale surrender of U.S. troops. SS *Standartenführer* (Lieutenant-Colonel) Joachim Peiper commanded the 1st SS Regiment of the 1st SS Division, and personally selected 5,000 elite troops to spearhead the German offensive. Peiper's regiment demonstrated fanatical dedication to the Third Reich and exceptional desire to reverse the setbacks experienced in the west.

By 17 December, American units in the Ardennes were in complete disarray. Surrounded, B Battery of the 285th Field Artillery Observation Battalion, consisting of American soldiers from Pennsylvania, Maryland, Virginia, and West Virginia, surrendered to the advancing Germans. Numerically, they represented but a small proportion of Allied prisoners taken during the Ardennes offensive, but, sadly, they became the most infamous.

Soldiers from Peiper's unit disarmed the Americans and marched them into a nearby field. The precise sequence of events is not entirely clear, but the SS troops fired on the prisoners, killing between 50 and 60 of them. Some 30 others escaped and fled under cover of darkness, evading the mobile forces that overran Allied positions. Reports of German atrocities spread quickly throughout the ranks on both sides, intensifying fighting in the Ardennes.

The Malmédy massacre was not an isolated incident, and calls for retribution for the activities of the SS gained momentum following the war. In May 1946, 74 SS officers and men stood trial in the former German concentration camp of Dachau, charged with the murders of American POWs around Malmédy. In the trial, Peiper assumed responsibility for the actions of his men; although he was 15 miles from Malmédy at the time of the massacre, he was convicted of the murders and sentenced to death, along with 42 of the other accused. However, serious irregularities in the interrogations of the defendants and the trial itself later came to light, and all of the death sentences handed down were eventually commuted. One by one, the defendants were paroled, with Peiper remaining in prison the longest. He was finally released in 1956.

See also Katyń Massacre; Meyer, Kurt; Le Paradis Massacre; Peiper, Joachim; War Crimes Wormhout Massacre

References

John M. Bauserman, *The Malmédy Massacre* (Shippensburg, PA: White Mane, 1995).

Trevor N. Dupuy, David L. Bongard, and Richard C. Anderson, Jr., *Hitler's Last Gamble: The Battle of the Bulge, December 1944–January 1945* (New York: HarperCollins, 1994).

James J. Weingartner, *Crossroads of Death: The Story of the Malmédy Massacre and Trial* (Berkeley: University of California Press, 1979).

Charles Whiting, *Massacre at Malmédy: The Story of Jochen Peiper's Battle Group, Ardennes, December, 1944* (New York: Stein and Day, 1971).

—*Scott Blanchette*

The Manchurian Candidate

This remarkable 1962 film, starring Angela Lansbury, Frank Sinatra, Laurence Harvey, and James Gregory, is the world's best-known visualization of brainwashing. It concerns a man who kills on command, then remembers nothing. This story about the ultimate domination of a human being drew on popular fears of communism abroad and modern society at home.

The film begins during the Korean War. Communist scientists in Manchuria, China, brainwash an American POW to assassinate a presidential candidate. Just the sight of the queen of diamonds triggers a robotic trance in the man and renders him totally obedient. Although fictional, the plot seemed only partly outlandish at the time. One film reviewer reassured the public that real brainwashing was not so precise and efficient, but the U.S. Army seemed to offer tacit confirmation of brainwashing when it confined returned POWs to a psychiatric unit. Further scientific validation came from some medical doctors, who believed that the Soviets really could manipulate minds, just as Ivan Pavlov had conditioned dogs.

Communism was the greatest fear mirrored in this film, but American life also contained threats to individualism. Director John Frankenheimer believed the whole country was brainwashed by television commercials, politicians, and a censored press. Indeed, the movie playfully shows people completely absorbed, almost entranced, in television viewing. By the same token, the film's eerie similarity to the assassination of U.S. President John F. Kennedy in 1963 suggested master plots by sinister puppeteers.

Some critics see the film primarily as anticommunist hysteria. It is revealing, however, that the Joseph McCarthy character is presented as a buffoon. The communists in the film are not the most immediate danger to liberty. In the plot's intricate structure, that threat comes from politicians who fan anticommunist paranoia in order to seize power themselves.

The film was remade by director Jonathan Demme in 2004, with a cast that included Liev Schreiber, Meryl Streep, and Denzel Washington. However, the POW element was removed, the new plot revolving around American soldiers who were brainwashed during the Gulf War by shadowy scientists connected to a corporation known as Manchurian Global.

See also Film; Indoctrination

References

Susan L. Carruthers, "*The Manchurian Candidate* and the Cold War Brainwashing Scare," *Historical Journal of Film, Radio, and Television* 18 (1998): 75–94.

John D. Marks, *Search for the Manchurian Candidate* (New York: Times Books, 1979).

Joost A.M. Meerloo, *The Rape of the Mind: The Psychology of Thought Control, Menticide, and Brainwashing* (New York: World Publishing, 1956).

Nora Sayre, *Running Time: Films of the Cold War* (New York: Dial Press, 1982).

—*Charles S. Young*

Maori Wars (1843–1872)

This series of colonial conflicts, fought by the British against the aboriginal peoples of New Zealand in the second half of the nineteenth century, revealed the complex nature of captivity during such conflicts. Britain formally annexed New Zealand in 1840, and campaigns to open up Maori homelands to white settlement were soon underway. In 1843, a group of white settlers trying to enforce a land claim at Wairau were set upon by Maori warriors; nearly half of the British party were killed, including a number of prisoners who were slain after capture. Fortunately, this did not prompt the British to respond in kind, and when they captured 183 warriors and a number of female camp followers after the Battle of Rangiriri in 1863, they interned the prisoners along with warriors who had been captured in smaller engagements on Kawau Island, north of Auckland. On 10 September 1864, however, 200 of these Maori prisoners escaped and began to build a fortification near the site of their internment, giving every indication that they were prepared to offer further resistance to the British. Not wishing to see a repetition of this embarrassing escape, the British moved 200 other Maori prisoners to the Chatham Islands, roughly 400 miles east of New Zealand, in the hopes that this distance would forestall another escape attempt. However, in a remarkable operation on 4 July 1868, a group of Maori warriors overpowered their 16 guards, seized a British schooner, and sailed back to New Zealand, taking with them virtually all of the prisoners-163 men, 64 women, and 71 children. Their leader, a man named Te Kooti, planned the operation brilliantly and ensured that no violence occurred during the escape; his warriors treated their former captives with perfect civility and even freed the crew of the seized schooner with a gift of £150.

Sadly, Te Kooti followed up this heroic epic with a reign of terror against British and Maori settlements in the Bay of Poverty area of New Zealand in November 1868. In that campaign, Te Kooti captured some 300 local Maori settlers; he executed dozens, and allowed many more of the prisoners to starve to death. He also murdered 54 European and Maori settlers whom he had captured in a night raid on the area. Unfortunately, these atrocities had a serious impact on the treatment of prisoners in future engagements. The British and their Maori allies made it clear that no quarter would be given to Te Kooti's warriors, a threat that they quickly acted upon. In January 1869, after 140 of Te Kooti's warriors and 135 women and children had surrendered at Ngatapa, their captors systematically put to death over 120 men, women, and children. British officers who were involved attempted to stop the murder of noncombatants, but concurred entirely that the male prisoners should be killed. Thereafter, the situation deteriorated into a series of retaliatory killings of prisoners by both sides until hostilities finally petered out in 1872.

Clearly, the treatment of prisoners in these conflicts was conditioned by racial factors, but other factors were involved as well. A feeling among European armies that imperial wars were not governed by the laws or customs of European wars, particularly where prisoners were involved, together with a simple tendency to retaliate in kind when atrocities occurred, all too often set in motion an escalating spiral of abuse against POWs and civilian prisoners.

References
James Belich, *The New Zealand Wars and the Victorian Interpretation of Racial Conflict* (Auckland: Auckland University Press, 1986).
Tim Ryan and Bill Parham, *The Colonial New Zealand Wars* (Wellington: Grantham House, 1986).

—Jonathan F. Vance

MASCHKE COMMISSION

In 1956, the last German prisoners of war returned home from the Soviet Union, ending the experience of captivity in World War II and providing the impetus for the establishment by the West German government of the Scientific Commission for the History of Prisoners of War, commonly known as the Maschke Commission. Founded in 1957, it aimed to collect systematically documents and reports pertinent to the experience of POWs, to evaluate these sources, and to compile the documentation. Cooperation with other countries was intended, but only the government of France initiated a similar project, the Commission d'Histoire de la Captivité, chaired by Fernand Braudel.

The commission was not the first of its kind in Germany. After World War I the Entente powers had prepared white papers concerning the treatment of POWs, to which the German government had not been able to respond satisfactorily. In order to avoid a repetition of this situation, in the late 1940s the Office for Peace Issues in Stuttgart compiled a series of studies on the fate of German POWs. In addition, the tracing services that searched for the millions of people missing after the war soon recognized that their fates could only be determined if the general course of events was understood. This led to the publication of a four-volume monograph by Kurt Böhme, the most important author of the Maschke Commission, in 1954–1962.

The first chairman of the commission, Professor Dr. Hans Koch, an East European historian in Munich who had been a prisoner himself, died unexpectedly in April 1959. He was succeeded by Professor Dr. Erich Maschke, whose main field of research was the history of the German east. In 1945, six months after the end of the war, the Russian occupiers of eastern Germany declared him to be a POW and ordered him deported to the Soviet Union. Returning in 1953, he was appointed to the chair for economic and social history at the University of Heidelberg in 1956, where he stayed until his retirement in 1969. The commission itself was based in Munich and managed by Kurt Böhme. Initially provided with a staff of four, the commission eventually employed 16 persons, including clerks and assistants. Involved in the research and writing were specialists from the tracing services, historians, and eyewitnesses like Henry Faulk, who wrote the volume on the British reeducation program. Its mandate lasted until 1972, although the final work was not concluded until the end of 1974.

Based on the evaluation of some 400,000 POW questionnaires, 2,000 eyewitness reports, and 45,000 documents, the commission produced a series of 22 volumes (over 10,000 pages in total) dealing with the following issues: German POWs in Yugoslavia (two volumes), German POWs in the Soviet Union, including camp life, forced labor, and penal camps (eight volumes), spiritual and cultural life in prison camps, German POWs in Poland and Czechoslovakia, German POWs in American hands (two volumes) and in British hands (two volumes), German POWs in Belgium, Luxembourg, and the Netherlands, German POWs in French hands, a general summary, and two diary volumes. Some topics were not covered, such as the fate of civilian deportees in the Soviet Union, which was dropped in 1958 for financial reasons. The same applied to the medical aspects of captivity, which were to be the subject of a parallel project. For political reasons, the war crimes trials were excluded, too; they were to be the subject of a Department of State study, which has not yet been completed.

Publication of the volumes, always the intent of the participating historians, was delayed by the need to secure approval from the German government. The first two volumes on captivity in Yugoslavia were published in 1962 and 1964, but in 1969, foreign minister Willy Brandt stated that the German government did not want to burden East-West relations by reproaches about the treatment of the German POWs. For this reason, the series was only accessible at university libraries for research purposes; not until 1975 was it made available for sale without restriction. Due to these circumstances, the series was widely ignored by the social science community, yet it provoked polemic responses from the left and the right wing. Although incomplete in some aspects, the series can still be regarded as the definitive study of German captivity during World War II.

References

Rolf Steininger, "Some Reflections on the Maschke Commission," in *Eisenhower and the German POWs: Facts Against Falsehood*, ed. Günter Bischof and Stephen Ambrose (Baton Rouge: Louisiana State University Press, 1992).

—*Rüdiger Overmans*

MATHER, COTTON (1663–1728)

Cotton Mather, one of the greatest Harvard-educated Puritan authors and preachers, published 450 works on wide-ranging topics, including Congregationalism, natural science, ecclesiastical history, witchcraft, and captivity among American Indians. He opposed the outcome of the Salem witchcraft trials (1693) in New England in *Magnalia Christi Americana* (1702), although in *Memorable Providences, Relating to Witchcrafts and Possessions* (1689) he supported the justice of the extreme verdicts.

Like other Puritan preachers, Mather understood the travails of white captivity among the Indians to be journeys of initiation from death to rebirth and considered captivity as a way for God to test or punish his creatures. Thus captivity for Puritans became a terrible experience, a world of darkness where catastrophe was normal and normalcy was both chaotic and surely Satan-inspired. The Puritans incorporated these fears into the sermons known as the jeremiad and focused on the ancient rule of justified retaliation, *lex talionis,* an eye for an eye. One example of the vengeance-jutice theme appears in Mather's *Decennium Luctuosum* (1699), in which he chronicled Hannah Dustin's difficult captivity and violent escape from her Indian captors, including the fact that she killed all of her captors with a tomahawk and carried their scalps back to Massachusetts. To Mather and other Puritans, former captives' strange post-captivity behavior represented a form of witchcraft that had to be driven out by religious exercise. The natural world became the feared domain of the hated enemy and required subjugation and conquest in order to establish and maintain the physical, political, economic, emotional, and cultural world of colonial civilization. In Mather's view, people taken captive by Indians had little hope of being restored to full commnity life and could only rely on God to sustain the will to live.

See also Colonial Captivity Narratives

References
Ronald A. Bosco, ed., *Paterna: The Autobiography of Cotton Mather* (Delmar, NY: Scholars' Facsimiles and Reprints, 1976).
Kenneth Silverman, *The Life and Times of Cotton Mather* (New York: Harper and Row, 1984).

—*Robert C. Doyle*

MAU MAU REBELLION (1952–1960)

One of the first significant anti-colonial uprisings in sub-Saharan Africa, the Mau Mau Rebellion in Kenya was also distinguished by the use of tactics that had proven so controversial in an earlier imperial conflict.

The Mau Mau was a secret paramilitary group connected to a variety of legal organizations dedicated to ridding Kenya of Europeans and Asians. Under its charismatic leader KaMau wa Ngenga, better known as Jomo Kenyatta, it spread discontent among the Gikuyu people and a number of other tribes, and on 20 October 1952 the governor of Kenya, Sir Evelyn Baring, declared a state of emergency. He ordered the detention of 183 known Mau Maus, including Kenyatta, but the movement retaliated with a wave of killings that targeted European and Asian residents of Kenya, but mostly Gikuyu people who remained loyal to the government. Indeed, over the course of the rebellion, the vast majority of Mau Mau victims were their fellow Kenyans.

The British response to the deepening crisis was to return to a policy that had been used in South Africa during the Boer War: mass detentions of civilians. In secret, the authorities began building dozens of large camps and then detaining tens of thousands of people. The vigor of the British operation convinced a number of Mau Mau leaders to contemplate encouraging their followers to surrender, but they soon had a change of heart and the mass arrests continued. As Gikuyu men and women were arrested and placed in the detention camps, the incidence of violence dropped dramatically, apparently vindicating the policy of leaving at liberty only those people whose loyalty to the government was beyond question. In April 1955 a new British commander, General Gerald Lathbury (who had himself been a prisoner of war during World War II), arrived to take over the operations, which continued until 1960. By that time, over 10,000 Mau Mau had been killed and over 80,000 Mau Mau and their supporters had been captured and placed in the camps.

Typically, they went first to the Langata reception camp near Nairobi to be classified by agents known as *gakonia* (little sacks), so called because they were clothed from head to toe in burlap to conceal their identities.

Suspects were classed as either Black (later Z1 or Z2) for hard-core Mau Mau, Grey (Y1) for Mau Mau who were candidates for re-education, or White (Y2) for civilians who could safely be released back to their villages to be supervised by their chiefs. Y1 detainees were sent to camps in their home districts to be "rehabilitated," while the Z1 and Z2 prisoners were transferred to special camps where the treatment was intended to break them down and force them to renounce their allegiance to the Mau Mau.

Conditions in those camps were brutal. The commandant at Mackinnon Road Camp told newcomers that the facility was also known as *Kufa na Kupona* (Life and Death)-inmates who cooperated lived; those who did not died. The camp at Manyani, which one critic called the African Belsen, housed more than 15,000 prisoners in aluminum huts behind electrified fences. The inmates slept on cement floors and spent their days in backbreaking labor or re-education classes; all the while, anti-Mau Mau propaganda blared from loudspeakers in every hut. Beatings were common-just one of the many tactics used to achieve the British aim of gradually splitting waverers away from the hardcores.

Over time, this policy proved to be successful and the dwindling number of recalcitrant Mau Mau were transferred to Hola Camp. There, they refused to work because of the terrible food and living conditions, but on the tenth day of their strike, the commandant responded by bringing in hundreds of heavily armed soldiers. The detainees immediately agreed to return to work, but instead, the commandant ordered the soldiers to attack; in the ensuing battle, 11 detainees were killed and dozens more wounded. The incident at Hola was followed by the abrupt closure of all of the 50-odd camps that made up what historian Marshall Clough has called the Kenyan gulag. However, the closure had more to do with a general British policy of disengaging from Africa than with a change of heart over the brutal treatment of over 80,000 Kenyan detainees.

References

Marshall S. Clough, *Mau Mau Memoirs: History, Memory and Politics* (Boulder, CO: Lynne Rienner, 1998).

Josiah Mwangi Kariuki, *Mau Mau Detainee: The Account of a Kenya African of His Experiences in Detention Camps,* 1953–1960 (London: Oxford University Press, 1963).

Ngugi wa Thiong'o, *Detained: A Writer's Prison Diary* (London: Heinemann, 1981).

Gakaara wa Wanjau, *Mau Mau Author in Detention* (Nairobi: Heinemann, 1988).

—*Jonathan F. Vance*

McCain, John (1936–)

The son and grandson of prominent four-star admirals in the U.S. Navy, John McCain was graduated from the United States Naval Academy in 1958 and served as a naval aviator in the Vietnam War. On 26 October 1967, operating from the carrier USS *Oriskany* (CVA-34), Lieutenant Commander John McCain was on his twenty-third bombing run over North Vietnam when the A-4 Skyhawk attack aircraft he was piloting was hit by a surface-to-air missile. Suffering serious injuries as he ejected from his aircraft, McCain landed in Truc Bach Lake in central Hanoi. He was captured and taken to the nearby Hoa Lo prison (the "Hanoi Hilton"). McCain spent the next five and a half years as a POW, mostly at the Hoa Lo, a period which included two years of solitary confinement and frequent beatings and other torture. Upon learning that McCain's father, Admiral John S. McCain, Jr., was Commander-in-Chief, Pacific (a command he held from 1968 to 1972), McCain's captors offered him early release, which he refused.

Following the signing of the peace accords ending the war, McCain was released on 15 March 1973. He continued to serve in the navy until 1981, retiring with the rank of captain. The following year he was elected to the U.S. Congress to represent the state of Arizona, serving two terms in the House of Representatives (1982–1986). In 1986, he was elected to the United States Senate. In 2000 Senator McCain campaigned unsuccessfully for the Republican party presidential nomination against Texas Governor George W. Bush. In 2004 he was courted by Democratic presidential nominee John Kerry as a potential running mate.

Senator McCain served as a member of the Senate Select Committee on POW/MIA Affairs (1991–1993). In 2005, he backed a measure to outlaw torture by American soldiers in the form of an amendment to a bill funding the wars in Iraq and Afghanistan.

See also Hanoi Hilton; POW/MIA Issue; Vietnam War

References
John McCain and Mark Salter, *Faith of My Fathers: A Family Memoir* (New York: HarperCollins, 1999).
Robert Timberg, *John McCain: An American Odyssey* (New York: Simon and Schuster, 1999).

—*Aldona Sendzikas*

Merchant Seamen

Not until this century has the status of captured merchant seamen been an issue. Previously, belligerent nations gave little thought to deciding whether merchant seamen were combatants or noncombatants. If the victorious forces felt so inclined, they imprisoned mariners; if they felt magnanimous, they released them. The Brussels Declarations of 1874 and the Hague Convention of 1899 both recognized that captured merchant mariners should be accorded POW status, but the 1907 Hague Convention went further to stipulate that merchant seamen should not be detained at all but should be released upon pledging not to participate in hostilities. During World War I, this article was ignored. Occasionally, captured merchant mariners were released, but more often they were detained as civilian internees rather than POWs. As such, they were responsible for their own upkeep, a fact that left some merchant seaman in civilian internment camps near destitution. Furthermore, at least one British merchant captain, Charles Fryatt, was treated as a guerrilla and executed for attempting to ram a German submarine.

The drafters of the 1929 Geneva Convention Relative to the Treatment of Prisoners of War tried to address this situation by proposing an article identifying merchant seamen as POWs, but this position was rejected in favor of an article that specifically stated that they were not POWs. This confusion meant that, during World War II, merchant seamen were neither POWs nor civilian internees. They were kept in separate camps away from those two groups, although they did benefit from the superintendence of the Protecting Power and the International Committee of the Red Cross (ICRC).

With the Geneva Convention of 1949, lawmakers finally enshrined the position that merchant seamen are indeed POWs, but even this was not always heeded in subsequent conflicts. During the India-Pakistan Wars of 1965 and 1971, both sides detained enemy merchant seamen without granting them POW status. As a result, the ICRC was unable to visit their camps to monitor their well-being. At present, the articles governing the status of merchant mariners in captivity also apply to the crews of civilian aircraft who are captured.

See also Fryatt, Charles Algernon

References
John Joel Culley, "A Troublesome Presence: World War II Internment of German Sailors in New Mexico," *Prologue* 28 (1996): 278–295.
Charles Dana Gibson, "Prisoners of War vs. Internees: The Merchant Marine Experience of World War II," *American Neptune* 54 (1994): 187–193.

—*Jonathan F. Vance*

Merry Christmas, Mr. Lawrence

This 1983 UK/Japan co-production was the first English-language project of Japanese director Nagisa Oshima. Based on the novel *The Seed and the Sower* by Laurens van der

Post, the film focuses on a war of wills between a rebellious British POW (David Bowie) and a Japanese camp commandant (Ryuichi Sakomoto) in 1942 Java. The commandant is impressed by the POW's defiance because he views the other prisoners' unwillingness to protest their cruel treatment as a sign of weakness. But part of the prisoner's motive is his tremendous guilt over his cowardice years earlier, when he failed to help his younger brother in a similar situation. Contrasted with this strange spiritual and intellectual relationship is a more standard conflict between bilingual prisoner Colonel John Lawrence (Tom Conti) and a sadistic sergeant (Takeshi Kitano). Lawrence is an astute observer of the cultural codes of his captors and even forms a sort of friendship with his adversary.

The film is ambitious, attempting to describe larger cultural differences between East and West within this POW-camp setting. It suffers from certain weaknesses, most notably its poor title, but it is an interesting contrast with similar films made by English-language directors. Where other filmmakers might have settled for teasing ironies out of the clash between captor and captive or between different cultures (Japanese/British) or charismas (Bowie and Sakamoto are more familiar as rock musicians than actors), Oshima also infuses the film with elements of mysticism and spirituality. Though these elements are common in Japanese cinema, English audiences are less familiar with them. This cultural difference may explain why critical opinion is so sharply divided on this film and why it remains an overlooked example of the POW genre.

See also Film; Post, Laurens van der

—*Darryl Wiggers*

MÉTIS REBELLIONS

During the first two decades after Confederation in 1867, the Dominion of Canada faced two uprisings of the Métis, or mixed blood, population of the Northwest Territories. Descended from European fur traders and their aboriginal wives, the Métis were predominantly French-speaking and Roman Catholic, and this brought them into conflict with the predominantly English-speaking and Protestant migrants from Ontario who settled in the Northwest beginning in the 1860s. In 1869, angered at not having been consulted concerning the transfer of Hudson's Bay Company territories to Canada, the Métis of the Red River Settlement frustrated the efforts of Canadian surveyors and road construction crews. This escalated to the seizure of Fort Garry (present-day Winnipeg) on 2 November 1869, and the proclamation of a Métis provisional government under the leadership of Louis Riel. The Canadian government dispatched a military force under the command of Colonel Garnet Wolseley, but the confrontation was diffused by the creation of the province of Manitoba, with safeguards in its constitution for Métis linguistic, religious, and property rights. In the spring of 1885, however, the Métis under Riel rose again, this time further to the west in the Saskatchewan Valley. The second rebellion effectively ended with the seizure of the Métis capital at Batoche by British Canadian forces under General Frederick Middleton on 12 May 1885.

Métis leader Louis Riel, who was imprisoned and executed after the Rebellion of 1885.

Prisoners figure prominently in the history of the Métis Rebellions. During the 1869 rebellion, Riel's provisional government imprisoned several Canadians, including John Christian Schultz, the editor of Red River's newspaper, and Thomas Scott, a surveyor from Ontario. These prisoners escaped in January 1870 and organized a militia to liberate Fort Garry. Scott was later recaptured, and because of the disrespect he showed his captors and his refusal to swear allegiance to the provisional government, he was executed by a Métis firing squad on 4 March 1870. During the 1885 rebellion, the Métis held prisoners at Batoche and the government forces sent to quell the rebellion saw the liberation of these prisoners as an important part of their mission. Riel's aboriginal allies also took prisoners, most famously following the battles of Frog Lake and Fort Pitt. The rebel internment of prisoners provoked considerable anger in eastern Canada. Infuriated by inaccurate images of Riel himself shooting a blindfolded Thomas Scott in the back of the head, the public, particularly in Ontario, demanded vengeance. When Riel was elected to parliament as a member for the new Manitoba constituency of Provencher, an angry mob prevented him from taking his seat and he went into exile in the United States until 1884. During the 1885 rebellion, the fate of two prisoners, Theresa Delaney and Theresa Gowanlock, captured by the Cree chief Big Bear after the battle of Frog Lake, elicited considerable speculation and concern among eastern Canadians. Upon their liberation, Delaney and Gowanlock reported that they had been treated well by their captors. However, the account they later published under the title *Two Months in the Camp of Big Bear* conformed to the sensationalist conventions of the colonial captivity narrative genre.

Of course, the Canadian government also took prisoners in the aftermath of the rebellions. After the first rebellion, Ambroise Lépine, the presiding officer of the Métis court martial that had tried Thomas Scott, was arrested, convicted of murder, and sentenced to death. With jurisdictional issues and ethnic and sectarian peace at stake, the Canadian government responded to the Lépine sentence by issuing a general amnesty for the rebels, except for Lépine and W.B. O'Donoghue, who, along with Riel, were exiled for five years. Following the second rebellion, the Cree chiefs Big Bear and Poundmaker were tried and imprisoned, while other aboriginal allies of the Métis were sentenced to death. However, the most important prisoner was Riel himself. After his capture at Batoche, Riel stood trial at Regina for high treason. Refusing to enter an insanity defense, he was convicted and sentenced to death. Despite pleas for clemency, especially from French Canadians, he was hanged on 16 November 1885. In his trial and the subsequent public discussion of his sentence, Métis treatment of prisoners was an important subtext. It has become a truism among Canadian historians that, while Riel may have been convicted of high treason, he was hanged for the execution of Thomas Scott.

See also Colonial Captivity Narratives.

References

J.M. Bumsted, "The Trial of Ambroise Lépine." *The Beaver* 77/2 (1997): 9–19.

Theresa Delaney and Theresa Gowanlock, *Two Months in the Camp of Big Bear,* ed. Sarah Carter (Regina, SK: Canadian Plains Research Centre, 1999).

Gerald Friesen, *The Canadian Prairies: A History* (Toronto: University of Toronto Press, 1984).

Jonathan F. Vance, *Objects of Concern: Canadian Prisoners of War though the Twentieth Century* (Vancouver: UBC Press, 1994).

—*Forrest D. Pass*

MEXICAN-AMERICAN WAR (1846–1848)

The Mexican-American War began because of American territorial expansion in the western part of the continent, including the annexation of Texas. When Mexico refused the United States' diplomatic efforts to purchase California and New Mexico, war fever seized the territory. Imperialists and slavery proponents supported the Mexican War, and volunteers from the south and west enlisted. Patriotic fervor was intensified by memories of the Mexican annihilation of American prisoners at the Alamo in 1836, as well as other incidents involving the capture and imprisonment of Americans living in Mexican territories. Before the Mexican War started, the Mexican army already had a reputation for being brutal to prisoners, both military and civilian.

American troops captured from several hundred to several thousand prisoners in each battle of the war. Most reports told only of military prisoners, although civilians serving the troops were also detained, including Mexican priests who acted as guerrillas and directed attacks on Americans and on any Mexicans who assisted them. The Americans usually exchanged or paroled prisoners because sheltering and supplying them was a burden and because prisoners slowed the advance. American officers hoped paroled prisoners would dissuade other Mexicans from fighting by telling them of the Americans' strength. Some Mexican officers refused parole, forcing the U.S. government to transport them to the United States, at considerable cost, but most prisoners taken at Vera Cruz and Cerro Gordo were paroled. However, because many violated their parole and reenlisted, the Americans eventually changed their policy and detained more prisoners.

The number of Americans seized by Mexican soldiers is not so well documented, although it is known that the Mexicans used American prisoners for labor. One U.S. soldier, Ralph W. Kirkham, wrote in his journal about seeing a monument outside Tacubaya (now part of Mexico City) that read: "This road was constructed by the Texan prisoners under General Santa Anna." The Mexicans also paraded prisoners through towns to boost public support for the war and to try to lower the morale of Americans. Many of these POWs were held at El Encarnacíon, and rescue efforts failed to liberate them.

Many of the details on the treatment of POWs appeared in newspaper articles, which described columns of prisoners marching behind lines while fire and smoke from battles lingered in the air. Soon after the Battle of Resaca de la Palma on 9 May 1846, American newspapers printed a drawing depicting the capture of Mexican General Rómulo La Vega, falsely crediting Captain Charles May, rather than soldiers of the 8th Infantry, with capturing the officer. Newspapers commented on the treatment of prisoners, with each side casting the other as cruel while praising their own soldiers as being humane. When Major Frederick D. Mills, of the 15th Infantry, was killed while trying to surrender, his hometown newspaper, the Burlington (Iowa) *Hawk-Eye,* protested: "Instead of treating him as they should have done, as a prisoner of war, the Mexicans basely fell upon him and lanced him to death . . . [he was] barbarously murdered by the enemy while a prisoner, and contrary to the laws and usages of war." At the same time, soldiers on both sides eagerly accepted spoils of war. Kirkham wrote to his wife that after the successful attack on Chapultepec Castle, he was allowed to choose a horse that belonged to an imprisoned Mexican officer.

Many prisoners held by Mexico were deserters from the U.S. Army who had been enticed by offers of money, property, and increased rank to enlist in the Mexican army. Court-martialed, these men were held at the Acordada and Citadel prisons where citizens of Mexico City visited them, brought them gifts, and asked for their release. "There are many Mexicans, prisoners of war, in our hands, who were taken on the field of battle fighting for their country's cause. Such men we honor and respect on their misfortune," John Peoples, editor of the *American Star,* wrote, "but for the apostatized and toad-spotted traitors who were taken in arms against their country, feelings of loathing and disgust take possession of us whenever we think of them." Some deserters were drummed out of camp while fifes and drums played the "Rogue's March." The *Hawk-Eye* reported that Major General Zachary Taylor favored this punishment because "such rascals, he said, might do for Santa Anna-they would not suit him-and it would be wasting powder and shot to shoot them."

As early as August 1847, American and Mexican leaders discussed the issue of prisoners of war and eventually agreed that all American POWs still in Mexican hands would be immediately exchanged for an equal number (taking rank into account) of Mexican prisoners in American hands. They also agreed that wounded prisoners should be transferred to healthier locations to assist in their convalescence, although they would officially remain prisoners. Despite these discussions, most prisoners remained confined, and by November 1847, Archbishop Juan Manuel of Mexico City wrote American commander Major-General Winfield Scott, offering to administer an oath to prisoners, swearing that they would not fight if paroled. Scott replied that many Mexicans had not honored their parole before and that his requests for the exchange of several American prisoners had been ignored. He said he would only free prisoners if the church informed them that parolees who reenlisted would be executed if caught by American troops. The archbishop agreed and administered the oath to more than 800 prisoners.

The war was finally brought to a close with the Treaty of Guadalupe Hidalgo, signed on 2 February 1848. According to Article 4 of the treaty, "all prisoners of war taken on either side, on land or on sea, shall be restored as soon as practicable after the exchange of the ratifications of this treaty." The document revealed that not only had prisoners been taken at sea, but that Native Americans, particularly the Comanches, had captured Mexicans. It specifically stated that such prisoners were to be released as well: "It is also agreed that if any Mexicans should now be held as captives by any savage tribes within the limits of the United States, as about to be established by the following article, the government of the United States will exact the release of such captives, and cause them to be restored to their country." In accordance with the treaty's provisions, Scott's successor, Major General William O. Butler, issued General Order 116 on 1 June 1848, freeing all prisoners. Guards read the order, shaved the heads of the remaining prisoners, removed the buttons from the uniforms of the American deserters at the Citadel (many of whom remained in Mexico, some begging on the streets to survive), and freed the rest.

See also Scott, Winfield

References

K. Jack Bauer, *The Mexican War 1846–1848* (New York: Macmillan, 1974).

John S.D. Eisenhower, *So Far From God: The U.S. War with Mexico 1846–1848* (New York: Random House, 1989).

George Wilkins Kendall, *Dispatches from the Mexican War,* ed. Lawrence Delbert Cress (Norman: University of Oklahoma Press, 1999).

Robert Ryal Miller, *Shamrock and Sword: The Saint Patrick's Battalion in the U.S.-Mexican War* (Norman: University of Oklahoma Press, 1989).

———, ed., *The Mexican War Journal and Letters of Ralph W. Kirkham* (College Station: Texas A&M University Press, 1991).

Peter F. Stevens, *The Rogue's March: John Riley and the St. Patrick's Battalion* (Washington, DC: Brassey's, 1999).

—*Elizabeth D. Schafer*

MEYER, KURT (1910–1961)

Kurt Meyer was a German officer who was tried and convicted of the murder of Canadian POWs during World War II. The son of a German World War I veteran, Meyer joined the Nazi party in the 1920s and in 1931 became a member of the SS (*Schutzstaffeln*). His career in the SS was meteoric, and he steadily rose through the officer ranks. By mid-1944, Kurt Meyer had become a highly decorated veteran and commander of the 12th SS Panzer (Hitler Youth) Division of the Waffen-SS.

Between 7 and 18 June 1944, while Meyer was still a regimental commander in the 12th Division, elements of his unit captured dozens of Canadian soldiers. A number of these prisoners were taken to Meyer's headquarters, where they were executed. In September 1944, Meyer was captured by Allied forces, and in December 1945 he went on trial, accused of being

Kurt Meyer (center, without hat) faces a Canadian military court in December 1945 (National Archives of Canada PA 41890)

responsible for the executions of 48 Canadian POWs. Although acquitted on two of the charges brought against him, Meyer was convicted on three others; he was deemed to have borne ultimate responsibility for the crimes and was sentenced to death. The sentence was later commuted to life imprisonment and he was transferred to Canada for incarceration. In 1951 Meyer was returned to West Germany to reside in a German prison, from which he was released in 1954. He published a popular memoir of his military career and spent his remaining years as a salesman for a brewery; ironically, one of his clients was a Canadian military base. In 1961 he died of a stroke.

Meyer's case raised the interesting issue of the degree of a commander's responsibility for his men's actions. The court, in the end, felt that it was impossible for Meyer not to have known of the killings when they occurred, and so he bore some responsibility for them. It has been suggested, though, that part of the reason for the commutation of his death sentence lay in the fact that some Canadian officers did not wish to hold a commander totally responsible for what his men did, fearing the consequences for Canadian commanders if it turned out that some German prisoners had been killed by their Canadian captors. Whatever the reason for this commutation, Meyer's conviction and sentence helped mark both the Canadian and the German boundaries for the treatment of POWs.

See also Malmédy Massacre; Le Paradis Massacre; Peiper, Joachim; Wormhout Massacre

References
Tony Foster, *Meeting of Generals* (Toronto: Methuen, 1986).
B.J.S. Macdonald, *The Trial of Kurt Meyer* (Toronto: Clarke, Irwin, 1954).
Howard Margolian, *Conduct Unbecoming: The Story of the Murder of Canadian Prisoners of War in Normandy* (Toronto: University of Toronto Press, 1998).
Kurt Meyer, *Grenadiers,* trans. Michael Mende (Winnipeg: J. J. Fedorowicz, 1994).

—*Daniel German*

MI9

MI (military intelligence) 9 was a branch of the British War Office charged with assisting Allied servicemen in captivity during World War II. Created on 23 December 1939, the office originally dealt with captured enemy soldiers as well; those duties were transferred to a separate department in December 1941. This left MI9 with a wide range of responsibilities: communicating with prisoners of war using coded letters; smuggling maps, money, clothing, compasses, hacksaws, and other escape equipment into prison camps; training servicemen how to behave while in enemy hands and how to escape; and establishing escape lines to convey Allied prisoners to neutral territory. Agents from MI9 operated in Western Europe, the Pacific theater, and the Mediterranean, either cooperating with local resistance organizations or creating their own, sometimes in conjunction with the office's American counterpart, MIS-X. At the end of the war, MI9 estimated that some 23,000 British, Commonwealth, American, and European POWs had escaped from captivity and reached neutral territory. To be sure, not all of these individuals required or received MI9 aid. Nevertheless, in making available to prisoners the information, equipment, and networks to help them regain their freedom, MI9 played a significant role in the underground war in Europe and the Far East.

See also MIS-X

References
M.R.D. Foot, *Resistance* (London: Eyre Methuen, 1976).
Clayton Hutton, *Official Secret* (London: Max Parrish, 1960).

—*Jonathan F. Vance*

MIS-X

Part of the U.S. government's Military Intelligence Department, Military Intelligence Section X, or MIS-X, was created in October 1942 to assist members of the U.S. forces in evading capture and escaping from captivity. It eventually grew to include a number of subsections, which were responsible for conducting debriefing interviews of returned escapers and evaders, handling coded correspondence with POWs, recording the locations and characteristics of prison camps, training and briefing servicemen about what to do in case of capture, and distributing escape material to servicemen and prison camps. Another related office in the Military Intelligence Department dealt with the interrogation of enemy prisoners of war. In the European theater, MIS-X worked in close cooperation with its British equivalent, MI9, and in 1945 sent a team to Odessa to assist in the extrication of Western POWs who had been liberated by Soviet forces. However, its organization was late getting started in the Pacific theater. A Southwest Pacific Headquarters was established in Brisbane, Australia, in late 1943, and not until November 1944 was a Pacific Ocean Area Office opened. This delay was partly due to the realization that one of the most effective means of clandestine contact with POWs-letters and packages-could not be used because the Japanese generally refused to forward mail to their prisoners. Still, postwar estimates suggest that MIS-X was responsible for helping as many as 12,000 American escapers and evaders return to friendly lines; even if that figure is slightly exaggerated, it is still an impressive result.

See also MI9

References

M.R.D. Foot and J.M. Langley, *MI9: Escape and Evasion, 1939–1945* (London: Bodley Head, 1979).

Lloyd R. Shoemaker, *The Escape Factory: The Story of MIS-X* (New York: St. Martin's, 1990).

A.R. Witrich, *MIS-X: Top Secret* (Raleigh, NC: Pentland Press, 1997).

—*Jonathan F. Vance*

MIXED MEDICAL COMMISSIONS

International law in the twentieth century has provided for the repatriation of sick or wounded POWs to their home country, and it stipulates that Mixed Medical Commissions be created to determine which prisoners are eligible for release on these grounds.

Many thousands of POWs were repatriated on medical grounds during World War I, but the process for determining who was repatriable was notoriously capricious. The Hague Convention of 1907, which protected prisoners in World War I, did not provide for impartial commissions to examine eligible prisoners. Instead, this was covered by the agreements concluded between the belligerent governments. A July 1917 agreement between Britain and Germany, for example, stated that the first medical commission struck by each side should consist of three doctors from the detaining power and three from Switzerland; in the event of a tie vote, the senior Swiss doctor would have the deciding vote. However, the agreement also stated that subsequent commissions, which would visit each camp every three to four months, should only have two Swiss doctors and three from the detaining power. As a result, a number of the commissions examining British POWs in Germany were known to be erratic in their decisions; it was far from certain that a grievously wounded man would be passed for repatriation, or that a fit, lightly wounded man would be rejected.

This inconsistency was addressed in the 1929 Geneva Convention Relative to the Treatment of Prisoners of War, which stated that all commissions were to consist of three doctors: one to be appointed by the detaining power and the other two to be appointed by the International Committee of the Red Cross, in consultation with the Protecting Power, the neutral body responsible for monitoring the conditions of captivity (Article 69). One of the neutral doctors was to act as chair of the commission. The commission's decisions were arrived at by simple minority vote, and the detaining power was asked to effect the repatriation of the eligible prisoners. There were a number of ways a prisoner could arrange to come before the commission. He could be recommended by the medical officer of his camp, by another senior prisoner, or by his own government. There was also provision for a prisoner to present himself before a commission on his own initiative (Article 70).

During the course of the examination by the commission, the prisoner was entitled to be accompanied by his own medical officer and another senior prisoner if he so desired. The conditions that justified repatriation were laid out in the Geneva Convention: loss of a limb, paralysis, other wounds that would render the prisoner an invalid for at least a year, tuberculosis, emphysema, cardiovascular and gastrointestinal disorders, nephritis, cystitis, neurasthenia, epilepsy, blindness, deafness, psychological disorders, poisoning, arthritis, rheumatism, cancer, malaria, chronic skin diseases, or avitaminosis. Self-inflicted wounds did not make the prisoner eligible for repatriation (although underlying psychological disorders could), nor did injuries or conditions that predated the outbreak of war. For example, Douglas Bader, the famed legless British fighter pilot, was never passed for repatriation by a mixed medical commission because he had lost his legs before the war.

Obviously, it was in the prisoner's best interests to make his claim as strong as possible. A Canadian officer with a badly injured arm, for example, was advised to hold his hand under ice-cold water before meeting the commission; after an hour's immersion, the hand was blue and shriveled, and the officer was approved for repatriation. Medical officers knew many other tricks that could make a patient appear more sick than he actually was. A brisk run before the examination would increase the heart rate, perhaps convincing the doctors that one was in cardiovascular distress. Tea leaves could be rubbed in the eyes, which would make them bloodshot and streaming. Some prisoners even tried substituting an infected friend's sputum or urine for their own, or feigning insanity to win a ticket home. Outright deception practiced by a healthy POW, however, was usually frowned on by their own medical officers for two reasons: should a fraudulent repatriate be discovered, it might jeopardize the entire exchange, and if any sort of quota was in operation, a fraudulent repatriate could be taking a place that should go to a genuinely sick prisoner.

See also Health; Repatriation

—*Jonathan F. Vance*

MLADIĆ, RATKO (1943–)

As leader of the Bosnian Serb Army during the war in Bosnia (1992–1995), General Ratko Mladić is among the few who have come to symbolize the Bosnian Serb campaign of "ethnic cleansing." Among his most infamous campaigns was the massacre of nearly 8 000 Bosnian Muslim males in the town of Srebrenica in July 1995. The Srebrenica massacre is considered to be Europe's worst atrocity since WWII.

Mladić was born on March 12, 1943 during WWII, a tumultuous period in the history of his native Yugoslavia. He was born in the Bosnian village of Kalinovik that was then a part of the Nazi Independent State of Croatia which was created in 1941 following the German and Italian invasion and dismemberment of Yugoslavia. After the Nazi defeat and establishment of communist Yugoslavia in 1945, the adult Mladić went on to become a regular officer of the Yugoslav People's Army.

When nationalist independence movements threatened the unity of Yugoslavia in 1991, Mladić was posted in Knin, Croatia to lead the Yugoslav Army's 9th Corps against local Croatian forces. The following year, Mladić assumed command of the Yugoslav Army's Second Military District, based in Sarajevo, Bosnia, then a constituent republic of Yugoslavia. In 1992, the pro-Yugoslav Bosnian Serb Assembly voted to establish the Bosnian Serb Army for which Mladić assumed command until late 1996.

It was during the 1990s war in Bosnia that the Commander led campaigns of terror and internment against Bosnians, civilian and military. Beginning in 1992, Mladić's Bosnian Serb forces besieged Sarajevo, shelling and terrorizing the civilian population from the hillside surrounding the city. In order to establish Serb areas of control, Mladić's forces deported thousands of non-Serbs from areas in northwestern and eastern Bosnia. Some of these non-Serbs were either killed or detained in special internment facilities where they were physically and psychologically abused.

Mladić's most infamous act during the war was as the overseer of the execution of nearly 8,000 Bosnian Muslim males in the town of Srebrenica in eastern Bosnia in July 1995. Seeing the Srebrenica region as strategically important, Mladić and the Bosnian Serb Army advanced onto Srebrenica where tens of thousands of Bosnian Muslim civilian refugees, together with some of the Bosnian forces, had fled. After five days of shelling and rocket fire, Mladić's forces entered the town. They separated the men from the women, took the men out to neighbouring fields and rivers, and summarily executed them. Most were of military age, but occasionally boys and the elderly were also killed. Mass executions also took place for those thousands of men who had attempted to escape Srebrenica during the Serb advance. The mass executions followed an established pattern. The men were either bussed or taken by truck to empty schools or warehouses where they were detained for several hours. They were then taken to relatively isolated fields for execution. In order to minimize resistance, prisoners were often blindfolded, their hands tied behind their backs and their shoes removed. Once arriving at the execution sites, the prisoners were taken into smaller groups, lined up and shot. Thereafter, they were buried into mass graves.

Although Mladić has since been indicted by the International Criminal Tribunal for the Former Yugoslavia (ICTY) on various war crimes, including genocide, crimes against humanity and sniping campaigns against the civilians of Sarajevo, he is, as of 2005, still at large.

References

Christopher Bennett, *Yugoslavia's Bloody Collapse: Causes, Course and Consequences* (Washington Square, New York: New York University Press, 1995).

Ljiljana Bulatovic, *General Mladic* (Belgrade: Nova Evropa, 1996).

Norman Cigar and Paul Williams, *Indictment at the Hague* (New York: New York University Press, 2002).

James Gow, *The Serbian Project and Its Adversaries: A Strategy of War Crimes* (Ithaca: McGill-Queen's University Press, 2003).

Bianca Jagger, "The Betrayal of Srebrenica," *The European*, 25 September–1 October, 1995, pp. 14–19.

Carole Rogel, *The Breakup of Yugoslavia and the War in Bosnia* (Westport, Connecticut: Greenwood Press, 1998).

David Rohde, Endgame: *The Betrayal and Fall of Srebrenica, Europe's Worst Massacre Since World War II* (New York: Farrar, Straus and Giroux, 1997).

Laura Silber and Allan Little, *The Death of Yugoslavia* (London: Penguin Books, 1997).

—*Jelica Zdero*

MONGOLS

One of the most crucial events in human history was the Mongol onslaught on Eurasia in the Middle Ages. After having united the Mongol tribes in 1206, Chinggis (Genghis) Khan began his conquest of the known world. In only a few decades, from 1215 to 1241, Chinggis and his successors led Mongol armies that devastated northern China, Persia, Turkestan, the Caucasus, Russia, and Poland. Western, Chinese, and other Asian sources described the invaders as barbarians, more resembling beasts than human beings, who left behind pyramids of skulls in the towns they conquered.

Brutality was a characteristic of warriors' behavior in traditional nomadic cultures and in the rivalries among tribal clans. Moreover, it stemmed from a permanent struggle for survival against the harshness of nature in the steppes. Mugging, kidnapping, murder, and rape were all part and parcel of the "law of the steppes." Nor was there any difference between male and female behavior. Mongol women did command troops and, in taking prisoners, did not hesitate to resort to violence. Captives—soldiers and civilians - alike—were tortured and murdered, and women were frequently raped. In some cases, people preferred to commit suicide rather than face being captured. Brutality against prisoners could be expected if besieged towns did not give up their resistance or if occupied regions ventured uprisings. Revenge was also taken when Mongol emissaries were killed. For example in 1218, when Mohammed II, shah of Khwarazm, whose territory stretched from the Caucasus to the Aral Sea, robbed and massacred a Mongol caravan, Chinggis Khan took revenge by torturing and murdering captives.

Not all captives fared so badly. Women of the Mongol nobility often received war prisoners as a special reward and used them as servants in their households. Captives could also avoid torture or death by voluntarily submitting to slavery or buying their freedom by paying a tribute of money, gold, or furs. This option was often taken by captured noblemen and merchants; common people were seldom able to buy their way out of captivity. If the Mongols decided to execute captured noblemen, they did so in the manner that was reserved for royal personages: without bloodshed. The captives were buried alive under a floor of planks on which the Mongols held a feast to celebrate their victory over the enemy. Nor did the Mongol invaders force Christian and Islamic captives to renounce their faith; such prisoners generally considered their captivity to be divine punishment for their sins.

Due to a shortage of women and the prevalence of polygamy in nomadic society, military campaigns played a significant role in providing Mongol warriors with wives; for example, many of Chinggis Khan's wives were former captives. However, these "alien" wives were treated with a great deal of respect and enjoyed the same rights as the Mongol women. Also worth mentioning is the fate of children, who were often kidnapped as war booty. Captive children lived with Mongol families in the Mongol camps, were acculturated to nomadic traditions, and grew up like Mongol children; in this way, they became fully integrated into Mongol society.

When the first waves of devastation were over, the Mongols began to treat prisoners with more tolerance, although treason and attempted escape still brought heavy punishment (blinding or beheading) for a prisoner. Capturing people brought prestige to the Mongol warrior; captives were living "war booty" that enlarged the captor's own power. Such tolerance was essential because, over time, the Mongol empire came to depend on the skill and labor of prisoners taken in battle. Subjugated peoples were often used as auxiliary troops in Mongol campaigns, and traders and craftsmen were often kidnapped so that their skills could contribute to the economic prosperity of the Mongol empire. For example, the Mongols learned the technique for besieging fortifications from Chinese and Persian specialists they had captured. The Mongols also forced captured soldiers to practice espionage among the enemy troops. When the Caucasian city of Derbent refused to surrender, the Mongols promised to spare the town if they were given the services of 10 soldier guides to lead the way through the Caucasus Mountains. The Mongols warned the guides not to play any tricks and, with typical brutality, beheaded one of them to show what fate awaited the rest if they did not point out the right way.

The employment of captives in the Mongol economy was widespread and varied. Prisoners were enlisted, both voluntarily and by force, for enormous construction projects, including building towns, streets, and viaducts. Although the sources do not relate in any detail the living conditions endured by prisoners of the Mongols, it is known that captives built the capital of the Mongol empire in Karakorum and were employed as interpreters and educators at the khan's court. Sources reveal that, during the reign of Kublai Khan (1260–1294), the palace guards in occupied Beijing consisted of captured soldiers from faraway Russia. Captives could even hold the post of minister, general, or personal advisor. This reflected the rapid process of Mongol acculturation to the conquered cultures, particularly the more advanced sedentary civilizations like China and Persia. Moreover, the Mongols sold captives (especially those from occupied Turkey and the Caucasus) to the Italian republics or to Egypt as part of a slave trade that was both lucrative and widespread. Without captives, both civilian and military, the conquest and administration of such a vast empire in Eurasia would not have been possible.

See also Tamerlane

References

Thomas Allsen, *Mongol Imperialism: The Policies of the Grand Qan Möngke in China, Russia, and the Islamic Lands, 1251–1259* (Berkeley: University of California Press, 1987).

James Chambers, *The Devil's Horsemen: The Mongol Invasion of Europe* (London: Weidenfeld and Nicolson, 1979).

Leo de Hartog, *Genghis Khan, Conqueror of the World* (New York: I. B. Tauris, 1989).

David O. Morgan, *The Mongols* (Oxford: Blackwell, 1986).

—*Eva-Maria Stolberg*

Montesquieu, Charles-Louis De Secondat, Baron De La Brède Et De (1689–1755)

The French jurist, historian, and philosopher known as Montesquieu is often seen as the first figure of the French Enlightenment and the precursor of modern sociology. Influenced by John Locke's benevolent rationalism, Montesquieu's 1748 magnum opus *The Spirit of the Laws* consisted of a comparison between types of government. Interpreted as a muffled attack against absolutism, *The Spirit of the Laws* suggested that the most efficient form of governance was a rational, constitutional monarchy incorporating a balance between the executive, legislative, and judiciary powers.

Ostensibly disputing Hobbes and Spinoza while heralding Rousseau, Montesquieu saw war as a perverse consequence of despotism, recognizing at the same time the need of liberal societies to arm and defend themselves against aggressive neighbors. He argued that a republic should do well to keep its soldiers away from political offices and conversely believed despots to be natural military leaders. He specified that, should such a tyrant be captured in combat, he be considered dead and replaced, lest the state collapse. Cunningly critiquing ancient laws to better comment on contemporary practices and issues, he refuted the theory that prisoners of war are mere slaves. While in antiquity prisoners could choose servitude over death, modern-day warfare demanded of prisoners simply that they no longer be in a position to harm victors. Considering parole and ransom as practical (i.e., economical) alternatives to the mistreatment of prisoners, Montesquieu was also one of the first cultural relativists to condemn overtly the practice of race-based slavery.

References

Louis Althusser, *Montesquieu, Rousseau, Marx: Politics and History* (London: Verso, 1982).

Melvin Richter, *The Political Theory of Montesquieu* (Cambridge: Cambridge University Press, 1977).

—*Laurent Ditmann*

MORE, THOMAS (1478–1535)

The epitome of the English Humanist, Thomas More (Sir Thomas More after 1521) was among the most renowned jurists of his time. Initially a trusted advisor of King Henry VIII as diplomat (1510–1517), member of the Privy Council (1518–1534), and Lord Chancellor (1529–1534), he ran afoul of his sovereign due to his defense of Papal authority over the Crown. This stance cost him his life but earned him his beatification in 1935. More's major contribution to Renaissance philosophy and literature is his essay *Utopia* (1516), the description of an ideal regime predicated on reason and moderation. The essay has been interpreted as upholding religious toleration, free and generalized education, and common ownership of land. More, however, may have been inclined to satirize his country rather than advocate far-reaching reform. While war and its proper conduct were Renaissance obsessions, More did not address the issue in great detail. He saw the practice of war as economically detrimental to the well-regulated state. In keeping with the scholastic concept of just war, he suggested that war be waged only defensively. Thus war waged in the defense of Utopia's commercial rights would be just, as trade was the basis of Utopia's supremacy. War thus became an obligation if Utopian traders were killed or maimed. Again in the context of the just war, More stated explicitly that prisoners of war, including captured merchants, should in no way be treated as slaves, but should be returned to their original country at the end of hostilities.

References

Peter Ackroyd, *The Life of Thomas More* (New York: Nan A. Talese, 1998).

Russell Abbot Ames, *Citizen Thomas More and His Utopia* (Princeton, NJ: Princeton University Press, 1949).

Gerard Wegemer, *Thomas More on Statesmanship* (Washington, DC: Catholic University of America Press, 1996).

—*Laurent Ditmann*

MOZAMBICAN CIVIL WAR

Mineral-rich Mozambique, strategically located on Africa's southeast coast, was for centuries under Portuguese colonial rule. A Marxist-Leninist pro-independence group known as Frelimo (the Front for the Liberation of Mozambique) began an armed struggle in September 1964 and its efforts, combined with

Children in their teens were often kidnapped and forced to serve with rebel armies. The boy on the right was liberated in 2000 (Molly Bingham)

political instability in Portugal, brought Mozambique independence in June 1975. But the country's troubles were far from over. Frelimo agreed to shelter rebels fighting for independence of neighboring Rhodesia, and in March 1976 implemented United Nations sanctions against the country, which involved closing its borders to trade and cutting off Rhodesia's access to the sea. In response, the Rhodesian government agreed to assist Frelimo's rival for control of Mozambique, the anti-Marxist Renamo (the Mozambican National Resistance). Through the late 1970s, then, Mozambique was the target of two attacking forces: Renamo fighters operating in the country, and Rhodesian soldiers launching raids across the border on Mozambican villages and agricultural settlements. When the Rhodesian war ended and that country gained independence as Zimbabwe in 1980, South Africa took over the role of Renamo's supporter, supplying arms and personnel to aid the struggle against Frelimo. Despite a 1984 non-aggression pact between Mozambique and South Africa, Renamo operations continued to escalate until a cease-fire was reached in 1992, bringing to an end the country's long civil war. Now one of the world's poorest countries, Mozambique has held on to a fragile peace, with Frelimo in government and Renamo in the role of the discontented opposition.

Crimes against prisoners were a distinguishing feature of the conflict; a 1988 report compiled for the U.S. State Department concluded that Renamo was responsible for the lion's share, as much as 95 percent, of the war crimes committed against civilians. Massacres such as the one that occurred at Homoíne in July 1987, when Renamo fighters slaughtered 424 civilians, including many women and children, were relatively common, and Renamo's attempts to avoid responsibility were unconvincing. In the case of Homoíne, an American missionary who witnessed the attack interviewed survivors and confirmed that the deaths had not occurred in a clash between local militias and government forces, as Renamo had claimed. Sources estimate that, over the course of the war, Renamo was responsible for the deaths of up to 100,000 Mozambican civilians.

Renamo was also interested in taking Western hostages, the first being a British zoologist and several Portuguese citizens in 1981. However, the object was not to kill or ransom them, but to win public relations victories by releasing them in carefully choreographed media events. It seems unlikely that this tactic achieved anything for Renamo's cause.

Finally, Renamo itself could not have existed without prisoners, for the bulk of its army consisted of Mozambican peasants (including children) who had been abducted, sometimes in groups as large as 200, and taken away to military training camps. They were considered prisoners while they were undergoing training, and were often bound together to prevent them from escaping. They enjoyed more freedom once they were inducted into the army, but many of the reluctant soldiers simply took advantage of that freedom to escape. They would then be replaced by other abductees, in a cycle that continued as long as the civil war lasted.

See also Angolan Civil War

References

Africa Watch, *Conspicuous Destruction: War, Famine and the Reform Process in Mozambique* (New York: Human Rights Watch, 1992).

William Finnegan, *A Complicated War: The Harrowing of Mozambique* (Berkeley: University of California Press, 1992).

Robert Gersony, *Summary of Mozambican Refugee Accounts of Principally Conflict-Related Experience in Mozambique* (Washington: State Department, 1988).

William Minter, *Apartheid's Contras: An Inquiry Into the Roots of War in Angola and Mozambique* (New York: Zed Books, 1994).

—*Jonathan F. Vance*

MURMAN RAILWAY

During World War I, prisoners of the Central Powers built a railway under notoriously hard conditions through northern Russia's polar zone. The Tsarist government considered this line to be essential to its war effort, which in 1915 suffered a serious setback. After the blockade of Russia's Baltic and Black Sea harbors, only two ports remained for the shipment of war material and industrial equipment from Britain and the United States. The far eastern harbor of Vladivostok on the Pacific Ocean came into heavy use, as did Russia's oldest port, Arkhangelsk in the north. The latter, however, was blocked by pack ice for half the year during the long winter. The construction of a railway to the ice-free Murman coast, which had been discussed before the war, was given a hasty go-ahead in the summer of 1915. The line was to be completed by the end of 1916, using Finnish inhabitants, Russian draftees, and prisoners of war as a labor force. It would extend over 1,400 kilometers from Lake Ladoga in the south, along the western coast of the White Sea, and eventually through the Kola Peninsula. The area it crossed was scarcely populated and lacked almost all infrastructure, changing from barren tundra to rocky highlands, and from woodlands to huge marshes.

Due to poor organization and avitaminosis, most of the war captives working there in 1915 were stricken by scurvy and were replaced by new prisoners from Siberia in spring 1916. During the successful Russian summer offensive of 1916, tens of thousands more POWs were shipped to the Murman area. The majority of them were ethnic Germans and Hungarians; an order of the Russian headquarters of June 1916 had decreed that only Germans and Hungarians (mostly out of Austria-Hungary's multinational army) be used for the hard and unhealthy labor. At the climax of the construction work in the autumn of 1916, they composed some 80 percent of all captive laborers on the line. Their extreme hardship, which contravened all prewar agreements regarding the use of POWs as a labor force, became known to the Central Powers by the summer of 1916. Immediate plans for reprisals to force an end to the suffering of these captives were postponed by the German government until October 1916, when 500 captive Russian officers were interned in a marshland camp in northern Germany, to be treated as enlisted men. Russia retaliated against its captive German officers from mid-November, but after negotiations involving the Tsar and his cousin, the German emperor, mutual reprisals were suspended in mid-December, on two conditions: that the POWs be evacuated immediately from the now-completed railway, and that the Russian captives in the war zones occupied by the Central Powers be inspected by neutral welfare delegations. As many as 40,000 prisoners were evacuated from the Murman area in 1917, leaving some 6,000 engaged in various labors, including the running of the line.

Because Russia left the war after the October Revolution of 1917, the railway was not brought into regular service for the war effort. Since many of the scurvy-stricken prisoners did not perish at the construction sites, but died later in their new internment places, it is difficult to say how many of the 70,000 prisoners sent to the Murman area died. Estimates run as high as 25,000, making the Murman Railway one of the worst horrors of captivity in Russia during World War I.

See also Burma-Thailand (Death) Railway; Labor; World War I—Eastern Front

References

Alfred W.F. Knox, *With the Russian Army 1914–1917,* 2 vols. (New York: Arno Press, 1971 [1922]).

Reinhard Nachtigal, *Die Murmanbahn: Die Verkehrsanbindung eines kriegswichtigen Hafens und das Arbeitspotential der Kriegsgefangenen (1915 bis 1918)* (Grunbach, Germany: Verlag Bernhard Albert Greiner, 2001).

Norman Stone, *The Eastern Front, 1914–917* (London: Scribner, 1975).

—*Reinhard Nachtigal*

Music

The soothing quality of music has been recognized for centuries, and prisoners of war through the ages have found great consolation in it. Even before humanitarian organizations began shipping musical instruments to prison camps in the twentieth century, prisoners made their own instruments to entertain themselves and their fellow inmates. Even in the most brutal of camps, the human voice could give comfort and hope where there was little else.

Prisoners have spent many hours singing hymns, love songs, and patriotic pieces, accompanied by violins, fifes, and flutes. At the U.S. Civil War prison in Rock Island, Illinois, Private E. Purdee of the 7th Florida Infantry made and sold violins. Corporal William Wall of the 2nd Kentucky Cavalry wrote, "I take my fiddle and Dick Cooper, of Covington, who is a capital jig dancer, furnish amusement for our room for an hour or two." In a grim prison camp, much-loved music could transport a prisoner back home for a short time.

During the wars of the twentieth century, philanthropic organizations have been active in supplying POWs with musical instruments, scores and sheet music, and other related supplies. As a result, the quality of playing in some camps was very high. Khabarovsk camp in Siberia, which held Austro-Hungarians captured by the Russians in World War I, had two choirs and two orchestras; they held concerts and recitals and also played for the camp theater, which was the prisoners' pride and joy. Wakefield, a camp in England for interned German civilians in World War I, had an orchestra that gave two performances each week and would tour around the camp's three compounds so that all internees could enjoy the music. Camp Shelby in Mississippi, which held German POWs in World War II, enjoyed 23 musical performances in an eight-month period in 1944, ranging from a piano solo to a concert by the 35-man camp orchestra, which played to an audience of 1,200 in the camp's amphitheater. In February 1944, the prisoners of Oflag 7B in Germany held

Bands made up of POWs were common in World War II prison camps. This one was in a camp in Germany (Jonathan F. Vance)

a two-week music festival that included 33 performances by 120 musicians and singers, and a total audience of over 6,000.

POWs have also found that music is a way of engaging in covert psychological warfare. Union prisoners in Andersonville camp in Georgia during the U.S. Civil War would sing patriotic songs, in the full knowledge that they irritated their Confederate guards. In Stalag Luft 3 in eastern Germany, a labor detachment often marched by the camp, lustily singing German martial songs. Not to be outdone, the prisoners' choir stationed themselves near the wire every day and serenaded them with "Hi Ho, Hi Ho, It's Off to Work We Go." After a few days, the labor battalion found a new route to its destination.

The most poignant accounts of music's ability to brighten the darkest hell come from the concentration camps of Nazi Germany. In Buchenwald, the French violinist Maurice Hewitt led a string quartet, and in Flossenbürg, Czech violinist Zdeněk Kolářský (former teacher at the Prague Conservatory of Music) performed Beethoven sonatas. Gleiwitz I, a subcamp of Auschwitz, had a small orchestra that played classical music. Terezín, the transit camp for Czech Jews facing deportation, had an even more vibrant music scene. Over two dozen prominent Czech and European musicians, composers, and conductors were interned there, and they produced and performed original compositions for piano, cello, string quartet, chorus, viola, and clarinet, as well as a full opera. Even in Auschwitz, music provided some solace. Under conductor Alma Rosé (a niece of Gustav Mahler), 41 women of varying musical abilities performed anywhere and anytime their guards wanted them to. They played together until November 1944, when the SS broke up the orchestra. Some of the women survived the war; others were not so lucky.

References
Josef Bor, *The Terezín Requiem* (New York: Alfred A. Knopf, 1963).
Fania Fénelon and Marcelle Routier, *Playing for Time,* trans. Judith Landry (New York: Atheneum, 1977).
Gerald Green, *The Artists of Terezín* (New York: Hawthorne Books, 1969).
Joža Karas, *Music in Terezín,* 1941–1945 (New York: Beaufort Books, 1985).
Bell I. Wiley, *The Life of Billy Yank, the Common Soldier of the Union* (Indianapolis: Bobbs-Merrill, 1952).
———, *The Life of Johnny Reb, the Common Soldier of the Confederacy* (Indianapolis: Bobbs-Merrill, 1943).

—*Elizabeth D. Schafer*

MUSSOLINI, BENITO (1883–1945)

Benito Mussolini, known as *il Duce,* founded Italian fascism and led Italy from 1922 to 1943. He was born on 29 July 1883 in the foothills of the Romagnole Apennines, and his father and grandfather were both peasants who spent time in prison for their socialist sympathies. Mussolini's earliest political leanings, as activist and journalist, mirrored theirs; in 1911, for example, he was imprisoned for opposing Italy's war in Libya. World War I initiated a major shift in Mussolini's ideology away from socialism and increasingly to the nationalist right. He favored Italian involvement and when he expressed as much in *Avanti!*, which he edited and which was the mouthpiece of the Italian Socialist Party, he was expelled from the Party. In 1915 Mussolini was called up to serve his country and did so with little distinction. In 1919 he founded the *Fasci Italiani di Combattimento.* The new movement's ideology was ill-defined but its call for action and its use of terror appealed to many. He was legally made prime minister in October 1922 by King Vittorio Emanuele III in response to his threat to march on Rome. Four short years later, all opposition parties, newspapers, and independent political activity were banned.

In the 1930s, Mussolini embarked upon an expansionist agenda, leading Italy into a war against Abyssinia (1935–1936) and actively intervening in the Spanish Civil War (1936–1939) on General Francisco Franco's side. He threw in his lot with Adolf Hitler and signed the Pact of Steel in 1936. Mussolini brought Italy into World War II in 1940. Following the Allied invasion of Sicily in July 1943, the Fascist Grand Council, frustrated with a series of Italian defeats, deposed him. The king imprisoned Mussolini first on the island of Ponza, then at the naval base at La Maddalena off Sardinia, and finally at the *Campo Imperatore,* a ski resort on the Gran Sasso Mountain. Mussolini's health, already in decline prior to his arrest, continued to deteriorate in prison. On 12 September 1943, Mussolini was rescued from his mountaintop exile by an SS glider team. For the next two years he ruled the Nazi-puppet Salò Republic in Northern Italy. Near war's end, he was captured, along with his mistress, by partisans while trying to escape to Switzerland. He was summarily executed and hung by his heels in Milan's Piazza Loreto on 28 April 1945.

References
R.J.B. Bosworth, *Mussolini* (London: Arnold, 2002).
Denis Mack Smith, *Mussolini* (New York: Knopf, 1982).

—*J. Peters Mersereau* and *Nathan Andrew Wilson*

MUTILATION

The practice of systematically mutilating prisoners, either to prevent them from returning to combat or as a means of psychological warfare, has a long pedigree stretching back thousands of years. It should be distinguished from casual abuse in that it follows a set pattern and is sometimes ritualistic.

At Medinet-Habu in Egypt, there is a relief sculpture of Egyptian soldiers amputating the hands or penises of their captured enemies. A scribe counted the body parts as they were removed so a record could be kept of the scale of the victory. The scalping of prisoners, which was a prominent feature of wars between Europeans and Amerindians in North America, should be seen in a similar light. The number of scalps taken by a warrior was an indication of his military prowess. An example from Mesoamerica may be similar in nature. In a campaign against Xochomilco, the Aztec king Ilzcoatl ordered that one ear be cut from each captive, although it is not clear if this was for accounting or ritual purposes.

Of a different order was the action of Byzantine Emperor Basil II, who ordered that 99 out of every 100 Bulgar prisoners he captured at the Battle of Cimbalongus in 1014 be blinded. Each one hundredth man was left with one eye. This barbaric tactic was clearly designed to cow his enemy, and in this regard it succeeded completely; the Bulgar Tsar Samuel dropped dead when confronted with his horribly mutilated soldiers.

Italian soldiers who were defeated at the Battle of Adowa in 1896 were also mutilated. Some 1,865 Italians were captured during the battle, and 30 of them had their genitals removed, according to the custom in Abyssinian warfare, and were returned to Italy emasculated. This was apparently done against the wishes of the Abyssinian leader, Menelik, who did however order that captured Ascari warriors (African allies of Italy) be released after their right hands and left feet had been amputated.

See also Torture

References

G.F.-H. Berkeley, *The Campaign of Adowa and the Rise of Menelik* (New York: Negro Universities Press, 1969 [1902]).

J. Bitschai and M. Leopold Brodny, *A History of Urology in Egypt* (Cambridge, MA: Riverside Press, 1956).

—Jonathan F. Vance

My Lai Massacre

The mass murder of 504 South Vietnamese civilians in the village of Son My by a company of American soldiers in March 1968 represents one of the worst atrocities committed by United States military personnel during the Vietnam War. Situated in Quang Ngai Province, Son My comprises a number of smaller hamlets including My Lai 4. This area was considered to have been a long-established political and military stronghold for the National Liberation Front (NLF).

On 16 March 1968, Charlie Company, 1st Battalion, 20th Infantry, 11th Infantry Brigade (Light) of the 23rd (American) Division descended upon Son My in order to locate and destroy main-force combat units of the 48th Local Force Battalion of the People's Liberation Armed Forces, which was believed to be regrouping in the hills to the north and northwest of the village. The previous day, the company had been informed by its commanding officer, Captain Ernest L. Medina, that the operation had been scheduled to occur at a time when all civilians would be away at the market. While Captain Medina never explicitly ordered the slaughter of women and children, he nevertheless left his troops with the distinct impression that this would be the opportunity for the company to exact revenge for those who had been killed or wounded, and no one was to be spared.

At 8:00 a.m., Charlie Company's 1st Platoon, commanded by Lieutenant William L. Calley, led the assault on My Lai 4, along with the 2nd Platoon. Believing that he was following the orders of Medina, Calley had the hamlet's unarmed civilians systematically rounded up and gunned down. Over the next four hours, the American troops raped, brutalized, and executed My Lai's old men, women, and children, including infants and the bedridden.

In the midst of the slaughter, Warrant Officer Hugh C. Thompson, Jr., a helicopter pilot in a unit assigned to cover the ground assault on the village, became aware that unarmed civilians were being indiscriminately murdered. In an effort to intervene, he landed his helicopter, had his crewmen train their weapons on the men of Charlie

Company, and attempted to rescue as many of the villagers that he could. Upon returning from the mission he immediately filed a formal complaint. The complaint was not investigated by brigade or division headquarters. Instead, the incident was covered up and reported officially as the "battle" of My Lai, listing 128 enemies killed with only three weapons recovered.

On 29 March 1969 Ron Ridenhour, a Vietnam veteran who was neither a member of Charlie Company nor involved in the massacre, wrote to several members of Congress about what he had heard while serving in Vietnam the previous year. Some members of Charlie Company had confided in Ridenhour of their involvement in the incident. Ridenhour's letter resulted in a preliminary investigation by the army which led to the filing of court-martial charges against William Calley in September 1969 alleging his responsibility for the deaths of 109 civilians at My Lai. The story broke in mid-November and gathered widespread attention when the 5 December 1969 issue of *Life* magazine printed a series of grisly color photographs of the massacre taken by Ron Haeberle, a journalist who had been accompanying Charlie Company on the operation.

The Army Chief of Staff, former commander of American forces in Vietnam, General William C. Westmoreland, created a special investigation panel headed by Lieutenant General William R. Peers to investigate whether or not the atrocity had been covered up by the military. The Peers report, which was released on 14 March 1970, called for the indictment of 28 officers for their involvement in the cover-up. Twelve officers were accused of covering up the incident, but only one stood trial, and he was later acquitted when several witnesses failed to recall the events about which they were being questioned. Only 13 members of Charlie Company, including Captain Medina, were charged with murder; all were acquitted or had the charges dropped except for Calley, who on 19 March 1971 was found guilty by a military court of six officers of the premeditated murder of at least 22 South Vietnamese civilians.

Calley was initially sentenced to life imprisonment at hard labor at the military prison at Fort Benning. President Richard M. Nixon, responding to public criticism of the fact that only Calley was being made the scapegoat of the crime, transferred Calley from the stockade to house arrest four and a half months later. He was eventually paroled on 9 November 1974.

See also Vietnam War

References

David L. Anderson, ed., *Facing My Lai: Moving Beyond the Massacre* (Lawrence: University Press of Kansas, 1998).

Michael Bilton and Kevin Sim, *Four Hours in My Lai: A War Crime and Its Aftermath* (New York: Viking, 1992).

Richard Hammer, *One Morning in the War: The Tragedy at Son My* (New York: Coward-McCann, 1970).

Seymour M. Hersh, *Cover-Up: The Army's Secret Investigation of the Massacre at My Lai 4* (New York: Random House, 1972).

——, *My Lai 4: A Report on the Massacre and Its Aftermath* (New York: Random House, 1970).

James S. Olson and Randy Roberts, eds., *My Lai: A Brief History with Documents* (Boston: Bedford Books, 1998).

Lieut.-Gen. W.R. Peers, *The My Lai Inquiry* (New York: W.W. Norton, 1979).

—*Geoffrey C. Stewart*

N

Nanking Massacre

The Nanking Massacre (also known as the Rape of Nanking) is considered one of the worst Japanese atrocities of the Sino-Japanese War (1937–1945). Japanese troops entered the Chinese capital of Nanking on 13 December 1937 and order was not restored until March 1938. During the initial weeks of Japanese occupation, there was widespread looting, mass killings of captives and civilians, and thousands of rapes. Statistics for deaths of POWs and civilians and rapes committed by the Japanese forces during the Nanking Massacre are still imprecise, but the significance of the event lies in the scale of the atrocities and the barbaric methods of execution. Nonetheless, estimates of 200,000 POW and civilian deaths are regarded as reasonable. Tabulating rapes presents a greater difficulty; the conservative minimum figure of 20,000 (to a higher estimate of 80,000) provides an indication of the scale of the Nanking Massacre.

In early December 1937, as Japan's Kwantung Army captured towns near Nanking, Generalissimo Chiang Kai-shek, under the local command of General Tang Sheng-shi of the Nanking Defense Force, evacuated most of his troops from the city. They left the 36th Division to provide cover for the Chinese army as it crossed the Yangtze River. About 50,000 troops were left to defend the city of as many as 500,000 people. On the morning of 13 December, after a brief but stiff resistance of five days, Japanese troops entered the walled city. Many Chinese soldiers laid down their arms and surrendered, while others attempted to flee.

The Japanese Imperial Headquarters ordered its army to take no prisoners. Beyond that, troops under the leadership of General Matsui Iwane and Prince Asaka were left to their own devices. POWs were rounded up and bound with their hands behind their backs. Many Chinese soldiers reportedly removed their uniforms to avoid capture, but the Japanese held all men of military age captive. On the first day alone, approximately 30,000 POWs and fleeing soldiers were killed. Orders to make the city safe for the arrival of Prince Asaka during a triumphal parade on 17 December resulted in more mass killings.

The Japanese forces used various methods of execution. Machine-gunning prisoners was the preferred method for executing hundreds or thousands of captives in a short period. In one incident near Mufu Mountain in mid-December, Japanese soldiers bound prisoners and led them to the banks of the Yangtze River. The prisoners were lined up for a few hours before realizing the Japanese had set up machine guns. The slaughter took an hour and many bodies were dumped in the Yangtze, but, as not all bodies could be disposed of in the river, the remaining corpses were doused with gasoline and set on fire. Figures for this particular massacre range from 15,000 to 57,400, depending on whether civilians are included in the tally.

Japanese troops devised barbarous and cruel punishments to execute their captives. Chinese POWs were burned alive in holding pens constructed with barbed wire around the perimeter to prevent escape; hundreds of prisoners at a time were executed in this fashion. In another form of execution, pits were dug and POWs were buried alive, sometimes with only their heads above ground to inflict a slow and tortuous death.

Chinese POWs were also used for training and entertainment purposes. Ostensibly to toughen new recruits for battle, soldiers bayoneted POWs who had been tied to posts. Bayoneting was often done poorly, wounding rather than killing, thus prolonging the victim's misery. Beheading was a common form of execution used both as training and entertainment. This method of execution was considered part of the *bushido* (way of the warrior) code, albeit a corrupted form of this traditional *samurai* ideal. POWs were forced to kneel with their hands tied behind their backs as other soldiers looked on and cheered on the executioner. The entertainment value reached a peak with the "100-man killing contest." Two sub-lieutenants, Toshiaki Mukai and Takeshi Noda, held a contest to see who would be the first to behead 100 Chinese POWs. This contest was famously covered in the *Tokyo Nichi Nichi Shimbun* after both had surpassed the 100-man mark. There were other instances of the Japanese executing POWs in games and training exercises, such as soldiers comparing the effectiveness of Chinese and Japanese rifles, with a blindfolded POW as the target.

Amidst the orgy of killing and looting of the Nanking residents' possessions, Japanese officers and troops committed tens of thousands of rapes. Girls as young as 10 and elderly women over 70 were victimized. They were often abducted in broad daylight and raped in front of their own family, or were taken away as sex slaves. Sex slaves received exceptionally harsh treatment as they were raped repeatedly in the same day, for days and weeks on end. To avoid possible senior officers' retribution (which never materialized), Japanese troops frequently killed their rape victims.

There is no single accepted cause for the widespread killings and rapes. Before entering Nanking, the Japanese Army had already killed POWs in Shanghai. However, possible reasons why events in Nanking escalated to wholesale slaughter include the breakdown of tight discipline, racial hatred, a desire to seek revenge against a spirited enemy, and the celebratory mood that accompanied the capture of the capital. These reasons, coupled with the Headquarters' "take no prisoners" order, likely triggered the massacre.

As the Nanking Massacre unfolded, it was reported in the world's newspapers, including journalists' first-hand accounts in the *New York Times*. Testimony concerning the massacre was later provided at the International Military Tribunal for the Far East (IMTFE) by survivors and foreign residents of Nanking, including Rev. John Magee and John Rabe, a Nazi who set up the Nanking International Safety Zone for refugees. In recent years, some former Japanese soldiers have confessed to their participation in the massacre. Most significantly, Prince Mikasa (1915–), Emperor Hirohito's younger brother and a witness to the massacre, decried the Japanese Army's conduct against the Chinese. He published a damning indictment of the military's policy in China during the war, entitled *Reflections as a Japanese on the Sino-Japanese War* (1943), which was suppressed and all copies supposed destroyed by the military. However, in 1994, one copy of this document resurfaced.

The Nanking Massacre remains a sore point between the two nations. The Chinese government claims the Japanese government has failed to offer sincere apologies and compensation for events in Nanking, one major atrocity among many others committed during the Sino-Japanese War. While the Japanese government delivers the occasional expression of "regret" over Japanese wartime actions in China (not just the Nanking Massacre), some influential members of Japanese society deny the severity, or even the existence, of the massacre. They believe the IMTFE handed "victor's justice" to General Matsui and Foreign Minister Hirota Koki, the two leaders held primarily responsible for the Nanking Massacre, and thus refuse to accept the scale of the event. Every four years, most recently in 2005, Japan's Education Ministry approves history textbooks that airbrush out the Nanking Massacre from Japan's history or minimize the scale of the massacre by referring to it as the "Nanking Incident." The controversy is compounded by leading Japanese politicians' denial of the Nanking Massacre, most notably Tokyo Governor Ishihara Shintaro, whose high position lends a veneer of respectability to these politicians' extremist beliefs.

References

Timothy Brook, ed., *Documents on the Rape of Nanking* (Ann Arbor: University of Michigan Press, 1999).

Iris Chang, *The Rape of Nanking: The Forgotten Holocaust of World War II* (New York: Basic Books, 1997).

Joshua A. Fogel, ed., *The Nanking Massacre in History and Historiography* (Berkeley: University of California Press, 2000).

James Yin and Shi Young. *The Rape of Nanking: An Undeniable History in Photographs* (Chicago: Innovative Publishing Group, 1996).

—*Simon Nantais*

Napoleonic Wars (1799–1815)

Napoleon Bonaparte—known to his supporters and enemies as a man of destiny, the Corsican bandit, or simply as "Boney"—ruled France with an iron fist for over a decade, from 1799 until his final defeat in 1815. For better or worse, his imperial court became the central focus of European affairs, and through his military genius and tenacity he made France the leading power in Europe. Not only was Napoleon heir to the legacy of the French Revolution, but he also felt he was predestined to rule both France and Europe. From the year he became emperor at the age of 35, he oversaw every aspect of government, from waging war and making political appointments to supervising the writing of his Code Napoléon and administering the national treasury.

Napoleon and his political allies seized power from the Directory government on 9–10 November 1799 (18–19 Brumaire). The collapse of the bourgeois Directory, coupled with the creation of the new Consulate government, effectively brought the French Revolution to an end. After a short period of consolidation, Napoleon's rejuvenated army defeated Austria and forced the Hapsburg government to sue for peace, officially bringing the French Revolutionary Wars to a close. Napoleon subsequently completed his skillful climb to power by crowning himself emperor of the French in May 1804.

The frequent wars of the Napoleonic period forced both the French and their enemies to turn to mass conscription to fill the ranks of their armies. With unprecedented numbers of troops fighting in untold battles across Europe, it became necessary to imprison captured troops in massive prison camps and offshore hulks for eventual exchange. In practice, captive officers were treated well and exchanged or paroled in the countries that captured them; the British settled into a gambling colony at Verdun and the French at British spas, giving language and etiquette lessons. While individual officers might be exchanged for their captured counterparts, repeated efforts at large-scale swaps fell through because of the mutual distrust between France and her enemies. Prisoner exchanges required a tremendous amount of negotiation and coordination between the involved parties. For example, Marshal Nicolas-Jean de Dieu Soult and Arthur Wellesley, the first Duke of Wellington, spent much of 1813 haggling over the exchange rate for three Frenchmen: Must it be three Englishmen or could it be one Englishman and two Spaniards? With this type of negotiation commonplace, it is not surprising that until the end of hostilities, most officers were simply paroled in the country that captured them.

Unfortunately, the captured troops of the Napoleonic Wars did not enjoy the same comforts as their officers. The common soldier could, and usually did, suffer great hardships and abuse at the hands of his captor. The French and English were generally hard but correct in their treatment of prisoners; neither provided particularly elaborate accommodations, but everyone was regularly fed and received limited medical attention. Prisoners of Russia and Spain however, faired much worse. Officially, Russia followed the accepted rules governing the treatment of prisoners of war, but unofficially, the

The dormitory for British prisoners in the French fortress of Bitche during the Napoleonic Wars (from Seacome Ellison, Prison Scenes; and Narratives of Escape from France *[London, 1838])*

government provided no food, no shelter, and plenty of beatings. French prisoners reportedly received no medical care and were routinely beaten, robbed, and murdered by both Russian soldiers and peasants.

The poor treatment of prisoners of war, however, was not a uniquely Russian phenomenon. Of the 24,000 French troops captured in Spain in 1808, barely one man in ten survived. According to eyewitness accounts, these prisoners were routinely robbed, beaten, and murdered by their Spanish captors. Originally, they were held in large prisons on the mainland. Later, after sickness and deprivation had thinned their ranks, they were moved to prison hulks in Cádiz harbor. Most captives recognized the cramped and diseased prison ships as their last stop before death. On several occasions, the infamous hospital hulk *Argonaute* was without food for days at a time, the sick and dying prisoners gnawing on their shoes and packs in an effort to gain sustenance. In the later stages of the war, Spanish prisons began to overflow with French prisoners, leading the Spanish to simply abandon some 5,500 Frenchmen in the Balearic Islands. On the tiny island of Cabrera the men struggled with nightmarish conditions, as they were marooned without adequate water, shelter, or even tools to bury their dead. With the conclusion of hostilities in 1814, French ships picked up the surviving prisoners from the island. An observer reported that the remaining French soldiers numbered "approximately two thousand walking skeletons, naked and almost dehumanized, many of them crazed."

Following Napoleon's disastrous Russian campaign in 1812, the newly allied coalition of Austria, Great Britain, Portugal, Prussia, Russia, Spain, and Sweden began wearing down the remaining French armies. By 1814 allied armies were advancing into France, and despite continuing French resistance, Paris surrendered on 31 March 1814. A few days later, Napoleon surrendered and was exiled to the Mediterranean island of Elba. Growing restless in isolation, Napoleon escaped from Elba in 1815 and returned to reclaim his throne in France. With news of the emperor's return, the allied powers quickly created a new military coalition and mobilized for war against France. Napoleon's campaign was cut short—brought to an abrupt end by the climactic battle of Waterloo. The allied victory at Waterloo marked the ultimate defeat of France and definitively closed the Napoleonic Wars by exiling Napoleon to the South Atlantic Island of Saint Helena. He died there, the last prisoner of the Napoleonic Wars, in 1821.

See also Dartmoor; Exchange; French Revolution, Wars of the; Bonaparte, Napoleon

References

Edward Boys, *Narrative of a Captivity and Adventures in France and Flanders: Between the Years 1803 and 1809* (London: R. Long, 1827).

David Chandler, *The Campaigns of Napoleon* (New York: Macmillan, 1966).

Gavin Daly, "Napoleon's Lost Legions: French Prisoners of War in Britain, 1803–1814," *History* 89 (361–380).

Seacome Ellison, *Prison Scenes; and Narratives of Escape from France, during the Late War* (London: Whittaker and Co., 1838).

Michael Lewis, *Napoleon and His British Captives* (London: George Allen and Unwin, 1962).

Martyn Lyons, *Napoleon and the Legacy of the French Revolution* (New York: St. Martin'sPress, 1994).

Gunther Rothenberg, *The Art of Warfare in the Age of Napoleon* (Bloomington: University of Indiana Press, 1978).

Jack Sweetman, "A Floating Prison Break," *Naval History* 19 (2005): 46–51.

—*Christopher Blackburn*

NEUTRAL INTERNEES

In time of war, neutral nations have often served as havens for refugees fleeing from the battle zones. During the twentieth century, Holland, Switzerland, Sweden, Spain, and the Republic of Ireland all housed prisoners of war and civilian internees from the combatant powers, in conditions that varied tremendously.

During World War I, POWs benefited from a series of exchanges that allowed certain classes of prisoners to spend their captivity in neutral Holland or Switzerland, rather than in the prison camps of their enemies. Exchanges of seriously wounded French and German prisoners began in March 1915, but other classes of prisoners were excluded until August 1915, when the French government agreed that less seriously wounded POWs, while not released outright, could be placed in the care of neutral governments. In January 1916, the first such exchange occurred when 200 French and German tubercular cases were transferred to Switzerland. By the middle of February, over a thousand such prisoners had arrived. In May 1916, the British government struck a similar agreement with Germany, and British and Empire prisoners began arriving in Switzerland.

A major breakthrough came in May 1917, when the French and German governments agreed on a reciprocal release of prisoners who had been held captive for more than 18 months or who were over 55 years of age (for officers) or 48 years of age (for enlisted men). In June 1917, the British government concluded a similar agreement with Germany, with the added proviso that POWs of less than 18 months' standing could be lodged in a neutral country if they exhibited signs of a captivity neurosis known as barbed-wire disease. If their condition did not improve within three months, they would be eligible to be released to their home country. To make room for these internees, the Swiss government agreed to release all tubercular patients and any other men whose recovery was expected to be prolonged. The Dutch government agreed to intern up to 16,000 combatants, as long as the British and German governments refunded the costs involved.

The agreement was a real boon to the POWs. While in Switzerland and Holland, they enjoyed comparative freedom of movement and were visited by representatives of their own governments, who could arrange for relief supplies if necessary. In Switzerland, British and Empire prisoners were housed in numerous hotels and guest houses (paid for by the British government), and recreational and educational programs were available. In Holland, prisoners lived in a number of large seaside hotels, and enjoyed sight-seeing

This carpentry shop provided job training to British prisoners interned in Switzerland in World War I (from J. Harvey Douglas, Captured: Sixteen Months as a Prisoner of War *[Toronto, 1918])*

trips, cycling outings, and dinner parties. By the end of the war, many thousands of POWs from both sides had enjoyed a temporary sojourn in neutral countries: 67,726 in Switzerland, 13,000 in Holland, and 65,000 in Sweden.

No comparable agreement was reached during World War II, but many thousands of civilian and military prisoners were interned in neutral nations for a variety of reasons. The Republic of Ireland was temporary home to dozens of airmen of all nationalities who had crash-landed there, and the conditions were hardly arduous. The main camp was at Curragh, and Allied and Axis airmen were held in adjoining compounds separated by heavy barbed-wire. Many internees had their own bicycles and made weekly trips into Dublin; they kept pets, became engaged to local girls, and held memberships in nearby tennis clubs. This liberal treatment did not, however, prevent them from attempting to escape. On 9 February 1942, all but one of the 33 Allied airmen (the other airman was on parole at the time) tried to breach the camp fence using ladders and wire cutters. All were apprehended before they got over the last fence, but on 17 August 1942 there was another mass escape involving 16 airmen, who rushed the main gate when the guards were opening it to let some bicycles through. Most were quickly recaptured, but at least two were helped to reach Northern Ireland, where they rejoined British forces.

The internment policy was a sore point with the Irish government. There were thousands of Irish nationals serving in the British forces, and Irish Prime Minister Eamon de Valera realized that it was only a matter of time before his government would be forced to intern one of its own citizens. In 1943, the government decided to intern only those airmen who crashed while on operational flights; airmen who claimed they were on non-operational flights were not detained.

Despite much abuse of this provision (particularly by American aircrew), it was adhered to, and in September 1943, the Irish government decided to make it retroactive: when the internees were transferred to a new camp at Gormanstown, any who had crashed while on non-operational flights were released. Thereafter, the internment policy was slowly loosened further, so that in June 1944 the last of the Allied internees were released.

Switzerland housed almost 300,000 military and civilian refugees during World War II. The civilian contingent was for the most part fleeing fascist persecution. Military internees were housed in camps and civilian houses and subject to military conventions. However, Swiss authorities quickly determined that civilian refugees should not be covered by these rules under war conditions and would have to earn their keep; this requirement was in line with public work required of Swiss civilians to help the war economy. It was also in response to a dual concern, on the one hand a desire for tighter political control, and on the other hand concern for the strain that Swiss refugee organizations were experiencing in border registration camps early in the war. The official creation of work camps stems from a 12 March 1940 decree of the Federal Council (the seven-member executive power in Switzerland); the first of 10 work camp was opened in Felsberg (Canton Graubünden) on 4 April 1940. By war's end, there were 88 work camps under the control of a private organization called *Zentralleitung der Arbeitslager*. Women, children, and the elderly were not required to work and were housed in separate refugee houses throughout Switzerland. Conditions in these camps varied according to camp leaders, refugee groups, and war conditions. Federal authorities soon discovered that camp leaders, who were all army officers, had no experience in dealing with civilians who had suffered persecution, and several camps acquired a notorious reputation. Some camp leaders eventually adjusted their expectations of civilians and succeeded in maintaining stability within and outside of their camps, while others, affected by anti-Semitism and xenophobia, mistreated internees, threatening some with deportation from Switzerland. In some cases, internees were sent back to their country of origin, but such cases were rare; this kind of repatriation required authorization by federal authorities and could not be ordered by the camp commander. There is no evidence that Jews were sent back once they had been brought into Swiss work camps. Generally, refugees who worked in these camps experienced a strict military regimen, but it was not violent and outings and correspondence were authorized and limited salaries were paid out. The total number of refugees in these work camps never exceeded 4,000 (in 1944 and 1945) out of an average of 25,000 civilian internees.

The government of neutral Sweden also found itself detaining thousands of combatants. In September 1939, three Polish submarines with some 180 men came to Sweden, where the crews were interned for the rest of the war. On 17 April 1940, some 5,700 Norwegians fled from advancing Germans. Roughly 3,000 of them stayed in Sweden and, together with 3,300 Danish internees and civilian refugees, began in 1943 to form "police-brigades," armed and trained by Swedish authorities. During 1940, some 500 other foreign servicemen were interned in Sweden, including British and French from the failed Norwegian campaign of 1940, Germans, and Poles. Most of them were sent home before 1941. The outbreak of the German-Soviet war in 1941 saw the arrival of 180 Russian sailors, while the number of British and, from 1942, American air crews in Sweden grew steadily. Polish, Soviet, and Yugoslav POWs who had escaped from German work camps in Norway were also interned in Sweden. Most internees were not detained for long periods; in 1944, 975 British and Americans were released, together with some Germans, Soviets, and Poles. In May 1945, a large number of Germans (as well as Estonians and Latvians who had served in German units) came to Sweden from Norway and Courland. In late 1945 and early 1946, 3,000 German and 146 Baltic internees were repatriated to the Soviet zone; other Germans were sent to the British sector in Germany.

Treatment of the internees in Sweden varied enormously. The German camps were strictly controlled throughout the war, as were the Soviet camps, which were often ruled by Soviet political commissars. In contrast, American and British Commonwealth internees were allowed frequent contact with local civilians and could choose their own accommodation outside the camp, at the Swedish government's expense. Even the largest internment camp was a prison in name only, since the hinges of the main gate were rusted off and the guards' rifles had brass caps welded over the muzzles to keep the rain out. By the same token, the Danish and Norwegian camps were in reality military training camps, not internment facilities.

The tables were turned somewhat in Spain, officially neutral but sympathetic to Nazi Germany. Allied airmen who crashed there, or escaping POWs who crossed the border from occupied France, found conditions to be similar to those encountered in German camps. Evaders or escapers who fell into the hands of the Spanish police could expect to be roughly treated: they would be searched and their valuables confiscated, interrogated at length as to their experiences, confined in tiny, dank cells, and issued little in the way of food. The lucky ones would shortly be brought to the attention of American or British consular officials; others might spend weeks or even months in Miranda de Ebro prison camp, a dismal compound that held refugees, political prisoners (mostly communists), evaders, and escaped POWs and slave laborers, before they could be rescued by their own government. In October 1941, there were some 600 prisoners in Miranda, including Poles, Belgians, Dutch, Czechs, Yugoslavs, French, Bulgarians, Hungarians, and Latin Americans. German officials visited the camp periodically to recruit workers to serve the Nazi state, but most declined. The British government also attempted to secure the freedom of sympathetic prisoners, even offering to supply visas to any French or Belgian prisoner who would claim he was Canadian. Prisoners willing to take part in this ruse were released from Miranda (and from a smaller camp at Palencia) at various times during the war.

References

Carl Geiser, *Prisoners of the Good Fight: The Spanish Civil War, 1936–1939* (Westport, CT: Lawrence Hill, 1986).

Wing Commander F. C. Griffiths, "Spanish Prisoners," *Blackwood's Magazine* 259 (1946): 1–18.

Alfred A. Häsler, *The Lifeboat Is Full: Switzerland and the Refugees, 1933–1945* (New York: Funk and Wagnall's, 1969).

Andre Lasserre, *Frontières et camps: Le refuge en Suisse de 1933 à 1945* (Lausanne, 1995).

Ralph Keefer, *Grounded in Eire: The Story of Two RAF Fliers Interned in Ireland during World War II* (Montreal: McGill-Queen's University Press, 2001).

Colonel H. A. Picot, *The British Interned in Switzerland* (London: Edward Arnold, 1919).

Bo Widfeldt, *The Luftwaffe in Sweden, 1939–1945* (Boylston, MA: Monogram Aviation Publishers, 1983).

—*Guillaume de Syon* and *Lars Ericson*

Neutral Nations Repatriation Commission

Established on 8 June 1953 during negotiations to end the Korean War, the Neutral Nations Repatriation Commission (NNRC) was a custodial body intended to ensure prisoners of war the right to freely accept or refuse repatriation to their original commands. Composed of member nations India, Sweden, Switzerland, Poland, and Czechoslovakia and under the command of Lieutenant-General K.S. Thimayya of India, the NNRC assumed control on 23 September 1953 of 23,000 POWs who had refused repatriation, including 23 Americans and 22,604 North Koreans and Chinese. These prisoners, known as "nonrepatriates," were hotly contested symbols of ideological illegitimacy in the Cold War struggle, and each combatant wanted to maximize the number of enemy prisoners who refused repatriation while minimizing "defectors" on its own side. Because each side suspected the other of coercion, they agreed to hand over all nonrepatriates to the NNRC for 90 days so that the prisoners could receive "explanations" from their original commands in the presence of neutral observers.

By the end of the explanation period, it was clear that the NNRC had failed to provide a neutral, noncoercive environment for the nonrepatriates. Explanations occurred on only 10 of the allotted 90 days, and only 3,224 of the 23,000 nonrepatriates ever appeared before the NNRC to express their wishes. The rest of the time was consumed in ceaseless maneuvering and mutual recrimination. Part of the problem was internal to the NNRC itself. The commission was neutral in name only, with Sweden and Switzerland favoring the UN position while Poland and Czechoslovakia consistently backed the Chinese and North Koreans. Only the Indian delegation made any genuine attempt at neutrality, and even it was overly dependent on the UN for logistical support. Above all, though, the NNRC was kept from succeeding by the warring parties, each more concerned with claiming a propaganda victory than ensuring the free expression of its own citizens being held captive. On 20 January 1954, the NNRC returned the remaining POWs to their detaining powers, and on 22 February 1954, it officially ceased to exist.

See also Forcible Repatriation; Korean War; Repatriation

References

Rosemary Foot, *A Substitute for Victory: The Politics of Peacemaking at the Korean Armistice Talks* (Ithaca, NY: Cornell University Press, 1990).

Kodendera Subayya Thimayya, *Experiment in Neutrality* (New Delhi: Vision Books, 1981).

United Nations, General Assembly, *The Korean Question: Report of the United Nations Command on the Operation of the Neutral Nations Repatriation Commission* (Eighth Session, Supplement No. 19, 1954).

—Michael J. Allen

NIGERIAN CIVIL WAR

See Biafran War

NONFORCIBLE REPATRIATION

See Forcible Repatriation

NORTHERN IRELAND

The 1972 Irish Republican Army (IRA) hunger strikes emanated out of a conflict over the status of terrorists in British prisons and changed the political context of the Troubles in Northern Ireland. The episodes demonstrated that Nationalist prisoners were willing to suffer for their cause rather than just inflicting suffering. The hunger strike began as a result of a change in the status of convicted terrorists from prisoners of war to common criminals.

In 1971, the British government began internment without trial. Internees were allowed to wear their own clothes, live in huts, segregate themselves according to paramilitary allegiance, and practice military drills; in short, they were treated in most respects like POWs. Convicted terrorists, on the other hand, were treated like common criminals, required to wear prison uniforms and confined to cells. In 1972, approximately 40 IRA prisoners launched a hunger strike for POW status. During the strike, the rumored death of a striker (the rumor was in fact false) caused widespread rioting, which prompted the British government to grant Special Category Status—essentially POW status—to the prisoners. Several years later, the British initiated a new strategy called criminalization, which phased out Special Category Status, thus removing the formal distinction between paramilitary prisoners and ordinary criminals. After 1 March 1976, convicted terrorists were criminals, not POWs. To Nationalist prisoners, Ireland's 800-year fight for freedom was being branded a crime.

The Irish prisoners were determined to regain their status as POWs, and a new battle began later in 1976, when prisoners refused to wear prison uniforms. These prisoners were confined to their cells, where they huddled naked on bare mattresses with only a blanket to cover them. By 1981 approximately 400 prisoners were involved in the "blanket protest," which evolved quickly into the "no wash protest." The prisoners, having no clothes, wore only a towel when going to the washroom. The wardens insisted that the towel be placed on a rack while washing, leaving the prisoner naked. A request for a second towel was refused and the prisoners boycotted washing. Wardens later prohibited trips to use the toilets unless prisoners wore their uniforms. Prisoners responded by throwing their waste out the windows. Wardens threw it back in. Later the windows were blocked, so prisoners smeared waste on the walls. As prisoners sat in their stinking cells, wrapped only in a blanket, they prepared their next strategy—the hunger strike.

The first hunger strike began in October 1979 when seven prisoners refused to eat until British authorities conceded five demands: the right to wear their own clothes and to refrain from prison work, free association with other prisoners, and organized recreation and leisure activity, including one letter, parcel, and visit per week. The strike ended when the government transferred a dying striker to the hospital. Believing that a colleague might die and aware that a document was on its way from London with enough concessions to form the basis for a settlement, the strike leadership ordered an end to the hunger strike. The document, however, was meaningless. The major concession was that prisoners did not have to wear uniforms but rather could wear the "civilian clothes" provided by the wardens; to the prisoners it amounted to the same thing. Betrayed and furious, they planned for a second strike almost immediately.

The second hunger strike started 1 March 1981, the fifth anniversary of the phasing out of Special Category Status. It lasted for 217 days and led to the deaths of 10 strikers, the first of whom was Bobby Sands. The impact of the 1981 strike on the Nationalist population in Ireland became clear when Sands was elected a Member of Parliament just 25 days before he died.

The irony of the whole affair was that prior to the deaths, the prisoners had won most of their demands, at least *de facto* if not *de jure*. The strike also had far-reaching consequences for Northern Ireland and proved to be a key turning point of the Troubles. The Republican movement achieved a propaganda victory over the British government and obtained a great deal of international sympathy. Support for the IRA's political wing, Sinn Féin, influenced the British government's signing of the Anglo-Irish Agreement in 1985.

See also Interrogation in Depth

References

David Beresford, *Ten Men Dead: The Story of the 1981 Irish Hunger Strike* (New York: Atlantic Monthly Press, 1989).

John Conroy, *Belfast Diary: War as a Way of Life* (Boston: Beacon Press, 1987).

Padraig O'Malley, *Biting at the Grave: The Irish Hunger Strikes and the Politics of Despair* (Boston: Beacon Press, 1990).

—*Craig T. Cobane*

Nuremberg Trials

The Bavarian city of Nuremberg, in southern Germany, first became associated with Adolf Hitler's National Socialist German Workers' Party in 1933, with the first meetings of the Nazi Party's annual congresses, which would continue through 1938. After World War II, it was chosen as the site for war crimes trials of the major Nazi leaders, many of whom were indicted in part for their involvement in atrocities against POWs and civilian internees.

Having been the cultural center of the German Renaissance in the fifteenth and sixteenth centuries, the city retained a medieval atmosphere, making it a suitable national shrine for the Nazi Party and its ideology of a return to the early glories of Germany. Not surprisingly, the city soon became the locus for the development of anti-Semitic propaganda. Jews were prohibited from legal professions and government service in 1933, and on 15 September 1935 at Nuremberg, the Nazis decreed that Jews were no longer citizens, could no longer serve in the armed forces, could not display Reich colors or the flag, and were forbidden to have marital or sexual relations with Gentiles. On 14 November, the so-called *Mischlinge* ("mixed blood") laws were passed, which identified criteria for genealogical racial identification of Aryans and non-Aryans. While these laws were supplemented at various times, the enforcement of the measures did not take full effect until after the 1936 Olympic Games hosted by Germany.

The atrocities committed by the Nazis had been publicized as early as 1942, and by 1944 the Allies (represented by British, Soviet, French, and American leaders) were discussing options for punishing offenders for their criminal actions in the war. Ultimately, they chose Nuremberg as the location for the International Military Tribunal, partly because of its symbolic connection with the Nazi movement and partly because its courthouse remained intact, despite the heavy Allied bombing of the city. Despite the knowledge that no effective trial mechanism had emerged after World War I, and amidst much disagreement over how to proceed and with what intensity, the tribnal opened its first full meeting at Nuremberg on 29 October 1945, with the trial to begin on 20 November 1945.

Although Adolf Hitler and Joseph Goebbels, among others, had committed suicide at the end of the war, the tribunal sought action against Hitler's SS, the Gestapo, the Reich Cabinet, and the German Armed Forces High Command on four counts: conspiracy, crimes against peace, war crimes, and crimes against humanity. Atrocities committed against prisoners of war and civilian internees were so prominent in the trial that virtually none of the major defendants were untouched by them. Among the incidents that figured in the proceedings were the operation of the concentration camps, the extermination of the Jewish population, the Commando Order, which decreed the execution of captured Allied commandos, even if they were captured while in uniform, the Commissar Order, which directed the execution of captured political leaders who had been attached to Red Army units, the execution of 50 Allied airmen after the escape from Stalag Luft 3 in March 1944, the systematic abuse of Soviet POWs, the treatment of captured partisans, and the use of POWs and civilian prisoners as slave labor.

Within one year, the trial's 403 sessions brought in 93 witnesses, interrogation documents from 143 more, and thousands of affidavits from across the world. From December 1946 to April 1949, 12 trials continued under the authority of the American forces. Many defendants were sentenced to hang or spend life in prison, a few were acquitted, and several thousand Nazi sympathizers remained in Europe after the war. The trials at Nuremberg have served as a historical marker for the punishment of war crimes, set legal precedents for future generations, and documented one of the most brutal periods of human history.

References

George Ginsburgs and V.N. Kudriavtsev, *The Nuremberg Trial and International Law* (Dordrecht: Martinus Nijhoff, 1990).

International Military Tribunal, *Trial of the Major War Criminals before the International Military Tribunal, Nuremberg, 14 November 1945–1 October 1946*, 42 vols. (Nuremberg: International Military Tribunal, 1947).

Michael R. Marrus, *The Nuremberg War Crimes Trial 1945–1946: A Documentary History* (Boston: Bedford Books, 1997).

Joseph E. Persico, *Nuremberg: Infamy on Trial* (New York: Viking, 1994).

Jacob Robinson and Henry Sachs, *The Holocaust: The Nuremberg Evidence* (Jerusalem: Yad Vashem, 1976).

Bradley F. Smith, *The Road to Nuremberg* (New York: Basic Books, 1981).

—Brad Lucas

Nurses

Nurses, both male and female, have tended sick and wounded soldiers in military conflicts since the earliest times, and they have been vulnerable to capture and imprisonment by enemy soldiers. Despite being considered noncombatants protected by international military protocol, some civilian and military nurses have been killed in service, punished for alleged war crimes, or held as prisoners of war.

Prior to the twentieth century, nurses were captured in both minor conflicts and major wars and were often expected to attend to enemy patients. However, newspaper accounts, diaries, and histories only briefly mention these nurse prisoners. Perhaps the first widely known nurse POW was Edith Cavell, a British woman who was accused of being a spy and executed by the Germans in World War I.

After Cavell's death, the largest groups of nurse war prisoners were seized in the Pacific theater during World War II. These prisoners' experiences were documented in magazine articles, books, plays, and movies, and they are probably the best known nurse prisoners of war. Immediately after the Japanese bombed Pearl Harbor, nurses stationed in Guam and the Philippines retreated with American troops to safer areas, where they tended to wounded soldiers while under enemy attack. Five Navy nurses were captured by the Japanese when Guam surrendered on 10 December 1941. They were held in Zentsuji Prison on Shikoku Island before being transferred to Kobe, where they remained until their release in August 1942. Other nurse prisoners were not as fortunate. Army nurses captured in the Philippines were kept at Santo Tomas Internment Camp until rescued in February 1945, and Navy nurses, also seized in the Philippines, remained in Los Baños Internment Camp through early 1945. These 99 nurses are considered to be the first U.S. military women held as prisoners of war.

American servicemen who survived the Bataan Death March called these nurses the "Angels of Bataan and Corregidor," and they dedicated a plaque in honor of their service in the Philippines. The women accompanied troops from their bases in Manila first to Bataan, where they established jungle hospitals to operate on casualties, then in the underground hospital in the rocky Malinta Tunnel of Corregidor, where they surrendered in 1942 to the Japanese when supplies dwindled. These nurses spent three years in prison camp, where they endured starvation and suffered from diseases like scurvy (caused by nutritional deficiencies) and malaria (transmitted by tropical parasites). They treated fellow prisoners in the camp hospitals, making medical tools and pharmaceuticals from scraps and plants as possible, and tried to boost morale among themselves and civilians. The nurse prisoners also smuggled out medicine hidden in fruit for delivery to male prisoners in nearby camps. War posters featured patriotic images of these nurse prisoners to encourage defense workers to increase war production. After liberation, the women continued to experience illnesses caused by their internment while they adjusted to peacetime life.

Thirty-two nurses from the Australian Army Nursing Service were also captured and imprisoned by the Japanese at Sumatra. They experienced deprivations and exhaustion similar to that experienced by the American nurse prisoners, and they also formed a supportive community in order to survive and sustain routine activities such as haircuts. The nurses suffered from dysentery, tooth decay, and muscle loss; after their repatriation, physical examinations led doctors to estimate that they had physically matured at least one decade more than the typical women their chronological age. Several of the women testified at the Australian War Crimes Board of Inquiry and the Tokyo War Trials, where the administrator of their camp was sentenced to prison.

Nurses were also imprisoned in the European theater. Sylvia M. Oiness wrote in the *American Journal of Nursing* about her five weeks of imprisonment aboard the German ship *Dresden* in the spring 1941.

She had been aboard an Egyptian medical relief vessel sunk by German naval units. Another captured nurse was Lieutenant Reba Whittle of the Army Nurse Corps, who was shot down by German aircraft while she was performing an air evacuation mission in September 1941. The wounded Whittle was transported to a prison camp, where she nursed inmates until she was freed. She received a Purple Heart; indeed, many of the nurse POWs were commended with citations and medals for bravery in captivity.

The World War II prisoner nurses have been featured in movies that often falsely dramatize their imprisonment with events that never happened, such as being shot by Japanese guards, accompanying men on the Bataan Death March, or developing a hierarchy of prisoners. In reality, no nurses were shot by Japanese guards, none were present on the Bataan Death March, and the nurses interned together regarded each other as equals, regardless of rank, cooperating and sharing work assignments to ease the stress of prison life. Most of the prisoners returned to nursing careers after the war.

Monika Schwinn was the next prominent nurse prisoner of war. A German nurse employed by the pediatric wing of the Aid Service of Malta's hospital in An Hoa, South Vietnam, Schwinn joined four coworkers on a Sunday jeep ride in April 1969. Ambushed by North Vietnamese soldiers, Schwinn and two other nurses, Marie-Luise Kerber and Hindrika Kortmann, and medical personnel Bernhard Diehl and Georg Batsch were captured. Forced to march on the Ho Chi Minh Trail and denied adequate food sources and medical care, Kerber, Kortmann, and Batsch died in the jungle and mountain prisons where they were held. Schwinn and Diehl were moved to the Hanoi Hilton after the Paris Accords, which stipulated female prisoners were supposed to be freed first. Schwinn's captors ignored this provision, and she remained the sole female prisoner at the Hanoi Hilton, sharing food with American captives until she was released in 1973. She wrote her memoirs of captivity as a memorial to the nurses who died while imprisoned.

See also Cavell, Edith; Los Banos Raid; Women; Zentsuji

References

Dorothy Still Danner, *What a Way to Spend a War: Navy Nurse POWs in the Philippines* (Annapolis, MD: Naval Institute Press, 1997).

Katherine Kenny, *Captives: Australian Army Nurses in Japanese Prison Camps* (St. Lucia: University of Queensland Press, 1986).

Judy Barrett Litoff and David C. Smith, *We're in This War, Too: World War II Letters from American Women in Uniform* (New York: Oxford University Press, 1994).

Elizabeth M. Norman, *We Band of Angels: The Untold Story of American Nurses Trapped on Bataan by the Japanese* (New York: Random House, 1999).

Monika Schwinn and Bernhard Diehl, *We Came to Help*, trans. Jan van Heurck (New York: Harcourt Brace Jovanovich, 1976).

Christina Twomey, "Australian Nurse POWs: Gender, War and Captivity," *Australian Historical Studies* 35 (2004): 255–274

—*Elizabeth D. Schafer*

O

Ōoka Shōhei (1909–1988)

Ōoka Shōhei was a Japanese novelist interned by the Americans at the Tanauan POW camp on Leyte Island, the Philippines, from March to November 1945. Shōhei, sick with malaria, was abandoned by his squad during an American attack on the island of Mindoro. After several abortive attempts to end his own life, he collapsed onto the ground, where his captors later found him, still asleep. He was sent to two U.S. Army hospitals, where he spent two months, and thence to the POW camp. His experiences provide the setting for his award-winning first novel, *Taken Captive: A Japanese POW's Story*, published between 1948 and 1951.

The novel explores two major issues: why Shōhei prepared to shoot an American soldier when he had resolved not to sully his hands with the blood of another, and how the defeated Japanese soldier went about recreating, within the context of internment, a social structure essential to self-definition. While *Taken Captive* is a lucid, penetrating treatment of life as a POW and the ethical conditions of war, it is also an allegorical depiction of Japan under American occupation. As such, its publication was delayed by occupation censors fearful of its message.

Shōhei's oeuvre represents numerous genres in addition to war-related fiction: love stories, novels of manners, literary criticism, essays, and historical fiction. It was on this last that Shōhei focused his efforts during his later years. He died on Christmas Day, 1988.

References

Ōoka Shōhei, *Fires on the Plain* (Rutland, VT: Charles E. Tuttle Company, 1967).

———, *Taken Captive: A Japanese POW's Story* (New York: J. Wiley and Sons, 1996).

David C. Stahl, *The Burdens of Survival: Ōoka Shōhei's Writings on the Pacific War* (Honolulu: University of Hawai'i Press, 2003).

—*Erik R. Lofgren*

Oradour-sur-Glane Massacre

The execution of virtually the entire population of Oradour-sur-Glane by SS troops in the summer of 1944 was one of the most brutal reprisals taken against civilian hostages in World War II. In the spring of 1944, the activities of the Maquis, a guerrilla army with strongholds in the south of France, were becoming a serious threat to the German forces occupying France. Because the Maquisards themselves were difficult to apprehend, the occupation forces embarked upon a reign of terror directed at the civilian population.

On 10 June 1944, a large force of Waffen-SS troops entered Oradour, a town near Limoges in southwestern France, and collected the inhabitants in the village square. The German commander demanded that a cache of arms and ammunition be turned over, but when no one came forward with weapons, he ordered the mayor to provide 30 hostages. When the mayor refused, the men of the village were taken to a number of barns, ostensibly to be held while the troops searched for the store of weapons. Instead, the men were shot with automatic weapons and pistols, and the barns were set alight. The women and children were herded into a church, which was barricaded shut and dynamited. In total, 642 men, women, and children perished; only seven people from the village survived. The German police later claimed that the massacre had been carried out in retaliation for the murder of a German officer and his driver by the

Maquis. This fact has never been proven and may well have been a complete fabrication; indeed, Robin Mackness has argued that the story was concocted to divert attention from the real reason for the massacre, that SS officers were looking for a cache of gold they believed was hidden in the village.

Attempts to bring the perpetrators to justice were largely unsuccessful. Unable to try the officers they believed were responsible, the French government instead indicted 21 soldiers who carried out the executions. However, the trial was a disaster. It raised a host of difficult questions about wartime collaboration with the Nazis and ended with the government voting amnesty to the majority of the defendants. The bitterness created by the trial was such that most local residents boycotted the French government's memorial at Oradour.

See also Ardeatine Caves Massacre; Lidice Massacre; Reprisals

References

Philip Beck, *Oradour: Village of the Dead* (London: Leo Cooper, 1979).

Sarah Farmer, *Martyred Village: Commemorating the 1944 Massacre at Oradour-sur-Glane* (Berkeley: University of California Press, 1999).

Jean-Jacques Fouche, ed., *Massacre at Oradour, France, 1944: Coming to Grips with Terror* (DeKalb: Northern Illinois University Press, 2004).

Robin Mackness, *Massacre at Oradour* (New York: Random House, 1988).

—*Jonathan F. Vance*

"Other Losses"

A category used in U.S. Army tallies of the millions of German military prisoners held in camps along the Rhine and elsewhere in the immediate aftermath of World War II in Europe, the phrase "other losses" is better known to the public as the title of a controversial best-seller by Canadian author James Bacque. He contends that the term refers to deaths, and that nearly one million Germans died as a result of a policy of deliberate starvation and neglect undertaken by American and French authorities at the behest of the Supreme Allied Commander, Dwight D. Eisenhower.

Published in the United States and Britain after its 1989 Canadian debut and translated into several foreign languages (including French and German), *Other Losses* has attracted a good deal of critical scrutiny. A variety of German, Canadian, and American military and diplomatic historians have drawn attention to key documents that Bacque overlooked, which indicate that "Other Losses" meant—among other things—transfers and releases, and have noted the author's misquotation of a number of printed and oral sources. Critics have also pointed to the absence of mass graves on the scale that would be required by such an atrocity and have found evidence of unwarranted statistical manipulation by the author of figures provided in various documents he cites. Support from a number of right-wing fringe groups involved in Holocaust denial has also damaged Bacque's credibility, though he himself draws no parallels between the Holocaust and Allied treatment of German captives.

Bacque, meanwhile, supported by a few academics and journalists, continues to maintain that such criticisms are only evidence of a cover-up and that those people who question his work are part of a vast conspiracy. Critics have in turn pointed out that such a conspiracy theory is by its very nature impossible to disprove, and they have questioned the accuracy of figures Bacque later received orally from a Russian source that he claimed verified his original numbers. Bacque has recently extended his condemnation of Allied policy to include the treatment of the German civilian population in *Crimes and Mercies* (1997), which has also drawn fire.

That German prisoners were treated very badly in the months immediately after the war—something that earlier historians had already documented at some length—is beyond dispute. That tens of thousands died who might have been saved is also beyond a shadow of a doubt. All in all, however, Bacque's thesis and mortality figures cannot be taken as accurate.

References

James Bacque, *Other Losses: An Investigation into the Mass Deaths of German Prisoners at the Hands of the French and Americans After World War II* (Toronto: Stoddart, 1989).

Günter Bischof and Stephen E. Ambrose, eds., *Eisenhower and the German POWs: Facts against Falsehood* (Baton Rouge: Louisiana State University Press, 1992).

S.P. MacKenzie, "Essay and Reflection: On the *Other Losses* Debate," *International History Review* 14 (1992): 661–680.

—*S. P. MacKenzie*

OTTOMAN EMPIRE

The status and treatment of prisoners of war and captives in the Ottoman Empire did not change drastically from the emergence of the Ottoman state in the early fourteenth century until after the Russo-Turkish War of 1828–1829. Generally, the Ottoman sultan would select one of four possible fates for captured enemies, whether they were soldiers or civilians, men, women, or children—execution; freedom on the condition of ransom, the release of Muslim captives taken by the enemy, or both; freedom without any conditions; or enslavement in the Ottoman Empire. Executions were rare, and until about 1830, most captives were enslaved. In fact, the Ottoman word for prisoner, *esir*, has the same meaning as slave, which makes it impossible to determine whether a slave was acquired through warfare or in some other fashion. Sometimes non-Muslim subjects of the empire who had openly rebelled against the state were also considered war captives and enslaved. According to Islamic legal tradition, only non-Muslims could be enslaved in war. Therefore, in wars against other Islamic states the enslaving of captured Muslims was not legally possible. As a general rule, one-fifth of enemy captives belonged to the Sultan and the rest were shared by his high-ranking subjects. War prisoners could also be sold in Anatolia either by the state or by their individual owners.

In general, the captured able-bodied men, especially soldiers, remained in the hands of the state. As they were capable of escape, the state felt the need to guard them closely. Consequently, they were usually kept at one of the prisons in Istanbul. Those who were held in the Arsenal Prison were used as galley slaves, a common practice in Mediterranean societies, or as laborers in the shipbuilding industry. They could also be employed in other jobs, which sometimes included service in the government as interpreters or as helpers in the Ottoman palace.

Ottomans made use of the captured males in another way: men and young boys were pressed into military and diplomatic service after some training. The Ottoman army, especially the Janissary (*Yeniçeri*) corps—elite Ottoman infantry units—recruited extensively from among captured war prisoners. In fact, some sources suggest that non-Muslims captured in battle formed the nucleus of the Ottoman army in the early to mid-fourteenth century. Slowly, the impressment of captured men into Ottoman service gave way to the *devshirme*, a system of forced recruitment or enslavement of Christian male children from among the conquered and captured non-Muslim populations who had not yet been given status as *dhimmi* (protected peoples, Christians, and Jews). Even those who had been designated as *dhimmi* were not always exempt, but those non-Muslims who had given up their sons to the Ottoman state became exempt from the *jizya* (poll tax) that others had to pay to maintain their *dhimmi* status.

Prisoners (but not *devshirme* recruits) were usually exchanged at the end of wars. However, a prisoner who was enslaved could possibly be manumitted even before war ended. This was usually, but not always, the result of conversion to Islam; since Muslims could not be enslaved legally, prisoners who converted were eventually released. As long as the prisoners remained Christians, their exchange or release by the state after a general peace agreement had been reached did not pose any problems. Those who had converted to Islam, though, could not legally be sent to their native states to live under Christian rule. Sometimes, especially during long wars, some prisoners could end up in private hands as slaves and were used in various areas. When a peace treaty was signed that called for the exchange of prisoners, the state would institute a general collection of these POWs-turned-slaves from their private owners in return for a small compensation. Some owners did not want to part with their slaves for a small compensation and attempted to keepthem, but the state was usually very vigilantin collecting the enslaved prisoners for exchange. Those prisoners who had remained in the state's control and had been put to work by the state were usually released from captivity after serving for several years.

After the Russo-Turkish War of 1828–1829, the Ottoman government discontinued the practice of enslaving prisoners of war. The Russian prisoners captured during the next major war, the Crimean War (1853–1856), for example, were not enslaved. Enslavement of those non-Muslim Ottoman subjects (*dhimmi*) who rebelled against the state was also discontinued after 1856.

Unfortunately, there is much less information available on those Ottomans who became prisoners in the hands of the enemy; what little we know of the Ottomans in enemy hands relates to those captured by the Austrians during the sieges of Vienna. It seems that the treatment of the captured Ottomans was much like that of prisoners captured by the Ottomans themselves, and sometimes even worse. According to Austrian sources, for example, most of the Ottomans captured during the Hapsburg-Ottoman Wars of 1683–1699 were forced, apparently through torture, to renounce Islam and accept Christianity. While some remained in the hands of the capturing commanders, most were sold into slavery. It is unlikely that the treatment of the Ottomans captured during other wars in Europe was any different than the treatment they received from the Austrians at the end of the seventeenth century. On certain occasions, just like in the Ottoman Empire, a single randomly chosen or a volunteer prisoner was released for a certain period of time to fetch ransom money from relatives and friends for himself and his POW friends so that the prisoners could buy themselves out of captivity.

Ottomans, whether civilians or soldiers, who were captured by Mediterranean states were generally used as galley slaves. As the detaining powers were usually most interested in money, the practice of releasing prisoners after payment of ransom money was also common among the Mediterranean powers.

In the late nineteenth century, during the Russo-Turkish War of 1878–1888, large numbers of Ottomans fell into Russian captivity both on the Caucasian front and after the surrender of the town of Pleven, in present-day Bulgaria. While we do not know how many men were taken captive and how many actually returned home, both western and Ottoman sources agree that the Ottomans received very cruel treatment both from the Russians and their allies. Some of those who did not die while they were being marched into captivity lost their lives while in POW camps. During the Balkan Wars, large numbers of Ottomans were taken captive. While each power treated enemy prisoners terribly, it seems that the worst treatment endured by the Ottomans came from the Bulgarians. Accounts of a few survivors compiled in a report of an international commission established after the war related that hundreds of prisoners were simply lined up and gunned down after the capture of Adrianople (Edirne). Those who were lucky enough to escape the massacre ended up in various POW camps. While some were treated reasonably well, many others, especially those on an islet in the river Tundzha, suffered terribly, many dying of hunger, cold, and disease. Some accounts reported that the starving Ottoman prisoners were reduced to eating grass and the bark of trees.

References

Y. Hakan Erdem, *Slavery in the Ottoman Empire and Its Demise, 1800–1909* (New York: St. Martin's Press, 1996).

Konstantin Mihailovic, *Memoirs of a Janissary*, trans. Benjamin Stolz (Ann Arbor: University of Michigan Press, 1975).

Halil Sahilionlu, "Slaves in Social and Economic Life of Bursa in the Late 15th and Early 16th Centuries," *Turcica* 17 (1985): 43–112.

Karl Teply, "Vom los Osmanischer Gefangenen aus dem Grossen Turkenkrieg 1683–99 ," *Sudost-Forschungen Jahrbuch* 32 (1973): 33–72.

Report of the International Commission to Inquire into the Causes and Conduct of the Balkan Wars (Washington, DC: Carnegie Endowment for International Peace, 1914).

— *Yücel Yanīkdağ*

P

Paradis Massacre Le

The massacre of 97 British POWs at a small village in northern France was one of the first atrocities committed against prisoners after the German invasion of France during World War II. On the morning of 27 May 1940, the 2nd Battalion Royal Norfolk Regiment was withstanding a strong attack from elements of the *SS Totenkopf* (Death's Head) Division at a hamlet called Le Paradis. Surrounded and out of ammunition, the senior surviving officer decided to surrender the remnants of the battalion. After one unsuccessful surrender attempt, when three Norfolks without weapons and holding white towels were killed, the SS unit took the 99 survivors prisoner. They were searched, subjected to severe ill-treatment, and were then marched into a field where two machine guns had been mounted. On orders from company commander Fritz Knöchlein, the guns fired; soldiers with fixed bayonets and officers and NCOs with revolvers and rifles finished off the wounded. Nevertheless, two badly wounded privates, Albert Pooley and William O'Callaghan, somehow survived. They crawled away at nightfall but were quickly recaptured. Pooley was repatriated in 1943; O'Callaghan returned to Britain in 1945.

The bodies were buried, but they were later exhumed by the French in 1942 and placed in Le Paradis churchyard. Fifty were identified; many had already been wounded before the massacre, for they bore traces of bandages on hands, arms, and legs, and some had rough splints. The incident was reported to 16th Army Headquarters, but no action was taken in Berlin. It was believed that this was due to the personal intervention of *Reichsführer* Heinrich Himmler, the head of the Waffen-SS, who had visited the *Totenkopf* Division on 29 May 1940. Knöchlein, a former officer at Dachau concentration camp, was tried by British military court in October 1948 and sentenced to death, in large part due to the testimony of Pooley and O'Callaghan. He was hanged in Hamburg on 28 January 1949.

See also Katyń Forest Massacre; Malmédy Massacre; Waffen-SS; Wormhout Massacre

References

Cyril Jolly, *The Vengeance of Private Pooley* (London: Heinemann, 1956).

—*David Ray*

Parole

While the idea of paroling prisoners extends at least back to classical times, widespread employment of this practice in Europe did not occur until the seventeenth century. The first reference in English to military parole, for example, appears in 1648 with a British soldier offering his word of honor, or *parole d'honneur*, that he would neither attempt to escape nor assist his own forces unless he was set free by appropriate means—usually in exchange for a prisoner of equal rank held by the other side. For a variety of reasons, chief among them the rise of the nation-state during the seventeenth century, soldiers who surrendered were no longer immediately subjected to enslavement, wholesale murder, or ransoming. Hugo Grotius, in his 1625 work *The Law of War and Peace*, observed that ordinary prisoners—as well as "personages of extraordinary rank"—were now more frequently considered to be in the custody of the enemy state, rather than at the disposal of individual captors.

The long-term maintenance of large numbers of captives, however, could prove troublesome as well as expensive. The military parole system provided a solution that was attractive for a variety of reasons. For the victors in any contest, parole meant that captives became responsible for their own care, a very important consideration when commissariats had great difficulty feeding and housing armies. The advantages to the prisoners were also obvious. They gained a large measure of liberty by asserting they would not take up arms again unless authorized to do so by officials from both sides. But there were, of course, problems. For the victors there was always the possibility that parole might be broken, that the former combatant would escape and engage in hostilities. For the losers, as well, the innovation could mean hardship. Soldiers on parole were required to provide their own upkeep and frequently had to find room and board in foreign lands. So long as family funds permitted, life could be tolerable or even very enjoyable, though wartime inflation meant difficulties for destitute officers and, over time, it became customary to allow prisoners to refuse parole.

While originally the preserve of higher-ranking officers, the parole system proved extremely flexible. By 1804, for example, the British permitted parole for all army officers down to sous-lieutenant, and for naval officers to the rank of midshipman. In a number of North American campaigns during the War of 1812, captured militiamen, including thousands of rank and file, simply returned to their prewar civilian pursuits after being granted parole. And during the Mexican War, General Winfield Scott said that occasionally he released all captives, whether officers or not, and allowed them to return to their homes. Ordinarily, senior officers remained behind enemy lines but were granted a tremendous amount of liberty until exchanged. Regulations published by the British government in the 1800s stipulated that parolees would remain within one mile of their abode, not trespass on fields, not leave the lodgings in the evening, behave decently, obey the law, and not write home unless the mail was examined first. Parolees stationed in Verdun, France, during the Napoleonic Wars enjoyed even greater freedom. Some had their families join them from England, money was funneled via the banking firm Perregaux in Paris, access to *Bells Weekly Magazine* was guaranteed, and roll call was required only once every five days.

During the twentieth century, the practice of parole was enshrined in various international agreements. Articles 10 through 12 of the 1907 Hague Convention, for example, detailed the right of prisoners to "be set at liberty on parole if the laws of their country allow," but they also noted that governments were not obliged to offer parole, that prisoners were not to be compelled to take it, and that parolees who broke their word "forfeited their right to be treated as prisoners of war, and can be brought before the courts." Similarly, the 1949 Geneva Convention concisely noted that "prisoners of war may be partially or wholly released on parole or promise, in so far as is allowed by the laws of the Power on which they depend. Such measures shall be taken particularly in cases where this may contribute to their state of health. No prisoner of war shall be compelled to accept liberty on parole or promise."

Despite such stipulations, belligerents rarely employed the system during the 1900s. When a suggestion was made that both sides release prisoners on parole during World War I, for example, the British prime minister responded that this was not practicable. Yet, at times, the practice has continued. A 25 March 1915 report noted that German prisoners had been permitted to go to America on parole, and the Japanese required all Filipinos to sign a parole in 1942 that was eventually recognized by the American government. But these were exceptions, and parole today has become almost exclusively associated with the criminal justice system. The abandonment of this custom by the military is likely related to several points: modern logistics have made the maintenance of large groups of prisoners far more practical, the goal of depriving the other side of trained professional soldiers has made exchanges undesirable for the detaining state, and portrayals of enemy soldiers in propaganda make it unlikely that civilians will accept them at liberty in their territory.

References

G.D. Brown, "Prisoner of War Parole: Ancient Concept—Modern Utility," *Military Law Review* 156 (1998): 200–223.

W.E.S. Flory, *Prisoners of War: A Study in the Development of International Law* (Washington, DC: American Council in Public Affairs, 1942).

Howard S. Levie, *Prisoners of War in International Armed Conflicts* (Newport, RI: Naval War College Press, n.d.).

Gerald J. Prokopowicz, "Word of Honor: The Parole System in the Civil War," *North and South* 6 (2003): 24–33.

—*George Sheppard*

Pavie, Marie-Marguerite Fabre (ca. 1762–1834)

The experiences of Marie Pavie are representative of the hardships endured by women prisoners during the French Revolution. She was married to Louis-Victor Pavie, journalist and publisher of a newspaper in Angers, France, where the couple operated a press out of their home. Her tribulations reflect the complexity and danger of life in western France, where Catholic Royalists remained faithful to the king despite the efforts of republican armies to destroy the monarchy. Because both parties wanted the Pavies to publish their bulletins, the Pavie press was ransacked and destroyed. Accused of counterrevolutionary activities and labeled an émigré (an enemy of the revolutionary government who had illegally taken flight), Louis-Victor was arrested. He escaped to Spain while Marie remained under house arrest in Angers. Early in the revolution, women were relatively safe, but nine months after revolutionaries beheaded King Louis XVI, his wife Marie Antoinette was also guillotined. Following this example, revolutionaries throughout France threw women into prison for their husbands' "crimes." In 1794, Marie Pavie, deemed guilty of being the wife of an émigré, was imprisoned in the chateau at Amboise, where she was awaiting the guillotine when the overthrow of revolutionary leader Maximilien Robespierre ended the revolution. She returned to Angers, where her heartbroken husband soon died. Widowed, Marie Pavie courageously rebuilt the press by publishing religious material and horticulture books. She passed the firm to her son, Louis, who published his son Théodore's American travel journal, *Souvenirs atlantiques*, in 1832. The "Marie Pavy" is a fragrant rose popular in the southern United States, probably in commemoration of this brave woman whose son became a recognized journalist and horticulturist.

See also French Revolution, Wars of the; Women

References

Betje Black Klier, "Pavie," in *The New Handbook of Texas*, ed. Ron Tyler (Austin: Texas State Historical Association, 1996).

———, *Tales of the Sabine Borderlands* (College Station: Texas A&M University Press, 1998).

———, *Pavie in the Borderlands* (Baton Rouge: Louisiana State University Press, 1999).

—*Betje Black Klier*

Pay

The practice of paying prisoners of war their regular military wages in addition to any pay they receive for work was eventually codified into international law. In the early modern era, it was customary for captured officers to be released on parole while they were awaiting exchange; they would be responsible for arranging and paying for their own board and lodging until negotiations were completed and they were able to return home. Because it was essential that they have money for their own upkeep, officers without private means received advances on their regular pay through agents appointed by their own government. When the use of parole declined, however, the practice of

A specimen of the money paid to Allied prisoners in Germany in World War I. The bottom line notes that the money could be used only in Bischofswerda camp (from John C. Thorn, Three Years a Prisoner in Germany *[Vancouver, 1919])*

paying officers remained in place, with certain revisions. According to the Hague Convention of 1907, officer POWs were to be paid by their captors the same wage received by officers of the same rank in the captor's army; the money was to be reimbursed by the prisoner's own government at the conclusion of hostilities. The system functioned reasonably well during World War I, and many prisoners were thus able to buy food or comforts in prison camp canteens. As a result, the practice was retained in the Geneva Convention of 1929, with the added proviso that the wage not exceed that which the POW would ordinarily receive from his own government.

During World War II, however, pay was distributed irregularly, if at all, with some governments being more careful about distribution than others. The U.S. government, for example, established a wage scale that ranged from $20 a month for German and Italian lieutenants to $40 for officers above the rank of major; Japanese officer POWs were paid on a slightly different scale. Enlisted men received a monthly allotment of $3. These amounts were paid in vouchers that could be used in prison camp canteens or were kept on account to be drawn on when necessary; only in special circumstances were prisoners permitted to possess cash. There was no such uniformity in the payment of Allied POWs in German hands, and policy differed greatly from camp to camp. Some prisoners received their pay on a regular basis, according to a set scale, although deductions for food and clothing were frequently made; generally, the pay was given in German currency (until the fall of 1944) or camp money. In other camps, pay was not distributed at all and, unlike in the United States, enlisted men in German camps received no pay unless they worked. By the same token, pay was uncertain in Japanese camps. Most prisoners received nothing, but some commandants (in Cabanatuan, in the Philippines, for example) lived up to the obligations of the Geneva Convention by distributing pay according to set scales to both officers and enlisted men, again with deductions for food and lodging; payments were usually made in the form of credited postal savings accounts. In the fall of 1944, what few payments had been made were stopped altogether.

Because of this spotty record, the Geneva Convention of 1949 moved to normalize the situation. Signatories agreed to a common scale that set rates of pay in five categories, from private to general. The rates were set in Swiss francs but were to be paid in local currencies at the prevailing rate of exchange. This was a significant advance over the 1929 Convention, in that it stipulated pay for other ranks as well as officers and ended the practice of linking pay to the rates of individual governments.

Recently, the pay issue has stirred another minor controversy. During World War II, the British government deducted from the accounts of officer POWs the amount of pay stipulated under the Geneva Convention, whether or not the POWs were actually receiving that money in captivity. A number of British former POWs have mounted a campaign to press their government to reimburse these amounts.

References
Walter Rundell, Jr., "Paying the POW in World War II," *Military Affairs* 22 (1958): 121–134.

—Jonathan F. Vance

PEACEKEEPING MISSIONS

Modern peacekeeping emerged in the late 1940s, when the United Nations dispatched personnel to observe ceasefires in the Middle East and along the border between India and Pakistan. Since then, the United Nations has mounted close to 60 peacekeeping operations in the Americas, Europe, Africa, Asia, and the Middle East. In addition to the U.N., the North Atlantic Treaty Organization (NATO) and the Organization of African Unity (OAU) are examples of other international organizations and alliances to have engaged in peacekeeping. Some peacekeeping operations are not dispatched under the auspices of any particular international body but in response to a specific crisis or peace settlement. For example, international observers were used in Indochina following the negotiation of the 1954 Geneva Accords and again in the early 1970s, in the aftermath of the Vietnam War. Similarly, peacekeepers were sent to Nigeria to monitor the Biafra crisis and, following the 1979 Israel-Egypt peace treaty, a multinational force was used to monitor the withdrawal of Israeli forces and to ensure compliance with that treaty's provisions.

However, the very definition of what constitutes peacekeeping is ambiguous. The earliest peacekeeping missions were characterized by small groups of unarmed, military observers who were expected not to influence the outcome of a conflict. Rather, their presence was intended as a confidence-building measure and as a deterrent to potential ceasefire violations. When the United Nations responded to the 1956 Suez Crisis, it did so with its first, large military operation, employing at its peak over 6,000 peacekeepers. The United Nations Emergency Force (UNEF) set important precedents for future peacekeeping missions, including the applicability to U.N. peacekeepers of the Convention on the Privileges and Immunities of the United Nations (1946), intended to secure the safety of U.N. personnel and to ensure their freedom of movement. Significantly, UNEF's rules of engagement permitted the use of force only in self-defense. Until the late 1980s, most peacekeeping operations followed the pattern of UNEF by using limited, if any, force in support of peaceful resolutions to interstate conflict.

With the end of the Cold War, U.N. peacekeeping multiplied, and some mission mandates demonstrated the Security Council's increased willingness to authorize the use of force not simply to "keep" peace but to enforce it, even within states, to protect and support civilians affected by civil war and unrest. While earlier peacekeeping was typically justified under chapter six of the U.N. Charter (Pacific Settlements of Disputes), this new generation of peacekeeping—sometimes termed peacemaking or peace enforcement—was often rooted in chapter seven (Action with Respect to Threats to the Peace, Breaches of the Peace, and Acts of Aggression). This muscular approach to peacekeeping has increased the chances of peacekeepers being perceived not as neutral observers but as combatants, and they are, therefore, more vulnerable to capture; conversely, this approach also empowers peacekeepers to use the requisite force needed to detain those who could jeopardize a mission's objectives.

The United Nations Protection Force (UNPROFOR), dispatched to the former Yugoslavia in 1992, is an example of a peacekeeping operation that rapidly evolved from "peacekeeping" to "peace enforcement," broadly interpreting and readily exercising its right to use force in self-defense. Its primary tasks were the defense of U.N.-protected areas; ceasefire verification; security for the delivery of humanitarian aid, including protection of the Sarajevo airport; and enforcement of no-fly zones. At close to 40,000 personnel, it is the largest peacekeeping operation in U.N. history; the more than 200 mission fatalities speak to the dangerous conditions under which it operated. To achieve its objectives, UNPROFOR worked in concert with NATO, particularly in the enforcement of no-fly zones. When NATO carried out air strikes against Bosnian Serb positions in May 1995,

370 U.N. peacekeepers were captured and illegally detained for one month so that they could be used as "human shields" against further air strikes. By the end of 1995, and following the successful negotiation of the Dayton Peace Agreement, the U.N. transferred authority for the operation to NATO, and it was recast as the Implementation Force (IFOR).

Even in the pre-Cold War period, peacekeepers were sometimes detained in the course of carrying out their duties. In the early 1960s, during the deployment of the Opération des Nations Unies au Congo (ONUC), the Armée Nationale Congolaise detained several peacekeepers, usually on unfounded charges of espionage. Following U.N. protests and the actions of senior officers in the field who negotiated their release, the peacekeepers were freed, though not before many were beaten so severely as to need hospitalization.

Such incidents highlight the complex legal status of peacekeepers. In theory, personnel deployed on chapter six peacekeeping operations are protected not only by the previously noted Convention on the Privileges and Immunities of the United Nations (1946), but now also by the U.N. Convention on the Safety of U.N. and Associated Personnel (1994); in addition, protection against detention or capture would be augmented by any status of forced agreement negotiated with the host country and the provisions under the law of international armed conflict that pertain to all civilians. But, when the Security Council creates a peacekeeping operation to enforce peace under chapter seven, the 1994 Convention is considered not to apply to any personnel who are engaged as combatants against organized armed forces and to whom the law of international armed conflicts applies. The Convention *is* deemed to apply, though, when the enforcement action is carried out in situations of internal armed conflict. This patchwork of international law, intended to protect peacekeepers should they be captured, is indicative of the fluid and evolving nature of peacekeeping itself.

Similarly, peacekeepers have operated in something of a legal gray area when it comes to their detention of people during operations. Because nation states and not international organizations signed the Geneva Conventions, peacekeepers have not been strictly bound by this international law. During the U.N.'s missions to Somalia (UNOSOM I and II), Canadian, Belgian, Italian, and Pakistani peacekeepers were variously accused of the abuse, torture, and murder of Somali detainees. In Canada, one accused peacekeeper was tried and found guilty of the torture and manslaughter of a Somali teenager, and the Canadian Airborne Regiment, the unit sent to Somalia, was disbanded. In the wake of such controversies, U.N. Secretary-General Kofi Annan clarified peacekeepers' responsibilities toward detained persons in a 1999 executive order that requires detainees to be treated in accordance with the provisions of the Geneva Convention of 1949. The order explicitly forbids "any form of torture or ill-treatment" of detainees.

One final point might be made with regard to peacekeeping and prisoners of war. In some cases, peacekeeping operations have been assigned the task of overseeing prisoner exchange. For example, in May 1974, the United Nations Disengagement Observer Force (UNDOF) was created, in part, to facilitate POW exchange between Israel and Syria. Outside U.N. auspices, the International Commission for Supervision and Control (ICSC) and the International Commission of Control and Supervision (ICCS) assisted with the exchange of prisoners in Indochina.

References

Paul F. Diehl, *International Peacekeeping* (Baltimore: Johns Hopkins University Press, 1994).

William J. Durch, ed., *The Evolution of U.N. Peacekeeping* (New York: St. Martin's Press, 1993).

Alan James, *Peacekeeping in International Politics* (New York: St. Martin's Press, 1990).

United Nations, *The Blue Helmets*, 3rd ed. (New York: United Nations Department of Public Information, 1996).

—*Kevin A. Spooner*

PEARL, DANIEL (1963–2002)

An American journalist for the *Wall Street Journal* was kidnapped and murdered by a radical Islamic group in Karachi, Pakistan. His kidnapping captured worldwide headlines and his subsequent murder, which was videotaped, produced global revulsion and horror. Pearl's captors used his Jewish ancestry to link him, erroneously, to the Israeli government and its intelligence agency Mossad.

Pearl was born in Princeton, New Jersey, and attended Stanford University in the early 1980s, graduating with a bachelor's degree in communications. He secured a position with the *Wall Street Journal* in 1990. In 1996, Pearl moved to the London Bureau as a Middle East correspondent, and in 2000, he became the newspaper's South Asia Bureau Chief and moved to Mumbai to take up his duties.

On 23 January 2002, Pearl disappeared in the Pakistani city of Karachi while researching possible links between Islamic militant groups and the "shoe bomber" Richard Reid. Four days later, a group calling itself The National Movement for the Restoration of Pakistani Sovereignty sent an e-mail intended for the United States and Israeli governments. Attached to the e-mail were several photos of the journalist in chains and with a gun to his head. The group claimed that Pearl was an Israeli spy and made several demands, including the release of all Pakistani terror detainees.

Some of Pearl's captivity was recorded on a videotape titled "The Slaughter of the Spy-Journalist, the Jew Daniel Pearl." In the video, Pearl stated his captors' demands while pictures of dead Muslims were superimposed around him. At times, Pearl appeared disoriented and unsure of his words (for instance, when condemning his country's actions), while at others (such as when affirming his Judaism), he appeared entirely sure of himself. Pearl's parents suggest that their son tried to get a message across to them by referring to a street named after his grandfather near Tel-Aviv, of which

Daniel Pearl (Daniel Pearl Foundation)

only the family was aware. Despite pleas from the international community and from his pregnant wife, Daniel Pearl's captors slit his throat on or about 29 January. Although the video did not display Pearl's death, one of his captors was shown severing Pearl's head, which was then held up by the hair as the group's demands scrolled across the screen. His body was recovered on 16 May and returned to the United States for burial. In July 2002, Ahmad Omar Saeed Sheikh, a British-born Islamic militant, was sentenced to death in a Pakistani court for Pearl's murder. Three other men were also found guilty and sentenced to 25 years in prison. Their appeals are pending. Khalid Shaikh Mohammed, believed to be one of the 9/11 planners and who was apprehended in Pakistan in 2003, has also been linked to the crime. A sixth suspect, Hashim Qadeer, awaits trial in Pakistan.

After Pearl's death, the *Wall Street Journal* noted that "(p)aradoxically, though he appears to have suffered at the hands of Islamic militants angry at the West, he was particularly sensitive to sentiments in the Islamic world and committed to explaining them to his readers in the West."

References
Bernard Herni Lévy, *Who Killed Daniel Pearl?* (Chicago: Independent Publishers Group, 2004).
Mariane Pearl, *A Mighty Heart: The Brave Life and Death of My Husband Danny Pearl* (New York: Scribner's, 2003).

—*John Maker*

PEIPER, JOACHIM (JÖCHEN) (1915–1976)

Tried and convicted for one of the most famous massacres of POWs during World War II, Joachim Peiper lived the rest of his life under the cloud of his crimes. Born in Berlin on 30 January 1915, he joined the SS in October 1933 and later, at 29 years of age, became one of the youngest regimental commanders in the German army. During the December 1944 German offensive in the Ardennes forest, in Belgium, soldiers of his regiment executed an undetermined number of unarmed American POWs in an atrocity that became known as the Malmédy Massacre. Following the war, he was tried as a war criminal for the actions of his troops. In May 1946, Peiper and 73 other former German military officers stood before an American military tribunal in the former concentration camp of Dachau. The questionable conduct of the trial reflected poorly on the American military justice system, but guilty verdicts were returned to all of the accused. On 16 July 1946, 43 men were sentenced to death, including Peiper. The condemned men awaited execution on death row in Landsberg, Germany, but eventually all of the death sentences were commuted. Peiper was released in December 1956.

Plagued by the notoriety of the Peiper legend, he unsuccessfully attempted to salvage a new life at the age of 41. Peiper's international reputation as an SS member and convicted war criminal hampered his efforts in business, and he eventually left Germany in disgrace. He was assassinated in France on 14 July 1976 and subsequently buried in his family tomb in Schondorf am Ammersee, Germany. The perpetrators were never apprehended.

See also Malmédy Massacre; Meyer, Kurt

References
Leo Kessler, *SS Peiper: The Life and Death of SS Colonel Jöchen Peiper* (London: Leo Cooper, 1986).
Jean Paul Pallud, *Ardennes, 1944: Peiper and Skorzeny* (London: Osprey, 1987).
Michael Reynolds, *The Devil's Adjutant: Jochen Peiper, Panzer* Leader (Stroud, UK: Spellmount, 2004).
James J. Weingartner, *Crossroads of Death: The Story of the Malmédy Massacre and Trial* (Berkeley University of California Press, 1979).
Charles Whiting, *Massacre at Malmédy: The Story of Jochen Peiper's Battle Group, Ardennes, December, 1944* (New York: Stein and Day, 1971).

—*Scott Blanchette*

PELOPONNESIAN WAR (431–404 B.C.E.)

In the fifth century B.C.E., Sparta and its allies, the Peloponnesian League, fought Athens and its allies, the Delian League, in a war that led ultimately to the defeat of Athens, the imposition of an oligarchic government therein (the Council of Thirty), and Athens's loss of its navy, its trade, and its empire.

In the years after it led coalitions that defeated the attempts of the Persian Empire under Darius and later under Xerxes to conquer Greece (499–479 B.C.E.), Athens became the economic, intellectual, and political leader of the Greek world, while its navy dominated the eastern Mediterranean. Sparta, fearing this growing Athenian power, engaged in a rivalry with Athens that eventually grew into the Peloponnesian War. The immediate trigger was Athens's alliance with Megara, a rebellious Spartan ally.

The first 10 years of this war became known as the Archidamian War, which ended with the Peace of Nicias. The Second Peloponnesian War involved the catastrophic Athenian expedition against Syracuse (415–413 B.C.E.), followed by the so-called Ionian War. The single most famous military action of the war was the attempt of Athens to capture Syracuse, with its invaluable silver mines, as a means of financing further operations against the Peloponnesian League. This project ended in disaster with thousands of Athenian soldiers enslaved as prisoners.

In ancient Greece, the rules of war did not prescribe precisely the treatment of prisoners of war. In general, the rule seems to have been that it was at the discretion of the victors to decide the fate of the defeated. Prisoners might be sold as slaves, kept as slaves of the state, exchanged, or executed. Sometimes, within individual conflicts, opponents would adopt ad hoc arrangements that provided for better treatment of prisoners. As the struggle between these two powers became more desperate, however, the treatment of prisoners deteriorated, and many of the customary rules of war were violated. Heralds, who alone guaranteed the possibility of communication between enemies, remained sacrosanct, but the custom of sparing the olive trees from the general destruction of crops, on account of the long period (30 years) required for them to bear fruit, was abandoned, and Spartan troops eventually destroyed the groves of Attica.

The worst instances of ruthlessness toward prisoners involved the populations of cities that repudiated their alliances. Pericles, the great Athenian statesman, had advocated relative leniency toward rebelling allies, but the demagogue Cleon pressed a policy of utmost severity. In 423 B.C.E.., Cleon persuaded the Athenians to put to death the population of Scione in punishment for their rebellion, and in 422 he sold the women and children of Torone into slavery following the collapse of that revolt. It was the fate of Mytilene, however, that has captured the interest of history. Originally, in response to the revolt of that city, Cleon convinced the Athenians to condemn all the people of Mytilene to death. Eventually, however, Diodatus and the moderates prevailed upon the assembly to rescind that order and to execute only the 1,000 leaders who had been detained.

The devastation wrought by the Peloponnesian War helped to destroy the prominence of the polis in classical Greece and to prepare the way for the conquests of Philip and Alexander and the Hellenistic age that arose therewith.

See also Greece—Bronze Age to the Hellenistic Period; Sphacteria, Battle of

References

Donald Kagan, *A New History of the Peloponnesian War*, 4 vols. (Ithaca, NY: Cornell University Press, 1969–1987).

Thucydides, *The Peloponnesian War*, trans. Rex Warner (Baltimore: Penguin Books, 1954).

—Patrick M. O'Neil

Percival, Arthur Ernest (1887–1966)

General A. E. Percival has gone down in history as the man who surrendered Singapore to the Japanese during World War II. Enlisting in the British army as a private before World War I, Percival rose to the rank of major-general by the outbreak of World War II. As a result of his prior service in Malaya, Percival was given command of all Commonwealth forces in Malaya in the spring of 1941. All of the defenses for the port city of Singapore, the principal city of Malaya, were pointed seaward, leaving the Malayan Peninsula undefended. The jungle conditions of the Malayan Peninsula had long been considered a sufficient defensive barrier, but Percival realized the shortsightedness of that thinking and requested six reinforced divisions and sufficient numbers of aircraft for support. Instead, he was given two and a half understrength, ill-trained, and badly led divisions and almost no air support.

The Japanese invaded Malaya on 8 December 1941 and forced Percival to withdraw his troops to the island of Singapore on 27 January 1942. The island, however, had not been prepared for defense, because it was thought that the defenses on the peninsula would be sufficient. As a result of both his own mistakes and the interference of his superiors, Percival was forced to surrender approximately 130,000 British, Australian, Indian, and Malayan troops on 15 February 1942. This surrender was the largest in British history, and many of these men would die from disease or malnutrition while in captivity. After surviving three and a half years of brutal imprisonment in Japanese-occupied Manchuria, Percival was freed in August 1945. Though American General Douglas MacArthur honored him by having him present for the surrender ceremonies on the USS Missouri in Tokyo Bay on 2 September 1945, Percival was reviled in his own country and died a broken man in 1966.

See also World War II—Far East

References

Peter Elphick, *Singapore: The Pregnable Fortress—A Study in Deception, Discord, and Desertion* (London: Coronet, 1995).

Clifford Kinvig, *Scapegoat: General Percival of Singapore* (London: Brassey's, 1996).

Arthur E. Percival, *War in Malaya* (London: Eyre and Spottiswoode, 1949).

Sir John G. Smyth, *Percival and the Tragedy of Singapore* (London: Macdonald, 1971).

—Alexander M. Bielakowski

Persian Gulf War

See Gulf War

Philippine-American War (1899–1902)

The Philippine-American War, also known as the Philippine Insurrection, was a direct result of Spain ceding control over the Philippine Islands to the United States following the Spanish-American War. The United States formally proclaimed possession of the Philippines in January 1899, which angered Emilio Aguinaldo, who vowed to lead a movement to resist American control and to proclaim the Filipino republic's independence. A clash between Filipinos and Americans in February 1899 escalated into a battle, as the American forces drove the insurgents back and inflicted heavy losses. This was the beginning of a war that would see more casualties than the conflict with Spain.

By 1900, there were 70,000 American soldiers stationed in the Philippines, under the control of Major General Arthur MacArthur. By that time, reports from the Philippines were already trickling back to the United States, as newspapers began to reprint letters sent from the battlefield that relayed gruesome accounts about what was really happening. In one letter, Corporal Sam Gillis of the 1st California Division wrote about instructing natives to return to their houses. If the natives refused, wrote Corporal Gillis, they were shot. In his first night, he wrote, he witnessed the killing of 300 natives. In other letters, the war was referred to as a "GooGoo Hunt," while Filipinos were referred to as "niggers." A similar account related the experiences of General Lloyd Wheaton. After General Wheaton and two of his companions were rescued from a Filipino trap, Wheaton ordered his men to burn every Filipino town and village in a 12-mile radius. On another occasion, when a soldier from New York was found shot, General Wheaton ordered his men to burn the nearest town and kill every native in sight. In the end, over 1,000 Filipinos were reported killed.

While the reports of brutality sent shockwaves throughout the United States, it was with horror that Americans reacted to the news of concentration camps. In 1901, Brigadier General J. Franklin Bell ordered the concentration of Filipino civilians into barrios. These barrios were an effective means of coercion for the Americans, as they separated the civilians from the insurgents. Bell ordered civilians to bring their animals, rice, and possessions to the barrios; all food, property, and livestock that remained outside after this would be confiscated. In order to discourage the spread of disease, Bell instituted a vaccination program for an estimated 300,000 Filipinos. He also attempted to establish a plentiful supply of food and instructed his commanders to build storehouses, set fair food prices, and prevent hoarding and speculation. However, despite all of Bell's efforts, human suffering in the barrios was severe. They were overcrowded, the food supply was short, and sanitation ranged from poor to appalling. In the end, malnutrition, poor sanitation, disease, and demoralization claimed at least 11,000 Filipino lives. It also made the population susceptible to the cholera epidemic of 1902.

The *barrios* cut off the guerrillas from their former village havens, making it impossible for them to maintain any type of organization. Aguinaldo, the leader of the insurgents, was captured in 1901, after which time he issued a proclamation for peace. While scattered resistance continued throughout the archipelago, the insurrection had ended by the summer of 1902.

Although never officially sanctioned by the American forces, physical mistreatment and torture played a definitive role in the Philippine-American War, what one general summed up perfectly as a "nasty little war."

See also Concentration Camps

References

David Haward Bain, *Sitting in Darkness: Americans in the Philippines* (Boston: Houghton Mifflin, 1984).

Brian McAllister Linn, *The U.S. Army and Counterinsurgency in the Philippine War, 1899–1902* (Chapel Hill: University of North Carolina Press, 1989).

T. Harry Williams, *The History of American Wars: From 1745 to 1918* (New York: Alfred A. Knopf, 1981).

—*Matthew E. Pearson*

PLAINS INDIAN WARFARE

Throughout the history of native warfare on the Great Plains of North America, prisoners, internees, slaves, and adoptees have been a part of the larger cycle of life. After the changes ushered in by the introduction of the horse and contact with whites, the taking and disposition of captives took on new significance. The appearance of European disease also altered the tempo, if not the basic character, of human bondage on the Plains. Likewise, the white society that spread ever farther over native lands brought its own special hue to long-standing patterns as Plains Indian warfare assumed a new complexion.

From earliest times, the peoples occupying the Great Plains and its fringes have raided neighboring and distant villages to exact revenge, gain wealth, achieve status, and take prisoners. Some have likened these early manifestations of warfare on the Plains to a game in which there was little bloodshed and a lot of ceremony. But recent scholarship has demonstrated more clearly the level of killing that sometimes took place, the motivation for carrying off captives, and the fate of those prisoners.

Archaeological evidence now shows a ferocity of warfare on the Plains that had never been presumed before. Field research has uncovered large-scale massacres of villagers dating back to 1300, with some evidence going as far back as 1100. During such raids across the Plains, it was not unusual to see the slaughter of the adult male population and the carrying off of women and children of both sexes as captives. Trophies—such as scalps, heads, noses, and feet—were taken from the bodies of the men, while women and children were returned to the attacker's villages to be adopted into the tribe, enslaved, or sacrificed.

The adoption of captives by Plains tribes was inspired normally by the need to replace tribal members who had been lost to war, disease, or injury. There were no tribal limitations to such adoptions. In prehistoric times, members of various enemy tribes were seized and adopted. Similarly, in later years it was common to capture and adopt white women and children. Those people thus adopted became full tribal members with all associated privileges and honors as well as responsibilities. Many adapted well to their new lives and made significant contributions to their new communities. For example, Quanah Parker, the great Comanche chief, was the son of Cynthia Ann Parker, a white woman who was captured by the Comanches on the Anglo-Texas frontier in 1836.

Those captives not chosen for adoption might be killed or impressed into slavery. There were already slave trade systems among the Plains Indians and their eastern neighbors in prehistoric times. These expanded and intensified after contact with whites. The Illinois, for example, had long-standing patterns of raiding the Plains for captive slaves, preying particularly on the Quapaws and the Pawnees. Indeed, the French word for Indian captives, *pani,* is cited by some as the origin of the name of the Pawnee tribe. Likewise, the Assiniboine enslaved Blackfeet and Gros Ventres, the Wichitas captured Apache, Osage, and Tonkawa women for use as slaves, and the Comanches raided the Lipan Apaches, particularly for female captives.

After the appearance of European disease, the intensity of raiding for new tribal members and slaves increased. Many native tribes suffered terribly from epidemics of smallpox, cholera, and measles that swept the Plains in the eighteenth and nineteenth centuries. Some tribes experienced losses of 80 percent or more of their populations; others, like the Mandan, were nearly exterminated by disease. The result was a desperate grasp by some to maintain tribal cultures by adopting new members wherever they could be seized and by lessening their burden of labor through the increased utilization of slaves. Some slaves were in turn traded for economic gain. The usual pattern here was for captured Indians, especially women, to be traded ever further eastward, sometimes ending up with European or, later, American masters.

The fate of still other captives was even more bleak. There are accounts of cannibalism and ritual sacrifice among some Plains Indian tribes. Such occurrences were not widespread, but they did occur. For example, there are several accounts of Wichitas consuming the flesh of their Indian prisoners. There was an air of magic associated with this practice and the belief that those who partook might gain the strength and bravery of their enemies. The Pawnees performed an elaborate ritual sacrifice of a captive young woman as the central part of their Morning Star Ceremony, a rite designed to ensure the fertility of the soil and the success of their crops.

The expansion of white exploration and settlement across the Plains saw the taking of Indian captives by a new and alien culture and acquainted Plains Indians with the practice of taking hostages. As early as 1601, the Spaniard Don Juan de Oñate seized the Wichita chief, Catarax, to prevent further Indian hostilities against the Spaniards in his expedition. In 1872, Colonel Ranald Slidell Mackenzie and his 4th Cavalry captured more than 100 Comanche women and children who were held as hostages for several months to ensure the good behavior of other Comanches. Other Indian prisoners were taken by white authorities to be dealt with by formal judicial processes. In 1871, the leading Kiowa chiefs Satank, Satanta, and Big Tree were arrested, convicted for raids from Indian Territory into Texas, and incarcerated in the state penitentiary at Huntsville, Texas. Many other Indian prisoners were sent to the army prison at Fort Marion, Florida, where some soon became ill and died. As the army campaigned throughout the Plains region, a major objective was the freeing of white captives held by Indians. At Washita in 1868, Custer's 7th Cavalry freed two white women captives. General Eugene Carr's 5th Cavalry rescued Mrs. Maria Weichell from the Cheyennes at the Battle of Summit Springs in 1869, while Mrs. Susanna Alderdice was killed in the Indian camp that day.

In the end, Indian resistance on the Plains was crushed before the close of the nineteenth century, and tribal peoples acknowledged their fate on the reservations set aside for them by the federal government. Most of these reserves were reduced to pitifully small size and generally located on less desirable lands.

They became virtual internment camps where the once proud native inhabitants of the land were confined. On these reservations, morale was dashed and there emerged a festering social malaise. But the spirit of those interned on the reservations was never fully destroyed, nor could the deep sense of Indian cultural value be erased.

See also Apache Wars; Seminole Wars; Sioux Wars; Wounded Knee Massacre

References

John C. Ewers, *Plains Indian History and Culture: Essays on Continuity and Change* (Norman: University of Oklahoma Press, 1997).

Stan Hoig, *Tribal Wars of the Southern Plains* (Norman: University of Oklahoma Press, 1993).

Brad D. Lookingbill, *War Dance at Fort Marion: Plains Indian War Prisoners* (Norman: University of Oklahoma Press, 2006).

Douglas W. Owsley and Richard L. Jantz, eds., *Skeletal Biology in the Great Plains: Migration, Warfare, Health, and Subsistence* (Washington, DC: Smithsonian Institution, 1994).

Robert M. Utley, *Frontiersmen in Blue: The United States Army and the Indian, 1848–1865* (Lincoln: University of Nebraska Press, 1967).

———, *Frontier Regulars: The United States Army and the Indian, 1866–1891* (Lincoln: University of Nebraska Press, 1973).

—William S. Reeder, Jr.

PLEASENCE, DONALD (1919–1995)

A veteran of more than 100 films, the English-born actor was accepted at the Royal Academy of Dramatic Art as a young man, but had to decline because his family was unable to afford the fees. Instead, Pleasence worked as a railway stationmaster until finally breaking onto the stage in *Wuthering Heights* in May 1939. World War II interrupted his acting career and Pleasence, a pacifist, declared himself to be a conscientious objector and was assigned to a lumber camp in northern England to perform alternative service. In time, his views changed and he decided to join the Royal Air Force, eventually qualifying as a wireless operator. On 31 August 1944, Pleasence's Lancaster bomber of 166 Squadron was shot down on a raid on a German V-weapons site in northern France and he was captured, spending the rest of the war in Stalag Luft 1, at Barth on the Baltic coast of Germany. While a prisoner, he became involved in the camp's theater company—perhaps his most memorable role was in *Petrified Forest*, in which he played the Leslie Howard character opposite a tall Canadian airmen in the Bette Davis role.

Liberated in 1945, Pleasence returned to acting, first on the stage and eventually in films. He achieved fame for his portrayal of Ernst Blofeld in the James Bond film *You Only Live Twice* (1967), but drew particular praise for his sensitive characterization of Colin Blythe, the Forger, in John Sturges' 1963 epic *The Great Escape*. One of two actors in the film who had actually been POWs themselves, Pleasence assisted Sturges with advice on matters of historical authenticity as production proceeded. He was the only actor from the original film to appear in the inferior made-for-television sequel *The Great Escape II: The Untold Story* (1988), this time portraying one of the Gestapo executioners; he had also played SS and Gestapo chief Heinrich Himmler in *The Eagle Has Landed* (1976). Known as an actor who brought skill and class to many a dreadful film, Pleasence never commented on the irony of an ex-POW portraying his former captors.

See also The Great Escape; Theater

—Jonathan F. Vance

POW/MIA ISSUE

One of the consequences of war is that soldiers on each side of the conflict will be captured and held as prisoners of war and that other soldiers will be missing in action (MIA) and become unaccounted for. Over the centuries, nations have addressed the issue of POW/MIA status differently. After many premodern conflicts, many nations did not return enemy soldiers who had been captured but instead maintained their claim on them and used them as forced laborers to repair the destruction of war. Soldiers whose fate was never determined were listed as MIAs and became just an asterisk in the statistics of each war. Very little effort was made to locate soldiers in this category. The passage of time, inadequate financial resources, diplomatic intransigence, and euphoria over a conflict's conclusion all diminished the desire to achieve the fullest possible accounting. Not until the twentieth century were steps taken to address this matter. The experience of prisoners of war held by the Japanese and Germans during World War II was directly responsible for the formation and implementation of the Missing Persons Act of 1942 and the Geneva Convention Relative to the Treatment of Prisoners of War in 1949.

The Vietnam War is also significant because it created a tremendous backlash against previous governments' unwillingness or inability to achieve the fullest possible accounting. It established in the American psyche the promise that all possible measures would be taken to repatriate the POWs/MIAs, or their remains, or to provide substantial explanations if this is not possible. Increasingly, that promise emerged as a model adopted by other nations. Out of the Vietnam experience came such prisoner advocate organizations as Radio of Free Asia (RFA), Voices in Vital America (VIVA), and the National League of Families (NLF). The POW/MIA Remembrance Bracelet and the POW/MIA Flag became symbols of the fullest possible accounting. Veterans' service organizations established standing committees and gave the matter very high priority. At the same time, a challenge came from family members who spoke out and demanded answers from governments on both sides of this war. They drew support from all segments of society—regardless of political persuasion, demographics, race, or creed—for the POWs and MIAs were drawn from across the spectrum of society.

The importance of this issue throughout the world can be seen through the American model. An autonomous agency, the Defense Prisoner of War/Missing Personnel Office, has been established to deal with all questions about prisoners of war and missing in action from all American wars; it is funded by congressional mandate through the budgetary process. Another agency, the Joint Task Force for Full Accounting, was established to handle the field excavation of human remains. To support these agencies, the Central Identification Laboratory—Life Science and the Armed Forces DNA Laboratory work as separate entities to identify and resolve cases of American servicemen and women whose remains have been recovered.

The American model is helping to reestablish the value of an individual soldier by affirming that the soldier's life is important and not expendable. This model is keeping faith with its citizen-soldiers and the families who must share a loved one to respond to the obligations imposed by today's world. It is an example worthy of emulation by all nations.

References

John M.G. Brown, *Moscow Bound: Policy, Politics and the POW/MIA Dilemma* (Eureka, CA: Veteran Press, 1993).

P.M. Cole, *POW/MIA Issues,* 3 vols. (Santa Monica, CA: Rand Corporation, 1994).

Craig Howes, *Voices of the Vietnam POWs: Witnesses to Their Fight* (New York: Oxford University Press, 1993).

Dorothy Howard McDaniel, *After the Hero's Welcome: A POW Wife's Story of the Battle Against a New Enemy* (Chicago: Bonus Books, 1991).

Chimp Robertson, *POW/MIA: America's Missing Men – The Men We Left Behind* (Walters, KS: Starburst Publishers, 1995).

Mark A. Sauter and Jim Sanders, *The Men We Left Behind: Henry Kissinger, The Politics of Deceit, and the Tragic Fate of POWs After the Vietnam War* (Washington, DC: National Press Books, 1993).

—Robert D. Necci

PRISON SHIPS

By the late eighteenth century, both the British civilian and military penal system had invested heavily in the use of prison hulks for housing prisoners. In the main, these prison ships were older vessels unfit for active ocean-going service, and rather than discard or destroy them, good use was found for them in England and her colonies as jails for civilian criminals and military prisoners of war. Conditions were designed to be horrible; the principle of less eligibility—conditions in a prison hulk must be worse than anything imaginable—was in place mainly as a deterrent to crime against the Crown.

During the American Revolution, the British Royal Navy established a fleet of military prison hulks designed to hold enemy soldiers and sailors captured in rebellion against the Crown. Based mostly in Wallabout Bay near Brooklyn, New York, from 1776 to 1782, the prison fleet included the *John, Whitby, Jersey, Preston, Lord Dunlace, Good Intent, Prince of Wales, Grosvenor, Falmouth, Glasgow, Good Hope, Judith, Scheldt, Frederick, Kitty, Woodlands, Clyde, Chatham, Felicity, Myrtle,* and *Scorpion.* Along with these ships, the Royal Navy also placed three hospital ships in Wallabout Bay, the *Hunter,* the *Perseverance,* and the *Bristol Packet,* for the enemy sick and wounded, and two hulks in Charleston Harbor, South Carolina, the *Torbay* and the *Pack Horse.* For the duration of the war, these ships were constantly busy housing thousands of Americans captured on land and at sea.

Few prisoners escaped from these hulks, and about 8,000 died from ill-treatment and the diseases of close confinement. The negative sentiment against the British hulks grew to become a seething obsession. During the war, Philip Freneau, a civilian passenger on an armed American ship captured by the British in 1780, published a scathing condemnation of his brief incarceration in the Scorpion in a poem entitled "The British Prison Ship." It was followed in 1829 by Captain Thomas Dring's *Recollections of the Jersey Prison Ship.* Narrators pointed out with regularity that in the prison hulks, the German troops were the kindest jailers, the Refugees or Loyalists the meanest, and the British, although generally harsh, varied from turnkey to turnkey.

Internationally, the new American government reacted strongly against the use of prison hulks. In 1783, Benjamin Franklin, Thomas Jefferson, and John Adams formed an American delegation to create a lasting Treaty of Amity (1785) between the United States and Frederick the Great of Prussia in which the prison hulk problem was directly addressed. Feeling wronged by the losses suffered in the British prison hulks, the new American government sought to eliminate even the slightest possibility that such things might happen again. In England, however, the Royal Navy continued its policy of using prison hulks like the *Hector* and *La Brave* to store its many prisoners of war, the practice lasting until Britain's second war with the United States, the War of 1812. This time, however, conditions improved and few prisoners died because both nations recognized each other's political sovereignty, and so prisoner-of-war status was no longer an issue. In England, the civilian prison hulk system survived until 1857, and prison ships were even employed by France and England during World War I. However, the ships used were generally modern, fully functional troop ships, and their use was clearly a temporary expedient; when camps on land were constructed, the prison ships were returned to duty as troop carriers.

References

Charles Campbell, *The Intolerable Hulks: British Shipboard Confinement, 1776–1857* (Bowie, MD: Heritage Press, 1994).

Albert Green, *Recollections of the Jersey Prison Ship from the Manuscript of Captain Thomas Dring* (New York: Corinth, 1961).

—*Robert C. Doyle*

PRISONERS OF THE SUN

An Australian movie by Siege Productions, *Prisoners of the Sun* was based on accounts of Japanese atrocities committed against Australian POWs on the island of Ambon, Dutch East Indies (now Indonesia), during World War II. The camp portrayed is probably Tantui, which was operated by the Japanese navy. The plot concerns the trial by the Australian military of three Japanese naval officers accused of decapitating four airmen. Captain Robert Cooper (Bryan Brown), the prosecutor, faces numerous obstacles, including the desire of the American military to protect the former camp commander, Vice Admiral Baron Takahashi (George Takei), for whom they have important peacetime plans. Takahashi is unjustly exonerated. However, Cooper is able to pursue two others: Captain Ikeuchi (Tetsu Watanabe), the second in command; and Lieutenant Tanaka (Toshi Shioya), a signals officer. Tanaka is returned to Ambon for the trial, and he corroborates the testimony of a surviving camp inmate, Private Jimmy Fenton (John Polson). Fenton agonizingly reveals that the airmen, one of whom was his brother, were beheaded by Takahashi, Ikeuchi, Tanaka, and others. After violently confronting Tanaka because he broke silence, which other Japanese refused to do, Ikeuchi commits suicide. Unable to retry the vice admiral and with Ikeuchi dead, the court makes Tanaka its scapegoat. He maintains that the Australians were legally court-martialed, but a Japanese sailor explains that Tanaka was duped and it becomes clear that he was following direct orders. Cooper, who reluctantly pursues the lieutenant, enters an eloquent plea of mercy for him, but the court finds Tanaka guilty and orders him shot. He is taken to the area where the four airmen had been killed and is placed before a firing squad. Despite its dramatic presentation, the movie is a realistic and plausible treatment of the issues surrounding the abuse of POWs and the search for justice.

See also Film

—*Robert S. La Forte*

PROTECTED PERSONNEL

"Protected personnel" is a category of combatant created under international law to include all medical staff, including doctors, dentists, nurses, and medical orderlies, as well as chaplains. In the prisoner of war conventions of the twentieth century, these personnel have enjoyed special rights should they fall into enemy hands.

The 1906 Geneva Convention for the Amelioration of the Condition of the Wounded and Sick of Armies in the Field stipulated that medical personnel and chaplains "shall be respected and protected under all circumstances. If they fall into the hands of the enemy they are not to be considered as prisoners of war" (Article 9). Instead, they were to be returned home as soon as possible. In World War I, the International Committee of the Red Cross (ICRC) devoted much effort to convincing belligerent states to abide by this provision. Success, however, came in fits and starts. A German-French agreement for the release of all medical personnel was suspended in November 1914, and by March 1915 only about 600 personnel from each side had been sent to Switzerland. There was a breakthrough in July 1915, when 4,000 French and 1,000 German protected personnel were released through Switzerland, and another in October 1916 that freed 3,000 French and 1,150 German medical staff. At the same time, the ICRC brokered agreements between the combatants on how many protected personnel would be retained in captivity to care for their fellow prisoners. Germany and Russia agreed to retain one doctor and 10 medical orderlies for every 2,500 POWs; a similar agreement was reached between Britain and Turkey with respect to Turkish prisoners, but these two governments agreed that one doctor and five orderlies would be retained for every 1,000 British prisoners. Austria-Hungary and Russia agreed on one doctor for every 1,500 POWs.

The 1929 Geneva Convention for the Amelioration of the Condition of the Wounded and Sick of Armies in the Field again stated that individuals engaged exclusively in caring for casualties were not to be retained as POWs. Arrangements were to be made without delay to return them to their own forces, and in the interim they could be engaged in caring for their own fellow prisoners. While they awaited release, they were to enjoy all the protection of international law. However, the convention also allowed that belligerents could conclude agreements for the retention of protected personnel. Indeed, in September 1941, the governments of Britain and Italy reached an agreement that allowed both sides to detain medical personnel and chaplains if they were needed to attend to their fellow prisoners. It became clear early in World War II that Germany also had every intention of retaining protected personnel, even in the absence of any agreements. Many such personnel were captured in the fall of France in 1940, and in November 1941, virtually the entire medical service of the New Zealand Division was captured in North Africa. In short order, they were transferred to captivity in Europe. There is no denying that, while in captivity, they performed heroic and essential services for their fellow prisoners. This fact suggests that the flexibility written into the Geneva Convention was wise.

The position of protected personnel with respect to repatriation was also unclear. Technically, surplus protected personnel were to be repatriated without delay; the spirit of international law suggested that the decision should be up to the personnel concerned. Both Germany and Italy, however, made it clear that they would decide how many enemy protected personnel would be retained in captivity. This position was bolstered by the argument, implicit in much of the government correspondence surrounding these repatriations, that any doctor or chaplain worth his salt should stay with his men. Another problem involved the certification of protected personnel. Early in the war, most belligerents accepted a simple letter as proof that an individual qualified for protected personnel status, but as the war dragged on, the German government became less willing to accept these letters of certification. There are a number of instances of medical personnel being forced to labor in work camps and being sentenced to solitary confinement if they refused.

The 1949 Geneva Convention Relative to the Treatment of Prisoners of War restated the provisions for protected personnel (Article 33), but there have been numerous examples of the contravention of this article. During the Vietnam War, North Vietnamese doctors refused to treat South Vietnamese soldiers; the Saigon government concluded that, by this action, the doctors had renounced their profession and were no longer entitled to special treatment. In 1972, during the India-Pakistan War, a number of Pakistani doctors were prohibited from performing medical duties because of the discovery of two escape tunnels in their camp. Although they had no personal involvement with the tunnels, they were stripped of their protected status.

See also Nurses

—*Jonathan F. Vance*

PROTECTING POWER

Before the twentieth century, it was usually up to each government to ensure that its citizens were being well treated in enemy hands. Typically, each government employed an agent in the enemy's capital, who would travel around to the places of internment, arrange for extra supplies of food, clothing, and recreational equipment, carry letters to and from prisoners, deal with complaints about treatment, and generally monitor their well-being. These agents did not have the force of international law behind them for support. Instead, they relied on force of personality, personal relations, common sense, and the good will of the detaining power to achieve their aims. There were, of course, occasional exceptions to this practice. In the thirteenth century, the Vatican Resident in Constantinople acted as a monitor for the well-being of Armenians and Jews, and the Capitulations of the Ottoman Empire of the 1500s used the term Protecting Power. However, the informal use of one's own nationals as agents was much more common.

In the Franco-Prussian War of 1870–1871, the warring states were represented by Protecting Powers for the first time in history: Great Britain acted on behalf of France, and the United States, Russia, and Switzerland acted for Germany. The employment here of citizens of nonbelligerents was necessitated by the expulsion of diplomats from Paris and Berlin, and by the severe restrictions on the liberty of other enemy aliens who remained. This practice was continued in subsequent conflicts: in the Sino-Japanese War (1894–1895), the United States represented both belligerents; in the Greek-Turkish War (1897), Germany acted for Turkey, while England, France, and Russia acted for Greece; and in the Italo-Turkish War (1911–1912), Germany served as Protecting Power for both sides.

During the Spanish-American War (1898) there came an innovation that would later become the cornerstone of the work of a Protecting Power: the prison camp inspection. For the first time, one government requested that its Protecting Power inspect the living conditions of its prisoners in the enemy's camps. So effective was this innovation that it has been used, with varying success, in all subsequent conflicts. In the Russo-Japanese War (1904–1905), for example, an American diplomat was able to visit a camp for Japanese POWs in Russia, and reported very favorably on the conditions there. Despite the wide approval of the Protecting Power's work, however, the institution was not featured in the 1899 or 1907 Hague Conventions, an omission that has mystified later scholars like Howard Levie.

Nevertheless, Protecting Powers were fully active during World War I, despite some initial resistance. The German government, for example, placed numerous restrictions on the movement of neutral inspectors and it took some years of negotiations to get them lifted. Similarly, the U.S. government refused in April 1917 to allow Switzerland to act as Protecting Power for German interests in the United States, at least until president Woodrow Wilson overruled his subordinates and allowed Swiss visits to go ahead. Switzerland, Holland, Denmark, Spain, and, until it entered the war in 1917, the United States all acted as Protecting Powers during World War I. Delegates from Spain, for example, visited over 200 prison camps and 250 work detachments over the course of the war.

The 1929 Geneva Convention Relative to the Treatment of Prisoners of War entrenched in international law the work of the Protecting Powers, in particular, the rules surrounding prison camp inspections. According to Article 86, "delegates shall be permitted to go to any place, without exception, where prisoners of war are interned. They shall have access to all places occupied by prisoners and may interview them, as a general rule without witnesses, personally or through interpreters." In effect, only Switzerland, Spain, and Sweden were able to act as Protecting Powers after the United States entered the war in December 1941.

The visits performed by the Protecting Power delegates in both world wars took place according to strictly observed guidelines, at least in the European theater. A schedule of visits had to be supplied well in advance to the detaining power, so that a liaison officer could be appointed. Generally, only three visits to each camp per year were permitted, because of the number of camps involved, but this limit could be stretched in exceptional circumstances. The visit usually began with a meeting with the commandant and his staff, who provided the delegate with all the statistics regarding the camp. Then, the inspector began his tour with the liaison officer and a member of the camp staff; in this way, the delegate was able to raise immediately any complaints or observations that occurred to him in the course of the visit. Every section of the camp was inspected, from the barracks to the kitchens to the latrine facilities, and careful notes were made of the conditions in each area. After the tour, the delegate was entitled to speak privately to the camp leaders, chaplain, and medical officers, and to any prisoners who wished to be interviewed; this gave the inmates an opportunity to make protests without fear of retaliation from their captors.

The delegate noted any needed supplies, received special messages for transmission to next of kin, and then returned to meet with the commandant, to resolve any minor issues that had come up. More significant matters were held over for discussion with higher authorities, while matters of great import would be dealt with directly by the belligerent governments, with the Protecting Power acting as an intermediary.

The situation was very different in the Pacific theater. The Japanese were extremely reluctant to allow any neutral delegates to visit their prison camps, and even after the government in Tokyo relented, the inspectors' freedom of action was severely constrained. Only two hours could be spent in any camp, and the delegate was prevented from talking with any prisoner except the appointed camp leader, and even then the discussion was monitored by camp officials. Many commandants refused to allow even a supervised interview, and some declined to answer any questions put to them by the inspector. In some cases, neutral inspections took place only after the Japanese had stocked the camp with extra food, clothing, medical supplies, and recreational equipment; once the inspector left, all of the extras were taken away again. So it is clear that the Protecting Power in the Far East was seriously hindered; it is difficult to say if any good came of their visits, and it is even possible that the Japanese tampered with their reports to create a false impression of conditions in the camps.

There were also problems in parts of Europe. The German government refused to allow Protecting Power intervention on behalf of POWs from Poland, Yugoslavia, France, Belgium, and Italy (after September 1943) on the grounds that those states had ceased to exist. Russia also declined to allow Protecting Powers to operate on its territory. As a result, the International Committee of the Red Cross estimated that only 30 percent of POWs during World War II benefited from the intervention of Protecting Power delegates.

Because of this low success rate, the 1949 Geneva Convention Relative to the Treatment of Prisoners of War strengthened the provisions that related to the Protecting Power, but this revision was to no avail. Rarely in post-1945 conflicts have Protecting Powers been able to act in the way that international lawmakers intended. The International Committee of the Red Cross has often taken on this role by default, but its work, laudable though it has been, is not a substitute for the Protecting Power as defined by international law.

References

William McHenry Franklin, *Protection of Foreign Interests: A Study in Diplomatic and Consular Practice* (Washington, DC: Government Printing Office, 1946).

Howard S. Levie, "Prisoners of War and the Protecting Power," *American Journal of International Law* 55 (1961): 374–397.

—*Jonathan F. Vance*

PSYCHOLOGY

See Barbed-Wire Disease

PUEBLO INCIDENT

On 23 January 1968, at the height of American involvement in the Vietnam War, North Korea created an international incident designed to humiliate the United States by seizing the USS *Pueblo* and imprisoning its crew as hostages. The *Pueblo*, an electronic surveillance ship, was patrolling off the coast of North Korea in international waters when six North Korean vessels surrounded it. After the Pueblo attempted to flee, the North Koreans opened fire upon the ship, killing one American and wounding three others. As North Korean soldiers boarded the vessel, the panicked crew attempted to burn or throw overboard classified files and secret intelligence equipment. Unprepared and ill-equipped to offer resistance, the remaining 82 crew members of the *Pueblo* surrendered.

Although the United States considered using military force to retaliate, President

Lyndon Johnson responded to this act of piracy by using diplomatic means to resolve the conflict. Johnson felt that military measures would jeopardize the lives of the crew. The attention of the United States was shifted to Vietnam after the South Vietnamese launched the Tet Offensive the following week. On 2 February, after attempting to resolve the conflict by making diplomatic appeals to the United Nations and the Soviet Union for assistance, the United States began to negotiate directly with North Korea for the release of the crewmen. The negotiations, however, quickly stalled, as the North Koreans wanted nothing short of an American admission of guilt, an apology, and a promise not to conduct further spy missions before they would release their prisoners.

The North Koreans utilized terror to get the maximum propaganda value out of their prisoners. Through psychological intimidation, food deprivation, and physical violence, the North Koreans slowly broke the spirit of the crew. The prisoners were forced to sign false confessions, to write letters to President Johnson, and to participate in staged press conferences, all of which were released to the international press. These measures were designed to humiliate the Americans and rob them of their self-respect. The Americans, however, resisted their captors in subtle ways, such as making an obscene gesture with their middle fingers, which they claimed was a Hawaiian good luck sign, during a group photo.

A breakthrough finally came in December after 10 months of negotiations between the United States and North Korea. The United States agreed to sign a North Korean document admitting guilt in return for the release of the prisoners; however, before signing the document, the United States would issue a public renunciation of the document as bogus. Realizing that they had received the maximum propaganda value from their prisoners and that they would soon have to begin negotiations with a new administration, the North Koreans did not object to the prior American denial. All 82 members of the crew were safely returned on 23 December 1968. Upon the crew's return to the United States, a Naval Court of Inquiry recommended courts-martial for two of the ship's officers, but the secretary of the navy overturned the recommendations, stating that "they had suffered enough."

See also Indoctrination; Vietnam War

References

Trevor Armbrister, *A Matter of Accountability: The True Story of the Pueblo Affair* (Guilford, CT: Lyons Press, 2004).

Ed Brandt, *The Last Voyage of USS Pueblo* (New York: W.W. Norton, 1969).

Lloyd M. Bucher, *Bucher: My Story* (Garden City, NY: Doubleday, 1970).

Russell D. Buhite, *Lives at Risk: Hostages and Victims in American Foreign Policy* (Wilmington, DE: Scholarly Resources, 1995).

Daniel V. Gallery, *The Pueblo Incident* (Garden City, NY: Doubleday, 1970).

—*William T. Hartley*

Punic Wars (264–146 B.C.E.)

The three Punic Wars (264–241; 218–201; and 149–146 B.C.E.) mobilized an enormous portion of the populations of two powerful and wealthy polities, the Roman Republic in central Italy and the state of Carthage on the coast of what is now Tunisia, as well as the people and resources of states allied to either side in Spain, Gaul, Italy, Sicily, and North Africa. The Punic Wars necessarily caused the detention of many thousands of combatants and civilians on both sides of the conflict.

Unfortunately, we have little direct testimony regarding the numbers, treatment, and ultimate fate of military prisoners during the Punic Wars. Roman and Greek writers have left almost nothing in the way of study or commentary on this aspect of war, despite the fact that war figured so prominently in Roman culture. Carthaginian documents are nonexistent. What little we do know comes from Latin or Greek sources, principally the Greek historian Polybius's *Histories,* and the Roman historian Livy's *Books from the Foundation of the City,* often recorded in final form long after the events occurred. This is further complicated because Polybius, Livy, and other sources often do not distinguish military from civilian prisoners. Nevertheless, it is possible to observe in these sources both the Romans and Carthaginians treating prisoners of war in a number of customary and often mutually agreed upon ways.

The persons of war captives (Latin *captivi*) belonged to the victor according to the conventions of nearly all Mediterranean cultures of the day. Polybius relates (3.84–85) how 15,000 Roman soldiers surrendered at the battle of Lake Trasimeno in 217, on the condition that their lives be spared. The Carthaginians accepted the offer, but their general Hannibal later told the Roman POWs that the commander who had accepted their surrender acted without authorization, and that he himself still held right of life and death over them.

When POWs' lives were spared, they became chattel property and were theoretically subject to any form of treatment, ranging from torture to sale. In fact, the practice of enslaving POWs seems to have so common at later periods of Roman history that it may well be that ancient sources assume this as the default method of dealing with POWs during the Punic Wars and accordingly fail to highlight it for our benefit. In the majority of cases where mention is made of prisoners taken, their fate is simply not told. The likelihood that many prisoners of war were enslaved during the Punic Wars is based on three factors: the almost complete absence of rights for POWs, later practice, especially Roman practice, and the frequent mention in our sources of the enslavement of whole populations of hostile cities.

In fact, these populations may be regarded as usually having a large component of POWs in the strict sense, since every free male was theoretically a combatant during the siege of a city. In this category we should put particularly the mass enslavements by the Romans during the Second Punic War noted by Livy, such as the 30,000 enslaved in Sicilian Agrigentum in 210 (26.40), 30,000 in Italy at Bruttium in 209 (27.16), and 30,000 at Tarentum in the same year (27.16).

However, the most frequently specified form of treatment of POWs during this period was the practice of ransom, the exchange of money or precious metal for the freedom and safe conduct of a prisoner. In his recounting the aftermath of the battle of Cannae in 214, one of Rome's most serious military defeats of any period, Livy notes that Hannibal set three different ransom prices for Roman POWs, according to social status: one for cavalry, one for infantry, and a third for slaves, who followed the army in the baggage train (22.58). According to both Polybius (6.58) and Livy (22.58–61), Hannibal sent a delegation of Roman POWs to Rome to propose this ransom. The Roman senate refused, since ransom would supply Hannibal with sorely needed funds, and declared that Roman soldiers were to fight to the death for the duration of the war. Livy's account relates—or, more probably, invents—a debate in the senate over this issue, including an impassioned speech by a POW leader who cites precedents from Roman history for ransoming captives.

Captives could of course be released without ransom by treaty or as a goodwill gesture. Polybius records a provision in the treaty between Rome and Carthage at the end of the First Punic War as saying that the Carthaginians must return prisoners to the Romans without ransom. According to Livy, after the battles of Lake Trasimeno, Trebia, and Cannae, Hannibal released without ransom captives of Rome's Italian allies (22.58) in order to win their states away from Rome. Prisoner exchange was not unknown either, although it seems to have been comparatively rare. Livy (23.7) gives an example of one such exchange under the auspices of Hannibal after the defection of the large Italian city of Capua to him in 216.

Noncombatants were effectively treated as POWs, particularly if their cities had been allied with or even unwillingly sheltered the enemy. While male citizens might be considered combatants, it is clear that much of the population, including women, the very old and very young, and slaves, were not. Polybius reports that the Romans took a large number of captives as early as 262 at Agrigentum during the First Punic War, although the Carthaginian garrison had secretly withdrawn (1.20). The Greek antiquarian Diodorus of Sicily records the number of enslaved as 25,000 (*Historical Library* 23.9). The Roman general Regulus took as captive 20,000 slaves of the Carthaginians in 256 from the Carthaginian countryside (Polybius 1.29). The Byzantine compiler Zonaras (8.12) tells us that many of these were Roman and Italian prisoners of war. Needless to say, if a whole city was captured, its free population, its movable wealth, including slaves, and its land belonged to the victors; it was unlikely that many of its citizens could ransom themselves. The Romans had other treatment for cities that offered particularly stubborn resistance: the male citizens might be put to the sword and the women and children only enslaved. If an order for no quarter was given, then all inhabitants, and often domestic animals as well, were slaughtered.

It is uncertain under what conditions either Romans and Carthaginians detained their POWs before they sold or ransomed them. Polybius (6.31) does describe an area of a typical Roman camp in which booty was stored (between the walls and the soldiers' tents), but he makes no specific mention of prisoners. Livy makes the point of saying (21.48) that Hannibal did not treat cruelly the prisoners taken in an action before the battle of Trebia (218); he did this in order to spread the repute of his goodwill, apparently toward Rome's Italian allies.

It would be close to accurate to say that prisoners of war during the Punic Wars, as with most other ancient wars, lost their human rights simply by the act of capture. What was done with them depended on the discretion of the victorious commander and the economic or political needs of the conquering army or state.

—Alexander Ingle

R

Race

The term *race* has little scientific use today, for there is no compelling evidence to link biologically distinctive human groups with variations in personal ability, social character, or cultural institutions. Simply put, there are no pure races of humankind. In a strict zoological sense, race is a subdivision of a species, but given the vast intermingling of peoples in the past five centuries, classifying *Homo sapiens* into simplistic structures is not only analytically reductive but also has proven to have deadly consequences.

From the beginnings of recorded history, there is evidence of conceptual definitions of people identified as "other," but the notion of races—different species of humans rather than just one humankind—emerged as a vehicle for scientific inquiry in the seventeenth century, when scientists began to develop a taxonomy of flora and fauna. As the concept of a nation became more closely identified as a biological unit, race theories emerged from attempts to explain why European civilization was ostensibly more developed and elevated than other peoples and cultures. In a 1684 article in *Journal des sçavans*, François Bernier published one of the first systematic constructions of a racial classification of humankind, based primarily on physical characteristics. And in 1817, Georges Cuvier identified the three subspecies of humans as Caucasian, Mongoloid, and Negroid. The idiom of race gained popular acceptance in European and American culture throughout the nineteenth century, but perhaps it drew the most interest following the revolutions of 1848, when discussions of Europe's "downfall" found an easy explanation in racial plurality and anticipated action for the future: the preservation of Caucasians through racial isolation.

In 1850, Herbert Spencer developed the theory that humans are in a constant struggle in which the strongest win, while Charles Darwin's *Origin of Species* (1858) argued that various life forms survived and developed as a result of adapting to a changing environment. Spencer's theory of survival of the *strongest,* different from the survival of the *fittest,* is commonly called *Social Darwinism.* Count Joseph-Arthur de Gobineau, in his 1854 *Inequality of Human Races,* assigned personality and psychological attributes to various races and articulated a vision of his own people as the "Aryan" race, superior in physical constitution, developed culture, and moral stature. Gobineau was joined by a host of other writers in considering race as an essential variable in interpreting history and biography. Gobineau, Houston Stewart Chamberlain, and other pseudoscientists argued that the "superiority" of their own culture and people was racially determined. Their approach ushered in the ideology known as *racism.*

In addition to physical characteristics such as skin pigmentation, stature, head shape, and hair color and form, numerous other variables have been used as erroneous bases of racial classification, from language and culture to geography and religion. As a result, and perhaps not surprisingly, other taxonomies and new vocabularies emerged during the nineteenth century that sought to marginalize particular groups while elevating others: Karoly Benkert's theories of "homosexuals" (1869) and Wilhelm Marr's coining of the term anti-Semitism (1879)—based on Christian Lassen's linguistic classification system from the 1840s—connected various hatreds of different groups under the larger rubric of "race theory." The culmination of Western race theories is exemplified in the rise of Nazi Germany, wherein ideologies based on blood purity, Aryan ancestry, and inevitable world domination fueled a war machine that initially sought enslavement of "lesser" races and aimed for the destruction of Jewish peoples everywhere. When the Nazis took power, they began a program of eugenics: the attempted "improvement" of the population through forced sterilization and marriage controls, including a euthanasia program that killed some 70,000 Germans—of all backgrounds—because of mental deficiencies and physical peculiarities. In the Holocaust, perhaps the ultimate ideological genocide, the Nazi powers deported, incarcerated, and slaughtered approximately 6 million Jews, roughly half a million Gypsies, and unknown thousands of homosexuals for reasons of "racial impurity." Unfortunately, the Holocaust does not stand alone as an atrocity fueled by racial ideology. The doctrine of Manifest Destiny in North America resulted in the near elimination of Native American "savages," and both Britain and the United States implemented their own national and cultural racial ideologies during World Wars I and II. While the images of apartheid in South Africa recede from cultural memory, the United States still contends with the repercussions of African slavery resulting in the bitter racism and prejudice that continues against African-Americans to this very day. Through ongoing research and critical inquiry, the dangerous consequences of race theories and the dangers of racist agendas continue to be exposed.

As a field of social scientific inquiry, the study of race was informed by evidence that race-based prejudice was learned rather than inherited behavior. From the 1920s to the 1930s, Franz Boas and his colleagues at Columbia University disproved claims that there was any significant correlation between race and sociocultural patterns. Similarly, Robert E. Park and others working in the University of Chicago disproved earlier race theories and set forth an "ecological theory" of race, claiming that competition and migration developed prejudice in various peoples as a type of defense mechanism. Social science has since offered a multitude of theoretical and analytical approaches to race, viewing it historically as a justification for capitalist exploitation and imperialism and turning attention to the current shift in racial ideologies: what was once deeply rooted in nationalism and exploitation has now been joined by an enhanced focus on ethnic, religious, and lifestyle identification processes, particularly as a global consciousness develops. The end of the Cold War, however, has re-ignited deep-seated sentiments that often return to race-based thinking as a means for group solidarity.

Scientific inquiry, ironically, may provide a better understanding of the common origins and differences among humans across the planet. Population geneticists L.L. Cavalli-Sforza, Paolo Menozzi, and Alberto Piazza, in *The History and Geography of Human Genes*, synthesized over 50 years of population genetics research to produce the first genetic atlas of the world. Such research, in addition to the Human Genome Diversity Project and other endeavors, will undoubtedly tell us more about the complex varieties among humans and help to undermine the erroneous racial theories that continue to murmur in various corners of every community.

Despite the illegitimacy of race in scientific terms, the concept has exercised considerable influence over the treatment of prisoners of war and internees since it became popular in the nineteenth century. Indeed, it should come as no surprise that racial assumptions often governed certain aspects of captivity. During the colonial wars waged by the European powers in North and South America, Africa, and Asia, captured natives were frequently put to death on the grounds that they were lower forms of life who did not deserve to live; the fact that these natives often murdered European prisoners was, paradoxically, taken as proof of their inherent barbarism. Racial considerations were also prominent in the U.S. Civil War. In 1863, the Confederacy announced that it would treat captured black Union soldiers, not as POWs, but as rebellious slaves, and that white officers who were captured while in command of black troops would be executed. Reports from Andersonville Prison in Georgia, however, suggest that the Confederate guards treated the black POWs the same as the whites; they did, however, reserve special ire for the white officers who had commanded black units.

Interestingly, in Nazi Germany, where racism and race theory were particularly virulent, the picture was more complex. There is conflicting evidence as to whether the Nazis treated blacks, whether they were French colonial troops or African-American soldiers or airmen, differently on grounds of race. There are many documented cases of the summary execution of French colonial troops after the fall of France in 1940, but such abuses seem to have been largely confined to the period immediately following capture. Efforts were made to seduce Moroccan or Algerian POWs away from their allegiance to France, but once they reached permanent camps, there is little indication of systematic abuse. Similarly, black pilots shot down during World War II were regarded as objects of curiosity by their German captors but were rarely singled out for special treatment. The fact that there were relatively few blacks in German camps may have prevented them from being singled out for special treatment. The Germans did, however, segregate some POWs by race; for example, soldiers from the Indian Army, captured in North Africa, were segregated into special camps and subjected to special efforts to encourage them to renounce their allegiance to the British Empire. The situation on the eastern front, of course, was entirely different. There, racism intermingled with a deep hatred of Communism to produce exceptionally brutal treatment of captured Soviets, treatment that was fully reciprocated. In the Pacific theater during World War II, a similar situation existed. One of the motives behind Japanese ill-treatment of western POWs seemed to have been decades of resentment against Western imperialism in the Far East and the racist assumptions that underpinned it; indeed, historians have argued that the Pacific war was a race war and that the atrocities committed against POWs should be seen in that context.

References

L.L. Cavalli-Sforza et al, *The History and Geography of Human Genes* (Princeton, NJ: Princeton University Press, 1994).

David Killingray, "Africans and African Americans in Enemy Hands," in *Prisoners of War and Their Captors in World War II*, ed. Bob Moore and Kent Fedorowich (Oxford: Berg, 1996).

Roger Lambo, "Achtung! The Black Prince: West Africans in the Royal Air Force, 1939–1946," in *Africans in Britain*, ed. David Killingray (London: Frank Cass, 1994).

Jonathan M. Marks, *Human Biodiversity: Genes, Race, and History* (New York: Aldine de Gruyter, 1995).

Ashley Montagu, *Man's Most Dangerous Myth: The Fallacy of Race* (Walnut Creek, CA: AltaMira Press, 1997).

Raffael Scheck, *Hitler's African Victims: The German Army Massacres of 1940* (Cambridge: Cambridge University Press, 2006).

Elisabeth Young-Bruehl, *The Anatomy of Prejudices* (Cambridge, MA: Harvard University Press, 1996).

—*Brad Lucas*

RANSOM

In the medieval world, the ancient practice of enslaving defeated enemies came to be seen as inappropriate in wars between Christians, and it was largely replaced by a system based on the payment of ransoms. Instances of this practice are attested in even the earliest periods of the Middle Ages. Ransom's incorporation into the laws of war was related both to the diffusion of Christian values and to a style of warfare in which identifiable individuals confronted each other in close combat. By the twelfth century, the practice was well established across Europe.

When a surrender was accepted, captor and captive entered into a relationship similar to that between feudal lord and vassal.

Until a ransom had been paid, the prisoner's status was essentially servile; his captor became his master. Even if he was not actually confined, the prisoner of war remained within the power of this master, compelled to obey his summons immediately. The captor, for his part, could undertake any reasonable action to obtain his payment, but he was obliged to protect the life of his prisoner and could not force him to do anything contrary to law or honor. Captives might be imprisoned, but more often they were released on parole to raise their ransoms. Technically, they and their lands enjoyed immunity from war until this was paid.

The process could be fraught with complexities. The act of surrender was often confused. In principle, a legally binding bond was created when one man simply pledged to another "I yield myself your prisoner." This might be accompanied by the surrender of the right gauntlet as a physical token of the captor's incontrovertible rights over the particular prisoner. However, amidst the confusion of battle, it was often not clear who had actually accepted an individual's surrender. For example, at the Battle of Poitiers in 1356, the French Count of Dammartin was abandoned by a succession of men to whom he had given his pledge, and consequently his life remained in danger. He continued, therefore, to give his pledge to others until finally he was safe in the custody of the English Earl of Salisbury. Dammartin was eventually recognized as Salisbury's prisoner, but not before the earl had incurred substantial legal costs establishing his claim in court.

The amount of ransom to be paid varied according to the wealth of an individual. David II of Scotland, imprisoned after his defeat at Neville's Cross in 1346, was held captive until 1357 and was finally released for a ransom of 100,000 marks, to be paid in 10 annual installments. By tradition, a nobleman's ransom would be equivalent to a year's revenue of his estate. In practice, the size of the ransom depended mostly on the inclination of the captor. The sixteenth-century Gascon captain Blaise de Lasseran Massencôm, Seigneur de Monluc, made moderate ransom demands, commenting that "it is unworthy to skin [prisoners] when they are honourable men of war." Yet on the whole, ransom demands were excessive; for rich and poor alike they could be a cripplingly onerous burden. Ordinary soldiers were generally ransomed for between one to three months' wages, leaving many with no means to support themselves in the meantime. In 1515 an English soldier, Thomas Cressy, was granted a license to beg for alms to pay the ransom he owed his French captor.

The consequences of defaulting on a ransom payment were, inevitably, serious. A poor man who could not afford his ransom would be expected to enter the service of his captor. Thus, whatever the religious objections, in practice some prisoners were reduced to a state close to slavery. The wealthy, too, might struggle to pay ransoms. A nobleman on parole would usually leave kinsmen or servants as sureties with his captor. If installments of the ransom were not forthcoming, the conditions of imprisonment for these sureties would rapidly deteriorate. If hostilities had ceased, legal proceedings to recover ransom payments could be instigated. If hostilities continued, direct reprisals could be taken, usually against the land and property of the defaulting party, which would no longer be considered immune. Perhaps the most potent weapon used against high-status prisoners who failed to pay ransoms was to dishonor them. This might, for example, involve the public display of their heraldic arms reversed or tied to the tail of a horse. In such a status-conscious society, the threat of dishonor would force all but the most recalcitrant to pay.

The prospect of receiving a fortune in ransom money was real enough to induce medieval soldiers to endure the hazards of life on campaign. Yet military ordinances strictly controlled the system of ransom. Prisoners of royal blood and from the leading noble households belonged to the king, regardless of who had captured them. The man who had actually accepted their surrender would be entitled only to an appropriate reward. The same applied to traitors who were captured in the service of the enemy. Even in those cases where a man had uncontested claim to a prisoner, the ordinances demanded that a third of the ransom he collected be paid to his immediate superior. This officer would, in turn, pay a share of all the ransom money he had received to the crown.

Yet the arrangements for ransom remained essentially personal, between captor and captive. As such, there was always a danger that they could be inimical to discipline. As early as the fourteenth century, soldiers were being ordered not to spend too much time pursuing captives for ransom purposes when they should be fighting to gain tactical objectives. By the seventeenth century, there were concerted attempts to stamp out the practice of ransoming. Oliver Cromwell, the Parliamentarian general and eventual victor of the English Civil War, promulgated regulations in 1644 that decreed that "No officer or soldier shall ransom or conceal a prisoner." Increasingly, it was accepted that a sovereign could claim the right to dispose of all prisoners as he wished, since he was paying for the war. By the end of the seventeenth century, the system of prisoner exchange, a practice with a long pedigree which had become increasingly common since the sixteenth century, was generally preferred to that of ransom.

See also Exchange

References

Philippe Contamine, *War in the Middle Ages*, trans. Michael Jones (Oxford: Blackwell, 1984).

Charles Cruikshank, *Henry VIII and the Invasion of France* (Stroud, UK: Alan Sutton, 1990).

Viscount Dillon, "Ransom," *Archaeological Journal* 61 (1904): 102–119.

Evan Haefili, "Ransoming New England Captives in New France," *French Colonial History* 1 (2002): 113-127.

M. H. Keen, *The Laws of War in the Late Middle Ages* (London: Routledge and Kegan Paul, 1965).

Michael Prestwich, *Armies and Warfare in the Middle Ages: The English Experience* (New Haven, CT: Yale University Press, 1996).

—*Gervase Phillips*

RAPE

See Sexual Violence

RATIONS

One of the constants in accounts of captivity is food. Prisoners of war and civilian internees have usually been obsessed with it, and for good reason. Captivity is usually a time of deprivation, and often food is the commodity that, next to liberty, is in shortest supply. It is hardly surprising that prisoners have spent hours discussing fantasy meals they would eat after the war and have filled their diaries with meticulous lists of food items received or traded. When the rations provided by the captor are insufficient to sustain life, the prisoner has to rely on other sources of sustenance to survive.

A number of factors have influenced the rations that detaining powers have made available to prisoners. A key determinant is the overall food supply available to the detaining power. During World War II, food was relatively plentiful in Canada, the United States, and Australia, so rations for prisoners held in those countries were quite generous. German POWs in Lethbridge camp, in western Canada, enjoyed a diet that offered roughly 3,000 calories per day; the average prisoner in the camp gained 12 pounds during his first 10 months in the camp. At Camp Clinton, Mississippi, a facility for German POWs in World War II, prisoners breakfasted on corn flakes, cake or bread, marmalade, and coffee with milk and sugar. A typical lunch consisted of potato salad, roast pork, and carrots, while dinner might be meat loaf, scrambled or boiled eggs, bread, milk, and coffee. The camp also had a canteen where prisoners could purchase candy, soft drinks, local produce, and perhaps even beer or wine. This was certainly a better diet than the prisoners would have enjoyed had they been in Germany.

In contrast, in Germany at the end of World Wars I and II and in Japan at the end of World War II, food shortages were severe and the civilian population often went

The kitchens at the Alexandra Palace in London, which held German POWs during World War I (from German Prisoners in Great Britain *[London, n.d.])*

hungry. As a consequence, POWs suffered severely, for it was unlikely that any detaining power would ensure that enemy prisoners ate better than its own civilians. British officers imprisoned in Rastatt in 1918 lived on coffee and a small chunk of bread for breakfast, a bowl of thin soup for lunch, and more soup for dinner, with perhaps a beet or a couple of baked potatoes. By 1945, Allied POWs in Japanese camps were existing on as little as 600 calories a day, less than half what captives in Germany received, and one-fifth of what POWs in Allied camps were receiving. It was not uncommon for prisoners in the Far East to lose 100 pounds in body weight over the duration of their captivity.

To some degree, international law has recognized that a detaining power will not always have limitless food supplies at its disposal. The Lieber Code of 1863, which regulated captivity during the U.S. Civil War, stipulated that prisoners should receive "plain and wholesome food" but added "whenever practicable" as a caveat. This effectively admitted that there would be occasions when the detaining power simply lacked the resources to feed prisoners adequately. Union POWs in the camp in Macon, Georgia, for example, were issued cornmeal with corn husks, rancid and maggoty bacon, salt, vinegar, and watery soup—an unappetizing fare to be sure, but no different from the rations their guards received. The 1907 Hague Convention held that POWs should receive the same rations as the troops that captured them, while other agreements reached in World War I attempted to lay down minimum calorie levels: 2,000 calories per day for nonworking prisoners, 2,500 for working prisoners, and 2,850 for prisoners doing hard labor. The 1929 Geneva Convention Relative to the Treatment of Prisoners of War altered this practice slightly by stating that prisoners should be fed on the same ration scale as the detaining power's own garrison troops, but there was no consistency in rations given to garrison troops of different nations. Figures ranged from 3,300 calories per day (for U.S. troops) to 1,500 calories (for Japanese troops), so that it was possible for a detaining power to abide by the letter of international law and yet still subject POWs to considerable suffering. The 1949 Geneva Convention Relative to the Treatment of Prisoners of War addressed this problem by eliminating the reference to garrison troops, stating that the daily ration should be "sufficient in quantity, quality, and variety to keep prisoners of war in good health and to prevent loss of weight or the development of nutritional deficiencies" (Article 26).

The decision to link prisoners' rations to those of the detaining power's garrison troops was significant in another respect as well. There are distinct cultural differences in diet, and those differences have sometimes proven deadly for POWs. The clearest example of this was in the Pacific theater in World War II. The Japanese diet is heavily based on rice, so POW rations were also based on rice. Western prisoners, however, were unused to such a high proportion of rice in their diets. Their bodies could not extract sufficient nutritional value from it, and the rice-based diet made them more susceptible to disease. A small quantity of rice per day was enough to sustain the average Japanese soldier, but it was not enough for the average Westerner. The 1949 Geneva Convention Relative to the Treatment of Prisoners of War attempted to resolve this conundrum by stipulating that detaining powers take into account the "habitual diet" of their captives when determining rations.

Prisoners living on short rations had two options to augment their diet: they could rely on external sources or turn to illicit means. The former was more satisfactory, and in many cases a food parcel from home made a prisoner's existence bearable. Until after World War I, friends or relatives could usually dispatch parcels of foodstuffs to prison camps with a reasonable expectation that they would reach the addressee intact. However, this was a system with built-in inequities: the wealthier or more influential a prisoner, the better he ate. Furthermore, it was not unknown for detaining powers to reduce rations if there were large quantities of food coming into a camp from external sources. Indeed, during World War I, it became clear that the system was grossly unfair. Some British prisoners in Germany received no extra food at all, while others received as many as 16 parcels in a fortnight; it was not unknown for a prisoner to receive over 100 pounds of food parcels each week. Consequently, British officials took the unpopular but understandable decision to place limits on food shipments: each prisoner could receive a maximum of 30 pounds of food per week. This smoothed out the inequalities and reduced the number of parcels going through the already taxed postal system.

From here, it was only a small step to the most successful program, the provision of unaddressed food parcels to POWs by the International Committee of the Red Cross (ICRC) during World War II. The plan was instituted early in the war, when the Canadian government agreed to provide 5,000 food parcels weekly, to be shipped to prison camps in Europe via New York. Later in the war, other nations, particularly the United States, Australia, and New Zealand, joined in. The parcels were initially carried to Lisbon by the U.S. Postal Service, but in December 1941, the ICRC created the Foundation for the Organization of Red Cross Transport; for the rest of the war, all relief supplies were carried in 43 Spanish, Swedish, Swiss, and Portuguese vessels. They entered the European continent at various ports, primarily Marseille, Lisbon, or Gothenburg, and were then transported to ICRC depots in Geneva or Lübeck in trucks or specially chartered trains. From there, they were moved to a number of Red Cross–operated central facilities for distribution to prison camps. Different countries produced slightly different parcels. The Canadian parcel, for example, was formulated by a doctor at the University of Toronto and provided 2,070 calories per day for seven days, from 13 food items: whole milk powder, butter, cheese, corned beef, pork luncheon meat, salmon, sardines, dried apples, dried prunes, sugar, jam, biscuits, and chocolate. Other items were salt, tea, and soap. The only inequity in the program was the fact that it was directed primarily at American and British Commonwealth POWs, not prisoners from other Allied nations. In fact, American figures showed that for every 10,000 grams of food shipped to a British POW, a Frenchman received 850 grams, a Belgian 500, a Pole 280, and a Yugoslav a mere 175 grams. Furthermore, the program was a limited success in the Far East. Despite many months of difficult negotiations, the Allies were only able to persuade Japan to accept about 225,000 parcels, which were delivered through ports in Russia; even then, only a fraction of these parcels ever reached the prisoners. Despite these problems, the program was a huge success and a considerable achievement in logistical terms. Canada alone produced 16 million food parcels over the course of the war.

When food from external sources was not available, prisoners could augment their rations on their own initiative. It was relatively easy for prisoners to barter for food with civilians or their own guards, assuming that they had something, like a watch or some cigarettes, to trade. By the same token, prisoners who worked on farms often ate the produce they helped raise, and others who worked unloading railway cars would take any opportunity to steal food as they unloaded it. Many camps had gardens in which they could grow vegetables or even raise chickens. At the other end of the spectrum, prisoners who existed on the brink of starvation were forced to become less discerning in their eating habits. At Belle Isle, a U.S. Civil War camp operated by the Confederacy in Richmond, Virginia, the prisoners captured the commandant's pet poodle and made a meal of it. POWs in the Pacific during World War II trapped cats, dogs, birds, snakes, or rats to eat. One prisoner passed a swamp on his way to work in a Japanese coal mine and took to stuffing his pockets with as many frogs as he could catch; he roasted and ate them during the day. Others caught grasshoppers or locusts to add protein to their rice ration. Soviet POWs in Germany in World War II were even more malnourished, and there are numerous accounts of their captors releasing guard dogs into the compounds to quell disturbances. Invariably, the dogs would not return to their masters, and a few days later the skin would be tossed over the wire.

Shortages of food brought out the best and the worst in prisoners. Some stole from their fellow prisoners out of sheer desperation, in the full knowledge that, next to treason, stealing food from a campmate was the worst crime a POW could commit. More often, shortages bred cooperation. Prisoners often joined together into small groups (prisoners in Germany during World War II called them combines) to pool their rations and make them go farther. Great care was taken to ensure that everything was shared out equally. One expedient was to assign a different person to cut the combine's bread ration each day. The process of ensuring that each slice was equal could take up to an hour, then each prisoner chose his own slice according to a predetermined order. To ensure that the cutter gained no unfair advantage, he selected his slice last. Practices like this suggest that the greatest skill a prisoner could possess to survive captivity was adaptability.

See also Avitaminosis; Health; International Committee of the Red Cross

References

Frederick F. Tisdall et al, "Final Report on the Canadian Red Cross Society Food Parcels for Prisoners-of-War," *Canadian Medical Association Journal* 60 (1949): 279–286.

—*Jonathan F. Vance*

REEDUCATION

For the purposes of this volume, the term *reeducation* refers to the attempt to alter the political beliefs of a group of individuals in order to influence and possibly reshape the political and ideological fabric of the country they hail from. It is largely a phenomenon of World War II. Determined to eradicate National Socialism in Germany, officials in the United States, Great Britain, and the Soviet Union devised educational programs designed to induce Germans to abandon Nazi philosophy and embrace democratic or, in the case of the Soviet program, communist, ideals. Naturally, their efforts were aimed first at those Germans who were readily accessible to them: captured *Wehrmacht* soldiers.

Prior to the twentieth century, prisoners of war were generally regarded as inactivated troops who would be of no further relevance to the course of events. Their mentalities and political beliefs seemed of no concern to the captors. Two factors, however, led to the full-scale emergence of reeducational programs for war prisoners during World War II: first, the war was universally understood as a contest between ideologies, and second, it coincided with the rise of modern social science and its growing influence in the field of education. From the outset, many people in the West felt that the widespread popularity that the governments of Germany and Japan enjoyed domestically was a sign of cultural deficiencies in the "national character" of the people of both countries. Thus, military victory was only a first step, to be followed by a reorientation of Germans and Japanese away from militarism and authoritarianism. Most notably in the United States, psychiatrists, sociologists, and anthropologists cooperated with government agencies to develop up-to-date educational strategies of democratic indoctrination. As long as the war lasted, the prime target of these efforts were captured enemy troops who, it was hoped, would eventually figure prominently in the establishment of a new type of government in their home countries.

Desperately defending itself against the German onslaught of June 1941, the Soviet Union was the first Allied nation to engage in reeducation. The purpose was twofold: the Red Army needed Germans for psychological warfare and propaganda purposes at the front, and the large and influential group of German émigré Communists in Moscow already planned to recruit personnel for a future Marxist German state in the case of Allied victory. As early as May 1942, the first "anti-fascist" school, or Antifa, began to offer courses. In 1943, when the number of German prisoners began to increase, the two largest and most famous Antifa schools began operations in Krasnogorsk and Talica. The curricula emphasized theoretical Marxism-Leninism and strict discipline. At the regular prison camps, Antifa activists wielded considerable authority over their fellow POWs and often backed their demands for political reorientation with force, thus giving the Soviet program a highly coercive character. Therefore, the program's success in genuinely altering the political beliefs of a significant proportion of the captured German soldiers is difficult to assess; the Soviets did, however, score a number of propaganda victories, most notably with the formation of the controversial National Committee Free Germany. Holding German prisoners until 1956 and practicing communist reeducation as a weapon in the emerging Cold War, the Soviet Union continued its Antifa activities longer than any other Allied nation, up to about 1950. Just as German émigrés had hoped, many of its graduates did indeed assume positions of power in communist East Germany after 1949.

In the United States, the question of a reeducation program for prisoners of war gained considerable urgency during the summer of 1943, when, following the Allied victory in North Africa, the number of Axis prisoners held in the United States surged to over 150,000. Despite public pressure to devise a program, however, the U.S. War Department remained reluctant, fearing German reprisals against Allied prisoners of war. The Geneva Convention did not explicitly prohibit reeducation, yet it made clear that any form of education in POW camps would have to work on a voluntary basis only. With these concerns in mind, in mid-1944 the Provost Marshal General's Office (PMGO) finally initiated a secret "intellectual diversion program," which refrained from open indoctrination as long as the war lasted and instead tried to familiarize the POWs with the English language and the nature of American democracy. In January 1945, the arrival of so-called assistant executive officers in almost all camps intensified these activities. Making use of various media, including films, lectures, and publications, these officers were supposed to deepen the prisoners' understanding of American political culture and thus provide them with an alternative to Nazism. Their success was limited, however, as they often faced opposition from camp commanders who favored efficient employment over education. Nonetheless, almost all of the roughly 375,000 German POWs interned in the United States came into contact with some sort of reeducational effort. Those genuinely in search for a new political outlook were certainly assisted. This holds especially true for prisoners selected to receive instruction at five special reeducation camps established by the Special Projects Branch of the PMGO between 1944 and 1946. When the last German prisoners left the United States in July 1946, about 30,000 of them had received some form of Special Projects instruction.

British reeducation began later than its American and Soviet equivalents, but here, too, proposals had been forwarded as early as 1940. Holding only small numbers of German prisoners until the Normandy invasion in June 1944, the British began their program in earnest only after the war had ended. Even more than the Americans, they emphasized the exposure of the prisoners to the way of life in a democratic society rather than the teaching of political principles. Training advisers of the Prisoner of War Division of the Foreign Office (POWD) encouraged and organized educational courses and cultural activities and arranged contacts between POWs and British civilians. Their success varied according to local conditions, the ability of the British staff, and the importance of the labor program at a particular camp. In January 1946, the POWD opened Camp 300, Wilton Park, as a special reeducation center that offered six-week courses of academic discussion to selected prisoners of different political affiliation. By mid-1948, about 4,000 German prisoners of war and 500 German civilians had graduated from courses at Wilton Park. In addition, the British in June 1946 undertook the ambitious project to reeducate a number of young and outspokenly fascist prisoners at Camp 180, Radwinter, later known as the Youth Camp.

Unlike the efforts directed at German prisoners, reeducational programs for Italian and Japanese personnel never made much headway. The United States had devised plans for both, but the Italian program lost most of its rationale after Italy had declared itself an Allied cobelligerent in September 1943. A lack of trained experts and widespread prejudice against a supposedly incorrigible Asian militarism hampered the Japanese program and limited it to an instructional course at Camp Huntsville, Texas, in 1945–1946. The Axis nations, on the other side, never really attempted to reeducate Allied POWs on their behalf—a clear reminder that Germany and Japan fought wars of conquest, not of moral persuasion.

See also Indoctrination

References

Henry Faulk, *Group Captives: The Re-education of German Prisoners of War in Britain, 1945–1948* (London: Chatto and Windus, 1977).

Uta Gerhardt, "A Hidden Agenda of Recovery: The Psychiatric Conceptualization of Re-education for Germany in the United States during World War II," *German History* 14 (1996): 297–324.

Andrew Rettig, "A De-Programming Curriculum: Allied Reeducation and the Canadian-American Psychological Warfare Program for German POWs, 1943–1947," *American Review of Canadian Studies* 29 (1999): 593–619.

Ron Robin, *The Barbed-Wire College: Reeducating German POWs in the United States during World War II* (Princeton, NJ: Princeton University Press, 1995).

Arthur L. Smith, *The War for the German Mind: Re-Educating Hitler's Soldiers* (Providence, RI: Berghahn Books, 1996).

—Rafael A. Zagovec

REHABILITATION

The notion that prisoners of war might require assistance in readjusting to a life of freedom after being released from captivity is relatively recent. There are two aspects to this problem: the necessity of integrating the former prisoner into the postwar economy by finding him suitable useful employment, and overcoming any physical or psychological problems that may be associated with captivity. Both areas saw significant improvements through the twentieth century.

In some ways, POWs were better placed for postwar employment than others in military service. The training regime for an infantryman produces skills that are not necessarily useful in peacetime society, so strictly in terms of future career options, service in the army might well be time wasted. Time in captivity is somewhat different. Certainly for career soldiers it is devastating; every year in captivity is another year of missing out on possibilities for command and promotion. But a prisoner who will be returning to civilian life at the end of hostilities and who has the desire and the means can use the time in captivity to plan for the future and, more importantly, to learn useful skills. The POW who uses his captivity carefully might well be better placed to enter the postwar job market than a demobilized soldier. This fact lay behind the educational schemes that have been mounted for prisoners of war. During World War I, the schemes put in place for POWs in enemy hands, as well as those interned in neutral countries, were explicitly intended to train prisoners to "get on with the battle of life" after the war. In World War II, the educational campaign was even more extensive and allowed prisoners to learn basic literacy, a trade, or even a professional qualification while behind barbed-wire. Many prisoners thus gained a distinct advantage in postwar society, for captivity allowed them to get job training that would not otherwise have been available to them.

One of the reasons job training was deemed so essential was because it would reduce the psychological difficulties that returned prisoners were expected to experience. Despite A.L. Vischer's pioneering work on barbed-wire disease in World War I, there were few doctors who understood the long-term effects of captivity, either in psychological or physical terms. One of the few who did was a Canadian, Dr. J.P.S. Cathcart, who reported on the matter in 1932. He argued that poor prison camp conditions over the long term were more likely to cause significant mental and physical problems than specific incidents of mistreatment. In examining former POWs, Cathcart found a host of physical and nervous complaints, from bronchitis to dizziness to insomnia, which he attributed to neurasthenia or nutritional deprivation. He concluded that many physical problems experienced by POWs after their release had a significant psychological component, based on confinement for long periods under conditions of unusual mental strain. But Cathcart was a lone voice; most doctors disregarded the aches, pains, and phobias of former POWs, assuring them that a few months of good food and family life would put them right. In many cases, it did not, and former POWs of World War I suffered badly from neglect by their own governments.

Because of this failure to address the rehabilitation of former POWs after World War I, Allied officials began to consider the problem very early in World War II. Discussions began in 1941, and by 1943, there was wide agreement on what was needed to smooth the transition to civilian life for former POWs. Job training was a large part of it; former prisoners needed to have something useful to do after years of feeling, often subconsciously, that they were doing nothing. But counseling was also a factor. Released POWs, it was realized, faced different problems than other soldiers, and so they required different solutions. They were liable to be highly strung, resistant to authority, prone to feelings of guilt, easily distracted, and deeply concerned about what they had missed while in captivity. To overcome these problems, many of the Allied governments drew up rehabilitation programs, which included frequent physical and psychological checkups, courses to fill them in on events that had occurred while they were captive, counseling sessions for former prisoners and their families, and opportunities for peer reinforcement through socializing with other former prisoners.

Even with these measures, applied more broadly in some countries than in others, former POWs experienced difficulties reintegrating into civilian society. Many of them found that restlessness prevented them from holding down a job. Others developed phobias of traffic, crowds, or open spaces. The obsession with food often lasted for years; one British woman discovered in the 1950s that her husband, a former prisoner, had been burying cans of food in their backyard since 1945, so they would have a reserve in the event of shortages. Some turned to alcohol or drugs to ease the transition, and some withdrew from society altogether, becoming hermits in rural or undeveloped areas. People like this, in spite of all the efforts at rehabilitation, would spend the rest of their lives held captive by their experiences.

See also Barbed-Wire Disease; Families

References

Joan Beaumont, "Gull Force Comes Home: The Aftermath of Captivity," *Journal of the Australian War Memorial* 14 (1989): 43–52.

George F. Collie, "Returned Prisoners of War: A Suggested Scheme for Repatriates," *The Fortnightly* 153 (1943): 407–411.

T.F. Main, "Clinical Problems of Repatriates," *Journal of Mental Science* 93 (1947): 354–363.

A.T.M. Wilson et al, "Group Techniques in a Transitional Community," *Lancet,* 31 May 1947, 735–738.

—*Jonathan F. Vance*

RELIGION

Religion has played a significant, though poorly understood, role in the life of prisoners of war and interned individuals during wartime. In general, religious belief can be linked to three issues: the close relationship between religion and ethnicity in twentieth-century wars, religion as a reason for internment, and the religious life of those interned in camps.

While taking prisoners according to faith has a long history—going back, for example, to the Crusader wars for Jerusalem, fought between Muslims and Christians—the link between internment and religion appears most overtly in the twentieth century. In many conflicts, religious faith has become synonymous with ethnicity and nationality.

Nationalism and the desire for national self-determination have become one of the most important reasons for the outbreak of war in the past two centuries. In order to differentiate one group from another, belligerents have used religion as a kind of signature that quickly identifies potential allies and enemies. The first large-scale campaign to round up prisoners of a distinct ethnic and religious type may have been during World War I, when Turkish authorities rounded up 1.5 million Armenian Christians. These Turkish subjects were then placed into camps or labor battalions and finally executed. Protests from diplomatic and religious leaders, especially Armenian Catholics, had little effect.

The most horrific use of religion (and ethnicity) during wartime, of course, occurred during World War II, when six million Jews were murdered by the Nazi regime in organized death camps. The Holocaust, however, points out the problems of separating religion from ethnicity or race. Nazi officials had little interest in the religious activity of Jews inside their borders. Rather, Nazis identified Jews through pseudoscientific research into individuals' lineage, looking for "Jewish blood." In this way, the Nazi regime conflated religious, ethnic, and racial biases into one general hatred of Jewish people, whether they were religious or not.

Wars in the Balkans have reinforced the problem of religious identification among combatants. During the war in Bosnia in the 1990s, for example, both the warring parties and outsiders consistently differentiated among groups by using the terms *Serb, Croat,* and *Muslim.* Only the third name had a religious meaning, and this contributed to confusion between ethnic and religious

The chapel at Dorchester prison camp in England in World War I (from German Prisoners in Great Britain *[London, n.d.])*

identities. Nevertheless, strong evidence exists that civilians were taken into custody by all sides based on their perceived religious-ethnic identity: Orthodox Christian, Roman Catholic, or Muslim.

Communist governments have actively targeted religious leaders for exile to concentration and "reeducation" camps, both during wartime and periods of peace. Beginning with the Russian Revolution of 1917, communists hoped to rid their lands of the "opiate of the masses" (as Marx called religion) by sending religious believers to labor camps. During the Russian Civil War (1917–1921), for example, the Red Army condemned Russian Orthodox clergy, monastics, and lay believers because of their religious faith. In all, some 40,000 clergy died in prison or from assassination in the USSR before the beginning of World War II.

The most infamous linkage between internment camps and religion may be communist Russia's first labor camp, located near the Arctic Circle on the Solovetski Islands. Solovki (as it was popularly called) had been a thriving monastery for almost 500 years when it was taken over by the Soviet regime. Thereafter monks and priests became prisoners of the state, and thousands of believers (along with political prisoners, prisoners of war, and common criminals) joined their ranks in the labor camp. Finally closed just before the outbreak of World War II, the Solovki Labor Camp has served as a constant reminder of religious persecution during wartime and peace.

During the 1960s, other communist governments sought out religious believers for persecution through exile to labor and reeducation camps. Few hard numbers are available, but the Castro regime clearly sent foreign missionaries and local religious leaders to work camps during the mid-1960s, hoping to rid Cuba of religious activity.

These actions, however, paled next to the wholesale internment of religious believers during the Chinese Cultural Revolution of 1966–1976. During this period, Mao Tse-tung's Red Guards actively sought out Buddhists, Daoists, Christians, and others in China and Tibet. Uncounted thousands were forced out of their homes and sent to learn "proper Socialism" and to forget their religious beliefs. Thousands of believers died during this campaign to cleanse China of religious influences.

More frequently, however, combatants have sought religious solace while being held prisoner. The 1929 Geneva Convention Relative to the Treatment of Prisoners of War confirmed the right of POWs to satisfy their intellectual and moral needs, proclaiming that "prisoners of war shall be permitted complete freedom in the performance of their religious duties, including attendance at the services of their faith, on the sole condition that they comply with the routine and police regulations prescribed by the military authorities. Ministers of religion, who are prisoners of war, whatever may be their denomination, shall be allowed freely to minister to their co-religionists" (chapter 4, article 16). Other international treaties and conventions have outlined similar freedoms of religion for combatants and civilians during wartime.

Such international laws, however, have often been ignored by authorities. Jewish believers certainly received no religious freedom in the Nazi death camps, and ministers have been turned away from camps in Cuba, among other places. Even without organized leadership in the camps, however, religion has played an important role in the life of prisoners. In some cases, the lack of personal freedom intrinsic to prison existence provided a sort of spiritual freedom for the prisoner. Prisoners have often described the most profound spiritual growth occurring just when all other rights were stripped from them. One Russian prisoner wrote that "nowhere else is there such a freedom for thought, such a deliverance from worldly concerns" as in a forced labor camp.

Most frequently, however, prisoners have turned to religion as a personal solace. Memoirs from many prisoners of war have recounted the development and strengthening of their religious faith during their time as prisoners. With their life regimented and controlled by outside forces, religion has helped to keep prisoners of war from mental breakdown, even as it has sometimes provided a reason for their original imprisonment.

See also Chaplains; Indoctrination

—*Roy R. Robson*

Reparations

The notion that former POWs should be entitled to reparations payments from their former captors in compensation for maltreatment first surfaced after World War I. Section 232 of the Treaty of Versailles ordered the German government to make reparations payments to various classes of Allied citizens, including civilians who had been interned and POWs who had suffered any form of maltreatment. The sums available for this purpose varied from country to country; the British government, for example, allotted roughly £5 million to be distributed to deserving claimants. To administer the reparations program, most Allied countries established commissions to contact eligible individuals, accept statements of claim from citizens who felt they qualified, hear individual cases, and determine the amount of money to be paid to each claimant. The greatest controversy in the process was the fact that civilian internees and former POWs were judged on different criteria. Civilians could make claims for general injury to health, while ex-POWs had to prove that a specific incident of maltreatment had resulted in a reduced earning capacity. Because of this variance, the difference in amounts awarded was striking. A theology student interned in relative comfort for much of the war was awarded $5,000 by the Canadian commission, despite the fact that the worst indignity he suffered was being slapped on the face by a German officer. In contrast, a former Boer War veteran who suffered frequent beatings and contracted eczema, neuritis, and dermatitis while being forced to clean camp latrines received only $600.

Such inequities moved Allied officials to improve the process of allotting reparations payments after World War II. Article 16 of the peace treaty with Japan made available certain assets to compensate Allied POWs for maltreatment while in captivity. This time, it was decided that reparations would be paid out according to fixed scales, rather than according to the decision of a judge. The amounts paid out varied from nation to nation. New Zealand paid each Far East POW £75, plus £5 for having worked as a forced laborer on the Burma-Thailand (Death) Railway. Australia made lump sum payments of £86 and gave ex-POWs in exceptional need access to a large trust fund. The Canadian government was the most generous. Far East POWs received $1 for each day of captivity (this amounted to roughly $1,000 for prisoners captured at Hong Kong), and they also had recourse to a large trust fund in emergencies. In most nations, prisoners who were held in the European theater did not receive reparations payments, but rather were compensated as part of their own government's pension package.

However, former Far East POWs only accepted these reparations on the understanding that they were to compensate for maltreatment; they expected further payments to be made for having been used as slave labor. When these payments were not forthcoming, former Far East POWs took their battle to a higher court, the United Nations Human Rights Commission, where they lodged claims for billions of dollars in reparations payments. In May 1991, the Japanese prime minister issued an official apology for the mistreatment of Allied POWs, but they refused to be mollified and pressed their claim for further reparations payments.

References

Ivy Lee, "In Search of Redress for Historical Injustice: The Slave Labor Lawsuits Against Japanese Corporations," *East Asia: An International Quarterly* 19 (2001): 143–154.

—*Jonathan F. Vance*

REPATRIATION

The term *repatriation* generally refers to the release of prisoners of war and internees on medical grounds while hostilities are still in progress. It came into widespread use in the twentieth century, after the exchange of able-bodied prisoners ceased to be the norm, and offered a means by which sick and wounded prisoners, those most vulnerable to deterioration of health, could be returned to their homelands for convalescence. It should be distinguished from an exchange of prisoners, a long-established practice that typically involved able-bodied captives traded according to principles of numerical equality. Exchanged prisoners were usually permitted to return to military service; repatriates of the twentieth century are prohibited by international law from further service.

Before the twentieth century, it had long been customary to allow the release of injured and infirm prisoners on humanitarian grounds, and on the grounds that they were of little military value to their own government. During the Napoleonic Wars, for example, after negotiations for a general exchange of prisoners had collapsed, both sides agreed instead to the exchange of sick and wounded, very elderly, and very young prisoners.

Though the 1907 Hague Convention did not provide for the repatriation of sick and wounded prisoners, repatriations were negotiated on an ad hoc basis during World War I, when relative goodwill between the combatant nations allowed them to reach a number of mutually beneficial agreements. In late 1914, the Swiss government raised the possibility of a mutual release of seriously wounded POWs between Germany and France, and in February 1915, after the Papacy had lent its support to the plan, France and Germany reached an accord. The first exchange occurred on 2 March 1915; by November 1916, over 10,000 German and French prisoners had been exchanged. The success of this scheme convinced International Committee of the Red Cross (ICRC) president Gustave Ador to suggest the exchange of less seriously

In this repatriation operation, at Smyrna in 1943, Italian POWs board the repatriation ship to the left of the photo while British POWs disembark at the right (Jonathan F. Vance)

wounded prisoners. France rejected the plan but agreed to the internment of such prisoners in Switzerland. In August 1915, again after the pope's intervention, the Kaiser personally acceded to the plan, and in January 1916, the first group of POWs, 200 French and German tubercular cases, reached Switzerland. By the middle of February, over a thousand such prisoners had arrived.

The British Foreign Office began to take an interest in these exchanges in December 1915, and in the spring of 1916, the British government elected to enter into negotiations with Germany. At the end of May 1916, the first group of British soldiers reached Switzerland. For the rest of the war, small parties of British and Empire prisoners would leave Germany, either to be repatriated directly to England (for the most serious medical cases) or to be interned in neutral countries (for other cases of repatriables). The earliest prisoner exchanges were arranged according to a schedule of ailments that justified repatriation, including tuberculosis; diabetes; pernicious anemia; malaria; poisoning by chlorine, carbon monoxide, or mercury; emphysema; bronchitis; asthma; digestive, vision, or circulatory disorders; gout; rheumatism; epilepsy; paralysis; sciatica; loss of limb; diphtheria; and neurasthenia. As the war progressed, the criteria expanded to include other ailments, and for many POWs the hope of repatriation became a vital source of sustenance.

When it came time to frame the 1929 Geneva Convention Relative to the Treatment of Prisoners of War, international lawmakers stipulated that belligerent governments were required to repatriate sick and wounded POWs without giving consideration to rank and number. This principle, that repatriations should be negotiated with respect to groups of prisoners rather than numbers, became a key factor behind the relative lack of success in negotiating repatriations during World War II, despite the greater number of eligible POWs. In May 1940, Britain and Germany agreed upon the appointment of Mixed Medical Commissions to examine prospective repatriates. These commissions, made up of three doctors—one appointed by the detaining power and the other two by the International Committee of the Red Cross—examined sick and wounded POWs and determined if they met the criteria for repatriation; those criteria had been laid out in the 1929 Geneva Convention. By March 1941, the commissions had passed 66 German and 1,153 British prisoners for repatriation. However, the first round of negotiations broke off in October 1941 because the German government demanded numerical equality in the exchange. Unfortunately, the talks collapsed while a group of Commonwealth prisoners was on its way out of Germany with high hopes of returning home; when they learned that the repatriation had been canceled, the disappointment was a bitter blow. Before the negotiations reopened, over 50 of these prisoners had died in captivity.

There was more success in negotiations between Britain and Italy, and an agreement was reached in late 1941. On 8 April 1942, the first exchange occurred at Smyrna. British and Italian ships had anchored in the harbor, and a ferry boat was used to effect the exchange of 1,229 Commonwealth and 919 Italian prisoners. Negotiations continued, and after some prodding from the Vatican, another exchange was set for 19 April 1943, again at Smyrna, involving roughly 150 Commonwealth and 1,211 Italian POWs. This operation was followed in quick succession by two other exchanges: on 9 May 1943, roughly 150 sick and wounded and 350 medical personnel were exchanged for 400 Italian sick and wounded and 2,000 medical personnel; and on 2 June 1943, 140 British sick and wounded and 290 medical personnel were exchanged for 2,676 Italian prisoners. The following month, realizing that the German army might well take over Italy if the government there collapsed, the British government sent 550 Italian repatriables and a few German civilians to Lisbon to be exchanged for about 100 British prisoners. Unfortunately, the latter group fell into German hands; Germany canceled the exchange and returned the POWs to captivity.

While this was going on, Germany and Britain had reached a new tentative agreement in June 1942. The accord allowed the repatriation of all sick and wounded POWs (known as *grands blessés*), all surplus medical personnel, and all civilians who wished to leave, whether or not they were interned, except those serving penal sentences or deemed to be dangerous to the detaining power. The German government withdrew from the negotiations before the agreement was finalized, and repatriation negotiations remained in abeyance for much of the fall and winter of 1942–1943 because of an unrelated dispute involving reprisals against prisoners. In the spring of 1943 discussions reopened. These talks continued for the rest of the war, resulting in four multilateral repatriations. The first took place at Gothenburg, Sweden, in October 1943 and involved some 5,000 British, Commonwealth, and American POWs for a similar number of Germans. The Allies had agreed to release medical personnel so that the numbers involved were roughly equal, in order to avoid a repetition of the October 1941 debacle. The second exchange, at Barcelona in May 1944, included just over a thousand Allied and 800 German prisoners; the third operation, in September 1944, again at Gothenburg, involved 2,560 Allied nationals and 2,100 Germans; and the last, at Marseille in January 1945, brought home some 2,500 Allied POWs.

In contrast, no repatriations were negotiated in the Pacific theater. The United States and Britain made a number of separate and unsuccessful proposals to Japan for the exchange of sick and wounded POWs, and in May 1944 the two powers arrived at a common repatriation plan to present to Japan: a series of continuing exchanges at Bikini until all military repatriables were released, after which time civilians would be turned over. To make the plan more appealing, the Allies agreed to free all interned

Japanese civilians who wished to return home. The common front was soon breached, however. In June 1944, the United States announced its intention to offer Japan an exchange of the isolated garrisons on Wake, Wotje, Mili, Maloelap, Jaluit, Ocean, and Nauru Islands for 25,000 sick and wounded American POWs. Realizing that it might be difficult to dissuade the United States from making the proposal, the British War Cabinet decided to ask the Americans to expand it to embrace all Allied POWs on a proportionate basis. If that failed, the Commonwealth would devise a similar exchange plan to present to Japan.

In September, the United States announced another unilateral approach, the exchange of 25,000 Japanese civilians captured on Saipan for an equal number of American, Latin American, and Canadian POWs and civilians. In November, the Americans rejected the Commonwealth's exchange plan, agreeing to include other Allied prisoners in its original scheme, but not on a proportionate basis. Reluctantly, the British government acceded, though still lamenting the way that events had transpired. In the end, all the agonizing was fruitless, as no military exchange was ever achieved. This was partly due to the fact that the Allies had so few Japanese POWs to offer in exchange, but perhaps more to the fact that Japan probably did not want them back in any case.

The articles relating to repatriation, restated in the 1949 Geneva Convention, were used to good effect in the Korean War. In April 1953, after the United Nations Command and the governments of China and North Korea concluded an agreement, Operation Little Switch occurred. In this exchange, some 6,640 Chinese and North Korean sick and wounded prisoners were traded for 684 soldiers from the UN Command. There were similar repatriations in the Arab-Israeli War of 1956 and the conflict between China and India in 1962, but an attempted repatriation during the Vietnam War was unsuccessful. In April 1971, after prolonged negotiations, the South Vietnamese authorities announced that they would unilaterally repatriate some 600 sick and wounded North Vietnamese POWs. As they surely expected, the vast majority of these captives declined repatriation when they were interviewed by delegates from the International Committee of the Red Cross. Furthermore, when the 13 willing repatriates were taken into North Vietnamese waters to be released, the Hanoi government announced that it did not want the prisoners back. Repatriation is a laudable goal in humanitarian terms but, like so many other aspects of the captivity experience, it has become highly politicized since World War II.

See also Big Switch, Operation; Mixed Medical Commissions

References

Bertram Bright, "Blinded and a Prisoner of War," *Blackwood's* 257 (1945): 242–250.

Arieh J. Kochavi, "Why None of Britain's Long Term POWs in Nazi Germany Were Repatriated During World War II," *Canadian Journal of History* 39 (2004): 63–85.

John C. Mustardé, *The Sun Stood Still* (London: Pilot Press, 1944).

Jonathan F. Vance, "The Trouble with Allies: Canada and the Negotiation of Prisoner of War Exchanges," in *Prisoners of War and Their Captors in World War II*, ed. Bob Moore and Kent Fedorowich (Oxford: Berg, 1996).

—*Jonathan F. Vance*

REPRISALS

A reprisal is most broadly considered as an act of retaliation taken in response to a wrongful act, or an act perceived to be wrongful. Reprisals can be private, as when individuals carry out reprisals as a form of vigilantism or to settle private claims. Public reprisals are the acts of a state or its representatives. They can be political, economic, or physical in form. Both public and private reprisals encompass notions of coercion, enforcement, deterrence, punishment, and revenge. Public reprisals also operate on the principle of collective responsibility, by which an entire group is held responsible for the acts of one or some.

Public reprisals take place during both peace and war. Examples of peacetime reprisals include physical acts, such as blockades and military attack or occupation, and economic acts, such as seizing or freezing of the assets of another state or its citizens, as the United States did against Iran in response to the abduction of American hostages. Peacetime reprisals frequently occur when war has not been declared but warlike conditions exist—either between states, as in the case of Arab-Israeli relations, or within a single state, as in Northern Ireland.

Reprisals are most often associated with declared war, however, and have even been considered a subcategory or form of warfare. They are illegal acts of warfare or retaliation carried out in response to an enemy's own illegal acts of warfare, to compel the enemy to comply with the rules of law. Reprisals have been particularly plentiful during the wars of nineteenth and twentieth centuries, especially during World War II. Although reprisals long predate the laws of war, since the nineteenth century they have been intimately connected to the international law of war, in that reprisals are both violations of law and the impetus for enactment of new law regulating or prohibiting them.

During World War II, reprisals took every conceivable form. The British government issued explicit economic reprisal orders in 1939 and 1940, in response to the German sinking and mining of belligerent and neutral merchant ships. Under such orders, all enemy exports were liable to seizure, whether shipped from enemy or neutral ports. When Italy entered the war on the side of Germany in 1940, the order was extended to apply to Italian commerce, even though Italy had not attacked British ships. Imports from neutral countries that were (or might be) intended for enemy ports also became subject to regulation and seizure.

In response to an appeal from U.S. President Franklin D. Roosevelt, Germany and Britain had agreed at the beginning of the war that they would not engage in unrestricted air warfare. However, Germany's offensive against the Netherlands and France in May 1940 and the bombing of Rotterdam on 14 May effectively ended the agreement. On 15 May, the British War Cabinet authorized the beginning of the strategic air offensive against Germany. It was several months before Germany was in a position to retaliate, with the Battle of Britain beginning in mid-August. British bombers promptly attacked Berlin. Reprisal followed reprisal as the bombing of cities and civilian and industrial targets spiraled.

Reprisals against prisoners of war are often imposed because they are held collectively responsible for their government's actions. Despite the work of the International Committee of the Red Cross at the end of the World War I to ensure better treatment for prisoners of war, and despite the 1929 Geneva Convention, which prohibited reprisals against prisoners (never ratified by Japan or the USSR), reprisals against POWs were frequent and serious during World War II. In the Allied raid on Dieppe on 19 August 1942, a number of captured German soldiers had their hands bound. When the German government learned of the incident, it protested and threatened to retaliate. The Germans did tie and later handcuff some British and Canadian prisoners, and German prisoners in certain British and Canadian camps were then also handcuffed.

Some of the many other reprisals against prisoners of war included Hitler's order that British commandos captured on missions in German-occupied territory be killed, the killing of German prisoners of war held by the French Forces of the Interior, the Waffen-SS's killing of Soviet prisoners on the eastern front, German treatment of Soviet prisoners in general, and Japanese treatment of POW work gangs.

Civilians in German-occupied territory were the most frequent victims of reprisal during World War II. Men, women, and children, most of whom had no connection to local resistance forces and who had not themselves engaged in acts of resistance against the German occupiers, were taken hostage, displaced, deported, or killed in retaliation for acts of sabotage or for attacks on German soldiers. German actions went well beyond any traditional bounds of proportional reprisal, into the realm of massacre and atrocity. Ratios were set at 10, 50, or 100 civilians to be killed for every German soldier wounded or killed. Entire villages in Poland, Italy, France, Czechoslovakia, and the USSR were destroyed.

Not until the end of World War II, with the International Military Tribunals at Nuremberg and Tokyo, the United Nations War Crimes Commission, and the postwar conventions, were reprisals against prisoners of war and the civilian populations of enemy occupied territory seriously discussed and outlawed. The four Geneva Conventions of 1949 all included provisions against reprisals: the first and third conventions banned reprisals with regard to categories of sick and wounded on land and sea; the third convention treated at length protections for prisoners of war, and prohibited reprisals against them; and the fourth convention's broad protections for civilians in occupied territory included specific prohibitions against hostage taking, pillage, collective punishments, and all measures of intimidation or terrorism. It left open, however, the question of whether reprisals against civilians in enemy territory were prohibited, as they were in enemy-occupied territory. The 1977 Additional Protocols to the Geneva Convention addressed this issue by extending the prohibition of reprisals to civilians and their objects in enemy territory, not only in enemy-occupied territory.

See also Ardeatine Caves Massacre; Lidice Massacre; Oradour-sur-Glane Massacre; Shackling Incident

References

Frits Kalshoven, *Belligerent Reprisals* (Leiden: A. W. Sijthoff, 1971).

———, "Belligerent Reprisals Revisited," *Netherlands Yearbook of International Law* 21 (1990): 43–80.

Adam Roberts and Richard Guelff, eds., *Documents on the Laws of War*, 2nd ed. (Oxford: Clarendon Press, 1989).

—*Victoria C. Belco*

ROMAN WORLD

The ancient Romans were infamous for forcing POWs to fight to the death in the arena as gladiators. This tradition, founded by the Etruscans, came to Rome in 264 B.C.E. for the funeral of Junius Brutus Pera. The names of two specific types of gladiator, the *Samnis* (Samnite) and the *Thrax* (Thracian), tell us how Romans used these peoples when they captured them. However, Romans captured POWs before 264 and treated them in a variety of ways. Unlike other contemporary societies, the Romans were very systematic in determining whether to spare, enslave, or execute POWs.

In archaic times, Romans were equally likely to execute POWs, enslave them, hold them for ransom, or set them free. POWs served as an excellent source of military intelligence, for which reason alone they were often spared. The other deciding factor was reciprocity. If the enemy held Roman POWs, better treatment was allotted. As late as 217, the second year of the Second Punic War, the Romans negotiated a man-for-man exchange of prisoners with Hannibal, instead of enslaving those they had captured, just as they had during the war with Pyrrhus, 280–275 B.C.E. The historian Dionysius of Halicarnassus tells us that it was the duty of a Roman patron to ransom his client should the client be captured, indicating the frequency of this misfortune during war. W. K. Pritchett says that among Greeks, economic gain was the deciding factor whether to ransom or enslave POWs. Among Romans, advantage was the determining factor, but advantage had political and personal elements beyond economic gain.

Ill-treatment of POWs was a very common fact of ancient war. Sometimes POWs were massacred as an intimidation tactic to discourage rebellion or to cow opposition. Romans generally spared POWs the first time a city rebelled, but were far more likely to massacre the males and enslave the women and children the second time a city rebelled. One early example occurred under Tarquin I (ca. 600), who attacked and captured the cities of Apiolae and Corniculum, massacring the adult males and enslaving the women and children. Livy says the POWs were sent to Rome, where they were sold at auction.

Fear of ill-treatment of fellow Romans and vision for future security had some benevolent results. In one case, Romulus forced POWs from Veii to walk in his triumph, but afterwards set them free without ransom. Some POWs went home, while others stayed in Rome and became citizens. Livy tells us that when Privernum was captured (for the second time), the enemy leader was sent to Rome, thrashed, and beheaded (a ritual punishment), but the rest of the Privernates were given citizenship. This is one of many examples of the genius that made the Roman Empire strong: the willingness to give citizenship to conquered foes. However, for every such example of wise statecraft, there are at least three times as many cases of enslaving the POWs. It is not always immediately apparent to the modern scholar why certain cities were spared and others enslaved, but for the Romans there were strategic considerations based on size, location, consanguinity, or wealth.

By the era of the Punic Wars, Rome's economy was driven by rural, agricultural slave labor. Cato the Elder, writing ca. 160 B.C.E., advised his fellow countrymen to get the most work out of slaves and then get rid of them. Gallic POWs, evidently, made good slaves, capable of hard work (Britons, on the other hand, were regarded as bad slaves. They were stubborn, had difficulty with Latin, and were poor workers). Hannibal's efforts to lure slaves to join his army against Rome won a few adherents, but far more significant is the Roman decision to set free and enroll 10,000 slaves in the army in 216 B.C.E. after the defeat of Cannae. This tells us there was already a considerable slave presence in Rome.

Between 200 and 150 B.C.E., the number of slaves in both rural regions and urban centers in Italy skyrocketed. Male POWs were usually captured on campaign or in battle, women and children when a city fell. The vast number of POWs from the east and Spain completely redrew the lines of Roman society. Literate Greek POWs were a highly prized commodity; they were sold to wealthy Roman families to tutor the children. Illiterate but physically fit prisoners unlikely to cause trouble were sold as farm or ranch hands, or if they were unlucky, they went to the mines. Only a few became gladiators, especially those who were considered dangerous. During Julius's conquest of Gaul, auctioneers followed the army to purchase POWs and manage their transport to market. This practice probably long predated the fall of the Republic.

The effect of this advantage-based policy of managing POWs dramatically changed Roman society. A proper education required a thorough mastery of Greek culture, acquired from the tutoring of a Greek-born slave, the *paedagogus*. The upper class of Rome began to assume a mixed Greco-Roman outlook that separated it from the lower class. Simultaneously, to earn popularity and votes, politicians began to stage circus games, especially gladiatorial matches. This required a steady influx of POWs, for it was too expensive to train gladiators and then allow half of the team to die. Most matches featured trained professionals against novices, recent POWs who stood little or no chance against professionals. Such contests were necessary to distract the poor from their economic woes, because slave labor was now competing so successfully against hired, free labor that hired labor was marginalized. Only skilled professional free labor (smiths, carpenters, etc.) could survive, and many large estates, called *latifundia*, began to train slaves to do skilled labor, as well. As long as the Romans kept winning foreign wars, slaves were plentiful and easily replaced: Almost every home could afford one. Terrence's comedies, written ca. 150 B.C.E., include slave characters whom the audience would immediately recognize as POWs sold into slavery (rather than born into slavery). The crisis came in the 130s when two slaves named Eunus and Cleon revolted in Sicily and raised a force of over 60,000 rebel slaves. Almost simultaneously, Tiberius Gracchus challenged the current economic system whereby poor Romans were made landless and penniless, unable to compete for jobs with slaves, while their land was sold from under them. However, the government defeated the slave rebels in 130 and accepted temporary solutions to the problems Gracchus had protested (being killed in the process). Two more great slave rebellions followed, that of Athenion and Tryphon in 103–101, and that of Spartacus (73–71).

Shakespeare's Mark Antony says of Julius Caesar at the funeral oration, "He hath brought many captives home to Rome whose ransoms did the general coffers fill." The first part of this is correct, for Julius's conquest of Gaul added tens of thousands of slaves to the Roman market. However, these slaves were seldom ransomed. Most were put to work in the fields, and many ended their lives in the arena.

Rome's economy continued to depend on slaves for the next three hundred years. Many emperors used conquest to establish legitimacy and to intimidate would-be aggressors. The prisoners generated by these wars generally continued to serve two functions. They provided the labor that made Rome great, building the Colosseum, numerous temples, bridges, aquaducts, city centers, and walls. The other function of prisoners was the "circenses" in the expression *panem circensesque*. On an ever-increasing level, the emperors used games to placate the populace of Rome. The mob's favorite form of entertainment was gladiatorial combat, so more and more prisoners were diverted to the arena. Since it was too expensive to train them as professional gladiators, thousands were simply slaughtered by professional gladiators or animals to endear the emperor to the crowd.

The reliance upon prisoners eroded the will of the emperor during the crisis of the third century because Rome was no longer winning foreign wars. The decrease of prisoners and increased pressure on the borders of the Empire made gladiatorial combat less frequent and emperors less popular. In 404 the emperor Honorius banned gladiatorial games, meaning that any prisoners the Roman army took were more likely to be sent to work farmland, or possibly be drafted into the army.

The other side of this issue is the way Romans reacted when their fellow countrymen became POWs. After 216 B.C.E., Romans refused to ransom their own people taken prisoner by the enemy. This bizarre policy strikes us as cruel and heartless, but Greek writers of Roman history mentioned it with awe and respect. This policy arose overnight after the Romans lost the Battle of Cannae to Hannibal on 2 August 216 B.C.E., and deeply changed the way Romans conducted war thereafter.

Early Romans surrendered to the enemy and ransomed prisoners as often as any other ancient people before 216. Several early heroes of the Republic were prisoners who turned the tables on their captors, such as C. Mucius Scaevola, Cloelia, and M. Atilius Regulus. Mucius Scaevola vowed to assassinate Lars Porsenna, and when he failed and was captured, he placed his own hand in a fire in defiance, an act that awed his captors so much they freed him. Cloelia, an imprisoned Roman maiden, escaped and swam across the Tiber, astounding her captors and her fellow Romans alike. The legend of Regulus deserves special note. Taken prisoner during the First Punic War by Carthage, he was held captive for five years and then sent to Rome to endorse a prisoner exchange and to open peace talks. He was to be the first Roman exchanged if his mission succeeded. However, he denounced the treaty on the Senate floor, arguing that the Carthaginians would gain the advantage from such an exchange. Then, to keep his word to return if the mission failed, he returned to Carthage, knowing he would be tortured to death.

In conquering the Italian peninsula, the Romans contended with the Etruscans, Umbrians, Gauls, Samnites, Greeks, and Carthaginians. As the identities of their foes changed from neighboring peoples to less familiar opponents, Roman willingness to surrender and to recover POWs dramatically diminished. At first, Romans had great sympathy for the plight of their countrymen taken as POWs by the Etruscans, who used to bind a living man and a dead in an "embrace of death" until the living perished. (This was the very crime for which Vergil's Mezentius was driven out by his outraged Etruscan subjects. According to Livy, the Etruscans also engaged in human sacrifice. When the embrace of death came to be regarded as excessively savage, the Etruscans switched to forcing POWs to fight as gladiators until only one survived. Romans inherited the tradition of gladiators from the Etruscans.) At some later, unknown time they ceased to feel pity and simply regarded Roman POWs taken by the Umbrians, Gauls, and Germans as lost altogether (recently deciphered tablets in Gubbio reveal that the Umbrians conducted a ritual human sacrifice of POWs, while the Gauls were headhunters and displayed their victims' heads on their saddles). Most infamous of all were the Carthaginians. Diodorus Siculus and Polybius both comment on their excessive, gratuitous cruelty to hapless POWs. In one instance, the victims' hands were cut off and stacked on spits before the victims were paraded and executed. The Romans had an uncommonly high respect for the integrity of the human body, even a prisoner's. Their horror at such barbarism merits emphasis, both because they almost never tortured POWs, and because this may account for their determination not to fall into the hands of the enemy.

The turning point in attitudes to prisoners was a result of evolution. The first crucial incident occurred in 321 when the Roman army walked into a trap at the Caudine Forks during the Second Samnite War. The Samnites took the entire Roman army prisoner, forced them to walk under the yoke (an Italic humiliation custom) and then, holding certain nobles as hostages, released the rest of the army. This deep humiliation resonated in the Roman psyche for generations, and was the first step in hardening the Roman martial spirit towards the ethos of never surrendering.

In 217 sources record the Romans' last POW exchange, when Q. Fabius Maximus Cunctator and Hannibal traded prisoners until there were no Carthaginian POWs left. Fabius had to dip into his own financial resources to ransom the remaining 240 Romans. This action apparently displeased the Senate, which allegedly no longer concerned itself with POWs. Some time later, Fabius nearly trapped Hannibal. In order to escape undetected, the Carthaginians executed all their POWs. This action was criticized in Roman sources for its cruelty, although the Senate had not taken the opportunity to ransom them. On another instance, Roman writers accuse Hannibal (probably falsely) of executing Roman POWs from the Battle of Cannae by forcing elephants to trample them.

The battle of Cannae changed everything. Hannibal offered to ransom the 10,000 POWs he had captured, but the Senate refused and abandoned them to their fate for two reasons. Firstly, they decided to deprive Hannibal of much-needed revenues, and secondly, to draw a line in the sand of irrevocable opposition. Livy has T. Manlius Torquatus denounce the POWs as cowards, saying that soldiers who have surrendered once will do so again, and as such are worthless to the state; they were no longer Romans. The speech in Livy is idealized and probably misattributed. The speaker was more likely M. Atilius Regulus, son of the Regulus from the First Punic War, whose motives better match the economics of the situation). Rebuffed, Hannibal sold the POWs into slavery in Africa and the Greek East. About 20 years later in 197, after the battle of Cynoscephalae, T. Quinctius Flamininus liberated some of these POWs.

Even with the conflicting accounts, the break with the past in refusing to ransom the POWs from Cannae is striking. While a POW, a Roman lost his citizenship and his rights as a property owner were assumed by another. But if he returned, by *postliminium,* he could resume all of those rights, even his marriage (upon the consent of both parties). While returning POWs suffered some measure of disgrace and reduction of status, they had never before been denied a return when the capacity existed to bring them home.

The bitter fate of the POWs from Cannae invoked such pity and compassion from many that the Senate agreed to receive POWs if a foreign power volunteered them. POWs suffered the stigma of *diminutio capite*, a reduction of social standing, but they could return. After Zama, Scipio Africanus brought home those POWs whom he could find in Africa, one of whom marched in Scipio's triumph wearing a *pilleus*, the cap of a freedman. Flamininus also rescued enslaved POWs provided by the Greeks.

Inevitably, when POWs languished in captivity for years, it created a crisis for their families who lacked their *paterfamilias*. Two major issues were the release of children from the legal jurisdiction of the father, and the status of his wife. After five years, his wife was considered a widow and entitled (in some cases even encouraged) to remarry. If he returned before the end of the five-year period, he could resume his marriage without interruption. Following the *lex Cornelia*, a POW was considered slain upon capture. This meant that his sons were released immediately from his *patrias potestas* (literally, father's power) and that his will was read. If the POW actually returned after this, a whole host of family problems erupted.

During the civil wars, captured troops often received the choice of defecting or perishing. Julius Caesar was highly unusual for his famed sense of *clementia* (mercy). He lured over many of the troops he captured, but allowed those who refused to defect to go free, even the armies of M. Afranius and L. Petreius in Spain when they did not join him. The Republicans, on the other hand, executed all captured Caesarians who would not defect. The Caesarian C. Scribonius Curio, when faced by superior Republican forces, preferred to die fighting from his shame at failure.

Two curious incidents arose during Augustus's reign that did much to change the established precedent for Roman POWs abroad. In 19 B.C.E., when Augustus received back the Eagles (the standards that identified military formations and whose capture was regarded as a disgrace to the unit) from M. Licinius Crassus's disastrous campaign of 53 B.C.E., he also had the opportunity to negotiate for the return of the men taken POW during Crassus's and Antony's failed Parthian invasions. Horace's famous Ode 3.5 invokes Regulus to argue against recovering the POWs. The opinion prevailed that a good Roman did not surrender, so the POWs did not deserve repatriation. Evidently Augustus was so determined to prove his Republicanism that he evoked a sterner Republican precedent than was necessary. Those prisoners given back for free were accepted—and they suffered *diminutio capitis*—but the Romans refused to ransom any of the POWs.

On a second occasion, nearly three decades later, he showed himself less rigid. In 9 C.E., the Germans revolted and ambushed three Roman legions and auxiliaries in the Teutoburger Wald. The legions were cut to pieces and the survivors captured. Some were ritually executed, while others were held as thralls and in some cases offered for ransom. Though inclined to appear severe, Augustus consented to allow the POWs' families to ransom them, provided the POWs did not return to Italy. In reality, the Empire was so badly shaken by the loss of three of its finest legions that Augustus had to find a proper way of concealing the severity of the loss from the Germans and even from other Romans, lest its full extent be discovered and exploited. By barring any state ransom, he was attempting to minimize the real jeopardy of the situation, but he realized the unpopularity he would incur by allowing so many Romans to suffer torture at the hands of the Germans. Those whose ransom could be paid by private resources were rescued. One suspects that the imperial coffers loaned some families capital, but had to make selective decisions as to whom they could help. This adopted policy of Julian clemency began to take precedence over "traditional" Republican values.

After Augustus, the emperors became more sympathetic to POWs. Claudius welcomed home those he could recover from Germany. Most of the POWs in the Year of Four Emperors were spared, aside from Otho's centurions from the First Battle of Bedriacum. Vitellius's execution of these brave officers earned him much contempt and played a role in his downfall and the destruction of Cremona at the hands of the Flavian troops after the Second Battle of Bedriacum. Imperial generosity to POWs soon became a standard, though it was always described in terms of an exception to the rule, accounted for by the emperor's exalted sense of *clementia*.

In the ancient world, the victor often executed captured males and auctioned off women and children. The Romans were no exception, but perhaps one in three captives were eventually set free and made citizens. The playwright Terrence may have been one such manumitted slave. On the other side is the Roman POW. The legend of the soldier unwilling to surrender and steeled for victory or death served a dual purpose. It intimidated the enemy and served to exaggerate the threat of fighting against Roman troops who knew only one conclusion to war. It also served to toughen the Roman soldier to live up to these expectations, or suffer shame and rejection by one's own family. It was irrelevant that by Livy's day, this notion had passed into the realm of legend. In fact, given that Romans prior to Hannibal's day fell captive often enough, even Livy's virtuous "good old days" were not so virtuous. Much of our evidence suggests it was not fear of shame, but the ferocity of Rome's enemies which built the Roman army's invincible reputation for death before capture.

References

J.P.V.D. Balsdon, *Romans and Aliens* (Chapel Hill: University of North Carolina Press, 1979).

Clarence Eugene Brand, *Roman Military Law* (Austin: University of Texas Press, 1968).

William V. Harris, *War and Imperialism in Republican Rome* (Oxford: Clarendon Press, 1979).

W. Kendrick Pritchett, *The Greek State at War* (Berkeley: University of California Press, 1971).

—*Gaius Stern*

ROUSSEAU, JEAN-JACQUES (1712–1778)

The Enlightenment is recognized as having had a significant impact on attitudes toward captivity, and the Swiss-born essayist, novelist, and philosopher Jean-Jacques Rousseau is generally categorized with thinkers of the liberal French Enlightenment, such as Voltaire and Diderot, because of his participation in their joint *Encyclopedia* project. The first commentators of his political philosophy, predicated on individual subservience to the common good, saw it as the foundation of modern deliberative democracy, in which the contractual link between society and its members guarantees freedom. Recent analysts, however, have interpreted his theoretical construct of society as foretelling authoritarian forms of government ranging from the French Revolution's Terror of 1793–1794 to Stalinism.

Germane to Rousseau's thought, as illustrated in *Discourse on the Origin of Inequality* (1754) and *The Social Contract* (1762), is a conceptual State of War existing between all members of the precontractual society. In contrast to that described by Thomas Hobbes, Rousseau's State of War is not characteristic of the State of Nature. It results from centuries of cultural customs originating in the Stronger's need for control of the means of subsistence and concomitant desire to dominate the Weaker. Motivated by self-interest and greed, the Stronger must expand his dominion by brute force, establishing a perverted Compact whereby obedience becomes the legal obligation of the Vanquished. In war, the Vanquished is indistinguishable from the slave, deprived of natural freedom and coerced into abject dependence on the Victor's resources.

To avoid the alienating effects of generalized war, Rousseau advocated a pacified society warranted by the veritable Social Contract in which property is limited by general consensus while community needs outweigh particular ones.

References

Jim Miller, *Rousseau: Dreamer of Democracy* (New Haven, CT: Yale University Press, 1984).

Zev M. Trachtenberg, *Making Citizens: Rousseau's Political Theory of Culture* (London: Routledge, 1993).

—*Laurent Ditmann*

Ruhleben

A suburb of western Berlin, Ruhleben was the site of the main internment camp for British and Empire civilians during World War I. Shortly after the beginning of the war, on 6 November 1914, the German government ordered British male subjects between the ages of 17 and 55 to be interned for the duration of the war. At Ruhleben, a horse-racing track was converted into a camp that eventually housed some 4,400 internees. Initially they lived in the stables, six internees being allotted to each horse box; hundreds more lived in the lofts above the stables, and 400 lived in the track's restaurants. In 1915, 12 temporary barracks were added to reduce congestion, but other amenities remained inadequate. Sanitary facilities were poor, the drainage of sewage and rainwater being hampered by the fact that the camp lay on reclaimed marshland. The electric system was confined to a few bulbs in each stable, and the only heat in the stables was provided by a traction engine hooked up to a boiler and an improvised series of pipes, which provided a few hours of heat each day.

Despite this gloomy setting, Ruhleben soon became a hive of activity. In January 1915, university graduates formed the Arts and Science Union, which gave advanced-level lectures on a wide range of subjects; more basic education was provided by the Ruhleben Camp School. Also in 1915, the Ruhleben Drama Society was established, and soon it spawned a number of other theatrical clubs. Thereafter, dozens of societies sprang up, including musical groups, debating clubs, sports teams, special interest groups, and religious circles. Indeed, Ruhleben was something of an intellectual crucible, for it counted among its alumni such future celebrities as Nobel laureate in physics James Chadwick, conductor and

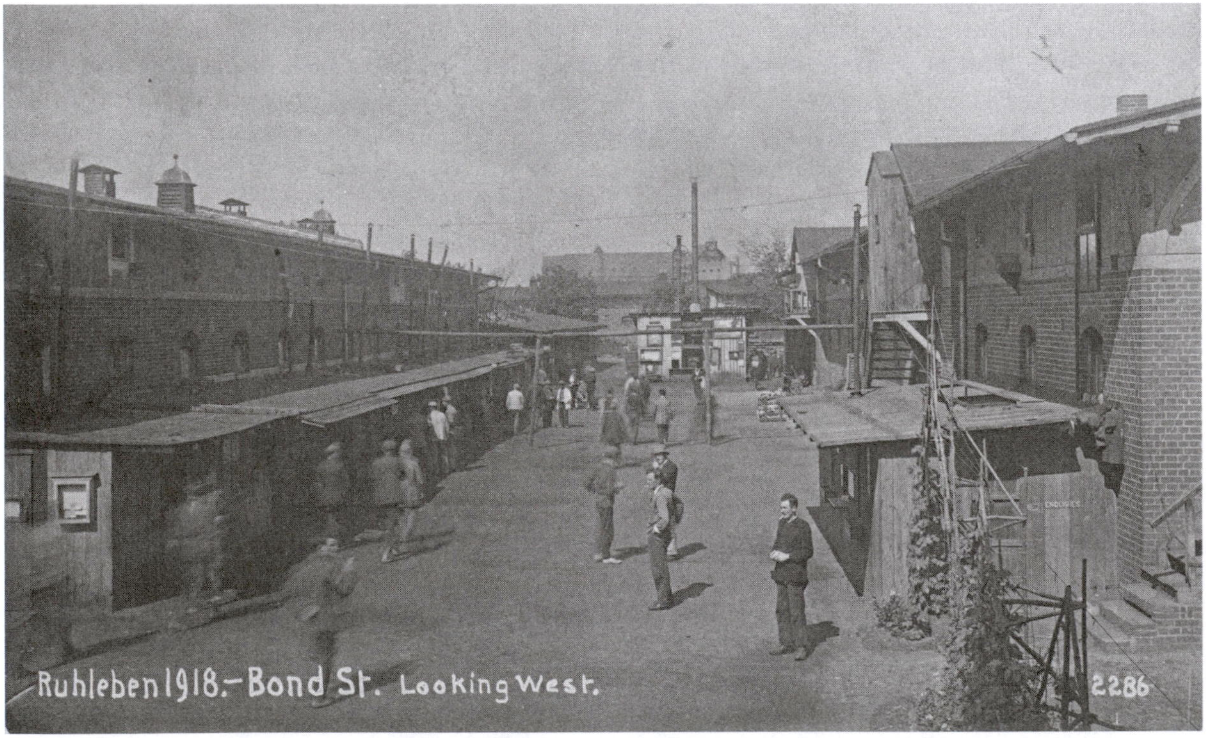

Ruhleben internment camp in Berlin. The stables that housed the prisoners are on either side of the central street (National Archives of Canada PA182553)

composer Sir Ernest MacMillan, Oxford historian and future World War II intelligence chief Sir John Masterman, and social psychologist J. Davidson Ketchum.

The camp's character began to change in January 1918, when a large group of internees over the age of 45 was transferred to Holland under a prisoner exchange scheme negotiated by Britain and Germany. Transfers continued intermittently through the year, and morale in the camp dropped appreciably for those who were left behind. When the armistice was announced, the prisoners were free to travel around Berlin, although many elected to wait in the camp until they were evacuated. Transportation to Britain was arranged promptly, and by the end of November 1918, Ruhleben had been emptied of internees. The racecourse stood until 1958, when it was demolished to make way for a new sewage plant.

See also Civilian Internees—World War I

References

Israel Cohen, *The Ruhleben Prison Camp* (London: Methuen, 1917).

Wallace Ellison, *Escapes and Adventures* (London: William Blackwood, 1928).

J. Davidson Ketchum, *Ruhleben: A Prison Camp Society* (Toronto: University of Toronto Press, 1965).

H.C. Mahoney, *Interned in Germany* (New York: Robert M. McBride, 1918).

Geoffrey Pyke, *To Ruhleben – And Back* (New York: McSweeney's Books, 2003).

—Jonathan F. Vance

Russian Civil War (1917–1921)

One of the most bitter and costly internal conflicts in modern history, the Russian Civil War took a ghastly toll in human lives. All combatants, and particularly prisoners of war, suffered from relentless hunger, disease, shortages, and inadequate medical care. The exact number of casualties is unknown, but estimates are as high as four million. The two principal combatants in the war were the Bolshevik Party, or the Reds, and their main domestic opponents, known collectively as the Whites. The conflict also involved peasant and outlaw bands, as well as troops from foreign countries, including Great Britain, France, Japan, and the United States. The Bolsheviks, who had seized power in Petrograd in November 1917, were revolutionary followers of socialist theorist Karl Marx. They overthrew a provisional government established in the aftermath of the March Revolution of 1917, which had forced Czar Nicholas II to abdicate the throne of Russia.

Full-scale civil war did not begin until May 1918, although opposition to the new Bolshevik government had surfaced almost immediately after the November Revolution. Leon Trotsky's rigorous leadership soon transformed the Red Army from a motley guard of workers and peasants into a highly disciplined and well-trained fighting force. The White Armies consisted largely of former czarist military officers and the Cossacks, bands of horsemen from the south of Russia who were fiercely loyal to the czarist government. Over 70,000 czarist officers served in the Red Army. They were, however, subject to a hostage system that kept their families prisoner to insure loyalty.

The major fronts were in Siberia and in the southern regions of the former Russian empire, particularly Ukraine, the Caucasus, and the Crimean peninsula. The great turning point in the war was 1919, when the Whites failed to take the cities of Moscow and Petrograd. Subsequently one front after another fell to the Reds. The conflict ended with the evacuation of the last White Army from the south of Russia in November 1920, although popular revolts and armed resistance continued in some areas until the mid-1920s.

From the beginning, brutality marked this war. Law, order, and humanity broke down as central authority disintegrated. A Red official chillingly summed up the philosophy on both sides—"Kill so that you will not be killed." The treatment of prisoners by both Reds and Whites was notoriously cruel and capricious. Many were shot or hanged without trial. Each side issued decrees that effectively sentenced to death all officers taken prisoner. The Bolsheviks alone carried out a minimum of 200,000 official executions. White commanders, due to manpower shortages, conscripted Red prisoners into their armies, often after having shot a certain number at random to ensure cooperation from the survivors. The Bolsheviks put prisoners into forced labor camps, where untold thousands worked and died from disease, exposure, starvation, and mass shootings. By the end of the Civil War, they held an estimated 40,913 POWs and suspected White supporters in over 120 camps.

Flagrant acts of inhumanity occurred on both sides. Prisoners were beaten and mutilated, and shockingly barbaric methods of execution were reported, from drowning and crucifixion to live burials and immersion in boiling water. There were cases of prisoners being loaded on a barge, which was then sunk by rounds of gunfire, or herded into freight cars similarly barraged with machine-gun fire. Each army also conducted campaigns of terror against civilians, as well as forced requisitions of food, housing, and transportation. Both sides took hostages freely and just as freely executed them without trial; entire villages went up in flames in retaliation for resistance or simply because they were suspected of sympathizing with the enemy. The violent excesses stemmed from the deep ideological passions driving each side. The Bolsheviks justified terror because it was perceived to be against "class enemies" in defense of a new order to be based on equality and social justice. The Whites fanatically despised Bolshevism, some because they favored a restored monarchy and others because they considered the Bolsheviks to be undemocratic or too radical.

The Red Army proved victorious in the end due to a series of factors, namely superior numbers, leadership, discipline, unity, and purpose. Sharply divided in goals and ideals, the Whites were united only by their opposition to Bolshevism. White commanders continually failed to coordinate military strategies and troop movements. Foreign military aid to the Whites proved insufficient to turn the tide of war, but it was substantive enough to allow the Bolsheviks to depict themselves as patriots defending Russia against outside intervention. White leaders were military men and not politicians. They failed to produce a viable economic or political program to win popular support, whereas the Bolsheviks offered a vision of the future that proved appealing on a mass scale.

The cruelty and harshness of the Russian Civil War left a bitter legacy. It ravaged Russia economically, but even more tragically, it laid the foundations for the authoritarian and highly militarized Soviet regime built by the victorious Bolsheviks. The conflict exacerbated centralizing, autocratic, and intolerant tendencies within Bolshevism and thereby set the stage for the one-party dictatorship that ruled the Soviet Union until its collapse in 1991.

References

Vladimir N. Brovkin, *Behind the Front Lines of the Civil War: Political Parties and Social Movements in Russia, 1918–1922* (Princeton, NJ: Princeton University Press, 1994).

Peter Kenez, *Civil War in South Russia, 1919–1920: The Defeat of the Whites* (Berkeley: University of California Press, 1977).

W. Bruce Lincoln, *Red Victory: A History of the Russian Civil War* (New York: Simon and Schuster, 1989).

Evan Mawdsley, *The Russian Civil War* (Boston: Allen and Unwin, 1987).

Richard Pipes, *Russia under the Bolshevik Regime* (New York: Alfred A. Knopf, 1994).

—Elaine McKinnon

Russo-Japanese War (1904–1905)

The Russo-Japanese War, the first major modern conflict pitting European against Asian peoples, was remarkable for the generous treatment of POWs. As many as 70,000 Russian soldiers and sailors were captured (613 of whom died in captivity), and only 1,728 Japanese enlisted men and 59 officers. In virtually every respect, their treatment by both sides was exemplary.

On 14 February 1904, the Japanese government, keen to demonstrate its humanitarian spirit, issued regulations for the treatment of wounded and able-bodied prisoners that owed much to the recently signed Hague Convention of 1899. The regulations were very liberal, guaranteeing parole walks for officers, spacious barracks, free postage, and the exchange or release of sick and wounded prisoners. Every indication is that these provisions were widely observed. The sick and wounded were ably cared for by relief detachments of the Japanese Red Cross, while able-bodied POWs were dispersed to 27 camps across Japan, many in infantry barracks. Officers enjoyed considerably better living conditions than enlisted men, but few of these prisoners had anything to complain about. Indeed, the Russian official who went to Japan to assist with the release of prisoners after the war's end was lavish in his praise of the Japanese for the kindness shown to Russian prisoners.

This beneficent treatment may have had an unintended consequence. When it came time to revise the Hague Convention in 1907, some international lawmakers argued, based in large part upon events of the Russo-Japanese War, that the legal protection of POWs was as good as it could be and that little else needed to be done on their behalf. The experience of World War I proved how wrong they were.

See also Hague Conventions of 1899 and 1907

References

Eliza Ruhamah-Scidmore, *As The Hague Ordains: Journal of a Russian Prisoner's Wife in Japan* (New York: H.Holt, 1907).

P. Towle, "Japanese Treatment of Prisoners in 1904–05," *Military Affairs* 39 (1975): 115–117.

—*Jonathan F. Vance*

RWANDAN CIVIL WAR (1990–1994)

In 1962, the small African country of Rwanda gained formal independence from its Belgian rulers. The colonial era, however, had left behind a poisonous legacy of ethnic division that would plague the country for decades. The tensions between the country's Hutu and Tutsi populations erupted in the early 1990s with a civil war and, ultimately, the worst case of genocide in recent history.

A degree of ethnic hierarchy predated colonial rule. Rwanda's three principal ethnic groups have historically been the Twa, Hutu, and Tutsi. The indigenous Twa have traditionally consisted of only one percent of the general population. Politically marginalized, they occupied the lowest rung on the social ladder. Second in overall status were the middle-class Hutu. Predominantly agriculturalists, the Hutu make up some 80-85 percent of the population. The Tutsi, roughly 15 percent of the population throughout the history of the region, were normally pastoralists, and owned most of the region's cattle. Over time they gradually came to occupy the upper strata of the Rwandan political, economic, and social hierarchies. Tutsi leaders consolidated their position by amalgamating local chieftaincies into two centralized kingdoms, first in Rwanda, and later in neighboring Burundi.

Prior to colonial rule, however, the labels Hutu and Tutsi constituted more of a loosely defined socioeconomic division than an ethnic one. Many Tutsi cultivated the land in addition to their raising of livestock, while many Hutu both had cattle and cultivated. Social mobility was flexible; through marriage, military prowess, or simply by acquiring enough wealth, a Hutu could, in fact, become Tutsi. Tutsi could likewise descend the social ladder if they fell from favor or lost wealth. The complex political order of pre-colonial Rwanda was equally flexible. Local chiefs, for instance, could be either Tutsi or Hutu.

The dynamic between Hutu and Tutsi changed with the colonial regime. In 1899 Rwanda became a German colony, and was transferred to Belgium as a League of Nations mandate after World War I. To explain away the origins of the colony's sophisticated political system, Europeans asserted that Tutsi ancestry was not truly African, but rather a people from biblical times who had somehow migrated south into sub-Saharan Africa. Racial hierarchy theory proved receptive in Rwandan society: Tutsis applied it to legitimize their authority, while Hutus used it to excuse their subservience and foster bitter feelings toward Tutsis.

German and Belgian authorities ruled Rwanda indirectly through the Tutsi elite. They began a process of centralization that increased the power of Tutsi rulers at the expense of the local Hutu chiefs. In the church and the education system, Tutsis enjoyed favored status. Already deprived of political power, the Hutu lost much of their economic influence when in 1932 the Belgians introduced a compulsory cultivation system of cash crops. In 1933, completing the transition to a race-based system of personal identity, the Belgians issued racial identity cards; 60 years later these would serve to help the perpetrators of genocide select their victims.

The post-colonial era witnessed an intensification of ethnic tensions. As the Tutsi elite had increasingly demanded independence, Belgian authorities shifted their allegiance to the Parmehutu, a sectarian ethnic party of the Hutu majority. In 1962, Belgium granted formal independence to Rwanda and the Parmehutu assumed power, abolishing Rwanda's Tutsi monarchy. In the ensuing decades, Rwandan extremists oversaw periodic massacres of Tutsi civilians. In 1973, General Juvénal Habyarimana, a Hutu of the Mouvement Révolutionnaire National pour le Développement (MRND), came to power in a coup. Ethnic tensions remained and violent acts against Tutsis continued to be tolerated. By the late 1970s, some two million Tutsis had fled the small African republic for the remote regions of neighboring Uganda, Tanzania, and Zaire (today the Democratic Republic of the Congo, or DRC). In 1979, members of the diaspora formed the Rwandese Patriotic Front (RPF) to negotiate better terms for the Tutsi population, but diplomatic channels offered little potential for success under Habyarimana's dictatorship.

Civil war broke out in October 1990 when the RPF launched a military campaign against the MRND forces in Rwanda. The RPF had little infrastructure for keeping prisoners. Instead, they often incorporated captured MRND soldiers into their own ranks through training and reindoctrination. A temporary ceasefire in March 1991 saw an exchange of prisoners of war and the withdrawal of foreign troops, Congolese soldiers, and some 600 French paratroopers backing the MRND counterinsurgency. The peace negotiations failed, however, and the civil war intensified. In Rwanda, intermittent massacres of small groups of Tutsi civilians by Hutu extremists went unpunished.

On 4 August 1993, a second peace agreement was finally signed. Negotiated at Arusha in Tanzania, the agreement called for power-sharing between the RPF and MRND, repatriation of refugees, and the integration of armed forces. A United Nations peacekeeping force was brought in to oversee the agreement, but Hutu extremists in the MRND refused to accept the terms for power-sharing and the fighting continued. On 6 April 1994, a plane carrying President Habyarimana was shot down by unknown forces, sparking a genocide that would last nearly four months.

The death of Habyarimana proved only to be a pretext for what had been a long-planned genocide. Years before the genocide, it had become commonplace for extremist Rwandan political leaders—including members of Habyarimana's Cabinet—to denounce Tutsis as "foreigners" and foment resentment among disaffected Hutus. For at least a year before the genocide, the extremist Hutu Power group's radio station had been inciting civilians to "cleanse" their country of the Tutsi "cockroaches." Much of the organization of the genocide was done years earlier by extremists in the Rwandan government and military. Between 1990 and 1994 the country spent $112 million (US) to purchase arms from South Africa, France, and Egypt, and increased its military to 28,000 men. In 1992, the MRND formed its notorious militia wing, the Interahamwe, made up mostly of roving bands of underemployed young Hutu men, trained in secret camps operated by Rwandan army officers, and armed with Kalashnikov rifles, grenades, and machetes. Having drawn up ahead of time their lists of Tutsi leaders and political opponents, the militias were well prepared to begin the killing when Habyarimana's death was announced.

Hutu extremists moved quickly to eliminate moderate elements in the Rwandan society and government. Agathe Uwilingiyimana, a moderate Cabinet member and a Hutu, was among the first officials murdered during the genocide. The assassination of her 10 Belgian U.N. guards brought international attention to the genocide, prompting Western countries to evacuate resident and vacationing citizens and embassy staff.

The incident ultimately paralyzed U.N. decision-makers and the international community. For months, General Romeo Dallaire, commander of the U.N.'s modest contingent of 2,500 peacekeepers in Rwanda, had warned that a genocide was being planned. When the killing began, Kofi Annan, then Undersecretary General for Peacekeeping, denied Dallaire permission to protect any other moderates and barred him from taking any concrete action to halt the genocide. The U.N. Security Council dismissed Dallaire's allegations of genocide as "unconfirmed" and refused to intervene. Dallaire's contingent was only capable of protecting a small number of Tutsis who fled to his headquarters.

From April through July 1994, the world stood by as some 800,000 Tutsis were murdered. This represented roughly 75 percent of Tutsis and over 10 percent of Rwanda's entire population. Many Hutus who opposed the killings, as well as those mistaken as Tutsis, were also among the victims. Most of the killings were committed by Interahamwe militias armed with machetes, though members of the Rwandan military, including the Presidential Guard, also participated directly. Leaders of the genocide used radio to incite hatred and coordinate the attacks.

The perpetrators of the genocide took few prisoners. People who did not possess a Hutu identity card, or could not prove that they were not Tutsi, were promptly executed. In some cases, individuals with enough cash could buy their own freedom or, more likely, secure a quick death by bullet instead of machete. Tens of thousands of women were taken prisoner and raped by their captors prior to being killed. The Interahamwe went directly to Tutsi homes, often identified by local informants, including neighbors and even family members. In order to prevent Tutsis from escaping, the Interahamwe set up roadblocks and checkpoints. Many Tutsis fled for the shelter of schools, churches, or football stadiums. Tragically, the concentration of Tutsis in such locations only facilitated the genocide. Those who escaped to remote regions of the country and mounted an armed resistance were more likely to survive.

The RPF had continued its offensive against the MRND during the genocide, and on 19 July, the capital city of Kigali finally fell and a new government was installed. The RPF had occasionally continued its practice of reincorporating enemy prisoners into its own ranks, but committed a number of retaliatory killings against enemy captives and Hutu civilians as they advanced toward the capital. Fearing further reprisals, some three million Hutus fled to Tanzania and the DRC, including unknown numbers of the perpetrators and organizers of the genocide.

Since 1994, the present government has had to deal with a staggering 120,000 genocide suspects held in overcrowded prisons. In 2003, some 40,000 prisoners were released, half of whom were elderly and infirm. The other 20,000 were among those who had already confessed and had been sentenced to attend solidarity camps for training and re-education. For its part, the international community established the International Criminal Tribunal for Rwanda (ICTR) in Arusha, designed to prosecute the leaders and organizers of the genocide. By 2004, however, the ICTR had completed only 15 trials. By the same time, local courts had tried only 5,500 individuals.

In 2002, the Rwandan government introduced a participatory form of justice called "gacaca" in an attempt to speed up the trial of the remaining tens of thousands of internees. Meaning "justice on the grass," gacaca is a judicial process whereby members of the public are invited to try accused perpetrators of genocide. The process is modeled loosely after pre-colonial practices directed by village elders and community members for resolving local disputes through consensus. Under the present system, individuals are tried in the communities in which they committed the alleged crime. Judges with informal legal training oversee the cases, and members of the community are invited to participate and provide input. No physical evidence is required, as verdicts can be based on testimony alone. Sentences range from community service to life imprisonment. The Rwandan government anticipated that within five years most of the accused will have been tried. Some observers worry, however, about the professional capacities and impartiality of judges and community participants. The ultimate success or failure of the process, and of national reconciliation in general, remains to be seen.

Colonialism stripped Rwanda of a longstanding equilibrium based on a complex social, political, and economic order. The new social order resulted in decades of bitter ethnic division between Hutus and Tutsis, culminating in the 1990-1994 civil war and genocide. While few captives were taken throughout the conflict, the postwar peace has left the small African country with the staggering task of bringing to justice the tens of thousands of remaining suspects of genocide and reintegrating them into a scarcely rehabilitated society.

References

Allison Corey and Sandra F. Joireman, "Retributive Justice: The *Gacaca* Courts in Rwanda," *African Affairs* 103 (2004): 73–89.

René Lemarchand, *Rwanda and Burundi* (New York: Praeger Publishers, 1970).

Malkki, Liisa H. *Purity and Exile: Violence, Memory, and National Cosmology Among Hutu Refugees in Tanzania* (Chicago: University of Chicago Press, 1995).

Edward L. Nyankanzi, *Genocide: Rwanda and Burundi* (Rochester, VT: Schenkman Books, 1998).

Gérard Prunier, *The Rwanda Crisis: History of a Genocide* (New York: Columbia University Press, 1995).

Aimable Ruzindana, "L'historiographie comme outil génocidaire: le cas du Rwanda," in *History in the Making VI*, eds. Reine Perreault and Bruce Cartledge (Montreal: Concordia University Press, 2000).

Gregory H. Stanton, "Could the Rwandan Genocide Have Been Prevented?" *Journal of Genocide Research* 6 (2004): 211–228.

Christopher C. Taylor, *Sacrifice as Terror: The Rwandan Genocide of 1994* (New York: Berg, 1999).

Philip Verwimp, "Death and Survival During the 1994 Genocide in Rwanda," *Population Studies* 58 (2004): 233–245.

David Waller, *Rwanda: Which Way Now?* (Oxford: Oxfam, 1996).

—*Robert Talbot*

S

St. John Ambulance

The St. John Ambulance Association (later the St. John Ambulance Brigade), founded in Britain in 1877 as an outgrowth of the medieval Order of St. John, was deeply involved in the provision of relief supplies to POWs during both world wars.

Early in World War I, the provision of aid to POWs was carried out by a number of different groups, a situation that resulted in considerable confusion and duplication of effort. To improve matters, the British War Office decided in September 1916 to compel the two major philanthropic organizations interested in prisoners, the Order of St. John of Jerusalem in England and the British Red Cross Society, to join forces. Accordingly, the Central Prisoners of War Committee was established, with representatives from each body, to assume complete control of all aspects of the relief effort, including the provision of food parcels. There was some resentment on the part of smaller groups that did not wish to work under the umbrella of the Central POW Committee, but the arrangement produced the desired improvement in efficiency. Over the course of the war, the St. John Ambulance and the British Red Cross worked together to dispatch literally millions of parcels of food and clothing to British and Empire POWs in Germany and Turkey.

During World War II, the St. John Ambulance again joined with the British Red Cross to form the Joint War Organization, which was responsible for a wide range of humanitarian tasks, including the provision of relief supplies to prisoner of war camps. The brigade was particularly active in supplying reading and educational materials to camps and assisting prisoners who wished to use their captivity to improve their education. Members of the brigade also played a significant role in work detachments. They taught their fellow prisoners basic first aid, hygiene, and home nursing, first from memory and later using textbooks provided by the London office of the St. John Ambulance. In one camp alone, Stalag 383 at Hohenfels in Bavaria, 500 first-aid certificates were awarded and over 1,500 minor accidents dealt with by prisoner-medics. After the war, the St. John Ambulance remained active, dispatching a detachment of women to provide humanitarian assistance at airstrips in Belgium that were being used for the evacuation of former prisoners.

The brigade was less active among POWs in the Far East, due to the Japanese unwillingness to accept relief supplies for prison camps. Furthermore, a number of members who were captured at Hong Kong were summarily executed by the Japanese, along with members of the Royal Army Medical Corps. However, members of the brigade were able to assist in the operation to bring home prisoners after their liberation in 1945. Lady Louis Mountbatten, superintendent in chief of the Nursing Corps and Divisions of the St. John Ambulance, was very active in this regard, and played a significant role in shipping supplies to recently liberated camps and expediting their evacuation.

See also International Committee of the Red Cross; Young Men's Christian Association

References

Ronnie Cole-Mackintosh, *A Century of Service to Mankind: A History of the St. John Ambulance Brigade* (London: Century Benham, 1986).

G.W.L. Nicholson, *The White Cross in Canada: A History of St. John Ambulance* (Montreal: Harvest House, 1967).

—*Jonathan F. Vance*

SANDAKAN–RANAU DEATH MARCH

The Sandakan–Ranau march represents the worst atrocity ever committed against Australian servicemen. After being captured by Japanese forces on Singapore in 1942, a group of 1,494 Australian POWs was sent to Sandakan in British North Borneo to construct an airfield. The following June, they were joined by a further 500 Australians and a similar number of British prisoners. Soon after, all but a few officers were removed to an internment compound in Kuching, leaving the men virtually leaderless.

The prisoners in Sandakan camp, under the administration of Lieutenant Susumi Hoshijima, were systematically and deliberately starved or beaten to death. By 1945 just over a thousand prisoners were fit enough to take part in two arduous marches to Ranau, an isolated camp 250 kilometers to the west. The first death march began on 28 January 1945, and the second on 29 May 1945. Nearly 300 prisoners, those too ill to be evacuated, were slaughtered soon after the last prisoners left Sandakan.

During the marches through thick jungle and swamp, those men who were too exhausted or ill to continue were killed by the guards. Once they reached Ranau, a deliberate plan of annihilation by starvation and brutality was carried out, with the Japanese captors under orders to exterminate every POW on the island. Only six of the men who set out for Ranau, all Australians, managed to escape and reach Allied troops. They were the only survivors of this systematic massacre of 2,500 POWs.

See also Bataan Death March; World War II—Far East

References

Lynette Ramsay Silver, *Sandakan: A Conspiracy of Silence* (Bowral, Australia: Sally Milner Publishing, 2000).

Don Wall, *Sandakan: The Last March* (Sydney: Griffin Press, 1988).

—*Colin Burgess*

SCAPINI, GEORGES (1893–1976)

The ambassador for French prisoners of war in Berlin from 1940 to 1944, Georges Scapini served as private in the 5th Infantry Division during World War I. He was blinded in battle in 1915 and was cited for bravery under fire. After recovering, he studied law, became a member of the Paris Bar, and, from 1928, served as an independent deputy from Paris in the Third Republic. Scapini strongly promoted Franco-German reconciliation throughout the interwar era. Despite Hitler's takeover in 1933, Scapini quickly joined the *Comité France-Allemagne,* constituted in 1935, which worked to bring together the two countries' elites.

The Germans held nearly two million French soldiers when an armistice ended the Battle of France on 25 June 1940. Under the Geneva Convention, the United States became Protecting Power for the French POWs, but in the fall of 1940, Germany proposed that the French State at Vichy protect its own prisoners. Leaders at Vichy accepted the proposal and head of state Philippe Pétain selected Scapini to serve as ambassador, in charge of the *Service Diplomatique des Prisonniers de Guerre* (SDPG, Diplomatic Service for the Prisoners of War), the so-called Scapini Mission.

In a December 1940 speech, Scapini argued that it served both countries' interests to collaborate in the reconstruction of a new Europe. After the liberation, Scapini justified his decision by pointing out that Germany might have retaliated against the prisoners had France refused Germany's offer to serve as its own Protecting Power. He insisted that the SDPG did at least as well if not better than the United States would have done in protecting the French prisoners' interests.

In the fall of 1940, Scapini attempted to persuade Germany simply to liberate all the French prisoners so as to encourage pro-German public opinion in France. When that failed, Scapini suggested that voluntary French laborers replace the POWs, a policy that would demonstrate the mutual interests of the two countries and win popular support for collaboration in France. But in 1940, the Germans had no intention of releasing a potentially hostile force that itself provided adequate labor for their needs. By 1942, having learned the limits of German good will, Scapini opposed then head of the government Pierre Laval's implementation of a laborer-POW exchange.

The SDPG inspected prison camps for compliance with international law (many former French POWs have noted the irony of a blind man running camp inspections) and provided prisoners with additional food, clothing, medicine, books, sports equipment, and musical instruments. The SDPG oversaw all correspondence between the prison camps and France, and it handled requests from prisoner representatives. Scapini did prevent the Germans from sending France's Jewish POWs to separate camps. However, on other issues, he proved less willing to resist German pressure. After seven French POWs protested German violations of Geneva Convention provisions prohibiting POW labor in war industries, Scapini took up the matter with General Hermann Reinecke, but he eventually backed down.

In December 1944, after Scapini informed the German government that he no longer recognized the authority of the remnants of the Vichy regime, then forcibly relocated to a German castle at Sigmaringen, he and the SDPG staff were arrested and sent to Silesia. Scapini eventually escaped and returned to Berlin with a group of POWs.

In May 1945, Scapini returned to Paris, was arrested and detained for two months, fled to Switzerland, and in June 1952 returned to face trial. The accusations against him focused on his many procollaboration statements from his years as ambassador and on his promotion of "Pétain circles" in the prison camps. Scapini countered by documenting protests he had lodged with the Germans and improvements he obtained for the POWs. After a three-day trial in July 1952, he was acquitted.

See also Vichy France; World War II—Western Europe

References

François Cochet, *Les Exclus de la victoire: Histoire des PG, déportés et STO, 1945–1985* (Paris: SPM-Kronos, 1992).

Yves Durand, *La Captivité: Histoire des prisonniers de guerre français, 1939–1945* (Paris: FNCPG-CATM, 1980).

Sarah Fishman, *We Will Wait: Wives of French Prisoners of War, 1940–1945* (New Haven, CT: Yale University Press, 1991).

Georges Scapini, *A Challenge to Darkness: The Life Story of J. Georges Scapini* (Garden City, NY: Doubleday, 1929).

———, *Mission sans gloire* (Paris: Morgan, 1960).

———, *"Prisoners,"* in *France during the German Occupation, 1940–1944*, trans. Philip Whitcomb (Stanford, CA: The Hoover Institution on War Revolution and Peace, 1957): 203–208.

—Sarah Fishman

SCOTT, WINFIELD (1786–1866)

A dominant figure in American military history of the nineteenth century, Winfield Scott was also at the center of a protracted reprisal involving prisoners of war during the War of 1812. Born in Virginia, Scott was commissioned in the army in 1808, and when the war began, he was second-in-command of an artillery regiment. In October 1812, he and nearly a thousand American regulars and militiamen were captured by British forces after the Battle of Queenston in the Niagara Peninsula. The vast majority of the prisoners were soon paroled (Scott himself reached Boston on 5 January 1813), but the British commander in Canada ordered that any of the American prisoners who appeared to be British-born should be transported to England; accordingly, 23 American soldiers of Irish birth left Canada to be tried for treason. In response, Scott recommended to his government the incarceration of a similar number of British soldiers in May 1813, which in turn moved the British to order the imprisonment of a further 46 Americans. In November 1813, American

President James Madison jailed another 46 British officers "as a pledge for the safety of those on whom the British government seems disposed to wreak its vengeance." The British responded in kind yet again, so that well over 200 POWs on both sides were imprisoned, often in appalling conditions. Protracted negotiations were required to secure the release of all of the hostages, including the original 23 Irish-Americans, who had never been tried for treason at all.

After being released from his parole, Scott returned to action in the War of 1812 and later led campaigns against Native Americans in the West, in Florida, and in Georgia. Promoted to commanding general of the U.S. Army in 1841, he led the invasion of Mexico in 1847 and was involved in the early actions of the U.S. Civil War. Scott retired from the army in 1861 and died at West Point, Connecticut, in 1866.

See also Mexican-American War; Reprisals; War of 1812

References

John S.D. Eisenhower, *Agent of Destiny: The Life and Times of General Winfield Scott* (New York: Free Press, 1997).
Timothy D. Johnson, *Winfield Scott: The Quest for Military Glory* (Manhattan: University Press of Kansas, 1998).
Ralph Robinson, "Retaliation for the Treatment of Prisoners of War in the War of 1812," *American Historical Review* 49 (1943): 65–70.
Winfield Scott, *Memoirs of Lieut.-General Scott*, 2 vols. (New York: Sheldon and Co., 1864).

—*Andrea Vandenberg*

SEMINOLE WARS (1817–1819, 1835–1842)

The Seminoles, an amalgam of Upper Creek refugees who fled to Florida during the early 1800s and Yamasees, Guales, Hitchitis, and Oconees with whom they mixed, fought a series of wars during the early 1800s against the United States in a desperate bid to remain in Florida. In these wars, the treatment of native prisoners became a contentious issue, as it did in most wars between European and non-European peoples.

The First Seminole War (1817–1819) erupted after rebellious Creek warriors joined the Seminoles in Spanish-controlled Florida rather than submit to the authority of the United States. The angry natives attacked exposed southern settlements and offered refuge to black slaves willing to join them. Southern planters responded by organizing raiding parties that invaded the Seminole heartland in search of escaped slaves.

In 1817 General Andrew Jackson received orders to put an end to the troublesome raids. Convinced that the Spanish had encouraged the frequent ambushes, he responded to the incursions by leading an invasion of the Florida peninsula in November 1817. Jackson and his motley army eventually defeated the Seminoles living west of the Suwannee River and successfully captured Pensacola and St. Marks. He justified these high-handed measures on the grounds that they were designed to secure the tranquillity of the exposed southern settlements. He also hoped that the display of military force would cow the renegade warriors who opposed him. His successful invasion ultimately convinced Spanish leaders to part with Florida in 1819. Two years later, the United States took formal possession of the region and land-hungry Americans poured into the peninsula.

During the 1820s, southern planters scrambled to find new lands for their crops. The Seminoles, like the other tribes of the southeast, recognized the threat and united in a desperate attempt to preserve their territory. After he became president in 1829, Andrew Jackson moved ahead with his removal strategy. A preliminary agreement to relocate the tribe west of the Mississippi was reached at the Treaty of Payne's Landing in 1832. However, the Seminoles as a whole did not approve the subsequent Treaty of Fort Gibson (28 March 1833) that cemented the deal to move onto Creek lands reserved for them in Indian Territory. Despite overwhelming tribal opposition to the treaty, U.S. officials announced plans to enforce it.

The diplomatic treachery infuriated the Seminoles. An overwhelming number of Seminoles did not believe the treaties were just and they vowed to fight removal. They gathered around patriot leaders like Osceola, Jumper, Alligator, Tiger Tail, Billy Bowlegs, and Holata Mico. Many of their black allies, realizing that removal would lead to their own enslavement, also joined forces with the Seminoles.

The decision of Wiley Thompson, a Florida Indian agent, to push ahead with the government's removal policies in December 1835 precipitated the Second Seminole War. Osceola, an outspoken foe of Thompson and opponent of removal, responded by killing the agent on 28 December 1835. That same day a party of Seminoles murdered Major Francis L. Dade and his company of troops. The Florida frontier was in a panic and the Seminoles, who frustrated their pursuers with guerrilla warfare tactics, were in control.

The elusive Seminoles complicated matters by retreating to the Everglades. For the first few years, one commander after another failed to subdue the Seminoles and their black allies. The outlook for the U.S. forces improved in 1837, when General Joseph M. Hernandez captured two Seminole chiefs, King Philip and Vehee Billy. The two leaders and their followers were detained at Fort Marion, an ancient casemate located near St. Augustine, until their transfer to Indian Territory could be arranged. News of the capture prompted Coacoochee, Philip's son, to surrender his band. During his detention, Coacoochee informed his captors that Osceola also wanted to discuss surrender terms.

A short time later, General Hernandez met Osceola under a flag of truce near Fort Peyton, Florida. Although he had promised the Seminole leaders protection during the negotiations, Hernandez arrested Osceola and 13 other Seminole chiefs on 22 October 1837. Then, all 95 Seminole prisoners were hastily marched to Fort Marion. Following the escape of several prominent Seminole prisoners, Osceola was transferred to Fort Moultrie, South Carolina; weakened by malaria, he died a prisoner of war on 30 January 1838. Army officers continued to violate flags of truce and promises of safe conduct in order to secure other prominent Seminole leaders.

By 1838 General Thomas S. Jesup concluded that the Seminole removal policy was flawed in that it would only prolong the bloody and costly war. Jesup informed his superiors that some 3,000 Seminoles had already moved west and that the remaining Seminole lands were not required for agricultural purposes. Although the natives did not block the path of American expansion of the Florida peninsula, politicians ignored Jesup's recommendations and pushed ahead with plans to remove all Seminoles from the region.

As the prolonged conflict continued, Seminole bands surrendered and grudgingly agreed to move west. Military leaders managed to bribe some chiefs into relocating, but a small band of hostile Seminoles continued to harass soldiers with well-organized ambushes. In February 1842, Colonel William Jenkins Worth convinced his superiors to end all military operations against the Indians. He believed that all attempts to remove the 300 to 500 Seminoles remaining in Florida were impractical. President John Tyler agreed and the Second Seminole War officially ended on 14 August 1842.

The Second Seminole War was the most violent chapter in the history of Indian removal. Defiant Seminoles fought valiantly to remain in Florida. In the end all but a few intransigent Seminoles had been removed or killed. The government paid a heavy price for its decision to relocate the Seminoles. Some 1,500 soldiers died during the seven-year conflict that cost taxpayers more than $20 million.

See also Apache Wars; Plains Indian Warfare; Sioux Wars

References

Alvin M. Josephy, Jr., *Now That the Buffalo's Gone* (Norman: University of Oklahoma Press, 1989).

John K. Mahon, *History of the Second Seminole War, 1835–1842* (Gainesville: University of Florida Press, 1967).

Francis Paul Prucha, *Sword of the Republic: The United States Army on the Frontier, 1783–1846* (Lincoln: University of Nebraska Press, 1969).

—*Jon Brudvig*

SEVEN YEARS' WAR (1756–1763)

The Seven Years' War was essentially two distinct conflicts, fought on a variety of fronts, ranging from the dynastic struggles of central Europe to the colonial conflicts of North America and India. The European theater involved the dispute between Frederick II (the Great) of Prussia and his opponents, Austria, France, Russia, Hanover, and Sweden; the colonial theater focused on the maritime and colonial conflicts between Great Britain and its Bourbon enemies, France and Spain.

The eighteenth-century Enlightenment had a direct impact on all aspects of European society, including combat in the Age of Reason. A guiding aspiration of the Enlightenment was to construct a society for human beings who would be rational, tolerant, and ultimately enlightened. With this in mind, an eighteenth-century concept of prisoners of war developed as Europeans struggled to embrace the complex notions of natural rights and the dignity of humankind.

Eighteenth-century armies typically reflected the spirit of the era by signing agreements or cartels with their adversaries. Cartels often allowed for the lavish treatment of prisoners, particularly captured aristocratic officers, and the rapid exchange or ransom of prisoners of war. Accordingly, in the Seven Years' War cartels were drawn up by Prussia and Austria in 1757, France and Russia in 1759, and Great Britain and France at the Convention of Sluys in 1759. The rates of exchange or ransom were assessed in cash or kind. A general could thus be exchanged for another general in a straight swap, or for a specified number of soldiers or officers. Any discrepancy in the exchange could be made up by monetary payments, ranging from as high as £2,500 for a field marshal to as low as eight shillings for a private soldier. While waiting for their repatriation, prisoners were typically tended by their own doctors, and their home government was held responsible for reimbursing their captors for the total cost of the prisoner's upkeep.

Under this system, military captivity was nothing more than a temporary condition, as prisoners were returned to their regiments as soon as arrangements were made for their ransom or exchange. On the battlefields of western Germany, "it was something of a joke in the English and French armies to be taken prisoner.... You had supper with Prince Ferdinand of Brunswick and the next day you were back with your regiment." Until their exchange, captured officers were usually quartered in private homes and were free to roam about on parole. Consequently, "Prussian prisoners of the Austrians might be seen taking the air in the park at Schönbrunn, or strolling along the banks of the Danube at Krems. In Berlin the high-ranking Russian and French officers entranced the ladies through their wealth and splendid manners, and wherever they appeared in the Prussian dominions the allied officers gave a valued stimulus to local trade." Unfortunately, while aristocratic officers enjoyed the generosity of their enlightened captors, common soldiers usually fared much worse. Captured troops were usually impressed into service by their captor or imprisoned in disease-ridden prison ships and overcrowded fortresses, from where thousands of bodies were carried to unmarked graves or simply thrown into the sea.

The Treaty of Paris brought an end to the Seven Years' War on 10 February 1763. Arguably, the most significant provisions of the treaty turned over virtually all French colonial territories in North America to Great Britain. The British also acquired Florida from Spain, while France retained a tenuous hold on her meager possessions in India. Generally, continental Europe remained free from territorial changes, and the treaty merely reaffirmed Prussian control of the disputed Silesian area.

References

John Childs, *Armies and Warfare in Europe, 1648–1789* (New York: Holmes and Meier, 1982).

Christopher Duffy, *The Military Experience in the Age of Reason* (New York: Routledge and Kegan Paul, 1987).

———, *The Army of Frederick the Great* (New York: Hippocrene Books, 1974).

—*Christopher Blackburn*

Sexual Relations

There is little objective research available on heterosexual sexual relations of prisoners of war and internees. Instead, there is a mass of anecdotal evidence, some of it undoubtedly sensationalized or even invented. Two trends do emerge, however: that sexual appetite declines along with the prisoners' food supply, and that prisoners who enjoy a certain amount of freedom, particularly those on work detachments, have had relatively easy access to members of the opposite sex.

A prisoner who rarely emerges from within the confines of the barbed-wire has almost no chance of engaging in heterosexual relations. This would apply to most Allied officers detained in World Wars I and II, and to American and British Commonwealth POWs during the Korean and Vietnam Wars. There may have been some homosexual activity, but the consensus among these prisoners is that sex became relatively insignificant in light of the other challenges they faced. According to an apocryphal but accurate comment, after the first six months in captivity, the only appetites left were for food and freedom. Indeed, POWs seem to have been more concerned about the effects of captivity (particularly nutritional deficiencies) on their postwar sexual performance than they were about their lack of sexual outlets while in prison camp.

That there is a relationship between diet and sexual appetite is supported by the suggestion that there was more sexual activity, or at least greater sexual drive, among German and Italian POWs in North America and Australia, who were in better physical condition because of better rations. Most prisoners who escaped from the camp at Evansville, Indiana, headed straight to the local brothel; military police and camp guards usually checked there first before widening their search for escapers. Work parties and parole walks also afforded German POWs the opportunity of interacting with civilian women, a fact that was well known to the authorities. In Canada, the Royal Canadian Mounted Police was frequently called in to investigate liaisons between POWs and civilians. As a weapon of last resort, it was not unknown for camp officials to transfer prisoners who were deemed to be getting too close to local women.

Sexual relations between POWs and civilians was likely more prevalent in North America and Australia because punishment for such interaction was less severe there than it was in Germany. A Polish prisoner, Marian Piotrowski, recalls that part of his initiation process into a German stalag was being read a notice giving the penalties for intercourse with German women; they ranged from 10 years in prison to death, and the notice was appended with the name and sentence of a recent offender. Prisoners were required to sign a form stating that they had read and comprehended the regulations. Nevertheless, it seems likely that the Nazi command took these regulations more seriously than the camp officials. Piotrowski reports that a number of prisoners were permitted to marry German women they had impregnated; if the prisoners were already married when the offense occurred, they received a salutary sentence of eight weeks in confinement. Indeed, the women involved were likely to face punishment that was more severe than the men. They, too, were liable to imprisonment if the affair was uncovered; even if it did not come to the attention of the civil authorities, they might face the wrath of their townspeople. Robin Campbell, a British officer captured in North Africa in 1941, recalls hearing of a German woman being led through her village with a sign around her neck that read "I have been the whore of a prisoner while my husband was fighting on the eastern front."

Despite the risk to both parties, prisoners who had some freedom of movement generally seem to have found that sex was readily available. The anecdotal evidence runs the gamut from hurried encounters in a haystack or storeroom in which any physical attraction was accentuated by a few cigarettes or a bar of chocolate, to long-term relationships involving genuine reciprocal affection. John Elwyn, a British airman posted to a work camp in Upper Silesia, in eastern Germany, met a young Polish woman while working on a construction site in November 1941. The two fell in love, and Elwyn frequently slipped out of his camp to spend time with her. At Christmas, the two went through a form of marriage and saw each other regularly until she fell ill and died in the late summer of 1942. This couple surely took their relationship farther than most, but there is no reason to doubt that many such couplings involved real love.

It is by no means clear that the prisoners always initiated these relationships. Indeed, more than one POW reported that the advances often came from the women, many of whom had been without male company for as long as the prisoners had been deprived of female company. By the same token, there were also many desperate women who were willing to sell their bodies for food or cigarettes.

See also Homosexuality

References

Robin Campbell, "Prisoner in Germany," *Atlantic Monthly* 173 (1944): 53–57.

John Elwyn, *At the Fifth Attempt: An Escape Story* (London: Leo Cooper, 1987).

Marian Piotrowski, *Adventures of a Polish Prisoner* (London: Lindsay Drummond, 1943).

—*Jonathan F. Vance*

Sexual Violence

Sex crimes during wartime occur in a variety of contexts. Often the perpetrators commit mass rape and leave the victims to suffer or die where the crime occurred. In other instances, perpetrators arrest or recruit victims and keep them in prisons, houses, or other areas where sexual crimes occur. Even though female and male POWs have been used as sexual slaves for their captors for centuries, the majority of victims of sexual violence throughout history are female. The longstanding disregard and silence by witnesses, lawmakers, military leaders, and others regarding the issue has served perpetrators well and hampered efforts to reduce the amount of sexual violence that occurs during armed conflicts today. Furthermore, societal and cultural mechanisms ensure the silence of a majority of victims, despite the physical and psychological horror of sexual abuse to them and their loved ones. Prostitution, a form of sexual abuse, thrives during armed conflict with little action by leaders to prevent the massive sexual exploitation of desperate women and children. Alcohol and other substances contribute greatly to the extent of sexual violence that occurs during armed conflicts. The motives for rape, gang rape, mass rape, forced prostitution, forced pregnancy, and other forms of sex crimes vary. In some instances, mass rape is a formal military strategy, while in other cases it can be the result of cultural attitudes, sexual drive, drunkenness, or an undisciplined soldiery.

According to historian Gerda Lerner, the first evidence of the enslavement and sexual abuse of captured women after military conquest dates from the third millennium B.C.E. With the establishment of slavery as an institution, slave owners rented out their slaves as prostitutes or worked them in commercial brothels. The Hebrew Scriptures and the Koran describe the rape of the women of conquered tribes as routine. Foreign women were often kidnapped as spoils of war, and forced to marry their captors/rapists. Kings of conquered tribes in biblical times were sometimes raped by the invading army. In the *Annals of Fulda*, there are references to women taken by warring tribes to be used for sexual purposes, as there are in studies of medieval Scandinavia. Genghis Khan used captured women as sexual slaves. However, not all peoples have employed sexual violence as a war measure. For example, in North America, although the Europeans raped Amerindian women, the Amerindians typically did not rape European women.

By the twentieth century, enforced heterosexuality of armies was a norm of military life, in contrast to ancient and medieval customs of homosexuality in the military. During World War I, the Germans had military brothels, some surrounded by barbed wire to contain the women who served the German soldiers. There is also much evidence of wartime rape revealed, for example, in the Bryce Report (1916) on German atrocities in Belgium and France.

By World War II, state organized, regulated, and enforced sexual slavery of captured women became major institutions of Germany and Japan. The institution of Japanese military "comfort stations" began in 1931 and was in full force by 1937 after the Japanese raped and murdered tens of thousands of Chinese women in Nanking. At least 200,000 rural and poor, Korean and other Asian women, as well as some Europeans, were recruited under false pretences or were forcibly abducted, made to serve up to 90 soldiers a day, were beaten, and kept in seclusion. Some women served for as long as nine years. It is estimated that between 70 and 90 percent died in captivity. Until 1993, the Japanese government denied any coercion in the recruitment of women into the *Yoja Chongsindae* (Women's Voluntary Labor Service Corps). Despite recent acknowledgment of the wrongs committed against them, the women have not received any form of compensation from the Japanese government.

Even less researched are the 500 or more Nazi brothels set up by the German state for the use of soldiers, forced laborers, and concentration camp inmates. Tens of thousands of women and some men of all nationalities worked as prostitutes for the German state, including Jewish, Gypsy, and Slavic women, despite National Socialist racial laws. As in the Japanese case, many women were forced into sexual slavery, many died, and the German government has never acknowledged these grave human rights abuses that were committed in its name.

Bosnian Serbs used rape as part of the military strategy of ethnic cleansing during the war in the former Yugoslavia. As Serbian soldiers invaded cities and towns, they raped women and girls. Between 150,000 to 300,000 female and male inmates were held in rape concentration camps, where they were repeatedly sexually assaulted one another, starved, buried alive, and murdered. Another form of sexual slavery was the rape/death prisons or brothels where Serbian soldiers held and daily gang raped captive women. The number of prisons is unknown, as is the number of women held there, most of whom were murdered and buried in mass graves. Only a handful of suspects charged with rape and sexual assault during the war have been arrested, and leaders in the Serbian army continue to deny the charges.

In addition to Bosnia-Herzegovina, the examples of sex crimes in twentieth- and twenty-first-century conflicts are endless: Japanese troops against women in the Philippines following Japan's invasion of that country; U.S. troops against Vietnamese women; and armed men against women and girls in the Bangladesh war of independence. Iraqi soldiers raped Kuwaiti women en masse during the invasion of Kuwait. In Africa, the widespread abuse of free, displaced, or captured women and girls has killed, maimed, and ruined an untold number of lives. For example: in the ethnic conflict in Rwanda, Hutu leaders ordered their troops to rape Tutsi women; according to Amnesty International, in Sudan's western Darfur region "Janjawid militiamen have sexually abused thousands of women and girls as young as eight years old. Abducted women have had their arms and legs broken to stop them escaping. In camps of displaced people around towns and villages in Darfur, the Janjawid have patrolled the periphery, raping women who venture out for food and water." In Uganda and in the Congo, widespread rape by armed militia has also been documented.

Ironically, even though the sexual abuse of men and boys usually is hardly mentioned, the world learned about sexual abuse of male Iraqi prisoners by U.S. troops, but there has been relative silence about the abuse of female prisoners. Even though the U.S. Congress has seen photos of abuse against Iraqi women, these have not been released. According to Amnesty International there was a sharp rise in violence against Iraqi women after the U.S.-led invasion and occupation, and the Australian SBS World News and Britain's newspaper *The Guardian* reported in May 2004 that U.S. forces tortured and raped Iraqi women held at the Abu Ghraib prison. Others have reported that U.S. forces have committed sexually violent abuses of imprisoned women who were arrested only because of their relationship to an alleged terrorist. Lawyers working inside Iraq and the American Civil Liberties Union have verified that U.S. troops have committed more than a few isolated incidents of sexual violence against Iraqi females, but the offenses remain outside the mainstream press and remain unpunished.

One of the main problems for prosecutors, scholars, and others is the longstanding and pervasive silence surrounding the topic of sexual violence that has served well the perpetrators and others inclined to disbelief. Because of the silence, many survivors endure a second tragedy: the painful denial and lack of acknowledgment following the crimes they experienced. Survivors live with their memories alone, often believing that most people would not want to know about their suffering. As one scholar writes on the sexual violence in Serbia, "even though women in rape/death camps know that the same things are being done to other women, and sometimes are even forced to watch them, still the sense of isolation is total." In some areas of the world, it is tribal custom to murder a woman who has been raped, and women practicing prostitution are often beaten as a punishment. An Amnesty International report on the sex crimes committed in Darfur states that "The social and economic effects can be equally lethal. The destructive effect on family ties and community relations is frequently devastating. Women who have suffered sexual violence are also made to bear the community's sense of shame. The survivors of rape and their children are sometimes shunned. Husbands may reject wives, and unmarried women may never be able to marry. Such women, forced to provide for themselves in a society that traditionally has no place for a woman to live independently of a man, face destitution and increasing vulnerability to further human rights abuses." The shame and other forms of discrimination ensure the silence of survivors.

Yet victims of sex crimes need survivors, witnesses, peacekeepers, and leaders in the international community to be anything but silent. Being raped is a horrific experience. Rape causes physical and psychological distress for years after the violation. Because of the force used, the skin in and around the vagina or anus is often ripped and abraded. In addition to internal injuries, such as a prolapsed uterus and bruising, there can be a massive loss of blood. This, in combination with the intense pain, can cause a person to lose consciousness or die. Such violence can leave a woman or girl sterile, kill a fetus if she happens to be pregnant, and could leave the survivor with severe abdominal pain for years. In times of war, rape often turns into gang rape, making it even more traumatic and life-threatening. In addition to the pain to the woman, injured breasts often no longer can be used to nurse, which can deprive an infant of life-saving milk, especially in times of hardship. Similarly, to be forced into prostitution means enduring multiple rapes each day for as many days as one survives. Those who do survive experience physical, psychological, and emotional injury from the repetitive assaults to their bodies and psyches, to an extent that is rarely overcome. Women and girls often commit suicide after they have been raped. The emotional and psychological trauma from all sexual crimes, especially in more conservative cultures where women were viewed as having been tarnished, is enormous. Even in the less conservative West, one study showed that over 200 women and girls committed suicide in Pankow alone and many more throughout Berlin in the final days of World War II.

Historically, military personnel, historians, witnesses, and other international observers have ignored the plight of wartime victims of sexual slavery, or have referred to such women as "camp followers," "prostitutes," "whores," or "comfort women." However, research and testimony reveal that many women were forced to act as sexual slaves, either coerced into the work by deception or physical force. Other women strategically "chose" this type of work over other forced labor in a concentration camp, or were forced into prostitution by their own or their families' starvation. The disregard of leading officials throughout the international community is baffling. For example, despite the alleged attempt by the U.S. military to educate servicemen about sexually transmitted diseases, the movie *Where the Girls Are: VD in Southeast Asia* (1969) clearly shows the main character as a victim (called "the victim" in the script) who faces a multitude of sexually available Asian women.

More recently, Brigadier-General Janis Karpinski, the commanding general of the 800th Military Police Brigade, stated in relation to the widespread sexual assaults against U.S. servicewomen: "The attitude of Lieutenant General Ricardo Sanchez [the ground commander in Iraq] permeated the entire chain of command: The women asked to be here, so now let them take what comes with the territory." Hundreds of sexual assault cases within the U.S. armed forces just during the Iraq War have gone unpunished, because military commanders, not prosecutors, decide whether a soldier should face criminal proceedings. Furthermore, in the United States the military definition of rape does not conform with any civilian federal statute. Servicewomen who become pregnant as a result of rape are forced to pay for their own abortions because they are not covered under military health insurance. If military commanders have these attitudes about women who are serving on their side of a conflict, then it is not surprising that there is a lack of concern of the rights of women from the "other" side, whether the conflict is in 2005 or 1942. Similarly, although in 2005 the U.S. Congress did tackle the issue of unpunished sexual assault against American servicewomen by American servicemen, Congress has remained silent on the sexual abuse committed by Americans against Iraqi women and girls.

Continuing a trend among the lawsuits from China, Korea, and other Asian countries, in late 2004 Japan's top court dismissed four Chinese women's demand for reparations and an apology from the government of Japan for forcing them into sexual slavery during World War II. Despite the fact that sexual violence probably has been the most prevalent among human rights abuses during the civil war in Sierra Leone, Human Rights Watch reported in 2001 that although the United Nations and the British Army have provided human rights education and training, there has been absolutely no education provided on the rights of women. Furthermore, in 2005 the United Nations is investigating sexual offenses committed by peacekeeping troops stationed throughout the world where young children are raped or forced into prostitution with no other means to survive.

Another aspect of sexual slavery is the prostitution that victims are forced into because of wartime deprivation, starvation, unemployment, and the willingness of occupying forces to take advantage of those forced into such choices (which are not really choices). Despite the long history of this subjugation, modern armies take few steps to prevent the abuse. Rather, it is common for military leaders to provide their male soldiers with condoms to prevent the spread of disease. This is seen in the present conflict in Iraq where condoms are flown in during stock time, and during World War II the Germans provided condoms through the entire conflict despite experiencing a massive shortage of rubber.

Sexually transmitted diseases have concerned military leaders for centuries because of the inevitable spread through the military forces. Before the introduction of penicillin after World War II, treatment of venereal diseases required considerable time. During World War II, the average length of gonorrhea treatment was three weeks. A soldier infected with syphilis was away from the front for up to half a year. At any given time, the average number of those away from duty being treated was the same as 14 battalions of Wehrmacht soldiers. Approximately 7,000 soldiers were constantly in treatment. Yet the focus of military leaders has not been to curb sexual activity or the sexual abuse and exploitation of local women and girls, but to provide safe sexual outlets for servicemen, regardless of the effects on women and girls.

Related to sex crimes is the widespread use and abuse of alcohol and the societal acceptance of this behavior. Concerning the abuse of alcohol on the Eastern Front during World War II, one study, based on an array of archival sources, clearly shows that the consumption of alcohol was widespread and contributed to the ubiquity of sexual violence. Researcher Wendy Gertjejanssen argues that with alcohol people were more willing to break regulations, such as the German racial laws, and they could have experienced heightened sexual desire. Furthermore, in various armed conflicts, biological factors are similar, such as alcohol, men, extended periods of sexual abstinence, life-threatening situations, high stress levels, and unarmed females who became victims of sexual torture. Military culture, peer pressure, and large groups of armed, exhausted, relieved, terrified, or intoxicated men together pose grave dangers to unarmed and often starving civilians. Furthermore, numerous studies in the medical and biological fields document the strong correlation between alcohol consumption, sexual violence, and the spread of sexually transmitted diseases.

Finally, Gertjejanssen argues in her study of sexual violence during World War II that in analyzing the Eastern Front, sexual violence seems to have been more often a case of armed men targeting women and girls because they were unarmed women and girls and therefore exploitable. Armed men on the Eastern Front did not seem to target women and girls merely because they belonged to a certain "enemy" group, or because the men viewed a woman of the enemy side as an "other," therefore, a "whore," and, hence, fair game. That is, the sexual violence in the east during World War II undermines the traditional feminist argument that rape has nothing to do with sexual desire and occurs only because of a desire to feel powerful. The fact that rape and sexual harassment are abuses of power aside, the evidence from the Eastern Front does not indicate that a desire for more power or more feelings of power were the only motives in rape.

Furthermore, neither Soviet nor German military leaders used rape as a military tactic. There does not seem to have been a specific order from either the German or the Soviet side that rape be used as a terror tactic or a weapon to destroy a population. Nevertheless, in 1941 with what became known as the Commissar Order, Hitler gave specific instructions to treat the population in the east with complete ruthlessness, and Stalin, for the most part, laughed about the "fun" his men were having. Although rape was not a formal military tactic by either army, it was used as a means of terror by both sides, and there was a tacit understanding that armed men had a right or even permission to rape women and girls. Indeed, although rape was not a formal military tactic, German men received what we could call a blessing to rape. A regulation from the Main SS Court Office declared that the lack of sexual intercourse and the large amount of alcohol consumed should be considered "extenuating circumstances" in rape trials, which should not be punished severely, especially if it was a first offense. The arrogant belief in one's right to sexual activity with another, often as a "reward" for having risked one's life, along with the widespread abuse of alcohol among the military, are main threads connecting rape for both the German and the Soviet military, and in other conflicts as well. These beliefs and motives contrast with the reasons behind sexual violence in other armed conflicts, such as in Bosnia-Herzegovina and Rwanda, where sexual violence was part of a formal military strategy.

Organizations such as Women, Law & Development International, People for Peace (Kenya), Restore Hope (Burundi), Isis of Uganda, Women's Feature Service, and the Korean Council for the Women Drafted for Sexual Slavery by Japan, along with other activists, scholars, and survivors, are working toward obtaining international and national legislation to ensure the prevention of gender violence during war. In the last century, when rape was defined as a crime in international humanitarian law, it was not viewed as a brutal attack, but as a provocation to honor. In addition to minimizing the brutal assault to the body and psyche, when rape is defined merely as a violation of a woman's honor, not her person, victims are discouraged from coming forward and prosecutors are less likely to litigate. Astrid Aafjes explains, "The 1907 Hague Convention Regulations Respecting the Laws and Customs of War on Land and its accompanying Regulations do not mention rape or other forms of sexual assault at all. Instead, Article 46 of the Convention's Regulations states obliquely that "family honor and rights, the lives of persons, and private property, as well as religious convictions and practice, must be respected . . . .'" This is also seen in the Fourth Geneva Convention of 1949, the 1977 Geneva Protocols protecting civilians in war, and the 1958 Red Cross Commentary on the Fourth Geneva Convention. For example, the Fourth Convention states that "Women shall be especially protected against any attack on their honor, in particular against rape, enforced prostitution, or any form of indecent assault." Article 147 of the same convention, however, states that "torture or inhuman treatment" and "willfully causing great suffering or serious injury to body or health" are war crimes. Although the latter describes a rape, rape was not intended to be included.

Legal scholar Rhonda Copelon explains that the problem in legal texts is the ambiguity over whether rape is defined as a "grave breach," the most serious crime under international law. Article 2 of the Geneva Convention defined grave breaches as "(a) wilful killing; (b) torture or inhuman treatment, including biological experiments; (c) willfully causing great suffering or serious bodily injury to body or health." According to Astrid Aafjes, the International Committee of the Red Cross (ICRC) "declared that the grave breach of Article 147 [of the Fourth Geneva Convention] covers rape" and cites the ICRC Aide-Memoire of 3 December 1992. Furthermore, according to Aafjes, "the U.S. Department of State also declared that rape is a war crime or a grave breach under customary international law and the Geneva Conventions and can be prosecuted as such."

For the first time, in various international documents in the 1990s the connection between rape and honor has been eradicated, and rape has been defined as a brutal crime against humanity without any reference to honor. For example, the statute of the International Tribunal for the Prosecution of Persons Responsible for Serious Violations of International Humanitarian Law Committed in the Territory of the Former Yugoslavia since 1991, the U.N. Declaration on the Elimination of Violence Against Women, and other international documents have no mention of honor in connection to the war crime rape. Also, the June 2000 International Federation of Human Rights newsletter *La Lettre* reported that "The Declaration on the Elimination of Violence to Women pronounced by the United Nations General Assembly in December 1993 (article 2) defined 'forced prostitution' as a form of violence . . . . Since [the 1995 International Women's Conference in] Beijing, the notion of 'forced prostitution' . . . seems to encompass the spirit of the Human Rights High Commission which compares 'forced prostitution' to a contemporary form of slavery. Finally, the statutes of the International Court of Justice recognizes 'forced prostitution' and 'sexual slavery' as war crimes."

Despite this progress, massive sex crimes committed in present-day conflicts, and countries, including the United States, are unabashedly ignoring international human rights regulations for armed conflicts. War crime trials fail to indict war criminals on charges of mass rape and sexual slavery, and peace agreements rarely address the issue of the sexual violence committed during a conflict. Moreover, in post-conflict periods, women are rarely involved in negotiations concerning conflict management or conflict prevention. On the national level, both legally and culturally, the connection between rape and honor still needs to be abolished. Astrid Aafjes writes that "The ultimate goal is the elimination of violence and not merely its prosecution. Combating sexual violence during time of war will require breaking the link between sexual assault and victim morality at the national level. It will require changing many countries' domestic law, and changing the way that members of many communities think about victims of sexual assault."

Greater funding for international tribunals to prosecute violators of human rights, as well as human rights training for judges, prosecutors, military and law enforcement personnel, and soldiers is needed. Discussions need to take place concerning the undeniable sexual desire that those in the armed services experience. The desire to escape the stresses of armed conflict is inevitable, but the shameful and widespread use of sexual violence as a means of escape demands innovative action. Furthermore, serious consideration needs to be taken to curb the use and abuse of alcohol and other mood-altering substances that contribute to widespread sexual violence and torture of both civilians and POWs.

References

Amnesty International, *Stop Violence Against Women: Sudan – Mass Rape, Abduction and Murder* (London: Amnesty International, 2004).

Astrid Aafjes, *Gender Violence: The Hidden War Crime* (Washington, DC: Women, Law and Development International, 1998).

Annales Fuldenses (The Annals of Fulda), trans. Timothy Reuter (Manchester: Manchester University Press, 1992).

Rhonda Copelon, "Surfacing Gender: Reengraving Crimes Against Women in Humanitarian Law," in *Women and War in the Twentieth Century: Enlisted With or Without Consent*, ed. Nicole Ann Dombrowski (New York: Garland, 1999): 332–359.

Wendy Jo Gertjejanssen, "Victims, Heroes, Survivors: Sexual Violence on the Eastern Front During World War II" (Ph.D. diss., University of Minnesota, 2004).

Ruth Matzo Karras, "Concubinage and Slavery in the Viking Age," *Scandinavian Studies* 62 (1990): 141–62.

Gerda Lerner, *The Creation of Patriarchy*, vol. 1, *Women and History* (New York: Oxford University Press, 1986).

John Lie, "The State as Pimp: Prostitution and the Patriarchal State in Japan in the 1940s," *Sociological Quarterly* 38 (1997): 251–263.

Catharine A. MacKinnon, "Turning Rape into Pornography: Postmodern Genocide," in *Mass Rape: The War against Women in Bosnia-Herzegovina*, ed. Alexandra Stiglmayer (Lincoln: University of Nebraska Press, 1994): 73–81.

Catherine N. Niarchos, "Women, War and Rape: Challenges Facing the International Tribunal for the Former Yugoslavia," *Human Rights Quarterly* 17 (1995): 649–690.

Christa Paul, *Zwangsprostitution: staatliche bordelle im Nationalsozialismus* (Berlin: Edition Hentrich, 1994).

Franz Seidler, *Prostitution, Homosexualität, Selbstverstümmelung: Probleme der deutschen Sanitätsführung* 1939–1945 (Neckargemünd: Kurt Vowinkel Verlag, 1977).

Chunghee Sarah Soh, "The Korean 'Comfort Women': Movement for Redress," *Asian Survey* 36 (1996): 1226–1241.

Richard Trexler, *Sex and Conquest: Gendered Violence, Political Order, and the European Conquest of the Americas* (Ithaca: Cornell University Press and Polity Press, 1995).

Seada Vranic, *Breaking the Wall of Silence: The Voices of Raped Bosnia* (Zagreb: Izdanja Antibarbarus, 1996).

—*Wendy-Jo Gertjejanssen*

SHACKLING INCIDENT

In one of the lengthiest reprisals of World War II, thousands of POWs in camps in Germany and Canada were placed in handcuffs, some for as long as a year. The reprisal had its roots in the failed Canadian raid on the French port of Dieppe in August 1942. After the raid, German soldiers recovered operational orders that directed Canadian troops to bind the hands of prisoners to prevent them from destroying documents. In response, the German government threatened to handcuff all soldiers captured at Dieppe unless the order was rescinded. Britain sent a mollifying reply, but in October the crisis escalated. Citing further investigation into the Dieppe case and another instance of the binding of prisoners during a British commando raid on the island of Sark, the German government announced on 7 October 1942 that 1,376 Canadian POWs would be shackled.

For the affected prisoners, this was little more than an inconvenience. The handcuffs were easily removed, and the prisoners scored a minor psychological warfare victory by making it immensely difficult for their guards to enforce the orders. The British government, however, reacted more vigorously, threatening to begin retaliatory shackling if Berlin did not back down. This threat put the government of Canada in an awkward position. Most of the German POWs captured thus far, about 16,000, were detained in Canada, yet the Canadian government strongly opposed the suggested reprisal. However, to prevent an open breach with Britain, Ottawa acquiesced and on 10 October ordered the shackling of German POWs.

The German government quickly raised the stakes by announcing it would handcuff three times the number of prisoners shackled by Canada; with this, 4,128 Allied prisoners in seven camps were involved. British Prime Minister Winston Churchill, the main supporter of the reprisal, wanted to match the German action, but public opinion, not only in the Commonwealth but in the United States as well, had swung strongly against the retaliation. Canadian officials, therefore, turned their efforts toward finding a way out of the situation. Eventually, they informed Churchill that Canada would not continue the reprisal and intended to take unilateral action in

In this photo a prisoner in Germany shows off his shackles (Jonathan F. Vance)

unshackling German prisoners in Canadian hands. A very public disagreement was prevented only when London and Ottawa agreed that the government of Switzerland, the Protecting Power charged with safeguarding the interests of Allied prisoners in Germany, be called upon to ask both sides to end the retaliation at the same time.

The Swiss request was transmitted in early December 1942, and Canadian officials immediately unshackled their German POWs. The German government, however, refused to cooperate and held to its original position: the shackling would not end until Allied governments publicly prohibited the binding of prisoners in the field. The Allies were unwilling to make this concession, and a year-long stalemate ensued. Not until October 1943 did the International Committee of the Red Cross believe that tempers had cooled sufficiently to permit another approach to Germany. This time, the Swiss proposed that the shackling in German camps be ended discreetly; neutral officials would be on hand to monitor the situation, but no public announcement would be made. The German government agreed to these terms and removed the shackles from the remaining Canadian and British prisoners in November and December 1943.

See also Reprisals; World War II—Western Europe

References

S.P. MacKenzie, "The Shackling Crisis: A Case-Study in the Dynamics of Prisoner-of-War Diplomacy in the Second World War," *International History Review* 17 (1995): 78–98.

Jonathan F. Vance, "Men in Manacles: The Shackling of Prisoners of War, 1942–43," *Journal of Military History* 59 (1995): 483–504.

—*Jonathan F. Vance*

SIERRA LEONE CIVIL WAR

Throughout the 1990s, several African nations were torn by civil war. Angola, Liberia, Rwanda, Somalia, and Sudan experienced brutal bouts of strife, famine, and, in the case of Rwanda, horrific acts of genocide. One of the bloodiest civil wars, however, occurred in the West African state of Sierra Leone. Beginning in 1991 and fueled by trade in illicit gems, particularly diamonds, Sierra Leone disintegrated into chaos until 2002 when a United Nations (U.N.) peacekeeping mission supported by British military force was able to enforce peace after a number of failed ceasefires. During this period, more than 17,000 foreign troops disarmed tens of thousands of rebels and militiamen in the biggest U.N. peacekeeping success in Africa after appalling failures in Angola, Rwanda, and Somalia. Despite the success, the conflict left approximately 50,000 dead and was characterized by horrific atrocities committed by the rebels and government soldiers. The rebels in particular had a brutal habit of recklessly amputating the limbs of captured civilians and executing captured soldiers. To a lesser but still considerable degree, the government militias developed a reputation for committing similar abuses. Indeed, the shockingly brutal treatment of prisoners of war illustrates the horror of the civil war in Sierra Leone.

Civil war began in 1991 when former army Corporal Foday Sankoh led the Revolutionary United Front (RUF) to begin a campaign to overthrow President Joseph Saidu Momoh, a former Major-General in the army. The RUF quickly began to capture towns along the border with Liberia, which itself was increasingly wracked by civil strife, exacerbating regional instability and adding to the chaos in Sierra Leone. By 1992, Momoh was ousted in a military coup led by a military captain, Valentine Strasser, who was apparently frustrated by Momoh's inability to deal with the rebels. Four years later, Strasser suffered the same fate and was overthrown in a military coup led by his defense minister, Brigadier Julius Maada Bio, who authorized previously planned elections. By late 1995 alone, about 10 percent of the population were refugees in neighboring countries, and at least 30 percent were internally displaced. Despite the fractious political environment, however, elections were held and Ahmad Tejan Kabbah was elected president in February 1996.

His administration signed a peace accord with Sankoh and the RUF, but this peace deal soon dissolved. Kabbah was toppled in 1997 and fled to neighboring Guinea to mobilize international support as violent fighting resumed. Civilian casualties increased considerably following the collapse of the ceasefire and military abuses intensified. An RUF-allied militia, the Armed Forces Revolutionary Council (AFRC), executed 35 soldiers and civilians by firing squad between October and December 1997. The international community slowly began to react, but bitter fighting continued to wreak havoc across the nation. By October 1998, the number of Sierra Leonese refugees in Guinea was 357,000, an estimated 217,000 of whom had arrived since February 1998. There were an additional 100,000 refugees scattered throughout Liberia, the Ivory Coast, Gambia, and

Senegal. Vital infrastructure was destroyed or crumbling, and over 75 percent of the national budget was spent on defense.

In February 1998, Nigeria led a West African intervention force (ECOMOG) into Sierra Leone and drove the RUF rebels out of the capital of Freetown, only to have the RUF recapture it in January 1999. A terror campaign was launched against civilians suspected of opposing the RUF, and against ECOMOG and government forces. There are several accounts of RUF forces executing ECOMOG and other soldiers who were attempting to surrender. Other prisoners were executed immediately, or after having been abused and tortured. A few were taken into captivity. In the meantime, the U.N. Security Council established the United Nations Observer Mission in Sierra Leone (UNOMSIL), with an authorized strength of 70 military observers, and sought to encourage a diplomatic solution in conjunction with ECOMOG. During the late summer and autumn, UNOMSIL received reliable reports and evidence of atrocities ranging from mutilations, amputations, summary executions, abductions, and house burnings of civilians and suspected government militia or supporters. UNOMSIL also observed that the government-allied militia, the Civil Defence Force (CDF), and ECOMOG personnel occasionally exhibited poor discipline, as indicated in their treatment of POWs. Reports suggested that ECOMOG personnel did not consistently ensure full respect for the provisions of international humanitarian law, such as those regarding the protection of noncombatants in combat situations and the proper treatment of combatants during surrender or after capture. The CDF appeared far more cavalier than ECOMOG in its treatment of POWs, and it appears that a take-no-prisoners approach was widespread. One prominent nongovernmental organization documented cases of the CDF or related factions summarily executing AFRC/RUF soldiers and collaborators. Some reports suggested that POWs were even set ablaze while still alive.

Despite such egregious acts, the efforts of UNOMSIL and ECOMOG led to a ceasefire with the RUF in May 1999, and in July a peace accord, known as the Lome agreement, was reached in the Togolese capital, Lome. The peace agreement stipulated that the rebels would receive posts in government and assurances that they would not be prosecuted for war crimes. There were also promises of rehabilitation for the rebels. However, peace remained fragile. In early August, a rebel group known as the Armed Forces Revolutionary Council (AFRC) and allied with the RUF took a group of UNOMSIL military and civilian personnel hostage, along with their ECOMOG escort. They were released unscathed within a week but all were robbed of personal possessions and verbally abused during their captivity. In this case, POWs were subjected to mental abuse and intimidation. Ironically, this occurred while UNOMSIL chaired a committee on the Release of Prisoners of War and Non-Combatants and illustrated the fluidity of the security situation and the disregard for the rights of POWs. In September 1999, the U.N. estimated that the rebel groups were still holding several thousand civilians and called on the RUF and AFRC to release all people detained by them. By December, U.N. troops began to arrive to police the peace agreement, even though one RUF leader promised to disobey their authority.

The government of Sierra Leone, ECOMOG, and the allied militia Civil Defense Force (CDF) assured UNOMSIL that they had released all persons detained by them. Still, in early 2000, Human Rights Watch expressed concern about credible reports that both the RUF and government-allied units continued to commit acts of brutality against civilians and prisoners. The RUF was cited for conducting the majority of atrocities, such as rape, murder, abduction, forced conscription, and amputation. The CDF was also criticized for torturing, mutilating, and summarily executing suspected members of the RUF, including RUF fighters who had surrendered their weapons and entered into U.N.-sponsored rehabilitation programs. Despite the presence of U.N. peacekeepers and a peace agreement, some rebel factions continued to attack ECOMOG and Sierra Leonese government troops. As rebels moved closer to the capital, Freetown, the British government deployed 800 paratroopers to evacuate British citizens and to assist in securing the airport for U.N. peacekeepers. The rebel leader, Foday Sankoh, was also captured, giving an added glimmer of hope that hostilities would end. Soon after, though, a renegade militia group called the West Side Boys took 11 British soldiers hostage, prompting British forces to mount an operation to rescue these hostages.

Peace was gradually but firmly restored in 2001 as U.N. troops began for the first time to deploy peacefully into rebel-occupied territory. In May, formal disarmament of the rebels began and the British-trained elements of a new Sierra Leone army began to deploy in rebel-held areas. By January 2002, Sierra Leone had finally achieved a measure of stability, unprecedented in over a decade, and war was declared over. Approximately 45,000 fighters had been disarmed, according to U.N. figures, and the Sierra Leonese government agreed (with U.N. support) to establish a war crimes court. This ended one of the bloodiest chapters in modern African history, although the ongoing war crimes trials continue to bring justice to those participants on both sides of the conflict who brutalized a nation for so long.

References

Adekeye Adebjo, *Building Peace in West Africa: Liberia, Sierra Leone, and Guinea-Bissau* (International Peace Academy Occasional Paper Series, 2002).

Corinne Dufka, "Getting Away With Murder, Mutilation, Rape: New Testimony from Sierra Leone," *Human Rights Watch* 11 (July 1999).

—*Esmorie Miller*

Sikh Wars (1845–1846, 1848–1849)

The British fought two separate but connected wars against the Sikhs in north-central India in the mid-nineteenth century, both motivated by a determination to guarantee British control in the area. In both cases, the treatment of prisoners was conditioned by the expectations of soldiers on each side. The Sikhs were accustomed to fighting on to the death; they did not expect to be taken prisoner themselves, and so they rarely took prisoners. At the Battle of Moodkee (18 December 1845), for example, Sikh soldiers promptly killed any wounded British soldiers they came across, as they did after the battles of Ferozeshah (21 December 1845) in the First Sikh War and Chillianwalla (13 January 1849) in the Second Sikh War. The British had been inclined to adopt a lenient policy toward Sikh prisoners but, angered by the murder of their wounded, they, too, began to deny quarter. In the last battle of the First Sikh War, at Sobraon on 10 February 1846, as many as 10,000 Sikhs were killed, many of them slaughtered by British soldiers after the battle had concluded. At least one British unit, the 3rd Light Dragoons, always charged into battle with the cry "Remember Moodkee!"

There were some exceptions to this cycle of violence. A lieutenant of the Bengal Artillery who fell into Sikh hands before Moodkee was treated civilly, if not generously, before being released and sent back to his unit by his captors. Another lieutenant, captured with serious wounds at Ferozeshah, was carefully tended by a Sikh soldier who carried him from the battle area and remained at his side until the lieutenant succumbed to his wounds. A number of wounded British soldiers captured at Bhudowal (21 January 1846) were saved by the intervention of a former member of the Bengal Artillery who had deserted nearly 20 years earlier; when the deserter was later captured at the Battle of Aliwal (28 January 1846), his intervention on behalf of the prisoners was, in turn, probably the only thing that saved him from the gallows.

References

Hugh Cook, *The Sikh Wars: The British Army in the Punjab, 1845–1849* (London: Leo Cooper, 1975).

—*Jonathan F. Vance*

SINCLAIR, ALBERT MICHAEL (1918–1944)

Lieutenant A.M. "Mike" Sinclair of the 60th King's Royal Rifle Corps made nine escape attempts from various camps during World War II, prompting the German security officer at Colditz Castle, Reinhold Eggers, to call him "the greatest escaper of all time." When he arrived at Colditz in January 1942, he already had a reputation as a wily, inveterate escaper. Captured at Calais in May 1940, he first spent time in Oflag 7C Laufen. He escaped from his next camp in Poland and crossed several borders before his recapture in Bulgaria five months later. In Czechoslovakia, as he was returning to camp under escort, he escaped once again. On his recapture he was held for a time by the Gestapo and then sent to Colditz, which provided Sinclair with a new challenge. Desperate for freedom, he made one attempt after another, and several times he actually got clear of the camp. On different occasions he got as far as Cologne and the Swiss and Dutch frontiers before being caught. He then tried impersonating the sergeant major of the German guard company at Colditz, but the escape attempt failed, and he was wounded when a guard discharged his rifle in the resultant melee.

Mike Sinclair died trying to escape from Colditz on 25 September 1944. Having scaled the wire enclosing a small park, he was frantically running through the trees when a guard's bullet struck him down, this time fatally. Two days later he was buried with full honors in the town's military cemetery. Sinclair, a man without peer as an escaper, was 26 years old when he made his final, desperate bid for freedom.

See also Colditz; Escape

References

Reinhold Eggers, *Colditz: The German Story* (London: Robert Hale, 1961).

P.R. Reid, *The Colditz Story* (London: Hodder and Stoughton, 1952).

———, *Colditz: The Full Story* (London: Macmillan, 1984).

J.E.R. Wood, ed., *Detour: The Story of Oflag IVC* (London: Falcon Press, 1946).

—*Colin Burgess*

SINO-JAPANESE WAR (1937–1945)

Sometimes referred to as the unknown campaign in the Pacific during the Second World War, the Sino-Japanese War began with an engagement between Japanese and Chinese troops at the Marco Polo Bridge in July 1937 (although some historians date the beginning of the conflict as the Mukden Incident of September 1931, after which the Japanese occupied Manchuria and established the puppet state of Manchukuo). The war, which continued until the western Allies defeated the Japanese in August 1945, cost as many as 21 million lives, the majority of them civilians.

In terms of the treatment of prisoners, the early years of the war foreshadowed the larger campaign in the Pacific, which began in December 1941 with the Japanese attack on Pearl Harbor. Shortly after the Marco Polo Bridge incident, the International Committee of the Red Cross (ICRC) offered its services to both sides, to monitor the treatment of POWs and detained civilians. The Japanese government declined, and over the course of the conflict, ICRC delegates were only able to make contact with about 100 military and civilian prisoners interned on the island of Amoy (now Xiamen), 32 Chinese POWs in two other camps, and 21 Japanese POWs.

The reluctance to allow the intercession of the ICRC had much to do with Japanese attitudes towards POWs, whom they regarded as having brought disgrace upon themselves, their families, and their country by surrendering. But it was also due to the fact that both sides were engaging in conduct that was prohibited under international law, particularly the Geneva Convention of 1929 (which Japan had not signed, in any case). The official policy of the Chinese Communist Party (CPP), for example, was to "re-educate" Japanese POWs and turn them into Communist sympathizers, a policy that was both pragmatic and philosophical. The CPP's 8th Route Army lacked the facilities to hold POWs, so could only execute or release them (in some cases, Chinese units forced Japanese POWs to execute their own officers and renounce their allegiance to the Japanese emperor as conditions of being taken into captivity). But realizing that freed Japanese prisoners were often punished when they returned to their own forces, the CPP began a concerted campaign to indoctrinate them. In May 1940, a chapter of the Japanese Anti-War Alliance was established in Ya'an by three POWs, at the urging of noted Japanese communist Sanzo Nosaka, who had been sent from Moscow by the Comintern. Later that year, Nosaka created the Japanese Workers and Farmers Group, which became the focus of the re-education campaign. Before long, dozens of branches of the organization were operating among Japanese POWs throughout China. By all accounts, they had considerable success and many Japanese prisoners embraced communism, realizing that the alternative was severe punishment at the hands of their own government and disgrace in their home communities.

The other distinguishing feature of the Sino-Japanese War was the astonishing brutality of the Japanese towards Chinese captives. The most notorious incident has become known as the Rape of Nanking, which began when Japanese troops entered the city of Nanking in December 1938. By the time order was restored to the city in March 1938, Japanese soldiers had slaughtered an estimated 240,000 POWs and civilians and committed as many as 80,000 rapes. Thousands of other soldiers and civilians were taken into captivity, where a variety of fates awaited them. Many of the female captives were turned into sex slaves, or "comfort women," and were forced to work in Japanese-run brothels set up for soldiers; many spent years enduring sexual and physical abuse in these brothels.

The other notorious use that the Japanese found for POWs and civilian detainees was as guinea pigs in their experiments in biological and chemical warfare. The secret Unit 731 operated in Manchukuo for much of the war, testing weaponized substances on prisoners to determine the most effective killing agents. It is impossible to determine how many prisoners died as a result of these experiments, but conservative estimates number around 30,000.

Atrocities such as the Rape of Nanking, the incidence of sexual slavery, and chemical and biological experiments have had a profound impact on Sino-Japanese relations, largely because successive Japanese governments have been reluctant to accept responsibility for the crimes in China. The other legacy of the war was the prolonged detention of Japanese POWs in China. In the early 1950s, there were still 1,062 prisoners in Chinese captivity. The first group (of roughly a thousand) was not released until 1956, and the remaining 45 were tried for war crimes by various military tribunals the same year. They received sentences that ranged from eight to 29 years; all publicly confessed their guilt and asked for the death penalty. However, no death sentences were handed down and in April 1964 the Chinese government released the 45 remaining prisoners.

See also Nanking Massacre; Sexual Violence; Vivisection

References

James C. Hsiung and Stephen I. Levine, eds., *China's Bitter Victory: The War With Japan, 1937–1945* (Armonk, NY: M. E. Sharpe, 1992).

Hsi-cheng Shi, *Nationalist China at War: Military Defeats and Political Collapse, 1937–1945* (Ann Arbor: University of Michigan Press, 1982).

Dick Wilson, *When Tigers Fight: The Story of the Sino-Japanese War, 1937–1945* (New York: Viking, 1982).

—*J.W. Smith*

SIOUX WARS (1854–1890)

The Sioux Wars began with a fight between a U.S. Army detachment and a band of Brulé Sioux over a cow in 1854 and it ended on the snowy ground of Wounded Knee, South Dakota, in 1890. In the interval raged the Santee (or Dakota Sioux) uprising in Minnesota in 1862, the 1866–1868 Red Cloud War, and the Great Sioux War of 1876. During this period, the Sioux seized white men, women, and children as captives, and the Army took large numbers of native prisoners.

A dispute over a cow near Fort Laramie, Wyoming, in August 1854 caused a detachment of soldiers under Lieutenant John Grattan to kill Brulé Sioux chief Conquering Bear. The detachment was then destroyed by Conquering Bear's enraged tribespeople. The army responded with a punitive expedition under General William Harney the following year that killed 85 Sioux and captured 70 women and children who were imprisoned at Fort Kearney, Nebraska.

The next outbreak did not occur until a Santee Sioux uprising began in August 1862. Desperate, starving natives raided first for food and then continued a rampage of unfettered revenge against agency personnel and settlers on and near their Minnesota reservation. When the affair concluded in late September, the Santees had killed hundreds of whites and taken 269 white and mixed-blood prisoners. The U.S. Army, after defeating the belligerents and freeing the captives, detained close to 2,000 Santees. Of these, 392 were tried as criminals and 307 condemned to death by hanging. In the end, 38 were actually hung for their participation in the conflict. During subsequent years, punitive army expeditions were mounted against those who had escaped into Dakota Territory after the uprising as well as the Lakota Sioux peoples living in that region. On one 1863 expedition, 250 Santee women and children were taken captive.

Three years later, in 1866, Red Cloud's War erupted over white incursions onto Sioux hunting grounds. It raged until 1868 when the United States agreed to abandon its string of forts along the Bozeman Trail and recognized Lakota Sioux suzerainty over a large domain in Dakota Territory and allowed their continued hunting on lands further west and south. Relative peace ensued, but some raiding continued against settlers and especially against native foes such as the Pawnees. In December 1875, however, a government directive stated that all natives remaining off the Dakota reserve after 1 January 1876 would be considered hostile. The result was the Great Sioux War of 1876 and Custer's defeat at the Little Bighorn on 25 June. At the Battle of Slim Buttes, which marked the end of the summer phase of that campaign, 12 native women and six children were taken prisoner by the 5th Cavalry. They were released at the end of the battle, but a number of Sioux men were also captured and held; one of them, Charging Bear, later became a scout for the U.S. Army. Sitting Bull and Crazy Horse, two principal Sioux chiefs, remained at large after the end of the campaign; both later surrendered, only to die under questionable circumstances.

The final phase of the Sioux Wars concluded with the capture of Chief Big Foot's band of Miniconjous en route to the Pine Ridge Agency in South Dakota. While the 7th Cavalry attempted to disarm its prisoners at Wounded Knee on the morning of 29 December 1890, a rifle fired and carnage ensued. More than 150 natives were killed and 50 wounded, while 25 U.S. soldiers died and 39 were wounded. The Sioux Wars were over and major armed native resistance in the United States had ended.

See also Apache Wars; Plains Indian Warfare; Seminole Wars

References

John S. Gray, *Centennial Campaign: The Sioux War of 1876* (Norman: University of Oklahoma Press, 1988).

Robert M. Utley, *Frontiersmen in Blue: The United States Army and the Indian, 1848–1865* (Lincoln: University of Nebraska Press, 1967).

———, *Frontier Regulars: The United States Army and the Indian, 1866–1891* (Lincoln: University of Nebraska Press, 1973).

Henry Woodhead, ed., *War for the Plains* (Alexandria, VA: Time-Life Books, 1994).

—*William S. Reeder, Jr.*

SKORZENY, OTTO (1908–1975)

Born in Vienna, Otto Skorzeny joined the Austrian Nazi party in 1931, and subsequently donned a brown shirt for membership in the SA (*Sturmabteilung*, or Storm Division, a Nazi paramilitary organization). Upon the outbreak of World War II in 1939, Skorzeny volunteered for the Waffen-SS and served with distinction in the 1st SS Division. After recovering from wounds suffered on the Eastern Front, the ambitious officer was recommended for special service as a commando. Skorzeny was present during the rescue of ousted dictator Benito Mussolini from a mountain stronghold. This was actually a Luftwaffe operation, but SS propagandists exaggerated Skorzeny's involvement and transformed him into a national hero. In May 1944, Skorzeny led operations against Yugoslav partisans, and narrowly missed capturing Josip Broz Tito. That summer he helped to crush the July plot against Adolf Hitler before traveling to Hungary in October to dissuade the country's regent, Miklós Horthy, from negotiating a separate peace with the Soviets.

During the German counteroffensive in the Ardennes in December 1944, Skorzeny led about two dozen commandos dressed in American uniforms behind Allied lines. The ruse was less successful than planned, but the infiltrators managed to sow confusion among American troops. It was, however, costly. The tactic was a clear violation of international law, but Skorzeny was led to believe that the Americans would regard the wearing of enemy uniforms as an acceptable *ruse de guerre*, so long as the individuals did not engage in any actual combat. It was poor advice. All 18 of his commandos who fell into American hands were executed shortly after capture.

After leading conventional forces in the defense of eastern Germany during the last months of the Reich, Skorzeny surrendered in May 1945 and was held prisoner until 1947, when he was brought to trial for his treacherous involvement in the Ardennes operations. Although acquitted—thanks in part to the testimony of Allied officers—Skorzeny remained in captivity until July 1948, when he escaped and fled to Spain.

The Franco regime issued Skorzeny a passport and allowed him to resume his prewar occupation of civil engineer; in 1952 he was granted amnesty by German authorities. The former SS officer amassed a fortune after the war, partly through dealings with Egyptian leader Gamel Abder Nasser and Juan Peron of Argentina. It is also suspected that he helped fugitive Nazi war criminals escape capture. Like other highly propagandized German commanders, Skorzeny achieved a sort of demigod status among his former enemies. He was especially popular with British commando officers who sought a greater role for their forces in the Cold War against the Soviet Union, and his "exploits" were celebrated in Charles Foley's gushing *Commando Extraordinary*.

References

Charles Foley, *Commando Extraordinary* (London: Pann, 1956).

Charles B. MacDonald, *A Time for Trumpets: The Untold Story of the Battle of the Bulge* (New York: William Morrow, 1985).

Otto Skorzeny, *My Commando Operations: The Memoirs of Hitler's Most Daring Commando*, trans. David Johnson (Atglen, PA: Schiffer, 1995).

—*Andrew Iarocci*

SLAUGHTERHOUSE–FIVE

Slaughterhouse-Five, or the Children's Crusade, Kurt Vonnegut's 1969 novel, was based on the author's experience in captivity in Germany during World War II. Vonnegut served as an infantry scout and was taken prisoner while on a patrol behind enemy lines during the Battle of the Bulge in December 1944. After his capture, Vonnegut was placed in a temporary camp and then transferred to a permanent camp in the city of Dresden. The camp was housed in a meat packing plant, and the soldiers barracked in the slaughterhouses, which gave the book its title. While in the camp, Vonnegut and the other 99 prisoners were put to work making a vitamin-enriched malt syrup for pregnant women.

Like Vonnegut, Billy Pilgrim, the novel's main character, was captured by the Germans during the Battle of the Bulge and was then transferred to a POW camp in Dresden. During the captivity of Pilgrim/Vonnegut, the Allies firebombed Dresden. Housed in underground facilities in the packing plants, the Allied POWs were among the few survivors of the firestorm, which claimed the lives of as many as 200,000 civilians. After the air raid, the POWs were used by the Germans to recover bodies and search for survivors.

In 1972, George Roy Hill produced and directed a critically acclaimed screen adaptation of the novel, starring Michael Sacks as Billy Pilgrim, Ron Liebman as a fellow prisoner, and Valerie Perrine. The movie, reasonably true to the novel, won the Jury Prize at the Cannes film festival.

See also Film; Vonnegut, Kurt, Jr.

—*Thomas L. Smith*

SLAVERY

Warfare and slavery have been inextricably intertwined throughout human history; indeed, slavery may have its very origins in the sparing of conquered enemies by victorious armies. Throughout the world, slavery has often been the price paid for military defeat. Reducing the captive's status from that of prisoner to that of property served a clear economic function. The victorious could henceforth reap the fruits of the vanquished's labor. Yet slavery served a deeper purpose, as a perpetual triumph for the victor and a perpetual humiliation for the enslaved. Furthermore, both triumph and humiliation could be hereditary. Historically, highly stratified societies with a large servile class often had their origins in the wartime enslavement of entire populations.

This, for example, was the fate of the Judeans, deported to Babylon after the destruction of Jerusalem in 587 B.C.E. The Helots, an indigenous people of the Peloponnese, were a similar case; they were conquered and held for centuries as a servile class by the Spartans. Yet the Helots also demonstrate that there existed degrees of slavery; as Greeks, they enjoyed some rights, such as to marry and maintain families. Others taken prisoner in war were reduced to the status of chattel slaves, essentially regarded as little more than livestock.

For the Romans, enslavement was the just punishment for those who had the audacity to bear arms against them. As the empire expanded, the Romans acquired influence in regions that had also long practiced slavery. Thus, the facilities of an organized slave trade already existed, helping to traffic and distribute prisoners of war taken by the victorious legions, such as those thousands of Gauls enslaved during Julius Caesar's Gallic War of 59–52 B.C.E.

The tradition of enslaving enemies survived in Europe for some time after the fall of the Roman Empire. During his campaigns Clovis (466–511 C.E.), king of the Franks, enslaved large numbers of Goths, who were then shared out among the people of the provinces he ruled. However, the influence of the Church militated against the enslaving of Christian captives, and the practice became rare by the eleventh century. The situation in Muslim countries was similar; Islamic law prohibited the enslaving of coreligionists. Yet in wars between opponents of different religions, the practice of enslaving captives continued.

Thus slavery persisted in the Balkans and the regions surrounding the Mediterranean, reinforced by the contact between Christendom and the Islamic world. Most enslaved prisoners faced the prospect of exhausting physical labor, degradation, and brutality. Perhaps the worse fate was that of the galley slave. Chained six to a bench and required to row 10, 12, even 20 hours at a stretch, only the most resilient prisoners survived any length of time at the oars. Yet for those who could endure long enough, there was occasionally hope of eventual release. Jean Parisot de la Valette, later Grand Master of the Knights of St. John, was captured in 1541. He spent a year as an Ottoman galley slave before being released in a prisoner exchange arranged between his order and the Barbary corsairs. Similarly, the Spanish soldier and author Miguel de Cervantes was captured and enslaved in 1575. True to form, he attempted a number of escapes from Algiers, until he was finally ransomed in 1580.

Both Christian and Muslim captives were generally subjected to pressure to convert, although some Islamic masters were tolerant of their slaves' religious beliefs. Conversion did offer some prospect of higher status or even freedom. It has been estimated that between 50 and 75 percent of Christian captives converted to Islam; some of them then went on to serve in Arab or Ottoman military forces. Indeed, it is probable that by the mid-fourteenth century Christian captives formed the nucleus of the Ottoman standing army. By 1438, slave soldiers were being recruited via the enforced enrollment of a levy of boys from the conquered Christian provinces of the Balkans. Converted to Islam and trained from childhood, these soldier slaves formed one of the most professional and formidable military corps in the late medieval world, the Janissaries.

Military slavery played an even more significant role in the history of Egypt. Not only was the country politically dominated by the Mamelukes (a caste of slave soldiers) from 1254 to 1811, but Egyptian military forces continued to raise units from among enslaved captives until as late as 1885. In 1820, the desire for slaves to form new, disciplined regiments led the viceroy, Muhammad 'Alī, to undertake the conquest of Sudan; the sole purpose of the entire campaign was to gather captives.

In Europe, too, the practice of enslaving prisoners of war reemerged in the early modern period. Despite the religious injunctions against enslaving fellow Christians, certain categories of prisoners were not considered suitable for exchange or ransom. This was particularly true in civil wars and the bitter conflicts arising from rebellion. In these circumstances, captives were sometimes enslaved. Thus, for example, some defeated Royalists of the British civil wars of 1642–1651 were transported to the West Indies and sold into servitude. They were followed by rebels who marched with James, Duke of Monmouth, to defeat at Sedgemoor in 1685 and by Jacobites taken at Preston in 1715.

Such captives were a useful source of labor on the plantations of the West Indies. For the most part, however, labor for Europe's colonies in the New World came from Africa. Both the trans-Saharan and the Atlantic slave trades provided a demand for captives that influenced patterns of warfare in Africa. Although outsiders rarely actually initiated wars, they did provide economic and political inducements to Africans to escalate conflicts and generate captives who could be enslaved. The situation on Africa's Atlantic coast provides a telling example. Some West Africans recognized the link between levels of warfare and the external slave trade. In the late seventeenth and early eighteenth century, two popular Islamic reform movements, led by Nasr al-Din and Abd al-Kadir, attempted to curb the practice of enslaving captives for foreign purchase. However, the emergent new regional powers of the late seventeenth century, such as the Dahomey, saw the enslavement of prisoners of war not just as a commercial strategy but also as a political one. In a process known as "eating the country," mass enslavement and deportations weakened the strength of enemies who could not otherwise be entirely conquered. By selling their captives to slave traders, victorious leaders could then finance further campaigns.

The suppression of the Atlantic slave trade, beginning with its abolition by the British Parliament in 1807, did not immediately end the practice of enslaving prisoners of war in Africa, for there remained an established internal slave system, and healthy markets to the north across the Sahara. Indeed, the institution of slavery has, to the shame of the modern world, survived to the present day in some areas of the globe. The link between warfare and slavery in Africa was largely broken by the end of the nineteenth century, when colonial rule made slave raiding a costly and clandestine business. In Europe, however, the phenomena would make a ghastly reappearance with the enslaving of millions of those judged racially inferior or politically undesirable by Hitler's Germany and Stalin's Soviet Union.

References

R.H. Barrow, *Slavery in the Roman Empire* (London: Methuen, 1928).

John W. Blassingame, *The Slave Community* (Oxford: Oxford University Press, 1972).

Ernle Bradford, *The Great Siege, Malta 1565* (London: Hodder and Stoughton, 1961).

Alan Burns, *History of the British West Indies* (London: Allen and Unwin, 1954).

Philippe Contamine, *War in the Middle Ages*, trans. Michael Jones (Oxford: Blackwell, 1984).

Seymour Drescher and Stanley L. Engerman, eds., *A Historical Guide to World Slavery* (Oxford: Oxford University Press, 1998).

Geoffrey Goodwin, *The Janissaries* (London: Saqi, 1997).

M.H. Keen, *The Laws of War in the Late Middle Ages* (London: Routledge and Kegan Paul, 1965).

Daniel Pipes, *Slave Soldiers and Islam: The Genesis of a Military System* (New Haven, CT: Yale University Press, 1981).

Gerard Prunier, "Military Slavery in the Sudan during the Turkiyya (1820–1885)" in *The Human Commodity: Perspectives on the Trans-Saharan Slave Trade*, ed. Elizabeth Savage (London: Frank Cass, 1992).

John Thornton, "Warfare, Slave Trading and European Influence: Atlantic Africa 1450–1800" in *War in the Early Modern World, 1450–1815*, ed. Jeremy Black (London: UCL Press, 1999).

—*Gervase Phillips*

SOMALI CIVIL WAR

The Somali Republic was created in 1960, when British Somaliland and Italian Somaliland were united and made independent. Because of its strategic significance, the country became a key pawn in the Cold War, and was flooded with American and Soviet-bloc weapons in the 1970s. It fought two brief wars with neighboring Ethiopia, and in the early 1980s slid into civil war, when the Somali National Movement began making hit-and-run attacks on government forces. The government responded in May 1988 by slaughtering tens of thousands of civilians in the northern part of the country, and soon Somalia had ceased to function as a state; it was simply a territory that rival warlords fought to control. In the early 1990s, the United Nations began sending in forces to mediate a ceasefire, ensure the security of humanitarian aid, and help the country to return to stability. During the civil war, thousands of captives were murdered by both sides, but ironically it was the U.N. intervention that resulted in the two most well-known incidents involving prisoners.

One of the units deployed to Somalia was the Canadian Airborne Regiment Brigade Group, which established a base at Belet Huen in December 1992 to protect the distribution of humanitarian aid in the area. As the weeks passed, the base was frequently targeted by Somali civilians, who infiltrated the perimeter under cover of darkness to steal supplies. Officially, orders stated that captured Somalis be detained overnight and then released to civilian authorities the next day; they were not technically considered prisoners of war, but they were to be treated as such. Unofficially, it became common knowledge among Canadian troops that captured Somalis could be abused as a way to discourage further incidents.

On the night of 16 March 1993, a 16-year-old Somali named Shidane Arone was captured by members of the Canadian Airborne Regiment. For two hours, he suffered extreme physical abuse at the hands of Master-Corporal Clayton Matchee, who beat him with an aluminum pipe, burned him with cigarettes, and had a photograph taken holding a gun to Arone's head. Some time around midnight, the teenager died of his injuries. Matchee was promptly arrested, but an attempted suicide left him unfit to stand trial; he returns to court for an assessment every two years, and on each occasion has been found unfit for trial. Six other members of the unit, however, were court-martialed on various charges relating to the prisoner's death. Two were acquitted, but one was found guilty of manslaughter and torture and sentenced to five years in prison. The other three were found guilty of negligent performance of duty, with sentences ranging from reduction in rank, to discharge from the Canadian Forces, to one year in prison.

The Arone case had severe repercussions in Canada. In 1995, to address public outrage over the brutal act, the federal government ordered that the Canadian Airborne Regiment be disbanded. It also established a commission of inquiry into the Canadian deployment to Somalia that ultimately found fault at various levels of the military hierarchy for, among other things, failures to ensure the maintenance of discipline.

The second incident involved an assault mounted by U.S. military units to capture associates of warlord Mohamed Farrah Aidid, who were sheltered in a compound outside the city of Mogadishu. The plan was to insert Special Forces soldiers by helicopter to capture the warlord's foreign minister and top political advisor; they would then be loaded into a ground convoy and driven back to the U.S. compound. But Somali civilians and local militiamen quickly gathered to oppose the operation; using rocket-propelled grenades, they downed two of the Black Hawk helicopters and sealed off the area with roadblocks constructed of boulders and burning tires. About 90 U.S. soldiers were trapped, and were only able to avoid capture with the aid of continuous air strikes against Somali positions. They were rescued by U.S., Malaysian, and Pakistani U.N. forces the following morning. But the pilot of one of the helicopters, Chief Warrant Officer Michael Durant of Berlin, New Hampshire, had already been taken prisoner by Somali militiamen, despite the efforts of two Special Forces snipers to protect him (both snipers were lynched by the mob that overran the helicopter crash site). The badly wounded Durant was held for 11 days before his captors released him.

Durant was the only official POW of the Battle of Mogadishu, although there are unconfirmed reports that Somali warlords have captured other U.S. servicemen to hold them for ransom. The battle was the subject of a number of books, and later a film by Ridley Scott in which actor Ron Eldard played the role of Mike Durant.

References

David Bercuson, *Significant Incident: Canada's Army, the Airborne, and the Murder in Somalia* (Toronto: McClelland & Stewart, 1996).

Mark Bowden, *Black Hawk Down: A Story of Modern War* (Boston: Atlantic Monthly Press, 1999).

Commission of Enquiry into the Deployment of Canadian Forces to Somalia, *Dishonoured Legacy: The Lessons of the Somalia Affair*, 5 vols. (Ottawa: Minister of Public Works, 1997).

Michael Durant and Steven Hartov, *In the Company of Heroes* (New York: Putnam, 2003).

Sherene H. Razack, *Dark Threats and White Knights: The Somalia Affair, Peacekeeping, and the New Imperialism* (Toronto: University of Toronto Press, 2004).

—Jonathan F. Vance

SON TAY RAID

The Son Tay Raid, or Operation King Pin, was a failed mission of 21 November 1970 to rescue Americans POWs in the heart of North Vietnam. The joint U.S. Army–Air Force rescue team executed a nearly flawless raid, but the commandos were unable to liberate any Americans because the Son Tay camp was empty of prisoners.

The POW camp, located approximately 23 miles west of Hanoi, consisted of four main buildings in a compound surrounded by a seven-foot-high wall and three observation towers. Photographs from SR-71 reconnaissance aircraft had indicated that over 50 Americans were interned at the site, but unfortunately for the United States, the prisoners were relocated weeks before the raid due to the flooding of the adjacent Song Con River.

Although the raid was essentially a failure, it nevertheless was a remarkable penetration into North Vietnam. Led by Lieutenant Colonel Arthur D. "Bull" Simons, the 59 army raiders and 42 air-support personnel conducted a 27-minute assault, resulting in the death of 60 prison guards. No Americans were killed.

Afterwards there was much heated discussion about the prudence of such a mission. But evidence suggests that it influenced improved conditions for the 450 American prisoners in Vietnam. Furthermore, POW morale was boosted when news of the raid became known.

The commander of the Son Tay Raid went on to accomplish a successful rescue mission elsewhere. In 1979, the then-retired Simons was hired by Ross Perot to rescue two employees of Electronic Data Systems who were wrongfully imprisoned in Tehran, Iran, an exploit mythologized in Ken Follet's *On Wings of Eagles (1983).*

See also Vietnam War

References

Heather David, *Operation Rescue: The First Complete Account of the Daring Drop into North Vietnam to Rescue American Prisoners of War* (New York: Pinnacle, 1971).

Lee A. Hassig, *The New Face of War: Special Forces and Missions* (Alexandria, VA: Time-Life Books, 1990).

William H. McRaven, *Special Operations—Case Studies in Special Operations Warfare: Theory and Practice* (Novato, CA: Presidio, 1995).

Benjamin F. Schemmer, *The Raid: The Son Tay Prison Rescue Mission* (New York: Ballantine, 2002).

—*Roger Chapman*

South African War

See Boer War

Soviet Special Camps in Germany

At the end of World War II, the NKVD, the Soviet secret service, established in the Soviet Zone of Occupation in Germany 10 special camps for the internment of German civilians. Between 1945 and 1950, 189,000 individuals were held prisoner in these camps, about 35 percent of whom died in captivity.

When the Red Army entered the territory of the German Reich in January 1945, Lavrentii Beriia, head of the NKVD, issued Top Secret Order No. 0016. In this order, Beriia enumerated those "elements" who were to be arrested: spies, terrorists, officials, economic leaders, and also "members of fascist organizations." This meant that virtually every German could be imprisoned. Between January and April 1945, about 215,000 people were detained, the majority of whom were deported. The initial intention of these arrests was twofold: to levy forced laborers for ailing Soviet industry, and to secure the hinterland of the front. Soon, the Soviets realized that only a minority of the prisoners were physically capable of forced labor. In addition, the rigorous arrest policy strengthened the German will to resist, while at the same time the Western allies had succeeded in moving forward rapidly. On the eve of the battle for Berlin, Beriia stopped the deportations and revised his list of wanted persons. From then on, only "active members" of the Nazi Party were to be arrested and sent into camps on German territory.

As the category "active members" was still vague, the majority of the prisoners were only minor functionaries of the Nazi Party who were not subjected to legal proceedings by the Soviets. In December 1946, Soviet leader Josef Stalin was notified that the NKVD expected to discover no incriminating evidence on these individuals; it was suggested that 35,000 prisoners should be released, for they had to be "fed needlessly." By this time, the disastrous hygiene situation and shortage of food was exacting an extraordinarily high death toll among the prisoners. Although Soviet leaders frequently turned to Stalin for a decision on that matter, a greater number of releases was not sanctioned until August 1948. Then, 27,749 internees accused of Nazi crimes were set free, but 16,104 of this category remained in the camps.

From 1948 onwards, another group of prisoners dominated the population of the camps: those people who had been charged with crimes against the regime of occupation and who had been convicted by Soviet Military Tribunals (SMT). Among them were numerous members of democratic parties who defied the oppressive policy of Communism. When the German Democratic Republic was coming into being in the autumn of 1949, Soviet leaders decided to dissolve the camps. The majority of the internees were released at the beginning of 1950, while the majority of the SMT convicts were handed over to East German prisons to serve their sentences.

The prisoners of the Soviet special camps were entirely isolated from the outside world. They were not allowed to write or to receive letters, so their relatives had no knowledge of their whereabouts. As the special camps were not labor camps, the prisoners were condemned to agonizing inactivity. Notwithstanding that in fact numerous Nazis and war criminals were interned in the camps, the majority of the inmates had been arbitrarily arrested, among them a large number of adolescents and even children.

As two of the Soviet special camps—Sachsenhausen and Buchenwald—were established on the sites of former Nazi concentration camps, a comparison with the Nazi camps seems obvious. There were, however, significant differences. Physical abuses in the camps by Soviet guards have only rarely been reported, although maltreatment and torture usually occurred immediately after arrest. Furthermore, the special camps were not labor camps. Finally, documented evidence that the Soviets deliberately aimed at exterminating the internees has not been detected. There is, however, little doubt that Stalin knowingly condoned the deaths of more than 60,000 individuals as result of his arrest and internment policy in postwar Germany.

See also Buchenwald

References
Sergej Mironenko et al, eds., *Sowjetische Speziallager in Deutschland, 1945 bis 1950,* 2 vols. (Berlin: Akademie, 1998).
Norman M. Naimark, *The Russians in Germany: A History of the Soviet Zone of Occupation, 1945–1949* (Cambridge, MA: The Belknap Press of Harvard University Press, 1995).

—Wolfram von Scheliha

SOYINKA, WOLE (1934–)

Wole Soyinka, the Nigerian playwright, poet, novelist, and Nobel laureate (1986), was imprisoned for almost two years by the Nigerian military authorities in 1967 at the outbreak of the Nigerian Civil War for allegedly attempting to secure a fighter-bomber for the rebels. Although not a combatant and never formally charged or tried, Soyinka was seen as a dangerous provocateur by the military government that had seized power in 1966.

Soyinka chronicles his imprisonment in two volumes: a book of poems, *A Shuttle in the Crypt,* written secretly while in prison, and a memoir, *The Man D*ied, composed after his release in 1969 but based on notes written in the margins of the few books he was permitted to have in prison. *The Man Died* is a mix of history, political analysis, and personal testimony to the horrors of prison. Focused on the gross injustice of what he views as a questionable war carried on by a thoroughly corrupt and illegitimate regime, the most compelling and beautifully composed portions of the book relate how he slowly began to lose his sanity during the 15 months he spent in solitary confinement: his tortured imagination and paranoia periodically overcoming his rational mind, it also unleashed a torrent of hallucinations and imagery that give artistic shape to the book.

Soyinka was quietly released in 1969. He writes, "It was sad no longer to be considered a dangerous man." Through his subsequent writings (both creative and otherwise), speeches and political action, Soyinka has worked for political and social reform in a Nigeria ruled almost exclusively by the military. In 1995, having fled Nigeria a year earlier, he was sentenced to death in absentia, a sentence since annulled.

References
Wole Soyinka, *A Shuttle in the Crypt* (New York: Hill and Wang, 1972).
———, *The Man Died* (New York: Noonday Press, 1988 [1972]).

—*Mark L. Lilleleht*

SPANDAU PRISON

Spandau Prison in West Berlin housed the seven Nazi war criminals who escaped the noose at Nuremberg. Built in 1876, the red brick prison was located in the borough of Spandau and designed to hold 500 to 600 prisoners. During the Third Reich period, the National Socialists used it as a way station for political prisoners being deported to concentration camps. After World War II, following the proceedings of the International Military Tribunal at Nuremberg, the seven members of the Nazi hierarchy who were not executed were sentenced to serve their terms in Spandau: Rudolf Hess, Deputy Führer; Erich Raeder, commander and chief of the German navy from 1928 to 1943; and Walther Funk, Nazi economics minister from 1937 to 1945, were sentenced to life; Albert Speer, architect and Reich Minister of Armaments and War Production from 1942 to 1945; and Baldur von Shirach, Nazi youth leader and governor of Vienna, were sentenced to 20 years; Konstantin Freiherr von Neurath, German foreign minister from 1932 to 1938, was sentenced to 15 years; and Karl Dönitz, Grand Admiral and German Chancellor after Hitler's death, was sentenced to 10 years. On 18 July 1946, these inmates arrived to begin their respective sentences behind the prison's walls.

Spandau, as part of the postwar settlement among the Allies, was jointly administered by the United Kingdom, the United States, France, and the Soviet Union. The day-to-day operation of the prison rotated among the four powers every three months. Even at the height of the Cold War, the prison remained a site of mutual cooperation between East and West. The majority of the prison's maintenance costs were paid for by West Germany.

The life of the inmates was highly structured, with visits and correspondence closely monitored and controlled. Schirach, Dönitz, Neurath, Raeder, Speer, Funk, and Hess were numbered one through seven, respectively, and referred to only as such. Of the seven, only four served their whole terms. On the grounds of health and age, Neurath was released on 6 November 1954, Raeder on 26 September 1955, and Funk on 14 May 1957. Dönitz served his term and was released on 1 October 1956. Ten years later Speer and Shirach were released. From that point on, Hess, once Hitler's third in command, remained the lone inmate in a giant prison. The cost of maintaining a prison for one person, coupled with the impression that Hess had served his time, increasingly became a contentious issue for Germans. While the three Western powers were sympathetic to Hess' release, the Soviet Union insisted that he serve out his sentence. Moscow believed that his continued incarceration was a symbolic reminder of the crimes and punishments of the Nazi past. Hess' sentence ended in 1987 when, at the age of 93, he committed suicide. Spandau Prison was subsequently demolished to prevent it from becoming a shrine for right-wing and neo-Nazi groups.

See also Hess, Rudolf; Nuremberg Trials

References
Jack Fishman, *Long Knives and Short Memories: The Spandau Prison Story* (London: Souvenir Press, 1986).
Albert Speer, *Spandau: The Secret Diaries*, trans. R. and C. Simpson (New York: Macmillan, 1976).

—*J. Peters Mersereau* and *Nathan Andrew Wilson*

SPANISH ARMADA

When the Spanish Armada came to grief during an abortive invasion of England in May 1588, over 500 Spanish sailors and soldiers fell into English hands. They included

397 men from the *Rosario*, which was captured after it was crippled by a collision with another Spanish ship, 17 from the *San Salvador*, which was captured after it was badly damaged by an explosion, and 158 from the *San Pedro Mayor*, which wrecked on the English coast. When the prisoners reached Devon, local authorities sorted them into "those of name and quality," who were to be transferred to "safe prisons", and "the rest of baser sort," who were to be held wherever accommodations could be found. Accordingly, some 200 men of this first group were sent to the prison at Exeter, while the rest were confined locally (in a building still known as the Spanish Barn) until their ship was repaired enough to serve as a floating prison. Members of this latter group were also put to work as agricultural laborers on local estates. A small group of prisoners of a higher rank, who were likely to command a good ransom, were sent to London for safekeeping. Those officers who remained in Devon had considerable freedom; one was given parole to work as a doctor in the area, and three others took advantage of their relative liberty to escape to Spain in February 1589.

Negotiations to ransom the prisoners began shortly after their arrival in England. Spanish authorities were willing to pay the equivalent of one month's pay (plus a small allowance for expenses) for the return of ordinary soldiers and seamen, and other amounts, ranging from 100 crowns for captains to 15 crowns for other officers, for officers. But English demands for a greater ransom meant that the prisoners remained in custody until 24 November 1589, when the majority of them were officially freed. Another group of 15 prisoners were freed at a later date; their captors had demanded as much as 20,000 crowns in ransom, but they were forced to relent when the Spanish arrested some English merchants on the continent as hostages. Don Pedro de Valdés, the commander of the *Rosario*, was freed in February 1593 upon payment of a ransom of £3550. The last Spanish captive in custody appears to have been an apothecary, who remained in England until 1597.

References

Paula Martin, *Spanish Armada Prisoners: The Story of the Nuestra Señora del Rosario and her Crew, and of the Other Prisoners in England, 1587–97* (Exeter: Exeter University Publications, 1988).

—*Jonathan F. Vance*

Spanish–American War (1898)

During the Spanish-American War of 1898, the United States held over 39,000 Spanish prisoners of war in America, the Philippines, Cuba, and outlying Spanish possessions. Spain, in contrast, held only a very few Americans, all of whom were exchanged during the conflict. The United States based its POW policy on the Geneva Convention of 1864, which it had signed in 1882, and so it faced several issues surrounding repatriation and the protection of Spanish prisoners from America's Cuban and Filipino allies.

In Cuba and surrounding Spanish territories, the U.S. military captured over 26,000 prisoners. Held with minimal restrictions after they surrendered their weapons and awaited transportation back to Spain, the Spanish prisoners openly fraternized with their American captors, much to the Cubans' dismay. Of the 1,774 naval prisoners—the entire surviving Spanish fleet after the Battle of Santiago Bay of 3 June 1898—nearly 360 of the sick and injured (half of whom died) went to Norfolk, Virginia, 79 officers and 14 enlisted men were held at the U.S. Naval Academy at Annapolis, Maryland, and 20 were imprisoned at Fort McPherson, Georgia. The remaining POWs were secured at Seavey Island off of Portsmouth, New Hampshire.

The navy placed its prisoners under marine guard but overall treated its captives in a humane manner. The only recorded exception took place on 4 July on the USS *Harvard*, when six prisoners were killed en route to New Hampshire when they did not respond promptly to orders in English. The best treatment was found at Annapolis, where officers who signed a parole promising not to escape or take up arms again against the United States were allowed liberty in town. The navy's most notable prisoner, Admiral Pascual Cervera y Topete, refused to sign a parole because he claimed that it was forbidden by Spanish law, and the navy granted him liberty based on his word as a gentleman to abide by American orders. Rear Admiral Frederick V. McNair was appointed superintendent to the academy so that the Spanish rear admiral would not be insulted by being under the command of a lower-ranked officer; McNair provided Cervera with servants (other Spanish POWs) and a house on the grounds of the academy, where he lived with his son. Cervera not only traveled freely in Annapolis, socializing with the local residents at church services and parties, but was also given permission on more than one occasion to visit his men at Norfolk and Portsmouth and even to travel to New York to arrange for the prisoners' passage back to Spain. They were returned home on 12 August 1898, a little over a month after their capture.

While the Spanish government did not pay for the transportation of the prisoners held by the U.S. Navy, it did so for those held by the U.S. Army. American President William McKinley had considered creating a POW camp at Galveston, Texas, for the Spanish troops, but canceled his plans after the United States agreed before the surrender of Santiago to pay for the transportation back to Spain of all army regulars held in Cuba and surrounding Spanish territories. Originally some American negotiators had hoped to use the repatriation issue of Spanish prisoners in the Philippines as a means to force Spain to concede territory, but the United States quickly agreed to pay for the transportation of the additional 13,000 prisoners in order to rid itself of the difficult duty of protecting Spanish personnel from Emilio Aguinaldo's rebel forces, who were brutalizing captives under their care.

References

P.H. Magruder, "The Spanish Naval Prisoners of War at Annapolis, 1898," *U.S. Naval Institute Proceedings* 56 (1930): 489–523.

David F. Trask, *The War with Spain in 1898* (New York: Macmillan, 1981).

Barrie Ernest Zais, "The Struggle for a Twentieth-Century Army: Investigation and Reform of the United States Army after the Spanish-American War, 1898–1903" (Ph.D. diss., Duke University, 1981).

—*Lori Bogle*

SPANISH CIVIL WAR (JULY 1936–MARCH 1939)

The Spanish Civil War was fought by Republican loyalists and left-wing groups against right-wing nationalist insurgents led by General Francisco Franco. The origins of the civil war lay in the discontent of rightist military officers toward Spain's Second Republic (1931–1936), opposition that culminated in a military coup on 17–18 July 1936. Strong resistance from the working class and military loyalists prevented a quick victory, embroiling the country in a bloody war. The Republicans retained control over much of urban and southern Spain, including Barcelona and Madrid, while the Nationalists—the name adopted by the right-wing military rebels—successfully overran large areas of rural northern and central Spain along with Morocco. Franco's Army of Africa sided with the Nationalists but could not cross the straits of Gibraltar as most of the navy had remained loyal to the Republic. However, Nazi Germany and Fascist Italy intervened by transporting these forces to Spain in German and Italian aircraft.

On 21 September 1936 the Nationalists united behind Franco, making him their commander-in-chief. In April 1937, Franco forcibly merged José Antonio Primo de Rivera's *Falange Española*—a party strongly influenced by European fascism—and the Catholic *Carlists* into a single party in order to subordinate all right-wing political organizations under his control and further unify the Nationalist war effort. The new party, the

Falange Española Tradicionalista y de las Juntas de Ofensiva Nacional Sindicalista (Traditionalist Spanish Falange and the Juntas of the National Syndicalist Offensive), was to be Spain's only legal party. Furthermore, the Catholic Church threw its wholehearted support behind the Francoist cause. Germany and Italy continued their crucial intervention by supplying arms and men. In contrast, the Republicans were far more fractured. The military insurrection effectively unleashed a social revolution, with working-class militias and committees organizing to run local affairs in the Republican zone. Tension over how to handle the war and revolution threatened to divide the *Confederación Nacional del Trabajo* (National Labor Confederation), the *Partido Obrero de Unificación Marxista* (United Marxist Workers' Party), and leftist Socialists on the one hand, from the Popular Front, reformist Socialists, and the *Partido Comunista de España* (Spanish Communist Party or PCE) on the other. In addition, socialists, communists, and anti-fascists from Europe and North America came to Spain to join International Brigades, formed to assist in the Republic's defense. Although from various socialist backgrounds, these groups were led primarily by the PCE. After the Soviet Union began intervening on behalf of the Republicans in November 1937, the PCE quickly eclipsed the other organizations in power and imposed their agenda.

Fearing the fall of Madrid, the Republican government temporarily vacated the capital on 6 November 1936 for Valencia, leaving the defense of the city in the hands of the PCE. In the spring and summer of 1937 the Nationalists drove through northern Spain. These new territories allowed the Nationalists to access the much-needed steel and mining resources in these parts. In March 1938, Catalonia was cut off from the rest of the Republic in the Nationalists' push to the sea, culminating in a December offensive against Catalonia itself. On 4 March 1939, tensions within the Republican camp finally boiled over. The remaining Republican factions attempted to throw off PCE dominance and reach a negotiated settlement with Franco. Fighting ensued in the capital of Madrid, resulting in PCE defeat. Yet Franco rebuffed all attempts to negotiate and took Madrid unopposed on 27 March. On 1 April 1939, a victorious Franco formally declared an end to the civil war.

Terror tactics, brutal subjugation of occupied areas, and the systematic execution and torture of prisoners inside and outside of newly established concentration camps occurred on both sides of the conflict. In the Republican zones, the Catholic clergy and other enemies were persecuted and murdered in the thousands for their support of Franco. According to accepted figures, approximately 6,800 clergy members were massacred, including 280 nuns. Some were hunted down individually while others were rounded up in groups and then shot *en masse*; sometimes a mock trial preceded executions. A number of victims were tortured before being hanged, drowned, suffocated, burned to death, or buried alive. Republican propaganda justified these killings as the outraged reactions of mobs against insurgent priests and clerics. Other principal targets were those directly involved in the rebellion, as well as those who could be identified as class enemies. Dubbed fascists or pro-fascists, potentially as many as 80,000 people were summarily executed after being hastily convicted by revolutionary courts.

In the Nationalist zones, Franco's desire to institutionalize his regime resulted in the indiscriminate shooting of all left-wing sympathizers and Republican supporters. Some referred to these actions as rearguard clean-up operations. As a reflex action to stamp out opposition in newly acquired territories, Franco's rebels principally targeted workers and middle-class professionals like journalists and lawyers, while throwing all known Republicans, anarchists, socialists, and communists in prison. Even conservative estimates place the number of civilian deaths near 100,000. A catch-all group, "enemies of the rebellion," was also rounded up and most certainly executed, as insurgent leaders believed they represented a potential fifth-column threat. Like their Republican counterparts, the Nationalists established a number of prison camps. During the course of the war, these camps overflowed with captured soldiers. In both their disciplinary brigades and concentration camps, Nationalist administrators segregated political prisoners and common criminals and subjected the former to intensive political and religious propaganda. Prisoners were also engaged in forced labor, a practice likewise employed by Republican guards in their camps. Many industrial enterprises found the use of slave labor to be extremely profitable and continued the practice into 1940. The physical intimidation and other terror tactics used by both sides to quash all forms of social and political dissent during the war became a mainstay of Franco's Spain.

For the major powers that became directly involved (Germany, Italy, and the Soviet Union) or that remained neutral (Britain, France, and the United States), the Spanish Civil War presaged World War II. For many of these countries, Spain provided a testing ground for new technologies and tactics. Military attacks on civilians, characterized most famously by the German bombing of the Basque village of Guernica, became a standard practice in war. Finally, the Nationalist notion that a concentration camp prisoner was redeemed through labor frighteningly foreshadowed the Nazi message "Work makes you free" written above the main gate of Auschwitz.

References

Julio de la Cueva, "Religious Persecution, Anticlerical Tradition and Revolution: On Atrocities against the Clergy during the Spanish Civil War," *Journal of Contemporary History* 33 (1998): 355–69.

George Esenwein and Adrian Shubert, *Spain at War: The Spanish Civil War in Context, 1931-1939* (Essex: Longman, 1995).

Carl Geiser, *Prisoners of the Good Fight: The Spanish Civil War, 1936–1939* (Westport, CT: Lawrence Hill, 1986).

Arthur Koestler, *Dialogue with Death*, trans. T. and P. Blewit (London: Hutchinson, 1966).

Michael Seidman, *Republic of Egos: A Social History of the Spanish Civil War* (Madison: University of Wisconsin Press, 2002).

—*J. Peters Mersereau* and *Nathan Andrew Wilson*

SPHACTERIA, BATTLE OF

The battle of Sphacteria took place during the Second Peloponnesian War (431–404 B.C.E.) between the Greek city-states of Athens and Sparta. In the course of a failed Spartan operation against an Athenian fort, the Athenians were able to capture a great number of elite Spartan troops and to use their lives as bargaining chips to extract military concessions from the enemy. Sphacteria remains one of the earliest and most detailed accounts of the use of prisoners of war as hostages for strategic gains.

Both Athens and Sparta had hoped the war between them would be a short one, but because neither side could strike directly at the main forces of the other—the Athenian navy ruled the seas, but the Spartan army was supreme on land—the war dragged on. Each year, the Athenians would remain behind their fortified walls, the Spartans would destroy Athenian lands outside those walls, and the Athenians would then replenish their losses from their great wealth. After over two years of fighting, each side began to grow intensely frustrated with the inconclusive course of the conflict.

The Athenian leader Pericles, hoping to contain the scale of the conflict, had refused to allow Athenian forces to attempt sustained attacks on Spartan territory. But when Pericles died in a plague that swept Athens in 420, another general, Cleon, was elected to take his place. The Greek historian Thucydides describes Cleon as "the most violent man at Athens," and Cleon quickly pressed for a policy of taking the war directly to Sparta. In 425, a small Athenian naval expedition landed, perhaps inadvertently during a storm, at the town of Pylos, deep in Spartan territory. While there, they built a small fort. The Athenian admirals left a small contingent of men in this stronghold under the command of one of their leading citizens and generals, Demosthenes, and then set sail to continue another mission.

This area was home to the Messinians, a group the Spartans had enslaved, and the Athenian presence was an encouragement to these slaves, known generally as Helots, to escape Sparta's grasp. When word of the fort reached the Spartan army, they sensibly feared an uprising of the slave population, and they quickly left their attacks on Athens to return home and confront the threat at Pylos.

The actual fortification was located on the edge of the shore, very near a small island named Sphacteria. The Spartans intended to cut off any retreat when they attacked Demosthenes' position from the front and, to this end, Spartan troops were transported across a small channel to Sphacteria. A small Spartan fleet guarded the harbor. The Athenians, however, had sent a runner to bring word to their nearby fleet, which quickly turned back to Pylos, defeated the Spartan ships, and trapped the Spartan troops on Sphacteria. A truce was quickly arranged: the men trapped on the island were the sons of the some of the most prominent families in Sparta and the Spartans were desperate not to lose them.

The Spartans felt that Sphacteria had been such a disaster that they sent a peace delegation to Athens. This was rebuffed by Cleon, and the truce quickly collapsed. Eventually Cleon personally assumed command of the situation and took a force to the island. By a combination of superior generalship, luck, and surprise, Cleon and Demosthenes defeated the Spartans, captured 292 of the elite troops (some 130 died in the siege and battle), and returned them to Athens as prisoners of war.

The Spartans now urgently sued for peace. Not only were Helots escaping through the Athenian-held area, but they could not bear to lose any more of what they considered to be the very finest of their young men. Rather than propose terms, however, Cleon bluntly informed the Spartan leadership that any further attacks on Athenian lands would result in the immediate execution of the prisoners and promptly launched further attacks against other Spartan possessions. The prisoners remained in Athenian hands until 421, when a temporary peace was arranged and the captured troops were returned according to the terms of a treaty.

The use of the Spartan hostages altered the course of the war dramatically, ending any Spartan attacks on Athenian property and turning the war in favor of Athens for the time being. Although Sparta was the stronger power on land, the Athenian threat to kill the hostages effectively neutralized this Spartan advantage and forced Sparta to seek other means to fight the Athenians besides direct assaults against Athens itself. The taking of civilian prisoners from vanquished enemies was common in the Greek world; they were often used as slaves, as collateral to enforce terms of surrender, or even as examples to be executed as a lesson to rebellious colonies or defeated powers. The battle of Sphacteria, however, was unusual in that it was a purely strategic act, designed to force military concessions from the enemy by holding troops and promising their safe return in exchange for very specific terms.

See also Greece—Bronze Age to the Hellenistic Period; Peloponnesian Wars

References
W. Robert Connor, *Thucydides* (Princeton, NJ: Princeton University Press, 1984)
Donald Kagan, *The Archidamean War* (Ithaca: Cornell University Press, 1974).
Robert B. Strassler, ed., *The Landmark Thucydides* (New York: Touchstone, 1998).

—*Tom Nichols*

Sports

Sports have offered prisoners of war a form of physical and emotional release throughout the history of warfare. Traditional images of prisoners of war depict them confined in small spaces either inside buildings or in stockades. Few illustrations, whether woodcuts, paintings, or photographs, show prisoners engaging in sporting activities,

POWs in Oflag 9A/H in Germany in World War II prepare for a boxing match (Jonathan F. Vance)

but documents, including letters, memoirs, and reports, refer to prisoners being allowed by their captors and guards to engage in some amusements. Prisoners have participated in sports and games requiring minimal equipment and space, regardless of when or where they were incarcerated. The type of sports and frequency of recreation varies from camp to camp according to enemy policies, local conditions, and the status of the war. Each prisoner's health also determines whether he or she can participate. Recreational periods provide prisoners an opportunity to move outside their cells and to escape, at least temporarily, the monotony of imprisonment and to relieve the stress of confinement. Some prisoners consider the time they devote to scheming how to escape to be sport, and actual attempts have often required physical prowess honed during exercise sessions in prison camps. Prisoners have occasionally used a sporting activity to escape, running out of camp or concealing a tunnel by pretending to play in an area.

Prisoners have relied on recreation, whether playing alone and or in groups, to maintain their sense of humor, reinforce their self-confidence, and improve their morale. Sports bond prisoners who play together and give them a sense of unity in an environment that promotes isolation. Such companionship is essential to preserve emotional health and physical vigor. Recreation offers prisoners feelings of normality as they perform familiar movements and actions from their precaptivity past; it gives prisoners the courage to endure their confinement by reminding them of peacetime life. Exercise improves prisoners' outlook on life by releasing endorphins and other naturally occurring pain-relieving chemicals into their bloodstreams. Outdoor sports gives some prisoners access to cleaner air than that available in their poorly ventilated cells. Many prisoner sports are informal, unorganized, and spontaneous (such as snowball fights); they relieve tension and give prisoners some control and freedom while performing the activity.

During centuries of warfare, prisoners have enjoyed participating in both games of chance and skill. Some prisoners have made dice and marbles. They test their mental acuity against others in chess and checkers matches. Prisoners also display their agility, strength, and speed by challenging each other to races and boxing or wrestling matches. Prisoners enjoy having the occasion to show off as well as to place bets on their favorite competitor. Hessian prisoners during the American Revolution drunkenly gambled, brawled, and cheered for fighting camp followers. Many prisoners have considered preparing and smoking cigars and pipes a favorite amusement. Some prisoners celebrate the release of a prisoner or stay of execution, while other enjoy watching others being punished. Prisoners enjoy playing pranks and practical jokes on each other and the guards and make sport of gesturing rudely at the latter. When inclement weather prevents outdoor activities, prisoners have staged lice and cockroach races. They also engage in storytelling, especially tall tales, humorous stories, and ghost stories, which are often set in the prison camp.

World War II prisoners in camps around the world participated in different recreational pursuits. Civilians at the Santo Tomas Internment Camp at Manila in the Philippines established a Recreation Committee that arranged teams for games after work around the camp was completed. Adults and children competed in baseball, softball, soccer, football, and basketball leagues. They also played croquet and field hockey. Golfers sought to win the camp's championship game on a three-hole golf course. Favorite games included chess, bridge, mah-jongg, cribbage, and pinochle, each with its own tournament. Similar sports were permitted among German prisoners held in camps in the United States and among imprisoned Japanese civilians. Allied prisoners in Europe managed to pursue some sports, but prisoners in Asia experienced brutally restrictive camps that limited recreation. Similarly, American prisoners held by North Vietnam in the 1960s and 1970s also were prohibited from engaging in sports. At the Hanoi Hilton, prisoners were allowed recreation time, which they used to speak to other prisoners and stretch their muscles to prevent them from atrophying. Most exercising occurred in individuals' cells as a way to maintain strength and discipline as far as possible and to feel in control of at least one aspect of their lives.

The escape of Italian prisoners from a British camp is perhaps one of the best-known examples of World War II POW sport. Felice Benuzzi, an Italian officer serving in Ethiopia, was interned by the British in 1941 when those forces secured Ethiopia from Benito Mussolini. Living in a camp at the base of Mount Kenya, Benuzzi disliked the passive existence he led in camp. "In order to break the monotony," he wrote, "one had only to start taking risks again." Realizing that the camp was too distant from any neutral nations he could escape to, Benuzzi decided to engineer an escape from what he called "this awful travesty of life." He resolved to escape from the camp, climb Mount Kenya, and return to the compound. With two other prisoners, Benuzzi prepared for six months, making climbing tools from pieces of metal and tents and backpacks from fabric scraps. Successfully escaping camp, the trio began a mountaineering adventure that included encounters with elephants and extreme temperatures. Scaling to Point Lenana at a height of 16,300 feet, they raised a flag they had sewn before descending to the camp to resume their imprisonment. After the war, a film, *The Ascent*, was based on Benuzzi's escape. Other films feature prisoners playing sports, such as the soccer match between World War II prisoners and Nazi guards in *Victory*, and television shows such *as Hogan's Heroes* also depict prisoners' recreational activities.

References

Felice Benuzzi, *No Picnic on Mount Kenya* (New York: Lyons Press, 1999 [1953]).

A.V.H. Hartendorp and Frank H. Golay, *The Santo Tomas Story* (New York: McGraw-Hill, 1964).

Phil Marchildon and Brian Kendall, *Ace: Phil Marchildon, Canada's Pitching Sensation and Wartime Hero* (Toronto: Viking, 1993).

Bell I. Wiley, *The Life of Billy Yank, the Common Soldier of the Union* (Indianapolis: Bobbs-Merrill, 1952).

———, *The Life of Johnny Reb, the Common Soldier of the Confederacy* (Indianapolis: Bobbs-Merrill, 1943).

Tim Wolter, *POW Baseball in World War II: The National Pastime Behind Barbed Wire* (Jefferson, NC: McFarland & Co., 2002).

—*Elizabeth D. Schafer*

SREBERNICA MASSACRE

The Srebrenica massacre of July 1995 refers to the killing of nearly 8, 000 Bosnian Muslim (also called Bosniak) males in and around the town of Srebrenica in eastern Bosnia by the Bosnian Serb Army during the war in Bosnia-Herzegovina (1992–1995). Under the command of the Bosnian Serb General Ratko Mladić (1943–) and with the aid of the "Scorpions," special forces sent from Serbia, Bosnian Muslim men were methodically executed over a period of just a few days and buried in mass graves. A massacre of this scale has not been seen in Europe since World War II.

The massacre took place in the backdrop of the Yugoslav wars of national independence (1991–1995). The former Yugoslavia had been composed of six constituent republics: Serbia, Croatia, Slovenia, Montenegro, Macedonia and Bosnia-Herzegovina. After Slovenia and Croatia declared their independence in 1991, it was clear that the country was going to break apart. The Bosnian parliament followed suit in October 1991, declaring its independence and later received international recognition both from the European Community and the United States in April 1992.

Not all of the inhabitants of Bosnia-Herzegovina—an ethnically heterogeneous population of Serbs, Croats and Muslims—desired to separate from Yugoslavia. The Bosnian Serbs, in particular, desired that Bosnia-Herzegovina remain in Yugoslavia, thus permitting them to inhabit a state where the majority of other Serbs lived. Therefore, in 1991 they established the Bosnian Serb Assembly, a representative body intended to look after the interests of the Bosnian Serbs. After Bosnia-Herzegovina received international recognition as an independent state in April 1992, the Bosnian Serb Assembly, now calling itself the Serbian Republic of Bosnia-Herzegovina and which later came to be known as simply Republika Srpska (the Serbian Republic), declared its independence, thus separating itself from the sovereign state of Bosnia-Herzegovina. In May 1992, Republika Srpska placed Bosnian Serb General Ratko Mladić in command of its newly formed Bosnian Serb Army.

The territorial division of the country, whose ethnic groups were scattered throughout the country, was, however, not settled through peaceful declarations of sovereignty. Although the international community made various attempts to establish peace, Bosnia-Herzegovina descended into a war that was fought between various combinations of ethnic groups, all fighting for territorial control of the country.

Among the fiercest fighting took place in the Srebrenica region of eastern Bosnia-Herzegovina, where Bosnian Serbs and Bosnian Muslims fought for territorial control. The Republika Srpska strongly believed that the area of Central Podrinje—where there was a Bosnian Muslim majority and wherein lay the town of Srebrenica—was of the greatest strategic importance. Taking control of the area would maintain the territorial integrity of Serb ethnic territories, linking Republika Srpska with neighbouring Serbia. Serb forces gained control of the region for several weeks in 1992, but by May Bosnian forces managed to recapture Srebrenica. They were, however, unable to link up with Bosnian-held lands further west, thus remaining within territory still under Serb control. By January 1993, Bosnian Serb forces managed to reduce considerably the size of the enclave to approximately an area of 150 square kilometers. As the Bosnian Serbs slowly advanced, civilians were forced to converge on Srebrenica whose population had increased to about 60, 000.

In March 1993 General Philippe Morillon, Commander of the UN Protection Force

(UNPROFOR) visited Srebrenica where conditions had quickly deteriorated. The town was overcrowded, had very little running water, food and medicine. At a public meeting the General promised that the town was to be under UN protection from then on. In March and April approximately 9, 000 Bosnian Muslims were evacuated. In April, the United Nations Security Council declared Srebrenica a "safe area," namely free from any armed or hostile attacks. Both the Bosnian Serb Army and the Bosnian forces violated the agreement. While some of the Bosnian forces refused to demilitarize the town, opening fire on Serb lines, the Bosnian Serb forces continued to advance through this so-called "safe area." Conditions continued to deteriorate over the next several months as Bosnian Serb forces prevented supplies of food, medicine, ammunition and fuel from reaching the town.

In March 1995 the President of Republika Srpska, Radovan Karadžić, issued a directive to the Bosnian Serb Army known as "Directive 7," instructing them to take immediate control of the situation in Srebrenica, whatever the cost. The Directive instructed the Army to make conditions so unbearable, so hopeless as to impress upon the inhabitants of Srebrenica that there would be no hope for survival. By mid-1995 conditions there had become catastrophic. Civilians were now dying of starvation.

The stage was now set for a major military advance. On July 9, the Bosnian Serb Army advanced on the town of Srebrenica, stopping just one kilometer short of it. NATO responded by bombing advancing Serb tanks. But following Serb threats to kill the Dutch UN troops held in custody, NATO ceased its bombing and the remaining UN forces could do little to protect the civilians at Srebrenica, having run extremely low on fuel and ammunition.

Now that NATO and the UN were rendered ineffective, the Bosnian Serb Army began to carry out summary executions at Srebrenica. There were a number of small- and large-scale executions that took place over a six-day period (July 11–16). The large-scale search and executions of Bosnian Muslim men occurred in roughly three stages. The first took place at Potočari, the Dutch UN compound near Srebrenica. Faced with the knowledge that Srebrenica was going to fall to the Serbs, thousands of Bosnian Muslims fled to the UN compound of Potočari looking for UN protection. On the evening of July 11 there were approximately 25, 000 refugees there. While women, children and the elderly constituted the vast majority, there were hundreds of men there as well. Refugees who could not fit into the UN compound found shelter in neighbouring factories where from July 11–13 they were subjected to days of terror. Beginning on the morning of July 12 and under the direction of General Ratko Mladić, the Bosnian Serb Army separated the men from the women, took the men out to neighbouring fields and rivers, and summarily executed them the following day. Most of these men were of military age, but occasionally younger and older men were executed. Few survived. The fate of the women was no less frightening as some were raped and killed.

The second stage of executions took place in the surrounding woods of Srebrenica. On the evening of July 11 and the morning of July 12, thousands of men had decided to form a column and flee the advancing army through the woods heading for the town of Tuzla. About one-third of these men were from the Bosnian Army, though not all were armed. The column was ambushed by the Bosnian Serb Army. While some were killed then and there, most were taken into captivity. On July 13, approximately 1, 500 Bosnian Muslim men were taken to a neighbouring warehouse, where the Serbs began throwing grenades. Few survived.

The third stage of executions involved prisoners who had been detained in the nearby town of Bratunac and subsequently taken to two locations beginning on 14 July. In the first, approximately 1, 000 prisoners were bussed to a school gymnasium, already occupied by other prisoners, in the nearby town of Grahovac. After being detained for a few hours, the prisoners were led out into smaller groups to a nearby field. Each was blindfolded and given a drink of water before setting off for the execution field. Once there, the prisoners were lined up, shot in the back and buried in two mass graves. Few survived. A second group of Bratunac prisoners were taken to a school in a village north of the town of Zvornik. They were held there for two nights. On July 16, with their hands tied behind their backs, the prisoners were taken to a neighbouring farm where, in groups of ten and totaling 1,200 men, they were lined up and shot.

The war in Bosnia-Herzegovina officially came to an end with the signing of the Dayton Peace Accords in November 1995. The International Criminal Tribunal of Yugoslavia has since indicted several individuals including the commander of the Bosnian Serb Army General Ratko Mladić and former president of Republika Srpska Radovan Karadžić for various war crimes including genocide, crimes against humanity and violations of the laws and customs of war. As of 2005, Mladić and Karadžić are still at large.

It was not until 2004 that Republika Srpska publicly apologized for the massacre. And although Serbia officially condemned the massacre from the beginning, it denied any involvement. It was not until the June 2, 2005 broadcast on Serbian television of a secret videotape showing the "Scorpions," a Serbian paramilitary force, executing six Bosnian Muslim males at Srebrenica that the denial of Serbian involvement could finally be put to rest. Besides the moral dimensions, the reluctance to acknowledge participation in the Srebrenica massacre had something to do with the slow progress of gathering evidence. Locating the bodies of victims has been slow and as of 2005 6, 000 have been exhumed and just over 2, 000 have been identified. As a result, some Serbs have disputed the actual numbers killed and do not consider the massacre to be a case of genocide, but a consequence of war. Still others have pointed to cases across Bosnia and Croatia where Serbs were similarly targeted for extermination and/or relocation. The expulsion of 200, 000 Serbs from Croatia in August 1995 that was accompanied by the killing of hundreds of mainly elderly persons is among the most significant. While true, the scale of the Srebrenica massacre is unmatched by any other during the Yugoslav wars and is today considered one of the largest mass executions in Europe since WWII.

References

Steven L. Burg and Paul S. Shoup, *The War in Bosnia-Herzegovina* (Armonk, New York: M.E. Sharpe, 1999).

Norman Cigar and Paul Williams, *Indictment at the Hague* (New York: New York University Press, 2002).

James Gow, *The Serbian Project and Its Adversaries: A Strategy of War Crimes* (Ithaca: McGill-Queen's University Press, 2003).

Bianca Jagger, "The Betrayal of Srebrenica," *The European,* 25 September–1 October, 1995, pp. 14–19.

Carole Rogel, *The Breakup of Yugoslavia and the War in Bosnia* (Westport, Connecticut: Greenwood Press, 1998).

David Rohde, *Endgame: The Betrayal and Fall of Srebrenica, Europe's Worst Massacre Since World War II* (New York: Farrar, Straus and Giroux, 1997).

Laura Silber and Allan Little, *The Death of Yugoslavia* (London: Penguin Books, 1997).

Jan Willem Honig and Norbert Both, *Srebrenica: Record of a War Crime* (New York: Penguin Books, 1996).

—*Jelica Zdero*

Stalag 17

Written for the screen by Billy Wilder and Edwin Blum, directed by Wilder, and based on the stage play of the same name by Donald Bevan and Edmund Trzcinski, *Stalag 17,* released in 1953, has long been considered one of the classic POW movies of film history. Less dramatic than Jean Renoir's *The Grand Illusion* and less action-packed than *The Great Escape, Stalag 17* uses doses of both drama and comedy to present the story of Sefton (William Holden), a wheeler-dealer American POW who is accused of selling out to the Germans. Although he is a prisoner, Sefton seldom wants for anything, and the failure of several escape attempts leads Sefton's fellow prisoners to believe that he might be a traitor. Unknown to them, however, a recently arrived prisoner, Price (Peter Graves), is actually an English-speaking German planted in the camp. In the end, Sefton is proven innocent, but the damage has already been done; he knows that his fellow prisoners were quite willing to punish him without any proof of his guilt.

The crux of the story, therefore, is an examination of the human tendency to look for scapegoats during difficult periods. Director Billy Wilder was clearly trying to draw parallels to Senator Joseph McCarthy's House Committee on Un-American Activities, which was conducting investigations into the activities of alleged communist sympathizers in the United States while the film was being made. Though Wilder was nominated for Best Director and Robert Strauss for Best Supporting Actor, *Stalag 17* won only one Academy Award, the Best Actor Oscar, which went to William Holden for his portrayal of Sefton.

See also Film

References

Billy Wilder, *Stalag 17* (Berkeley: University of California Press, 1999).

—*Alexander M. Bielakowski*

Stalag Luft 3

Stalag Luft 3, located near the town of Sagan in the German province of Silesia, became the largest and most famous prison camp for Allied airmen in World War II. It was opened in April 1942, after the Luftwaffe decided that all captured airmen should be confined in a single camp. In its original incarnation, Stalag Luft 3 consisted of two compounds: East, which held some 500 officers, and Center, housing roughly 1,000 noncommissioned officers. These compounds and all subsequent additions were of a standardized construction: prefabricated wooden huts, a cement punishment block, double barbed-wire fences, and guard towers around the perimeter. From these humble beginnings, Stalag Luft 3 soon grew. The populations of East and Center nearly doubled, and new compounds were added: North, for officers, in April 1943; South, for American officers, in September 1943; an auxiliary camp at Belaria, in January 1944; and West, also for Americans, in March 1944. At its peak, well over 10,000 Allied airmen lived in Stalag Luft 3.

The camp boasted a wide range of amenities intended to make captivity more bearable: a fully equipped theater, a number of orchestras, a library and educational program, sports teams, and religious services. In addition, Stalag Luft 3, especially East, Center, and North Compounds, was a hive of escape activity. The Wooden Horse escape of October 1943 and the Great Escape of March 1944 both occurred at Sagan, and the NCOs of Center compound were also very active. Literally hundreds of tunnels (most of them abortive) were dug in Stalag Luft 3, and hundreds of escapers got away from the camp; dozens reached the safety of neutral territory.

Because of the camp's location in eastern Germany, it was vulnerable to the advance of the Soviet army and in January 1945, the commandant announced that Stalag Luft 3 would be evacuated. Beginning on 28 January 1945, the compounds were emptied of prisoners, who were formed up in ranks and marched west, to a nearby railroad. The columns went in different directions: most of the Americans were taken to southern Germany, the prisoners of East and Belaria were moved to a camp near Berlin, and the inmates of North traveled to Lübeck, in northwest Germany. Despite fears that the Nazis would execute the inmates of Stalag Luft 3, the majority of the POWs survived the forced marches to be liberated in April and May 1945.

A small museum has been erected near Sagan (now Zagan in western Poland), and the foundations of some of the camp's buildings are still visible in the undergrowth that has taken over the camp site.

See also Bushell, Roger Joyce; Great Escape; Wooden Horse

References
Kingsley Brown, *Bonds of Wire: A Memoir* (Toronto: Collins, 1989).
Robert Buckham, *Forced March to Freedom* (Stittsville, ON: Canada's Wings, 1984).
Albert P. Clark, *33 Months as a POW in Stalag Luft III: A World War II Airman Tells His Story* (Golden, CO: Fulcrum Publishing, 2005).
Arthur A. Durand, *Stalag Luft III: The Secret Story* (London: Patrick Stephens, 1988).
Ken Rees, *Lie in the Dark and Listen: The Remarkable Exploits of a WWII Bomber Pilot and Great Escaper* (London: Grub Street, 2004).
Jonathan F. Vance, "The War Behind the Wire: The Battle to Escape from a German Prison Camp," *Journal of Contemporary History* 28 (1993): 675–693.

—*Jonathan F. Vance*

STOCKDALE, JAMES BOND (1923–2005)

The senior ranking Navy POW for his entire captivity in North Vietnam, James Stockdale graduated from the U.S. Naval Academy in 1946 and began flight training in 1949. While serving as Carrier Air Group commander on the USS *Oriskany,* he was shot down on 9 September 1965 and was held in solitary confinement or isolation in Hanoi for most of the next five years.

Although tortured repeatedly from early 1966 until late 1969, whenever possible Stockdale used the covert POW communications system to establish a chain of command, to maintain military discipline, and to regulate captor-captive relations. He was so successful that in late 1967 his captors moved him and 10 "die-hard" resisters into an isolated camp they called Alcatraz. As senior ranking officer there, Stockdale organized such resistance that he was removed in early 1969. Some time later, when pressured to appear in a propaganda film, he mutilated his face and attempted suicide to avoid collaborating. After the POWs were reorganized in late 1970 into the group compounds they called Camp Unity, Stockdale held a high command position. One of the first POWs released during Operation Homecoming, he left Hanoi on 12 February 1973.

For his "valiant leadership" and "extraordinary courage," Stockdale was awarded the Congressional Medal of Honor in 1976. He retired from the navy as a vice admiral in 1979; his memoir *In Love and War,* co-authored with his wife Sybil, appeared in 1984. During the 1992 presidential election, he was Ross Perot's running mate.

See also Homecoming, Operation; Vietnam War

References
James Stockdale, *A Vietnam Experience: Ten Years of Reflection* (Stanford, CA: Hoover Press, 1984).
James and Sybil Stockdale, *In Love and War: The Story of a Family's Ordeal and Sacrifice During the Vietnam Years* (Annapolis, MD: Naval Institute Press, 1990 [1984]).

—*Craig Howes*

SULMONA

Campo 78 at Sulmona, in central Italy, served as a POW camp in both world wars. During World War I, it housed Austrian prisoners captured in the Isonzo and Trentino campaigns; during World War II, it was home to as many as 3,000 British and Commonwealth officers and other ranks captured in North Africa.

The camp itself was built on a hillside and consisted of a number of brick barracks surrounded by a high wall. During World War II, conditions in Sulmona, as in many Italian camps, were good, especially in the two officers' compounds. Regular rations of macaroni soup and bread were augmented by fresh fruit and cheese in the summer, and food parcels from the International Committee of the Red Cross were distributed regularly. For recreation, the prisoners laid out a football field, and they also had equipment for cricket and basketball. There was a theater, a small lending library, at least one band, and a newspaper produced by a group of prisoners.

In September 1943, as the Italian government neared collapse, the inmates of Sulmona heard rumors that the evacuation of the camp was imminent. They awoke one morning to discover that their guards had deserted them.

On 14 September, German troops arrived to escort the prisoners northwards, to captivity in Germany, but not before hundreds of them had escaped into the hills.

See also Chieti

References

Donald I. Jones, *Escape from Sulmona* (New York: Vantage Press, 1980).

Edward Ward, *Give Me Air* (London: John Lane, 1946).

J.H. Witte, *The One that Didn't Get Away* (Bognor Regis, UK: New Horizons, 1983).

—*Tony Dawes*

SULTANA DISASTER

One of the worst accidents involving prisoners of war occurred in 1865, at the end of the U.S. Civil War, just as released Union captives were being returned to their homes.

The prison camp in Cahaba, Alabama, the first capital of the state, had been established in 1863 in a partially completed warehouse that had been built to hold corn and cotton. It was closed again within a year when the camp at Andersonville, Georgia, was opened, but remained in use as an unofficial transfer facility and overflow camp. Nine months before the end of the war, to deal with a new influx of POWs, Confederate military authorities reopened the Cahaba Federal Prison, as it was officially known; its unofficial name was Castle Morgan. Conditions there were typical of many Civil War prisons: poor sanitation, inadequate food, and cramped sleeping arrangements. Authorities admitted that the camp's capacity was between 500 and 700 men, but at one time there may have been as many as 3,000 Union POWs held there; in total, some 5,000 prisoners passed through the camp. Furthermore, it was situated on the banks of the Alabama River and was subject to periodic flooding. Still, with a death rate of only about 5 percent, it compared favorably with the more notorious Andersonville.

In February 1865, with the Confederate forces rapidly losing the ability to feed their own troops, let alone prisoners of war, negotiators from the Union and the Confederacy agreed that prisoners from Cahaba, Andersonville, and Macon camps would be held at a neutral site near Vicksburg, Mississippi, where they would be fed and cared for by the better equipped Union Army until negotiations for their exchange were concluded. From Vicksburg, they would be taken north by steamboat up the Mississippi River to Cairo, Illinois, and from there would be returned to their homes. One of the steamboats contracted to carry the released prisoners was the *Sultana*, a 260-foot-long paddle-wheeler built in Cincinnati in 1863.

The *Sultana* arrived at Vicksburg in April 1865 and began loading prisoners. By this time, most of the men from Andersonville and Macon had already left Vicksburg, and the majority of the remaining prisoners were from Cahaba. They were anxious to get home, and the owners of the *Sultana* were anxious to transport them, because they were being paid $5 for each soldier and $10 for each officer. The boat was only rated to carry 376 passengers and crew, but by the time it left the wharf in Vicksburg on 24 April, there were as many as 2,300 passengers on board, most of them released POWs but also a number of civilians, including women and children.

The *Sultana* steamed north, the spirits of the former prisoners rising as they drew closer to their homes. Then, early on the morning of 27 April 1865, about eight miles north of Memphis, one of the *Sultana*'s boilers exploded, quickly followed by two others; the boilers had always been troublesome and one of them, the only one that did not explode, had required emergency repairs while the boat was docked in Vicksburg. Hundreds of passengers were either killed by the blasts, scalded to death, or crushed by debris; those who survived the initial explosions had to face the fire that quickly enveloped the boat. The survivors jumped into the river but many of them could not swim, and quickly drowned; even those who could swim had a difficult time,

The Sultana, photographed at Helena, Arkansas, on 25 April 1865 (from Joseph Taylor Elliott, "The Sultana Disaster," Indiana Historical Society Publications *5/3 [1913])*

because the Mississippi River was in flood and there was very little dry land nearby. Other river boats were quick to reach the scene and pick up survivors, but they found more dead bodies than live ones. A precise death toll was never calculated, but best estimates are that more than 1,600 passengers, the majority of them from Cahaba prison camp, perished in the disaster.

The town of Cahaba fell into a slump after the Civil War and eventually disappeared from the map; a government plaque now marks the location of the prison camp. The site of the tragedy, however, is more difficult to determine. The Mississippi River has changed its course a number of times since the 1860s, and present historians believe that whatever remains of the *Sultana* now lies under about 20 feet of loam and soybean field.

See also Andersonville Prison Camp; U.S. Civil War

References

Chester D. Berry, *Loss of the Sultana and Reminiscences of Survivors* (Knoxville: University of Tennessee Press, 2005 [1892]).

William O. Bryant, *Cahaba Prison and the Sultana Disaster* (Tuscaloosa: University of Alabama Press, 1990).

James Elliott, *Transport to Disaster* (New York: Holt, Rinehart & Winston, 1962).

Jerry O. Potter, *The Sultana Tragedy: America's Greatest Maritime Disaster* (Gretna, LA: Pelican Publishing, 1992).

Gene Eric Salecker, *Disaster on the Mississippi: The Sultana Explosion, April 27, 1865* (Naval Institute Press, 1996).

—Jonathan F. Vance

Swedish–Russian Wars (1323–1809)

Sweden and Russia fought a number of wars between 1323, when the two nations concluded their first peace treaty, and 1809,

Swedish POWs working on the construction of the new Russian capital, St. Petersburg (Detail of C.F. Coyet's plan of 1721, Military Archives, Stockholm, Sweden)

when they concluded their last. A small number of POWs were taken during the fourteenth, fifteenth, and sixteenth centuries, but during the seventeenth century the number grew dramatically. When the Russians besieged the Swedish city of Riga in Livonia (now Latvia) in 1656, several hundred civilian and military prisoners were taken from the surrounding countryside and forced into Russia and Siberia. During the Great Northern War (1700–1721), tens of thousands of POWs were taken on both sides, most of whom were placed in rural towns in Sweden or Siberia, as well as in Voronezh and the newly founded city of St. Petersburg.

During the war of 1788–1790, a large number of Swedish soldiers and at least 800 naval officers and sailors fell into captivity. Many of them had to walk long distances to captivity and were fed and sheltered for short periods in a number of small towns and villages along the way. Instead of being placed in large camps, the POWs were marched from Reval (now Tallinn in Estonia) to Tartu, Smolensk, and eventually to Orenburg in Siberia. After five months in Siberia they were forced to continue via Moscow, Tver, and Tsarskoje Selo to St. Petersburg. Once the peace treaty was signed in the autumn of 1790, several POW columns were assembled around St. Petersburg for the journey across the Carelian isthmus to Finland, where the survivors were released. In Sweden the Russian POWs, as before, were deployed in small towns and villages, as well as in the capital, Stockholm. A number of them also elected to stay in Sweden after the war.

The war of 1808–1809 resulted in Russia's conquest of Sweden's eastern part, Finland, and the capture of almost 7,000 officers and soldiers by the Russians. In an attempt to divide their enemy, the Russians released all Finnish soldiers, while the Swedish soldiers were taken to captivity in St. Petersburg. Here more than 1,500 Swedish soldiers and sailors were forced to work on construction projects on the city's canals. Smaller groups of officers were sent deep into Russia, to Rostov and Yaroslav (Jarossaw), and several unsuccessful attempts were made to persuade the POWs to join Russian military service. Not all prisoners were treated so badly, however. A few high-ranking officers, once they had given their word of honor not to escape, were allowed to attend parties arranged by the nobility of St. Petersburg. In late 1809, once the peace treaty was signed, the last contingents of the POWs were sent home to Sweden.

See also Fraustadt-Grodno Massacres

References

Lars Ericson, *Swedish Soldiers: Allotment Soldiers, Cavalry Men and Naval Sailors in War and Peace* (Lund: Historiska Media, 1995).

—Lars Ericson

T

Taiping Rebellion

The Taiping Rebellion, the largest uprising in nineteenth-century China, pitted the Manchu Qing dynasty that had ruled China since the seventeenth century against a coalition of forces that sought to overthrow it, led by a messianic Christian convert named Hung Hsiu-ch'üan. The rebellion was a purely Chinese affair until the early 1860s, when the Ever-Victorious Army, made up of Chinese and Western volunteers, intervened on the side of the Qing.

A notable feature of the rebellion was the enlistment of POWs and civilian captives into the forces of the opposing side. The Taiping rebels adopted a simple policy toward prisoners. Any who offered resistance were killed and, as Franz Michael notes, there were numerous occasions when the Taiping slaughtered every man, woman, and child in towns that resisted them. However, anyone who was willing to join them or support their cause was well treated, a fact that explains in part the tremendous growth of the Taiping movement in the 1850s. When the rebels captured the city of Wu-ch'ang in January 1853, for example, virtually the entire population, male and female, joined the Taiping army.

Despite rumors that captured rebels faced immediate execution, the anti-Taiping forces also enlisted prisoners into their own ranks. American Frederick Townsend Ward, who first led the Ever-Victorious Army, made only limited efforts to enlist captured rebels, but his successor, the British Major Charles Gordon, was driven by high casualty and desertion rates to be more assiduous in this regard. In May 1863, after a battle at T'ai-ts'ang, Gordon enlisted roughly 700 rebel soldiers whom his army had captured. When K'un-shan was captured in June 1863, some 2,000 more rebel POWs were taken into the Ever-Victorious Army, to make up for losses through desertion. In December 1863, another thousand captured rebels were impressed into service by Gordon, although half were sent home within weeks when it became clear they were more of a liability than an asset. To Li Hung-chang, the leader of the anti-Taiping force that fought alongside the Ever-Victorious Army in the Yangtze Delta region, this was hardly surprising. He had used POWs on a limited basis in his own army in the past, but was disturbed by Gordon's reliance on them and feared they would turn against their new commanders.

The rebellion finally ended in July 1864, when the fall of Nanking was followed by the virtual extermination of the remaining rebels. Thousands who refused to surrender committed mass suicide; even had they been willing to give themselves up, Tseng Kuo-fan, commander of the Qing anti-Taiping forces, had already determined that their surrender would not be accepted. As many as 100,000 rebels died in the fall of Nanking; the total death toll for the 14-year rebellion may have been as high as 30 million.

References

Franz Michael, *The Taiping Rebellion: History and Documents*, 3 vols. (Seattle: University of Washington Press, 1966).

Richard J. Smith, *Mercenaries and Mandarins: The Ever-Victorious Army in Nineteenth-Century China* (Millwood, NY: KTO Press, 1978).

—Jonathan F. Vance

TAJIKISTAN CIVIL WAR

Of the four central Asian republics that were once part of the Soviet Union, only Tajikistan descended into civil war shortly after the dissolution of the Soviet Union. In May 1992, an odd grouping of democrats, liberals, secularists, and Islamic fundamentalists allied against the new government, which collapsed in short order. But before the new coalition could assume power, warlords from the southwestern part of the country took over the capital, Dushanbe, and continued to control the country long after the civil war ended in June 1997, with a United Nations-brokered agreement among rival groups. Despite the accord, low-intensity warfare has continued, occasionally flaring up into more serious clashes and preventing the country from rebuilding. As many as 70,000 people were killed in the conflict, and 650,000 were forced from their homes by the fighting. Most of the civilian casualties were in the south, where militias allied to the ruling party waged a war of ethnic cleansing against local ethnic minorities.

The United Nations has long been active in attempting to keep the peace in the country, but the lawlessness of Tajikistan was made evident in December 1996, when elements of the Presidential Guard captured a party of U.N. military observers. Officers prepared them for execution, but a party of rankers stepped in to prevent the killings. The following week a similar incident occurred, but again the U.N. observers were released, this time when the Tajik commander was distracted by a passing vehicle. Later in December, yet another group of seven U.N. monitors was taken prisoner by a local warlord who demanded the return of some of his fighters stranded in Afghanistan as the price for their lives. Fortunately, bloodshed was again averted and the monitors released. In 1997, a semi-independent rebel group abducted two French citizens, one of whom was freed after two weeks, but the other was killed during an attempted rescue.

The abductors have not only targeted foreigners. In April 1999, an opposition army commander kidnapped six policemen and held them as hostages to force the government to release a number of his own imprisoned fighters. Two years later, in June 2001, another opposition commander captured four policemen and 15 German aid workers, and demanded the release of suspects in the assassination of the Tajik deputy interior minister; the hostages were eventually released.

Despite the chaos in the country, from January 1993 the International Committee of the Red Cross was able to gain access to prisoners detained by the new rulers of Tajikistan, within certain limits: convicted prisoners could be visited regularly to monitor their living conditions, but individuals who were deemed to be security suspects could only receive visits after the permission of a government official had been secured. As in all conflicts of this nature, an inspection by Red Cross delegates does not constitute an admission on the part of the detaining power that the detainees have been granted official prisoner of war status. Indeed, human rights groups remain concerned about the fate of political prisoners held in Tajikistan.

References

Mohammed-Reza Djalili, Frédéric Grare, and Shirin Akiner, eds., *Tajikistan: The Trials of Independence* (New York: St. Martin's Press, 1997).

—*Jonathan F. Vance*

TAMERLANE (1336–1405)

Mongol leader Tamerlane (the name is a corruption of Timur the Lame, or Timurlenk, which refers to an infirmity caused by an arrow wound to a foot) was a descendant of Genghis Khan; his armies ravaged Persia, Egypt, Syria, and India.

Tamerlane was known for his brutality toward the citizens of captured cities. Populations that had the temerity to rebel against him were ruthlessly slaughtered, and towers of skulls were erected as a warning to others. In 1401, he captured Baghdad and massacred 20,000 of its inhabitants, and on 20 July 1402, he decisively defeated the Ottoman Turks at the Battle of Angora, capturing the Ottoman Sultan Bayezid I (c. 1360–1403, reigned 1389–1402) and his wife Despina, daughter of Serbian Prince Lazar. Tamerlane initially treated Bayezid with the honors due a sovereign but soon began a humiliation of his Ottoman prisoner. Tamerlane is reputed to have had him carried through Anatolia in a barred litter, called by some a cage, and to have kept him in chains at night. He is also said to have forced Despina to be his cupbearer and to serve at his table naked, in front of Bayezid. After eight months of captivity, Bayezid died, either of an apoplectic seizure or by suicide. Three years later, Tamerlane himself died, while on the march toward China.

See also Mongols

References

A. D. Alderson, *The Structure of the Ottoman Dynasty* (New York: Oxford University Press, 1956).

Lord Kinross, *The Ottoman Centuries—The Rise and Fall of the Turkish Empire* (New York: Quill, 1977).

—*B. Alan Guthrie III*

THEATER

Since the eighteenth century, and perhaps earlier, POWs and internees have mounted theatrical productions as a way to ease the boredom of captivity. Indeed, a number of prominent actors and directors, including Derek Bond, Henry Mollison, Cameron Mackintosh, John Casson, and Roy Kinnear, gained valuable experience in prison camp theaters. Because both the Hague and Geneva Conventions stipulated that detaining powers were to provide recreational opportunities for their prisoners, camp theatricals became particularly sophisticated in the twentieth century. During World War I, productions ranged from recitations or simple plays performed in small work camps, to full-scale, professional-quality shows. At first, productions were primitive and amateurish. Costumes and scenery were assembled from whatever material could be found in the camp, and scripts were written by prisoners with dramatic leanings. The plays, often variety shows or light comedies, were performed in any large room that happened to be available in the camp. From these humble beginnings, prison camp theater grew. Ruhleben camp in Berlin, which housed British civilian internees, had a theater society whose work rivaled anything seen on the London stage. Prospective directors had to submit their scripts, not only to German censors, but to the program committee of the Ruhleben Dramatic Society, which judged their artistic merit, and the camp's Entertainments Committee, which judged their commercial promise. If a script was approved, the director hired costumes from Berlin shops, commissioned the printing of posters and programs, auditioned actors, and assembled props and sets. The process was complicated, but the Ruhleben Dramatic Society was still able to mount 31 productions over 10 months in 1916.

During World War II, humanitarian agencies were much more active in sending supplies into the camps, so that by 1944 most large prison camps in Germany and North America boasted impressive, specially built theaters. Stalag Luft 3, a camp for Allied airmen in eastern Germany, had a theater in each of its five compounds, and all were fully equipped with orchestra pit, rheostated lighting, scenery flats, and a broad range of professional-quality props and costumes. Scripts, too, were provided by aid groups like the YMCA, so that the prisoners could produce everything from light comedies to costume dramas to Shakespearean tragedies.

Even in camps with less sophisticated facilities, theater provided a wonderful diversion to POWs. The German prisoners in Yelabuga camp in the Soviet Union mounted plays by Chekhov, Gogol, and Gorky, with the blessing of their captors, and sometimes performed their own works as well; these were often procommunist in tone, to convince the Soviets to allow them to continue their theatricals. In Japanese

During World War II the theater at Stalag Luft 3, as portrayed by artist and former POW Ley Kenyon, boasted particularly sohisticated facilities. (Jonathan F. Vance)

camps, prisoners also mounted plays as a way to turn attention away from their plight. Even in Dachau concentration camp, the inmates put on theatrical productions, albeit without the permission of their captors.

References
"In German Prison Camps," *Theater Arts* 28 (1944): 253–254.
Joe Klaas, "Barbed Wire Theatre," *Theater Arts* 28 (1944): 743–744.

—*Jonathan F. Vance*

THIRTY YEARS' WAR (1618–1648)

The Thirty Years' War, part of the military revolution that took place roughly between 1500 and 1800, began as a religious struggle and quickly evolved into a political conflict that enveloped much of Europe. It was particularly noteworthy for the lack of any legal framework to protect POWs and for the large number of mercenary units involved. Both of these factors had considerable influence on captivity issues.

Swedish King Gustavus Adolphus's Military Laws (*krigslagar*) notwithstanding, there was no internationally recognized legal framework for the treatment of prisoners of war during this period, and this meant that captivity was often a brutal experience during the Thirty Years' War. In the years preceding the war, there were many instances of harsh treatment of prisoners. There seems to have been a general consensus that towns and cities could be legitimately sacked if they refused to surrender before the besiegers brought up their artillery. For example, after the capture of Haarlem in Holland in 1573, in spite of promises that none of the defenders would be harmed, the Spanish army hanged, beheaded, or drowned many burghers. Such conduct was the norm during the Thirty Years' War, and often no quarter was given.

In the 1630s, the Finnish cavalry of the Swedish army was known for its ferocity. After the Battle of Oldendorf, in 1633, the Scottish mercenary James Turner saw "a great many kill'd in cold blood by the Finns, who profess to give no quarter."

However, the existence of large mercenary forces also meant that POWs could save themselves by changing sides. The largest armies enlisted nearly 1,000 mercenary units. (In the Swedish language, these soldiers were called "enlisted," because their names were entered on a list upon recruitment.) The army of the Holy Roman Empire had around 550 mercenary regiments of infantry, cavalry, and dragoons (pertinent data exist for around 450 of them), which were owned by approximately 600 generals and colonels known as military enterprisers. The Swedish army had around 350 regiments (beside the national conscript army) owned by 200 enterprisers, while the third largest army, that of the Catholic League, had 175 regiments owned by 150 military enterprisers.

The mercenary trade involved huge sums of money, and the units were, for all intents and purposes, the personal property of the enterpriser. The dominant nationality among mercenaries was German, but there were also large numbers of Scots, Irish, and English. Religion, however, did not play an important role for these soldiers. Many Catholics, for example, served in the Protestant Swedish army. Because the mercenary units were so flexible, it was typical for the victor to recruit enemy prisoners of war into his own army, with the probable exception of Swedish or Finnish indigenous soldiers who were captured. Where POWs were detained, their personal effects became the property of the captor, and any ransoms paid would be divided between the captor and his commander in fixed proportions.

The wholesale enlistment of enemy prisoners was a feature of many later battles of the war. The Battle of Breitenfeld in 1631 produced around 9,000 prisoners of war for the victorious Protestant army, and historians believe that the majority of the prisoners subsequently enlisted in the Protestant army. In northern German cities like Rostock and Wismar, prisoners of war from the defending Catholic force were divided up among the Swedish regiments. The Battle of Nördlingen in September 1634, a great imperial victory, saw Spanish and German Catholic forces decimate their Swedish and German Protestant enemies, who retreated in disorder. Around 6,000 dead were left on the battlefield, and about the same number of prisoners were taken, including the Swedish commander in chief, Gustav Horn. Many German Protestant prisoners then changed sides and fought alongside their former enemies in later battles.

The Thirty Years' War was brought to a conclusion by the Peace of Westphalia in 1648. This agreement was significant for the subsequent treatment of POWs, for it normalized the practice of releasing all prisoners, without ransom, at the end of hostilities.

References

Geoffrey Parker, *The Military Revolution: Military Innovation and the Rise of the West, 1500–1800*, rev. ed. (Cambridge: Cambridge University Press, 1996).

———, ed., *The Thirty Years' War* (London: Routledge, 1997).

Fritz Redlich, *The German Military Enterpriser and His Work Force: A Study in European Economic and Social History*, vol. 1 (Wiesbaden, Germany: Franz Steiner Verlag, 1964).

William Watts, *The Swedish Discipline*, vol. 2 (London: John Dawson, 1632): 39–69.

—Bertil Häggman

THOMPSON, CAPTAIN FLOYD J. "JIM" (1933–)

Captain Floyd Thompson was the longest held POW in American history, having been in captivity in Vietnam for nearly nine years, from 26 March 1964 to 16 March 1973. The distinction is sometimes mistakenly given to navy Lieutenant Everett Alvarez, Jr., who was the first American pilot shot down over North Vietnam on 5 August 1964; Thompson was held over four months longer than Alvarez.

On 26 March 1964, Thompson, commander of Detachment A31, 7th Special Forces Group at Khe Sahn, Republic of Vietnam, was flying in an L-19 observation airplane to reconnoiter enemy positions within his area of responsibility. As the aircraft flew low to gain information on a previously unknown enemy bridge, it came under intense enemy ground fire and was shot down. The pilot was killed and Captain Thompson was severely injured and lost consciousness. He awoke four days later to find himself a prisoner of the communist Viet Cong. In the years ahead, he suffered through 12 communist detention camps. Throughout this ordeal, Thompson survived torture, starvation, and other physical and mental abuse while resisting enemy interrogation, making numerous escape attempts, and actively undermining the enemy's efforts to break other prisoners.

During his internment, he was held in solitary confinement for over four years before being placed with other prisoners. At one camp he was handcuffed, placed in leg irons, and continually blindfolded. At another he was crammed into a small cage measuring two feet by two feet by five feet and fed only cold rice and gruel. He was also hung from rafters by his wrists for days on end and beaten. He was exposed to the weather, to deadly insects and snakes, and to the horror of having rats run over his body at night. Even under these most devastating conditions, he repeatedly attempted escape. He was recaptured shortly after each attempt, severely tortured, and placed in solitary confinement.

He was returned to American control on 16 March 1973 and continued his military career after a period of medical treatment and recovery. Jim Thompson retired from the United States Army as a full colonel on 31 December 1981 after being totally disabled by a major stroke.

See also Vietnam War

References

Tom Philpott, *Glory Denied: The Saga of Jim Thompson, America's Longest-Held Prisoner of War* (New York: Penguin, 2003).

—*William S. Reeder, Jr.*

Tibet, Invasion and Occupation of

The mountainous country of Tibet, in central Asia, has long been the subject of Chinese claims, the government in Beijing frequently asserting its sovereignty over the country. In October 1950, while much of the world was diverted by the war in Korea, the Chinese army took advantage of the opportunity to invade Tibet. The speed of the Chinese advance easily overwhelmed the Tibetan defenders, and a number of garrisons promptly surrendered. On 19 October, units of the Chinese army surrounded a body of Tibetan troops near the monastery of Drukha, and Ngabo, the governor of Kham province, had no option to surrender; the Chinese turned this debacle into a propaganda occasion, filming Ngabo signing the surrender documents. Then, all of the Tibetan POWs were gathered together for lectures on socialism and the unity of the Chinese motherland, given money and provisions, and sent home. At this stage, China preferred to use the velvet-glove approach and saw little to be gained by mistreating soldiers who, in a philosophical sense, Beijing wished to consider as fellow Chinese.

Tibet had few alternatives but to accept Chinese terms, but in late 1955 the Kanding Rebellion, as Beijing called it, broke out as a series of spontaneous risings against forced collectivization. This time, the Chinese responded more firmly, bombing monasteries in which dissidents had sheltered and imprisoning rebel leaders. Stories circulated that religious and secular leaders were being tortured and killed in Chinese captivity, and by late 1957, what began as a revolt in the eastern region of Tibet had become a nationwide rebellion, led by Tibetans from Kham province.

It was a low-intensity conflict at first, but it flared up in 1959, in part because of rumors that the Chinese planned to abduct the Dalai Lama, Tibet's revered spiritual and political leader. The Chinese army subdued the rebels with relative ease, arresting some 4,000 Tibetans. Continuing their advance, they gradually pushed the Khampa fighters towards India, where many of them took refuge. It was the end of Tibet's existence as an autonomous region within the People's Republic of China, but China experienced one major setback as a result of the rebellion: In March 1959, the Dalai Lama slipped across the border into India, to live in exile as a continual thorn in Beijing's side.

The willingness of India to shelter Tibetan refugees and fighters also brought that nation into the conflict. In October 1962, after border negotiations between Delhi and Beijing collapsed, Chinese troops attacked Indian posts in the western region, easily overwhelming them. To mark their triumph, the Chinese army transported the exhausted and bedraggled Indian POWs back to Lhasa, the Tibetan capital, where they were marched through the streets as symbols of China's victory.

With Tibet now firmly under China's control, Beijing set about bringing the region under the influence of the Cultural Revolution: Tibetan culture and religion was systematically destroyed, and dissidents murdered or imprisoned. This strategy lasted until 1974, when Chinese policy shifted. Political prisoners were released, some cultural and religious institutions were restored, and the country was opened to foreign tourists. But the more lenient policy only encouraged pro-independence Tibetans, and a series of demonstrations, mostly led by monks, began in September 1987. This brought a swift crackdown from Chinese authorities, and many protestors were arrested. Another series of riots in March 1988 was followed by a wave of arrests, as many as 2,000 this time, and in March 1989 Beijing declared martial law in Lhasa. Within three days, as many as 300 Tibetans had been arrested.

The detention policy continues to be a major obstacle to peace in Tibet. Non governmental organizations such as Asia Watch and Human Rights Watch constantly document the practice of arresting Tibetans who call for independence (an ideology the Chinese refer to as "splittism"), but are frustrated by China's refusal to release information on the charges laid against individuals, the length of their sentences, where they are being held, or their physical condition. Details of a few high-profile prisoners, however, have emerged. One is activist monk Tenzin Delek Rinpoche, who was arrested with another dissident, Lobsang Dondrup, in April 2002 and charged with a series of bombings (the official charges were "incitement to separatism" and "crimes of terror"). The latter was executed, but Tenzin Delek's death sentence was suspended for two years. In Chinese practice, if a prisoner under this sentence behaves, the sentence is often commuted to life imprisonment; in Tenzin Delek's case, the commutation occurred in January 2005. Another important case involved the imprisonment of a group known as "the Singing Nuns," so called because they smuggled out of captivity an audiotape of songs expressing their commitment to Tibetan independence. These and other cases have been well publicized by human rights groups, but the fact that Chinese authorities continue to deal with protests by arresting dissidents en masse means that the abuse of prisoners will persist as long as Tibetans continue to be thwarted in their struggle for independence.

References

Robert Ford, *Captured in Tibet* (Oxford: Oxford University Press, 1990 [1958]).

"Trials of a Tibetan Monk: The Case of Tenzin Delek," *Human Rights Watch* 16/1 (February 2004).

Tsering Shakya, *The Dragon in the Land of Snows: A History of Modern Tibet Since 1947* (New York: Columbia University Press, 1999).

—*Jonathan F. Vance*

Tokyo War Crimes Trials

Immediately after World War II, all of the Allied nations that had been involved in the Pacific war (the United States, Britain, Australia, Canada, New Zealand, Russia, China, the Netherlands, and France) instituted legal proceedings against Japanese defendants for war crimes, including atrocities committed against prisoners of war and civilians. The United States took the leading role in these prosecutions, because it had taken the leading role in the war in the Pacific theater.

Fairly early on, the Allies knew of Japanese war crimes in the campaign in China, of which the so-called Rape of Nanking was only the most notorious, and very shortly after the bombing of Pearl Harbor on 7 December 1941, the Allies began receiving reports of further atrocities committed against POWs and civilians. As a result, in January 1942, the Inter-Allied Declaration on Punishment for War Crimes, which dealt mostly with the European war, stated that the Japanese military and government would be held accountable after the war. Further warnings of the consequences of illegal warfare were given over the next three years, culminating in the Potsdam Declaration of 26 July 1945, which delineated the policy for the trial and punishment of alleged war criminals in Europe and the Far East. By this time, the United Nations War Crimes Commission was already in operation, as was its subcommission in Chungking, China, so prosecutions could begin within months of the end of the war in the Pacific. Accordingly, on 19 January 1946, the International Military Tribunal for the Far East (IMTFE) was established, and the Tokyo War Crimes Trials, as the IMTFE came to be known, began on 29 April 1946. On that day, 28 Japanese defendants were formally indicted on 55 counts, in three categories: crimes against peace (counts 1 to 36); murder (counts 37 to 52); and other conventional war crimes and crimes against humanity (counts 53 to 55).

With respect to the crimes committed against POWs and civilians, the prosecution held that they were so widespread and frequent that the defendants must have, or should have, known of them and so were legally culpable. To support their case, counsel made much of the fact that four percent of British and American POWs had died in German hands, while 27 percent had died in Japanese hands. Furthermore, the deaths of POWs and civilians constituted murder because they occurred in a war that was both aggressive and illegal. The defense countered that the crimes were in fact sporadic; had the ill-treatment of prisoners been a general policy, it would have been consistently applied. The judges accepted the prosecution's case and all 25 defendants (two of the original group had died during the proceedings, and another had been declared mentally unfit to stand trial) were found guilty and received sentences ranging from death to seven years in prison.

The Tokyo trials involved only the architects of the war, the so-called Class A defendants. Class B defendants, who were accused of personally committing war crimes, and Class C defendants, accused of ordering war crimes or failing to stop them, were prosecuted in dozens of other smaller trials held in Yokohama, Singapore, Rabaul, Batavia (Djakarta), Manila, and elsewhere. The Yokohama trials, the largest single group of trials, were divided into seven categories: POW command responsibility trials, POW camp trials, trials for ceremonial murders, trials for atrocities committed against downed airmen, cases involving the denial of a fair trial, trials for acts of revenge, and trials for medical experiments on POWs. The defendants ranged from senior commanders like Tomoyuki Yamashita and Masaharu Homma (executed for war crimes in the Philippines, including the Bataan Death March) to camp administrators and interpreters. At least two Japanese who were born in North America were accused of committing crimes against POWs and were eventually executed for treason.

The IMTFE was slightly different from the Nuremberg Trials of the major Nazi leaders in that it claimed legitimation from the recognized body of international law rather than the Potsdam Declaration. In total, the war crimes trials in the Far East handed down 920 death sentences and some 3,000 prison terms.

See also Bataan Death March; Nuremberg Trials; Nanking Massacre

References
Arnold C. Brackman, *The Other Nuremberg: The Untold Story of the Tokyo War Crimes Trials* (New York: Morrow, 1987).
Richard H. Minear, *Victor's Justice: The Tokyo War Crimes Trials* (Princeton, NJ: Princeton University Press, 1971).
Philip R. Piccigallo, *The Japanese on Trial: Allied War Crimes Operations in the East, 1945–1951* (Austin: University of Texas Press, 1979).
John R. Pritchard and Sonia Zaide, eds., *The Tokyo War Crimes Trials* (New York: Garland, 1981).

—*Jonathan F. Vance*

TORTURE

Prisoners of war and civilian captives have been the victims of torture for millennia. In some societies, such as certain North and South American aboriginal communities, the torture of prisoners had a ritual meaning; it was part of the process of celebrating victory over an enemy, demonstrating one's superiority as a warrior, or propitiating the gods who made the victory possible. It might also be used as punishment; the Japanese during the Second World War, for example, had a range of tortures that they were willing to inflict on prisoners who attempted to escape or committed other infractions. More frequently, torture has been a means to extract information from a prisoner, and captors have devised a terrifying variety of ways to cause unimaginable pain to convince prisoners to reveal sensitive information. This has been effective in some instances, but on other occasions the torture has been so severe that the prisoner died before revealing any information of value. Furthermore, there are countless cases in which torture has simply stiffened the prisoner's resolve to resist; indeed, captured members of resistance movements during World War II were known to commit suicide rather than reveal information to their Nazi captors under torture. Finally, it must be admitted that many instances of torture have occurred simply because of the sadistic impulses of guards; sadly, as some U.S. POWs in Vietnam discovered, one cannot underestimate the tendency of certain people to gain pleasure from inflicting pain on their fellow human beings.

The practice of torture has been condemned by jurists for as long as there has been international law covering the conduct of warfare, and various nations have been assiduous in tracking down and trying individuals accused of torture. Many of the war crimes trials that followed World War II, for example, related to the torture of military or civilian prisoners. Furthermore, in 1975 the World Medical Association adopted the Declaration of Tokyo, by which physicians pledged not to "countenance, condone or participate in the practice of torture or other forms of cruel, inhuman or degrading procedures." In the view of many observers, this was a belated recognition that doctors, either in Nazi concentration camps or in Japanese-occupied Manchuria during World War II, had performed unspeakable experiments in the name of science, experiments that were in fact nothing more than torture.

The debate over torture, however, returned to the headlines in the aftermath of the Iraq War, with the revelation that detainees at the Abu Ghraib Detention Facility in Baghdad had been subject to violent and degrading treatment that could be interpreted as torture. Despite the fact that the United States had ratified the 1994 Convention Against Torture and Other Cruel, Inhuman or Degrading Treatment or Punishment and the military was prohibited from such practices by the Uniform Code of Military Justice, the waters had been muddied by the insistence of the White House after the 9/11 attacks that the 1994 Convention did not apply to foreign nationals being held abroad by U.S. forces. This, coupled with the fact that military units charged with guarding detainees received unclear and conflicting directives as to how detainees should be treated, meant that prisoner abuse was widespread in U.S.-run detention facilities in Iraq, Afghanistan, and Cuba. A number of officers and other ranks have been charged with and tried for committing offenses against prisoners, but many claim that they are being singled out for prosecution for public relations reasons; the real problems, they maintain, were due to inadequate training of military prison guards, unclear or conflicting orders, inadequate supervision from superiors, and the presence of civilian contractors (in most cases CIA operatives) in the prisons, who seemed to be outside of any military command structure.

The focus for a change in policy was Arizona Senator John McCain, who proposed an amendment to the 2006 military appropriations bill that would prohibit the cruel, inhumane, and degrading treatment of individuals held by U.S. authorities anywhere in the world. McCain's amendment was motivated by a number of factors. He was aware that the images of prisoners being subjected to degrading treatment at Abu Ghraib had done incalculable damage to the international image of the United States, damage far greater than the value of the information that might have been gained by the practices. He also realized that permitting torture would essentially declare open season on American nationals who might be captured in future conflicts; if it was acceptable for U.S. officials to abuse prisoners to gain information, then logically it was acceptable for others to abuse American prisoners to the same end. Furthermore, as probably the only person involved in the debate who had actually undergone torture at the hands of the enemy (McCain was a POW in Vietnam for over five years), McCain knew that information secured under duress was often of little value, because the prisoner would say anything to convince his captors to stop the brutalizing. McCain himself recalled one instance when his Vietnamese interrogators were determined to discover the names of members of his squadron; realizing that telling them something would end the torture, if only temporarily, he gave them the names of the offensive linemen of the Green Bay Packers football team. That similar things occurred in the War on Terror seems indisputable. Ibn Al-Shaykhal-Libi, a top Al Qaeda official, revealed under rigorous questioning (observers have assumed that the interrogation was accompanied by practices that might be considered torture) by Egyptian authorities that Al Qaeda terrorists had traveled to Iraq to learn about chemical and biological weapons. He later admitted that the confession was false, and that it had been given under duress. Subsequent events proved that there were no chemical and biological weapons in Iraq at the time that Al-Shaykhal-Libi claimed to have been there to study them. This case seemed to bear out the warning that is written into the U.S. Army Field Manual on Intelligence Interrogation, which states that "the use of force is a poor technique, for it yields unreliable results."

The McCain amendment, however, was strongly opposed by the White House, and particularly by Vice President Dick Cheney, who insisted that interrogators needed every tool available to extract information from terror suspects, and felt that the amendment could make the U.S. government vulnerable to lawsuits filed by detainees. Cheney had already clashed with Matthew Waxman, appointed as the Pentagon's chief advisor on detainee issues, because of Waxman's insistence on drawing up new standards of conduct that would prohibit cruel, humiliating, or degrading treatment; the *New York Times* saw little coincidence in the fact that Waxman resigned in December 2005, at the height of the debate over McCain's amendment. The Bush Administration threatened to veto any legislation that contained the amendment, but when McCain drew support from 90 senators, including 46 from President Bush's own party, former Secretary of State Colin Powell, and the U.S. Conference of

Catholic Bishops, the White House softened its stand, insisting only on exemption for operatives of the Central Intelligence Agency and for any interrogations that occurred abroad.

In the view of McCain's supporters, this made the amendment meaningless; it would not allow the United States to regain the moral high ground on the issue, and would still give interrogators *carte blanche* in dealing with suspected terrorists. Under the proposed revisions, abuses such as those committed at Abu Ghraib would still be deemed acceptable.

But in December 2005, President Bush, in the face of mounting pressure domestically and internationally, withdrew his objection to McCain's amendment. The about-face was widely regarded as a setback for both Bush and Cheney, but supporters insisted that it would do much to repair the damaged image of the U.S. in the world. For McCain, who had said that the amendment would win "the hearts and minds" of doubters in the war against terror and that it would convince them that the United States was not like the terrorists, it was a personal, political, and moral victory.

References

Thomas S. Abler, "Scalping, Torture, Cannibalism and Rape: An Ethnohistorical Analysis of Conflicting Cultural Values in War," *Anthropologica* 34 (1992): 3–20.

Mark Danner, *Torture and Truth: America, Abu Ghraib, and the War on Terror* (New York: New York Review Books, 2004).

Karen J. Greenberg, ed., *The Torture Debate in America* (Cambridge: Cambridge University Press, 2005).

Karen J. Greenberg and Joshua L. Dratel, eds., *The Torture Papers: The Road to Abu Ghraib* (Cambridge: Cambridge University Press, 2005).

Sanford Levinson, ed., *Torture: A Collection* (New York: Oxford University Press, 2004).

Rod Morgan and Malcolm Evans, eds., *Protecting Prisoners: The Standards of the European Committee for the Prevention of Torture in Context* (Oxford: Oxford University Press, 1999).

—*Jonathan F. Vance*

TOWER OF LONDON

Despite the Tower of London's long and bloody history, in the beginning, the simple garrison was just one of many keeps erected during the eleventh century to protect a fledgling Norman monarchy. Construction on what was then known as the "White Tower" began in 1078 and work to expand the stronghold continued for centuries. The structure was William the Conqueror's chief defense in London and, although it was a relatively modest fortress in its original form, the White Tower remained the centerpiece of the larger palatial complex. Although the Tower has served many functions, its role as a national garrison and prison defined its place in British history.

The first prisoner incarcerated in the Tower of London was Ranulf Flambard, Bishop of Durham. Flambard, Justiciar of William II, was despised by the public who suffered under the economic strain of early Norman fiscal policies. The hatred ran so deep that, upon the death of William II, Flambard was hastily sent to the Tower. Ironically, Flambard was also the first to escape his captivity, which tells us something of life within the Tower. As both a prominent and wealthy state prisoner, Flambard secured for himself a position of relative comfort as a detainee. Surrounded by his own servants and indulging in many extravagances, Flambard created an opulent atmosphere within the Tower. It was his ability to purchase these luxuries that led to his easy escape. Indeed, on the night of his escape in 1101 Flambard held a banquet for his guards, and once they were suitably intoxicated he slipped out the window to freedom. Although this tale is somewhat atypical, it nonetheless illustrated that fortune and privilege promised a reasonably decent lifestyle within the Tower.

Flambard was a political prisoner, but his experience as an inmate was also common among prisoners of war. Unlike the state criminals housed in the Tower, prisoners of war who had not been convicted of any specific offense were held there until their

"The prison room in the Beauchamp Tower, part of the Tower of London" (from William Hepworth Dixon, Her Majesty's Tower, vol. 1 [London: Cassell, 1900]

ransoms could be paid or pardon was granted. In the late thirteenth century, as the Scottish waged war with the British for their independence, King John Baliol was captured and held in the Tower for three years, his healthy living allowance paid for by King Edward I. Unfortunately, not all were so lucky. The famous William Wallace, Scottish patriot, was arrested in 1305 and, unlike Baliol, was tried at Westminster Hall and condemned. His stay in the Tower, therefore, was short and ended with a brutal public execution. Thus, an important distinction was made between prisoners of war who were deemed honorable and worthy, and those ignoble captives who too seriously threatened the English monarchy.

Although Wallace was certainly not the only prisoner of war to suffer a terrible death at the hands of the English, his story illustrates that the nature of captivity depended, in large part, on external factors. Political context, social stature, and personal affluence would determine life in the Tower for many POWs. This was particularly true in the late fourteenth and early fifteenth centuries as war with France and Scotland brought many stately captives, carrying large ransoms, to the royal prison. The most celebrated of these was King John II, who was captured at Poitiers by the Black Prince. Entering the city on a white horse surrounded by his court, the King's procession was much celebrated for the money it would bring the British crown. Held captive for several years, the king was released when the ransom was delivered. Although prisoners of war could be held for very long periods of time while waiting for their dues to be paid, it is also important to note that honored captives were often permitted to leave their royal apartments in the Tower and participate in activities outside the complex. King James I of Scotland, for example, was captured at the age of 12 and lived for 17 years in the hands of the English. Here he was cared for and educated by the crown, and became an active writer and poet. However, only part of his time was spent in the Tower and, in the fifteenth century, he even followed King Henry V on one of his campaigns in France. Certainly, such long stays away from their homelands could produce a great deal of sorrow and yearning, but for many prisoners of war the struggles of captivity were eased by a relatively tolerable environment within the Tower.

Despite the often comfortable surroundings permitted prisoners of war, the Tower also appeared quite menacing at times, particularly under Tudor authority in the fifteenth and sixteenth centuries. With the introduction, and popularization, of various devices of torture, among them the rack, the Tower entered what was an exceptionally bloody era. In particular, it was King Henry VIII who sent many individuals, both innocent and guilty, to the Tower, never to be seen alive again. The most famous of these was Anne Boleyn, whose inability to bear Henry a male heir significantly shortened her life. It was this "dark age" that provided fodder for the stories that have made the Tower a national legend.

Periods of political strife—both civil and international—would determine the role of the Tower for three more centuries until, in the 1800s, it began the transformation from a prison to a monument. This restorative work continued into the twentieth century and the Tower slowly emerged as a national icon. It was during this period that the Tower housed its last prisoner. In 1941 Rudolf Hess, a leading member of the Nazi Party, landed in Scotland with the ultimate goal of negotiating a lasting peace. Unwilling to accept the demands, however, British officials labeled Hess a prisoner of war, and he was detained until his trial at Nuremberg in 1945. Though only part of this time was spent in the Tower, Hess was a notable prisoner and his stay in England was reasonably comfortable. Since holding this final prisoner, the Tower has settled into its role as a museum. A popular tourist attraction today, the Tower of London is renowned for its sordid past as a setting for national intrigue. Indeed, rumors of ancient ghosts continue to draw visitors looking for gruesome tales of torture and painful death.

See also Hess, Rudolf; Jean II of France

References

Russell Chamberlin, *The Tower of London: An Illustrated History* (Exeter, UK: Webb & Bower, 1989).

William Hepworth Dixon, *Her Majesty's Tower* (Philadelphia: J. B. Lippincott, 1896).

Derek Wilson, *The Tower: 1078–1978* (London: Hamish Hamilton, 1978).

—Liam van Beek

Townshend, Sir Charles Vere Ferrers (1861–1924)

Sir Charles Townshend was a much decorated British general whose surrender of the large garrison at Kut during World War I overshadowed his earlier accomplishments. Born in Southwark on 29 February 1861, Townshend embarked upon a military life and proved his ability as a commander in a number of imperial expeditions undertaken during the late Victorian era. When World War I broke out, Townshend was with the Indian Army, and in April 1915 he was given command of a division in Mesopotamia. He scored a number of impressive victories against the Turkish army, but in December 1915 he found his division trapped in Kut-al-Amara, near the Tigris River in present-day Iraq. The expected relief column never came, and on 29 April 1916, Townshend surrendered the garrison, which was then over 13,000 strong. His troops suffered terribly in captivity (nearly 5,000 died in Turkish hands), but Townshend was well treated during his internment on Prinkipo Island (Büyükada) off Constantinople; indeed, he lived in conditions that can only be described as luxurious. In October 1918, the Turks released him on the understanding that he would plead their case for favorable armistice terms to his political masters.

The British government established a commission to investigate the Mesopotamia disaster, and it exonerated Townshend of wrongdoing; indeed, many contemporary observers praised his conduct of operations. However, his conduct in captivity, particularly his apparent lack of concern for the welfare of his soldiers in Turkish prison camps, severely damaged his reputation and cost him any chance of advancement in the army after World War I. Townshend retired from the military and took up politics, but with only limited success. He died in Paris on 18 May 1924.

See also World War I—Middle East

References

A.J. Barker, *Townshend of Kut* (London: Cassel, 1967).

Paul K. Davis, *Ends and Means: The British Mesopotamian Campaign and Commission* (Rutherford, NJ: Fairleigh Dickinson University Press, 1994).

C.V.F. Townshend, *My Campaign in Mesopotamia* (London: Thornton Butterworth, 1920).

—*Tanya Demjanenko*

Transit Camps

In the Nazi concentration camp system during World War II, there existed a type of facility known alternately as *Sammellager* (assembly camp) or *Durchgangslager* (transit camp). Usually on German-occupied territory, these camps served as central points of collection of Jews before their shipment to death camps. The length of internment in these camps varied, however; many detainees remained there for months, while others were promptly tortured and killed. Furthermore, the exact number of these camps is difficult to determine, as some installations served as transit camps for a brief time period before becoming another type of camp. Bergen-Belsen, in Germany, for example, ended up doubling as concentration and transit camp when shipments of Jews to the east stopped and prisoners were brought back to Germany. Some camps, like Nexon and Vénissieux in central and eastern France, were specifically defined as assembly camps by the Vichy authorities and housed both Jews and non-Jews. Among the most notorious installations for Jews, however, were Berg in Norway, Drancy in France, Malines in Belgium, Fossoli di Carpi in Italy, Westerbork in the Netherlands, and Zabikow, near Poznan in Poland. The typology of transit camps is ill-defined, except for the fact that they were usually located near a railroad and originally managed by local authorities before the Nazis took over. Beyond this, each camp activity, size, and length of function varied.

In the isolated area of Westerbork, in the Netherlands, for example, the camp began its existence under Dutch control in 1939 and served to house Jewish refugees from Germany, who built the facility, a collection of 200 cottages and barracks to house up to 3,000 people. The Dutch Jewish community, led by a council, paid for maintenance and supplies for those housed there and continued to do so after the SS took over the installation in July 1942. There followed an awkward division of responsibility, along the lines of the Kapo system in other Nazi camps, whereby German Jews managed the installation and processed Dutch Jews onto Auschwitz-bound trains (the first left 15 July 1942), in exchange for staving off their own fate. Led by Albert Konrad Gemmeker, commandant from October 1942, the camp became the site where some 80,000 Jews were processed onto death trains until the fall of 1944, when transports to death camps ended. During that time, Jews also served in nearby work camps. When Canadian troops liberated the camp on 12 April 1945, there were still 900 Jews living there.

In Drancy, north of Paris, the French interned Austrian and German citizens as of September 1939, but between the fall of France in June 1940 and the summer of 1941, French POWs were processed by Nazi authorities for shipment to German prison camps. On 20 August 1941, Drancy became a transit camp for Jews following the arrest by Paris police of some 3,500 Jews. Until July 1942, Drancy counted only male Jews in its ranks, then began to house women, children, and elderly detainees. Although French officials administered the camp, leadership belonged to a German officer. The Germans assumed complete control in the summer of 1943, with French prisoners carrying out duties previously assigned to French bureaucrats. The first trains to Auschwitz left the Bourget-Drancy train station in the spring of 1942 and continued to run until two weeks before the camp's liberation, on 17 August 1944. Some 65,000 Jews died as a result.

See also Concentration Camps; Extermination Camps

References
Jacob Boas, *Boulevard des Misères: The Story of Transit Camp Westerbork* (Hamden, CT: Archon Books, 1985).
M. Felstiner, "Commandant of Drancy: Alois Brunner and the Jews of France," *Holocaust and Genocide Studies* 2 (1987): 21–47.
Anne Grynberg, *Les camps de la honté: Les internés juifs des camps français, 1939–1944* (Paris: La Découverte, 1991).
Alfred Konieczny, "The Transit Camp for Breslau Jews at Riebnig in Lower Silesia (1941–1943)," *Yad Vashem Studies* 25 (1996): 317–342.

—*Guillaume de Syon*

TRANSPORTATION BY SEA

Prisoners of war and internees who are transported by sea have faced two different hazards: the conditions on the ships themselves, and the possibility of being sunk, often by their own forces. Both of these risks were apparent during World War II.

When the Japanese government realized that it needed POWs on the home islands to serve as slave laborers, it began shipping them from Singapore, Hong Kong, Java, and the Philippines to ports in Japan. Almost invariably, these voyages involved weeks of misery aboard rusting and decrepit freighters. In August 1942, British Lieutenant Douglas Allison left Changi Prison in Singapore to join a draft of 1,400 POWs being shipped to Japan. Their transport was a small steamer, the *Fukkai Maru*, which had four small holds into which the prisoners were packed. Those who would not fit below were forced to find space on the deck, which they shared with four flimsy wooden shacks that the Japanese had erected to use as lavatories. Before the ship sailed, however, the Japanese decided to remove about 400 prisoners to sail on another ship; this cleared the decks but did nothing to ease the crowding in the holds. Wooden platforms had been erected on all sides of the holds, so most of the POWs had to spend their days in a crouching position either on top of or beneath the platform. Allison's space in the hold measured 15 feet long, 11 feet wide, and 3.5 feet high, a space he shared with 14 other prisoners, rats, lice, and human excreta. They were allowed out for roughly 90 minutes each day, but they spent the rest of the voyage crammed into the holds. On some sunny days, the deck got so hot that it could not be walked upon; temperatures in the holds were well in excess of 100 degrees Fahrenheit. In these hellish conditions, Allison and his fellow prisoners existed from 19 August to 24 September 1942.

Allison's experiences were entirely typical of those endured by thousands of other prisoners who were transported on Japanese "death ships" or "hell ships." Already weakened by long periods on short rations, malnourished and sick prisoners were packed tightly into aged transports and given little in the way of food or water. Sanitation facilities were often nonexistent, so within days the holds would be fouled with excreta from dysentery-plagued POWs. Disease spread quickly, and many prisoners died. The fortunate ones received a hasty burial at sea; the bodies of others were simply left in the holds to be cleared out after the living were disembarked.

The hell ships were also vulnerable to another hazard, attack from enemy submarines or surface vessels, a hazard that eventually claimed more lives than the hell ships themselves. The first such tragedy occurred in July 1940, when the British steamer *Arandora Star* was torpedoed by the German submarine U-47 and sank, claiming the lives of hundreds of German and Italian civilian internees who had been bound for Canada. In light of this, the International Committee of the Red Cross (ICRC) pushed belligerent governments to come to an arrangement that would prevent such sinkings, either by following prearranged routes or by providing sailing schedules for such ships, but when no agreement was reached, the matter was allowed to lapse. Then, on 8 August 1942, the Italian ship *Nino Bixio* was sunk on its way from Benghazi to Italy with a load of Australian POWs; 37 died. In September 1942, the German submarine U-156 torpedoed the British liner *Laconia*, with its cargo of 1,800 prisoners. This was followed by the sinking of the *Lisbon Maru*, with 1,000 British POWs on board, in the China Sea in October 1942, and of the *Nova Scotia*, with 645 Italian internees, off Mozambique on 29 November 1942. Another ship carrying civilian internees to Japan, the *Montevideo Maru*, was torpedoed by an American submarine. The ICRC continued to attempt to conclude an agreement that would prevent such occurrences, and in May 1943, the Italian government proposed that all sides give advance notice of the sailing of POW ships, so that naval units could avoid them. This proposal, like all others, was rejected by the Allies on the grounds that it might yield some strategic advantage to the Axis powers, who, it was suspected, could not be trusted.

Sadly, the sinkings only increased in frequency after this failure. On 7 September 1943, the *Shinyo Maru* was sunk by the American submarine *Paddle* west of Mindanao, killing over 600 American prisoners. On 24 October, the *Arisan Maru* was torpedoed east of Hong Kong, probably by the USS *Snook*, and sank with hundreds more American POWs. On 12 September 1944, the *Kachidoki Maru* (which, ironically, was constructed in New Jersey and began life as an American passenger liner called the *Wolverine State*) and the *Rokyu Maru*, together carrying over 2,200 British and Australian prisoners who had survived the horrors of the Death Railway, were attacked and sunk by American submarines off Hainan. Fewer than half of the prisoners survived. On 21 September 1944, the *Hofoku Maru*, carrying a load of Allied POWs, was sunk by American aircraft off Manila. All told, it is estimated that 15,000 POWs and civilian internees died when their transports were lost due to enemy action during World War II.

See also Altmark Incident

References

Douglas Allison, "The Voyage of the *Fukkai Maru*," *Blackwood's* 259 (1946): 135–143.

Joan Beaumont, "Victims of War: The Allies and the Transport of Prisoners-of-War by Sea, 1939–45," *Journal of the Australian War Memorial* 2 (1983): 1–7.

Joan and Clay Blair, Jr., *Return from the River Kwai* (New York: Simon and Schuster, 1979).

Spence Edge and Jim Henderson, *No Honour, No Glory* (Auckland: Collins, 1983).

Gregory F. Michno, *Death on the Hellships: Prisoners at Sea in the Pacific War* (Annapolis, MD: Naval Institute Press, 2001).

Bob Moore, "The Last Phase of the Gentleman's War: British Handling of German Prisoners of War on Board HMT *Pasteur*, March 1942," *War and Society* 17 (1999): 41–55.

Judith L. Pearson, *Belly of the Beast: A POW's Inspiring True Story of Faith, Courage, and Survival Aboard the Infamous WWII Japanese Hell Ship "Oryoku Maru"* (New York: New American Library, 2001).

—*Jonathan F. Vance*

TREATY OF AMITY AND COMMERCE (1785)

The United States attempted to regulate the treatment of prisoners of war from its earliest experiences as a nation. During the American Revolution (1775–1783), the political problem was sovereignty, and this problem had implications for the status of prisoners of war. Because the British frequently considered captives as rebels or traitors rather than as legitimate POWs, their treatment was often harsh. As a result, more Americans died in British captivity than on the battlefield. In 1783, Benjamin Franklin, Thomas Jefferson, and John Adams formed an American delegation to devise a treaty between the United States and Frederick the Great of Prussia. Feeling aggrieved by the losses suffered in the British prison hulks, the new American government sought to eliminate even the slightest possibility of such things happening again and addressed the issue squarely for the first time in Article 24 of this treaty: "to prevent the destruction of prisoners of war by crowding them into close and noxious places, the two parties solemnly pledge themselves to each other and to the world that they will not adopt any such practice." Ratified in 1785 by the Prussians and the Congress of the United States, the Treaty of Amity, replete with benevolence, was lauded by statesmen like George Washington and others as the most progressive international agreement of its age, and it marked a new era in negotiations between sovereign nations. Its intention was to lessen the horrors of bloodshed and relieve the distress of enemies in the event of war. However, no war took place between the two signatory countries until the outbreak of hostilities in 1917, so the Treaty of Amity and Commerce was never put to the test. It was later superseded by the Hague Conventions of 1899 and 1907.

References

Karl J. R. Arndt, *The Treaty of Amity and Commerce of 1785 between His Majesty the King of Prussia and the United States of America* (Munich: Heinz Moos, 1977).

—*Robert C. Doyle*

U

Uganda–Tanzania War (1978–1979)

The short war between Uganda and Tanzania is a rarity in postcolonial conflicts in Africa, in that the abuse of prisoners was neither widespread nor unanimously condoned. There certainly were incidences of violence and ill treatment, but there were also instances of tolerance toward prisoners that are unusual in such wars.

In September 1978, the brutal dictator of Uganda, Idi Amin, sent his army into neighboring Tanzania. It was an ill-advised and in some ways inexplicable move; it may be that the increasingly unpopular Amin, who for years had relied on the arrest, execution, and torture of opponents to secure his control of the country, was trying to prevent his army from rising up against him by sending it outside the country to fight. The Ugandan army slaughtered some 1,500 Tanzanian civilians in Kagera province; several hundred more, mostly women, were taken prisoner and sent to a forced-labor camp at Kalisizo in southern Uganda.

The Tanzanian army, though small and unprepared, quickly expanded and pushed Amin's forces out of Kagera. Then, determined to rid its neighbor of the troublesome dictator, it moved into Uganda on a war of liberation. Augmented by anti-Amin Ugandan soldiers, the Tanzanian army showed remarkable skill in the campaign, given its poor state of readiness when the war began. It reached the Ugandan capital of Kampala in April 1979 and installed a new government to replace Amin. It also showed remarkable restraint in dealing with prisoners. Ugandan soldiers were often given the opportunity to join the fight against their former leader, and after the fall of Kampala, there was a week-long amnesty to allow Amin's men to surrender without penalty. After that amnesty expired, however, there was rather less tolerance. Tanzanian units were unpredictable; they would either execute or release POWs from Amin's army as the spirit moved them. But anti-Amin Ugandan troops usually murdered any of Amin's former soldiers they captured. The former dictator having escaped to Saudi Arabia, his soldiers were the only symbols of the old regime upon which Ugandans could take revenge.

The Tanzanian army also encountered a considerable number of Libyans, sent by Mohamar Gaddafi to prop up his old friend and fellow dictator. They were not regular army troops, but rather poorly trained militiamen who had been led to believe that they were going to Uganda for further training exercises; others were not even Libyan citizens, but had merely gone to Uganda from Libya to look for work. In the early battles, Tanzanian soldiers were not inclined to take the Libyans prisoner, because their political education instructors had drilled it into them that the Libyans were the advance guard of a larger Arab force that was going to reintroduce slavery to Tanzania. In one engagement, for example, some 200 Libyan soldiers were killed and only one captured.

Soon, however, the Tanzanian army began to take a more lenient attitude toward the Libyans, after it became clear that the latter were in Uganda very reluctantly. After the capture of Entebbe in April 1979, Tanzania found itself with 59 able-bodied Libyan prisoners (wounded Libyan POWs had been immediately returned to their homeland). Ten who were not Libyan citizens were freed after three months, while the rest were released after nine months of captivity in Tanzania. Despite Gaddafi's claims that Tanzania had demanded a ransom, the prisoners were returned to Libya without condition. It is unlikely that Gaddafi would have paid a ransom in any case, because he appeared to have little interest in the fate of his soldiers who fell into enemy hands, but more importantly, Tanzanian president Julius Nyerere made it very clear that he was not in the business of selling prisoners. "Libya will get all her prisoners back. We will not sell them. We will never trade human lives for money," he declared.

References
Tony Avirgan and Martha Honey, *War in Uganda: The Legacy of Idi Amin* (Westport, CT: Lawrence Hill & Co., 1982).
Wycliffe Kato, *Escape from Idi Amin's Slaughterhouse* (New York: Quartet Books, 1989).

—*Jonathan F. Vance*

UNITED STATES CIVIL WAR (1861–1865)

The war between the Union and the Confederacy, which lasted from 1861 to 1865, produced some of the most notorious instances of the abuse of prisoners of war in American history. From the outbreak of war in 1861 until the middle of 1863, the problems presented by POWs proved manageable for both the Union and the Confederacy. Many prisoners were exchanged immediately after capture or paroled within hours or days. Those subjected to longer terms of imprisonment—over weeks or months—were generally housed in such buildings as warehouses or civilian jails. It was not until 22 July 1862 that the Dix-Hill cartel regulating exchanges on a nationwide basis was concluded. Union authorities were reluctant to deal directly with their Confederate counterparts for fear of seeming to recognize the Confederacy as a legitimate government, and therefore the cartel was explicitly between armies; the Confederate Robert Ould and Union Major General Benjamin Franklin Butler were the most active agents under the cartel.

The cartel broke down in mid-1863 because of issues of race, specifically the growing Union emphasis on emancipation of slaves as a necessary war aim to destroy Southern resistance, and the resulting Confederate reaction. The Emancipation Proclamation and the Union decision to raise black regiments angered Confederates and raised fears of insurrection. The Confederates announced a policy of summarily executing white officers leading black troops and turning captured black soldiers over to state authorities to be dealt with as rebellious slaves, even if the soldier had been free before the war. Union authorities insisted that all their soldiers be treated alike when captive (although for much of the war, black Union soldiers were paid less than their white comrades). It is difficult to generalize about the fates of blacks taken prisoner by Confederate troops; some ended up as part of the general population in prison camps, others undoubtedly were executed upon or before capture. However, it is clear that at a series of battles—such as Fort Pillow, Tennessee; Poison Spring, Arkansas; Saltville, Virginia; and the Crater in Virginia—black soldiers died in numbers and under circumstances that suggest that they feared dire consequences if captured, more so than white troops might face.

The suspension of the cartel was particularly ill-timed. Tens of thousands of soldiers were taken prisoner in 1863 and 1864, overwhelming the small scale and makeshift arrangements of both sides, especially the Confederacy. The Union, under the leadership of Colonel William Hoffman, commissary of prisoners, opened or expanded large camps in Elmira, New York, Columbus (Camp Chase), Indianapolis (Camp Morton), Chicago (Camp Douglas), Point Lookout, Maryland, and elsewhere; Johnson's Island, in Lake Erie off Sandusky, Ohio, was reserved for officers. The Confederacy, under the leadership of John H. Winder, opened or

The view from the main gate of the prison camp at Andersonville, Georgia, during the Civil War (from Augustus C. Handin, Martyria; or, Andersonville Prison *[Boston, 1866])*

expanded facilities at Richmond's Libby Prison and on Belle Isle, outside Richmond; at Salisbury, North Carolina; Macon, Georgia; most notoriously at Andersonville, Georgia; and elsewhere. Conditions were barely acceptable at best, with Southern prison camps for Union soldiers being particularly ill-planned, ill-run, and ill-supplied, and guarded by castoff troops.

An April 1864 exchange of the sickest prisoners led to widespread outrage in the North, as the "living skeletons" returned by the Confederates confirmed fears that Union troops were suffering terribly. Engravings of the most emaciated returnees filled the Northern press, and the Joint Congressional Committee on the Conduct of the War and the semiofficial Sanitary Commission were among those who seized the opportunity to accuse the Confederacy of deliberately starving Union troops. In May 1864, Union Secretary of War Edwin Stanton cut the rations of Confederates held prisoner in retaliation. Many in the North thought that easing the plight of prisoners and punishing those responsible should be an additional aim of the Union war. George F. Root's 1864 hit song, "Tramp! Tramp! Tramp! The Boys Are Marching," was reflective of the unforgiving and hyper-patriotic mood of most people in the North as they imagined what was happening to POWs. Others in the North blamed president Abraham Lincoln and his advisers for allowing almost all exchanges to stop over the issue of the treatment of black troops (Lincoln's fear that this issue might adversely affect his reelection in 1864 was unfounded). On the other hand, white Southern commentators have argued, on slender evidence, that General U. S. Grant, military commander of all Union troops from late 1863, urged that exchanges remain suspended to aggravate severe manpower problems in the South.

In January 1865, the Confederates, in serious military difficulty and perhaps looking to the desperate measure of recruiting large numbers of blacks into their own forces, agreed to rapid exchange of all prisoners, including black Union soldiers. After the major surrenders of April 1865, Confederate soldiers, rather than being taken into captivity, were allowed to return home on parole, and the remaining military prisoners on both sides were released. With the return of prisoners, demands that the perpetrators of abuses against POWs be brought to justice grew louder. Henry Wirz, a Swiss-born Confederate captain who had commanded the stockade at Andersonville, was hanged in November 1865 after trial by a Union military commission. Wirz seems to have been guilty mostly of inefficiency and lassitude in dealing with insurmountable logistical and supply problems, as well as being a foreign-born martinet.

Through the half-century after 1865, Northern commentators, particularly surviving POWs, continued to write vicious critiques, attacking the Confederates for their treatment of wartime prisoners. Confederate partisans were slower to organize a counterattack because of the greater disruption of life in the South and the facts of Union victory. Over two-thirds of the more than 400 narratives by or about former prisoners were from Yankees. Many of these narratives were formulaic, drawing upon the literary tradition of American captivity narratives, and some were exaggerated. Prison camps thus provided a contentious issue among whites as they remembered the war after 1865.

Of the 195,000 Union soldiers who lost their lives during the war, about 30,000 (or over 15 percent) died while prisoners; roughly 26,000 (or about 12 percent) of the 215,000 fatal Confederate casualties died in captivity. In total, almost nine percent of the 630,000 men who died during the U.S. Civil War perished in prison camps.

See also Andersonville; Elmira; Libby Prison; Lieber Code

—Douglas G. Gardner

V

Van der Post, Sir Laurens (1906–1996)

For three and a half years, British writer Laurens van der Post endured the world of Japanese POW camps in Java, and forever after his experience there played a substantial role in his writings. Born of a distinguished Boer family in the Orange River Colony in southern Africa on 13 December 1906, van der Post opposed racial discrimination, a stance that led to his emigration from the Union of South Africa and to a widely varied career as anthropologist, philosopher, novelist, poet, explorer, and soldier. While serving as commanding officer of Britain's 43rd Special Military Mission in Java, he was taken prisoner by the Japanese in 1942. A lieutenant-colonel, van der Post had earlier served in Abyssinia (now Ethiopia), North Africa, and Syria. He had also spent time in Japan in the 1930s and his knowledge of Japanese language and customs served him well during captivity. Although he suffered the usual physical and psychological tortures associated with prison camp life in the Pacific theater, he believed that knowledge of the Japanese mind and the ability to speak their language saved his and his fellow prisoners' lives on several occasions.

Van der Post's first important literary expression of this view is in the novella, *A Bar of Shadow*, published in 1954. In 1963 this novella, with two other short works, was issued as *The Seed and the Sower.* The main characters are John Lawrence and Jacques Celliers, both of whom are patterned after van der Post. They, like the author, are subject to harsh treatment; Celliers is killed, but Lawrence outwits his adversaries by understanding them. In 1983, part of this work was incorporated into a play and then into a successful, surrealistic film, *Merry Christmas, Mr. Lawrence.* In 1970, van der Post published the autobiographical *The Night of the New Moon,* republished in North America as *The Prisoner and the Bomb.* Although the title is meant to emphasize 6 August 1945, when the atomic bomb was dropped on Hiroshima, the book is a vehicle that allows van der Post to probe his own feelings on captivity and the importance of the bomb as a cultural force. Other autobiographical accounts include *About Blady: A Pattern Out of Time, A Memoir* (1991) and *The Admiral's Baby* (1996).

After the war, van der Post refused to take part in war crimes trials in Southeast Asia and Japan, but he did feel that the use of the atomic bomb was justified. He believed that he had irrefutable proof that all prisoners of the Japanese would have been killed or otherwise died if the bomb had not abruptly ended the fighting. He served on Lord Mountbatten's staff in Indonesia and was made commander of the Order of the British Empire in 1947 for his wartime service. He was knighted by Queen Elizabeth II in 1981. Van der Post died on 15 December 1996, by which time he had written 25 works of fiction and nonfiction and had been involved in a variety of other literary and cultural activities. He was a mentor of Prince Charles, godfather of Prince William, and a confidant of British Prime Minister Margaret Thatcher.

See also Merry Christmas, Mr. Lawrence

References

Frederic I. Carpenter, *Laurens van der Post* (New York: Twayne Publishers, 1969).

J.D.F. Jones, *Teller of Many Tales: The Lives of Laurens van der Post* (New York: Carroll and Graf, 2002).

Kenneth A. Robb, "Laurens van der Post," in *Dictionary of Literary Biography*, 204.
———, *British Travel Writers, 1940–1997* (Detroit: Gale, 1999).
Laurens van der Post, *The Night of the New Moon* (London: Hogarth Press, 1970).

—Robert S. La Forte

Vattel, Emmerich De (1714–1767)

Emmerich de Vattel, a Swiss diplomat and legal scholar, made major contributions to the theory of international law through his work *Le droit des gens; ou, Principes de la loi naturelle* (1758) (*The Law of Nations; or, The Principles of Natural Law*), which was in turn heavily influenced by Christian Wolff's *Jus Gentium Methodo Scientifica Pertractum* (1754).

Although Vattel continued the natural law approach that had long dominated thinking in international law, he tended to emphasize the role of the agreement of nations to clear principles of law, established in treaties and in custom alike. Vattel saw men and nations as essentially rational, creating rights and duties out of their striving for self-preservation. He reasoned that belligerents had a duty to spare the lives of those who surrendered, unless they had seriously violated the rules of war. Prisoners should not ordinarily be put to death, but belligerents could execute traitors and deserters and could punish insubordination. Unarmed enemy civilians should not be maltreated or made prisoners, and the ransoming of prisoners was to be encouraged. The conditions of passports, safe-conducts, and paroles were to be scrupulously observed by both sides, and sovereigns must not cause their subjects to violate paroles. Captors had a right to secure prisoners, if necessary, but only for the duration of the war and under humane conditions. The killing of innocent hostages was to be avoided if possible, and if a prisoner died, one hostage held for his safety was to be freed.

Vattel rejected the rationale that was generally used by philosophers to justify slavery, for he denied that, in general, one had the right to kill or to enslave those defeated in just war.

References

Peter Pavel Remec, *The Position of the Individual in International Law According to Grotius and Vattel* (The Hague: Martinus Nijhoff, 1960).
Emmerich de Vattel, *The Law of Nations; or, The Principles of Natural Law Applied to the Conduct and to the Affairs of Nations and of Sovereigns*, trans. Charles G. Fenwick (Washington, DC: Carnegie Institute of Washington, 1916).

—Patrick M. O'Neil

Vichy France

In July 1940, Marshal Philippe Pétain, who became the prime minister of France during the disastrous Battle of France in May-June 1940, destroyed the Third Republic and created a new government, the French State, with its capital located (in theory only temporarily) in the central French spa town of Vichy.

The nearly two million French POWs captured in June were central to the plans of the Vichy government, in part justifying its existence and remaining a constant factor in Franco-German relations. The armistice of 25 June 1940 specified that the French POWs would remain in German hands until a final peace treaty had been signed. However, many of France's new leaders, including Pétain and Pierre Laval, considered the armistice only a step toward reestablishing normal relations between France and Germany. They played a game of anticipating German demands in the hopes of winning favorable concessions, a policy that POW negotiations well illustrate. Under the Geneva Convention, the United States, then neutral, was appointed Protecting Power for the French POWs. But Vichy accepted a German proposal to substitute itself for the United States as protector of its own prisoners. Under a protocol signed in November 1940, Vichy established a mission in Berlin and appointed Georges Scapini as ambassador.

Scapini and others at Vichy believed that by working outside the rules, placing the POWs within the framework of friendlier Franco-German relations, and demonstrating to Germany their mutual interests, they would be able to get the prisoners home. Vichy's rhetoric of cooperation and collaboration and its refusal to confront Germany on violations of the Geneva Convention left many French POWs, held as enemy soldiers and exploited for labor, bewildered and unsure where their duty lay.

While Vichy took credit for all POW liberations (numbering some 500,000), in fact its policies were responsible for liberating about 220,000 POWs before the end of the war. In June 1942, Pierre Laval announced a program called the *Relève*: for every three skilled workers who volunteered to work in Germany, one POW was repatriated. Laval masterminded this policy, hoping to avoid forced labor and encourage a procollaboration attitude by using the POWs as a reward. In February 1943, since the *Relève* failed to produce enough workers, Germany imposed forced labor on France, but the POWs continued to be inducements. Under a policy called Transformation, every compulsory laborer who went to Germany enabled one POW to be "transformed" into a civilian laborer in Germany, working alongside other forced laborers, wearing civilian clothes, and earning real money rather than camp currency.

In addition to its foreign policy of collaboration, Vichy had a domestic program, the National Revolution, that was to restore France to glory through an authoritarian government and a return to a society based on small farms and shops led by a natural elite. Vichy worked to instill in the French population the virtues of sacrifice and hard work. Vichy propaganda made abundant use of the POWs in Germany to illustrate the virtues it hoped to instill in the French public at home-redemption through suffering, hard work, order, hierarchy, and obedience. Vichy propaganda portrayed the prison camps in a positive light, either as an extended summer camp for adults, stressing the musical groups, classes, sports and other activities POWs engaged in, or as a sort of monastic retreat where the POWs lived a harsh and simple but healthy life of contemplation and labor.

All governments that hold POWs can be expected to use them for their own advantage. The Vichy regime stands apart in the extent to which it tried to exploit its own POWs for its own political advantage.

See also Scapini, Georges

References

Jean-Pierre Azéma, *From Munich to the Liberation, 1938–1944*, trans. Janet Lloyd (Cambridge: Cambridge University Press, 1984).

Yves Durand, *La Captivité histoire des prisonniers de guerre français, 1939–1945* (Paris: FNCPG-CATM, 1980).

Sarah Fishman, "Grand Delusions: The Unintended Consequences of Vichy France's Prisoner of War Propaganda," *Journal of Contemporary History* 26 (1991): 229–254.

Robert Paxton, *Vichy France: Old Guard and New Order* (New York: Columbia University Press, 1982).

—*Sarah Fishman*

VIETNAM WAR (1959–1975)

The longest war in the history of the United States, the Vietnam War produced a number of prisoners of war, civilian detainees, and internees. One of the first prisoners taken was Army Special Forces Major James N. Rowe, captured on 29 October 1963. Nick Rowe was one of the very few to escape his captors successfully, regaining his freedom on 31 December 1968. A few months after Rowe's capture, Special Forces Captain Floyd J. Thompson was taken prisoner in South Vietnam in March 1964 and would emerge at the end of the war as the longest held prisoner of war in American history. Some months later Lieutenant Everett Alvarez, the first American pilot to be shot down in raids over North Vietnam, was captured, and he was the first American "guest" at Hoa Lo Prison, known as the Hanoi Hilton. Over the course of the war, several hundred more soldiers, sailors, airmen, and marines were taken into captivity by the communist forces in North and South Vietnam and Laos. At war's end, 587 American prisoners were released.

An aerial view of Hoa Lo Prison, better known as the Hanoi Hilton. (Department of the U.S. Air Force)

The typical American prisoner in the Vietnam War was an air force or navy pilot shot down over North Vietnam, captured by the local populace or militia, transferred to army control, and then quickly transported to a facility in the extensive network of prisons in the city of Hanoi or in the outlying countryside. Such prisoners were interrogated and tortured, and indoctrinated with communist propaganda and a very biased version of Vietnamese history. They withstood extraordinary adversity over a period of many years. On 6 July 1966, 52 of them were paraded down the streets of Hanoi, being kicked and beaten as they went. Although treatment improved somewhat after 1969, beatings and torture continued.

Less typical, but comprising roughly 20 percent of the total POW population, were those men captured inside South Vietnam or Laos; this group included army and Marine Corps infantrymen and Special Forces soldiers captured in the field, a smattering of officers and warrant officers taken captive after their helicopters were shot down, and a few air force and Marine Corps fighter pilots. These prisoners endured indescribable hardship; housed in small bamboo cages in crude jungle camps with their feet often held in wooden stocks, they existed on a starvation diet of nothing but rice and water. Sanitary conditions in these jungle camps were deplorable, disease was rife, medical care was generally unavailable, and many died. Only a handful ever successfully escaped. One primary reason for the poor conditions was that the government of North Vietnam never recognized the Geneva Convention on the treatment of prisoners as applying to American captives. They contended that the war was an undeclared belligerency and that U.S. servicemen were "criminals" and "air pirates." Red Cross visits were never allowed.

Roughly 100 of the more than 120 prisoners captured in South Vietnam and Laos were ultimately moved to the capital of North Vietnam, many along the infamous Ho Chi Minh Trail. This fact raises a perplexing question: if the war in the south was truly a civil war being waged by the people of South Vietnam against their own government (as North Vietnam claimed), how then did so many captured Americans find their way into the hands of the North Vietnamese? The government of North Vietnam never came to grips with this contradiction during the war, so these special prisoners were kept isolated from other Americans in the north, either in separate camps or eventually in a sequestered corner of the Hanoi Hilton known as Las Vegas. Most of these men were also listed as missing in action (MIA) throughout the war, largely because the communists did not want to admit to a total that would reveal how few of the prisoners of war detained in the south had actually survived.

Since the return of American POWs and the end of U.S. involvement in the Vietnam War in 1973, the remains of 502 MIAs have been accounted for in Southeast Asia, but 2,081 are still missing. Three prisoners of war received the Medal of Honor for their actions during captivity. Navy Rear Admiral James B. Stockdale and Air Force Colonel George E. Day were presented their medals by President Gerald Ford on 4 March 1976. Air Force Captain Lance P. Sijan's was given posthumously to his parents; he died in captivity, a model of resistance.

Besides the well-publicized American prisoners of war, there were also thousands of

South Vietnamese and North Vietnamese prisoners as well. The exact numbers will never be known. Many of these prisoners were killed by their captors, and others died in captivity of disease, starvation, or ill-treatment. Many of the North Vietnamese prisoners held in South Vietnam were kept in exemplary camps, largely in the hope that the example might be copied by the North Vietnamese. Captured South Vietnamese soldiers were held under the same deplorable conditions as American prisoners in the southern jungles. Only some of them were ever moved to camps in North Vietnam.

Besides the military prisoners of war in Vietnam, there was also a large number of civilian internees. South Vietnam imprisoned civilians who were suspected of belonging to or collaborating with the insurgent Communist Viet Cong. Many of these were identified through the CIA-assisted intelligence-sharing apparatus known as Phoenix. The Phoenix program itself was not responsible for the atrocities commonly associated with it; nonetheless, many of those identified by the program were later apprehended by police or the South Vietnamese Army and tortured or killed outright; many of the survivors faced years of incarceration in horrendously poor conditions.

The communist side, too, imprisoned, tortured, and murdered civilians and minority mountain tribespeople. Their goal sometimes was to reeducate and return them to village life, but other internees, particularly after the fall of South Vietnam, were doomed to years in reeducation/labor camps. And the communists detained not only Vietnamese civilians, but a substantial number of Americans and Europeans as well. Of the 587 American prisoners returned at the end of the war, 24 were civilians who had been working in South Vietnam for U.S. contractors or government agencies. Two other prisoners not counted among the returning Americans were German nurses working for the Knights of Malta when they were captured in 1969 along with three others who did not survive the ordeal of captivity. These two, one male and one female, spent their four years of internment in some of the worst of the camps with American prisoners of war.

See also Hanoi Hilton; Ho Chi Minh Trail; Homecoming, Operation; Pueblo Incident; Son Tay Raid; Stockdale, James Bond; Thompson, Captain Floyd J. "Jim"

—*William S. Reeder, Jr.*

VIKINGS

The term *Vikings* refers to Nordic warriors who engaged in raids throughout Europe between the eighth and the twelfth centuries. They were Scandinavian in origin, although not all Scandinavians were Vikings—many in the region considered them to be outlaws—and not all Vikings come from Scandinavia. From their first recorded raid in 787 AD to the twelfth century, the Vikings terrorized large parts of the Western world, from Newfoundland in the west to Russia in the east, and as far south as the Mediterranean.

Viking raiders were interested in plundering precious metals and weapons, but they also placed a very high premium on captives; indeed, they were among the most active participants in the slave trade of the period. Typically, after sacking a town, Viking chieftains would determine which of the survivors were worth taking prisoner; one's chances of survival, then, depended on whether one was deemed saleable on the slave market, or desirable as the personal servant or concubine to a Viking warrior. Those whose lives were spared were carried away by boat—chronicles record that the warrior Haesten needed 200 ships to transport back to Scandinavia all of the plunder, including captives and goods, taken in raids on France in 882 AD—but where the number of captives was large, it was more common to march them overland to the nearest slave market for sale.

Slaves, then, constituted one of the Vikings' primary export commodities (the other was furs), but not all prisoners were sold at these slave markets; others became part of Viking society as household servants or agricultural laborers. Neither was a particularly secure existence. When a chieftain died, a female slave from his household either volunteered or was chosen to die with him. Contemporary accounts describe that she would be expected to have sexual intercourse with all male members of the clan before being ritually executed and burned alongside her master. Slave laborers, on the other hand, could be called upon at any time to join a raiding party, something that offered the opportunity for escape but was just as likely to end in death.

Furthermore, not all prisoners became slaves. Archaeologists have noted that some Viking military fortifications bear a striking resemblance to the defenses of Constantinople, suggesting that the Vikings captured Byzantine engineers and brought them north to work on their own defenses. These captives would have been held in relatively high esteem because of their skill and education and, despite the fact that they were technically prisoners, may well have been considered among the elites of Viking society.

Still, they were the exception rather than the rule, and the Vikings were known for their tireless pursuit of potential slaves. As the contemporary chronicler Adam of Bremen put it, they were quite happy to take advantage of those nearest to them: "As soon as one has caught his neighbor, he sells him ruthlessly as a slave, to either friend or stranger."

References
Johannes Brøndsted, *The Vikings* (Harmondsworth, UK: Penguin, 1973).
Paddy Griffith, *The Viking Art of War* (Mechanicsburg, PA: Stackpole Books, 1995).

—Jonathan F. Vance

VIVISECTION

Vivisection, meaning in this context the performance of medical experiments or procedures on unwilling human subjects, was carried out by members of the Axis powers in all theaters during World War II. Instances ranged from elaborate experimental programs by both the Japanese and the Germans involving thousands of individuals to the almost naive dissection of a living Allied pilot, carried out by a Japanese surgeon for the edification of his medical orderlies. This dissection took place on a small island of the south Pacific but the surgeon involved never came to trial; most likely, he died in the ensuing months of the war.

Similarly, Japanese bacteriological warfare experiments, carried out on a massive scale in Manchuria, remained untried after the war. These experiments, performed by Unit 731 and related elements of the Imperial Japanese Army in Manchuria, constitute a heinous example of illegal and murderous experimentation. The central figure in this extensive bacteriological-warfare experimentation program is Dr. Ishii Shirō (1892–1959). In 1933, Ishii began his experiments in this field. His first laboratory was in Harbin, Manchuria, in a former soy sauce factory, but the widespread experimental enterprise eventually comprised many units. Enormous funds must have been provided to support these activities, money that the Japanese government supplied generously, if indirectly, through army funds. One can only speculate as to how much government officials—or the monarchy—knew about Ishii's work.

Experimentation was conducted into ways of infecting humans with organisms that cause a remarkably wide range of diseases, including typhus, plague, dysentery, and particularly anthrax. Ishii considered anthrax the most effective bacterial agent because it could be produced in quantity, was resistant to destruction over time, retained its virulence, and was 80 to 90 percent fatal. He considered the "best" epidemic disease for warfare to be plague, and the most reliable vector-borne disease to be epidemic encephalitis. One of the chief Manchurian research sites was at a village called Pingfan. At least 3,000 victims, mostly Chinese and Manchurian, died here as a result of the experiments of Ishii and his associates. Experimental subjects were referred to as *maruta* or logs. One type of experiment involved tying the subjects to posts in an open field and then detonating small germ-filled canisters above or around them. The total number of victims killed in these types of experiments in all locations between 1933 and 1945 may be as high as 30,000, though precision is not possible. Because of the dearth of documentation, the proportion of prisoners of war to civilians used as test subjects also cannot be determined. The POWs were largely Chinese, though some Western ex-POWs claim to have been among this group; most victims did not survive.

Regrettably, there was no trial of Unit 731 activities. The reason was cold-blooded. The Japanese information was the only data in existence that was based on more or less scientifically controlled experiments into the effects of bacteriological warfare agents on humans. U.S. government officials granted immunity to the Japanese researchers in return for full and exclusive access to this mass of unique data.

Several of the Far East war crime trials that did occur created great interest after the war, perhaps none more so than that involving the Kyūshū Imperial University Faculty of Medicine. In May 1945, an American B-29 bomber was shot down over the Japanese island of Kyushu. Eleven parachutes were seen to open, but after the war ended, no record was found to reveal the fate of any of these men. Eight men had died after vivisection at Kyushu Imperial University and could not be identified by name; American authorities concluded that these men were part of the missing group. The university is located in the city of Fukuoka on Kyushu, the westernmost of the Japanese main islands. Its Faculty of Medicine was considered first-rate in 1945, among the best outside the environs of Tokyo. One of the potential defendants, Dr. Ishiyama Fukujirū (who committed suicide before trial), was chief of the First Surgery Clinic.

The trial revealed that the doomed fliers were first placed in detention barracks until one defendant, Komori Taku, persuaded the officer in charge to release the fliers for medical experimentation. Komori contacted Ishiyama at the surgical clinic, offering him use of the men "for the advancement of medicine." (It should be noted that physicians at another hospital had rejected the offer.) On four dates in May and June 1945, various operations were performed. None of the POWs had any injury requiring surgical treatment. The operative procedures were varied. Lungs were removed from each of two POWs, while the purported object of another operation was to reach the trigeminal nerve "from the top of the brain"—not a possibility; this flier died from hemorrhage and brain damage. One airman had his stomach removed, a second was exsanguinated and infused with sea water, while another had several operations involving his gall bladder, liver, and heart. All eight fliers died before leaving the operating theater, which was simply a dissecting room in the anatomy department. No records were kept of these "experimental" operations at the time or later. Japanese author Endo Shusaku wrote a challenging novel based on this episode, entitled in translation *The Sea and Poison*.

There was no dearth of similar offenses against humanity taking place in Nazi Germany at the time. The horrendous experiments conducted on tens of thousands of concentration camp victims became fully documented, to the horror of the world, via explicit, detailed, first-hand evidence during a lengthy postwar trial. Most victims had been prisoners in concentration camps across Europe. Many of these men, women, and children were Jews, some were Gypsies, and others were nationals of numerous countries. Many were prisoners of war, particularly from the Soviet Union and Poland.

The Luftwaffe studies of Dr. Sigismund Rascher at Dachau examined the effects of high altitudes and freezing on the human body; experiments at Sachsenhausen and Natzweiler studied malaria and mustard gas; Dr. Ernst Fisher studied the effects of sulfanilamide at Ravensbrück, where bone, muscle, and nerve regeneration was also studied; epidemic jaundice and sterilization experiments were conducted at Auschwitz and Ravensbrück; typhus was studied by Dr. Ding at Buchenwald and Dr. Eugen

Haagen at Natzweiler; poisons and the destructive effects on humans of incendiary bombs were studied at Buchenwald. Most of these experiments were scientifically crude, and all were barbarous. In the cold experiments at Dachau, for example, prisoners were simply immersed in icy waters for prolonged periods, many until they died, so that time of survival could be measured. For those who did not die during the experiments, resuscitation was sometimes attempted, reputedly including the frivolous technique of placing the male victim's body beside that of a naked woman. Most of the approximately 500 experiments done at Dachau were conducted in 1941 and 1942.

In the major war crimes trial conducted against alleged vivisectors, docketed as *United States of America v. Karl Brandt et al.* but known widely as "The Doctors Trial," almost all of the 23 defendants were members of the German medical profession; Karl Brandt, for example, had been personal physician to Adolf Hitler. Those convicted and ultimately hanged included Brandt; Karl Gebhardt, SS chief Heinrich Himmler's personal physician; Joachim Mrugowsky, chief of the Hygienic Institute of the Waffen-SS; Rudolph Brandt, personal administrative officer to Himmler; Wolfram Sievers, not a physician, but rather director of the Ahnenerbe Society's Institute for Military Scientific Research; Victor Brack, chief administrative officer in the Chancellory of the Führer; and Waldemar Hoven, chief doctor at Buchenwald concentration camp. Eight other defendants were sentenced to prison terms, and seven were acquitted. Few other instances of vivisection saw alleged perpetrators brought to trial. Some of these, most notably Joseph Mengele, escaped from Europe and successfully evaded trial. Others were reported to have died in the late stages of the war or to have vanished into Soviet camps. But survivors have published accounts of many of the Nazi vivisection crimes. For example, research on twins carried out at Auschwitz by Mengele had received much attention, and indeed, the entire Auschwitz experience has been written up voluminously.

The men were found guilty on charges of murder and crimes against humanity rather than on breaches of ethical behavior. Nevertheless, the subject of the ethics of human experimentation was discussed at length throughout the trial. Ultimately, the military tribunal judges enunciated what has become known as the Nuremberg Code, a 10-point exposition of mandatory principles to be adhered to in order for human experimentation to be ethically founded. Based in natural law, this widely publicized code has been central to discussions on the ethics of medical experimentation since that time.

See also Concentration Camps; Torture

References

Sheldon H. Harris, *Factories of Death: Japanese Biological Warfare, 1932–45, and the American Cover Up* (New York: Routledge, 1994).

Charles G. Roland, "Human Vivisection: The Intoxication of Limitless Power in Wartime," in *Prisoners of War and Their Captors in World War II*, ed. Bob Moore and Kent Fedorowich (Oxford: Berg, 1996).

Lore Shelley, ed., *Criminal Experiments on Human Beings in Auschwitz and War Research Laboratories: Twenty Prisoners' Accounts* (San Francisco: Mellen Research University Press, 1991).

—Charles G. Roland

VLASOV, LIEUTENANT GENERAL ANDREI (1900–1946)

Vlasov was a prominent officer in the Soviet Army whose exemplary service early in World War II was overshadowed by his defection to Germany and complicity with the enlistment of Russian POWs in the German Army.

The son of a peasant, Vlasov was conscripted in 1919 and remained in the Red Army through the interwar years. He showed great promise as a soldier and was justly rewarded for transforming his first command, the 99th Infantry Division, from a notoriously ill-disciplined unit into the best division in the Kiev military district. He served ably during the first months of the German invasion of Russia in 1941, but he was captured in July 1942 after the army group he had been sent to command was left in an untenable position by his superiors.

He was well treated by his captors, who soon realized that he might be turned against his own country. Indeed, Vlasov eagerly offered his assistance in encouraging Soviet prisoners to join with the Germans in defeating Soviet leader Josef Stalin. Vlasov eventually became associated with two initiatives: the Eastern Propaganda Section, which trained Russian POWs who had volunteered to serve in German units; and the Smolensk Committee, which waged an anti-Stalinist propaganda campaign aimed at Russian units. In April 1943, the POWs trained by the Eastern Propaganda Section were brought together as the Russian Liberation Army, with Vlasov as the figurehead commander. However, Vlasov soon learned that his captors little trusted him; furthermore, the army he hoped to lead into battle was equipped with obsolete weapons and led by German officers who did not speak Russian. Then, in September 1943, Adolf Hitler, believing that the turncoat POWs constituted a threat, ordered that all Russian units in the German Army be disbanded. Manpower shortages prevented this step, so instead Hitler decreed that the Russian units, roughly 30 divisions of nearly a million men in total, be shifted to northwest Europe and Italy. There, the units proved so unreliable that they were eventually converted into labor battalions.

By this time the German government, desperate for more soldiers, gave Vlasov greater authority in the hopes that he could recruit more POWs. He was placed at the head of a provisional government for Russia and was given titular command of the 800,000-man Russian Liberation Army. Recruits did indeed pour in, at a rate of thousands per week, but Vlasov himself was still prevented from commanding his units in battle. In April 1945, one of his divisions was thrown into battle on the Oder River, but ironically it ended the war fighting its one-time allies: in May 1945, the division, having changed sides again, helped Czech partisans to liberate Prague from the Nazis.

This action, however, could not save Vlasov. His erstwhile Czech allies soon disowned him, and he surrendered to U.S. forces. Within days he was taken into Soviet custody, and he was hanged in 1946.

See also British Free Corps; Defection

References

Catherine Andreyev, *Vlasov and the Russian Liberation Movement: Soviet Reality and Émigré Theories* (New York: Cambridge University Press, 1987).

Sven Steenberg, *Vlasov* (New York: Alfred A. Knopf, 1970).

Wilfried Strik-Strikfeldt, *Against Stalin and Hitler* (London: Macmillan, 1970).

Jürgen Thorwald, *The Illusion: Soviet Soldiers in Hitler's Army*, trans. Richard and Clara Winston (New York: Harcourt, Brace, Jovanovich, 1975).

—*Kara Brown*

VON RYAN'S EXPRESS

Set in a World War II prisoner-of-war camp in Italy, this 1965 American film (directed by Mark Robson and written by Wendall Mayes from a novel by David Westheimer) starts as a solemn version of *The Bridge on the River Kwai* but is soon transformed into an exciting and suspenseful adventure story. Frank Sinatra plays a resourceful American air force colonel who is placed in charge of the mostly British prisoners. He quickly earns the contempt of the other prisoners, who accuse him of cooperating with the enemy and dub him "*Von Ryan*." Their scorn turns to respect when he is placed in the camp sweatbox for demanding better conditions. Later, when the Italian war effort collapses, the prisoners escape and sneak onto a German train bound for Switzerland. For a time, with the help of sympathetic Italians, their ruses are successful. Eventually the Germans catch on and send an armored train and fighter planes after them.

Critics praised the action-filled conclusion for its good special effects and impressive stunt work, culminating in a final scene that is the film's most memorable. Frank Sinatra makes an effective action hero, aided by veteran actor Trevor Howard as the British officer who is the prisoners' unofficial leader until Ryan takes over. The story possesses few historically accurate details (no such escape ever occurred) and also lacks an overt morality lesson of the kind usually offered by other films of the POW genre. *Von Ryan's Express* is mostly notable as a fun-filled adventure story with exciting scenes and an appealing cast. The film received an Academy Award nomination for Best Sound Effects.

See also Film; Westheimer, David

—*Daryl Wiggers*

VONNEGUT, KURT, JR. (1922–)

Kurt Vonnegut, Jr., the author of *Slaughterhouse-Five*, one of the most well-known novels of captivity during World War II, was born in Indianapolis, educated in public schools, and attended Cornell University. During World War II, he joined the U.S. Army and was assigned as an infantry scout. Vonnegut was sent to the Army Specialized Training program at Alabama Polytechnic Institute in Auburn, Alabama, but his training there was interrupted because of the need for frontline troops.

During the Battle of the Bulge in December 1944, Vonnegut's patrol was captured by the Germans. Vonnegut was placed in a temporary facility and then sent to a permanent POW camp in Dresden. He and fellow prisoners were housed in a meatpacking plant; the prisoners' barracks were underground slaughterhouses. Vonnegut was put to work making vitamin-enriched malt syrup for use as a dietary supplement for pregnant women. On 14 February 1945, the Allied air forces mounted a devastating firebomb raid on Dresden. The POWs, housed in underground shelters, were among the few survivors of the firestorm, which may have killed as many as 200,000 civilians. After the air raid, Vonnegut was enlisted in the effort to find survivors and recover bodies.

After his liberation from prison camp, Vonnegut returned to the United States and briefly worked as a crime reporter and in public relations for General Electric before becoming an author. In 1969, he published *Slaughterhouse-Five*, which in 1972 was made into a critically acclaimed and award-winning film by director George Roy Hill. Vonnegut has written 14 novels and countless short stories and essays.

See also Film; *Slaughterhouse-Five*

References

Kurt Vonnegut, *Fates Worse than Death* (New York: Berkley Books, 1992).

———, *Palm Sunday: An Autobiographical Collage* (New York: Dell, 1981).

———, *Slaughterhouse-Five, or the Children's Crusade: A Duty-Dance with Death* (New York: Dell, 1969).

———, *Wampeters, Foma, and Granfalloons* (New York: Dell, 1974).

W

Waffen-SS

As the armed elite of the Nazi state, the Waffen-SS provided specially trained military units for use in battle under the field command of the German armed forces during World War II. As soon as the war began, however, the influence of Nazi ideology was producing significant differences in military behavior. As a result of the German army's prompt court-martial of a Waffen-SS soldier for shooting 50 Jews in September 1939, Heinrich Himmler, as *Reichsführer-SS*, lobbied and won from Adolf Hitler the right to set up his own court system, independent of the German military, for the investigation of crimes alleged against members of the Waffen-SS. This accounts for significant gaps in the historical record concerning Waffen-SS crimes against POWs. Even so, evidence indicates that POWs were ill-treated and killed by the Waffen-SS.

Almost as soon as the war began, the first reported atrocity against Allied prisoners occurred. Nearly 100 British soldiers taken prisoner in northern France in May 1940 were rounded up at Le Paradis by members of the Waffen-SS *Totenkopf* (Death's Head) Division and subsequently shot. Attempts by the German army to bring the perpetrators to justice at the time were frustrated by Himmler, and no action was taken by Germany against these men. After the end of fighting in the west, the next major scenes of mistreatment of prisoners of war occurred in the eastern front. During the end of the summer of 1941, the SS *Kavallerie Brigade* executed 259 captured Soviet soldiers and over 6,500 civilians in the area of the Pripet Marshes. And in reprisal for the killing of six captured SS officers by the Soviets in early 1942, the Waffen-SS *Division Leibstandarte Adolf Hitler* shot and killed every Russian POW who fell into their hands over the next three days, approximately 4,000 in all. In similar instances, thousands of Soviet prisoners were killed by the Waffen-SS during the war in the east, to say nothing of the murders of civilians committed in the region as well. When the Waffen-SS was engaged against Western allied troops after the invasion of Normandy in June 1944, reports of the killing of POWs began anew. In the two most notable incidents, as many as 156 Canadian and British soldiers, many of whom were wounded, were murdered by members of the 12th SS Hitler Youth Division 10 days after the Allies established a beachhead, and in December 1944, 82 Americans taken prisoner during the German counteroffensive in the Ardennes were shot by elements of the 1st SS Panzer Division, at Malmédy, Belgium. Only one American, an officer, survived, and he later testified against his attackers.

In the years after the war, attempts were made to rehabilitate the image of the Waffen-SS, claiming they were not part of the rest of the SS but were simply crack soldiers under the command of the military. Quite apart from the many instances in which the Waffen-SS was proved to have committed mass murders of civilians in all parts of occupied Europe, enough evidence of their killing of prisoners of war of all nationalities was presented at later war crimes trials to render these apologetic claims empty.

See also Ardeatine Caves Massacre; Lidice Massacre; Malmédy Massacre; Meyer, Kurt; Oradour-sur-Glane Massacre; Le Paradis Massacre; Peiper, Joachim

References

George H. Stein, *The Waffen-SS: Hitler's Elite Guard at War, 1939–1945* (Ithaca, NY: Cornell University Press, 1984).

Bernd Wegner, *The Waffen-SS: Organization, Ideology, and Function* (Oxford: Basil Blackwell, 1989).

—Vasilis Vourkoutiotis

WAINWRIGHT, JONATHAN MAYHEW (1883–1953)

American general Jonathan Wainwright was responsible for surrendering the garrison of the Philippines to the Japanese during World War II. Born in Walla Walla, Washington, on 2 August 1883, Wainwright counted army and navy officers on both sides of his family. Nicknamed "Skinny" by his classmates, he graduated from the U.S. Military Academy at West Point in 1906 and was commissioned a second lieutenant in the cavalry. Wainwright held various posts until he was promoted to major general and took command of the Philippine Division in September 1940. After the Japanese invasion of the Philippines on 8 December 1941, he commanded the North Luzon Force in its withdrawal to the Bataan Peninsula. Promoted to lieutenant-general in March 1942, Wainwright was appointed commander of U.S. Forces Far East after General Douglas MacArthur was ordered to Australia. Forced to withdraw the remnants of his combined American/Filipino army to the island of Corregidor in Manila harbor, Wainwright was compelled to surrender on 6 May 1942.

After surviving the Bataan Death March, Wainwright was transported to Japanese-occupied Manchuria, where he spent the next three years as a prisoner of war. Forced to watch the horrible mistreatment of his men at the hands of the Japanese, Wainwright often attempted to intervene on their behalf but his efforts were almost always unsuccessful. For three years, he was starved and mistreated by his captors, who forced him to perform menial tasks in an effort to humiliate him. Liberated on 25 August 1945, Wainwright had expected to be court-martialed and imprisoned for surrendering his forces in the Philippines. Instead, he was honored—first, on 2 September 1945, when he stood behind Douglas MacArthur at the surrender ceremonies on the USS *Missouri* in Tokyo Bay, and next, upon his return to the United States, where he was promoted to full general and awarded the Congressional Medal of Honor by President Harry S Truman. His health shattered by his long and harsh imprisonment, Wainwright retired in August 1947, and died on 2 September 1953, the eighth anniversary of the Japanese surrender.

See also Bataan Death March; World War II—Far East

References

John J. Beck, *MacArthur and Wainwright: Sacrifice of the Philippines* (Albuquerque: University of New Mexico Press, 1974).

Eva J. Matson, ed., *Heroes of Bataan, Corregidor, and Northern Luzon* (Carlsbad, NM: M. Griffin, 1994).

Duane P. Schultz, *Hero of Bataan: The Story of General Jonathan M. Wainwright* (New York: St. Martin's Press, 1981).

Jonathan M. Wainwright, *General Wainwright's Story: The Account of Four Years of Humiliating Defeat, Surrender, and Captivity* (Garden City, NY: Doubleday, 1949).

—Alexander M. Bielakowski

WAITE, TERRY (1939–)

A British hostage negotiator working for the Church of England, Terry Waite endured nearly five years as a Hizb'Allah captive in Lebanon.

As the Archbishop of Canterbury's Assistant for Anglican Communion Affairs, Waite had extensive experience negotiating the humanitarian release of hostages in the Muslim world, including Iranian Anglicans (1981) and British nationals held in Libya (1985). After an increase in the capture of Western hostages by the militant Shi'a Muslim organization Hizb'Allah (then operating under the name Islamic Jihad for the Liberation of Palestine) in 1985, Waite traveled to Lebanon to mediate for their release.

On 20 January 1987, while attempting to meet alone with representatives of the hostage takers, Waite was himself kidnapped. Although ostensibly held as a bargaining chip to effect the release of Shi'ites and other Hizb'Allah sympathizers detained in Kuwait, Israel, and Western Europe, a false rumor that Waite had been involved in the Iran-Contra Affair may have been behind his capture.

For the first four years of his imprisonment, Waite was chained to a wall in solitary confinement. He endured a mock execution, beatings, and interrogations seeking to link him to the actions of the United States government. Often moved between different Hizb'Allah safe houses in civil war-torn Beirut, the poor conditions of various prison cells hastened his development of respiratory problems. He survived through recourse to his Christian faith, intense self-discipline, and by immersing himself in the occasional books provided by his captors. Waite was eventually placed together with three other Western hostages held by Hizb'Allah, and the conditions of his incarceration improved. Following the conclusion of the Lebanese Civil War, the United Nations negotiated Waite's release in November 1991.

Since his return to Great Britain, Waite has spoken and written widely, and he continues to be active in a number of charities. He produced a moving memoir of his experiences entitled *Taken on Trust: Recollections from Captivity*.

See also Intifada; Lebanese Civil War

References

Magnus Ranstorp, *Hizb'allah in Lebanon: The Politics of the Western Hostage Crisis* (London: Macmillan, 1997).

Terry Waite, *Taken on Trust: Recollections from Captivity* (London: Hodder & Stoughton, 1993).

—*Andrew Theobald*

WALKER, DR. MARY EDWARDS (1832–1919)

A promoter of women's dress reforms and an avid participant in the women's suffrage movement, Mary Edwards Walker was born in Oswego, New York, on the family's 33-acre farm, where she and her four elder sisters provided much of the labor. With doctors high in demand at the time, she obtained her medical degree from Syracuse Medical College in 1855, the only woman in her class, and later took a second medical degree from Hygeia Therapeutic College in 1862. Mary Edwards Walker began her medical practice in Columbus, Ohio, in 1855. Her marriage to Dr. Albert Miller that same year ended in divorce in 1869.

As a woman, Walker was denied a commission as a surgeon in the Union Army during the U.S. Civil War. Despite this difficulty, in 1861 she became a civilian contract surgeon for the Union Army. Walker, like many medical practitioners of the time, had strong opinions about the effectiveness of amputations and believed that many soldiers were unnecessarily maimed and suffered death due to infection.

In February 1864, Walker became a civilian contract surgeon assigned to the Fifty-second Ohio Volunteers, stationed in Tennessee; this was the first official recognition of her status as a doctor. Two months later she was captured by Confederate soldiers while en route to aid civilians in the surrounding area, and was made a prisoner of war. She spent the next five months in Castle Thunder Prison in Richmond, Virginia, where she suffered from health problems due to poor nutrition and the terrible living conditions. Her complaints about the lack of an adequate prison diet led Confederate authorities to add wheat bread and cabbage to the rations. In August, Walker was exchanged for a male Confederate officer, a further recognition of her important position.

After the war, Walker continued to press for a commission as a military surgeon, but to no avail. On 11 November 1865, President Andrew Johnson presented her with the Congressional Medal of Honor, but in 1918 the U.S. government rescinded the Medal of Honor from individuals who were not involved in actual conflict, including Mary Edwards Walker. However, she defied the government and refused to return the medal, wearing it until her death on 21 February 1919. Mary Edwards Walker was inducted into the Women's Hall of Fame at Seneca Falls, New York, in 2000.

See also U.S. Civil War

References
Margaret Beethman and Kay Boardman, *Victorian Women Magazines: An Anthology* (Manchester: Manchester University Press, 2001).
Elizabeth D. Leonard, *Yankee Women: Gender Battles in the Civil War* (New York: Norton, 1994).
Charles McCool Snyder, *Dr. Mary Walker: The Little Lady in Pants* (New York: Vantage Press, 1962).
Dale L. Walker, *Mary Edwards Walker: Above and Beyond* (New York: Forge, 2005).
Helen Beal Woodward, *The Bold Women* (Freeport, NY: Books for Libraries Press, 1971).

—*Anne M.E. Millar*

WALKER LYNDH, JOHN (1981–)

Referred to as the Taliban American or Johnny Jihad by the media, Walker Lyndh was the first U.S. citizen captured in Afghanistan while fighting with the Taliban forces.

Born in Washington, DC, raised in San Francisco, and baptized as a Roman Catholic, Walker Lyndh converted to Islam at age 16 and in 1998 spent 10 months in Yemen learning Arabic. He returned to Yemen in February 2000 and probably entered Afghanistan in early 2001. He later claimed to have trained in an Al Qaeda training camp before joining Al Ansar, a terrorist cell funded by Al Qaeda leader Osama bin Laden.

Walker Lyndh was captured by Northern Alliance forces in November 2001 and detained in Qala-i-Jangi prison, where he was wounded in an uprising that resulted in the deaths of hundreds of Taliban and Al Qaeda captives. At first, he gave his name as Abdul Hamid, but later revealed his identity to a television reporter. He was quickly transferred to a U.S. naval vessel for detention, and signed a confession (there remains some question whether the confession was coerced, or whether he was unjustly denied the benefit of legal counsel) admitting that he was a member of Al Qaeda.

In February 2002, Walker Lyndh was indicted in a federal court in Alexandria, Virginia, on 10 charges, including conspiracy to murder U.S. nationals and contributing services to Al Qaeda. However, prosecutors negotiated a plea bargain with Walker Lyndh's lawyers—there are unconfirmed reports that the deal was struck to avoid Walker Lyndh testifying in court that he had been tortured while in custody—and in July 2002 he pleaded guilty to two of the lesser charges. In return for the other eight being dropped, he agreed to refrain from making public statements on his captivity and to accept a 20-year prison sentence. With that, the medium-security prison in Victorville, California, became home to the man to whom President George W. Bush once allegedly referred as "some misguided Marin County hot-tubber."

See also Afghan Wars; War on Terror

—*Jonathan F. Vance*

WAR CRIMES

Criminal acts have always taken place during war. It was not until the twentieth century that certain criminal acts committed in wartime became punishable offenses under international humanitarian law. War crimes, however, do not encompass any and all criminal acts perpetrated during times of war. As Steven Ratner has stated, war crimes are violations of the laws of war, laid down by international humanitarian law, that carry with them individual criminal responsibility. It is also noteworthy, although apparently obvious, that war crimes take place by definition during times of war. Other heinous crimes commonly attributed as war crimes, such as genocide and crimes against peace, have their own legal definitions as distinct from war crimes.

Throughout history, attempts have been made to place limitations on the conduct of warfare beginning at least as far back as the sixth century B.C.E., when the Chinese military theorist Sun-Tzu proposed the placing of such limitations. Until the late nineteenth century, wars were largely governed by the "customary" rules of war. Further, as Timothy McCormack notes, "the concept of war crimes and the practice of trial and punishment for those guilty of such crimes not only predate any notion of international law, but are also evident in the histories of diverse cultural and religious traditions." Some such customs have always been governed to some degree by common sense. One did not poison the common stream.

In the Middle Ages, European warfare was supposedly governed by decorous codes of conduct. One, the code of chivalry, was at base a warrior code that developed in the hope that knights would protect society, not despoil it. However, such idealized and mythologized martial codes did not often mitigate the brutality and suffering that was, and is, so often attendant upon warfare; witness, for example, the sacking of Constantinople in 1204 during the Fourth Crusade. The Middle Ages did, however, witness some of the first prosecutions for aggression and atrocities, such as that which tried the Scottish rebel William Wallace. Nevertheless, prior to the twentieth century, few rules existed for the official protection of civilians. The term "rape and pillage" was not (and *is* not) an anachronism. There were few structures in place that could punish gross abuses of the customary rules of war except, perhaps, war itself. During the nineteenth century, governments and military tribunals increasingly tried certain persons for what they considered to be violations of the customary laws of war. What seems clear, according to McCormack, is that historical "constraints on the waging of war across cultural and religious divides is fundamental to the relatively recent attempts to identify and develop a universalist corpus of international law."

However, the codification and expansion of the customary laws of war throughout the twentieth century (and the criminalization of breaching such rules) does not suggest that humanity finally eradicated the worst abuses it had inflicted upon itself. On the contrary, the repeated attempts of the previous century to limit wartime behavior were in large measure the result of an intensification of warlike behavior and human suffering. Ironically, it was due to this unprecedented intensification, along with the possibility for modern weaponry to inflict even greater suffering, that legal limits began to be taken seriously.

Customary international law and treaty law form the basis of modern international law. At the beginning of the twenty-first century, the United Nations (U.N.) established the International Criminal Court (ICC). The Rome Statute of the International Criminal Court of 17 July 1998, which governs the jurisdiction and functioning of the ICC, stipulates that the court's jurisdiction "shall be limited to the most serious crimes of concern to the international community as a whole." The statute covers four umbrella categories: the crime of genocide, crimes against humanity, war crimes, and the crime of aggression. This recent development was built upon centuries of wartime conduct and, more importantly, a twentieth century replete with war crimes. The development of international humanitarian law, and the criminalization of wartime atrocities, had its practical beginnings, however, in the mid-nineteenth century.

Historians have often claimed that the nineteenth century was an era of unprecedented peace in European history. However the lack of a general European war does not mean that major and costly wars did not take place. The Greek Revolution (1821–1828), the First Carlist War in Spain (1832–1840), and the various Russo-Turkish Wars are all relevant examples. Russo-Turkish tensions also played a role in the outbreak of the Crimean War (1853–1856), in which nearly 300,000 people died. However, during the War of Italian Unification (1859), Swiss businessman Henri Dunant witnessed first-hand the suffering of sick and wounded soldiers and later wondered whether "some international principle, sanctioned by a convention and inviolate in character, which, once agreed upon and ratified, might constitute the basis for societies for the relief of the wounded in the different European countries?" This question formed the basis of the First Geneva Convention. The International Committee for Relief to the Wounded was thus struck in 1863 and was subsequently renamed the International Committee of the Red Cross (ICRC). The ICRC has since acted as the chief international arbiter and interpreter of the Geneva Conventions. On 22 August 1864, the First Geneva Convention was signed.

Following the numerous wars of the late nineteenth century, and on the eve of the Boer War, the First Peace Conference was convened in The Hague, Netherlands, in 1899. The Second Peace Conference followed in 1907. These resulted in the Hague Conventions, which were among the first formal statements concerning the laws of war and war crimes. Article 2 of the 1899 Hague Convention stipulates that "(t)he right of belligerents to adopt means of injuring the enemy is not unlimited." Article 23 enunciates what were agreed upon as war crimes. It was especially prohibited for armies "to employ poison or poisoned arms; to kill or wound treacherously individuals belonging to the hostile nation or army; to kill or wound an enemy who … has surrendered at discretion; to declare that no quarter will be given; to employ arms … of a nature to cause superfluous injury; to make improper use of a flag of truce … as well as the distinctive badges of the Geneva Convention [that is, ICRC symbols]; [or] to destroy or seize the enemy's property, unless such destruction or seizure be imperatively demanded by the necessities of war." In essence, the Hague Conventions built upon the edifice constructed in 1864; their main and stated purpose being to limit the severity and means by which armies could wound each others' combatants. Significantly, these limitations still form the basis upon which war crimes are founded.

The First World War (1914–1918) provided the first major test for the Hague Conventions. However, the absence of an international body with jurisdiction over war crimes meant that, in the aftermath of the war, alleged war criminals were most often tried under separate national jurisdictions. The Great War also provided abundant examples of criminal activity. The violation of Belgian neutrality, the first employment of poison gas (in clear violation of the Hague Conventions), and the employment of unrestricted submarine warfare were but a few of the charges leveled against Germany. Allied governments also participated in "outlawed" behavior such as retaliatory gas attacks and the starvation of the German population by "distant" blockade. The trial of men drawn almost exclusively from the Central Powers, however, raised questions regarding judicial impartiality (or lack thereof). The legitimacy of war crimes prosecutions has suffered from a perception that such trials represent "victor's justice." In fact, there remains a vast gulf between those accused of war crimes from defeated nations and those drawn from victorious ones. After the Great War, truly international trials designed to punish those responsible for war crimes never materialized.

A continuing debate also exists over what is generally considered to be the twentieth century's first genocide. The Armenian Massacre took place mainly between 1915 and 1917. It is generally agreed that hundreds of thousands (perhaps over one million) people were killed as a result of the systematic deportation and murder of Armenian civilians. This episode remains a matter of ongoing dispute because the Turkish government denies that genocide occurred since the deportations did not constitute a state-sponsored policy. Instead, Turkey claims that the deaths resulted from conditions caused more generally by the First World War. Turkey's hoped-for entry into the European Union also exacerbates this issue and illustrates quite effectively that contemporary politics, which are in many ways divorced from the original commission of the crime in question, often complicate issues of criminal responsibility in war.

In 1928, the Kellogg-Briand Pact was signed in Paris. The pact was an international treaty "providing for the renunciation of war as an instrument of national policy." Despite the pact's failure, it remains an important treaty in the development of international law. The pact helped establish the international "belief" (though not commonly practiced) that military force should only be used as a last resort. The idea that the waging of aggressive war is a criminal act is an important one. The Crime of Aggression, however, is not currently defined. A review of the Rome Statute will take place in 2009, and will hopefully define exactly what constitutes a Crime of Aggression.

Few would argue, however, that Adolf Hitler's invasion of Poland was anything but an aggressive crime. World War II was exponentially more "criminal" than the First World War. German and Japanese war crimes were many and varied (as were those that have been attributed to the Allies, such as the bombing of Dresden, the targeting of Germany's civilian population, and the atomic annihilation of Hiroshima and Nagasaki, acts for which no one was held criminally responsible). Suffice it to say that Nazi Germany's state-sponsored genocidal policy resulted in the deaths of around 9 million to 12 million people (reliable figures are difficult to tabulate). Japanese war crimes took place across the Far East and were exemplified by the Rape of Nanking, which began on 13 December 1937.

The nature of Axis war crimes was suspected early in the war and, therefore, various Allied governments established the United Nations War Crimes Commission (UNWCC) in 1943 to investigate war crimes. After the surrender of Nazi Germany in May 1945 and Japan in September of the same year, two military tribunals were established to prosecute German and Japanese war criminals. As writer Jackson Maogoto put it, "These tribunals . . . represented the very first practical manifestation of the international penal process in modern times." The Germans were tried at the International Military Tribunal at Nuremberg (IMT) and the Japanese at the International Military Tribunal for the Far East at Tokyo (IMTFE). In order to ensure that these courts would command legitimacy, the Allied governments agreed that the definition of war crimes had to be limited, in writer Timothy MacCormack's words , "as offenses 'against the laws and customs of war' rather than to be defined more broadly." A number of those accused were sentenced to death, several were given prison terms, and others were acquitted. These trials helped the world come to terms with the horrors of the war, but they also had a more lasting effect in the area of international law. The Nuremberg and Tokyo trials established, in Roger Clark's view, that "there are certain crimes which are of international concern or are crimes under international law."

The International Military Tribunals set in motion a number of treaties and conventions that have been ratified since 1945. These have included the Geneva Conventions of 1949, two additional protocols to the Geneva Convention (1977), the International Convention Against the Taking of Hostages (1979), and the Convention Against Torture and other Cruel, Inhuman or Degrading Treatment or Punishment (1984), among many others. Missing, among all of these laudable conventions, is the concept that infractions must be tried by an international criminal court. Instead, war crimes jurisdiction fell to individual states. This led to a system whereby states were compelled either to try suspected war criminals or extradite them to a country willing to do so, a system that failed to prosecute many alleged war criminals. By the 1990s, the treaty practices of the previous 45 years had constructed what Clark calls a "firmly established set of rules and principles for international cooperation in dealing with crimes under international law" but the *machinery* of international justice was not yet created.

Recent outrages against human decency in the former Yugoslavia and in Rwanda, however, seem to have belatedly garnered legal attention from the international community. Here we return to the Rome Statute of 1998 by which the International Criminal

Court was established. The Rome Statute's definition of war crimes mirrors that defined in 1899 at the First Peace Conference. Twentieth-century barbarity, however, has necessitated the inclusion of a broader range of criminal offenses, many of which were codified in the Geneva Conventions of 1949, including willful killing, torture, hostage-taking, biological experimentation, and compelling a prisoner of war to serve in the forces of a hostile power. Events in the second half of the century resulted in an even broader range of war crimes which includes "ethnic cleansing," rape, forced prostitution, forced pregnancy, the use of human shields, civilian starvation, the conscription of children, and attacks upon civilians, humanitarian missions, and peacekeepers.

The International Criminal Court (ICC), which came into effect on 1 July 2002, describes itself as "the first ever permanent, treaty-based, international criminal court established to promote the rule of law and ensure that the gravest international crimes do not go unpunished." It remains to be seen if the ICC will live up to its praiseworthy, if lofty, mandate. The current trial of former Iraqi President Saddam Hussein (taking place in Iraq), however, provides evidence that the legitimacy of the ICC has yet to be fully recognized. The current War on Terror also provides evidence that the definition of "war crimes" (for example, acts of terrorism or, conversely, the questionable combatant status of yet-to-be-charged detainees at the U.S. base at Guantánamo Bay) is still debatable. But what remains virtually incontestable is that, however one describes them, war crimes continue to occur every day.

See also Human Shields; International Law; Lynching; Nuremberg Trials; Tokyo War Crimes Trials

References

Roy Gutman and David Rieff, eds., *Crimes of War* (New York: Norton, 1999).

Jackson Nyamuya Maogoto, *War Crimes and Realpolitik* (Boulder, CO: Lynne Rienner, 2004).

Timothy McCormack and Gerry Simpson, eds., *The Law of War Crimes* (The Hague: Kluwer Law International, 1997).

Norman E. Tuterow, ed., *War Crimes, War Criminals, and War Crimes Trials: An Annotated Bibliography and Source Book* (New York: Greenwood Press, 1986).

—*John Maker*

WAR OF 1812 (1812–1815)

The War of 1812, fought by Britain and the United States, provides interesting examples of how military prisoners were dealt with early in the nineteenth century. During the conflict some captives were simply massacred, hundreds were ransomed or held hostage, thousands were imprisoned then exchanged, many more were granted parole to remain at liberty behind enemy lines, but others were placed in isolated prisons or naval hulks. On the whole, the War of 1812 generally witnessed humane treatment of captured combatants and both sides expected their men to be treated well and protected from harm.

When hostilities broke out in June 1812, no formal agreements existed regarding prisoners. Yet events after the British victory at Detroit in August 1812 set a pattern for most engagements in the conflict. Some 1,600 Ohio militiamen were immediately granted parole to return to their homes by British authorities and were escorted beyond possible danger from Amerindian warriors. Meanwhile, the 582 American regular troops were shipped to Quebec City as prisoners of war. In general this was the normal practice followed by both sides during the conflict. Members of volunteer units and militia companies who surrendered were normally dismissed with a promise that they would not serve again, while regular troops were held for longer periods. Officers, after being held for a time, were typically given a parole that provided them with freedom of movement within a town or larger area. Enlisted men, however, were often incarcerated for years before they could be exchanged for prisoners from the other side, and some remained behind bars long after the war ended. The British used a variety of prisons in North America, the

American general William Hull surrenders to British general Isaac Brock at Detroit in 1812 (National Archives of Canada C 16404)

Caribbean, and at home to house American prisoners, while the U.S. government housed most of its captives in state institutions in Massachusetts and Kentucky.

The two warring nations negotiated a series of POW conventions, with the first signed at Halifax, Nova Scotia, in November 1812. Both sides agreed to keep accurate lists of any men who had been captured. If each power consented, an exchange of lists would occur and soldiers in confinement or on parole behind enemy lines would once again be free to serve their country. The document even specified the comparative worth of various individuals; in keeping with the stratified nature of the military, two privates were considered the equivalent of a sergeant, three were equal to a colonel, and 30 were needed to free a brigadier-general. Subsequent negotiations led to a second agreement in 1813 whereby both nations pledged to treat captives with "humanity, conformable to the usage and practice of the most civilized nations during the war." Corporal punishment was prohibited, minimum rations were outlined, and places for exchanges were established. In the end, Britain failed to ratify this agreement, apparently disagreeing with both the type of foods required by Americans and their insistence on the paroling of maritime captives, but the main principles of both conventions were generally adhered to nonetheless.

One major problem arose when British authorities decided to prosecute for treason 23 U.S. soldiers captured during the invasion of Queenston, Upper Canada, in October 1812. It was argued that the individuals had been born as British subjects and remained so despite naturalization. The Americans, of course, argued otherwise, but the captives were sent to England anyway early the next year. Then, in May 1813, U.S. forces on the Niagara frontier put in close confinement an equivalent number of British soldiers as hostages and the British responded by taking 46 prisoners and putting them in close confinement at Quebec City. The Americans retaliated by threatening to execute two prisoners for every one of their soldiers put to death. Meanwhile, an additional 59 Americans taken prisoner at the Battle of Beaver Dams were deported to England because it was claimed they were British subjects. Orders were then issued for another 59 British officers to be held in close confinement in response. In the end, calmer heads prevailed and the British abandoned the plan for treason trials. The spiral of retaliation was officially brought to a close with an April 1814 agreement. Under it, all POWs held in North America were to be exchanged and were permitted to rejoin the service of their respective countries after 15 May.

Another nasty incident involving prisoners occurred in present-day Michigan when an American army was defeated at the River Raisin on 22 January 1813. After the battle ended, most of the regular soldiers were marched back to British territory, but some 80 prisoners who were unable to walk were left behind without sufficient protection. Native warriors attached to the British forces, under the command of a Wyandot named Roundhead, then immediately massacred about 30 of the unfortunate individuals, tortured a handful of others, and held the rest for ransom. That this event led to the creation of the patriotic cry "Remember the Raisin!" indicates how atypical it was.

It has been estimated that some 20,000 Americans—mostly sailors or privateers—were held in various institutions by British authorities over the course of the war. About a third of them were kept in Dartmoor Prison, located 17 miles from Plymouth, England. Basic necessities were provided by both the British and American governments, and only 275 inmates died during the course of the war, mostly from pneumonia and smallpox. The prison became a thriving community, with two theater companies and opportunities for dancing, music, gambling, and fencing, as well as an itinerant Methodist service and a regular Sunday market for agricultural goods and crafts produced by prisoners. Nonetheless, the institution suffered a postwar riot that made the name Dartmoor notorious in the United States.

The third article of the December 1814 Treaty of Ghent that concluded the War of

1812 provided for the immediate release of prisoners "as soon as practicable," but American officials failed to provide adequate transportation in a timely fashion. The deaths of seven prisoners finally convinced British authorities they had to arrange for repatriation with the details of costs to be worked out later.

See also Dartmoor; Scott, Winfield

References
Donald R. Hickey, *The War of 1812: A Forgotten Conflict* (Chicago: University of Illinois Press, 1989).
J. Mackay Hitsman, *The Incredible War of 1812: A Military History* (Toronto: University of Toronto Press, 1965).
Reginald Horsman, "The Paradox of Dartmoor Prison," *American Heritage* 26 (1975): 12–17, 85.
George Sheppard, *Plunder, Profit and Paroles: A Social History of the War of 1812 in Upper Canada* (Montreal: McGill-Queen's University Press, 1994).

—*George Sheppard*

WAR ON TERROR

After the 11 September 2001 terrorist attacks on targets in the United States, the government of President George W. Bush inaugurated what became known as the War on Terror, a rhetorical rather than a legal characterization, since most scholars agree that it does not constitute an armed conflict under international law (jurist Joan Fitzpatrick calls the Bush Administration's legal characterization of the war "remarkably ambiguous"). Nevertheless, the goal of the War on Terror is to eliminate the terrorist network of Al Qaeda and groups linked to it. The war has a number of distinct elements: the invasion of Afghanistan to oust the Taliban regime, which was known to be sympathetic to Al Qaeda and which refused to cooperate by turning over terrorist suspects to the United States; the war on Iraq, to remove another regime that was believed to be offering safe haven to terrorists and that was presumed to possess weapons of mass destruction that might be unleashed against civilian targets (a presumption that was later proven to be incorrect); and the campaign to uncover and break up Al Qaeda cells around the world, imprison their members, and prevent further terrorist attacks.

In each of these contexts, a particularly thorny issue was what protection detainees should enjoy under international law, and more specifically, whether they should be considered prisoners of war under the Geneva Convention. The invasion of Afghanistan produced a number of different kinds of prisoners: members of the Afghani regular armed forces; militiamen and other irregular soldiers; and individuals who were presumed to be Al Qaeda fighters. The response of the White House to the question of POW status for all of these groups was unequivocal: On 7 February 2002, a White House Fact Sheet announced that all prisoners then held at the Guantánamo Bay detention facility in Cuba (including those taken in Afghanistan) would be treated humanely and in the spirit of the Geneva Convention of 1949. However, while the statement declared that the Geneva Convention applied to Taliban detainees, those detainees did not qualify as POWs under the Convention, and it did not apply at all to the Al Qaeda detainees. The announcement had been preempted, however, by Secretary of Defense Donald Rumsfeld during a press conference en route to the newly opened U.S. detention facility at Guantánamo Bay, Cuba, on 27 January. When a journalist asked one of the U.S. military officials about the detainees' rights under the Geneva Convention, Rumsfeld quickly jumped in to point out that the captives were not POWs, and therefore any discussion of the Geneva Convention was irrelevant.

Legal scholars were quick to open a debate on the legitimacy of this determination. Judge George Aldrich questioned the wisdom of denying POW status to Taliban fighters on the grounds that they did not meet the criteria for combatant status as laid out in the Geneva Convention. On the contrary, argued Aldrich, both international law and the U.S. Army Field Manual on the Law of Land Warfare specifically stipulated that, even if an enemy fighter did not appear to be entitled to POW status, that status should be presumed until such time as a competent tribunal could make a definitive determination. This practice had been followed by the British government when dealing with interned Iraqis during the Gulf War. Aldrich found his government's decision particularly disturbing because the United States had been outraged by the tendency of both North Korea and North Vietnam to deny POW status to U.S. servicemen on the grounds that they were more properly considered criminals. "Time," wrote Aldrich, reflecting on how the roles were apparently now reversed, "evidently dulls memory."

Other scholars have agreed. Yasmin Naqvi of the International Committee of the Red Cross (ICRC) concurs that the U.S. position contradicted its own military law, as reiterated as late as 1997 in the U.S. Army's regulation "Enemy Prisoners of War, Retained Personnel, Civilian Internees and Other Detainees," in not giving Taliban fighters the benefit of the doubt and appointing a tribunal to determine whether they should be accorded POW status. She points out that the United States' two strongest allies in the War on Terror, the United Kingdom and Australia, have similar articles in their military regulations, a fact that might prove problematic in the case of intended transfer of prisoners between countries. Avril McDonald, of the TMC Asser Institute for International Law at The Hague, argues that the denial of POW status to Taliban fighters was "legally flawed and at variance" with U.S. law. She surmises that the decision was taken to avoid being constrained by certain articles of the Geneva Convention. For example, once the armed conflict between the United States and Afghanistan ended, under the Convention all POWs were to be released as soon as possible, assuming that they had not been charged with specific crimes. However, the U.S. government has declared that it intended to detain, without charges, certain Taliban prisoners for an indefinite period for interrogation purposes.

Prisoners suspected of being Al Qaeda fighters, whether captured in Afghanistan, Iraq, or any other nation, are in a very different position. Most observers agree that they constitute illegal combatants, or "unprivileged belligerents"; they are neither entitled to any protection under the Geneva Convention as POWs, nor are they entitled to the presumption of POW status that Taliban fighters should enjoy. The most they can expect is to be treated humanely and according to the general precepts of international law.

However, even this level of treatment has not always been assured. Indeed, there has been growing concern over U.S. detention policies, beginning with the declaration that suspected terrorists could be held, indefinitely and without charge, for the purposes of interrogation (a practice that the U.S. Supreme Court had rejected in a June 2004 decision). The prisoner abuse scandal at Abu Ghraib prison added to fears that detainees were not being treated humanely, and in 2005 the ICRC expressed concern that a small number of captives were being held incommunicado at a facility in Charleston, South Carolina. To address these growing concerns, the U.S. Senate passed a resolution in October 2005 that would regulate the handling of detainees by establishing a set of rules that accorded with the spirit of the Geneva Convention. The White House, led by Vice President Dick Cheney, mounted strong opposition to this suggestion.

But in November 2005 came even more serious allegations, when the *Washington Post* reported that the Central Intelligence Agency (CIA) was holding key Al Qaeda suspects at secret detention centers, known as "black sites," in nations such as Thailand, Bulgaria, Poland, Romania, and Russia. The report suggested that 30 top Al Qaeda leaders were being held in CIA-run "black sites," while another 70 had been turned over for interrogation purposes to the intelligence services of Egypt, Jordan, Morocco, and other countries. The lobby group Human Rights Watch came forward with evidence, taken from flight logs, of an unusual number of CIA-controlled flights among Iraq, Afghanistan, Cuba, the United States, and suspected "black sites." By December this practice, known as "rendition," had implicated not only countries in the former Soviet bloc and the Middle East, but nations such as Ireland, Canada, and Germany as well. Flight logs showed CIA-operated aircraft stopping in these countries, leading some journalists to wonder if other governments were complicit in the practice of rendition. To address mounting pressure, the European Union's top human rights body, the Council of Europe, pledged to investigate the allegations, while the ICRC continues to request access to all detainees to ensure they are being treated humanely, a request that the U.S. government, as of December 2005, continued to deny.

The other controversial matter has been the U.S. decision, announced by President Bush in November 2001, to try terror suspects in military commissions rather than civilian courts. Before 9/11, the preferred option was to try terror suspects in district court, under federal statute. But, as legal scholar Ruth Wedgwood points out, this practice carried with it certain dangers: Sensitive intelligence information could not be protected once it was entered into evidence; the rules of evidence would disallow much of the material gathered; and that evidence was rarely gathered under a warrant, something that would make it inadmissible in court. As a result, convictions were anything but guaranteed. According to Wedgwood, this is why the U.S. government declined an offer from Sudan in 1996 to turn over Osama bin Laden: because there was considerable doubt that he could be convicted in court. Furthermore, Wedgwood notes that there are many precedents for the use of military commissions to try suspected war criminals or terror suspects. To cite just one example, some 2,500 Nazi and Japanese defendants were tried by military commissions after World War II, and there were few complaints about the justice of the process.

But others claim that the analogy is flawed; in both cases after World War II, the United States was acting as an occupying power, which is not the case in the War on Terror, and to use military commissions instead of federal courts is, according to Joan Fitzpatrick, "unprecedented and legally insupportable." These philosophical objections were soon accompanied by practical problems. The commissions began work at Guantánamo Bay in the fall of 2004, but ran into problems with translation, legal challenges, the resignation of two military prosecutors who claimed the system was unfair, and finally a federal district court ruling in November that they violated U.S. obligations under the Geneva Convention. In August 2005, the government, admitting that the use of military commissions had damaged American credibility with potential allies, announced changes to the system to address the gravest criticisms.

However, many legal scholars continue to maintain that suspected terrorists are best dealt with by bringing suspects to trial openly and transparently, according to the laws of individual countries. This has been the policy of the German government, which in August 2005 secured the conviction of a Moroccan man on the charge of belonging to an illegal organization (Al Qaeda). Two months later, a court in Düsseldorf sentenced two Jordanians, a Palestinian, and an Algerian to between five and eight years in prison for plotting attacks on two Jewish-owned nightclubs in the city, for belonging to a terrorist organization, and for possessing forged documents. Significantly, three of the most notable Al Qaeda suspects, the "Taliban American" John Walker Lyndh, Richard Reid, who tried to blow up an airliner with a bomb concealed in his shoe, and Zacarias Moussaoui, the alleged twentieth hijacker of the 9/11 attacks, have been prosecuted in federal court rather than by military commission. In sum, there seems little to be gained by creating a detention regime that, because of its secretiveness, invites scrutiny and criticism.

See also Abu Ghraib Prison; Afghan Wars; Guantánamo Bay; International Law; Iraq War; Walker Lyndh, John

References

George H. Aldrich, "The Taliban, al Qaeda, and the Determination of Illegal Combatants," *Humanitäres Völkerrecht* 15 (2002): 202–206.

Erin Chlopak, "Dealing with the Detainees at Guantanamo Bay: Humanitarian and Human Rights Obligations Under the Geneva Convention," *Human Rights Brief* 9 (2002): 6–9, 13.

Joan Fitzpatrick, "Jurisdiction of Military Commissions and the Ambiguous War on Terror," *American Journal of International Law* 96 (2002): 345–354.

Avril McDonald, "Defining the War on Terror and the Status of Detainees," *HEFT* 4 (2002): 206–209.

Sean D. Murphy, "Decision Not to Regard Persons Detained in Afghanistan as POWs," *American Journal of International Law* 96 (2002): 475–480.

Yasmin Naqvi, "Doubtful Prisoner-of-War Status," *International Red Cross Review* 84 (September 2002): 571–594.

Ruth Wedgwood, "Al Qaeda, Terrorism, and Military Commissions," *American Journal of International Law* 96 (2002): 328–337.

—*Jonathan F. Vance*

Wars of the Roses (1455–1485)

This series of struggles to gain control of the English throne saw great variations in the treatment of prisoners by the opposing sides, the houses of York and Lancaster. In the early battles, prisoners were usually treated with care and respect. After the Battle of St. Albans on 22 May 1455, for example, the Yorkist Earls of Devon, Dorset, and Pembroke and the Duke of Buckingham were taken prisoner and all were spared by their Lancastrian captors. At the Battle of Blore Heath (23 September 1459), three Yorkist knights were captured when they became separated from the main army; they were imprisoned in Chester Castle for nine months and then released. This relative mercy is noteworthy because, since the struggle was at various times a civil war and a rebellion, all prisoners might just as easily have been executed for treason immediately upon capture.

Indeed, after the Lancastrian defeat at Wakefield (30 December 1460), attitudes toward captives hardened. The Yorkists executed a number of noblemen captured during the battle, including Richard Neville, the Earl of Salisbury, and this series of ruthless killings set a precedent for the indiscriminate execution of prisoners by both sides. So, the Battle of Towton (29 March 1461) was followed by the execution of 42 Lancastrian knights (a number of others were pardoned), a situation that was repeated after the Battle of Hexham (25 April 1464). King Edward pardoned the noblemen he captured at the Battle of Tewkesbury (4 May 1471) but later had a change of heart; about a dozen nobles were tried for treason and executed.

Common soldiers experienced the same variations in treatment. It is recorded that at Towton, Edward and the Earl of Warwick shouted "Spare the commons! Kill the lords!" but their calls for partial mercy went unheeded; no quarter was given, and many soldiers who might have been captured were slaughtered where they stood. The same thing happened after Tewkesbury, when the Yorkist troops killed and looted any Lancastrian soldiers they captured. However, on other occasions, the victorious side believed that the commoners should not pay with their lives for the crimes of their nobles. So, after Hexham, the fortresses of Alnwick and Dunstanburgh capitulated when the Yorkists offered full pardon to all defenders. After Tewkesbury, Edward pardoned all common soldiers who had fought against him, and after the Battle of Stoke (16 June 1487) some 700 rebel soldiers were captured; a handful of them, mostly Irishmen, were executed, but the majority, including a number of German mercenaries, were allowed to go free.

It seems likely that these variations in treatment were more due to pragmatic rather than philosophical reasons. Some scholars have suggested that the rebels were freed after Stoke so that they could carry back to their villages news of the impossibility of further resistance. Furthermore, mercy was shown to captured nobles where there were allies to be made. If, on the other hand, there was a previous crime to be avenged, or a charge of treason was necessary to set an example, or if the unfortunate captive owned lands that were coveted by his captors, then his execution usually came swiftly.

References
Philip A. Haigh, *The Military Campaigns of the Wars of the Roses* (London: Alan Sutton, 1995).
Alison Weir, *Lancaster and York: The Wars of the Roses* (London: Jonathan Cape, 1995).

—*Jonathan F. Vance*

WERRA, FRANZ VON (1914–1941)

A Swiss-born fighter ace who was shot down over England during the Battle of Britain on 5 September 1940, Franz von Werra became the only German prisoner of war to escape from the west and reach home. Three weeks after his capture, the 26-year-old pilot was sent to a POW camp at Grizedale Hall in northern England, where he slipped away during an exercise walk 12 days later. Recaptured after three days, he was then sent to a more secure camp, the Hayes at Stanwick, near Derby. Once there, he and four friends dug a tunnel, which they breached successfully. Now on the run, he tried to steal a Hurricane fighter from a British airfield by pretending to be a Dutch pilot named van Lott. From the fighter's cockpit he told the duty officer he was based in Aberdeen, had been shot down, and wanted to return to his unit. The ruse did not succeed, and von Werra surrendered at gunpoint.

Sent to Canada with other German prisoners in January 1941, von Werra jumped from the train taking him to his new camp and walked south in appalling winter conditions, eventually crossing the frozen St. Lawrence River into the still neutral United States. He returned home to Germany a national hero. Franz von Werra resumed combat flying, but died on 25 October 1941 when his aircraft suffered engine failure and crashed into the North Sea.

See also Escape

References
Kendal Burt and James Leasor, *The One That Got Away* (London: Michael Joseph, 1956).
Fritz Wentzel, *Single or Return: The First Escape of a German POW from England* (London: William Kimber, 1954).

—*Colin Burgess*

WESTHEIMER, DAVID (1917–2005)

Born in Houston, Texas, Westheimer joined the Army Air Corps in 1941 and trained as a navigator in Florida before going overseas in July 1942 with the 344th Squadron of the 98th Bombardment Group (Heavy). The squadron flew Consolidated Liberator four-engine bombers, and Westheimer was on his twenty-ninth mission when his aircraft was shot down during a raid on Naples in December 1942. Seven of the 10 crew members survived to become POWs, initially at the quarantine camp at Poggio Mirteto and then at the prison camps at Chieti and Sulmona, Italy. Westheimer and his fellow prisoners enjoyed a brief taste of freedom when the Italian government capitulated in September 1943, but they were soon rounded up by German troops and sent north, first to Stalag 7A at Moosburg near Innsbruck, and then to Stalag Luft 3 at Sagan. That camp was evacuated in January 1945 as Russian troops approached, and Westheimer joined a column of American POWs that was sent south, back to Moosburg. He was finally liberated in April 1945.

Westheimer had studied creative writing at Rice University before the war, and filled his idle hours in captivity with reading. He took up writing after the war and published his first novel, *Summer on the Water*, in 1948. Five more novels followed before the publication of what would become his biggest seller, *Von Ryan's Express* (1964), about an American airman who leads a group of British POWs in an audacious escape scheme;

a year after the book was published, it was turned into a successful film starring Frank Sinatra. A sequel, *Von Ryan's Return*, which saw the main character escape from internment in neutral Switzerland to return to Italy on a covert mission, was published in 1980. Westheimer wrote many other novels and screenplays, and in 1992 published *Sitting It Out*, perhaps the best memoir to emerge from the American POW experience during World War II. In 2000, his collected poems appeared under the title *The Great Wounded Bird*, a volume that included many verses written in and about captivity. Westheimer died in Los Angeles in November 2005 of heart failure.

See also *Von Ryan's Express*

References
David Westheimer, *Von Ryan's Express* (New York: Doubleday, 1964).
——, *Von Ryan's Return* (New York: Coward, 1980).
——, *Sitting It Out: A World War II POW Memoir* (Houston: Rice University Press, 1992).
——, *The Great Wounded Bird and Other Poems* (Huntsville: Texas Review Press, 2000).

—*Jonathan F. Vance*

WIESENTHAL, SIMON (SZYMON) (1908–2005)

Known as the "Nazi Hunter," Holocaust survivor Simon Wiesenthal devoted his life to locating and collecting evidence against former Nazi war criminals. Wiesenthal grew up in Buczacz, formerly part of Austria-Hungary and now part of the Ukraine. In 1928 he applied to the Polytechnic Institute in Lvov, but his admission was denied because the quota of Jewish students had already been filled. Wiesenthal went on to the Technical University of Prague where he graduated with a degree in architectural engineering in 1932. In 1936, he married Cyla Mueller and together they resided in Lvov until their life changed with the signing of the Non-Aggression Pact between Germany and Russia.

Under Russian occupation, Wiesenthal's stepfather and stepbrother died in purges, while Wiesenthal was forced to vacate his architectural business. When in 1941 German occupiers replaced the Russians, Wiesenthal and his wife were forced into labor camps. With the implementation of the Final Solution in 1942, Wiesenthal's wife managed to escape the labor camps and to live out the rest of the war as a Pole, due to her blonde hair and false papers provided by the Polish Underground. Wiesenthal himself would spend the rest of the war being shuffled among 12 concentration camps, eventually being liberated from Mauthausen on 5 May 1945. The Wiesenthals were reunited in 1946, but together they lost 89 relatives in the Holocaust.

In the war's aftermath, Wiesenthal worked for the War Crimes section of the United States Army, where he was tasked with collecting evidence of wartime atrocities. With the completion of this assignment in 1947, he opened the Jewish Historical Documentation Center in Linz, Austria, once again devoting himself to evidence collection. The office eventually closed in 1954, but Wiesenthal continued his work privately. He described himself as being instrumental in the capture of Adolf Eichmann, although this fact has been disputed by Israeli agents responsible for the actual arrest. Following the capture of Eichmann, Wiesenthal was inspired to reopen the Jewish Documentation Center in Vienna, devoting his work strictly to the capture of war criminals. High-profile captures included Karl Silberbauer, the Gestapo officer who arrested Anne Frank, and Franz Stangl, former commandant of Treblinka and Sobibor concentration camps.

Wiesenthal went on to publish his memoirs, *The Murderers Among Us*, in 1967. He died 20 September 2005 at age 96, after having been credited with the capture of up to 1,100 war criminals.

References
Alan Levy, *The Wiesenthal File* (London: Constable, 1993)
Simon Wiesenthal, *The Murderers Among Us: The Simon Wiesenthal Memoirs* (New York: Bantam, 1967).
——, *Justice Not Vengeance* (London: Weidenfeld & Nicolson, 1989).

—*Teresa Iacobelli*

WODEHOUSE, SIR PELHAM GRENVILLE (1881–1975)

P. G. Wodehouse, the creator of Jeeves, the quintessential British valet, and author of novels, short stories, and Broadway lyrics, was captured by German forces on 22 May 1940 in Le Touquet, France, in the Channel coast. Initially placed under house arrest, Wodehouse was deported to the prison at Lille with other enemy nationals. Over the next year, he was transferred to prisons in Liège, Huy, and finally to a lunatic asylum at Tost, in southeast Germany. While there, Wodehouse mailed postcards to his American literary agent, requesting his agent send five-dollar checks to individuals in Canada. Upon receiving these checks, parents of missing Canadian airmen learned that their sons were alive and incarcerated with Wodehouse.

After an American Associated Press correspondent discovered Wodehouse in Tost, his American friends began to lobby the German government for his release. After allowing him to publish his story, "My War with Germany," the Germans confined Wodehouse to a hotel in Berlin and asked him to broadcast radio programs to America. The programs were heard in London, creating great controversy; Wodehouse was branded a traitor in the House of Commons and the newspaper columnist "Cassandra" launched a smear campaign. A government investigation cleared Wodehouse, but it was not released until 1980. Because of the controversy over his broadcasts, he was not welcome back in England, so he emigrated to the United States, becoming a U.S. citizen in 1955. Wodehouse was finally exonerated in January 1975 and granted a knighthood. He died the following month at the age of 93.

P. G. Wodehouse

See also Civilian Internees—World War II

References

Frances Donaldson, *P. G. Wodehouse: A Biography* (New York: Alfred A. Knopf, 1982).
Robert McCrum, *Wodehouse: A Life* (New York: W.W. Norton, 2004).
Kristin Thompson, *Wooster Proposes, Jeeves Disposes: or Le Mot Juste* (New York: Heinemann, 1992).
P. G. Wodehouse with William Townend, "Performing Flea," in *Wodehouse on Wodehouse* (London: Penguin, 1981).

—*Thomas L. Smith*

WOMEN

Women civilians and military personnel have been prisoners of war in various geographic regions and historical eras. Female residents living near war zones have been seized and held against their will by enemy troops. Other women became prisoners while voluntarily accompanying military forces; these camp followers were captured along with the soldiers when armies surrendered. Female combatants entered warfare knowing they could be seized as prisoners of war like male soldiers. Although fighting forces were expected to respect international protocol developed during the nineteenth and twentieth centuries regarding the treatment of prisoners, even in modern times, many women prisoners of war have suffered abuse, mistreatment, and sexual assaults by enemy captors who disregarded these conduct codes. Critics of countries that allow women to serve in combat argue that women should not be placed at risk of becoming prisoners of war. Ignoring the fact that for centuries there have been women war prisoners, these naysayers insist that female prisoners of war would detrimentally affect the morale of their male comrades, especially if they were aware that the women had been injured and suffered physical or emotional pain.

Since ancient times, literary and historical texts have alluded to women prisoners of war. Female captives were often considered spoils of war by their captors, who used the women as servants or prostitutes or sold them in exchange for desired goods. Their captors used women prisoners of war to bargain with opponents. Some of the better known cases of women prisoners of war include frontier residents abducted by Native Americans who were at war with settlers. Indian captivity narratives were popular from the late seventeenth through the nineteenth century, and women who survived and were rescued often printed a memoir or made public appearances at fairs and public meetings. Women were also prisoners during colonial conflicts, including the French and Indian War. Both colonial and British-allied women were prisoners in the American Revolution. Most women taken captive were British camp followers, including wives, daughters, and maids, although cases of civilian colonial women being held by British troops were publicized, often to cast the British in a negative manner.

During the American Civil War several prominent women became prisoners of war. Not only did surgeon Dr. Mary Walker oversee the women prisoners held at the Confederate prison in Louisville, Kentucky, but she also was imprisoned there herself. Serving four months, Walker was held under suspicion that she had spied for the Union Army. She later became the only woman to receive the Medal of Honor for her wartime service and was well-known nationwide. Pauline Cushman was also arrested by Confederates for allegations of spying. Union troops saved her from being executed. On the other side, Belle Boyd spent time in a Union prison because she engaged in espionage for the Confederacy. Nancy Hart was imprisoned by Union forces because she aided Confederate forces, and she disarmed her guard to shoot him and return to Confederate service.

The world wars produced both famous and anonymous female prisoners of war. Edith Cavell and Mata Hari were imprisoned and executed, based on accusations that they were spies in World War I. In World War II, large groups of military nurses were interned by the Japanese in the Philippines, Sumatra, and Japan. Civilian women, many of whom had been living in Asia or were traveling there when the war began, were captured with their children and confined to internment camps in the Philippines and the East Dutch Indies.

At the Santo Tomas Internment Camp on a college campus near Manila, several thousand female war prisoners, like many internees, experienced a drastic change in lifestyle. Many of the women had been upper-class residents, and the loss of their social status and privileges was demoralizing. All prisoners were expected to work, and women often performed tasks they considered beneath their dignity. Women prisoners were forced to abandon their roles, living standards, and expectations. While imprisoned, they did not receive recognition for their talents and social graces or enjoy their husbands' ample salaries. They fought to retain their individuality while coping with daily issues and survival in the camp's tense atmosphere. Women slept on mattresses on the floor in a building filled with prisoners. A 6:30 curfew required everyone to go inside, with lights out a half hour later.

Child care proved challenging for women in these camps, especially those who had relied on servants and now had to learn how to cook, clean, and communicate with their children. Most of the women's husbands had been sent to other camps or were fighting in the war, and pregnant women faced childbirth away from friends and family. Other women secured male partners in the camp and became pregnant. During the first six months of internment, the prisoners received minimal food and had to obtain food by foraging, trading with natives, and growing their own gardens. Many of the women were unfamiliar with such procedures, although the more fortunate prisoners could avoid them because they had external contacts who sent them supplies and money. Women had to wait in line for the few supplies provided by camp officials; while they conducted these and other chores, their children played together on camp playgrounds.

Everyone worked for several hours each day, and many women aimed to get the sought-after jobs as teachers and clerks. The camp school offered classes for adults who wanted to learn languages or improve their business skills for postwar employment. There were English-language classes so that non–English speakers could converse with their neighbors. Women served on educational committees and raised funds for supplies. After work, women could participate in recreational activities, playing cards or board games, or could attend dances and observe ball games and theatrical performances organized by the male prisoners. Some women preferred to knit, sew, tend the garden, or learn carpentry skills. These familiar routines kept women busy and helped them to avoid the depression and despair provoked by internment. If a woman became physically or mentally ill, a boarding school in the camp took care of her children. Suffering from dysentery and malnutrition, as well as other diseases, many women stopped menstruating. Some women were hospitalized because they failed to respond to medical treatment.

Isolated from the world, women often risked death or other punishment from guards by listening to radios. Passing notes between camps was also forbidden, but women prisoners managed to send and receive messages to and from friends and spouses. Few letters arrived by mail, and those that did were often a year old and severely censored. Women prisoners often learned the location of their husbands only months, even years, after their capture. Others were informed their spouse had died. Suddenly single parents, many women prisoners focused their attention on their children. Many women became religious and many found their faith intensified. Finally, in February 1945, the women prisoners at Santo Tomas saw paratroopers landing outside their compound to rescue them.

Approximately, 80,000 Dutch, British, and Australian women and children who had been living in a Dutch colony were interned in Japanese prisoner-of-war camps in the Dutch East Indies when the Japanese army occupied those islands in March 1942. Segregated by gender, these civilians experienced abrupt lifestyle changes similar to those experienced by the women in Santo Tomas. Although the guards took most prisoners' possessions, some women managed to secure paper and pencils to draw scenes of camp life. The women lived in a variety of buildings, ranging from monasteries to huts. They were expected to perform labor in camp. Like the women at Santo Tomas, the women lived in crowded conditions and suffered starvation and illness. The extreme heat and humidity of the tropical climate made life miserable. Mosquitoes transmitted malaria, and women also developed dysentery because of their poor diet and because water sources were contaminated. An estimated 10,000 women and children died while imprisoned by the Japanese in the Dutch East Indies. When rations were reduced in 1944 as the Japanese war effort faltered, women prisoners relied on gardens they planted. They also bartered with local residents for food and sometimes ate reptiles for protein. Women were expected to perform all necessary tasks around the camp, from planting to digging graves. Exhausted, many women relied on religion to strengthen them spiritually, singing "The Captives' Hymn" at Sunday services.

In Europe, women prisoners of war included well-known individuals such as Lieutenant Reba Whittle, a nurse who was shot down on an air evacuation mission in September 1944. Resistance workers, including Mildred Harnack-Fish and Sophie Scholl, were captured, imprisoned, and executed for their efforts to impede the German military and disseminate anti-Nazi material. Other women were arrested for hiding Allied soldiers and Jews, helping prisoners to escape, or sabotaging military machinery. The millions of women imprisoned during the Holocaust, many of them killed, represent the largest group of women prisoners of war. Many survivors have written memoirs of their years in the camps, providing us with first-hand accounts of the women who died while imprisoned.

Many movies document the internment of World War II women prisoners of war. Some treatments are fictional, while others are based on individuals' stories or commonly shared experiences. For example, *Three Came Home* depicts the incarceration of Agnes Newton Keith, who lived in Japanese prison camps throughout the war. *Paradise Road* portrays the female colonists held prisoner in Sumatra. And *Sophie's Choice* portrays the agonizing situations encountered by Jewish female prisoners during the Holocaust.

In conflicts after World War II, several women have been known to be prisoners of war, and others probably were also held, as individuals or in groups, but not reported. German nurses Monika Schwinn, Marie-Luise Kerber, and Hindrika Kortmann were captured by North Vietnamese troops in 1969 during the Vietnam War. Kerber and Kortmann died in captivity, and Schwinn became the only female captive at the infamous North Vietnamese prison camp known as the Hanoi Hilton. Liberated in 1973, she wrote a book about her experiences, her friends who died, and the American prisoners she met. Several female missionaries were prisoners in Laos and Vietnam. Evelyn Anderson and Beatrice Kosin were captured and set on fire in 1972. Betty Ann Olsen and Eleanor Ardel Vietti were imprisoned during the Tet Offensive at the leprosarium where they worked in Ban Me Thuot. Olsen died and was buried on the Ho Chi Minh Trail, and Vietti is considered a missing prisoner of war whose whereabouts are unknown.

Two American women were prisoners of war in the Persian Gulf War. Major Rhonda L. Cornum and Melissa Rathbun-Nealy were captured by Iraqi soldiers and held for several weeks. Cornum wrote a book about her imprisonment, divulging that a soldier had sexually attacked her. In the 1990s, Yugoslavian women were seized by enemy troops and assaulted while being held captive.

Probably more women have been prisoners of war than reports indicate. Some countries do not reveal who they have captured and where they are held, and other nations engage in covert action in which such information and statistics are not recorded. Women have also been political prisoners, jailed for speaking out against victorious military leaders. Cultural attitudes toward women, including those that see women as property or deny them civil rights, have often determined how they are treated while imprisoned and whether their existence is publicly acknowledged. Few female prisoners of war have received recognition or military awards for their captivity. Those who survived to be liberated have returned home, where they attempt to adjust to nonprison careers and domestic responsibilities. Ironically, many women considered their imprisonment as a time of growth in which they had the freedom and time to learn who they were and discover their strengths while encountering adversity.

See also Camp Followers; Cavell, Edith; Children; Families; Nurses; Walker, Mary Edwards

—Elizabeth D. Schafer

Wooden Horse

One of the most innovative escapes of World War II, the Wooden Horse escape was also one of the most successful. In the summer of

1943, a group of British airmen in Stalag Luft 3 Sagan devised an ingenious escape plan: they would sink a tunnel from the middle of the compound, thereby reducing by about half the required length of the tunnel. To camouflage the shaft, they proposed to construct a wooden vaulting horse that would be carried into the compound and used for exercise by the prisoners. The interior of the horse was constructed so that two or even three men, with all the necessary digging equipment, could be carried inside. Each day, prisoners carried the horse to a spot in the compound and took turns vaulting over it; beneath the horse, workers sunk a short shaft and started to dig toward the wire. Beginning on 8 July 1943, the daily routine continued until the tunnel reached a shallow ditch outside the wire. On 29 October 1943, three POWs, Eric Williams, Michael Codner, and Oliver Philpot, crept out of the tunnel and away from the camp. Williams and Codner, disguised as French businessmen, traveled to Stettin (now Szczecin in Poland); there, they stowed away on a neutral ship and reached neutral Sweden on 11 November. Philpot, disguised as a Norwegian Nazi, headed for Danzig, where he too smuggled himself aboard a neutral ship; he reached Sweden on 3 November.

After the war, both Williams and Philpot published accounts of their escape. Williams's fictionalized account, *The Wooden Horse*, became a best-seller and was made into a motion picture by the same name in 1950. He then embarked on a profitable writing career and spent his retirement sailing European waters on his yacht Escaper. He died in 1983. Philpot lived a quiet life until his death in London in 1993. Codner joined the British colonial service after the war and died at the hands of guerrillas in Malaya in March 1952.

See also Escape; Great Escape; Stalag Luft 3

References

Oliver Philpot, *Stolen Journey* (London: Hodder and Stoughton, 1950).

Eric Williams, *The Wooden Horse* (Barnsley, UK: Pen and Sword Books, 2005 [1949]).

—Jonathan F. Vance

WORLD WAR I—AFRICA

The campaigns in Africa in World War I were some of the most unusual of the war in terms of combatants, tactics, and events. The situation in the German colonies in east, west, and southwest Africa also revealed the degree to which race affected captivity issues.

In September 1914, at the urging of the British government, a South African army under Louis Botha invaded German South-West Africa (present-day Namibia), but the offensive ended in an embarrassing reverse at the Battle of Sandfontein. A number of South African soldiers were captured in this engagement, and they were eventually joined by men taken in subsequent actions. The prisoners were held in two camps, at Tsumeb and Namutoni, in the north end of the colony, and appear to have been well treated. Wood-carving supplies, theatrical materials, and musical instruments were available for recreation, and the prisoners organized sports and a small library. They were permitted to work for pay and could buy clothing, liquor, and other amenities in local shops. Rations included beef and rum and anything else they could steal from the railway yard and warehouses where many of them worked. They exercised strict discipline in the camp and seem to have been most aggrieved at the fact that they were guarded by blacks. Botha repaid the fair treatment when the last German forces in South-West Africa surrendered in July 1915. Indeed, he was criticized at the time for being "generous to a fault" to the vanquished enemy.

In German East Africa, there was also controversy over the use of natives to guard white prisoners. British and Belgian POWs captured early in the campaign there were held at Kilimatinde, where the treatment was generally good. As in South-West Africa, rations included meat and potatoes, and the prisoners could purchase extras—like tea, tobacco, sugar, and liquor—with an allowance paid to them by their captors. The camp guards did not hold roll calls, and they permitted the prisoners to take regular walks outside the camp. When typhoid struck the compound, German doctors were brought in and dealt with the crisis quickly and efficiently. In April 1916, the prisoners were moved to Tabora, where their numbers eventually totaled some 2,000 Belgian and British POWs, 100 British missionaries, and around 30 British women and children. At Tabora, the prisoners enjoyed clean quarters (complete with native servants), decent food (again, served by natives), and many opportunities for educational improvement. One incident, however, affronted the contemporary press: the white prisoners were allegedly forced to pull a heavy wagon while blacks looked on and jeered. There were also allegations that Belgian soldiers abused German civilians after Tabora was captured in September 1916; these charges brought a reprisal from Germany, which ordered the imprisonment of 23 prominent Belgians in Germany. Subsequent investigation revealed that the German civilians had not been mistreated; they had, however, asked to be moved to internment camps in France because they feared that native soldiers in the Belgian army were cannibalistic.

References

Percy Close, *A Prisoner of the Germans in South-West Africa* (Capetown: T. Maskew Miller, n.d. [1919]).

Byron Farwell, *The Great War in Africa, 1914–1918* (New York: Norton, 1986).

E. C. Holtom, *Two Years Captivity in German East Africa* (London: Hutchinson, n.d.).

Charles Miller, *The Battle for the Bundu: The First World War in East Africa* (New York: Macmillan, 1974).

—*Jonathan F. Vance*

World War I—Eastern Front

Captivity was one of the most characteristic aspects of warfare on the eastern front during World War I. In contrast to the static trench combat of the western front, warfare in the east was mobile, with the front shifting back and forth hundreds of miles. As a result, from the very first battles of the war, the armies of Russia (a member of the Allied Entente), Germany, and Austria-Hungary (the Central Powers) captured a very large number of enemy soldiers. In the battle of Tannenberg alone (August 1914), 92,000 Russian soldiers were taken captive by the German army, while at Przemyśl (March 1915) and Luts'k (June 1916) the Austro-Hungarian army lost to captivity 117,000 and 240,000 soldiers respectively. Overall, during three and a half years of fighting on the eastern front, roughly five million soldiers were taken captive: Russia captured 2.27 million enemy soldiers (2.11 million from Austria-Hungary and 167,000 from Germany), Germany captured 1.43 million Russian soldiers, and Austria-Hungary captured 1.27 million Russian soldiers.

All three belligerent powers on the eastern front were signatories of the Hague Conventions of 1899 and 1907, which had codified the treatment of POWs. This meant that they accepted the obligation to behave "humanely" toward the prisoners and to treat them "on the same footing as the troops of the Government who had captured them." In general terms, Russia, Germany, and Austria-Hungary all attempted to abide by the specific provisions of the Hague Conventions, and in contrast to other twentieth-century conflicts, one seldom finds examples of torture and deliberate violence inflicted upon prisoners. Nevertheless, the complete lack of preparedness to house, feed, and clothe the massive numbers of POWs meant that living conditions in the camps—especially in Russia—dipped at times below acceptable standards. During the first two years of the war (1914–1916) rank-and-file prisoners were often interned in makeshift and overcrowded quarters without basic sanitary and medical facilities. As a result, cases of typhus, typhoid fever, and dysentery were common, and outbreaks of epidemics were recorded in camps in Wittenberg (Germany), Mauthausen (Austria-Hungary), and many camps in Russia. The POW camp at Totskoye, near Samara, Russia, was probably the most disease-ridden camp of the war, with a typhus

Austrian soldiers guarding a group of bedraggled Serbian POWs captured in the fighting in the east (from Collier's Photographic History of the European War *[New York: 1916])*

epidemic in the winter of 1915–1916 claiming the lives of over 9,000 of the camp's 17,000 inmates. The living conditions of the rank-and-file POWs began to improve gradually from the second year of the war, due to accelerated construction of permanent camps, widespread usage of POW labor (which gave many POWs better access to food, improved lodgings, and supplemental income), and the distribution of relief by Red Cross societies from the fall of 1915 onward. The March 1917 Revolution in Russia brought with it a less restrictive regime in the rank-and-file camps, and many prisoners were allowed to interact freely with the Russian population. Following the Bolshevik Revolution in November of that year, rank-and-file prisoners were officially promised by the new government the same rights as Soviet citizens. However, the descent of Russia into political chaos and civil war meant that the treatment and condition of the prisoners were decided on a local level rather than prescribed from above.

In contrast to the overall harsh living conditions of rank-and-file prisoners, POW officers were treated generally as "gentlemen." This meant superior lodgings, a monthly salary paid by the captor state, and an exemption from any kind of labor. POW officers were also granted permission to organize self-improvement courses, pursue sports, raise theatrical productions, and use their salaries for additional purchases outside of camp. From 1917 onward, the inflationary pressures in Germany, Austria-Hungary, and Russia reduced the purchasing power of POW officers' salaries and limited their ability to ameliorate their living conditions. The overall scarcity of foodstuffs at the end of the war, especially in Germany and Austria, significantly affected the diet of POW officers and reduced the gap between them and the rank-and-file prisoners.

All three belligerent powers on the eastern front attempted to induce POWs to become disloyal to their home state. This was done by targeting prisoners from specific national groups and encouraging them to volunteer for national military formations. Special "propaganda camps" were designated for specific nationalities with improved living conditions, a national cultural program, and frequent visits by émigré national politicians. Rastatt, Salzwedel, and Wetzlar in Germany, Freistadt and Kenyermezo-Tabor in Austria-Hungary, and Darnitsa, Tyumen', Kirsanov, and Odessa in Russia served as "propaganda camps" during various stages of the war. Apart from the Czech Legion, which managed to recruit some 40,000 Czech and Slovak POWs to fight on the side of Russia, all other national formations failed to attract a significant number of prisoners. This failure was the result of the general unwillingness of POWs to return to the front, the higher priority placed by captor states on the usage of POWs as agricultural and industrial labor, and the rather lukewarm support given to the recruitment drives by government officials in the multinational states of Russia and Austria-Hungary. Attempts to recruit POWs to fight with the Red Army in 1918 were also generally unsuccessful. Nevertheless, in one significant case, that of ethnic Hungarian POWs, the Red Army did manage to find many volunteers. During the short-lived Hungarian Soviet Republic in 1919, the Hungarian Communist leadership consisted of a significant number of former POWs.

The negotiations between the Bolsheviks and the Central Powers in Brest-Litovsk during the winter of 1917–1918 did not result in a quick and orderly repatriation of POWs. The ensuing treaty (March 1918) accepted repatriation in general terms, but further negotiations were needed during the summer of 1918 to hammer out the details. As a result of the delay, about 500,000 POWs were trapped in Siberia and Central Asia for the duration of the Russian Civil War (1918–1920) and close to 200,000 Russian POWs were prevented by the Entente Powers from returning home after the war had ended in the west. Repatriation resumed in earnest only in 1920, with the last prisoners returning home by the spring of 1922. The Norwegian explorer Fridtjof Nansen, who had been appointed by the Council of the League of Nations to coordinate repatriation efforts, received the Nobel Peace Prize for 1922 for his work in this regard.

See also Brändström, Elsa; Czech Legion; Murman Railway

—*Alon Rachamimov*

WORLD WAR I—FAR EAST

At the outbreak of World War I, the German colonies in the Pacific were virtually undefended. There were a few native police-soldiers, but the German colonists themselves were both physically and temperamentally unsuited for military service. As a result, the colonies were occupied by Allied forces with little opposition: New Zealand troops took over Samoa in August 1914; Australian forces occupied New Guinea in September 1914; and Japanese forces took possession of German Micronesia in October 1914.

There was no general internment of German colonists, but individuals were imprisoned for specific reasons. On 30 November 1914, four German colonists on Rabaul were arrested and publicly whipped for an alleged assault on an Australian missionary. Later in the war, there was a general internment of all Germans on Rabaul, including women, but it was short-lived; most prisoners were soon released, although colonists who refused to swear an oath of neutrality were deported to Australia.

German officials on Samoa were sent to New Zealand for internment in a damp and drafty compound on Motuihi Island off Auckland, and later on Somes Island in Wellington Bay, where other Germans from New Zealand were interned. Eventually, the Somes Island camp held nearly 300 internees, and local officials declared that they could accept to more. However, the apparently unstable New Zealand administrator on Samoa, Colonel Robert Logan, was determined to detain all Germans in the territory, and built Sogi Internment Camp to hold Germans who were arrested for such minor offenses as flying German flags or singing German songs. Later, Logan was denied permission to execute a number of recaptured escapers, and only the war's end prevented him from interning every single German on Samoa.

Also noteworthy are the experiences of the crew of the German gunboat *Cormoran*, which had taken refuge on U.S.-controlled Guam when the war began. When the United States entered the war in April 1917, the German crewmen were deported to U.S. prison camps, while 28 Melanesian crewmen were held as POWs on Guam. However, they were treated less generously than their white shipmates, receiving sharply reduced rations (American officials believed they worked better on less food) and living in a ramshackle camp that was known as Cannibal Town, a reference to local misconceptions about the Melanesians' taste in food. The prisoners remained on Guam until January 1919, when they were returned to Rabaul.

The largest groups of prisoners in the Far East was in Japan, which had agreed to act as detaining power for some 4,600 Germans captured in China at the outbreak of hostilities. Held in 12 camps (later reduced to eight), they were treated generously: they had orchestras, gardens, parole walks, canteens, recreation facilities, and adequate food. The prisoners also received much aid from the Japanese YMCA. At Christmas, YMCA delegates went to great trouble to procure Christmas trees for the POWs, and also supplied 2,500 candles, 50,000 sheets of writing paper, and 1,500 envelopes. Indeed, there seems to have been considerable sympathy for the German POWs, not just on the part of their captors but within the civilian population around the camps in which they were interned.

References

Charles Burdick and Ursula Moessner, *The German Prisoners of War in Japan, 1914–1920* (Lanham, MD: University Press of America, 1984).

Olive Checkland, *Humanitarianism and the Emperor's Japan, 1877–1977* (New York: St. Martin's Press, 1994).

Gerhard Fischer, *Enemy Aliens: Internment and the Homefront Experience in Australia, 1914–1920* (St. Lucia: Queensland University Press, 1989).

Hermann Joseph Hiery, *The Neglected War: The German South Pacific and the Influence of World War I* (Honolulu: University of Hawai'i Press, 1995).

S.S. Mackenzie, *The Australians at Rabaul: The Capture and Administration of German Possessions in the Southern Pacific* (Melbourne: Angus and Robertson, 1927).

F.A. Maguire and R.W. Cilento, "The Occupation of German New Guinea," in *The Official History of the Australian Army Medical Services in the War of 1914–1918*, vol. 1, ed. A.G. Butler (Melbourne: Australian War Memorial, 1930).

C. D. Rowley, *The Australians in German New Guinea, 1914–1921* (Carlton: Melbourne University Press, 1958).

Herbert T. Ward, *Flight of the Cormoran* (New York: Vantage Press, 1970).

—*Jonathan F. Vance*

WORLD WAR I—MIDDLE EAST

Contemporary polemicists and later historians agree that captivity in Turkish hands during World War I was an experience of almost unequaled brutality. When Sir Charles Townshend surrendered the garrison of Kut-al-Amara to Turkish forces in April 1915, nearly 13,000 British and Indian officers and other ranks became prisoners. For the officers, as well as for members of the Royal Flying Corps who fell into Turkish hands during aerial operations, conditions were spartan but acceptable. The majority of them were confined in Anatolia, in empty buildings that had been requisitioned from local civilians. Rations were generally poor, but the prisoners were largely left to their own devices; the Turks believed there was little danger of escape, given the fact that the camps were so isolated. Even the senior British officers discouraged escape; one airmen was told by a superior that, if he persisted in planning an escape, he would be turned over to the Turks. Nevertheless, by 1917 a number of the officers began serious preparations for escape; in August 1917 a group of three succeeding in reaching British lines after escaping from Kastamuni, and in August 1918 a group of eight successfully escaped from Yozgat.

In contrast to this relative comfort and despite promises that they would be treated as honored guests of the Turkish Sultan, the troops suffered appalling ill-treatment and died by the thousands. Their agony began on the march from Kut to Baghdad, when a combination of disease, battle wounds, lack of food and water, and exhaustion thinned the ranks of the captives. The sickest were left in Baghdad, and 345 of these were eventually exchanged for a similar number of wounded Turkish prisoners. The rest were put through another long march to Ras al 'Ain, where primitive camps had been established for them; by the time they arrived, however, over 3,000 of the POWs had died. The survivors were put to work on the Baghdad railway, but by September, disease, heat exhaustion, overwork, and poor rations had rendered them ineffective as a labor force. American medical and consular officials were able to collect a few of the stragglers and some of the sickest POWs, but the rest endured another long march to camps in Asia Minor and another litany of abuses at the hands of their captors. To add to their physical discomforts, the Indian prisoners were also subject to coercive measures, as the Turks pressured them (unsuccessfully) into joining the Turco-German forces fighting against the Allies. For months, the Turks refused to allow neutral observers access to the camps; only after much effort were American diplomatic officials permitted to do what they could to ameliorate conditions in the camps. By then, it was too late for many prisoners; 2,500 of the 9,300 Indian POWs and fully 70 percent of the British POWs died in Turkish camps.

That there was studied brutality is beyond question, but cultural factors also conspired against the British prisoners. Overcrowding, poor rations, infestations of vermin, and primitive living quarters were their lot, but Turkish soldiers probably lived in conditions that were not markedly different. In some sense, then, the Turks probably did observe one of the fundamentals of international law pertaining to captivity at the time: that prisoners be fed and housed at the standards of the detaining power's own garrison troops. That this was considerably less than British prisoners needed for survival says as much about the inadequacy of international law as it does about the Turkish attitude toward prisoners.

See also Townshend, Sir Charles Vere Ferrers

References

A.J. Barker, *The Neglected War: Mesopotamia, 1914–1918* (London: Faber, 1967).

R.S. Gwatkin-Williams, *Prisoners of the Red Desert, Being a Full and True History of the Men of the "Tara"* (London: Thornton Butterworth, 1919).

C.W. Hill, *The Spook and the Commandant* (London: William Kimber, 1975).

M.A.B. Johnston and K.D. Yearsley, *450 Miles to Freedom* (London: William Blackwood, 1919).

E.H. Jones, *The Road to En-Dor* (London: John Lane, 1919).

Sir Thomas White, *Guests of the Unspeakable* (London: John Hamilton, 1928).

—Jonathan F. Vance

World War I—Ottoman Empire

Although the somewhat chaotic nature of the war in the Ottoman Empire makes it impossible to determine with any accuracy the number of Ottomans—mostly Turks, but also Arabs and other ethnic groups in smaller numbers—captured by the Entente during World War I, it is estimated that approximately 250,000 Ottomans became POWs. The British by far captured the most Ottomans (150,000), followed by the Russians (estimates range between 61,000 and 90,000), while the French had 2,000 at most. The Ottoman POWs captured by the British were interned in places such as India, Burma, and Cyprus, but a great majority of them were in various camps in Egypt.

While the overwhelming majority of the Ottoman prisoners in Russia were captured on the Turco-Russian front in the Caucasus, a significant number of them became prisoners on the Galician front. As the Russian Empire was unprepared to deal with the large numbers of prisoners it captured, the soldiers of the Central Powers were generally quartered in makeshift, overcrowded, and unsanitary conditions. The result was outbreaks of typhus and various other diseases, which cost many prisoners their lives. A few contemporaries point out that Turkish prisoners suffered considerably, some freezing to death during transport to prison camps because of Russian neglect and indifference. The majority of the Ottoman POWs in Russian captivity were interned in Siberia, where conditions for POWs were worse than in European Russia. In contrast to the officers, the rank and file were employed in various branches of Russian industry and suffered from harsh conditions and treatment, especially before the Russian Revolution.

In Egypt, Ottomans captured by the British were kept in newly constructed barbed-wire camps. As the climate allowed it, the prisoners were first quartered in tents, then moved into more permanent buildings. Better climate, hygienic conditions, and generally more adequate camps made the lives of these Ottoman prisoners easier as compared to their comrades in Russia. Unfortunately, our knowledge about the roughly 18,000 Ottoman POWs in India and Burma is even more fragmentary.

Whether in Russia, Egypt, India, Burma, or France, the prisoners managed to devise activities to deal with their boredom and make their lives in captivity more productive. For these purposes, the prisoners organized schools and workshops to teach or learn foreign languages, gain new skills, or simply to learn how to read and write. Both the British and the Russians separated the Turks from the Arabs in hopes of widening the division among the two groups. The British especially recruited from among the Arab POWs to join the forces of Sherif Hussein, who revolted against the Ottoman government. It is clear that the Ottoman POWs in Russia suffered more than those in British and French captivity, many dying as a result of cold, hunger, or disease. Unfortunately, the available sources do not allow us to give precise numbers, but close to 25 percent of Ottoman POWs died in Russian captivity. About 10 percent (15,000) of the Turks in British captivity were blind at least in one eye when they returned. While the POWs and the Turkish government blamed inadequate British medical services, the blindness was most likely the result of trachoma, an eye disease prevalent in the area. Repatriation of the POWs dragged on for a few years after the war ended; some prisoners were not able to return home until 1922–1923.

References

Mehmet Arif Ölçen, *Vetluga Memoir: A Turkish Prisoner of War in Russia* (Gainesville: University of Florida Press, 1995).

Turkish Prisoners in Egypt: A Report by the Delegates of the International Committee of the Red Cross (London: HMSO, 1917).

Yücel Yanīdağ, "Ottoman Prisoners of War in Russia, 1914–22," *Journal of Contemporary History* 34 (1999): 69–85.

— *Yücel Yanīkdağ*

WORLD WAR I—WESTERN FRONT

On the western front, World War I was largely static, with the combatants facing each other in long lines of trenches. Groups of prisoners were captured during this phase, in trench raids and limited offensives, but the large groups of POWs were taken during the open-warfare phases in 1914 and 1918.

Very early in the war, the German government found itself having to cope with a deluge of POWs: 141,000 French, 31,000 Belgian, and 9,000 British soldiers were captured by the middle of October 1914. These numbers grew in fits and starts as the war progressed. By February 1915, for example, the numbers had grown to 245,000 French, 39,000 Belgian, and 18,000 British. In the winter of 1917, there were about 40,000 British POWs in Germany. The Battle of Cambrai in November 1917 resulted in the capture of another 9,000, but the largest group fell into German hands in March 1918, during the German spring offensive. At that time, roughly 100,000 British soldiers were taken prisoner, the majority from the disintegrated 5th Army. By the time the war ended, there were 6,577 British officers and 161,026 enlisted men in German camps, in addition to some 10,000 soldiers from the dominions and colonies of the British Empire, 1,100 members of the Royal Navy, and 3,073 officers and other ranks from the Royal Naval Division. At the same time, German camps held 350,000 French and 43,000 American POWs.

British forces captured about 328,000 German POWs during the war, some 184,000 of whom were held in British-run camps in France. There were also 400,000 German prisoners in France who had been captured by the French armies. The French government also held a number of Turkish and Bulgarian POWs, whom they interned on the island of Corsica.

These figures include a number of unusual groups of POWs. Some 65,000 Austro-Hungarian prisoners were captured by Serbia, but disease, wounds, and accidents so thinned their ranks that by the time they reached prison camps in France, there were only about 20,000 left. The French separated those who clearly had enemy sympathies from those who were apparently serving under duress. Included in this group were Danes from Schleswig, Franco-Germans from Alsace-Lorraine, Bulgarians, and a number of anti-German Austro-Hungarians. Deserted by their governments, they were viewed sympathetically by the French, who gave them favored prisoner status and allowed them greater freedom and more privileges than other POWs enjoyed. Another unusual group of prisoners was the 20,000-strong Russian Expeditionary Force, which was promptly interned when the Russian-German armistice was signed. They were later joined in captivity in France by 45,000 Russians released from prison camps in the Rhineland.

In general, conditions were best in the camps for German POWs in Britain and in the camps that the American Expeditionary Force operated for the POWs it captured. Conditions were slightly less favorable in the French-run camps, while the worst conditions were undoubtedly found in the work camps in Germany. As in most conflicts, officers lived rather better than enlisted men, regardless of the nation in which they were detained.

Without question, the most favorable conditions prevailed in Britain. Officers lived in a number of stately former homes like Grizedale Hall and Donington Hall, where conditions were cramped but quite comfortable. Some 11,000 POWs were held on prison ships. These were not nineteenth-century-style hulks, however, but troopships with excellent facilities. Fewer than half of the POWs in Britain were put to work; those who did labor tended to work on farms, or in ports or forests in France. In terms of diet, a working prisoner in the early years of the war received roughly 4,600 calories per day, and even when food shortages struck Britain later in the war, working POWs still received some 3,000 calories per day. By any stretch of the imagination, this was generous, for POW rations like this have rarely been matched in any war.

The French government was initially overwhelmed by the number of German prisoners and had to find space for them in prison ships and tented cities; some were even transferred to camps in North Africa. Once the first influx was accommodated, however, the French began building prefabricated prison camps, and conditions improved greatly. Of particular concern was reciprocal treatment with respect to French prisoners in Germany. The French extended parole to German officer prisoners but stopped the practice upon learning that the Germans were not extending parole to French officers. By the same token, French officials abided by the Hague Convention and did not force prisoners to work in enterprises connected to the war effort until they learned Germany was forcing French POWs to labor in war-related industries. Furthermore, there were three ration scales for POWs in France: favored, for soldiers captured after they had been impressed into service by the German army; normal, for Turkish or Austro-Hungarian prisoners; and reciprocal, for German POWs, a diet that had been reduced to match the caloric intake of French POWs in Germany. Nevertheless, the conditions of captivity in France were generally good, even among the 75 percent of POWs who worked. The fact that France did not release its last POWs until 1920, but rather kept them at work repairing war damage, must be balanced against the reality of life in postwar Germany, which suggests that many POWs were in fact better off staying in France.

When the United States entered the war in April 1917, they had had nearly three years of experience in inspecting prison camps and trying to ensure that POWs were as well treated as possible. In light of this, it is striking that the standards of living in the U.S.-run camps in France were so inadequate. The American forces had initially transferred the POWs they captured to French control, but they stopped this practice when American soldiers started falling into German hands; U.S. officials believed it important to retain some German POWs to ensure that American POWs were well treated. However, the American camps were plagued by overcrowding, inadequate facilities—some POWs were even sheltered in tents, years after the other belligerent states had stopped this practice—and dangerous work. In one incident involving POWs who had been ordered to help dispose of munitions, an explosion killed 25 prisoners. The survivors mounted a work stoppage, but the authorities maintained their right to put prisoners to this type of work. It would later be outlawed by international lawmakers.

The most brutal conditions, though, were in German work camps. Some prisoners were lucky enough to be sent to agricultural labor camps or farms, where the work was pleasant and there was the opportunity to procure extra food. Others were sent to industrial concerns managed by businessmen who realized that a contented work force is an efficient work force. Such prisoners enjoyed relatively good food, spartan but clean living quarters, adequate recreational opportunities, and safe working conditions. But many more POWs were forced to work in dangerous conditions under the supervision of vicious overseers. Ten- or 12-hour days were the rule, and the pay and rations were poor. One prisoner worked in a lumber camp in East Prussia for a wage that was the equivalent of a cent an hour. The dangers were ever present. In mines or factories, minor cuts often went untreated, often leading to blood poisoning. Arms and legs were caught in machinery, causing frightful injuries. Prisoners working in salt mines developed painful open sores on their arms and legs; others were killed by rock falls in coal mines. Supervisors would beat prisoners whom they deemed to be working too slowly and conferred severe punishments for minor infractions. Many POWs found that the physical affects of these abuses remained with them for decades after the war.

For the adventurous prisoner, escape offered a means to regain one's freedom. Compared to World War II, escape was easier, less dangerous, and had a higher chance of success. In the first place, anti-escape techniques were more primitive, so it was relatively easy to get out of camp in the first place. Police forces were also less vigilant, so escapers were less likely to be recaptured; if they were apprehended, punishments were generally lighter in all countries. For POWs in Germany, neutral havens were available in Holland and Switzerland; prisoners who escaped from camps in Britain could take advantage of the Dutch ships that were frequent visitors to British ports. It seems likely that thousands of POWs of all nations were able to make successful escapes during World War I.

Those prisoners who lacked the energy or courage to attempt escape had no choice but to await repatriation, exchange, or liberation. The belligerent governments in western Europe reached a number of agreements that allowed prisoners who were seriously wounded or sick, over a certain age, or who had spent more than 18 months in captivity to be released to their own country or, more frequently, to sit out the war in neutral Switzerland, Holland, or Sweden. These agreements, which involved about 145,000 prisoners of all sides, made the difference between life and death for many of the most vulnerable POWs.

The rest had to wait until the end of hostilities to return home, and even then the process was protracted and confused. POWs in Britain and France were kept working, in part as a form of punishment; many people on the Allied side believed that German prisoners should clean up the damage their war had caused. Prisoners in Germany also found that their captivity extended well after the armistice. To a large degree, central authority in Germany broke down, and prisoners were at the mercy of local military or civil leaders. In some cases, they were simply ignored altogether: a good number of British prisoners found that their guards had deserted them, and they had to make their own way out of Germany. This was easier said than done. POWs in western Germany could walk to reach friendly forces, but those in the east had to locate a means of transport; prisoners in Stralsund camp on the Baltic coast were forced to charter a special train to take them to Denmark. Even unluckier were prisoners in some of the harsher work camps, many of whom were forced to labor for weeks after the armistice had been signed.

See also Exchange; Holzminden; Repatriation

—*Jonathan F. Vance*

World War II—Eastern Front

The war between Nazi Germany and Soviet Russia (1941–1945) was arguably the largest and most brutal theater of land warfare in the twentieth century. Fueled by bitter ideological antagonism, the enormous cruelty at the front extended directly into the treatment of prisoners of war on both sides. Of 5.7 million captured Red Army soldiers, about 3.3 million died in German captivity—a staggering mortality rate of 57 percent. By comparison, the mortality rate of British and American POWs in German hands lay between 3.5 and 5.1 percent. On the other side, almost one-third of up to three million German and Austrian prisoners of war perished in Soviet captivity. And Germany's allies fared little better: Two million of their soldiers, mainly Hungarians, Rumanians, Czechs, and Italians, were captured by the Red Army during the war and suffered mortality rates at times comparable to that among the Germans. In Soviet and German POW camps, years of hard labor and almost unbearable living conditions shaped the lives of those who were to survive. Facing this prospect, many soldiers on both sides decided to fight to the bitter end rather than to give up, thus intensifying and prolonging what already was a savage war.

In the early morning hours of 22 June 1941, the German Wehrmacht (armed forces) and its allies invaded the Soviet Union. Taken by surprise, the Red Army initially offered only sporadic resistance. In the first week of July alone, the German army encircled and captured over 320,000 Russian troops at Biasystok and Minsk. Heading further east, it continued to capture huge numbers of Soviet soldiers, most notably at Smolensk, Kiev, and Bryansk. By the time the Wehrmacht's advance came to its first significant standstill near Moscow in December 1941, over 3.2 million Soviet soldiers had fallen into German captivity. By February 1942, two million of them had lost their lives. This mass death had been clearly premeditated. Prior to the German attack, in March 1941, Hitler had relieved his troops from allegiance to the traditional code of military honor: "The Communist is from first to last no comrade. It is a war of extermination." And despite occasional criticism out of its ranks, the Wehrmacht generally complied with the regime's genocidal premises.

Thus, for many Soviet soldiers, death came immediately after their capture: according to German orders, political officers (commissars) were to be shot on the spot and others, especially Jewish soldiers, were handed over to SS execution squads. Undernourished and liable to be shot if they were physically unable to carry on, tens of thousand then perished during the seemingly endless marches from the front to camps in Poland and Germany. Prisoners who made it to their permanent camp locations usually found nothing but a barren field surrounded by barbed-wire. For shelter, they were forced to dig holes into the ground. With no sanitary facilities, these "camps" soon became breeding grounds for typhus and dysentery. Then the coming of winter hit the inmates in their makeshift shelters. The most common cause of death among the POWs at that time, however, was starvation. In order to maintain the food supply of their own troops and that of the German civilian population, the leadership of the Third Reich had decided to induce a "natural" decimation of the Russian prisoners, whom they branded "subhumans" and "worthless eaters." Some Soviet POWs even became the first victims of the gas chambers at a number of concentration camps, including Auschwitz. Clearly, the treatment of the Soviet POWs in 1941–1942 fell into line with Nazi designs of a racist war of conquest and

In the early summer of 1943, some 52,000 German soldiers were marched through the streets of Moscow on their way to Soviet POW camps (Bundesarchiv Koblenz)

annihilation in which no rules, be they legal or ethical, were recognized.

In early 1942, however, pressure mounted to make use of prisoners of war in industry and agriculture. Following the anticipated victory, the German leadership had initially planned to demobilize large portions of the Wehrmacht in order to create a manpower pool for the defense industry. But with the advance stalled, demobilization became impossible. Instead, a first batch of 400,000 Soviet prisoners in Germany were forced to toil on projects such as highway construction and mining. Requiring a healthy workforce, the labor program led to the gradual betterment of the prisoners' living conditions. In the spring of 1942, the death rate in the POW camps began to drop, though this was not entirely due to sudden German benevolence: by now, so many prisoners had died that in many cases the meager allotments of food became sufficient for those who remained. Yet, not until July 1944 did the food supply for the working Soviet prisoners reach a level comparable to that of other Allied prisoners in German captivity.

In addition to labor, service in the German army seemed to offer a way of survival for Soviet prisoners. In 1942, the Wehrmacht and the SS began to recruit volunteers among the POWs. Appealing to anticommunist sentiment and the will to survive among the captives, their efforts had some success. Tens of thousands of former Soviet soldiers served in special German-led battalions, in the army of Lieutenant General Andrei Vlasov, a former Red Army commander who had switched sides, and in German work battalions. The total number of former Soviet prisoners in the German armed services is unknown, with estimates ranging from 250,000 to about one million. The remaining POWs became part of the gigantic slave labor pool that propped up the Third Reich's industry in the later years of the war. Their living conditions remained harsh, and another 1.3 million perished in German captivity between 1942 and 1945. Furthermore, in spite of Allied victory, the plight of many Soviet prisoners did not end in 1945. Of approximately 1.8 million prisoners eventually repatriated to the USSR, 150,000 were sentenced to six years forced labor for "aiding the enemy," and almost all others experienced the hostility engendered by Soviet leader Josef Stalin's infamous Order 270, which had called all Red Army soldiers who allowed themselves to be captured alive "traitors to the motherland."

To fall into enemy captivity on the eastern front turned out to be highly perilous for German soldiers as well. Here too, legal considerations made no impact. Even though the USSR had not signed the Geneva Convention, it had indicated that it would observe the Hague Order and the Second Geneva Convention for the protection of the wounded. Nevertheless, retreating Red Army forces more often than not executed their wounded POWs. But during the Wehrmacht's initial advance in 1941 and 1942, the number of German soldiers in Soviet hands remained relatively low. Until the battle of Stalingrad, which ended in January 1943, the number of German POWs did not exceed 100,000. At Stalingrad, however, another 93,000 fell into Soviet captivity, of whom barely 6,000 were to survive their internment. The mortality rate among German POWs at the time rose to 90 percent, as the majority never made it to permanent prison camps. But unlike their Soviet counterparts in 1941–1942, the German prisoners were not subjected to a policy of systematic mass murder. Instead, they fell victim to the unorganized state of the Soviet POW camp system (GUPVI), to the chaotic conditions of a country ravaged by war, and to individual acts of retaliation. In addition, after months of winter fighting, many German soldiers went into captivity in pitiful physical state, at least one-third of them in need of medical attention, which the Russians generally failed to provide.

Following the defeat at Kursk in the summer of 1943, the German army began its final retreat from Russia. The rising number of POWs now entirely overwhelmed Soviet capacities. The number of base camps in the Soviet Union tripled from 52 to 156 in 1944, yet scarcities remained everywhere, especially in food provision, winter clothing, and medical supplies. At the end of the war in May 1945, another 1.5 million Axis soldiers who had failed to reach American or British front lines flooded into Russian temporary POW camps. Once in camps in the Soviet Union, they were put to work to reconstruct the war-torn country. In fact, the USSR's first five-year economic plan after the war depended heavily on POW labor. For many years and under often gruesome conditions, German and Austrian prisoners built power plants and railway tracks, the Metro in Moscow, defense industries in the Ural mountains, gold mines in eastern Siberia, and much more. Even the Russian atomic bomb program owed much to the labor and technical expertise of German prisoners of war.

Given their suffering, the German prisoners showed little positive reaction to Soviet propaganda efforts. Attempts to organize them into an opposition to Hitler's regime largely fell on deaf ears, even though small groups such as the National Committee for a Free Germany served as recruiting grounds for administrative personnel for the Soviet occupied zone of Germany after the war. The majority of the prisoners, however, experienced Soviet political influence as oppressive. Most infamous were the camp hierarchies established by the Antifa, groups of anti-fascist, mainly communist, German POWs who had been handpicked by Soviet authorities in order to control their fellow inmates. Usually, these selected prisoners occupied privileged positions in the camps and could be easily identified among their undernourished comrades by their healthy, well-fed appearance.

The living conditions in Soviet captivity failed to improve after the war. Constant hunger, slave labor, and a lack of medical care led the prisoners to develop specific strategies of survival. The German prisoners adopted the "plenny-step," a mode of slow movement designed to conserve the body's energy that soon turned the camp inhabitants into a mass of bent, crawling figures. The "hunger winter" of 1946–1947, which followed a Russian crop failure, took yet another heavy toll on them. Soviet authorities had to declare a state of emergency for the entire GUPVI camp system in order to battle the dramatically decreasing labor output and the surging mortality rates. And given the importance of prisoner labor, repatriations began only gradually. In mid-1947, when the first mass repatriations of Austrian and Hungarian prisoners commenced, there were still over one million German POWs in the Soviet Union whose repatriation did not begin until a year later. By 1950, their number had slowly dropped to 30,000.

The story of those last 30,000 German prisoners constitutes the final chapter of the sad history of POW internment on what had been the eastern front. Stripped of their status as prisoners of war and instead considered as convicted war criminals, these internees became a lever used by the Soviets in the Cold War, particularly with respect to the newly established Federal Republic of Germany. While some of these former German soldiers had undoubtedly committed war crimes, many others had received their original sentences—25 years of hard labor—for petty offenses or simply out of bad luck. For another five years, German prisoners toiled in the Soviet Union until that country finally repatriated them in 1955–1956 in exchange for the establishment of diplomatic relations with the Federal Republic. The last German POW did not return home until 1956, more than 10 years after the end of the war.

See also Commissar Order; Katyń Massacre

References

Omer Bartov, *Hitler's Army: Soldiers, Nazis, and War in the Third Reich* (New York: Oxford University Press, 1991).

S.P. MacKenzie, "The Treatment of Prisoners of War in World War II," *Journal of Modern History* 66 (1994): 487–520.

Robert G. Moeller, "War Stories: The Search for a Usable Past in the Federal Republic of Germany," *American Historical Review* 101 (1996): 1008–1048.

Christian Streit, "The German Army and the Policies of Genocide," in *The Policies of Genocide: Jewish and Soviet Prisoners of War in Nazi Germany*, ed. Gerhard Hirschfeld (Boston: Allen and Unwin, 1986).

—Rafael A. Zagovec

WORLD WAR II—FAR EAST

The exact number of prisoners taken by opposing forces in the Far East during World War II is impossible to ascertain. The figure most often used for Allied soldiers captured is 320,000: 140,000 Europeans and North Americans and 180,000 Chinese, Filipino, Indian, Indonesian, and other Asian colonial troops. Most of these prisoners were seized early in 1942, the bulk in the capitulations of Singapore, Bataan, Corregidor, Hong Kong, and Java. Many nonwhites, if they survived their initial ordeal, were released within a few months of capture, although some were used in nearby work camps as slave labor. White captives, except the very few who escaped or were liberated earlier, were held until Japan surrendered in 1945.

The largest groups of white POWs were from the United Kingdom and Northern Ireland, the United States, and the Netherlands East Indies (Dutch and Euro-Indonesian Dutch). The Japanese took 93,000 prisoners at the fall of the Netherlands East Indies in March 1942, but the most commonly used figure for Dutch POWs taken is 40,000. Whether some Indonesians, whom other POWs called "Black Dutch," are included in this figure is unclear. They most certainly constituted the majority of the other 53,000 captives. American prisoners numbered 25,600, excluding 11,000 Filipino Scouts who were part of the U.S. Army. British captives constituted the largest number, approximately 50,000. The total number of British personnel surrendering, including United Kingdom, Northern Ireland, and colonial forces, was 130,000, of which more than half were Indian. The number of Canadians seized by the Japanese was 1,733; the majority of them were members of the Royal Rifles of Canada and the Winnipeg Grenadiers, captured at Hong Kong, but a handful of airmen and seamen were taken prisoner as well. Australian POWs numbered 22,376 and New Zealanders, 121.

Again, all of these numbers are imprecise, but they are important in determining survival rates. The approximate number and percentages of white POWs who died in Japanese captivity of all causes are: Americans, 8,288 or 35.6 percent; Australians, 7,777 or 34.7 percent; British, 13,432 or 26 percent; Canadians, 290 or 16.7 percent; Dutch, 8,000 or 20 percent; and New Zealanders, 31 or 25.6 percent. Overall, 37,800 men or 26.9 percent perished by war's end.

Uncertainties also exist regarding the number of Japanese military personnel taken prisoner by the Allies. Russia, which entered the war against Japan after the atomic bomb was dropped on Hiroshima, claimed to have taken 594,000 Japanese captive, with 70,880 freed on the spot. Japanese scholars maintain that 850,000 of their troops were seized by the Soviets and shipped mainly to Siberia, where they remained for the next several years. Since Japan's military law forbade surrender, during most of the war other Allied powers took far fewer prisoners than the Russians. For example, in 1945, after months of fighting in Burma, only 1,400 of 30,000 Japanese troops survived an effort to break out of Allied encirclement. At Saipan there were virtually no survivors, at Iwo Jima just 216 remained out of a 21,000-man garrison, and only about 7,400 out of 114,939 Japanese soldiers were alive after the battle of Okinawa. At Peleliu, in Borneo, on Tinian, and elsewhere, similar circumstances prevailed.

Some historians have attributed the paucity of captives to more than Japanese military law, suggesting that once Allied troops learned of Japanese atrocities against POWs, they stopping taking prisoners. Instances of Japanese being shot when surrendering are not well documented but anecdotal evidence suggests that we can assume they occurred. Some attribute the practice of shooting potential prisoners to the logic of the Far East phase of World War II, which is deemed to have been a "race war."

Certainly, at the beginning of the war, feelings of racial superiority caused European and American troops to discount Japanese fighting skill, a view that was later modified. Race and a desire to demonstrate superiority to whites played a role in the

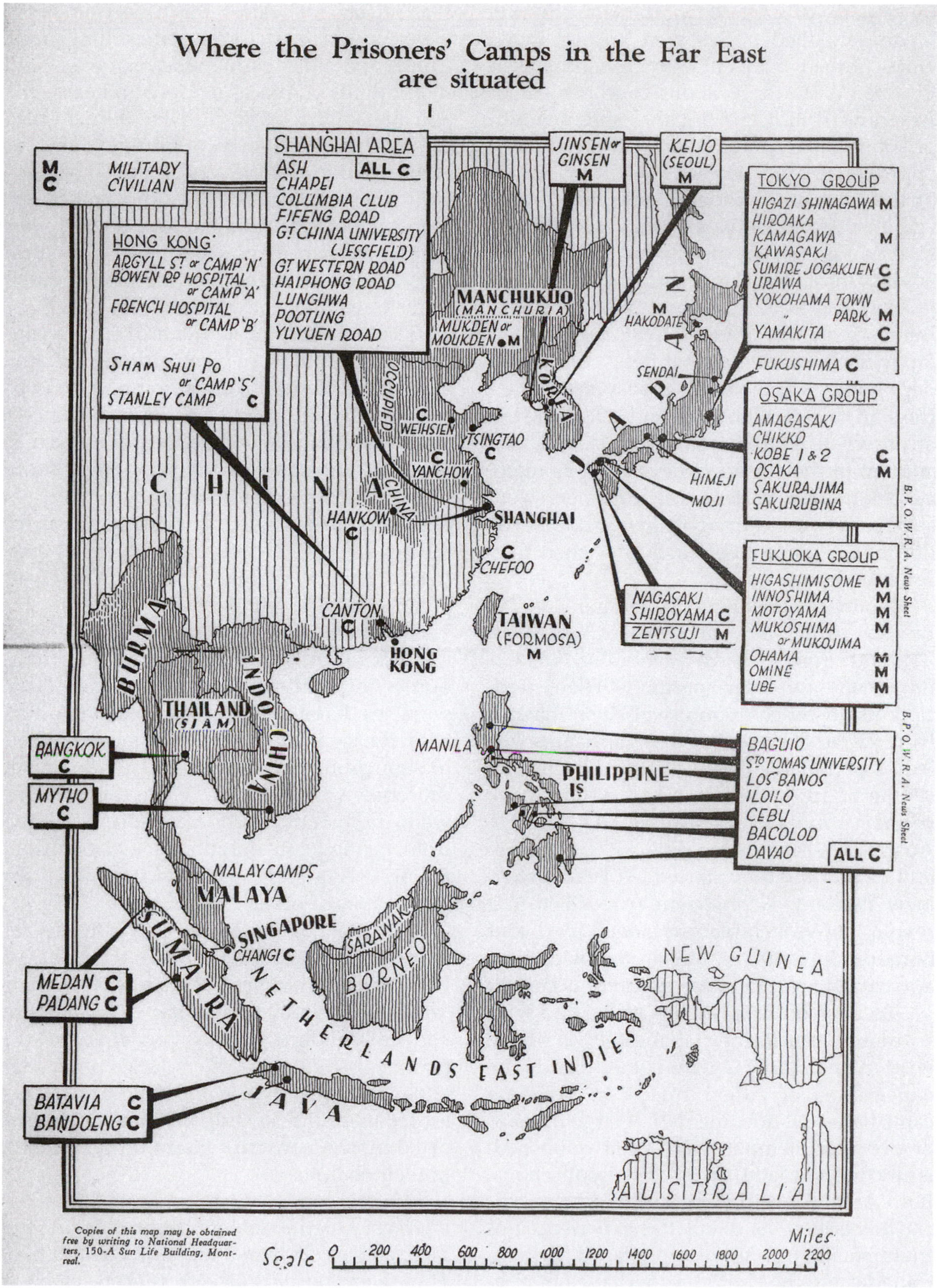

This map, showing the location of Japanese prison camps during World War II, was prepared for a charitable organization in Canada (Jonathan F. Vance) See additional maps at back of book.

treatment of Allied prisoners by the Japanese. Allied troops were treated much worse in the Far East than by the Germans in Europe. While only about four percent of American, British, and British Commonwealth prisoners died while held by the Germans, approximately 27 percent died in the hands of the Japanese. (A major exception to this "gentler" treatment was German handling of eastern Europeans, especially troops of the Soviet Union. Russian treatment of German POWs was equally, if not more, brutal.) Interestingly, the Soviets' treatment of their Japanese captives, while considered deplorable, was the same as that received by Russian citizens who lived and labored in the areas where POWs were held. In fact, one student of the subject believes that as many as one-quarter of Japanese prisoners were successfully radicalized by Soviet indoctrination and became leftist activists when they returned home.

Japanese prisoners in camps run by British, American, and Australian/New Zealand forces were generally treated humanely, although spartanly. There were riots in prison compounds in Australia and New Zealand. Causes of these uprisings varied, but fanatical zeal coupled with the shame of surrender seem to have been the primary motivating forces. At Cowra, Australia, 234 inmates died, 31 by suicide and 12 in a fire they started. At Featherston, New Zealand, 48 prisoners were killed in a revolt. POWs complained about food and boredom in camps in the United States, but apparently no organized resistance occurred.

Because of the dishonor associated with surrender, few former Japanese POWs have written memoirs. On the other hand, the experiences of Allied troops in Japanese camps are well documented. A large number of prisoner memoirs have been published, either individually or in edited collections. Both Australia and New Zealand have official histories that detail the experiences of their men. The governments of Britain, Canada, and the United States have not published official histories, but many monographs have been written.

The largest camps for Allied prisoners were located in the Philippines, Singapore, China, and Japan proper, but men were held in hundreds of places across Southeast Asia and the southwest Pacific. Field-grade officers were normally removed from their commands, but junior officers often stayed with their troops. Conditions in almost all camps were miserable—inadequate food, poor shelter, inferior or no clothing, few medical supplies or little medical treatment, harsh punishment, and often hard labor.

Japan did not observe normal rules concerning prisoners of war, although it had signed the Hague Convention of 1907 concerning the laws and customs of war. In 1942, the Japanese government promised to observe, mutatis mutandis, the more detailed 1929 Geneva Convention, which its delegates had signed but its government refused to ratify. However, for the most part, this promise was unkept. Early in the war, Japanese Prime Minister and War Minister Hideki Tojo issued orders that POWs were to work for their keep. Afterwards, in violation of international law and practice, they were used regularly in war-related industries. By the same token, POWs were forced to sign promises not to escape. When such promises were violated, which they seldom were, punishment upon recapture ranged from beatings to executions. On occasion, fellow POWs were also shot in reprisal for the escapes of others.

Despite the existence of a Prisoner of War Administrative Division in the Japanese War Ministry, camp commanders or their senior NCOs ran the camps. The Japanese had no standard way of behaving toward prisoners. Treatment often varied according to the attitude or whim of the highest or lowest Japanese officer, enlisted man, or Korean or Formosan conscript guard who had men in their charge.

No one can adequately impart the suffering most Allied prisoners endured during the three and a half years they were held captive. They were beaten, kicked, robbed, clubbed with rifles and sticks, shot, had swordsmanship practiced on them, and were buried alive. Sadistic physicians experimented on them, and their corpses were mutilated. Some Japanese even practiced cannibalism on their bodies. POWs endured the "water treatment" and were made to stand at attention looking into a blistering sun or shivering in a freezing rain. When transported, they were herded along in "death marches" at Bataan, Sandakan, and elsewhere, were crowded into insufferably hot boxcars, or were placed for days in the sweltering holds of "death ships" with little room to move and nowhere to perform bodily functions.

Worst of all they were starved and, as a consequence, suffered from almost every disease known to humanity. They had fever, chills, malaise, pain, anorexia, tropical ulcers, abdominal cramps from recurrent malaria, and dysentery that pained and killed. Beriberi caused feet to ache, cardiac failure, and loss of vision. Xerophthalmia meant sore eyes, corneal ulcers, and impaired vision. Diphtheria, flu, typhoid fever, tuberculosis, and pneumonia were commonplace. And their health suffered ever after. As one writer has put it, the overwhelming majority endured "hell on earth: aging faster, dying sooner."

See also Bataan Death March; Bicycle Camp; Burma-Thailand (Death) Railway; Cabanatuan; Changi; Cowra Incident; Featherston Incident; Sandakan-Ranau Death March; Wainwright, Jonathan Mayhew; Zentsuji

—Robert S. La Forte

WORLD WAR II—JAPANESE-AMERICANS AND JAPANESE-CANADIANS

The evacuation of people of Japanese descent from the West Coast of the United States and Canada during World War II remains one of the most controversial aspects of wartime on the home front. Not all of the evacuees were actually interned, but they all suffered serious infringements of their liberties as a result of their ethnicity.

On 15 December 1941, just a week after the Japanese bombing of Pearl Harbor, Frank Knox, the U.S. secretary of the navy, stated that fifth columnists among ethnic Japanese in Hawai'i had been active in helping to prepare for the attack. Such statements exacerbated preexisting anti-Japanese sentiment in the United States, especially on the West Coast, and eventually induced president Franklin D. Roosevelt to sign Executive Order #9006 on 19 February 1942, which authorized the exclusion of any individuals from certain "military areas" of the United States. On 22 March, the first evacuation orders, pertaining to the Los Angeles area, were promulgated, followed the next day by orders covering people of Japanese descent in parts of Washington state. In time, the orders were expanded to affect some 120,000 people: 41,000 Issei (immigrants born in Japan), 72,000 Nisei (born in the United States of Japanese parents), and 9,000 Kibei (educated in Japan).

These evacuees went first to a number of assembly centers in California, Washington, Oregon, and Arizona, which were in operation from 21 March to 31 October 1942. These spartan compounds provided temporary accommodation until the inmates were transferred to relocation centers in Wyoming, Colorado, California, Arizona, Idaho, and Arkansas. The evacuees had been told that the relocation was for their own protection and would last for the duration of the war, but instead the War Relocation Authority (WRA) viewed the centers, not as internment camps, but as temporary accommodation for evacuees until they could be permanently resettled elsewhere in the United States. There was resistance to this policy among evacuees, who had been led to believe that they could return to their homes once the war was over, and the ill-feeling, coupled with poor living conditions at some of the centers, led to disturbances at various relocation centers. Of greater long-term consequence were a number of court challenges launched against the government's relocation policy. One decision, rendered in December 1944, decided that the WRA had no authority to intern an American citizen who was "concededly loyal." With this judgment, the WRA announced that all centers would be closed by the end of 1945. In fact the last center, at Tule Lake, California, closed in February 1946.

There was a similar evacuation in Canada, although it was much smaller in scale. Faced with a combination of local anti-Asian hostility, wartime paranoia, and legitimate military justification, the federal government announced on 26 February 1942 the evacuation of all Japanese nationals and Japanese-Canadians from the West Coast; in all, some 21,000 people were uprooted, the vast majority of them in British Columbia. Roughly 8,000 of these were temporarily held at the Hastings Park Exhibition Grounds in Vancouver, which served as a transit center from 16 March to 30 September 1942; there, they were guarded by Japanese-Canadian veterans who had served in the Canadian Expeditionary Force in World War I. The bulk of the evacuees were eventually relocated to isolated communities in the interior of British Columbia or elsewhere in Canada; about 2,200 males were sent to work camps. None of these people were, strictly speaking, interned. They were under surveillance and required permits to travel, but they did not live behind barbed-wire and were not held by armed guards, and indeed they were free to arrange their own accommodation elsewhere in Canada if they so desired. In fact, only about 800 Japanese-Canadians were actually interned, at a remote camp in Angler, Ontario, north of Lake Superior. Some of them had been unjustly arrested for minor infractions, but others were ardently pro-Japanese and made no secret of their hope for a Japanese victory.

Opinion on the internment of Japanese in the United States and Canada is still sharply divided. Some scholars believe it was totally unjust, pointing to the fact that not a single act of sabotage in North America or Hawai'i can be traced to people of Japanese descent. Others contend that this merely proves the evacuation did what it was intended to do. While they admit that the episode was lamentable, they insist that it be seen in the context of the war, as a justifiable security measure based on the information that was available at the time.

See also Civilian Internees—World War II—North America

References

Ken Adachi, *The Enemy That Never Was: A History of Japanese Canadians* (Toronto: McClelland and Stewart, 1976).

Allan R. Bosworth, *America's Concentration Camps* (New York: W.W. Norton, 1967).

Jeffery F. Burton et al, *Confinement and Ethnicity: An Overview of World War II Japanese Relocation Sites* (Seattle: University of Washington Press, 2002).

Tetsuden Kashima, *Judgment Without Trial: Japanese American Imprisonment during World War II* (Seattle: University of Washington Press, 2003).

Dillon S. Myer, *Uprooted Americans: The Japanese Americans and the War Relocation Authority during World War II* (Tucson: University of Arizona Press, 1971).

Patricia E. Roy et al, *Mutual Hostages: Canadians and Japanese during the Second World War* (Toronto: University of Toronto Press, 1990).

Page Smith, *Democracy on Trial: The Japanese American Evacuation and Relocation in World War II* (New York: Simon and Schuster, 1995).

—*Jonathan F. Vance*

WORLD WAR II—LATIN AMERICA

From 1941 to 1945, the U.S. government, fearing that Nazi-organized uprisings would be the prelude to Axis invasion of the Western Hemisphere, orchestrated the expulsion and internment of several thousand Germans, Japanese, and Italians from Latin America. These allegedly "dangerous enemy aliens" were selected by U.S. diplomats and undercover FBI agents who had little training and scant knowledge of the language or social conditions of the countries in which they worked. Relying on local police or anonymous informants for denunciations of suspected Axis agents, the officials' work brought mixed results.

In the course of the war, some 4,058 Germans, 2,264 Japanese, and 288 Italians from more than a dozen Latin American countries were shipped to the United States and interned at Camp Kenedy, Camp Seagoville, and Camp Crystal City, Texas; Camp Blanding, Florida; Stringtown, Oklahoma; Fort Lincoln, North Dakota; Camp Forrest, Tennessee; and others. Most of the Japanese were sent by Peru, whose government asked the United States to accept all of its 30,000 Japanese immigrants for internment, a request denied because of inadequate shipping. Few if any of the Japanese internees had been politically active. Among the Italians were some supporters of Italy's dictator Benito Mussolini who were accused of spreading fascist propaganda, but most were selected on the basis of their nationality alone.

The Department of Justice described the German contingent as "an ill-assorted miscellany of individuals representing a complete cross-section of every political and national strain to be found in prewar Germany." About one in five German internees was a member of the Nazi Party. Several dozen were active recruiters for the party or had distributed pro-Nazi propaganda, and about 10 were involved in espionage. At the other end of the spectrum were more than 80 Jewish refugees who had fled Europe for Latin America, only to find themselves labeled "dangerous" and sent to camps designed to hold their persecutors. The bulk of the German group was made up of German immigrants who had lived for years or decades in Latin American countries. Most sympathized with their former homeland but did nothing to further the German war effort. Some were deported by corrupt Latin American officials who then seized their property. There were internment camps for Axis nationals in Brazil, Venezuela, Colombia, Costa Rica, Nicaragua, the Dominican Republic, Cuba, Mexico, Curaçao, and the Panama Canal Zone as well.

After an initial period of disorganization, the U.S. internment camps were improved to provide living conditions that compared favorably to the War Relocation Authority camps for Japanese and Japanese-Americans. Internees were well fed, could work if they wished, and had access to a commissary and Sears Roebuck mail-order catalogs. Single women and married couples without children were housed at Seagoville, a former minimum-security women's prison that resembled a college campus and was the most comfortable of the camps. The worst facility was the state prison at Stringtown, where internees slept in filthy, overcrowded cells and had inadequate drinking water. (Stringtown was closed in May 1943.) Interned families lived in simple shacks at Crystal City, where children could attend school in their native languages and play sports or use the large swimming pool built by volunteer internee labor.

By the end of the war, about three-quarters of the internees had been repatriated to their countries of birth, in exchange for Americans held by the Axis. Those Germans still in the camps returned to their homes in Latin America. Many of the remaining Japanese and the German Jews stayed on and eventually became U.S. citizens.

See also Civilian Internees—World War II; Civilian Internees—World War II—Britain; Civilian Internees—World War II—North America

References

Edward N. Barnhart, "Japanese Internees from Peru," *Pacific Historical Review* 31 (1962): 169–178.

Max Paul Friedman, *Nazis and Good Neighbors: The United States Campaign Against the Germans of Latin America in World War II* (Cambridge: Cambridge University Press, 2003).

C. Harvey Gardiner, *Pawns in a Triangle of Hate: The Peruvian Japanese and the United States* (Seattle: University of Washington Press, 1981).

—Max Paul Friedman

WORLD WAR II—NORTH AMERICA

When the United States entered World War II, the problem of maintaining prisoners of war was among the last considerations of a country reeling from a Japanese attack. Because the Unites States had not held large numbers of foreign prisoners since British soldiers were interned in 1812, past experience could provide little guidance. The remaining alternative was the 1929 Geneva Convention Relative to the Treatment of Prisoners of War, an as yet unproved document whose application had to be tested at every step. Beyond an acceptance of these basic principles, the United States was in no way prepared for more than 425,000 German and Italian prisoners of war who would inundate the country between the spring of 1943 and the spring of 1945. They began arriving in May 1943, with the collapse of the Afrika Korps, at a rate that averaged 20,000 a month. Following the Normandy invasion of June 1944, the numbers soared to 30,000 Germans a month, peaking at 60,000 prisoners in April and May of 1945. A trickle of POWs, protected personnel (such as chaplains, physicians, or veterinarians), and the badly wounded went in the other direction, to Germany, usually aboard the famous neutral Swedish ships *Drottningholm* or *Gripsholm*.

Despite some planning by the Provost Marshal General's Office (PMGO) and the Justice Department in the months before the United States entered the war, American unpreparedness was reflected at the outset by the government's inefficient division of responsibility: the War Department was charged with feeding, guarding, and housing the POWs, while the State Department was charged with negotiating for their repatriation via neutral nations. The War Department, in turn, reassigned some responsibilities to the Army Service Forces, headed by General Brenhom Somervell, which in turn controlled the PMGO under Major-General Allen Gullion. The State Department, meanwhile, established an Internees Section in the Office of Special War Problems Division. To complicate the situation still further, the PMGO was responsible for the Aliens Division, the reorganization of which finally led, in June 1943, to the creation of the Prisoner of War Division, under the able direction of the new assistant provost marshal general, Brigadier-General Blackshear M. Bryan. Policy decisions, therefore, were rerouted through several administrative levels, any one of which might have had a different opinion or interpretation. Despite these bureaucratic entanglements, however, the first order of business at the end of 1942 was to establish camps to contain the sudden and seemingly unending deluge of arriving enemy prisoners.

The PMGO authorized the creation of two types of camps: permanent base camps and branch camps, numbering 141 and 319 respectively, by May 1945. The War Department stipulated that the camp sites be isolated, easily guarded, and away from blackout areas, which extended 150 miles inland from the Mexican and Canadian borders, 75 miles inland from both coasts, and near shipyards or vital war industries. Whenever possible, two types of camps, permanent base camps and branch camps, were to be located at or near existing military bases, two-thirds of which were located in the South and Southwest. The capacity of each camp ranged between 1,000 and 5,000 men, averaging 2,500. All camps were guarded by military personnel, which grew to 47,000 in number, although overseas priorities often led to the assignment of less than competent soldiers to POW camp duty. There was a continual, critical shortage of German and Italian-speaking administrators.

Since the beginning of the war, the United States had been facing a labor shortage as the military draft drained the manpower pool. Foreign workers were being recruited from Mexico, Jamaica, and the Bahamas when Washington decided, in March 1943, to turn to the incoming POWs. The program was placed under the direction of the War Manpower Commission and the War Food Administration within the War Department. Pay scales were adjusted to rank, and although officers were not obligated to work, many elected to fill at least supervisory positions. Paid labor existed in two forms: labor at American military installations, and labor contracted out to private business. Despite the initial public fear of hiring enemy POWs, the protests from American trade unions, and the complications caused by Italy's change to the Allied side after the fall of Benito Mussolini's fascist government, the work program was hugely successful and, thanks to the $22 million paid into the U.S. Treasury by the contractors who hired the POWs, it was nearly self-sufficient. By the end of the war, of the 370,000 prisoners held in the United States, nearly 200,000 were employed in jobs outside the military sector, largely harvesting crops in almost every agricultural state.

Despite the decent living conditions, the handicraft and educational programs promoted by the YMCA and various charities, and the demanding work schedules, groups of hard-core Nazis could be found in nearly every camp. The problem stemmed from the American failure to take advantage of the critical period immediately following the prisoners' capture. The first several weeks are critical because military prisoners are dazed and display a universal vulnerability. It is at this moment that the prisoner must be interrogated, segregated by political persuasion, processed, and assigned to a camp—yet it was precisely at this point that American concern with the prisoners' political views ceased. Only the most basic division of captives took place. First, naval prisoners were separated from army prisoners, and officers were segregated from enlisted men. The most visibly rabid Nazis, 4,500 by 1945, were interned at Alva, Oklahoma, and the most visibly dedicated anti-Nazis, 3,300 in number, were shipped to Fort Devens, Massachusetts, and Camp Campbell, Kentucky. Although an innovative program was later initiated to "democratize" the prisoners, the best opportunity to segregate the various shades of political ideology had passed. One tragic result was a reign of violence through the camps between September 1943 and April 1944 that saw six murders, two forced suicides, 43 "voluntary" suicides, a general camp riot, and hundreds of beating and death threats by secret Nazi kangaroo courts.

An issue related to camp violence and POW control, and one that caused the public the greatest concern, was that of POW escapes. From 21 April 1942, when the first prisoners arrived in the United States, to the end of the war three years later, there were a total of 1,073 escapes. The work camps were maintained with minimum security, a calculated risk, in an effort to free the greatest number of army personnel for combat overseas, and a small number of escapes was considered acceptable. The overwhelming majority of escapees (907) were recaptured within three days. Twenty-one managed to remain on the loose for more than 14 days, and only 17 were still at large when the last German POW was shipped back to Europe on 30 June 1947. One by one, each of the 17 was arrested by the FBI over the next decades. The final fugitive German prisoner of war, Georg Gaertner, surrendered on national television in September 1986, as part of a plan to promote his book, *Hitler's Last Soldier in America*.

The end of the war brought the prisoners some unwanted changes. First, the quality of food deteriorated sharply. The reasons are many: American captives in enemy hands were being liberated, freeing Washington of the fear of retaliation; the shocking extent of concentration camp horrors was coming clear; available resources were being shifted to the Pacific to support the planned invasion of Japan; and the government was smarting from a recent series of newspaper articles that sharply criticized the "coddling" of POWs. The second change was more serious. In an agreement with Britain and France and as an alternative to returning the POWs to a devastated Germany, the German prisoners were turned over to America's allies for use as raw labor. They worked in mines and helped clear bombed roads and cities. Most were held for an average of one year and were repatriated to Germany in late 1947 or early 1948, many malnourished and embittered by their postwar treatment.

A large portion of those returning to the American and British zones of occupation fared well. Since many had learned English while in captivity, they were readily employed by either the U.S. Army or the American Military Government. Others joined the civilian municipal governments as interpreters, clerks, civil servants, or liaison personnel to the American forces. Some few rose to dizzying heights—Karl Janisch became a justice on the Austrian Supreme Court; General Hans A. Link became the German military representative to the United States and Canada; and Baron Rüdiger von Wechmar became the president of the General Assembly of the United Nations, and later the head of European Parliament—although it is debatable if their success can be directly traced to their years of captivity in America. What can be stated is that, despite a lack of preparation and guidelines, the United States successfully transported some 370,000 battle-hardened German prisoners of war across the oceans to hastily constructed camps, where they were well fed, educated, worked, and often entertained, with a minimum of escapes and, aside from the violence perpetrated by their fellow POWs, without the serious discomfort found in other POW camp systems maintained by many U.S. friends and foes alike.

See also Livingston, Camp; Werra, Franz von

—*Arnold C. Krammer*

World War II—Western Europe

World War II in Europe saw an enormous number of soldiers, sailors, and airmen fall into their enemy's captivity. All told, in the European and North African campaigns, between 8,500,000 and nine million Allied POWs (approximately six million of whom were Soviets) were taken by the Axis powers. Conversely, some 8.25 million Germans and Italians were taken captive by the Allies, almost 3.4 million of whom surrendered their arms after the final capitulations on the western front. A word of caution about these figures, however: given the mutual antipathy of Germany and the Soviet Union and the disregard of international convention this engendered, the figures from the eastern front are imprecise. The scale of the logistical efforts involved in maintaining this number of disarmed soldiers, however poorly in some circumstances, was quite unprecedented in the history of warfare.

The groundwork for the behavior of the belligerents toward POWs grew out of dissatisfaction with the plight of POWs in World War I. Soon after the conclusion of hostilities in 1918, the Grotius Society (a group studying aspects of international law) led an investigation and assessment of the shortcomings of the Hague Conventions of 1907 in protecting prisoners during the 1914–1918 conflict. Their results were taken up by the International Committee of the Red Cross (ICRC), which invited the signatories to the earlier treaties to open discussions on the issue in the early to mid-1920s. The result of these consultations and negotiations was an international conference in Geneva in 1928 that produced the Convention Relative to the Treatment of Prisoners of War, signed in July 1929. This treaty was different from previous efforts in several ways: it formally recognized the ICRC as a relief agency to be given full access to the prisoners of the warring parties; it formalized the diplomatic protection of the rights of prisoners by a neutral Protecting Power; and ratifying signatories to the convention were to be bound by its provisions, whether or not their enemy had signed the convention as well (Article 82). In practice, however, the belligerents in World War II fell far short of living up to the idealism of the conference and the convention.

In western Europe, major problems ensued for those prisoners whose countries had been overrun by Germany. For instance, the German-appointed French Ambassador Georges Scapini "negotiated" away many protections that should have been afforded to French POWs. The most notable consequence was the use of French and also Belgian captive soldiers in labor endeavors (such as the armaments industry) that directly benefited the German war effort. The British Commonwealth nations (Great Britain, Canada, Australia, New Zealand, South Africa, and India), along with the United States after its entrance into the war, had one significant bargaining chip that other European nations lacked: significant numbers of German prisoners of war in their possession. Threats of reciprocal reprisals were a significant factor in the relatively better treatment afforded these countries' soldiers in German captivity.

Nevertheless, a few incidents served as reminders of just how fragile the balance could be. For example, Canadian and British troops were handcuffed for a year during the infamous Shackling Incident after Germany accused these countries of binding the hands of German captives and killing Germans caught during the raid on Dieppe, France, in 1942. Furthermore, the German government was willing to cut corners as often as possible to reduce the burden on their resources that came from providing for tens of thousands of western Allied POWs. An early example of this was the decision by German authorities—based on the frequency and bounty of food parcels from the British Commonwealth and the United States being distributed to their POWs by the ICRC—to reduce the rations given to Commonwealth and U.S. POWs by one-third, thus forcing the home countries to subsidize Germany's obligations under the convention. With regard to Italy, no major problems were reported concerning their treatment of Western Allied prisoners, nor were Italian POWs in Allied hands the subject of much controversy.

After the entrance of the United States into the war, both sides made good use of the Swiss government as the official Protecting Power and allowed their delegates relatively unfettered access in inspecting the prisoner of war camps. The same could be said of the ICRC delegates, who visited the camps of most of the Western countries throughout the war. The reports of these two different agencies constituted the belligerents' main sources of information about how their captured soldiers were being treated by the enemy power.

The most vulnerable stage for the soldier becoming a prisoner was at capture, and it was here that accusations of war crimes flew from all sides. The war in the east, following an ideological agenda rather than the terms of the Geneva Convention, saw significant mass killings on both sides. In North Africa, Italy, and the main western campaign, the accusations focused for the most part on smaller engagements, with some notable exceptions being mass killings conducted by some units of the Waffen-SS. Hitler's Commando Order of October 1942 led to the killing of small groups of Allied commandos by both the SS and regular German military units in most theaters of the war in the west, and this comprised one of the foundations for accusations of war crimes at the later Nuremberg Trials. By the same token, the German government accused the British of killing their soldiers instead of taking them prisoner on several occasions during the Greek campaign, especially during small skirmishes in the Aegean. At the very least, the details of evidence collected by the Wehrmacht's own War Crimes Branch surrounding these events makes the British denials of any wrongdoing appear somewhat hasty. Though both the British and American forces committed fewer violations of international law during the war than did Germany, with no evidence of a general policy that ran counter to established conventions, it is nonetheless probable that some excesses committed by the forces of both Allies went underinvestigated and were therefore unpunished.

In general then, with regard to prisoners of war, World War II in Europe saw mass violations of the Geneva Convention on the eastern front and significant violations on the western front. The overrunning and occupation of Allied countries in western Europe usually resulted in their captured soldiers being put to illegal use by Germany in the armaments industries. That this did not often occur with American and British POWs was due to the great numbers of German POWs held by those countries. And though some historians question the treatment of German prisoners by the Allies in the months immediately after the cessation of hostilities in Europe, no consensus has developed concerning consistent or significant American or

British mistreatment of German POWs during the war itself.

See also Arbeitskommandos; Colditz; Commando Order; Dulag Luft; Extermination Camps; Great Escape; Lamsdorf; "Other Losses"; Scapini, Georges; Shackling Incident

—*Vasilis Vourkoutiotis*

WORMHOUT MASSACRE

Along with a similar incident at Le Paradis, France, the Wormhout Massacre was an early example of the systematic abuse of POWs by SS troops during World War II. On 28 May 1940, elements of the 2nd Battalion, Royal Warwickshire Regiment, were captured by troops of the SS *Leibstandarte Adolf Hitler* Regiment after an engagement near Wormhout, south of Dunkirk, in northern France. The fighting had been bitter, and the wounding of the *Leibstandarte* commander may have convinced the SS troops that revenge was called for. They began executing individual prisoners shortly after the battle ended, and then marched a large group of roughly 100 POWs to a barn just west of Wormhout. When the senior British officer present demanded better care for the wounded, the SS officer responded by tossing a hand grenade among the prisoners. The survivors were then brought out of the barn in groups of five and shot; this process continued until the barn had been emptied. Between 80 and 90 prisoners in all were executed; there were 15 survivors, most of whom spent the rest of the war in captivity.

In 1944, the *Leibstandarte* Regiment was involved in the massacre of American troops at Malmédy, a crime for which 74 members of the unit were eventually tried by the Allied War Crimes Commission. No separate trial was held for the Wormhout Massacre.

See also Malmédy Massacre; Meyer, Kurt; Le Paradis Massacre; Peiper, Joachim

References

Leslie Aitken, *Massacre on the Road to Dunkirk: Wormhout 1940* (London: William Kimber, 1977).

—*Jonathan F. Vance*

WOUNDED KNEE MASSACRE

The Wounded Knee Massacre took place on 29 December 1890, near the Pine Ridge Reservation in South Dakota. The armed engagement, in which some 150 American Indian men, women, and children perished, culminated nearly 30 years of warfare on the Great Plains.

The tragedy of the Wounded Knee Massacre, also called the Ghost Dance (or Messiah) War, grew out of a messianic movement that swept the plains during the late 1880s. In their anger and despair, many reservation Indians turned to the teachings of Wovoka, a Paiute prophet who promised converts a life free of hunger and misery, and embraced the ghost dance.

In November 1890, Daniel Royer, the new and inexperienced agent at Pine Ridge, requested military assistance when antagonism toward whites continued to spread. Fearing a violent confrontation, a few thousand Lakota ghost dancers fled to the security of "the Stronghold," a natural Badlands fortress located in an isolated northwestern corner of the Pine Ridge Reservation, where they prayed for the renewal of their people. Peace advocates responded by appealing to the dancers to return to the agency.

Shortly after the dancers' return was negotiated, however, news reached the agency that Sitting Bull, a respected Hunkpapa chief and Ghost Dance supporter, had been killed on 15 December 1890. Sitting Bull's grieving followers immediately set off for the Cheyenne River Reservation to warn Minneconjou Chief Big Foot. Realizing that he would be detained or killed if he remained at his camp, Big Foot led nearly 350 followers on a 150-mile winter journey to Pine Ridge. On 28 December, the military finally found the elusive band. Rather than fight the pursuing soldiers, Big Foot surrendered to Major Samuel Whitside and set up camp along the Wounded Knee Creek, some 20 miles east of Pine Ridge.

Attempts by members of the 7th Cavalry to disarm and arrest Big Foot's followers prompted the massacre. During the search for weapons, a rifle discharged and both sides began fighting. When the shooting finally subsided, 146 Sioux (84 men and boys, 44 women, and 18 children) lay dead. Within a short time another seven of the 51 wounded survivors died in a makeshift reservation hospital.

The tragic events of 29 December 1890 infuriated the dancers who had surrendered at Pine Ridge. In their anger they bolted the reservation and sought vengeance by attacking the agency and any troops they encountered. General Nelson A. Miles's successful combination of diplomacy and military superiority convinced the rebels to surrender on 15 January 1891. By the end of the month General Miles left Pine Ridge with 25 leading ghost dancers. These prisoners of the Ghost Dance War were to be held as captives at Fort Sheridan, Illinois, to ensure the good behavior of those left behind at the agency. Instead, Buffalo Bill Cody persuaded government officials to let the captives participate in his Wild West Show's European tour.

See also Sioux Wars

References

Robert M. Utley, *The Lance and the Shield: The Life and Times of Sitting Bull* (New York: Henry Holt, 1993).

———, *The Last Days of the Sioux Nation* (New Haven, CT: Yale University Press, 1963).

Herbert J. Viola, *Trail to Wounded Knee: The Last Stand of the Plains Indians, 1860–1890* (Washington, DC: National Geographic, 2004).

—*Jon Brudvig*

Y

Yalta Conference

From 4 February to 11 February 1945 the three major Allied leaders, Franklin D. Roosevelt of the United States, Winston Churchill of Great Britain, and Josef Stalin of the Soviet Union, debated the outstanding questions of war and peace at Yalta in the Crimea. Although not the key issue, one subject for discussion was the treatment of prisoners of war. The most crucial point concerned the repatriation of Soviet citizens, civilians and soldiers alike, forcibly deported by the Nazis to Germany and German-occupied countries and liberated as a result of military operations undertaken by the Western Allies. The Soviet government considered that these citizens should be regarded, not as war prisoners, but as free nationals of an Allied (Soviet) power, and consequently should be placed in camps separate from German POWs.

The Western Allies repatriated two million Russians to the Soviet Union in the years 1945–1947. Repatriation operations took place in Germany proper and in Norway, the Netherlands, Belgium, France, and even in North Africa. Soviet citizens, soldiers and civilians alike, were handed over to the Soviet security agencies—the NKVD and SMERSH (literally, *SMERt' SHpionov*, or "Death to Spies"). In addition, thousands of Tsarist exiles were surrendered against their will to the Soviet Union; these people had never lived in the Soviet Union, having fled Russia in 1919 as allies of the British and Americans, and therefore were not covered by the Yalta Agreement. The policy adopted by the U.S. and British governments was that all claimants to Soviet nationality were to be released to the Soviet government irrespective of their wishes. Once repatriated to the Soviet Union, most of the Russian prisoners vanished in the Gulag system. For Stalin, these repatriates were traitors; to fall into German captivity, instead of dying in battle, was considered an act of treason against the Soviet Motherland.

The U.S. and British governments kept the repatriation operations secret, fearing a public revolt against the brutal measures toward Russian prisoners, particularly in view of the large numbers of women and children involved. Moreover, U.S. and British officials did not want to endanger the alliance with the Soviet Union: to refuse the Soviet government's request for the return of its citizens would lead to serious trouble. The Soviets would not understand Western humanitarian motives and would protest that they were being treated differently than other Allied countries. Furthermore, Allied intelligence estimated that there were 40,000 British and 75,000 Americans imprisoned by the Soviets in eastern Europe and the Soviet Union, and the Western Allies feared that their own prisoners would not be released if they protested Soviet repatriation. In this regard, the POW question became a bargaining chip between the western Allies and the Soviet Union.

See also Forcible Repatriation; Keelhaul, Operation; Repatriation

References

Foreign Relations of the United States. Diplomatic Papers. The Conferences at Malta and Yalta 1945 (Washington, DC: Government Printing Office, 1955).

Nicholas Bethell, *The Last Secret: Forcible Repatriation to Russia, 1945–1947* (London: Andre Deutsch, 1974).

Mark R. Elliot, "The United States and Forced Repatriation of Soviet Citizens," *Political Science Quarterly* 58 (1973): 253–275.

Julius Epstein, *Operation Keelhaul: The Story of Forced Repatriation from 1944 to the Present* (Greenwich, CT: Devin-Adair, 1973).
Nikolai Tolstoy, *Victims of Yalta* (London: Hodder and Stoughton, 1977).

—*Eva-Maria Stolberg*

Yeo-Thomas, Forest Frederick Edward (1901–1964)

A much decorated resistance fighter and concentration camp escaper, Wing Commander Forest Frederick Edward "Tommy" Yeo-Thomas was born 17 June 1901 in London but was educated for the most part in France. He served in World War I and then fought with the Poles against the Russians. During World War II, he joined the French Resistance, and as an operative with the Special Operations Executive (SOE) was parachuted into France in February 1943, using the code name "the White Rabbit." A formidable and resourceful agent, he undertook a second mission into France later that year. Parachuted into France a third time in February 1944, he was betrayed and captured by the Gestapo, who subjected him to two months of beatings and torture. He only survived by claiming to be Squadron Leader Kenneth Dodkin, a downed airman.

After two escape attempts, Yeo-Thomas was transported to Buchenwald concentration camp. Here he met two SOE agents known to him, and he teamed up with them to coordinate escape attempts and camp resistance. In September 1944, the camp commandant received orders to eliminate all 37 SOE operatives held in the camp. Yeo-Thomas and two others were saved when they managed to change identities with three dead French inmates. Four more agents were hidden by sympathetic inmates and survived; the other 30 were hanged using piano-wire nooses.

Yeo-Thomas and his two companions were able to leave Buchenwald on a work party, from which they escaped and reached the safety of Allied lines. Tommy Yeo-Thomas returned to Paris after the war but died on 26 February 1964 from illnesses directly related to his brutal treatment at the hands of the Gestapo.

See also Buchenwald

References
Colin Burgess, *Destination: Buchenwald* (Kenthurst, Australia: Kangaroo Press, 1995).
Bruce Marshall, *The White Rabbit* (London: Evans Brothers, 1952).

—*Colin Burgess*

Young Men's Christian Association (YMCA)

The YMCA has emerged as one of the most influential humanitarian organizations involved in the relief effort for POWs and civilian internees in the twentieth century. A nonsectarian and nonpolitical organization devoted to developing high standards of Christian character, it originated in England in 1844, moving to Australia in 1850 and North America in 1851. In 1855, various local bodies affiliated into the World Alliance of YMCAs, headquartered in Geneva, Switzerland.

The World's Committee of YMCAs realized early in World War I that it could play a vital role in assisting prisoners and accepted an offer by the American branch, under John R. Mott, to play the major role in this endeavor. In January 1915, Mott dispatched two officials to Europe to lay the groundwork for the service. Visiting London, Paris, Berlin, St. Petersburg, Rome, and Vienna, they eventually secured the concurrence of all of the major belligerent governments, and so the War Prisoners Aid (WPA) of the YMCA was established, using the personnel and resources of the national YMCAs wherever possible.

Like the International Committee of the Red Cross (ICRC) and the Protecting Power, the YMCA used camp visits to ascertain the educational, recreational, moral, and religious needs of prisoners. (It left to other agencies the provision of food, clothing, and money.) Not surprisingly, the supply of religious materials was a priority for the WPA, and it shipped to prison camps large quantities of bibles, icons, vestments, communion vessels, and church furnishings. Despite its name, the YMCA was completely nonsectarian in its work with POWs; it responded to all requests, regardless of religion. In Wieselberg camp in Austria, for example, it erected two churches, one Russian Orthodox and one Roman Catholic, and also furnished a number of prayer rooms for Jewish prisoners. But the WPA was just as concerned with the physical and moral well-being of prisoners as it was with the spiritual. Consequently, it also provided sports equipment, musical instruments and sheet music, theatrical supplies, books and library materials, educational supplies, and stationary. Wherever possible, WPA camp inspectors also acted to mediate disputes between prisoners and their captors.

The obstacles to the WPA were great. Often, belligerent states refused access to certain types of camps. YMCA delegates were barred, for example, from work camps in Germany and civilian internment camps in France. Also, there were rarely enough delegates to do the work required; in Germany, the YMCA was allowed only 13 delegates to work on behalf of nearly three million POWs. Furthermore, when the United States entered the war in April 1917, the YMCA was forced to withdraw its American inspectors and find neutral replacements, no easy task given the fact that hundreds of the most qualified neutral citizens were already working for the Protecting Powers or the ICRC. Nevertheless, the WPA located able replacements and was able to continue its work until the end of the war. After the armistice of November 1918, it staffed relief depots to assist prisoners on their way home and provided refreshments at ports and railway junctions used by large groups of recently liberated prisoners.

Early in World War II, the World's Committee again approached the Swiss government with the request that it be authorized to work on behalf of prisoners of all nations. The government gave its blessing, and YMCA officials were sent to the capitals of the major belligerent states to secure the cooperation of other governments. This was quick in coming: by November 1939, the governments of Britain, Germany, and France had all agreed to allow the YMCA to carry on its mission in prison camps. The WPA was duly reconstituted and began work almost immediately, eventually supervising 40 delegates in 26 countries. To understand the scope of the global effort, it is sufficient to consider the WPA's work in one country. In Canada, where some 35,000 German POWs were held, a WPA Committee of prominent Canadians was organized to supervise the work of WPA delegates, to act as a public relations center, and to serve as liaison between the WPA and the Canadian public. The leading lights behind the work in Canada were Conrad Hoffman, who had directed WPA work in Germany during World War I, and Jerome Davis. Later, when Davis went to Moscow to attempt to initiate YMCA work with prisoners there, he was replaced by Louis Boschenstein, a Swiss professor at the University of Toronto. Since many of the Canadian prison camps were in isolated locations, the YMCA delegates had long distances to travel, which tended to make their visits even more meaningful to the detainees. When they brought along sports equipment or reading material without requiring that the prisoners attend prayer meetings, it was further proof that their aims were strictly humanitarian and that they had no deeper agenda.

A noteworthy success for the Canadian YMCA came in Hong Kong. A YMCA supervisor, George Porteous, had accompanied the Canadian units when they were first dispatched to the colony, and he was arranging recreational and educational opportunities before the Japanese attack. When the bulk of Hong Kong's garrison was captured in December 1941, Porteous merely continued his work. He reorganized the YMCA library of 300 books, adding to it as new volumes were received from local philanthropists or humanitarian organizations. At its peak, the library had over 1,000 books and a sophisticated bookbinding and repair facility operated by self-taught prisoners. Porteous also organized handicrafts as a way for prisoners to pass the time by making such useful items as wooden clogs, chess boards, cigarette holders, and sweaters. Educational classes were arranged in such subjects as algebra, physics, shorthand, Ukrainian, civics, and music theory, with the YMCA providing the materials. The Japanese allowed the YMCA to send musical instruments into Hong Kong camps, and sports equipment was also made available. In their weakened physical condition, however, comparatively few POWs were able to take part in sports. Ironically, Porteous received little credit from the Canadian government upon his return to Canada. Though treated as a POW, he had never been officially listed as being in military service, so he returned home to find that the government had billed him for income tax while he was in captivity.

See also International Committee of the Red Cross; St. John Ambulance

References

Chris Christiansen, *Seven Years Among Prisoners of War*, trans. Ida Egede Winther (Athens: Ohio University Press, 1994).

Frederick Harris, ed., *Service with Fighting Men: An Account of the Work of the American Young Men's Christian Associations in the World War*, vol. 2 (New York: Association Press, 1922).

Conrad Hoffman, *In the Prison Camps of Germany: A Narrative of 'Y' Service among Prisoners of War* (New York: Association Press, 1920).

Alan M. Hurst, *The Canadian Y.M.C.A. in World War II* (Toronto: National War Services Committee of the National Council of YMCAs of Canada, n.d.).

Clarence Prouty Shedd, *History of the World's Alliance of Young Men's Christian Associations* (London: S.P.C.K., 1955).

André Vuliet, *The YMCA and Prisoners of War: War Prisoners Aid of the YMCA during World War II* (New York: Internment Committee of the YMCA, 1946).

—*Jonathan F. Vance*

Z

Zentsuji

Zentsuji prison camp, on the island of Shikoku, was typical of the facilities operated by Japan during World War II. The first POW camp established in Japan, it opened on 16 January 1942, and its first inmates were 234 Americans captured on Guam and Wake Island. Later, some Australians, a few civilians, and crew members of a number of British, American, and Dutch naval vessels arrived. In July 1943, a large group of American soldiers was transferred from a camp near Tokyo, and through 1944 the camp population remained stable at around 700 American and British Commonwealth POWs. When the war ended in August 1945, however, only 109 prisoners remained in the camp, the rest having been transferred to other facilities.

Zentsuji's principal camp consisted of a two-story barracks in a five-acre compound. Compared to other camps operated by the Japanese, conditions at Zentsuji were fairly good. Some members of the camp staff were relatively lenient, although their discipline became more brutal as the war dragged on. For at least part of the time that the camp was in operation, prisoners enjoyed a weekly bath and the occasional walk through the town and environs, so morale was as good as could be expected under the circumstances. The camp's greatest distinction was that it possessed the library of former American Ambassador to Tokyo, Joseph Grew, which provided the prisoners with a wide variety of reading material and made possible the establishment of Zentsuji College, an educational program run by the prisoners.

Zentsuji was also the administrative headquarters for a number of other camps nearby. Records are incomplete, but there may have been as many as 10 subcamps (some considerably larger than the main camp) controlled from Zentsuji. Prisoners in these camps were sent to work in a variety of concerns, including farms, railways, and mines.

See also World War II—Far East

References

Donald T. Giles, Jr., ed., *Captive of the Rising Sun: The POW Memoirs of Rear Admiral Donald T. Giles* (Annapolis, MD: Naval Institute Press, 1994).

—*E. P. Smith*

Bibliography & Suggested Readings

Bibliography

Note: Additional readings appear with individual articles.

General

Ronald H. Bailey, *Prisoners of War* (Alexandria, VA: Time-Life Books, 1981).

A.J. Barker, *Behind Barbed Wire* (London: B.T. Batsford, 1974).

Joan Beaumont, "Rank, Privilege and Prisoners of War," *War & Society* 1 (1983): 67–94.

Tim Bird, *American POWs of World War II: Forgotten Men Tell Their Stories* (Westport, CT: Praeger, 1992).

Bill Bunbury, *Rabbits and Spaghetti: Captives and Comrades – Australians, Italians and the War* (Fremantle: Fremantle Arts Centre Press, 1995).

Lewis H. Carlson, *We Were Each Other's Prisoners: An Oral History of World War II American and German Prisoners of War* (New York: Basic Books, 1997).

Hugh Clarke, Colin Burgess, and Russell Braddon, *Prisoners of War* (North Sydney: Time-Life Books, 1988).

Hugh Clarke and Colin Burgess, *Barbed Wire and Bamboo: Australian POW Stories* (St. Leonards: Allen & Unwin, 199).

Daniel G. Dancocks, *In Enemy Hands: Canadian Prisoners of War, 1939–45* (Edmonton, AB: Hurtig, 1983).

Robert C. Doyle, *Voices from Captivity: Interpreting the American POW Narrative* (Manhattan: University Press of Kansas, 1994).

Niall Ferguson, "Prisoner Taking and Prisoner Killing in the Age of Total War: Towards a Political Economy of Military Defeat," *War in History* 11 (2004): 148–192.

Herbert C. Fooks, *Prisoners of War* (Federalsburg, MD: J.W. Stowell, 1924).

Richard Garrett, *P.O.W.: The Uncivil Face of War* (London: David & Charles, 1981).

John Laffin, *The Anatomy of Captivity* (London: Abelard-Schuman, 1968).

George Q. Lewis and John Mewha, *History of Prisoner of War Utilization by the United States Army 1776–1945* (Washington, DC: United States Center for Military History, 1988).

Bob Moore and Kent Fedorowich, eds., *Prisoners of War and their Captors in World War II* (Oxford: Berg, 1996).

P.R. Reid and Maurice Michael, *Prisoner of War* (London: Hamlyn Publishing, 1984).

Claire Swedberg, ed., *In Enemy Hands: Personal Accounts of Those Taken Prisoner in World War II* (Mechanicsburg, PA: Stackpole Books, 1997).

Patrick Wilson, *The War Behind the Wire: Experiences in Captivity during the Second World War* (Barnsley, UK: Pen & Sword Books, 2000).

Escape

J.R. Ackerley, *Escapers All* (London: John Lane, 1932).

Paul Brickhill, *Escape - or Die* (London: Evans Brothers, 1952).

Colin Burgess, *Freedom or Death: Australia's Greatest Escape Stories from Two World Wars* (St. Leonards: Allen & Unwin, 1994).

Graeme Cook, *Breakout!: Great Wartime Escape Stories* (London: Hart-Davis, MacGibbon, 1974).

Aidan Crawley, *Escape from Germany: The Methods of Escape Used by RAF Airmen during the Second World War* (London: HMSO, 1985).

Basil Davenport, *Great Escapes* (New York: Sloane, 1952).

John Dominy, *The Sergeant Escapers* (London: Ian Allan, 1974).

Robert C. Doyle, *A Prisoner's Duty: Great Escapes in U.S. Military History* (Annapolis, MD: Naval Institute Press, 1997).

A.J. Evans, *Escape and Liberation, 1940–1945* (London: Hodder & Stoughton, 1945).

Ian Fellowes-Gordon, *The World's Greatest Escapes* (London: Odhams Books, 1966).

Burton Graham, *Escape from the Nazis* (Secaucus, NJ: Castle Books, 1975).

Robert Jackson, *When Freedom Calls: Great Escapes of the Second World War* (London: Arthur Barker, 1973).

P.R. Reid, *My Favourite Escape Stories* (London: Lutterworth Press, 1975).

A.I. Shuster, *Great Civil War Escapes* (New York: G.P. Putnam's Sons, 1967).

They Got Back: The Best Escape Stories from the RAF Flying Review (London: Herbert Jenkins, 1961).

Eric Williams, ed., *The Escapers* (London: Collins, 1953).

——, *Great Escape Stories* (London: Arthur Barker, 1958).

Andrew S. Winton, *Open Road to Faraway: Escapes from Nazi POW Camps, 1941–1945* (Dunfermline, UK: Cualann Press, 2001).

Korea

Albert D. Biderman, *March to Calumny: The Story of American POWs in the Korean War* (New York: Macmillan, 1963).

Wallace L. Brown, *The Endless Hours: My Two and a Half Years as a Prisoner of War of the Chinese Communists* (New York: Norton, 1961).

Cyril Cunningham, *No Mercy, No Leniency: Communist Mistreatment of British and Allied Prisoners of War in Korea* (Barnsley, UK: Pen & Sword Books, 2000).

Philip Deane, *I Was a Captive in Korea* (New York: Norton, 1953).

Anthony Farrar-Hockley, *The Edge of the Sword* (Stroud, UK: Alan Sutton, 1993 [1954]).

Peter Gaston, *Korea, 1950–1953: Prisoners of War, The British Army* (Uckfield, UK: Naval & Military Press, 2002).

David Green, *Captured at the Imjin River: The Korean War Memoirs of a Gloster* (Barnsley, UK: Pen & Sword Books, 2003).

Kenneth K. Hansen, *Heroes Behind Barbed Wire* (Princeton, NJ: Van Nostrand, 1957).

Laurence Jolidon, *Last Seen Alive: The Search for Missing POWs from the Korean War* (Rochester, NY: Ink-Slinger Press, 1995).

Eugene Kinkead, *In Every War But One* (New York: Norton, 1959).

Derek G. Kinne, *The Wooden Boxes* (London: Muller, 1955).

Dennis Lankford, *I Defy!* (London: Wingate, 1954).

Raymond B. Lech, *Broken Soldiers* (Urbana: University of Illinois Press, 2000).

Samuel M. Meyers and Albert Biderman, eds., *Mass Behavior in Battle and Captivity: The Communist Soldier in the Korean War* (Chicago: University of Chicago Press, 1968).

Ward M. Millar, *Valley of the Shadow* (New York: David McKay, 1955).

H.K. Shin, *Remembering Korea 1950: A Boy Soldier's Story* (Reno: University of Nevada Press, 2001).

Harry Spiller, ed., *American POWs in Korea: 16 Personal Accounts* (Jefferson, NC: McFarland, 1998).

Sandy Strait, *What Happened to American Prisoners of War in Korea* (Unionville, NY: Royal Fireworks Press, 1998).

Treatment of British Prisoners of War in Korea (London: HMSO, 1955).

Stanley Weintraub, *The War in the Wards: Korea's Unknown Battle in a Prisoner-of-War Hospital Camp* (New York: Doubleday, 1964).

William Lindsay White, *The Captives of Korea* (New York: Scribner's, 1957).

Larry Zellers, *In Enemy Hands: A Prisoner in North Korea* (Lexington: University Press of Kentucky, 1991).

U.S. Civil War

Flavel C. Barber, *Holding the Line: The Third Tennessee Infantry, 1861–1864* (Kent, OH: Kent State University Press, 1994).

Arch Fredric Blakey, *General John H. Winder, CSA* (Gainesville: University of Florida Press, 1990).

Benjamin F. Booth, *Dark Days of the Rebellion: Life in Southern Military Prisons*, ed. Steve Meyer (Garrison, IA: Meyer Publishing, 1996 [1897]).

Frances H. Casstevens, *Out of the Mouth of Hell: Civil War Prisons and Escapes* (Jefferson, NC: McFarland & Co., 2005).

John Cimprich and Robert C. Mainfort, "The Fort Pillow Massacre: A Statistical Note," *Journal of American History* 79 (1989): 830–7.

Robert E. Denney, *Civil War Prisons and Escapes: A Day-by-Day Chronicle* (New York: Sterling, 1993).

James R. Hagood, *The Immortal Six Hundred: A Story of Cruelty to Confederate Prisoners of War* (Little Rock, AK: Eagle Press, 1986 [1905].

William Best Hesseltine, *Civil War Prisons: A Study in War Psychology* (Columbus: Ohio State University Press, 1930).

Randolph W. Kirkland, Jr., *Dark Hours: South Carolina Soldiers, Sailors and Civilians Who Were Held in Federal Prisons during the War for Southern Independence, 1861–1865* (Charleston: South Carolina Historical Society, 2002).

Muriel Phillips Joslyn, *Immortal Captives: The Story of 600 Confederate Officers and the United States Prisoner of War Policy* (Shippensburg, PA: White Mane, 1996).

George Levy, *To Die in Chicago: Confederate Prisoners at Camp Douglas, 1862–1865* (Gretna, LA: Pelican Publishing, 1995).

John Lynn, *800 Paces to Hell: Andersonville* (Fredericksburg, VA: Sergeant Kirkland's Press, 1998).

William Marvel, *Andersonville: The Last Depot* (Chapel Hill: University of North Carolina Press, 1994).

Richard Masterson, *Salisbury: Civil War Death Camp in North Carolina* (Shippensburg, PA Burd Street Press, 2005).

Charles W. Sanders, Jr., *While in the Hands of the Enemy: Military Prisons of the Civil War* (Baton Rouge: Louisiana State University Press, 2005).

Mark A. Snell and Ezra Hoyt Ripple, eds., *Dancing Along the Deadline: The Andersonville Memoir of a Prisoner of the Confederacy* (Novato, CA: Presidio, 1996).

Lonnie R. Speer, *Portals to Hell: Military Prisons of the Civil War* (Mechanicsburg, PA: Stackpole Books, 1997).

Francis Benson Thompson, ed., *Berry Benson's Civil War Book: Memoirs of a Confederate Scout and Sharpshooter* (Athens: University of Georgia Press, 1991).

The War of the Rebellion: A Compilation of the Official Records of the Union and Confederate Armies (Washington: Government Printing Office, 1880–1901), series II.

Ronald G. Watson, ed., *From Ashby to Andersonville: The Civil War Diary and Reminiscences of George A. Hitchcock* (Mason City, IA: Savas Publishing, 1997).

Vietnam

Everett Alvarez, Jr., and Anthony S. Pitch, *Chained Eagle* (New York: Donald I. Fine, 1990).

Laurence Bailey, *Solitary Survivor: The First American POW in Southeast Asia* (New York: Brassey's, 1995).

Richard Blakely, *Prisoner at War: The Survival of Commander Richard A. Stratton* (Garden City, NJ: Doubleday, 1978).

Ernest Brace, *A Code to Keep: The True Story of America's Longest-Held Civilian POW in Vietnam* (Central Point, OR: Hellgate Press, 2001).

Nigel Cawthorne, *Bamboo Cage: The Full Story of the American Servicemen Still Held Hostage in South-East Asia* (London: Leo Cooper, 1991).

Larry Chesley, *Seven Years in Hanoi: A POW Tells His Story* (Salt Lake City: Book Craft, 1973).

Rod Colvin, *First Heroes: The POWs Left Behind in Vietnam* (New York: Irvington, 1987).

Dieter Dengler, *Escape from Laos* (Novato, CA: Presidio Press, 1979).

Jeremiah A. Denton, Jr., *When Hell Was In Session* (New York: Readers Digest Press, 1976).

Zalin Grant, *Survivors: American POWs in Vietnam* (New York: Berkley Books, 1985).

Larry Guarino, *A POW's Story: 2801 Days in Hanoi* (New York: Ivy, 1990).

John G. Hubbell, *P.O.W.: A Definitive History of the American Prisoner of War Experience in Vietnam, 1964–1973* (New York: Reader's Digest Press, 1976).

Sam Johnson and Jan Winebrenner, *Captive Warriors: A Vietnam POW's Story* (College Station: Texas A&M University Press, 1992).

Taylor Baldwin Kiland and Jamie Howren, *Open Doors: Vietnam POWs Thirty Years Later* (Dulles, VA: Potomac Books, 2005).

Malcolm McConnell, *Into the Mouth of the Cat: The Story of Lance Sijan, Hero of Vietnam* (New York: Norton, 1985).

John M. McGrath, *Prisoners of War: Six Years in Hanoi* (Annapolis, MD: Naval Institute Press, 1975).

Mark Moyar, *Phoenix and the Birds of Prey: The CIA's Secret Campaign to Destroy the Viet Cong* (Annapolis, MD: Naval Institute Press, 1997).

Robinson Risner, *The Passing of the Night: My Seven Years as a Prisoner of the North Vietnamese* (New York: Random House, 1973).

Stuart I. Rochester and Frederick Kiley, *Honor Bound: The History of American Prisoners of War in Southeast Asia, 1961–1973* (Washington, DC: Office of the Secretary of Defense, 1998).

James N. Rowe, *Five Years to Freedom* (Boston: Little, Brown, 1971).

George J. Veith, *Code-Name Bright Light: The Untold Story of U.S. POW Rescue Efforts during the Vietnam War* (New York: Free Press, 1998).

War Crimes

Allen Andrews, *Exemplary Justice* (London: Harrap, 1976).

Patrick Brode, *Casual Slaughters and Accidental Judgements: Canadian War Crimes Prosecutions, 1944–1948* (Toronto: University of Toronto Press, 1997).

Frank Buscher, *The U.S. War Crimes Trial Program in Germany, 1946–1955* (Westport, CT: Greenwood Press, 1989).

Robert E. Conot, *Justice at Nuremberg* (New York: Harper & Row, 1983).

Syzmon Datner, *Crimes Against POWs: Responsibility of the Wehrmacht* (Warsaw: Zachodnia Agencja Prasowa, 1964).

Eugene Davidson, *The Nuremberg Fallacy: Wars and War Crimes since World War II* (New York: Macmillan, 1973).

Alfred M. de Zayas, *The Wehrmacht War Crimes Bureau, 1939–1945* (Lincoln: University of Nebraska Press, 1989).

Knut Dörmann, *Elements of War Crimes Under the Rome Statute of the International Criminal Court: Sources and Commentary* (Cambridge: Cambridge University Press, 2003).

Michael J. Goodwin, *Shobun: A Forgotten War Crime in the Pacific* (Mechanicsburg, PA: Stackpole Books, 1995).

Hamburg Institute, *The German Army and Genocide: Crimes Against War Prisoners, Jews and Other Civilians in the East, 1939–1944* (New York: New Press, 1999).

Chester Hearn, *Sorties Into Hell: The Hidden War on Chichi Jima* (Westport, CT: Praeger, 2003).

R.W.D. Jones, *The Practice of the International Criminal Tribunals for the Former Yugoslavia and Rwanda* (Ardsley, NY: Transnational Publishers, 2000).

Theodor Meron, "War Crimes in Yugoslavia and the Development of International Law," *American Journal of International Law* 88 (1994): 84–87.

Lord Russell of Liverpool, *The Scourge of the Swastika: A Short History of Nazi War Crimes* (London: Cassell, 1954).

——, *The Knights of Bushido: The Shocking History of Japanese War Atrocities* (New York: E.P. Dutton, 1958).

A.P. Scotland, *The London Cage* (London: Evans Brothers, 1957).

Bradley F. Smith, *Reaching Judgement at Nuremberg* (New York: Basic Books, 1977).

Yuki Tanaka, *Hidden Horrors: Japanese War Crimes in World War II* (Boulder, CO: Westview Press, 1996).

Women

Peggy Abkhazi, *A Curious Cage: A Shanghai Journal, 1941–1945* (Victoria, BC: Sono Nis Press, 1981).

Pamela Bhagat, *War: What Price are Women Paying?* (New Delhi: Women's Feature Service, 2002).

Lynn Z. Bloom, "Escaping Voices: Women's South Pacific Internment Diaries and Memoirs," *Mosaic* 23 (1990): 101–12.

Sheila Bruhn, *Diary of a Girl in Changi, 1941–1945* (Kenthurst, Australia: Kangaroo Press, 1996).

Helen Colijn, *Song of Survival: Women Interned* (Ashland, OR: White Cloud Press, 1995).

Kristin Conrey, "Remembering the Forgotten: A Look at the Women POWs of World War II," *Minerva: Quarterly Report on Women and the Military* 16 (1998): 25–75.

Natalie Crouter, *Forbidden Diary: A Record of Wartime Experience, 1941–45* (New York: Franklin, 1980).

Linda Grant De Pauw, *Battle Cries and Lullabies: Women in War from Prehistory to the Present* (Norman: University of Oklahoma Press, 1998).

Ustinia Dolgopol, "Women's Voices, Women's Pain," *Human Rights Quarterly* 17 (1995): 127–154.

Mercedes Herrera-Graf, "Stress, Suffering and Sacrifice: Women POWs in the Civil War," *Minerva: Quarterly Report on Women and the Military* 16 (1998): 1–24.

Ronny Herman, *In the Shadow of the Sun* (Surrey, BC: Vanderheide Publishing, 1992).

Human Rights Watch, *The War Within the War: Sexual Violence Against Women and Girls in Eastern Congo* (New York: Human Rights Watch, 2002).

Human Rights Watch/Africa and Human Rights Watch Women's Rights Project, *Shattered Lives: Sexual Violence during the Rwandan Genocide and its Aftermath* (New York: Human Rights Watch, 1996).

Judith S. Hyland, *In the Shadow of the Rising Sun* (Minneapolis: Augsburg, 1984).

Charlotte Lindsey, "Women and War: The Detention of Women in Wartime," *International Review of the Red Cross* 83 (June 2001): 505–520.

Celia Lucas, *Prisoners of Santo Tomas: A True Account of Women POWs Under Japanese Control* (Conshohocken, PA: Combined Books, 1997).

Fern Miles, *Captive Community: Life in a Japanese Internment Camp* (Jefferson City, TN: Mossy Creek, 1987).

Carolyn Paine Miller, *Captured: A Mother's True Story of Her Family's Imprisonment by the Viet Cong* (Chappaqua, NY: Christian Herald Books, 1977).

Bessy Myers, *Captured: My Experiences as an Ambulance Driver and as a Prisoner of the Nazis* (London: George G. Harrap, 1941).

Luise Rinser, *A Woman's Prison Journal: Germany, 1944* (New York: Schocken Books, 1987).

Darlene Deibler Rose, *Evidence Not Seen: A Woman's Miraculous Faith in the Jungles of World War II* (San Francisco: Harper, 1990).

Margaret Sams, *Forbidden Family: A Wartime Memoir of the Philippines, 1941–1945* (Madison: University of Wisconsin Press, 1997).

Dorothy Davis Thompson, *The Road Back: A Pacific POW's Liberation Story* (Lubbock: Texas Tech University Press, 1996).

Elizabeth Vaughan, *The Ordeal of Elizabeth Vaughan: A Wartime Diary of the Philippines* (Athens: University of Georgia Press, 1985).

Lavinia Warner and John Sandilands, *Women Beyond the Wire: A Story of Prisoners of the Japanese* (London: Michael Joseph, 1982).

Kate Webb, *On the Other Side: 23 Days With the Viet Cong* (New York: Quadrangle Books, 1972).

Denny Williams, *To the Angels* (San Francisco: Denson Press, 1985).

World War I

Norman Archibald, *Heaven High, Hell Deep, 1917–18* (North Stratford, NH: Ayer, 1979).

Carl P. Dennett, *Prisoners of the Great War: Authoritative Statement of Conditions in the Prison Camps of Germany* (Boston: Houghton Mifflin, 1919).

J. Harvey Douglas, *Captured: Sixteen Months as a Prisoner of War* (Toronto: McClelland, Goodchild and Stewart, 1917).

Edwin Erich Dwinger, *The Army Behind Barbed Wire: A Siberian Diary* (London: G. Allen & Unwin, 1930).

Roman Dyboski, *Seven Years in Russia and Siberia, 1914–1921* (Cheshire, CT: Cherry Hill Books, 1971 [1922]).

A.J. Evans, *The Escaping Club* (London: Jonathan Cape, 1921).

Christopher J. Gallagher, *The Cellars of Marcelcave: A Yank Doctor in the BEF* (Shippensburg, PA: Burd Street Press, 1998).
Duncan Grinnell-Milne, *An Escaper's Log* (London: John Lane, 1926).
Malcolm Hall, *In Enemy Hands: A British Territorial Soldier in Germany, 1915–1919* (Stroud, UK: Tempus Publishing, 2002).
J.L. Hardy, *I Escape!* (London: John Lane, 1928)
M.C.C. Harrison and H.A. Cartwright, *Within Four Walls* (London: Edward Arnold, 1930).
Robert Jackson, *The Prisoners, 1914–18* (New York: Routledge, 1989).
Daniel J. McCarthy, *The Prisoner of War in Germany: The Care and Treatment of the Prisoner of War with a History of the Development of the Principle of Neutral Inspection and Control* (New York: Moffat, Yard, 1918).
Desmond Morton, *Silent Battle: Canadian Prisoners of War in Germany, 1914–1919* (Toronto: Lester, 1992).
Michael Moynihan, *Black Bread and Barbed Wire: Prisoners in the First World War* (London: Leo Cooper, 1978).
Reinhard Nachtigal, "German Prisoners of War in Tsarist Russia: A Glance at Petrograd St. Petersburg," *German History* 13 (1995): 198–204.
Gilbert Nobbs, *Englishman, Kamerad* (Uckfield, UK: Naval & Military Press, 2005).
Gunther Plüschow, *My Escape from Donington Hall* (London: John Lane, 1929).
Alon Rachamimov, "Imperial Loyalties and Private Concerns: Nation, Class and State in the Correspondence of Austro-Hungarian POWs in Russia," *Austrian History Yearbook* 31 (2000).
Richard B. Speed, *Prisoners, Diplomats and the Great War: A Study in the Diplomacy of Captivity* (New York: Greenwood Press, 1990).
W.A. Tucker, *The Lousier War* (London: NEL, 1974).
Richard van Emden, *Prisoners of the Kaiser: The Last POWs of the Great War* (Barnsley, UK: Pen & Sword Books, 2000).
Samuel R. Williamson and Peter Pastor, eds., *Essays on World War I: Origins and Prisoners of War* (New York: Columbia University Press, 1983).

World War II - European Theater

B. Arct, *Secret Journal: Life in a World War II Prison Camp* (Oxford: Past Times, 1995).
Noel Barber, *Prisoner of War: The Story of British Prisoners Held by the Enemy* (London: George G. Harrap, 1944).
Mitchell G. Bard, *Forgotten Victims: The Abandonment of Americans in Hitler's Camps* (Boulder, CO: Westview Press, 1994).
Ron Baybutt, *Camera in Colditz* (London: Hodder & Stoughton, 1982).
Art and Lee Beltrone, *A Wartime Log: A Remembrance from Home through the American YMCA* (Charlottesville, VA: Howell Press, 1995).
T.D. Calnan, *Free As a Running Fox* (New York: Dial Press, 1970).
The Earl of Cardigan, *I Walked Alone* (London: Routledge & Kegan Paul, 1950).
Adrian Carton de Wiart, *Happy Odyssey* (London: Jonathan Cape, 1950).
Nigel Cawthorne, *The Iron Cage: Are British Prisoners of War Abandoned in Soviet Hands Still Alive in Siberia?* (London: Fourth Estate, 1993).
William Chapin, *Milk Run: Prisoner of War, 1944 – An American Flier in Stalag 17-B* (Sausalito, CA: Windgate Press, 1992).
Roger Cohen, *Soldiers and Slaves: American POWs Trapped by the Nazis' Final Gamble* (New York: Alfred A. Knopf, 2005).
J. Frank Diggs, *Americans Behind the Barbed Wire, World War II: Inside a German Prison Camp* (Arlington, VA: Vandamere Press, 2000).
Florimond Duke, *Name, Rank and Serial Number* (New York: Meredith Press, 1969).
Donald Edgar, *The Stalag Men* (London: John Clare, 1982).
Ian English, *Assisted Passage: Walking to Freedom, Italy, 1943* (Uckfield, UK: Naval & Military Press, 2004).
David A. Foy, *For You the War Is Over: American Prisoners of War in Nazi Germany* (New York: Stein and Day, 1984).

Victor F. Gammon, *Not All Glory!: True Accounts of RAF Airmen Taken Prisoner in Europe, 1939–1945* (London: Arms and Armour, 1996).

Robert Garioch, *Two Men and a Blanket: A Prisoner of War's Story* (Edinburgh: Southside, 1975).

C. Ross Greening, *Not As Briefed: From the Doolittle Raid to a German Stalag* (Pullman: Washington State University Press, 2001).

Robert L. Grupp and Henry Oehmsen, *The Tracks of God: The Story of Henry Oehmsen, Waffen SS Soldier of World War II and Prisoner of the Soviets* (Philadelphia: Xlibris Corporation, 2000).

Eugene E. Halmos, Jr., *The Wrong Side of the Fence: A United States Army Air Corps POW in World War II* (Shippensburg, PA: White Mane, 1996).

Ned Handy and Kemp Battle, *The Flame Keepers: The True Story of an American Soldier's Survival Inside Stalag 17* (New York: Hyperion, 2004).

James Hargest, *Farewell Campo 12* (London: Michael Joseph, 1945).

George Harsh, *Lonesome Road* (London: Longman, 1971).

Otis Hays, *Home from Siberia: The Secret Odysseys of Interned American Airmen in World War II* (College Station: Texas A&M University Press, 1990).

B.A. James, *Moonless Night: One Man's Struggle for Freedom, 1940–1945* (London: William Kimber, 1983).

David James, *Escaper's Progress* (London: Blackwoods, 1947).

Alexander Jefferson and Lewis H. Carlson, *Red Tail Captured, Red Tail Free: Memoirs of a Tuskegee Airman and POW* (New York: Fordham University Press, 2005).

Ewart C. Jones, *Germans Under My Bed* (London: Arthur Barker, 1957).

Martin Jordan, *For You the War Is Over* (London: Peter Davies, 1946).

J.M. Langley, *Fight Another Day* (London: Collins, 1974).

E.H. Larive, *The Man Who Came in from Colditz* (London: Robert Hale, 1975).

John F. Leeming, *Always Tomorrow* (London: George G. Harrap, 1951).

Donald MacDonell, *From Dogfight to Diplomacy: A Spitfire Pilot's Log, 1932–1958* (Barnsley, UK: Pen & Sword Books, 2005).

Guy Morgan, *P.O.W.* (New York: McGraw-Hill, 1945).

Walter Morison, *Flak and Ferrets: One Way to Colditz* (London: Sentinel, 1995).

Derrick Nabarro, *Wait for the Dawn* (London: Cassel, 1952).

John Nichol and Tony Rennell, *The Last Escape: The Untold Story of Allied Prisoners of War in Germany, 1944–45* (New York: Viking, 2002).

Alfred Novotny, *The Good Soldier: From Austrian Social Democracy to Communist Captivity with a Soldier of Panzer-Grenadier Division "Grossdeutschland"* (Bedford, PA: Aberjona Press, 2002).

Richard Pape, *Boldness Be My Friend* (New York: Elek Books, 1953).

Julie M. Phend and Stanley E. Edwards, Jr., *D-Day and Beyond: The True Story of Escape and POW Survival* (Shippensburg, PA: White Mane, 2004).

Jack A. Poolton, *Destined to Survive: A Dieppe Veteran's Story* (Toronto: Dundurn Press, 1998).

T.C.F. Prittie and W. Earle Edwards, *Escape to Freedom* (London: Hutchinson, 1946).

Ian Ramsay, *P.O.W.: A Digger in Hitler's Prison Camps, 1941–45* (Melbourne: Macmillan, 1985).

Miles Reid, *Last on the List* (London: Leo Cooper, 1974).

——, *Into Colditz* (Wilton: Michael Russell, 1983).

Roland Rieul, *Escape into Espionage: The True Story of a French Patriot in World War Two* (New York: Walker and Company, 1987).

Harry Roberts, *Capture at Arnhem: A Diary of Disaster and Survival* (Moreton-in-Marsh, UK: Windrush Press, 1999).

Charles Robinson, *Journey Into Captivity* (Canberra: Australian War Memorial, 1991).

David Rolf, *Prisoners of the Reich: Germany's Captives, 1939–1945* (London: Leo Cooper, 1988).

Giles Romilly and Michael Alexander, *The Privileged Nightmare* (London: Weidenfeld and Nicolson, 1954).

Norman Rudi, *An Iowa Pilot Named Hap: Hartley A. "Hap" Westbrook* (Ames, IA McMillen Publishing, 2001).

Jerry Sage, *Sage: The Man They Called "Dagger" of the OSS* (Wayne, PA: Tobey Publishing, 1985).

Armin Scheiderbauer, *Adventures in My Youth: A German Soldier on the Eastern Front, 1941–45* (Solihull, UK: Helion and Company, 2003).

Ralph E. Sirianni and Patricia I. Brown, *POW #3959: Memoir of a World War II Airman Shot Down Over Germany* (Jefferson, NC: McFarland & Co., 2005).

Edward Sniders, *Flying In, Walking Out: Memories of War and Escape* (Barnsley, UK: Pen & Sword Books, 1999).

Harry Spiller, *Prisoners of Nazis: Accounts by American POWs in World War II* (Jefferson, NC: McFarland & Co, 1997).

Delmar T. Spivey, *POW Odyssey: Recollections of Center Compound, Stalag Luft III, and the Secret German Peace Mission in World War II* (Attleboro, MA: Colonial Lithograph, 1984).

Geoff Taylor, *Return Ticket* (London: Peter Davies, 1972).

W.B. Thomas, *Dare to Be Free* (London: Allan Wingate, 1953).

Bob Vanderstok, *War Pilot of Orange* (Missoula, MT: Pictorial Histories, 1987).

John A. Vietor, *Time Out: American Airmen in Stalag Luft I* (Fallbrook, CA: Aero Publishers, 1951).

Vasilis Vourkoutiotis, *Prisoners of War and the German High Command: The British and American Experience* (London: Palgrave Macmillan, 2003).

H.E. Woolley, *No Time Off For Good Behaviour* (Burnstown, ON: General Store, 1990).

John Worsley and Kenneth Giggal, *John Worsley's War: An Official War Artist in World War II* (Shrewsbury: Airlife, 1993).

World War II - North America

Robert D. Billinger, *Hitler's Soldiers in the Sunshine State: German POWs in Florida* (Lanham, MD: University Press of America, 2000).

Anita Buck, *Behind Barbed Wire: German Prisoners of War in Minnesota* (St. Cloud, MN: North Star Press, 1998).

David J. Carter, *Behind Canadian Barbed Wire: Alien, Refugee and Prisoner of War Camps in Canada, 1914–1946* (Elkwater, AB: Eagle Butte Press, 1998).

Judith M. Gansberg, *Stalag U.S.A.: The Remarkable Story of German POWs in America* (New York: Thomas Y. Crowell, 1977).

Georg Gartner and Arnold Krammer, *Hitler's Last Soldier in America* (New York: Stein and Day, 1985).

Jeffrey E. Geiger, *German Prisoners of War at Camp Cooke, California: Personal Accounts of 14 Soldiers, 1944–1946* (Jefferson, NC: McFarland & Co., 1996).

Wesley Harris, *Fish Out of Water: Nazi Submariners as Prisoners in North Louisiana During World War II* (Rushton, LA: Roughedge Publications, 2004).

Helmut Horner, *A German Odyssey: The Journal of a German Prisoner of War* (Golden, CO: Fulcrum Publishing, 1991).

Ted Jones, *Both Sides of the Wire: The Fredericton Internment Camp*, 2 volumes (Fredericton, NB: New Ireland Press, 1989).

L.E. Keefer, *Italian Prisoners of War in America, 1942–1946* (New York: Praeger, 1992).

Kathy Kirkpatrick, *Prisoners of War in Utah During World War II* (Salt Lake City: GenTracer, 2004).

Allen V. Koop, *Stark Decency: German Prisoners of War in a New England Village* (Hannover, NH: University Press of New England, 1988).

Arnold Krammer, *Nazi Prisoners of War in America* (New York: Stein and Day, 1979).

Lowell A. May, *Camp Concordia: German POWs in the Midwest* (Manhattan, KS: Sunflower University Press, 1995).

John Melady, *Escape from Canada!: The Untold Story of German POWs in Canada, 1939–1945* (Toronto: Macmillan, 1981).

John Hammond Moore, *The Faustball Tunnel: German POWs in America and Their Great Escape* (New York: Random House, 1978).

Hans-Georg Neumann, *A Man Worth Knowing: The Memoirs of Hans-Georg Neumann* (Toronto: Natural Heritage / Natural History, 1996).

Reinhold Pabel, *Enemies Are Human* (Philadelphia: John C. Winston, 1955).

Cecil Porter, *The Gilded Cage: Gravenhurst German Prisoner-of-War Camp 20, 1940–1946* (Gravenhurst, ON: Gravenhurst Book Committee, 2003).

Walter Schmid, *A German POW in New Mexico* (Albuquerque: University of New Mexico Press, 2000).

Ulrich Steinhilper and Peter Osborne, *Ten Minutes to Buffalo: The Story of Germany's Great Escaper* (Bromley, UK: Independent Books, 1991).

——, *Full Circle: The Long Way Home from Canada* (Bromley, UK: Independent Books, 1992).

Carol Van Valkenburg, *An Alien Place: The Fort Missoula, Montana, Detention Camp, 1941–44* (Missoula, MT: Pictorial Histories, 1995).

Richard Paul Walker, *The Lone Star and the Swastika: Prisoners of War in Texas* (Austin, TX: Eakin Press, 2000).

Michael R. Waters et al, *Lone Star Stalag: German Prisoners of War at Camp Hearne* (College Station: Texas A&M University Press, 2004).

World War II - Pacific Theater

William Allister, *Where Life and Death Hold Hands* (Toronto: Stoddart, 1989).

Kenneth G. Baird, *Letters to Harvelyn from Japanese POW Camps: A Father's Letters to His Young Daughter During World War II* (Toronto: HarperCollins, 2002).

Joan Beaumont, *Gull Force: Survival and Leadership in Captivity* (Sydney: Allen & Unwin, 1988).

William A. Berry, *Prisoner of the Rising Sun* (Norman: University of Oklahoma Press, 1993).

Geoffrey Blain, *Huryo: The Emperor's Captives* (New York: Vantage, 1995).

Jack Chalker, *Burma Railway Artist: An Artist at War in Singapore, Thailand and Burma, 1942–45* (London: Leo Cooper, 1994).

Les Chater, *Behind the Fence: Life as a POW in Japan, 1942–1945* (St. Catharines, ON: Vanwell, 2001).

Anthony Cowling, *My Life with the Samurai* (Kenthurst, Australia: Kangaroo Press, 1996).

Gavan Daws, *Prisoners of the Japanese: POWs of World War II in the Pacific* (New York: William Morrow, 1994).

A.B. Feuer, ed., *FDR's Prisoner Spy: The POW Diary of Cdr Thomas Hayes, USN* (Pacifica, CA: Pacifica Press, 1999).

John Fletcher-Cooke, *The Emperor's Guest, 1942–45* (London: Leo Cooper, 1972).

Frank J. Grady and Rebecca Dickson, *Surviving the Day: An American POW in Japan* (Annapolis, MD: Naval Institute Press, 1997).

Bill Griffiths, *Blind to Misfortune: A Story of Great Courage in the Face of Adversity* (Barnsley, UK: Pen & Sword Books, 2006).

James Home, *Their Last Tenko* (Huddersfield, UK: Quoin Publishing, 1989).

Gene S. Jacobsen, *We Refused to Die: My Time as a Prisoner of War in Bataan and japan, 1942–1945* (Salt Lake City: University of Utah Press, 2004).

D. Clayton James, ed., *South to Bataan, North to Mukden: The Prison Diary of Brigadier General W.E. Brougher* (Athens: University of Georgia Press, 1971).

E. Bartlett Kerr, *Surrender and Survival: The Experience of American POWs in the Pacific, 1941–1945* (New York: William Morrow, 1985).

S. Woodburn Kirby, *The War Against Japan*, vol. 5, *The Surrender of Japan* (London: HMSO, 1969).

Robert S. La Forte and Ronald E. Marcello, eds., *Building the Death Railway: The Ordeal of American POWs in Burma, 1942–1945* (Wilmington, DE: SR Books, 1993).

Robert S. La Forte et al, eds., *With Only the Will to Live: Accounts of Americans in Japanese Prison Camps, 1941–1945* (Wilmington, DE: SR Books, 1994).

Eric Lomax, *The Railway Man: A POW's Searing Account of War, Brutality and Forgiveness* (New York: Norton, 1995).

W. Wynne Mason, *Prisoners of War: Official History of New Zealand in the Second World War 1939–45* (Wellington: War History Branch, Department of Internal Affairs, 1954).

Brian MacArthur, *Surviving the Sword: Prisoners of the Japanese, 1942–45* (London: Time Warner Books, 2005).

John McEwan, *Out of the Depths of Hell: A Soldier's Story of Life and Death in Japanese Hands* (Barnsley, UK: Pen & Sword Books, 1999).

Tom McGowran, *Beyond the Bamboo Screen: Scottish Prisoners of War Under the Japanese* (Dunfermline, UK: Cualann Press, 2000).

David McIntosh, *Hell on Earth: Aging Faster, Dying Sooner — Canadian Prisoners of the Japanese During World War II* (Whitby, ON: McGraw-Hill Ryerson, 1997).

Steve Mellnik, *Philippine Diary, 1939–1945* (New York: Van Nostrand Reinhold, 1969).

John J.A. Michel, *Mr. Michel's War, From Manila to Mukden: An American Naval Officer's War with the Japanese, 1941–1945* (Novato, CA: Presidio Press,).

Hank Nelson, *Prisoners of War: Australians Under Nippon* (Sydney: ABC Enterprises, 1985).

William F. Nimmo, *Behind a Curtain of Silence: Japanese in Soviet Custody, 1945–1956* (New York: Greenwood Press, 1988).

John Playter, *Survivor* (Bolivar, MO: Southwest Baptist University Press, 2000).

Ralph Rentz, *They Can't Take That Away From Me: Odyssey of a POW* (East Lansing: Michigan State University Press, 2003).

Charles G. Roland, "Stripping Away the Veneer: P.O.W. Survival in the Far East as an Index of Cultural Atavism," *Journal of Military History* 53 (1989): 79–94.

——,"Massacre and Rape in Hong Kong: Two Case Studies Involving Medical Personnel and Patients," *Journal of Contemporary History* 32 (1997): 43–61.

——, *Long Night's Journey Into Day: Prisoners of War in Hong Kong and Japan, 1941–1945* (Waterloo, ON: Wilfrid Laurier University Press, 2001).

Iwao Peter Sano, *One Thousand Days in Siberia: The Odyssey of a Japanese-American POW* (Lincoln: University of Nebraska Press, 1997).

Tilak Raj Sareen, *Japanese Prisoners of War in India, 1942–46: Bushido and Barbed War* (Honolulu: University of Hawai'i Press, 2005).

Ulrich Straus, *The Anguish of Surrender: Japanese POWs of World War II* (Seattle: University of Washington Press, 2003).

Lester I. Tenney, *My Hitch in Hell: The Bataan Death March* (New York: Brassey's, 1995).

Philip Towle, Margaret Kosuge, and Yoichi Kibata, eds., *Japanese Prisoners of War* (New York: Hambledon, 2000).

Douglas Valentine, *The Hotel Tacloban* (Westport, CT: Lawrence Hill, 1984).

Van Waterford, *Prisoners of the Japanese in World War II* (Jefferson, NC: McFarland & Co., 1994).

William Jacob Weissinger, *Attention Fool!: A USS Houston Crewman Survives the Burma Death Camps* (Austin, TX: Eakin Press, 1997).

Lionel Wigmore, *Australia in the War of 1939–1945*, vol. 4, *The Japanese Thrust* (Canberra: Australian War Memorial, 1957).

Bob Wodnik, *Captured Honor: POW Survival in the Philippines and Japan* (Pullman, WA: Washington State University Press, 2003).

Readings

Introduction to Readings

Jonathan Vance, 2006

One of the most important developments in the history of prisoners of war and internment has been the progressive improvement in international law covering the conditions of captivity. From the *Lieber Code* to the *Geneva Convention Additional Protocols of 1977*, governments and lawmakers have striven to learn from history and address the changing nature of warfare, all in an effort to ensure that the international conventions safeguarding prisoners worked to the mutual satisfaction of captor and captive alike. These conventions have grown larger to deal with the new realities of conflict; in this section, the reader will find all of the essential international agreements, but only those portions of them that deal specifically with POWs and internees.

Since the terrorist attacks of 11 September 2001, public interest has focused more intensely on the status and treatment of captives than it ever has before. As a consequence, the debate has moved far beyond international lawmakers, and the second group of readings, new to this second edition, reflects that growing interest. In selecting just a few documents from a huge number of newspaper editorials, government statements, press accounts, and nongovernmental organization reports, I have attempted to present as wide a range of opinion as possible, with the greatest possible variety of authorship.

The Lieber Code of 1863 was the first document covering the protection of POWs that was embraced by military authorities, although its impact must be set against the appalling conditions endured by Confederate and Union prisoners during the U.S. Civil War. *The Hague Convention of 1907* built on the foundations of the Lieber Code, but took into account lessons learned from wars that occurred in the interim. Sadly, the inability of the Hague Convention to deal with many controversies surrounding captivity necessitated the creation of the first international agreement directly relating to the treatment of

POWs, the *Geneva Convention of 1929*. But again, the convention's shortcomings were made apparent by the experience of World War II, and motivated international lawmakers to come together again to formulate the *Geneva Convention of 1949*. It remains an important benchmark in international law concerning captivity, although the Geneva Convention Additional Protocols of 1977 revealed that there remained areas of concern for jurists; the protocols indicate that lawmakers continue to attempt to learn from the past, and to address issues that might be crucial in future conflicts.

But the fact that there was considerable debate over how to deal with captives in future conflicts was made clear by *William Safire's 1984 article in the New York Times*, which was deeply critical of the Additional Protocols and argued that they would give the upper hand to suspected terrorists. At the time, this was largely an academic debate, but after the attacks of 11 September 2001, the treatment of terror suspects under international law became an immediate concern of governments, the military, jurists, and the general public. There are a number of elements to this ongoing debate, beginning with the legal status of individuals captured in the War on Terror. The White House made its position clear in a *press release in February 2002*, but that position was almost immediately attacked by jurists; *Judge George Aldrich's essay* on the Taliban, Al Qaeda, and the determination of combatant status and *Erin Chlopak's article* on the detainees at Guantánamo Bay represent two responses. In August 2004, *the International Committee of the Red Cross* offered its own interpretation of the status of prisoners taken in the war against terrorism.

The other significant part of the debate revolves around the use of torture. *The World Medical Association's Declaration of Tokyo* (1975, revised 2005) and *the International Convention Against Torture* (1987) were pledges by the international community that POWs and other detainees would not be subjected to physical or mental abuse while in captivity. However, allegations that terror suspects were routinely tortured has called into question the efficacy of these documents. Arguments for and against the use of torture have addressed both philosophical and practical issues, but perhaps the most eloquent addition to the discussion *is Senator John McCain's essay "Torture's Terrible Toll,"* written by perhaps the only person involved in the debate who had actually experienced torture at the hands of an enemy captor. The lobbying eventually secured the inclusion in the *Defense Appropriations Act*, 2006 of articles prohibiting "cruel, inhuman, or degrading treatment or punishment" of captives, but some observers have since expressed concern that *President George W. Bush's signing statement* that accompanied the passage of the legislation rendered it toothless, by giving the president a considerable degree of freedom in interpreting the act.

The final set of documents endeavors to paint a broader picture. *The International Committee of the Red Cross's paper Deprived of Freedom* sets out the goals and methods that the committee uses in attempting to do as much as possible on behalf of detainees. However, *Alex Perry's account* of the battle inside the prison camp at Qala-i-Jangi demonstrates that some incidents are simply beyond the power of non-governmental organizations to resolve. And finally, it is fitting that the last word should go to a POW, *Sergeant Chris Stone*, who was captured by Serb soldiers while serving with NATO forces in Macedonia. Stone's account affirms that, after centuries of experience with captivity, some things remain entirely unchanged.

There is no indication that public interest in the subject of captivity is waning, and new and important voices join the debate every day. Readers who wish to follow the discussion of the status of prisoners, the use of torture, the rights of internees, the judicial prosecution of suspected terrorists, and any other theme can so do on the internet, through the websites of governments, news agencies, universities, and nongovernmental organizations like Human Rights Watch, Amnesty International, and the International Committee of the Red Cross.

EXTRACTS FROM INSTRUCTIONS FOR THE GOVERNMENT OF THE ARMIES OF THE UNITED STATES IN THE FIELD (THE "LIEBER CODE") (24 APRIL 1863)

48.
Deserters from the American Army, having entered the service of the enemy, suffer death if they fall again into the hands of the United States, whether by capture, or being delivered up to the American Army; and if a deserter from the enemy having taken service in the Army of the United States, is captured by the enemy, and punished by them with death or otherwise, it is not a breach against the law and usages of war, requiring redress or retaliation.

49.
A prisoner of war is a public enemy armed or attached to the hostile army for active aid, who has fallen into the hands of the captor, either fighting or wounded, on the field or in the hospital, by individual surrender or by capitulation.

All soldiers, of whatever species of arms; all men who belong to the rising en masse of the hostile country; all those who are attached to the army for its efficiency and promote directly the object of the war, except such as are hereinafter provided for; all disabled men or officers on the field or elsewhere, if captured; all enemies who have thrown away their arms and ask for quarter, are prisoners of war, and as such exposed to the inconveniences as well as entitled to the privileges of a prisoners of war.

50.
Moreover, citizens who accompany an army for whatever purpose such as sutlers, editors, or reporters of journals, or contractors, if captured, may be made prisoners of war, and be detained as such.
The monarch and members of the hostile reigning family, male or female, the chief, and chief officers of the hostile government, its diplomatic agents, and all persons who are of particular and singular use and benefit to the hostile army or its government, are, if captured on belligerent ground, and if unprovided with a safe conduct granted by the captor's government, prisoners of war.

51.
If the people of that portion of an invaded country which is not yet occupied by the enemy, or of the whole country, at the approach of a hostile army, rise, under a duly authorized levy, en masse to resist the invader, they are now treated as public enemies, and, if captured, are prisoners of war.

52.
No belligerent has the right to declare that he will treat every captured man in arms of a levy en masse as a brigand or bandit. If however, the people of a country, or any portion of the same, already

occupied by an army, rise against it, they are violators of the laws of war, and are not entitled to their protection.

53.
The enemy's chaplains, officers of the medical staff, apothecaries, hospital nurses and servants, if they fall into the hands of the American Army, are not prisoners of war, unless the commander has reasons to retain them. In this latter case, or if, at their own desire, they are allowed to remain with their captured companions, they are treated as prisoners of war, and may be exchanged if the commander sees fit.

54.
A hostage is a person accepted as a pledge for the fulfillment of an agreement concluded between belligerents during the war, or in consequence of a war. Hostages are rare in the present age.

55.
If a hostage is accepted, he is treated like a prisoner of war, according to rank and condition, as circumstances may admit.

56.
A prisoner of war is subject to no punishment for being a public enemy, nor is any revenge wreaked upon him by the intentional infliction of any suffering, or disgrace, by cruel imprisonment, want of food, by mutilation, death, or any other barbarity.

57.
So soon as a man is armed by a sovereign government and takes the soldier's oath of fidelity, he is a belligerent; his killing, wounding, or other warlike acts are not individual crimes or offenses. No belligerent has a right to declare that enemies of a certain class, color, or condition, when properly organized as soldiers, will not be treated by him as public enemies.

58.
The law of nations knows of no distinction of color, and if an enemy of the United States should enslave and sell any captured persons of their army, it would be a case for the severest retaliation, if not redressed upon complaint.
The United States can not retaliate by enslavement; therefore death must be the retaliation for this crime against the law of nations.

59.
A prisoner of war remains answerable for his crimes committed against the captor's army or people, committed before he was captured, and for which he has not been punished by his own authorities.
All prisoners of war are liable to the infliction of retaliatory measures.

60.
It is against the usage of modern war to resolve, in hatred and revenge, to give no quarter. No body of troops has the right to declare that it will not give, and therefore will not expect, quarter; but a commander is permitted to direct his troops to give no quarter, in great straits, when his own salvation makes it impossible to cumber himself with prisoners.

61
Troops that give no quarter have no right to kill enemies already disabled

on the ground, or prisoners captured by other troops.

62.
All troops of the enemy known or discovered to give no quarter in general, or to any portion of the army, receive none.

63.
Troops who fight in the uniform of their enemies, without any plain, striking, and uniform mark of distinction of their own, can expect no quarter.

64.
If American troops capture a train containing uniforms of the enemy, and the commander considers it advisable to distribute them for use among his men, some striking mark or sign must be adopted to distinguish the American soldier from the enemy.

65.
The use of the enemy's national standard, flag, or other emblem of nationality, for the purpose of deceiving the enemy in battle, is an act of perfidy by which they lose all claim to the protection of the laws of war.

66.
Quarter having been given to an enemy by American troops, under a misapprehension of his true character, he may, nevertheless, be ordered to suffer death if, within three days after the battle, it be discovered that he belongs to a corps which gives no quarter.

67.
The law of nations allows every sovereign government to make war upon another sovereign state, and, therefore, admits of no rules or laws different from those of regular warfare, regarding the treatment of prisoners of war, although they may belong to the army of a government which the captor may consider as a wanton and unjust assailant.

71.
Whoever intentionally inflicts additional wounds on an enemy already wholly disabled, or kills such an enemy, or who orders or encourages soldiers to do so, shall suffer death, if duly convicted, whether he belongs to the Army of the United States, or is an enemy captured after having committed his misdeed.

72.
Money and other valuables on the person of a prisoner, such as watches or jewelry, as well as extra clothing, are regarded by the American Army as the private property of the prisoner, and the appropriation of such valuables or money is considered dishonorable, and is prohibited.

Nevertheless, if large sums are found upon the persons of prisoners, or in their possession, they shall be taken from them, and the surplus, after providing for their own support, appropriated for the use of the army, under the direction of the commander, unless otherwise ordered by the government. Nor can prisoners claim, as private property, large sums found and captured in their train, although they have been placed in the private luggage of the prisoners.

73.
All officers, when captured, must surrender their side arms to the captor. They may be restored to the prisoner in marked cases, by the commander, to signalize admiration of his distinguished bravery or approbation of his humane treatment of prisoners before his capture. The captured officer to whom they may be restored can not wear them during captivity.

74.
A prisoner of war, being a public enemy, is the prisoner of the government, and not of the captor. No ransom can be paid by a prisoner of war to his individual captor or to any oficer in command. The government alone releases captives, according to rules prescribed by itself.

75.
Prisoners of war are subject to confinement or imprisonment such as may be deemed necessary on account of safety, but they are to be subjected to no other intentional suffering or indignity. The confinement and mode of treating a prisoner may be varied during his captivity, according to the demands of safety.

76.
Prisoners of war shall be fed upon plain and wholesome food, whenever practicable, and treated with humanity.

They may be required to work for the benefit of the captor's government, according to their rank and condition.

77.
A prisoner of war who escapes may be shot or otherwise killed in his flight but neither death nor any other punishment shall be inflicted upon him simply for his attempt to escape, which the law of war does not consider a crime. Stricter means of security shall be used after an unsuccessful attempt to escape.

If, however, a conspiracy is discovered, the purpose of which is a united or general escape, the conspirators may be rigorously punished, even with death; and capital punishment may also be inflicted upon prisoners of war discovered to have plotted rebellion against the authorities of the captors, whether in union with fellow prisoners or other persons.

78.
If prisoners of war, having given no pledge nor made any promise on their honor, forcibly or otherwise escape, and are captured again in battle after having rejoined their own army, they shall not be punished for their escape, but shall be treated as simple prisoners of war, although they will be subjected to stricter confinement.

79.
Every captured wounded enemy shall be medically treated, according to the ability of the medical staff.

80.
Honorable men, when captured, will abstain from giving to the enemy information concerning their own army, and the modern law of war permits no longer the use of any violence against prisoners in order to

extort the desired information or to punish them for having given false information.

81.
Partisans are soldiers armed and wearing the uniform of their army, but belonging to a corps which acts detached from the main body for the purpose of making inroads into the territory occupied by the enemy. If captured, they are entitled to all the privileges of the prisoner of war.

82.
Men, or squads of men, who commit hostilities, whether by fighting, or inroads for destruction or plunder, or by raids of any kind, without commission, without being part and portion of the organized hostile army, and without sharing continuously in the war, but who do so with intermitting returns to their homes and avocations, or with the occasional assumption of the semblance of peaceful pursuits, divesting themselves of the character or appearance of soldiers—such men, or squads of men, are not public enemies, and, therefore, if captured, are not entitled to the privileges of prisoners of war, but shall be treated summarily as highway robbers or pirates.

83.
Scouts, or single soldiers, if disguised in the dress of the country or in the uniform of the army hostile to their own, employed in obtaining information, if found within or lurking about the lines of the captor, are treated as spies, and suffer death.

84.
Armed prowlers, by whatever names they may be called, or persons of the enemy's territory, who steal within the lines of the hostile army for the purpose of robbing, killing, or of destroying bridges, roads, or canals, or of robbing or destroying mail, or of cutting the telegraph wires, are not entitled to the privileges of the prisoner of war.

85.
War-rebels are persons within an occupied territory who rise in arms against the occupying or conquering army, or against the authorities established by the same. If captured, they may suffer death, whether they rise singly, in small or large bands, and whether called upon to do so by their own, but expelled, government or not. They are not prisoners of war; nor are they if discovered and secured before their conspiracy has matured to an actual rising or armed violence.

105.
Exchanges of prisoners take place—number for number—rank for rank—wounded for wounded—with added condition for added condition—such, for instance, as not to serve for a certain period.

106.
In exchanging prisoners of war, such numbers of persons of inferior rank may be substituted as an equivalent for one of superior rank as may be agreed upon by cartel, which requires the sanction of the government, or of the commander of the army in the field.

107.
A prisoner of war is in honor bound truly to state to the captor his rank;

and he is not to assume a lower rank than belongs to him, in order to cause a more advantageous exchange, nor a higher rank, for the purpose of obtaining better treatment.
Offenses to the contrary have been justly punished by the commanders of released prisoners, and may be good cause for refusing to release such prisoners.

108.
The surplus number of prisoners of war remaining after an exchange has taken place is sometimes released either for the payment of a stipulated sum of money, or, in urgent cases, of provision, clothing, or other necessities.
Such arrangement, however, requires the sanction of the highest authority.

109.
The exchange of prisoners of war is an act of convenience to both belligerents. If no general cartel has been concluded, it can not be demanded by either of them. No belligerent is obliged to exchange prisoners of war.
A cartel is voidable as soon as either party has violated it.

110.
No exchange of prisoners shall be made except after complete capture, and after an accurate account of them, and a list of the captured officers, has been taken.

119.
Prisoners of war may be released from captivity by exchange, and, under certain circumstances, also by parole.

120.
The term 'parole' designates the pledge of individual good faith and honor to do, or to omit doing, certain acts after he who gives his parole shall have been dismissed, wholly or partially, from the power of the captor.

121.
The pledge of the parole is always an individual, but not a private act.

122.
The parole applies chiefly to prisoners of war whom the captor allows to return to their country, or to live in greater freedom within the captor's country or territory, on conditions stated in the parole.

123.
Release of prisoners of war by exchange is the general rule; release by parole is the exception.

124.
Breaking the parole is punished with death when the person breaking the parole is captured again.
Accurate lists, therefore, of the paroled person must be kept by the belligerents.

125.
When paroles are given and received there must be an exchange of two written documents, in which the name and rank of the paroled individuals are accurately and truthfully stated.
126.
Commissioned officers only are allowed to give theft parole, and they can give it only with the permission of their superior, as long

as a superior in rank is within reach.

127.
No non-commissioned officer or private can give his parole except through an officer. Individual paroles not given through an officer are not only void, but subject the individuals giving them to the punishment of death as deserters. The only admissible exception is where individuals, properly separated from their commands, have suffered long confinement without the possibility of being paroled through an officer.

128.
No paroling on the battlefield; no paroling of entire bodies of troops after a battle; and no dismissal of large numbers of prisoners, with a general declaration that they are paroled, is permitted or of any value.

129.
In capitulations for the surrender of strong places or fortified camps the commanding officer, in cases of urgent necessity, may agree that the troops under his command shall not fight again during the war, unless exchanged.

130.
The usual pledge given in the parole is not to serve during the existing war, unless exchanged.
This pledge refers only to the active service in the field, against the paroling belligerent or his allies actively engaged in the same war. These cases of breaking the parole are patent acts, and can be visited with the punishment of death; but the pledge does not refer to internal service, such as recruiting or drilling the recruits, fortifying places not besieged, quelling civil commotions, fighting against belligerents unconnected with the paroling belligerents, or to civil or diplomatic service for which the paroled officer may be employed.

131.
If the government does not approve of the parole, the paroled officer must return into captivity, and should the enemy refuse to receive him, he is free of his parole.

132.
A belligerent government may declare, by a general order, whether it will allow paroling, and on what conditions it will allow it. Such order is communicated to the enemy.

133.
No prisoner of war can be forced by the hostile government to parole himself, and no government is obliged to parole prisoners of war, or to parole all captured officers, if it paroles any. As the pledging of the parole is an individual act, so is paroling, on the other hand, an act of choice on the part of the belligerent.

146.
Prisoners taken in the act of breaking an armistice must be treated as prisoners of war, the officer alone being responsible who gives the order for such a violation of an armistice. The highest authority of the belligerent aggrieved may demand redress for the infraction of an armistice.

Extracts from the 1907 Hague Convention IV with Respect to the Laws and Customs of War on Land (18 October 1907)

Preamble:

Until a more complete code of the laws of war has been issued, the High Contracting Parties deem it expedient to declare that, in cases not included in the Regulations adopted by them, the inhabitants and the belligerents remain under the protection and the rule of the principles of the law of nations, as they result from the usages established among civilized peoples, from the laws of humanity, and the dictates of the public conscience.

Convention:
Article 1.
The Contracting Powers shall issue instructions to their armed land forces which shall be in conformity with the Regulations respecting the Laws and Customs of War on Land, annexed to the present Convention.

Article 3.
A belligerent party which violates the provisions of the said Regulations shall, if the case demands, be liable to pay compensation. It shall be responsible for all acts committed by persons forming part of its armed forces.

Regulations:

Regulations respecting the laws and customs of war on land.

Section I.—On Belligerents.
Chapter I.—The Qualifications of Belligerents.

Article 1.
The laws, rights, and duties of war apply not only to armies, but also to militia and volunteer corps fulfilling the following conditions:—
1. To be commanded by a person responsible for his subordinates;
2. To have a fixed distinctive emblem recognizable at a distance;
3. To carry arms openly; and
4. To conduct their operations in accordance with the laws and customs of war.
In countries where militia or volunteer corps constitute the army, or form part of it, they are included under the denomination "army."

Article 2.
The inhabitants of a territory which has not been occupied, who, on the approach of the enemy, spontaneously take up arms to resist the invading troops without having had the time to organize themselves in accordance with Article 1, shall be regarded as belligerents if they carry arms openly and if they respect the laws and customs of war.

Article 3.
The armed forces of the belligerent parties may consist of combatants and noncombatants. In the case of capture by the enemy, both have a right to be treated as prisoners of war.

Chapter II.—Prisoners of War.

Article 4.
Prisoners of war are in the power of the hostile Government, but not of

the individuals or corps who capture them.

They must be humanely treated.

All their personal belongings, except arms, horses, and military papers, remain their property.

Article 5.
Prisoners of war may be interned in a town, fortress, camp, or other place, and bound not to go beyond certain fixed limits; but they cannot be confined except as an indispensable measure of safety and only while the circumstances which necessitate the measure continue to exist.

Article. 6.
The State may utilize the labour of prisoners of war according to their rank and aptitude, officers excepted. The tasks shall not be excessive and shall have no connection with the operations of the war.

Prisoners may be authorized to work for the public service, for private persons, or on their own account.

Work done for the State is paid at the rates in force for work of a similar kind done by soldiers of the national army, or, if there are none in force, at a rate according to the work executed.

When the work is for other branches of the public service or for private persons the conditions are settled in agreement with the military authorities.
The wages of the prisoners shall go towards improving their position, and the balance shall be paid them on their release, after deducting the cost of their maintenance.

Article 7.
The Government into whose hands prisoners of war have fallen is charged with their maintenance.

In the absence of a special agreement between the belligerents, prisoners of war shall be treated as regards board, lodging, and clothing on the same footing as the troops of the Government who captured them.

Article 8.
Prisoners of war shall be subject to the laws, regulations, and orders in force in the army of the State in whose power they are. Any act of insubordination justifies the adoption towards them of such measures of severity as may be considered necessary.

Escaped prisoners who are retaken before being able to rejoin their own army or before leaving the territory occupied by the army which captured them are liable to disciplinary punishment.

Prisoners who, after succeeding in escaping, are again taken prisoners, are not liable to any punishment on account of the previous flight.

Article 9.
Every prisoner of war is bound to give, if he is questioned on the subject, his true name and rank, and if he infringes this rule, he is liable to have the advantages given to prisoners of his class curtailed.

Article 10.
Prisoners of war may be set at liberty on parole if the laws of their country allow, and, in such cases, they are bound, on their personal honour, scrupulously to fulfil, both towards their own Government and the Government by whom they were made prisoners, the engagements they have contracted.

In such cases their own Government is bound neither to require of nor accept from them any service incompatible with the parole given.

Article 11.
A prisoner of war can not be compelled to accept his liberty on parole; similarly the hostile Government is not obliged to accede to the request of the prisoner to be set at liberty on parole.

Article 12.
Prisoners of war liberated on parole and recaptured bearing arms against the Government to whom they had pledged their honour, or against the allies of that Government, forfeit their right to be treated as prisoners of war, and can be brought before the Courts.

Article 13.
Individuals who follow an army without directly belonging to it, such as newspaper correspondents and reporters, sutlers and contractors, who fall into the enemy's hands and whom the latter thinks expedient to detain, are entitled to be treated as prisoners of war, provided they are in possession of a certificate from the military authorities of the army which they were accompanying.

Article 14.
An inquiry office for prisoners of war is instituted on the commencement of hostilities in each of the belligerent States, and, when necessary, in neutral countries which have received belligerents in their territory. It is the function of this office to reply to all inquiries about the prisoners. It receives from the various services concerned full information respecting internments and transfers, releases on parole, exchanges, escapes, admissions into hospital, deaths, as well as other information necessary to enable it to make out and keep up to date an individual return for each prisoner of war. The office must state in this return the regimental number, name and surname, age, place of origin, rank, unit, wounds, date and place of capture, internment, wounding, and death, as well as any observations of a special character. The individual return shall be sent to the Government of the other belligerent after the conclusion of peace.

It is likewise the function of the inquiry office to receive and collect all objects of personal use, valuables, letters, &c., found on the field of battle or left by prisoners who have been released on parole, or exchanged, or who have escaped, or died in hospitals or ambulances, and to forward them to those concerned.

Article 15.
Relief societies for prisoners of war, which are properly constituted in accordance with the laws of their country and with the object of serving as the channel for charitable effort shall receive from the belligerents, for themselves and their

duly accredited agents every facility for the efficient performance of their humane task within the bounds imposed by military necessities and administrative regulations. Agents of these societies may be admitted to the places of internment for the purpose of distributing relief, as also to the halting places of repatriated prisoners, if furnished with a personal permit by the military authorities, and on giving an undertaking in writing to comply with all measures of order and police which the latter may issue.

Article 16.
Inquiry offices enjoy the privilege of free postage. Letters, money orders, and valuables, as well as parcels by post, intended for prisoners of war, or dispatched by them, shall be exempt from all postal duties in the countries of origin and destination, as well as in the countries they pass through.

Presents and relief in kind for prisoners of war shall be admitted free of all import or other duties, as well as of payments for carriage by the State railways.

Article 17.
Officers taken prisoners shall receive the same rate of pay as officers of corresponding rank in the country where they are detained, the amount to be ultimately refunded by their own Government.

Article 18.
Prisoners of war shall enjoy complete liberty in the exercise of their religion, including attendance at the services of whatever Church they may belong to, on the sole condition that they comply with the measures of order and police issued by the military authorities.

Article 19.
The wills of prisoners of war are received or drawn up in the same way as for soldiers of the national army.

The same rules shall be observed regarding death certificates as well as for the burial of prisoners of war, due regard being paid to their grade and rank.

Article 20.
After the conclusion of peace, the repatriation of prisoners of war shall be carried out as quickly as possible.

Chapter III.—The Sick and Wounded.

Article 21.
The obligations of belligerents with regard to the sick and wounded are governed by the Geneva Convention.

GENEVA CONVENTION RELATIVE TO THE TREATMENT OF PRISONERS OF WAR (27 JULY 1929)

Part I
General Provisions
Article 1. The present Convention shall apply without prejudice to the stipulations of Part VII:
(1) To all persons referred to in Articles 1, 2 and 3 of the Regulations annexed to the Hague Convention (IV) of 18 October 1907, concerning the Laws and Customs of War on Land, who are captured by the enemy.
(2) To all persons belonging to the armed forces of belligerents who are captured by the enemy in the course of operations of maritime or aerial war, subject to such exceptions (derogations) as the conditions of such capture render inevitable. Nevertheless these exceptions shall not infringe the fundamental principles of the present Convention; they shall cease from the moment when the captured persons shall have reached a prisoners of war camp.

Art. 2. Prisoners of war are in the power of the hostile Government, but not of the individuals or formation which captured them. They shall at all times be humanely treated and protected, particularly against acts of violence, from insults and from public curiosity. Measures of reprisal against them are forbidden.

Art. 3. Prisoners of war are entitled to respect for their persons and honour. Women shall be treated with all consideration due to their sex.

Prisoners retain their full civil capacity.

Art. 4. The detaining Power is required to provide for the maintenance of prisoners of war in its charge.

Differences of treatment between prisoners are permissible only if such differences are based on the military rank, the state of physical or mental health, the professional abilities, or the sex of those who benefit from them.

Part II

Capture
Art. 5. Every prisoner of war is required to declare, if he is interrogated on the subject, his true names and rank, or his regimental number.

If he infringes this rule, he exposes himself to a restriction of the privileges accorded to prisoners of his category.

No pressure shall be exercised on prisoners to obtain information regarding the situation in their armed forces or their country. Prisoners who refuse to reply may not be threatened, insulted, or exposed to unpleasantness or disadvantages of any kind whatsoever.

If, by reason of his physical or mental condition, a prisoner is incapable of stating his identity, he shall be handed over to the Medical

Service.

Art. 6. All personal effects and articles in personal use—except arms, horses, military equipment and military papers—shall remain in the possession of prisoners of war, as well as their metal helmets and gas-masks.

Sums of money carried by prisoners may only be taken from them on the order of an officer and after the amount has been recorded. A receipt shall be given for them. Sums thus impounded shall be placed to the account of each prisoner.

Their identity tokens, badges of rank, decorations and articles of value may not be taken from prisoners.

Part III
Captivity
Section I
Evacuation of Prisoners of War
Art. 7. As soon as possible after their capture, prisoners of war shall be evacuated to depots sufficiently removed from the fighting zone for them to be out of danger.

Only prisoners who, by reason of their wounds or maladies, would run greater risks by being evacuated than by remaining may be kept temporarily in a dangerous zone.

Prisoners shall not be unnecessarily exposed to danger while awaiting evacuation from a fighting zone.

The evacuation of prisoners on foot shall in normal circumstances be effected by stages of not more than 20 kilometres per day, unless the necessity for reaching water and food depôts requires longer stages.

Art. 8. Belligerents are required to notify each other of all captures of prisoners as soon as possible, through the intermediary of the Information Bureaux organised in accordance with Article 77. They are likewise required to inform each other of the official addresses to which letters from the prisoners' families may be addressed to the prisoners of war.

As soon as possible, every prisoner shall be enabled to correspond personally with his family, in accordance with the conditions prescribed in Article 36 and the following Articles.

As regards prisoners captured at sea, the provisions of the present article shall be observed as soon as possible after arrival in port.

Section II
Prisoners of War Camps
Art. 9. Prisoners of war may be interned in a town, fortress or other place, and may be required not to go beyond certain fixed limits. They may also be interned in fenced camps; they shall not be confined or imprisoned except as a measure indispensable for safety or health, and only so long as circumstances exist which necessitate such a measure.

Prisoners captured in districts which are unhealthy or whose climate is deleterious to persons coming from temperate climates shall be removed as soon as possible to a more favourable climate.

Belligerents shall as far as possible avoid bringing together in the same camp prisoners of different races or nationalities.

No prisoner may at any time be sent to an area where he would be exposed to the fire of the fighting zone, or be employed to render by his presence certain points or areas immune from bombardment.

Chapter 1
Installation of Camps

Art. 10. Prisoners of war shall be lodged in buildings or huts which afford all possible safeguards as regards hygiene and salubrity.

The premises must be entirely free from damp, and adequately heated and lighted. All precautions shall be taken against the danger of fire.

As regards dormitories, their total area, minimum cubic air space, fittings and bedding material, the conditions shall be the same as for the depot troops of the detaining Power.

Chapter 2
Food and Clothing of Prisoners of War

Art. 11. The food ration of prisoners of war shall be equivalent in quantity and quality to that of the depot troops.

Prisoners shall also be afforded the means of preparing for themselves such additional articles of food as they may possess.

Sufficient drinking water shall be supplied to them. The use of tobacco shall be authorized. Prisoners may be employed in the kitchens.

All collective disciplinary measures affecting food are prohibited.

Art. 12. Clothing, underwear and footwear shall be supplied to prisoners of war by the detaining Power. The regular replacement and repair of such articles shall be assured. Workers shall also receive working kit wherever the nature of the work requires it.

In all camps, canteens shall be installed at which prisoners shall be able to procure, at the local market price, food commodities and ordinary articles.

The profits accruing to the administrations of the camps from the canteens shall be utilised for the benefit of the prisoners.

Chapter 3
Hygiene in Camps

Art. 13. Belligerents shall be required to take all necessary hygienic measures to ensure the cleanliness and salubrity of camps and to prevent epidemics.

Prisoners of war shall have for their use, day and night, conveniences which conform to the rules of hygiene and are maintained in a constant state of cleanliness.

In addition and without prejudice to the provision as far as possible of baths and shower-baths in the camps, the prisoners shall be provided with a sufficient quantity of water for their bodily cleanliness.

They shall have facilities for

engaging in physical exercises and obtaining the benefit of being out of doors.

Art. 14. Each camp shall possess an infirmary, where prisoners of war shall receive attention of any kind of which they may be in need. If necessary, isolation establishments shall be reserved for patients suffering from infectious and contagious diseases.

The expenses of treatment, including those of temporary remedial apparatus, shall be borne by the detaining Power.

Belligerents shall be required to issue, on demand, to any prisoner treated, and official statement indicating the nature and duration of his illness and of the treatment received.

It shall be permissible for belligerents mutually to authorize each other, by means of special agreements, to retain in the camps doctors and medical orderlies for the purpose of caring for their prisoner compatriots

Prisoners who have contracted a serious malady, or whose condition necessitates important surgical treatment, shall be admitted, at the expense of the detaining Power, to any military or civil institution qualified to treat them.

Art. 15. Medical inspections of prisoners of war shall be arranged at least once a month. Their object shall be the supervision of the general state of health and cleanliness, and the detection of infectious and contagious diseases, particularly tuberculosis and venereal complaints.

Chapter 4
Intellectual and Moral Needs of Prisoners of War
Art. 16. Prisoners of war shall be permitted complete freedom in the performance of their religious duties, including attendance at the services of their faith, on the sole condition that they comply with the routine and police regulations prescribed by the military authorities.

Ministers of religion, who are prisoners of war, whatever may be their denomination, shall be allowed freely to minister to their co-religionists.

Art. 17. Belligerents shall encourage as much as possible the organization of intellectual and sporting pursuits by the prisoners of war.

Chapter 5
Internal Discipline of Camps
Art. 18. Each prisoners of war camp shall be placed under the authority of a responsible officer.

In addition to external marks of respect required by the regulations in force in their own armed forces with regard to their nationals, prisoners of war shall be required to salute all officers of the detaining Power.

Officer prisoners of war shall be required to salute only officers of that Power who are their superiors or equals in rank.

Art. 19. The wearing of badges of

rank and decorations shall be permitted.

Art. 20. Regulations, orders, announcements and publications of any kind shall be communicated to prisoners of war in a language which they understand. The same principle shall be applied to questions.

Chapter 6
Special Provisions Concerning Officers and Persons of Equivalent Status

Art. 21. At the commencement of hostilities, belligerents shall be required reciprocally to inform each other of the titles and ranks in use in their respective armed forces, with the view of ensuring equality of treatment between the corresponding ranks of officers and persons of equivalent status.

Officers and persons of equivalent status who are prisoners of war shall be treated with due regard to their rank and age.

Art. 22. In order to ensure the service of officers' camps, soldier prisoners of war of the same armed forces, and as far as possible speaking the same language, shall be detached for service therein in sufficient number, having regard to the rank of the officers and persons of equivalent status.

Officers and persons of equivalent status shall procure their food and clothing from the pay to be paid to them by the detaining Power. The management of a mess by officers themselves shall be facilitated in every way.

Chapter 7
Pecuniary Resources of Prisoners of War

Art. 23. Subject to any special arrangements made between the belligerent Powers, and particularly those contemplated in Article 24, officers and persons of equivalent status who are prisoners of war shall receive from the detaining Power the same pay as officers of corresponding rank in the armed forces of that Power, provided, however, that such pay does not exceed that to which they are entitled in the armed forces of the country in whose service they have been. This pay shall be paid to them in full, once a month if possible, and no deduction therefrom shall be made for expenditure devolving upon the detaining Power, even if such expenditure is incurred on their behalf.

An agreement between the belligerents shall prescribe the rate of exchange applicable to this payment; in default of such agreement, the rate of exchange adopted shall be that in force at the moment of the commencement of hostilities.

All advances made to prisoners of war by way of pay shall be reimbursed, at the end of hostilities, by the Power in whose service they were.

Art. 24. At the commencement of hostilities, belligerents shall determine by common accord the maximum amount of cash which prisoners of war of various ranks and categories shall be permitted to retain in their possession. Any excess

withdrawn or withheld from a prisoner, and any deposit of money effected by him, shall be carried to his account, and may not be converted into another currency without his consent.
The credit balances of their accounts shall be paid to the prisoners of war at the end of their captivity.

During the continuance of the latter, facilities shall be accorded to them for the transfer of these amounts, wholly or in part, to banks or private individuals in their country of origin.

Chapter 8
Transfer of Prisoners of War
Art. 25. Unless the course of military operations demands it, sick and wounded prisoners of war shall not be transferred if their recovery might be prejudiced by the journey.

Art. 26. In the event of transfer, prisoners of war shall be officially informed in advance of their new destination; they shall be authorized to take with them their personal effects, their correspondence and parcels which have arrived for them.

All necessary arrangements shall be made so that correspondence and parcels addressed to their former camp shall be sent on to them without delay.

The sums credited to the account of transferred prisoners shall be transmitted to the competent authority of their new place of residence.
Expenses incurred by the transfers shall be borne by the detaining Power.

Section III
Work of Prisoners of War
Chapter I
General
Art. 27. Belligerents may employ as workmen prisoners of war who are physically fit, other than officers and persons of equivalent status, according to their rank and their ability.
Nevertheless, if officers or persons of equivalent status ask for suitable work, this shall be found for them as far as possible.

Non-commissioned officers who are prisoners of war may be compelled to undertake only supervisory work, unless they expressly request remunerative occupation.

During the whole period of captivity, belligerents are required to admit prisoners of war who are victims of accidents at work to the benefit of provisions applicable to workmen of the same category under the legislation of the detaining Power. As regards prisoners of war to whom these legal provisions could not be applied by reason of the legislation of that Power, the latter undertakes to recommend to its legislative body all proper measures for the equitable compensation of the victims.

Chapter 2
Organization of Work
Art. 28. The detaining Power shall assume entire responsibility for the maintenance, care, treatment and the payment of the wages of prisoners of war working for private individuals.

Art. 29. No prisoner of war may be employed on work for which he is physically unsuited.

Art. 30. The duration of the daily work of prisoners of war, including the time of the journey to and from work, shall not be excessive and shall in no case exceed that permitted for civil workers of the locality employed on the same work. Each prisoner shall be allowed a rest of twenty-four consecutive hours each week, preferably on Sunday.

Chapter 3
Prohibited Work
Art. 31. Work done by prisoners of war shall have no direct connection with the operations of the war. In particular, it is forbidden to employ prisoners in the manufacture or transport of arms or munitions of any kind, or on the transport of material destined for combatant units.

In the event of violation of the provisions of the preceding paragraph, prisoners are at liberty, after performing or commencing to perform the order, to have their complaints presented through the intermediary of the prisoners' representatives whose functions are described in Articles 43 and 44, or, in the absence of a prisoners' representative, through the intermediary of the representatives of the protecting Power.

Art. 32. It is forbidden to employ prisoners of war on unhealthy or dangerous work. Conditions of work shall not be rendered more arduous by disciplinary measures.

Chapter 4
Labour Detachments
Art. 33. Conditions governing labour detachments shall be similar to those of prisoners-of-war camps, particularly as concerns hygienic conditions, food, care in case of accidents or sickness, correspondence, and the reception of parcels.

Every labour detachment shall be attached to a prisoners' camp. The commander of this camp shall be responsible for the observance in the labour detachment of the provisions of the present Convention.

Chapter 5
Pay
Art. 34. Prisoners of war shall not receive pay for work in connection with the administration, internal arrangement and maintenance of camps.

Prisoners employed on other work shall be entitled to a rate of pay, to be fixed by agreements between the belligerents.

These agreements shall also specify the portion which may be retained by the camp administration, the amount which shall belong to the prisoner of war and the manner in which this amount shall be placed at his disposal during the period of his captivity.
Pending the conclusion of the said agreements, remuneration of the work of prisoners shall be fixed according to the following standards:
(a) Work done for the State shall be paid for according to the rates in force for soldiers of the national forces doing the same work, or, if no such rates exist, according to a tariff

corresponding to the work executed.
(b) When the work is done for other public administrations or for private individuals, the conditions shall be settled in agreement with the military authorities.
The pay which remains to the credit of a prisoner shall be remitted to him on the termination of his captivity. In case of death, it shall be remitted through the diplomatic channel to the heirs of the deceased.

Section IV
Relations of Prisoners of War with the Exterior
Art. 35. On the commencement of hostilities, belligerents shall publish the measures prescribed for the execution of the provisions of the present section.

Art. 36. Each of the belligerents shall fix periodically the number of letters and postcards which prisoners of war of different categories shall be permitted to send per month, and shall notify that number to the other belligerent. These letters and cards shall be sent by post by the shortest route. They may not be delayed or withheld for disciplinary motives.

Not later than one week after his arrival in camp, and similarly in case of sickness, each prisoner shall be enabled to send a postcard to his family informing them of his capture and the state of his health. The said postcards shall be forwarded as quickly as possible and shall not be delayed in any manner.
As a general rule, the correspondence of prisoners shall be written in their native language. Belligerents may authorize correspondence in other languages.

Art. 37. Prisoners of war shall be authorized to receive individually postal parcels containing foodstuffs and other articles intended for consumption or clothing. The parcels shall be delivered to the addressees and a receipt given.

Art. 38. Letters and remittances of money or valuables, as well as postal parcels addressed to prisoners of war, or despatched by them, either directly or through the intermediary of the information bureaux mentioned in Article 77, shall be exempt from all postal charges in the countries of origin and destination and in the countries through which they pass.

Presents and relief in kind intended for prisoners of war shall also be exempt from all import or other duties, as well as any charges for carriage on railways operated by the State.

Prisoners may, in cases of recognized urgency, be authorized to send telegrams on payment of the usual charges.

Art. 39. Prisoners of war shall be permitted to receive individually consignments of books which may be subject to censorship.

Representatives of the protecting Powers and of duly recognized and authorized relief societies may send works and collections of books to the libraries of prisoners' camps. The transmission of such consignments to libraries may not be delayed under pretext of difficulties of censorship.

Art. 40. The censoring of correspondence shall be accomplished as quickly as possible. The examination of postal parcels shall, moreover, be effected under such conditions as will ensure the preservation of any foodstuffs which they may contain, and, if possible, be done in the presence of the addressee or of a representative duly recognized by him.
Any prohibition of correspondence ordered by the belligerents, for military or political reasons, shall only be of a temporary character and shall also be for as brief a time as possible.

Art. 41. Belligerents shall accord all facilities for the transmission of documents destined for prisoners of war or signed by them, in particular powers of attorney and wills.

They shall take the necessary measures to secure, in case of need, the legalisation of signatures of prisoners.

Section V
Relations between Prisoners of War and the Authorities

Chapter I
Complaints of Prisoners of War Respecting the Conditions of Captivity
Art. 42. Prisoners of war shall have the right to bring to the notice of the military authorities, in whose hands they are, their petitions concerning the conditions of captivity to which they are subjected.

They shall also have the right to communicate with the representatives of the protecting Powers in order to draw their attention to the points on which they have complaints to make with regard to the conditions of captivity.

Such petitions and complaints shall be transmitted immediately.

Even though they are found to be groundless, they shall not give rise to any punishment.

Chapter 2
Representatives of Prisoners of War
Art. 43. In any locality where there may be prisoners of war, they shall be authorized to appoint representatives to represent them before the military authorities and the protecting Powers.

Such appointments shall be subject to the approval of the military authorities.

The prisoners' representatives shall be charged with the reception and distribution of collective consignments. Similarly, in the event of the prisoners deciding to organize amongst themselves a system of mutual aid, such organization shall be one of the functions of the prisoners' representatives. On the other hand, the latter may offer their services to prisoners to facilitate their relations with the relief societies mentioned in Article 78.

In camps of officers and persons of equivalent status the senior officer prisoner of the highest rank shall be recognized as intermediary between the camp authorities and the officers and similar persons who are prisoners. For this purpose he shall have the power to appoint an officer prisoner to assist him as interpreter in the course of conferences with the authorities of the camp.

Art. 44. When the prisoners' representatives are employed as workmen, their work as representatives of the prisoners of war shall be reckoned in the compulsory period of labour.

All facilities shall be accorded to the prisoners' representatives for their correspondence with the military authorities and the protecting Power. Such correspondence shall not be subject to any limitation.

No prisoners' representative may be transferred without his having been allowed the time necessary to acquaint his successors with the current business.

Chapter 3
Penal Sanctions with Regard to Prisoners of War
I. General Provisions
Art. 45. Prisoners of war shall be subject to the laws, regulations and orders in force in the armed forces of the detaining Power.

Any act of insubordination shall render them liable to the measures prescribed by such laws, regulations, and orders, except as otherwise provided in this Chapter.

Art. 46. Prisoners of war shall not be subjected by the military authorities or the tribunals of the detaining Power to penalties other than those which are prescribed for similar acts by members of the national forces.

Officers, non-commissioned officers or private soldiers, prisoners of war, undergoing disciplinary punishment shall not be subjected to treatment less favourable than that prescribed, as regards the same punishment, for similar ranks in the armed forces of the detaining Power.

All forms of corporal punishment, confinement in premises not lighted by daylight and, in general, all forms of cruelty whatsoever are prohibited. Collective penalties for individual acts are also prohibited.

Art. 47. A statement of the facts in cases of acts constituting a breach of discipline, and particularly an attempt to escape, shall be drawn up in writing without delay. The period during which prisoners of war of whatever rank are detained in custody (pending the investigation of such offences) shall be reduced to a strict minimum.

The judicial proceedings against a prisoner of war shall be conducted as quickly as circumstances will allow. The period during which prisoners shall be detained in custody shall be as short as possible.

In all cases the period during which a prisoner is under arrest (awaiting punishment or trial) shall be deducted from the sentence, whether disciplinary or judicial, provided such deduction is permitted in the case of members of the national forces.
Art. 48. After undergoing the judicial or disciplinary punishment which has been inflicted on them, prisoners of war shall not be treated differently from other prisoners.

Nevertheless, prisoners who have been punished as the result of an attempt to escape may be subjected to a special regime of surveillance, but this shall not involve the suppression of any of the safeguards accorded to prisoners by the present Convention.

Art. 49. No prisoner of war may be deprived of his rank by the detaining Power.

Prisoners on whom disciplinary punishment is inflicted shall not be deprived of the privileges attaching to their rank. In particular, officers and persons of equivalent status who suffer penalties entailing deprivation of liberty shall not be placed in the same premises as non-commissioned officers or private soldiers undergoing punishment.

Art. 50. Escaped prisoners of war who are re-captured before they have been able to rejoin their own armed forces or to leave the territory occupied by the armed forces which captured them shall be liable only to disciplinary punishment.

Prisoners who, after succeeding in rejoining their armed forces or in leaving the territory occupied by the armed forces which captured them, are again taken prisoner shall not be liable to any punishment for their previous escape.

Art. 51. Attempted escape, even if it is not a first offence, shall not be considered as an aggravation of the offence in the event of the prisoner of war being brought before the courts for crimes or offences against persons or property committed in the course of such attempt.

After an attempted or successful escape, the comrades of the escaped person who aided the escape shall incur only disciplinary punishment therefor.

Art. 52. Belligerents shall ensure that the competent authorities exercize the greatest leniency in considering the question whether an offence committed by a prisoner of war should be punished by disciplinary or by judicial measures.

This provision shall be observed in particular in appraising facts in connexion with escape or attempted escape.

A prisoner shall not be punished more than once for the same act or on the same charge.

Art. 53. No prisoner who has been awarded any disciplinary punishment for an offence and who fulfils the conditions laid down for repatriation shall be retained on the ground that he has not undergone his punishment.

Prisoners qualified for repatriation against whom any prosecution for a criminal offence has been brought may be excluded from repatriation until the termination of the proceedings and until fulfilment of their sentence, if any; prisoners already serving a sentence of imprisonment may be retained until the expiry of the sentence.

Belligerents shall communicate to each other lists of those who cannot be repatriated for the reasons indicated in the preceding paragraph.

II. Disciplinary Punishments
Art. 54. Imprisonment is the most severe disciplinary punishment which may be inflicted on a prisoner of war.
The duration of any single punishment shall not exceed thirty days.

This maximum of thirty days shall, moreover, not be exceeded in the event of there being several acts for which the prisoner is answerable to discipline at the time when his case is disposed of, whether such acts are connected or not.

Where, during the course or after the termination of a period of imprisonment, a prisoner is sentenced to a fresh disciplinary penalty, a period of at least three days shall intervene between each of the periods of imprisonment, if one of such periods is of ten days or over.

Art. 55. Subject to the provisions of the last paragraph of Article 11, the restrictions in regard to food permitted in the armed forces of the detaining Power may be applied, as an additional penalty, to prisoners of war undergoing disciplinary punishment.

Such restrictions shall, however, only be ordered if the state of the prisoner's health permits.

Art. 56. In no case shall prisoners of war be transferred to penitentiary establishments (prisons, penitentiaries, convict establishments, etc.) in order to undergo disciplinary sentence there.

Establishments in which disciplinary sentences are undergone shall conform to the requirements of hygiene.

Facilities shall be afforded to prisoners undergoing sentence to keep themselves in a state of cleanliness.

Every day, such prisoners shall have facilities for taking exercise or for remaining out of doors for at least two hours.

Art. 57. Prisoners of war undergoing disciplinary punishment shall be permitted to read and write and to send and receive letters.

On the other hand, it shall be permissible not to deliver parcels and remittances of money to the addressees until the expiration of the sentence. If the undelivered parcels contain perishable foodstuffs, these shall be handed over to the infirmary or to the camp kitchen.

Art. 58. Prisoners of war undergoing disciplinary punishment shall be permitted, on their request, to present themselves for daily medical inspection. They shall receive such attention as the medical officers may consider necessary, and, if need be, shall be evacuated to the camp infirmary or to hospital.

Art. 59. Without prejudice to the competency of the courts and the superior military authorities, disciplinary sentences may only be awarded by an officer vested with disciplinary powers in his capacity as commander of the camp or detachment, or by the responsible officer acting as his substitute.

III. Judicial Proceedings
Art. 60. At the commencement of a judicial hearing against a prisoner of war, the detaining Power shall notify the representative of the protecting Power as soon as possible, and in any case before the date fixed for the opening of the hearing.

The said notification shall contain the following particulars:
(a) Civil status and rank of the prisoner.
(b) Place of residence or detention.
(c) Statement of the charge or charges, and of the legal provisions applicable.
If it is not possible in this notification to indicate particulars of the court which will try the case, the date of the opening of the hearing and the place where it will take place, these particulars shall be furnished to the representative of the protecting Power at a later date, but as soon as possible and in any case at least three weeks before the opening of the hearing.

Art. 61. No prisoner of war shall be sentenced without being given the opportunity to defend himself.

No prisoner shall be compelled to admit that he is guilty of the offence of which he is accused.

Art. 62. The prisoner of war shall have the right to be assisted by a qualified advocate of his own choice and, if necessary, to have recourse to the offices of a competent interpreter. He shall be informed of his right by the detaining Power in good time before the hearing.

Failing a choice on the part of the prisoner, the protecting Power may procure an advocate for him. The detaining Power shall, on the request of the protecting Power, furnish to the latter a list of persons qualified to conduct the defence.

The representatives of the protecting Power shall have the right to attend the hearing of the case.

The only exception to this rule is where the hearing has to be kept secret in the interests of the safety of the State. The detaining Power would then notify the protecting Power accordingly.

Art. 63. A sentence shall only be pronounced on a prisoner of war by the same tribunals and in accordance with the same procedure as in the case of persons belonging to the armed forces of the detaining Power.

Art. 64. Every prisoner of war shall have the right of appeal against any sentence against him in the same manner as persons belonging to the armed forces of the detaining Power.

Art. 65. Sentences pronounced against prisoners of war shall be communicated immediately to the protecting Power.

Art. 66. If sentence of death is passed on a prisoner of war, a communication setting forth in detail the nature and the circumstances of the offence shall be addressed as soon as possible to the representative of the protecting Power for transmission to the Power in whose armed forces the prisoner served.

The sentence shall not be carried out before the expiration of a period of at least three months from the date of the receipt of this communication by the protecting Power.

Art. 67. No prisoner of war may be deprived of the benefit of the provisions of Article 42 of the present Convention as the result of a judgment or otherwise.

Part IV
End of Captivity
Section I
Direct Repatriation and Accommodation in a Neutral Country

Art. 68. Belligerents shall be required to send back to their own country, without regard to rank or numbers, after rendering them in a fit condition for transport, prisoners of war who are seriously ill or seriously wounded.

Agreements between the belligerents shall therefore determine, as soon as possible, the forms of disablement or sickness requiring direct repatriation and cases which may necessitate accommodation in a neutral country. Pending the conclusion of such agreements, the belligerents may refer to the model draft agreement annexed to the present Convention.

Art. 69. On the opening of hostilities, belligerents shall come to an understanding as to the appointment of mixed medical commissions. These commissions shall consist of three members, two of whom shall belong to a neutral country and one appointed by the detaining Power; one of the medical officers of the neutral country shall preside. These mixed medical commissions shall proceed to the examination of sick or wounded prisoners and shall make all appropriate decisions with regard to them.

The decisions of these commissions shall be decided by majority and shall be carried into effect as soon as possible.

Art. 70. In addition to those prisoners of war selected by the medical officer of the camp, the following shall be inspected by the mixed medical commission mentioned in Article 69, with a view to their direct repatriation or accommodation in a neutral country:
(a) Prisoners who make a direct request to that effect to the medical officer of the camp;
(b) Prisoners presented by the prisoners' representatives mentioned in Article 43, the latter acting on their own initiative or on the request of the prisoners themselves;
(c) Prisoners nominated by the Power in whose armed forces they served or by a relief society duly recognized and authorized by that Power.

Art. 71. Prisoners of war who meet with accidents at work, unless the injury is self-inflicted, shall have the benefit of the same provisions as regards repatriation or accommodation in a neutral country.

Art. 72. During the continuance of hostilities, and for humanitarian reasons, belligerents may conclude agreements with a view to the direct repatriation or accommodation in a neutral country of prisoners of war in good health who have been in captivity for a long time.

Art. 73. The expenses of repatriation or transport to a neutral country of prisoners of war shall be borne, as from the frontier of the detaining Power, by the Power in whose armed forces such prisoners served.

Art. 74. No repatriated person shall be employed on active military service.

Section II
Liberation and Repatriation at the End of Hostilities

Art. 75. When belligerents conclude an armistice convention, they shall normally cause to be included therein provisions concerning the repatriation of prisoners of war. If it has not been possible to insert in that convention such stipulations, the belligerents shall, nevertheless, enter into communication with each other on the question as soon as possible. In any case, the repatriation of prisoners shall be effected as soon as possible after the conclusion of peace.

Prisoners of war who are subject to criminal proceedings for a crime or offence at common law may, however, be detained until the end of the proceedings, and, if need be, until the expiration of the sentence. The same applies to prisoners convicted for a crime or offence at common law.

By agreement between the belligerents, commissions may be instituted for the purpose of searching for scattered prisoners and ensuring their repatriation.

Part V
Deaths of Prisoners of War

Art. 76. The wills of prisoners of war shall be received and drawn up under the same conditions as for soldiers of the national armed forces.

The same rules shall be followed as regards the documents relative to the certification of the death.

The belligerents shall ensure that prisoners of war who have died in captivity are honourably buried, and that the graves bear the necessary indications and are treated with respect and suitably maintained.

Part VI
Bureaux of Relief and Information Concerning Prisoners of War

Art. 77. At the commencement of hostilities, each of the belligerent Powers and the neutral Powers who have belligerents in their care, shall institute an official bureau to give information about the prisoners of war in their territory.

Each of the belligerent Powers shall inform its Information Bureau as soon as possible of all captures of prisoners effected by its armed forces, furnishing them with all particulars of identity at its disposal to enable the families concerned to be quickly notified, and stating the official addresses to which families may write to the prisoners.

The Information Bureau shall transmit all such information immediately to the Powers concerned, on the one hand through the intermediary of the protecting Powers, and on the other through the Central Agency contemplated in Article 79.

The Information Bureau, being charged with replying to all enquiries relative to prisoners of war, shall receive from the various services concerned all particulars respecting internments and transfers, releases on parole, repatriations, escapes, stays in hospitals, and deaths, together with all other particulars necessary for establishing and keeping up to date an individual record for each prisoner of war.

The Bureau shall note in this record, as far as possible, and subject to the provisions of Article 5, the regimental number, names and surnames, date and place of birth, rank and unit of the prisoner, the surname of the father and name of the mother, the address of the person to be notified in case of accident, wounds, dates and places of capture, of internment, of wounds, of death, together with all other important particulars.

Weekly lists containing all additional particulars capable of facilitating the identification of each prisoner shall be transmitted to the interested Powers.

The individual record of a prisoner of war shall be sent after the conclusion of peace to the Power in whose service he was.

The Information Bureau shall also be required to collect all personal effects, valuables, correspondence, pay-books, identity tokens, etc., which have been left by prisoners of war who have been repatriated or released on parole, or who have escaped or died, and to transmit them to the countries concerned.

Art. 78. Societies for the relief of prisoners of war, regularly constituted in accordance with the laws of their country, and having for their object to serve as intermediaries for charitable purposes, shall receive from the belligerents, for themselves and their duly accredited agents, all facilities for the efficacious performance of their humane task within the limits imposed by military exigencies. Representatives of these societies shall be permitted to distribute relief in the camps and at the halting places of repatriated prisoners under a personal permit issued by the military authority, and on giving an undertaking in writing to comply with all routine and police orders which the said authority shall prescribe.

Art. 79. A Central Agency of information regarding prisoners of war shall be established in a neutral country. The International Red Cross Committee shall, if they consider it necessary, propose to the Powers concerned the organization of such an agency.

This agency shall be charged with the duty of collecting all information regarding prisoners which they may be able to obtain through official or private channels, and the agency shall transmit the information as rapidly as possible to the prisoners' own country or the Power in whose service they have been.

These provisions shall not be interpreted as restricting the humanitarian work of the International Red Cross Committee.

Art. 80. Information Bureaux shall enjoy exemption from fees on postal matter as well as all the exemptions prescribed in Article 38.

Part VII
Application of the Convention to Certain Categories of Civilians
Art. 81. Persons who follow the armed forces without directly belonging thereto, such as correspondents, newspaper reporters, sutlers, or contractors, who fall into the hands of the enemy, and whom the latter think fit to detain, shall be entitled to be treated as prisoners of war, provided they are in possession of an authorization from the military authorities of the armed forces which they were following.

Part VIII
Execution of the Convention
Section I
General Provisions
Art. 82. The provisions of the present Convention shall be respected by the High Contracting Parties in all circumstances.

In time of war if one of the belligerents is not a party to the Convention, its provisions shall, nevertheless, remain binding as between the belligerents who are parties thereto.

Art. 83. The High Contracting Parties reserve to themselves the right to conclude special conventions on all questions relating to prisoners of war concerning which they may consider it desirable to make special provisions.

Prisoners of war shall continue to enjoy the benefits of these agreements until their repatriation has been effected, subject to any provisions expressly to the contrary contained in the above-mentioned agreements or in subsequent agreements, and subject to any more favourable measures by one or the other of the belligerent Powers concerning the prisoners detained by that Power.

In order to ensure the application, on both sides, of the provisions of the present Convention, and to facilitate the conclusion of the special conventions mentioned above, the belligerents may, at the commencement of hostilities, authorize meetings of representatives of the respective authorities charged with the administration of prisoners of war.

Art. 84. The text of the present Convention and of the special conventions mentioned in the preceding Article shall be posted, whenever possible, in the native language of the prisoners of war, in places where it may be consulted by all the prisoners.
The text of these conventions shall be communicated, on their request, to prisoners who are unable to inform themselves of the text posted.

Art. 85. The High Contracting Parties shall communicate to each other, through the intermediary of the Swiss Federal Council, the official translations of the present

Convention, together with such laws and regulations as they may adopt to ensure the application of the present Convention.

Section II
Organization of Control
Art. 86. The High Contracting Parties recognize that a guarantee of the regular application of the present Convention will be found in the possibility of collaboration between the protecting Powers charged with the protection of the interests of the belligerents; in this connexion, the protecting Powers may, apart from their diplomatic personnel, appoint delegates from among their own nationals or the nationals of other neutral Powers. The appointment of these delegates shall be subject to the approval of the belligerent with whom they are to carry out their mission.

The representatives of the protecting Power or their recognized delegates shall be authorized to proceed to any place, without exception, where prisoners of war are interned. They shall have access to all premises occupied by prisoners and may hold conversation with prisoners, as a general rule without witnesses, either personally or through the intermediary of interpreters.

Belligerents shall facilitate as much as possible the task of the representatives or recognized delegates of the protecting Power. The military authorities shall be informed of their visits.
Belligerents may mutually agree to allow persons of the prisoners' own nationality to participate in the tours of inspection.

Art. 87. In the event of dispute between the belligerents regarding the application of the provisions of the present Convention, the protecting Powers shall, as far as possible, lend their good offices with the object of settling the dispute.

To this end, each of the protecting Powers may, for instance, propose to the belligerents concerned that a conference of representatives of the latter should be held, on suitably chosen neutral territory. The belligerents shall be required to give effect to proposals made to them with this object. The protecting Power may, if necessary, submit for the approval of the Powers in dispute the name of a person belonging to a neutral Power or nominated by the International Red Cross Committee, who shall be invited to take part in this conference.

Art. 88. The foregoing provisions do not constitute any obstacle to the humanitarian work which the International Red Cross Committee may perform for the protection of prisoners of war with the consent of the belligerents concerned.

Section III
Final Provisions
Art. 89. In the relations between the Powers who are bound either by The Hague Convention concerning the Laws and Customs of War on Land of 29 July 1899, or that of 18 October 1907, and are parties to the present Convention, the latter shall be complementary to Chapter 2 of the Regulations annexed to the above-mentioned Conventions of The

Hague.

Art. 90. The present Convention, which shall bear this day's date, may be signed up to 1 February 1930, on behalf of any of the countries represented at the Conference which opened at Geneva on 1 July 1929.

Art. 91. The present Convention shall be ratified as soon as possible.

The ratifications shall be deposited at Berne.

In respect of the deposit of each instrument of ratification, a procès-verbal shall be drawn up, and copy thereof, certified correct, shall be sent by the Swiss Federal Council to the Governments of all the countries on whose behalf the Convention has been signed or whose accession has been notified.

Art. 92. The present Convention shall enter into force six months after at least two instruments of ratification have been deposited.

Thereafter it shall enter into force for each High Contracting Party six months after the deposit of its instrument of ratification.

Art. 93. As from the date of its entry into force, the present Convention shall be open to accession notified in respect of any country on whose behalf this Convention has not been signed.

Art. 94. Accessions shall be notified in writing to the Swiss Federal Council and shall take effect six months after the date on which they have been received.

The Swiss Federal Council shall notify the accessions to the Governments of all the countries on whose behalf the Convention has been signed or whose accession has been notified.

Art. 95. A state of war shall give immediate effect to ratifications deposited and to accessions notified by the belligerent Powers before or after the commencement of hostilities. The communication of ratifications or accessions received from Powers in a state of war shall be effected by the Swiss Federal Council by the quickest method.

Art. 96. Each of the High Contracting Parties shall have the right to denounce the present Convention. The denunciation shall only take effect one year after notification thereof has been made in writing to the Swiss Federal Council. The latter shall communicate this notification to the Governments of all the High Contracting Parties.

The denunciation shall only be valid in respect of the High Contracting Party which has made notification thereof.

Such denunciation shall, moreover, not take effect during a war in which the denouncing Power is involved. In this case, the present Convention shall continue binding, beyond the period of one year, until the conclusion of peace and, in any case, until operations of repatriation shall have terminated.

Art. 97. A copy of the present Convention, certified to be correct, shall be deposited by the Swiss Federal Council in the archives of the League of Nations. Similarly, ratifications, accessions and denunciations notified to the Swiss Federal Council shall be communicated by them to the League of Nations.

EXTRACTS FROM THE GENEVA CONVENTION RELATIVE TO THE TREATMENT OF PRISONERS OF WAR (12 AUGUST 1949)

The undersigned Plenipotentiaries of the Governments represented at the Diplomatic Conference held at Geneva from April 21 to August 12, 1949, for the purpose of revising the Convention concluded at Geneva on July 27, 1929, relative to the Treatment of Prisoners of War, have agreed as follows:

Part I
General Provisions
Article 1
The High Contracting Parties undertake to respect and to ensure respect for the present Convention in all circumstances.

Article 2
In addition to the provisions which shall be implemented in peace time, the present Convention shall apply to all cases of declared war or of any other armed conflict which may arise between two or more of the High Contracting Parties, even if the state of war is not recognized by one of them.

The Convention shall also apply to all cases of partial or total occupation of the territory of a High Contracting Party, even if the said occupation meets with no armed resistance.

Although one of the Powers in conflict may not be a party to the present Convention, the Powers who are parties thereto shall remain bound by it in their mutual relations. They shall furthermore be bound by the Convention in relation to the said Power, if the latter accepts and applies the provisions thereof.

Article 3
In the case of armed conflict not of an international character occurring in the territory of one of the High Contracting Parties, each Party to the conflict shall be bound to apply, as a minimum, the following provisions:

(1) Persons taking no active part in the hostilities, including members of armed forces who have laid down their arms and those placed hors de combat by sickness, wounds, detention, or any other cause, shall in all circumstances be treated humanely, without any adverse distinction founded on race, colour, religion or faith, sex, birth or wealth, or any other similar criteria.
To this end the following acts are and shall remain prohibited at any time and in any place whatsoever with respect to the above-mentioned persons:
(a) violence to life and person, in particular murder of all kinds, mutilation, cruel treatment and torture;
(b) taking of hostages;
(c) outrages upon personal dignity, in particular, humiliating and degrading treatment;
(d) the passing of sentences and the carrying out of executions without previous judgment pronounced by a regularly constituted court affording all the judicial guarantees which are recognized as indispensable by civilized peoples.

(2) The wounded and sick shall be collected and cared for.

An impartial humanitarian body, such as the International Committee of the Red Cross, may offer its services to the Parties to the conflict.

The Parties to the conflict should further endeavour to bring into force, by means of special agreements, all or part of the other provisions of the present Convention.

The application of the preceding provisions shall not affect the legal status of the Parties to the conflict.

Article 4

A. Prisoners of war, in the sense of the present Convention, are persons belonging to one of the following categories, who have fallen into the power of the enemy:

(1) Members of the armed forces of a Party to the conflict, as well as members of militias or volunteer corps forming part of such armed forces.

(2) Members of other militias and members of other volunteer corps, including those of organized resistance movements, belonging to a Party to the conflict and operating in or outside their own territory, even if this territory is occupied, provided that such militias or volunteer corps, including such organized resistance movements, fulfil the following conditions:
(a) that of being commanded by a person responsible for his subordinates;
(b) that of having a fixed distinctive sign recognizable at a distance;
(c) that of carrying arms openly;
(d) that of conducting their operations in accordance with the laws and customs of war.

(3) Members of regular armed forces who profess allegiance to a government or an authority not recognized by the Detaining Power.

(4) Persons who accompany the armed forces without actually being members thereof, such as civilian members of military aircraft crews, war correspondents, supply contractors, members of labour units or of services responsible for the welfare of the armed forces, provided that they have received authorization from the armed forces which they accompany, who shall provide them for that purpose with an identity card similar to the annexed model.

(5) Members of crews, including masters, pilots and apprentices, of the merchant marine and the crews of civil aircraft of the Parties to the conflict, who do not benefit by more favourable treatment under any other provisions of international law.

(6) Inhabitants of a non-occupied territory, who on the approach of the enemy spontaneously take up arms to resist the invading forces, without having had time to form themselves into regular armed units, provided they carry arms openly and respect the laws and customs of war.

B. The following shall likewise be treated as prisoners of war under the present Convention:

(1) Persons belonging, or having belonged, to the armed forces of the occupied country, if the occupying

Power considers it necessary by reason of such allegiance to intern them, even though it has originally liberated them while hostilities were going on outside the territory it occupies, in particular where such persons have made an unsuccessful attempt to rejoin the armed forces to which they belong and which are engaged in combat, or where they fail to comply with a summons made to them with a view to internment.

(2)The persons belonging to one of the categories enumerated in the present Article, who have been received by neutral or non-belligerent Powers on their territory and whom these Powers are required to intern under international law, without prejudice to any more favourable treatment which these Powers may choose to give and with the exception of Articles 8, 10, 15, 30, fifth paragraph, 58–67, 92, 126 and, where diplomatic relations exist between the Parties to the conflict and the neutral or non-belligerent Power concerned, those Articles concerning the Protecting Power. Where such diplomatic relations exist, the Parties to a conflict on whom these persons depend shall be allowed to perform towards them the functions of a Protecting Power as provided in the present Convention, without prejudice to the functions which these Parties normally exercise in conformity with diplomatic and consular usage and treaties.

C. This Article shall in no way affect the status of medical personnel and chaplains as provided for in Article 33 of the present Convention.

Article 5
The present Convention shall apply to the persons referred to in Article 4 from the time they fall into the power of the enemy and until their final release and repatriation.

Should any doubt arise as to whether persons, having committed a belligerent act and having fallen into the hands of the enemy, belong to any of the categories enumerated in Article 4, such persons shall enjoy the protection of the present Convention until such time as their status has been determined by a competent tribunal.

Article 6
In addition to the agreements expressly provided for in Articles 10, 23, 28, 33, 60, 65, 66, 67, 72, 73, 75, 109, 110, 118, 119, 122, and 132, the High Contracting Parties may conclude other special agreements for all matters concerning which they may deem it suitable to make separate provision. No special agreement shall adversely affect the situation of prisoners of war, as defined by the present Convention, nor restrict the rights which it confers upon them.

Prisoners of war shall continue to have the benefit of such agreements as long as the Convention is applicable to them, except where express provisions to the contrary are contained in the aforesaid or in subsequent agreements, or where more favourable measures have been taken with regard to them by one or other of the Parties to the conflict.

Article 7
Prisoners of war may in no

circumstances renounce in part or in entirety the rights secured to them by the present Convention, and by the special agreements referred to in the foregoing Article, if such there be.

Article 8
The present Convention shall be applied with the cooperation and under the scrutiny of the Protecting Powers whose duty it is to safeguard the interests of the Parties to the conflict. For this purpose, the Protecting Powers may appoint, apart from their diplomatic or consular staff, delegates from amongst their own nationals or the nationals of other neutral Powers. The said delegates shall be subject to the approval of the Power with which they are to carry out their duties.

The Parties to the conflict shall facilitate to the greatest extent possible the task of the representatives or delegates of the Protecting Powers.

The representatives or delegates of the Protecting Powers shall not in any case exceed their mission under the present Convention. They shall, in particular, take account of the imperative necessities of security of the State wherein they carry out their duties.

Article 9
The provisions of the present Convention constitute no obstacle to the humanitarian activities which the International Committee of the Red Cross or any other impartial humanitarian organization may, subject to the consent of the Parties to the conflict concerned, undertake for the protection of prisoners of war and for their reflief.

Article 10
The High Contracting Parties may at any time agree to entrust to an organization which offers all guarantees of impartiality and efficacy the duties incumbent on the Protecting Powers by virtue of the present Convention.

When prisoners of war do not benefit or cease to benefit, no matter for what reason, by the activities of a Protecting Power or of an organization provided for in the first paragraph above, the Detaining Power shall request a neutral State, or such an organization, to undertake the functions performed under the present Convention by a Protecting Power designated by the Parties to a conflict.

If protection cannot be arranged accordingly, the Detaining Power shall request or shall accept, subject to the provisions of this Article, the offer of the services of a humanitarian organization, such as the International Committee of the Red Cross, to assume the humanitarian functions performed by Protecting Powers under the present Convention.

Any neutral Power or any organization invited by the Power concerned or offering itself for these purposes, shall be required to act with a sense of responsibility towards the Party to the conflict on which persons protected by the present Convention depend, and shall be required to furnish sufficient assurances that it is in a position to undertake the appropriate functions and to discharge them impartially.

No derogation from the preceding provisions shall be made by special agreements between Powers one of which is restricted, even temporarily, in its freedom to negotiate with the other Power or its allies by reason of military events, more particularly where the whole, or a substantial part, of the territory of the said Power is occupied.

Whenever in the present Convention mention is made of a Protecting Power, such mention applies to substitute organizations in the sense of the present Article.

Article 11
In cases where they deem it advisable in the interest of protected persons, particularly in cases of disagreement between the Parties to the conflict as to the application or interpretation of the provisions of the present Convention, the Protecting Powers shall lend their good offices with a view to settling the disagreement.

For this purpose, each of the Protecting Powers may, either at the invitation of one Party or on its own initiative, propose to the Parties to the conflict a meeting of their representatives, and in particular of the authorities responsible for prisoners of war, possibly on neutral territory suitably chosen. The Parties to the conflict shall be bound to give effect to the proposals made to them for this purpose. The Protecting Powers may, if necessary, propose for approval by the Parties to the conflict a person belonging to a neutral Power, or delegated by the International Committee of the Red Cross, who shall be invited to take part in such a meeting.

Part II
General Protection of Prisoners of War
Article 12
Prisoners of war are in the hands of the enemy Power, but not of the individuals or military units who have captured them. Irrespective of the individual responsibilities that may exist, the Detaining Power is responsible for the treatment given them.

Prisoners of war may only be transferred by the Detaining Power to a Power which is a party to the Convention and after the Detaining Power has satisfied itself of the willingness and ability of such transferee Power to apply the Convention. When prisoners of war are transferred under such circumstances, responsibility for the application of the Convention rests on the Power accepting them while they are in its custody.

Nevertheless, if that Power fails to carry out the provisions of the Convention in any important respect, the Power by whom the prisoners of war were transferred shall, upon being notified by the Protecting Power, take effective measures to correct the situation or shall request the return of the prisoners of war. Such requests must be complied with.

Article 13
Prisoners of war must at all times be

humanely treated. Any unlawful act or omission by the Detaining Power causing death or seriously endangering the health of a prisoner of war in its custody is prohibited, and will be regarded as a serious breach of the present Convention. In particular, no prisoner of war may be subjected to physical mutilation or to medical or scientific experiments of any kind which are not justified by the medical, dental or hospital treatment of the prisoner concerned and carried out in his interest.

Likewise, prisoners of war must at all times be protected, particularly against acts of violence or intimidation and against insults and public curiosity.

Measures of reprisal against prisoners of war are prohibited.

Article 14
Prisoners of war are entitled in all circumstances to respect for their persons and their honour.

Women shall be treated with all the regard due to their sex and shall in all cases benefit by treatment as favourable as that granted to men.

Prisoners of war shall retain the full civil capacity which they enjoyed at the time of their capture. The Detaining Power may not restrict the exercise, either within or without its own territory, of the rights such capacity confers except in so far as the captivity requires.

Article 15
The Power detaining prisoners of war shall be bound to provide free of charge for their maintenance and for the medical attention required by their state of health.

Article 16
Taking into consideration the provisions of the present Convention relating to rank and sex, and subject to any privileged treatment which may be accorded to them by reason of their state of health, age or professional qualifications, all prisoners of war shall be treated alike by the Detaining Power, without any adverse distinction based on race, nationality, religious belief or political opinions, or any other distinction founded on similar criteria.

Part III
Captivity
Section I
Beginning of Captivity
Article 17
Every prisoner of war, when questioned on the subject, is bound to give only his surname, first names and rank, date of birth, and army, regimental, personal or serial number, or failing this, equivalent information.

If he wilfully infringes this rule, he may render himself liable to a restriction of the privileges accorded to his rank or status.

Each Party to a conflict is required to furnish the persons under its jurisdiction who are liable to become prisoners of war, with an identity card showing the owner's surname, first names, rank, army, regimental, personal or serial number or equivalent information, and date of birth. The identity card may, furthermore, bear the signature or the fingerprints, or both, of the owner, and may bear, as well, any other information the Party to the conflict may wish to add concerning the persons belonging to its armed forces. As far as possible the card shall measure 6.5 x 10 cm. and shall be issued in duplicate. The identity card shall be shown by the prisoner of war upon demand, but may in no case be taken away from him.

No physical or mental torture, nor any other form of coercion, may be inflicted on prisoners of war to secure from them information of any kind whatever. Prisoners of war who refuse to answer may not be threatened, insulted, or exposed to unpleasant or disadvantageous treatment of any kind.

Prisoners of war who, owing to their physical or mental condition, are unable to state their identity, shall be handed over to the medical service. The identity of such prisoners shall be established by all possible means, subject to the provisions of the preceding paragraph.

The questioning of prisoners of war shall be carried out in a language which they understand.

Article 18
All effects and articles of personal use, except arms, horses, military equipment and military documents, shall remain in the possession of prisoners of war, likewise their metal helmets and gas masks and like articles issued for personal protection. Effects and articles used for their clothing or feeding shall likewise remain in their possession, even if such effects and articles belong to their regulation military equipment.

At no time should prisoners of war be without identity documents. The Detaining Power shall supply such documents to prisoners of war who possess none.

Badges of rank and nationality, decorations and articles having above all a personal or sentimental value may not be taken from prisoners of war.

Sums of money carried by prisoners of war may not be taken away from them except by order of an officer, and after the amount and particulars of the owner have been recorded in a special register and an itemized receipt has been given, legibly inscribed with the name, rank and unit of the person issuing the said receipt. Sums in the currency of the Detaining Power, or which are changed into such currency at the prisoner's request, shall be placed to the credit of the prisoner's account as provided in Article 64.

The Detaining Power may withdraw articles of value from prisoners of war only for reasons of security; when such articles are withdrawn, the procedure laid down for sums of money impounded shall apply.

Such objects, likewise sums taken away in any currency other than that of the Detaining Power and the conversion of which has not been asked for by the owners, shall be kept in the custody of the Detaining Power and shall be returned in their initial shape to prisoners of war at the end of their captivity.

Article 19
Prisoners of war shall be evacuated, as soon as possible after their capture, to camps situated in an area far enough from the combat zone for them to be out of danger.

Only those prisoners of war who, owing to wounds or sickness, would run greater risks by being evacuated than by remaining where they are, may be temporarily kept back in a danger zone.

Prisoners of war shall not be unnecessarily exposed to danger while awaiting evacuation from a fighting zone.

Article 20
The evacuation of prisoners of war shall always be effected humanely and in conditions similar to those for the forces of the Detaining Power in their changes of station.

The Detaining Power shall supply prisoners of war who are being evacuated with sufficient food and potable water, and with the necessary clothing and medical attention. The Detaining Power shall take all suitable precautions to ensure their safety during evacuation, and shall establish as soon as possible a list of the prisoners of war who are evacuated.

If prisoners of war must, during evacuation, pass through transit camps, their stay in such camps shall be as brief as possible.

Section II
Internment of Prisoners of War

Chapter I
General Observations
Article 21
The Detaining Power may subject prisoners of war to internment. It may impose on them the obligation of not leaving, beyond certain limits, the camp where they are interned, or if the said camp is fenced in, of not going outside its perimeter. Subject to the provisions of the present Convention relative to penal and disciplinary sanctions, prisoners of war may not be held in close confinement except where necessary to safeguard their health and then only during the continuation of the circumstances which make such confinement necessary.

Prisoners of war may be partially or wholly released on parole or promise, in so far as is allowed by the laws of the Power on which they depend. Such measures shall be taken particularly in cases where this may contibute to the improvement of their state of health. No prisoner of war shall be compelled to accept liberty on parole or promise.

Upon the outbreak of hostilities, each Party to the conflict shall notify the adverse Party of the laws and regulations allowing or forbidding its own nationals to accept liberty on parole or promise. Prisoners of war who are paroled or who have given their promise in conformity with the laws and regulations so notified, are bound on their personal honour scrupulously to fulfill, both towards the Power on which they depend and towards the Power which has captured them, the engagements of their paroles or promises. In such cases, the Power on which they depend is bound neither to require nor to accept from them any service incompatible with the parole or promise given.

Article 22
Prisoners of war may be interned only in premises located on land and affording every guarantee of hygiene and healthfulness. Except in particular cases which are justified by the interest of the prisoners themselves, they shall not be interned in penitentiaries.

Prisoners of war interned in unhealthy areas, or where the climate is injurious for them, shall be removed as soon as possible to a more favourable climate.

The Detaining Power shall assemble prisoners of war in camps or camp compounds according to their nationality, language and customs, provided that such prisoners shall not be separated from prisoners of war belonging to the armed forces with which they were serving at the time of their capture, except with their consent.

Article 23
No prisoner of war may at any time be sent to, or detained in areas where he may be exposed to the fire of the combat zone, nor may his presence be used to render certain points or areas immune from military operations.

Prisoners of war shall have shelters against air bombardment and other hazards of war, to the same extent as the local civilian population. With the exception of those engaged in the protection of their quarters against the aforesaid hazards, they may enter such shelters as soon as possible after the giving of the alarm. Any other protective measure taken in favour of the population shall also apply to them.

Detaining Powers shall give the Powers concerned, through the intermediary of the Protecting Powers, all useful information regarding the geographical location of prisoner of war camps.

Whenever military considerations permit, prisoner of war camps shall be indicated in the day-time by the letters PW or PC, placed so as to be clearly visible from the air. The Powers concerned may, however, agree upon any other system of marking. Only prisoner of war camps shall be marked as such.

Article 24
Transit or screening camps of a permanent kind shall be fitted out under conditions similar to those described in the present Section, and the prisoners therein shall have the same treatment as in other camps.

Chapter II
Quarters, Food and Clothing of Prisoners of War
Article 25
Prisoners of war shall be quartered under conditions as favourable as those for the forces of the Detaining Power who are billeted in the same area. The said conditions shall make allowance for the habits and customs of the prisoners and shall in no case be prejudicial to their health.
The foregoing provisions shall apply in particular to the dormitories of prisoners of war as regards both

total surface and minimum cubic space, and the general installations, bedding and blankets.

The premises provided for the use of prisoners of war individually or collectively, shall be entirely protected from dampness and adequately heated and lighted, in particular beween dusk and lights out. All precautions must be taken against the danger of fire.

In any camps in which women prisoners of war, as well as men, are accommodated, separate dormitories shall be provided for them.

Article 26
The basic daily food rations shall be sufficient in quantity, quality and variety to keep prisoners of war in good health and to prevent loss of weight or the development of nutritional deficiencies. Account shall also be taken of the habitual diet of the prisoners.

The Detaining Power shall supply prisoners of war who work with such additional rations as are necessary for the labour on which they are employed.

Sufficient drinking water shall be supplied to prisoners of war. The use of tobacco shall be permitted.

Prisoners of war shall, as far as possible, be associated with the preparation of their meals; they may be employed for that purpose in the kitchens. Furthermore, they shall be given the means of preparing, themselves, the additional food in their possession.

Adequate premises shall be provided for messing.

Collective disciplinary measures affecting food are prohibited.

Article 27
Clothing, underwear and footwear shall be supplied to prisoners of war in sufficient quantities by the Detaining Power, which shall make allowance for the climate of the region where the prisoners are detained. Uniforms of enemy armed forces captured by the Detaining Power should, if suitable for the climate, be made available to clothe prisoners of war.

The regular replacement and repair of the above articles shall be assured by the Detaining Power. In addition, prisoners of war who work shall receive appropriate clothing, wherever the nature of the work demands.

Article 28
Canteens shall be installed in all camps, where prisoners of war may procure foodstuffs, soap and tobacco and ordinary articles in daily use. The tariff shall never be in excess of local market prices.

The profits made by camp canteens shall be used for the benefit of the prisoners; a special fund shall be created for this purpose. The prisoners' representatives shall have the right to collaborate in the management of the canteen and of this fund.

When a camp is closed down, the credit balance of the special fund shall be handed to an international welfare organization, to be employed for the benefit of prisoners of war of the same nationality as those who have contributed to the fund. In case of a general repatriation, such profits shall be kept by the Detaining Power, subject to any agreement to the contrary between the Powers concerned.

Chapter III
Hygiene and Medical Attention
Article 29
The Detaining Power shall be bound to take all sanitary measures necessary to ensure the cleanliness and healthfulness of camps and to prevent epidemics.

Prisoners of war shall have for their use, day and night, conveniences which conform to the rules of hygiene and are maintained in a constant state of cleanliness. In any camps in which women prisoners of war are accommodated, separate conveniences shall be provided for them.

Also, apart from the baths and showers with which the camps shall be furnished, prisoners of war shall be provided with sufficient water and soap for their personal toilet and for washing their personal laundry; the necessary installations, facilities and time shall be granted them for that purpose.

Article 30
Every camp shall have an adequate infirmary where prisoners of war may have the attention they require, as well as appropriate diet. Isolation wards shall, if necessary, be set aside for cases of contagious or mental disease.

Prisoners of war suffering from serious disease, or whose condition necessitates special treatment, a surgical operation or hospital care, must be admitted to any military or civilian medical unit where such treatment can be given, even if their repatriation is contemplated in the near future. Special facilities shall be afforded for the care to be given to the disabled, in particular to the blind, and for their rehabilitation, pending repatriation.

Prisoners of war shall have the attention, preferably, of medical personnel of the Power on which they depend and, if possible, of their nationality.

Prisoners of war may not be prevented from presenting themselves to the medical authorities for examination. The detaining authorities shall, upon request, issue to every prisoner who has undergone treatment, an official certificate indicating the nature of his illness or injury, and the duration and kind of treatment received. A duplicate of this certificate shall be forwarded to the Central Prisoners of War Agency.

The costs of treatment, including those of any apparatus necessary for the maintenance of prisoners of war in good health, particularly dentures and other artificial appliances, and spectacles, shall be borne by the Detaining Power.

Article 31
Medical inspections of prisoners of war shall be held at least once a month. They shall include the checking and the recording of the

weight of each prisoner of war. Their purpose shall be, in particular, to supervise the general state of health, nutrition and cleanliness of prisoners and to detect contagious diseases, especially tuberculosis, malaria and venereal disease. For this purpose the most efficient methods available shall be employed, e.g., periodic mass miniature radiography for the early detection of tuberculosis.

Article 32
Prisoners of war who, though not attached to the medical service of their armed forces, are physicians, surgeons, dentists, nurses or medical orderlies, may be required by the Detaining Power to exercise their medical functions in the interests of prisoners of war dependent on the same Power. In that case they shall continue to be prisoners of war, but shall receive the same treatment as corresponding medical personnel retained by the Detaining Power. They shall be exempted from any work under Article 49.

Chapter IV
Medical Personnel and Chaplains Retained to Assist Prisoners of War
Article 33
Members of the medical personnel and chaplains while retained by the Detaining Power with a view to assisting prisoners of war, shall not be considered as prisoners of war. They shall, however, receive as a minimum the benefits and protection of the present Convention, and shall also be granted all facilities necessary to provide for the medical care of, and religious ministration to prisoners of war.

They shall continue to exercise their medical and spiritual functions for the benefit of prisoners of war, preferably those belonging to the armed forces upon which they depend, within the scope of the military laws and regulations of the Detaining Power and under control of its competent services, in accordance with their professional etiquette. They shall also benefit by the following facilities in the exercise of their medical or spiritual functions:
(a) They shall be authorized to visit periodically prisoners of war situated in working detachments or in hospitals outside the camp. For this purpose, the Detaining Power shall place at their disposal the necessary means of transport.
(b) The senior medical officer in each camp shall be responsible to the camp military authorities for everything connected with the activities of retained medical personnel. For this purpose, Parties to the conflict shall agree at the outbreak of hostilities on the subject of the corresponding ranks of the medical personnel, including that of societies mentioned in Article 26 of the Geneva Convention for the Amelioration of the Condition of the Wounded and Sick in Armed Forces in the Field of August 12, 1949. This senior medical officer, as well as chaplains, shall have the right to deal with the competent authorities of the camp on all questions relating to their duties. Such authorities shall afford them all necessary facilities for correspondence relating to these questions.
(c) Although they shall be subject to the internal discipline of the camp in which they are retained, such personnel may not be compelled to

carry out any work other than that concerned with their medical or religious duties.

During hostilities, the Parties to the conflict shall agree concerning the possible relief of retained personnel and shall settle the procedure to be followed.

None of the preceding provisions shall relieve the Detaining Power of its obligations with regard to prisoners of war from the medical or spiritual point of view.

Chapter V
Religious, Intellectual and Physical Activities
Article 34
Prisoners of war shall enjoy complete latitude in the exercise of their religious duties, including attendance at the service of their faith, on condition that they comply with the disciplinary routine prescribed by the military authorities.

Adequate premises shall be provided where religious services may be held.

Article 35
Chaplains who fall into the hands of the enemy Power and who remain or are retained with a view to assisting prisoners of war, shall be allowed to minister to them and to exercise freely their ministry amongst prisoners of war of the same religion, in accordance with their religious conscience. They shall be allocated among the various camps and labour detachments containing prisoners of war belonging to the same forces, speaking the same language or practising the same religion. They shall enjoy the necessary facilities, including the means of transport provided for in Article 33, for visiting the prisoners of war outside their camp. They shall be free to correspond, subject to censorship, on matters concerning their religious duties with the ecclesiastical authorities in the country of detention and with international religious organizations. Letters and cards which they may send for this purpose shall be in addition to the quota provided for in Article 71.

Article 36
Prisoners of war who are ministers of religion, without having officiated as chaplains to their own forces, shall be at liberty, whatever their denomination, to minister freely to the members of their community. For this purpose, they shall receive the same treatment as the chaplains retained by the Detaining Power. They shall not be obligated to do any other work.

Article 37
When prisoners of war have not the assistance of a retained chaplain or of a prisoner of war minister of their faith, a minister belonging to the prisoners' or a similar denomination, or in his absence a qualified layman, if such a course is feasible from a confessional point of view, shall be appointed, at the request of the prisoners concerned, to fill this office. This appointment, subject to the approval of the Detaining Power, shall take place with the agreement of the community of prisoners concerned and wherever necessary, with the approval of the local religious authorities of the same

faith. The person thus appointed shall comply with all regulations established by the Detaining Power in the interests of discipline and military security.

Article 38
While respecting the individual preferences of every prisoner, the Detaining Power shall encourage the practice of intellectual, educational, and recreational pursuits, sports and games amongst prisoners, and shall take the measures necessary to ensure the exercise thereof by providing them with adequate premises and necessary equipment.

Prisoners shall have opportunities for taking physical exercise, including sports and games, and for being out of doors. Sufficient open spaces shall be provided for this purpose in all camps.

Chapter VI
Discipline
Article 39
Every prisoner of war camp shall be put under the immediate authority of a responsible commissioned officer belonging to the regular armed forces of the Detaining Power. Such officer shall have in his possession a copy of the present Convention; he shall ensure that its provisions are known to the camp staff and the guard and shall be responsible, under the direction of his government, for its application.

Prisoners of war, with the exception of officers, must salute and show to all officers of the Detaining Power the external marks of respect provided for by the regulations applying in their own forces.

Officer prisoners of war are bound to salute only officers of a higher rank of the Detaining Power; they must, however, salute the camp commander regardless of his rank.

Article 40
The wearing of badges of rank and nationality, as well as of decorations, shall be permitted.

Article 41
In every camp the text of the present Convention and its Annexes and the contents of any special agreement provided for in Article 6, shall be posted, in the prisoners' own language, in places where all may read them. Copies shall be supplied, on request, to the prisoners who cannot have access to the copy which has been posted.

Regulations, orders, notices and publications of every kind relating to the conduct of prisoners of war shall be issued to them in a language which they understand. Such regulations, orders and publications shall be posted in the manner described above and copies shall be handed to the prisoners' representative. Every order and command addressed to prisoners of war individually must likewise be given in a language which they understand.
Article 42
The use of weapons against prisoners of war, especially against those who are escaping or attempting to escape, shall constitute an extreme measure, which shall always be preceded by warnings appropriate to the circumstances.

Chapter VII
Rank of Prisoners of War
Article 43
Upon the outbreak of hostilities, the Parties to the conflict shall communicate to one another the titles and ranks of all the persons mentioned in Article 4 of the present Convention, in order to ensure equality of treatment between prisoners of equivalent rank. Titles and ranks which are subsequently created shall form the subject of similar communications.

The Detaining Power shall recognize promotions in rank which have been accorded to prisoners of war and which have been duly notified by the Power on which these prisoners depend.

Article 44
Officers and prisoners of equivalent status shall be treated with the regard due to their rank and age.

In order to ensure service in officers' camps, other ranks of the same armed forces who, as far as possible, speak the same language, shall be assigned in sufficient numbers, account being taken of the rank of officers and prisoners of equivalent status. Such orderlies shall not be required to perform any other work.

Supervision of the mess by the officers themselves shall be facilitated in every way.

Article 45
Prisoners of war other than officers and prisoners of equivalent status shall be treated with the regard due to their rank and age.

Supervision of the mess by the prisoners themselves shall be facilitated in every way.

Chapter VIII
Transfer of Prisoners of War after Their Arrival in Camp
Article 46
The Detaining Power, when deciding upon the transfer of prisoners of war, shall take into account the interests of the prisoners themselves, more especially so as not to increase the difficulty of their repatriation.

The transfer of prisoners of war shall always be effected humanely and in conditions not less favourable than those under which the forces of the Detaining Power are transferred. Account shall always be taken of the climatic conditions to which the prisoners of war are accustomed and the conditions of transfer shall in no case be prejudicial to their health.

The Detaining Power shall supply prisoners of war during transfer with sufficient food and drinking water to keep them in good health, likewise with the necessary clothing, shelter and medical attention. The Detaining Power shall take adequate precautions especially in case of transport by sea or by air, to ensure their safety during transfer, and shall draw up a complete list of all transferred prisoners before their departure.

Article 47
Sick or wounded prisoners of war shall not be transferred as long as their recovery may be endangered by the journey, unless their safety imperatively demands it.

If the combat zone draws closer to a camp, the prisoners of war in the said camp shall not be transferred unless their transfer can be carried out in adequate conditions of safety, or unless they are exposed to greater risks by remaining on the spot than by being transferred.

Article 48
In the event of transfer, prisoners of war shall be officially advised of their departure and of their new postal address. Such notifications shall be given in time for them to pack their luggage and inform their next of kin.

They shall be allowed to take with them their personal effects, and the correspondence and parcels which have arrived for them. The weight of such baggage may be limited, if the conditions of transfer so require, to what each prisoner can reasonably carry, which shall in no case be more than twenty-five kilograms per head.

Mail and parcels addressed to their former camp shall be forwarded to them without delay. The camp commander shall take, in agreement with the prisoners' representative, any measures needed to ensure the transport of the prisoners' community property and of the luggage they are unable to take with them in consequence of restrictions imposed by virtue of the second paragraph of this Article.

The costs of transfers shall be borne by the Detaining Power.

Section III
Labour of Prisoners of War
Article 49
The Detaining Power may utilize the labour of prisoners of war who are physically fit, taking into account their age, sex, rank and physical aptitude, and with a view particularly to maintaining them in a good state of physical and mental health.

Non-commissioned officers who are prisoners of war shall only be required to do supervisory work. Those not so required may ask for other suitable work which shall, so far as possible, be found for them.

If officers or persons of equivalent status ask for suitable work, it shall be found for them, so far as possible, but they may in no circumstances be compelled to work.

Article 50
Besides work connected with camp administration, installation or maintenance, prisoners of war may be compelled to do only such work as is included in the following classes:
(a) agriculture;
(b) industries connected with the production or the extraction of raw materials, and manufacturing industries, with the exception of metallurgical, machinery and chemical industries; public works and building operations which have no military character or purpose;
(c) transport and handling of stores which are not military in character or purpose;
(d) commercial business, and arts and crafts;
(e) domestic service;
(f) public utility services having no military character or purpose.
Should the above provisions be

infringed, prisoners of war shall be allowed to exercise their right of complaint in conformity with Article 78.

Article 51
Prisoners of war must be granted suitable working conditions, especially as regards accommodation, food, clothing and equipment; such conditions shall not be inferior to those enjoyed by nationals of the Detaining Power employed in similar work; account shall also be taken of climatic conditions.

The Detaining Power, in utilizing the labour of prisoners of war, shall ensure that in areas in which such prisoners are employed, the national legislation concerning the protection of labour, and, more particularly, the regulations for the safety of workers, are duly applied.

Prisoners of war shall receive training and be provided with the means of protection suitable to the work they will have to do and similar to those accorded to the nationals of the Detaining Power. Subject to the provisions of Article 52, prisoners may be submitted to the normal risks run by these civilian workers.

Conditions of labour shall in no case be rendered more arduous by disciplinary measures.

Article 52
Unless he be a volunteer, no prisoner of war may be employed on labour which is of an unhealthy or dangerous nature.

No prisoner of war shall be assigned to labour which would be looked upon as humiliating for a member of the Detaining Power's own forces.

The removal of mines or similar devices shall be considered as dangerous labour.

Article 53
The duration of the daily labour of prisoners of war, including the time of the journey to and fro, shall not be excessive, and must in no case exceed that permitted for civilian workers in the district, who are nationals of the Detaining Power and employed on the same work.

Prisoners of war must be allowed, in the middle of the day's work, a rest of not less than one hour. This rest will be the same as that to which workers of the Detaining Power are entitled, if the latter is of longer duration. They shall be allowed in addition a rest of twenty-four consecutive hours every week, preferably on Sunday or the day of rest in their country of origin. Furthermore, every prisoner who has worked for one year shall be granted a rest of eight consecutive days, during which his working pay shall be paid him.

If methods of labour such as piece work are employed, the length of the working period shall not be rendered excessive thereby.

Article 54
The working pay due to prisoners of war shall be fixed in accordance with the provisions of Article 62 of the present Convention.

Prisoners of war who sustain accidents in connection with work, or who contract a disease in the course, or in consequence of their work, shall receive all the care their condition may require. The Detaining Power shall furthermore deliver to such prisoners of war a medical certificate enabling them to submit their claims to the Power on which they depend, and shall send a duplicate to the Central Prisoners of War Agency provided for in Article 123.

Article 55
The fitness of prisoners of war for work shall be periodically verified by medical examinations at least once a month. The examinations shall have particular regard to the nature of the work which prisoners of war are required to do.

If any prisoner of war considers himself incapable of working, he shall be permitted to appear before the medical authorities of his camp. Physicians or surgeons may recommend that the prisoners who are, in their opinon, unfit for work, be exempted therefrom.

Article 56
The organization and administration of labour detachments shall be similar to those of prisoner of war camps.

Every labour detachment shall remain under the control of and administratively part of a prisoner of war camp. The military authorities and the commander of the said camp shall be responsible, under the direction of their government, for the observance of the provisions of the present Convention in labour detachments.

The camp commander shall keep an up-to-date record of the labour detachments dependent on his camp, and shall communicate it to the delegates of the Protecting Power, of the International Committee of the Red Cross, or of other agencies giving relief to prisoners of war, who may visit the camp.

Article 57
The treatment of prisoners of war who work for private persons, even if the latter are responsible for guarding and protecting them, shall not be inferior to that which is provided for by the present Convention. The Detaining Power, the military authorities and the commander of the camp to which such prisoners belong shall be entirely responsible for the maintenance, care, treatment, and payment of the working pay of such prisoners of war.

Such prisoners of war shall have the right to remain in communication with the prisoners' representatives in the camps on which they depend.

Section IV
Financial Resources of Prisoners of War
Article 58
Upon the outbreak of hostilities, and pending an arrangement on this matter with the Protecting Power, the Detaining Power may determine the maximum amount of money in cash or in any similar form, that prisoners may have in their possession. Any amount in excess, which was properly in their

possession and which has been taken or withheld from them, shall be placed in their account, together with any monies deposited by them, and shall not be converted into any other currency without their consent.

If prisoners of war are permitted to purchase services or commodities outside the camp against payment in cash, such payments shall be made by the prisoner himself or by the camp administration who will charge them to the accounts of the prisoners concerned. The Detaining Power will establish the necessary rules in this respect.

Article 59
Cash which was taken from prisoners of war, in accordance with Article 18, at the time of their capture, and which is in the currency of the Detaining Power, shall be placed to their separate accounts, in accordance with the provisions of Article 64 of the present Section.

The amounts, in the currency of the Detaining Power, due to the conversion of sums in other currencies that are taken from the prisoners of war at the same time, shall also be credited to their separate accounts.

Article 60
The Detaining Power shall grant all prisoners of war a monthly advance of pay, the amount of which shall be fixed by conversion, into the currency of the said Power, of the following amounts:
Category I: Prisoners ranking below sergeants: eight Swiss francs.
Category II: Sergeants and other non-commissioned officers, or prisoners of equivalent rank: twelve Swiss francs.
Category III: Warrant officers and commissioned officers below the rank of major or prisoners of equivalent rank: fifty Swiss francs.
Category IV: Majors, lieutenant-colonels, colonels or prisoners of equivalent rank: sixty Swiss francs.
Category V: General officers or prisoners of war of equivalent rank: seventy-five Swiss francs.

However, the Parties to the conflict concerned may by special agreement modify the amount of advances to pay due to prisoners of the preceding categories.

Furthermore, if the amounts indicated in the first paragraph above would be unduly high compared with the pay of the Detaining Power's armed forces or would, for any reason, seriously embarrass the Detaining Power, then, pending the conclusion of a special agreement with the Power on which the prisoners depend to vary the amounts indicated above, the Detaining Power:
(a) shall continue to credit the accounts of the prisoners with the amounts indicated in the first paragraph above;
(b) may temporarily limit the amount made available from these advances of pay to prisoners of war for their own use, to sums which are reasonable, but which, for Category I, shall never be inferior to the amount that the Detaining Power gives to the members of its own armed forces.

The reasons for any limitations will be given without delay to the

Protecting Power.

Article 61
The Detaining Power shall accept for distribution as supplementary pay to prisoners of war sums which the Power on which the prisoners depend may forward to them, on condition that the sums to be paid shall be the same for each prisoner of the same category, shall be payable to all prisoners of that category depending on that Power, and shall be placed in their separate accounts, at the earliest opportunity, in accordance with the provisions of Article 64. Such supplementary pay shall not relieve the Detaining Power of any obligation under this Convention.

Article 62
Prisoners of war shall be paid a fair working rate of pay by the detaining authorities direct. The rate shall be fixed by the said authorities, but shall at no time be less than one-fourth of one Swiss franc for a full working day. The Detaining Power shall inform prisoners of war, as well as the Power on which they depend, through the intermediary of the Protecting Power, of the rate of daily working pay that it has fixed.

Working pay shall likewise be paid by the detaining authorities to prisoners of war permanently detailed to duties or to a skilled or semi-skilled occupation in connection with the administration, installation or maintenance of camps, and to the prisoners who are required to carry out spiritual or medical duties on behalf of their comrades.

The working pay of the prisoners' representatives, of his advisers, if any, and of his assistants, shall be paid out of the fund maintained by canteen profits. The scale of this working pay shall be fixed by the prisoners' representative and approved by the camp commander. If there is no such fund, the detaining authorities shall pay these prisoners a fair working rate of pay.

Article 63
Prisoners of war shall be permitted to receive remittances of money addressed to them individually or collectively.

Every prisoner of war shall have at his disposal the credit balance of his account as provided for in the following Article, within the limits fixed by the Detaining Power, which shall make such payments as are requested. Subject to financial or monetary restrictions which the Detaining Power regards as essential, prisoners of war may also have payments made abroad. In this case payments addressed by prisoners of war to dependents shall be given priority.
In any event, and subject to the consent of the Power on which they depend, prisoners may have payments made in their own country, as follows: the Detaining Power shall send to the aforesaid Power through the Protecting Power, a notification giving all the necessary particulars concerning the prisoners of war, the beneficiaries of the payments, and the amount of the sums to be paid, expressed in the Detaining Power's currency. The said notification shall be signed by the prisoners and countersigned by

the camp commander. The Detaining Power shall debit the prisoners' account by a corresponding amount; the sums thus debited shall be placed by it to the credit of the Power on which the prisoners depend.

To apply the foregoing provisions, the Detaining Power may usefully consult the Model Regulations in Annex V of the present Convention.

Article 64
The Detaining Power shall hold an account for each prisoner of war, showing at least the following:
(1) The amounts due to the prisoner or received by him as advances of pay, as working pay or derived from any other source; the sums in the currency of the Detaining Power which were taken from him; the sums taken from him and converted at his request into the currency of the said Power.
(2) The payments made to the prisoner in cash, or in any other similar form; the payments made on his behalf and at his request; the sums transferred under Article 63, third paragraph.
Article 65
Every item entered in the account of a prisoner of war shall be countersigned or initialled by him, or by the prisoners' representative acting on his behalf.

Prisoners of war shall at all times be afforded reasonable facilities for consulting and obtaining copies of their accounts, which may likewise be inspected by the representatives of the Protecting Powers at the time of visits to the camp.

When prisoners of war are transferred from one camp to another, their personal accounts will follow them. In case of transfer from one Detaining Power to another, the monies which are their property and are not in the currency of the Detaining Power will follow them. They shall be given certificates for any other monies standing to the credit of their accounts.

The Parties to the conflict concerned may agree to notify to each other at specific intervals through the Protecting Power, the amount of the accounts of the prisoners of war.

Article 66
On the termination of captivity, through the release of a prisoner of war or his repatriation, the Detaining Power shall give him a statement, signed by an authorized officer of that Power, showing the credit balance then due to him. The Detaining Power shall also send through the Protecting Power to the government upon which the prisoner of war depends, lists of all appropriate particulars of all prisoners of war whose captivity has been terminated by repatriation, release, escape, death or any other means, and showing the amount of their credit balances. Such lists shall be certified on each sheet by an authorized representative of the Detaining Power.

Any of the above provisions of this Article may be varied by mutual agreement between any two Parties to the conflict.

The Power on which the prisoner of war depends shall be responsible for settling with him any credit balance due to him from the Detaining Power on the termination of his captivity.

Article 67
Advances of pay, issued to prisoners of war in conformity with Article 60, shall be considered as made on behalf of the Power on which they depend. Such advances of pay, as well as all payments made by the said Power under Article 63, third paragraph, and Article 68, shall form the subject of arrangements between the Powers concerned, at the close of hostilities.

Article 68
Any claim by a prisoner of war for compensation in respect of any injury or other disability arising out of work shall be referred to the Power on which he depends, through the Protecting Power. In accordance with Article 54, the Detaining Power will, in all cases, provide the prisoner of war concerned with a statement showing the nature of the injury or disability, the circumstances in which it arose and particulars of medical or hospital treatment given for it. This statement will be signed by a responsible officer of the Detaining Power and the medical particulars certified by a medical officer.

Any claim by a prisoner of war for compensation in respect of personal effects, monies or valuables impounded by the Detaining Power under Article 18 and not forthcoming on his repatriation, or in respect of loss alleged to be due to the fault of the Detaining Power or any of its servants, shall likewise be referred to the Power on which he depends. Nevertheless, any such personal effects required for use by the prisoners of war whilst in captivity shall be replaced at the expense of the Detaining Power. The Detaining Power will, in all cases, provide the prisoner of war with a statement, signed by a responsible officer, showing all available information regarding the reasons why such effects, monies or valuables have not been restored to him. A copy of this statement will be forwarded to the Power on which he depends through the Central Prisoners of War Agency provided for in Article 123.

Section V
Relations of Prisoners of War with the Exterior
Article 69
Immediately upon prisoners of war falling into its power, the Detaining Power shall inform them and the Powers on which they depend, through the Protecting Power, of the measures taken to carry out the provisions of the present Section. They shall likewise inform the parties concerned of any subsequent modifications of such measures.

Article 70
Immediately upon capture, or not more than one week after arrival at a camp, even if it is a transit camp, likewise in case of sickness or transfer to hospital or to another camp, every prisoner of war shall be enabled to write direct to his family, on the one hand, and to the Central Prisoners of War Agency provided for in Article 123, on the other hand, a card similar, if possible, to the model annexed to the present

Convention, informing his relatives of his capture, address and state of health. The said cards shall be forwarded as rapidly as possible and may not be delayed in any manner.

Article 71
Prisoners of war shall be allowed to send and receive letters and cards. If the Detaining Power deems it necessary to limit the number of letters and cards sent by each prisoner of war, the said number shall not be less than two letters and four cards monthly, exclusive of the capture cards provided for in Article 70, and conforming as closely as possible to the models annexed to the present Convention. Further limitations may be imposed only if the Protecting Power is satisfied that it would be in the interests of the prisoners of war concerned to do so owing to difficulties of translation caused by the Detaining Power's inability to find sufficient qualified linguists to carry out the necessary censorship. If limitations must be placed on the correspondence addressed to prisoners of war, they may be ordered only by the Power on which the prisoners depend, possibly at the request of the Detaining Power. Such letters and cards must be conveyed by the most rapid method at the disposal of the Detaining Power; they may not be delayed or retained for disciplinary reasons.

Prisoners of war who have been without news for a long period, or who are unable to receive news from their next of kin or to give them news by the ordinary postal route, as well as those who are at a great distance from their homes, shall be permitted to send telegrams, the fees being charged against the prisoners of war's accounts with the Detaining Power or paid in the currency at their disposal. They shall likewise benefit by this measure in cases of urgency.

As a general rule, the correspondence of prisoners of war shall be written in their native language. The Parties to the conflict may allow correspondence in other languages.

Sacks containing prisoner of war mail must be securely sealed and labelled so as clearly to indicate their contents, and must be addressed to offices of destination.

Article 72
Prisoners of war shall be allowed to receive by post or by any other means individual parcels or collective shipments containing, in particular, foodstuffs, clothing, medical supplies and articles of a religious, educational or recreational character which may meet their needs, including books, devotional articles, scientific equipment, examination papers, musical instruments, sports outfits and materials allowing prisoners of war to pursue their studies or their cultural activities.

Such shipments shall in no way free the Detaining Power from the obligations imposed upon it by virtue of the present Convention.

The only limits which may be placed on these shipments shall be those proposed by the Protecting Power in the interest of the prisoners themselves, or by the International Committee of the Red Cross or any other organization giving assistance to the prisoners, in respect of their own shipments only, on account of exceptional strain on transport or communications.

The conditions for the sending of individual parcels and collective relief shall, if necessary, be the subject of special agreements between the Powers concerned, which may in no case delay the receipt by the prisoners of relief supplies. Books may not be included in parcels of clothing and foodstuffs. Medical supplies shall, as a rule, be sent in collective parcels.

Article 73
In the absence of special agreements between the Powers concerned on the conditions for the receipt and distribution of collective relief shipments, the rules and regulations concerning collective shipments, which are annexed to the present Convention, shall be applied.

The special agreements referred to above shall in no case restrict the right of prisoners' representatives to take possession of collective relief shipments intended for prisoners of war, to proceed to their distribution or to dispose of them in the interest of the prisoners.

Nor shall such agreements restrict the right of representatives of the Protecting Power, the International Committee of the Red Cross or any other organization giving assistance to prisoners of war and responsible for the forwarding of collective shipments, to supervise their distribution to the recipients.

Article 74
All relief shipments for prisoners of war shall be exempt from import, customs and other dues.

Correspondence, relief shipments and authorized remittances of money addressed to prisoners of war or despatched by them through the post office, either direct or through the Information Bureaux provided for in Article 122 and the Central Prisoners of War Agency provided for in Article 123, shall be exempt from any postal dues, both in the countries of origin and destination, and in intermediate countries.

If relief shipments intended for prisoners of war cannot be sent through the post office by reason of weight or for any other cause, the cost of transportation shall be borne by the Detaining Power in all the territories under its control. The other Powers party to the Convention shall bear the cost of transport in their respective territories.

In the absence of special agreements between the Parties concerned, the costs connected with transport of such shipments, other than costs covered by the above exemption, shall be charged to the senders.

The High Contracting Parties shall endeavour to reduce, so far as possible, the rates charged for telegrams sent by prisoners of war, or addressed to them.

Article 75
Should military operations prevent

the Powers concerned from fulfilling their obligation to assure the transport of the shipments referred to in Articles 70, 71, 72 and 77, the Protecting Powers concerned, the International Committee of the Red Cross or any other organization duly approved by the Parties to the conflict may undertake to ensure the conveyance of such shipments by suitable means (railway wagons, motor vehicles, vessels or aircraft, etc.). For this purpose, the High Contracting Parties shall endeavour to supply them with such transport and to allow its circulation, especially by granting the necessary safe-conducts.

Such transport may also be used to convey:
(a) correspondence, lists and reports exchanged between the Central Information Agency referred to in Article 123 and the National Bureaux referred to in Article 122;
(b) correspondence and reports relating to prisoners of war which the Protecting Powers, the International Committee of the Red Cross or any other body assisting the prisoners, exchange either with their own delegates or with the Parties to the conflict.
These provisions in no way detract from the right of any Party to the conflict to arrange other means of transport, if it should so prefer, nor preclude the granting of safe-conducts, under mutually agreed conditions, to such means of transport.

In the absence of special agreements, the costs occasioned by the use of such means of transport shall be borne proportionally by the Parties to the conflict whose nationals are benefited thereby.

Article 76
The censoring of correspondence addressed to prisoners of war or despatched by them shall be done as quickly as possible. Mail shall be censored only by the despatching State and the receiving State, and once only by each.

The examination of consignments intended for prisoners of war shall not be carried out under conditions that will expose the goods contained in them to deterioration; except in the case of written or printed matter, it shall be done in the presence of the addressee, or of a fellow-prisoner duly delegated by him. The delivery to prisoners of individual or collective consignments shall not be delayed under the pretext of difficulties of censorship.

Any prohibition of correspondence ordered by Parties to the conflict, either for military or political reasons, shall be only temporary and its duration shall be as short as possible.

Article 77
The Detaining Powers shall provide all facilities for the transmission, through the Protecting Power or the Central Prisoners of War Agency provided for in Article 123, of instruments, papers or documents intended for prisoners of war or despatched by them, especially powers of attorney and wills.

In all cases they shall facilitate the preparation and execution of such documents on behalf of prisoners of war; in particular, they shall allow them to consult a lawyer and shall take what measures are necessary for the authentication of their signatures.

Section VI
Relations Between Prisoners of War and the Authorities
Chapter I
Complaints of Prisoners of War Respecting the Conditions of Captivity
Article 78
Prisoners of war shall have the right to make known to the military authorities in whose power they are, their request regarding the conditions of captivity to which they are subjected.

They shall also have the unrestricted right to apply to the representatives of the Protecting Powers either through their prisoners' representative or, if they consider it necessary, direct, in order to draw their attention to any points on which they may have complaints to make regarding their conditions of captivity.

These requests and complaints shall not be limited nor considered to be a part of the correspondence quota referred to in Article 71. They must be transmitted immediately. Even if they are recognized to be unfounded, they may not give rise to any punishment.

Prisoners' representatives may send periodic reports on the situation in the camps and the needs of the prisoners of war to the representatives of the Protecting Powers.

Chapter II
Prisoner of War Representatives
Article 79
In all places where there are prisoners of war, except in those where there are officers, the prisoners shall freely elect by secret ballot, every six months, and also in case of vacancies, prisoners' representatives entrusted with representing them before the military authorities, the Protecting Powers, the International Committee of the Red Cross and any other organization which may assist them. These prisoners' representatives shall be eligible for re-election.

In camps for officers and persons of equivalent status or in mixed camps, the senior officer among the prisoners of war shall be recognized as the camp prisoners' representative. In camps for officers, he shall be assisted by one or more advisers chosen by the officers; in mixed camps, his assistants shall be chosen from among the prisoners of war who are not officers and shall be elected by them.

Officer prisoners of war of the same nationality shall be stationed in labour camps for prisoners of war, for the purpose of carrying out the camp administration duties for which the prisoners of war are responsible. These officers may be elected as prisoners' representatives under the first paragraph of this Article. In such a case the assistants to the prisoners' representatives shall be chosen from among those prisoners of war who are not officers.

Every representative elected must be approved by the Detaining Power before he has the right to commence his duties. Where the Detaining Power refuses to approve a prisoner of war elected by his fellow prisoners of war, it must inform the Protecting Power of the reason for such refusal.

In all cases the prisoners' representative must have the same nationality, language and customs as the prisoners of war whom he represents. Thus, prisoners of war distributed in different sections of a camp, according to their nationality, language or customs, shall have for each section their own prisoners' representative, in accordance with the foregoing paragraphs.

Article 80
Prisoners' representatives shall further the physical, spiritual and intellectual well-being of prisoners of war.
In particular, where the prisoners decide to organize amongst themselves a system of mutual assistance, this organization will be within the province of the prisoners' representative, in addition to the special duties entrusted to him by other provisions of the present Convention.

Prisoners' representatives shall not be held responsible, simply by reason of their duties, for any offences committed by prisoners of war.

Article 81
Prisoners' representatives shall not be required to perform any other work, if the accomplishment of their duties is thereby made more difficult.

Prisoners' representatives may appoint from amongst the prisoners such assistants as they may require. All material facilities shall be granted them, particularly a certain freedom of movement necessary for the accomplishment of their duties (inspection of labour detachments, receipt of supplies, etc.).

Prisoners' representatives shall be permitted to visit premises where prisoners of war are detained, and every prisoner of war shall have the right to consult freely his prisoners' representative.

All facilities shall likewise be accorded to the prisoners' representatives for communications by post and telegraph with the detaining authorities, the Protecting Powers, the International Committee of the Red Cross and their delegates, the Mixed Medical Commissions and the bodies which give assistance to prisoners of war. Prisoners' representatives of labour detachments shall enjoy the same facilities for communication with the prisoners' representatives of the principal camp. Such communications shall not be restricted, nor considered as forming a part of the quota mentioned in Article 71.

Prisoners' representatives who are transferred shall be allowed a reasonable time to acquaint their successors with current affairs.

In case of dismissal, the reasons therefore shall be communicated to the Protecting Power.

Chapter III
Penal and Disciplinary Sanctions
I. General Provisions
Article 82
A prisoner of war shall be subject to the laws, regulations and orders in force in the armed forces of the Detaining Power; the Detaining Power shall be justified in taking judicial or disciplinary measures in respect of any offence committed by a prisoner of war against such laws, regulations or orders. However, no proceedings or punishments contrary to the provisions of this Chapter shall be allowed.

If any law, regulation or order of the Detaining Power shall declare acts committed by a prisoner of war to be punishable, whereas the same acts would not be punishable if committed by a member of the forces of the Detaining Power, such acts shall entail disciplinary punishments only.

Article 83
In deciding whether proceedings in respect of an offence alleged to have been committed by a prisoner of war shall be judicial or disciplinary, the Detaining Power shall ensure that the competent authorities exercise the greatest leniency and adopt, wherever possible, disciplinary rather than judicial measures.

Article 84
A prisoner of war shall be tried only by a military court, unless the existing laws of the Detaining Power expressly permit the civil courts to try a member of the armed forces of the Detaining Power in respect of the particular offence alleged to have been committed by the prisoner of war.

In no circumstances whatever shall a prisoner of war be tried by a court of any kind which does not offer the essential guarantees of independence and impartiality as generally recognized, and, in particular, the procedure of which does not afford the accused the rights and means of defence provided for in Article 105.

Article 85
Prisoners of war prosecuted under the laws of the Detaining Power for acts committed prior to capture shall retain, even if convicted, the benefits of the present Convention.

Article 86
No prisoner of war may be punished more than once for the same act or on the same charge.

Article 87
Prisoners of war may not be sentenced by the military authorities and courts of the Detaining Power to any penalties except those provided for in respect of members of the armed forces of the said Power who have committed the same acts.

When fixing the penalty, the courts or authorities of the Detaining Power shall take into consideration, to the widest extent possible, the fact that the accused, not being a national of the Detaining Power, is not bound to it by any duty of allegiance, and that he is in its power as the result of circumstances independent of his own will. The said courts or authorities shall be at liberty to reduce the penalty provided for the violation of which the prisoner of war is accused, and shall therefore not be bound to apply the minimum penalty prescribed.

Collective punishment for individual acts, corporal punishment, imprisonment in premises without daylight and, in general, any form of torture or cruelty, are forbidden.

No prisoner of war may be deprived of his rank by the Detaining Power, or prevented from wearing his badges.

Article 88

Officers, non-commissioned officers and men who are prisoners of war undergoing a disciplinary or judicial punishment, shall not be subjected to more severe treatment than that applied in respect of the same punishment to members of the armed forces of the Detaining Power of equivalent rank.

A woman prisoner of war shall not be awarded or sentenced to a punishment more severe, or treated whilst undergoing punishment more severely, than a woman member of the armed forces of the Detaining Power dealt with for a similar offence.

In no case may a woman prisoner of war be awarded or sentenced to a punishment more severe, or treated whilst undergoing punishment more severely, than a male member of the armed forces of the Detaining Power dealt with for a similar offence.

Prisoners of war who have served disciplinary or judicial sentences may not be treated differently from other prisoners of war.

II. Disciplinary Sanctions

Article 89

The disciplinary punishments applicable to prisoners of war are the following:

(1) A fine which shall not exceed 50 per cent of the advances of pay and working pay which the prisoner of war would otherwise receive under the provisions of Articles 60 and 62 during a period of not more than thirty days.

(2) Discontinuance of privileges granted over and above the treatment provided for by the present Convention.

(3) Fatigue duties not exceeding two hours daily.

(4) Confinement.

The punishment referred to under (3) shall not be applied to officers.

In no case shall disciplinary punishments be inhuman, brutal or dangerous to the health of prisoners of war.

Article 90

The duration of any single punishment shall in no case exceed thirty days. Any period of confinement awaiting the hearing of a disciplinary offence or the award of disciplinary punishment shall be deducted from an award pronounced against a prisoner of war.

The maximum of thirty days provided above may not be exceeded, even if the prisoner of war is answerable for several acts at the same time when he is awarded punishment, whether such acts are related or not.

The period between the pronouncing of an award of disciplinary punishment and its execution shall not exceed one month.

When a prisoner of war is awarded a further disciplinary punishment, a period of at least three days shall elapse between the execution of any two of the punishments, if the duration of one of these is ten days or more.

Article 91
The escape of a prisoner of war shall be deemed to have succeeded when:
(1) he has joined the armed forces of the Power on which he depends, or those of an allied Power;
(2) he has left the territory under the control of the Detaining Power, or of an ally of the said Power;
(3) he has joined a ship flying the flag of the Power on which he depends, or of an allied Power, in the territorial waters of the Detaining Power, the said ship not being under the control of the last named Power.
Prisoners of war who have made good their escape in the sense of this Article and who are recaptured, shall not be liable to any punishment in respect of their previous escape.

Article 92
A prisoner of war who attempts to escape and is recaptured before having made good his escape in the sense of Article 91 shall be liable only to a disciplinary punishment in respect of this act, even if it is a repeated offence.

A prisoner of war who is recaptured shall be handed over without delay to the competent military authority.

Article 88, fourth paragraph, notwithstanding, prisoners of war punished as a result of an unsuccessful escape may be subjected to special surveillance. Such surveillance must not affect the state of their health, must be undergone in a prisoner of war camp, and must not entail the suppression of any of the safeguards granted them by the present Convention.

Article 93
Escape or attempt to escape, even if it is a repeated offence, shall not be deemed an aggravating circumstance if the prisoner of war is subjected to trial by judicial proceedings in respect of an offence committed during his escape or attempt to escape.

In conformity with the principle stated in Article 83, offences committed by prisoners of war with the sole intention of facilitating their escape and which do not entail any violence against life or limb, such as offences against public property, theft without intention of self-enrichment, the drawing up or use of false papers, or the wearing of civilian clothing, shall occasion disciplinary punishment only.

Prisoners of war who aid or abet an escape or an attempt to escape shall be liable on this count to disciplinary punishment only.

Article 94
If an escaped prisoner of war is recaptured, the Power on which he depends shall be notified thereof in the manner defined in Article 122, provided notification of his escape has been made.

Article 95
A prisoner of war accused of an offence against discipline shall not be kept in confinement pending the hearing unless a member of the armed forces of the Detaining Power would be so kept if he were accused of a similar offence, or if it is essential in the interests of camp order and discipline.

Any period spent by a prisoner of war in confinement awaiting the disposal of an offence against discipline shall be reduced to an absolute minimum and shall not exceed fourteen days.

The provisions of Articles 97 and 98 of this Chapter shall apply to prisoners of war who are in confinement awaiting the disposal of offences against discipline.

Article 96
Acts which constitute offences against discipline shall be investigated immediately.

Without prejudice to the competence of courts and superior military authorities, disciplinary punishment may be ordered only by an officer having disciplinary powers in his capacity as camp commander, or by a responsible officer who replaces him or to whom he has delegated his disciplinary powers.

In no case may such powers be delegated to a prisoner of war or be exercised by a prisoner of war.

Before any disciplinary award is pronounced, the accused shall be given precise information regarding the offences of which he is accused, and given an opportunity of explaining his conduct and of defending himself. He shall be permitted, in particular, to call witnesses and to have recourse, if necessary, to the services of a qualified interpreter. The decision shall be announced to the accused prisoner of war and to the prisoner's representative.

A record of disciplinary punishments shall be maintained by the camp commander and shall be open to inspection by representatives of the Protecting Power.

Article 97
Prisoners of war shall not in any case be transferred to penitentiary establishments (prisons, penitentiaries, convict prisons, etc.) to undergo disciplinary punishment therein.
All premises in which disciplinary punishments are undergone shall conform to the sanitary requirements set forth in Article 25. A prisoner of war undergoing punishment shall be enabled to keep himself in a state of cleanliness, in conformity with Article 29.

Officers and persons of equivalent status shall not be lodged in the same quarters as non-commissioned officers or men.

Women prisoners of war undergoing disciplinary punishment shall be confined in separate quarters from male prisoners of war and shall be under the immediate supervision of women.

Article 98
A prisoner of war undergoing

confinement as a disciplinary punishment, shall continue to enjoy the benefits of the provisions of this Convention except in so far as these are necessarily rendered inapplicable by the mere fact that he is confined. In no case may he be deprived of the benefits of the provisions of Articles 78 and 126.

A prisoner of war awarded disciplinary punishment may not be deprived of the prerogatives attached to his rank.

Prisoners of war awarded disciplinary punishment shall be allowed to exercise and to stay in the open air at least two hours daily.

They shall be allowed, on their request, to be present at the daily medical inspections. They shall receive the attention which their state of health requires and, if necessary, shall be removed to the camp infirmary or to a hospital.

They shall have permission to read and write, likewise to send and receive letters. Parcels and remittances of money, however, may be withheld from them until the completion of the punishment; they shall meanwhile be entrusted to the prisoners' representative, who will hand over to the infirmary the perishable goods contained in such parcels.

III. Judicial Proceedings
Article 99
No prisoner of war may be tried or sentenced for an act which is not forbidden by the law of the Detaining Power or by international law, in force at the time the said act was committed.

No moral or physical coercion may be exerted on a prisoner of war in order to induce him to admit himself guilty of the act of which he is accused.

No prisoner of war may be convicted without having had an opportunity to present his defence and the assistance of a qualified advocate or counsel.

Article 100
Prisoners of war and the Protecting Powers shall be informed as soon as possible of the offences which are punishable by the death sentence under the laws of the Detaining Power.

Other offences shall not thereafter be made punishable by the death penalty without the concurrence of the Power on which the prisoners of war depend.

The death sentence cannot be pronounced on a prisoner of war unless the attention of the court has, in accordance with Article 87, second paragraph, been particularly called to the fact that since the accused is not a national of the Detaining Power, he is not bound to it by any duty of allegiance, and that he is in its power as the result of circumstances independent of his own will.

Article 101
If the death penalty is pronounced on a prisoner of war, the sentence shall not be executed before the expiration of a period of at least six months from the date when the

Protecting Power receives, at an indicated address, the detailed communication provided for in Article 107.

Article 102
A prisoner of war can be validly sentenced only if the sentence has been pronounced by the same courts according to the same procedures as in the case of members of the armed forces of the Detaining Power, and if, furthermore, the provisions of the present Chapter have been observed.

Article 103
Judicial investigations relating to a prisoner of war shall be conducted as rapidly as circumstances permit and so that his trial shall take place as soon as possible. A prisoner of war shall not be confined while awaiting trial unless a member of the armed forces of the Detaining Power would be so confined if he were accused of a similar offence, or if it is essential to do so in the interests of national security. In no circumstances shall this confinement exceed three months.

Any period spent by a prisoner of war in confinement awaiting trial shall be deducted from any sentence of imprisonment passed upon him and taken into account in fixing any penalty.

The provisions of Articles 97 and 98 of this Chapter shall apply to a prisoner of war whilst in confinement awaiting trial.

Article 104
In any case in which the Detaining Power has decided to institute judicial proceedings against a prisoner of war, it shall notify the Protecting Power as soon as possible and at least three weeks before the opening of the trial. This period of three weeks shall run as from the day on which such notification reaches the Protecting Power at the address previously indicated by the latter to the Detaining Power.

The said notification shall contain the following information:
(1) Surname and first names of the prisoner of war, his rank, his army, regimental, personal or serial number, his date of birth, and his profession or trade, if any;
(2) Place of internment or confinement;
(3) Specification of the charges on which the prisoner of war is to be arraigned, giving the legal provisions applicable;
(4) Designation of the court which will try the case, likewise the date and place fixed for the opening of the trial.

The same communication shall be made by the Detaining Power to the prisoners' representative.

If no evidence is submitted, at the opening of a trial, that the notification referred to above was received by the Protecting Power, by the prisoner of war and by the prisoners' representative concerned, at least three weeks before the opening of the trial, then the latter cannot take place and must be adjourned.

Article 105
The prisoner of war shall be entitled to assistance by one of his prisoner comrades, to defence by a qualified

advocate or counsel of his own choice, to the calling of witnesses and, if he deems necessary, to the services of a competent interpreter. He shall be advised of these rights by the Detaining Power in due time before the trial.

Failing a choice by the prisoner of war, the Protecting Power shall find him an advocate or counsel, and shall have at least one week at its disposal for the purpose. The Detaining Power shall deliver to the said Power, on request, a list of persons qualified to present the defence. Failing a choice of an advocate or counsel by the prisoner of war or the Protecting Power, the Detaining Power shall appoint a competent advocate or counsel to conduct the defence.

The advocate or counsel conducting the defence on behalf of the prisoner of war shall have at his disposal a period of two weeks at least before the opening of the trial, as well as the necessary facilities to prepare the defence of the accused. He may, in particular, freely visit the accused and interview him in private. He may also confer with any witnesses for the defence, including prisoners of war. He shall have the benefit of these facilities until the term of appeal or petition has expired.

Particulars of the charge or charges on which the prisoner of war is to be arraigned, as well as the documents which are generally communicated to the accused by virtue of the laws in force in the armed forces of the Detaining Power, shall be communicated to the accused prisoner of war in a language which he understands, and in good time before the opening of the trial. The same communication in the same circumstances shall be made to the advocate or counsel conducting the defence on behalf of the prisoner of war.

The representatives of the Protecting Power shall be entitled to attend the trial of the case, unless, exceptionally, this is held in camera in the interest of State security. In such a case the Detaining Power shall advise the Protecting Power accordingly.

Article 106
Every prisoner of war shall have, in the same manner as the members of the armed forces of the Detaining Power, the right of appeal or petition from any sentence pronounced upon him, with a view to the quashing or revising of the sentence or the reopening of the trial. He shall be fully informed of his rights to appeal or petition and of the time limit within which he may do so.

Article 107
Any judgment and sentence pronounced upon a prisoner of war shall be immediately reported to the Protecting Power in the form of a summary communication, which shall also indicate whether he has the right of appeal with a view to the quashing of the sentence or the reopening of the trial. This communication shall likewise be sent to the prisoners' representatives concerned. It shall also be sent to the accused prisoner of war in a language he understands, if the sentence was not pronounced in his presence. The Detaining Power shall

also immediately communicate to the Protecting Power the decision of the prisoner of war to use or to waive his right of appeal.

Furthermore, if a prisoner of war is finally convicted or if a sentence pronounced on a prisoner of war in the first instance is a death sentence, the Detaining Power shall as soon as possible address to the Protecting Power a detailed communication containing:
(1) the precise wording of the finding and sentence;
(2) a summarized report of any preliminary investigation and of the trial, emphasizing in particular the elements of the prosecution and the defence;
(3) notification, where applicable, of the establishment where the sentence will be served.
The communications provided for in the foregoing sub-paragraphs shall be sent to the Protecting Power at the address previously made known to the Detaining Power.

Article 108
Sentences pronounced on prisoners of war after a conviction has become duly enforceable, shall be served in the same establishment and under the same conditions as in the case of members of the armed forces of the Detaining Power. These conditions shall in all cases conform to the requirements of health and humanity.

A woman prisoner of war on whom such a sentence has been pronounced shall be confined in separate quarters and shall be under the supervision of women.

In any case, prisoners of war sentenced to a penalty depriving them of their liberty shall retain the benefit of the provisions of Articles 78 and 126 of the present Convention. Furthermore, they shall be entitled to receive and despatch correspondence, to receive at least one relief parcel monthly, to take regular exercise in the open air, to have the medical care required by their state of health, and the spiritual assistance they may desire. Penalties to which they may be subjected shall be in accordance with the provisions of Article 87, third paragraph.

Part IV
Termination of Captivity
Section I
Direct Repatriation and Accommodation in Neutral Countries
Article 109
Subject to the provisions of the third paragraph of this Article, Parties to the conflict are bound to send back to their own country, regardless of number or rank, seriously wounded and seriously sick prisoners of war, after having cared for them until they are fit to travel, in accordance with the first paragraph of the following Article.

Throughout the duration of hostilities, Parties to the conflict shall endeavour, with the cooperation of the neutral Powers concerned, to make arrangements for the accommodation in neutral countries of the sick and wounded prisoners of war referred to in the second paragraph of the following Article. They may, in addition, conclude agreements with a view to the direct repatriation or internment in a neutral country of able-bodied prisoners of war who have undergone a long period of captivity.

No sick or injured prisoner of war who is eligible for repatriation under the first paragraph of this Article, may be repatriated against his will during hostilities.

Article 110
The following shall be repatriated direct:
(1) Incurably wounded and sick whose mental or physical fitness seems to have been gravely diminished.
(2) Wounded and sick who, according to medical opinion, are not likely to recover within one year, whose condition requires treatment and whose mental or physical fitness seems to have been gravely diminished.
(3) Wounded and sick who have recovered, but whose mental or physical fitness seems to have been gravely and permanently diminished.

The following may be accommodated in a neutral country:
(1) Wounded and sick whose recovery may be expected within one year of the date of the wound or the beginning of the illness, if treatment in a neutral country might increase the prospects of a more certain and speedy recovery.
(2) Prisoners of war whose mental or physical health, according to medical opinion, is seriously threatened by continued captivity, but whose accommodation in a neutral country might remove such a threat.
The conditions which prisoners of war accommodated in a neutral country must fulfil in order to permit their repatriation shall be fixed, as shall likewise their status, by agreement between the Powers concerned. In general, prisoners of war who have been accommodated in a neutral country, and who belong to the following categories, should be repatriated:
(1) Those whose state of health has deteriorated so as to fulfil the conditions laid down for direct repatriation;
(2) Those whose mental or physical powers remain, even after treatment, considerably impaired.

If no special agreements are concluded between the Parties to the conflict concerned, to determine the cases of disablement or sickness entailing direct repatriation or accommodation in a neutral country, such cases shall be settled in accordance with the principles laid down in the Model Agreement concerning direct repatriation and accommodation in neutral countries of wounded and sick prisoners of war and in the Regulations concerning Mixed Medical Commissions annexed to the present Convention.

Article 111
The Detaining Power, the Power on which the prisoners of war depend, and a neutral Power agreed upon by these two Powers, shall endeavour to conclude agreements which will enable prisoners of war to be interned in the territory of the said neutral Power until the close of hostilities.

Article 112

Upon the outbreak of hostilities, Mixed Medical Commissions shall be appointed to examine sick and wounded prisoners of war, and to make all appropriate decisions regarding them. The appointment, duties and functioning of these Commissions shall be in conformity with the provisions of the Regulations annexed to the present Convention.

However, prisoners of war who, in the opinion of the medical authorities of the Detaining Power, are manifestly seriously injured or seriously sick, may be repatriated without having to be examined by a Mixed Medical Commission.

Article 113
Besides those who are designated by the medical authorities of the Detaining Power, wounded or sick prisoners of war belonging to the categories listed below shall be entitled to present themselves for examination by the Mixed Medical Commissions provided for in the foregoing Article:
(1) Wounded and sick proposed by a physician or surgeon who is of the same nationality, or a national of a Party to the conflict allied with the Power on which the said prisoners depend, and who exercises his functions in the camp.
(2) Wounded and sick proposed by their prisoners' representative.
(3) Wounded and sick proposed by the Power on which they depend, or by an organization duly recognized by the said Power and giving assistance to the prisoners.

Prisoners of war who do not belong to one of the three foregoing categories may nevertheless present themselves for examination by Mixed Medical Commissions, but shall be examined only after those belonging to the said categories.
The physician or surgeon of the same nationality as the prisoners who present themselves for examination by the Mixed Medical Commission, likewise the prisoners' representative of the said prisoners, shall have permission to be present at the examination.

Article 114
Prisoners of war who meet with accidents shall, unless the injury is self-inflicted, have the benefit of the provisions of this Convention as regards repatriation or accommodation in a neutral country.

Article 115
No prisoner of war on whom a disciplinary punishment has been imposed and who is eligible for repatriation or for accommodation in a neutral country, may be kept back on the plea that he has not undergone his punishment.

Prisoners of war detained in connection with a judicial prosecution or conviction and who are designated for repatriation or accommodation in a neutral country, may benefit by such measures before the end of the proceedings or the completion of the punishment, if the Detaining Power consents.

Parties to the conflict shall communicate to each other the names of those who will be detained until the end of the proceedings or the completion of the punishment.

Article 116
The cost of repatriating prisoners of war or of transporting them to a neutral country shall be borne, from the frontiers of the Detaining Power, by the Power on which the said prisoners depend.

Article 117
No repatriated person may be employed on active military service.

Section II
Release and Repatriation of Prisoners of War at the Close of Hostilities

Article 118
Prisoners of war shall be released and repatriated without delay after the cessation of active hostilities.

In the absence of stipulations to the above effect in any agreement concluded between the Parties to the conflict with a view to the cessation of hostilities, or failing any such agreement, each of the Detaining Powers shall itself establish and execute without delay a plan of repatriation in conformity with the principle laid down in the foregoing paragraph.

In either case, the measures adopted shall be brought to the knowledge of the prisoners of war.

The costs of repatriation of prisoners of war shall in all cases be equitably apportioned between the Detaining Power and the Power on which the prisoners depend. This apportionment shall be carried out on the following basis:
(a) If the two Powers are contiguous, the Power on which the prisoners of war depend shall bear the costs of repatriation from the frontiers of the Detaining Power.
(b) If the two Powers are not contiguous, the Detaining Power shall bear the costs of transport of prisoners of war over its own territory as far as its frontier or its port of embarkation nearest to the territory of the Power on which the prisoners of war depend. The Parties concerned shall agree between themselves as to the equitable apportionment of the remaining costs of the repatriation. The conclusion of this agreement shall in no circumstances justify any delay in the repatriation of the prisoners of war.

Article 119
Repatriation shall be effected in conditions similar to those laid down in Articles 46 to 48 inclusive of the present Convention for the transfer of prisoners of war, having regard to the provisions of Article 118 and to those of the following paragraphs.

On repatriation any articles of value impounded from prisoners of war under Article 18, and any foreign currency which has not been converted into the currency of the Detaining Power, shall be restored to them. Articles of value and foreign currency which, for any reason whatever, are not restored to prisoners of war on repatriation, shall be despatched to the Information Bureau set up under Article 122.

Prisoners of war shall be allowed to take with them their personal effects, and any correspondence and parcels which have arrived for them. The weight of such baggage may be limited, if the conditions of repatriation so require, to what each prisoner can reasonably carry. Each prisoner shall in all cases be authorized to carry at least twenty-five kilograms.

The other personal effects of the repatriated prisoner shall be left in charge of the Detaining Power which shall have them forwarded to him as soon as it has concluded an agreement to this effect, regulating the conditions of transport and the payment of the costs involved, with the Power on which the prisoner depends.

Prisoners of war against whom criminal proceedings for an indictable offence are pending may be detained until the end of such proceedings, and, if necessary, until the completion of the punishment. The same shall apply to prisoners of war already convicted for an indictable offence.

Parties to the conflict shall communicate to each other the names of any prisoners of war who are detained until the end of the proceedings or until punishment has been completed.

By agreement between the Parties to the conflict, commissions shall be established for the purpose of searching for dispersed prisoners of war and of assuring their repatriation with the least possible delay.

Section III
Death of Prisoners of War
Article 120

Wills of prisoners of war shall be drawn up so as to satisfy the conditions of validity required by the legislation of their country of origin, which will take steps to inform the Detaining Power of its requirements in this respect. At the request of the prisoner of war and, in all cases, after death, the will shall be transmitted without delay to the Protecting Power; a certified copy shall be sent to the Central Agency.

Death certificates, in the form annexed to the present Convention, or lists certified by a responsible officer, of all persons who die as prisoners of war shall be forwarded as rapidly as possible to the Prisoner of War Information Bureau established in accordance with Article 122. The death certificates or certified lists shall show particulars of identity as set out in the third paragraph of Article 17, and also the date and place of death, the cause of death, the date and place of burial and all particulars necessary to identify the graves.

The burial or cremation of a prisoner of war shall be preceded by a medical examination of the body with a view to confirming death and enabling a report to be made and, where necessary, establishing identity.

The detaining authorities shall ensure that prisoners of war who have died in captivity are honourably buried, if possible according to the rites of the religion to which they belonged, and that their graves are respected, suitably maintained and marked so as to be found at any time. Wherever possible, deceased prisoners of war who depended on the same Power shall be interred in the same place.

Deceased prisoners of war shall be buried in individual graves unless unavoidable circumstances require the use of collective graves. Bodies may be cremated only for imperative reasons of hygiene, on account of the religion of the deceased or in accordance with his express wish to this effect. In case of cremation, the fact shall be stated and the reasons given in the death certificate of the deceased.

In order that graves may always be found, all particulars of burials and graves shall be recorded with a Graves Registration Service established by the Detaining Power. Lists of graves and particulars of the prisoners of war interred in cemeteries and elsewhere shall be transmitted to the Power on which such prisoners of war depended. Responsibility for the care of these graves and for records of any subsequent moves of the bodies shall rest on the Power controlling the territory, if a Party to the present Convention. These provisions shall also apply to the ashes, which shall be kept by the Graves Registration Service until proper disposal thereof in accordance with the wishes of the home country.

Article 121
Every death or serious injury of a prisoner of war caused or suspected to have been caused by a sentry, another prisoner of war, or any other person, as well as any death the cause of which is unknown, shall be immediately followed by an official enquiry by the Detaining Power.

A communication on this subject shall be sent immediately to the Protecting Power. Statements shall be taken from witnesses, especially from those who are prisoners of war, and a report including such statements shall be forwarded to the Protecting Power.

If the enquiry indicates the guilt of one or more persons, the Detaining Power shall take all measures for the prosecution of the person or persons responsible.

Part V
Information Bureaux and Relief Societies for Prisoners of War
Article 122
Upon the outbreak of a conflict and in all cases of occupation, each of the Parties to the conflict shall institute an official Information Bureau for prisoners of war who are in its power. Neutral or non-belligerent Powers who may have received within their territory persons belonging to one of the categories referred to in Article 4, shall take the same action with respect to such persons. The Power concerned shall ensure that the Prisoners of War Information Bureau is provided with the necessary accommodation, equipment and staff to ensure its efficient working. It shall be at liberty to employ prisoners of war in such a Bureau under the conditions laid down in the Section of the present Convention dealing with work by prisoners of war.

Within the shortest possible period, each of the Parties to the conflict shall give its Bureau the information referred to in the fourth, fifth and sixth paragraphs of this Article regarding any enemy person belonging to one of the categories referred to in Article 4, who has fallen into its power. Neutral or non-belligerent Powers shall take the same action with regard to persons belonging to such categories whom they have received within their territory.

The Bureau shall immediately forward such information by the most rapid means to the Powers concerned, through the intermediary of the Protecting Powers and likewise of the Central Agency provided for in Article 123.

This information shall make it possible quickly to advise the next of kin concerned. Subject to the provisions of Article 17, the information shall include, in so far as available to the Information Bureau, in respect of each prisoner of war, his surname, first names, rank, army, regimental, personal or serial number, place and full date of birth, indication of the Power on which he depends, first name of the father and maiden name of the mother, name and address of the person to be informed and the address to which correspondence for the prisoner may be sent.

The Information Bureau shall receive from the various departments concerned information regarding transfer, releases, repatriations, escapes, admissions to hospital, and deaths, and shall transmit such information in the manner described in the third paragraph above.

Likewise, information regarding the state of health of prisoners of war who are seriously ill or seriously wounded shall be supplied regularly, every week if possible.

The Information Bureau shall also be responsible for replying to all enquiries sent to it concerning prisoners of war, including those who have died in captivity; it will make any enquiries necessary to obtain the information which is asked for if this is not in its possession.

All written communications made by the Bureau shall be authenticated by a signature or a seal.

The Information Bureau shall furthermore be charged with collecting all personal valuables, including sums in currencies other than that of the Detaining Power and documents of importance to the next of kin, left by prisoners of war who have been repatriated or released, or who have escaped or died, and shall forward the said valuables to the Powers concerned. Such articles shall be sent by the Bureau in sealed packets which shall be accompanied by statements giving clear and full particulars of the identity of the person to whom the articles belonged, and by a complete list of the contents of the parcel. Other personal effects of such prisoners of war shall be transmitted under arrangements agreed upon between the Parties to the conflict concerned.

Article 123

A Central Prisoners of War Information Agency shall be created in a neutral country. The

International Committee of the Red Cross shall, if it deems necessary, propose to the Powers concerned the organization of such an Agency.

The function of the Agency shall be to collect all the information it may obtain through official or private channels respecting prisoners of war, and to transmit it as rapidly as possible to the country of origin of the prisoners of war or to the Power on which they depend. It shall receive from the Parties to the conflict all facilities for effecting such transmissions.

The High Contracting Parties, and in particular those whose nationals benefit by the services of the Central Agency, are requested to give the said Agency the financial aid it may require.

The foregoing provisons shall in no way be interpreted as restricting the humanitarian activities of the International Committee of the Red Cross, or of the relief societies provided for in Article 125.

Article 124
The national Information Bureaux and the Central Information Agency shall enjoy free postage for mail, likewise all the exemptions provided for in Article 74, and further, so far as possible, exemption from telegraphic charges or, at least, greatly reduced rates.

Article 125
Subject to the measures which the Detaining Powers may consider essential to ensure their security or to meet any other reasonable need, the representatives of religious organizations, relief societies, or any other organization assisting prisoners of war, shall receive from the said Powers, for themselves and their duly accredited agents, all necessary facilities for visiting the prisoners, for distributing relief supplies and material, from any source, intended for religious, educational or recreative purposes, and for assisting them in organizing their leisure time within the camps. Such societies or organizations may be constituted in the territory of the Detaining Power or in any other country, or they may have an international character.

The Detaining Power may limit the number of societies and organizations whose delegates are allowed to carry out their activities in its territory and under its supervision, on condition, however, that such limitation shall not hinder the effective operation of adequate relief to all prisoners of war.

The special position of the International Committee of the Red Cross in this field shall be recognized and respected at all times.

As soon as relief supplies or material intended for the above-mentioned purposes are handed over to prisoners of war, or very shortly afterwards, receipts for each consignment, signed by the prisoners' representative, shall be forwarded to the relief society or organization making the shipment. At the same time, receipts for these consignments shall be supplied by the administrative authorities responsible for guarding the prisoners.

Protocol Additional to the Geneva Conventions of 12 August 1949, and relating to the Protection of Victims of International Armed Conflicts (Protocol 1)

Adopted on 8 June 1977 by the Diplomatic Conference on the Reaffirmation and Development of International Humanitarian Law applicable in Armed Conflicts, entry into force 7 December 1979, in accordance with Article 95

Preamble

The High Contracting Parties,

Proclaiming their earnest wish to see peace prevail among peoples,
Recalling that every State has the duty, in conformity with the Charter of the United Nations, to refrain in its international relations from the threat or use of force against the sovereignty, territorial integrity or political independence of any State, or in any other manner inconsistent with the purposes of the United Nations;
Believing it necessary nevertheless to reaffirm and develop the provisions protecting the victims of armed conflicts and to supplement measures intended to reinforce their application,;
Expressing their conviction that nothing in this Protocol or in the Geneva Conventions of 12 August 1949 can be construed as legitimizing or authorizing any act of aggression or any other use of force inconsistent with the Charter of the United Nations;
Reaffirming further that the provisions of the Geneva Conventions of 12 August 1949 and of this Protocol must be fully applied in all circumstances to all persons who are protected by those instruments, without any adverse distinction based on the nature or origin of the armed conflict or on the causes espoused by or attributed to the Parties to the conflicts;

Have agreed on the following:

PART I

GENERAL PROVISIONS

Article 1.- General principles and scope of application

1. The High Contracting Parties undertake to respect and to ensure respect for this Protocol in all circumstances.

2. In cases not covered by this Protocol or by other international agreements, civilians and combatants remain under the protection and authority of the principles of international law derived from established custom, from the principles of humanity and from the dictates of public conscience.

3. This Protocol, which supplements the Geneva Conventions of 12 August 1949 for the protection of war victims, shall apply in the situations referred to in Article 2 common to those Conventions.

4. The situations referred to in the preceding paragraph include armed conflicts in which peoples are

fighting against colonial domination and alien occupation and against racist regimes in the exercise of their right of self-determination, as enshrined in the Charter of the United Nations and the Declaration on Principles of International Law concerning Friendly Relations and Co-operation among States in accordance with the Charter of the United Nations ....

Article 3. Beginning and end of application

Without prejudice to the provisions which are applicable at all times:
(a) The Conventions and this Protocol shall apply from the beginning of any situation referred to in Article 1 of this Protocol;
(b) The application of the Conventions and of this Protocol shall cease, in the territory of Parties to the conflict, on the general close of military operations and, in the case of occupied territories, on the termination of the occupation, except, in either circumstance, for those persons whose final release, repatriation or re-establishment takes place thereafter. These persons shall continue to benefit from the relevant provisions of the Conventions and of this Protocol until their final release, repatriation or re-establishment.

Article 4. Legal status of the Parties to the conflict

The application of the Conventions and of this Protocol, as well as the conclusion of the agreements provided for therein, shall not affect the legal status of the Parties to the conflict. Neither the occupation of a territory nor the application of the Conventions and this Protocol shall affect the legal status of the territory in question.

Article 5. Appointment of Protecting Powers and of their substitute

1. It is the duty of the Parties to a conflict from the beginning of that conflict to secure the supervision and implementation of the Conventions and of this Protocol by the application of the system of Protecting Powers, including inter alia the designation and acceptance of those Powers, in accordance with the following paragraphs. Protecting Powers shall have the duty of safeguarding the interests of the Parties to the conflict.

2. From the beginning of a situation referred to in Article each Party to the conflict shall without delay designate a Protecting Power for the purpose of applying the Conventions and this Protocol and shall, likewise without delay and for the same purpose, permit the activities of a Protecting Power which has been accepted by it as such after designation by the adverse Party.

3. If a Protecting Power has not been designated or accepted from the beginning of a situation referred to in Article 1, the International Committee of the Red Cross, without prejudice to the right of any other impartial humanitarian organization to do likewise, shall offer its good offices to the Parties to the conflict with a view to the designation without delay of a Protecting Power to which the Parties to the conflict

consent. For that purpose it may, inter alia, ask each Party to provide it with a list of at least five States which that Party considers acceptable to act as Protecting Power on its behalf in relation to an adverse Party, and ask each adverse Party to provide a list of at least five States which it would accept as the Protecting Power of the first Party; these lists shall be communicated to the Committee within two weeks after the receipt of the request; it shall compare them and seek the agreement of any proposed State named on both lists.

4. If, despite the foregoing, there is no Protecting Power, the Parties to the conflict shall accept without delay an offer which may be made by the International Committee of the Red Cross or by any other organization which offers all guarantees of impartiality and efficacy, after due consultations with the said Parties and taking into account the result of these consultations, to act as a substitute. The functioning of such a substitute is subject to the consent of the Parties to the conflict; every effort shall be made by the Parties to the conflict to facilitate the operations of the substitute in the performance of its tasks under the Conventions and this Protocol.

5. In accordance with Article 4, the designation and acceptance of Protecting Powers for the purpose of applying the Conventions and this Protocol shall not affect the legal status of the Parties to the conflict or of any territory, including occupied territory.

6. The maintenance of diplomatic relations between Parties to the conflict or the entrusting of the protection of a Party's interests and those of its nationals to a third State in accordance with the rules of international law relating to diplomatic relations is no obstacle to the designation of Protecting Powers for the purpose of applying the Conventions and this Protocol.

7. Any subsequent mention in this Protocol of a Protecting Power includes also a substitute.

Article 6. Qualified persons

1. The High Contracting Parties shall, also in peacetime, endeavour, with the assistance of the national Red Cross (Red Crescent, Red Lion and Sun) Societies, to train qualified personnel to facilitate the application of the Conventions and of this Protocol, and in particular the activities of the Protecting Powers.

2. The recruitment and training of such personnel are within domestic jurisdiction.

3. The International Committee of the Red Cross shall hold at the disposal of the High Contracting Parties the lists of persons so trained which the High Contracting Parties may have established and may have transmitted to it for that purpose.

4. The conditions governing the employment of such personnel outside the national territory shall, in each case, be the subject of special agreements between the Parties concerned.

Article 7. Meetings

The depositary of this Protocol shall convene a meeting of the High Contracting Parties, at the request of one or more of the said Parties and upon the approval of the majority of the said Parties, to consider general problems concerning the application of the Conventions and of the Protocol....

PART II
WOUNDED, SICK AND SHIPWRECKED
SECTION I. GENERAL PROTECTION

Article 11. Protection of persons

1. The physical or mental health and integrity of persons who are in the power of the adverse Party or who are interned, detained or otherwise deprived of liberty as a result of a situation referred to in Article I shall not be endangered by any unjustified act or omission. Accordingly, it is prohibited to subject the persons described in this Article to any medical procedure which is not indicated by the state of health of the person concerned and which is not consistent with generally accepted medical standards which would be applied under similar medical circumstances to persons who are nationals of the Party conducting the procedure and who are in no way deprived of liberty.

2. It is, in particular, prohibited to carry out on such persons, even with their consent:
(a) Physical mutilations;
(b) Medical or scientific experiments;
(c) Removal of tissue or organs for transplantation, except where these acts are justified in conformity with the conditions provided for in paragraph 1 ....

4. Any wilful act or omission which seriously endangers the physical or mental health or integrity of any person who is in the power of a Party other than the one on which he depends and which either violates any of the prohibitions in paragraphs 1 and 2 or fails to comply with the requirements of paragraph 3 shall be a grave breach of this Protocol....

PART III
COMBATANT AND PRISONER-OF-WAR STATUS

Article 37. Prohibition of perfidy

1. It is prohibited to kill, injure or capture an adversary by resort to perfidy. Acts inviting the confidence of an adversary to lead him to believe that he is entitled to, or is obliged to accord, protection under the rules of international law applicable in armed conflict, with intent to betray that confidence, shall constitute perfidy. The following acts are examples of perfidy:
(a) The feigning of an intent to negotiate under a flag of truce or of a surrender;
(b) The feigning of an incapacitation by wounds or sickness;
(c) The feigning of civilian, non-combatant status; and
(d) The feigning of protected status by the use of signs, emblems or uniforms of the United Nations or of

neutral or other States not Parties to the conflict.

2. Ruses of war are not prohibited. Such ruses are acts which are intended to mislead an adversary or to induce him to act recklessly but which infringe no rule of international law applicable in armed conflict and which are not perfidious because they do not invite the confidence of an adversary with respect to protection under that law. The following are examples of such ruses: the use of camouflage, decoys, mock operations and misinformation ....

Article 40. Quarter

It is prohibited to order that there shall be no survivors, to threaten an adversary therewith or to conduct hostilities on this basis.

Article 41. Safeguard of an enemy hors de combat

1. A person who is recognized or who, in the circumstances, should be recognized to be hors de combat shall not be made the object of attack.

2. A person is hors de combat if:
(a) He is in the power of an adverse Party;
(b) He clearly expresses an intention to surrender; or
(c) He has been rendered unconscious or is otherwise incapacitated by wounds or sickness, and therefore is incapable of defending himself, provided that in any of these cases he abstains from any hostile act and does not attempt to escape.

3. When persons entitled to protection as prisons of war have fallen into the power of an adverse Party under unusual conditions of combat which prevent their evacuation as provided for in Part m, Section I, of the Third Convention, they shall be released and all feasible precautions shall be taken to ensure their safety.

Article 42. Occupants of aircraft

1. No person parachuting from an aircraft in distress shall be made the object of attack during his descent.

2. Upon reaching the ground in territory controlled by an adverse Party, a person who has parachuted from an aircraft in distress shall be given an opportunity to surrender before being made the object of attack, unless it is apparent that he is engaging in a hostile act.

3. Airborne troops are not protected by this Article.

SECTION. COMBATANT AND PRISONER-OF-WAR STATUS

Article 43. Armed forces

1. The armed forces of a Party to a conflict consist of all organized armed forces, groups and units which are under a command responsible to that Party for the conduct of its subordinates, even if that Party is represented by a government or an authority not recognized by an adverse Party. Such armed forces shall be subject to an internal disciplinary system which, inter alia, shall enforce compliance with the rules of

international law applicable in armed conflict.

2. Members of the armed forces of a Party to a conflict (other than medical personnel and chaplains covered by Article 33 of the Third Convention) are combatants, that is to say, they have the right to participate directly in hostilities.

3. Whenever a Party to a conflict incorporates a paramilitary or armed law enforcement agency into its armed forces it shall so notify the other Parties to the conflict.

Article 44. Combatants and prisoners of war

1. Any combatant, as defined in Article 43, who falls into the power of an adverse Party shall be a prisoner of war.

2. While all combatants are obliged to comply with the rules of international law applicable in armed conflict, violations of these rules shall not deprive a combatant of his right to be a combatant or, if he falls into the power of an adverse Party, of his right to be a prisoner of war, except as provided in paragraphs 3 and 4.

3. In order to promote the protection of the civilian population from the effects of hostilities, combatants are obliged to distinguish themselves from the civilian population while they are engaged in an attack or in a military operation preparatory to an attack. Recognizing, however, that there are situations in armed conflicts where, owing to the nature of the hostilities an armed combatant cannot so distinguish himself, he shall retain his status as a combatant, provided that, in such situations, he carries his arms openly:
(a) During each military engagement, and
(b) During such time as he is visible to the adversary while he is engaged in a military deployment preceding the launching of an attack in which he is to participate.
Acts which comply with the requirements of this paragraph shall not be considered as perfidious within the meaning of Article 37, paragraph 1 (c).

4. A combatant who falls into the power of an adverse Party while failing to meet the requirements set forth in the second sentence of paragraph 3 shall forfeit his right to be a prisoner of war, but he shall, nevertheless, be given protections equivalent in all respects to those accorded to prisoners of war by the Third Convention and by this Protocol. This protection includes protections equivalent to those accorded to prisoners of war by the Third Convention in the case where such a person is tried and punished for any offences he has committed.

5. Any combatant who falls into the power of an adverse Party while not engaged in an attack or in a military operation preparatory to an attack shall not forfeit his rights to be a combatant and a prisoner of war by virtue of his prior activities.

6. This Article is without prejudice to the right of any person to be a prisoner of war pursuant to Article 4 of the Third Convention.

7. This Article is not intended to change the generally accepted practice of States with respect to the wearing of the uniform by combatants assigned to the regular, uniformed armed units of a Party to the conflict.

8. In addition to the categories of persons mentioned in Article 13 of the First and Second Conventions, all members of the armed forces of a Party to the conflict, as defined in Article 43 of this Protocol, shall be entitled to protection under those Conventions if they are wounded or sick or, in the case of the Second Convention, shipwrecked at sea or in other waters.

Article 45. Protection of persons who have taken part in hostilities

1. A person who takes part in hostilities and falls into the power of an adverse Party shall be presumed to be a prisoner of war, and therefore shall be protected by the Third Convention, if he claims the status of prisoner of war, or if he appears to be entitled to such status, or if the Party on which he depends claims such status on his behalf by notification to the detaining Power or to the Protecting Power. Should any doubt arise as to whether any such person is entitled to the status of prisoner of war, he shall continue to have such status and, therefore, to be protected by the Third Convention and this Protocol until such time as his status has been determined by a competent tribunal.

2. If a person who has fallen into the power of an adverse Party is not held as a prisoner of war and is to be tried by that Party for an offence arising out of the hostilities, he shall have the right to assert his entitlement to prisoner-of-war status before a judicial tribunal and to have that question adjudicated. Whenever possible under the applicable procedure, this adjudication shall occur before the trial for the offence. The representatives of the Protecting Power shall be entitled to attend the proceedings in which that question is adjudicated, unless, exceptionally, the proceedings are held in camera in the interest of State security. In such a case the detaining Power shall advise the Protecting Power accordingly.

3. Any person who has taken part in hostilities, who is not entitled to prisoner-of-war status and who does not benefit from more favourable treatment in accordance with the Fourth Convention shall have the right at all times to the protection of Article 75 of this Protocol. In occupied territory, an such person, unless he is held as a spy, shall also be entitled, notwithstanding Article 5 of the Fourth Convention, to his rights of communication under that Convention.

Article 46. Spies

1. Notwithstanding any other provision of the Conventions or of this Protocol, any member of the armed forces of a Party to the conflict who falls into the power of an adverse Party while engaging in espionage shall not have the right to the status of prisoner of war and may be treated as a spy.

2. A member of the armed forces of a

Party to the conflict who, on behalf of that Party and in territory controlled by an adverse Party, gathers or attempts to gather information shall not be considered as engaging in espionage if, while so acting, he is in the uniform of his armed forces.

3. A member of the armed forces of a Party to the conflict who is a resident of territory occupied by an adverse Party and who, on behalf of the Party on which he depends, gathers or attempts to gather information of military value within that territory shall not be considered as engaging in espionage unless he does so through an act of false pretences or deliberately in a clandestine manner. Moreover, such a resident shall not lose his right to the status of prisoner of war and may not be treated as a spy unless he is captured while engaging in espionage.

4. A member of the armed forces of a Patty to the conflict who is not a resident of territory occupied by an adverse Party and who has engaged in espionage in that territory shall not lose his right to the status of prisoner of war and may not be treated as a spy unless he is captured before he has rejoined the armed forces to which he belongs.

Article 47. Mercenaries

1. A mercenary shall not have the right to be a combatant or a prisoner of war.

2. A mercenary is any person who:
(a) Is specially recruited locally or abroad in order to fight in an armed conflict;
(b) Does, in fact, take a direct part in the hostilities;
(c) Is motivated to take part in the hostilities essentially by the desire for private gain and, in fact, is promised, by or on behalf of a Party to the conflict, material compensation substantially in excess of that promised or paid to combatants of similar ranks and functions in the armed forces of that Party;
(d) Is neither a national of a Party to the conflict nor a resident of territory controlled by a Party to the conflict;
(e) Is not a member of the armed forces of a Party to the conflict; and
(f) Has not been sent by a State which is not a Party to the conflict on official duty as a member of its armed forces.

PART IV
CIVILIAN POPULATION
SECTION I.-GENERAL PROTECTION AGAINST EFFECTS OF HOSTILITIES...

Article 50. Definition of civilians and civilian population

1. A civilian is any person who does not belong to one of the categories of persons referred to in Article 4 A (1), (2), (3) and (6) of the Third Convention and in Article 43 of this Protocol. In case of doubt whether a person is a civilian, that person shall be considered to be a civilian.

2. The civilian population comprises all persons who are civilians.

3. The presence within the civilian population of individuals who do not come within the definition of civilians does not deprive the

population of its civilian character.

Article 51. Protection of the civilian population

1. The civilian population and individual civilians shall enjoy general protection against dangers arising from military operations. To give effect to this protection, the following rules, which are additional to other applicable rules of international law, shall be observed in circumstances.

2. The civilian population as such, as well as individual civilians, shall not be the object of attack. Acts or threats of violence the primary purpose of which is to spread terror among the civilian population are prohibited.

3. Civilians shall enjoy the protection afforded by this Section, unless and for such time as they take a direct part in hostilities.

4. Indiscriminate attacks are prohibited. Indiscriminate attacks are:
(a) Those which are not directed at a specific military objective;
(b) Those which employ a method or means of combat which cannot be directed at a specific military objective; or
(c) Those which employ a method or means of combat the effects of which cannot be limited as required by this Protocol; and consequently, in each such case, are of a nature to strike military objectives and civilians or civilian objects without distinction.

5. Among others, the following types of attacks are to be considered as indiscriminate:
(a) An attack by bombardment by any methods or means which treats as a single military objective a number of clearly separated and distinct military objectives located in a city, town, village or other area containing a similar concentration of civilians or civilian objects; and
(b) An attack which may be expected to cause incidental loss of civilian life, injury to civilians, damage to civilian objects, or a combination thereof, which would be excessive in relation to the concrete and direct military advantage anticipated.

6. Attacks against the civilian population or civilians by way of reprisals are prohibited.

7. The presence or movements of the civilian population or individual civilians shall not be used to render certain points or areas immune from military operations, in particular in attempts to shield military objectives from attacks or to shield, favour or impede military operations. The Parties to the conflict shall not direct the movement of the civilian population or individual civilians in order to attempt to shield military objectives from attacks or to shield military operations.

8. Any violation of these prohibitions shall not release the Parties to the conflict from their legal obligations with respect to the civilian population and civilians, including the obligation to take the precautionary measures provided for in Article 57 ....

SECTION III.-TREATMENT OF PERSONS IN THE POWER OF A PARTY TO THE CONFLICT
CHAPTER 1.-FIELD OF

APPLICATION AND PROTECTION OF PERSONS AND OBJECTS

Article 73. Refugees and stateless persons

Persons who, before the beginning of hostilities, were considered as stateless persons or refugees under the relevant international instruments accepted by the Parties concerned or under the national legislation of the State of refuge or State of residence shall be protected persons within the meaning of Parts I and III of the Fourth Convention, in all circumstances and without any adverse distinction.

Article 75. Fundamental guarantees

1. In so far as they are affected by a situation referred to in Article 1 of this Protocol, persons who are in the power of a Party to the conflict and who do not benefit from more favourable treatment under the Conventions or under this Protocol shall be treated humanely in all circumstances and shall enjoy, as a minimum, the protection provided by this Article without any adverse distinction based upon race, colour, sex, language, religion or belief, political or other opinion, national or social origin, wealth, birth or other status, or on any other similar criteria. Each Party shall respect the person, honour, convictions and religious practices of all such persons.

2. The following acts are and shall remain prohibited at any time and in any place whatsoever, whether committed by civilian or by military agents:

(a) Violence to the life, health, or physical or mental well-being of persons, in particular:
(i) Murder;
(ii) Torture of all kinds, whether physical or mental;
(iii) Corporal punishment ; and
(iv) Mutilation;
(b) Outrages upon personal dignity, in particular humiliating and degrading treatment, enforced prostitution and any form of indecent assault;
(c) The taking of hostages;
(d) Collective punishments; and
(e) Threats to commit any of the foregoing acts.

3. Any person arrested, detained or interned for actions related to the armed conflict shall be informed promptly, in a language he understands, of the reasons why these measures have been taken. Except in cases of arrest or detention for penal offences, such persons shall be released with the minimum delay possible and in any event as soon as the circumstances justifying the arrest, detention or internment have ceased to exist.

4. No sentence may be passed and no penalty may be executed on a person found guilty of a penal offence related to the armed conflict except pursuant to a conviction pronounced by an impartial and regularly constituted court respecting the generally recognized principles of regular judicial procedure, which include the following:
(a) The procedure shall provide for an accused to be informed without delay of the particulars of the offence alleged against him and shall afford

the accused before and during his trial all necessary rights and means of defence;
(b) No one shall be convicted of an offence except on the basis of individual penal responsibility;
(c) No one shall be accused or convicted of a criminal offence on account of any act or omission which did not constitute a criminal offence under the national or international law to which he was subject at the time when it was committed; nor shall a heavier penalty be imposed than that which was applicable at the time when the criminal offence was committed; if, after the commission of the offence, provision is made by law for the imposition of a lighter penalty, the offender shall benefit thereby;
(d) Anyone charged with an offence is presumed innocent until proved guilt according to law;
(e) Anyone charged with an offence shall have the right to be tried in his presence;
(f) No one shall be compelled to testify against himself or to confess guilt;
(g) Anyone charged with an offence shall have the right to examine, or have examined, the witnesses against him and to obtain the attendance and examination of witnesses on his behalf under the same conditions as witnesses against him;
(h) No one shall be prosecuted or punished by the same Party for an offence in respect of which a final judgement acquitting or convicting that person has been previously pronounced under the same law and judicial procedure;
(i) Anyone prosecuted for an offence shall have the right to have the judgement pronounced publicly; and
(i) A convicted person shall be advised on conviction of his judicial and other remedies and of the time-limits within which they may be exercised.

5. Women whose liberty has been restricted for reasons related to the armed conflict shall be held in quarters separated from men's quarters. They shall be under the immediate supervision of women. Nevertheless, in cases where families are detained or interned, they shall, whenever possible, be held in the same place and accommodated as family units.

6. Persons who are arrested, detained or interned for reasons related to the armed conflict shall enjoy the protection provided by this Article until their final release, repatriation or re-establishment, even after the end of the armed conflict.

7. In order to avoid any doubt concerning the prosecution and trial of persons accused of war crimes or crimes against humanity, the following principles shall apply:
(a) Persons who are accused of such crimes should be submitted for the purpose of prosecution and trial in accordance with the applicable rules of international law; and
(b) Any such persons who do not benefit from more favourable treatment under the Conventions or this Protocol shall be accorded the treatment provided by this Article, whether or not the crimes of which they are accused constitute grave breaches of the Conventions or of this Protocol.

8. No provision of this Article may be construed as limiting or infringing any other more favourable provision granting greater protection, under any applicable rules of international law, to persons covered by paragraph 1.

CHAPTER 11.-MEASURES IN FAVOUR OF WOMEN AND CHILDREN

Article 76. Protection of women

1. Women shall be the object of special respect and shall be protected in particular against rape, forced prostitution and any other form of indecent assault.

2. Pregnant women and mothers having dependent infants who are arrested, detained or interned for reasons related to the armed conflict, shall have their cases considered with the utmost priority.

3. To the maximum extent feasible, the Parties to the conflict shall endeavour to avoid the pronouncement of the death penalty on pregnant women or mothers having dependent infants, for an offence related to the armed conflict. The death penalty for such offences shall not be executed on such women.

Article 77. Protection of children

1. Children shall be the object of special respect and shall be protected against any form of indecent assault. The Parties to the conflict shall provide them with the care and aid they require, whether because of their age or for any other reason.

2. The Parties to the conflict shall take all feasible measures in order that children who have not attained the age of fifteen years do not take a direct part in hostilities and, in particular, they shall refrain from recruiting them into their armed forces. In recruiting among those persons who have attained the age of fifteen years but who have not attained the age of eighteen years, the Parties to the conflict shall endeavour to give priority to those who are oldest.

3. If, in exceptional cases, despite the provisions of paragraph 2, children who have not attained the age of fifteen years take a direct part in hostilities and fall into the power of an adverse Party, they shall continue to benefit from the special protection accorded by this Article, whether or not they are prisoners of war.

4. If arrested, detained or interned for reasons related to the armed conflict, children shall be held in quarters separate from the quarters of adults, except where families are accommodated as family units as provided in Article 75, paragraph 5.

5. The death penalty for an offence related to armed conflict shall not be executed on persons who had not attained the age of eighteen years at the time the offence was committed

....

CHAPTER III. JOURNALISTS

Article 79. Measures of protection for journalists

1. Journalists engaged in dangerous

professional missions in areas of armed conflict shall be considered as civilians within the meaning of Article 50, paragraph 1.

2. They shall be protected as such under the Conventions and this Protocol, provided that they take no action adversely affecting their status as civilians, and without prejudice to the right of war correspondents accredited to the armed forces to the status provided for in Article 4 A (4) of the Third Convention.

3. They may obtain an identity card similar to the model in Annex II of this Protocol. This card, which shall be issued by the government of the State of which the journalist is a national or in whose territory he resides or in which the news medium employing him is located, shall attest to his status as a journalist.

PART V EXECUTION OF THE CONVENTIONS AND OF THIS PROTOCOL
SECTION I. GENERAL PROVISIONS...

Article 81. Activities of the Red Cross and other humanitarian organizations

1. The Parties to the conflict shall grant to the International Committee of the Red Cross all facilities within their power so as to enable it to carry out the humanitarian functions assigned to it by the Conventions and this Protocol in order to ensure protection and assistance to the victims of conflicts; the International Committee of the Red Cross may also carry out any other humanitarian activities in favour of these victims, subject to the consent of the Parties to the conflict concerned.

2. The Parties to the conflict shall grant to their respective Red Cross (Red Crescent, Red Lion and Sun) organizations the facilities necessary for carrying out their humanitarian activities in favour of the victims of the conflict, in accordance with the provisions of the Conventions and this Protocol and the fundamental principles of the Red Cross as formulated by the International Conferences of the Red Cross.

3. The High Contracting Parties and the Parties to the conflict shall facilitate in every possible way the assistance which Red Cross (Red Crescent, Red Lion and Sun) organizations and the League of Red Cross Societies extend to the victims of conflicts in accordance with the provisions of the Conventions and this Protocol and with the fundamental principles of the Red Cross as formulated by the International Conferences of the Red Cross.

4. The High Contracting Parties and the Parties to the conflict shall, as far as possible, make facilities similar to those mentioned in paragraphs 2 and 3 available to the other humanitarian organizations referred to in the Conventions and this Protocol which are duly authorized by the respective Parties to the conflict and which perform their humanitarian activities in accordance with the provisions of the Conventions and this Protocol.

SECTION II. REPRESSION OF BREACHES OF THE CONVENTIONS AND OF THIS PROTOCOL

Article 85. Repression of breaches of this Protocol

1. The provisions of the Conventions relating to the repression of breaches and grave breaches, supplemented by this Section, shall apply to the repression of breaches and grave breaches of this Protocol.

2. Acts described as grave breaches in the Conventions are grave breaches of this Protocol if committed against persons in the power of an adverse Party protected by Articles 44, 45 and 73 of this Protocol, or against the wounded, sick and shipwrecked of the adverse Party who are protected by this Protocol, or against those medical or religious personnel, medical units or medical transports which are under the control of the adverse Party and are protected by this Protocol.

3. In addition to the grave breaches defined in Article 11, the following acts shall be regarded as grave breaches of this Protocol, when committed wilfully, in violation of the relevant provisions of this Protocol, and causing death or serious injury to body or health:
(a) Making the civilian population or individual civilians the object of attack;
(b) Launching an indiscriminate attack affecting the civilian population or civilian objects in the knowledge that such attack will cause excessive loss of life, injury to civilians or damage to civilian objects, as defined in Article 57, paragraph 2 (a) (iii);
(c) Launching an attack against works or installations containing dangerous forces in the knowledge that such attack will cause excessive loss of life, injury to civilians or damage to civilian objects, as defined in Article 57, paragraph 2 (a) (iii);
(d) Making non-defended localities and demilitarized zones the object of attack;
(e) Making a person the object of attack in the knowledge that he is hors de combat;
(f) the perfidious use, in violation of Article 37, of the distinctive emblem of the red cross, red crescent or red lion and sun or of other protective signs recognized by the Conventions or this Protocol.

4. In addition to the grave breaches defined in the preceding paragraphs and in the Conventions, the following shall be regarded as grave breaches of this Protocol, when committed wilfully and in violation of the Conventions of the Protocol;
(a) The transfer by the Occupying Power of parts of its own civilian population into the territory it occupies, or the deportation or transfer of all or parts of the population of the occupied territory within or outside this territory, in violation of Article 49 of the Fourth Convention;
(b) Unjustifiable delay in the repatriation of prisoners of war or civilians;
(c) Practices of apartheid and other inhuman and degrading practices involving outrages upon personal dignity, based on racial discrimination;

(d) Making the clearly-recognized historic monuments, works of art or places of worship which constitute the cultural or spiritual heritage of peoples and to which special protection has been given by special arrangement, for example, within the framework of a competent international
organization, the object of attack, causing as a result extensive destruction thereof, where there is no evidence of the violation by the adverse Party of Article 53, sub-paragraph (b), and when such historic monuments, works of art and places of worship are not located in the immediate proximity of military objectives:
(e) Depriving a person protected by the Conventions or referred to in paragraph 2 of this Article of the rights of fair and regular trial.

5. Without prejudice to the application of the Conventions and of this Protocol, grave breaches of these instruments shall be regarded as war crimes.

Article 86. Failure to act

1. The High Contracting Parties and the Parties to the conflict shall repress grave breaches, and take measures necessary to suppress all other breaches, of the Conventions or of this Protocol which result from a failure to act when under a duty to do so.

2. The fact that a breach of the Conventions or of this Protocol was committed by a subordinate does not absolve his superiors from penal or disciplinary responsibility, as the case may be, if they knew, or had information which should have enabled them to conclude in the circumstances at the time, that he was committing or was going to commit such a breach and if they did not take all feasible measures within their power to prevent or repress the breach.

Article 87. Duty of commanders

1. The High Contracting Parties and the Parties to the conflict shall require military commanders, with respect to members of the armed forces under their command and other persons under their control, to prevent and, where necessary, to suppress and to report to competent authorities breaches of the Conventions and of this Protocol.

2. In order to prevent and suppress breaches, High Contracting Parties and Parties to the conflict shall require that, commensurate with their level of responsibility, commanders ensure that members of the armed forces under their command are aware of their obligations under the Conventions and this Protocol.

3. The High Contracting Parties and Parties to the conflict shall require any commander who is aware that subordinates or other persons under his control are going to commit or have committed a breach of the Conventions or of this Protocol, to initiate such steps as are necessary to prevent such violations of the Conventions or this Protocol, and, where appropriate, to initiate disciplinary or penal action against violators thereof.

Article 88. Mutual assistance in criminal matters

1. The High Contracting Parties shall afford one another the greatest measure of assistance in connexion with criminal proceedings brought in respect of grave breaches of the Conventions or of this Protocol.

2. Subject to the rights and obligations established in the Conventions and in Article 85, paragraph 1, of this Protocol, and when circumstances permit, the High Contracting Parties shall co-operate in the matter of extradition. They shall give due consideration to the request of the State in whose territory the alleged offence has occurred.

3. The law of the High Contracting Party requested shall apply in all cases. The provisions of the preceding paragraphs shall not, however, affect the obligations arising from the provisions of any other treaty of a bilateral or multilateral nature which governs or will govern the whole or part of the subject of mutual assistance in criminal matters.

Article 89. Co-operation

In situations of serious violations of the Conventions or of this Protocol, the High Contracting Parties undertake to act, jointly or individually, in co-operation with the United Nations and in conformity with the United Nations Charter ....

Protocol Additional to the Geneva Conventions of 12 August 1949, and Relating to the Protection of Victims of Non-International Armed Conflicts (Protocol II)

Adopted on 8 June 1977 by the Diplomatic Conference on the Reaffirmation and Development of International Humanitarian Law applicable in Armed Conflicts, entry into force 7 December 1978, in accordance with Article 23

Preamble

The High Contracting Parties,

Recalling that the humanitarian principles enshrined in Article 3 common to the Geneva Conventions of 12 August 1949 constitute the foundation of respect for the human person in cases of armed conflict not of an international character;

Recalling furthermore that international instruments relating to human rights offer a basic protection to the human person;

Emphasizing the need to ensure a better protection for the victims of those armed conflicts;

Recalling that, in cases not covered by the law in force, the human person remains under the protection of the principles of humanity and the dictates of the public conscience;

Have agreed on the following:

PART I
SCOPE OF THIS PROTOCOL

Article 1. Material field of application

1. This Protocol, which develops and supplements Article 3 common to the Geneva Conventions of 12 August 1949 without modifying its

existing conditions of application, shall apply to all armed conflicts which are not covered by Article 1 of the Protocol Additional to the Geneva Conventions of 12 August 1949, and relating to the Protection of Victims of International Armed Conflicts (Protocol I) and which take place in the territory of a High Contracting Party between its armed forces and dissident armed forces or other organized armed groups which, under responsible command, exercise such control over a part of its territory as to enable them to carry out sustained and concerted military operations and to implement this Protocol.

2. This Protocol shall not apply to situations of internal disturbances and tensions, such as riots, isolated and sporadic acts of violence and other acts of a similar nature, as not being armed conflicts.

Article 2. Personal field of application

1. This Protocol shall be applied without any adverse distinction founded on race, colour, sex, language, religion or belief, political or other opinion, national or social origin, wealth, birth or other status, or on any other similar criteria (hereinafter referred to as "adverse distinction") to all persons affected by an armed conflict as defined in Article 1.

2. At the end of the armed conflict, all the persons who have been deprived of their liberty or whose liberty has been restricted for reasons related to such conflict, as well as those deprived of their liberty or whose liberty is restricted after the conflict for the same reasons, shall enjoy the protection of Articles 5 and 6 until the end of such deprivation or restriction of liberty ....

PART II
HUMANE TREATMENT

Article 4. Fundamental guarantees

1. All persons who do not take a direct part or who have ceased to take part in hostilities, whether or not their liberty has been restricted, are entitled to respect for their person, honour and convictions and religious practices. They shall in all circumstances be treated humanely, without any adverse distinction. It is prohibited to order that there shall be no survivors.

2. Without prejudice to the generality of the foregoing, the following acts against the persons referred to in paragraph I are and shall remain prohibited at any time and in any place whatsoever:
(a) Violence to the life, health and physical or mental well-being of persons, in particular murder as well as cruel treatment such as torture, mutilation or any form of corporal punishment;
(b) Collective punishments;
(c) Taking of hostages;
(d) Acts of terrorism;
(e) Outrages upon personal dignity, in particular humiliating and degrading treatment, rape, enforced prostitution and any form of indecent assault;
(f)Slavery and the slave trade in all their forms;
(g) Pillage;

(h) Threats to commit any of the foregoing acts.

3. Children shall be provided with the care and aid they require, and in particular:
(a) They shall receive an education, including religious and moral education, in keeping with the wishes of their parents, or in the absence of parents, of those responsible for their care;
(b) All appropriate steps shall be taken to facilitate the reunion of families temporarily separated;
(c) Children who have not attained the age of fifteen years shall neither be recruited in the armed forces or groups nor allowed to take part in hostilities;
(d) The special protection provided by this Article to children who have not attained the age of fifteen years shall remain applicable to them if they take a direct part in hostilities despite the provisions of sub-paragraph (c) and are captured;
(e) Measures shall be taken, if necessary, and whenever possible with the consent of their parents or persons who by law or custom are primarily responsible for their care, to remove children temporarily from the area in which hostilities are taking place to a safer area within the country and ensure that they are accompanied by persons responsible for their safety and well-being.
Article 5. Persons whose liberty has been restricted

1. In addition to the provisions of Article 4, the following provisions shall be respected as a minimum with regard to persons deprived of their liberty for reasons related to the armed conflict, whether they are interned or detained:
(a) The wounded and the sick shall be treated in accordance with Article 7;
(b) The persons referred to in this paragraph shall, to the same extent as the local civilian population, be provided with food and drinking water and be afforded safeguards as regards health and hygiene and protection against the rigours of the climate and the dangers of the armed conflict;
(c) They shall be allowed to receive individual or collective relief;
(d) They shall be allowed to practise their religion and, if requested and appropriate, to receive spiritual assistance from persons, such as chaplains, performing religious functions;
(e) They shall, if made to work, have the benefit of working conditions and safeguards similar to those enjoyed by the local civilian population.

2. Those who are responsible for the internment or detention of the persons referred to in paragraph I shall also, within the limits of their capabilities, respect the following provisions relating to such persons:
(a) Except when men and women of a family are accommodated together, women shall be held in quarters separated from those of men and shall be under the immediate supervision of women;
(b) They shall be allowed to send and receive letters and cards, the number of which may be limited by the competent authority if it deems necessary;
(c) Places of internment and detention shall not be located close to the combat zone. The persons

referred to in paragraph 1 shall be evacuated when the places where they are interned or detained become particularly exposed to danger arising out of the armed conflict, if their evacuation can be carried out under adequate conditions of safety;
(d) They shall have the benefit of medical examinations;
(e) Their physical or mental health and integrity shall not be endangered by an unjustified act or omission. Accordingly, it is prohibited to subject the persons described in this Article to any medical procedure which is not indicated by the state of health of the person concerned, and which is not consistent with the generally accepted medical standards applied to free persons under similar medical circumstances.

3. Persons who are not covered by paragraph I but whose liberty has been restricted in any way whatsoever for reasons related to the armed conflict shall be treated humanely in accordance with Article 4 and with paragraphs 1 (a), (c) and (d), and 2 (b) of this Article.

4. If it is decided to release persons deprived of their liberty, necessary measures to ensure their safety shall be taken by those so deciding.
Article 6. Penal prosecutions

1. This Article applies to the prosecution and punishment of criminal offences related to the armed conflict.
2. No sentence shall be passed and no penalty shall be executed on a person found guilty of an offence except pursuant to a conviction pronounced by a court offering the essential guarantees of independence and impartiality. In particular:
(a) The procedure shall provide for an accused to be informed without delay of the particulars of the offence alleged against him and shall afford the accused before and during his trial all necessary rights and means of defence;
(b) No one shall be convicted of an offence except on the basis of individual penal responsibility;
(c) No one shall be held guilty of any criminal offence on account of any act or omission which did not constitute a criminal offence, under the law, at the time when it was committed; nor shall a heavier penalty be imposed than that which was applicable at the time when the criminal offence was committed; if, after the commission of the offence, provision is made by law for the imposition of a lighter penalty, the offender shall benefit thereby;
(d) Anyone charged with an offence is presumed innocent until proved guilty according to law;
(e) Anyone charged with an offence shall have the right to be tried in his presence;
(f) No one shall be compelled to testify against himself or to confess guilt

3. A convicted person shall be advised on conviction of his judicial and other remedies and of the time-limits within which they may be exercised.

4. The death penalty shall not be pronounced on persons who were under the age of eighteen years at the time of the offence and shall not be carried out on pregnant women

or mothers of young children.

5. At the end of hostilities, the authorities in power shall endeavour to grant the broadest possible amnesty to persons who have participated in the armed conflict, or those deprived of their liberty for reasons related to the armed conflict, whether they are interned or detained ....

RIGHTS FOR TERRORISTS?

William Safire

New York Times
November 15, 1984

WASHINGTON - In the murky depths of the Reagan bureaucracy, where _ the light of landslides never penetrates and the sound of Cabinet voices cannot be heard, a move is afoot that would enhance the international status of terrorist organizations and give individual terrorists new rights in war.

This anti-humanitarian step bears the imprimatur of the International Red Cross and the fine-sounding title of "Protocols Additional to the Geneva Convention of 1949 and Relating to the Protection of Victims of Armed Conflicts."

President Carter signed this treaty, negotiated by détentenik Republicans, in 1977, but the United States Senate has never ratified it.

Now the State Department Legal Adviser, Davis R. Robinson, has urged in a secret memo that the Reagan Administration "move toward effective international humanitarian protection, consistent with Western military interests," by submitting the protocols to the Senate for ratification.

These protocols, purporting to protect the victims of war, are designed — in the first article's telltale language — to help "peoples fighting against colonial domination and against racist regimes in the exercise of their right to self-determination." That's third-worldese for the P.L.O. and Swapo, which want to be treated as what the treaty calls "parties to an armed conflict," entitled to rights of a recognized state at war.

One tenet of "civilized" war is that combatants openly wear uniforms and do not conceal their weapons. That distinguishes soldiers from civilians. But terrorists don't operate that way; those combatants often seek to appear to be civilians, thereby using innocents as their shield. When terrorist attacks draw retaliation, that disguise causes civilian casualties.

These protocols treat as a soldier the guerrilla who masquerades as a civilian. Although the treaty pays lip service to the centuries-old requirement that an armed combatant separate himself from the civilian population, and solemnly admonishes the terrorist to display his weapon openly as he opens fire, the protocols add: "Recognizing, however, that there are situations in armed conflicts where, owing to the nature of the hostilities an armed combatant cannot so distinguish himself, he shall retain his status as a combatant."

That's a loophole wide enough to permit those who organize a truck-bomb blast at an embassy leeway to claim the status of prisoners of war, if captured — with all the interrogation limits, visits and exchange benefits accorded to uniformed soldiers of a nation captured by its opponent. Terrorists — who regularly flout those rules of warfare that seek to protect civilians — would gain the rights of soldiers who are obliged to try to limit the effects of war on noncombatant victims.

Once the line between civilian and soldier is blurred, no civilian is safe. This treaty, which contains many laudable provisions, blurs that fundamental line. For all its language about protecting victims, it would create more victims by legitimizing the terrorist who claims to be fighting "colonialism" and "racism."

Why, then, are interagency memos flying out of the belly of Foggy Bottom to press the Senate for ratification? Mr. Robinson, the Legal Adviser, proposes to festoon the treaty with "reservations" reflecting objections to these points, summarized by William Clark back when he was at State.

Ratification munchkins think that our reservations satisfy our legal position, missing the point: As the crisis of terror worsens, the P.L.O. and Swapo will achieve their treaty, with world approval, while the U.S. will be yes-butting its head into the propaganda wall.

The Joint Chiefs of Staff, which was suckered seven years ago into approving this on the promise of reservations, belatedly sees its real portent and has drafted 300 pages opposing the protocols. The Secretary of State, who recently took a-gutsy stand against helplessness in the face of terror attacks, cannot be in favor of giving new rights to terrorists.

It may be that some people just don't get the word. Others may be persuaded that the protocols require the renunciation of terrorism. Worst, the move may be caused by inertia—tidy bureaucrats reacting to a tickler file that reminds them to get all signed treaties ratified.
Now that the subject has been raised, it should be disposed of decisively: the Senate should pass a resolution of intent not to ratify a treaty that creates more victims than it helps.

WHITE HOUSE FACT SHEET ON STATUS OF DETAINEES AT GUANTANAMO

The White House
Office of the Press Secretary

February 7, 2002

(www.whitehouse.gov/news/releases/2002/02/20020207-13.html)

United States Policy.

- The United States is treating and will continue to treat all of the individuals detained at Guantanamo humanely and, to the extent appropriate and consistent with military necessity, in a manner consistent with the principles of the Third Geneva Convention of 1949.
- The President has determined that the Geneva Convention applies to the Taliban detainees, but not to the al-Qaida detainees.
- Al-Qaida is not a state party to the Geneva Convention; it is a foreign terrorist group. As such, its members are not entitled to POW status.
- Although we never recognized the Taliban as the legitimate Afghan government, Afghanistan is a party to the Convention, and the President has determined that the Taliban are covered by the Convention. Under the terms of the Geneva Convention, however, the Taliban detainees do not qualify as POWs.
- Therefore, neither the Taliban nor al-Qaida detainees are entitled to POW status.
- Even though the detainees are not entitled to POW privileges, they will be provided many POW privileges as a matter of policy.

All detainees at Guantanamo are being provided:

- three meals a day that meet Muslim dietary laws
- water
- medical care
- clothing and shoes
- shelter
- showers
- soap and toilet articles
- foam sleeping pads and blankets
- towels and washcloths
- the opportunity to worship
- correspondence materials, and the means to send mail
- the ability to receive packages of food and clothing, subject to security screening

The detainees will not be subjected to physical or mental abuse or cruel treatment. The International Committee of the Red Cross has visited and will continue to be able to visit the detainees privately. The detainees will be permitted to raise concerns about their conditions and we will attempt to address those concerns consistent with security.

Housing. We are building facilities in Guantanamo more appropriate for housing the detainees on a long-term basis. The detainees now at Guantanamo are being housed in temporary open-air shelters until these more long-term facilities can be arranged. Their current shelters are reasonable in light of the serious security risk posed by these detainees and the mild climate of Cuba.

POW Privileges the Detainees will not receive. The detainees will receive much of the treatment normally afforded to POWs by the Third Geneva Convention. However, the detainees will not receive some of the specific privileges afforded to POWs, including:

- access to a canteen to purchase food, soap, and tobacco
- a monthly advance of pay
- the ability to have and consult personal financial accounts
- the ability to receive scientific equipment, musical instruments, or sports outfits

Many detainees at Guantanamo pose a severe security risk to those responsible for guarding them and to each other. Some of these individuals demonstrated how dangerous they are in uprisings at Mazar-e-Sharif and in Pakistan. The United States must take into account the need for security in establishing the conditions for detention at Guantanamo.

Background on Geneva Conventions. The Third Geneva Convention of 1949 is an international treaty designed to protect prisoners of war from inhumane treatment at the hands of their captors in conflicts covered by the Convention. It is among four treaties concluded in the wake of WWII to reduce the human suffering caused by war. These four treaties provide protections for four different classes of people: the military wounded and sick in land conflicts; the military wounded, sick and shipwrecked in conflicts at sea; military persons and civilians accompanying the armed forces in the field who are captured and qualify as prisoners of war; and civilian non-combatants who are interned or otherwise found in the hands of a party (e.g. in a military occupation) during an armed conflict.

THE TALIBAN, AL QAEDA, AND THE DETERMINATION OF ILLEGAL COMBATANTS

By George H. Aldrich[1]

*Extract from "Humanitäres Völkerrecht", No 4/2002, a review published by the German Red Cross (*www.drk.de*) and the "Institute for International Law of Peace and Armed Conflict" in Bochum (*www.ifhv.de).

Originally published in 2002

Last September 11, a small number of men who were members of a fanatical group known as "al Qaeda" carried out a suicidal armed attack upon the United States that resulted in very substantial material damage and the loss of life by some three thousand persons, the great majority of whom were civilians. In response, the United States and a number of allies have taken action to find, capture or kill as many members of that al Qaeda organization as possible and deprive it of funds, support and sanctuary.

As the leaders of al Qaeda and a large part of its membership and facilities were located within the territory of Afghanistan, the Taliban, who controlled all but a small part of Afghanistan and were, consequently, the effective government of Afghanistan, were requested to assist in this effort. The Taliban refused to do so and made clear that they would continue to give sanctuary to al Qaeda. As a result, the United States and its allies attacked the armed forces of the Taliban, as well as those of al Qaeda, in the process killing and capturing a considerable number of soldiers belonging to both entities. As these persons were captured in the course of an international armed conflict, questions immediately arose as to their legal status and as to the protections to which they might be entitled pursuant to international humanitarian law, particularly as it was clear that at least some of them were bound to face criminal proceedings for terrorist acts and other crimes.

While these questions were most often phrased in terms of entitlement to the status of, or protection as, prisoners of war (POWs), the real issue was whether they were legal or illegal combatants. In other words, were they persons who had a legal right to take part in hostilities, or, to the contrary, were they persons who could be prosecuted and punished for murder and other crimes under national law simply for their participation in an armed conflict?[2]

---

[1] Judge at the Iran-US Claims Tribunal.

[2] While members of the Armed forces of Parties to the Geneva Conventions who are not combatants, such as medical personnel and chaplains, as well as certain categories of persons who accompany the armed forces are entitled to POW status if captured, other persons who are not members of the armed forces are civilians and, as such, are not privileged by law to take part legally in hostilities. See Regulations Respecting the Laws and Customs of War on Land, Art. 1, annexed to Convention [No. IV] Respecting the Laws and Customs of War on Land, Oct.18, 1907, 36 Stat. 2277, 1 Bevans 631; Convention [No. III] Relative to the Treatment of Prisoners of War, Aug. 12, 1949, Art. 4, 6 UST 3316, 74 UNTS 135 [hereinafter Geneva Convention No. III]; Protocol Additional to the Geneva Conventions of 12 August 1949, and Relating to the Protection of

In February of this year, President Bush determined the position of the United States concerning at least some of these questions. In essence, as announced by the White House Press Secretary on February 7, 2002, he decided that:

(1) The 1949 Geneva Convention concerning the treatment of prisoners of war, to which both Afghanistan and the United States are Parties, applies to the armed conflict in Afghanistan between the Taliban and the United States;

(2) That same Convention does not apply to the armed conflict in Afghanistan and elsewhere between al Qaeda and the United States;

(3) Neither captured Taliban personnel nor captured al Qaeda personnel are entitled to be POWs under that Convention; And

(4) Nevertheless, all captured Taliban and al Qaeda personnel are to be treated humanely, consistent with the general principles of the Convention, and delegates of the International Committee of the Red Cross may visit privately each detainee.[3]

Victims of International Armed Conflicts, opened for signature Dec. 12, 1977, Arts. 43 & 44, 1125 UNTS 3 [hereinafter Protocol I]. From this analysis I exclude the archaic "levée en masse" provided for in Article 2 of the Hague Regulations, supra, and retained in Article 4A(6) of Geneva Convention No. III, supra.

Let us examine these decisions in light of applicable international humanitarian law. In that connection, I must begin by noting the curious fact that I have not seen any public legal defense of those decisions by the United States other than by the Presidential Press Spokesman. If the State Department Legal Adviser, the Defense General Counsel, or the Attorney General has published any analytical justification of them, I am not aware of it. Perhaps there has not been enough public or Congressional criticism of the President's decisions to make such an analytical defense necessary as a matter of public relations, but those of us in the international legal community would certainly appreciate it. I know from my experience years ago as a lawyer for the United States that such analyses most certainly have been prepared, hopefully in time to assist the President in making his decisions, but, in any event, to defend those decisions.

Turning to the applicable law and the choices the President faced, I suggest that the decision to consider that there are two separate armed conflicts is correct. One is the conflict with al Qaeda that is not limited to the territory of Afghanistan. Al Qaeda is evidently a clandestine organization with elements in many countries and composed apparently of people of various nationalities, which has the purpose of advancing

[3] See Press Release, Status of Detainees at Guantanamo, Fact Sheet and Statement (7 February 2002)

certain political and religious objectives by means of terrorist acts directed against the United States and other, largely Western, nations. As such, al Qaeda is not in any respect like a State and lacks international legal personality. It is not a Party to the Geneva Conventions, and it could not be a Party to them or to any international agreement. Its methods brand it as a criminal organization under national laws and as an international outlaw. Its members are properly subject to trial and punishment under national criminal laws for any crimes that they commit.

The armed attack against the Taliban in Afghanistan analytically is a separate armed attack that was rendered necessary because the Taliban, as the effective government of Afghanistan, refused all requests to expel al Qaeda and instead gave sanctuary to it. While the United States, like almost all other countries, refused to extend diplomatic recognition to the Taliban, both Afghanistan and the United States are Parties to the Geneva Conventions of 1949, and the armed attacks by the United States and other nations against the armed forces of the Taliban in Afghanistan clearly constitute an international armed conflict to which those Conventions, as well as customary international humanitarian law, apply.

This analysis must recognize that practical problems are likely to arise in some circumstances, for example, when al Qaeda personnel are captured while accompanying Taliban armed forces; but, once the al Qaeda personnel are identified, they clearly would not be entitled to POW status.[4] As persons who have been combatants in hostilities and are not entitled to POW status, they are entitled, under customary international law to humane treatment of the same nature as that prescribed by Article 3 common to the four Geneva Conventions of 1949 and, in more detail, by Article 75 of Geneva Protocol I of 1977; but they may lawfully be prosecuted and punished under national laws for taking part in the hostilities and for any other crimes, such as murder and assault, that they may have committed.[5] They have been illegal combatants, or, as my friend the late Professor and Judge Richard

---

[4] I know of no evidence that would suggest that al Qaeda personnel were incorporated in Taliban military units as part of Taliban armed forces.

[5] With respect to illegal combatants to whom the Geneva Conventions apply, it may be argued that such persons enjoy some additional protections as "protected persons" under the Geneva Convention Relative to the Protection of Civilian Persons of 1949, but such status would not preclude their prosecution and punishment under national laws. See Convention [IV] Relative to the Protection of Civilian Persons in Time of War, Aug. 12, 1949, Part III, 6 UST 3516, 75 UNTS 287; US Department of the Army, The law of land warfare: United States army field manual, FM 27–10, para. 73 (1956). However, the negotiating history of the Convention is unclear on that question. In any event, the question seems academic in the context of al Qaeda personnel, as the Conventions do not apply to them and as virtually all of them appear to be nationals of States with which the United States has normal diplomatic relations, and such nationals are excluded from the definition of protected persons by Article 4 of the Convention.

Baxter once described such persons, they are "unprivileged belligerents",[6] that is, belligerent persons who lack the privilege enjoyed by the armed forces of a State to engage in warfare with immunity from any liability under national law or under international law, except as prescribed by the international laws of war. This vulnerability to prosecution for simply taking part in an armed conflict and for injuries that may have been caused in that connection is the sanction prescribed by the law to deter illegal combatants.

I find it quite difficult to understand the reasons for President Bush's decision that all Taliban soldiers lack entitlement to POW status. The White House Press Secretary gave the following, cryptic explanation of that decision:
"Under Article 4 of the Geneva Convention, however, Taliban detainees are not entitled to POW status. To qualify as POWs under Article 4, al Qaeda and Taliban detainees would have to have satisfied four conditions: they would have to be part of a military hierarchy; they would have to have worn uniforms or other distinctive signs visible at a distance; they would have to have carried arms openly; and they would have to have conducted their military operations in accordance with the laws and customs of war. The Taliban have not effectively distinguished themselves from the civilian population of Afghanistan. Moreover, they have not conducted their operations in accordance with the laws and customs of war. Instead, they have knowingly adopted and provided support to the unlawful terrorist objectives of the al Qaeda."[7]

Members of the press attending a press conference probably do not carry with them copies of the Geneva Convention. If they had, they might well have asked the Press Secretary what happened to the first provision of Article 4. As many of you know, it provides as follows:
"A. Prisoners of war, in the sense of the present Convention, are persons belonging to one of the following categories, who have fallen into the power of the enemy:
Members of the armed forces of a Party to the conflict as well as members of militias or volunteer corps forming part of such armed forces."[8]

Are the Taliban soldiers not members of the armed forces of a Party to the conflict? Or, at least, are they not members of militias or volunteer corps forming part of those armed forces? It is only with respect to the second category of POWs that we come to the four conditions referred to by the Press Secretary as justifying the President's decision, and that category relates only to militias and volunteer corps that do not, repeat not, form part of

[6] Baxter, R., "So-called "Unprivileged Belligerency": Spies, Guerillas and Saboteurs", (1951) 28 British Yearbook of International Law 323, reprinted in (1975) Military Law Review Bicentennial Issue 501.

[7] See Press Release, supra note 2.

[8] Geneva Convention No. III, supra note 1, at Art. 4.

the armed forces of a Party to the conflict. On the basis of the public record to date, we cannot know the answer of the President to those questions. We are forced to speculate. Perhaps the United States might argue that Afghanistan has no armed forces within the meaning of that sub-paragraph 1, but rather only armies of competing warlords; but that would, I suggest, not be fully convincing given the general perception that, when the attacks began, the Taliban was the government in effective control of most of Afghanistan.

Perhaps the same argument could be phrased differently, for example, that no armed forces in Afghanistan "belong to" Afghanistan, which is the "Party to the conflict" and that only armed forces belonging to a Party to the conflict are entitled to POW status; but the different language would give me no greater confidence in the force of the argument. Certainly the protections of the Convention would be eroded if it were accepted that they need not be accorded to the armed forces of a government in effective control of the territory of a State by another State that declines to recognize the legitimacy of that government.

Another possible argument might be that the conditions specified for POW status by Article 4A(2) for militias and volunteer corps that are not part of the armed forces are somehow also applicable to all armed forces. While contrary to textual logic, the assertion has occasionally been made that those four requirements are inherent in the nature of armed forces of States.[9] I consider that to be a dangerous argument, however, one that States should be reluctant to put forward, because the fourth condition – that the militia or corps conducts its operations in accordance with the laws of war – can easily be abused, as it was by North Korea and by North Vietnam, to deny POW treatment to all members of a State's armed forces on the ground that some of its members allegedly committed war crimes. Even in a conflict where substantial war crimes were committed by the armed forces of a State, this would be a bad idea. Those who commit war crimes should be punished, but their crimes should not be used as an excuse to deprive others of the protections due POWs.

It seems clear to me that it would be much easier and more convincing for the United States to conclude that the members of the armed forces of the effective government of most of Afghanistan should, upon capture, be treated as POWs. That causes me to suspect that there may have been some unexplained reason behind the decision. I am forced to ask why the United States would wish to deprive all Taliban soldiers of POW status when they have been defending the government whose armed forces they are? Does it intend to prosecute

---

9 See, e.g., Rosas, A., The Legal Status of Prisoners of War, Suomalanine Tiedeakatemia, Helsinki, 1976, p. 328; Mallison,W. T. & Mallison, S.V., "The Juridical Status of Irregular Combatants under the International Humanitarian Law of Armed Conflict", (1977) 9 Case Western Reserve Journal of International Law 44–48.

them simply for participating in the conflict? I must doubt that. Does it intend to prosecute them for crimes under United States law? For crimes under some Afghan law? If a few of them are guilty of war crimes or crimes against humanity, they could be prosecuted while remaining POWs. I have questions, but no answers. I would suggest that a necessary first step would be for the United States to explain publicly what is the basis and the reason for denial of POW status to all Taliban prisoners, not simply by asserting that the Taliban armed forces did not distinguish themselves adequately from the civilian population and did not conduct their military operations in accordance with the laws of war, but by evidence documenting such assertions accompanied by a convincing explanation of the gravity of these matters and by some explanation of the evidently felt need to deprive them of POW status.

When I prepared the first draft of these remarks, I assumed that the rejection of POW status for Taliban soldiers must have been the result of some unexplained central purpose, probably one related to the ultimate prosecution of some of them. The longer I ponder the question of the reasons that might have inspired this decision by the President, the more I am inclined to suspect that there may well not have been any such unexplained purpose. Might it not be the case that the present administration in Washington believes precisely what the White House Press Spokesman said, that is, that the failure of the Taliban soldiers to wear uniforms of the sort worn by the members of modern armies and the support by the Taliban government of the unlawful terrorist objective of al Qaeda suffice to justify, or even require, denial of POW status to all members of the Taliban armed forces? Certainly, one can imagine such a determination being urged by those who, in the Reagan Administration, grotesquely described Geneva Protocol No. I as law in the service of terrorism.[10] Without a doubt the most difficult element to defend of the decisions made by President Bush in February with respect to the status of prisoners taken in Afghanistan is the blanket, all-encompassing nature of the decision to deny POW status to the Taliban prisoners. By one,

---

[10] See, e.g., Feith, D. J., "Law in the Service of Terror – The Strange Case of the Additional Protocol", National Interest, No. 1, Fall 1985, at 36; Sofaer, A. D., "Terrorism and the Law", (1986) 64 Foreign Affairs 901; Roberts, G. B., "The New Rules for Waging War: The Case Against Ratification of Additional Protocol I", (1985) 26 Virginia Journal of International Law 109; Safire,W., "Rights for Terrorists? A 1977 Treaty Would Grant Them", New York Times, 15 November 1984, at A31, col. 5.
For responses to these comments, see Aldrich, G. H., "Progressive Development of the Laws of War: A Reply to Criticisms of the 1977 Geneva Protocol I", (1986) 26 Virginia Journal of International Law 693; Solf, W. A., "A Response to Feith's Law in the Service of Terror – The Strange Case of the Additional Protocol", (1986) 20 Akron Law Review 261; Gasser, H.-P., "An Appeal for Ratification by the United States", (1987) 81 American Journal of International Law 912 and Aldrich, G. H., "Prospects for United States Ratification of Additional Protocol I to the 1949 Geneva Conventions", (1991) 85 American Journal of International Law 1.

sweeping determination, President Bush determined that not a single Taliban soldier, presumably not even the army commander, could qualify for POW status under the Geneva Convention. While decisions by armed forces in the past doubtless included some decisions about army units or other groups as a whole, one cannot help but question the all-encompassing nature of this one. Can it possibly exclude any doubt? Moreover, can it legitimately preclude any contest by an individual prisoner?

Article 5 of the Convention states the following cautionary rule: "Should any doubt arise as to whether persons, having committed a belligerent act and having fallen into the hands of the enemy, belong to any of the categories enumerated in Article 4, such persons shall enjoy the protection of the present Convention until such time as their status has been determined by a competent tribunal."[11]

Given that provision, either the United States must maintain that no doubt could arise with respect to any Taliban prisoner, or it must preserve the option of a determination by a tribunal in the event that any doubt does arise concerning a group or an individual prisoner. I have been informed that the Press Spokesman of the Department of State indicated in his press briefing on February 8 of this year that the United States would be prepared to review its determination about the applicability of Article 4 of the Convention should any genuine doubt about status arise in individual cases. I do not know whether such "review" would be made by a tribunal, as required by the Convention, or by the President. Review in individual cases is helpful and meaningful. Only if reviews occur in practice can that be determined. Given the broad and definitive nature of the President's determination, there would appear to be a risk that any review might well have to be limited to resolving doubts as to whether a prisoner was, in fact, a member of the Taliban armed forces, not whether those armed forces meet the standards of Article 4. If so limited, a right to individual review would fall far short of a right to determination of POW entitlement by an Article 5 tribunal.

The United States probably believes that its screening of Taliban captives prior to their transfer to the camp in Cuba is thorough and as fully adequate as a tribunal to ensure that they are legitimately detained for purposes of further criminal investigation. That may well be true, but, in view of the President's determination, such screening could have no effect on their entitlement to POW status.

There are, in my view, all too few places where international humanitarian law provides for the rights of individuals to challenge State action, but one of those few is the right of access to a tribunal granted by Article 5. It would be regrettable if in practice it proves to have been effectively negated for Taliban prisoners.

---

[11] Geneva Convention No. III, supra note 1, at Art. 4.

In this connection, I note that the United States Army Field Manual on the Law of Land Warfare makes the following interpretation of Article 5 of the Convention:
"b. *Interpretation*. The foregoing provision applies to any person not appearing to be entitled to prisoner-of-war status who has committed a belligerent act or who has engaged in hostile activities in aid of the armed forces and who asserts that he is entitled to treatment as a prisoner of war or concerning whom any other doubt of a like nature exists."[12]

This interpretation clearly indicates that doubt arises and a tribunal is required whenever a captive who has participated in hostilities asserts a right to be a POW. That is a point that we were careful to state in Article 45, paragraph 1 of Protocol No. I when we negotiated it in the seventies, and, in my view, it is now part of customary international law. In that connection, I should point out that, when the armed forces of countries that are Parties to the Geneva Protocol capture Taliban soldiers, they will obviously be required by Article 45, paragraph 1 to give them POW status unless and until a tribunal decides otherwise. This obligation might also prevent transfer of such prisoners to the United States.[13]

Also relevant to prisoners facing criminal prosecution is paragraph 2 of Article 45 of Protocol I which establishes a separate right of any person who has fallen into the power of an adverse Party and is to be tried by that Party for an offense arising out of the hostilities to have his entitlement to POW status determined by a judicial tribunal.

When that text was negotiated, the United States Government was painfully aware of the experiences in Korea and Vietnam where many American military personnel were mistreated by their captors and were denied POW status by mere allegations that they were all criminals. Time evidently dulls memory.

---

[12] United States Army Field Manual, supra note 4, at para. 71(b).

[13] 12 Article 45, para. 1 provides: "A person who takes part in hostilities and falls into the power of an adverse Party shall be presumed to be a prisoner of war, and therefore shall be protected by the Third Convention, if he claims the status of prisoner of war, or if he appears to be entitled to such status, or if the Party on which he depends claims such status on his behalf by notification to the detaining Power or to the Protecting Power.
Should any doubt arise as to whether any such person is entitled to the status of prisoner of war, he shall continue to have such status and, therefore, to be protected by the Third Convention and this Protocol until such time as his status has been determined by a competent tribunal." Protocol I , supra note 1, at Art. 45. Article 12 of Geneva Convention No. III includes the following restriction:
"Prisoners of war may only be transferred by the Detaining Power to a Power which is a party to the Convention and after the Detaining Power has satisfied itself of the willingness and ability of such transferee Power to apply the Convention. When prisoners of war are transferred under such circumstances, responsibility for the application of the Convention rests on the Power accepting them while they are in custody." Geneva Convention No. III, supra note 1, at Art. 12.

In conclusion, I should stress that the legal difficulties I have indicated with the actions taken by the United States concerning prisoners captured in Afghanistan exist only with respect to persons who served in the armed forces of the Taliban, not with respect to those who were members of the al Qaeda terrorist group. The latter are, in my view, international outlaws who are entitled to humanitarian treatment, but nothing more.

This conclusion flows from the fact – that there are two armed conflicts involved in Afghanistan – one with the Taliban, to which the Geneva Conventions and, for Parties to it, Protocol No. I, apply, and another with al Qaeda, to which those treaties do not apply. Al Qaeda and its personnel do not belong to any Party to the Geneva Conventions and al Qaeda is not itself capable of being a Party to a conflict to which those Conventions and Protocol No. 1 apply. Members of al Qaeda are not entitled to be combatants under international law and are subject to trial and punishment under national laws for their crimes.

DEALING WITH THE DETAINEES AT GUANTANAMO BAY: HUMANITARIAN AND HUMAN RIGHTS OBLIGATIONS UNDER THE GENEVA CONVENTIONS

Erin Chlopak
Human Rights Brief Volume 9, Issue 3, beginning at page 6 is: 9 No. 3 Hum. Rts. Brief 6 (2002)

Controversy has surrounded the United States' detention and treatment of nearly two hundred alleged members of the Taliban and al-Qaeda at the U.S. naval base in Guantanamo Bay, Cuba. At issue is the scope of applicability of the Geneva Conventions, a series of treaties that provide international humanitarian legal standards for states parties during armed conflicts. In particular, the Third Geneva Convention relative to the Treatment of Prisoners of War and the Fourth Geneva Convention relative to the Protection of Civilian Persons in Time of War extend a variety of procedural and substantive legal rights to prisoners of war and other victims of armed conflicts. As states parties to the Conventions, both the United States and Afghanistan are legally bound to afford the protections guaranteed in the treaties to prisoners detained as a result of the present conflict between the two countries.

In January 2002, shortly after their detention, U.S. Secretary of Defense Donald Rumsfeld labeled the Guantanamo Bay prisoners "unlawful combatants" who "do not have any rights under the Geneva Convention[s]," indicating that the prisoners would be treated "for the most part . . . in a manner that is reasonably consistent with the Geneva Conventions, to the extent they are appropriate." In response to this and similar statements, as well as footage of the detainees incarcerated in metal cages and wearing shackles, blacked-out goggles, surgical face masks, and sound--blocking earmuffs, other governments and human rights groups have condemned the U.S. for failing to respect human rights and humanitarian law. Perhaps in acquiescence to this international pressure, the U.S. has modified its position on the application of the Geneva Conventions, announcing in early February that prisoners who fought for the Taliban in Afghanistan would be covered by the Conventions. In spite of U.S. efforts to allay international criticism, human rights groups and international legal scholars continue to charge that this latest decision fails to conform fully to the duties of the U.S. under the Geneva Conventions. Specifically, while the U.S. accurately acknowledged the general applicability of the Conventions to Taliban detainees, the government's unilateral decision to deny all detainees prisoner of war (POW) status, and its decision categorically to except al-Qaeda detainees from any coverage by the Conventions, suggest the U.S. government has improperly interpreted its legal obligations under the Conventions.

The Geneva Conventions and the Scope of Their Protection

There are four Geneva Conventions, signed in 1949 and supplemented by two additional Protocols, signed in 1977. Convention I, For the Amelioration of the Condition of the Wounded and Sick in Armed Forces in the Field, and Convention II, For the Amelioration of the Condition of Wounded, Sick and Shipwrecked Members of Armed Forces at Sea, enumerate protections guaranteed to members of the armed forces who fall ill or are injured during an armed conflict. Convention III, Relative to the Treatment of Prisoners of War, and Convention IV, Relative to the Protection of Civilian Persons in Time of War, describe protections guaranteed to persons who are taken into enemy custody during an armed conflict. Protocol I, relating to the Protection of Victims of International Armed Conflicts, and Protocol II, relating to the Protection of Victims of Non-International Armed Conflicts, extend protections of the Geneva Conventions to persons combating foreign occupation or internally racist regimes, as well as to victims of internal conflicts.

Most relevant to the Guantanamo Bay detainees are the Third and Fourth Conventions. The Third Convention defines categories of persons entitled to POW classification, articulates the procedure for classifying a prisoner whose -status is unclear, and enumerates the rights of detainees classified as POWs. Article 4 of the Third Convention defines several categories of persons entitled to classification as prisoners of war, including persons "who have fallen into the power of the enemy" and who are (1) members of armed forces of a party to the conflict; or (2) members of other militias or volunteer corps, which are commanded by a person responsible for subordinates; have a fixed and distinctive -symbol, recognizable at a distance; carry arms openly; and conduct operations in accordance with the laws of war. Article 5 explains that "[s]hould any doubt arise as to whether persons, having committed a belligerent act and having fallen into the hands of the enemy, belong to any of the categories enumerated in Article 4, such persons shall enjoy the protection of the present Convention until such time as their status has been determined by a competent tribunal." The U.S. government is therefore obliged to recognize the POW status of detainees who clearly fit into an Article 4 category, and must allow a competent tribunal to determine the status of those whose status is ambiguous.

Defining the Status of the Detainees

The U.S. government's classification of the Guantanamo Bay detainees as "unlawful combatants" has generated confusion and controversy. Secretary Rumsfeld's early statement that all of the detainees were "unlawful combatants" who lacked any rights under the Geneva Conventions seemed to imply that "unlawful combatants" inherently are not protected by the Geneva Conventions. "Unlawful combatants," often referred to as "unprivileged combatants" are those fighters who are not entitled to the privileges of POW status. Unlawful combatants, however, are not persons lacking all rights under the Conventions. Indeed, rather than suggest that certain categories of aggressors may be excepted from the protection of the Conventions, Article 4 of the Fourth Convention professes a broad protection of persons "who, at a given moment and in any manner whatsoever, find themselves, in case of a conflict or occupation, in the hands of a Party to the conflict or Occupying Power of which they are not nationals." The only caveat to this encompassing protection is that the prisoners must be nationals of a state bound by the Convention.

The International Committee of the Red Cross (ICRC) and the International Criminal Tribunal for the Former Yugoslavia (ICTY) have interpreted the Third and Fourth Conventions jointly to embrace all persons who fall into enemy custody during an armed conflict, and neither has recognized an exception for so-called unlawful combatants. Quoting both sources, Human Rights Watch (HRW) explained that "'nobody in enemy hands can fall outside the law,'" and prisoners detained by an enemy in an armed conflict either are protected by the Third Convention as prisoners of war, or by the Fourth Convention as civilians.

The United States' Application of the Geneva Conventions

After initially refusing to guarantee full application of the Geneva Conventions to any of the detainees, the U.S. has recently compromised, and conceded that the Conventions apply to Taliban detainees. Nevertheless, the U.S. continues to deny the application of the Geneva Conventions to al-Qaeda prisoners, has refused to grant any of the detainees POW status, and has denied the prisoners the right to a determination of such status by a competent tribunal. The U.S. government's basis for distinguishing between Taliban and al-Qaeda detainees was its recognition of Afghanistan's status as a signatory to the Conventions in contrast to al-Qaeda, which, as a non-state actor, has not and could not have signed the treaties. Such a categorical exception of al-Qaeda detainees results from a flawed interpretation of the express language of Article 4 of the Fourth Convention, and contradicts customary interpretations of the broad scope of the Conventions. Similarly, the executive decision categorically to deny all detainees POW status directly violates Article 5 of the Third Convention, which provides for the determination of such status by competent tribunals.

Refusal of the U.S. Government to Apply the Geneva Conventions to al-Qaeda Detainees

In early February, White House Press Secretary Ari Fleischer commented that al-Qaeda fighters "do not qualify [for protection under the Geneva Conventions] because they do not represent any country that is party to the treaty." Article 4 of the Fourth Convention does not except combatants on the basis of their representation of a state not party to the Conventions, but rather it excludes persons who are nationals of a state not bound by the Conventions. Thus, the language of the Conventions seems to indicate that persons who fought on behalf of al-Qaeda, and who are nationals of a state party to the Conventions, would be within the scope of their protections.

According to HRW, the detainees encompass a variety of nationalities, including Afghans, Pakistanis, and, in lesser numbers, Saudis, Yemenis, Uzbeks, Chechens from Russia, Chinese, and others. Each of these nations has both signed and ratified the Conventions, or joined the Conventions by accession. The United States ratified the Conventions in 1955. Although China, Pakistan, the Russian Federation, Yemen, and the U.S. entered reservations and/or declarations upon signing the Conventions, none of the reservations or declarations provides a basis for excluding their nationals from the general protections afforded by the Conventions, or from the benefits of POW status in particular. In addition, these reservations and declarations do not provide a basis for denying such -protections. Thus, the U.S. government's current policy of -categorically refusing to apply the Geneva Conventions to non--Taliban detainees contradicts customary legal interpretations of the scope of the Conventions, as well as the explicit language of the Fourth Convention. Members of either the -Taliban or al-Qaeda, who are nationals of a country that has signed the Geneva Conventions, expressly are within the scope of the treaties. Current U.S. policy at best misinterprets, and at worst ignores, this legal reality and potentially -renders the U.S. in breach of its treaty obligations for any actions against detainees which contradict the Conventions' guarantees.

Denying All Detainees Prisoner of War Status

Although the U.S. has correctly recognized that the Geneva Conventions apply to Taliban fighters captured during the present conflict in Afghanistan, its unilateral decision to deny such detainees POW status violates the procedures established by the Conventions for determining the status of prisoners -captured by an enemy in an armed conflict. Moreover, the refusal of the U.S. even to recognize the Geneva Conventions with respect to al-Qaeda detainees precludes a proper determination of their legal status.

Article 4 of the Third Convention confers POW status on persons who fall into enemy power and who are members of armed forces of a party to the conflict. Alternatively, Article 4 characterizes as POWs members of irregular forces, such as militias or volunteer corps who: (1) adhere to an established chain of command; (2) wear a uniform or otherwise have some fixed and distinctive symbol, which is recognizable at a distance; (3) carry arms openly; and (4) conduct operations in accordance with the laws of war.

The Crimes of War Project, a collaborative organization of journalists, lawyers, and scholars formed in 1999 and headquartered at

American University in Washington, D.C., seeks to educate the public about international humanitarian legal issues. The Project recently surveyed international legal and humanitarian experts on their opinions about the applicability of the Geneva Conventions to the Guantanamo Bay detainees. Most of the survey's respondents believed Taliban detainees, and possibly al-Qaeda detainees, should be accorded POW status. Most of the experts characterized the Taliban detainees as members of Afghanistan's armed forces, entitling them to POW status under Article 4(1) of the Third Convention. Among such experts, Washington College of Law Professor Robert Goldman criticized the Bush Administration's classification of the Taliban as irregular forces under Article 4(2), which requires them to meet the four criteria enumerated under that category. Similarly, during a recent interview on National Public Radio, David Scheffer, Senior Fellow at the U.S. Institute of Peace, emphasized the importance of recognizing that captured Taliban fighters are part of the organized, armed force of Afghanistan, and thus entitled to POW status. Nevertheless, even under the four criteria enumerated for irregular forces, most of the experts surveyed by the Crimes of War Project believed that the Taliban detainees would be entitled to POW status. Curtis Doebbler, Professor of Human Rights Law at the American University in Cairo, asserted that the Taliban do meet the four criteria mandated for irregular forces, although he, like many others, was less confident about the ability of al-Qaeda detainees to satisfy the criteria.

Indeed, there is less support for classifying al-Qaeda fighters as POWs under the Geneva Conventions. Even HRW has suggested that "ultimately the al-Qaeda fighters would likely not be accorded POW status." However, as HRW, the Crimes of War Project, and other experts have highlighted, the principal criticism of the U.S. position is not the government's improper categorization of the detainees under Article 4 of the Third Convention. Rather, critics emphasize the government's failure to make individualized determinations about the status of each prisoner, and its outright neglect of Article 5, which requires that a competent tribunal resolve such controversial determinations. Article 5 further provides that detainees whose legal status is in doubt "shall enjoy the protection of the present Convention" until a tribunal makes the final determination. Thus, even if, as the U.S. presently claims, none of the detainees ultimately would be entitled to POW status, Article 5 requires that each detainee whose status is in doubt be treated as a POW until a competent tribunal makes a final determination.

Under U.S. military regulations, a "competent tribunal" pursuant to Article 5 of the Third Convention consists of three commissioned officers. As HRW explained, the regulations require that persons whose status is to be determined be advised of their rights; be permitted to attend all open sessions, call witnesses, question witnesses called by the tribunal; be permitted, but not compelled, to testify or otherwise address the tribunal; and be provided with an interpreter, if necessary. The regulations provide for the tribunal's determination of the detainee's status in closed session by a majority vote and require a preponderance of evidence to support the tribunal's finding.

The clear purpose of Article 5, and the corresponding procedures set forth in U.S. military law, is to ensure that the assessment of a prisoner's status is a fair and objective determination. Beyond violating its explicit, legal obligations under Article 5, the executive branch's unilateral determination of the prisoners' collective status, absent a finding by an objective tribunal, renders the U.S. susceptible to charges of unfairness, corruption, and dishonesty.

The Significance of Recognizing the Geneva Conventions

The Geneva Conventions confer a variety of protections to prisoners detained during an international conflict. Among them are protections relating to humane treatment (Convention III, Article 3; Convention IV, Article 3), interrogation (Convention III, Article 17; Convention IV, Article 31), and prosecution (Convention III, Articles 87, 99-108; Convention IV, Articles 146-47). The legal status of individual prisoners dictates the scope of their protections under the Conventions. Nevertheless, all persons detained in an armed conflict may be prosecuted for war crimes, crimes against humanity, and other crimes unrelated to armed conflict. Similarly, all detainees must be treated humanely, in accordance with international human rights norms, and as recommended by the ICRC.

Humane Treatment in the Context of International Human Rights Law

To provide a context for the Conventions' requirement of "humane treatment," HRW explained that torture and ill-treatment of prisoners are prohibited by customary law and international human rights treaties. Article 7 of the International Covenant on Civil and Political Rights, ratified by the United States in 1992, sets forth the non-derogable principle that "[n]o one shall be subjected to torture or to cruel, -inhuman or degrading treatment or punishment." Similarly, the Convention against Torture and other Cruel, Inhuman or Degrading Treatment or Punishment, to which the U.S. became a party in 1994, prohibits, under all circumstances, the use of torture and other excessive forms of punishment.

The Ramifications of POW Status: Humane Treatment and Interrogation

Although all of the Guantanamo Bay detainees are entitled to humane treatment under the broad provisions of the Geneva Conventions and the more specific provisions of international human rights treaties, those entitled to POW status are guaranteed further protections. Regarding interrogation and prosecution, for example, the

Third Convention extends additional protections to POWs. Under Article 17, POWs are required only to disclose their last names, first names, rank, birth dates, and military serial numbers. Although both POWs and unprivileged combatants are protected by the Conventions' general prohibitions against torture, Article 17 provides that POWs who refuse to answer interrogations "may not be threatened, insulted, or exposed to unpleasant or disadvantageous treatment of any kind." Article 21 prohibits holding POWs in close confinement except as necessary to safeguard their health, and in such circumstances, the nature and duration of confinement also must be limited to what is necessary. Similarly, Article 25 requires that POWs be accommodated in conditions as favorable as those provided for the forces of the detaining power stationed in the same area. Such conditions must allow for the habits and customs of the prisoners, and may not be prejudicial to their health. Article 34 guarantees POWs "complete latitude" in the enjoyment and exercise of their religious duties. Prisoners who are properly determined not to be POWs are not entitled to these and other guarantees enumerated in the Third Convention.

In the absence of a proper determination of the status of each detainee at Guantanamo Bay, and in light of the ICRC's inability to disclose its findings publicly, it is difficult to analyze whether any of the detainees are entitled to these specific POW privileges, let alone whether their rights have been violated. Foreign governments and media, and international human rights groups, have articulated a general concern regarding the apparent nature of the prisoners' detention. Their critiques have suggested that depriving the detainees of their senses of sight and hearing by requiring them to wear blacked-out goggles and sound-blocking earmuffs constitutes inhumane treatment, in violation of the general human rights principles embodied in the Geneva Conventions.

The U.S. government has defended its detention practices as necessary security measures. On January 18, 2002, delegates of the ICRC visited the Guantanamo Bay detainees, but ICRC standard procedures prohibit public comment on the treatment or conditions of prisoners. Rather, ICRC delegates submit recommendations to detaining authorities and encourage such authorities to take measures necessary to resolve any humanitarian problems.

The Ramifications of POW Status: Prosecution and Punishment

Perhaps the most significant rights accorded to prisoners of war are in the context of prosecution and punishment. Generally speaking, POWs may not be prosecuted or punished for mere participation in the armed conflict, although they may be tried for war crimes, crimes against humanity, and crimes unrelated to the conflict. Article 83 of the Third Convention requires that a detaining power exercise "the greatest leniency" in determining whether an offense alleged to have been committed by a POW be adjudged by judicial or disciplinary proceedings and provides that "wherever possible, disciplinary rather than judicial measures" shall be taken. Article 84 enunciates that "[i]n no circumstances whatever shall a prisoner of war be tried by a court of any kind which does not offer the essential guarantees of independence and impartiality as generally recognized, and in particular, the procedure of which does not afford the accused the rights and means of defence provided for in Article 105." Article 105 correspondingly guarantees POWs the assistance of a legal defense by a qualified advocate or counsel of his choice. It further requires that the detaining power deliver to the protecting power a list of persons qualified to present the POW's defense, and ultimately obliges the detaining power to appoint a competent advocate or counsel if the POW does not choose his own. Article 86 guarantees POWs the right against double jeopardy. Article 87 limits the penalties to which POWs may be subjected to those that would be imposed upon members of the armed forces of the detaining power who have committed the same acts. Article 106 provides that every POW shall have the same rights of appeal or petition of a sentence as are guaranteed to the members of the armed forces of the detaining power. Moreover, POWs must be fully informed of such rights, as well as the time limit within which they may appeal.

In light of these and the numerous other rights guaranteed to prisoners of war, it is clear that the Guantanamo Bay detainees are not being treated in accordance with the Third Convention. Moreover, absent an objective determination of their legal status by a competent tribunal, the nature of their detention violates the requirement in Article 5 that detainees whose status is uncertain be treated in accordance with the Third Convention until such status is determined.

The Consequences of Selectively Applying the Geneva Conventions

Beyond noting the sheer illegality of selectively applying the Geneva Conventions, some experts question why the U.S. would violate its duties in the absence of any apparent gain. Most of the experts surveyed by the Crimes of War Project believe that the U.S. has little to gain from denying POW status to qualified prisoners. Such experts noted that POWs and unprivileged combatants are equally subject to prosecution for fundamental human rights violations. Perhaps the government's primary concern is the apparent conflict between its noted intention to try those detained in military tribunals, where procedural rights are limited and the rules of evidence are more indulgent, and the provisions in the Third Convention requiring that POWs be prosecuted and punished in a manner consistent with the treatment of members of the armed forces of the detaining country who violate similar laws.

Regardless of the government's underlying objectives, setting a standard for selectively applying the provisions of an international treaty poses serious consequences to citizens of all states parties to the agreement. In particular, some have expressed concern over the future treatment of U.S. special forces, who usually do not wear uniforms and therefore could be denied POW status for failing to meet the conditions enumerated in Article (4)(2) of the Third Convention.

Conclusion

The Geneva Conventions set forth legal standards and procedures for the treatment of all nationals of states parties who fall into enemy custody during an armed conflict. In particular, the Third Convention articulates a duty of a detaining power to convene a competent tribunal to determine the legal status of persons detained in such a conflict. Moreover, where the status of detainees is in doubt, a detaining power is required to accord them the rights and privileges enumerated in the Third Convention until such status is determined by an objective tribunal. The circumstances of the detention and treatment by the United States of the prisoners currently detained at Guantanamo Bay fail to-conform to the Geneva Conventions in several respects. The refusal to recognize the Conventions with respect to prisoners classified as members of al-Qaeda violates the text and customary interpretations of the Fourth Convention. The -unilateral determination that no prisoner is entitled to POW status violates the Third Convention's guarantee that such determinations are to be made by competent tribunals. Finally, in light of the likelihood that at least some of the prisoners should be entitled to POW status, the nature of their detention violates the various provisions of the Third Convention, which guarantee privileged treatment to POWs.

As one of the most powerful nations in the world, the U.S. is setting a dangerous precedent for the future application and interpretation of the Geneva Conventions. In the interest of its own credibility, as well as the future safety of its own armed forces, the U.S. government would be well advised to reconsider its position and comply with all of its obligations under the Conventions.

THE WORLD MEDICAL ASSOCIATION DECLARATION OF TOKYO

The World Medical Association Declaration of Tokyo

Guidelines for Physicians Concerning Torture and other Cruel, Inhuman or Degrading Treatment or Punishment in Relation to Detention and Imprisonment.

Adopted by the 29th World Medical Assembly, Tokyo, Japan, October 1975, and editorially revised at the 170th Council Session, Divonne-les-Bains, France, May 2005.

(http://www.wma.net/e/policy/c18.htm)

PREAMBLE

It is the privilege of the physician to practise medicine in the service of humanity, to preserve and restore bodily and mental health without distinction as to persons, to comfort and to ease the suffering of his or her patients. The utmost respect for human life is to be maintained even under threat, and no use made of any medical knowledge contrary to the laws of humanity.

For the purpose of this Declaration, torture is defined as the deliberate, systematic or wanton infliction of physical or mental suffering by one or more persons acting alone or on the orders of any authority, to force another person to yield information, to make a confession, or for any other reason.

DECLARATION

1. The physician shall not countenance, condone or participate in the practice of torture or other forms of cruel, inhuman or degrading procedures, whatever the offense of which the victim of such procedures is suspected, accused or guilty, and whatever the victim's beliefs or motives, and in all situations, including armed conflict and civil strife.

2. The physician shall not provide any premises, instruments, substances or knowledge to facilitate the practice of torture or other forms of cruel, inhuman or degrading treatment or to diminish the ability of the victim to resist such treatment.

3. The physician shall not be present during any procedure during which torture or any other forms of cruel, inhuman or degrading treatment is used or threatened.

4. A physician must have complete clinical independence in deciding upon the care of a person for whom he or she is medically responsible. The physician's fundamental role is to alleviate the distress of his or her fellow human beings, and no motive, whether personal, collective or political, shall prevail against this higher purpose.

5. Where a prisoner refuses nourishment and is considered by the physician as capable of forming an unimpaired and rational judgment concerning the consequences of such a voluntary refusal of nourishment, he or she shall not be fed artificially. The decision as to the capacity of the prisoner to form such a judgment should be confirmed by at least one other independent physician. The consequences of the refusal of nourishment shall be explained by the physician to the prisoner.

6. The World Medical Association will support, and should encourage the international community, the National Medical Associations and fellow physicians to support, the physician and his or her family in the face of threats or reprisals resulting from a refusal to condone the use of torture or other forms of cruel, inhuman or degrading treatment.

CONVENTION AGAINST TORTURE AND OTHER CRUEL, INHUMAN OR DEGRADING TREATMENT OR PUNISHMENT

(http://www.unhchr.ch/html/menu3/b/h_cat39.htm)

Adopted and opened for signature, ratification and accession by General Assembly resolution 39/46 of 10 December 1984, entry into force 26 June 1987, in accordance with article 27 (1)

The States Parties to this Convention,

Considering that, in accordance with the principles proclaimed in the Charter of the United Nations, recognition of the equal and inalienable rights of all members of the human family is the foundation of freedom, justice and peace in the world;

Recognizing that those rights derive from the inherent dignity of the human person;

Considering the obligation of States under the Charter, in particular Article 55, to promote universal respect for, and observance of, human rights and fundamental freedom;

Having regard to article 5 of the Universal Declaration of Human Rights and article 7 of the International Covenant on Civil and Political Rights, both of which provide that no one shall be subjected to torture or to cruel, inhuman or degrading treatment or punishment;

Having regard also to the Declaration on the Protection of All Persons from Being Subjected to Torture and Other Cruel, Inhuman or Degrading Treatment or Punishment, adopted by the General Assembly on 9 December 1975;

Desiring to make more effective the struggle against torture and other cruel, inhuman or degrading treatment or punishment throughout the world;

Have agreed as follows:

PART I
Article 1

1. For the purposes of this Convention, the term "torture" means any act by which severe pain or suffering, whether physical or mental, is intentionally inflicted on a person for such purposes as obtaining from him or a third person information or a confession, punishing him for an act he or a third person has committed or is suspected of having committed, or intimidating or coercing him or a third person, or for any reason based on discrimination of any kind, when such pain or suffering is inflicted by or at the instigation of or with the consent or acquiescence of a public official or other person acting in an official capacity. It does not include pain or suffering arising only from, inherent in or incidental to lawful sanctions.

2. This article is without prejudice to any international instrument or national legislation which does or may contain provisions of wider application.

Article 2

1. Each State Party shall take effective legislative, administrative, judicial or other measures to prevent acts of torture in any territory under its jurisdiction.

2. No exceptional circumstances whatsoever, whether a state of war or a threat of war, internal political in stability or any other public emergency, may be invoked as a justification of torture.

3. An order from a superior officer or a public authority may not be invoked as a justification of torture.

Article 3

1. No State Party shall expel, return ("refouler") or extradite a person to another State where there are substantial grounds for believing that he would be in danger of being subjected to torture.

2. For the purpose of determining whether there are such grounds, the competent authorities shall take into account all relevant considerations including, where applicable, the existence in the State concerned of a consistent pattern of gross, flagrant or mass violations of human rights.

Article 4

1. Each State Party shall ensure that all acts of torture are offences under its criminal law. The same shall apply to an attempt to commit torture and to an act by any person which constitutes complicity or participation in torture.

2. Each State Party shall make these offences punishable by appropriate penalties which take into account their grave nature.

Article 5

1. Each State Party shall take such measures as may be necessary to establish its jurisdiction over the offences referred to in article 4 in the following cases:

(a) When the offences are committed in any territory under its jurisdiction or on board a ship or aircraft registered in that State;
(b) When the alleged offender is a national of that State;
(c) When the victim is a national of that State if that State considers it appropriate.

2. Each State Party shall likewise take such measures as may be necessary to establish its jurisdiction over such offences in cases where the alleged offender is present in any territory under its jurisdiction and it does not extradite him pursuant to article 8 to any of the States mentioned in paragraph I of this article.

3. This Convention does not exclude any criminal jurisdiction exercised in accordance with internal law.

Article 6

1. Upon being satisfied, after an

examination of information available to it, that the circumstances so warrant, any State Party in whose territory a person alleged to have committed any offence referred to in article 4 is present shall take him into custody or take other legal measures to ensure his presence. The custody and other legal measures shall be as provided in the law of that State but may be continued only for such time as is necessary to enable any criminal or extradition proceedings to be instituted.

2. Such State shall immediately make a preliminary inquiry into the facts.

3. Any person in custody pursuant to paragraph I of this article shall be assisted in communicating immediately with the nearest appropriate representative of the State of which he is a national, or, if he is a stateless person, with the representative of the State where he usually resides.

4. When a State, pursuant to this article, has taken a person into custody, it shall immediately notify the States referred to in article 5, paragraph 1, of the fact that such person is in custody and of the circumstances which warrant his detention. The State which makes the preliminary inquiry contemplated in paragraph 2 of this article shall promptly report its findings to the said States and shall indicate whether it intends to exercise jurisdiction.

Article 7

1. The State Party in the territory under whose jurisdiction a person alleged to have committed any offence referred to in article 4 is found shall in the cases contemplated in article 5, if it does not extradite him, submit the case to its competent authorities for the purpose of prosecution.

2. These authorities shall take their decision in the same manner as in the case of any ordinary offence of a serious nature under the law of that State. In the cases referred to in article 5, paragraph 2, the standards of evidence required for prosecution and conviction shall in no way be less stringent than those which apply in the cases referred to in article 5, paragraph 1.

3. Any person regarding whom proceedings are brought in connection with any of the offences referred to in article 4 shall be guaranteed fair treatment at all stages of the proceedings.

Article 8

1. The offences referred to in article 4 shall be deemed to be included as extraditable offences in any extradition treaty existing between States Parties. States Parties undertake to include such offences as extraditable offences in every extradition treaty to be concluded between them.

2. If a State Party which makes extradition conditional on the existence of a treaty receives a request for extradition from another State Party with which it has no extradition treaty, it may consider this Convention as the legal basis for extradition in respect of such

offences. Extradition shall be subject to the other conditions provided by the law of the requested State.

3. States Parties which do not make extradition conditional on the existence of a treaty shall recognize such offences as extraditable offences between themselves subject to the conditions provided by the law of the requested State.

4. Such offences shall be treated, for the purpose of extradition between States Parties, as if they had been committed not only in the place in which they occurred but also in the territories of the States required to establish their jurisdiction in accordance with article 5, paragraph 1.

Article 9

1. States Parties shall afford one another the greatest measure of assistance in connection with criminal proceedings brought in respect of any of the offences referred to in article 4, including the supply of all evidence at their disposal necessary for the proceedings.

2. States Parties shall carry out their obligations under paragraph I of this article in conformity with any treaties on mutual judicial assistance that may exist between them.

Article 10

1. Each State Party shall ensure that education and information regarding the prohibition against torture are fully included in the training of law enforcement personnel, civil or military, medical personnel, public officials and other persons who may be involved in the custody, interrogation or treatment of any individual subjected to any form of arrest, detention or imprisonment.

2. Each State Party shall include this prohibition in the rules or instructions issued in regard to the duties and functions of any such person.

Article 11

Each State Party shall keep under systematic review interrogation rules, instructions, methods and practices as well as arrangements for the custody and treatment of persons subjected to any form of arrest, detention or imprisonment in any territory under its jurisdiction, with a view to preventing any cases of torture.

Article 12

Each State Party shall ensure that its competent authorities proceed to a prompt and impartial investigation, wherever there is reasonable ground to believe that an act of torture has been committed in any territory under its jurisdiction.

Article 13

Each State Party shall ensure that any individual who alleges he has been subjected to torture in any territory under its jurisdiction has the right to complain to, and to have his case promptly and impartially examined by, its competent authorities. Steps shall be taken to ensure that the complainant and witnesses are protected against all ill-treatment or intimidation as a consequence of his complaint or any evidence given.

Article 14

1. Each State Party shall ensure in its legal system that the victim of an act of torture obtains redress and has an enforceable right to fair and adequate compensation, including the means for as full rehabilitation as possible. In the event of the death of the victim as a result of an act of torture, his dependants shall be entitled to compensation.

2. Nothing in this article shall affect any right of the victim or other persons to compensation which may exist under national law.

Article 15

Each State Party shall ensure that any statement which is established to have been made as a result of torture shall not be invoked as evidence in any proceedings, except against a person accused of torture as evidence that the statement was made.

Article 16

1. Each State Party shall undertake to prevent in any territory under its jurisdiction other acts of cruel, inhuman or degrading treatment or punishment which do not amount to torture as defined in article I, when such acts are committed by or at the instigation of or with the consent or acquiescence of a public official or other person acting in an official capacity. In particular, the obligations contained in articles 10, 11, 12 and 13 shall apply with the substitution for references to torture of references to other forms of cruel, inhuman or degrading treatment or punishment.

2. The provisions of this Convention are without prejudice to the provisions of any other international instrument or national law which prohibits cruel, inhuman or degrading treatment or punishment or which relates to extradition or expulsion.

PART II

Article 17

1. There shall be established a Committee against Torture (hereinafter referred to as the Committee) which shall carry out the functions hereinafter provided. The Committee shall consist of ten experts of high moral standing and recognized competence in the field of human rights, who shall serve in their personal capacity. The experts shall be elected by the States Parties, consideration being given to equitable geographical distribution and to the usefulness of the participation of some persons having legal experience.

2. The members of the Committee shall be elected by secret ballot from a list of persons nominated by States Parties. Each State Party may nominate one person from among its own nationals. States Parties shall bear in mind the usefulness of nominating persons who are also members of the Human Rights Committee established under the International Covenant on Civil and Political Rights and who are willing to serve on the Committee against

Torture ....

Article 19

1. The States Parties shall submit to the Committee, through the Secretary-General of the United Nations, reports on the measures they have taken to give effect to their undertakings under this Convention, within one year after the entry into force of the Convention for the State Party concerned. Thereafter the States Parties shall submit supplementary reports every four years on any new measures taken and such other reports as the Committee may request.

2. The Secretary-General of the United Nations shall transmit the reports to all States Parties.

3. Each report shall be considered by the Committee which may make such general comments on the report as it may consider appropriate and shall forward these to the State Party concerned. That State Party may respond with any observations it chooses to the Committee.

4. The Committee may, at its discretion, decide to include any comments made by it in accordance with paragraph 3 of this article, together with the observations thereon received from the State Party concerned, in its annual report made in accordance with article 24. If so requested by the State Party concerned, the Committee may also include a copy of the report submitted under paragraph I of this article.

Article 20

1. If the Committee receives reliable information which appears to it to contain well-founded indications that torture is being systematically practised in the territory of a State Party, the Committee shall invite that State Party to co-operate in the examination of the information and to this end to submit observations with regard to the information concerned.

2. Taking into account any observations which may have been submitted by the State Party concerned, as well as any other relevant information available to it, the Committee may, if it decides that this is warranted, designate one or more of its members to make a confidential inquiry and to report to the Committee urgently.

3. If an inquiry is made in accordance with paragraph 2 of this article, the Committee shall seek the co-operation of the State Party concerned. In agreement with that State Party, such an inquiry may include a visit to its territory.

4. After examining the findings of its member or members submitted in accordance with paragraph 2 of this article, the Commission shall transmit these findings to the State Party concerned together with any comments or suggestions which seem appropriate in view of the situation.

5. All the proceedings of the Committee referred to in paragraphs I to 4 of this article shall be confidential, and at all stages of the proceedings the cooperation of the

State Party shall be sought. After such proceedings have been completed with regard to an inquiry made in accordance with paragraph 2, the Committee may, after consultations with the State Party concerned, decide to include a summary account of the results of the proceedings in its annual report made in accordance with article 24.

Article 21

1. A State Party to this Convention may at any time declare under this article that it recognizes the competence of the Committee to receive and consider communications to the effect that a State Party claims that another State Party is not fulfilling its obligations under this Convention. Such communications may be received and considered according to the procedures laid down in this article only if submitted by a State Party which has made a declaration recognizing in regard to itself the competence of the Committee. No communication shall be dealt with by the Committee under this article if it concerns a State Party which has not made such a declaration. Communications received under this article shall be dealt with in accordance with the following procedure;

(a) If a State Party considers that another State Party is not giving effect to the provisions of this Convention, it may, by written communication, bring the matter to the attention of that State Party. Within three months after the receipt of the communication the receiving State shall afford the State which sent the communication an explanation or any other statement in writing clarifying the matter, which should include, to the extent possible and pertinent, reference to domestic procedures and remedies taken, pending or available in the matter;

(b) If the matter is not adjusted to the satisfaction of both States Parties concerned within six months after the receipt by the receiving State of the initial communication, either State shall have the right to refer the matter to the Committee, by notice given to the Committee and to the other State;

(c) The Committee shall deal with a matter referred to it under this article only after it has ascertained that all domestic remedies have been invoked and exhausted in the matter, in conformity with the generally recognized principles of international law. This shall not be the rule where the application of the remedies is unreasonably prolonged or is unlikely to bring effective relief to the person who is the victim of the violation of this Convention;

(d) The Committee shall hold closed meetings when examining communications under this article;

(e) Subject to the provisions of subparagraph (c), the Committee shall make available its good offices to the States Parties concerned with a view to a friendly solution of the matter on the basis of respect for the obligations provided for in this Convention. For this purpose, the Committee may, when appropriate, set up an ad hoc conciliation commission;

(f) In any matter referred to it under this article, the Committee may call upon the States Parties concerned, referred to in subparagraph (b), to

supply any relevant information;
(g) The States Parties concerned, referred to in subparagraph (b), shall have the right to be represented when the matter is being considered by the Committee and to make submissions orally and/or in writing;
(h) The Committee shall, within twelve months after the date of receipt of notice under subparagraph (b), submit a report:

(i) If a solution within the terms of subparagraph (e) is reached, the Committee shall confine its report to a brief statement of the facts and of the solution reached;

(ii) If a solution within the terms of subparagraph (e) is not reached, the Committee shall confine its report to a brief statement of the facts; the written submissions and record of the oral submissions made by the States Parties concerned shall be attached to the report.

In every matter, the report shall be communicated to the States Parties concerned ....

Article 22

1. A State Party to this Convention may at any time declare under this article that it recognizes the competence of the Committee to receive and consider communications from or on behalf of individuals subject to its jurisdiction who claim to be victims of a violation by a State Party of the provisions of the Convention. No communication shall be received by the Committee if it concerns a State Party which has not made such a declaration.

2. The Committee shall consider inadmissible any communication under this article which is anonymous or which it considers to be an abuse of the right of submission of such communications or to be incompatible with the provisions of this Convention.

3. Subject to the provisions of paragraph 2, the Committee shall bring any communications submitted to it under this article to the attention of the State Party to this Convention which has made a declaration under paragraph I and is alleged to be violating any provisions of the Convention. Within six months, the receiving State shall submit to the Committee written explanations or statements clarifying the matter and the remedy, if any, that may have been taken by that State.

4. The Committee shall consider communications received under this article in the light of all information made available to it by or on behalf of the individual and by the State Party concerned.

5. The Committee shall not consider any communications from an individual under this article unless it has ascertained that:
(a) The same matter has not been, and is not being, examined under another procedure of international investigation or settlement;
(b) The individual has exhausted all available domestic remedies; this shall not be the rule where the application of the remedies is unreasonably prolonged or is unlikely to bring effective relief to the person who is the victim of the

violation of this Convention.

6. The Committee shall hold closed meetings when examining communications under this article.

7. The Committee shall forward its views to the State Party concerned and to the individual ....

Article 23

The members of the Committee and of the ad hoc conciliation commissions which may be appointed under article 21, paragraph I (e), shall be entitled to the facilities, privileges and immunities of experts on mission for the United Nations as laid down in the relevant sections of the Convention on the Privileges and Immunities of the United Nations.

Article 24

The Committee shall submit an annual report on its activities under this Convention to the States Parties and to the General Assembly of the United Nations ....

PART III
Article 26

This Convention is open to accession by all States. Accession shall be effected by the deposit of an instrument of accession with the Secretary-General of the United Nations ....

Article 28

1. Each State may, at the time of signature or ratification of this Convention or accession thereto, declare that it does not recognize the competence of the Committee provided for in article 20 ....

Article 29

1. Any State Party to this Convention may propose an amendment and file it with the Secretary- General of the United Nations. The Secretary-General shall thereupon communicate the proposed amendment to the States Parties with a request that they notify him whether they favour a conference of States Parties for the purpose of considering an d voting upon the proposal. In the event that within four months from the date of such communication at least one third of the States Parties favours such a conference, the Secretary-General shall convene the conference under the auspices of the United Nations. Any amendment adopted by a majority of the States Parties present and voting at the conference shall be submitted by the Secretary-General to all the States Parties for acceptance.

2. An amendment adopted in accordance with paragraph I of this article shall enter into force when two thirds of the States Parties to this Convention have notified the Secretary-General of the United Nations that they have accepted it in accordance with their respective constitutional processes.

3. When amendments enter into force, they shall be binding on those States Parties which have accepted them, other States Parties still being bound by the provisions of this Convention and any earlier

amendments which they have accepted.

Article 30

1. Any dispute between two or more States Parties concerning the interpretation or application of this Convention which cannot be settled through negotiation shall, at the request of one of them, be submitted to arbitration. If within six months from the date of the request for arbitration the Parties are unable to agree on the organization of the arbitration, any one of those Parties may refer the dispute to the International Court of Justice by request in conformity with the Statute of the Court ....

Article 31

1. A State Party may denounce this Convention by written notification to the Secretary-General of the United Nations. Denunciation becomes effective one year after the date of receipt of the notification by the Secretary-General.

2. Such a denunciation shall not have the effect of releasing the State Party from its obligations under this Convention in regard to any act or omission which occurs prior to the date at which the denunciation becomes effective, nor shall denunciation prejudice in any way the continued consideration of any matter which is already under consideration by the Committee prior to the date at which the denunciation becomes effective ....

TORTURE'S TERRIBLE TOLL

Senator John McCain

Reprinted with permission of
Senator John McCain.
Originally published by Newsweek
November 21, 2005

The debate over the treatment of enemy prisoners, like so much of the increasingly overcharged partisan debate over the war in Iraq and the global war against terrorists, has occasioned many unserious and unfair charges about the administration's intentions and motives. With all the many competing demands for their attention, President Bush and Vice President Cheney have remained admirably tenacious in their determination to prevent terrorists from inflicting another atrocity on the American people, whom they are sworn to protect. It is certainly fair to credit their administration's vigilance as a substantial part of the reason that we have not experienced another terrorist attack on American soil since September 11, 2001.

It is also quite fair to attribute the administration's position—that U.S. interrogators be allowed latitude in their treatment of enemy prisoners that might offend American values—to the president's and vice president's appropriate concern for acquiring actionable intelligence that could prevent attacks on our soldiers or our allies or on the American people. And it is quite unfair to assume some nefarious purpose informs their intentions. They bear the greatest responsibility for the security of American lives and interests. I understand and respect their motives just as I admire the seriousness and patriotism of their resolve. But I do, respectfully, take issue with the position that the demands of this war require us to accord a lower station to the moral imperatives that should govern our conduct in war and peace when they come in conflict with the unyielding inhumanity of our vicious enemy.

Obviously, to defeat our enemies we need intelligence, but intelligence that is reliable. We should not torture or treat inhumanely terrorists we have captured. The abuse of prisoners harms, not helps, our war effort. In my experience, abuse of prisoners often produces bad intelligence because under torture a person will say anything he thinks his captors want to hear—whether it is true or false—if he believes it will relieve his suffering. I was once physically coerced to provide my enemies with the names of the members of my flight squadron, information that had little if any value to my enemies as actionable intelligence. But I did not refuse, or repeat my insistence that I was required under the Geneva Conventions to provide my captors only with my name, rank and serial number. Instead, I gave them the names of the Green Bay Packers' offensive line, knowing that providing them false information was sufficient to suspend the abuse. It seems probable to me that the terrorists we interrogate under less than humane standards of treatment are also likely to resort to deceptive answers that are perhaps less provably false than that which I once offered.

Our commitment to basic humanitarian values affects—in part—the willingness of other nations to do the same. Mistreatment of enemy prisoners endangers our own troops who might someday be held captive. While some enemies, and Al Qaeda surely, will never be bound by the principle of reciprocity, we should have concern for those Americans captured by more traditional enemies, if not in this war then in the next. Until about 1970, North Vietnam ignored its obligations not to mistreat the Americans they held prisoner, claiming that we were engaged in an unlawful war against them and thus not entitled to the protections of the Geneva Conventions. But when their abuses became widely known and incited unfavorable international attention, they substantially decreased their mistreatment of us. Again, Al Qaeda will never be influenced by international sensibilities or open to moral suasion. If ever the term "sociopath" applied to anyone, it applies to them. But I doubt they will be the last enemy America will fight, and we should not undermine today our defense of international prohibitions against torture and inhumane treatment of prisoners of war that we will need to rely on in the future.

To prevail in this war we need more than victories on the battlefield. This is a war of ideas, a struggle to advance freedom in the face of terror in places where oppressive rule has bred the malevolence that creates terrorists. Prisoner abuses exact a terrible toll on us in this war of ideas. They inevitably become public, and when they do they threaten our moral standing, and expose us to false but widely disseminated charges that democracies are no more inherently idealistic and moral than other regimes. This is an existential fight, to be sure. If they could, Islamic extremists who resort to terror would destroy us utterly. But to defeat them we must prevail in our defense of American political values as well. The mistreatment of prisoners greatly injures that effort.

The mistreatment of prisoners harms us more than our enemies. I don't think I'm naive about how terrible are the wages of war, and how terrible are the things that must be done to wage it successfully. It is an awful business, and no matter how noble the cause for which it is fought, no matter how valiant their service, many veterans spend much of their subsequent lives trying to forget not only what was done to them, but some of what had to be done by them to prevail.

I don't mourn the loss of any terrorist's life. Nor do I care if in the course of serving their ignoble cause they suffer great harm. They have pledged their lives to the intentional destruction of innocent lives, and they have earned their terrible punishment in this life and the next. What I do mourn is what we lose when by official policy or official neglect we allow, confuse or encourage our soldiers to forget that best sense of ourselves, that which is our greatest strength—that we are different and better than our enemies, that we fight for an idea, not a tribe, not a land, not a king, not a twisted interpretation of an ancient religion, but for an idea that all men are created equal and endowed by their Creator with inalienable rights.

Now, in this war, our liberal notions are put to the test. Americans of good will, all patriots, argue about what is appropriate and necessary to combat this unconventional enemy. Those of us who feel that in this war, as in past wars, Americans should not compromise our values must answer those Americans who believe that a less rigorous application of those values is regrettably necessary to prevail over a uniquely abhorrent and dangerous enemy. Part of our disagreement is definitional. Some view more coercive interrogation tactics as something short of torture but worry that they might be subject to challenge under the "no cruel, inhumane or degrading" standard. Others, including me, believe that both the prohibition on torture and the cruel, inhumane and degrading standard must remain intact. When we relax that standard, it is nearly unavoidable that some objectionable practices will be allowed as something less than torture because they do not risk life and limb or do not cause very serious physical pain.

For instance, there has been considerable press attention to a tactic called "waterboarding," where a prisoner is restrained and blindfolded while an interrogator pours water on his face and into his mouth—causing the prisoner to believe he is being drowned. He isn't, of course; there is no intention to injure him physically. But if you gave people who have suffered abuse as prisoners a choice between a beating and a mock execution, many, including me, would choose a beating. The effects of most beatings heal. The memory of an execution will haunt someone for a very long time and damage his or her psyche in ways that may never heal. In my view, to make someone believe that you are killing him by drowning is no different than holding a pistol to his head and firing a blank. I believe that it is torture, very exquisite torture.

Those who argue the necessity of some abuses raise an important dilemma as their most compelling rationale: the ticking-time-bomb scenario. What do we do if we capture a terrorist who we have sound reasons to believe possesses specific knowledge of an imminent terrorist attack?

In such an urgent and rare instance, an interrogator might well try extreme measures to extract information that could save lives. Should he do so, and thereby save an American city or prevent another 9/11, authorities and the public would surely take this into account when judging his actions and recognize the extremely dire situation which he confronted. But I don't believe this scenario requires us to write into law an exception to our treaty and moral obligations that would permit cruel, inhumane and degrading treatment. To carve out legal exemptions to this basic principle of human rights risks opening the door to abuse as a matter of course, rather than a standard violated truly *in extremis*. It is far better to embrace a standard that might be violated in extraordinary circumstances than to lower our standards to accommodate a remote contingency, confusing personnel in the field and sending precisely the wrong message abroad about America's purposes and practices.

The state of Israel, no stranger to terrorist attacks, has faced this dilemma, and in 1999 the Israeli Supreme Court declared cruel, inhumane and degrading treatment illegal. "A democratic, freedom-loving society," the court wrote, "does not accept that investigators use any means for the purpose of uncovering truth. The rules pertaining to investigators are important to a democratic state. They reflect its character."

I've been asked often where did the brave men I was privileged to serve with in North Vietnam draw the strength to resist to the best of their abilities the cruelties inflicted on them by our enemies. They drew strength from their faith in each other, from their faith in God and from their faith in our country. Our enemies didn't adhere to the Geneva Conventions. Many of my comrades were subjected to very cruel, very inhumane and degrading treatment, a few of them unto death. But every one of us—every single one of us—knew and took great strength from the belief that we were different from our enemies, that we were better than them, that we, if the roles were reversed, would not disgrace ourselves by committing or approving such mistreatment of them. That faith was indispensable not only to our survival, but to our attempts to return home with honor. For without our honor, our homecoming would have had little value to us.

The enemies we fight today hold our liberal values in contempt, as they hold in contempt the international conventions that enshrine them. I know that. But we are better than them, and we are stronger for our faith. And we will prevail. It is indispensable to our success in this war that those we ask to fight it know that in the discharge of their dangerous responsibilities to their country they are never expected to forget that they are Americans, and the valiant defenders of a sacred idea of how nations should govern their own affairs and their relations with others—even our enemies.

Those who return to us and those who give their lives for us are entitled to that honor. And those of us who have given them this onerous duty are obliged by our history, and the many terrible sacrifices that have been made in our defense, to make clear to them that they need not risk their or their country's honor to prevail; that they are always—through the violence, chaos and heartache of war, through deprivation and cruelty and loss—they are always, always, Americans, and different, better and stronger than those who would destroy us.

109TH CONGRESS - REPORT
HOUSE OF REPRESENTATIVES
1ST SESSION / 109-359

-MAKING APPROPRIATIONS FOR THE DEPARTMENT OF DEFENSE FOR THE FISCAL YEAR ENDING SEPTEMBER 30, 2006, AND FOR OTHER PURPOSES

December 18, 2005- Ordered to be printed

Mr. YOUNG of Florida, from the committee of conference, submitted the following

CONFERENCE REPORT
[To accompany H.R. 2863]

The committee of conference on the disagreeing votes of the two Houses on the amendment of the Senate to the bill (H.R. 2863) 'making appropriations for the Department of Defense for the fiscal year ending September 30, 2006, and for other purposes', having met, after full and free conference, have agreed to recommend and do recommend to their respective Houses as follows:

That the House recede from its disagreement to the amendment of the Senate, and agree to the same with an amendment, as follows:

In lieu of the matter stricken and inserted by said amendment, insert:

DIVISION A

DEPARTMENT OF DEFENSE APPROPRIATIONS ACT, 2006

That the following sums are appropriated, out of any money in the Treasury not otherwise appropriated, for the fiscal year ending September 30, 2006, for military functions administered by the Department of Defense and for other purposes, namely:

[. . .]

TITLE X--MATTERS RELATING TO DETAINEES

SEC. 1001. SHORT TITLE.

This title may be cited as the 'Detainee Treatment Act of 2005'.

SEC. 1002. UNIFORM STANDARDS FOR THE INTERROGATION OF PERSONS UNDER THE DETENTION OF THE DEPARTMENT OF DEFENSE.

(a) In General- No person in the custody or under the effective control of the Department of Defense or under detention in a Department of Defense facility shall be subject to any treatment or technique of interrogation not authorized by and listed in the United States Army Field Manual on Intelligence Interrogation.

(b) Applicability- Subsection (a) shall not apply with respect to any person in the custody or under the effective control of the Department of Defense pursuant to a criminal law or immigration law of the United States.

(c) Construction- Nothing in this section shall be construed to affect the rights under the United States Constitution of any person in the custody or under the physical jurisdiction of the United States.

SEC. 1003. PROHIBITION ON CRUEL, INHUMAN, OR DEGRADING TREATMENT OR PUNISHMENT OF PERSONS UNDER CUSTODY OR CONTROL OF THE UNITED STATES GOVERNMENT.

(a) In General- No individual in the custody or under the physical control of the United States Government, regardless of nationality or physical location, shall be subject to cruel, inhuman, or degrading treatment or punishment.

(b) Construction- Nothing in this section shall be construed to impose any geographical limitation on the applicability of the prohibition against cruel, inhuman, or degrading treatment or punishment under this section.

(c) Limitation on Supersedure- The provisions of this section shall not be superseded, except by a provision of law enacted after the date of the enactment of this Act which specifically repeals, modifies, or supersedes the provisions of this section.

(d) Cruel, Inhuman, or Degrading Treatment or Punishment Defined- In this section, the term 'cruel, inhuman, or degrading treatment or punishment' means the cruel, unusual, and inhumane treatment or punishment prohibited by the Fifth, Eighth, and Fourteenth Amendments to the Constitution of the United States, as defined in the United States Reservations, Declarations and Understandings to the United Nations Convention Against Torture and Other Forms of Cruel, Inhuman or Degrading Treatment or Punishment done at New York, December 10, 1984.

SEC. 1004. PROTECTION OF UNITED STATES GOVERNMENT PERSONNEL ENGAGED IN AUTHORIZED INTERROGATIONS.

(a) Protection of United States Government Personnel- In any civil action or criminal prosecution against an officer, employee, member of the Armed Forces, or other agent of the United States Government who is a United States person, arising out of the officer, employee, member of the Armed Forces, or other agent's engaging in specific operational practices, that involve detention and interrogation of aliens who the President or his designees have determined are believed to be engaged in or associated with international terrorist activity that poses a serious, continuing threat to the United States, its interests, or its allies, and that were officially authorized and determined to be lawful at the time that they were conducted, it shall be a defense that such officer, employee, member of the Armed Forces, or other agent did not know that the practices were unlawful and a person of ordinary sense and understanding would not know the practices were unlawful. Good faith reliance on advice of counsel should be an important factor, among others, to consider in assessing whether a person of ordinary sense and understanding would have known the practices to be unlawful. Nothing in this section shall be construed to limit or extinguish any defense or protection otherwise available to any person or entity from suit, civil or criminal liability, or damages, or to provide immunity from prosecution for any criminal offense by the proper authorities.

(b) Counsel- The United States Government may provide or employ counsel, and pay counsel fees, court costs, bail, and other expenses incident to the representation of an officer, employee, member of the Armed Forces, or other agent described in subsection (a), with respect to any civil action or criminal prosecution arising out of practices described in that subsection, under the same conditions, and to the same extent, to which such services and payments are authorized under section 1037 of title 10, United States Code.

SEC. 1005. PROCEDURES FOR STATUS REVIEW OF DETAINEES OUTSIDE THE UNITED STATES.

(a) Submittal of Procedures for Status Review of Detainees at Guantanamo Bay, Cuba, and in Afghanistan and Iraq-

(1) IN GENERAL- Not later than 180 days after the date of the enactment of this Act, the Secretary of Defense shall submit to the Committee on Armed Services and the Committee on the Judiciary of the Senate and the Committee on Armed Services and the Committee on the Judiciary of the House of Representatives a report setting forth--

(A) the procedures of the Combatant Status Review Tribunals and the Administrative Review Boards established by direction of the Secretary of Defense that are in operation at Guantanamo Bay, Cuba, for determining the status of the detainees held at Guantanamo Bay or to provide an annual review to determine the need to continue to detain an alien who is a detainee; and

(B) the procedures in operation in Afghanistan and Iraq for a determination of the status of aliens detained in the custody or under the physical control of the Department of Defense in those countries.

(2) DESIGNATED CIVILIAN OFFICIAL- The procedures submitted to Congress pursuant to paragraph (1)(A) shall ensure that the official of the Department of Defense who is designated by the President or Secretary of Defense to be the final review authority within the Department of Defense with respect to decisions of any such tribunal or board (referred to as the 'Designated Civilian Official') shall be a civilian officer of the Department of Defense holding an office to which appointments are required by law to be made by the President, by and with the advice and consent of the Senate.

(3) CONSIDERATION OF NEW EVIDENCE- The procedures submitted under paragraph (1)(A) shall provide for periodic review of any new evidence that may become available relating to the enemy combatant status of a detainee.

(b) Consideration of Statements Derived With Coercion-

(1) ASSESSMENT- The procedures submitted to Congress pursuant to subsection (a)(1)(A) shall ensure that a Combatant Status Review Tribunal or Administrative Review Board, or any similar or successor administrative tribunal or board, in making a determination of status or disposition of any detainee under such procedures, shall, to the extent practicable, assess--

(A) whether any statement derived from or relating to such detainee was obtained as a result of coercion; and

(B) the probative value (if any) of any such statement.

(2) APPLICABILITY- Paragraph (1) applies with respect to any proceeding beginning on or after the date of the enactment of this Act.

(c) Report on Modification of Procedures- The Secretary of Defense shall submit to the committees specified in subsection (a)(1) a report on any modification of the procedures submitted under subsection (a). Any such report shall be submitted not later than 60 days before the date on which such modification goes into effect.

(d) Annual Report-

(1) REPORT REQUIRED- The Secretary of Defense shall submit to Congress an annual report on the annual review process for aliens in the custody of the Department of Defense outside the United States. Each such report shall be submitted in unclassified form, with a classified annex, if necessary. The report shall be submitted not later than December 31 each year.

(2) ELEMENTS OF REPORT- Each such report shall include the following with respect to the year covered by the report:

(A) The number of detainees whose status was reviewed.

(B) The procedures used at each location.

(e) Judicial Review of Detention of Enemy Combatants-

(1) IN GENERAL- Section 2241 of title 28, United States Code, is amended by adding at the end the following:

'(e) Except as provided in section 1005 of the Detainee Treatment Act of 2005, no court, justice, or judge shall have jurisdiction to hear or consider--

'(1) an application for a writ of habeas corpus filed by or on behalf of an alien detained by the Department of Defense at Guantanamo Bay, Cuba; or

'(2) any other action against the United States or its agents relating to any aspect of the detention by the

Department of Defense of an alien at Guantanamo Bay, Cuba, who--

'(A) is currently in military custody; or

'(B) has been determined by the United States Court of Appeals for the District of Columbia Circuit in accordance with the procedures set forth in section 1005(e) of the Detainee Treatment Act of 2005 to have been properly detained as an enemy combatant.'.

(2) REVIEW OF DECISIONS OF COMBATANT STATUS REVIEW TRIBUNALS OF PROPRIETY OF DETENTION-

(A) IN GENERAL- Subject to subparagraphs (B), (C), and (D), the United States Court of Appeals for the District of Columbia Circuit shall have exclusive jurisdiction to determine the validity of any final decision of a Combatant Status Review Tribunal that an alien is properly detained as an enemy combatant.

(B) LIMITATION ON CLAIMS- The jurisdiction of the United States Court of Appeals for the District of Columbia Circuit under this paragraph shall be limited to claims brought by or on behalf of an alien--

(i) who is, at the time a request for review by such court is filed, detained by the Department of Defense at Guantanamo Bay, Cuba; and

(ii) for whom a Combatant Status Review Tribunal has been conducted, pursuant to applicable procedures specified by the Secretary of Defense.

(C) SCOPE OF REVIEW- The jurisdiction of the United States Court of Appeals for the District of Columbia Circuit on any claims with respect to an alien under this paragraph shall be limited to the consideration of--

(i) whether the status determination of the Combatant Status Review Tribunal with regard to such alien was consistent with the standards and procedures specified by the Secretary of Defense for Combatant Status Review Tribunals (including the requirement that the conclusion of the Tribunal be supported by a preponderance of the evidence and allowing a rebuttable presumption in favor of the Government's evidence); and

(ii) to the extent the Constitution and laws of the United States are applicable, whether the use of such standards and procedures to make the determination is consistent with the Constitution and laws of the United States.

(D) TERMINATION ON RELEASE FROM CUSTODY- The jurisdiction of the United States Court of Appeals for the District of Columbia Circuit with respect to the claims of an alien under this paragraph shall cease upon the release of such alien from the custody of the Department of Defense.

(3) REVIEW OF FINAL DECISIONS OF MILITARY COMMISSIONS-

(A) IN GENERAL- Subject to

subparagraphs (B), (C), and (D), the United States Court of Appeals for the District of Columbia Circuit shall have exclusive jurisdiction to determine the validity of any final decision rendered pursuant to Military Commission Order No. 1, dated August 31, 2005 (or any successor military order).

(B) GRANT OF REVIEW- Review under this paragraph--

(i) with respect to a capital case or a case in which the alien was sentenced to a term of imprisonment of 10 years or more, shall be as of right; or

(ii) with respect to any other case, shall be at the discretion of the United States Court of Appeals for the District of Columbia Circuit.

(C) LIMITATION ON APPEALS- The jurisdiction of the United States Court of Appeals for the District of Columbia Circuit under this paragraph shall be limited to an appeal brought by or on behalf of an alien--

(i) who was, at the time of the proceedings pursuant to the military order referred to in subparagraph (A), detained by the Department of Defense at Guantanamo Bay, Cuba; and

(ii) for whom a final decision has been rendered pursuant to such military order.

(D) SCOPE OF REVIEW- The jurisdiction of the United States Court of Appeals for the District of Columbia Circuit on an appeal of a final decision with respect to an alien under this paragraph shall be limited to the consideration of--

(i) whether the final decision was consistent with the standards and procedures specified in the military order referred to in subparagraph (A); and

(ii) to the extent the Constitution and laws of the United States are applicable, whether the use of such standards and procedures to reach the final decision is consistent with the Constitution and laws of the United States.

(4) RESPONDENT- The Secretary of Defense shall be the named respondent in any appeal to the United States Court of Appeals for the District of Columbia Circuit under this subsection.

(f) Construction- Nothing in this section shall be construed to confer any constitutional right on an alien detained as an enemy combatant outside the United States.

(g) United States Defined- For purposes of this section, the term 'United States', when used in a geographic sense, is as defined in section 101(a)(38) of the Immigration and Nationality Act and, in particular, does not include the United States Naval Station, Guantanamo Bay, Cuba.

(h) Effective Date-

(1) IN GENERAL- This section shall take effect on the date of the enactment of this Act.

(2) REVIEW OF COMBATANT STATUS TRIBUNAL AND MILITARY COMMISSION DECISIONS- Paragraphs (2) and (3) of subsection (e) shall apply with respect to any claim whose review is governed by one of such paragraphs and that is pending on or after the date of the enactment of this Act.

SEC. 1006. TRAINING OF IRAQI FORCES REGARDING TREATMENT OF DETAINEES.

(a) Required Policies-

(1) IN GENERAL- The Secretary of Defense shall ensure that policies are prescribed regarding procedures for military and civilian personnel of the Department of Defense and contractor personnel of the Department of Defense in Iraq that are intended to ensure that members of the Armed Forces, and all persons acting on behalf of the Armed Forces or within facilities of the Armed Forces, ensure that all personnel of Iraqi military forces who are trained by Department of Defense personnel and contractor personnel of the Department of Defense receive training regarding the international obligations and laws applicable to the humane detention of detainees, including protections afforded under the Geneva Conventions and the Convention Against Torture.

(2) ACKNOWLEDGMENT OF TRAINING- The Secretary shall ensure that, for all personnel of the Iraqi Security Forces who are provided training referred to in paragraph (1), there is documented acknowledgment of such training having been provided.

(3) DEADLINE FOR POLICIES TO BE PRESCRIBED- The policies required by paragraph (1) shall be prescribed not later than 180 days after the date of the enactment of this Act.

(b) Army Field Manual-

(1) TRANSLATION- The Secretary of Defense shall provide for the United States Army Field Manual on Intelligence Interrogation to be translated into arabic and any other language the Secretary determines appropriate for use by members of the Iraqi military forces.

(2) DISTRIBUTION- The Secretary of Defense shall provide for such manual, as translated, to be provided to each unit of the Iraqi military forces trained by Department of Defense personnel or contractor personnel of the Department of Defense.

(c) Transmittal of Regulations- Not less than 30 days after the date on which regulations, policies, and orders are first prescribed under subsection (a), the Secretary of Defense shall submit to the Committee on Armed Services of the Senate and the Committee on Armed Services of the House of Representatives copies of such regulations, policies, or orders, together with a report on steps taken to the date of the report to implement this section.

(d) Annual Report- Not less than one year after the date of the enactment of this Act, and annually thereafter, the Secretary of Defense shall submit to the Committee on Armed Services of the Senate and the Committee on Armed Services of the House of Representatives a report on the implementation of this section.

[. . .]

# # #

PRESIDENT'S STATEMENT ON SIGNING OF H.R. 2863, THE "DEPARTMENT OF DEFENSE, EMERGENCY SUPPLEMENTAL APPROPRIATIONS TO ADDRESS HURRICANES IN THE GULF OF MEXICO, AND PANDEMIC INFLUENZA ACT, 2006"

Office of the Press Secretary
December 30, 2005

Today, I have signed into law H.R. 2863, the "Department of Defense, Emergency Supplemental Appropriations to Address Hurricanes in the Gulf of Mexico, and Pandemic Influenza Act, 2006." The Act provides resources needed to fight the war on terror, help citizens of the Gulf States recover from devastating hurricanes, and protect Americans from a potential influenza pandemic.

Sections 8007, 8011, and 8093 of the Act prohibit the use of funds to initiate a special access program, a new overseas installation, or a new start program, unless the congressional defense committees receive advance notice. The Supreme Court of the United States has stated that the President's authority to classify and control access to information bearing on the national security flows from the Constitution and does not depend upon a legislative grant of authority. Although the advance notice contemplated by sections 8007, 8011, and 8093 can be provided in most situations as a matter of comity, situations may arise, especially in wartime, in which the President must act promptly under his constitutional grants of executive power and authority as Commander in Chief of the Armed Forces while protecting certain extraordinarily sensitive national security information. The executive branch shall construe these sections in a manner consistent with the constitutional authority of the President.

Section 8059 of the Act provides that, notwithstanding any other provision of law, no funds available to the Department of Defense for fiscal year 2006 may be used to transfer defense articles or services, other than intelligence services, to another nation or an international organization for international peacekeeping, peace enforcement, or humanitarian assistance operations, until 15 days after the executive branch notifies six committees of the Congress of the planned transfer. To the extent that protection of the U.S. Armed Forces deployed for international peacekeeping, peace enforcement, or humanitarian assistance operations might require action of a kind covered by section 8059 sooner than 15 days after notification, the executive branch shall construe the section in a manner consistent with the President's constitutional authority as Commander in Chief.

A proviso in the Act's appropriation for "Operation and Maintenance, Defense-Wide" purports to prohibit planning for consolidation of certain offices within the Department of Defense. Also, sections 8010(b), 8032, 8037(b), and 8100 purport to specify the content of portions of future budget requests to the Congress. The executive branch shall construe these provisions relating to planning and making of budget recommendations in a manner consistent with the President's constitutional authority to require the opinions of the heads of departments, to supervise the unitary executive branch, and to recommend for congressional consideration such measures as the President shall judge necessary and expedient.

Section 8005 of the Act, relating to requests to congressional committees for reprogramming of funds, shall be construed as calling solely for notification, as any other construction would be inconsistent with the constitutional principles enunciated by the Supreme Court of the United States in INS v. Chadha.

The executive branch shall construe section 8104, relating to integration of foreign intelligence information, in a manner consistent with the President's constitutional authority as Commander in Chief, including for the conduct of intelligence operations, and to supervise the unitary executive branch. Also, the executive branch shall construe sections 8106 and 8119 of the Act, which purport to prohibit the President from altering command and control relationships within the Armed Forces, as advisory, as any other construction would be inconsistent with the constitutional grant to the President of the authority of Commander in Chief.

The executive branch shall construe provisions of the Act relating to race, ethnicity, gender, and State residency, such as sections 8014, 8020 and 8057, in a manner consistent with the requirement to afford equal protection of the laws under the Due Process Clause of the Constitution's Fifth Amendment.

The executive branch shall construe Title X in Division A of the Act, relating to detainees, in a manner consistent with the constitutional authority of the President to supervise the unitary executive branch and as Commander in Chief and consistent with the constitutional limitations on the judicial power, which will assist in achieving the shared objective of the Congress and the President, evidenced in Title X, of protecting the American people from further terrorist attacks. Further, in light of the principles enunciated by the Supreme Court of the United States in 2001 in Alexander v. Sandoval, and noting that the text and structure of Title X do not create a private right of action to enforce Title X, the executive branch shall construe Title X not to create a private right of action. Finally, given the decision of the Congress reflected in subsections 1005(e) and 1005(h) that the amendments made to section 2241 of title 28, United States Code, shall apply to past, present, and future actions, including applications for writs of habeas corpus, described in that section, and noting that section 1005 does not confer any constitutional right upon an alien detained abroad as an enemy combatant, the executive branch shall construe section 1005 to preclude the Federal courts from exercising subject matter jurisdiction over any existing or

future action, including applications for writs of habeas corpus, described in section 1005.

Language in Division B of the Act, under the heading "Office of Justice Programs, State and Local Law Enforcement Assistance," purports to require the Attorney General to consult congressional committees prior to allocating appropriations for expenditure to execute the law. Because the President's constitutional authority to supervise the unitary executive branch and take care that the laws be faithfully executed cannot be made by law subject to a requirement to consult with congressional committees or to involve them in executive decision-making, the executive branch shall construe the provision to require only notification. At the same time, the Attorney General shall, as a matter of comity between the executive and legislative branches, seek and consider the views of appropriate committees in this matter as the Attorney General deems appropriate.

Certain provisions in the Act purport to allocate funds for specified purposes as set forth in the joint explanatory statement of managers that accompanied the Act or other Acts; to make changes in statements of managers that accompanied various appropriations bills reported from conferences in the past; or to direct compliance with a committee report. Such provisions include section 8044 in Division A, and sections 5022, 5023, and 5024 and language under the heading "Natural Resources Conservation Service, Conservation Operations" in Division B, of the Act. Other provisions of the Act, such as sections 8073 and 8082 in Division A, purport to give binding effect to legislative documents not presented to the President. The executive branch shall construe all these provisions in a manner consistent with the bicameral passage and presentment requirements of the Constitution for the making of a law.

GEORGE W. BUSH

THE WHITE HOUSE,

December 30, 2005.

# # #

Deprived of Freedom

The International Committee of the Red Cross
Central Tracing Agency and Protection Division

ICRC publication 2002
Reference: 0685

(www.icrc.org/web/eng/siteeng0.nsf/iwpList265/B462B98285B30773C1256C79004D4EE7)

Protection of prisoners: a necessity.

Even in societies where the rule of law prevails, the authorities may, if they feel threatened, be tempted to use undue force in order to attain their political or military objectives.

The same is true of opposition factions. People deprived of their freedom in such circumstances are particularly vulnerable, for they are in danger of disappearing or being subjected to torture or ill-treatment.

Under international humanitarian law and the mandate entrusted to it by the international community, the International Committee of the Red Cross (ICRC) is responsible for helping the victims of both internal and international armed conflicts and of other situations of violence. Since 1915 the ICRC has progressively developed procedures for visiting and subsequently monitoring the conditions in which people deprived of their freedom are detained. On the basis of the Geneva Conventions or with the prior consent of the detaining authorities, it regularly visits prisoners of war, civilian internees and security prisoners, and keeps a check on their situation until they are released. By making repeated visits, it is able to assess the psychological and material conditions of detention.

The ICRC reports its findings to the authorities and, if necessary, asks them to take steps to halt any abuses noted or remedy shortcomings in the prison system.
Although the risk of purely arbitrary arrest is high, particularly during internal unrest, the ICRC remains strictly neutral: it does not comment on the grounds for imprisonment, but confines its observations and requests to the treatment of detainees, particularly during interrogation, and to the conditions of detention. However, it does make sure that people facing prosecution benefit by the minimum legal safeguards laid down in international law.

Through its work the ICRC supports the efforts made by the international community to promote respect for international humanitarian law and the general principles of human rights.

Visits to prisoners: a practice established in the early twentieth century.

Ever since 1915, the ICRC has been visiting people deprived of their freedom in times of conflict. It became concerned about the situation of prisoners of war and civilian internees in the early months of the First World War, once it was clear that the conflict would be of long duration: on its own initiative, and with the belligerents' consent, it started visiting them.

Its objective was to encourage the parties to improve the prisoners' conditions of detention wherever necessary, and to be able to inform their governments and families how they were faring. This practice was subsequently codified in international humanitarian law, in the 1929 Geneva Convention on prisoners of war. In 1918 and 1919, ICRC delegates also visited security prisoners for the first time in Petrograd (Russia) and in Hungary. During the Second World War they made over 11,170 visits to camps housing prisoners of war and civilian internees in the hands of States party to the 1929 Geneva Convention.

After 1945 the ICRC adapted its activities to the needs created by new forms of conflict, offering its humanitarian services to the belligerents and visiting people in captivity during the wars in Viet Nam and Afghanistan and the internal conflicts in Mozambique, El Salvador and Nicaragua, and in situations of internal tension such as the one that prevailed in South Africa. At the same time, the ICRC has continued to protect and assist prisoners of war during and after international armed conflicts (Falklands/Malvinas Islands, Iran/Iraq, Panama/United States, the Gulf war, Ecuador/Peru and Eritrea/Ethiopia).

International humanitarian law: protection for people deprived of their freedom.

International humanitarian law contains many provisions relating to the situation of people deprived of their freedom.

In international armed conflicts, the following persons are protected by the Geneva Conventions of 1949 and Additional Protocol I:

prisoners of war, by the Third Geneva Convention which is devoted entirely to them (for instance, during the Gulf war, Iraqi prisoners detained by the Coalition forces and prisoners from Coalition countries in the hands of the Iraqi authorities);

civilian internees (i.e. civilians deprived of their freedom for security reasons), by the Fourth Geneva Convention on the protection of civilians in wartime (for instance, Iraqi nationals living in the United Kingdom, Italy and France and interned there from the start of the Gulf war);

in the event of territorial occupation, persons suspected or accused of committing acts hostile to the occupying power, persons tried for such acts and criminal law prisoners, by the provisions of the Fourth Geneva Convention (for instance, Palestinians detained or interned by Israel).

The States party to the Geneva Conventions have formally undertaken to allow ICRC delegates to visit the above-mentioned persons in the event of international armed conflict.

In non-international armed conflicts, on the other hand, people who are not or are no longer taking part in the hostilities, particularly those deprived of their freedom, are protected by Article 3 common to the Geneva Conventions and by Additional Protocol II.

The ICRC steps in on their behalf by virtue of the right of initiative assigned to it by the Conventions. In practice, it draws on the concepts applicable to international armed conflicts to define the categories of prisoners to whom it wants access: members of government armed forces, armed rebels captured by enemy forces, and civilians arrested by the government or the armed opposition because of their real or presumed support for the other side. The ICRC likewise visits people who are likely to be persecuted because of their ethnic origin, religions, belief, etc.

The ICRC may also offer its services to the authorities in the event of internal tension or disturbances. In such cases it acts, according to the gravity and urgency of the humanitarian needs observed, on the basis of the humanitarian right of initiative laid down in the Statutes of the International Red Cross and Red Crescent Movement and accepted by the States. For its detention-related activities those two criteria are determined by factors such as the number of arrests, the effectiveness of supervisory mechanisms within the country, the conduct of police and security forces and allegations of ill-treatment and disappearances.

Then again, the ICRC may offer its services to the authorities in other situations such as serious disruptions of law and order or the lack of minimum guarantees of individual safety, for instance, if many people are affected or if it believes that its intervention may reduce tension.

Over the years the ICRC has steadily extended the scope of its activities: criminal law offenders are included in its representations and visits if they share the same premises as persons arrested in connection with internal tension or disturbances, or if they are suffering as a direct result of that situation. For example, if prison food supplies are inadequate (thus affecting all prisoners, regardless of their status or the reasons for their arrest), the ICRC asks the authorities to take the necessary steps to remedy the shortage. Any additional assistance provided by the ICRC is distributed to all prisoners alike.

Visits to prisoners captured during internal armed conflict.

The Russian civil war (1917-1921) was the first internal armed conflict during which the ICRC visited prisoners; its delegates modelled their activities on the practice established for prisoners of war in international armed conflicts.

With the spate of internal conflicts after the Second World War, this work assumed particular importance. The ICRC's objective was to gain access to all people captured and held by all parties to the conflict, but it did not always manage to do so. In other situations, ICRC visits have helped to protect people held not only by the government authorities but also by liberation or opposition movements.

ICRC visits: facts are established, then the authorities are approached.

ICRC teams visiting people deprived of their freedom consist of at least one delegate and one doctor or sometimes a nurse.

The size of the team and the length of the visits depend on the scale of the problems anticipated and the size of the premises to be visited: two people are enough to visit a police station in Sri Lanka, but one or more teams working together over several weeks will be required for the same task in large prisons divided into many sections holding thousands of prisoners, such as that of Shibergan in Afghanistan.

All ICRC visits follow a standard procedure and take place only if certain conditions are fulfilled. ICRC visits to places of detention start with a preliminary exchange of views with the people in charge there to explain how the visits themselves are organized and carried out. Together with the prison authorities, the delegates then inspect the entire premises (cells, dormitories, latrines, showers, exercise yards, visiting rooms, kitchens, workshops, sports areas, places of worship, infirmary, punishment and solitary confinement cells, etc.).

The most important part of the visit is the private conversations the delegates have with each prisoner who so requests, as well as with those to whom the delegates themselves wish to speak in private, at which neither the authorities nor the guards are present. In this way the ICRC team tries to find out what the prisoners regard as their main problems.

After analysing the information gathered and their own observations, the delegates submit their findings, conclusions and recommendations to the people in charge of the place of detention and make a note of their comments. In many cases, problems can be solved by establishing an ongoing working relationship with the local prison authorities.

The next step is to approach the higher authorities. Problems such as overcrowding, medical care and water or food supplies very often depend not only on the prison director but also on other authorities such as the Prisons Department or the Ministry of Health. Such approaches may take the form of interviews at various levels or of correspondence or written reports, depending on how great and how urgent the problem is.

The ICRC regularly provides the national authorities with a summary report on its findings over a given period or in a specific category of places of detention, which covers not only the problems identified but also any improvements observed or measures taken.

Prior conditions -
Drawing on the experience acquired over the years, the ICRC has thus established guidelines enabling it to evaluate a prison system with maximum objectivity and submit concrete and realistic proposals which take local customs and standards into account.

Whatever the circumstances, the ICRC visits people deprived of their freedom only if the authorities allow it:

to see all prisoners who come within its mandate and to have access to all places at which they are held;

to speak with prisoners in private, without any third parties being present;

to draw up a list of prisoners during its visit whom it considers to come within its mandate, or to receive such a list from the authorities and to check and supplement it if necessary;

to repeat its visits to all prisoners of its choice if it considers that the situation so warrants, and to do so as often as it wishes.

Confidential reports -
Until the late 1940s, the ICRC used to publish its reports on visits to prisoners. However, because its reports were sometimes used polemically for political purposes, thereby jeopardizing further dialogue with the authorities, the ICRC had to stop publishing them. Since then, ICRC reports have been submitted solely to the authorities concerned. The ICRC nevertheless reserves the right to publish its entire report if a detaining authority issues an abridged and consequently incomplete version of it.

Place of detention: one reality, three perceptions -
Steps taken by ICRC delegates on behalf of people deprived of their freedom are based on an analysis and consolidation of information obtained chiefly from three sources:

the authorities, who explain their view of the prison system and conditions of detention and tell of any problems encountered;

prisoners, who describe their own experiences and difficulties;

the delegates, who gather full information from these two sources and their own observations to form their own conclusions.

Private interviews with prisoners: the cornerstone of ICRC action

Conversations in strict privacy between delegates and individual prisoners, without any authorities present, are the cornerstone of ICRC action on behalf of people deprived of their freedom.

Such interviews without witnesses, as they are sometimes called, serve a dual purpose: they give the prisoners a break from prison routine, during which they can speak freely about what matters most to them and be sure of being heard; and they enable the ICRC to find out all about the conditions of detention and the treatment of prisoners. The interviewing delegate also enquires how the arrest and the subsequent questioning took place, and about the conditions of detention at the various places where the prisoner was temporarily held before arriving at the place visited.

In addition, the delegate may be given information about fellow prisoners whose arrest has not yet been notified to the ICRC or whom it has not been able to contact. He or she will ensure that the interview takes place without interference from other prisoners, who might seek to exert pressure.

The task of conducting such interviews is all the more delicate because they often revive painful memories of traumatic experiences, and there can be no question of subjecting the prisoners to a fresh interrogation. There are no precise rules for interviewing detainees: it is up to the delegate to assess the situation on a case-by-case basis and adjust to it to create an atmosphere of trust. Sometimes the chance to speak to somebody from outside is enough for the individual prisoners to confide in the delegate, while for others it may take several visits before they will tell their story. Then again, they may open up only to the ICRC doctor. On the strength of the information thus gathered and after cross-checking, the ICRC decides what action should be taken.

Whenever necessary, interpreters are used to communicate with the prisoners. They are recruited by the ICRC itself and, to avoid any pressure, they are never nationals of the country in which the visits take place. If it has no suitable interpreters available, the ICRC may ask the prisoners to appoint one or more from among themselves; this practice is seldom adopted, however, since the prisoner interpreting a fellow inmate's remarks may be endangered by doing so or may distort what he or she says.

A professional code of conduct drawn up with the prisoner's interests in mind

To the ICRC, the interests of the individual prisoners visited prevail over all other considerations. Their situation may lead to diplomatic approaches or some other intervention, but must always be handled with the utmost caution.

A risk of reprisals against prisoners if allegations of ill-treatment are reported to the prison authorities may cause the ICRC to postpone its call for an investigation. Delegates will nevertheless contact other officials often at a higher level to prevent such situations from recurring. On no account will the ICRC quote a prisoner's statements without his or her express permission. It takes care to see that its interventions do not have any negative impact on the day-to-day life of inmates, and adapts them accordingly. This is monitored by regular visits to the same place of detention.

The ICRC is also careful not to disrupt the prisoners' own internal organization. To withstand the pressures of prison life to the best of its ability, every group of prisoners sets up its own structures which sometimes reflect the social hierarchy and political movements of the outside world. To request the transfer of prisoners from one block to another may upset that internal structure and have serious repercussions such as fights, rivalries between groups or the deprival of certain advantages linked to residence in a given block. On the other hand, the ICRC may ask for prisoners to be transferred because they are being taunted or ill-treated by cellmates for political or other reasons.

Individual monitoring to prevent extrajudicial executions and forced disappearances of people under arrest

Any situation of conflict or violence within a country brings with it the risk of disappearances and extrajudicial executions.

In order to prevent disappearances, the identity of people arrested must be established as soon as possible and their cases kept under observation. The ICRC therefore asks to be informed promptly of all people arrested and detained and to see them without delay. When visiting such prisoners, the ICRC registers their names and all other personal data and transmits them to their families. It can thus keep track of these people throughout their imprisonment, for each time it visits their place of detention it asks to see them again. If this is not possible, it will want to know why, and ask to be informed of the missing prisoner's whereabouts. If a prisoner is transferred, the ICRC will try to visit him or her at the new place of detention.

Such visits will continue until the danger is significantly reduced or until the person is released, and individual monitoring may not stop even then, for families sometimes have to be contacted to check that a prisoner really has been released. If the situation so requires, particularly when the ICRC cannot gain access to a person whom it has previously visited, it repeatedly contacts the highest authorities both orally and in writing until it receives satisfactory information as to that person's situation and whereabouts.

The ICRC also contacts the authorities when its delegates are given eyewitness accounts of arrests, or at the request of families who report that a relative is missing.

A step-by-step approach

The ICRC analyses each item of information gathered by its delegates in the field in order to ensure that it really does see all detainees.

If it feels that it is not being given access to all the prisoners it wishes to see, the ICRC contacts the authorities to enquire about them. Its work is therefore not confined to the prisoners it visits, but is also based on statements made to its delegates by people who themselves witnessed an arrest, by the families of missing persons or by prisoners who report that a fellow inmate has disappeared.

Prisoners sometimes tell delegates that they have been held at places which the authorities have not reported to the ICRC. In such cases, the ICRC will negotiate access to the places in question and ask to be systematically informed of their existence.
However, if it believes that unofficial detention and hence the danger of disappearances may increase if it steps in, it may decide to postpone its intervention. It will nonetheless try, on the basis of any information it can obtain and especially the testimony of credible fellow prisoners, to keep a check on the situation of people detained in such places.

Registration and notification:
a safeguard -
The risk of extrajudicial execution or disappearance is frequently greater when the authorities have no reliable system for monitoring the prisoners' presence at, transfer to or release from places of detention.

To lessen that risk the ICRC stresses the need for such a system; in particular, it recommends that registers be kept or that the authorities in the capital be systematically notified of each arrest, transfer or release. It also points out the advantages to the detaining authorities of doing so, i.e. being able to improve the organization, whether food supplies or security arrangements, of everyday life in places of detention.

ICRC delegates have sometimes helped to establish a monitoring system at the national level, for instance, by training local officials or providing material assistance.

The ICRC systematically checks information provided by the authorities against the lists it draws up during its visits or eyewitness accounts provided by the population.

Long-term dialogue and presence: a strategic choice

The ICRC has chosen to work on the basis of dialogue with parties to conflict and with the authorities, seeking to influence their behaviour and persuade them to comply with humanitarian law and principles.

But to do so a climate of confidence, which can only be created in the long term and through sustained work in the field, has to be established with all concerned. That is one reason for the ICRC's discretion. In exchange, it expects its contacts to show that they are willing to take the political steps required to improve the situation.

The limits of confidentiality -
Dialogue with the authorities, and not the systematic denunciation of violations of international law and humanitarian principles, is the course of action adopted by the ICRC. It does not allow itself to be swayed by the media or any other form of public pressure. But if serious and repeated violations occur and its own confidential approaches are in vain, or if it finds that the authorities clearly have no intention of respecting international humanitarian law, it may decide to speak out.

Parties to the conflict shall record as soon as possible, in respect of each wounded, sick or dead person of the adverse Party falling into their hands, any particulars which may assist in his identification. (...) Parties to the conflict shall prepare and forward to each other through the same bureau,* certificates of death or duly authenticated lists of the dead.

First Geneva Convention of 1949, Article 16

** i.e. ICRC Central Tracing Agency*

Dialogue, not compromise

All ICRC action on behalf of people deprived of their freedom is based on dialogue with prisoners, but also with the authorities.

Getting the most objective picture possible of a place of detention or a prison system means listening to what everyone concerned has to say about it.

Dialogue with the prison officials helps the ICRC to find out whether the problems observed are due to shortcomings in the system or occasional malfunction, or are obviously intentional. Such dialogue also serves to determine the level in the chain of command at which the problem originates, and the authorities to be contacted about it.
Depending on circumstances, it may be necessary to call for a budget allocation, promote food self-sufficiency, make the local civilian or medical authorities aware of their responsibilities, restore a dialogue between guards and authorities or, in some cases, appeal to outside States for specific forms of assistance.

Malnutrition among prisoners may, for example, reflect widely differing problems ranging from deliberate policy on the part of the detaining authorities to difficulties of a purely logistical nature. In one African country, the ICRC urgently requested the Ministries of the Interior and Transport to provide a prison with food and have the lorry used to deliver the prison's supplies repaired; they responded, and the prisoners soon showed no further sign of malnutrition.

Problems among prisoners may also reflect the attitude of a guard or official. Initially the ICRC will try to persuade those responsible to modify their behaviour but, if that fails, it will contact the authorities at a higher level.

Engaging in dialogue does not mean accepting a compromise: the ICRC will adamantly continue to press for a solution to the humanitarian problems observed.
Using all possible channels open to it, it will try to reach all members of the administrative, judicial, military and political systems who are capable of influencing the situation, from the prison director right up to the head of State. If the ICRC finds that it is making no headway and concludes that a new approach would be in the interest of the persons it visits, it may decide to suspend or discontinue its activities, or even publicly appeal to the States party to the Geneva Conventions to ensure that international humanitarian law is respected.

Restoring family contact: a vital task.

To maintain decent conditions of detention, it is essential to preserve contact between prisoners and their families. Such contact is essential to their psychological well-being. Moreover, the family can provide the prisoner with often vital material support.

In many contexts, family links are severed by conflict or unrest. The ICRC will then step in to restore them, asking that prisoners be authorized to communicate with their kin by means of Red Cross messages (the content of which is restricted to personal and family news) and to receive family visits throughout their detention.
If necessary the ICRC may, in cooperation with the National Red Cross or Red Crescent Society, provide financial assistance or organize transport to help families travel to the prison, since prisoners are often held thousands of kilometres away from their homes and would otherwise be totally cut off from their loved ones.

Everyday prison life.

One of the ICRC's objectives when visiting places of detention is to ensure that prisoners are detained in conditions which show due respect for human dignity.

Such conditions depend first and foremost on the detaining authorities. However well-intentioned they may be, they do not always have the necessary resources to meet all the relevant international standards. To obtain appropriate living conditions and treatment, humane principles must be firmly upheld and imaginative solutions found. Above all, this means listening
to the needs expressed by prisoners, and taking the local social and cultural context into account. For example, some prisoners do not want to be housed in individual cells as required by international agreements. The concept of living space may therefore vary widely from one culture to another and the ICRC must adapt its approaches accordingly.

One of the ICRC's priorities is to get to know the prisoners' everyday environment. After an interview with the director of the place of detention, the visit starts with an inspection of all premises and facilities used by the prisoners. In the presence of the authorities, delegates have the daily routine explained to them, from how the kitchens are run and the sanitary installations cleaned to the ventilation of dormitories and the storage of food; they also check on facilities for family visits and access to the exercise yard, etc. The same subjects are taken up again during the conversations held in private with the prisoners and the results are rounded off by the delegates' own observations.

Ad hoc emergency aid -
The ICRC's aim is to persuade the detaining authorities to take the necessary steps to ensure decent conditions of detention, not to shoulder their responsibilities for them. However, the ICRC will itself

provide material assistance if the situation so requires and particularly if the survival of prisoners is at stake. This may take the form of additional food, medicines for the prison dispensary, sanitation work or various other repairs. At the same time the ICRC will ask the detaining authorities to assume their obligations as such, reminding them that they themselves are responsible for providing decent material and psychological conditions of detention.

An extreme case: Rwanda -
The situation in Rwanda's prisons after the genocide of 1994 was so acute – the government in place lacked the means to perform its duties as the detaining authority, the prisons were overcrowded to an unprecedented degree and the local population was clamouring for mass arrests – that the ICRC took exceptional action. In order to save the lives of tens of thousands of prisoners, the ICRC decided to equip new places of detention. It also took over the task of feeding the prisoners, at the same time calling on the authorities to progressively assume their responsibilities in that respect.

Looking beneath the surface

ICRC delegates are aware that their visits may have been prepared, if not adroitly orchestrated, by the authorities.

There may be freshly painted walls, mended sanitary facilities, larger helpings of food on that particular day, and medical care for the sick. The ICRC naturally welcomes all improvements which are lasting and of true benefit to the prisoners. But only regular visits can show whether they are permanent or not.

The delegates' own experiences enable them to see through such stratagems and to identify any problems regarding treatment or living conditions that are not immediately obvious. To do so, they must compare the differing versions given by prisoners and the authorities with their own personal observations. It is only by looking beneath the surface and analysing the situation in greater depth, thanks to their knowledge of the prison environment, that they will be able to form an accurate picture of the real conditions of detention and take appropriate steps in agreement with the authorities.

To assess the conditions of detention, specific parameters must be taken into account.

These parameters are as follows:

the prison facilities (buildings, dormitories, bedding, sanitary facilities, drainage, ventilation and exercise yard);

the prisoners' access to these facilities (the official or customary routine in the place of detention, e.g. frequency of access to showers and length of the exercise period, as the fact that a facility exists does not mean that prisoners can use it);

internal regulations (timetables, family visits, correspondence, leisure activities, etc.);

treatment and discipline (relations between prisoners and authorities, possibility for prisoners to speak with the prison officials, duration and conditions of solitary confinement, etc.);

the training and the working conditions of the prison staff;

contacts with the outside;

the internal organization of prisoners (political disputes, gangs, internal reprisals, collaboration with the authorities, etc., and delegates must be familiar with this aspect of prison life, otherwise any proposal they make may endanger the very people they are trying to help).

Role of medical personnel - ICRC visiting teams include doctors and nurses whose primary role is not to treat prisoners but to ensure that the detaining authorities guarantee them a state of health consistent with local standards. They assess the detainees' nutritional status, hygiene and living conditions (drinking water, ventilation of premises, latrines, overcrowding and its consequences on the prisoners' mental and physical health, etc.), as well as the personnel and facilities available for medical care; they will also check whether the prison population really does have access to them. Here, too, the private interviews play a crucial part.

Combating torture and ill-treatment.

In situations of conflict or violence, anyone deprived of freedom may be subjected to torture and other ill-treatment at each stage of his or her detention.

To prevent and try to put a stop to such practices is one of the ICRC's main concerns. Even when ICRC delegates are allowed to visit prisoners during the interrogation period, which is often considered the most dangerous, they are very rarely able to do so in the places where such acts are committed.

The ICRC's work to combat torture and ill-treatment is largely based on convergent accounts by prisoners of everything that has happened to them since their arrest. Any physical and psychological after-effects observed by the ICRC doctor, which may or may not corroborate their statements, are also taken into account. All this information is gathered during conversations in private with the prisoners. It is then analysed, compared and evaluated in the light of statements from other sources to check intrinsic consistency and authenticity, for the ICRC is well aware that the strength of its representations lies in their credibility. Subject to the individual prisoners' permission, the ICRC passes on allegations of torture or ill-treatment to the authorities. In some cases it calls for an enquiry to establish the facts and prevent the recurrence of such acts. In others, it goes straight to the top and asks the highest authorities to put a stop to them. If, when a case is cited, the prisoner concerned does not want to be named in connection with it or the delegates fear that their intervention might be followed by reprisals, the ICRC will proceed differently. If, however, the lives of prisoners are directly threatened, it will contact the authorities at the next level of responsibility, calling for warnings that acts of torture will be punished and for improvements in the training of prison guards.

Torture and ill-treatment may indicate a deliberate intention to punish, deter, interrogate or even terrorize. In such situations only the delegate's ability to convince and influence people, which requires tenacity and patience, will yield results. But unless the highest authorities show the necessary political will, the ICRC's effectiveness will be limited. In practice, its work and that of the human rights agencies which is based on public opinion campaigns complement one another.

A disorganized prison system may also give rise to torture and ill-treatment. In such cases the ICRC will try to identify the causes of any malfunction and act upon them. In a prison where ill-treatment was regularly inflicted, for instance, delegates noticed that the untrained guards were too few in number to maintain security and believed that violence was the only means they had to do their job. The ICRC alerted the relevant ministry and persuaded it to increase the number of guards and train them properly. As a result, there were far fewer complaints of ill-treatment.

Torture: no definition broad enough

To give itself sufficient scope for action, the ICRC has never defined the term "torture". There are always two aspects to torture, one physical and the other psychological; they are interlinked and inseparable. The psychological effects often go far deeper than the physical effects. For instance, seeing torture inflicted on one's children or other loved ones, or even on somebody else, may prove much more traumatic than actually undergoing physical torture oneself.

Torture also has a strong cultural connotation. Its significance within a given social order and the intention behind it vary widely. Some behaviour may be regarded as "benign" in one culture, whereas in another it may violate, for example, a religious taboo.

The ICRC has therefore decided not to adopt any of the definitions of torture formulated by the international community in recent years, although it may refer to them if it feels that doing so might help to combat the phenomenon of torture.

The doctor's role in visits to torture victims -

In principle, every ICRC team visiting prisoners who may have been tortured includes a doctor to examine them and assess their physical and psychological condition. For people who have been brutalized and humiliated by torture, this meeting with a doctor from the outside is often invaluable, for they can be reassured as to their state of health. It is particularly important for victims of sexual torture: they will often confide more readily in a doctor than in another delegate.

The doctor examines the prisoners and the results go on file, possibly to serve as supporting evidence. With the respective prisoners' consent, detailed allegations may be used in representations to put a stop to torture. The ICRC doctor acts as a "neutral medical intermediary". As such, he or she may remind the prison doctors of medical ethics by drawing their attention to the World Medical Association's Declaration of Tokyo, which prohibits any active or passive participation by doctors in torture and any other forms of cruel, inhuman or degrading treatment.

Special protection for women and children in prison

Women and children in prison are particularly vulnerable and therefore need specific protection.

Admittedly, women are generally less likely than men to be deprived of their freedom on account of a conflict but, when they are, their conditions of detention are sometimes worse than those of other prisoners. Women may be deprived of their freedom during armed conflicts for various reasons. There are detailed rules in the four Geneva Conventions of 1949 and their two Additional Protocols of 1977 concerning the treatment of persons deprived of their freedom in connection with situations of armed conflict. These rules include specific provisions on the treatment of women in detention. The aim of these specific provisions is to provide additional protection for women with regard to their particular medical and physiological needs, which are often, but not always, related to their child-bearing role, and to give consideration for their privacy.

The accommodation provided for women may be too cramped if only one detention centre is set aside for them. The fact that prisons often have no female staff may have serious consequences, including certain forms of harassment by guards. During its visits, the ICRC pays special attention to the situation of women prisoners, who are moreover usually visited by female delegates. Specific rules regarding women and expectant or nursing mothers are laid down in the Geneva Conventions. Also, standards set out in other international instruments require particular care to ensure that women deprived of their freedom are held in a safe and decent custodial environment: mixed gender staffing, separate accommodation, equality of access to activities, ante-natal and postnatal care, hygiene and health care, protection from ill-treatment, family visits, etc.

Children and detention of a mother.

Also of relevance is the prohibition on the execution of the death penalty on pregnant women or mothers with dependent infants.

Women often play the central role in the family unit, and detained women often suffer acutely from separation from their children (especially babies and young children) and from lack of information as to their well-being. Women therefore need to have contact with their children, including physical contact. Women may have to be given assistance to have such contact because of the distance of the place of detention from their homes, because contacts outside the prison are restricted, or because they do not know the whereabouts of their children.

In some cases, women may enter the prison pregnant or become pregnant while in detention.
Babies may also be taken away from their mothers immediately after birth or when the mother is discharged from hospital. Many women (especially nursing mothers) find enforced separation from their children particularly traumatic and one of the most difficult aspects of their detention. The effects on the children could also be psychologically damaging.
Nursing mothers should therefore be able to keep their newborn babies with them in detention if this is in the best interests of the children. If separated from them, nursing mothers must be informed of their whereabouts and be allowed to maintain frequent physical contact with them.

Special protection for children

During its visits, the ICRC pays special attention to the situation of detained minors. Children are imprisoned too, either for criminal law offences or because they have been caught up in the turmoil of events, or even because they have been enrolled as combatants.

For them, the loss of freedom may be very hard to bear and have lasting effects on their development. They should also be protected against indecent assault. The ICRC insists on the psychological and emotional equilibrium, development and education of young prisoners being ensured as far as possible, and urges the detaining authorities to see that the following requirements are met:

juveniles in detention should, as a rule, be accommodated separately from adults except when children and parents are held in the same place;

juveniles should be offered as many purposeful activities as possible, such as sport, vocational training, recreation, physical education;

if they are not released and their detention is extended, children must be transferred as soon as possible to a specialized establishment for minors;

children must receive food, hygiene and medical care suited to their age and general condition;

children must be able to continue their schooling;

children must be able to keep in regular contact with their families and the outside world;

disciplinary procedures and sanctions must be adjusted;

regarding the death penalty, the States party to the Fourth Geneva Convention (Art. 68, para. 4) and the Additional Protocols (Art. 77, para. 5, API and Art. 6, para. 4, APII) should take legislative measures under penal and military law to prohibit the pronouncement or execution of a death sentence against anyone aged less than 18 years at the time of the offence.

An important aspect of protection: upholding legal safeguards .

The ICRC intervenes to ensure that certain universally recognized principles enshrined in the Geneva Conventions and their Additional Protocols are respected by all parties to an armed conflict.

No person may be deprived of his or her freedom except on legal grounds and in accordance with procedures provided for by law.
The ICRC has therefore acted in conflict situations to see that judicial guarantees are applied. Judicial guarantees, also known as fair trial rights, are an integral part of international humanitarian law. They are provided for in the Geneva Conventions, and in their two Additional Protocols. These provisions are a key component of the notion of humane treatment and their very aim is to protect the life, health and dignity of persons subjected to penal sanctions. Judicial guarantees were considered to be so important by the drafters of the Geneva Conventions and their Additional Protocols that their violation constitutes a grave breach or a war crime under the Conventions and under customary international law.
The ICRC has thus, for example, requested that prisoners of war accused of criminal offences be informed of the charges and evidence against them and that the right of such prisoners not to testify against themselves be respected. One State holding prisoners of war under investigation for the murder of another prisoner was reminded by the ICRC of the ban on extorting confessions, the right of the accused prisoners to be defended by a lawyer qualified to prepare their defence, their right to the services of an interpreter, etc.

The basic provision on judicial guarantees is contained in Article 3 common to the four Geneva Conventions which prohibits "the passing of sentences and the carrying out of executions without previous judgment pronounced by a regularly constituted court, affording all the judicial guarantees which are recognized as indispensable by civilized peoples".

The Third Geneva Convention contains detailed safeguards that must be applied in criminal proceedings against prisoners of war, whereas the Fourth Geneva Convention contains judicial guarantees for civilians in international armed conflict. Judicial guarantees for any person affected by an international armed conflict who is not entitled to more favorable treatment under the Conventions are elaborated in Additional Protocol I, while the safeguards that must be applied in penal proceedings carried out in relation to an internal armed conflict are provided for in Additional Protocol II (see below).

In the past few years the ICRC has extended its interventions in this domain to other situations of violence, drawing on the rules and principles of international humanitarian law or other relevant provisions of international law.

Penal prosecutions

Article 6 of Protocol II additional to the Geneva Conventions

1. This Article applies to the prosecution and punishment of criminal offences related to the armed conflict.

2. No sentence shall be passed and no penalty shall be executed on a person found guilty of an offence except pursuant to a conviction pronounced by a court offering the essential guarantees of independence and impartiality. In particular:

a) the procedure shall provide for an accused to be informed without delay of the particulars of the offence alleged against him and shall afford the accused before and during his trial all necessary rights and means of defence;

b) no one shall be convicted of an offence except on the basis of individual penal responsibility;

c) no one shall be held guilty of any criminal offence on account of any act or omission which did not constitute a criminal offence, under the law, at the time when it was committed; nor shall a heavier penalty be imposed than that which was applicable at the time when the criminal offence was committed; if after the commission of the offence, provision is made by law for the imposition of a lighter penalty, the offender shall benefit thereby;

d) anyone charged with an offence is presumed innocent until proved guilty according to law;

e) anyone charged with an offence shall have the right to be tried in his presence;

f) no one shall be compelled to testify against himself or to confess guilt.

3. A convicted person shall be advised on conviction of his judicial and other remedies and of the time-limits within which they may be exercised.

4. The death penalty shall not be pronounced on persons who were under the age of eighteen years at the time of the offence and shall not be carried out on pregnant women or mothers of young children.

5. At the end of hostilities, the authorities in power shall endeavour to grant the broadest possible amnesty to persons who have participated in the armed conflict, or those deprived of their liberty for reasons related to the armed conflict, whether they are interned or detained.

ICRC action: a means at the international community's disposal

For several decades the international community has been intensifying its efforts, both in terms of legislation and in the field, to protect people deprived of their freedom.

The ICRC's presence in the prison environment is one way of promoting respect for human dignity. Its intervention, which takes place in situations of acute crisis, must then gradually be supplemented by the human rights activities of other agencies.

While pursuing its own approach, which is based on dialogue with the authorities and on confidentiality, the ICRC has strengthened its operational cooperation in this field with national, international and non-governmental organizations, such as the Office of the United Nations High Commissioner for Human Rights, UNICEF and *Médecins sans frontières*, so as to avoid duplication of efforts and inconsistency in any action undertaken. Other components of the International Red Cross and Red Crescent Movement sometimes do welfare work in prisons in peacetime; some National Red Cross and Red Crescent Societies, for instance, provide material, psychological and social support for their countries' prisoners.

"What matters [...]"

"What matters is not only the good the ICRC brings, but even more the bad it prevents."

Nelson Mandela
(Registration No. 220/82, Robben Island Prison, 1962-1990)

It is hard for the ICRC to assess the true impact of its visits to people deprived of their freedom; it would also be difficult to say how things might have been if the ICRC had been unable to operate in a given situation. Nelson Mandela qualified the ICRC's work in these terms: "What matters is not only the good the ICRC brings, but even more the bad it prevents". All conversations with prisoners show that a visit by the ICRC has at least one result: it offers them a lifeline, an opportunity to talk and be listened to, to voice their tensions and frustrations (sometimes quite aggressively), and to express their anxieties and fears to someone who is well-disposed towards them. The psychological effect of contact with the outside world is very important and should not be underestimated.

Moreover, the regular presence of the ICRC and its constant contacts at all levels of power have a dissuasive effect: they help to forestall and contain such phenomena as forced disappearances, torture and ill-treatment. Working as it does in times of armed conflict, disturbances, tensions and other situations of violence within a country, the ICRC is well aware that its activities are part of a longer-term process, for although rapid improvements can certainly be made, its mere presence in places of detention does not mean that abuses will stop.

If such phenomena are to be eradicated completely, the situation must return to normal and nongovernmental organizations and other components of civil society must be able to resume their regulatory functions, particularly those which enable the judicial system to work properly and arbitrary practices to be effectively curbed.

Mission

The International Committee of the Red Cross (ICRC) is an impartial, neutral and independent organization whose exclusively humanitarian mission is to protect the lives and dignity of victims of war and internal violence and to provide them with assistance. It directs and coordinates the international relief activities conducted by the Movement in situations of conflict. It also endeavours to prevent suffering by promoting and strengthening humanitarian law
and universal humanitarian principles. Established in 1863, the ICRC is at the origin of the International Red Cross and Red Crescent Movement.

IRAQ POST 28 JUNE 2004: PROTECTING PERSONS DEPRIVED OF FREEDOM REMAINS A PRIORITY

International Committee of the Red Cross Copyright © 2006

May 8, 2004

(http://www.icrc.org/web/eng/siteeng0.nsf/iwpList322/89060107D77D7299C1256EE7005200E8)

In view of the continuing hostilities in Iraq, the protection of persons deprived of freedom remains one of the ICRC's priorities. The ICRC's main objective is to visit all persons detained in connection with the hostilities in order to monitor whether their treatment, their conditions of detention and the judicial guarantees accorded correspond to the requirements of applicable law.

In order to determine what body of law applies to different categories of persons deprived of their freedom and what the legal obligations of the powers detaining them are the ICRC needs to continuously assess the situation on the ground.

After the hand-over of power from the Coalition Provisional Authority to the interim Iraqi Government on 28 June 2004, following the United Nations Security Council resolution 1546 stating the end of the foreign occupation, the legal situation has changed.

As stated in the resolution, the presence and the military operations of the Multinational Forces in Iraq are based on the consent of the Interim Government of Iraq. The ICRC therefore no longer considers the situation in Iraq to be that of an international armed conflict between the US-led coalition and the state of Iraq and covered by the Geneva Conventions of 1949 in their entirety. The current hostilities in Iraq between armed fighters on one hand opposing the Multinational Force (MNF-I) and/or the newly established authorities on the other, amount to a non-international armed conflict. This means that all parties including MNF-I are bound by Article 3 common to the four Geneva Conventions, and by customary rules applicable to non-international armed conflicts.

All parties must ensure at all times that those not or no longer taking part in the fighting – including persons deprived of their freedom in connection with the continuing hostilities - are protected in accordance with these rules.

The change in the legal situation means that most persons deprived of their freedom in relation to the hostilities are now no longer protected by the whole of the Third or Fourth Geneva Convention but by common Article 3 of the Geneva Conventions and by customary rules applicable in non-international armed conflicts. It has the following implications for persons deprived of their freedom:

- Those persons arrested before 28 June and currently interned by the MNF-I should either be released, charged and tried or placed within another legal framework that regulates their continued internment. They remain protected by the Third Geneva Convention – for prisoners of war - or the Fourth Geneva Convention - for interned and detained civilians - until they are released or handed over to Iraqi authorities.

- Persons arrested prior to 28 June who have been handed over to Iraqi authorities and continue to be detained in connection with the ongoing non-international armed conflict are protected by Article 3 common to the Geneva Conventions, and customary rules applicable to non-international armed conflicts; other applicable international law and relevant Iraqi law would apply to them as well. The same rules apply to persons arrested since 28 June 2004 by Iraqi authorities or the MNF-I in connection with the ongoing non-international armed conflict.

- Persons arrested prior to 28 June, handed over to the Iraqi authorities and then detained for reasons unrelated to the now ongoing non-international armed conflict are protected by Iraqi law and other applicable international law, e.g. human rights law, but no longer by international humanitarian law.

- Persons arrested and detained by Iraqi authorities since 28 June for reasons unrelated to the ongoing non-international conflict are protected by Iraqi law and other applicable international law, e.g. human rights law, but no longer by international humanitarian law.

Regardless of their status, charges against any detainee or internee are to be properly investigated. They can be prosecuted and, if proven guilty, sentenced. Whatever the crimes committed, they have the right to a fair trial, including the right to defend themselves and to be assisted by a lawyer.

ICRC continues to visit thousands of people deprived of freedom and detained by the MNF-I. It plans to also visit detainees held by Iraqi authorities in connection with the internal armed conflict underway. However, its ability to do so depends on the security situation on the ground.

INSIDE THE BATTLE AT QALA-I-JANGI

Alex Perry

December 01, 2001

In Afghanistan, nothing is ever what it seems. Including surrender.

On Nov. 24, a bright, warm Saturday, 300 Taliban soldiers who had fled the American bombardment of Kunduz, their last stronghold in the north of Afghanistan, laid down their weapons in the desert a few miles to the north of Mazar-i-Sharif. They surrendered to Northern Alliance General Abdul Rashid Dostum, who crowed that his forces had achieved a "great victory" as the pows were herded 50 at a time onto flatbed trucks.

Even by the standards of Afghanistan's warlords, Dostum has an unsavory reputation. In earlier episodes of Afghanistan's wars, he was reputed to have killed those of his soldiers who broke the rules by tying them to the tracks of his tanks. But outside Mazar, his soldiers told their prisoners that Dostum wanted to make a gesture of reconciliation to help unite Afghanistan's warring tribes. Afghan members of the Taliban would be free to return to their homes, while foreigners would be detained before being handed over to the U.N. Dostum didn't search his prisoners; that was a mistake, one he would bitterly regret. "If we had searched them, there would have been a fight," he said Wednesday, surveying hundreds of dismembered, blackened and crushed bodies. "But perhaps it wouldn't have been as bad as this."

The Taliban fighters, many of whom were foreigners, were transported from the field of surrender to a holding site in Qala-i-Jangi, a sprawling 19th century prison fortress to the west of Mazar, where Dostum stabled his horses. The convoy of prisoners had to pass through the city center; two weeks before, the Taliban had ruled the streets. The prisoners now peered out from under their blankets with shell-shocked, bloodshot eyes. The people of Mazar stared back at them with open hatred.

Things went wrong almost immediately. Once inside Qala-i-Jangi, the Taliban soldiers were asked to turn out their pockets. A prisoner, waiting until Alliance commander Nadir Ali was near, suddenly produced a grenade and pulled the pin, killing himself and the commander. In a similar attack the same night, another prisoner killed himself and senior Hazara commander Saeed Asad. The remaining men were led into underground cells to join scores of other captured Taliban fighters. Despite the grenade attacks, the Alliance guards were not reinforced.

Sunday Morning

The next morning, two Americans went to meet the prisoners at Qala-i-Jangi. Their mission at the fortress: to identify any members of al-Qaeda among the prisoners. But the

Americans didn't conduct the interviews one by one--another mistake. Instead, at 11:15 a.m., the pair--Johnny Micheal Spann, 32, one of the CIA agents who had been active in Afghanistan since the war's beginning, the other identified by colleagues only as "Dave"--were taken to an open area outside the cells and a group of prisoners brought to meet them. According to members of a German television crew who were later trapped in the fort with Dave, Spann asked the prisoners who they were and why they joined the Taliban. They massed around him. "Why are you here?" Spann asked one. "To kill you," came the reply as the man lunged at Spann's neck. Spann drew his pistol and shot the man dead. Dave shot another, then grabbed an AK-47 from an Alliance guard and opened fire. According to eyewitness accounts given to the German team, the Taliban fighters launched themselves at Spann, scrabbling at his flesh with their hands, kicking and beating him. Spann killed two more with his pistol before he disappeared under the crush. An Alabaman with a wife and three children, Spann became the first American to die in combat in Afghanistan.

The Taliban then overpowered the Alliance guards, killing them with their own weapons. Dave mowed down three more Taliban, then sprinted to the main building along the north wall, where two Red Cross workers had just begun a meeting with the prison governor. "He burst in and told us to get out of there," says Simon Brooks, a Briton and a Red Cross staff member. "He was really shaken up. He said there were 20 dead Northern Alliance guys, and the Taliban were taking control of the fort." As Dave stayed behind to try to rescue Spann, the two Red Cross workers climbed up to the fort's parapet, hoisted themselves over the wall and slid 60 ft. down the other side. Meanwhile, the firing had alerted a pair of TV crews. They too ran to the main building; there they found Dave and were pinned down in the ensuing fire fight.

A few hundred yards to the south, in the prison block, the Taliban freed its comrades. Three escaped through a drain under the southern wall; all were soon shot by Alliance soldiers outside the fort. The Taliban fighters, trapped in the southwestern quarter of the fort, stormed a nearby armory, making off with AK-47s, grenades, mines, rocket launchers, mortars and ammunition. Alliance soldiers held on to the southeastern corner, which included an arched gateway, a courtyard and the gatekeeper's house. Other fighters took positions on the north wall and the roof of the main building. A vicious exchange of fire across the grassy parade ground followed. Two Alliance tanks along the north wall started firing into the Taliban area.

SUNDAY AFTERNOON At 2 p.m. two minivans and a pair of open-sided white Land Rovers mounted with machine guns pulled up outside the fortress gates. From the minivans jumped nine American special-operations men wearing wraparound sunglasses and baseball caps and carrying snub-nosed M-4 automatic rifles. The Land Rovers disgorged six British SAS soldiers armed with M-16s and dressed in jeans, sweaters, Afghan scarves and pakuls, the distinctive woolen hats of the Afghan mujahedin. The Americans and British quickly convened a conference with the Alliance leaders. "I want satcom [satellite communications] and JDAMS [guided munitions]," said the American commander. "Tell them there will be six or seven buildings in a line in the southwest half. If they can hit that, then that would kill a whole lot of these motherf______."

A bearded American in a Harley-Davidson cap and mirrored sunglasses raised Dave on the radio. "Shit...shit...O.K....Shit...O.K. Hold on, buddy, we're coming to get you," he said. Then, cutting the radio, he turned to his commander: "Mike is MIA. They've taken his gun and his ammo. We have another guy. He managed to kill two of them with his pistol, but he's holed up in the north side with no ammo." As a hurried discussion of tactics began, Harley-Davidson went back to his radio. Then he cut in: "Shit. Let's stop f___ing around and get in there." Pointing to the sky, he added, "Tell those guys to stop scratching their balls and fly."

Outside the fort, Alliance soldiers began pouring out of the northeast battlements, skidding over the walls and down the ramparts. The wounded were whisked away in commandeered taxis. A fire fight raged through the afternoon. Two American fighter planes began circling the area. Inside, TIME's translator, Nagidullah Quraishi, was ordered to the gatekeeper's roof and told to translate conversations between the Western soldiers and their Afghan allies. Alliance General Majid Rozi told the Americans and the British that a white single-story building inside the Taliban area needed to be hit, and the visitors proceeded to spot the target for the planes far above. "Thunder, Ranger," said the American radio operator, speaking to the airplanes above. "The coordinates are: north 3639984, east 06658945, elevation 1,299 ft." He turned to his comrades. "Four minutes."

"Three minutes."

"Two minutes."

"Thirty seconds."

"Fifteen seconds." From the sky, a great, arrow-shaped missile appeared, zeroing in on its target a hundred yards away and sounding like a car decelerating in high gear. The spotters lay flat. Alliance commanders and soldiers crouched against the door leading to the roof. The missile hit at 4:05 p.m. For a split second, as the concussive sound waves radiated outward, lungs emptied. Shrapnel whistled by. Then Alliance soldiers burst into applause. A U.S. soldier picked up a fallen piece of metal. "Souvenir," he said, grinning. Six more strikes followed before the British SAS commander re-established contact with Dave, still penned in with the TV crews. The SAS soldier told the Alliance commander that after two more strikes, his men should fire all their weapons. "Our guy is going to try to make a break for it," said the Briton. The conversation turned to Spann.

"From what I understand, he was already gone before we got here," said an American.

"Three minutes," said the SAS guy. "Two minutes...30 seconds." Everyone crouched once more against the wall. Again a glistening white arrow screamed down, again the split-second blackout. "One more," said the SAS man.

MONDAY The American and British teams stayed in position overnight. Fighting was constant, red tracers shooting off into Mazar city. Sometime after dark, Dave and the journalists escaped over the north wall. "He just climbed over and hitched a ride into town," a special-operations soldier later explained. "The first thing we have to do now is get our other guy out."

By Monday morning the Alliance had established a new command post at the northeast tower on top of what an American commander described as "10 tons of munitions, rockets, mortars, the works." A tank was driven onto the tower. From his seat on the garrison roof, commander Mohammed Akbar guided mortar and tank fire to Taliban positions in the southwest. "Excellent--right on the nose!" he shouted, as bullets from Taliban snipers whizzed just over his head. Then came the next mistake.

Around 10 a.m. four more special-operations soldiers and eight men from the 10th Mountain Division arrived at a position about 300 yds. outside the fort to the northeast. Inside the fort, bomb spotters were preparing three more strikes. A pilot circled overhead, radioing instructions to the spotters, his voice clearly audible on handsets held by the soldiers posted outside the fort. "Be advised," he said to the soldiers in the fort, "you are dangerously close. You are about a hundred yards away from the target." "I think we're perhaps a little too close," came the spotter's reply. "But we have to be, to get the laser on the target." Pause. Bomb spotter: "We are about ready to pull back." Pilot: "We are about to release." Spotter: "Roger." Spotter: "Be advised we have new coordinates: north 3639996, east 06658866." Pilot: "Good. Copy." Spotter: "Mitch and Siberson are making their run now." Spotter again: "Two minutes."

At 10:53 a.m. the missile slammed into the north wall, perhaps 10 yds. from the Alliance's command center in the northeast tower. Much more powerful than previous strikes, it sent clouds of dust hundreds of feet into the air. "No, no!" Alliance commander Olim Razum yelled at the 10th Mountain soldiers. "This is the wrong place! Tell them to cut it!" A special-operations man glanced up at the cloud and shouted, "Incoming shrapnel--get down!" As the dust cloud cleared, a U-shaped hole the size of a small swimming pool appeared in the wall next to the northeast tower. The tank had flipped onto its back, its gun turret blown off. Alliance soldiers, bleeding, coated in dust, began sliding down the side of the fort and staggering across the surrounding cotton fields. "It missed," said a soldier named Afiz, blood dripping from his eyes and ears. "I don't know where my friends are." From under the fort's entrance arch, SAS and American soldiers emerged choking and spitting. "We have one down, semiconscious, no external bleeding," a radio crackled. "We have men down," a special-operations soldier told TIME. "Get out of here. Please."

Within 20 min., the casualties and walking wounded were loaded into seven jeeps and minibuses, which sped off to the U.S. base. Nine men were airlifted out. Nik Mohammed, 24, an Alliance soldier on the northeast tower at the time of the strike, said he helped pull three uniformed soldiers he believed to be Americans from the rubble of the collapsed wall and claimed that two of them were dead. On Tuesday the Pentagon said that there had been no military deaths but that five U.S. service members had been seriously injured and had been evacuated to Landstuhl Regional Medical Center in Germany. Four British soldiers were also reported wounded over the previous 22 hours, one seriously, though British officials--who never comment on the SAS--will not confirm that they were wounded at Qala-i-Jangi. On the Alliance side, there were said to be as many as 30 dead and 50 injured.

At 4:50 p.m. a small group of special-operations soldiers returned. Dave was with them. He climbed up the northeast tower to confer with Alliance General Rozi. "You don't want to leave here tonight," an American soldier told TIME, checking his night-vision goggles. "There's going to be quite a show." The soldier used a reporter's satellite phone to call his wife and tell her he might be on the TV news that night--"Tape it all day, will you? O.K. Love you, babe." At midnight an American AC-130 gunship began lazily circling Qala-i-Jangi. It flew five times over the same spot, spraying the southern end of the fort with a golden stream of fire. Later a massive ball of flame lifted up from the fort, kicking off a fireworks display as mortar rounds and ammunition belts fired off into the night sky. Explosions sounded through the night; the blast blew open doors 10 miles away.

TUESDAY By the next morning the surviving Taliban troops were beginning to flag; Rozi estimated that there were only about 50 survivors from the original 600 or so in the fort and that they had no water or ammunition left. Their only food was horsemeat from Dostum's cavalry. A fighter who had escaped during the night was caught by local residents and hanged from a tree. Alliance forces were so confident of victory that at one frontline position, three shared a powerful joint of hashish. Others tucked into peanut butter and jelly from the American food drops. At 10 a.m. a group of 17 special-operations and SAS men returned to the gatekeeper's house. Harley-Davidson was there, along with Dave, who was wearing a black shalwar kameez (the traditional Afghan pants and long shirt) and carrying an AK-47. After talking to Rozi, Dave told his men, "We're going to close in on these guys pretty hard. The one thing the general said to watch out for is a mortar still operating in there."

At 10:50 a.m. U.S. and British troops

positioned themselves along the parapets to the east of the Taliban compound. "Did you see the show last night?" one asked TIME, grinning. "We watched for two hours. Really something." Around 100 Alliance soldiers scaled the southwest tower and lay down along the walls, firing on the Taliban below. Others manned the western tower. Before long, wounded and dead Alliance soldiers were being ferried through the gates. A U.S. soldier ran back to greet an SAS comrade who had felt the full force of Monday's air strike. "How's your hearing today?" he bellowed. Pause. "I said, 'How's your hearing?'"

By 1:25 p.m. from the southwest tower, commander Akbar estimated Taliban strength at "1 1/2" men. On the field below lay hundreds of dead and dying. Two embraced in death. Alliance soldiers stepped gingerly over the bodies. Some of the dead had their hands bound, and Alliance soldiers used scissors to snip off the strings. At 2:10 p.m. Akbar decided all the Taliban fighters were dead and walked down onto the field. His men, by now plainly spooked by the suicidal bravery of the Taliban, had to be forced to break cover. One wounded Taliban soldier, lying in the long grass, was shot to pieces. Alliance soldiers started looting, taking guns and ammunition and rifling the pockets of the dead for money, pens and cigarettes. The Taliban's new-looking sneakers were a particular target. Within minutes, the Alliance fighters had thrown away their shoes and yanked the sneakers from the cold, gray feet of the Taliban dead. The bloated carcasses of 30 horses, with entrails spilling, added a thick stench to the smoke and gunpowder. All the dead were described by the Alliance as "terrorists" and "dangerous foreigners." "I killed four Chechens, four," said Mohammed Yasin excitedly. "I can show you the bodies." The occasional explosion from the smoldering arms depot sent Alliance men scampering across the field, hurdling bodies as they ran for cover.

In a basement under one pock-marked house, five Taliban fighters were trapped alive. Grenades were thrown in the tiny windows and AK-47s fired after them. With Alliance soldiers too afraid to enter the stables, a tank was brought in, crushing bodies under its tracks before firing five rounds into the block. In a ditch on the main parade ground, a young Taliban fighter, lying sprawled on his side, was still breathing. An Alliance soldier dropped a rock on his head. A few yards away lay a bloodied prayer book.

Even in the heat of battle, warriors can be rational; few fight to the death. But the Taliban at Qala-i-Jangi truly did, and beyond it. Spann's body, recovered by a special-operations squad, had been booby-trapped; a grenade had been hidden under the corpse of a Taliban fighter that lay on top of the American. As late as Thursday, those removing bodies were still taking fire from Taliban fighters who had somehow survived in the basements underneath the fort. On Saturday the basements were flooded; Northern Alliance observers expected perhaps five or six surviving Taliban to come out. In fact, at 11 a.m. no fewer than 86 filthy and hungry prisoners emerged; they were given bananas, apples and pomegranates, clothing and shoes. Three trucks took the wounded away. One of the 86 told Alliance fighters he was an American. The 20-year-old, who had been wounded in the leg, said he was from Washington. He would not give his name but said he was a convert to Islam who had come to Afghanistan--after a spell at a madrasah in Pakistan--to help the Taliban build a perfect Islamic government.

The battle was finally over. It had ended as it started, with a surrender. And its story held within its chapters a brutal lesson. The war against terrorism, they like to say, is a new form of war. But at Qala-i-Jangi, as the blood of horses and dead young men snaked into the dust, the oldest form of war imaginable seemed to have made a cruel and bitter return.

FRONTLINE
INTERVIEW WITH SERGEANT CHRISTOPHER STONE

From WGBH Educational Foundation

What you were actually doing on the Macedonian-Serbian border that day? What sort of operations were you involved in?

We had just recently changed from a UN observing mission to a NATO mission. Primarily, we were observing the border between Yugoslavia and Macedonia. Our job was basically to ensure if Yugoslavia did send troops south of the border in some of kind of retaliation for the air strikes, that we would give warning to the other NATO troops that were serving in Macedonia at the time.

Did you regard it as a particularly dangerous place to be? Did you know about the level of hostility in that area towards what the Americans were doing?

I don't think that initially we did. As part of the UN mission that we had been performing for the month before, the people were generally friendly to us. They would wave and smile at us as we went through. However, when we did change to the NATO mission, we also changed our uniforms. We went to green Humvees, and green helmets, and that's when we began to see a very drastic change in the attitude of the people in the area towards our presence there.

Was this also after the war stopped? Were they, in a sense, reacting to what American air power was inflicting on Serbia?

I don't think it was wholly when the conflict began--it was even prior. A lot of it started as soon as there was talk that the strikes appeared imminent. We'd get protests from the locals, and some threw rocks. So it wasn't only after the strikes began, but mainly when we changed our position.

There's been considerable uncertainty over what you were doing there that day, and especially, where you were. There are some suggestions that you may have strayed at times across into Yugoslavia--therefore from the Serb point of view, you'd be a legitimate target in time of war. Tell me what happened, and where were you when it happened?

On March 31, myself and the two other soldiers, Andy and Steve, were conducting a reconnaissance mission of a route that we would use as sort of an escape route--a secondary escape route in case something did happen, if troops did come across the border from Yugoslavia. This was an area that we'd operating in for about a month now. The villages were all familiar to us. The roads were all familiar to us. As we were coming back from performing that reconnaissance, we had just gone through a village and we ran into what turned out to be a deliberate ambush. It was set up to perhaps accomplish exactly what did happen.

How did the skirmish actually unfold?

As we drove past the village, we began hearing pings on the back of our Humvee, which we felt were rocks. That was common. . . . So we brought our gunner, Steve Gonzales down into the truck, and decided to drive out of the area. . . . to get away from whatever was happening. But after that point, we began taking rounds from all sides, and we began to see soldiers appearing from behind haystacks or rocks or boulders. There were about 30 of them, and they just appeared out of nowhere. That's what led us to believe that it was deliberately planned.

At that point, you radioed to your base to tell them that you were under attack. Tell me about that dialogue. What did your base say to you?

That's correct. The other guys had their own responsibilities. As commander, my job was to call. So I grabbed the radio, and called up my platoon sergeant, who was back at one of the positions. I told him that we were surrounded, and we were taking fire. I also gave him the position where we were. Evidently they didn't get all the coordinates of whatever our global positioning system said, and they only heard the first three digits.

My platoon sergeant asked me if I was joking. I told him I wasn't joking, and that this was really happening. That's the last I heard, because something went wrong with the radio transmission--maybe the antenna was shot off, or some other condition happened that it was broken.

At that point, were you fighting back? Or was it obvious that that was hopeless, given the scale of the ambush?

It certainly was hopeless. We'd already pulled our gunner down back into the vehicle, and that was basically our only defensive weapon on top of the Humvee. Also, in the peacekeeping mode that we were in, as a safety precaution, we didn't have our weapons loaded and ready to fire.

You surrendered at that point?
It wasn't in the Hollywood sense where we put the white flag out, but we did exit the truck after we became immobile. We couldn't move any longer, so our decision was to get out. We were immediately surrounded by probably 30 soldiers on the three of us, so the odds were just a little too great.

Obviously, you couldn't resist 30 of them. What was their reaction to the fact that you were clearly giving up?

I think they saw us each as punching bags at that point. There were probably between five or six soldiers on each of us, kicking and beating us and generally stripping all our equipment from us, and putting a lot of abuse on all three of us.

Was it obvious to you these were Serb forces?

Yes, it was. They were dressed in Serbian uniforms, and we recognized the patches on their shoulders. While this was happening, there were a lot of villagers standing around, and they made no effort to help the soldiers. But they didn't obviously weren't interested in helping us, either.

What was going through your mind at that point? Did you think they were going to kill you, right there and then?

I did. And obviously I was in shock. We were driving through familiar territory. I'd been through that village probably ten times in the last month, so just to be thrust in that situation so quickly and have this happen was very surprising. Immediately after they pulled us out and roughed us up, they took us back into the village. We were all placed on our knees, the three of us with our hands behind our head. They put a rifle to the back of my head, so obviously my reaction was that this was a classic execution position. I really believed that was the end.

How long were you in that position, until it was obvious that they were not going to execute you?

I would say probably for about minute we were in that position, until they pushed us forward. Then we were laying on our stomachs as they continued to search and beat us, and they were all standing around at this point, just kind of watching.

Did they say anything to you that you understood?

Not particularly. There was some cursing. Obviously they were familiar with English slang. There was a lot of accusing us of invading their country. This was in real broken English, and we'd just pick up phrases. They asked us who we were and what we were doing, implying that we were not where we were supposed to be. But other than that, the English was very rare.

Do you think that they were under the mistaken impression that you had actually entered Yugoslavia?

I don't think they were, because it was such a deliberate ambush, and it was such an identifiable location that was clearly in Macedonia. In fact, that village is not in one of the contested areas--although the border is contested--so it was clear that we were in Macedonia. I don't know if their intent was to make us believe that we were in the wrong place. That would probably be the most likely thing. That's my opinion.

What happened to you next? You've gone through this mock execution. What happened then?

There was some more searching going on, with different people. That's when their senior leadership began to take over what was happening. As we laid there, we would continue to get beaten. Someone would come running up and kick us. The black eyes that I got were from a kick that I received while I was laying there, after the initial beating took place.

What did they actually do to you to

break your nose?

A man came up from my left side and just kicked me with full force, right in the face. My nose immediately began to gush blood. After that, they did bring up some gauze and put it on my nose after he kicked me. This stopped the bleeding, but that was probably the harshest blow.

What happened to you after that? At the moment you're not even in Yugoslavia. What happens next?

We were probably there in that position for 15 or 20 minutes. Then we were just thrown into the back of a truck. They drove for about an hour or so, at first through twisting, bumpy roads, and then what seemed to be a major highway.

Where did you end up at the end of this journey?

That's a good question. We're not exactly sure where. The first place we did stop looked like some kind of army barracks, and that's where we received our first medical attention. They looked at us and evaluated whatever wounds we had sustained. We stayed there for about a half an hour, then we drove for another couple hours. I believe we ended up in Nis, a city in southern Yugoslavia.

You were still together at this point?

We were together up until when we arrived in Nis. That's when we were separated, and didn't see each other much, except for the filming that you saw. . . .

What led up to the filming? What were you being told what to say? What was the purpose of it?

Once we got to Nis, we were individually in a room where they had sort of a press conference set up. There were cameras, and civilian and military officials there, and they began to question me. I assume they did the same with the others. The purpose of their questioning was not necessarily anything that was in our spectrum of knowledge. It was basically political questions, policies of the government, the purpose of the bombing, and things that really I had no knowledge of or any relevance in discussing with them. We weren't told what to say. It was more of an interview, a question-and- answer thing.

At that point, were they suggesting that you sign any documents indicating that you were opposed to US policy?

No, no. That was never presented. We were asked to make a statement a couple of days later. But all it told was that we were part of NATO in an effort to invade the peaceful people of Serbia. I'm not sure if it actually said "peaceful," but it said I had invaded the country of Yugoslavia.

Was it around this time that they began a fairly concerted effort to debrief you, but by using torture? Was that something that happened to you after you appeared before the cameras?

The cameras were there very early in

the capture, probably within the first six or seven hours. After that point, they began interrogations, which continued with the same line of questioning--not necessarily focusing on our mission or what our purpose was, but the greater picture of how our army operated, and what not. There was also a form of torture involved, in that we'd be left for hours and hours.

The whole time we were hooded and handcuffed, with bags over our head. That in itself was a form of torture, in that we would never know what was happening. We never knew when we'd be interrogated. We were watched with a guard maybe feet from us 24 hours a day. If we moved from a certain position, we'd be kicked or beaten. It was definitely an effort to break our will.

What was going through your mind at the time? Were you fearful that you weren't going to be able to resist this kind of interrogation, that you would break?

I didn't see exactly that they were looking from me to break personally, so that wasn't my main concern. My main concern throughout the whole time was if we would even get out of that situation, because there were so many different circumstances when it appeared to be a good time for them to kill us. Within that first seven days, I was just preparing myself for the fact that we may not make it out of there.

Were there any other occasions where they threatened you with execution, as they had in that first few minutes of your capture?

There was. At one point during the interrogation, they had asked me to give the address of my family back in the States. and I didn't give that to them. I didn't tell them, and at that point, one of the guys came around me with a baton. He brought it around my neck, and one of the other guys lifted up his coat showing a revolver, implying that if I didn't tell them, then obviously they'd kill us. But was something I just was not going to do, and it wasn't pressured after that point. I don't know if that was a bluff or what, but luckily they didn't pressure me anymore.

Did they make it clear to you that they didn't regard you as prisoners of war? Even their foreign ministry was referring to you as terrorists and spies--and that, therefore you didn't have the kind of protections that would be afforded to you under the Geneva Convention.

Right. They continued to imply that throughout the initial period. Throughout the interrogations, they believed we were either an effort sent in to find downed pilots, or we were the lead element of some kind of ground invasion. We were never specifically told we were POWs. In fact, they did mention at one point that we would be put on trial, and that would determine what would happen to us. That was obviously a question I asked many times--what was going to happen. They said that it's for the court to decide, that you'll be tried as a war criminal. . . . That was only mentioned once, and after that we never heard anything about it.

In this period, isolation one of their chief weapons. You didn't have the opportunity of talking to the other two?

Oh, certainly. We didn't have the opportunity at all to talk to anyone other than in the interrogations, which were not exactly conversations. So we were left in the dark with a bag over our head, handcuffed, laying on a wooden floor, 24 hours a day. Their intent was obviously that kind of torture.

Were you aware of the significant efforts made by the Cypriot government to try and seek your release? And Jesse Jackson was applying diplomatic pressure, before you actually met him, to try and get your release. Did you know there were efforts underway to try and get you out?

No, we had no idea what was happening, aside from my own personal belief that that was happening. At several points, they had told us that the government hadn't asked for our release. They asked why did I think that they hadn't asked for it? I didn't believe that, and I knew that wasn't the case. But as far as the Cypriot president's efforts and Reverend Jackson's efforts, we had no knowledge at all of what was happening in the political issues of our case.

When you were taken out of your cell and brought in to meet Reverend Jackson, did you know where you were going and for what reason?

No. We were brought to a new place at that time, moved from the prison where we had been at for several weeks, to a new building. Until we walked into the room, until they opened the door of the room where we met him, I had no idea what would happen in there. I wasn't sure if it was another interrogation, or if it was some kind of trial that they had threatened so long ago. Really, it could've been anything.

What was going through your mind when you walked through the door? Presumably, you recognized him immediately?

Right. Obviously, I was just shocked to see these faces. . . . I did recognize him immediately, and he introduced himself, which I found kind of strange. I was speechless at the time. I really didn't know what to say, because I had anticipated the worst could happen here. I wasn't expecting to see a friendly face or expecting to see someone who was there to offer some encouragement. So, at first I couldn't even talk. I was just speechless.

What did he tell you he was there to do? Did he give you the belief that perhaps he was going to be able to secure release, or he just wanted to come as a humanitarian gesture to buck up your spirits?

He didn't offer any kind of explanation as to why he was there. All he did was offer some words of encouragement. He gave some prayer, inspiration and some words from the Bible or some scripture. Other than that, it wasn't clear, and I wasn't expecting that he was there for that reason. In fact, I had anticipated he was there with the other people as some sort of humanitarian mission to find out how we were--to make sure of our treatment, and things like that. The next day, when we met with him the second time, he began to hint at the fact they were working on our release. That was the first I had any idea of why they were there.

What was going through your mind at that point? Did you think it was realistic?

I didn't. I had listened to the air raid sirens every day, several times a day, and I always believed that as long as the war was still going on, there was no reason for them to release us. So when the members were hinting that they were working for our release, I was filled with hope, but I was very skeptical. I was trying to keep myself from getting my hopes up too high.

How did you find out that you were going to be released?

That Saturday night that we had met with him earlier in the day, I was sitting in the cell. One of the senior prison officials came in, who we had only seen a couple of times, mainly when we were brought in there. He was in civilian clothes. It was late at night, right around bedtime when they'd usually to tell us to go to sleep. He came into the cell, told me to sit down, and he sat down next to me.

He didn't speak any English and, but he spoke a couple of words and he said "Home," and he made an ascent of an airplane with his hand. He said, "Home over the USA," or something like that. I finally really believed that maybe it would happen. That's when I first started to accept it a little bit. I wasn't saying, "Okay, it's over now, that's it," but it was definitely very encouraging that he was there, and it seemed like it was really going to happen.

You had another 12 hours to wait until you finally got out of the cell and were handed over to Jackson. That must have been a very hard night.

Yes, it was. It was probably the longest night that I've ever had. After his visit, they made a big production of getting all our stuff packed up--some books and some hygiene products that the Red Cross had brought. So we're all packed up. . . . I was sitting there on the bed waiting. . . . I think they were under the impression that that we'd be moved that night. But then around midnight one of the normal guards came in and said in broken English that it wouldn't happen until the morning--it was unsafe to go out that night because of the bombing. He told us to go to sleep and we'd leave in the morning. That was impossible. Sleep wasn't something that I could've done, and I didn't all that night, except for maybe an hour before sunrise. I lay there all night, hoping and praying that it was really going to happen.

You were finally handed over to Jesse Jackson. Do you remember what he told you when you finally realized that you were leaving that prison cell behind?

I do. We were standing against the wall after they had done the signing and he said, "The first thing I want you to do is take your hands from behind your back, because you are now free, you're free to embrace." That's what he said--his exact words--I remember it quite clearly. And so we did. We walked up to him and this huge religious delegation was there. They hugged us. We got to use the phone and call our families, so it was just terribly emotional. He would later dub me as "the weeping prophet" because often, throughout that course of time, I had trouble not crying. I was always so filled with emotion. It was just an unbelievable feeling. It wasn't quite over until we were out of Yugoslavia, and I think all three of us were still on edge until we were totally clear of the area.

Did you have any thoughts as you were leaving? It occurs to me that you may well have gone through towns that had been the victims of the American allied bombing campaign. You clearly were able to differentiate between the guards and civilians, the Serb people. Did you have any feelings of what is all this about, and what have we inflicted on these people? Did those thoughts go through your mind?

As a human being, you do think things like that. You can recognize the fact that nations war against each other, armies war against each other, and the people of an entire nation are not always enemies. With the kind of person I am, there was a sense of regret that this terrible conflict was still happening. Clearly, it was no good for anyone. No war is, but the outcome was just. I had to keep that in perspective--that what we were fighting for was right, and it was just. The implications of that had to be accepted.

Is there any sort of overwhelming memory that comes back from that? Is there a lesson that you felt you took away from it that in some way mitigates the suffering you went through?

I do. When I look back on it and see all the hardship that we had to go through, it makes it easier to think that you may have gotten stronger. I became a better person because of it, and I'll be able to deal with adversity in my life in a better way, using that as a reference. For the rest of my life, I'll be able to say that no matter what hardships I face, if I had the strength to go through that, I can certainly deal with this.

Historical Timeline of entries

This time-line includes most of the entries contained in this encyclopedia, with the exception of some of the thematic entries, such as "Labor," "Slavery," "War Crimes," and "Women," that have been a feature of captivity through the ages. Entries that are relevant to more than one conflict are listed more than once; Dartmoor, for example, was used as a prison during the Napoleonic Wars and the War of 1812, and so appears under both headings. Biographical entries appear according to the individual's involvement with captivity, rather than their birth or death date: the entry for "Winston Churchill," then, appears with the Boer War, when he was a civilian internee in South Africa. Because of the number of entries covering World War II, that section of the time-line has been arranged thematically as well as chronologically, to make it as functional as possible to the reader.

ANCIENT & CLASSICAL WORLD

Greece - Bronze Age to the Hellenistic Period		3500 B.C.E.-300 B.C.E.
	Sphacteria, Battle of	425 B.C.E.
	Peloponnesian Wars	431-404 B.C.E.
Ancient Egypt		3200 B.C.E.-350 B.C.E.
Hittites		1800-1175 B.C.E.
Greece - Hellenistic Period		300 B.C.E.
	Punic Wars	264-146 B.C.E.
Roman World		100 B.C.E.-500 C.E.
Attila the Hun		453

DARK & MIDDLE AGES

Karbala	629
Imma	679
Vikings	8th - 12th centuries
Basil II Bulgaroctonus	958-1025
Crusades	11th - 13th centuries
Ransom	11th - 17th centuries
Tower of London	1078-1945
Plains Indian Warfare	1100-1890

Renaissance & Age of Exploration

Age of Revolutions & Empires

Lieber Code 1863
Sultana Disaster 1865
Dr. Mary Walker.......... 1832-1919

Geneva Convention of 1864
Information Bureaus 1866-
Métis Rebellions 1869-1870, 1885
Central POW Agency 1870-
Franco-Prussian War 1870-1871
Brussels Declaration 1874
International Committee of the
Red Cross (ICRC) 1876-
St. John Ambulance 1877-
Wounded Knee Massacre 1890
Concentration Camps 1896-
Spanish-American War 1898

Boer War 1899-1902
Winston Leonard
Spencer Churchill 1874-1965

Hague Convention of 1899
Philippine-American War 1899-1902

TWENTIETH CENTURY

Boxer Rising 1900
Russo-Japanese War 1904-1905
Geneva Convention of 1906
Protected Personnel 1906
Hague Convention of 1907
Avitaminosis 1914-
Mixed Medical Commissions 1914-

World War I 1914-1918
Elsa Brändström 1888-1948
Roger David 1864-1916
Casement ....
Edith Cavell.................. 1865-1915
Civilian Internees

Edward Estlin (e.e.) Cummings 1894-1962
Czech Legion
Charles Algernon Fryatt.............................. 1872-1916
Charles-André-Marie Joseph de Gaulle 1890-1970
James Watson Gerrard, III 1867-1951
Henri-Honoré Giraud........................... 1879-1949
Grand Illusion La Grande Illusion 1937
Holzminden
Isle of Man
Lamsdorf
Lubyanka Prison
Murman Railway
Neutral Internees
Ruhleben
Sulmona
Sir Charles Vere Ferrers Townshend...... 1861-1924

Russian Civil War... 1917-1921
Barbed-wire Disease 1919-
Reparations... 1919-
Chinese Civil War.. 1927-1949
Geneva Convention of 1929
Gulag 1934-1991
Spanish Civil War.. 1936-1939

Sino-Japanese War.. 1937-1945
Nanking Massacre 1937-1938

World War II 1939-1945

Events
Altmark Incident.......... 1940
Defence Regulation 18B................................ 1940
Commissar Order 1941
Commando Order 1942

Doolittle Raid 1942
Shackling Incident 1942-1943
Featherston Incident 1943
Wooden Horse 1943
Bullet Decree 1944
Cowra Incident 1944 1944
Great Escape................. 1944
Los Baños Raid 1945
Yalta Conference 1945
Nuremberg Trials 1945-1949
Operation Keelhaul 1945-19
Tokyo War Crimes
Trials.............................. 1946-1948
Maschke
Commission 1957-1974

Camps

Auschwitz
Bergen-Belsen
Bicycle Camp
Buchenwald
Cabanatuan
Changi
Chieti
Colditz
Concentration
Camps
Dachau
Dulag Luft
Extermination
Camps
Fresnes Prison
Holloway Prison
Island Farm
Isle of Man
Lamsdorf
Livingston, Camp
Spandau Prison
Stalag Luft 3
Transit Camps
Zentsuji

Film and Television

The Captive Heart........ 1946

Stalag 17	1953
The Colditz Story	1955
The Bridge on the River Kwai	1957
The Great Escape	1963
Hogan's Heroes	1965-1971
King Rat	1965
Von Ryan's Express	1965
Slaughterhouse-Five	1969
Merry Christmas, Mr. Lawrence	1983
Prisoners of the Sun	1990

Individuals

Douglas Robert Steuart Bader	1910-1982
Gottlob Berger	1896-1975
Pierre Boulle	1912-1994
Roger Joyce Bushell	1910-1944
Anne Frank	1929-1945
Rudolf Hess	1894-1987
Tadeusz Bor Komorowski	1895-1966
Eric Henry Liddell	1902-1945
Kurt Meyer	1910-1961
Benito Mussolini	1883-1945
Ooka Shohei	1909-1988
Joachim Jochen Peiper	1915-1976
Arthur Ernest Percival	1881-1966
Donald Pleasance	1919-1995
Georges Scapini	1863-1976
Albert Michael Sinclair	1918-1944
Otto Skorzeny	1908-1975
Sir Laurens van der Post	1906-1996
Andrei Vlasov	1900-1946
Kurt Vonnegut, Jr.	1922-
Jonathan Mayhew Wainwright	1883-1953
Franz von Werra	1914-1941
David Westheimer	1917-2005

Simon Wiesenthal......... 1908-2005
Sir Pelham Grenville Wodehouse.................... 1881-1975
Frederick Forest
Edward Yeo-Thomas ... 1901-1964

War Crimes

Le Paradis Massacre..... 1940
Wormhout Massacre.... 1940
Katyn Forest Massacre 1941
Bataan Death March..... 1942
Lidice Massacre 1942
Ardeatine Caves Massacre 1943

Malmédy Massacre 1944
Oradour-sur-Glane Massacre 1944
Sandakan-Ranau Death March................. 1945

Miscellaneous

Arbeitskommandos
Blue Division
British Army Aid Group
British Free Corps
Burma-Thailand Death Railway
Central Registry of War Criminals and Security Suspects (CROWCASS)
Civilian Internees
DEF/SEP Status............ 1945-1946
Gestapo
MI9
MIS-X
Neutral Internees
"Other Losses"
Vichy France
Waffen-SS

Torture.. In light of the prisoner abuse scandals surrounding detainees in Iraq, Guantanamo Bay and Afghanistan, the 109th US Congress wrote specific rules for the handling and interrogation of detainees in U.S. custody.
See the *Detainee Treatment Act of 2005*

Pentagon Appropriations Bill for 2006 (H.R. 2863)... Signed into law by President George W. Bush in December 2005
See *President's Statement on Signing of H.R. 2863*

INDEX

A

B

C

E

F

G

H

I

J

K

L

N

O

P

Q

R

S

T

U

V

W

X

Y

Z